Basic Marketing Research

Second Edition

Basic Marketing Research

Second Edition

Gilbert A. Churchill, Jr.

Arthur C. Nielsen, Jr., Chair of Marketing Research
University of Wisconsin

The Dryden Press
A Harcourt Brace Jovanovich College Publisher
Fort Worth   Philadelphia   San Diego   New York   Orlando   Austin   San Antonio
Toronto   Montreal   London   Sydney   Tokyo

Acquisitions Editor: Rob Zwettler
Developmental Editor: Millicent Treloar
Project Editor: Cate Rzasa
Production Manager: Bob Lange
Permissions Editor: Cindy Lombardo
Director of Editing, Design, and Production: Jane Perkins

Text and Cover Designer: Mercedes Santos
Copy Editor: Susan Baranczyk
Indexer: Margaret Jarpey
Compositor: The Clarinda Company
Text Type: 10/12 Janson

Library of Congress Cataloging-in-Publication Data
Churchill, Gilbert A.
　　Basic marketing research / Gilbert A. Churchill, Jr.—2nd ed.
　　　p. cm.
　　Includes bibliographical references and index.
　　ISBN 0-03-054017-8
　　1. Marketing research.　　I.　Title.
HF5415.2.C49　1992
　658.8′3—dc20　　　　　　　　　　　　　　　　　91–8862

Printed in the United States of America
123-032-987654321
Copyright © 1992, 1988 by The Dryden Press.

Requests for permission to make copies of any part of the work should
be mailed to: Permissions Department, Harcourt Brace Jovanovich,
Publishers, 8th Floor, Orlando, FL 32887.

Address orders:
The Dryden Press
Orlando, FL 32887

Address editorial correspondence:
The Dryden Press
301 Commerce Street, Suite 3700
Fort Worth, TX 76102

The Dryden Press
Harcourt Brace Jovanovich

To our grandchildren — Kayla Marie,
Johnathon Winston, and Kelsey Lynn

The Dryden Press Series in Marketing

Allvine
Marketing: Principles and Practices

Assael
Marketing: Principles and Strategy

Balsley and Birsner
Selling: Marketing Personified

Bateson
**Managing Services Marketing:
Text and Readings,** *Second Edition*

Blackwell, Johnston, and Talarzyk
**Cases in Marketing Management
and Strategy**

Blackwell, Talarzyk, and Engel
**Contemporary Cases in Consumer
Behavior,** *Third Edition*

Boone and Kurtz
Contemporary Marketing
Seventh Edition

Carter and Mentzer
Readings in Marketing Today

Churchill
Basic Marketing Research
Second Edition

Churchill
**Marketing Research:
Methodological Foundations**
Fifth Edition

Cummings
Contemporary Selling

Czinkota and Ronkainen
International Marketing
Second Edition

Dunn, Barban, Krugman, and Reid
**Advertising: Its Role in Modern
Marketing,** *Seventh Edition*

Engel, Blackwell, and Miniard
Consumer Behavior, *Sixth Edition*

Futrell
Sales Management, *Third Edition*

Ghosh
Retail Management

Green
Analyzing Multivariate Data

Harrell
Consumer Behavior

Hutt and Speh
**Business Marketing Management:
A Strategic View of Industrial and
Organizational Markets**
Fourth Edition

Ingram and LaForge
**Sales Management: Analysis and
Decision Making,** *Second Edition*

Kaufman
Essentials of Advertising
Second Edition

Kurtz and Boone
Marketing, *Third Edition*

Mentzer and Schwartz
Marketing Today, *Fourth Edition*

Park and Zaltman
Marketing Management

Patti and Frazer
**Advertising: A Decision-
Making Approach**

Rachman
Marketing Today, *Second Edition*

Rogers, Gamans, and Grassi
Retailing: New Perspectives
Second Edition

Rosenbloom
**Marketing Channels:
A Management View,** *Fourth Edition*

Schellinck and Maddox
**Marketing Research:
A Computer-Assisted Approach**

Schnaars
MICROSIM
*Marketing simulation available for
IBM PC® and Apple®*

Sellars
**Role Playing the Principles of
Selling,** *Second Edition*

Shimp
**Promotion Management and
Marketing Communications**
Second Edition

Talarzyk
Cases and Exercises in Marketing

Terpstra and Sarathy
International Marketing
Fifth Edition

Tootelian and Gaedeke
**Cases and Classics in
Marketing Management**

Weiers
Introduction to Business Statistics

Weitz and Wensley
**Readings in Strategic Marketing:
Analysis, Planning, and
Implementation**

Zikmund
Exploring Marketing Research
Fourth Edition

Preface

Basic Marketing Research is designed for the introductory, undergraduate course in marketing research and can be used either in one- or two-quarter sequences or in semester courses.

The topic of marketing research is a complex one. It involves a number of questions that need to be answered and a number of decisions that need to be made with respect to the choice of techniques used to solve a research problem. Without some overriding framework, which this book attempts to provide, it is easy for students to become lost in a maze; that is, to become so overwhelmed by the bits and pieces that they fail to see the interrelationships of the parts to the whole. Yet, an understanding of these interrelationships is essential both to the aspiring manager and the aspiring researcher, for in a very real sense, marketing research is one big trade-off.

Decisions made with respect to one stage in the research process have consequences for other stages. Managers need an appreciation of the subtle and pervasive interactions among the parts of the research process so that they can have the appropriate degree of confidence in a particular research result. Researchers also need to appreciate the interactions among the parts. The parts serve as the "pegs" on which to hang the knowledge accumulated about research methods. Researchers need to resist the temptation of becoming enamored of the parts to the detriment of the whole.

This book attempts to serve both the aspiring manager and the aspiring researcher by breaking the research process down into some basic stages that must be completed when answering a research question. The specific stages are

1. Formulate problem.
2. Determine research design.
3. Determine data-collection method.
4. Design data-collection forms.
5. Design sample and collect data.
6. Analyze and interpret the data.
7. Prepare the research report.

The organization of the book parallels these stages in the research process. Thus, the book is organized into seven corresponding parts. Each part (or stage) is then broken into smaller parts, so that a given stage is typically discussed in multiple chapters. This modular treatment allows students to negotiate the maze. It also allows instructors some latitude with respect to the order in which they cover topics.

Organization

Part One consists of four chapters and an appendix. Chapter 1 provides an overview of the subject of marketing research and describes the kinds of problems for which it is used, who is doing research, and how the research function is organized. Chapter 1 also provides a perspective on career opportunities available in marketing research.

Chapter 2, which is new, provides an overview of the various ways of gathering marketing intelligence. It emphasizes the increasingly important role played by decision support systems in providing business and competitive intelligence and contrasts the information system approaches to the project emphasis approach taken in the book. Chapter 3 then overviews the research process. The appendix to Chapter 3 discusses various ethical frameworks for viewing marketing research techniques. Chapter 4 discusses the problem-formulation stage of the research process and explains the issues that must be addressed in translating a marketing decision problem into one or more questions that research can address productively. It also covers the preparation of a research proposal.

Part Two concerns the choice of research design and consists of two chapters. Chapter 5 overviews the role of various research designs and discusses one of the basic types, the exploratory design. Chapter 6 then discusses the two other basic types, descriptive and causal designs.

Part Three discusses the general issue of selecting a data-collection method and contains five chapters and an appendix. Chapter 7 focuses on secondary data as an information resource, while the appendix to Chapter 7 discusses the many sources of published secondary data. Chapter 8 discusses the operations of and data supplied by standardized marketing information services. Chapter 9 describes the issues involved when choosing between the two primary means by which marketing information can be collected—through observing or questioning subjects. Chapter 10 then describes the main alternatives and the advantages and disadvantages of each when subjects are to be questioned. Chapter 11 does the same for observational techniques.

Part Four addresses the actual design of the data-collection forms that will be used in a study. Chapter 12 discusses a sequential procedure that can be used to design a questionnaire or observation form. Chapter 13 then discusses some basic measurement issues that researchers and managers need to be aware of so that they will neither mislead others nor be misled themselves when interpreting the findings. Chapter 14 describes some of the most popular techniques marketers currently use to measure customers' attitudes, perceptions, and preferences.

Part Five, which consists of four chapters, examines sample design and deals with the actual collection of data needed to answer questions. Chapter 15 overviews the main types of samples that can be used to determine the population elements from which data should be collected. It also describes the main types of nonprobability samples and simple random sampling, the most basic probability sampling technique. Chapter 16 discusses the use of stratified sampling and cluster sampling, which are more sophisticated probability sampling techniques. Chapter 17 treats the question of how many population elements need to be sampled for research questions to be answered with precision and confidence in the results. Chapter 18 discusses data collection and the many errors that can occur in completing this task from a perspective that allows managers to better assess the quality of information they receive from research.

Once the data have been collected, emphasis in the research process logically turns to analysis, which is a search for meaning in the collected information. The search for meaning involves many questions and several steps, and the three chapters in Part Six attempt to overview these steps and questions. Chapter 19 reviews the preliminary analysis steps of editing, coding, and tabulating the data. Chapter 20 discusses the procedures that are appropriate for examining whether the differences between groups are statistically significant. Chapter 21 describes the statistical procedures that can be used to examine the degree of relationship between variables.

Part Seven, which consists of two chapters and an epilogue, discusses the last, yet critically important, part of the research process: the research report. Because it often becomes the standard by which any research effort is judged, the research report must contribute positively to that evaluation. Chapter 22 discusses the criteria a written research report should satisfy and a form it can follow so that it does contribute positively to the research effort. Chapter 23 provides a similar perspective for oral reports. Chapter 23 also discusses some graphic techniques that can be used to communicate the important findings more forcefully. The epilogue ties together the elements of the research process by demonstrating their interrelationships in overview fashion.

Organizing the material in this book around the stages in the research process produces several significant benefits. First, it allows the subject of marketing research to be broken into very digestible bites. Second, it demonstrates and continually reinforces how the individual bits and pieces of research technique fit into a larger whole. Students can see readily, for example, the relationship between statistics and marketing research, or where they might pursue additional study to become research specialists. Third, the organization permits the instructor some flexibility with respect to the order in which the parts of the process may be covered.

Special Features

In addition to its pedagogically sound organization, *Basic Marketing Research* has several special features that deserve mention. First, the book is relatively complete with respect to its coverage of the most important techniques available for gathering marketing intelligence. The general approach employed when discussing topics is not only to provide students with the pros and cons of the various methods by which a research problem can be addressed, but also to develop an appreciation of why these advantages and disadvantages occur. The hope is that through this appreciation students will be able to creatively apply and critically evaluate the procedures of marketing research. Other important features include the following:

1. A set of learning objectives highlights the most important topics discussed in the chapter. The chapter summary then recaps the learning objectives point by point.
2. A "Case in Marketing Research" opens each chapter. These scenarios are adapted from actual situations and should prove to be very interesting to students. Furthermore, an end-of-chapter reference to the introductory case ("Back to the Case") illustrates how the scenario can be brought into sharper focus using the methods described in the chapter.
3. A running glossary appears throughout the text. Key terms in each chapter are boldfaced, and their definitions appear in the margin where the terms are discussed. Each key term is also indexed.
4. The "Research Windows" provide a view of what is happening in the world of marketing research. "Research Windows" describe what is going on at specific companies and offer some specific "how to" tips. Like the "Case in Marketing Research" features, they serve to breathe life into the subject and strongly engage the students' interest.
5. Extensive use of photos provides visual reinforcement to important concepts. Appearing throughout the book, the photos provide students with a tangible understanding of how various aspects of the research process are conducted.

6. Discussion questions, problems, and/or projects are found at the end of each chapter. This feature allows students the opportunity to apply the chapter topics to focused situations, thereby honing their analytical skills and developing firsthand knowledge of the strengths and weaknesses of various research techniques.

7. A worked-out research project is discussed throughout the book. This project is found at the end of each part and concerns retailers' attitudes toward advertising in various media. The project represents an actual situation faced by a group of radio stations in one community. It begins with a description of the radio stations' concerns and objectives. Each of the sections then describes how the research was designed and carried out, demonstrating the interrelationships of the stages in the research process and providing students with a real, hands-on perspective as to how research is actually conducted.

8. Several cases occur at the end of each part and deal with a stage in the research process. The twenty-eight cases assist students in developing their own evaluation and analytical skills. They are also useful in demonstrating the universal application of marketing research techniques. The methods of marketing research can be used not only by manufacturers and distributors of products, as is commonly assumed, but also by the private and public sectors to address other issues. The cases include such diverse entities or issues as the Big Brothers program, computerized bibliographic data services, banking services, and university extension programs. All cases represent actual situations, although some of them have been disguised to protect the proprietary nature of the information.

9. Raw data are provided for three of the cases to allow students to perform their own analyses to answer questions. The data are listed in the *Instructor's Manual* (*IM*) for the convenience of those who wish to enter the data into their computer systems. The data are also available on computer disk to adopters. The disk allows those who have statistical packages available to use them for analyses. Others may find it more convenient to upload the data from the disk onto the school's mainframe computer and have students use the larger systems for analyses. To obtain a copy of the disk, which is available for the IBM microcomputer, adopters must send the insert card in the *IM* to the nearest Dryden regional sales office.

Changes in the Second Edition

Several major changes have been made to the second edition of *Basic Marketing Research*. There is an increased emphasis on managing marketing research information throughout the book, as well as several organizational changes. For example, the discussion of decision support systems has been moved forward to Chapter 2, and the discussion has been expanded to highlight the provision of business and competitive intelligence. The new chapter, for example, discusses how to obtain competitive information and how to use the new electronic communication and software systems and a common server to tie together many different sources of data. It also contrasts the decision support system approach to marketing intelligence and the project approach taken in this book.

Another organizational change involves focus groups, which are now discussed with other exploratory research techniques rather than with alternative data collection methods. Further, the discussion has been expanded.

Another change is the new discussion of ethics in Appendix 3A, which presents alternative ethical models and establishes a framework for the new ethical dilemmas contained in each of the subsequent chapters. This organization resolves the problem of how to treat the topic of ethics. It is difficult to treat it early because students do not yet have the technical sophistication to appreciate alternative ways to approach ethical problems. Treating it late, as most books do for this reason, makes ethics appear as an afterthought. Treating the conceptual foundations early in the book and then interweaving ethical dilemmas with technical issues allows students to more readily appreciate the social consequences of proceeding in particular ways.

Profiles of marketing research professionals have been added as part openers. Each profile highlights the daily work of marketing research as it pertains to the main ideas of the part. The profiles motivate student interest by demonstrating the importance of marketing research in corporate decision making.

There has also been a major revision of the cases. Over 40 percent of the cases are new. Further, several of the old cases have been revised and updated.

Another significant addition to the second edition is the description, questionnaire, coding form, and raw data for a ground coffee study conducted by NFO. The study was used to generate a number of discussion questions and problems for the chapters, which give students the opportunity to work with "live" data. This should hone their skills in translating research problems into data analysis issues and in interpreting computer output. Moreover, the data base is rich enough for instructors to design their own application problems/exercises for their classes, thereby allowing even more opportunity for "hands-on" learning.

The addition of the SPSS/PC+ command structures for each of the cases containing raw data makes the second edition of the book even more "user-friendly." Instructors can now easily duplicate the analyses behind the cases and share that with the students, thereby giving them practice in interpreting computer output.

Finally, all of the chapters have been subjected to thorough scrutiny and rewrite. There has been a major updating of the examples, for instance. There are many more in-text examples and Research Windows than were found in the first edition, and the examples are as up-to-date as possible. These changes help the book reflect the current practice of marketing research. The discussion in some chapters has been expanded and in others it has been streamlined, always with the intention of making it as clear as possible. Some of the more significant chapter-by-chapter changes include the following:

- **Chapter 1** A new set of examples outlining the scope and thrust of marketing research. Changes in marketing research practices.
- **Chapter 2** New and expanded discussion of decision support systems.
- **Chapter 3** Increased emphasis on managing marketing research information. Increased emphasis on the respective roles of decision maker and researcher in defining the research problem. A new section on sources of decision problems and how research needs can change as the trigger for the decision problem changes. More emphasis on procedures for making sure that the true decision problem, not symptoms of a problem, is being addressed. A new section on choosing and using research suppliers. A new appendix on ethics.
- **Chapter 5** Reorganization to fully cover qualitative and exploratory research designs. Expanded discussions of focus groups, trade literature, secondary data, and the relationships between problem definition and research design.
- **Chapter 6** Enlarged discussion of simulated test markets, controlled test markets (including electronic test markets), and standard test markets. More descriptive information about each as well as their advantages and disadvantages and how to choose among them.

- **Chapter 7** Increased discussion on the use of internal data such as sales reports and prior studies. New material on locating external data including on-line services. Revised and expanded appendix regarding major government and private suppliers of data organized in a new structure by type of problem.
- **Chapter 8** Expanded discussion of the data available from the standardized marketing information services. A new organization that describes how the information available from these firms can be used to profile customers, measure product sales and market share, measure advertising exposure and effectiveness, and the like.
- **Chapter 10** New material on computer-assisted interviewing and mall intercepts.
- **Chapter 19** New material on banner formats for presenting tabular data. Revised discussion in the appendix on how to better frame a hypothesis. A more complete discussion of the trade-offs between Type I and Type II errors.
- **Chapter 22** New checklist of elements to include in reports.
- **Chapter 23** New tips for preparing effective presentation visuals.

Ancillaries

A complete, carefully developed ancillary package accompanies the second edition of *Basic Marketing Research*.

Instructor's Manual/Transparency Masters Developed with the assistance of Jacqueline C. Hitchon and Gregory D. Martin of the University of Wisconsin–Madison, the *Instructor's Manual* contains alternative course outlines, instruction suggestions for each chapter, answers to discussion questions, solutions to cases, and approximately 100 transparency masters with notes.

Test Bank The *Test Bank*, which is included in the *Instructor's Manual*, contains more than 2,100 questions, including true-false and multiple-choice questions.

Computerized Test Bank A computerized version of the text bank is available for the IBM PC® and IBM-compatible computers. The questions on the disks are identical to those that appear in the printed version of the *Test Bank*. This system also gives instructors the option of entering the program and adding or deleting questions.

Case Data Disk A disk containing research data necessary to solve certain text cases is available upon request for the IBM PC.

Computer-Based Experiential Exercises A number of the chapters also contain suggestions for computer-based experiential exercises that can be assigned to illustrate chapter notions. The exercises, which have been developed by D. A. Schellinck and R. N. Maddox, tend to be very involving for students. The exercises are available to adopters on disk for IBM microcomputers.

Edustat A comprehensive, menu-driven statistical software for the IBM PC and IBM-compatible computers is available on request.

Acknowledgments

While writing a book is never the work of a single person, one always runs the risk of omitting some important contributions when attempting to acknowledge the help of others. Nonetheless, the attempt must be made because this book has benefited immensely from the many helpful comments I have received along the way from interested colleagues.

I wish to acknowledge the following people who reviewed the manuscript for the first edition: David Andrus, Kansas State University; Donald Bradley, University of Central Arkansas; David Gourley, Arizona State University; D. S. Halfhill, California State University, Fresno; Vince Howe, University of Kentucky; Glen Jarboe, University of Texas, Arlington; Leonard Jensen, Southern Illinois University, Carbondale; Roland Jones, Mississippi State University; Subhash Lonial, University of Louisville; Douglas MacLachlan, University of Washington; Thomas Noordewier, University of Vermont; David Urban, Georgia State University; and Joe Welch, North Texas State University.

I would also like to thank the following individuals who reviewed the manuscript for the second edition. While much of the credit for the strengths of the book is theirs, the blame for any weaknesses is strictly mine. Thank you one and all for your most perceptive and helpful comments.

Joseph Ballenger
Stephen F. Austin State University

David Gourley
Arizona State University

Diana Grewal
University of Miami

Thomas S. Gruca
University of Massachusetts at Amherst

Doug Hausknecht
University of Akron

Deborah Roedder John
University of Minnesota

Ram Kesavan
University of Detroit

Daulatram Lund
University of Nevada

Tridib Mazumdar
Syracuse University

Debra Ringold
University of Baltimore

John H. Summey
Southern Illinois University

Linda Tischler worked closely with me on the first edition of *Basic Marketing Research* and Gini Hartzmark did the same on the second edition. Their editorial assistance was invaluable in fine-tuning the manuscript and developing the pedagogy.

My colleagues at the University of Wisconsin have my thanks for the intellectual stimulation and psychological support they have always provided.

I also wish to thank Janet Christopher who did most of the typing on the manuscript. She was efficient in her efforts and patient with mine. I also wish to thank students Tom Brown, Beth Bubon, Joseph Kuester, Jayashree Mahajan, Kay Powers, and David Szymanski for their help with many of the tasks involved in completing a book such as this. I would like to thank the editorial and production staff of The Dryden Press for their professional efforts on my behalf. I am also grateful to the Literary Executor of the late Sir Ronald A. Fisher, F.R.S., to Dr. Frank Yates, F.R.S., and to Longman Group Ltd., for permission to reprint Table III from their book *Statistical Tables for Biological, Agricultural and Medical Research* (6th Edition, 1974).

Finally, I once again owe a special debt of thanks to my wife, Helen, and our children. Their unyielding support and generous love not only made this book possible but worthwhile doing in the first place.

Gilbert A. Churchill, Jr.

Madison, Wisconsin
September 1991

About the Author

Gilbert A. Churchill, Jr., DBA (Indiana University), is the Arthur C. Nielsen, Jr., Chair of Marketing Research at the University of Wisconsin–Madison. He joined the Wisconsin faculty in 1966 and has taught there since, except for one year that he spent as a visiting professor at Bedriftsokonomisk Institutt in Oslo, Norway. Professor Churchill was named Distinguished Marketing Educator by the American Marketing Association in 1986, only the second individual so honored. The award recognizes and honors a living marketing educator for distinguished service and outstanding contributions in the field of marketing education.

Professor Churchill is a past recipient of the William O'Dell Award for the outstanding article appearing in the *Journal of Marketing Research* during the year. He has also been a finalist for the award four other times. He was named Marketer of the Year by the South Central Wisconsin Chapter of the American Marketing Association in 1981. He is a member of the American Marketing Association and has served as vice-president of publications and on its board of directors as well as on the association's Advisory Committee to the Bureau of the Census. In addition, he has served as consultant to a number of companies, including Oscar Mayer, Western Publishing Company, and Parker Pen.

Professor Churchill's articles have appeared in such publications as the *Journal of Marketing Research*, the *Journal of Marketing*, the *Journal of Consumer Research*, the *Journal of Retailing*, the *Journal of Business Research*, *Decision Sciences*, *Technometrics*, and *Organizational Behavior and Human Performance*, among others. He is a co-author of several other books, including *Marketing Research: Methodological Foundations*, Fifth Edition (Hinsdale: Ill.: Dryden, 1991); *Sales Force Management: Planning, Implementation, and Control*, Third Edition (Homewood, Ill.: Irwin, 1989); and *Salesforce Performance* (Lexington, Mass.: Lexington Books, 1984). He is a former editor of the *Journal of Marketing Research* and has served on the editorial boards of *Journal of Marketing Research*, *Journal of Marketing*, *Journal of Business Research*, and *Journal of Health Care Marketing*. Professor Churchill currently teaches undergraduate and graduate courses in marketing research and sales management and is a past recipient of the Lawrence J. Larson Excellence in Teaching Award.

Contents in Brief

Contents

Part 5   Sampling and Data Collection   453

Part 6   Data Analysis   605

Introduction to Marketing Research and Problem Definition

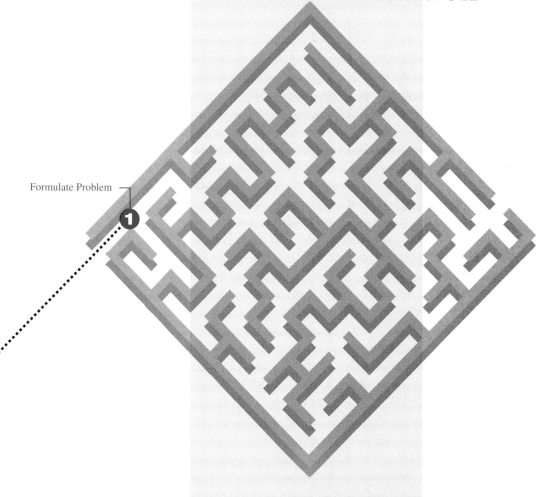

Formulate Problem

1

Part One gives an overview of marketing research. Chapter 1 looks at the kinds of problems for which marketing research is used, who is doing it, and how it is organized. Chapter 2 discusses alternative ways of providing marketing intelligence: through marketing information systems, decision support systems, or projects designed to get at specific issues. Chapter 3 provides an overview of the research process, and the appendix to Chapter 3 discusses some of the ethical questions that can arise when gathering information. Chapter 4 discusses in detail problem formulation, the first stage in the research process.

GAYLE FUGUITT
Vice-President of Marketing Research
and Quality Improvement
Yoplait USA

Gayle Fuguitt's job title is vice-president of Marketing Research and Quality Improvement for Yoplait USA, but to hear her tell it, that title could just as easily be "consumer advocate."

"In the strictest and the loosest sense," says Fuguitt, "I am the person at the company who is responsible for objectively representing the consumer."

Yoplait is a division of General Mills. It is strictly a yogurt company, and representing the yogurt-buying public is a responsibility that Fuguitt takes very seriously.

"I am the person at the meeting whom they turn to when they want to know what the consumer wants. This may be quite different from what I want or think as a businessperson," says Fuguitt. "And what the consumer wants may not always be practical. If you make a product that has all the features the consumer wants, it may be so expensive to produce that the consumer won't buy it.

"Conversely, I'm often the person who has to sit there at the meeting and say, 'Listen, if you present this new product in this way, 47 percent of consumers won't put it in their shopping cart.' "

Predicting who will and won't buy a new product is one of the biggest challenges of Fuguitt's job. Yoplait obtains data, much of it generated through grocery store scanners, on a continuous basis from an independent research supplier. Together with her team, Fuguitt chooses from a menu of data information she feels is most useful for Yoplait. For example, she routinely tracks information on market share and sales volume, demographic data on purchasers, as well as a variety of other data.

But Fuguitt's job involves a lot more than just keeping her eye on the numbers. She needs to decide what data are relevant to the particular problem she's working on. Then she and her team use sophisticated data-analysis techniques to make optimal use of the data. She is also responsible for presenting the data in a meaningful way so that it can be used to make real business decisions.

On a typical day Fuguitt, who is also the mother of a one-year-old boy, gets into work a little before 8:15 a.m. in order to prepare for the day's meetings. Every Friday morning she attends a management team meeting, where the nine people who report directly to the president of Yoplait sit down and discuss how they want to run the business. "On one particular Friday I discussed results of some 800-number research in which we asked Yoplait consumers to answer questions about our products," she reports.

Fuguitt also meets regularly with people in the marketing department at Yoplait as well as at the parent company, General Mills. Between meetings she answers phone calls. But when test results come in, she tends to drop everything and immediately calls her research team together to evaluate and disseminate the new data.

"It's close to real-time research," says Fuguitt. "Raw data are faxed to my office, and we try to move the information along to the appropriate people as fast as possible."

New problems come to her all the time. "People from the marketing department bring me technical problems. They say, 'We want to try a new product, and we need to run a four-panel test. . . .' My first reaction is to try to get them to back away from that and talk in their own language about what they're trying to accomplish, so that I have a sense of what they're really trying to find out. Most often a clear formulation of the problem simplifies finding the appropriate research design.

"If you've accurately framed your problem and your research design is problem specific, then the data you generate should accurately address the problem. Ideally, though, the data you generate should go beyond answering the initial question. They should reveal implications beyond the answer you sought. 'Is the product good? Yes. But the things that are best about it are the taste and the packaging. Consumers have misgivings about some of the following features. . . .'

"When I was in business school I probably couldn't have predicted that I'd be doing exactly what I'm doing now. But I would have told you that I wanted to do something where I had a lot of interaction with people and where I could see concrete results. That's exactly what I do now."

Adds Fuguitt, "I love it when I go to the grocery store and see something on the shelf that I helped create."

Chapter One

Role of Marketing Research

Learning Objectives

Upon completing this chapter, you should be able to

1. Define marketing research.

2. Cite the two factors that are most responsible for how the research function is organized in any given firm.

3. List some of the skills that are important for careers in marketing research.

Case in Marketing Research

Julie Sullivan told her secretary to hold her calls. She closed the door to her office and moved the box of Crunchy Chex off her desk. She was assistant manager of Marketing Research at Hallorhan Bold, a Chicago advertising agency, and she'd been putting in a lot of hours on the Crunchy Chex account, trying to figure out why its market share was slipping. She put the cereal box in her bottom desk drawer. For the next hour at least, she did not want to think about Crunchy Chex.

Sullivan had been invited to return to her college alma mater to speak at Career Night. She had been flattered to be asked and had gladly accepted. But it had never occurred to her how difficult it would be to put together a coherent presentation on career opportunities in marketing research.

The easiest thing would be just to talk about her own career. Sullivan loved working in advertising research. She loved the fast pace and the excitement of juggling several projects at once. In the four years she'd been at Hallorhan Bold, she'd

done everything. She'd polled eight-year-olds in shopping malls on their favorite bubble gum flavors. She'd squinted through a one-way mirror while groups of senior citizens discussed denture care products. There were days she spent in meetings, days she spent buried under piles of data while the phone rang off the hook with clients demanding to know what it all meant.

But describing only her own job, as diverse it might be, would show only a tiny part of the career picture in marketing research. All Sullivan had to do was think about a handful of friends whom she had graduated with and who had gone into marketing research. Bob Vaughn worked for one of the big research suppliers. In fact, Hallorhan Bold was one of his clients. Trina, her old roommate, had spent the last three years at Presto Products developing a new brand of fresh pasta sauces. Sullivan had noticed them at the grocery store the other day. She wondered whether they were performing up to expectations.

Interrupting that line of thought, Sullivan's secretary knocked on the office door and poked her head in apologetically. "I'm sorry to disturb you, Ms. Sullivan, but Mr. Bold wants you in the conference room right away. He's meeting with Don Meyerson from PK Perfumes, and he says he needs you right away."

Sullivan nodded. "I'm on my way."

Discussion Issues

1. If you were Sullivan, what kinds of things would you share with the college students at Career Night?
2. If you were a student thinking about a career in marketing research, what questions would you ask Sullivan?
3. If you were planning a career in marketing—as opposed to marketing research—do you think you would find Sullivan's presentation valuable? Why or why not?

Marketing research is a much broader activity than most people realize. There is much more to it than simply asking ultimate consumers what they think or feel about some product or ad. To be sure, consumer surveys and focus groups are very important marketing research tools. However, in an effort to learn about the consumer and compete effectively in the marketplace, an organization may need to employ other methods. Consider the following examples:

Example   The Eastman Kodak Company wanted to improve its relatively flat sales curve. Researchers at Kodak knew that amateur photographers goofed on more than two billion pictures a year, so they took a look at ten thousand photos to see what kinds of things the photographers were doing wrong. Their study led to a number of design ideas for the Kodak disc camera and helped eliminate almost one-half of out-of-focus and underexposed shots. First introduced in 1982, the disc camera has been one of the most successful new products in Kodak history.[1]

Example   "One Sunday morning in the summer of 1986, six Marriott employees on a secret intelligence mission checked into a cheap hotel outside the Atlanta airport. Once inside their $30-a-night rooms, decorated with red shag rugs and purple velour curtains, the team went into their routine. One called the front desk saying that his shoelace had broken—could someone get him a new one? Another carefully noted the brands of soap, shampoo, and towels. A third took off his suit jacket, lay down on the bed, and began moaning and writhing and knocking the headboard against the wall while a colleague in the next room listened for the muffled cries of feigned ecstasy and calmly jotted down that this type of wall wasn't at all soundproof. For six months this intelligence team had traveled the country, gathering information on the players in the economy hotel business, a market Marriott strongly wished to enter. Armed with detailed data about potential rivals' strengths and weaknesses, Marriott budgeted $500 million for a new hotel chain it felt would beat the competition in every respect, from soap to service to soundproof rooms. Fairfield Inn, launched in the fall of 1987, currently has an occupancy rate 10 percentage points higher than the rest of the industry.[2]

Example   Executives at Hoover became suspicious when their consumer surveys showed that on the average, people spent one hour a week vacuuming their houses. Consequently, the executives decided to hook up timers to some vacuum cleaners, and they exchanged these models with vacuums in people's homes. As the executives had expected, the timers showed that people spent less time vacuuming than they had previously claimed—actually only 35 minutes a week.[3]

As the preceding examples demonstrate, the scope of marketing research activities goes beyond simply asking individual consumers for their likes and dislikes. Observation, either personal observation (as was done by the Kodak researchers and the Marriott employees) or mechanical observation (à la Hoover), is also a legitimate marketing research activity. At the same time, some very productive research involves no more than the study of readily available data, and some involves the systematic testing of an ad, a new package, or a product. The fundamental point is that marketing research is a pervasive activity that can take *many forms*, because its basic purpose is to help marketing managers make better decisions in any of their areas of responsibility.

Role of Marketing Research in Marketing Management

Anyone planning a career in marketing management should understand what marketing research can do. Managers at all levels and in all areas of business must make decisions. Accurate, effective decision making is often dependent on the quality of information provided. Marketing research plays an essential role in providing accurate and useful information.

You may recall from your introductory course in marketing the emphasis that many organizations place on the marketing concept. In today's hotly competitive marketplace, the marketing concept has been gaining in importance. The marketing concept states that the principal task of the marketing function is to serve the interests of the customer rather than the interests of the business. Many organizations have failed to embrace this notion, though—sometimes with dire consequences. American auto manufacturers, for example, believed for decades that marketing was less important than engineering, finance, and manufacturing. But as sales figures fell in the face of high fuel prices, Japanese competition, and quality-conscious consumers, the industry had to reassess its beliefs. As one auto executive noted ruefully, "If there's a growing respect for the market, it's because we've learned that disrespecting it cost us an arm and a leg."[4]

Once an organization decides to focus its attention on marketing, it often discovers that satisfying customers means juggling a number of factors to achieve a balance that will enable its product to compete successfully in the marketplace. Marketing managers generally focus their efforts on the four Ps—price, product, place, and promotion.[5]

The marketing manager's essential task is to combine these variables, known as the *marketing mix*, into an effective marketing program in which all the elements complement each other. This task would be much simpler if all the elements that could affect customer satisfaction were under the manager's control and if consumer reaction to any contemplated change could be predicted. Usually, however, a number of factors affecting the success of the marketing effort are beyond the marketing manager's control, and the behavior of individual consumers is largely unpredictable. In addition, the objectives and internal resources of the firm may not coincide with the marketing manager's proposed strategy. The competitive, technological, economic, cultural, social, political, or legal environments may not be conducive to the marketing department's goals.

Figure 1.1 summarizes the task of marketing management. Customers are at the center of the figure because they are the focus of the firm's activities. Their satisfaction is achieved through simultaneous adjustments in the elements of the marketing mix, but the results of these adjustments are uncertain because the marketing task takes place within an uncontrollable environment. Consequently, as director of the firm's marketing activities, the marketing manager has an urgent need for information—and marketing research is traditionally responsible for providing it. Marketing research is the firm's formal communication link with the environment. It is the means by which the firm generates, transmits, and interprets information from the environment about or relating to the success of the firm's marketing plans.

The definition of **marketing research** emphasizes its information-linkage role.

> Marketing research is the function which links the consumer and the customer to the organization through information—information used to identify and define marketing problems; generate, refine, and evaluate marketing actions; monitor marketing performance; and improve our understanding of marketing as a process.[6]

Marketing research The function that links the consumer to the marketer through information—information used to identify and define marketing problems; generate, refine, and evaluate marketing actions; monitor marketing performance; and improve understanding of marketing as a process.

Figure 1.1   **Task of Marketing Management**

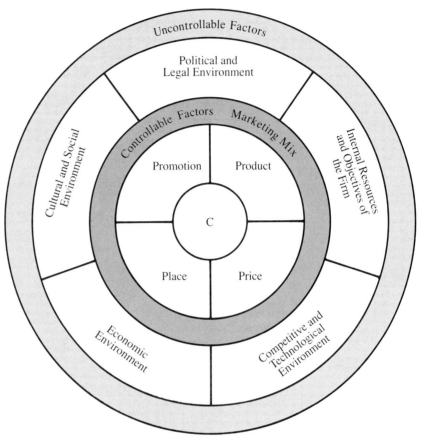

Source: Adapted from E. Jerome McCarthy and William D. Perreault, Jr., *Basic Marketing: A Managerial Approach*, 10th ed. (Homewood, Ill.: Richard D. Irwin, Inc., 1990), p. 48.

Note that this definition indicates that marketing research provides information to the organization for use in at least four areas: (1) the generation of ideas for marketing action, including the definition of marketing problems, (2) the evaluation of marketing ideas, (3) the comparison of performance versus objectives, and (4) the development of general understanding of marketing phenomena and processes. Further, marketing research is involved with all phases of the information-management process, including (1) the specification of what information is needed, (2) the collection and analysis of the information, and (3) the interpretation of that information with respect to the objectives that motivated the study in the first place.

The definition of marketing research implies a role in each of the sectors of Figure 1.1. A periodic survey (Table 1.1) conducted by the American Marketing Association details more specifically how many organizations use marketing research. [7] Although the table is organized somewhat differently from the figure, the relationship between the two is readily apparent. Much research, for example, is done to measure consumer wants and needs. Other research assesses the impact of previous adjustments in the marketing mix or gauges the potential impact of new changes.

Table 1.1   ***Research Activities of 587 Companies***

	Percentage Doing			Percentage Doing
A. Business/Economic and Corporate Research		**D. Distribution**		
1. Industry/market characteristics and trends	83%	1. Plant warehouse location studies		23%
2. Acquisition/diversification studies	53	2. Channel performance studies		29
3. Market share analyses	79	3. Channel coverage studies		26
4. Internal employee studies (morale, communication, etc.)	54	4. Export and international studies		19
		E. Promotion		
B. Pricing		1. Motivation research		37%
1. Cost analysis	60%	2. Media research		57
2. Profit analysis	59	3. Copy research		50
3. Price elasticity	45	4. Advertising effectiveness		65
4. Demand analysis:		5. Competitive advertising studies		47
a. Market potential	74	6. Public image studies		60
b. Sales potential	69	7. Sales force compensation studies		30
c. Sales forecasts	67	8. Sales force quota studies		26
5. Competitive pricing analyses	63	9. Sales force territory structure		31
		10. Studies of premiums, coupons, deals, etc.		36
C. Product				
1. Concept development and testing	68%	**F. Buying Behavior**		
2. Brand name generation and testing	38	1. Brand preference		54%
3. Test marketing	45	2. Brand attitudes		53
4. Product testing of existing products	47	3. Product satisfaction		68
5. Packaging design studies	31	4. Purchase behavior		61
6. Competitive product studies	58	5. Purchase intentions		60
		6. Brand awareness		59
		7. Segmentation studies		60

Source: Thomas C. Kinnear and Ann R. Root, *1988 Survey of Marketing Research*, 1988, p. 43. Reprinted with permission from American Marketing Association, Chicago, IL 60606.

Some research deals directly with the environment, such as studies of legal constraints on advertising and promotion and studies of social values, business policy, and business trends.

Another way of looking at the function of marketing research is to consider how management uses it. Some marketing research is used for planning, some for problem solving, and some for control. When used for planning, it deals largely with determining which marketing opportunities are viable and which are not promising for the firm. Also, when viable opportunities are uncovered, marketing research

Many companies pride themselves on how their products reflect their excellent marketing research.

Source: Courtesy of Fisher-Price.

provides estimates of their size and scope, so that marketing management can better assess the resources needed to develop them. Problem-solving marketing research focuses on the short- or long-term decisions that the firm must make with respect to the elements of the marketing mix. Control-oriented marketing research helps management to isolate trouble spots and to keep abreast of current operations. The

Table 1.2   ***Kinds of Questions Marketing Research Can Help Answer***

I. Planning
   A. What kinds of people buy our products? Where do they live? How much do they earn? How many of them are there?
   B. Are the markets for our products increasing or decreasing? Are there promising markets that we have not yet reached?
   C. Are the channels of distribution for our products changing? Are new types of marketing institutions likely to evolve?

II. Problem Solving
   A. Product
      1. Which of various product designs is likely to be the most successful?
      2. What kind of packaging should we use?
   B. Price
      1. What price should we charge for our products?
      2. As production costs decline, should we lower our prices or try to develop higher-quality products?
   C. Place
      1. Where, and by whom, should our products be sold?
      2. What kinds of incentives should we offer the trade to push our products?
   D. Promotion
      1. How much should we spend on promotion? How should it be allocated to products and to geographic areas?
      2. What combination of media—newspapers, radio, television, magazines—should we use?

III. Control
   A. What is our market share overall? In each geographic area? By each customer type?
   B. Are customers satisfied with our products? How is our record for service? Are there many returns?
   C. How does the public perceive our company? What is our reputation with the trade?

---

kinds of questions marketing research can address with regard to planning, problem solving, and control decisions are listed in Table 1.2. The relationship between each of these questions and a marketing manager's area of responsibility is easy to see.

Who Does Marketing Research?

Marketing research, as a sizable business activity, owes its existence to this country's shift from a production-oriented to a consumption-oriented economy at the end of World War II. However, some marketing research was conducted before the war, and the origins of formal marketing research predate the war by a good number of years.

> More by accident than foresight, N. W. Ayer & Son applied marketing research to marketing and advertising problems. In 1879, in attempting to fit a proposed advertising schedule to the needs of the Nichols-Shepard Company, manufacturers of agricultural machinery, the agency wired state officials and publishers throughout the country requesting information on expected grain production. As a result, the agency was able to construct a crude but formal market survey by states and counties. This attempt to construct a market survey is probably the first real instance of marketing research in the United States.[8]

There were even formal marketing research departments and marketing research firms before World War II.[9] However, marketing research really began to grow when

Marketing research that showed an increasing number of time-squeezed shoppers led Von's groceries to institute a drive-thru grocery window. Shoppers may order any ten items and pick them up three minutes later. In an industry with slim profit margins, consumer-responsive Von's is a profit leader.

Source: © Steve Smith/ONYX.

firms found they could no longer sell all they could produce, but rather had to gauge market needs and produce accordingly. Marketing research was called upon to estimate these needs. As consumer discretion became more important, many firms shifted their orientation to accommodate the new business climate. Marketing began to assume a more dominant role and production a less important one. The marketing concept emerged, and along with it a reorganization of the marketing effort. Many marketing research departments were born in these reorganizations. The growth of these departments was stimulated by a number of factors, including past successes, increased management sophistication, and the data revolution created by the computer. The success of firms with marketing research departments caused still other firms to establish departments.

While the growth in the number of new marketing research departments has slowed recently, the firm that does not have a formal department, or at least a person

Figure 1.2   **Organization for Marketing Research**

	Number Answering	Percentage Having Formal Department	One Person	No One Assigned
Manufacturers of Consumer Products	84	77	18	5
Publishing and Broadcasting	50	78	18	4
Manufacturers of Industrial Products	88	51	33	16
Financial Services	78	82	14	4
Retailing/ Wholesaling	25	72	12	16
Advertising Agencies	29	72	17	11
Health Services	81	42	42	16
All Others	130	55	30	15
All Companies Answering This Question*	565	63	26	11

*Excludes marketing research and consulting firms.
Source: Thomas C. Kinnear and Ann R. Root, *1988 Survey of Marketing Research*, p. 10. Reprinted with permission from American Marketing Association, Chicago, IL 60606.

assigned specifically to the marketing research activity, is now the exception rather than the rule (see Figure 1.2). Marketing research departments are very prevalent among industrial and consumer manufacturing companies, but they also exist in other types of companies. Publishers and broadcasters, for example, do a good deal of research. They attempt to measure the size of the market reached by their message and construct a demographic profile of this audience. These data are then used to sell advertising space or time (Figure 1.3). Also, financial institutions such as banks and brokerage houses do research involving forecasting, measurement of market potentials, determination of market characteristics, market share analyses, sales analyses, location analyses, and product-mix studies.

Much of the research conducted by advertising agencies deals directly with creating the advertisement itself. This may involve testing alternative approaches to the wording or art used in the ad or investigating the effectiveness of various celebrity spokespersons. However, many agencies also do marketing research for their clients to determine the market potential of a proposed new product or the client's market share.

The enterprises included in the "All Others" category shown in Figure 1.2 include public utilities, transportation companies, and trade associations, among

Figure 1.3   *Use of Marketing Research Data by a Magazine Publisher*

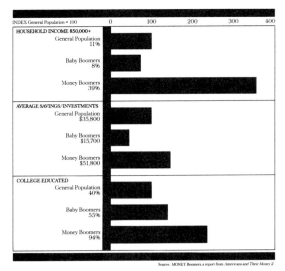

Money Boomers are better boomers.

Are things really booming for the baby boomers? Not really. Because as these charts show, most of America's 25 to 39's barely keep up with the entire U.S. population.

But there is an elite segment of baby boomers who are quite different. And clearly superior.

MONEY magazine's Executive Editor, Landon Jones (author of the definitive book on the baby boom generation, *Great Expectations*), has called them the Super Class. Others have labeled this elusive audience Yuppies, or Super Boomers. By any name, they are the rich topping that has given marketing allure to the plain vanilla of the baby boom.

And it is the members of this segment who are most likely to subscribe to MONEY. Here's how MONEY magazine's boomer-age subscribers stack up against their ordinary contemporaries and the U.S. as a whole.

First, consider a real yardstick of affluence—$50,000+ households. Only 11 per cent of the U.S. population earns that much. And just 8 per cent of baby boomers.

But for MONEY boomers, the figure is a startling 39 per cent.

Next, examine savings and investments. Where the general population controls $35,800, the typical baby boomer has just $15,700. But the MONEY boomers are working with a hefty $51,800.

As you might expect, these disparities in earnings/investments reflect differing levels of education. For though 55 per cent of all boomers are college educated, a whopping 94 percent of MONEY boomers are.

In sum, MONEY attracts a financially mature segment of the baby boomers. To learn more about these extraordinary consumers, please request a copy of *MONEY Boomers*, a report from *Americans and Their Money 2*. Just call: (212) 841-4925, or ask your MONEY representative.

MONEY boomers. For advertisers, these readers are themselves—the rewards of MONEY.

Money®
America's Financial Advisor

Source: © 1986, *Money* Magazine, Time Inc.

others. Public utilities and transportation companies often provide their customers with useful marketing information, particularly statistics dealing with area growth and potential. Trade associations often collect and disseminate operating data gathered from members.

The entire spectrum of marketing research activity also includes specialized marketing research and consulting firms, government agencies, and universities. While most specialized marketing research firms are small, a few are sizable enterprises.[10] Some of these firms provide syndicated research; they collect certain information on a regular basis, which they then sell to interested clients. The syndicated services include operations such as the A. C. Nielsen Company, which provides product-movement data for grocery stores and drug stores, and the National Purchase Diary consumer panel. Such services are distinguished by the fact that their research is not custom designed except in the limited sense that the firm will perform special analyses for a client from the data it regularly collects. Other research firms, though, specialize in custom-designed research. Some of these provide only a field service; they collect data and return the data-collection instruments directly to the research sponsor. Some are limited-service firms, which not only collect the data but also analyze them for the client. And some are full-service research suppliers, which help the client in the design of the research, as well as in collecting and analyzing data.

Government agencies provide much marketing information in the form of published statistics. Indeed, the federal government is the largest producer of marketing facts through its various censuses and other publications.

Much university-sponsored research of interest to marketers is produced by the marketing faculty or by the bureaus of business research found in many schools of business. Faculty research is often reported in marketing journals, while research bureaus often publish monographs on various topics of interest.

Organization of Marketing Research

The organizational form of marketing research depends largely on the size and organizational structure of the individual company. In small firms, where one person often handles all the organization's research needs, there are few organizational questions other than determining to whom the research director shall report. Most often, this will be the sales or marketing manager, although some marketing research managers report directly to the president or the executive vice-president. Larger research units can take a variety of organizational forms, although three types are common.

1. Organization by area of application, such as by product line, by brand, by market segment, or by geographic area.
2. Organization by marketing function performed, such as field sales analysis, advertising research, or product planning.
3. Organization by research technique or approach, such as sales analysis, mathematical and/or statistical analysis, field interviewing, or questionnaire design.

Many firms with very large marketing research departments combine two or more of these organizational structures.

Whether the firm is centralized or decentralized also affects the organization of the marketing research function. With decentralized companies—those in which authority and decision making are spread among a fairly large number of people—each division or operating unit might have its own marketing research department, or a single department in central headquarters might serve all operating divisions, or research departments might exist at both levels. The primary advantages of a corporate-level location are greater coordination and control of corporate research activity, economy, increased capability from an information system perspective, and greater usefulness to corporate management in planning. The primary advantage of a division or group-level location is that it allows research personnel to acquire valuable knowledge about divisional markets, products, practices, and problems. While shifting between the corporate and divisional structures occurs quite frequently, the recent trend is toward a mixed arrangement, in an attempt to secure the advantages of each.

For example, Kodak has a combination centralized/decentralized marketing research function. The research people in the divisions work directly with the managers of those business units. The centralized group is responsible for staying abreast of industry trends and changing technology, since changes here could affect a number of business units. Researchers assigned to corporate marketing research are also responsible for competitive analysis in order to ensure the most objective view. Finally, they serve as a quality-control center for the decentralized research activity, so division-initiated projects are passed before this group for possible changes in method. One benefit of this review is that it develops institutional memory in terms of better ways to approach specific tasks.

Kraft also uses a hybrid organizational structure. It has research groups assigned to each product group (e.g., grocery, refrigerated, frozen, and food-service) and a corporate group of researchers as well. Some of the advantages Kraft realizes from the centralized group are the consistent application of research methodology, opportunities to develop key learnings across departments and customer bases, the potential to minimize duplication (spending research funds to address the same consumer issue by two different research groups), and an ability to produce actionable, cost-effective research across all of the firm's customer bases.[11]

The organization of the marketing research function thus depends on the relative importance of the function within the firm and on the scale and complexity of the research activities to be undertaken. Moreover, the organizational form is subject to changes from time to time, some arising from changes within the firm. As the firm's size and market position change, the emphasis and organization of the marketing research function must also change, so that it is continually tailored to suit the firm's information needs. Research Window 1.1 describes the emphasis on and organization of the research function at the Quaker Oats Company.

Data indicate that large firms are likely to spend a larger proportion of the marketing budget on research than are small firms. Among firms with sales of $25 million and over, approximately $3\frac{1}{2}$ percent of the average marketing budget is spent on research, while among smaller firms, only about $1\frac{1}{2}$ percent of the average marketing budget is spent on research.[12] As Figure 1.4 indicates, a few firms spend a very large proportion of their total marketing budget on research.

One important change that has been occurring in marketing research in recent years is the transition from a specific-problem perspective to a total-marketing-intelligence perspective. This perspective is usually called a marketing information system (MIS) or decision support system (DSS). The emphasis in these systems is on diagnosing the information needs of each of the marketing decision makers so that they have the kinds of information they need, when they need it, to make the kinds of decisions they must make. We will discuss marketing intelligence systems in the next chapter.

Job Opportunities in Marketing Research

It is hard to generalize about the kinds of tasks a marketing researcher might perform. As previously suggested, the tasks will depend upon the type, size, and organizational structure of the firm with which the individual is employed. They will also depend upon whether the person works for a research supplier or for a consumer of research information.

Research Window 1.1
Marketing Research—On the Job at Quaker Oats

Most students beginning a course in marketing research have only a fuzzy idea of what a researcher actually does on the job or how that position fits with the rest of an organization. Obviously, the details of the position differ from one firm to another, but let us examine the place of the researcher in one giant consumer goods organization that has a healthy respect for what marketing research can offer—the Quaker Oats Company. This company willingly admits that its officers rarely make critical decisions without input from the marketing research department. Its philosophy regarding marketing research follows:

Marketing research exists at Quaker Oats for one reason: to recommend data-based courses of action that will improve corporate profits. More specifically, the stated mission of the Marketing Information Department is to contribute to Quaker's long-term grocery products' sales and profits through the collection and analysis of marketing information. This data—whether it is from survey research or the analysis of business problems—is used by the researcher to form points of view about likely consumer behavior to alternative marketing actions being considered by the company.

The importance of the marketing research function is recognized throughout the organization and primarily in the marketing area. In fact, according to the vice-president of marketing, "Quaker's Marketing Research Department is significantly involved in and makes substantial contributions toward identifying and addressing major marketing issues faced by Brand Management."

Quaker is one of the few companies to have its marketing research department led by a vice-president—another clear indication of the importance of the function to the company. Reporting to the vice-president are seven functional units designed to provide facilities for tracking existing markets, investigating new areas, and developing and executing consumer research. These reporting functions include three divisional research units, as well as marketing information systems, sales research, business development, and a project-administration function.

The typical entry-level position within the Marketing Information Department is that of a research analyst. The research analyst receives on-the-job training from the research supervisor or manager while learning the business of his or her assigned brand. Once the analyst has demonstrated a knowledge of the business and the ability to operate independently, the usual progression of positions in terms of responsibility and compensation is as follows: senior research analyst, research supervisor, research manager, group research manager, and director.

A position in marketing research at Quaker requires a high level of research and analytical ability and experience with survey research and statistical analysis (usually obtained through graduate-level studies or equivalent work experience). Good human relations and communications skills are also critical in dealing with professionals in other departments, as well as in ensuring that one's recommendations are included in marketing plans. Finally, a research analyst must be the type of person who will develop a sense of personal responsibility for the sales progress of assigned brands, even though final responsibility for a brand's success rests with product management.

Source: "Marketing Research, a Career for You . . . " The Quaker Oats Company, Chicago, IL.

The responsibilities of a marketing researcher could range from the simple tabulation of questionnaire responses to the management of a large research department. Research Window 1.2, for example, lists some common job titles and the functions typically performed by occupants of these positions. Figure 1.5 illustrates what they are likely to be paid and how that compares with salaries of those in similar positions in 1983.

Figure 1.4   **Share of Marketing Budgets Allocated to Research**

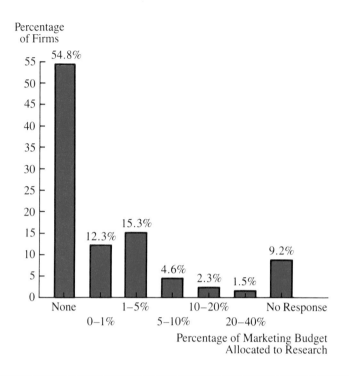

Source: Developed from data in A. Parasuraman, "Research's Place in the Marketing Budget," *Business Horizons*, 26 (March–April 1983), pp. 25–29.

As these job descriptions reveal, there are opportunities in marketing research for people with a variety of skills. There is room for technical specialists, such as statisticians, as well as for research generalists, whose skills are relevant to managing the people and resources needed for a research project rather than the mathematical detail any study may involve. The skills required to perform each job satisfactorily will, of course, vary.

In consumer-goods companies, the typical entry-level position is research analyst, usually for a specific brand. While learning the characteristics and details of the industry, the analyst will receive on-the-job training from a research manager. The usual career path for an analyst is to advance to senior analyst, then research supervisor, and on to research manager for a specific brand. At that time the researcher's responsibilities often broaden to include a group of brands.

Among research suppliers, the typical entry-level position is research trainee, a position in which the person will be exposed to the types of studies in which the supplier specializes and to the procedures required for completing them. Quite often, trainees will spend some time actually conducting interviews, coding completed data-collection forms, or possibly even assisting with the analysis. The goal is to expose trainees to the processes the firm follows so that when they become account representatives, they will be familiar enough with the firm's capabilities to respond intelligently to clients' needs for research information.

The requirements for entering the marketing research field include human-relation, communication, conceptual, and analytical skills. Marketing researchers

Research Window 1.2
Marketing Research Job Titles and Responsibilities

1. **Research Director/Vice-President of Marketing Research:** This is the senior position in research. The director is responsible for the entire research program of the company. Accepts assignments from superiors or from clients or may, on own initiative, develop and propose research undertakings to company executives. Employs personnel and exercises general supervision of research department. Presents research findings to clients or to company executives.

2. **Assistant Director of Research:** This position usually represents a defined "second in command," a senior staff member having responsibilities above those of other staff members.

3. **Statistician/Data Processing Specialist:** Duties are usually those of an expert consultant on theory and application of statistical technique to specific research problems. Usually responsible for experimental design and data processing.

4. **Senior Analyst:** Usually found in larger research departments. Participates with superior in initial planning of research projects and directs execution of projects assigned. Operates with minimum supervision. Prepares or works with analysts in preparing questionnaires. Selects research techniques, makes analyses, and writes final report. Budgetary control over projects and primary responsibility for meeting time schedules rest with the senior analyst.

5. **Analyst:** The analyst usually handles the bulk of the work required for execution of research projects. Often works under senior analyst's supervision. The analyst assists in preparation of questionnaires, pretests them, and makes preliminary analyses of results. Most library research or work with company data is handled by the analyst.

6. **Junior Analyst:** Working under rather close supervision, junior analysts handle routine assignments. Editing and coding of questionnaires, statistical calculations above the clerical level, and simpler forms of library research are among the duties. A large portion of the junior analyst's time is spent on tasks assigned by superiors.

7. **Librarians:** The librarian builds and maintains a library of reference sources adequate to the needs of the research department.

8. **Clerical Supervisor:** In larger departments, the central handling and processing of statistical data are the responsibility of one or more clerical supervisors. Duties include work scheduling and responsibility for accuracy.

9. **Field Work Director:** Usually only larger departments have a field work director, who hires, trains, and supervises field interviewers.

10. **Full-Time Interviewer:** The interviewer conducts personal interviews and works under direct supervision of the field work director. Few companies employ full-time interviewers.

11. **Tabulating and Clerical Help:** The routine, day-to-day work of the department is performed by these individuals.

Source: Thomas C. Kinnear and Ann R. Root, *1988 Survey of Marketing Research*, p. 4 of the appendix. Reprinted with permission from American Marketing Association, Chicago, IL 60606.

need to be able to interact effectively with others, for they rarely, if ever, work in isolation. They need to be good communicators, both orally and with the written word. They need to understand business in general and marketing processes in particular. When dealing with brand, advertising, sales, or other types of managers, they need to have some understanding of the issues with which these managers contend and the types of mental models the managers use to make sense of situations. Marketing researchers also should have some basic numerical and statistical skills, or at least they should have the capacity to develop those skills. They must be comfortable with numbers and with the techniques of marketing research. Their growth as professionals and their advancement within their organization will depend

Figure 1.5   ***Mean Compensation for All Marketing Research Positions***

Position	Number of Positions		Compared with 1983 Mean ($000)	Percent Change
Directors	314	$61,300	51.0	+20%
Assistant Directors	58	$50,700	44.7	+13
Senior Analysts	185	$40,300	34.0	+19
Statisticians	56	$45,400	30.7	+48
Analysts	175	$31,100	25.1	+24
Field Work Directors	10	$32,300	23.5	+37
Librarians	25	$31,200	20.8	+33
Junior Analysts	94	$24,900	18.8	+32
Clerical Supervisors	19	$22,600	16.8	+35
Full-Time Interviewers	8	$17,000	13.1	+30
Tabulating and Clerical Help	124	$19,700	14.0	+41
Total Number of Positions	**1,068**			

Source: Thomas C. Kinnear and Ann R. Root, *1988 Survey of Marketing Research*, p. 62. Reprinted with permission from American Marketing Association, Chicago, IL 60606.

upon their use of these skills and their acquiring other technical, management, and financial skills.

Successful marketing researchers tend to be proactive rather than reactive; that is, they tend to identify and lead the direction in which the individual studies and overall programs go rather than simply respond to the explicit requests for information given them. Successful marketing researchers realize that marketing research is conducted for only one reason—to help make better marketing decisions. Thus, they are comfortable in the role of staff person making recommendations to others rather than having responsibility for the decisions themselves.

The American Marketing Association's skills matrix for marketing researchers (Table 1.3), which is used to structure the association's professional development program, provides a useful overview of the full set of skills needed for a career in marketing research. As the matrix indicates, general managerial and financial skills become more important as a person moves up in the research department.

An increasingly common career path for those working in divisionalized structures is a switch from research to product or brand management. One advantage these people possess is that after working so intimately with marketing intelligence,

Table 1.3   **Skills Needed by Marketing Researchers**

	Entry/Junior Level (Less than 3 years' experience)	Mid-Level (3–7 years' experience)	Senior Level (More than 7 years' experience)
Technical Skills			
Computer literacy	*	*	*
Numerical skills	*	*	*
Sample design	*	*	*
Statistical analysis	*	*	*
Data base management		*	*
Model building		*	*
Project management		*	*
Research knowledge		*	*
System design		*	*
Marketing processes			*
Project conceptualization			*
Managerial Skills			
Communicating	*	*	*
Statistical analysis	*	*	*
Reporting	*	*	*
Coordinating projects	*	*	*
Coordinating people		*	*
Motivating		*	*
Defining tasks		*	*
Training/development		*	*
Planning/strategy			*
Financial administration			*

Source: *The American Marketing Association's Professional Development Program* (Chicago: American Marketing Association, 1988), p. 9.

they often know more about the customers, the industry, and the competitors than anyone in the company with the same years of experience. Note, though, that researchers desiring such a switch need more substantive knowledge about marketing phenomena and greater business acumen in general than those planning on staying in marketing research.

Back to the Case

Julie Sullivan took a deep breath and looked at the 60 or so undergraduates who were looking up expectantly at her. She wished she'd had more time to prepare for her Career Night speech, but yesterday the data had come in on Crunchy Chex and she'd been up half the night working on a research proposal for the PK Perfumes account. All she had on the lectern in front of her were a few notes she'd jotted down between phone calls two days before.

"At some point in every business enterprise," she began, "questions are asked to which there are no obvious answers. 'Would people buy more of our product if we made it cheaper? Why does our product sell better in the Southwest versus the Northeast? If we distribute a 25-cents-off coupon for our product, will we generate enough sales to make the discount pay?' The list of questions is limitless. The role of marketing research is to answer them.

"Marketing research takes many forms—from the guy who owns the corner diner and asks his friends to taste a new dish he's thinking of putting on the menu to the researchers who try to discover the emotional associations consumers have with household products.

"It is done in every possible setting. I work in an advertising agency, and I'm involved in a dozen accounts. Right now I'm working on a well-established cereal brand, trying to figure out what's causing a slump in its sales; I'm planning a research study to evaluate the effectiveness of an advertising campaign for a new line of women's fragrances; and I'm trying to find the best way to conduct taste tests for a new type of baby food. In my job I use my technical research skills, I use my

communication skills, and in some situations, I fall back on what I learned in the psychology courses I took in college.

"While I have to be an instant expert on any product that comes my way, I have a friend who for the last three years has worked solely on spaghetti sauce. She works for a large consumer foods conglomerate, and three years ago they were looking for ideas for a new product. Her team identified some new trends in how people were eating and shopping. People wanted food that was quick to prepare, preferably in the microwave, yet their tastes were becoming more sophisticated and they were becoming much more health conscious. The team developed a new line of fresh pasta sauces that can go straight from the dairy case into the microwave.

"Another friend of mine works for a big marketing research supplier. He was a real computer wizard in school, and he loves being able to quantify complex human behavior. He designs research studies and oversees their execution for some of the biggest companies in the United States. And he says that even though he works in an incredibly technical and analytical environment, he is

constantly reminded of how important his writing and communication skills are.

"I have another friend who is the marketing research manager for one of the biggest soft drink brands in the country. Behind his desk, instead of a painting, there hangs a sign. It reads, 'I am the consumer.' He says he wants every person who comes into his office to remember that his job is to give voice to what the people who buy the product think. Incidentally, he says, it also doesn't hurt to be reminded of the most satisfying aspect of his work every time he comes into his own office.

"Although all of us are in marketing research, we have dissimilar skills. We received different training. We do different things. If you asked us to describe what our typical day at the office is like, you would get four completely different descriptions. But all of us, when you asked us what we do, would eventually say the same thing. We are the voice of the consumer in corporate America."

Sullivan smiled at the warm applause when she had finished speaking. Then she opened up the floor for questions.

Summary

Learning Objective 1: Define marketing research.

Marketing research is the function that links the consumer to the marketer through information. The information is used to identify and define marketing problems; generate, refine, and evaluate marketing actions; monitor marketing performance; and improve understanding of marketing as a process.

Learning Objective 2: Cite the two factors that are most responsible for how the research function is organized in any given firm.

The two factors that are most significant in determining the organization of a firm's research function are the firm's size and the degree of centralization or decentralization of its operations.

Learning Objective 3: List some of the skills that are important for careers in marketing research.

Most positions in marketing research require analytical, communication, and human-relation skills. In addition, marketing researchers must be comfortable working with numbers and statistical techniques, and they must be familiar with a great variety of marketing research methods.

Discussion Questions, Problems, and Projects

1. Indicate whether marketing research is relevant to each of the following organizations and, if so, how each might use it.
   (a) Pepsico, Inc.
   (b) Your university
   (c) The Chase Manhattan Bank
   (d) The American Cancer Society
   (e) A small dry cleaner
2. Specify some useful sources of marketing research information for the following situation.

   Ethan Moore has worked for several years as the lead chef in a restaurant specializing in ethnic cuisine. Dissatisfied with his income, he has decided to start his own business. Based on his experiences in the restaurant, he recognizes a need for a local wholesale distributor specializing in hard-to-find ethnic foodstuffs. He envisions starting a firm that will handle items commonly used in Oriental and African recipes.

   With the help of a local accountant, Moore prepared a financial proposal that revealed the need for $150,000 in start-up capital for Ethan's Ethnic Foods. The proposal was presented to a local bank for review by their commercial loan committee, and Moore subsequently received the following letter from the bank:

   Mr. Moore:
   We have received and considered your request for start-up financing for your proposed business. While the basic idea seems sound, we find that your sales projections are based solely on your own experience and do not include any hard documentation concerning the market potential for the products you propose to carry. Until such information is made available for our consideration, we have no choice but to reject your loan application.

   Bitten hard by the entrepreneurial bug, Moore views this rejection as a minor setback. Given his extremely limited financial resources, where and how might he obtain the needed information? (Hint: First determine what types of information would be useful.)
3. What do the following two research situations have in common?
   Situation I: The Bugs-Away Company marketed successful insect repellents. The products were effective and leaders in the market. They were available in blue aerosol cans with red caps. The instructions, in addition to a warning to keep the product away from children, were clearly specified on the container. Most of the company's range of products were also produced in similar containers by competitors. The CEO was worried because of declining sales and shrinking profit margins. Another issue that perturbed him was that companies such as his were being severely criticized by government and consumer groups for their use of aerosol cans. The CEO contacted the company's advertising agency and requested that it do the necessary research to find out what was happening.
   Situation II: In early 1990 the directors of Adams University were considering an expansion of the business school due to increasing enrollments over the past ten years. Their plans included constructing a new wing, hiring five new faculty members, and increasing the number of scholarships from 100 to 120. The funding for this ambitious project was to be provided by some private sources, internally generated funds, and the state and federal governments. A prior research study (completed in 1981), using a sophisticated forecasting methodology, indicated that student enrollment would peak in 1989. Another study, conducted in November 1983,

indicated universities could expect gradual declining enrollments during the mid-1990s. The directors were concerned about the results of the later study and the talk it stimulated about budget cuts by the government. A decision was made to conduct a third and final study to determine likely student enrollment.

4. What do the following two research situations have in common?

Situation I: The sales manager of Al-Can, an aluminum can manufacturing company, was delighted with the increase in sales over the past few months. He was wondering whether the company's new cans, which would be on the market in two months, should be priced higher than the traditional products. He confidently commented to the vice-president of marketing, "Nobody in the market is selling aluminum cans with screw-on tops. We can get a small portion of the market and yet make substantial profits." The product manager disagreed with this strategy. In fact, she was opposed to marketing these new cans. The cans might present problems in preserving the contents. She thought to herself, "Aluminum cans are recycled, so nobody is going to keep them as containers." There was little she could do formally because these cans were the president's own idea. She strongly recommended to the vice-president of marketing that the cans should be priced in line with the other products. The vice-president thought a marketing research study would resolve this issue.

Situation II: A large toy manufacturer was in the process of developing a tool kit for children in the five-to-ten-year age-group. The tool kit included a small saw, screwdriver, hammer, chisel, and drill. This tool kit was different from the competitors', as it included an instruction manual with "101 things to do." The product manager was concerned about the safety of the kit and recommended the inclusion of a separate booklet for parents. The sales manager recommended that the tool kit be made available in a small case, as this would increase its marketability. The advertising manager recommended that a special promotional campaign be launched in order to distinguish it from the competitors' products. The vice-president thought that all the recommendations were worthwhile but that the costs would increase drastically. He consulted the market research manager, who further recommended that a study be conducted.

5. List the key attributes that an individual occupying the following positions must possess. Why are these attributes essential?
   (a) Senior analyst
   (b) Full-time interviewer
   (c) Research director

6. Suppose that you have decided to pursue a career in the field of marketing research. In general, what types of courses should you take in order to help yourself achieve your goal? Why? What types of part-time jobs and/or volunteer work would look good on your resume? Why?

Endnotes

1. John Koten, "You Aren't Paranoid If You Feel Someone Eyes You Constantly," *The Wall Street Journal* (March 29, 1985), pp. 1 and 21. See also "Credit Success of Kodak Disc Camera to Research," *Marketing News*, 17 (January 21, 1983), pp. 8 and 9.

2. Brian Dumaine, "Corporate Spies Snoop to Conquer," *Fortune*, 118 (November 7, 1988), pp. 66–69, 72, 76.

3. Koten, "You Aren't Paranoid," pp. 1 and 21.

4. "Chrysler Tries to Sharpen Its Brand Identity," *Business Week* (November 21, 1983), p. 104.

5. E. Jerome McCarthy and William D. Perreault, Jr., *Basic Marketing: A Managerial Approach*, 10th ed. (Homewood, Ill.: Richard D. Irwin, 1990).

6. Peter Bennett, ed., *Glossary of Marketing Terms* (Chicago: American Marketing Association, 1988), pp. 117–118.

7. Thomas C. Kinnear and Ann R. Root, *1988 Survey of Marketing Research* (Chicago: American Marketing Association, 1988). This survey is the eighth in a series begun in 1947. This latest survey was sent to 2,401 marketing research executives, and the tabulation in Table 1.1 is based on the returns from the 630 usable questionnaires.

8. Lawrence C. Lockley, "History and Development of Marketing Research," Section 1, p. 4, in Robert Ferber, ed., *Handbook of Marketing Research*. Copyright © 1974 by McGraw-Hill, 1974. Used with permission of McGraw-Hill Book Company.

9. The Curtis Publishing Company is generally conceded to have formed the first formal marketing research department with the appointment of Charles Parlin as manager of the Commercial Research Division of the Advertising Department in 1911, while the A. C. Nielsen Company, the largest marketing research firm in

the world, began operation in 1934. For a detailed treatment of the development of marketing research, see Robert Bartels, *The Development of Marketing Thought* (Homewood, Ill.: Richard D. Irwin, 1962), pp. 106–124, or Jack J. Honomichl, *Marketing Research People: Their Behind-the-Scenes Stories* (Chicago: Crain Books, 1984), especially Part II on pages 95–184, which deals with the evolution and status of the marketing research industry.

10. For a list of the largest marketing research firms, see Jack J. Honomichl, "Leading 50 Researchers Top $2.6 Billion," *Advertising Age*, 60 (June 5, 1989), pp. S1–S20.

11. Larry Stanek, "Keeping Focused on the Consumer While Managing Tons of Information," in *Presentations from the 9th Annual Marketing Research Conference* (Chicago: American Marketing Association, 1988), pp. 62–70.

12. A. Parasuraman, "Research's Place in the Marketing Budget," *Business Horizons*, 26 (March–April 1983), pp. 25–29.

Suggested Additional Readings

For a discussion of what is happening in the world of marketing research, see

Jack J. Honomichl, "Leading 50 Researchers Top $2.6 Billion," *Advertising Age*, 60 (June 5, 1989), pp. S1–S20.

Thomas C. Kinnear and Ann R. Root, *1988 Survey of Marketing Research* (Chicago: American Marketing Association, 1988).

For a historical perspective on the evolution of the marketing research industry, see

Jack J. Honomichl, *Marketing Research People: Their Behind-the-Scenes Stories* (Chicago: Crain Books, 1984).

For discussion of the careers available in marketing research, see

John R. Blair, "Marketing Research Offers Highly Visible, Action-Oriented Career with Growth Potential," *Student Edition Marketing News*, 2 (March 1984), pp. 1 and 3.

Lawrence Gibson, "Confused New Marketing Researchers Soon Feel Confidence, Then Challenge," *Student Edition Marketing News*, 2 (March 1984), pp. 1 and 3.

Neil Holbert, *Careers in Marketing* (Chicago: American Marketing Association, 1976), pp. 18–23.

2

Gathering Marketing Intelligence

Learning Objectives

Upon completing this chapter, you should be able to

1. Explain the difference between a project emphasis in research and a marketing information system (MIS) or decision support system (DSS) emphasis.

2. Define what is meant by an MIS.

3. Cite some of the problems inherent in an MIS.

4. Define what is meant by a DSS.

5. Specify what feature most clearly differentiates a DSS from an MIS.

Case in Marketing Research

Bruce Watley punched up the sales figures for Allied Food's Crispy Chip division. He instructed the computer to break down the data by region and then called up the figures for the San Antonio/Houston area. It was the third time that day he'd looked at them. Sales of Crispy Chip products were definitely slumping in that geographical region. All the snack products were being affected, but the tortilla chips seemed hardest hit. A check of the entire southwestern part of the country showed that so far the slump was limited to south Texas, but that there definitely was a problem. Why, though? And why only in that area?

Two years earlier, when Watley had first joined Allied, it might have taken him three months just to spot the problem. But Allied had recently put into place a sophisticated decision support system (DSS). On a daily basis, Allied's DSS gathered sales data from supermarket scanners na-tionwide, analyzed the data for important clues and local trends, and flagged executives about problems and opportunities in any of Allied's markets. The DSS was designed to allow executives like Watley to immediately take advantage of sales data from electronic scanners.

Scanners had been collecting data at supermarket checkout counters for almost a decade. At first, however, there had been no computer software to organize the information for marketing managers. When Watley first joined Allied he had had access to monthly scanner data, but it had been unwieldy to use. The data he would have needed to investigate the south Texas problem would have had to be delivered to his office by a forklift.

Software advances now made it possible for DSS users like Watley to track how many units of a particular product were purchased in a given store in a given week. And that was just the sort of data that Watley was going to take a hard look at for the whole of south Texas. The south Texas mystery would be a good test of whether the DSS was worth the big bucks Allied had paid for it, Watley thought.

Discussion Issues

1. If you were Watley, what types of information would you look for that might help explain the poor performance of Crispy Chip products in south Texas?

2. If you were the brand manager for Crispy Chips, what advantages do you think a tool like DSS would give you?

3. What are the relative advantages and disadvantages of using a DSS versus a traditional marketing research study to investigate the sales slump in south Texas?

It was suggested in the last chapter that the fundamental purpose of marketing research is to assist marketing managers with the decisions they must make within any of the domains of their responsibility. As directors of firms' marketing activities, marketing managers have an urgent need for information, or marketing intelligence. They might need to know about the changes that can be expected in customer purchasing patterns, the types of marketing institutions that might evolve, which of several alternative product designs might be the most successful, the shape of the firm's demand curve, or any of a number of other issues that could affect the way they plan, solve problems, or evaluate and control the marketing effort. We suggested that marketing research is traditionally responsible for this intelligence function. As the formal link with the environment, marketing research generates, transmits, and interprets feedback originating in the environment regarding the success of the firm's marketing plans and the strategies and tactics employed in implementing those plans.

This book takes a project approach to providing marketing intelligence. It discusses the steps that need to be executed to answer a specific problem faced by a marketing manager. An overview of the steps is provided in the next chapter, and the remainder of the book discusses each one in detail. It needs to be pointed out beforehand, though, that the project approach to research emphasized in this book is just one of the ways by which marketing intelligence is provided. Two other ways are through marketing information systems (MIS) and through decision support systems (DSS). The purpose of this chapter is to provide some appreciation for the differences between the project approach and these alternative schemes for providing marketing intelligence. The first section in this chapter highlights the fundamental difference between a project emphasis to research and the alternative approaches. The second section discusses the essential nature of marketing information systems; and the third section, decision support systems. This is followed by a discussion of the complementary roles of projects and information systems in providing marketing intelligence.

Fundamental Difference

The difference in perspective between a project emphasis to research and an information system emphasis was highlighted years ago in a useful analogy comparing a flash bulb and a candle.

> The difference between marketing research and marketing intelligence is like the difference between a flash bulb and a candle. Let's say you are dancing in the dark. Every 90 seconds you are allowed to set off a flash bulb. You can use those brief intervals of intense light to chart a course, but remember everybody is moving, too. Hopefully, they'll accommodate themselves roughly to your predictions. You might get bumped and you may stumble every so often, but you can dance along.
>
> On the other hand, you can light a candle. It doesn't yield as much light but it's a steady light. You are continually aware of the movements of other bodies. You can adjust your own course to the courses of others. The intelligence system is a kind of candle. It's no great flash on the immediate state of things, but it provides continuous light as situations shift and change.[1]

Historically, one of the problems of the project emphasis has been its nonrecurring nature. Often projects are devised in times of crises and carried out with urgency, and this has led to an emphasis on data collection and analysis instead of the development of pertinent information on a regular basis. One suggestion for closing the gap is to think of management in terms of an ongoing process of decision making that requires a flow of regular inputs rather than in terms of waiting for crisis situations to arise.

Marketing Information Systems

Marketing information system (MIS) A set of procedures and methods for the regular, planned collection, analysis, and presentation of information for use in making marketing decisions.

The earliest attempts at providing a steady flow of information inputs (i.e., candlelight) focused on **marketing information systems (MIS),** which were defined as "a set of procedures and methods for the regular, planned collection, analysis, and presentation of information for use in making marketing decisions."[2] The key word in the definition is *regular*, since the emphasis in an MIS is to produce information on a recurring basis rather than on the basis of one-time research studies.

The thrust in designing an MIS is a detailed analysis of each decision maker who might use the system, in order to secure an accurate, objective assessment of each person's decision-making responsibilities, capabilities, and style.

An MIS analysis focuses on determining the types of decisions each decision maker is called upon to make and the types of information each person needs to make those decisions. It looks at the information the individual receives on a regular basis and the special studies that are periodically needed. And it asks decision makers what improvements they would like to see in the current information system, both in the types of information they receive and in the form in which they receive it.

Given these information specifications, MIS designers then attempt to specify, get approval for, and subsequently generate a series of reports that would go to the various decision makers.[3] Research Window 2.1, for example, shows the sales analysis reports and sales expense and margin reports developed for an information system for a consumer food products company for which the author served as consultant. As might be obvious from Research Window 2.1, the purpose and form of each report typically meant designing it so that it might serve a number of managers with similar job titles. System design people spent a lot of time working with individual decision makers to develop good report formats and efficient systems for extracting and combining information from the various data banks, a typical occurrence when designing MIS's. It is not unusual to have separate data banks for general sales data, market data, product data, sales representative data, and consumer data in an MIS.[4]

While they might not be obvious from Research Window 2.1, several things had to be done to develop this information system. First, the decision makers affected by the planned system had to be identified. Then their information needs had to be determined, both with respect to the type of information each person needed and with respect to the form in which they could best use it. It was then necessary to specify the data that would be input to the system, how the data could be secured, how they would be stored, how the data in separate data banks would be accessed and combined, and what the report formats would look like. Only after these analyses and design steps were completed could the system be constructed, which was essentially a programming task. Programmers wrote and documented programs that made data retrieval as efficient as possible with respect to the use of computer time and memory. When all the procedures were debugged and the system was operating correctly, it was put on-line. Once on-line, any authorized manager could ask for any of the previously defined reports. In the earliest days of MIS, these requests would have had to go through the computer or information system department, which would issue a hard copy, or printed report. As the system evolved, managers at the company could access reports directly through computer terminals sitting on their desks.

Research Window 2.1
Sales Analysis and Sales Expense and Margin Reports
in a Consumer Food Products Company

Report Name	Purpose	Frequency	Distribution*
A. Sales Analysis Reports			
Region	To provide sales information in units and dollars for each sales office or center in the region as well as a regional total	Monthly	One copy of applicable portions to each regional manager
Sales Office or Center	To provide sales information in units and dollars for each district manager assigned to a sales office	Monthly	One copy of applicable portions to each sales office or center manager
District	To provide sales information in units and dollars for each account supervisor and retail salesperson reporting to the district manager	Monthly	One copy of applicable portions to each district manager
Salesperson Summary	To provide sales information in units and dollars for each customer on whom the salesperson calls	Monthly	One copy of applicable portions to each salesperson
Salesperson Customer/Product	To provide sales information in units and dollars for each product for each customer on whom the salesperson calls	Monthly	One copy of applicable portions to each salesperson
Salesperson/Product	To provide sales information in units and dollars for each product the salesperson sells	Quarterly	One copy of applicable portions to each salesperson

*To understand the report distribution, it is useful to know that salespeople were assigned accounts in sales districts. Salespeople were assigned one or, at most, a couple of large accounts and were responsible for all the grocery stores, regardless of geography, affiliated with these large accounts, or they were assigned a geographic territory and were responsible for all the stores within that territory. All sales districts were assigned to sales offices or sales centers. The centers were, in turn, organized into regions.

Decision Support Systems

When they were first proposed, MISs were held up as an information panacea. The reality, however, often fell short of the promise. The primary reasons are as much behavioral as they are technical. People tend to resist change, and with an MIS the changes are often substantial. Also many decision makers are reluctant to disclose to others what factors they use and how they combine these factors when making a decision about a particular issue, and without such disclosure it is next to impossible to design reports that will give them the information they need in the form they need

Report Name	Purpose	Frequency	Distribution*
Region/Product	To provide sales information in units and dollars for each product sold within the region. Similar reports would be available by sales office and by district.	Monthly	No general distribution; used for special sales analysis when needed
Region/ Customer Class	To provide sales information in units and dollars for each class of customer located in the region. Similar reports would be available by sales office and by district.	Monthly	No general distribution; used for special sales analysis when needed
B. Sales Expense and Margin Reports			
Salesperson Compensation and Expense Report	To provide a listing of salesperson compensation and expenses by district	Monthly	District managers
Salesperson Sales Expense Report	To provide comparative information regarding the ability of the salespeople to manage their expenses	Monthly	District managers
Salesperson Margin Report	To highlight the contribution to profit being made by the various salespeople	Monthly	District managers
Sales Office and Center Margin Report	To highlight the profitability of the various districts within a sales office or center	Monthly	Center managers
Region Margin Report	To highlight the profitability of the various centers within a region	Monthly	Regional managers

it. Even when managers are willing to disclose their decision-making calculus and information needs, there are problems.

Different managers typically emphasize different things and, consequently, have different data needs. There are very few report formats that are optimal for different users. Either the developers have to design "compromise" reports that are satisfactory for a number of users, although not ideal for any single user, or they have to engage in the laborious task of programming to meet each user's needs, one at a time. Sometimes top management provides less than enthusiastic support for the changes that necessarily accompany an MIS, a condition that seems to be particularly common among the more unsuccessful attempts to develop MISs. Equally troublesome, though, have been the problems associated with underestimating the costs and time required to establish such systems, caused by underestimating the size of the task, changes in organizational structure, key personnel, and electronic data-processing systems they require. By the time these systems can be developed, the personnel for which they are designed often have different responsibilities or the economic and competitive environments around which they are designed have changed. Thus, they are often obsolete soon after being put on-line, meaning that the whole process of analysis, design, development, and implementation has to be repeated anew.

Another fundamental problem with MISs is that the systems do not lend themselves to the solution of ill-structured problems, which are the most common kind of problems managers face. The notion of ill-structured problems can be understood through the description of decision making as a process involving three stages: intelligence, design, and choice.[5]

> Intelligence refers to the gathering of information from the decision-making system's environment and exploring that information in an effort to recognize the existence of problems. Design refers to the clarification of a problem, to the creation of potential solutions to the problem, and to the assessment of a potential solution's feasibility. Finally, the choice stage involves the act of choosing one of the feasible solutions and investigating the implementation of that solution. . . . . If a problem encountered in decision making cannot be fully clarified and if the exploration of potential solutions cannot be completed before a choice must be made, then the problem is said to be ill-structured. Otherwise, the problem is well-structured and can (in principle, at least) be programmed.[6]

Many of the activities performed by managers cannot be programmed, nor can they be performed routinely or delegated, because they involve personal choices. Since a manager's decision making is often ad hoc and addressed to unexpected choices, standardized reporting systems lack the necessary scope and flexibility to be useful. Nor can managers, even if they are willing to, specify in advance what they want from programmers and model builders, because decision making and planning are often exploratory. As decision makers and their staffs learn more about a problem, their information needs and methods of analysis evolve. Further, decision making often involves exceptions and qualitative issues that are not easily programmed.

As these problems with MISs became more apparent, the emphasis in regularly supplied marketing intelligence changed from the production of preformatted batch reports to a **decision support system (DSS)**, which has been defined as "a coordinated collection of data, systems, tools, and techniques with supporting software and hardware, by which an organization gathers and interprets relevant information from business and environment and turns it into a basis for marketing action."[7]

A DSS concentrates on the design of data systems, model systems, and dialog systems that can be used interactively by managers. (See Figure 2.1.)[8]

Data Systems

The **data system** in a DSS includes the processes used to capture and the methods used to store data coming from marketing, finance, and manufacturing, as well as information coming from any number of external or internal sources. The typical data system has modules containing customer information, general economic and demographic information, competitor information, and industry information, including market trends.

Decision support system (DSS) A coordinated collection of data, systems tools, and techniques with supporting software and hardware, by which an organization gathers and interprets relevant information from business and environment and turns it into a basis for marketing action.

Data system The part of a decision support system that includes the processes used to capture and the methods used to store data coming from a number of external and internal sources.

Figure 2.1   ***Components of a Decision Support System***

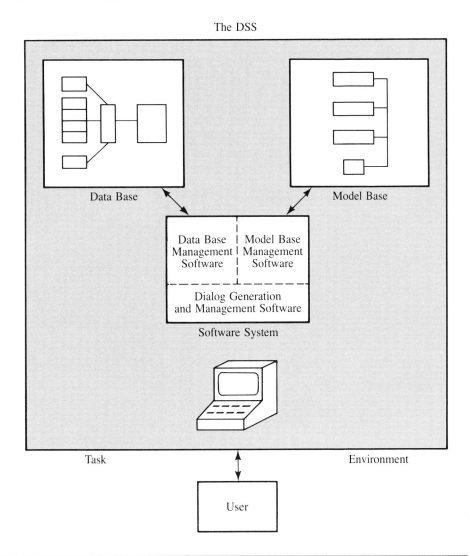

Source: Adapted from Ralph H. Sprague, Jr., and Eric D. Carlson, *Building Effective Decision Support Systems* (Englewood Cliffs, N.J.: Prentice-Hall, 1982), p. 29.

One of the significant trends in the development of DSS's is the explosion in data bases that provide such information. Over three thousand data bases can now be accessed on-line via computer, as compared with less than nine hundred in 1980. Some two to three hundred of these data bases apply to the information needs of business. The insights marketing managers can gather from commercially available data bases are almost mind boggling. They certainly dwarf the possibilities of even a half dozen years ago. Research Window 2.2, for example, describes the experience of how the Mead Corporation is staying abreast of its industry. Increasingly, companies are setting up systems to track and capture this information on a regular basis.[9]

Remote access to a company's computer via hand-held terminals provides up-to-date point of sales data for a company's decision support system.

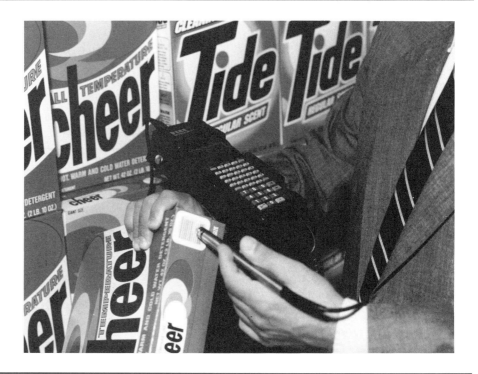

Source: Courtesy of BASS, Inc., Dayton, Ohio.

Model Systems

Model system The part of a decision support system that includes all the routines that allow the user to manipulate the data so as to conduct the kind of analysis the individual desires.

The **model system** in a DSS includes all the routines that allow the user to manipulate the data so as to conduct the kind of analysis the individual desires. Whenever managers look at data, they have a preconceived idea of how something works and, therefore, what is interesting and worthwhile in the data. These ideas are called models.[10] Most managers also want to manipulate data to gain a better understanding of a marketing issue. These manipulations are called procedures. The routines for manipulating the data may run the gamut from summing a set of numbers to conducting a complex statistical analysis to finding an optimization strategy using some kind of nonlinear programming routine. At the same time, "the most frequent operations are basic ones: segregating numbers into relevant groups, aggregating them, taking ratios, ranking them, picking out exceptional cases, plotting and making tables."[11]

In recent years, there has been an increase in the application of formal decision models to marketing situations. Formal models attempt to capture the issues managers deem most relevant when making particular decisions. Figure 2.2. shows the extent to which marketing decisions are being modeled among the Fortune 1000 companies. An examination of Figure 2.2. suggests the models are directed at various decision levels in these organizations.

The credit-approval and salesperson-routing models could be considered operational models. Operational models are usually used by lower-level managers to support the short-time-horizon (e.g., daily or weekly) decisions they are usually

Research Window 2.2
An Experience of the Mead Corporation with an On-Line Information Search

Dennis Rediker, director of strategy and planning at the Mead Corporation, uses on-line research to explore and track developments in the forest-products industry, which is the company's core business. Although papermaking is an ancient process, there have recently been rapid developments in pulp production abroad that are of keen interest to the company.

New technology has made it possible to get quality pulp never used before in papermaking from resources in many countries. Using fast-growing trees that can be converted cost effectively into quality pulp can give a paper manufacturer a considerable cost advantage.

Rediker went on-line, for example, to scan the big global NEXIS data base for information about eucalyptus pulp. An article in *The Economist* produced leads to companies using the special technology needed to mass-produce paper from this raw material. In particular, Rediker learned that B.A.T. Industries' subsidiary, Wiggins-Teape, had purchased Celulosa de Asturias, a Spanish eucalyptus pulper.

He next did a search on B.A.T. Industries in the Viewpoint Library Files of the Exchange service. A 1984 report by an analyst in the investment firm of Phillips & Drew produced useful information and led him to other companies involved in producing eucalyptus pulp, such as Aracruz Cellulose of Brazil.

Following these leads, Rediker identified several contacts in companies around the world with whom he could exchange views on this subject. Further research in the Dialog and NEXIS data bases brought up statistics on production and investments. Of particular interest was the discovery that many companies are linked through relationships not widely known. Rediker passed this intelligence along to the company's senior vice-president–international, James Van Vleck, who then established new contacts with people who could help him explore the options available to the company and the likely effect of future pulp developments on the company's business.

After the initial research, Rediker established a procedure for following future developments continuously through ECLIPSE (automatic electronic clipping service) searches on NEXIS. "Planning," says Rediker, "is the most external, information-conscious function in a company, so it's not surprising that external data bases are playing an increasingly important role for us planners. In fact, the same thing is happening with top management."

Source: James McGrane, "Using On-Line Information for Strategic Advantage," *Planning Review* (November-December 1987), p. 29.

called upon to make. These models normally use internal company data in their operation.

The pricing, sales territory assignment, and advertising media selection models could be considered more tactical. Tactical models are commonly used by middle managers to allocate and control the firm's resources. The time horizon built into tactical models is typically longer than that built into operational models, for several months up to a couple of years. While these models also make use of internal, objective data for the most part, they also rely on subjective and external data.

The new product-evaluation and product-deletion models could be considered more strategic in nature. Strategic models tend to be broad in scope. Much of the data for them comes from external sources and may be subjective in nature. They are used by top management to execute their strategic planning responsibilities, and consequently use years rather than months or days for the appropriate time horizon.

Figure 2.2   ***Use of Marketing Decision Models in Fortune 1000 Companies***

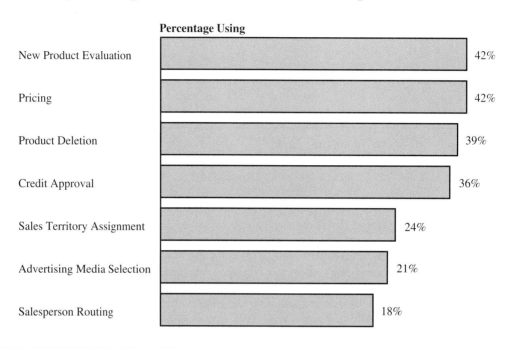

Percentage Using

New Product Evaluation	42%
Pricing	42%
Product Deletion	39%
Credit Approval	36%
Sales Territory Assignment	24%
Advertising Media Selection	21%
Salesperson Routing	18%

Source: Developed from information in Raymond McLeod, Jr., and John C. Rogers. "Marketing Information Systems: Their Current Status in *Fortune* 1000 Companies." *Journal of Management Information Systems*, 1 (Spring 1985), pp. 57–75.

Dialog Systems

Dialog system The part of a decision support system that permits users to explore the data bases by employing the system models to produce reports that satisfy their particular information needs. Also called *language systems.*

A **dialog system,** which is also called a language system, is most important in a DSS and clearly differentiates a DSS from an MIS. Dialog systems permit managers, who are not programmers themselves, to explore the data bases by using the system models to produce reports that satisfy their own particular information needs. The reports can be tabular or graphical, and the report formats can be specified by individual managers. The dialog systems can be passive, which means that the analysis possibilities are presented to the decision makers for selection via menu, a few simple key strokes, light pen, or a mouse device, or they can be active, requiring the users to state their requests in a command mode. A key feature is that managers, instead of funneling their data requests through a team of programmers, can conduct their analyses by themselves (or through one of their assistants) sitting at a computer terminal using the dialog system. This allows them to target the information they want and not to be overwhelmed with irrelevant data. Managers can ask a question and, on the basis of the answer, can ask a subsequent question, and then another, and another, and so on.

With the right DSS, for example, a marketing VP evaluating the sales of a recently introduced test instrument could "call up" sales by month, then by the year, breaking them out *at his option* by, say, customer segments. As he works at his CRT terminal, his inquiries could go in several directions depending on the decision at hand. If his train of thought raises questions about monthly sales last

A dialog system in a DSS permits managers to explore on their own the data bases using system models to produce reports that satisfy their own particular information needs.

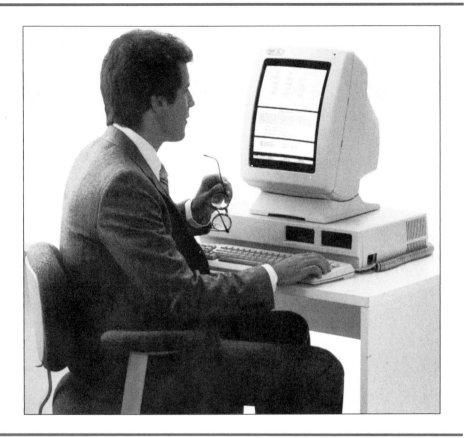

Source: Courtesy of CPT Corporation.

year compared to forecasts, he wants his information system to follow along and give him answers immediately.

He might see that his new product's sales were significantly below forecast. Forecasts too optimistic? He compares other products' sales to his forecasts, and finds that the targets were very accurate. Something wrong with the product? Maybe his sales department is getting insufficient leads, or isn't putting leads to good use? Thinking a minute about how to examine that question, he checks ratios of leads converted to sales—product by product. The results disturb him. Only 5% of the new product's leads generate orders compared to the company's 12% all-product average. Why? He guesses that the sales force isn't supporting the new product enough. Quantitative information from the DSS perhaps could provide more evidence to back that suspicion. But already having enough quantitative knowledge to satisfy himself, the VP acts on his intuition and experience and decides to have a chat with his sales manager.[12]

As the availability of on-line data bases has increased, so too has the need for better dialog systems. While that sounds simple enough, it is in fact a difficult task because of the large amount of data available, the speed with which they hit a company, and the fact that they come from a variety of sources. A relatively recent development in this area is distributed network computing. Such systems make use of a common interface or server. Through that server, the analyst can do data entry, data query, spreadsheet analysis, plots, statistical analysis, or even report preparation, all through some very simple commands. (See Figure 2.3.) For example, one of

Figure 2.3   *Use of Dialog Systems with Common Server or Interface Using Simplified, Standardized Instructions to Perform Multiple Tasks*

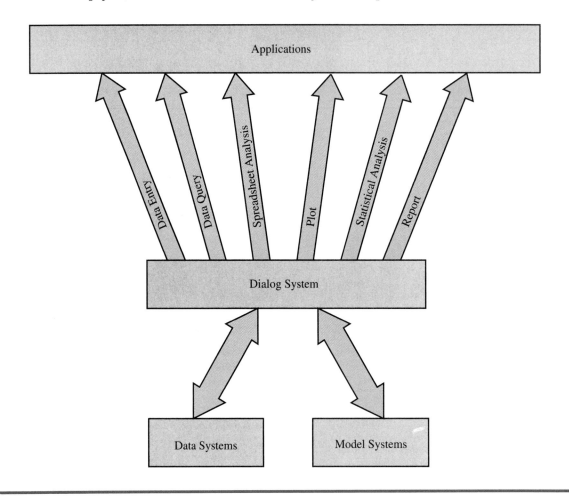

the more popular systems, Metaphor, uses a mouse to access needed documents.[13] Further, users can formulate complex queries through simple instructions. For example, they can join data elements simply by drawing a line between two boxes. Thus, if a user wanted to look at sales in the Southeast, he or she would simply draw a line between the data element marked "Sales" and the box labeled "Southeast." Users can build more elaborate routines by flowing data through a series of the available tools (word processing, spreadsheet, and graphics, for instance). They can specify sequences of operations by drawing arrows from one routine to the next. Once sequences are created, users can store them and launch similar analyses in the future with a single click of the mouse. Once the sequences are recalled, users can modify and restore them. Thus, managers have the ability to continuously improve their modeling of the problems they face, without needing to become computer experts or even very knowledgeable about what goes on behind the scenes.

Research Window 2.3 describes the experiences at Clorox before and after installing the Metaphor dialog system.

Research Window 2.3
Experience at Clorox in Using the Metaphor Dialog System

Getting all the data on computer systems at Clorox once taxed the company's MIS department beyond its resources. With new volumes of data rolling in all the time, the task was too complex and time-consuming to load all the information on mainframes. But that was often the only way that data from different geographic areas and time periods could be reconciled.

Before Clorox acquired the Metaphor system, brand managers sometimes would come to the MIS department "with requests that certain product data be looked at," according to Sean F. McKenna, Clorox's systems and data base administrator for Metaphor systems. He recalls that it sometimes took so long to honor the request that by the time the brand manager got the data, "no one was interested in looking at it anymore."

Today, Clorox brand managers are able to use all the data bought from the major services because Metaphor has written conversion routines that allow these data to be quickly loaded.

[Tim] Hensley [director of business systems] and McKenna have found that marketing teams for Clorox's many brands require little MIS support because the marketing personnel develop their own applications. "We give the brand people a 25-hour training course for the system, but we find that they can learn to use it for all practical purposes in five hours or so," says McKenna.

Clorox officials decline, for competitive reasons, to discuss how the Metaphor system is being used with any specific brands. But they talked generally about how it was employed when Kingsford with Mesquite charcoal was introduced last year.

The company got into the charcoal briquet business in 1973 when it acquired Kingsford Company. Kingsford later became the leading national charcoal briquet brand. In 1981, Clorox introduced Match Light, an instant-lighting charcoal that has a commanding lead in that niche.

When Clorox planned the introduction of Kingsford with Mesquite charcoal, briquets laced with mesquite wood to impart a mesquite flavor to food, it wanted to determine if Mesquite sales would siphon off sales from its two other charcoal brands. If so, the company could end up spending money for promotion and advertising without increasing its overall share of the $418 million U.S. (1985) market for charcoal briquets. That share stood at about 42 percent, according to analysts.

Kingsford with Mesquite charcoal was launched last year in about half the country and was not initially sold in many states where Clorox's two other charcoal brands were marketed. Sales data was then collected from all states, and marketers found that sales of Kingsford and Match Light declined only slightly in areas where Mesquite was being sold.

Further analysis of the sales data (on the Metaphor system) of competing charcoal brands disclosed that in areas where Mesquite was being sold, the sale of generic charcoal brands marketed by several large supermarket chains was declining. Clorox's overall share of the market rose several percentage points, and Mesquite was introduced nationally early in 1986.

When following sales of a mostly seasonal product like charcoal briquets, brand managers have to access data that may affect sales, such as weather conditions. That type of information can be easily retrieved and integrated with other data for analysis by Metaphor users at Clorox.

Hensley, who oversees business systems managers, client services, and user training and education at Clorox, is not readily given to endorsing vendor products. But his enthusiasm for the Metaphor system underscores many of his comments, especially when he discusses the graphics capabilities of the system:

> Metaphor has a graphics capability that other systems don't have. Prior to getting the system, our graphics were done primarily for presentations. You knew the answer. You just wanted to get it up graphically to show to someone else.
>
> Now, production of graphics is so simple, they can be used for analysis. You can take something and in maybe five seconds construct the graphic. You can turn it and look at it six different ways graphically and do in two or three minutes what it would take hours to do with another system. This has been made so easy that the system has become a true tool, not just a decision-support system.

Source: Bob Goligoski, "Brand Leaders," *Business Computer Systems*, 5 (June 1986), pp. 26–33.

DSS versus MIS

From the preceding discussion, it should be obvious that DSSs and MISs are both concerned with improving information processing so that better marketing decisions can be made. A DSS differs from an MIS, though, in a number of ways. First, a DSS tends to be aimed at the less well-structured, underspecified problems that managers face rather than at those problems that can be investigated using a relatively standard set of procedures and comparisons. Second, a DSS attempts to combine the use of models and analytical techniques and procedures with the more traditional data access and retrieval functions. Third, such systems specifically incorporate features that make them easy to use in an interactive mode by noncomputer people, including such things as menu-driven procedures for doing an analysis and graphic display of the results. Regardless of how the interaction is structured, these systems have the ability to respond to users' ad hoc requests in "real time," meaning the time available for making the decision. Fourth, a DSS emphasizes flexibility and adaptibility. It can accommodate different decision makers with diverse styles as well as changing environmental conditions.

The Future of DSS versus Traditional Marketing Research

There is no question that the explosion in data bases and computer software for accessing those data bases is changing the way marketing intelligence is secured. Not only are more companies building DSSs, but those that have them are becoming more sophisticated in using them for general business and competitive intelligence. This in turn has produced some changes in the organization of the marketing intelligence function. One relatively recent and important change has been the emergence of the position of chief information officer, or CIO.[14]

The CIO's major role is to run the company's information and computer systems like a business. The CIO serves as the liaison between the firm's top management and its information systems department. He or she has the responsibility for planning, coordinating, and controlling the use of the firm's information resources, and is much more concerned with the firm's outlook than the daily activities of the department. CIOs typically know more about the business in general than the managers of the information system departments, who are often stronger technically. In many cases, the managers of the information system department will report directly to the CIO. Research Window 2.4, for example, describes what has happened to the marketing intelligence function at Kraft in terms of providing competitive intelligence.

One noteworthy item in the Kraft example is that the explosion in data bases and the emergence of DSSs has not eliminated traditional marketing research projects for gathering marketing intelligence. Not only is this true at Kraft, but it is also true at other companies with established marketing research departments. This is because the two activities are not competitive mechanisms for marketing intelligence but, rather, complementary ones. While DSS's provide valuable input for broad strategic decisions, allow managers to stay in tune with what is happening in their external environments, and serve as an excellent early-warning system, they sometimes do not provide enough information as to what to do in specific instances, such as when the firm is faced with introducing a new product, changing distribution channels, evaluating a promotional campaign, and so on. When actionable information is required to address specific marketing problems or opportunities, the research project will likely continue to play a major role.[15]

Research Window 2.4
The Changing Nature of How Competitive Intelligence Is Provided at Kraft

Kraft's competitive intelligence gathering happens on lots of different levels and depends on how deep your definition is. Market-share monitoring, through Info-Scan . . . provides some information on competitors. And now, with scanners, we have a lot more competitive data than we used to. We can tell what prices competitors have been charging, what kind of product featuring they did, and what their promotional program was in comparison with ours. Then we can ask questions about changes: Why did that happen? What did the competition do? What should we do?

Another level of knowing what the competition is doing involves tracking studies, where you assess how familiar consumers are with your brands, what advertising they're familiar with, what messages they're receiving, how those messages became attitudes that affect evaluations of your products and competitors' products.

A third level is product testing—evaluating our products versus those of our competitors. All three are fairly standard tools that have been around for a long time.

In the last few years, we've started looking at some new things that can't really be measured in the marketplace. For example, we want to know when a competitor is opening a new plant or starting a new manufacturing process. We watch people changes. We note when the head of an organization moves from Company A to Company B. This is intelligence that tells you more about the company and what it's doing, as opposed to determining its performance in various markets.

We've identified a network of competitively knowledgeable employees throughout the company—each with a specialty. They are 30 or 40 people from all kinds of functions—manufacturing, operations, R&D, marketing—and usually managers and directors, in some cases analytical types. They're generally middle managers, not top management, definitely not clerical.

We found these people by going to department heads and division heads and asking them to suggest people who could monitor competitive activities and keep in touch with a central facility, which is the business research services group in my department.

The members of the network keep a watch on particular journals, newspapers, and magazines. It's almost like an internal clipping service. They send the clippings to the business research services people, and they prepare a very quick browse list with one- or two-sentence summaries of each article and an estimate of how long it would take to read the full article. The list goes to about 150 people—senior middle management and senior management. A senior manager or division president can scan down the list of articles and say, "Gee, there is something about the Campbell Soup Company that interests me." Then he can request a copy.

This system was actually developed outside our department. We originally had two information centers. We had a marketing information center, which is part of my department, working with general brand management, and a business research center, which reported into corporate strategy. That group worked with corporate-type departments—law, acquisition, finance, treasury—and it developed the surveillance system. We merged the two pieces into one group in my department about a year ago.

Source: Larry Stanek, Vice-President and Director of Marketing Information, "Kraft, Inc.: CI as Part of Marketing Research," in Howard Sutton, *Competitive Intelligence* (New York: The Conference Board, 1988), p. 25.

In sum, both traditional, or project-based, and DSS-based approaches to marketing intelligence can be expected to grow in importance.[16] In an increasingly competitive world, information is vital, and a company's ability to obtain and analyze information will largely determine its future. The light from both flash bulbs and candles is necessary.

Back to the Case

Bruce Watley hung up the telephone. His conversation with the San Antonio Crispy Chip sales rep had just confirmed what the DSS data had shown him earlier in the day. A regional chip manufacturer had recently introduced a white tortilla chip called El Rio. Its distribution was limited to the San Antonio/Houston area.

The chip, even the Crispy Chip rep had to admit, was pretty good. As a result El Rio's sales had sharply cut into the sales of Crispy Chip's traditional Spanish Moss brand tortilla chip. In addition, sales of all Crispy Chip's products were slipping as supermarkets devoted more and more shelf space to El Rio.

It would take some quick maneuvering to turn the situation around. Watley wondered how quickly Crispy Chips could get a white tortilla chip into production and onto the south Texas shelves. He guessed three to six months if they really hustled. Boy, in the old days it would have taken three months just to comb through the data to figure out what was going on in south Texas.

Watley had not been an enthusiastic supporter of the DSS system. It had been very expensive, and intially he had worried that it would be too hard for someone with only average computer skills to use. But after his experience with the sales slump in south Texas, he had to admit he was impressed.

Information was updated daily on hand-held terminals by the 10,000 or so Crispy Chip salespeople so that information on the 50 Crispy Chip product lines appeared on company computer screens in the form of easy-to-read charts. Yellow indicated a sales slowdown; red, a sales drop; and green, an upswing in sales.

As pleased as Watley was by the performance of the DSS in pinpointing the cause of the south Texas sales slump, he wasn't completely convinced of its value. He worried that the new DSS would make managers even more focused on short-term gains at the expense of building brand loyalty. He had read somewhere that using DSS data was a little like driving a car while looking through the rearview mirror. The danger seemed to be that by paying so much attention to what had happened yesterday, you would lose sight of what might happen tomorrow.

In this instance at least, though, the DSS had proved to be a useful tool.

The Crispy Chip problem is based on Frito-Lay's experience in south Texas, as reported by Jeffrey Rothfeder, Jim Bartimo, Lois Therrien, and Richard Brandt in *Business Week* (July 2, 1990), pp. 54–55.

Summary

Learning Objective 1: Explain the difference between a project emphasis in research and a marketing information system (MIS) or decision support system (DSS) emphasis.

The difference between the project emphasis to research and the marketing information system (MIS) or decision support system (DSS) emphases is that both of the latter rely on the continual monitoring of the firm's activities, competitors, and environment, while the former emphasizes the in-depth, but nonrecurring, study of some specific problem or environmental condition.

Learning Objective 2: Define what is meant by an MIS.

A marketing information system is a set of procedures and methods for the regular, planned collection, analysis, and presentation of information for use in making marketing decisions. The thrust in designing an MIS is a detailed analysis of each decision maker who might use the system, in order to secure an accurate, objective assessment of each manager's decision-making responsibilities, capabilities, and style—and, most important, each manager's information needs. Given the specification of information needs, system support people develop report formats and efficient systems for extracting and combining information from various data banks.

Learning Objective 3: Cite some of the problems inherent in an MIS.

People tend to resist change, and with an MIS, the changes are often substantial. Marketing information systems require managers to disclose their decision-making processes, which many managers are reluctant to do. Further, the report formats are typically compromises that try to satisfy the different styles of the different users. Also, the development time required for these systems often means that they quickly become obsolete.

Learning Objective 4: Define what is meant by a DSS.

A decision support system is a coordinated collection of data, systems' tools, and techniques with supporting software and hardware, by which an organization gathers and interprets relevant information from business and the environment and turns it into a basis for marketing action. A DSS concentrates on the design of data systems, model systems, and dialog systems.

Learning Objective 5: Specify what feature most clearly differentiates a DSS from an MIS.

The dialog systems are most important and most clearly differentiate a DSS from an MIS. They allow managers to conduct their own analyses while they, or one of their assistants, sit at a computer terminal. This allows managers to analyze problems using their own personal views of what might be happening in a given situation, relying on their intuition and experience rather than on a series of prespecified reports.

Discussion Questions, Problems, and Projects

1. Twenty years ago the marketing information system was emphasized as being the solution to a host of problems arising from irregular research efforts. The promise was never realized, and current emphasis is on the design of decision support systems rather than marketing information systems. How do you account for the gap between the promise and delivery of MIS? Do you think DSS's will suffer the same fate as MIS's? Why or why not?

2. In each of the following scenarios, identify the general type of DSS model (operational, tactical, or strategic) the decision maker is likely to use. Then explain why.
    (a) Louise Smith is brand manager for Procon power tools. It is her responsibility to decide where a series of ads promoting Procon's circular saws should be placed. The advertising agency that designed the ads has suggested that they be run over a nine-month period.
    (b) Ray Griffith is a district sales manager for Allied Grocery Wholesalers, Inc. His largest customer, Flora's Fine Foods, has informed him that it will need increased salesperson contact over the next month due to its "Super 50th" anniversary sale. Griffith must decide how to rearrange sales-call schedules to provide increased contact with Flora's.
    (c) Jill Andrews is vice-president of marketing for Rizzi Industries, a consumer packaged goods manufacturing company. Sales of one of Rizzi's product lines have been steadily decreasing for the last five years. Andrews must decide whether the product line has the potential to be rescued, or if it should be phased out of production.

3. You have been requested to design a DSS for a manufacturer of automotive parts.
    (a) What data should be included in the system (e.g., sales by sales area or by product line, age, and type of automobile driven)?
    (b) What data sources might be used to create the information system?
    (c) How will you structure the system conceptually, including the elements you will build into each of the subsystems?

4. Arrange an interview with a manager of a local business for the express purpose of discussing a DSS.
   (a) Complete the following:

   Name of the company: _____

   _____

   Name and title of the manager you interviewed: _____

   _____

   (b) Briefly describe the DSS that the company is currently using, emphasizing especially the functions that are served by it (e.g., production, sales management, etc.).
   (c) Write a brief assessment of the manager's familiarity with the concept. Is the manager more concerned with the technical questions (e.g., how information is stored) or with the overall concept and its impact on the organization's decision-making capabilities?
   (d) Briefly describe the company's use of the DSS, including how it determines which managers get what access to what data and how, its experience with the system, and so on.

5. Your company is in the process of installing its first DSS. The system has been designed, the hardware installed, and it is due to be up and running in two weeks. Your task is to provide system users with orientation and training. It is your feeling that the company's managers will initially be resistant to using the DSS. To help overcome this resistance, what specific capabilities of the DSS will you emphasize in your initial orientation presentations?

Endnotes

1. Statement by Robert J. Williams, who was the creator of the first recognized marketing information system at the Mead Johnson division of the Edward Dalton Company. "Marketing Intelligence Systems: A DEW Line for Marketing Men," *Business Management* (January 1966), p. 32.

2. Donald F. Cox and Robert E. Good, "How to Build a Marketing Information System," *Harvard Business Review*, 45 (May–June 1967), pp. 145–154.

3. See Raymond McLeod, Jr., and John C. Rogers, "Marketing Information Systems: Their Current Status in Fortune 1000 Companies," *Journal of Management Information Systems*, 1 (Spring 1985), pp. 57–75, for the results of a survey conducted among the executives of the Fortune 1000. The survey highlights the relative emphasis on MIS's and their use by management in the reporting firms. The paper also provides a historical perspective on the development and use of MIS's.

4. See Van Mayros and D. Michael Werner, *Marketing Information Systems* (Radnor, Penn.: Chitton, 1982), for a detailed list of the elements that might go into each one of these data banks.

5. Herbert A. Simon provided the description of decision making as a process involving intelligence, design, and choice. *The New Science of Management Decisions* (New York: Harper and Row, 1960).

6. Robert H. Bonczek, Clyde W. Holsapple, and Andrew B. Whinston, "Developments in Decision Support Systems," undated manuscript, Management Information Research Center, Krannert Graduate School of Management, Purdue University, pp. 3–4.

7. John D. C. Little, "Decision Support Systems for Marketing Managers," *Journal of Marketing*, 43 (Summer 1979), p. 11. See also John D. C. Little, Lakshmi Mohan, and Antoine Hatorin, "Yanking Knowledge from the Numbers: How Marketing Decision Support Systems Can Work for You," *Industrial Marketing*, 67 (March 1982), pp. 46, 50–56; and Martin D. Goslar and Stephen

W. Brown, "Decision Support System Models," *Information Processing and Management*, 2 (1988), pp. 429–448.

8. Figure 2.1 and the surrounding discussion are adapted from the excellent treatment of the subject by Ralph H. Sprague, Jr., and Eric D. Carlson, *Building Effective Decision Support Systems* (Englewood Cliffs, N.J.: Prentice-Hall, 1982), chapters 1 and 2. See also Jitender S. Deogun, "A Conceptual Approach to Decision Support Systems: Advantage in Consumer Marketing Settings," *Journal of Consumer Marketing*, 3 (Summer 1986), pp. 43–50.

9. Some of the more important sources of this information are described in Chapter 7. For a general discussion of the design of business intelligence systems, see Benjamin Gilad and Tamar Gilad, *The Business Intelligence System: A New Tool for Competitive Advantage* (New York: American Management Association, 1988). For an overview of what industry is actually doing, see Howard Sutton, *Competitive Intelligence* (New York: The Conference Board, 1988).

10. John D. C. Little and Michael N. Cassettari, *Decision Support Systems for Marketing Managers* (New York: American Management Association, 1984), p. 14.

11. Ibid., p. 15.

12. Michael Dressler, Ronald Beall, and Joquin Ives Brant, "What the Hot Marketing Tool of the '80s Offers You," *Industrial Marketing*, 68 (March 1983), pp. 51 and 54.

13. Some other popular systems are Express, Marksman, and Decision Master. For a general discussion on the use of these systems, see Valerie Free, "The Marketing War Gets Automated," *Marketing Communications*, 13 (June 1988), pp. 40–48, 79.

14. For general discussions of the office of CIO, see P. Declan O'Riordan, "The CIO: MIS Makes Its Move into the Executive Suite," *Journal of Information Systems Management* (Summer 1987),

pp. 54–56; and Jim Sielski, "Evolving Post of Chief of Info," *Chicago Tribune* (November 20, 1988), pp. 33 and 35.

15. Even with respect to the activity of providing competitive intelligence, a project-based approach can complement the insights gathered through ongoing monitoring. For a comparison of the benefits and costs of using each approach, see John E. Prescott and Daniel C. Smith, "A Project-Based Approach to Competitive Analysis," *Strategic Management Journal*, 8 (September–October 1987), pp. 411–423.

16. For discussion of the trends in DSS and marketing research, see M. C. Er, "Decision Support Systems: A Summary, Problems, and Future Trends," *Decision Support Systems*, 4 (September 1988), pp. 355–363; and Stephen K. Keiser, James R. Krum, and Pradeep A. Rau, "Changing Patterns in Marketing Research," *Marketing Intelligence and Planning*, 5 (Number 1), pp. 10–18. For a look at the factors affecting the usage of DSS's, see George M. Zinkhan, Erich A. Joachimsthaler, and Thomas C. Kinnear, "Individual Differences and Marketing Decision Support Systems Usage and Satisfaction," *Journal of Marketing Research*, 24 (May 1987), pp. 208–214.

Suggested Additional Readings

For useful discussions of the structure and use of decision support systems, see

Martin D. Goslar and Stephen W. Brown, "Decision Support System Models," *Information Processing and Management*, no. 4, 2 (1988), pp. 429–448.

John D. C. Little, "Decision Support Systems for Marketing Managers," *Journal of Marketing*, 43 (Summer 1979), pp. 9–27.

John D. C. Little and Michael N. Cassettari, *Decision Support Systems for Marketing Managers* (New York: American Management Association, 1984.)

Ralph H. Sprague, Jr., and Eric D. Carlson, *Effective Decision Support Systems* (Englewood Cliffs, N.J.: Prentice-Hall, 1982).

For a general discussion of the design of business intelligence systems, see

Benjamin Gilad and Tamar Gilad, *The Business Intelligence System: A New Tool for Competitive Advantage* (New York: American Management Association, 1988).

Process of Marketing Research

Learning Objectives

Upon completing this chapter, you should be able to

1. Explain the difference between a program strategy and a project strategy in marketing research.

2. Outline the steps in the research process and show how the steps are interrelated.

3. Cite the most critical error in marketing research.

Case in Marketing Research

According to Donald Lewicki, it had been like pulling teeth to get Central Bank to agree to a marketing research study in the first place. This thought wasn't exactly reassuring to Judy Isaacs as Lewicki ushered her through his bank's offices to meet with the private banking department.

The bank had just moved into its new corporate headquarters in a recently completed office tower downtown. It still smelled of fresh paint and new carpet. As Isaacs followed Lewicki down the high-tech hallway, they passed workers on ladders installing futuristic light fixtures overhead.

Central Bank was a very successful Pittsburgh bank that had taken advantage of banking deregulation to expand into other cities. It had moved into the Columbus area two years ago and was struggling to make its presence felt in a very competitive banking environment.

Lewicki had recently been transferred to the Columbus office to establish a private banking department. Private banking, as Lewicki had explained to Isaacs at their first meeting, was a service-oriented department designed to make banking easy for wealthy customers. To customers who deposited a minimum of $100,000 with Central Bank, the private banking department would provide free banking services, lines of credit at discount rates, and as much special attention as it could muster. Most transactions could be handled with a phone call.

Even though banking is a very customer-oriented business, banks as a rule don't spend much on marketing research. As Lewicki had told Isaacs, getting his people to agree to hire her firm had been a struggle. Entering the sleek conference room, Isaacs hoped that since they had now committed to using a marketing research firm, they would put their initial reluctance behind them.

"The most important thing I hope to accomplish today," began Isaacs once the handshaking was over, "is to articulate the problem for which you need my help. I know that sounds pretty elementary, but it could be quite difficult. The point is, unless I know what questions to ask, the answers I find aren't likely to be meaningful."

"Well," began Lewicki, eager to get the ball rolling, "we have to build a private banking clientele pretty much from zero. We basically know what services we can offer, though there's some flexibility there. We know which other area banks offer private banking. We know what they require in terms of minimum deposits and what services they offer."

Isaacs took the summary chart that was handed to her. At a glance there seemed to be a uniform menu of services that the city's banks offered to their most desirable customers. In the "minimum deposit" section, however, the amounts ranged from $100,000 to $500,000.

"Security National Bank has a minimum of half a million for a private banking account?" exclaimed Isaacs.

"Yes," answered one of Central's private bankers. "Security National is one of the oldest banks in town, and it's built strong relationships with some of the wealthiest people in Columbus. There's a certain element of status involved with its private accounts. Security prints "private banking" on the checks of its private banking customers, and since everyone knows how much you have to put in the bank . . ."

"Well, I still have no idea why we've engaged a marketing research firm," interjected one of the bank officers. "No offense to Ms. Isaacs, but I don't understand what the mystery is here. We know exactly what kind of clientele we're looking for—put crassly, they're millionaires. In other cities we've managed to build private banking by targeting our marketing at the very wealthy. We do direct mailings to residents of affluent neighborhoods, doctors, lawyers, and top employees of major corporations. That's how we should be spending our money, not by giving it to Ms. Isaacs' firm."

"But would your money be spent well?" asked Isaacs confidently. "Money for advertising is easy to spend. One of the things that marketing research can do is make sure that the money you're going to spend on advertising is spent in the most cost-effective way."

"I guess that's one of the reasons we've hired you," said Lewicki with a grin, "but I think that first we do need to go back a step. Since we're not a Columbus organization, we're not as well connected in this town as our competition is. I think the first thing we need to know from Ms. Isaacs is who our market is. How many people in Columbus fit the financial profile of a private banking customer? Who are they, and what is the best way to reach them?"

Discussion Issues

1. If you were Isaacs, what arguments would you present to convince Central Bank that its dollars will be well spent doing a research study?
2. What form do you think this research study might take?
3. What constraints might affect the form of the study?

Program strategy
A company's philosophy of how marketing research fits into its marketing plan.

Project strategy The design of individual marketing research studies that are to be conducted.

Chapter 1 highlighted the many kinds of problems that marketing research can be used to solve. It emphasized that marketing research is a firm's communication link with the environment and can help the marketing manager in planning, problem solving, and control. Every company has its own way of using marketing research. Some use it on a continuous basis to track sales or to monitor the firm's market share. Others resort to it only when a problem arises or an important decision—such as the launching of a new product—needs to be made. A company's overall philosophy of how marketing research fits into its marketing plan determines its **program strategy** for marketing research.[1] A program strategy specifies the types of studies that are to be conducted and for what purposes. It might even specify how often these studies are to take place.

How the individual studies are designed is the basis of a firm's **project strategy.** A look at how marketing research is handled at Procter & Gamble (P & G), one of the nation's leading consumer manufacturers, should help to clarify the difference between a program strategy and a project strategy.

It is P & G's policy that at least once a year marketing research will be conducted on each of its brands. These studies assess people's likes and dislikes about P & G products, the products' names, packaging, and hundreds of other details. This mountain of information is then funneled to every major segment of the company, including the executive suite, where it is sifted and resifted for implications for P & G's marketing, advertising, manufacturing, and research and development operations. This ongoing process may be thought of as P & G's program strategy for marketing research.

The *project* strategies P & G employs vary widely, however. In addition to the usual types of marketing research—such as extensive questionnaires about existing products and test marketing in supermarkets—P & G takes some further steps. For example, P & G's researchers might follow homemakers around while they do the laundry, noting how they sort the clothes, how many loads they do, and what temperature settings they use on their washing machines. This kind of research has led to some breakthroughs. Cheer, for example, was formulated in response to researchers' observations that homemakers needed one detergent that could handle all fabrics and all water temperatures.[2]

The details of this type of research, as well as the specific design of consumer questionnaires or the format in which a new product is sampled to customers in supermarkets, all reflect the company's project strategy.

Program strategy typically answers questions such as "Should we do marketing research?" and "How often?" and "What kind?" Project strategy addresses the issue of "Now that we've decided to go ahead with marketing research, how should we proceed? Should we use in-store surveys, self-administered printed questionnaires, or one of the new electronic interviewing devices? Should we question more people or fewer? More often or less often?" In sum, project strategy deals with how a study should be conducted, whereas program strategy addresses the question of what type of studies the firm should conduct.

Research Window 3.1 outlines the kinds of studies that constitute the Gillette Company's program strategy for marketing research. As you can see, each type of study is planned to meet a certain objective. The design of individual studies defines the firm's project strategy—for example, the use of personal interviews in the national consumer studies, mail questionnaires in the brand-tracking studies, and telephone interviews when measuring brand awareness. The goal of all this research is to help Gillette maintain its 60-percent share of the blade and razor market.

Research Window 3.1
Major Thrusts of Marketing Research at the Gillette Company

1. Annual National Consumer Studies

The objectives of these annual studies are to determine what brand of razor and blade was used for the respondents' last shave, to collect demographic data, and to examine consumer attitudes toward the various blade and razor manufacturers. These studies rely on personal interviews with national panels of male and female respondents, who are selected using probability sampling methods.

2. National Brand-Tracking Studies

The purpose of these studies is to track the use of razors and blades so as to monitor brand loyalty and brand switching tendencies over time. These studies are also conducted annually and use panels of male and female shavers. However, the information is collected via mail questionnaires.

3. Annual Brand-Awareness Studies

These studies are aimed at determining the "share of mind" Gillette products have. This information is collected by annual telephone surveys that employ unaided as well as aided recall of brand names and advertising campaigns.

4. Consumer-Use Tests

The key objectives of the use-testing studies are to ensure that "Gillette remains state of the art in the competitive arena, that our products are up to our desired performance standards, and that no claims in our advertising, packaging, or display materials are made without substantiation." At least two consumer-use tests are conducted each month by Gillette. In these tests, consumers are asked to use a single variation of a product for an extended period of time, at the end of which their evaluation of the product is secured.

5. Continuous Retail Audits

The purpose of the retail audits is to provide top management with monthly market share data, along with information regarding distribution, out-of-stock, and inventory levels of the various Gillette products. This information is purchased from the commercial information services providing syndicated retail audit data. The information is supplemented by special retail audits that Gillette itself conducts, which look at product displays and the extent to which Gillette blades and razors are featured in retailer advertisements.

Source: Adapted from "Mature Products Remain as the Mainstays in the Gillette Company," *Marketing News*, 17 (June 10, 1983), p. 17. Adapted with permission from *Marketing News*, published by the American Marketing Association; Chicago, IL 60606.

Research process The sequence of steps in the design and implementation of a research study, including problem formulation, determination of research design, determination of data-collection method, design of data-collection forms, design of the sample and collection of the data, analysis and interpretation of the data, and preparation of the research report.

All research problems require their own special emphases and approaches. Since every marketing research problem is unique in some ways, the research procedure is usually custom tailored. Nonetheless, there is a sequence of steps called the **research process** (see Figure 3.1), which can be followed when designing the research project. This chapter overviews the research process, and the remaining chapters discuss the stages in the process in more detail.

Sequence of Steps in Marketing Research

Formulate Problem

One of the more valuable roles marketing research can perform is helping to define the marketing problem to be solved. Only when the problem is precisely defined can research be designed to provide pertinent information. Part of the process of problem

Figure 3.1   ***Stages in the Research Process***

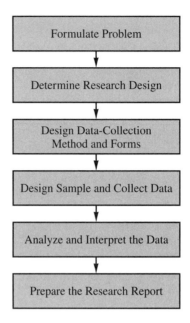

definition includes specifying the *objectives* of the specific research project or projects that might be undertaken. Each project should have one or more objectives, and the next step in the process should not be taken until these can be explicitly stated.

Determine Research Design

The choice of research design depends on how much is known about the problem. If relatively little is known about the phenomenon to be investigated, *exploratory research* will be warranted. Typically, exploratory research is used when the problem to be solved is broad or vague. It may involve reviewing published data, interviewing knowledgeable people, or investigating trade literature that discusses similar cases. In any event, one of the most important characteristics of exploratory research is its flexibility. Since researchers know little about the problem at this point, they must be ready to follow their intuition about possible areas and tactics of investigation.

If, instead of being broad or vague, a problem is precisely and unambiguously formulated, *descriptive* or *causal* research is needed. In these research designs, data collection is not flexible but rigidly specified, both with respect to the data-collection forms and the sample design. The descriptive design emphasizes determining the frequency with which something occurs or the extent to which two variables covary. The causal design uses experiments to identify cause-and-effect relationships between variables.

Determine Data-Collection Method

Secondary data Statistics not gathered for the immediate study at hand but for some other purpose.

Often the information that a firm needs to solve its problem already exists in the form of **secondary data,** or data that have already been collected for some purpose other than the question at hand. Such data may exist in the firm's own internal information

Today's small, lightweight, and easy-to-use camcorders are a product of new technology and effective marketing research.

Source: Courtesy of Sony Corporation of America.

system as feedback on warranty cards, call reports from the sales force, or orders from wholesalers. If the firm itself does not have the necessary information, it may be readily available from a good business library, in the form of government statistics or trade association reports. Finally, if neither of these sources prove fruitful, the data may have already been collected by a commercial research supplier. While the firm must pay for such information, the fee is usually less than the cost of an original study. In any case, for reasons of both cost and time, researchers should always look first at existing sources of data before launching a research project.

Primary data
Information collected specifically for the investigation at hand.

If the information needed is not readily available, or if it is available only in a form unsuitable for the problem at hand, then the research must depend on **primary data,** which are collected specifically for the study. The research questions here are several, including: Should the data be collected by observation or questionnaire? How should these observations be made—personally or electronically? How should the questions be administered—in person, over the telephone, or through the mail?

Design Data-Collection Forms

Once the researchers have settled on the method to be used for the study, they must decide on the type of observation form or questionnaire that will best suit the needs of the project. Suppose a questionnaire is being used. Should it be structured as a fixed set of alternative answers, or should the responses be open ended, to allow respondents to reply in their own words? Should the purpose be made clear to the respondents, or should the study objectives be disguised? Should some kind of rating scale be used? What type?

Design Sample and Collect Data

After determining how the needed information will be collected, the researchers must decide what group will be observed or questioned. Depending on the study, this group might be homemakers, preschoolers, sports car drivers, Pennsylvanians, or tennis players. The particular subset of the population chosen for study is known as a *sample*.

Sampling frame The list of sampling units from which a sample will be drawn; the list could consist of geographic areas, institutions, individuals, or other units.

In designing the sample, researchers must specify (1) the **sampling frame,** which is the list of population elements from which the sample will be drawn, (2) the sample-selection process, and (3) the size of the sample. While people often assume the frame is implicit in the research problem and thus take it for granted, that assumption can be dangerous.

> Take the case of the manufacturer of dog food . . . who went out and did an intensive market study. He tested the demand for dog food; he tested the package size, the design, the whole advertising program. Then he launched the product with a big campaign, got the proper distribution channels, put it on the market and had tremendous sales. But two months later, the bottom dropped out—no follow-up sales. So he called in an expert, who took the dog food out to the local pound, put it in front of the dogs—and they would not touch it. For all the big marketing study, no one had tried the product on the dogs.[3]

As this old but classic example illustrates, the dog population was not part of the sampling frame, probably because it is people who buy dog food and not the dogs themselves. Nevertheless, the careless specification of population elements had dire consequences. While the consequences may be less dire in other cases, it is important to realize that when we sample from, say, a phone book or a mailing list, we are not sampling from the population as a whole, but are only sampling from people whose names appear in the phone book or on the mailing list. Answers to a questionnaire on frequency of air travel would clearly be quite different if the sample were selected from the New York City phone book than if it were selected from the book covering rural West Virginia.

Probability sample
A sample in which each population element has a known, nonzero chance of being included in the sample.

Nonprobability sample
A sample that relies on personal judgment somewhere in the element selection process and therefore prohibits estimating the probability that any population element will be included in the sample.

The sample-selection process requires that the form of the sample be specified. Will it be a **probability sample,** in which each member of the population has a known chance of being selected? Or will it be a **nonprobability sample,** in which the researchers subjectively decide which particular group will be part of the study?

Sample size addresses the issue of how many institutions or subjects it is necessary to use in the project in order to get reliable answers without exceeding the time and money budgeted for it.

Once the dimensions of the sample design are specified, data collection can begin. Data collection requires a field force of some type, although field methods are largely dictated by the data-collection method, the kinds of information to be obtained, and the sampling requirements. The use of personnel to collect data raises a host of questions with respect to selection, training, and control of the field staff. For example, what kind of background should interviewers have in order to glean the most information from respondents? What specific training is necessary to ensure that interviewers administer the questionnaires accurately? How often, and in what way, should the accuracy of the answers on the questionnaires be checked by validation studies? These questions should be anticipated in designing the research.

Analyze and Interpret the Data

Researchers may amass a mountain of data, but it is useless unless the findings are analyzed and the results interpreted in light of the problem at hand. Data analysis generally involves several steps. First, the data-collection forms must be scanned to be sure that they are complete, consistent, and that the instructions were followed. This process is called **editing.** After being edited, the forms must be **coded,** which involves assigning numbers to each of the answers so that they may be analyzed by a computer. The final step in analyzing the data is **tabulation.** This refers to the orderly arrangement of data in a table or other summary format achieved by counting the frequency of responses to each question. At this point the data may also be cross-classified by other variables. Suppose researchers asked women if they like a certain new cosmetic. Their responses may be cross-classified by age-group, income level, and so forth.

The coding, editing, and tabulation functions are common to most research studies. Any statistical tests applied to the data are generally unique to the particular sampling procedures and data-collection instruments used in the research. These tests should be anticipated before data collection is begun, if possible, to assure that the data and analyses will be appropriate for the problem as specified.

Prepare the Research Report

The research report is the document submitted to management that summarizes the research results and conclusions. It is all that many executives will see of the research effort, and it becomes the standard by which that research is judged. Thus, it is imperative that the research report be clear and accurate, since no matter how well all previous steps have been completed, the project will be no more successful than the research report. One empirical study that investigated the factors determining the extent to which research results are used by firms found that the research report was one of the five most important determinants.[4]

Additional Comments on Marketing Research Steps

While the above discussion should provide some understanding of the steps in the research process, five additional points need to be made. First, each step in the process is more complex than the above discussion suggests. Each involves a number of issues rather than a single decision or even a few decisions. Table 3.1, for example, lists some of the typical questions that need resolving at each stage.

Second, although the stages have been presented as if one would proceed through them in a lockstep fashion when designing a research project, nothing could be further from the truth. Rather, Figure 3.1 could be drawn with a number of feedback loops suggesting a possible need to rethink, redraft, or revise the various elements in the process as the study proceeds. The process would begin with problem formulation, and then could take any direction. The problem may not be specified explicitly enough to allow the development of the research design, in which case the researchers would need to return to stage one to define the research objectives more clearly. Alternatively, the process may proceed smoothly to the design of the data-collection forms, the pretest of which may require a revision of the research objectives or the research design. Still further, the sample necessary to answer the problem as specified may be prohibitively costly, again requiring a revision of the earlier steps. Once the data are collected, no revision of the procedure is possible. It is possible, though, to revise the earlier steps on the basis of the *anticipated* analysis, so it is critical that the methods used to analyze the data be determined before the data are collected.

Although it is hard for beginning researchers to understand, the steps in the research process are highly interrelated. A decision made at one stage will affect decisions at each of the other stages, and a revision of the procedure at any stage often

Table 3.1   *Questions Typically Addressed at the Various Stages of the Research Process*

Stage in the Process	Typical Questions
Formulate problem	What is the purpose of the study—to solve a problem? identify an opportunity? Is additional background information necessary? What information is needed to make the decision at hand? How will the information be utilized? Should research be conducted?
Determine research design	How much is already known? Can a hypothesis be formulated? What types of questions need to be answered? What type of study will best address the research questions?
Determine data-collection method	Can existing data be used to advantage? What is to be measured? How? What is the source of the data to be collected? Can objective answers be obtained by asking people? How should people be questioned? Should the questionnaires be administered in person, over the phone, or through the mail? Should electronic or mechanical means be used to make the observations?
Design data-collection forms	Should structured or unstructured items be used to collect the data? Should the purpose of the study be made known to the respondents? Should rating scales be used in the questionnaires? What specific behaviors should the observers record?
Design sample and collect data	Who is the target population? Is a list of population elements available? Is a sample necessary? Is a probability sample desirable? How large should the sample be? How should the sample be selected? Who will gather the data? How long will the data gathering take? How much supervision is needed? What operational procedures will be followed? What methods will be used to ensure the quality of the data collected?
Analyze and interpret the data	Who will handle the editing of the data? How will the data be coded? Who will supervise the coding? Will computer or hand tabulation be utilized? What tabulations are called for? What analysis techniques will be used?
Prepare the research report	Who will read the report? What is their technical level of sophistication? What is their involvement with the project? Are managerial recommendations called for? What will be the format of the written report? Is an oral report necessary? How should the oral report be structured?

Marketing researchers test films with groups of consumers prior to the films' release on video cassette. Movies that have a high repeat viewing potential, like this children's movie, are targeted for video sales while movies that will most likely be seen only once are aimed at the rental market.

Source: © 1990 by Marianne Barcellona.

requires modifications of procedures at each of the other stages. Unfortunately, it seems that this lesson is only understood by those who have experienced the frustrations and satisfactions of being involved in an actual research project.

Third, the important error to be concerned about when designing a research project is the *total error* likely to be associated with the project. All the steps are necessary and vital, and it is dangerous to emphasize one to the exclusion of one or more others. Many beginning students of research, for example, argue for large sample sizes. What they fail to realize is that an increase in the sample size to reduce sampling error can often lead to an increase in the total error of the research effort, since other errors increase more than proportionately with sample size. For example, a study may require researchers to call people from a list of randomly selected phone numbers. Even if the numbers themselves represent an excellent cross section of the population, a funny thing may happen on the way to the study's results. Researchers working a nine-to-five day will doubtlessly have trouble connecting with families in which both spouses work or with households made up of single working people. If this potential error is not accounted for, the study may overly represent the homebound—the elderly, families with a baby or an invalid, or the unemployed.[5] The larger the sample size, of course, the larger would be the weight of this group's opinions. The magnitude of the error caused by a large sample would then have a significant effect on the total error associated with the project.

Total error, rather than errors incurred in any single stage, is the important error in research work, except insofar as those individual errors increase total error. Quite often, *part error*, or *stage error*, will be increased so that total error may be decreased. Questions such as those in Table 3.1 must be addressed so that total error can be minimized.

Fourth, the stages in the research process serve to structure the remainder of this book. The next chapter, for example, discusses the first stage, problem formulation, while each of the remaining stages warrants a special section in the book.

Fifth, the stages in the research process can also be used to direct additional study in research method. The aspiring research student needs more sophistication in at least some of the stages than this book could possibly provide. The sections and chapters will indicate where in-depth study might be most useful.

Back to the Case

Judy Isaacs entered the conference room at Central Bank more confidently than she had two weeks before. Holding a copy of the research proposal she and her staff had devised, she took her place in front of the flip chart that an associate had set up.

"Central Bank would like to establish a successful private banking group in the Columbus area," she began. "In the past, Central has started private banking programs in new cities with campaigns primarily targeted at easily identified millionaires. Our exploratory research has shown, however, that this might not be the most fertile group of potential private banking customers, and our

research suggests a different direction for the remainder of this study."

"At the most basic level, a potential private banking customer can be defined as someone who has $100,000 to deposit with the bank. This individual must also feel that depositing the money with a bank in exchange for special banking services is more attractive then other alternatives, such as buying stock or investing in mutual funds.

"You'll notice I don't refer to these potential customers as millionaires or wealthy individuals. I avoid these terms on purpose because I think they conjure up a mental image in each of us, and that mental image can be misleading. I think we all tend

to think of millionaires as people with big houses and BMWs in their garages. When I take a look at some of the marketing efforts Central Bank has made in the past, they seem to be geared to that preconception of a wealthy individual.

"But my preliminary research has led me to believe that there are some very good reasons for avoiding the stereotypes about millionaires. For example, 80 percent of the millionaires in this country are first-generation millionaires. They made their own wealth; they did not inherit it. The typical American millionaire owns, or once owned, a business generating annual receipts of between $500,000 and $10 million. His or her business is most likely in the top 10 percent of firms in its industry in terms of profitability. In addition, the millionaire population has increased at a rate almost 15 times faster than the household population in America.

"While a lot of Central Bank's past efforts have been focused on affluent neighborhoods, I suspect that a big house is a much better predictor of the size of an individual's mortgage than of his or her bank account. I'd like to focus not on the stereotypical millionaires but, rather, on individuals who are likely to have $100,000 plus to put in the bank.

"I propose that we identify the privately held businesses in the Columbus metropolitan area with sales of $1 million or more. We'll take a random sample of those companies and do a telephone survey of their owners or CEOs."

"Isn't a phone survey going to be very expensive? Why don't we just mail out a questionnaire? We could send one to every company on the list instead of having to do a sample," pointed out one of the bankers.

"I realize that a phone survey is much more expensive than mailing a written questionnaire," replied Isaacs, "but there are several reasons for incurring the expense. First of all, the people we've targeted put a very high value on their time and are not likely to spend their scarce time filling out a questionnaire that is of no immediate direct benefit to them-

selves or their company. We could try to compensate them for doing it, but frankly, I think it would take quite a bit to induce them to do it. Also, the turnaround time on a phone survey is much faster, and I gather that all of you are pretty anxious to get results in the shape of private banking customers.

"I'll work closely with your department to formulate the questionnaire we'll use for the telephone survey."

"Once we've tabulated the results," interjected Don Lewicki, "we'll have a profile of a Columbus private banking customer. Then we'll work with Ms. Isaacs to conduct some focus groups and try out some of the strategies we've been talking about in terms of building a niche for private banking with Central Bank."

"For example," said Isaacs, flipping through her charts, "you can see I've suggested four focus groups. Two are of individuals who fit our profile in terms of income and interest but who do not currently have a private banking relationship with an area bank, and two are of individuals who already have private banking accounts. You can see from the budget breakdown that even this limited number of focus groups will be expensive. Our experience is that with high-income individuals, you have to pay between $100 and $200 to get them to participate."

"What do you hope to learn for that kind of money?" demanded one of the bank officers.

"We figure that the focus groups will give us a chance to really hear what our customers and potential customers think," answered Lewicki.

Isaacs joined in, "It will also be a good opportunity for you to try out some of the marketing strategies that will certainly suggest themselves after we've looked at the telephone survey data. For example, this might be a good time to find out whether you'd attract more customers by lowering the minimum initial deposit. It might give you a chance to explore whether allowing someone to use the private banking services for a minimum deposit of, let's say, $75,000 would give you first crack at business owners on their way up—or whether you'd just be attracting individuals who are not potentially profitable for private banking."

"And then what happens?" asked the same banker.

"And then we are done with you?" asked the bank officer who had most strongly objected to a marketing research study in the first place— only this time his tone was full of good-natured teasing.

"Oh no," replied Isaacs, only half in jest. "I know that you're going to decide that using my firm was such a good investment that you want us to help you pretest your advertising campaign!"

To find out more about marketing to millionaires, see Thomas J. Stanley, "How to Sell to a Millionaire," *Sales & Marketing Management*, 141 (August 1988), pp. 62–66.

Summary

Learning Objective 1: Explain the difference between a program strategy and a project strategy in marketing research.

A company's overall philosophy of how marketing research fits into its marketing plan determines its *program strategy* for marketing research. A program strategy specifies the types of studies that are to be conducted, and for what purposes. It might even specify how often these studies are to take place. The design of the individual studies themselves constitutes the firm's *project strategy*.

Learning Objective 2: Outline the steps in the research process and show how the steps are interrelated.

The steps in the research process are: (1) formulate the problem, (2) determine the research design, (3) determine the data-collection method, (4) design the data-collection forms, (5) design the sample and collect the data, (6) analyze and interpret the data, and (7) prepare the research report. These steps are highly interrelated in that a decision made at one stage will affect decisions in every other stage, and a revision of the procedure in any stage often requires modification of procedures in every other stage.

Learning Objective 3: Cite the most critical error in marketing research.

Total error, rather than the size of an error that occurs in any single stage, is the most critical error in research work.

Discussion Questions, Problems, and Projects

1. What advantages are gained by marketing researchers who follow the research process illustrated in Figure 3.1?

2. For each of the situations described below, which type of research design is most appropriate? Why?
    (a) Frank's Flies is a fishing lure manufacturer. Frank's management has decided to enter the lucrative market for trout flies, an area in which the company has little experience. The fly development department has decided that it needs more information concerning trout fishing in general before it can begin designing the new product line.
    (b) The management team at Aardvark Audio strongly suspects that the company's current advertising campaign is not achieving its stated goal of raising consumer awareness of the company's name to a 75-percent recognition level in the target market. The team has decided to commission a research project to test the effectiveness of the various ads in the current campaign.
    (c) Ace Fertilizer Company is trying to decide where advertisements for its vegetable garden fertilizers should be placed. Management is contemplating a research project to determine which publications home gardeners read on a regular basis.

3. Using the steps of the research process to structure your thinking, evaluate the following marketing research effort.

    The FlyRight Airline Company was interested in altering the interior layout of its aircraft to suit the tastes and needs of an increasing segment of its market—businesspeople. Management was planning to reduce the number of seats and install small tables to enable businesspeople to work during long flights. Prior to the renovation, management decided to do some research to ensure that these changes would suit the needs of the passengers. To keep expenses to a minimum, the following strategy was employed.

    Questionnaires were completed by passengers during flights. Due to the ease of administration and collection, the questionnaires were distributed only on the short flights (those less than one hour). The study was conducted during the second and third week of December, as that was when flights were full. To increase the response rate, each flight attendant was responsible for a certain number of questionnaires. Management thought this was a good time to acquire as much information as possible; hence, the questionnaire included issues apart from the new seating arrangement. As a result, the questionnaire took 20 minutes to complete.

4. Schedule an interview with the marketing research director of a firm near your home or where you go to school. In the interview, try to develop an exhaustive list of the general types of studies the firm conducts and for what purposes. Pick two of the studies and secure as much detail as you can on their specifics, such as the type and

size of the sample, the data-collection instruments used, what is done with the data after they are collected, and so on. Report on what you find, organizing that report according to the firm's program and project strategies for research.

Endnotes

1. Walter B. Wentz, *Marketing Research: Management and Methods* (New York: Harper and Row, 1972), pp. 19–24. For an example of a program strategy for marketing research, see "Research Basic to Baby-Wear Business," *Marketing News*, 21 (February 13, 1987), pp. 26 and 28, which describes the use of marketing research by Soft Care Apparel, Inc., the manufacturer of Curity Children's Wear.

2. John A. Prestbo, "At P & G Success Is Largely Due to Heeding Consumer," *The Wall Street Journal* (April 29, 1980), pp. 1 and 35.

3. Joseph R. Hochstim, "Practical Uses of Sampling Surveys in the Field of Labor Relations," *Proceedings of the Conference on Business Application of Statistical Sampling Methods* (Monticello, Ill.: The Bureau of Business Management, University of Illinois, 1950), pp. 181–182. As should be obvious from the example, researchers need to access both constituencies (dogs *and* dogs' purchasing agents)

when assessing the appeal of a product like dog food. See Nancy J. Church, "Get the Dog's Opinion When Researching Dog Food," *Marketing News*, 22 (August 29, 1988), p. 41, for suggestions on how to go about this.

4. Rohit Deshpande and Gerald Zaltman, "A Comparison of Factors Affecting Researcher and Manager Perceptions of Market Research Use," *Journal of Marketing Research*, 21 (February 1984), pp. 32–38. See also Michael Y. Hu, "An Experimental Study of Managers' and Researchers' Use of Consumer Marketing Research," *Journal of the Academy of Marketing Science*, 14 (Fall 1986), pp. 44–51.

5. Bernice Kanner, "What Makes an Ad Work?" *New York*, 16 (May 23, 1983), p. 16.

Appendix 3A

Ethics A concern with the development of moral standards by which situations can be judged; applies to all situations in which there can be actual or potential harm of any kind (e.g., economic, physical, or mental) to an individual or group.

Marketing Research Ethics

Much of this text discusses the techniques for doing marketing research. Most of the time, the act of choosing a particular research technique will involve an implicit judgment about the **ethics** of the proposed procedure. Many researchers (and managers as well) fail to confront the issue of whether it is morally acceptable to proceed in a particular way or whether they are acting in a socially responsible manner by doing so. Many take the view that if it is legal, it is ethical. They fail to appreciate that there can be differences between what is ethical and what is legal. Even among those who do appreciate the distinction, there is often a reluctance to evaluate the ethical implications of their decisions, because they feel ill-equipped to do so. Like most professionals, they simply do not know how or where to start.[1]

Although ignorance may seem like bliss, ignoring ethics issues simply because they are difficult presents real and growing dangers to individual researchers and the marketing research profession itself. For one thing, there have been a number of recent cases in which members of the profession faced litigation for alleged unethical practices. For example, Atkinson Research was sued for using a survey questionnaire to rig TV ratings in Minneapolis on behalf of its client, KARE-TV.[2] The questionnaire contained instructions for respondents to watch a particular TV channel as often as possible for a week, ostensibly so that the firm could assess viewer reactions. The suit charged that the "survey" was taken during the May Nielsen ratings period to deliberately manipulate the TV ratings. In another instance, Beecham Products sought more than $24 million in court from the research company Yankelovich Clancy Shulman for negligent misrepresentation of research findings because its market share forecasts were not upheld during the 1986 launch of Delicare, a detergent for fine fabrics.[3] A further cause for concern resides in the increasing use of telephone "surveys" as a guise for sales ploys or fundraising.[4] This troublesome trend has resulted in approximately 20 states during the past two years considering legislation that would entirely ban various forms of unsolicited telephone calls, including genuine research calls.

As mentioned, ethics is not simply a matter of compliance with laws and regulations. Rather, a particular act may be legal but not ethical. For example, although abortion on

Source: This appendix is based largely on the unpublished paper by Jacqueline C. Hitchon and Gilbert A. Churchill, Jr., "The Three Domains of Ethical Concern for the Marketing Researcher."

demand is legal, many find it unethical. Similarly, even though it is perfectly legal to observe people without their consent when they are shopping, some would argue that it is unethical to do so. Ethics is more proactive than the law. It attempts to anticipate problems, whereas most laws and regulations emerge from social pressure for change in a slow, reactive fashion. Ethics is concerned with the development of moral standards by which situations can be judged. It focuses on those situations in which there can be actual or potential harm of some kind (for example, economic, physical, or mental) to an individual or group. It asks questions such as the following:

- Is the action or anticipated action arbitrary or capricious? Does it unfairly single out an individual or group?
- Does the action or anticipated action violate the moral or legal rights of any individual or group?
- Does the action or anticipated action conform to accepted moral standards?
- Are there alternative courses of action that are less likely to cause actual or potential harm?[5]

Marketing researchers need to recognize that (1) the effective practice of their profession depends a great deal on the good will of and participation by the public, and (2) currently, the American public is becoming more and more protective of its privacy. This makes it more difficult and costly to approach, recruit, and survey participants. "Bad" research experiences that violate the implicit trust of the participants in a study can only accentuate the trend. In addition to moral fairness issues, then, self-preservation issues dictate that marketing researchers develop a sense for the ethical issues involved in particular choices. The fact that good ethics is good business is one of the reasons associations whose members are involved in marketing research have developed codes of ethics to guide the behaviors of their members.[6]

The purpose of this appendix is to provide marketing researchers with a framework and some guidelines for making ethical judgments. To this end, the appendix first reviews two main approaches from moral philosophy for making ethical judgments—*deontology* and *teleology*. The two approaches offer different perspectives on ethical problems. They serve to illustrate that a judgment about the ethicality of some approach depends not only on the researcher's awareness of the ethical dilemma but also on his or her philosophical orientation or value system.[7] Then the appendix discusses some of the major ethical issues that arise within the researchers' three domains of ethical responsibility (pictured in Figure 3A.1): (1) the researcher–participant relationship, (2) the researcher–client relationship, and (3) the researcher–research team relationship. It is recognized that all these interactions take place within a larger environment and that they have potential implications for society as well as the research profession itself.

One of the many things that make ethical decisions difficult is that the researcher's duties and responsibilities toward one party in the three domains often conflict with the individual's responsibilities toward another, including one's self. The individual then must somehow balance these opposing obligations. Consider, for example, the dilemma faced by a researcher deciding whether to expose the true purpose of a study to potential respondents. The researcher believes that exposing the true purpose beforehand would increase noncooperation and would lower the accuracy and reliability of the data collected from those who participate. The researcher's obligation to the client suggests that the research purpose should be disguised. But that could be unfair to the respondents. As a compromise, the researcher might decide to withhold the purpose initially but then debrief each respondent after securing the data. Even though this might be perceived as being more fair than keeping the purpose hidden, it might also cause some of the respondents to feel that they have been duped. This, in turn, could cause them to refuse to participate in any research investigations in the future, thereby hurting the profession.

Figure 3A.1   ***A Structure for Evaluating Ethical Dilemmas***

	Participant	Client	Member of Research Team
Deontological-Based Analysis Impact of the contemplated action on the rights of each individual			
Teleological-Based Analysis Benefits or consequences to be realized from the contemplated action			

Ethical Frameworks

As mentioned previously, there are currently two major traditions providing different bases for evaluating the ethics of a given act that tend to dominate ethical reasoning in general and marketing ethics in particular: **deontology** and **teleology.**[8]

Deontology An ethical or moral reasoning framework that focuses on the welfare of the individual and that uses means, intentions, and features of an act itself in judging its ethicality; sometimes referred to as the rights or entitlements model.

Deontology   Deontological ethics focuses on the welfare of the individual and emphasizes means and intentions for justifying an act. Deontologists believe that features of the act itself make it right or wrong. Deontological thinking rests on two fundamental principles—the rights principle and the justice principle.

The *rights principle* focuses on two criteria for judging an action: (1) universality, which means that every act should be based on principles that everyone could act on, and (2) reversibility, which means that every act should be based on reasons that the actor would be willing to have all others use, even as a basis for how they treat the actor. The rights principle is the philosophical source of specific, generally acknowledged rights in society, such as the "right to know." Several rights have acquired the force of law and have become established in the literature with respect to the treatment of research participants.[9]

The *justice principle* reflects three categories of justice: (1) distributive, whereby resources are distributed according to some evaluation of just desserts; (2) retributive, whereby the wrongdoer is punished proportionally to the wrongdoing, provided that it was committed knowingly and freely; and (3) compensatory, whereby the injured party is restored to his or her original position. An example of the justice principle applied in a marketing research setting concerns the compensatory measures that researchers take in debriefing research participants who have been significantly changed by the research experience.

With its emphasis on the issue that every individual has a right to be treated in ways that ensure the person's dignity, respect, and autonomy, the deontological model is sometimes referred to as the rights or entitlements model.

Table 3A.1   ***Questions That Need Asking to Apply the Utilitarian Model***

What are the viable courses of action available?

What are the alternatives?

What are the harms and benefits associated with the courses of action available?

Can these harms and benefits be measured? Can they be compared?

How long will these harms and benefits last?

When will these harms and benefits begin?

Who will be directly harmed? Who will be indirectly harmed?

Who will be directly benefited? Who will be indirectly benefited?

What are the social and/or economic costs attached to each alternative course of action?

Which alternatives will most likely yield the greatest net benefit to all individuals affected by the decision? Or if no alternative yields a net benefit, which one will lead to the least overall harm?

Source: Robert A. Cooke, *Ethics in Business: A Perspective* (Chicago: Arthur Andersen & Co., 1988), p. 5.

Teleology An ethical or moral reasoning framework that focuses on the net consequences that an action may have. If the net result of benefits minus all costs is positive, the act is morally acceptable; if the net result is negative, the act is not morally acceptable.

Teleology   The most well-known branch of teleological ethics is *utilitarianism*, which focuses on society as the unit of analysis and stresses the consequences of an act, rather than the intentions behind it, in evaluating its ethical status. The utilitarian model emphasizes the consequences that an action may have on all those directly or indirectly affected by it. The utilitarian perspective holds that the correct course of action is the one that promotes "the greatest good for the greatest number." Utilitarianism requires that a social cost/benefit analysis be conducted for the contemplated action. All benefits and costs to all persons affected by the particular act need to be considered to "the degree possible and summarized as the net of all benefits minus all costs. If the net result is positive, the act is morally acceptable; if the net result is negative, the act is not."[10] Net benefits can be assessed by focusing on the questions listed in Table 3A.1.

Historically, social scientists for the most part have assumed that a cost/benefit analysis is appropriate in deciding whether or not to conduct a research study.[11] Usually, the costs of conducting the study, in terms of time, money, and harm to participants, are weighed against its benefits in terms of useful and valid information to society. Marketing researchers have operated similarly, but they have typically focused on the benefits to the client rather than society as a whole. Both have tended to neglect, or have seemingly been unaware of, other ethical perspectives or the possibility that the decision reached from applying a utilitarian perspective could conflict with one reached from applying some other perspective. This type of situation is illustrated in the ethical dilemmas in Table 3A.2.

The utilitarian (teleological) perspective, with its focus on the greatest good for the greatest number, would suggest that both the sheriff and the CEO acted correctly. By acting the way they did, they saved the most people. The deontological view, with its emphasis on fairness and justice to the individual, would suggest that both men acted unethically. The dilemmas illustrate one of the fundamental problems with the utilitarian view—namely, that individuals or small groups can suffer major harm because their "large costs" are averaged with small gains to a large number of other people, with the result that the net benefit for the act is positive.

Partly because small segments can pay a high price for the slight benefit to large numbers, the suggestion has recently been made that utilitarianism is appropriate only to very general planning when no specific harm to individuals is expected and that marketing activities having a foreseeable and potentially serious impact on individuals should be regulated by deontological reasoning.[12] This implies that since research participants, clients, and team members are identifiable individuals and the effect of the research on them can be anticipated, the criteria of universality and reversibility, rather than a broad cost/benefit analysis, should be applied.

Table 3A.2   *Two Ethical Dilemmas to Contrast Deontological and Teleological Analysis*

Consider the situation of a small-town sheriff in a "grade-B" Western movie: Twelve individual men are being held as suspects in a murder case. The town is upset, and a mob threatens to kill all 12, unless the individual who committed the heinous crime comes forward. The sheriff can't stop the mob, so he picks one person at random and turns him over to the crowd, thus saving the other 11.

Or consider this case: The CEO of a company is under attack because the company recently experienced some setbacks, which were caused entirely by external circumstances. Stockholders stand to lose much of their investments, and the entire leadership of the company is threatened. The CEO decides to blame one of his vice-presidents, picked at random and without any reason. The entire company is saved.

Here's the issue: Did the sheriff or the CEO act rightly in either or both cases?

Source: Taken from the comments made by Myles Brand, Provost and Vice-President for Academic Affairs at the Ohio State University, while serving as a moderator for the session "Academia: Fostering Values" at the Fourth Biannual W. Arthur Cullman Symposium, The Ohio State University, Columbus, Ohio, April 25, 1988.

Readers also need to be aware that although the two frameworks emphasize different perspectives by which the ethicality of some contemplated act can be evaluated, neither approach provides precise answers to ethical decisions. In a utilitarian analysis, for example, one still needs to quantify costs and benefits; in deontological reasoning, one needs to evaluate the seriousness of a right's infringement. What constitutes ethical conduct in the eyes of the marketing research profession is ultimately going to be a matter of consensus. That consensus can be reached only if individual researchers think about ethical issues and exchange views.

In part to redress the unbalance in a field dominated by a utilitarian approach to ethical decision making, deontological reasoning underlies the remainder of the discussion in this appendix—specifically, identifying rights violations and conflicts and evaluating their severity. As students of marketing research, you should form the habit of interpreting a rights violation, as identified here, as a cost to be integrated into a utilitarian cost/benefit analysis. Interpreting the issues from both perspectives should make you more informed researchers who are better able to see and to evaluate the ethical trade-offs in particular situations.

Researcher–Research Participant Relationship

One useful way of viewing the ethical dilemmas that arise in the domain of the researcher-research participant relationship is by categorizing them according to five rights of research participants.[13] The advantage of discussing these issues within such a framework is that the emphasis is on identifying why a procedure might be unethical (e.g., it violates participants' right to safety) and learning which procedures cause ethical controversy. Researchers are then in a better position to generalize to new situations as they arise.

On March 15, 1962, President Kennedy delivered a special message on protecting consumers' interests, in which he outlined the Consumers' Bill of Rights, enumerating the right to safety, the right to be informed, the right to choose, and the right to be heard. These four rights were given the force of law in the Privacy Act of 1974, which applies to the abuse of respondents in federal government surveys.[14] Moreover, because most marketing research participants are acting in their role as consumers, these rights are ethically (even where they are not legally) applicable to our discussion. Other rights have since been advocated by various interest groups (e.g., the right to a consumer education, the right to representation, the right to a healthy physical environment), but one right in

Table 3A.3   **Eight Key Problem Areas of Ethical Concern within the**
Domain of the Researcher–Research Participant Relationship

Ethical Issues	Rights Violations	Rights Compensation
1. Preserving participants' anonymity	Right to safety	
2. Exposing participants to mental stress	Right to safety	Right to be heard
3. Asking participants questions detrimental to their self-interest	Right to safety	
4. Using special equipment and techniques	Right to safety	Right to redress
5. Involving participants in research without their knowledge	Right to be informed	Right to redress
6. Using deception	Right to be informed	Right to be heard; right to redress
7. Using coercion	Right to choose	
8. Depriving participants of their right to self-determination	Right to choose	

particular has been generally accepted and seems appropriate within the domain of the researcher-research participant relationship: the right to redress.[15]

Not all rights violations are grievous, so once an infringement has been identified, subjective judgment is required to evaluate the seriousness of the offense. For example, many researchers have pointed out that the degree of deception involved in concealing the true purpose of an experiment (and disregarding the subjects' right to be informed) is usually of the same trivial order as the degree of deception involved in the "white lies" that are an inherent part of everyone's social and family life.

Table 3A.3 lists the eight areas of ethical concern that seem most relevant to the domain of the researcher-research participant relationship.[16] Each key issue primarily violates one of three rights: the right to safety, to be informed, or to choose. The fourth right, the right to be heard, is violated whenever a participant is not allowed to ask questions during and after the research procedure or to voice anxieties and misgivings. Moreover, compliance with the subject's right to be heard can sometimes compensate for an infringement of other rights. Where the right to be heard stresses the fundamental need for self-expression, the right to redress emphasizes restoration to an original or comparable position. Although it can be argued that compensatory measures are desirable in all eight situations, Table 3A.3 lists the use of the right to be heard and the right to redress where they are believed to be most pertinent.

Preserving Participants' Anonymity   Maintaining subjects' anonymity ensures that they are safe from invasions of privacy. The preservation of participants' anonymity is often a more serious obligation in the field of marketing research than in other behavioral disciplines because the information obtained by marketing researchers can be extremely useful to other agents. Purchase-related data, for example, are of interest to all kinds of sellers. Further, knowledge of participants' identities is often desirable for the client who wishes to compile a mailing list of survey respondents, particularly those who feel favorably disposed to the product concept being tested. Unless respondents agree ahead of time to have their identities disclosed to the sponsor, however, such information should not be provided.

Exposing Participants to Mental Stress   An effort should be made at all times to minimize any mental stress that the research procedures may inflict on participants. On an everyday procedural level, this includes arriving punctually for a prearranged interview, showing the subject consideration and respect, and promptly fulfilling one's commitments (e.g., payment for participating). In addition, subjects may be exposed to stress as a result of the subject matter of an experiment. For example, taste tests can be humiliating for participants who pride themselves on their ability to identify a certain brand, when they find themselves unable to do so in a blind taste test.

Debriefing is usually recognized as essential if the research experience is stressful or if deception is used, but it can be undertaken in other circumstances because it is consistent with the subject's right to be heard. Its main purpose is to give participants the opportunity to voice their views on the research experience and to have any anxieties dispelled.

Asking Participants Questions Detrimental to Their Self-Interest   Consider the situation in which a marketing researcher is employed to ask respondents how acceptable certain prices are for a product, when the client's objective is to raise the current price to the highest acceptable level. If respondents are informed of the purpose of the research and its sponsor, they are likely to hedge in their answers, which will reduce the quality of the research. If, on the other hand, they are not informed about the purpose and sponsor, their responses may be against their own self-interest, thereby violating their right to safety. Situations like this, which put the researcher's ethical standards against his or her technical standards, are particularly distressing. Although the simplest solution may be to refuse to undertake the project, it is up to the individual to consider all the issues involved and reach an informed decision with which he or she feels comfortable.

Using Special Equipment and Techniques   Special equipment and techniques deserve separate mention largely because they threaten subjects' safety in ways that other procedures do not. One class of equipment, recording devices, makes later identification of individual subjects much easier and thus threatens their anonymity. The potential audience for a participant's response is also broadened when recordings are used. In certain cases, such techniques may even render blackmail a possibility. Another class of special techniques to cause ethical concern is projective techniques, the renewed use of which is currently being advocated in consumer research.[17] Projective techniques are believed to be a means of revealing unconscious thoughts and motives. In situations in which the subject is not even aware of what he or she is revealing, it is evident that the researcher is doubly obliged to act discretely and responsibly.

If safety is interpreted primarily in physical rather than privacy terms, then equipment used to measure participants' physiological reactions is more likely to violate the right to safety. Although most measures in marketing research have traditionally been either self-report or human observation, there is growing interest in the use of physiological measures, particularly to measure the response to advertising.[18] When testing physiological reactions, the researcher is under obligation to ensure that the machines are used and maintained properly so that there is no threat to the participant's physical safety. In addition, it is important that the subject be psychologically comfortable with the procedure.

Involving Participants in Research without Their Knowledge   The importance of gaining subjects' "informed, expressed consent" was first articulated at the Nuremburg Trials in protest against the inhuman treatment of prisoners involved in research in Nazi concentration camps. The criterion of "informed, expressed consent" has subsequently been incorporated into many codes of ethics and has been amended to allow incompletely informed consent provided that (1) the research involves minimal risk to subjects and (2) the research could not be practically carried out otherwise. The grim source of the "informed, expressed consent" rule lends it particular importance; moreover, the general concept gives rise to two further areas of ethical concern: the use of coercion and the use of deception.

Three common procedures exist that involve subjects in research without their knowledge and therefore without their consent:

First, *participant observation* is the name given to procedures in which the researcher participates in the activity of interest in order to observe people's behavior in their natural environment. A relevant example would be a marketer living among and studying the WASP (White, Anglo-Saxon, Protestant) subculture for 18 months in order to better understand WASP consumption behavior.[19]

Few clear guidelines exist on how participant observers should balance ethical concerns against greater validity in observation. One suggestion is to reveal one's true identity and purpose to subjects once the data have been collected and to allow the subjects to read the final report on their activities.[20] This course of action is consistent with participants' right to be heard. It rests on the hope that they will endorse the researcher's efforts and conclusions. If they do not support the study's findings, however, the researcher is faced with two competing obligations: promoting the use of the research versus respecting the subjects' right to redress (i.e., to refuse to participate after the fact).

A second procedure, *observing people in public places*, is less intrusive than participant observation and is also more common among marketing researchers. It is helpful to watch shopper's reactions to new floor displays in a store, for example. For many researchers, any activity or conversation occurring in a public place is fair game and arouses no ethical scruples. Strictly speaking, however, the research participants are being involved without their knowledge or consent, and their rights are being infringed on. If the research cannot be practically carried out by any other means, the violation can be minimized in two ways: (1) by posting an obvious notice over the whole area (e.g., the store), stating that it is under observation by researchers, or (2) by approaching subjects individually once the data have been collected and asking their permission to use them.

Withholding benefits from control groups is an issue of particular concern in running field experiments. Indeed, Burroughs-Wellcome's AIDS-combating drug AZT was recently released for general use before testing was complete, precisely because it seemed ethically indefensible to deprive the tests' control groups of the hope of delaying the disease's progress.[21] Issues to consider in deciding whether to run a field experiment with a control group include the importance of the possible benefit to the participants and the crucial nature of the information to be provided by running the study.

Using Deception   Deception is commonly used in research with human participants in the belief that subjects try to guess what behavior the researcher is expecting to see and alter their behavior accordingly.[22] Even procedural information can provoke dysfunctional responses. If the researcher announces that a recall test will be given later, for example, subjects may make a conscious effort to memorize the stimuli, whereas the recall test may well have been intended to tap noneffortful remembrance. Because of such concerns, most research is given a cover story or guise, and subjects in experiments are not informed about what kinds of tests will be given to them later.

These precautions seem sensible from the point of view of preserving the validity of the research, but they violate the subjects' right to know. Once again, there is no single correct decision that can be generalized to all research. A legal framework is available in this instance to supplement other frameworks, however. The 1981 amendment to the Privacy Act sanctions incompletely informed consent, provided that the research involves minimal risk to the subject and cannot be practicably carried·out any other way.

Using Coercion   The use of coercion by Nazi doctors in World War II concentration camps to get subjects for their research experiments has been well publicized. Less overt forms of coercion operate frequently in today's research with human subjects, and the legitimate researcher needs to be alert to them.

Captive Subject Pools   Unlike many social scientists, marketers usually do not recruit prisoners or hospital patients, subjects who tend to think that it will count against them in their own institution if they refuse to participate. But marketing researchers do commonly use employees who may think that their success in the company is partially dependent on their compliance.

Persistent Harassment   Telephone interviewing currently is a popular data collection technique among marketing researchers. Unfortunately, its high usage level has provoked an ethical dispute that may lead to government regulation. Consumers are being harassed by an overload of telephone surveys, many of which are merely sales ploys in disguise and an increasing number of which, though genuine, are irritatingly impersonal computer-voiced interviews. As with all forms of coercion used in recruiting research subjects, harassment by telephone tends to result not only in an ethical dilemma but also in poor data. If people agree to answer questions, they will do so resentfully and without due care; it is also likely that many will refuse to participate at all, with the result that the final sample of respondents will be skewed and will have been relatively costly to obtain.[23]

Status of the Researcher   As an expert and authority figure, the researcher can use this status as another subtle source of coercion.[24] Sometimes individuals who initially agree to take part in the research later wish to change their minds but are too intimidated to voice their reluctance. Marketing researchers need to be particularly sensitive to this issue when dealing with children, the elderly, the poor, or the uneducated.

Depriving Participants of Their Right to Self-Determination   The experience of participating in research always has some effect on the individual, but usually it is of a trivial nature, such as when a person fills in a questionnaire in order to kill time before supper. In some instances, however, the subject is substantially changed by the research experience in ways that he or she could not have foreseen. The subject has thereby been deprived of choice in the matter of self-determination. For example, the objective of taste tests is to find the alternative that is preferred by most people or a particular segment of subjects, not to demonstrate to subjects that many of them cannot identify their "favorite" brand when the typical identification symbols (such as the label) have been removed. One nagging question is what this does to the individual's self-confidence. In situations like this, it is the experimenter's responsibility to restore the subject to his or her original, or a comparable, condition.

Researcher–Client Relationship

The ethical issues of researcher–participant are difficult in their own right, and they become even more troublesome when the researcher's obligations to the client are introduced into the picture. Many times the demands of how to best serve the client will compete with the demands placed on the researcher regarding the moral rights of participants. Ethical concerns in the domain of the marketing researcher–client relationship can be usefully organized around four main issues: confidentiality, technical integrity, administrative integrity, and research utilization.

Confidentiality   The researcher is obliged to be discrete in at least two respects: (1) in not revealing one client's affairs to another client who is a competitor, and (2) in some circumstances, in not revealing the sponsor of the research to participants. In both cases, the researcher's loyalties can be torn and compromises may be necessary.

It is difficult to serve well several clients who have similar business interests. Even if one keeps one's list of clients confidential so that overt inquiries from one customer about another are avoided, it is not always possible to keep information acquired about one client's interests from affecting work for another client. The collection of basic demographic and socioeconomic information on a particular area is a case in point. What if that information, gathered for one client, is useful in designing a study for another client? Should the researcher ignore the knowledge he or she has when this can raise the quoted cost of the research to the second client and thereby jeopardize the business for the researcher? The issue of when "background knowledge" stops and an ethical conflict begins because of the need for client confidentiality is a real one for independent research agencies.

A conflict of loyalties also exists if the sponsor of the research does not want to be identified to the research participants, for fear of biasing their responses or indirectly tipping off a competitor. Participants' right to be informed, however, includes knowledge of the research sponsor as well as of the research purpose. Not every obligation can be fulfilled in this instance, and the researcher must make decisions tailored to each situation. For example, greater weight can be given to participants' rights if they are providing information that could be used against their interests.

Technical Integrity   As Research Window 3A.1 indicates, marketing researchers personally feel that maintaining research integrity is the most difficult ethical problem they face. Violations of research integrity extend from designing studies without due care through the unnecessary use of complex analytical procedures to the deliberate fudging of data. It cannot be emphasized enough that in this pioneering stage of the profession's development, researchers must maintain the strictest technical integrity if they are to have credibility as professional experts. It is not only unethical but also shortsighted to take advantage of the client's lack of expertise in research design and methodology, because where trust fails, funding eventually does also.

Administrative Integrity   Research Window 3A.1 indicates that treating clients fairly is also a difficult ethical problem for marketing researchers. Unfair practices that have received particular mention can be generally grouped under the term *administrative integrity*, as distinguished from technical integrity. For independent research agencies, passing hidden charges to the client and conflicts in pricing are common problems.

Research Utilization   A researcher's ethical obligations to the client extend beyond the mere completion of the project. After the project is finished, the researcher has the responsibility to promote the correct use of the research and to prevent the misuse of the findings. To some extent, these obligations are fulfilled if the contributions and limitations of the research are clearly articulated in the research report. In addition to inadvertent misuse, however, the client might deliberately suppress or distort the research results. Empirical evidence, for example, indicates that dishonesty in reporting to higher-ups is perverting the results of market tests and that potentially successful products have been dropped and unwanted ones have been introduced because of the manipulation of marketing research results.[25] Distortion of the findings can create a serious dilemma for the researcher, because it raises the issue of with whom the researcher's loyalties rest: the manager who hired the researcher and to whom the research report was delivered but who is now distorting the findings to support his or her own preconceived beliefs, or the firm for which the manager works. In situations like this, the researcher will often want to set the record straight because it is the firm's (not the manager's) money that paid for the research, and the researcher's own integrity and reputation are also at stake.

Researcher–Research Team Relationship

At this point it may appear that researchers operate as individuals when making research decisions. That is incorrect. Rather, an authority structure that constrains the individual researcher's decision-making latitude is likely to exist. When subordinates are acting

Research Window 3A.1

Researchers' Own Perceptions of the Four Most Difficult Ethical Problems They Face*

Activity	Examples	Frequency
Maintaining their research integrity	Deliberately withholding information, falsifying figures, altering research results, misusing statistics, ignoring pertinent data	33%
Treating outside clients fairly	Passing hidden charges to clients, overlooking violations of the project requirements when subcontracting parts of the project	11
Maintaining research confidentiality	Sharing information among subsidiaries in the same corporation, using background data developed in a previous project to reduce the cost of a current project	9
Balancing marketing and social considerations	Conducting research for companies that produce products hazardous to one's health or research that improves the effectiveness of advertising to children	8

*Based on responses to the question, "In all professions (e.g., law, medicine, education, accounting, marketing, etc.), managers are exposed to at least some situations that pose a moral or ethical problem. Would you briefly describe the job situation that poses the *most difficult* ethical or moral problem for you?"

Source: Developed from the information in Shelby D. Hunt, Lawrence B. Chonko, and James B. Wilcox, "Ethical Problems of Marketing Researchers," *Journal of Marketing Research*, 21 (August 1984), pp. 309–324.

according to instructions, the supervisor is partly responsible for their ethical conduct. Moreover, in addition to the official hierarchy, there exists an unofficial sphere of influence that renders every team member partially responsible for the others' moral behavior. Three areas of primary concern in the domain of the researcher–research team are the individual's own belief system, association with others at work, and the opportunity to behave unethically.[26]

Researcher's Own Beliefs   Surprisingly, only a small correlation has been found between people's ethical behavior in organizations and their own ethical beliefs. Indeed, association with other people who are behaving unethically and the opportunity to behave likewise are better predictors of an individual's conduct than his or her own belief system.[27]

Association with Others at Work   Many studies indicate that superiors have a great deal of influence over juniors' ethical conduct. In fact, actions of top management have been found to be the best predictor of perceived ethical problems for marketing researchers.[28] The source of the boss's influence probably resides in subordinates' fear of reprisals for not conforming and in their acceptance of legitimate authority. As a consequence of poor examples seen by them, marketing practitioners do not see themselves as being under pressure to improve their own ethics.[29] Indeed, they view themselves as more ethical than their peers, top management, and corporate policy. When frequency of contact with superiors is low, peers will have more influence than superiors on ethical conduct.

Opportunity to Behave Unethically   Evidence suggests that the opportunity to engage in unethical behavior affects its occurrence; more behaviors are likely to be unethical when there is greater opportunity to engage in unethical behavior.[30] Moreover, the opportunity to behave unethically is greater for marketing researchers than for many workers because of their boundary-spanning roles. Marketers, in general, span the boundary between the company and the public; marketing researchers, specifically, bridge the gap between the participant and the client, and there is a great deal of room for dishonesty while playing the go-between. Punishments and rewards might be used to reduce the attractiveness of opportunities for unethical conduct, such as a special raise for acting ethically or a delayed promotion for acting unethically. Management could also issue a corporate code of ethics to announce its concern with ethical issues and to voice standards of conduct that it considers desirable. Other suggestions to reduce the acceptability of unethical conduct within the organization include the use of consultants and seminars on ethics.[31]

Needed: A Balanced Perspective

You are probably sensitive by now to the fact that ethical issues are indeed difficult to deal with. Even when one wants to do what is morally right, it is not always intuitively obvious what the correct course of action is. Actions that might benefit one of the parties in the three domains of ethical responsibility might harm another. Whose rights or what benefits should take precedence? There are no easy answers to this question, but there are some things researchers can do to assure themselves that they are operating ethically when making decisions on techniques.

Sensitivity to the issue helps in itself. Asking oneself about the ethical implications of each contemplated course of action is a useful posture in its own right. Those who do that regularly should behave more ethically because their actions then entail explicit rather than implicit judgments. It is also useful to develop experience and expertise in handling difficult ethical situations. To that end, each of the following chapters contains two or more ethical situations that you are asked to evaluate. These Ethical Dilemmas are strategically placed within the chapters to expose you to the technical elements of the situations before confronting you with the ethical issues.

You are strongly urged to evaluate formally each of these Ethical Dilemmas, using both deontological and teleological moral philosophies and taking into account the typical parties with whom researchers deal. Figure 3A.1 offers a structure that you might find useful for conducting these analyses.

Summary

Ethics is concerned with the development of moral standards that can be applied to situations in which there can be actual or potential harm of any kind (economic, physical, or mental) to an individual or group. When contemplating some action, the marketing researcher needs to be concerned with at least three parties: participants or subjects, clients, and members of the research team.

There are two major traditions providing different bases for evaluating the ethics of a given act that tend to dominate marketing ethics: deontology and teleology. Deontological ethics focuses on the welfare of the individual and emphasizes means and intentions in justifying an act. Deontologists argue that every individual has certain rights, and it is the features of the act itself, with regard to how the act affects these rights, that make the act right or wrong.

Teleological ethics focuses on the benefits to be derived from the act. The various teleological theories differ on the issue of whose benefits to focus on. The most well-known branch of teleological ethics, utilitarianism, focuses on society as the unit of analysis. It holds that the correct course of action is the one that promotes the greatest good for the greatest number.

If researchers are to behave ethically, they need to be vigilant. They must be aware that the use of certain techniques in certain instances may be morally questionable. A recommended posture is to evaluate each contemplated action from both the deontological and the teleological perspectives. That, at least, will make the judgment explicit rather than implicit.

Discussion Questions, Problems, and Projects

1. The opinion has sometimes been voiced, "If it's legal, it's ethical." Is there any difference between what is legally right and what is morally right? Explain.
2. What are the essential differences between the deontological and the teleological perspectives? Which do you embrace? Why?
3. What questions would need to be asked to apply the teleological perspective?
4. What are the basic rights of participants in research?
5. What are the areas of most ethical concern within the domain of the researcher-research participant relationship, from a deontological perspective? What rights are at issue in each area?
6. What are the chief ethical concerns of marketing researchers when dealing with clients?
7. What factors most affect a researcher's ethics when dealing with other research team members? What are the implications for how researchers behave?

Endnotes

1. Karen Berney, "Finding the Ethical Edge," *Nation's Business*, 75 (August 1987), pp. 18–24.

2. Gregg Cebrzynski, "TV Station Sued Over Alleged 'Phoney' Survey," *Marketing News*, 21 (August 28, 1987), pp. 1 and 42.

3. Ellen Neuborne, "Researchers See Chill from Suit," *Advertising Age*, 58 (July 20, 1987), pp. 3, 50.

4. Martha Brannigan, "Pseudo Polls: More Surveys Draw Criticism for Motives and Methods," *The Wall Street Journal* (January 27, 1987), p. 27.

5. Robert A. Cooke, *Ethics in Business: A Perspective* (Chicago: Arthur Andersen & Co., 1988), p. 2.

6. For an empirical study of how people's views on ethical behaviors in research affect their participation, see Eleanor Singer, "Public Reactions to Some Ethical Issues of Social Research," *Journal of Consumer Research*, 11 (June 1984), pp. 501–509.

7. This appendix approaches ethics from the micro, or individual, level. It can also be approached from a macro perspective, in which the focus is on the ethical rightness or wrongness of the system itself, or from a company or firm perspective. For discussion of the types of questions that arise from these alternative perspectives, see Cooke, *Ethics in Business*.

8. For general discussions of the differences between the perspectives, see Cooke, *Ethics in Business*; O. C. Ferrell and Larry G. Gresham, "A Contingency Framework for Understanding Ethical Decision Making in Marketing," *Journal of Marketing*, 49 (Summer 1985), pp. 87–96; Shelby D. Hunt and Scott Vitell, "A General Theory of Marketing Ethics," *Journal of Macromarketing*, 6 (Spring 1986), pp. 5–16; and Donald P. Robin and R. Eric Reidenbach, "Social Responsibility, Ethics, and Marketing Strategy: Closing the Gap between Concept and Application," *Journal of Marketing*, 51 (January 1987), pp. 44–58. For descriptions of other frameworks, see one of the general books on ethics, such as Richard De George, *Business Ethics*, 2nd ed. (New York: Macmillan, 1986), or Manuel Velasquez, *Business Ethics*, 2nd ed. (Englewood Cliffs, N.J.: Prentice-Hall, Inc., 1982). For a general treatment of ethics in marketing, including separate discussions of ethics in advertising, field sales, and marketing research, see Gene R. Laczniak and Patrick E. Murphy, eds., *Marketing Ethics: Guidelines for Managers* (Lexington, Mass.: D. C. Heath, 1985).

9. Alice M. Tybout and Gerald Zaltman, "Ethics in Marketing Research: Their Practical Relevance," *Journal of Marketing Research*, 11 (November 1974), pp. 357–368.

10. Robin and Reidenbach, "Social Responsibility, Ethics, and Marketing Strategy," p. 46.

11. Louise H. Kidder and Charles M. Judd, *Research Methods in Social Relations*, 5th ed. (New York: Holt, Rinehart and Winston, 1986), pp. 452–510.

12. Robin and Reidenbach, "Social Responsibility, Ethics, and Marketing Strategy."

13. This procedure is consistent with the approach used by Tybout and Zaltman. Their analysis concentrated on three of the four rights then established, rather than the five rights discussed here. See Tybout and Zaltman, "Ethics in Marketing Research: Their Practical Relevance."

14. Cynthia J. Frey and Thomas C. Kinnear, "Legal Constraints and Marketing Research: Review and Call to Action," *Journal of Marketing Research*, 16 (August 1979), pp. 295–302.

15. David A. Aaker and George S. Day, "A Guide to Consumerism," in David A. Aaker and George S. Day, eds., *Consumerism: Search for the Consumer Interest* (New York: Macmillan Publishing Co., Inc., 1982), pp. 4–8; and Lee E. Preston and Paul N. Bloom, "The Concerns of the Rich/Poor Consumer," in Paul N. Bloom and Ruth Belk Smith, eds., *The Future of Consumerism* (Lexington, Mass.: D. C. Heath and Co., 1986), pp. 38–40.

16. For background on the various rights of research participants, see Herbert C. Kelman, "Human Uses of Human Subjects: The Problem of Deception in Social Psychological Experiments," *Psychological Bulletin*, 67 (January 1967), pp. 1–11; Charles Mayer and Charles White, Jr., "The Law of Privacy and Marketing

Research," *Journal of Marketing*, 33 (April 1969), pp. 1–4; Herbert C. Kelman, "The Rights of the Subject in Social Research: An Analysis in Terms of Relative Power and Legitimacy," *American Psychologist*, 27 (November 1972), pp. 989–1016; Tybout and Zaltman, "Ethics in Marketing Research"; "Ethical Principles of Psychologists," *American Psychologist*, 36 (June 1981), pp. 633–638; Robert Rosenthal and Ralph L. Rosnow, *Essentials of Behavioral Research: Methods and Data Analysis* (New York: McGraw-Hill, 1984); and Kidder and Judd, *Research Methods in Social Relations.*

17. David G. Mick, "Consumer Research and Semiotics: Exploring the Morphology of Signs, Symbols, and Significance," *Journal of Consumer Research*, 13 (September 1986), pp. 196–213.

18. David W. Stewart, "Physiological Measurement of Advertising Effects," *Psychology and Marketing*, 1 (Spring 1984), pp. 43–48; John T. Cacioppo and Richard E. Petty, "Physiological Responses and Advertising Effects: Is the Cup Half Full or Half Empty," *Psychology and Marketing*, 2 (Summer 1985), pp. 115–126; Joanne M. Klebba, "Physiological Measures of Research: A Review of Brain Activity, Electrodermal Response, Pupil Dilation and Voice Analysis Methods and Studies," in *Current Issues and Research in Advertising* (Ann Arbor: University of Michigan, 1985), pp. 53–76; and Scott S. Liu, "Picture-Image Memory of TV Advertising in Low-Involvement Situations: A Psychophysiological Analysis," in *Current Issues and Research in Advertising* (Ann Arbor: University of Michigan, 1986), pp. 27–60.

19. Elizabeth C. Hirschman, "Humanistic Inquiry in Marketing Research: Philosophy, Method, and Criteria," *Journal of Marketing Research*, 23 (August 1986), p. 243.

20. Ibid., p. 244.

21. D. Grady, "Look, Doctor, I'm Dying. Give Me the Drug," *Discover* (August 1986), pp. 78–86.

22. Alan G. Sawyer, "Demand Artifacts in Laboratory Experiments," *Journal of Consumer Research*, 1 (March, 1975), pp. 20–30; and Leonard Berkowitz and Edward Donnerstein, "External

Validity Is More than Skin Deep: Some Answers to Criticisms of Laboratory Experiments," *American Psychologist*, 37 (March 1982), pp. 245–257.

23. Brannigan, "Pseudo Polls."

24. Tybout and Zaltman, "Ethics in Marketing Research."

25. Calvin L. Hodock, "Intellectual Dishonesty Is Perverting the Results from Various Market Tests," *Marketing News*, 18 (January 1984), p. 1.

26. Ferrell and Gresham, "A Contingency Framework for Understanding Ethical Decision Making in Marketing."

27. Mary Zey-Ferrell and O. C. Ferrell, "Role-Set Configuration and Opportunities as Predictors of Unethical Behavior in Organizations," *Human Relations*, 35 (July 1982), pp. 587–604; and O. C. Ferrell, Mary Zey-Ferrell, and Dean Krugman, "A Comparison of Predictors of Ethical and Unethical Behavior Among Corporate and Agency Advertising Managers," *Journal of Macromarketing*, 3 (Spring 1983), pp. 19–27.

28. Shelby D. Hunt, Lawrence B. Chonko, and James B. Wilcox, "Ethical Problems of Marketing Researchers," *Journal of Marketing Research*, 21 (August 1984), p. 314.

29. O. C. Ferrell and K. Mark Weaver, "Ethical Beliefs of Marketing Managers," *Journal of Marketing*, 42 (July 1978), pp. 69–73.

30. Zey-Ferrell and Ferrell, "Role-Set Configurations and Opportunities"; Ferrell and Gresham, "A Contingency Framework for Understanding Ethical Decision Making"; and Skinner, Dubinsky, and Ferrell, "Organizational Dimensions of Marketing-Research Ethics."

31. Patrick Murphy and Gene R. Laczniak, "Marketing Ethics: A Review with Implications for Managers, Educators and Researchers," in Ben M. Enis and Kenneth J. Roering, eds., *Review of Marketing 1981* (Chicago: American Marketing Association, 1981), pp. 251–266.

Problem Formulation

Learning Objectives

Upon completing this chapter, you should be able to

1. Specify the three sources of marketing problems or opportunities.

2. Describe the main purpose of marketing research for each of the three sources of marketing problems.

3. Describe a decision situation.

4. List the factors that make up a decision maker's environment.

5. Describe the various elements a researcher must understand in order to address the real decision problem.

6. Distinguish between a decision problem and a research problem.

7. Explain why a decision tree can be useful in problem solving.

8. Outline the various elements of the research proposal.

This was not a pleasure trip. Celia Cooper, the new marketing manager of the Lady Lillian Dress Company, was traveling with the company's president, Elliott Levinson, to Philadelphia. They were going to meet with the company's longtime customer, Hanna's, to find out why the department store chain no longer wanted to sell dresses made by the Lady Lillian Dress Company. Cooper, who had been with Lady Lillian for less than two months and had only met with the company's president on a few brief occassions, felt like she was taking a business trip with a grizzly bear—a very grumpy grizzly bear.

What Hanna's executives had to say at the meeting didn't do anything to cheer him up. They were as diplomatic as possible, but the bottom line was that Lady Lillian's dresses, which generally sold in the $100 range, were too drab and priced too low for the retailer's upscale image.

After meeting with Hanna's executives, Levinson and Cooper went down onto the sales floor. They found that while designer dresses had elaborate displays to entice the shopper, the Lady Lillian dresses were jammed onto steel racks with only the sleeves showing.

"This is an insult to the customer," declared Levinson in disgust.

In a restaurant across the street from Hanna's flagship store, Cooper faced Levinson over a plate of french fries. His face was grim but his attitude positive.

"I want today to mark the beginning of the transformation of the Lady Lillian Dress Company. Up until now we've basically been a Seventh Avenue dressmaker. I want to turn us into a marketer of sophisticated apparel. But I want to do that without turning our back on our ultimate customer—the woman who buys a dress for $100. A hundred dollars—think of it. For most American women, $100 is a lot of money. For that they should be able to buy a dress that makes them feel beautiful, and they shouldn't have to paw through a rack of dresses jammed into the back of the store to do it!"

"I agree," said Cooper. "I think the concept of a good dress for $100 is still a good one. But somewhere along the road we've gotten off track."

"That's why I hired you," replied Levinson with a wolfish grin. "How do you suggest we get back on track?"

"I think we need pay attention to what the people at Hanna's have told us. They're much closer to the consumer than we are. To be perfectly honest, I think we need to get much closer to the consumer. I think our next step should be to hire a marketing research firm to find out more about the woman who buys our dresses. We know that the people at Hanna's think that our dresses are drab, but do the customers? Hanna's is very frank about wanting to pursue an upscale image; maybe it doesn't want to sell any moderately priced dresses. Then there's the possibility that our dresses aren't drab but the customers are being turned off by the way Hanna's is displaying them."

Levinson nodded. "If you think we need a marketing research study, then I think that should be our first step. But I don't want to spend a fortune, and I don't want it to take forever. I agree that we probably need to know more about how our customers perceive us before we plan our strategy, but I don't want to spend our resources studying the problem, I want us to spend the resources doing something about it."

Discussion Issues

1. What was the decision problem facing the Lady Lillian Dress Company?
2. What are the research problems raised by the decision problem?
3. In what way are the research problems that Cooper must define affected by Levinson, the person who will eventually act on the results of the marketing research study?

Problem Formulation

An old adage says, "A problem well defined is half solved." This is especially true in marketing research, for it is only when the problem has been clearly defined and the objectives of the research precisely stated that research can be designed properly. "Properly" here means not only that the research will generate the kinds of answers needed, but that it will do so efficiently.

Problem definition (or problem formulation) is being used in the broadest sense of the term. It refers to those situations that might indeed represent real problems to the marketing decision maker, as well as to those situations that might be better described as opportunities. In order to understand the problem definition stage of the marketing research process, it is helpful to have some appreciation of how problems and opportunities arise.

There seem to be three fundamental sources for marketing problems or opportunities and, consequently, research problems: (1) unanticipated change, (2) planned change, and (3) serendipity in the form of new ideas.[1] Change in one form or another is the most important source by far.

One of the great sources of unanticipated change is the environment in which firms operate. There are simply many elements in a firm's external environment that can create problems or opportunities. These include demographic, economic, technological, competitive, political, and legal changes that can impact, often significantly, the marketing function. How the firm responds to new technology or a new product introduced by a competitor or a change in demographics or lifestyles largely determines whether the change turns out to be a problem or an opportunity. For example, "General Foods' . . . Maxim was the first, freeze-dried instant coffee. This put Nestlé under considerable pressure. Nestlé responded with Taster's Choice freeze-dried instant coffee and soon dominated Maxim in the market."[2]

Not all change is unanticipated. Much of it is planned. Most firms want to increase their business and contemplate various marketing actions for doing so. These actions include the introduction of new products, improved distribution, more effective pricing, and advertising. Planned change is oriented more toward the future, while unanticipated change is oriented more toward the past. The former is more proactive, while the latter is more reactive. Planned change is change that the firm wishes to bring about—the basic issue is *how*. The role of marketing research here is to investigate the feasibility of the alternatives being considered.

A third source of marketing problems or opportunities is serendipity, or chance ideas. The new idea might come from a customer in a complaint letter or by some other means. For example, Rubbermaid makes it a practice for its executives to read customer letters so as to find out how people like the company's products. These letters often lead to new product ideas. For example, complaints about the difficulty of storing traditional rack-and-mat sets because of their bulk led the company to develop a one-piece dish drainer for washing dishes by hand.[3] Strict attention to detail, including suggestions like this, has allowed the company to introduce about 100 new products a year. Marketing research plays an important role in the company's development process. Besides customers, other sources of good ideas are salespeople and their call reports. Similarly, comments from the trade might serve as the impetus for planned change, for which research might play a role.

Regardless of how problems or opportunities arise, most of them will require additional information for resolution. The information needed for their resolution will need to be identified and approaches for securing it determined. This requires good communication between the decision maker and the marketing researcher. The decision maker needs to understand what research can and cannot accomplish. The

"My mistake was in ignoring the effect that global marketing imperatives would have on local hot dog sales."

Source: Drawing by Ed Fisher. © 1990 *Advertising Age*. Reprinted by permission of Ed Fisher.

researcher needs to understand the nature of the decision the manager faces and what he or she hopes to learn from research, that is, the project objectives.

Researchers must avoid simply responding to managers' requests for information. To do so is akin to a doctor's letting a patient perform his or her own diagnosis and prescribe the treatment as well. Rather, the researcher needs to work with the manager much like a doctor works with a patient; both need to communicate openly in translating symptoms into underlying causal factors.

There is a general tendency to assume that managers have a clear understanding of the problems they face and that the only real difficulty lies in communicating that understanding. This assumption is false. To many managers, the problem is primarily a lack of important facts. They tend to define it as a broad area of ignorance. "They say in effect: 'Here are some things I don't know. When the results come in, I'll know more. And when I know more, then I can figure out what to do.'"[4] Research results based on such a mode of operation most often turn out to be "interesting," but not very actionable. All the results do is reduce the level of uncertainty, but they provide little understanding of the true problem. Both managers and researchers need to recognize that marketing research does not produce answers or strategies. It produces data—data that must be interpreted and converted into action plans by management. In order for the interpretation to be on target, the research needs to reflect management's business priorities and concerns, for "it is far better to resolve the right . . . problem partially than to resolve the wrong problem fully."[5]

Managers need to play an active role in communicating their information needs to researchers. They also need to be semiactive participants in the research process itself, interacting with the researchers when necessary to ensure that the research will provide the information they truly need to make the decisions with which they are faced. Sometimes this may mean using their own intuition when interpreting the research findings, as Research Window 4.1 demonstrates.

A proper understanding of the basic structure of decisions can help researchers do a better job of determining the information needs of managers. The simplest of decision situations can be characterized by the following conditions. See Figure 4.1.

Research Window 4.1
Managers as Active Participants in the Research Process

In the early days of pay-cable services, a television company was considering the establishment of a cultural cable channel as a logical extension of its business. A company executive commissioned a survey to determine the demand for such a channel, which would have carried a monthly fee similar to that charged by Home Box Office (HBO), at the time the only existing pay-cable outlet.

The survey appeared to give a green light to the project, indicating that 20 percent of all cable users would subscribe. But the executive, even though he could find no technical flaw in the questionnaire or the sampling technique, remained skeptical of the results. He remembered from his years of experience how focus group participants would often claim to be fans of public television but would rarely admit to watching "Dallas," "Dynasty," or other top-rated network shows. This phenomenon suggested to him that the survey data might not be realistic.

Pursuing his hunch, the executive hired another research firm to investigate the channel's potential. This firm knew that consumers have been known to tell white lies to an interviewer. They tend, for example, to exaggerate their involvement in socially desirable activities such as voting. Similarly, they are apt to overestimate their willingness to purchase attractive or glamorous new products or services. They may wish to please the interviewer, to appear open to new experiences, to appear financially capable of purchasing the offering, or—as in the case of the cable station—to appear intelligent and cultured. The new research team constructed its study to account for such tendencies.

Although the researchers asked many of the same questions that appeared in the first survey, they also included seemingly unrelated questions about respondents' recent participation in a range of activities, from attending the opera to going to the zoo to watching a ball game. Again, 20 percent said they were willing to pay for the cultural channel. But when respondents who had never before patronized cultural events were eliminated from the "yea sayers"—on the assumption that they were unlikely to undergo a sudden metamorphosis into highbrows—the research predicted that less than 1 percent of cable users were likely to subscribe. The company scrapped its plan for the station.

How did this cable executive avoid a calamity? First, his understanding of the market allowed him to recognize potential shortcomings in the initial research. Second, he was able to find a research company experienced in gauging consumers' real interest in new products. Obviously, had he commissioned the research only to support a decision he had already made, he would never have questioned the encouraging findings of the first study. His success underscores the importance of direct management's involvement in market research.

Source: Robert S. Duboff, "The Real Magic of Market Research," *Viewpoint*, 17 (Summer 1988), pp. 19–20.

Figure 4.1   **A Sample Decision Situation**

Barbara B., a high school student interested in a broadcasting career, must decide whether to go to **College A_1**—an inexpensive community college nearby, which will allow her to live at home and work part-time as a secretary at a local radio station in hopes of getting experience that will lead to a good job in her field, *or* **College A_2**—an expensive but excellent private college far from home, with a well-known communications department and a good track record in job placement and in percentage of students accepted to graduate school. What might be the advantages—and disadvantages—of each choice?

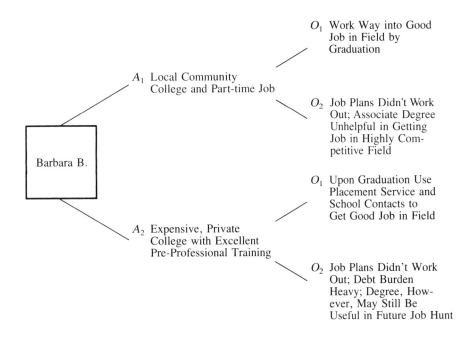

1. Person or organization X has a problem. That problem is the result of something that is taking place in X's environment (E).
2. There are at least two courses of action, A_1 and A_2, that X can follow.
3. If X chooses to follow A_2, for example, there are at least two possible outcomes of that choice $(O_1$ and $O_2)$. Of these outcomes, one is preferred to the other, so the decision process must have an objective.
4. There is a chance, but not an equal chance, that each course of action will lead to the desired outcome. If the chances were equal, the choice would not matter.[6]

To sum up, a person faces a decision situation if he or she has a problem, knows several good, but not equally good, ways of solving it, and must pick between the various choices available. Research can assist in clarifying any of these characteristics of the decision situation. Let us briefly consider how.

The Decision Maker and the Environment

It is important that the researcher understand the personality of the decision maker and the environment in which that person operates. Sometimes a decision maker will have preset ideas about a particular situation, and surprisingly, his or her position may not change, regardless of what is found by the researcher. Research merely represents "conscience money" in these cases. The results are readily accepted when they are consistent with the decision the individual wants to make, or with the person's perceptions of the environment or the consequences of alternative actions. Otherwise, the results are questioned, at best, or discarded as being inaccurate, at worst. The reason, of course, is that the individual's view of the situation is so strongly held that the research will do little to change it. When this is the case, research will be a waste of the firm's resources. The first task of the researcher, therefore, is to discover whether the decision maker is truly willing to consider the results of the research.

An example of pointless research was found by the Advertising Research Foundation in surveying financial service companies. Although such companies spend almost as much as other consumer goods industries on television ads, they spend relatively little on research to test the effectiveness of their ads ($28,300 median for banks, $45,800 for diversified financial companies, and only $22,500 for insurance companies, compared with upwards of $500,000 for other consumer goods industries). And among the 60 percent of this group who bother to test at all, 58 percent admit that the results of such research do not play an important part in their marketing decision making.[7]

Often the task of determining whether management's preferred opinion might change with research information is complicated by the fact that the researcher's contact is not the final decision maker but a liaison. Yet, this determination should be made before the researcher begins work.

As previously mentioned, the researcher also needs to understand the environment of the enterprise in which the decision maker operates. What are the constraints on that person's actions? What are the resources at the decision maker's disposal? What is the time frame in which the manager is operating? It does little good to design a study, however accurate, that costs $20,000 and takes six months to complete when the decision maker needs the results within one month and has only $2,000 for the research. Obviously, some compromises must be made, and it is the researcher's responsibility to anticipate them by carefully examining the decision environment.

The corporate culture, of course, is an important factor in the environment and should be carefully studied by the researcher.[8] In some firms, the process by which decisions are made is dominant, while in other firms the personality of management is more important. At General Mills, for example, the emphasis is on research that evaluates alternatives. Thus, instead of asking the question, "What proportion of potato chips is eaten at meals?" General Mills would ask, "How can we advertise our potato chips for meal consumption?" or "Will a 'meal commercial' sell more chips than our present commercial?" (both action questions). To design effective research for General Mills, therefore, a researcher would need to be aware of this aspect of the general corporate culture.

The environment will include the state of the economy in general and also the economic situation of the particular industry involved and the company itself. In the mid-1980s, for example, the environment for manufacturers of fast-selling products like videocassette recorders was quite different from that for the ailing steel industry, despite the fact that they were both part of the same national economy.

Even within the same company, decision makers' environments may differ. At the same time that Coleco Industries was deciding to dump its entire computer operation (after sales of its Adam home computers and ColecoVision video games fizzled), it was also struggling to fill the huge demand for its highly successful Cabbage Patch Kids.[9] Decision makers in these two divisions of the company faced very different challenges from their environments.

Figure 4.2   **The Best-Laid Models of Mice and Men . . .**

The late Bob Keith, while president of the Pillsbury Company, was once persuaded by Pillsbury's operations researchers to review one of his major marketing decisions using a formal decision model. He agreed to the outcomes, their values, and their probabilities, and chose the decision rule he felt most appropriate. The computer then calculated the expectations, compared them, and reported the alternative that should be chosen according to that rule. Mr. Keith disagreed, noting that another alternative was obviously the only correct choice—indeed, it was the choice that *had* been made not long before. "How can that be?" the researchers asked. "You accepted all the values and probabilities and chose the decision rule yourself. The rest is just arithmetic." "That's fine," Keith replied, "but you forgot to ask me about a few other things that were more important."

Source: Adapted from Charles Raymond, *The Art of Using Science in Marketing* (New York: Harper & Row, 1974), p. 17.

Alternative Courses of Action

Research can be properly designed only when the alternative courses of action being considered are known. The more obvious ones are typically given to the researcher by the decision maker, and the researcher's main task is to determine whether the list provided indeed exhausts the alternatives. Quite often the researcher will not be informed of some of the options being considered. The researcher should check to see that all implicit options have been made explicit, since it is important that the research be relevant to all alternatives.

Let us consider an example of the types of alternative courses of action that a company may consider. The Campbell Soup Company has a strong commitment to keeping pace with consumer and technological trends. As part of its ongoing research, the company's product managers team up with in-house and outside researchers to probe for openings in the market. In addition to Campbell's traditional family market, the research teams have investigated the eating habits and flavor preferences of career women, Hispanics, consumers over age 55, and owners of microwave ovens—each of these groups suggesting an alternative course of action. And now that the company's "Soup is Good Food" campaign is well established, the team has begun work on positioning soup as a convenient snack food. Some of the other alternatives the company is considering are to create other value-added food items, advertise heavily to attract consumers to try Campbell's products, and be a low-cost producer.[10]

Researchers at times must adopt the role of detective in order to uncover the hidden agendas and alternatives lurking beneath the surface in any decision situation. If a critical piece of information remains undiscovered, even the most sophisticated research techniques cannot solve the problem. Attempting to impress the company president, researchers at Pillsbury discovered this fact belatedly—to their embarrassment (Figure 4.2).

Objectives of the Decision Maker

As a part of understanding the decision maker, the researcher should be aware that individuals differ in their attitudes toward risk and that these differences influence their choices. Some people are willing to assume a good deal of risk for the chance of even a small gain.[11] Others are unwilling to assume any risk, even when the potential gain is great. And some individuals walk a middle ground.

A person's attitude toward risk changes with the situation. When feeling secure in his or her position in the company, a person may take greater risks than at another time, when feeling less secure.

Take the case of Jimmy Spradley, young president of Standard Candy of Nashville, manufacturers of Goo Goo Clusters—a gooey confection dear to the hearts of southerners. When Spradley took over Standard Candy, it was close to bankruptcy. The new president immediately turned his focus to marketing, offering brokers trips as incentives for improved sales performance and enticing retailers to stock the brand by offering appealing discounts. By the summer of 1983 sales were strong, and the company's debts were being paid off. It was then that Spradley took a big risk.

Impatient to boost sales even further, he doubled his discounts for certain customers. Sales soared, but profits plummeted, and the company began to lose money. Spradley quickly stopped the practice, admitting ruefully, "I've learned there's more to my company's health than fast growth."

Spradley could afford to take risks. After all, his father owned 50 percent of the company's stock, sales were on the upswing, and his decision could easily be reversed if initial results were bad. A year earlier, with the wolves at the door, Spradley's tactics were less risky. He knew that at that point one serious slip meant financial disaster for the company.[12]

It is the researcher's task to discover what attitude toward risk the decision maker has. Often some hint of the decision maker's posture can be gained from intensive probing, using "what if" hypothetical outcomes of the research.

Closely allied to the need to determine the decision maker's attitude toward risk is the need to determine the decision maker's specific objectives. It is unfortunate, but true, that these are rarely explicitly stated.

> Despite a popular misconception to the contrary, objectives are seldom given to the researcher. The decision maker seldom formulates his objectives accurately. He is likely to state his objectives in the form of platitudes which have no operational significance. Consequently, objectives usually have to be extracted by the researcher. In so doing, the researcher may well be performing his most useful service to the decision maker.[13]

The researcher must transform the platitudes into specific operational objectives that the research can be designed to serve.

> One effective technique for uncovering these objectives consists of confronting the decision maker with each of the possible solutions to a problem and asking him whether he would follow that course of action. Where he says "no," further probing will usually reveal objectives which are not served by the course of action.[14]

Once the objectives for the research are finally decided upon, they should be committed to writing. In the course of this effort, additional clarity in thinking and in communication between the decision maker and researcher is often achieved. They should then agree formally on their written expression (by each initialing each statement of purpose, by initialing the entire document, or by some other means). This tends to prevent later misunderstandings.

Consequences of Alternative Courses of Action

A great deal of marketing research is intended to determine the consequences of various courses of action. Much of the research highlighted in the tables in Chapter 1, for example, deals with the impact of manipulating one of the Ps in the marketing mix. This is not surprising since, as we have seen, the marketing manager's task basically involves manipulating the elements of the mix to achieve customer satisfaction. What is a more natural marketing research activity than seeking answers to such questions as, What will be the change in sales occasioned by a change in the product's package? If we change the sales compensation plan, what will be the effect on the sales representatives' performance and on their attitudes toward the job and company? Which ad is likely to generate the most favorable customer response?

Researchers are primarily responsible for designing research that accurately assesses the outcomes of past or contemplated marketing actions. In this capacity, they must gauge the actions against all the outcomes management deems relevant. Management, for example, may want to know the impact of the proposed change on sales as well as on consumer attitudes. If the research addresses only consumer attitudes, management will most assuredly ask for the relationship between attitudes and sales. Embarrassing questions of this nature can only be avoided if researchers painstakingly probe for all relevant outcomes before designing the research.

Ethical
Dilemma 4.1   The president of a small bank approaches you with plans to launch a special program of financial counseling and support for women and asks you to establish whether there is sufficient public interest to justify starting the program. No other bank in the city caters specifically to women, and you think that professional women, in particular, might be enthused. The president believes that if news of the plan leaks out, competitors may try to preempt him, so he asks you to keep the bank's identity secret from respondents and to inquire only into general levels of interest in increased financial services for women. However, as you read through the literature that he has left on your desk, you notice that the bank is located in the most depressed area of the city, where women might be harassed and feel unsafe.

- Would it be unethical to research the general problem of how much demand exists for a women's banking program, when the bank in question will interpret the demand as encouragement to launch such a program itself?
- What might be the costs to the researcher in voicing misgivings about the suitability of this particular bank's launching of the program? Would you voice your misgivings?
- Does it violate respondents' rights if you do not reveal the identity of the research sponsor? If so, is it a serious violation in this case? Is there a conflict of interest here with respect to respondents' right to be informed versus the client's right to confidentiality?

Translating the Decision Problem into a Research Problem

Decision problem The problem facing the decision maker for which the research is intended to provide answers.

Research problem A restatement of the decision problem in research terms.

A detailed understanding of the decision maker's personality, environment, objectives, and preconceived ideas of possible alternative courses of action should enable researchers to translate the **decision problem** into a **research problem.** A research problem is essentially a restatement of the decision problem in research terms. Consider, for example, the new product introduction for which sales are below target. The decision problem faced by the marketing manager is deciding what to do about the shortfall. Should the target be revised? Should the product be withdrawn? Should

Table 4.1   *Examples of the Relationship between*
Decision Problems and Research Problems

Decision Problems	Research Problems
Develop package for a new product	Evaluate effectiveness of alternative package designs
Increase market penetration through the opening of new stores	Evaluate prospective locations
Increase store traffic	Measure current image of the store
Increase amount of repeat purchasing behavior	Assess current amount of repeat purchasing behavior
Develop more equitable sales territories	Assess current and proposed territories with respect to their potential and workload
Allocate advertising budget geographically	Determine current level of market penetration in the respective areas
Introduce new product	Design a test market through which the likely acceptance of the new product can be assessed

one of the other elements in the marketing mix, such as advertising, be altered? Suppose the manager suspects that the advertising campaign supporting the new product introduction has been ineffective. This suspicion could serve as the basis for a research problem. For example, as the demand for denim jeans faded in the mid-1980s, Wrangler made the decision to expand its market beyond Western wear into a broad range of garments. To promote the line, Wrangler launched an advertising campaign with the theme "Live it to the Limit," featuring people in exciting situations wearing Wrangler shirts, pants, and swimwear. However, subsequent consumer research showed that shoppers continued to perceive Wrangler as a maker of jeans, and not other, non-denim apparel. Wrangler's decision to stay with an expanded clothing line remained firm, but it was clear that the advertising had failed to convey that message. Consequently, Wrangler revised its advertising again to feature mini-adventure movies in which the heroes and heroines wore fashionable Wrangler non-denim outfits.[15]

Some illustrations of the distinctions between decision problems and research problems can be found in Table 4.1. Though the two problems are obviously related, they are not the same. The decision problem involves what needs to be done. The research problem involves determining what information should be provided in order to make the decision on what needs to be done—and how that information can best be secured.

In making this determination, the researcher must make certain that the real decision problem, not just the symptoms, is being addressed. The landscape is dotted with examples where poor decision problem definition led to poor research problem definition with unfortunate consequences, some more dire than others. The debacle with Coca-Cola Classic is well known. What is perhaps less well known is that Miller did not invent Lite beer. Rather, it was first developed by Meister Bräu.[16] The taste tests indicated that people liked the beer. When it was introduced by Meister Bräu, though, it failed. The company in turn sold it to Miller, who defined the decision problem and subsequently the research problem as something more than having a

Figure 4.3   *Percentage of Research Users Who Believe that Researchers Engage in the Activity to Help Define the Decision Problem or "Preferably Should" Engage in the Activity*

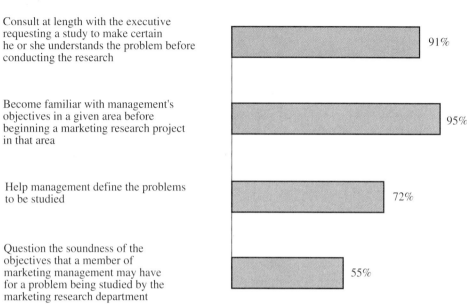

Activity

Consult at length with the executive requesting a study to make certain he or she understands the problem before conducting the research — 91%

Become familiar with management's objectives in a given area before beginning a marketing research project in that area — 95%

Help management define the problems to be studied — 72%

Question the soundness of the objectives that a member of marketing management may have for a problem being studied by the marketing research department — 55%

Source: Developed from the information in James R. Krum, Pradeep A. Rau, and Stephen K. Keiser, "The Marketing Research Process: Role Perceptions of Researchers and Users," *Journal of Advertising Research*, 25 (December 1987/January 1988), p. 14.

preferred taste. Rather, Miller's research suggested that the big beer drinkers tried to project macho images, and the very concept of a diet beer connoted "wimp." Miller's emphasis thus became one of changing the image of the brand through its use of famous sports personalities. Another not-so-well-known instance of poor problem definition leading to poor interpretation of research involved the Muppets. The producer of the show, Bernie Brillstein, originally pitched the show to CBS. CBS's marketing research indicated that there was no way to win an audience with a show having a *frog* for a host. The frog was Kermit; he and his fellow Muppets eventually became a hugely successful syndication.[17] In this case, neither the decision makers nor the researchers at CBS took into account the fact that every new show has to form a chemistry with its viewers, and that takes time.

How does one avoid the trap of researching the wrong decision problem? The main way is to delay research until the decision problem is properly defined.

There is an old saying that applies here: "If you do not know where you want to go, any road will get you there." It is the same in decision making. If the decision maker does not know what he or she wants to achieve, any alternative will be satisfactory and research will be of little use. Too often the researcher's initial step is to write a proposal describing the methods that will be used to conduct the research. Instead, the researcher should take the time to examine the situation carefully so as to acquire the necessary appreciation for (1) the decision maker and the environment, (2) the alternative courses of action, (3) the objectives of the decision maker, and (4) the consequences of alternative actions. As Figure 4.3 indicates, even marketing managers believe that researchers should take an active role in helping to define the decision problem and in specifying the information that will be useful for solving it.

One useful mechanism for making sure that the real decision problem will be addressed by the research is to execute a **research request step** before preparing the research proposal.[18] This step requires that the decision maker and researcher have a meeting in which the decision maker describes the problem and the information that is needed. The researcher then drafts a statement describing his or her understanding of the problem. The statement should include, but is not limited to, the following items:

Research request step
The initial step that sets the research process in motion; this statement, which is prepared by the researcher after meeting with the decision maker, summarizes the problem and the information that is needed to address it.

1. Action: The actions that are contemplated on the basis of the research.
2. Origin: The events that led to a need for the decision to act. While the events may not directly affect the research that is conducted, they help the researcher understand more deeply the nature of the research problem.
3. Information: The questions that the decision maker needs to have answered in order to take one of the contemplated courses of action.
4. Use: The way each piece of information will be used to help make the action decision. Supplying logical reasons for each piece of the research ensures that the questions make sense in the light of the action to be taken.
5. Targets and their subgroups: The groups from whom the information must be gathered. Specifying these groups helps the researcher design an appropriate sample for the research project.
6. Logistics: Approximate estimates of the time and money that are available to conduct the research. Both of these factors will affect the techniques finally chosen.

This written statement should be submitted to the decision maker for his or her approval. As mentioned earlier, the approval should be formalized by having the decision maker initial and date the entire document or each section. One interesting thing about the initialing is that it commits the manager and the researcher to an agreement a lot stronger than word of mouth. Lawrence Blagman, the director of marketing research for MasterCard International, found this out early in his research career. As he reports: "I learned a very big lesson once when conducting a communication test. The objectives for testing were not written. The results of the test came back, and when I proceeded to show how and why the advertising failed to communicate the intended message, the agency and marketing group were quick to point out all the other things that were communicated. Now although these other issues were of lesser importance and were not the purpose of the advertising, marketing proclaimed the test to be a success."[19] Consequently, the research department at MasterCard International requires those requesting research to sign the research request form prepared by the researchers before the department even will undertake the formal development of the procedures of the research.

Another way of ensuring that the true decision problem is addressed in the research is through the use of scenarios that attempt to anticipate the contents of the final report. The researcher is primarily responsible for preparing the scenarios. Based on his or her understanding of the total decision situation, the researcher tries to anticipate what the final report could look like and prepares hypothetical elements, admittedly in relatively crude form. The researcher then confronts the decision maker with tough questions like, "If I came up with this cross tabulation with these numbers in it, what would you do?"[20] One of the biggest payoffs that comes from this exercise

It is of the utmost importance that the problem to be investigated is precisely defined before research is carried out. Sophisticated technique cannot overcome poor problem specification.

Source: © 1990 Norm Bendell. Bendell Studio represented by David Goldman Agency, New York City, NY.

is improved communication between researcher and manager as to the exact parameters of the study. For example, one large electronics company wished to determine the knowledge of and preferences for stereo components among young consumers. It was only after the researchers prepared mock tables showing preference by age and sex that the client's wishes became truly clear. Based on their prior discussions, the researchers specified the age breakdowns for the tables as 13 to 16 and 17 to 20. Only after presenting this scenario to the company's managers did the researchers learn that to the client, "young" meant children age 10 or older. The client further believed that preteens are very volatile and undergo radical changes from year to year, especially as they approach puberty. Thus, not only was the contemplated research wrong from the standpoint of starting age it would attempt to access, but the planned categories were too gross to capture the client's basic concerns. Without the scenarios, the client's expectations may not have surfaced until the research was too far under way to change it.

Both the use of a formal research request and the use of hypothetical scenarios can help ensure that the *purpose* of the research is agreed upon before the research is designed.

Decision Trees

Decision tree A decision flow diagram in which the problem is structured in chronological order, typically with small squares indicating decision forks and small circles indicating chance forks.

One way for researchers to communicate their understanding of the decision problem and the alternatives being considered is to diagram the problem in a **decision tree.** The root of the decision tree is the problem at hand. It then branches off to show

Figure 4.4   ***Sample Decision Tree of Burger Delight's Alternatives***

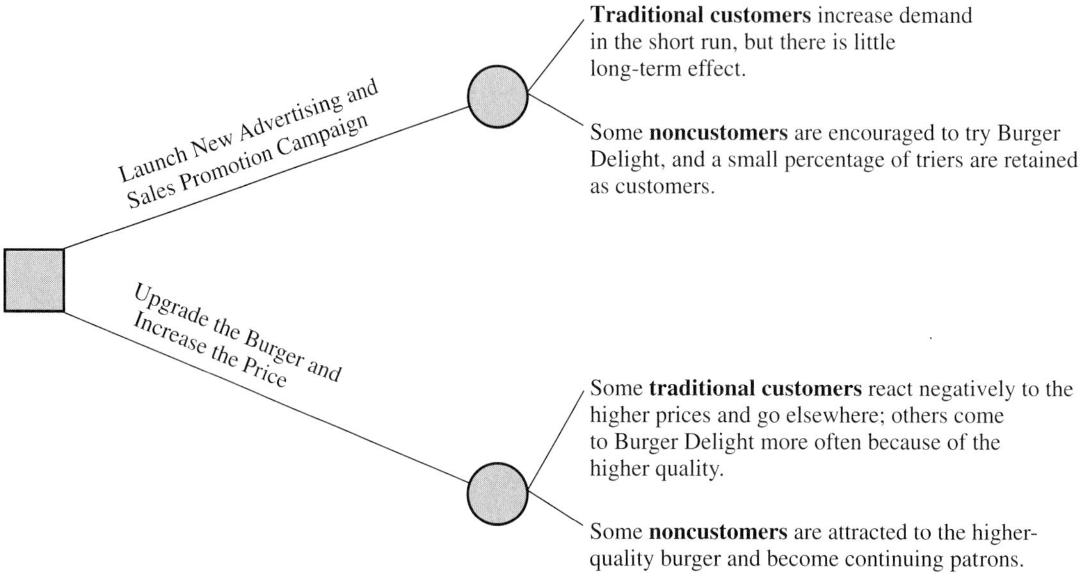

Traditional customers increase demand in the short run, but there is little long-term effect.

Some **noncustomers** are encouraged to try Burger Delight, and a small percentage of triers are retained as customers.

Launch New Advertising and Sales Promotion Campaign

Upgrade the Burger and Increase the Price

Some **traditional customers** react negatively to the higher prices and go elsewhere; others come to Burger Delight more often because of the higher quality.

Some **noncustomers** are attracted to the higher-quality burger and become continuing patrons.

various ways of approaching the problem. The tree's branches are connected by either *decision forks* or *chance forks*. A decision fork is usually depicted as a small square; a chance fork, as a small circle. The most important thing in using a decision tree is to lay out the problem completely before attempting to solve it by "pruning," or crossing off, the undesirable branches.

Figure 4.4 is a decision tree showing the possible consequences of two courses of action that a hamburger chain, Burger Delight, is considering in order to stem a continuing sales decline. The options are to launch a new promotional campaign or to upgrade the quality of the product through the use of better ingredients, which would mean an increase in its price. The choice will depend on the expected value of the two options. If, for example, the decision maker chooses the new advertising campaign, there is a chance that demand will increase and sales will improve for the duration of the campaign. However, once the campaign is over, sales may return to their previous levels. If, on the other hand, the company opts to upgrade its product with a corresponding price increase, demand may increase in certain locations but fall in others. An improved product may, however, assist in stemming a long-term sales decline.

In each case there are some encouraging possibilities and some serious risks. What happens ultimately depends on many factors beyond the decision maker's control. But it is not necessary to formally solve the problem diagrammed in the decision tree to benefit from the device. It helps conceptualize the problem and communicate its basic structure to others. In diagramming a problem, one reveals the interrelationship of the decisions that need be made. This illuminates the role of research in the decision and encourages communication between decision maker and researcher. A decision tree can cast a formerly murky decision problem into bold relief and make various options clearer.

The Research Proposal

Once the purpose and scope of the research are agreed upon, researchers can turn their attention to the *techniques* that will be used to conduct the research. The decision maker should be informed of these techniques before the research begins. Typically, this is done via a formal research proposal, which also affords the researcher another opportunity to make sure that the research being contemplated will provide the information needed to answer the decision maker's problem.

Research proposal A written statement that describes the marketing problem, the purpose of the study, and a detailed outline of the research methodology.

Some **research proposals** are very long and detailed, running twenty pages or more. Others are as short as a single page. Regardless of their length, however, most proposals contain the following elements.[21]

1. *Tentative project title.*
2. *Statement of the marketing problem.* This is a brief statement that outlines or describes the general problem under consideration. Its brevity gives the reader a general sense of the reason for the project before reading the proposal in detail.

   This section of the proposal sums up preliminary discussions that have taken place between the decision maker and the writer. From it the decision maker can determine whether the researcher accurately comprehends the problem and the decision maker's information needs. It is a good way for both parties to make sure they understand each other before committing further time and money to the project.
3. *Purpose and limits of the project.* In this section the writer states the purpose and scope of the project. *Purpose* refers to the project's goals or objectives. Often a *justification* for the project—a statement of why it is important to pursue research on this topic—is included here. *Scope* refers to the actual limitations of the research effort: in other words, what is *not* going to be investigated. In this section the writer spells out the various hypotheses to be investigated or the questions to be answered. At this point the writer may also want to address what effect time and money constraints may have on the project or what the potential limitations are of the applicability of the project's findings. Far from being a hedge, documenting these issues early in the project may help in avoiding misunderstandings and disagreements when the project is completed.
4. *Outline.* This is a tentative framework for the entire project. It should be flexible enough to allow for unforeseen difficulties. Statistical tables or graphs reflecting proposed hypotheses that the writer intends to incorporate should be shown in outline form.
5. *Data sources and research methodology.* The types of data to be sought (primary or secondary) are briefly identified here, and a brief explanation is given as to how the necessary information will be gathered (e.g., surveys, experiments, library sources). *Sources* for data may be government publications, company records, actual people, and so forth.

   If measurements, such as consumer attitudes, will be involved, the techniques to be used should be stated. Since this proposal is designed to be read by management, not fellow researchers, the language used in describing these techniques should be as nontechnical as possible. The nature of the problem will probably indicate the types of techniques to be employed.

   The population or sample to be studied and its size should be described. The writer should mention whether the group will be divided into segments (i.e., rather than studying 1,000 teenagers, a study may focus only on those who own cars). The writer should also justify why that kind of sampling strategy is necessary.

The kinds of data-collection forms the researcher plans to use should be discussed and included in the plan if possible. Depending on the nature of the study, these may be questionnaires, psychological tests, or observation forms. The proposal should indicate the reliability and validity of the measure to be used.

6. *Estimate of time and personnel requirements.* The number of people required to complete the study should be listed, along with an indication of their level of responsibility and rate of pay. The various phases of the study, and the amount of time required for each, should also be made clear. An example follows:

- Preliminary investigation: two months
- Final test of questionnaire: one month
- Sample selection: one month
- Mail questionnaire, field follow-up, etc.: four months

As mentioned earlier, if the project is to be completed under serious time constraints, the researcher may wish to indicate what effect this circumstance may have on the study's results.

7. *Cost estimates.* The cost of the personnel required should be combined with expenses for travel, materials, supplies, computer charges, printing and mailing costs, and overhead charges, if applicable, to arrive at a total cost for the project. As mentioned with regard to time, if the project is to be completed under serious financial constraints, the effect of this should be made clear at this point. It is better to face these potential problems early in the project rather than to run out of money or miss a deadline once a project has begun. The researcher, not the client, is usually the one to bear the responsibility for such shortcomings.

Once the decision maker has read and approved the proposal, he or she should formalize acceptance of it by signing and dating the document. Table 4.2 contains a portion of an actual research plan, with some authorization and budget information removed, that was prepared by the research department at General Mills. Note the clearly stated criteria that will be used to interpret the results and the carefully crafted action standards specifying what will be done depending upon what the research results indicate. The effort expended by the marketing research department in translating information requests into specific, action-oriented statements like this helps account for the wide acceptance of and enthusiastic support for the research function at General Mills.

Ethical Dilemma 4.2

A manufacturer of bolts and screws approaches you and outlines the following problem: "My friend owns a hardware store, and you used a technique called multidimensional scaling to produce what I think he called a 'perceptual map,' which positioned his operation in relation to his competitors and showed him where there was space in the market to expand his business. I don't understand the details of it, but I was very impressed with the map and I want you to do the same for me."

- What have you learned about the manufacturer's research problem?
- Is it likely that the development of a perceptual map will be useful to the manufacturer of bolts and screws?
- Is it ethical to agree to his proposal?

Table 4.2   *A Sample Proposal from General Mills for Protein Plus*

1. **Problem and Background.** Protein Plus has performed below objectives in test-market. New product and copy alternatives are being readied for testing. Three alternative formulations—Hi Graham (A), Nut (B), and Cinnamon (C)—that retain the basic identity of current Protein Plus but have been judged to be sufficiently different and of sufficient potential for separate marketing have been developed for testing against the current product (D).

2. **Decision Involved.** Which product formulations should be carried into the concept fulfillment test?

3. **Method and Design.** An in-home product test in which one product is tested at a time. Each of the four test-products will be tested by a separate panel of 150 households. Each household will have purchased adult ready-to-eat cereal within the past month and will be interested in the test-product, as evidenced by their selection of Protein Plus as one or more of the next ten cereal packages they say they would like to buy. They will be exposed to Protein Plus in a booklet that will also contain an ad for several competitive products such as Product 19, Special K, Nature Valley, and Grape Nuts. A Protein Plus ad will be constructed for each of the four test-products, differing primarily in the kind of taste appeal provided. Exposure to these various executions will be rotated so that each of the four test-panels is matched on ready-to-eat cereal usage. The study will be conducted in eight markets. Product will be packaged in the current Protein Plus package flagged with the particular taste appeal for that product.

   The criterion measure will be the homemakers' weighted share after their exposure to the product, adjusted to reflect the breadth of interest in the various Protein Plus taste appeals that have been promoted.

   Rather than trust a random sampling procedure to represent the population at large, a quota will be established to ensure that the sample of people initially contacted for each panel will conform as closely as possible to the division of homemakers under 45 (56 percent) and over 45 (44 percent) in the U.S. population.

4. **Criteria for Interpretation.** Each formulation generating a higher weighted homemaker share than standard will be considered for subsequent testing. If more than one formulation beats standard, each will be placed in concept fulfillment test unless one is better than the other(s) at odds of 2:1 or more.

5. **Estimated Project Expense:** within ±500: $22,000

6. Individual who must finally approve recommended action: _____

7. Report to be delivered by _____ if authorized by _____ and test materials shipped by _____.

When Is Marketing Research Justified?

While the benefits of marketing research are many, it is not without its drawbacks. There is no denying that the process is often time-consuming and expensive, and if it is done incorrectly, it can hurt more than help a company. In some ways, "research is like fire—it can illuminate and comfort: but if not managed properly, it can burn and hurt,"[22] badly in some instances, such as was the case with CBS and the Muppets. Even when done correctly, though, there are situations in which marketing research either cannot provide the answers a company seeks or poses disadvantages that outweigh its possible advantages (Table 4.3).

For example, ABC lavishly launched an experimental entertainment recording service called Telefirst in Chicago in January 1984. The service was designed to provide first-run movies, uncut concerts, children's programs, and so forth to homes equipped with videocassette recorders and special decoders. By June 11, 1984, ABC decided to cancel it for many reasons, including discount-pricing trends in the videocassette rental industry, technical problems, and competition from the local subscription-television service. Could marketing research have predicted—and prevented—such a disaster? Yes and no.

Table 4.3   *Ten Situations When Marketing Research May Not Help*

When you honestly know what you need to know without research.

When the information already exists.

When time is an enemy.

When conducting research would tip your hand to a competitor.

When a test doesn't represent future conditions.

When the cost of research would exceed its value.

When the budget is insufficient to do an adequate job.

When research findings would not affect the product's introduction.

When the problem is unclear and the objectives are vague.

When the research is not feasible technically.

Source: Lee Adler, "Secrets of When, and When Not, to Embark on a Marketing Research Project," *Sales and Marketing Management*, 124 (March 17, 1980), pp. 108 and 124, (May 19, 1980), p. 77.

ABC had conducted some consumer surveys prior to introduction but had failed to test the high price of Telefirst versus its convenience. ABC assumed people would rather pay for movies delivered to their homes than travel to and from stores to rent cassettes. That assumption proved false and was a major cause of Telefirst's failure.

But an ABC spokesman maintained that more thorough marketing research could not have prevented the death of Telefirst. According to him, "You can ask consumers about new technologies, but they really have to experience them before they can render a meaningful response. Also, ABC had to actually experiment with the system before it could decide whether it would work out."[23]

In other cases, the benefits of marketing research must be weighed against the risks of tipping off a competitor, who can then rush into the market with a similar product at perhaps a better price or with an added product advantage. Airwick Industries was especially proud of its new product Carpet Fresh, a rug and room deodorant. It did very well in test markets and was launched nationally. Unfortunately for Airwick, an initially skeptical competitor, Sterling Drug, had been carefully monitoring the product's test market performance and saw signs of its potential success. Sterling began a crash project to duplicate Carpet Fresh and within six months was on the market with a competing product, Love My Carpet.[24]

Some companies will forgo test marketing if there is little financial risk associated with a new product introduction. Or the expense and effort of marketing research may outweigh the influence its findings will have on company decisions. Such was the case in our earlier example of financial service advertisers.

Despite these reservations, few companies are willing to risk such endeavors as launching a new product or developing a major advertising campaign without doing preliminary marketing research. A. C. Nielsen data indicate that roughly three out of four test-marketed products succeed, whereas four out of five products not fully tested fail.[25] Telecom Research, a company that does advertising testing, estimates that half of the $65 billion spent by U.S. companies on advertising in 1982 was wasted. As the company's president notes, "Marketers don't want it to be their money, so they turn to research to find out how people see their sell."[26]

Table 4.4   ***Six Common Situations Where Marketing Research Can Help***

When you lack information needed to make a marketing decision.

When you are weighing alternatives and are not sure which one to choose.

When there is conflict within the organization over some policy, objective, or strategy.

When you detect symptoms of a problem, such as declining market share or weakening distribution.

When a marketing program is going well, and you want to know *why*, so that you can further exploit whatever it is that you're doing right.

When you undertake something different: a new product, revised price, new distribution channel, new package, new market segment.

Source: Lee Adler, "Secrets of When, and When Not, to Embark on a Marketing Research Project," *Sales and Marketing Management*, 123 (September 17, 1979), p. 108.

With such enormous money, time, and effort at stake, marketing research, despite its limitations, often seems the best way for a company to hedge its bets in a volatile marketplace (Table 4.4).

Besides, when it is good, marketing research can be very, very good. Based on marketing research, G. D. Searle developed a highly effective positioning strategy for Equal, its now popular sugar replacement; Kenner developed a Kissing Barbie Doll based on little girls' observed play habits; Sunset Books picked the title for a highly successful cookbook based on focus-group interviews; and designers at Berni Corporation changed the background color on Barrelhead Sugar-Free Root Beer cans after researchers found that people swore the drink tasted more like old-fashioned root beer in a frosty mug when it was served from beige cans instead of blue.[27]

Human nature, it seems, is nothing if not quirky and unpredictable. Often marketing research can reduce the risk inherent in that fact.

Choosing and Using a Research Supplier

Most sizable business organizations today have formal marketing research departments. However, except for the very largest consumer products companies, these departments tend to be small—sometimes consisting of one person. In such cases, the firm's researcher may spend less time conducting actual research than supervising projects undertaken by research suppliers hired by the firm. Marketing managers in many large companies also use outside suppliers.

There are many advantages to using research suppliers. If the research work load tends to vary over the course of the year, the firm may find it less expensive to hire suppliers to conduct specific projects when needed than to staff an entire in-house department that may sit idle between projects. Also, the skills required for various projects may differ. By hiring outside suppliers, the firm can match the project to the vendor with the greatest expertise in the particular area under investigation. In addition, hiring outside suppliers allows the sponsoring company to remain anonymous, and it avoids problems that might arise with regard to internal politics.

Although it has become increasingly common to buy marketing research, many managers are uncertain as to how one goes about selecting a research supplier.

***One Possible, but Not
Recommended, Method
for Choosing a
Research Supplier***

"All right, Miss Burton,
start the music and take
away another chair."

Source: Cartoon by Peter Steiner. Reprinted with permission.

Perhaps the first step is to decide when research is really necessary. Although there is no simple formula for assessing this need, most managers turn to research when they are unsure about their own judgment and other information sources seem inadequate. Before contacting research suppliers, it is important for the manager to identify the most critical areas of uncertainty and the issues that would benefit most from research.

Once a manager has determined the most critical area for research, he or she is ready to seek the right supplier for the job. The selection process is not easy, for there are thousands of qualified marketing research companies in the United States. Some are full-service "generalist" companies; others are specialists in qualitative research, advertising-copy testing, concept testing, and so on, and still others are services that only conduct interviews, process data, or work with statistics.

It is important that the manager carefully evaluate the capabilities of suppliers in light of the company's research needs. Some issues require small-scale qualitative studies while others require large-scale quantitative research projects. It is essential that the vendor selected understand the firm's information needs and have the expertise required to conduct the research.

Experts suggest that managers seek proposals from at least three companies. They also urge that the research user talk with the persons at the supplier company who will be processing and analyzing the data, writing the report, supervising the interviewers, and making presentations to management.

Marketing research is still an art, not a science. It benefits from heavy involvement of senior research professionals, who provide insights that come only from years of training and experience. The most important asset of a research firm is the qualifications of the research professional(s) who will be involved in the design, day-to-day supervision, and interpretation of the research.

Table 4.5   ***Criteria Used by Land O'Lakes, Inc., to Evaluate Research Suppliers***

General attitude and responsiveness: enthusiastic, helpful, prompt replies on cost estimates, proposals, etc.

Marketing insight: informative, understands study objectives, has ability to analyze data, provides recommendations

Fundamental design: questionnaire, study instructions, test plan, etc.

Questionnaire construction: format, order and wording of questions, appropriate scales

Tabulation design: format, accuracy

Day-to-day serving: responsive and informative on study progress, problems, etc.

Analysis: thorough, relates to objectives

Quality of report writing: concise, clear, accurate, executive summary

Presentation: well-planned, concise, materials organized, verbal skills

Delivery time: topline, tables, report

Cost: over, under, justified

Overall performance

    Excellent: outstanding performance in all phases of the project

    Very good: acceptable performance on all phases of the project

    Good: work is satisfactory; however, could improve performance in one or two phases of the project

    Fair: performance fell short in one or more phases of the project

    Poor: performance and quality of the work is unacceptable

Source: Courtesy of Stephen Lauring, Marketing Research Manager, Land O'Lakes, Inc.

The research user's responsibility is to communicate effectively with the prospective vendor and provide the necessary background and objectives for the study. Research users should also ask about the supplier's quality control standards. Most research firms are pleased when clients show concern about the quality of their work and will gladly explain their quality control steps in the areas of field work, coding, and data processing.

After reading the proposals and meeting key personnel, the manager should perform a comparative analysis. He or she should use the proposals to evaluate each vendor's understanding of the problem, how each will address it, and the cost and time estimates of each. In making this evaluation, the manager needs to keep in mind that the value of the information to be produced is determined by its use, not its mere presence. Thus, the manager needs to be forthright in addressing how he or she would use the information provided by executing the various proposals.

Many firms have formal evaluation systems with specified criteria for evaluating research suppliers. This is particularly true among those companies who use suppliers on a regular basis. Land O'Lakes, Inc., the dairy producer, for example, uses the criteria shown in Table 4.5 to evaluate the research suppliers it uses. The company has a formal set of written guidelines that it shares with potential research suppliers,

Research Window 4.2
How Clients and Marketing Research Firms Should Not Work Together

Both clients and marketing research firms may contribute to faulty designs, missed schedules, cost overruns, and inappropriate analyses. Client rules for creating such problems are as follows:

1. Keep the real purpose and objectives of the research hidden from the research firm.
2. Try to reduce the cost estimate by glossing over anticipated problems.
3. Change the questionnaire frequently. Include at least one change after interviewing has begun.
4. Delay the start of data collection. Cancel and restart the project, but insist upon receiving the report by the original deadline.
5. Delay approving analytical and tabulation plans as long as possible; then change the plan verbally without written confirmation.
6. Demand all possible cross tabulations, whether or not they are relevant to the purpose of the study.
7. Fail to pay for the research within a reasonable time.

Rules that a research firm can follow to reduce the likelihood of being burdened with client work in the future are as follows:

1. Modify the objectives of the research to fit the methodology that you find convenient.
2. Low-ball the cost estimate; then use minor changes in the project to raise the budget after being awarded the job.
3. Agree with the client on changes to be made; then after the project has been completed, tell the client it was just too late to make the changes.
4. Tell the client that all is on schedule when it is not.
5. Bill the client before submitting the final report. Make it more than the original estimate, but do not bother to explain why until asked.
6. Send the report late; then avoid the client's phone calls.

In the most successful client–research firm relationships, both sides treat each other as professionals, are open with one another, and work together in designing the project to meet objectives and in handling the problems that inevitably arise.

Source: Michael Hardin, "How Clients and Marketing Research Firms Should Not Work Together," *Marketing Today*, Volume 23; No. 1, 1985.

spelling out these criteria in more detail. Further, at the completion of each project, a research analyst, the manager, or the research director evaluates the supplier in terms of whether the provider was excellent, very good, good, fair, or poor in terms of each of the criteria. There is also a comment section for each criterion, where the evaluator can explain the basis of the evaluation. The firm applies as many of these criteria as it can when evaluating the proposals of new suppliers.

When evaluating suppliers that seem equally competent, a manager must rely on his or her intuitive assessment regarding the soundness of the research design proposed, the supplier's responsiveness to the manager's specific questions, and the vendor's understanding of the subtler aspects of the marketing problem.

In this section we have provided some guidelines for a successful partnership between research suppliers and users. As we all know, however, reality often seems to follow Murphy's Law rather than a textbook model. Research Window 4.2 suggests how to tailor a research partnership for a perfect fit with failure.

Back to the Case

Celia Cooper was again flying to Philadelphia with the president of the Lady Lillian Dress Company, and while it was a business trip this time, too, it was a pleasure. Eight months after hearing the executives at Hanna's tell them why they wanted to drop the Lady Lillian line, Cooper and Elliott Levinson were going back to Philadelphia to convince Hanna's to open, within its department stores, boutiques featuring Lady Lillian dresses.

After the first meeting at Hanna's, Lady Lillian had commissioned a marketing research study in order to find out as much as possible about their ultimate customers. Through focus groups, they had learned that Lady Lillian had a good reputation for quality but was considered old-fashioned.

As a result, Levinson had brought in new design talent to make the company's dresses more stylish. The designer had done a great job. Cooper was wearing a dress from the new spring line to the meeting.

In order to make sure that new line got maximum exposure, the company had decided to follow the lead of designers such as Liz Claiborne and Calvin Klein and open department store boutiques dedicated exclusively to Lady Lillian dresses. The boutiques, which were going into stores of several national retail chains, were just called "Lillian" because marketing research had shown that the name "Lady Lillian"

was perceived by younger women as being too old-fashioned.

While Cooper knew they would have a tough sell in convincing Hanna's that the Lillian boutique could generate enough volume in $100 dresses to justify a dedicated selling area, she had confidence in Burton West, the company's sales manager, who was traveling with Cooper and Levinson this trip. He was armed with sales figures from stores that had already established Lillian boutiques. For those retailers, sales of Lady Lillian dresses had more than doubled.

Based on the experience of the Leslie Fay Company as reported by Monica Roman, "Why Leslie Fay's Duds Aren't Duds Anymore," *Business Week* (June 16, 1990), p. 86.

Summary

Learning Objective 1: Specify the three sources of marketing problems or opportunities.

The three sources of marketing problems or opportunities, and consequently research problems, are (1) unanticipated change, (2) planned change, and (3) serendipity in the form of new ideas.

Learning Objective 2: Describe the main purpose of marketing research for each of the three sources of marketing problems.

For marketing problems caused by unanticipated change, the purpose of marketing research is to find out what is happening and why. For problems caused by planned change, it is how to bring about the desired change. For serendipity in the form of new ideas, it is how to capture and evaluate the promise of the new idea.

Learning Objective 3: Describe a decision situation.

A person faces a decision situation if he or she has a problem, knows several good, but not equally good, ways of solving it, and must pick between the various choices available.

Learning Objective 4: List the factors that make up a decision maker's environment.

A decision maker's environment includes not only the state of the economy in general, but the economic situation of the particular industry involved and the specific company in that industry. Researchers also need to be aware that the corporate culture can affect decision making and consequently the research that supports that decision making.

Learning Objective 5: Describe the various elements a researcher must understand in order to address the real decision problem.

In order for the research to address the real decision problem and not some symptom of it, the researcher working on the problem must develop an understanding of the personality of the decision maker and his or her environment; the alternative courses of action being considered; the objectives of the decision maker, including his or her attitude toward risk; and the potential consequences of the alternative courses of action.

Learning Objective 6: Distinguish between a decision problem and a research problem.

Decision problems involve what needs to be done. Research provides the necessary information to make an informed choice, so the research problem essentially involves determining what information to provide and how that information can best be secured.

Learning Objective 7: Explain why a decision tree can be useful in problem solving.

The decision tree is a useful device for conceptualizing a problem and communicating its basic structure to others. Diagramming a problem forces a focus on the interrelationship of the decisions that need to be made. A decision tree can cast the problem into bold relief and make various options clearer.

Learning Objective 8: Outline the various elements of the research proposal.

Most research proposals contain the following elements: tentative project title, statement of the marketing problem, purpose and limits of the project, outline, data sources and research methodology, estimate of time and personnel requirements, and cost estimates.

Discussion Questions, Problems, and Projects

1. Given the following decision problems, identify the research problems.
    (a) what pricing strategy to follow for a new product
    (b) whether to increase the level of expenditures on print advertising
    (c) whether to increase in-store promotion of existing products
    (d) whether to expand current warehouse facilities
    (e) whether to change the sales force compensation package
    (f) whether to change the combination of ticket price, entertainers, and security at the Indiana State Fair
    (g) whether to revise a bank's electronic payment service
2. Given the following research problems, identify corresponding decision problems for which they might provide useful information.
    (a) design a test market to assess the impact on sales volume of a particular discount theme
    (b) evaluate the stock level at the different warehouses
    (c) evaluate the sales and market share of grocery stores in a particular location
    (d) develop sales forecasts for a particular product line
    (e) assess the level of awareness among students, faculty, and staff about the benefits of IBM PS/2 ownership
    (f) assess attitudes and opinions of customers toward existing theme restaurants
3. Briefly discuss the difference between a decision problem and a research problem.
4. In each of the following situations, identify the fundamental source of the marketing problem or opportunity, a decision problem arising from the marketing problem or opportunity, and a possible research problem.
    (a) Apex Chemical Supply is a manufacturer of swimming pool maintenance chemicals. Recently, a malfunction of the equipment that mixes anti-algae compound resulted in a batch of the product that not only inhibits algae growth but also causes the pool water to turn a beautiful shade of light blue (with no undesirable side effects).

(b) State University's director of recruitment for the MBA program recently extended offers to 20 promising students. Only 5 offers were accepted. In the past, acceptance rates have averaged 90 percent. A survey of non-acceptors conducted by the director revealed that the primary reason for declining the offer was the perception that State's course requirements are too "restrictive."

(c) Montgomery Candy Company has enjoyed great success in its small regional market. Management attributes much of this success to Montgomery's unique distribution system, which ensures twice weekly delivery of fresh product to retail outlets. The directors of the company have instructed management to expand Montgomery's geographical market if it can be done without altering the twice weekly delivery policy.

5. Schedule an interview with the marketing manager of a firm near your home or your school. In the interview, attempt to isolate a problem with which the manager is wrestling and for which research information would be helpful. Explore each of the parts of a "research request step" with the manager. After the interview, prepare a short report that summarizes your discussion with respect to actions being considered, origin of the problem, information that would be useful to solve it, how each bit of information might be used in its solution, and the targets and subgroups for the study. Submit your report to the manager and secure an evaluation from him or her as to whether your report effectively captures the situation confronting the firm.

6. You are the marketing manager of a mid-size manufacturing firm. Recently you solicited proposals for an upcoming research project from three outside marketing research suppliers. You have the formal proposals in hand and must choose which supplier to use. In general, what criteria should you use in making your decision?

Endnotes

1. William F. O'Dell, Andrew C. Ruppel, Robert H. Trent, and William J. Kehoe, *Marketing Decision Making: Analytic Framework and Cases*, 4th ed. (Cincinnati: South-Western Publishing Co., 1988).

2. Glen L. Urban, John R. Hauser, and Nikhilesh Dholakia, *Essentials of New Products Management* (Englewood Cliffs, N.J.: Prentice-Hall, Inc., 1987), p. 6.

3. Andrew Kupfer, "Why the Bounce at Rubbermaid," *Fortune*, 115 (April 13, 1987), pp. 77–78.

4. Alan R. Andreasen, " 'Backward' Market Research," *Harvard Business Review*, 63 (May–June 1985), p. 176.

5. O'Dell et al., *Marketing Decision Making*, p. 14.

6. See Russell L. Ackoff, *The Art of Problem Solving* (New York: John Wiley & Sons, Inc., 1978).

7. Bill Abrams, "Financial Service Advertisers Seen Neglecting Ad Research," *The Wall Street Journal* (August 8, 1983), p. 23.

8. Joel Levine, while vice-president of marketing research at the Pillsbury Company in Minneapolis, suggested that awareness of the corporate culture is one of the most important factors that distinguishes researchers who affect strategic marketing decisions from those who do not. See "Six Factors Mark Researchers Who Sway Strategic Decisions," *Marketing News*, 17 (February 4, 1983), p. 1. See also Bernie Whalen, "Researchers Stymied by 'Adversary Culture' in Firms," *Marketing News*, 16 (September 17, 1982), pp. 1 and 7. For discussion of how changes in the corporate culture are affecting research at Sony, see Elizabeth Rubinfien, Yamiko Ono, and Laura Lundro, "A Changing Sony Aims to Own the 'Software' That Its Products Need," *The Wall Street Journal* (December 30, 1988), pp. A1 and A4.

9. "Adam Hits the Briar Patch," *Newsweek*, 107 (January 14, 1985), p. 61.

10. "Soup Maker Bets Future on Monitoring Technological Consumption Changes," *Marketing News*, 18 (October 12, 1984), pp. 44. See also Anthony Bianco, "Marketing's New Look: Campbell Leads a Revolution in the Way Consumer Products Are Sold," *Business Week* (January 26, 1987), pp. 64–69.

11. The types of decision makers are more formally defined in decision theory literature. See, for example, the classic work by Howard Raiffa, *Decision Analysis: Introductory Lectures on Choices under Uncertainty* (Reading, Mass.: Addison-Wesley, 1968), pp. 51–101.

12. John F. Persinos, "Sugar Baby," *Inc.*, (May 1984), pp. 85–92.

13. Russell L. Ackoff, *Scientific Method* (New York: John Wiley, 1962), p. 71.

14. Ibid., p. 71.

15. Pat Sloan, "Wrangler Campaign Soft-Pedals Denim," *Advertising Age*, 55 (November 1, 1984), p. 3, and Bernice Kanner, "Raiders of the Lost Market," *New York*, 17 (November 26, 1984), pp. 18–24.

16. Wayne A. Lemburg, "Past AMA President Hardin, Head of Market Facts, Looks Back at the Early Days of Marketing Research," *Marketing News*, 20 (December 19, 1986), p. 9.

17. Dennis Kneale, "CBS Frantically Woos Hollywood to Help It Win Back Viewers," *The Wall Street Journal* (February 9, 1989), p. A10.

18. Paul W. Conner, " 'Research Request Step' Can Enhance Use of Results," *Marketing News*, 19 (January 4, 1985), p. 41. See also

Paul D. Boughton, "Marketing Research and Small Business: Pitfalls and Potential," *Journal of Small Business Management*, 21 (July 1983), pp. 36–42, for a list of questions small business managers (any decision maker, actually) can ask to make sure that they are getting the most from their research.

19. Lawrence H. Blagman, "Managing Information," in *Presentations from the 9th Annual Marketing Research Conference* (Chicago: American Marketing Association, 1988), p. 134.

20. Andreasen, " 'Backward' Market Research," p. 180.

21. J. Paul Peter and James H. Donnelly, Jr., *A Preface to Marketing Management*, 4th ed. (Homewood, Ill.: Richard D. Irwin, Inc., 1988), pp. 48–49.

22. Blagman, "Managing Information," p. 126.

23. Bernie Whalen, "Why ABC's Telefirst Didn't Last," *Advertising Age*, 55 (November 9, 1984), p. 32.

24. Bill Abrams, "Some Tales of 'Copycat' Products Are Best Left Untold, Sterling Drug Learns," *The Wall Street Journal* (May 11, 1980), p. 18.

25. Lee Adler, "Test Marketing—It's the Pitfalls," *Sales and Marketing Management*, 128 (March 15, 1982), pp. 74–77.

26. Kanner, "Raiders of the Lost Market," p. 16.

27. "To Test or Not to Test Seldom the Question," *Advertising Age*, 55 (February 20, 1984), p. M–10; Daisy Maryles, "Market Research Sets Style, Content of Sunset Cookbook," *Publisher's Weekly* (October 8, 1982), p. 41; and Ronald Alsop, "Color More Important in Catching Consumer's Eyes," *The Wall Street Journal* (November 29, 1984), p. 37.

Suggested Additional Readings

For useful discussions on the nature of decision problems and how to go about problem solving, see

Russell L. Ackoff, *The Art of Problem Solving* (New York: John Wiley & Sons, Inc., 1978).

William F. O'Dell, Andrew C. Ruppel, Robert H. Trent, and William J. Kehoe, *Marketing Decision Making: Analytic Framework and Cases*, 4th ed. (Cincinnati: South-Western Publishing Co., 1988).

For useful discussions on how to translate decision problems into research problems, see the O'Dell et al. reading mentioned above as well as

Alan R. Andreasen, " 'Backward' Market Research," *Harvard Business Review*, 63 (May–June 1985), pp. 176, 180, 182.

Paul W. Conner, " 'Research Request Step' Can Enhance Use of Results," *Marketing News*, 19 (January 4, 1985), p. 41.

For more detailed treatment of the content of the various parts of a research proposal and some sample proposals, see

Kenneth W. Houp and Thomas E. Pearsall, *Reporting Technical Information*, 4th ed. (Encino, Calif.: Collier Macmillan Publishers, 1980), pp. 342–365.

Part One

Research Project

In the following description of an actual research project, note the kind of background information the researchers received when they first met their client, a group of radio station managers. Subsequent sections in this book will show how the researchers tackled the project and will analyze what they did well—or could have done better or differently.

In a small midwestern city, radio station owners and operators banded together to form a group called the Centerville Area Radio Association (CARA) to promote radio advertising. Station managers in the group were interested in finding out what their customers—specifically the local businesses who advertised on their stations—liked and disliked about radio advertising. They decided to commission a marketing research study to investigate the situation.

Members of CARA hoped the study would uncover ways that they could compete more effectively with the other major media: television and newspapers. They also hoped that the research could show them how they might better satisfy customers and thus increase their advertising sales volume.

When the study began, radio held a 13.5-percent share of the market in the Centerville area. CARA data showed that radio's sales volume had been growing at an annual rate of 9 to 10 percent for the past several years, and group members expected that this level of growth would continue for the foreseeable future.

CARA members thought that radio offered some advantages over newspapers and television. The group was especially proud of its sales philosophy, which embodied the marketing concept at its best. "The client comes first," was the watchword with CARA. CARA members thought that this philosophy, combined with their "consultant-sell" sales approach, made customers perceive radio sales representatives as more concerned, more cooperative, and better trained than other media reps. Hence, it was CARA's opinion that radio sales reps had a better image in the business than sales reps from other

media. These opinions, while widely held by CARA members, had never been tested for accuracy.

The groups that interested CARA the most were local businesspeople who were already their customers or those whom they would like to have as customers. Businesses that were not yet advertisers were included in the study if they showed an interest in using one of the three major media in the future.

Finally, CARA wanted to know (1) if the amount of money a given business spent every year on advertising had any effect on its attitudes toward media and sales representatives and (2) what characteristics businesspeople sought in these representatives.

The researchers formulated a number of hypotheses or conjectures from the information presented them by CARA managers. For example, it was hypothesized that there would be differences in businesspeoples' attitudes toward television, radio, and newspaper, and that differences would also be found in attitudes toward sales representatives of each of the media. The various characteristics of the advertising media, as well as the attributes of the salespeople for each medium, were hypothesized to vary in importance to businesspeople. It was also hypothesized that the attitudes of businesspeople who were not managers or owners, and who were not involved in buying advertising, would differ from those of the population of interest.

After further probing, researchers were able to translate these hypotheses into problems that could be addressed by research. Specifically, they restated the problem in the form of two objectives:

1. Identify business decision makers' attitudes toward the advertising media of newspaper, radio, and television.
2. Identify business decision makers' attitudes toward the advertising sales representatives of newspaper, radio, and television.

They pointed out to CARA members that the information acquired from investigating these two areas could subsequently be used to make informed choices about what strategy to pursue in competing with other media.

It is, of course, too early to know what the actual results of the study might be. However, we can speculate on how varying results might affect management decisions. What might management want to do if the study showed that businesspeople had a negative opinion of radio advertising? What might they do if they found that advertisers liked their sales approach? Using the steps in the research process as a guide, how would you suggest the research proceed?

Problem: How do we get more eligible males in the big brother organ.

Case 1.1 Big Brothers of Fairfax County

Big Brothers of America is a social service program designed to meet the needs of boys ages six to eighteen from single-parent homes. Most of the boys served by the program live with their mothers and rarely see or hear from their fathers. The purpose of the program is to give these boys the chance to establish a friendship with an interested adult male. Big Brothers of America was founded on the belief that association with a responsible adult can help program participants become more responsible citizens and better-adjusted young men.

The program was started in Cincinnati in 1903. Two years later, the organization was granted its first charter in New York State through the efforts of Mrs. Cornelius Vanderbilt. By the end of World War II, there were 30 Big Brothers agencies. Today there are 300 agencies across the United States, and 120,000 boys currently are matched with Big Brothers.

The Fairfax County chapter of Big Brothers of America was founded in Fairfax in 1966. In 1971, United Way of Fairfax County accepted the program as part of its umbrella organization and now provides about 85 percent of its funding. The remaining 15 percent is raised by the local Big Brothers agency.

Information about the Big Brothers program in Fairfax County reaches the public primarily through newspapers (feature stories and classified advertisements), radio, public service announcements, posters (on buses and in windows of local establishments), and word-of-mouth advertising. The need for volunteers is a key message emanating from these sources. The agency phone number is always included so that people wanting to know more about the program can call for information. Those calling in are given basic information over the telephone and are invited to attend one of the monthly orientation sessions organized by the Big Brothers program staff. At these meetings, men get the chance to talk to other volunteers and to find out what will be expected of

them should they decide to join the program. At the end of the session, prospective volunteers are asked to complete two forms. One is an application form and the other is a questionnaire in which the person is asked to describe the type of boy he would prefer to be matched with, as well as his own interests.

The files on potential Little Brothers are then reviewed in an attempt to match boys with the volunteers. A match is made only if both partners agree. The agency stays in close contact with the pair and monitors its progress. The three counselors for the Big Brothers program serve as resources for the volunteer.

The majority of the inquiry calls received by the Fairfax County agency are from women who are interested in becoming Big Sisters or from people desiring information on the Couples Program. Both programs are similar to the Big Brothers program and are administered by it. In fact, of 55 calls concerning a recent orientation meeting, only 5 were from males. Only 3 of the 5 callers actually attended the meeting—a typical response.

Although the informational campaigns and personal appeals thus seem to have some effect, the results are also generally disappointing and do little to alleviate the problem of a shortage of volunteer Big Brothers. There are currently 250 boys waiting to be matched with Big Brothers, and the shortage grows weekly.

Big Brothers of Fairfax County believes that a lack of awareness and accurate knowledge could be the cause of the shortage of volunteers. Are there men who would volunteer if only they were made aware of the program and its needs? Or is the difficulty a negative program image? Do people think of Little Brothers as problem children, boys who have been in trouble with the law or who have severe behavioral problems? Or could there be a misconception of the type of man who would make a good Big Brother? Do people have stereotypes with respect to the volunteers—for example, that the typical volunteer is a young, single, professional male?

Questions

1. What is (are) the marketing decision problem(s)?
2. What is (are) the marketing research problem(s)?

3. What types of information would be useful to answer these questions?
4. How would you go about securing this information?

Case 1.2   Supervisory Training at the Management Institute

University of Wisconsin–Extension is the outreach campus of the University of Wisconsin system. Its mission is to extend high-quality education to people who are not necessarily "college students" in the normal sense. The Management Institute (MI) is one of the departments within UW–Extension. It conducts programs aimed at providing education and training in at least a dozen areas of business and not-for-profit management.

The supervisory training area within MI designs and conducts continuing-education training programs for first-level supervisors. The training programs are designed to improve a trainee's managerial, communication, decision-making, and human-relation skills. They consequently cover a broad range of topics.

A continuing decline in enrollments in the various programs during the past several years had become a problem of increasing concern to the three supervisory program directors. They were at a loss to explain the decline, although informal discussions among the supervisors raised a number of questions to which they did not know the answers. Have people's reasons

for attending supervisory training programs changed? What are their reasons for attending them? Was the decline caused by economic factors? Was it because of increased competition among continuing-education providers? Was it due to the content or structure of MI's programs themselves? Was it because of the way the programs were promoted? Were the programs targeted at the right level of supervisor?

Typically, the major promotion for any program involved mailed brochures that described the content and structure of the course. The mailing list for the brochures was all past attendees of any supervisory training program conducted by MI.

Questions

1. What is (are) the decision problem(s)?
2. What is (are) the research problem(s)?
3. How would you recommend MI go about addressing the research problem(s)? That is, what data would you collect, and how might those data be used to answer the research question(s) posed?

 *How do we get more people coming thru program?*

Case 1.3   St. Andrews Medical Center (A)[1]

Since 1985, St. Andrews Medical Center has operated a special Eating Disorders Clinic to provide in-patient and out-patient treatment of anorexia nervosa and bulimia. Anorexia nervosa, often characterized by an intense obsession with dieting and weight loss, and bulimia, also known as the "binge and purge syndrome," typically afflict young women between the ages of 14 and 22. Both conditions can result in very

serious health problems (or even death) if left untreated.

The hospital marketing staff estimates that there are approximately 600 anorexic women in St. Andrews' primary service area (this is the "prevalence" of the condition); about 15 new cases will arise each year (the "incidence") based on current population estimates. The estimated prevalence and incidence of bulimia are also projected to be about 600 and 15, respectively.

[1]The contributions of Tom J. Brown to the development of this case are gratefully acknowledged.

Table 1   *St. Andrews Eating Disorders Clinic Cases of Anorexia Nervosa and Bulimia Treated 1985–1989*

Year	Number of Cases Treated		Percentage of Area Cases*	
	Anorexia	Bulimia	Anorexia	Bulimia
1985	112	87	18.5	14.4
1986	243	186	40.1	30.7
1987	235	161	38.3	26.6
1988	147	121	24.3	20.0
1989	123	118	20.3	19.5

*Assumes constant prevalence of 606 cases each of anorexia nervosa and bulimia.

As a general rule, women suffering from anorexia nervosa or bulimia are referred to an eating disorders program by a physician or psychologist. On occasion, women who recognize that they have a problem with one of these conditions will seek help directly through an eating disorders program. For instance, in 1989, of the 241 cases of bulimia or anorexia nervosa treated at the St. Andrews Eating Disorders Clinic, 198 patients (82 percent) were referred by other health-care providers.

During recent years, the program has witnessed a dramatic decrease in the number of cases of both anorexia nervosa and bulimia treated at the Eating Disorders Clinic. Table 1 presents the total number of women with each of the two conditions who were treated within the St. Andrews program since it was initiated in 1985. Assuming the prevalence of the conditions to be relatively stable from year to year (about 600 women with each condition), the approximate percentage of cases of each disorder treated at St. Andrews can be calculated. These percentages (essentially, "market shares") are also presented in Table 1.

Although the St. Andrews program was the first eating disorders program in the area, it is not the only program. City Hospital, located a few blocks away, also operates a special clinic for treating eating disorders, and has done so since 1986. City Hospital's program maintains a health-care staff of 20 people, roughly the same number of staff members maintained by the St. Andrews program. Although they cannot be certain, officials at St. Andrews believe that the program at City Hospital has treated a growing number of cases each year since its inception.

Costs for treatment at both programs are comparable; in addition, these costs have not escalated as rapidly as health-care costs in general. In fact, typical treatment costs in 1989 were only about 25 percent higher than those when the program was initiated at St. Andrews. Unfortunately, many types of health insurance and HMOs (health maintenance organizations) do not offer coverage for treatment of these conditions.

St. Andrews officials are very concerned about the future direction of the Eating Disorders Clinic.

Questions

1. As a marketing researcher, how would you define the decision problem(s)?
2. What is (are) the research problem(s)?
3. How, in general, would you propose that the research proceed? Who might provide useful input? How might you access these people?

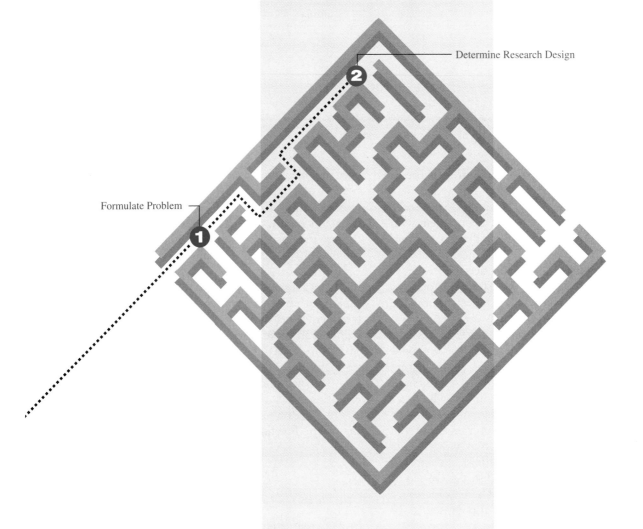

Part Two

Research Design

Formulate Problem

Determine Research Design

Part Two deals with the general issue of designing research so that it addresses the appropriate questions efficiently. Chapter 5 provides an overview of various research designs and discusses the exploratory design at some length. Chapter 6 then discusses descriptive and causal designs, two other primary types of research design.

MICHAEL BAKER
Director of Marketing Research
Coca-Cola Foods

Michael Baker thinks of himself as a marketer first. This business orientation puts Baker in the position to do more than just respond to problems. "We pride ourselves on being able to spot issues that help the company focus on smarter ways to use our marketing dollars."

Baker is in charge of all custom marketing research for existing and new products at Coca-Cola Foods, which includes Minute Maid®, Hi-C®, and Five Alive® brands. He has a staff of five research professionals and two clerical support people. He says that there are two ways that a marketing research department can be organized, either by methodology or by business unit. Baker feels that since it is important that his group be perceived as marketers and not just research specialists, his department is accordingly organized according to business units: breakfast beverages, children's beverages, and refreshment beverages.

Often a marketing brand manager will come to Baker with a particular problem for which he or she needs help. For example, the manager is curious about what would happen if he or she changed the package of a product or redirected the advertising. But Baker and his staff aren't shy about generating issues themselves. "We take a proactive role in marketing," declares Baker. "For example, a brand manager may decide he wants to do a consumer promotion. That could be anything from a 25-cents-off coupon to a 'frequent shopper' program that rewards consumers who buy your products frequently. But a lot of consumer promotions don't pay back—a dollar spent on promotion does not translate into a dollar of increased sales. The brand manager may have decided on a certain type of promotion. He's

happy. He hasn't come to us. But we may come to him and say, 'Listen, let's look at this.' We may show him, either with data we already have in hand or by designing a test of the proposed promotion, that there is a more effective way to structure the promotion to accomplish his objectives.

"In formulating research design, the absolute most important thing is to make sure that you understand the unique objective to the situation at hand," says Baker. "You have to be certain that you can articulate exactly what you want to find out and why.

"The biggest pitfall in research design is that there are a lot of standard approaches in marketing research. The danger is that you try to fit all the business problems that you run across into the standard approaches. You fall back onto what worked last time, and you try to make the problems fit the research norms as opposed to fitting the research to the problems.

"In addition, it is also easy to forget that the objective is not to do the test," warns Baker, "but to make smarter business decisions. It is incredibly important to design research that has a custom fit to the problem that you are studying."

Baker came to his career by an unusual path. In college he was interested in psychology but frustrated that so many theories were based on little experimental evidence. When

he took a social psychology course, he knew he'd found what he wanted to do. He loved the application of the experimental method on the study of human behavior where a hypothesis regarding human behavior could be tested experimentally. He also loved the creative outlet of designing problem-specific experiments.

Baker went on to get both a bachelor's and a master's degree in social psychology, but then realized that the sorts of problems he would be focusing on as an academic were largely of interest only to other academicians. The turning point for him came when one of the research projects he was involved in through a professor received Senator Proxmire's Golden Fleece Award. The award is given to draw attention to projects that are gross wastes of taxpayers' money. "I had to ask myself," remembers Baker, "I know that I love what I'm doing, but how can I turn my skills to problems that people want answers to? How can I do work that's useful and profitable? That's when I decided to get my MBA and go into marketing research.

"It's funny, but I'm really doing the same things at Coca-Cola that I was doing as a social psychologist," muses Baker. "I'm dealing with human behavior; I'm getting at questions of why people do what they do—in this case, make purchasing decisions. Even a lot of the reasons are the same. Often we buy things not just for what they are, but for what they say about us. For example, the foods we buy are often a statement to our families about how we feel about them, a way of telling them that we want to do our best for them. And there's the same central importance of creativity in formulating the research design."

Chapter Five

Types of Research Design and Exploratory Research

Learning Objectives

Upon completing this chapter, you should be able to

1. Explain what a research design is.

2. List the three basic types of research design.

3. Describe the major emphasis of each type of research design.

4. Cite the crucial principle of research.

5. Describe the basic uses of exploratory research.

6. Specify the key characteristic of exploratory research.

7. Discuss the various types of exploratory research and identify the characteristics of each.

8. Identify the key person in a focus group.

Case in Marketing Research

"The world has changed and we have not been changing with it," boomed Larry Grenfell as he paced in front of the flip chart that showed Beautique's falling market share. He had taken off his jacket and rolled up his sleeves. Top management sat in rows, giving him their complete attention like chastised schoolchildren.

"In 1972 Beautique was the biggest beauty company in the world. We 'owned' the direct-selling channel. We made quality products, we packaged them attractively, we priced them competitively, and we sold them door-to-door through a network of housewives earning extra money in their free time. In 1972 Beautique had sales of more than $1 billion a year. Our stock was selling for $140 a share—that's almost 63 times earnings. We were the darling of Wall Street, a highly decentralized organization led by a small, lean corporate staff.

"One year later," growled Grenfell, "our stock had plummeted to $18 a share. My predecessor looked at the situation and saw that Beautique had grown so big so fast that it lacked the internal structure and controls to manage what had grown into a complex international operation. He imposed a program of strict centralization, along with financial and operational controls.

"What Beautique's last president accomplished was necessary and important. But it hasn't done much to boost our sales. Our stock is still under $20 a share. Now," declared Grenfell, slamming both his hands on the conference table in front of him, "I want to know what we should do to change this state of affairs!"

There was silence in the room for more time than felt comfortable. Finally, Linda Seidel, the head of Beautique's direct-selling division, spoke up.

"One problem, as I see it," she began, "is that while Beautique has been focusing on tightening up the internal structure, there have been major changes in the marketplace that we seem to have been unaware of—or at least we've failed to develop strategies to deal with them. For example, historically Beautique has recruited housewives to be sales representatives. But as more women have entered the work force full-time, it has become harder and harder to recruit good sales reps. To compound the situation, when sales reps go door-to-door, there's no one home."

"Good point," barked Grenfell. "What else?"

"Well," replied Peter Bennington, who was in charge of new product development, "in the last ten years we've seen an increased diversity of taste in a population of consumers who seem to have more and more discretionary dollars to spend. In short, people's lifestyles have changed. Their needs have changed. We've stayed the same."

"Well then, we'd better change —and fast," retorted Grenfell.

"I don't think we know enough to start making changes," interjected John Boldt, Beautique's new director of marketing. Pete and Linda have identified two enormous changes in our market. It's safe to say that these cultural shifts have affected us adversely, but in what way? I think our biggest problem is that we're not in touch with our consumers. For years we've been thinking of our sales rep as our customer. There are good reasons for that. She places the order, we ship the product to her, she pays the bill. Not a bad definition of a customer, but it's wrong.

"We have no idea what the people who make the final buying decision think of us and our products. We need to commission a consumer research study. We need to ask our customers and potential customers what they want from beauty products and what they want from Beautique."

To everyone's surprise, Larry Grenfell smiled.

Discussion Issues

1. For Beautique, what are the potential benefits of an exploratory marketing research study?
2. What kinds of problems might the marketing researchers encounter?

The preceding chapters presented some of the kinds of problems marketing research can help to solve. As you may have noticed, there can be great variation in the nature of the questions research investigates. Some can be very specific: "If we change the advertising mix, what will happen to sales?" Others are much more general: "Why have sales fallen below target? How do customers feel about the product?" As you may have guessed, different formulations of a problem can lead to different research approaches.

In this chapter we will discuss the basic concepts central to research design. We will also outline the most common types of designs and show how they relate to each other. Exploratory research will be discussed in detail in this chapter, while descriptive and causal research will be explored more completely in the next chapter. The discussion should help to illuminate the first steps researchers take when they begin to tackle a marketing problem.

Research Design as a Plan of Action

Research design The framework or plan for a study that guides the collection and analysis of the data.

A **research design** is simply the framework or plan for a study used as a guide in collecting and analyzing data. It is the blueprint that is followed in completing a study. It resembles the architect's blueprint for a house. While it is possible to build a house without a detailed blueprint, the final product will more than likely be somewhat different from what was originally envisioned by the buyer. A certain room is too small; the traffic pattern is poor; some things really wanted are omitted, other, less important things are included, and so on. It is also possible to conduct research without a detailed blueprint. The research findings are also likely to differ widely from what was desired by the consumer or user of the research. "These results are interesting, but they do not solve the basic problem" is a common lament. Further, just as the house built without a blueprint is likely to cost more because of midstream alterations in construction, research conducted without a research design is likely to cost more than research properly executed using a research design.

Thus, a research design ensures that the study (1) will be relevant to the problem and (2) will use economical procedures. It would help the student learning research methods if there were a single procedure to follow in developing the framework or if there were a single framework to be learned. Unfortunately, this is not the case.[1]

> There is never a single, standard, correct method of carrying out research. Do not wait to start your research until you find out *the* proper approach, because there are many ways to tackle a problem—some good, some bad, but probably several good ways. There is no single perfect design. A research method for a given problem is not like the solution to a problem in algebra. It is more like a recipe for beef stroganoff; there is no one best recipe.

Exploratory research Research design in which the major emphasis is on gaining ideas and insights; it is particularly helpful in breaking broad, vague problem statements into smaller, more precise subproblem statements.

Rather, there are many research design frameworks, just as there are many unique house designs. Fortunately though, just as house designs can be broken into basic types (for example, ranch, split-level, two-story), research designs can be classified into some basic types. One very useful classification is in terms of the fundamental objective of the research: exploratory, descriptive, or causal.[2]

Types of Research Design

Descriptive research Research design in which the major emphasis is on determining the frequency with which something occurs or the extent to which two variables covary.

The major emphasis in **exploratory research** is on the discovery of *ideas* and *insights*.[3] The soft drink manufacturer faced with decreased sales might conduct an exploratory study to generate possible explanations. **Descriptive research** is typically concerned with determining the *frequency* with which something occurs or the relationship between two variables. It is typically guided by an initial hypothesis. Suppose the soft drink manufacturer thought that sales of his diet cola were slipping because the number of teenaged girls who constituted his primary market had declined over the past five years. He might decide to commission a study to see if trends in soft drink consumption were related to characteristics such as age or sex. This would be a descriptive study.

Causal research
Research design in which the major emphasis is on determining cause-and-effect relationships.

A **causal research** design is concerned with determining cause-and-effect relationships. Causal studies typically take the form of experiments, since experiments are best suited to determine cause and effect. For instance, our soft drink manufacturer may be interested in determining which of several different advertising appeals is most effective. One way for such a company to proceed would be to use different ads in different geographic areas and investigate which ad generated the highest sales. In effect, the company would perform an experiment, and if it was designed properly, the company would be in a position to conclude that one specific appeal caused the higher rate of sales.

Although it is useful to divide research designs into these neat categories— exploratory, descriptive, and causal research—as a way of helping to explain the research process, three warnings are in order. First, the distinctions among the three are not absolute. Any given study may serve several purposes. Nevertheless, certain types of research designs are better suited for some purposes than others. The crucial principle of research is that *the design of the investigation should stem from the problem.* Each of these types is appropriate to specific kinds of problems.

Second, in the remainder of this chapter and in the next chapter, we shall discuss each of the design types in more detail. The emphasis will be on their *basic characteristics* and *generally fruitful approaches.* Whether or not the designs are useful in a given problem setting depends on how imaginatively they are applied. Architects can be taught basic design principles; whether they then design attractive, well-built houses depends on how they apply these principles. So it is with research. The general characteristics of each design can be taught. Whether they are productive in a given situation depends on how skillfully they are applied. There is no single best way to proceed, just as there is no single best floor plan for, say, a ranch-type house. It all depends on the specific problem to be solved. Research analysts, then, need an understanding of the basic designs so that they can modify them to suit specific purposes.

Hypothesis A statement that specifies how two or more measurable variables are related.

Finally, it should be noted that the three basic research designs can be viewed as stages in a continuous process. Figure 5.1 shows the interrelationships. Exploratory studies are often seen as the initial step. When researchers begin an investigation, it stands to reason that they lack a great deal of knowledge about the problem. Consider: "Brand X's share of the disposable diaper market is slipping. Why?" This statement is too broad to serve as a guide for research. To narrow and refine it would logically be accomplished with exploratory research, in which the emphasis would be on finding possible explanations for the sales decrease. These tentative explanations, or **hypotheses,** would then serve as specific guides for descriptive or causal studies. Suppose the tentative explanation that emerged was that "Brand X is an economy-priced diaper, originally designed to compete with low-cost store-brand diapers. Families with children have more money today than when the brand was first introduced and are willing to pay more for higher-quality baby products. It stands to reason that our market share would decrease." The hypothesis that families with small children have more real income to spend, and that a larger proportion of that money is going toward baby products, could be examined in a descriptive study of trends in the baby products industry.

Figure 5.1   **Relationships among Research Designs**

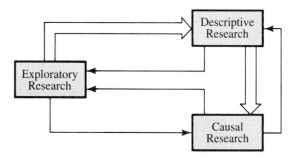

Suppose the descriptive study did support the hypothesis. The company might then wish to determine whether parents were, in fact, willing to pay more for higher-quality diapers and, if so, what features (such as better fit or greater absorbency) were most important to them. This might be accomplished through a test market study, a causal design.

Each stage in the process thus represents the investigation of a more detailed statement of the problem. Although we have suggested that the sequence would be from exploratory to descriptive to causal research, alternative sequences might occur. The "families with small children have more money to spend on baby products" hypothesis might be so generally accepted that the sequence would be from exploratory directly to causal. This sequence is more typical of what actually happened in the hard-fought battle between Procter & Gamble and Kimberly-Clark for shares of the lucrative diaper market.

Procter & Gamble (P & G), which had an enormous hit with Pampers, grew uncharacteristically complacent about the brand in the two decades following its introduction. By the early 1980s, Pampers had become P & G's single largest business, at $1 billion per year. But Kimberly-Clark spotted an opening in the market that P & G had neglected. In response to its perception that parents were willing to pay more for a diaper with greater absorbency and less leakage, Kimberly-Clark developed Huggies, a premium-priced diaper.

The introduction of Huggies had a drastic effect on Pampers' market share. In 1985, realizing it was rapidly being beaten at its own game, P & G poured $725 million into revamping production facilities and advertising a new generation of higher-quality, more expensive Pampers. Since the success of competing Huggies had already proved that parents were willing to pay extra for better diapers, P & G did not have to waste time or money testing that concept. Instead it could concentrate on causal research to refine design and fine-tune price and advertising approaches in its test market in Wichita, Kansas.[4]

The potential for conducting research in the reverse direction also exists. If a hypothesis is disproved by causal research (e.g., the product bombs in taste tests), the analyst may then decide that another descriptive study, or even another exploratory study, is needed. Also, not every research problem will begin with an exploratory study. It depends on how specific researchers can be in formulating the problem before them. A general, vague statement leads naturally to exploratory work, while a specific, cause-effect hypothesis lends itself to experimental work.

Originally a product of successful exploratory research, Pampers suffered a temporary sales decline when competitors acted on up-to-date research that showed a willingness by consumers to purchase more expensive and more effective diapers. Further research by Procter & Gamble led to today's high-selling Pampers designed and packaged separately for boys and girls.

Source: © Gropp/SIPA.

Ethical
Dilemma 5.1   Marketing Research Insights was asked to carry out the data-collection and analysis procedures for a study designed by a consumer goods company. After studying the research purpose and design, a consultant for Marketing Research Insights concluded that the design was poorly conceived. First, he thought that the design was more complex than was necessary, inasmuch as some of the data could be obtained through secondary sources, precluding the necessity of much primary data collection. Second, the proposed choice of primary data collection would not produce the kinds of information sought by the company.

Although the consultant advised the company of his opinions, the company insisted on proceeding with the proposed design. Marketing Research Insights' management was reluctant to undertake the study, as it believed that the firm's reputation would be harmed if its name were associated with poor research.

- What decision would you make if you were a consultant for Marketing Research Insights?
- In general, should a researcher advance his or her opinion of a proposed design, or should the researcher remain silent and simply do the work?
- Is it ethical to remain silent in such situations?

Exploratory Research

As previously stated, the general objective in exploratory research is to gain insights and ideas. The exploratory study is particularly helpful in breaking broad, vague problem statements into smaller, more precise subproblem statements, ideally in the form of specific hypotheses. In effect, a hypothesis is a statement that specifies how two or more measurable variables are related.[5]

In the early stages of research, we usually lack sufficient understanding of the problem to formulate a specific hypothesis. Further, there are often several tentative explanations for a given marketing phenomenon. For example, sales are off because our price is too high, our dealers or sales representatives are not doing the job they should or our advertising is weak, and so on. Exploratory research can be used to establish priorities in studying these competing explanations. Top priority would usually be given to whichever hypothesis appeared most promising in the exploratory study. Priorities may also be established according to the feasibility of researching the hypotheses. Exploratory studies should help to eliminate ideas that are not practical.

An exploratory study is also used to increase the analyst's familiarity with a problem. This is particularly true when the analyst is new to the problem arena, for example, a marketing research consultant going to work for a company for the first time.

The exploratory study may also be used to clarify concepts. For instance, if management is considering a change in service policy intended to increase dealer satisfaction, an exploratory study could be used to (1) clarify what is meant by dealer satisfaction and (2) develop a method by which dealer satisfaction could be measured.

The Reagan administration found itself facing the kind of broad, ill-defined problem that exploratory studies are designed to address when it set out to make the tax code more fair. The first issue to be resolved was what fairness in the tax code really meant. Several studies had supported the notion that a majority of Americans felt the system then in place was unfair; 82 percent responding to an Internal Revenue Service–sponsored survey felt this way, and two-thirds responding to a Louis Harris poll said they were "fed up" with the current system because of its unfairness. As Kent Smith, who headed a study of taxpayer compliance for the American Bar Association, commented, though, "the polls don't explain precisely why people think the current system is unfair. We've been frustrated by the way the fairness questions have been asked. . . . Is it tax enforcement that bothers people? Tax rates? The way laws are written? Tax avoidance by other people? Or is it because they believe their taxes are poorly spent by government?"[6] Exploratory research would play a particularly important role in clarifying a concept like this.

In sum, an exploratory study is used for any or all of the following purposes:[7]

- Formulating a problem for more precise investigation
- Developing hypotheses
- Establishing priorities for further research
- Gathering information about the practical problems of carrying out research on particular issues
- Increasing the analyst's familiarity with the problem
- Clarifying concepts

In general, exploratory research is appropriate for any problem about which little is known. It becomes the foundation for a good study.

Because so much is typically unknown at the beginning of an inquiry, exploratory studies are generally very flexible with regard to the methods used for gaining insight and developing hypotheses. "Formal design is conspicuous by its absence in exploratory studies."[8] Exploratory studies rarely use detailed question-naires or involve probability sampling plans. Rather, investigators frequently change the research procedure as the vaguely defined initial problem is transformed into one with more precise meaning. Investigators often follow where their noses lead them in an exploratory study. Ingenuity, judgment, and good luck inevitably play a part in leading to the one or two key hypotheses that, it is hoped, will account for the phenomenon. While exploratory research may be conducted in a variety of ways, experience has shown that literature surveys, experience surveys, focus groups, and the analysis of selected cases are particularly productive.[9]

Literature Search

Literature search
A search of statistics, trade journal articles, other articles, magazines, newspapers, and books for data or insight into the problem at hand.

One of the quickest and cheapest ways to discover hypotheses is in the work of others, through a **literature search.** The search may involve conceptual literature, trade literature, or, quite often, published statistics. The literature that is searched depends naturally on the problem being addressed. Miller Business Systems, Inc., of Dallas, for example, routinely monitors trade literature in order to keep track of its competitors. The information on each competitor is entered into the "competitor profiles" it keeps in its data base. The company regularly scans these profiles for insights on what the competition might be doing. One such scan indicated that a competitor had hired nine furniture salespeople in a 10-day period. This was a tip-off to a probable push by the competitor in the office-furniture market. With this early notice, Miller was able to schedule its salespeople to make extra calls on their accounts, thereby blunting the competitor's sales drive.[10]

Sometimes conceptual literature is more valuable than trade literature. For example, a firm with a dissatisfied field sales force would probably begin its study with a search of literature on concepts and ideas related to satisfaction in such personnel. The search might include research studies in psychology, sociology, and personnel management, in addition to marketing journals. The focus would be on the factors determining employee satisfaction and dissatisfaction. The analyst would keep a keen eye for those factors also found in the company's environment. The question of how to measure an employee's satisfaction would also be researched at the same time.

Suppose a firm's problem was one that typically triggers much marketing research: "Sales are off. Why?" Exploratory insights into this problem could easily and cheaply be gained by analyzing published data and trade literature. Such an analysis would quickly indicate whether the problem was an industry problem or a firm problem. For example, it was readily apparent to Procter & Gamble that the decline in Pampers' market share was a company problem, since the disposable diaper industry as a whole showed no signs of weakening.

Very different research is in order if the firm's sales are down but (1) the company's market share is up, since industry sales are down further; (2) the company's market share has remained stable; or (3) the company's market share has declined. The last situation would trigger an investigation of the firm's marketing mix variables, while the first condition would prompt an analysis to determine why industry sales are off.

A company's own internal data should be included in the literature examined in exploratory research, as Mosinee Paper Company found to its pleasant surprise. The company was contemplating dropping one of its products because of its dismal sales performance. Before doing so, though, the company tallied sales of the product per salesperson and found that only a single salesperson was selling that specific grade of industrial paper. Upon further investigation, Mosinee discovered how the buyers "were using the paper—an application that had been known only to the one salesman and his customers. This information enabled management to educate its other salesmen as to the potential market for the paper and sales rose substantially."[11]

It is important to remember that in a literature search, as in any exploratory research, the major emphasis is on the discovery of ideas and tentative explanations of the phenomenon and not on demonstrating which explanation is *the* explanation. The demonstration is better left to descriptive and causal research. Thus, the analyst must be alert to the hypotheses that can be derived from available material, both published material and the company's internal records.

Experience Survey

Experience survey
Interviews with people knowledgeable about the general subject being investigated.

Sometimes called the *key informant survey*, the **experience survey** attempts to tap the knowledge and experience of those familiar with the general subject being investigated. For example, Clearwood Building, Inc., of San Francisco, focused on architects and designers when trying to get a handle on its competitors. It asked these people to describe the worst features of builders that tended to turn off buyers of expensive homes. Some of the answers included bad manners, workers who tracked dirt across carpets, and beat-up construction trucks, which buyers objected to having parked in their driveways. The company used these insights for a major repositioning of its business to the Bay Area's upper crust. "The company bought a new truck and kept it spotless. Its estimators donned jackets and ties. And its work crews, now impeccably polite, began rolling protective runners over carpets before they set foot in clients' homes. In less than two years, Clearwood's annual revenue jumped to $1 million from $200,000."[12]

In studies concerned with the marketing of a product, anyone who has any association with the marketing effort is a potential source of information. This would include the top executives of the company, the sales manager, product manager, and sales representatives. It would also include wholesalers and retailers who handle the product, as well as consumers who use the product. It might even include individuals who are not part of the chain of distribution but who might, nevertheless, possess some insight into the phenomenon. For example, a children's book publisher gained valuable insights into the reason for a sales decline by talking with librarians and schoolteachers. These discussions indicated that an increased use of library facilities, both public and school, coincided with the product's drop in sales. The increase in library usage was, in turn, traced to an increase in federal funds, which had enabled libraries to buy more books for their children's collections.

Usually, a great many people know something about the general subject of any given problem. However, not all of them should be contacted.

> Research economy dictates that the respondents in an experience survey be carefully selected. The aim of the experience survey is to obtain insight into the relationships between variables rather than to get an accurate picture of current practices or a simple consensus as to best practices. One is looking for provocative ideas and useful insights, not for the statistics of the profession. Thus the respondents must be chosen because of the likelihood that they will offer the contributions sought. In other words, a *selected* sample of people working in the area is called for.[13]

Never, therefore, should a probability sample, in which respondents are chosen by some random process, be used in an experience survey. It is a waste of time to interview those who have little competence or little relevant experience in the subject under investigation. It is also a waste of time to interview those who cannot articulate their experience and knowledge. It is important, though, to include people with

Research Window 5.1
Use of Experience Survey to Gain Insight into a Declining Sales Situation

After several years of declining revenues followed ten years of revenue and profit growth, the firm's board of directors questioned the advisability of continuing with one line of business. A review of internal sales records revealed that its market for the service line was limited to approximately thirty large packaged goods manufacturers. No significant external secondary data sources were located. Executives of the firm were then asked to identify the three most knowledgeable persons in the country with respect to the service line's characteristics, its market, and the capabilities of competitive suppliers. All three persons nominated were executives of present or past customers of the firm. Appointments for personal interviews were made with each nominee by telephone, using the firm's president as a reference.

Each of the three personal interviews was conducted at the informant's place of business, and lasted from 1½ to 3½ hours. . . . The sessions ranged over a wide variety of topics. Informants were asked to assess the past, current, and probable future developments of the service line, the market, and the comparative strengths and weaknesses of the major suppliers of the service line, including the research sponsor.

The findings . . . revealed that there had been no decline in market activity during the past two years. There had been, however, a concerted effort by a number of packaged goods manufacturers to divert business to two new service suppliers during the period. This was done to assure additional sources of supply and capacity in order to handle a significant expansion of demand that was expected to occur within two years. As a result, established suppliers were allocated less business during the period but could expect a resumption of their previous growth in the near future. The manufacturers were reluctant to divulge these plans to the established suppliers for fear they would add excess capacity and act to limit the competitiveness of the new suppliers.

Source: William E. Cox, Jr., *Industrial Marketing Research* (New York: John Wiley, 1979), pp. 25–26.

differing points of view. The children's book publisher we mentioned earlier interviewed company executives, key people in the product group, sales representatives, managers of retail outlets in which the books were sold, teachers, and librarians in the process of investigating the sales decline.

The interviews were all unstructured and informal. The emphasis in each interview among those immediately concerned with the distribution of the product was, "How do you explain the sales decrease? In your opinion, what is needed to reverse the downward slide?"[14] Most of the time each interview was then devoted to exploring in detail the various rationales and proposed solutions. A number of sometimes conflicting hypotheses emerged. This provided the researchers with an opportunity to "bounce" some of the hypotheses off groups with differing vantage points and, in the process, get a feel for which of the hypotheses would be most fruitful to research. The interviews with librarians and teachers approached the problem from a different angle. Here the emphasis was on discovering changes in children's reading habits.

The respondents were given a great deal of freedom in choosing the factors to be discussed. This is consistent with the notion that the emphasis in exploratory research is on developing tentative explanations and not on demonstrating the viability of a given explanation. This emphasis, as well as the conduct of the experience survey, is reflected in the experience of an industrial goods manufacturer described in Research Window 5.1.

Focus Groups

Focus groups are another useful method for gathering ideas and insights.[15] In a **focus group,** a small number of individuals are brought together in a room to sit and talk about some topic of interest to the focus group sponsor. The discussion is directed by a moderator. The moderator attempts to follow a rough outline of issues while simultaneously having the comments made by each person considered in group discussion. Each individual is thereby exposed to the ideas of the others and submits his or her ideas to the group for consideration.

Focus groups are currently one of the most frequently used techniques in marketing research; they have proved to be productive for a variety of purposes, including the following:

- Generating hypotheses that can be further tested quantitatively.
- Generating information helpful in structuring consumer questionnaires.
- Providing overall background information on a product category.
- Securing impressions on new product concepts.

For example, American Express used the insights gathered from focus groups as an important input when developing the program that extended manufacturers'[16] warranties on products that were bought with an American Express Card. Similarly, Ray-O-Vac found through a series of focus groups that people wanted brighter, more modern, and more dependable flashlights. The company also discovered that people were willing to pay for added durability. These insights led to the development of their line of Workhorse flashlights, which regenerated a mature market.[17] Research Window 5.2 discusses the insights Oscar Mayer and the Buick Division of General Motors gleaned from focus groups.

Although focus groups do vary in size, most consist of eight to twelve members. Smaller groups are too easily dominated by one or two members; with larger groups, frustration and boredom can set in, as individuals have to wait their turn to respond or get involved. Respondents are generally selected so that the groups are relatively homogeneous, minimizing both conflicts among group members on issues not relevant to the study objectives and differences in perceptions, experiences, and verbal skills. Differences that are too great with respect to any of these characteristics can intimidate some of the group participants and stifle discussion. For example, the group for a project that involved a mixed group of architects, roofing contractors, and building owners included a person whose company was called Tony the Roofer. "Tony had all the experience and involvement with the product category the other participants had. But he was so intimidated by all the other people, he just would not say anything. Every so often we would ask what *he* thought of some subject, but he just would mumble that he agreed with what one of the 'bigger' people had said."[18]

Most firms conducting focus groups use screening interviews to determine the individuals who will compose a particular group. One type they try to avoid is the individual who has participated before in a focus group, since some of these people tend to behave as "experts." Their presence can cause the group to behave in dysfunctional ways as experienced participants continually try to make their presence felt. As focus groups have become more popular, problems in recruiting rookies have intensified. Firms also try to avoid groups in which some of the participants are friends or relatives, because this tends to inhibit spontaneity in the discussion as the acquaintances begin talking to each other.

Given that the participants in any one group should be reasonably homogeneous, how can a firm ensure that it is getting a wide spectrum of insights? The key way is

Research Window 5.2
Experiences of Oscar Mayer and the Buick Division
of General Motors with Focus Groups

Oscar Mayer When Oscar Mayer found that its Select Slices line of lunch meats was not meeting sales projections and was actually declining in sales, it launched a series of focus group studies to get some idea of why. One insight from the focus groups was that people perceived luncheon meats as being very high in calories. For example, participants in general estimated that a single ham slice had between 150 and 250 calories, which was more than they perceived a Snickers bar to have (in fact, the ham slice had fewer than 30).

Using this research as a basis, Oscar Mayer decided to launch a new line of low-fat cold cuts by repositioning many of its existing products from the Select Slices product line. The repositioning involved some new packaging, including adding a blue shield to the packaging that mentions the fat-free content of the cold cuts (e.g., 96-percent fat free for its corned beef); new flavors; grouping the products together on the supermarket shelves; and a new ad program emphasizing that the product was low in fat and calories in addition to tasting great.

Buick Division of General Motors The Buick Division of General Motors used focus groups to help develop the Regal two-door, six-passenger coupe it introduced in 1987. The effort had begun more than five years before, when Buick held about 20 focus groups across the country and asked what features customers wanted in a new car. Who were the customers? They were those wealthy enough to afford a $14,000 price tag, then about $1,000 to $2,000 more than the average new car, which meant annual incomes of $40,000 or above. All the participants, gathered in every major geographic region of the country, had purchased new cars within the last four years.

"What these groups told us was that the customers wanted a legitimate back seat, at least 20 miles per gallon, and 0-to-60-miles acceleration in 11 seconds or less," says Jay Qualman, Buick's general director of advertising. "They wanted a stylish car, but they didn't want it to look like it had just landed from outer space."

After Buick engineers created clay models of the car and mock-ups of the interior, the company went back to yet another focus group of target buyers. What the customers didn't like were the oversized bumper and the severe slope of the hood. What they did like were the four-wheel disk brakes and the four-wheel independent suspension. Focus groups also helped to refine the advertising campaign for the Regal. Participants were first asked which competing cars most resembled the Buick in terms of image and features. The answer was Oldsmobile, a sister General Motors division. "That made us realize we had to separate the two in the minds of the public," says Qualman. "So we repositioned Buick above Oldsmobile. How? By focusing on comfort and luxury features such as full six-passenger seating, wood-grain instrument panels, velour-type fabrics, and special stereo systems. We also learned that the driving experience was more important to Buick owners."

Buick and its agency, McCann-Erickson, created twenty ad concepts, which were later narrowed down to four. Focus groups were next shown various TV commercials and printed ad slicks. Participants then voiced their reactions as to which were most effective. "Among the things we were concerned with was selecting a music sound track that would attract younger customers without turning off their parents," says Qualman. The theme: "The new Buick Regal. There's nothing like it on the American road."

Source: Mary Jung, "Oscar Mayer Repositions Failing Line to Attract Health-Conscious Consumers," *Marketing News*, 22 (August 15, 1988), p. 6; and Jeffrey A. Trachtenberg, "Listening, the Old-Fashioned Way," *Forbes*, 140 (October 5, 1987), pp. 202, 204.

Exploratory research may include focus groups such as this one, where different toothpaste brands are compared and discussed.

Source: © Steve Smith/ONYX.

by having multiple groups. Not only can the characteristics of the participants vary across groups, but so can the issue outline. Ideas discovered in one group session can be introduced in subsequent group sessions for reaction. A typical project has four groups, but some may have up to twelve. The guiding criterion is whether the later groups are generating additional insight into the phenomenon under study. When they show diminishing returns, the groups are stopped.

The typical focus group session lasts from 1½ to 2 hours. Groups can be arranged at various sites, including the client's home office, a neutral site, the office of the research agency, or even one of the respondent's homes. Each site has its own advantages and disadvantages with respect to the ability to recruit respondents, the costs of the session, the rapport that can be established, and the ability to record the interviews for later transcription and analysis.[19]

The moderator in the focus group has a key role.[20] For one thing, the moderator typically translates the study objectives into a discussion guide. To do so, he or she needs to understand the background of the problem and the most important information the client hopes to glean from the research process. The moderator also needs to understand the parameters of all the focus groups in terms of their number, size, and composition, as well as how they might be structured to build on one another. Moreover, the moderator must lead the discussion so that all objectives of the study are met and do so in such a way that *interaction* among the group members is stimulated and promoted. The focus group session should not be allowed to dissolve into nothing more than a set of concurrent interviews in which the participants each take turns responding to a predetermined set of questions. This is an extremely delicate role. It requires someone who is intimately familiar with the purpose and objectives of the research and at the same time possesses good interpersonal

Table 5.1   Ten Criteria of Good Focus Group Moderators

1. Quick Learner

Moderator must be able to learn quickly and incorporate new material into his or her normal thinking and vocabulary. Must be able to absorb the content of the client briefing quickly and understand what the client is seeking to generate from the focus group sessions. Must be able to quickly absorb and understand the inputs from the group participants.

2. A "Friendly" Leader

Moderator can develop rapport with group respondents quickly (within ten minutes). Should be viewed by the group as the authority figure; also as the type of person with whom they would like to have a casual conversation. If moderator is perceived as being friendly, he or she will elicit more honest, in-depth responses from the group than one who is dictatorial or threatening.

3. Knowledgeable But Not All-Knowing

Moderator will communicate to the group that he or she has some knowledge about the subject at hand but is not an expert. If group members feel the moderator is an expert, they will ask questions about the topic rather than provide answers or discussion of their views. Participants also might respond to the moderator's direction from the perspective of an expert rather than that of the consumer, user, or potential customer for the product, service, or idea being covered, to impress the moderator with their knowledge.

4. Excellent Memory

Moderator needs to have a good memory to be able to tie together inputs that are generated during the early part of the session with others that come up toward the end. Must be able to recall key information volunteered by each participant throughout the session so that statements made later can be cross-checked for the consistency of the participants' viewpoints.

5. Good Listener

Moderator must be a good listener. Must have the ability to remember key information that individual participants say during the group and the ability to hear all the information that people say, in terms of both content and implication.

6. A Facilitator, Not a Performer

The objective of the group is to secure information from the participants rather than entertain the clients in the observation room. Some moderators perform for the clients who are observing the session. Observing focus groups can be tedious, particularly if one is participating in a series of groups, and comic relief can pass the time more quickly, but too much moderator-generated humor will result in less-than-satisfactory inputs from the participants.

7. Flexible

Must be flexible during the session with regard to the flow of the discussion. Some adhere so closely to their moderator's guide that they disrupt the natural flow of group discussion to ensure that each point on the outline is covered before going on to the next item. The guide is simply an outline, and it is often much more effective to deviate from the pre-arranged order to capitalize on the inputs of valuable discussion. An effective moderator is sufficiently flexible to do this.

8. Empathic

Moderator should be an empathic individual. Must be able to relate to the nervousness that some group respondents have as a result of being asked to talk before the others. If respondent believes that the moderator understands his or her situation, this person is much more likely to participate actively in the group discussions.

9. A "Big Picture" Thinker

Moderator must be able to separate the important observations on a group session from the less significant inputs. At the conclusion of each group session, the moderator must be able to draw together all the inputs received and be able to communicate to the client the overall ("big picture") message generated by the discussion.

10. Good Writer

Most clients who use the focus group technique require written reports to summarize the results of the groups. Therefore, the moderator should be skilled in writing clear, concise summaries of the sessions that provide clients with meaningful and action-oriented conclusions and recommendations.

Source: Reprinted by permission of the publisher, from *The Practical Handbook and Guide to Focus Group Research* by Thomas L. Greenbaum, pp. 50–54, (Lexington, Mass.: D. C. Heath and Company, Copyright 1988).

communication skills. One important measure of a focus group's success is whether the participants talk to each other, rather than the moderator, about the items on the discussion guide.

Some of the key qualifications moderators must have are described in Table 5.1. Moderating an industrial focus group is even more difficult than moderating one involving a consumer product. A moderator for a consumer good typically knows something about the product or service at issue. After all, moderators are consumers too. Not so with many industrial goods. This means that the moderator's briefing for an industrial good has to be longer and more detailed. It also means that many of the group participants will know a great deal more about the product or service being discussed than the moderator. Directing group discussion under these conditions can be a taxing job indeed.[21]

Sponsors can realize several advantages from the proper conduct of focus groups. For one thing, they allow for serendipity. Ideas can simply drop "out of the blue" during a focus group discussion. Further, the group setting allows them to be developed to their full significance, because it allows for snowballing. A comment by one individual can trigger a chain of responses from other participants. Often after a brief introductory warm-up period, respondents can "turn on" to the discussion. They become sufficiently involved that they want to express their ideas and expose their feelings. Some feel more secure in the group environment than if they were being interviewed alone, since they soon realize that they can expose an idea without necessarily having to defend or elaborate on it. Consequently, responses are often more spontaneous and less conventional than they might be in a one-on-one interview.

Group interviews do offer certain benefits not obtainable with individual depth interviews, but they also have their weaknesses. Although they are easy to set up, they are difficult to moderate and to interpret. It is easy to find evidence in one or more of the group discussions that supports almost any preconceived position. Because executives have the ability to observe the discussions through one-way mirrors or the opportunity to listen to tape recordings of the sessions, focus groups seem more susceptible to executive and even researcher biases than do other data-collection techniques, although sometimes the ability to study the tapes can be an advantage. Not only does the systematic study of the tapes allow those doing so to get a first hand sense of what the target group is feeling, but the tape also provides a vehicle for communicating that feeling to others. For example, Time, Inc., used focus groups when it noticed signs of rising dissatisfaction with customer service, whichthreatened renewal rates.

> Readers who had received poor service were invited to hour-long sessions to voice their complaints.
>
> "All of the people had some complaint about what had happened to them," McDonald (the director of research) said. "A premium promised but not delivered, a mix-up in billing, a payment not credited, an erroneous referral to a collection agency."
>
> Because of the bad service, he said, the readers were furious.
>
> McDonald taped the focus groups, edited the tape to a 25-minute video, and used it as a propaganda device to change the attitudes of the customer service staff.
>
> "Its impact upon the Time, Inc., staff was incredibly powerful," he said. "Suddenly, all of the faceless millions had faces. The customers became real people rather than abstractions."[22]

Putting faces on the faceless worked to advantage for Time, but it can just as easily become a disadvantage, for it makes it very easy to forget that the discussion, and consequently the results, are greatly influenced by the moderator and the specific direction he or she provides. Moderators possessing all of the desired skills listed in Table 5.1 are extremely rare. One has to remember that the results are not representative of what would be found in the general population and thus are *not* projectable. Further, the unstructured nature of the responses makes coding, tabulation, and analysis difficult. Focus groups should *not* be used, therefore, to develop head counts of the proportion of people who feel a particular way. Focus groups are better for generating ideas and insights than for systematically examining them.[23]

Analysis of Selected Cases

Analysis of selected cases Intensive study of selected examples of the phenomenon of interest.

Sometimes referred to as the analysis of *insight-stimulating examples*, the **analysis of selected cases** involves the intensive study of selected cases of the phenomenon under investigation. Researchers may examine existing records, observe the phenomenon as it occurs, conduct unstructured interviews, or use any one of a variety of other approaches to analyze what is really happening in a given situation. The focus may be on entities (individual people or institutions) or groups of entities (sales representatives or distributors in various regions).

The method is characterized by several features.[24] First, the attitude of the investigator is the key. The most productive attitude is one of alert receptivity, of seeking explanations rather than testing explanations. The investigator is likely to make frequent changes in direction as new information emerges. He or she may have to search for new cases or secure more data from previously contacted cases. Second, the success of the method depends heavily on how well the investigator can integrate the diverse bits of information he or she has amassed into a unified interpretation. Finally, the method is characterized by its intensity. The analyst attempts to obtain sufficient information to characterize and explain both the unique features of the case being studied and the features it has in common with other cases.

> In one study to improve the productivity of the sales force of a particular company, the investigator studied intensively two or three of the best sales representatives and two or three of the worst. Data was collected on the background and experience of each representative and then several days were spent making sales calls with them. As a result, a hypothesis was developed. It was that checking the stock of retailers and suggesting items on which they were low were the most important differences between the successful and the poor sales representatives.[25]

In this example, the key insight that good sales representatives had in common, and in which they differed from poor sales representatives, led them to check retailer inventory.

Some situations that are particularly productive of hypotheses are as follows:

1. *Cases reflecting changes and, in particular, abrupt changes.* For example, the way a market adjusts to the entrance of a new competitor can reveal a great deal about the structure of an industry.
2. *Cases reflecting extremes of behavior.* The case of the best and worst sales representatives just cited is an example. Similarly, to determine the factors responsible for the differences in sales performance among a company's territories, one could learn more by comparing the best and worst territories than by looking at all territories.
3. *Cases reflecting the order in which events occurred over time.* For example, in the case of the differing sales performance by territory, it may be that in one territory a branch office replaced a manufacturer's agent, while in another it replaced an industrial distributor.

Which cases will be most valuable depends, of course, on the problem in question. It is generally true, though, that cases that display sharp contrasts or have striking features are most useful. This is because minute differences are usually difficult to discern. Thus, instead of trying to determine what distinguishes the average case from the slightly above-average case, it is better to contrast the best and worst and thereby magnify whatever differences may exist.

Ethical

Dilemma 5.2   Prompted by an increasing incidence of homes for sale by owner, the president of a local real estate company asks you to undertake exploratory research to ascertain what kind of image realtors enjoy in the community. Unbeknownst to your current client, you undertook a similar research study for a competitor two years ago and, based on your findings, have formed specific hypotheses about why some homeowners are reluctant to sell their houses through realtors.

- Is it ethical to give information obtained while working for one client to another client who is a competitor? What should you *definitely* not tell your current client about the earlier project?
- Is it ethical to undertake a research project when you think that you already know what the findings will be? Can you generalize findings from two years ago to today?
- Should you help this company define its problem, and if so, how?

Back to the Case

Larry Grenfell was once again addressing a gathering of Beautique's top managers. In front of him on the conference table sat a copy of the research report on Beautique. It summarized the findings of one of the largest consumer research studies in the industry. The study relied on personal interviews with some of Beautique's most successful and least successful salespeople, several focus groups with customers, and mailed questionnaires sent to a sample of customers who had purchased from Beautique in the past. Moreover, the study was by no means over. A study like this one generated almost as many questions as answers. However, it had already brought into focus major problems that Beautique had to address.

"We wanted to know what consumers had to say," said Grenfell, pointing to the thick volume in front of him, "and boy did we get an earful. While each of you is going to need some time to study this, I wanted to take a minute to pique your interest.

"I was very surprised to find that our consumers feel that our pricing is inconsistent with our competitors'. Some of our prices are perceived as being too low. Consumers can't believe that these products are any good because they're so cheap. Other prices of ours are perceived as being too high, and in those cases we're seen as not delivering appropriate quality.

"We're going to have to start letting the market, not our costs, set

the price of our products," commented Linda Seidel, who was in charge of the direct-selling division.

"One finding that shouldn't surprise anyone is that we have an image problem. For the past several years our reputation has been declining in the public's eye," reported Grenfell.

"Hallelujah," declared John Boldt, from the marketing department.

"You've got to be kidding," groaned somebody else.

"Not at all," replied Boldt. "It's much better to have an image problem than to have a quality problem."

"Now here's an example of the sort of little gem of information that I hope this study holds for each of us," continued Beautique's president. "You all know that our SkinSilk skin cream is one of the largest-selling skin creams in the world. But how many of you know that it repels mosquitoes?"

"You've got to be kidding!" someone exclaimed.

"He's right," said Peter Bennington, from new product development. "There's an ingredient in it that mosquitoes hate. They won't land on skin after the lotion is applied."

"Now there has to be some way to capitalize on this," said Grenfell.

"I'm not sure that we want to muddy the waters by advertising that Skin-Silk makes your skin silky soft and also repels mosquitoes, but there has to be some way for us to use this to sell more SkinSilk."

"Maybe we could change the packaging to make it easier to apply all over your body instead of just on your hands. Maybe some sort of spray bottle?" suggested Bennington.

"Those are just the sort of ideas that I hope this report will generate.

But I want you to get reading and get thinking right away. Ideas like a packaging change for SkinSilk need specific marketing research. We don't want to spend months and years sifting through the information we've gathered. We're going to *do* something about it!"

Based on Paul Markovits, "Direct Selling Is Alive and Well," *Sales and Marketing Management* (August 1988), pp. 76–78.

Summary

Learning Objective 1: Explain what a research design is.

A research design is the framework or plan for a study that guides the collection and analysis of data.

Learning Objective 2: List the three basic types of research design.

One basic way of classifying designs is in terms of the fundamental objective of the research: exploratory, descriptive, or causal.

Learning Objective 3: Describe the major emphasis of each type of research design.

The major emphasis in *exploratory research* is on the discovery of ideas and insights. *Descriptive research* is typically concerned with determining the frequency with which something occurs or the relationship between variables. A *causal research* design is concerned with determining cause-and-effect relationships.

Learning Objective 4: Cite the crucial principle of research.

The crucial principle of research is that *the design of the investigation should stem from the problem*.

Learning Objective 5: Describe the basic uses of exploratory research.

Exploratory research is basically "general picture" research. It is quite useful in becoming familiar with a phenomenon, in clarifying concepts, in developing but not testing "if-then" statements, and in establishing priorities for further research. The output from exploratory research is ideas and insights, not answers.

Learning Objective 6: Specify the key characteristic of exploratory research.

Exploratory studies are characterized by their flexibility.

Learning Objective 7: Discuss the various types of exploratory research and identify the characteristics of each.

Among the various types of exploratory research are literature searches, experience surveys, focus groups, and analyses of selected cases. Literature searches may involve conceptual literature, trade literature, or, quite often, published statistics. Experience surveys, sometimes known as *key informant surveys*, attempt to tap the knowledge and experience of those familiar with the general subject being investigated. Focus groups are in a sense personal interviews conducted among a small number of individuals, normally eight to twelve, simultaneously. However, the interview relies more on group discussion than on a series of directed questions to generate data. The analysis of selected cases is sometimes referred to as the analysis of *insight-stimulating examples*. By either label, the approach involves the intensive study of selected cases of the phenomenon under investigation.

Learning Objective 8: Identify the key person in a focus group.

The moderator is key to successful functioning of a focus group. The moderator must not only lead the discussion so that all objectives of the study are met but must do so in such a way that interaction among group members is stimulated and promoted.

Discussion Questions, Problems, and Projects

1. The Communicon Company was a large supplier of residential telephones and related services in the southeast United States. The Department of Research and Development recently designed a prototype with a memory function that could store the number of calls and the contents of the calls for a period of 48 hours. A similar model, introduced by Communicon's competitor three months earlier, was marginally successful. However, both the models suffered from a technical flaw. It was found that a call lasting for over 20 minutes would result in a loss of the dial tone for 90 seconds. This was mainly attributable to the activation of the memory function. Notwithstanding the flaw, management was excited about the efforts of the research and development department. They decided to do a field study to gauge consumer reaction to the memory capability. A random sample of 1,000 respondents was to be chosen from three major metropolitan centers in the Southeast. The questionnaires were designed to find out respondents' attitudes and opinions toward this new instrument.

   In this situation, is the research design appropriate? If yes, why? If no, why not?

2. A medium-size manufacturer of high-speed copiers and duplicators was introducing a new desktop model. The vice-president of communications had to decide between two advertising programs for this product. He preferred advertising program Gamma and was sure it would generate more sales than its counterpart, advertising program Beta. The next day he was to meet with the senior vice-president of marketing to plan an appropriate research design for a study that would aid in the final decision as to which advertising program to implement.

   What research design would you recommend? Justify your choice.

3. A local mail-order firm was concerned with improving its service. In particular, management wanted to assess if customers were dissatisfied with current service and the nature of this dissatisfaction.

   What research design would you recommend? Justify your choice.

4. The Write-It Company was a manufacturer of writing instruments such as fountain pens, ballpoint pens, soft-tip pens, and mechanical pencils. Typically, these products were retailed through small and large chains, drugstores, and grocery stores. The company had recently diversified into the manufacture of disposable cigarette lighters. The distribution of this product was to be restricted to drugstores and grocery stores. The reason was that management believed that its target market of low- and middle-income classes would use these outlets. Your expertise is required in order to decide on an appropriate research design to determine if this would indeed be the case.

   What research design would you recommend? Justify your choice.

5. Feather-Tote Luggage is a producer of cloth-covered luggage, one of the primary advantages of which is its light weight. The company distributes its luggage through major department stores, mail-order houses, clothing retailers, and other retail outlets such as stationery stores, leather goods stores, and so on. The company advertises

rather heavily, but it also supplements this promotional effort with a large field staff of sales representatives, numbering around 400. The number of sales representatives varies, and one of the historical problems confronting Feather-Tote Luggage has been the large number of sales representatives' resignations. It is not unusual for 10 to 20 percent of the sales force to turn over every year. Since the cost of training a new person is estimated at $5,000 to $10,000, not including the lost sales that might result because of a personnel switch, Mr. Harvey, the sales manager, is rightly concerned. He has been concerned for some time and, therefore, has been conducting exit interviews with each departing sales representative. On the basis of these interviews, he has formulated the opinion that the major reason for this high turnover is general sales representatives' dissatisfaction with company policies, promotional opportunities, and pay. But top management has not been sympathetic to Harvey's pleas regarding the changes needed in these areas of corporate policy. Rather, it has tended to counter Harvey's pleas with arguments that too much of what he is suggesting is based on his gut reactions and little hard data. Before it would be willing to change things, top management desires more systematic evidence that job satisfaction, in general, and these dimensions of job satisfaction, in particular, are the real reasons for the high turnover. Harvey has called on the Marketing Research Department at Feather-Tote Luggage to assist him in solving his problem.

(a)   As a member of this department, identify the general hypothesis that would guide your research efforts.

(b)   What type of research design would you recommend to Harvey? Justify your answer.

6.   Cynthia Gaskill is the owner of a clothing store that caters to college students. Through informal conversations with her customers, she has begun to suspect that a video-rental store specifically targeting college students as customers would do quite well in the local market. While her informal conversations with students have revealed an overall sense of dissatisfaction with existing rental outlets, she hasn't been able to isolate specific areas of concern. Gaskill, thinking back to a marketing research course she took in school, has decided that focus group research would be an appropriate method to gather information that might be useful in deciding whether to pursue further development of her idea (e.g., a formal business plan, store policies, etc.).

(a)   What is the decision problem and resulting research problem apparent in this situation?

(b)   Who should Gaskill select as participants for the focus group?

(c)   Where should the focus group session be conducted?

(d)   Who should be the moderator of the focus group?

(e)   Develop a discussion outline for the focus group.

7.   The exploratory techniques of focus group research and experience surveys are similar in many ways, yet each offers distinct advantages, depending on the objectives of the research project. What are some of the similarities and differences in these techniques?

Endnotes

1. Julian L. Simon, *Basic Research Methods in Social Science: The Art of Empirical Investigation* (New York: Random House, 1969), p. 4.

2. Claire Selltiz, Lawrence S. Wrightsman, and Stuart W. Cook, *Research Methods in Social Relations*, 3rd ed. (New York: Holt, Rinehart and Winston, 1976), pp. 90–91. See also Fred N. Kerlinger, *Foundations of Behavioral Research*, 3rd ed. (New York: Holt, Rinehart and Winston, 1986), pp. 347–390.

3. The basic purposes are those suggested by Selltiz, Wrightsman, and Cook, *Research Methods*.

4. Nancy Giges and Laurie Freeman, "Wounded Lion? Trail of Mistakes Mars P & G Record," *Advertising Age*, 56 (July 29, 1985), pp. 1 and 50.

5. See Kerlinger, *Foundations of Behavioral Research*, for a discussion of the criteria of good hypotheses and of the value of hypotheses in guiding research.

6. Alan Murray, "To Revamp Tax Code, Reagan Will Tap Belief that System Is Unfair," *The Wall Street Journal* (April 15, 1985), p. 21.

7. Selltiz, Wrightsman, and Cook, *Research Methods*, p. 91.

8. Harper W. Boyd, Ralph Westfall, and Stanley F. Stasch, *Marketing Research: Text and Cases*, 7th ed. (Homewood, Ill.: Richard D. Irwin, 1989), p. 93.

9. Selltiz, Wrightsman, and Cook, *Research Methods.* Chapter 4 has a particularly informative discussion of the types of research that are productive at the exploratory stages of an investigation.

10. Steven P. Galante, "More Firms Quiz Customers for Clues About Competition," *The Wall Street Journal* (March 3, 1986), p. 17.

11. Jon G. Udell and Gene R. Laczniak, *Marketing in an Age of Change* (New York: John Wiley, 1981), p. 154.

12. Galante, "More Firms Quiz Customers."

13. Selltiz, Wrightsman, and Cook, *Research Methods*, p. 94.

14. Selltiz, Wrightsman, and Cook suggest that it is often useful in an exploratory study to orient questions toward "what works." That is, they recommend that questions be of the following form: "If (a given effect) is desired, what influences or what methods will, in your experience, be most likely to produce it?" (p. 95).

15. Focus groups grew out of focused interviews. For discussion of their origin and evolution, see Robert K. Merton, "The Focused Interview and Focus Groups: Continuities and Discontinuities," *Public Opinion Quarterly*, 51 (Winter 1987), pp. 550–566.

16. Jeffrey A. Trachtenberg, "Listening, the Old-Fashioned Way," *Forbes*, 140 (October 5, 1987), pp. 202, 204.

17. Jennifer Riddle, "Complaining Customers Get Firms' Attention," *Wisconsin State Journal* (June 22, 1986), p. 2.

18. Robert C. Inglis, "In-Depth Data: Using Focus Groups to Study Industrial Markets," *Business Marketing*, 72 (November 1987), p. 80.

19. Goldman and McDonald discuss the pros and cons of the various sites as well as a number of other operational questions that arise with the conduct of focus groups. See Alfred E. Goldman and

Susan Schwartz McDonald, *The Group Interview: Principles and Practice* (Englewood Cliffs, N.J.: Prentice-Hall, 1987). See also *Focus Groups: Issues and Approaches*, prepared by the Qualitative Research Council of the Advertising Research Foundation, 1985.

20. Thomas L. Greenbaum, *The Practical Handbook and Guide to Focus Group Research* (Lexington, Mass.: D. C. Heath and Company, 1988) has a particularly useful discussion on the requirements for moderators and how to go about selecting them.

21. Inglis, "In-Depth Data," has a useful discussion of the extra difficulties moderators of industrial focus groups face. For discussions of the use of focus groups for industrial goods, see Edward F. McQuarrie and Shelby H. McIntyre, "Focus Groups and the Development of New Products by Technologically Driven Companies: Some Guidelines," *Journal of Product Innovation Management*, 3 (March 1986), pp. 40–46.

22. Scott C. McDonald, Nancy E. Dince, and Larry P. Stanek, "Focus Groups Being Subverted by Clients," *Marketing News*, 18 (August 28, 1987), p. 48.

23. For an empirical assessment of the relative ability of individual interviews versus focus groups of various sizes and composition to generate ideas, see Edward F. Fern, "The Use of Focus Groups for Idea Generation: The Effects of Group Size, Acquaintanceship, and Moderator on Response Quantity and Quality," *Journal of Marketing Research*, 19 (February 1982), pp. 1–13.

24. These features are detailed further in Selltiz, Wrightsman, and Cook, *Research Methods*, pp. 98–99. See also Thomas V. Bonoma, "Case Research in Marketing: Opportunities, Problems, and a Process," *Journal of Marketing Research*, 22 (May 1985), pp. 199–208; and Robert K. Yin, *Case Study Research: Design and Methods* (Beverly Hills, Calif.: Sage Publications, 1989).

25. Harper W. Boyd, Ralph Westfall, and Stanley F. Stasch, *Marketing Research: Text and Cases*, 6th ed. (Homewood, Ill.: Richard D. Irwin, 1985), p. 51.

Suggested Additional Readings

For an excellent discussion of the three types of research designs, their basic purposes, and generally fruitful approaches, see

Claire Selltiz, Lawrence S. Wrightsman, and Stuart W. Cook, *Research Methods in Social Relations*, 3rd ed. (New York: Holt, Rinehart and Winston, 1976).

Fred N. Kerlinger, *Foundations of Behavioral Research*, 3rd ed. (New York: Holt, Rinehart and Winston, 1986).

For some illustrations of their use in the industrial marketing context see

William E. Cox, Jr., *Industrial Marketing Research* (New York: John Wiley, 1979).

For detailed discussion on how to go about conducting focus groups, see

Focus Groups: Issues and Approaches (New York: Advertising Research Foundation, 1985).

Alfred E. Goldman and Susan Schwartz McDonald, *The Group Depth Interview: Principles and Practice* (Englewood Cliffs, N.J.: Prentice-Hall, Inc., 1987).

Thomas L. Greenbaum, *The Practical Handbook and Guide to Focus Group Research*, (Lexington, Mass.: D. C. Heath and Company, 1988).

Jane Farley Templeton, *Focus Groups: A Guide for Marketing and Advertising Professionals* (Chicago: Probus Publishing Company, 1987).

Descriptive and Causal Research Designs

Learning Objectives

Upon completing this chapter, you should be able to

1. Cite three major purposes of descriptive research.

2. List the six specifications of a descriptive study.

3. Explain what a dummy table is.

4. Discuss the difference between cross-sectional and longitudinal designs.

5. Explain what is meant by a *panel* in marketing research and explain the difference between a traditional panel and an omnibus panel.

6. Explain what is meant by a turnover table, or brand-switching matrix.

7. Describe the emphasis in sample surveys.

8. Distinguish between the commonsense notion of causality and the scientific notion.

9. Define *concomitant variation*.

10. List three ways of determining a causal relationship.

11. Clarify the difference between laboratory experiments and field experiments.

12. Explain which of the two types of experiments has greater internal validity and which has greater external validity.

13. List the three major problems in test marketing.

14. Discuss the advantages and disadvantages of simulated test marketing.

15. Distinguish between a standard test market and a controlled test market.

Case in Marketing Research

Dr. Michael Biraldi knew that he had a good product, but he wasn't sure of what to do with it. He had developed his line of Aquaderm skin-care products specifically for his patients with diabetes. (One of the characteristic symptoms of the disease is severe dryness of the extremities.) He had begun by developing a hand and foot lotion from a peanut extract that was especially effective in combating dryness. It was so successful that he had branched out into facial moisturizers and cleansers.

But diabetics were a small and easily targeted market. If Biraldi wanted to sell his products to a broader population, clearly he needed some help.

He had approached Tim Meyer, a business consultant who specialized in helping start-up companies. Meyer had managed to raise a small amount of working capital on the basis of Biraldi's success in marketing to dia-

betics. Biraldi had anted up some of his own funds as well.

The dermatologist had wanted to spend the money on eye-catching packaging and advertising, but Meyer had pointed out that the amount of money they had on hand was insufficient to do either effectively. In addition, it was unlikely they'd be able to raise more until they had a clear idea of what they hoped to accomplish, how they hoped to accomplish it, and had some evidence of at least a reasonable chance of succeeding.

To this, Biraldi had responded, "Well, I know what I want to accomplish. I want to make a lot of money."

That was how he had come to be here, he mused, sitting in the dark, staring through a one-way mirror at twelve young women between the ages of 22 and 32 as they applied Aquaderm lotion to their faces. While they did so, a representative of

the marketing research firm that Meyer had hired asked them questions about the product.

Biraldi felt miserable sitting in the darkened room, listening to strangers sniff and make faces over Aquaderm. The products had taken him years to develop. They really were his baby.

Discussion Issues

1. If you were Biraldi, what questions would you want marketing research to answer before you launched the product?
2. In what circumstances might a marketer be justified in not doing research?
3. If you were Meyers, the business consultant, what questions might you like to ask Biraldi about his goals for Aquaderm?

In the last chapter we learned that research designs typically fall into one of three categories: exploratory, descriptive, or causal research. We examined exploratory research and noted that one of its primary uses is to generate ideas and insights for additional, more targeted research. In this chapter we will see how descriptive and causal research might be used to test the validity of the hypotheses that exploratory studies generate.

Descriptive Research Designs

A great deal of marketing research can be considered descriptive research, which is used for the following purposes:

1. To describe the characteristics of certain groups. For example, based on information gathered from known users of our particular product, we might attempt to develop a profile of the "average user" with respect to income, sex, age, educational level, and so on.
2. To estimate the proportion of people in a specified population who behave in a certain way. We might be interested, say, in estimating the proportion of people within a specified radius of a proposed shopping complex who would shop at the center.
3. To make specific predictions. We might be interested in predicting the level of sales for each of the next five years so that we could plan for the hiring and training of new sales representatives.

Descriptive research encompasses an array of research objectives. However, a descriptive study is more than a fact-gathering expedition.

> Facts do not lead anywhere. Indeed, facts, as facts, are the commonest, cheapest, and most useless of all commodities. Anyone with a questionnaire can gather thousands of facts a day—and probably not find much real use for them. What makes facts practical and valuable is the glue of explanation and understanding, the framework of theory, the tie-rod of conjecture. Only when facts can be fleshed to a skeletal theory do they become meaningful in the solution of problems.[1]

The researcher should not fall prey to the temptation of beginning a descriptive research study with the vague thought that the data collected should be interesting. A good descriptive study presupposes much prior knowledge about the phenomenon being studied. It rests on one or more specific hypotheses. These conjectural statements guide the research in specific directions. In this respect, a descriptive study design is very different from an exploratory study design. Whereas an exploratory study is characterized by its flexibility, descriptive studies can be considered rigid. Descriptive studies require a *clear specification* of the *who, what, when, where, why,* and *how* of the research.

Suppose a chain of food convenience stores is planning to open a new outlet, and the company wants to determine how people usually come to patronize a new outlet. Consider some of the questions that would need to be answered before data collection for this descriptive study could begin. Who is to be considered a patron? Anyone who enters the store? What if they do not buy anything but just participate in the grand-opening prize giveaway? Perhaps a patron should be defined as anyone who purchases anything from the store.

Should patrons be defined on the basis of the family unit, or should they be defined as individuals, even though the individuals come from the same family? What characteristics of these patrons should be measured? Are we interested in their age

Table 6.1   **Dummy Table**

| | Store Preference by Age | | |
Age	Prefer A	Prefer B	Prefer C
Less than 30			
30–39			
40 or more			

and sex, or perhaps in where they live and how they came to know about our store? When shall we measure them, while they are shopping or later? Should the study take place during the first weeks of operation of the store, or should it be delayed until the situation has stabilized somewhat? Certainly if we are interested in word-of-mouth influence, we must wait at least until that influence has a chance to operate.

Where shall we measure the patrons? Should it be in the store, immediately outside the store, or should we attempt to contact them at home? Why do we want to measure them? Are we going to use these measurements to plan promotional strategy? In that case the emphasis might be on measuring how people become aware of the store. Or are we going to use these measurements as a basis for locating other stores? In that case the emphasis might shift more to determining the trading area of the store.

How shall we measure the patrons? Shall we use a questionnaire, or shall we observe their purchasing behavior? If we use a questionnaire, what form will it take? Will it be highly structured? Will it be in the form of a scale? How will it be administered? By telephone? By mail? Perhaps by personal interview?

These questions are not the only ones that would be or should be asked. Certainly, some of the answers will be implicit in the hypothesis or hypotheses that guide the descriptive research. Others, though, will not be obvious. The researcher will be able to specify them only after some labored thought or even after a small pilot or exploratory study. In either case, the researcher is well advised to delay collecting that first item of information with which to test the hypotheses until clear judgments of the who, what, when, where, why, and how of descriptive research have been made.

Dummy table A table that will be used to catalog the collected data.

The researcher should also delay data collection until it has been clearly determined how the data are to be analyzed. Ideally, a set of dummy tables should be prepared before beginning the collection process. A **dummy table** is used to catalog the data that is to be collected. It shows how the analysis will be structured and conducted. Complete in all respects save for filling in the actual numbers, it contains a title, headings, and specific categories for the variables making up the table. All that remains after collecting the data is to count the number of cases of each type. Table 6.1 shows what might be used by a women's specialty store preparing to investigate whether its customers are predominantly from one age-group and, if so, how that group differs from the customers who frequent competitors' stores.

Note that the table lists the particular age segments the store's owner wishes to compare. It is crucial that the exact variables and categories to be investigated be specified before researchers begin to collect the data. The statistical tests that will be used to uncover the relationship between age and store preference in this case should also be specified before data collection begins. Inexperienced researchers often question the need for such hard, detailed decisions before collecting the data. They assume that delaying these decisions until after the data are collected will somehow make the decisions easier. Just the opposite is true, as any experienced researcher will attest.

> Most difficult for the beginning researcher to anticipate will be the analytical problems he may face after the data are gathered. He tends to believe that a wide variety of facts will be enough to solve anything. Only after struggling with sloppy, stubborn, and intractable facts, with data not adequate for the testing of hypotheses and with data that are interesting but incapable of supporting practical recommendations for action will he be fully aware that the big "mistakes" of research usually are made in the early stages. Each definition of a problem or problem variable will create different facts or findings, and a formulation once made serves to restrict the scope of analysis. No problem is definitively formulated until the researcher can specify how he will make his analysis and how the results will contribute to a practical solution.[2]

Once the data have been collected and analysis is begun, it is too late to lament, "If only we had collected information on that variable," or "If only we had measured the Y variable using a finer scale." Correcting such mistakes at this time is next to impossible. Rather, the analyst must take such considerations into account when planning the study. And dummy tables make such planning easier.

Another way of ensuring that the information collected in a descriptive study will address the objectives of the research is to specify in advance the objective each question addresses, the reason the question is included in the study, and the particular analysis in which the question will be used.

For example, a meat packer is interested in investigating the potential market for a new hot dog.[3] Before allowing the study to begin, he may well ask his researchers to justify the questions they seek to have answered. One question researchers plan to ask respondents is, "How many packages of hot dogs does your family eat every month?"

In keeping with the preliminary planning we have suggested, let us imagine a scenario between the meat packer (MP) and his head researcher (R).

MP: What objectives does this question address?

R: This question will give us the information we need to classify people who eat hot dogs into specific categories based on how many hot dogs they eat. This information can help us predict future patterns, and may be related to a group's interest in our new hot dog. If one of the study's objectives is to find the group most likely to buy our proposed new product, then this question may help us find that group and ultimately learn if its members share any characteristics, such as age, size of household, family income, etc.

MP: Are there any other reasons why this question is included in the study?

R: Yes, once we have developed a profile of our typical customer, we may be able to use that information to choose advertising media that will reach high-usage households at the least cost.

MP: How will the responses to this question be analyzed?

R: First, we will generate a frequency distribution. This will help us to sort respondents into three categories: light, moderate, and heavy users. Then we will try to relate usage types to such demographic variables as size of household, age of household shopper, total income, etc. We may also be able to determine how different prices would affect purchasing behavior.

Figure 6.1   ***Classification of Descriptive Studies***

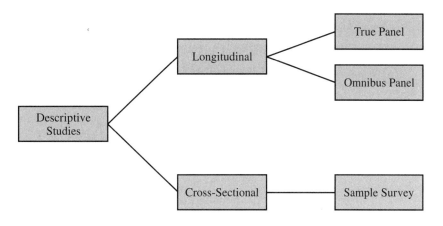

This kind of exercise is called *output planning*. It is especially useful if it is done before the study, in conjunction with the development of dummy tables, as suggested earlier. The dummy tables provide some additional clues on how to phrase the individual questions and code the responses.

Figure 6.1 is an overview of the various types of descriptive studies. The basic distinction is between *cross-sectional designs*, which are the most common and most familiar, and *longitudinal designs*. Typically, a **cross-sectional study** involves researching a sample of elements from the population of interest. If the population under investigation is hot dog eaters, the elements of the sample may include heavy users, moderate users, or people who eat hot dogs only on the Fourth of July. Most characteristics of the elements, or sample members, are measured only once. Researchers may ask sample members their age, sex, income, and education, for example.

A **longitudinal study,** on the other hand, involves a *panel*, which is a fixed sample of elements. The elements may be stores, dealers, individuals, or other entities. The panel, or sample, remains relatively constant through time, although members may be added to replace dropouts or to keep it representative. The sample members in a panel are measured repeatedly, in contrast with the one-time measurement in a cross-sectional study. Both cross-sectional and longitudinal studies have weaknesses and advantages.

Longitudinal Analysis

There are two types of panels. The older type (called a **true panel** in this text) relies on repeated measurements of the same variables. For example, the National Purchase Diary (NPD) maintains a consumer panel of 13,000 families.[4] On a monthly basis, each family records its purchases of each of a number of products. Similarly, the Nielsen Retail Store Audit involves a sample of 10,000 stores.[5] Each store is checked monthly for its sales of each of a number of products. The operations of these panels will be examined more thoroughly when we discuss secondary sources of information in Chapter 7, but the important point to note now is that analysts measure each sample member with regard to the same characteristics each time. In the NPD panel, researchers measure purchases; in the Nielsen Retail Store Audit, they measure sales.

Cross-sectional study Investigation involving a sample of elements selected from the population of interest which are measured at a single point in time.

Longitudinal study Investigation involving a fixed sample of elements that is measured repeatedly through time.

Panel (true) A fixed sample of respondents who are measured repeatedly over time with respect to the same variables.

Panel (omnibus) A fixed sample of respondents who are measured repeatedly over time but on variables that change from measurement to measurement.

In recent years, a new type of panel, called the **omnibus panel,** has sprung up. The information collected from the members selected for this type of panel varies. At one time, it may be attitudes with respect to a new product. At another time, the panel members might be asked to evaluate alternative advertising copy. In each case, a sample might be selected from the larger group, which is in turn a sample of the population. The subsample might be drawn randomly. More likely, though, participants with the desired characteristics will be chosen from a total panel. For example, the Parker Pen Company maintains a panel of 1,100 individuals, who were chosen because they expressed some interest in writing instruments and, of course, because of their willingness to participate. Parker Pen will often use selected members of this panel to evaluate new writing instruments. If the new instrument is a fountain pen, the company will probably choose individuals who prefer fountain pens to test the product. Those chosen and the information sought will vary from project to project.

R. J. Reynolds, manufacturer of Camel, Vantage, and Winston cigarettes, chooses its panel members based on ability rather than interest. The company maintains a panel of 350 of its employees, whose job it is to provide information for quality control and new brand development.[6] Only those employees who can successfully pass a screening test in which they smoke three cigarettes and can then identify which two were alike are allowed on the panel. As members of the panel, the employees are called upon to sniff, feel, and draw on unlit cigarettes, to smoke the cigarettes, and then to provide their sensory evaluations. While the information that is collected is fairly standardized, the cigarettes being evaluated vary from test to test.

The distinction between the traditional panel and the omnibus panel is important. True longitudinal analysis, also called *time series analysis*, can be performed only on the first type of data, repeated measurements of the same entities over time. We shall see why when we discuss the method of analysis unique to panel data—the turnover table. The turnover table can be used only when individuals and variables are held constant through time. This is not to deny the value of the newer types of panels. Rather, we wish only to raise a cautionary flag, because in other respects (for example, sample design, information collection, and so forth) both types of panels have about the same advantages and disadvantages when compared with cross-sectional studies. Consequently, we shall treat both types of panel studies together when discussing these general advantages and disadvantages.

Probably the single most important advantage of true panel data is the way it lends itself to analysis. Suppose we are presently subscribing to the type of service that generates consumer purchase data from a panel of 1,000 families. Suppose further that we manufacture a laundry detergent, which we will call Brand A, and our brand has two main competitors, Brands B and C. There are also a number of other smaller competitors, which we will classify together in the single category, Brand D.

We have recently changed the package design of our product, and we are now interested in determining what impact the new design has on sales. Let us consider the performance of our brand before the change (time period t_1), and after the package change (time period t_2).

We could perform several types of analyses on these data.[7] We could look at the proportion of those in the panel who bought our brand in period t_1. We could also calculate the proportion of those who bought our brand in period t_2. Suppose these calculations generated the data shown in Table 6.2, which indicates that the package change was successful. Brand A's market share increased from 20 percent to 25 percent. Further, Brand A seemed to make its gains at the expense of its two major competitors, whose market shares decreased.

Table 6.2   *Number of Families in Panel Purchasing Each Brand*

Brand Purchased	During First Time Period (t_1)	During Second Time Period (t_2)
A	200	250
B	300	270
C	350	330
D	150	150
Total	1,000	1,000

But that is not the whole story or even a completely accurate picture of the market changes that occurred. Look at what happens when, in assessing the impact of the package change, we maintain the identity of the sample members. Since we have repeated measures of the same individuals, we can count the number of families who bought Brand A in both periods, those who bought B or C or one of the miscellaneous brands in both periods, and those who switched brands between the two periods. Suppose Table 6.3 resulted from these tabulations. This table, which is a **turnover table,** or a **brand-switching matrix,** contains the same basic information as Table 6.2. That is, we see that 20 percent of the families bought Brand A in period t_1, while 25 percent did so in period t_2. But Table 6.3 also shows that Brand A did not make its market share gains at the expense of Brands B and C, as originally suggested, but rather captured some of the families who previously bought one of the miscellaneous brands; 75 families switched from Brand D in period t_1 to Brand A in period t_2. And, as a matter of fact, Brand A lost some of its previous users to Brand B during the period; 25 families switched from Brand A in period t_1 to Brand B in period t_2.

Table 6.3 also allows the calculation of brand loyalty. Consider Brand A, for example: 175 of the 200, or 87.5 percent, of those who bought Brand A in period t_1 remained "loyal to it" (bought it again) in period t_2. By dividing each cell entry by the row or previous period totals, one can assess these brand loyalties and can also throw the basic changes that occurred in the market into bolder relief. Table 6.4, produced

Brand-switching matrix
A two-way table that indicates which brands a sample of people purchased in one period and which brands they purchased in a subsequent period, thus highlighting the switches occurring among and between brands as well as the number of persons that purchased the same brand in both periods.

Table 6.3   *Number of Families in Panel Buying Each Brand in Each Period*

		During Second Time Period (t_2)				
		Bought A	**Bought B**	**Bought C**	**Bought D**	**Total**
	Bought A	175	25	0	0	200
During First Time Period (t_1)	Bought B	0	225	50	25	300
	Bought C	0	0	280	70	350
	Bought D	75	20	0	55	150
	Total	250	270	330	150	1,000

Table 6.4   **Brand Loyalty and Brand-Switching Probabilities among Families in Panel**

		During Second Time Period (t_2)				
		Bought A	**Bought B**	**Bought C**	**Bought D**	**Total**
During First Time Period (t_1)	Bought A	.875	.125	.000	.000	1.000
	Bought B	.000	.750	.167	.083	1.000
	Bought C	.000	.000	.800	.200	1.000
	Bought D	.500	.133	.000	.367	1.000

by such calculations, suggests, for example, that among the three major brands, Brand A exhibited the greatest buying loyalty and Brand B the least. This is important to know because it indicates whether families like the brand when they try it.[8]

Whether we can conclude that those who switched from one of the miscellaneous brands to Brand A were prompted to do so by the package change is open to question, for reasons that we will discuss later in the chapter. The point is that turnover, or brand-switching, analysis can be performed only when there are repeated measures over time for the same variables for the same subjects. It is not appropriate for omnibus panel data, in which the variables being measured are constantly changing, nor is it appropriate for cross-sectional studies, even if successive cross-sectional samples are taken.

Thus, the unique advantage of true longitudinal analysis is that since it reveals changes in individual members' behavior, researchers can determine the effect of a change in a particular marketing variable—a package design, for example—better than if they had conducted separate studies using samples made up of different individuals. Had two different groups been used to study a change in a particular variable, it would not be clear whether variations in the data were due to changes in the marketing variable or to differences between the two groups.

Although the major advantage of a panel is analytical, a panel also provides some advantages in the kind of information it yields. Panels are probably a researcher's best format for collecting classification information, such as respondents' incomes, ages, education levels, and occupations. And this information allows a more sophisticated analysis of a study's results.

Cross-sectional studies are limited in this respect, since respondents being contacted for the first and only time are rarely willing to give lengthy, time-consuming interviews. Panel members are usually compensated for their participation, so their interviews can be longer and more exacting, or there can be several interviews. Further, the sponsoring firm can afford to spend more time and effort securing accurate classification information, as this information can be used in a number of studies.

Panel data are also believed to be more accurate than cross-sectional data because panel data tend to be freer from the errors associated with reporting past behavior. Errors arise in reporting past behavior because humans tend to forget, partly because time has elapsed, but partly for other reasons. In particular, research has shown that events and experiences are forgotten more readily if they are inconsistent with attitudes or beliefs that are important to the person or that threaten the person's self-esteem. If, for example, subjects are asked how often they brush their teeth, they might overstate the number of times—either because they genuinely do not remember or because they fear the interviewer will think less of them for brushing too seldom. In a panel, on the other hand, behavior is recorded as it occurs, so less reliance is placed on a respondent's memory. When diaries are used to record purchases, the problems should be virtually eliminated because the respondent is instructed to record the purchases immediately upon returning home. When other behaviors, such as television viewing, are of interest, respondents are asked to record those behaviors as they occur, thus minimizing the possibility that they will be forgotten or misremembered.

In one study, for example, 261 mothers were asked to record the kinds of products and services—cereals, toys, fast foods, and so on—their children requested. Each mother was asked to keep three daily diaries: a product-request diary, a product-purchase diary, and a television-viewing log. The product-request diary is shown in Table 6.5.

Researchers chose the panel diary method for the study because they deemed it the most accurate. As mentioned earlier, errors often occur in cross-sectional studies because respondents say what they think the interviewers want to hear or what they feel will make them look good in the interviewers' eyes. The panel design helps reduce this interaction bias. First, respondents come to trust the interviewer to a greater degree because of repetitive contact. Second, more frequent contact creates rapport.

The main disadvantage of panels is that they are nonrepresentative. The agreement to participate involves a commitment on the part of the designated sample member, and many individuals refuse this commitment. They do not wish to be bothered with testing products, evaluating advertising copy, or filling out consumer diaries. Because these activities require a sizable time commitment, families in which both husband and wife work, for example, may be less well represented than those in which one partner works and the other is at home. Consumer panels that require households to keep a record of their purchases generally have cooperation rates of about 60 percent when members are contacted in person and lower participation rates if telephone or mail is used for the initial contact.[9]

The better ongoing panel operations select prospective participants very systematically. They attempt to generate and maintain panels that are representative of the total population of interest with respect to such characteristics as age, occupation, education, and so on. Quite often, to create a representative panel, they will use *quota samples*, in which the proportion of sample members possessing a certain characteristic is approximately the same as the proportion possessing that characteristic in the general population. As a very simplified example of this, consider an organization that wishes to study sports car owners. If the organization knows that of the people owning sports cars, 73 percent are men and 27 percent are women, then it will want its quota sample to reflect that percentage.

All the research organization can do, however, is designate the families or respondents that are to be included in the sample. Researchers cannot force individuals to participate, nor can they require continued participation from those who initially agreed to cooperate. True, they often encourage participation by offering some premium or by paying panel members for their cooperation. Nevertheless, a significant percentage of the individuals the organization may have hoped to include often refuse to cooperate—or drop out quickly once the panel has begun. Some individuals are lost to the panel because they move away or die. Depending on the type of cooperation needed, the refusal and *mortality*, or drop-out,

Table 6.5   **Product Request Diary**

Date:	1 Products	2 Where were you when your child asked? (check as many as apply)				3 How did your child try to get you to buy it? (check as many as apply)									4 If you said yes to child's request, did you: (check one and skip to column 8)			5 If you didn't say yes to child's request, did you (check one)				6 If you didn't say yes, how did your child react? (check one)			
		At home	On the way to the store	At the store	Other	Just asked, didn't nag about it	Really pleaded with you over and over	Said he/she had seen product on TV	Said brother, sister, or friend has or likes it	Bargained (offered to do chores, pay for part, etc.)	Gave bunch of ways he or she would use product	Just put in shopping basket at store	Other	Didn't mind buying it—said yes right away	Didn't mind buying it, but discussed with child before saying yes	Said yes, but not to the brand the child wanted	Said no, and that was that	Said no and explained why	Said no, but agreed to buy something else instead	Said maybe sometime, but not now	Seemed to take it okay	Disappointed, but didn't say anything more	Argued a little, then let it drop	Argued a lot, kept nagging	Got really angry with you
Product Type	Brand Name (if child asks for a specific brand)																								

Source: Leslie Isler, Edward Popper, and Scott Ward, *Children's Purchase Request and Parental Responses: Results from a Diary Study* (Cambridge, Mass.: Marketing Science Institute, 1979), pp. 26–27. Reprinted with permission.

rate might run over 50 percent. And, of course, the question then arises as to whether the panel is still representative of the population. Further, the payment of a reward for cooperation raises the question of whether particular types of people are attracted to such panels. It seems, for example, that "panel cooperation appears to be best in households with more than two members, in households having wives in the younger age groups, and in households with more education."[10] Unrepresentiveness may not be a problem in every study. It depends on the purpose of the study and the particular variables of interest.

In one of the more extensive studies investigating the "representativeness" of a continuing household panel, Market Facts compared data gathered from a mail panel against data gathered from randomly selected telephone samples. Research Window 6.1 shows that the differences were very small with respect to such issues as travel outside the United States, beer consumption, households with heart attack sufferers, and households with cigarette smokers. However, the study goes on to point out that "experimentation of this kind has revealed instances of significant differences between

7					8						9		10							11							12			13						
If child argued or got angry, how did you respond to the child's reaction? (check as many as apply)					Main reason(s) child asked for this (check as many as apply)						Has child asked for this product before?		If you said yes to #9: When was the last time child asked for it? (check one)							If you said yes to #9: How often does your child ask for this product? (check one)							Has your child asked for this specific brand before? (check one)			If you said yes to #12: How often does your child ask for this specific brand (check one)						
Ignored it	Repeated what you'd said before	Got angry with child	Made some compromise	Decided to buy what child asked for	Saw it in store	Saw TV commercial for it	Brother, sister, or friends have it	Saw other advertising for it (not TV)	Don't know	Other	Yes	No	Yesterday	Earlier this week	Last week	In last 2 weeks	In last month	Over a month ago	Don't know	3–4 times a week	1–2 times a week	Once every couple of weeks	About once a month	Once every few months	Once or twice a year	Don't know	Yes	No, child doesn't prefer any particular brands of this product	No	3–4 times a week	1–2 times a week	Once every couple of weeks	About once a month	Once every few months	Once or twice a year	Don't know

data generated by mail panel and through telephone interviewing . . . What these experiments strongly suggest, therefore, is that great care must continue to be exercised in the selection of research method, when methodological options exist. But they also suggest that many . . . marketing questions can be addressed very effectively through controlled mail panels. . . ."[11] The trouble with bias due to unrepresentativeness, of course, is that one never knows in advance whether it will affect the results, much less how.

Cross-Sectional Analysis

Despite the advantages of longitudinal analysis, in actual practice, cross-sectional designs are the best known and most important descriptive designs. The cross-sectional study has two distinguishing features. First, this study provides a snapshot of the variables of interest at a single point in time, as contrasted with the longitudinal study, which provides a series of pictures that, when pieced together, provide a movie

Research Window 6.1
Comparison of Responses of the Market Facts Mail Panel and Randomly Selected Telephone Samples

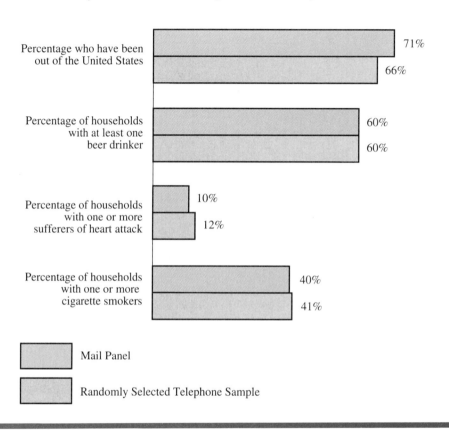

Source: Verne B. Churchill, "Learning to Live with Continuing Household Panels," *TeleNation Reports* (Summer 1988), p. 1. Published by Market Facts, Inc.

Sample survey Cross-sectional study in which the sample is selected to be representative of the target population and in which the emphasis is on the generation of summary statistics such as averages and percentages.

of the situation and the changes that are occurring. Second, in the cross-sectional study, the sample of elements is typically selected to be representative of some known universe. Therefore, a great deal of emphasis is placed on selecting sample members, usually with a probability sampling plan. That is one reason that the technique is often called **sample survey.** The probability sampling plan allows determination of the sampling error associated with the statistics, which are generated from the sample but used to describe the universe. Most sample surveys involve enough observations to allow for cross-classification of the variables.

The objective of cross-classification analysis is to establish categories such that classification in one category implies classification in one or more other categories. The method of cross-classification analysis will be detailed later, in the discussion of tabulation. For the moment, simply note that it involves counting the *simultaneous occurrence* of the variables of interest. For example, suppose management feels that occupation is an important factor in determining the consumption of its product.

Further, suppose the proposition to be examined is that white-collar workers are more apt to use the product than blue-collar workers. If this hypothesis were examined in a cross-sectional study, measurements would be taken from a representative sample of the population with respect to their occupation and use of the product. In cross tabulation, researchers would count the number of cases that fell in each of the following classes:

- White-collar and use the product
- Blue-collar and use the product
- White-collar and do not use the product
- Blue-collar and do not use the product

That is, the emphasis would be on the relative frequency of occurrence of the joint phenomenon "white-collar occupation and user of the product." If the hypothesis is to be supported by the sample data, the proportion of white-collar workers using the product should exceed the proportion of blue-collar workers using the product.

Ethical
Dilemma 6.1   The regional sales manager for a large chain of men's clothing stores asks you to establish whether increasing his salespeople's commission will result in better sales performance. Specifically, he wants to know whether increasing the commission on limited lines of clothing will result in better sales on those lines but with the penalty of fewer sales on the remaining lines, and whether raising the commission on all lines will produce greater sales on all lines. Suppose that you think that the best way to investigate the issue is through a field experiment in which some salespeople receive increased commission on a single line, others receive increased commission across the board, and still others make up a control group, whose members receive no increase in commission.

- Are there ethical problems inherent in such a design?
- Is the control group being deprived of any benefits?

Causal Research Designs

Often exploratory or descriptive research will turn up several cause-and-effect hypotheses that a marketing manager may want to examine. For example, if a price change is planned, a manager may want to test this hypothesis: "A 5-percent increase in the price of the product will have no significant effect on the amount of the product that customers will buy." If the marketing department is considering a change in packaging, planners may first want to test this hypothesis: "A redesign of the cereal package so that it is shorter and less likely to tip over will improve consumer attitudes toward the product."

When the research question can be framed this explicitly, the researcher is dealing with a situation ripe for causal analysis. Descriptive research is fine for testing hypotheses, but it is not as effective as causal designs for testing cause-and-effect relationships. To understand why, one must understand the notion of causality, the types of evidence that establish causality, and the effect of outside variables in a research setting.

Concept of Causality

The concept of causality is complex, and a detailed discussion of it would take us too far afield. However, a few essentials will allow us to properly determine the role of the experiment in establishing the validity of a hypothesis that X causes Y.

In nontechnical language, the statement that one thing (X) is the cause of another thing (Y) suggests that there is a single cause of an event. The scientific notion of causality differs from this commonsense notion in three respects. First, the scientific notion holds that X would only be one of a number of determining conditions rather than the single one. Second, it holds that X does not make the occurrence of Y certain but just makes it more likely. Finally, the scientific notion holds that we can never prove that X really is a cause of Y, but rather we only *infer* from some observed data (perhaps acquired in a very controlled experimental setting) that such a relationship exists.[12]

The scientific notion recognizes the fallibility of the procedures used to obtain data, or evidence, and for that reason, a causal statement is never demonstrated conclusively. Three basic kinds of evidence can be used to support scientific inferences: concomitant variation, time order of occurrence of variables, and elimination of other possible causal factors.[13]

Evidence of Causality

Concomitant variation
The extent to which a cause, X, and an effect, Y, occur together or vary together in the way predicted by the hypothesis.

One type of evidence for the scientific inference "X is a cause of Y" is **concomitant variation**—the extent to which a cause, X, and an effect, Y, occur together or vary together in the way predicted by the hypothesis.

Consider the example of a foreign car manufacturer who wants to test the relationship between the quality of its dealers and the company's market share in an area. The manufacturer's hypothesis is, "The success of our marketing efforts is highly dealer-dependent. Where we have good dealers, we have good market penetration, and where we have poor dealers, we have unsatisfactory market penetration." Now if X is to be considered a cause of Y, we should expect to find the following: In those territories where our good dealers are located, we should have satisfactory market shares, while in those territories where our poor dealers are located, we should have unsatisfactory market shares. However, if we find that in a large number of territories with good dealers we also have unsatisfactory market shares, we must conclude that our hypothesis is faulty.

Perfect evidence of concomitant variation would be provided, of course, if all good dealers were located in territories with satisfactory market shares, and all poor dealers were located in territories with unsatisfactory market shares. The "pure" case will rarely be found in practice, as other causal factors will produce some deviation from a one-to-one relationship between X and Y. Some good dealers, for example, may be located in territories where "Buy American" sentiment is very strong and hence foreign car sales are very low. A poor dealer may have no nearby competition in a territory where foreign cars are popular and thus have an excellent market share despite a reputation for poor service.

Suppose that when we analyzed the relationship between X and Y, we found evidence of concomitant variation. What can we say? All we can say is that *the association makes the hypothesis more likely; it does not prove it.*[14] We are always inferring, rather than proving, that a causal relationship exists. Similarly, the lack of an association between X and Y cannot be taken as conclusive evidence that there is no causal relationship between them.

We will explore the idea of concomitant variation more closely in a later chapter. For the moment, let us emphasize that concomitant variation is one type of evidence supporting the existence of a causal relationship between X and Y; but its absence does not necessarily negate a relationship between X and Y, nor does its presence guarantee one.

The time order of occurrence of variables is another type of evidence of a causal relationship between two variables. This evidence is based on the following simple concept:

> One event cannot be considered the "cause" of another if it occurs *after* the other event. The occurrence of a causal factor may precede or may be simultaneous with the occurrence of an event; by definition, an effect cannot be produced by an event that occurs only after the effect has taken place. However, it is possible for each term in the relationship to be both a "cause" and an "effect" of the other term.[15]

Though conceptually simple, time-order evidence requires the close attention of researchers. Sometimes it is difficult to establish the time sequence governing a phenomenon. For example, consider the relationship between a firm's annual advertising expenditures and its sales. Marketing managers often attribute a sales increase to an increase in spending on advertising. However, many companies follow a rule of thumb that uses past sales as a guide to allocating resources to advertising. For example, an amount equal to 10 percent of last year's sales may be earmarked for this year's advertising budget. This practice confuses the issue of which event is the cause and which is the effect. Does advertising lead to higher sales, or do higher sales lead to an increased ad budget? An intimate understanding of the way the company establishes the ad budget should resolve the dilemma in this situation.

The *elimination of other possible causal factors* is very much like the Sherlock Holmes approach to analysis. Just as Sherlock Holmes holds that "when you have eliminated the impossible, whatever remains, however improbable, must be the truth,"[16] this type of evidence of causality focuses on the elimination of possible explanations other than the one being studied. This may mean physically holding other factors constant, or it may mean adjusting the results to remove the effects of factors that do vary.

Take the situation of the divisional manager of a chain of supermarkets investigating the effects of end-of-aisle displays on orange sales. Suppose that the manager found that per-store sales of oranges increased during the past week and that a number of stores were using end-of-aisle displays for oranges. To conclude that the end displays were indeed the factor responsible for the sales increase, the manager would need to eliminate other possible variables such as price, size of store, and orange type and quality. This might involve looking at orange sales for stores of approximately the same size, checking to see if prices were the same in stores having an increase in sales and stores with no increase, and checking to determine if the type and quality of oranges were consistent with the previous week's.

A controversy over the 1983 Nielsen television ratings provided an interesting example of eliminating other possible causal factors. During the ratings period under investigation, the Nielsen ratings were so high that many people questioned the numbers. Some felt the dramatic increase in the number of people watching broadcast television had been affected by Nielsen's recent change to a larger sample of households. The Nielsen numbers were especially suspect because a study commissioned by the National Association of Broadcasters during the same period had indicated that people were dissatisfied with the offerings on broadcast television and were spending less time watching it. Were the Nielsen data wrong?

Investigators suggested that there were several other possible explanations for the phenomenon. Among them were (1) an increase in the amount of special-event

In order to conclude that the display was responsible for any observed increase in sales, the manager of the produce department would need to eliminate other possible reasons for the sales increase, such as a change in overall store traffic and the weather.

Source: Courtesy of Sunkist Growers, Inc.

programming, (2) the weather, (3) economic conditions, (4) a change in the proportion of working women, and (5) a change in the number of pay-cable homes. Through systematic investigation of each of these factors, it was discovered that broadcast television viewing was indeed up, and the most likely explanation was the especially foul weather the country experienced in 1983, particularly in the East Central, Pacific, and Northeast states.[17]

Experimentation as Causal Research

Experiment Scientific investigation in which an investigator manipulates and controls one or more independent variables and observes the dependent variable or variables for variation concomitant to the manipulation of the independent variables.

Because of the control it affords investigators, an **experiment** can provide more convincing evidence of causal relationships than an exploratory or descriptive design can. For this reason, experiments are often called causal research.

> An experiment is taken to mean a scientific investigation in which an investigator manipulates and controls one or more independent variables and observes the dependent variable or variables for variation concomitant to the manipulation of the independent variables. An *experimental design*, then, is one in which the investigator *manipulates* at least one independent variable.[18]

Because investigators are able to control at least some manipulations of the presumed causal factor, they can be more confident that the relationships discovered are so-called true relationships.

Laboratory experiment Research investigation in which investigators create a situation with exact conditions so as to control some, and manipulate other, variables.

Two types of experiments can be distinguished — the *laboratory experiment* and the *field experiment*. Since each has its own advantages and disadvantages, research analysts need to be familiar with both. A **laboratory experiment** is one in which an investigator creates a situation with the desired conditions and then manipulates some variables while controlling others. The investigator is thus able to observe and measure the effect of the manipulation of the variables while the effect of other factors is minimized.

In one laboratory experiment designed to measure the effect of price on the demand for coffee and cola, for example, 135 homemakers in a small town in Illinois

One objective of both laboratory and field experiments is to discover which choices consumers make among products. Laboratory experiments take place in an artificial setting, created by the investigators. Field experiments take place in a natural setting, although one or more variables may be manipulated there, too.

Source: Courtesy of Marketing Intelligence Service Ltd.

were asked to take part in simulated shopping trips.[19] On each of the eight simulated trips, which were conducted in subjects' homes, the homemakers could choose their favorite brands from a full assortment of coffees and colas listed on index cards. The only change on each trip was the products' prices. Each homemaker was free to switch brands to obtain the best product for the money. In this respect, the trial purchase was not unlike an actual purchase. In other respects, however, this trial was unlike conditions in a real supermarket. In the laboratory experiment, the homemakers were free from the distractions of other variables such as packaging, position on the shelf, and in-store promotions.

Field experiment
Research study in a realistic situation in which one or more independent variables are manipulated by the experimenter under as carefully controlled conditions as the situation will permit.

A **field experiment** is a research study in a realistic or natural situation, although it, too, involves the manipulation of one or more variables under as carefully controlled conditions as the situation will permit. The laboratory experiment is distinguished from the field experiment, then, primarily in terms of environment, although the distinction is one more of degree than of kind, as both involve some manipulation. The degree of control and precision afforded by each individual field or laboratory experiment varies.[20]

A similar investigation to test the effect of price on the demand for coffee and cola was also conducted in a field experiment. In this case, the experiment was conducted in two small towns in Illinois, ten miles apart. The manipulations here involved actual changes in price for the respective brands.

Four supermarkets were used in all, two from each town. Two units in one town were designated as control stores, where the price of each brand was maintained at its regular level throughout the experiment. In the experimental town, the prices were systematically varied in the two stores during the experiment. Prices were marked on the package of each brand so as to be clearly visible but not conspicuous. After each price change, a cooling-off period was introduced to offset any surplus accumulated by consumers. The impact of the price change was monitored by recording weekly sales for each brand. This allowed brand market shares for each price condition to be determined. No displays, special containers, or other devices were used to draw consumer attention to the fact that the relative prices of the brands had been altered. All other controllable factors were also held as constant as possible.

Note the distinction between the two studies. In the field experiment, no attempt was made to set up special conditions. The situation was accepted as found, and manipulation of the experimental variable—price—was imposed in this natural environment. The laboratory experiment, on the other hand, was contrived. Subjects were told to behave as if they were actively shopping for the product. The prices of the respective brands were varied for each of these simulated shopping trips.

The results of the two experiments were consistent for one product and inconsistent for the other. The laboratory experiment generated reasonably valid estimates of consumers' reactions to real-world (field experiment) price changes for brands of cola. However, the data for coffee was considered invalid since it tended to overstate the effects of the price changes.

Internal and External Validity of Experiments

Internal validity One criterion by which an experiment is evaluated; the criterion focuses on obtaining evidence demonstrating that the variation in the criterion variable was the result of exposure to the treatment, or experimental, variable.

Certain advantages and disadvantages result from the difference in procedure in laboratory and field experiments. The laboratory experiment typically has the advantage of greater **internal validity** because of the greater control of the variables that it affords. To the extent that we are successful in eliminating the effects of other factors that may obscure or confound the relationships under study, either by physically holding these other factors constant or by allowing for them statistically, we may conclude that the observed effect was due to the manipulation of the experimental variable. That is, we may conclude the experiment is internally valid. Thus, internal validity refers to our ability to attribute the effect that was observed to the experimental variable and not other factors. In the pricing experiment, internal validity focused on the need to obtain data demonstrating that the variation in the criterion variable—brand demanded—was the result of exposure to the experimental variable—relative price of the brand—rather than other factors, such as advertising, display space, store traffic, and so on. These other factors were nonexistent in the simulated shopping trips.

External validity One criterion by which an experiment is evaluated; the extent, to what populations and settings, to which the observed experimental effect can be generalized.

Whereas the laboratory experiment has the advantage in internal validity, the field experiment has the advantage in **external validity,** which focuses on how well the results of the experiment can be generalized to other situations.[21] The artificiality of laboratory experiments limits the extent to which the results can be generalized to other populations and settings.[22] In the simulated shopping trips, no real purchases took place. Further, we might suppose that the experimenter's calling attention to the price may have caused people to be more price conscious than they would have been in a supermarket. They may have attempted to act more "rationally" than they normally would. Further, those who agreed to participate in the laboratory experiment may not be representative of the larger population of shoppers, either because the location of the study was not typical or because those who willingly participated in such a study may be different in some significant way from those who declined to participate. Such problems would seriously jeopardize the external validity of the findings.

The controls needed for internal validity often conflict with the controls needed for external validity. A control or procedure required to establish internal validity may lessen the value of the results for generalization. The conditions needed to establish external validity may cast doubt on a study's internal validity. Both internal and external validity are matters of degree rather than all-or-nothing propositions.

Role of Experimentation in Marketing Research

Experiments in marketing were rare before 1960, but their growth since then has been steady. One of the most significant growth areas has been in market testing, or *test marketing*. Although some writers make a distinction between the terms, the essential

Popular Science magazine tested two different newsstand covers of its annual December "Best of What's New" feature. One cover uses several photos; the other is all type. The results will be used to determine the new look of the magazine.

Source: Reprinted with permission from *Popular Science* Magazine, copyright 1990, Times Mirror Magazines, Inc. Distributed by Los Angeles Times Syndicate.

Market test (test marketing) A controlled experiment done in a limited but carefully selected sector of the marketplace; its aim is to predict the sales or profit consequences, either in absolute or relative terms, of one or more proposed marketing actions.

feature of the **market test** is that "it is a controlled experiment, done in a limited but carefully selected part of the marketplace, whose aim is to predict the sales or profit consequences, either in absolute or relative terms, of one or more proposed marketing actions."[23] Very often the action in question is the marketing of a new product or an improved version of an old product. For example, Research Window 6.2 describes the experience of Wendy's in developing the "Big Classic" hamburger.

Notwithstanding previous tests of the product concept, the product package, the advertising copy, and so on, the test market is still the final gauge of consumer acceptance of the product. A. C. Nielsen data, for example, indicate that roughly three out of four products that have been test marketed succeed, while four out of five that have not been test marketed fail.[24]

Test marketing is not restricted to testing the sales potential of new products, but has been used to examine the sales effectiveness of almost every element of the marketing mix: for example, to measure the sales effectiveness of a new display, the responsiveness of food sales to supermarket shelf space changes, the impact of a change in retail price on the product's market share, the price elasticity of demand for a product, the effect of different commercials upon sales of a product, the sales effects of two different campaign themes, and the differential effects of price and advertising on demand in addition to their use in determining the sales potential of new products.

Experimentation is not restricted to test marketing. Rather, it can be used whenever the manager has some specific mix alternatives to consider—for example, package design A versus B—and when the researcher can control the conditions sufficiently to allow an adequate test of the alternatives. Experiments are often used, therefore, when testing product or package concepts and advertising copy, although they have also been used for such things as determining the optimal number of sales calls to be made upon industrial distributors.[25]

Research Window 6.2
Research Conducted by Wendy's for the "Big Classic" Hamburger

To find out what people want, Wendy's spent $1 million over nine months doing taste tests with 5,200 people in six cities. They tested:

Nine different buns: some hard, some soft; with sesame seeds or poppy seeds; cold, toasted, or warmed; square or round; and even croissants

Forty special sauces, including steak sauce, hot sauce, mustard, and salad dressing

Three types of lettuce: chopped, shredded, and leaf

Two sizes of tomato slices

Four boxes in ten earth-tone colors

The final product is a quarter-pound square beef patty topped with leaf lettuce, two tomato slices, raw onion rings, dill pickles, and extra dabs of ketchup and mayonnaise on a corn-dusted, hearth-baked kaiser bun. It comes in an almond-colored styrofoam box with a dome sculpted to resemble the bun's top. It can cost up to 10 cents more than the old burger, which is still on the menu.

The big news research showed was that the order of the condiments "makes a tremendous difference to consumers," Denny Lynch, a spokesperson for Wendy's, said. "Which is why the Big Classic will taste different rightside up or upside down, depending on the way the toppings hit your taste buds."

Wendy's came up with a color code to help its employees remember the correct order: white, red, green, white, red, green (mayonnaise, ketchup, pickle, onion, tomato, lettuce).

Source: "Wendy's Discovers—Old Burger," *The Wisconsin State Journal* (September 19, 1986), p. 6. Reprinted with permission.

Future and Problems of Experimentation

Although marketing experiments will probably be used more frequently in the future, particularly when the research problem is one of determining which is the best of an available set of limited marketing alternatives, experimentation is not without its problems. Test marketing, which has been described as a double-edged sword, is a useful vehicle for illustrating these problems. As Larry Gibson, former director of corporate marketing research for General Mills, states: "It costs a mint, tells the competition what you're doing, takes forever, and is not always accurate. . . . For the moment, it's the only game in town."[26] Although Gibson is referring specifically to test marketing, similar problems beset other types of experiments as well. Three of the more critical problems of experimentation in general, and test marketing in particular, are cost, time, and control.

Cost   Always a major consideration in test marketing, the cost includes the normal research costs associated with designing the data-collection instruments and the sample, the wages paid to the field staff that collects the data, and a number of other indirect expenses as well. For instance, the test market should reflect the marketing strategy to be employed on the national scale if the results are to be useful. So the test also includes marketing costs for advertising, personal selling, displays, and so on.

Philip Morris test marketed Like, its "99% caffeine-free" cola, in eight cities. Its ad budget for those eight cities, which contain approximately 5 percent of the U.S. population, was $2.3 million. If that level of advertising were done nationally, it would amount to $45 million, which is more than either Pepsi or Coke spends annually. The market test also included coupons, free samples, and other promotions, the cost of which was approximately equal to the ad budget.[27]

With new product introductions, there are also the costs associated with producing the merchandise. To produce the product on a small scale is typically inefficient. Yet to gear up immediately for large-scale production can be tremendously wasteful if the product proves a failure. It usually costs about $3.1 million to take a new product from the research and development stage through test marketing in 2 percent of the United States.[28]

Time   The time required for an adequate test market can also be substantial. It took Procter & Gamble nine years to go national with Pampers disposable diapers after they were first introduced in Peoria, Illinois.[29] One reason for extending the period of test marketing is that the empirical evidence indicates that a test market's accuracy increases directly with time. According to A. C. Nielsen data, after two months forecast accuracy is only 1 out of 7, meaning that when test market results were compared to national sales figures, the test market statistics predicted national sales accurately in only 13 percent of the cases. The odds steadily increased, though, to 5 out of 6 after ten months.[30] Consequently, a year is often recommended as a minimum before any kind of "go–no go" decision is made. The year allows researchers to account for possible seasonal variations and to study repeat-purchasing behavior. Such lengthy experiments are costly, and they raise additional problems of control and competitive reaction. However, experiments conducted over short periods do not allow the cumulative impact of marketing actions.[31] These disadvantages must be weighed against one another in each individual situation before deciding on the length of the test marketing period.

Control   The problems associated with control manifest themselves in several ways. First, there are the control problems in the experiment itself. What specific test markets will be used? How will product distribution be organized in those markets? Can the firm elicit the necessary cooperation from wholesalers? From retailers? Can the test markets and control cities be matched sufficiently to rule out market characteristics as the primary reason for different sales results? Can the rest of the elements of the marketing strategy be controlled so as not to cause unwanted aberrations in the experimental setting? Too much control can often be as much of a problem as too little. Precisely because the product is being test marketed, it may receive more attention than it would ever receive on a national scale. In the test market, for example, store shelves may be better stocked, the sales force more diligent, and the advertising more prominent than would normally be the case.

One example of this phenomenon is Pringle's potato chips, which were very successful in the test market but bombed nationally. Their failure has often been attributed to a decline in quality that occurred when the product had to be produced in quantities large enough for national distribution.[32]

There are control problems associated with competitive reaction, too. While the firm might be able to coordinate its own marketing activities, and even those of intermediaries in the distribution channel, so as not to contaminate the experiment, it can exert little control over its competitors. Competitors can, and do, sabotage marketing experiments by cutting the prices of their own products, gobbling up quantities of the test marketer's product—thereby creating a state of euphoria and false confidence on the part of the test marketer—and by other devious means. Test marketing has been called the most dangerous game in all of marketing because of the great opportunity it affords for misfires, as shown by the examples in Table 6.6.

Table 6.6   *Examples of Misfires in Test Marketing*

1. **Example:** When Campbell Soup first test marketed Prego Spaghetti sauce, Campbell marketers say they noticed a flurry of new Ragu ads and cents-off deals that they feel were designed to induce shoppers to load up on Ragu and to skew Prego's test results. They also claim that Ragu copied Prego when it developed Ragu Home-style spaghetti sauce, which was thick, red, flecked with oregano and basil, and which Ragu moved into national distribution before Prego.

2. **Example:** Procter & Gamble claims that competitors stole its patented process for Duncan Hines chocolate chip cookies when they saw how successful the product was in test market.

3. **Example:** A health and beauty aids firm developed a deodorant containing baking soda. A competitor spotted the product in test market, rolled out its own version of the deodorant nationally before the first firm completed its testing, and later successfully sued the product originator for copyright infringement when it launched its deodorant nationally.

4. **Example:** When Procter & Gamble introduced its Always brand sanitary napkin in a test market in Minnesota, Kimberly-Clark Corporation and Johnson & Johnson countered with free products, lots of coupons, and big dealer discounts, which caused Always not to do as well as expected.

5. **Example:** A few years ago, Snell (Booz Allen's design and development division, which does product develop-

ment and work under contract) developed a nonliquid temporary hair coloring that consumers used by inserting a block of solid hair dye into a special comb. "It went to market and it was a bust," the company's Mr. Schoenholz recalls. On hot days when people perspired, any hair dye excessively applied ran down their necks and foreheads. "It just didn't occur to us to look at this under conditions where people perspire," he says.

6. **Example:** Campbell Soup spent 18 months developing a blended fruit juice called Juiceworks. By the time the product reached the market, three competing brands were already on store shelves. Campbell dropped its product.

7. **Example** Spurred by its incredible success with Fruit 'N' Juice Bars, Dole worked hard to create a new fruity ice cream novelty product with the same type of appeal. Company officials expected that the product that resulted from this development activity, Fruit and Cream Bars, which it test marketed in Orlando, Florida, would do slightly less well because it was more of an indulgence-type product. However, the test market results were so positive that Dole became the number-one brand in the market within three months. The company consequently shortened the test market to six months. When it rolled out the product, though, the company unhappily found four unexpected entrants in the ice cream novelty category. Due to the intense competition, Fruit and Cream sales fell short of expectations.

Source: Example 1—Betty Morris, "New Campbell Entry Sets Off a Big Spaghetti Sauce Battle," *The Wall Street Journal* (December 2, 1982), p. 31; Example 2—Eleanor Johnson Tracy, "Testing Time for Test Marketing," *Fortune*, 110 (October 29, 1984), pp. 75–76; Example 3—Kevin Wiggins, "Simulated Test Marketing Winning Acceptance," *Marketing News*, 19 (March 1, 1985), pp. 15 and 19; Example 4—Damon Darden, "Faced with More Competition, P&G Sees New Products as Crucial to Earnings Growth," *The Wall Street Journal* (September 13, 1983), pp. 37 and 53; Example 5—Roger Recklefs, "Success Comes Hard in the Tricky Business of Creating Products," *The Wall Street Journal* (August 23, 1978), pp. 1 and 27; Example 6—Annetta Miller and Dody Tsiantor, "A Test for Market Research," *Newsweek*, 110 (December 28, 1987), pp. 32–33; Example 7—Leslie Brennan, "Test Marketing Put to the Test," *Sales and Marketing Management*, 138 (March 1987), pp. 65–68.

One could argue that the misfire reflected in the fifth example in Table 6.6 represents one of the fundamental reasons why test markets are desirable. It seems better to find out about product performance problems like this in a test market than after a product is introduced nationally. Consider, for example, the losses in company prestige that would have resulted if the following problems had not been discovered in test markets.[33]

1. Because packages would not stack, scouring pads fell off the shelf.
2. A dog food discolored on the store shelves.
3. In cold weather, baby food separated into a clear liquid and a sludge.
4. In hot weather, cigarettes in a new package dried out.
5. A pet food gave the test animals diarrhea.
6. When a product change in a liquid detergent was combined with a price reduction, consumers thought the product had been diluted with water.

7. Because of insufficient glue, over half of the packages came apart during transit.

8. Excessive settling in a box of paper tissues caused the box to be one-third empty at purchase.

9. Sunlight dishwashing liquid was confused with Minute Maid lemon juice by at least 33 adults and 45 children, who became ill after drinking it.

10. When a large packaged goods company set out to introduce a squirtable soft drink concentrate for children, it held focus groups to monitor user reaction. In the sessions children squirted the product neatly into cups. Yet once at home, few could resist the temptation to decorate their parents' floors and walls with colorful liquid. After a flood of parental complaints, the product was withdrawn from development.

Examples 1 through 4, 6, and 7 in Table 6.6, however, are of a different sort. By exposing the product to competitors through a test market, each of the firms lost much of its differential development advantage.

The simple point is that the marketing manager contemplating a market test must weigh the costs of such a test against its anticipated benefits. While it may serve as the final yardstick for consumer acceptance of the product, in some cases it may be less effective and more expensive than a carefully controlled laboratory or in-home test.[34]

Types of Test Markets

Standard test market A test market in which the company sells the product through its normal distribution channels.

Controlled test market An entire test program conducted by an outside service in a market in which it can guarantee distribution.

Electronic test market A market test done in a limited geographic area in which a supplier maintains a panel of households from which it collects demographic information, who are given an identification card, whose purchases are scanned, and whose television-viewing behavior is electronically monitored, thereby allowing the supplier to link demographic information with television-viewing and purchase behavior.

Figure 6.2 shows the most commonly used **standard test markets,** markets in which companies sell the product through their normal distribution channels. The results are typically monitored by one of the standard distribution services discussed in the next chapter.

An alternative to the standard test market is the **controlled test market,** sometimes called the *forced-distribution test market.* In the controlled market, the entire test program is conducted by an outside service. The service pays retailers for shelf space and can therefore guarantee distribution to those stores that represent a predetermined percentage of the marketer's total food store sales volume. A number of research firms operate controlled test markets, including Audits & Surveys' Burgoyne, Inc.; A. C. Nielsen; and Dancer, Fitzgerald, Sample.[35]

An increasingly popular variation of the controlled test market is the **electronic test market.** Electronic test markets differ from traditional controlled test markets in several ways. First, providers of the electronic services recruit a panel of households in the test market area from which they secure a great deal of demographic information. These households are given identification cards, which they show when checking out at grocery stores. Everything they purchase is automatically recorded and associated with the household through scanners found in all supermarkets in the area. Second, suppliers of the electronic services also have the capability to monitor each household's television-viewing behavior. They thus have the capability to correlate exposure to test commercials to purchase behavior, which in turn allows users of the electronic services to test not only consumer acceptance of a new or modified product but also various other parts of the marketing program. Del Monte, for example, uses electronic test markets for media-weight, pricing, and promotion tests, in addition to new product evaluations.[36] The leading suppliers of electronic test-marketing services are Nielsen, with its Electronic Research for Insights into Marketing (ERIM) and IRI, with BehaviorScan. Research Window 6.3 illustrates how the link between the demographic information of households and their purchase behavior can be used to advantage.

Figure 6.2   ***Most Popular Standard Test Markets***

Source: Data from Pat Seelig, "All Over the Map," *Sales and Marketing Management*, 142 (March 1989), pp. 65–66.

Simulated test market
A study in which interviews are conducted to determine consumer ratings of products: then consumers are given the opportunity to purchase the product in a simulated store environment.

Another relatively recent variation in test marketing is the **simulated test market** (STM). STM studies are usually employed prior to a full-scale test market. Typically an STM study begins with consumer interviews, either in shopping malls or occasionally in their homes. During the interview, consumers are shown the new product and asked to rate its features. They are then shown commercials for it and for competitors' products. In a simulated store environment, they are then given the opportunity to buy the product, often at a reduced price or with a cents-off coupon. Those who choose not to purchase the test product are typically given free samples.

After a predetermined use period, researchers conduct follow-up telephone interviews with the participants to assess their reactions to the product and their repeat-purchase intentions.

All the information is fed into a computer model, which has equations for the repeat purchase and market share likely to be achieved by the test model. The key to the simulation is the equations built into the computer model. Studies have indicated that in 80 percent of the cases, STM models can come within 10 percent of predicting actual sales.[37]

Choosing a Test Market Procedure

Those faced with the need to test market a new product or to fine-tune another element of the marketing program need to make a choice about which type of test

Research Window 6.3
Use of an Electronic Test Market by Ocean Spray

In an attempt to be perceived more broadly, Ocean Spray developed a totally new fruit beverage, Mauna La'i Hawaiian Guava Drink. The product represented a significant departure for Ocean Spray, in that it was different in color, taste, and aroma from any other fruit drink on the market.

Concerned about how consumers might respond to the product, Ocean Spray decided to test market it using BehaviorScan's facilities in Eau Claire, Wisconsin, and Midland, Texas. Ocean Spray believed that the target market for Mauna La'i was similar to that for its cranberry drink: older children and adults with average education and income.

After six months in test market, initial trial for Mauna La'i was good, but the rate of repurchase was far below what was needed to be profitable. It did not appear that Mauna La'i would survive the test to go national. But on analyzing BehaviorScan's data more closely, Ocean Spray found a few surprises: (1) the buyer base was smaller than expected, but these consumers were buying the product more frequently than was projected; (2) the product was not selling to the target market—yuppies (young urban professionals) were buying the Mauna La'i.

After analyzing this pattern for nearly a year, Ocean Spray decided that it would be profitable to market the product as long as it was marketed toward the heavily beverage-consuming yuppies. Mauna La'i's media plan was altered to reach the more upscale market, and the juice was rolled out nationally. After only three months in the national market, consumer demand was so high that Ocean Spray started to produce a 64-ounce size. John Tarsa, Ocean Spray's manager of marketing research, believes that the use of an electronic test market was key to Mauna La'i's success. "In a traditional test market, we wouldn't be rolling with Mauna La'i at all, because our repeat number was no good. The electronic test market was instrumental in helping us decide what we needed to change to make it a success."

Source: Leslie Brennan, "Test Marketing Put to the Test," *Sales and Marketing Management*, 138 (March 1987), p. 68; and David Kiley, "Small Firms Grow Strong on Steady Diet of Data," *Adweek's Marketing Week* (May 16, 1988).

market to use. One useful way to view that choice is to look at the alternatives as stages in a sequential process, with simulated test markets preceding controlled test markets, which in turn come before standard test markets. See Figure 6.3. The sequence is not always as pictured, however. A very promising STM or controlled test market can cause a firm to skip one or more intermediate stages, and perhaps to move directly to national rollout.

A prime advantage of STMs is the protection from competitors they provide. They are also good for assessing trial and repeat-purchasing behavior. They are faster and cheaper than full-scale tests and are particularly good for spotting weak products, which allows firms to avoid full-scale testing of these products. The Achilles' heel of STMs is that they do not provide any information about the firm's ability to secure trade support for the product or about what competitive reaction is likely to be. Thus, they are more suited for evaluating product extensions than for examining the likely success of radically different new products.

Controlled test markets are more expensive than simulated test markets but less costly than standard test markets. One reason why they cost less than standard test markets is that the research supplier secures distribution. The manufacturer does not need to use its own sales force to convince the trade that stocking the product is worthwhile. The manufacturer can rest assured that the new product will obtain the right level of store acceptance, will be positioned in the correct aisle in each store, will receive the right number of facings on the shelf, will have the correct everyday price,

Figure 6.3   *A Perspective on the Various Types of Test Markets*

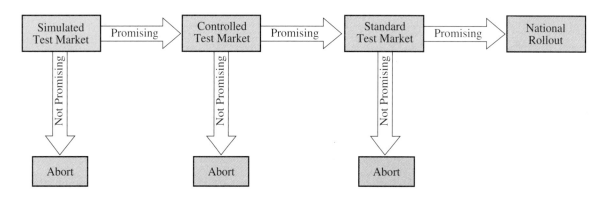

will not experience any out-of-stock problems, and will receive the planned level of promotional displays and price features.

This perfect implementation of the marketing plan also represents one of the weaknesses of the controlled test market. Acceptance or rejection of the new product by the trade in the "real world" is typically critical to the success of any new product.[38] A controlled test market guarantees acceptance by the trade for the duration of the test, but acceptance will not be guaranteed during the actual marketing of the product. When the manufacturer does not need to worry about this because the new product fits in nicely with its existing line, for which the company already has distribution, the controlled test market is a fairly good indicator. However, the problem of overcontrol of the marketing effort during the test market does need to be taken into account. At times, the real situation is still going to have out-of-stocks, poor aisle locations, inadequate displays, and less-than-perfect cooperation from the trade on pricing and trade promotions. When the manufacturer has sufficient experience to account for these adjustments, the controlled test market provides a useful laboratory for testing acceptance of the product and for fine-tuning the marketing program. When the product is novel or represents a radical departure for the manufacturer, the question of trade support is much more problematic, and the controlled test is much less useful under these circumstances.

The traditional, or standard, test market provides a more natural environment than either the simulated or the controlled test market. The standard test market plays a more vital role when

1. It is important for the firm to test its ability to actually sell to the trade and get distribution for the product.
2. The capital investment is significant and the firm needs a prolonged test market to accurately assess its capital needs or its technical ability to manufacture the product.[39]
3. The firm is entering new territory and needs to build its experience base so that it can play for real, but it wants to learn how to do so on a limited scale.

Ethical

Dilemma 6.2   The promotions manager of a soft drink company asks you to help him run an experiment to determine whether he should start advertising in cinemas showing movies rated R or NR-17. He explains that he has read a journal article indicating that viewers' responses to upbeat commercials are more favorable if the commercials follow very arousing film clips, and he believes that his soft drink commercial will stimulate more sales of the drink in the cinema if it follows previews of very violent or erotic films, such as are shown before the feature film.

- If you ran a laboratory experiment for this client, what kinds of manipulations would you use, and what are the ethical issues involved in their use?
- Is it feasible to run a field experiment, and would the ethical issues change if a field experiment were run rather than a laboratory experiment?
- If you found that increasing viewers' arousal levels did indeed make them more favorably disposed toward products advertised through upbeat commercials, what are the ultimate ethical implications for influencing television programming?

Back to the Case

Dr. Michael Biraldi and Tim Meyer sat in Biraldi's office. It was Wednesday afternoon and Biraldi had no patients scheduled. It was a time he usually set aside for work on his line of Aquaderm products. Before the two men were the results of the study the marketing researchers had conducted.

The study had been an eye-opening process for Biraldi, who had come to realize that it took a lot more than a good product and the desire to make a profit to make a success of a fledgling enterprise.

For example, a survey of consumers had shown that they preferred Aquaderm's present, no-frills packaging over the fancier mock-ups that had been tested. They also preferred the unscented products over the three different scents that had been tried.

A survey of retailers had helped Meyers and Biraldi decide that it would be better to try to introduce the entire line of products at once rather than to launch each item in the line separately.

Pricing had been determined by observing consumers on a simulated shopping trip, in which the prices of the Aquaderm products had been systematically varied in relation to the prices of competing products. Surprisingly, the Aquaderm products, which were very inexpensive to produce, had tended to appeal to consumers who were used to buying at the expensive range of cosmetic prices.

Perhaps the most significant finding had been the realization that without extensive advertising and a known brand name, it would be nearly impossible to sell the Aquaderm line in large drugstore chains.

Biraldi and Meyers began to discuss the alternatives. They could use what little was left of the money they had already raised and begin selling the Aquaderm line regionally in independent drugstores and pharmacies. On the other hand, they could try to raise additional funds for advertising, based on the product's strong performance in the consumer tests. A third alternative would be to

try to sell the line to a cosmetics or pharmaceutical company that was in a better position to market it.

Biraldi's experience in readying his products for the market shows the many ways marketing research can be used to fine-tune a concept. The marketing research firm in this case used both descriptive and causal research studies to answer Biraldi's questions about his product line. The many surveys the firm conducted concerning Aquaderm's appearance, performance, and packaging are all examples of descriptive research. The price tests with consumers are an example of causal research. In discussing how to proceed, Biraldi and Meyers might have based their final decision on published industry data that revealed competitors' advertising expenditures and distribution arrangements—a form of exploratory research.

Summary

Learning Objective 1: Cite three major purposes of descriptive research.

Descriptive research is used when the purpose is (1) to describe the characteristics of certain groups, (2) to estimate the proportion of people in a specified population who behave in a certain way, and (3) to make specific predictions.

Learning Objective 2: List the six specifications of a descriptive study.

Descriptive studies require a clear specification of the answers to who, what, when, where, why, and how in the research.

Learning Objective 3: Explain what a dummy table is.

A dummy table is used to catalog the data that is to be collected. It serves as a statement of how the analysis will be structured and conducted. Complete in all respects save for filling in the actual numbers, it contains a title, headings, and specific categories for the variables making up the table.

Learning Objective 4: Discuss the difference between cross-sectional and longitudinal designs.

A cross-sectional design involves researching a sample of elements from the population of interest. Various characteristics of the elements are measured once. Longitudinal studies involve panels of people or other entities whose responses are measured repeatedly over a span of time.

Learning Objective 5: Explain what is meant by a *panel* in marketing research and explain the difference between a traditional panel and an omnibus panel.

A panel is a fixed sample of elements. In a traditional panel, a fixed sample of subjects is measured repeatedly with respect to the same type of information. In an omnibus panel, a sample of elements is still selected and maintained, but the information collected from the members varies with the project.

Learning Objective 6: Explain what is meant by a turnover table, or brand-switching matrix.

A turnover table, or brand-switching matrix, is a two-way table that indicates which brands a sample of people purchased in one period and which brands they purchased in a subsequent period, thus highlighting the switches occurring among brands, as well as the number of persons who purchased the same brand in both periods.

Learning Objective 7: Describe the emphasis in sample surveys.

The sample survey involves the study of a number of cases at the same point in time. The survey attempts to be representative of some known universe, both in terms of the number of cases included and in the manner of their selection.

Learning Objective 8: Distinguish between the commonsense notion of causality and the scientific notion.

The commonsense notion of causality suggests that there is a single cause of an event. The scientific notion of causality holds that there may be a number of determining conditions that are probable causes for an event, but that said relationship can be only inferred, never proven conclusively.

Learning Objective 9: Define *concomitant variation*.

Concomitant variation is the extent to which a cause and an effect occur together or vary together in the way predicted by the hypothesis.

Learning Objective 10: List three ways of determining a causal relationship.

Three ways of determining a causal relationship are (1) through concomitant variation, (2) through time order of occurrence of variables, and (3) by eliminating other possible sources of explanation.

Learning Objective 11: Clarify the difference between laboratory experiments and field experiments.

Laboratory experiments are distinguished from field experiments primarily in terms of environment. The analyst creates a setting for a laboratory experiment, while a field experiment is conducted in a natural setting. The distinction is one more of degree than of kind, as both involve control and manipulation of one or more presumed causal factors.

Learning Objective 12: Explain which of the two types of experiments has greater internal validity and which has greater external validity.

The laboratory experiment typically has the advantage of greater internal validity because of the greater control of the variables that it affords. Field experiments are generally considered more externally valid, meaning that their results are better able to be generalized to other situations.

Learning Objective 13: List the three major problems in test marketing.

Three of the more critical problems in experimentation in general, and in test marketing in particular, are cost, time, and control.

Learning Objective 14: Discuss the advantages and disadvantages of simulated test marketing.

Simulated test marketing studies provide the following advantages: (1) they protect a marketer from competitors, (2) they are faster and cheaper than full-scale tests, and (3) they are particularly good for spotting weak products. However, they do have disadvantages in that they cannot provide any information about the firm's ability to secure trade support for a product, nor do they indicate what competitive reaction is likely to be.

Learning Objective 15: Distinguish between a standard test market and a controlled test market.

A standard test market is one in which companies sell the product through their normal distribution channels, and results are typically monitored by a standard distribution service. In a controlled test market, the entire program is conducted by an outside service. The service pays retailers for shelf space and therefore can guarantee distribution to those stores that represent a predetermined percentage of the marketer's total store sales volume.

Discussion Questions, Problems, and Projects

1. The management of a national book club was convinced that the company's market segment consisted of individuals in the 25- to 35-year-old age-group, while its major competitor's market segment seemed more widely distributed with respect to age. It attributed this difference to the type of magazines in which the competitor advertised. Management decided to do a study to determine the socioeconomic characteristics of its own market segment. Management formed a panel of 800 heads of households who had previously shown a strong interest in reading. Mail questionnaires would be sent to all the panel members. One month after receiving all the questionnaires, the company would again send similar questionnaires to all the panel members.

   In this situation, is the research design appropriate? If yes, why? If no, why not?

2. Mr. Pennymarch, as the advertising manager for *Chemistry Today* magazine, is charged with the responsibility for selling advertising space in the magazine. The magazine deals primarily with chemical processing technology and is distributed solely by subscription. Major advertisers in the magazine are the producers of chemical processing equipment, since the magazine is primarily directed at engineers and other technical people concerned with the design of chemical processing units.

   Since the size and composition of the target audience for *Chemistry Today* are key concerns for prospective advertisers, Pennymarch is interested in collecting more detailed data on the readership. While he presently has total circulation figures, he feels that these understate the potential exposure of an advertisement in *Chemistry Today*. In particular, he feels that for every subscriber, there are several others in the subscriber's firm to whom the magazine is routed for their perusal. He wishes to determine how large this secondary audience is and also wishes to develop more detailed data on *Chemistry Today* readers, such as degree of technical training, level in the administrative hierarchy, and so forth.

(a)   Does Pennymarch have a specific hypothesis? If yes, state the hypothesis.

(b)   What type of research design would you recommend? Justify your answer.

3. The Allure Company, a large manufacturer of women's beauty aids, conducted a study in 1990 in order to assess how its brand of hair dye was faring in the market. Questionnaires were mailed to a panel of 1,260 families. The Allure brand of hair dye had three major competitors: Brand A, Brand B, and Brand C. A similar study conducted in 1989 had indicated the following market shares: Allure, 31.75 percent (i.e., 400 families); Brand A, 25 percent (315 families); Brand B, 32.54 percent (410 families); and Brand C, 10.71 percent (135 families). The present study indicated that its market share had not changed during the one-year period, although Brand B had increased its market share to 36.5 percent (460 families). However, this increase could be accounted for by a decrease in Brand A's and Brand C's market shares. (Brand A now had a market share of 22.23 percent, or 280 families; Brand C now had a market share of 9.52 percent, or 120 families). The management of the Allure Company decided it had little to worry about.

The study of 1990 also revealed some additional facts. Over the one-year period 70 families from Brand A and 30 families from Brand C had switched to Allure. Five families from Brand B and 30 families from Brand C had switched to Brand A, while none of the Allure users had switched to Brand A. These facts further reassured management. Finally, 45 families switched from Brand B to Brand C, but none of the families using Allure or Brand A had switched to Brand C. Brand C's loyalty was estimated to be .556.

(a)   Do you think that management of the Allure Company was accurate in analyzing the situation? Justify your answer.

(b)   You are called upon to do some analysis. From the data given above, construct the brand-switching matrix. (Hint: Begin by filling in the row and column totals.)

(c)   Indicate what this matrix reveals for each of the brands over the one-year period.

(d)   Complete the following table and compute the brand loyalties.

		At Time (t_2)			
	Bought Allure	Bought A	Bought B	Bought C	Total
At Time (t_1): Bought Allure					
Bought A					
Bought B					
Bought C					

(e)   What can be said about the degree of brand loyalty for each of the four products?

4. The Nutri Company was a medium-size manufacturer of highly nutritional food products. The products were marketed as diet foods with high nutritional content. The company was considering marketing these products as snack foods but was concerned about its present customers' reaction to the change in the products' images. The company decided to assess customers' reaction by conducting a study using one of the established types of consumer panels.

What type of panel would you recommend in this situation? Why?

In this situation, would you recommend a field study or a sample survey? Why?

5. Super Savers is a chain of department stores located in large towns and metropolitan centers in the northeastern United States. In order to improve its understanding of the market, management has decided to develop a profile of the so-called average customer. You are requested to design the study.
   (a) What kind of research design will you select? Justify your choice.
   (b) List at least ten relevant variables.
   (c) Specify at least four hypotheses. (Note: A hypothesis is a conjecture as to how two or more variables are related. You should indicate the direction of the suggested relationship and how each of the variables would be measured.)
   (d) Construct dummy tables using four of the variables that you specified in part (b) of this problem.
6. Consider the following statement: "The increase in sales is due to the new sales personnel that we recruited from the vocational school over the last several years. Sales of the new salespeople are up substantially, while sales for longer-term salespeople have not increased."
   Identify the causal factor (X) and the effect factor (Y) in the above statement.
7. The research department of the company in Question 6 investigated the change in sales for each of the company's salespeople. Using criteria supplied by management, the department categorized all territory sales changes as "increased substantially," "increased marginally," or "no increase." Consider the following table, in which 260 sales personnel have been classified as old or new:

Salesperson Assigned	Territory Sales Change			
	Increased Substantially	Increased Marginally	No Increase	Total
New	75	30	5	110
Old	50	40	60	150

   (a) Does this table provide evidence of concomitant variation? Justify your answer.
   (b) What conclusions can be drawn about the relationship between X and Y on the basis of the preceding table?
8. Six months later, the research department in Question 7 investigated the situation once again. However, a new variable was considered in the analysis, namely, the type of territory to which the salesperson was assigned; more specifically, whether the salesperson was assigned to an essentially metropolitan or nonmetropolitan territory. The following table summarizes the research department's findings:

Salesperson Assigned	Metropolitan Territory			
	Territory Sales Change			
	Increased Substantially	Increased Marginally	No Increase	Total
New	70	20	—	90
Old	54	16	—	70

Salesperson Assigned	Nonmetropolitan Territory			
	Territory Sales Change			
	Increased Substantially	Increased Marginally	No Increase	Total
New	5	10	5	20
Old	20	40	20	80

(a) If the type of territory to which the salesperson was assigned is ignored, does this table provide evidence of concomitant variation between change in sales and whether the salespeople were new or old? Justify your answer.

(b) If type of territory is considered, does the table provide evidence of concomitant variation between sales changes and whether the salespeople were new or old? Justify your answer.

9. The product development team at Busby's Briquets has been working on several modifications of Busby's highly successful line of charcoal briquets. The most promising development is a new briquet that imparts a unique smoky flavor to grilled meat. Management, based on favorable feedback from a few employees who have tested the product in their homes, feels that the new briquet has the potential to become a major seller.

At a recent strategy session, the vice-president of marketing suggested a test-marketing program before committing to introduction of the new briquet. He pointed out that a test market would be a good way to evaluate the effectiveness of two alternative advertising and promotional campaigns that have been proposed by Busby's ad agency. He feels that effectiveness should be evaluated in terms of the trial and repeat-purchasing behavior engendered by each program. He also wants to gauge Busby's current distributors' acceptance of the new product.

The CEO of Busby's, however, is not very enthusiastic about the idea of test marketing. She pointed out several of her concerns, among them the fact that Busby's competitors could easily duplicate the new briquet, the fact that the company is nearing the limit of budgeted costs for developing the new briquet, and the fact that the seasonal nature of briquet sales makes it imperative to reach a "go–no go" decision on the new briquet by early April, only four months away.

The director of marketing research stated that she felt a test-marketing plan could be devised that would satisfy both the vice-president of marketing and the CEO. She was instructed to submit a preliminary proposal at the next strategy session.

(a) What information should be obtained from the test market in order to satisfy the vice-president of marketing?

(b) Under what constraints must the test-marketing plan operate in order to satisfy the CEO?

(c) Given your answers to (a) and (b), what method of test marketing should the director recommend? Why?

10. Schedule an interview with the marketing manager of a firm near your home or your school. In the interview, discuss the use of test marketing by the firm. Attempt to find answers to the following questions: How important is test marketing in the firm's product-development process? Does the firm normally progress through different types of test marketing for a specific product (as suggested in this text), or is only one type commonly used? What does your contact see as the advantages and disadvantages of various methods of test marketing? Have successful test-marketing episodes always led to successful product introductions for the firm? What does your contact perceive as the most promising avenue for future development of test-marketing procedures?

Write a report of your interview, highlighting information that you obtained that was not discussed in the text, or that seems at odds with the textbook discussion.

Endnotes

1. Robert Ferber, Donald F. Blankertz, and Sidney Hollander, Jr., *Marketing Research* (New York: The Ronald Press Co., copyright 1964), p. 153. See also "Marketing Research Needs Validated Theories," *Marketing News*, 17 (January 21, 1983), p. 14. For an alternative view, see Raymond J. Lawrence, "To Hypothesize or Not to Hypothesize? The Correct 'Approach' to Survey Research," *Journal of the Market Research Society*, 24 (October 1982), pp. 335–343.

2. Ferber, Blankertz, and Hollander, *Marketing Research*, p. 171.

3. Benjamin D. Sackmary, "Data Analysis & Output Planning Improve Value of Marketing Research," *Marketing News*, 17 (January 21, 1983), p. 6. Published by the American Marketing Association.

4. *We Make the Market Perfectly Clear* (New York: National Purchase Diary Panel, Inc., undated).

5. *Management with the Nielsen Retail Index System* (Northbrook, Ill.: A. C. Nielsen Company, undated).

6. Margaret Loeb, "Testers of Cigarettes Find On-Job Puffing Really Isn't a Drag," *The Wall Street Journal* (August 22, 1984), pp. 1 and 15.

7. Hans Zeisel, *Say It With Figures*, 5th ed. (New York: Harper and Row, 1968), pp. 200–239, has a highly readable version of the analyses that can be performed with panel data. See also David Rogosa, "Comparisons of Some Procedures for Analyzing Longitudinal Panel Data," *Journal of Economics and Business*, 32 (Winter 1980), pp. 136–151, and Gregory B. Markus, *Analyzing Panel Data* (Beverly Hills, Calif.: Sage Publications, 1979).

8. Table 6.4 can also be viewed as a transition matrix, because it depicts the brand-buying changes occurring from period to period. Knowing the proportion switching allows early prediction of the ultimate success of some new product or some change in market strategy. See, for example, Seymour Sudman and Robert Ferber, *Consumer Panels* (Chicago: American Marketing Association, 1979), pp. 19–27, which also provides an excellent review of the literature on facets of consumer panels such as their uses, sampling and sampling biases, data-collection methods, conditioning, data processing and file maintenance, costs of operating, and choosing a consumer panel service.

9. See Sudman and Ferber, *Consumer Panels*, p. 31. For suggestions on recruiting and maintaining cooperation from panel members, see William H. Motes, "How to Solve Common Problems in Longitudinal Studies," *Marketing News*, 18 (January 6, 1984), p. 3.

10. Sudman and Ferber, *Consumer Panels*, p. 31–32. Winer demonstrates the biasing effects of attrition on the parameters of models fit to panel data. See Russell S. Winer, "Attrition Bias in Econometric Models Estimated with Panel Data," *Journal of Marketing Research*, 20 (May 1983), pp. 177–186. See also Jennifer Waterton and Denise Lievesley, "Attrition in a Panel Study of Attitudes," *Journal of Official Statistics*, 3 (No. 3, 1987), pp. 267–282.

11. Verne B. Churchill, "Learning to Live with Continuing Household Panels," *TeleNation Reports* (Summer 1988), p. 2.

12. See Claire Selltiz, Lawrence S. Wrightsman, and Stuart W. Cook, *Research Methods in Social Relations*, rev. ed. (New York: Holt, Rinehart and Winston, 1959), pp. 80–82, for a brief but lucid discussion of the differences between the commonsense and scientific notions of causality. See also David A. Kenny, *Correlation and Causality* (New York: John Wiley, 1979), especially Chapter 1.

13. Selltiz, Wrightsman, and Cook, *Research Methods*, pp. 83–88.

14. In Chapter 18 we will discuss the various conditions that can arise when looking at evidence of concomitant variation. For the moment, we simply wish to emphasize through example that association between X and Y does not mean there is causality between X and Y and that the absence of such association does not mean there is no causality.

15. Selltiz, Wrightsman, and Cook, *Research Methods*, p. 85.

16. Arthur Conan Doyle, "The Sign of the Four," in *The Complete Sherlock Holmes*, (Garden City, N.Y.: Garden City Publishing Company, Inc., 1938), p. 94.

17. Kevin Burns, "TV Viewing Up—Maybe," *Media Message: An Ogilvy & Mather Commentary on Media Issues* (October 1983), pp. 1–7.

18. Fred N. Kerlinger, *Foundations of Behavioral Research*, 3rd ed. (New York: Holt, Rinehart and Winston, 1986), p. 293. See also Geoffrey Keppel, *Design and Analysis: A Researcher's Handbook*, 2nd ed. (Englewood Cliffs, N.J.: Prentice-Hall, 1982), especially Chapter 1 for a description of the essential ingredients in experiments.

19. John R. Nevin, "Using Controlled Experiments to Estimate and Analyze Brand Demand," unpublished Ph.D. dissertation, University of Illinois, 1972. See also John R. Nevin, "Laboratory Experiments for Estimating Consumer Demand: A Validation Study," *Journal of Marketing Research*, 11 (August 1974), pp. 261–268. Another area in which laboratory and field experiments have been used to examine the same phenomenon is comparative advertising. See George E. Belch, "An Examination of Comparative and Non-comparative Television Commercials: The Effects of Claim Variation and Repetition on Cognitive Response and Message Acceptance," *Journal of Marketing Research*, 18 (August 1981), pp. 333–349; and William R. Swinyard, "The Interaction between Comparative Advertising and Copy Claim Variation," *Journal of Marketing Research*, 18 (May 1981), pp. 175–186.

20. Laboratory and field experiments typically play complementary roles in providing managerially useful marketing information. For a discussion of their respective roles, see Alan G. Sawyer, Parker M. Worthing, and Paul E. Sendak, "The Role of Laboratory Experiments to Test Marketing Strategies," *Journal of Marketing*, 43 (Summer 1979), pp. 60–67.

21. Cook and Campbell distinguish four types of validity: (1) statistical conclusion, (2) internal, (3) construct, and (4) external. Their definitions of internal and external validity parallel ours. Statistical conclusion validity addresses the extent and statistical significance of the covariation that exists in the data; construct validity examines the operations used in the experiment and attempts to assess whether they indeed capture the construct they were supposed to measure. We will have more to say on construct validity in the measurement chapters and statistical conclusion validity in the analysis chapters. Thomas D. Cook and Donald T. Campbell, *Quasi-Experimentation: Design and Analysis Issues for Field Settings* (Chicago: Rand McNally College Publishing Company, 1979), pp. 37–94.

22. For a general discussion of how the usefulness of experimental results is affected by the researcher's treatment of unmanipulated background factors in the experiment, see John G. Lynch, Jr., "On the External Validity of Experiments in Consumer Research," *Journal of Consumer Research*, 9 (December 1982), pp. 225–244.

23. Alvin R. Achenbaum, "Market Testing: Using the Marketplace as a Laboratory," in Robert Ferber, ed., *Handbook of Marketing Research* (New York: McGraw-Hill, 1974), pp. 4-31 to 4-54. For recent assessments of what is happening in the test market arena, see "Test Marketing," *Sales and Marketing Management*, 136 (March 1986), pp. 87–117. See also "To Test or Not to Test Seldom the Question," *Advertising Age*, 55 (February 20, 1984), pp. M10–M11.

24. "Test Marketing: What's in Store," *Sales and Marketing Management*, 128 (March 15, 1982). pp. 57–85. See also "New Product Debuts Reach Record Levels, Creating Market Pressures," *The Wall Street Journal* (June 11, 1987), p. 1.

25. There are several references that provide useful overviews of marketing's use of experiments in general and test markets in particular. See, for example, David M. Gardner and Russell W. Belk, *A Basic Bibliography on Experimental Design in Marketing* (Chicago: American Marketing Association, 1980); and John R. Dickinson, *The Bibliography of Marketing Research Methods* (Lexington, Mass.: Lexington Books, 1986), pp. 261–273.

26. "To Test or Not to Test Seldom the Queston," pp. M10–M11.

27. "Seven-Up's No-Caffeine Cola," *The Wall Street Journal* (March 25, 1982), p. 27.

28. Eleanor Johnson Tracy, "Testing Time for Test Marketing," *Fortune*, 110 (October 29, 1984), pp. 75–76.

29. Julie B. Solomon, "P & G Rolls Out New Items at Faster Pace, Turning Away from Long Marketing Testing," *The Wall Street Journal* (May 11, 1984), p. 25. See also Dan Koeppel, "Will K-C

Ever Get Once Overs Out of Missouri?" *Adweek's Marketing Week* (February 27, 1989), p. 62.

30. "How to Improve Your Chances for Test-Market Success," *Marketing News*, 18 (January 6, 1984), pp. 12–13.

31. Some work has been done on early prediction of a new product's success, but these efforts still must have sufficient time to allow assessment of repeat-purchasing tendencies. See Chakravarthi Narasimhan and Subrata K. Sen, "New Product Models for Test Market Data," *Journal of Marketing*, 47 (Winter 1983), pp. 11–24, for a review of a number of these models. For an empirical comparison of the predictive power of five of them, see Vijay Mahajan, Eitan Muller, and Subhash Sharma, "An Empirical Comparison of Awareness Forecasting Models of New Product Introduction," *Marketing Science*, 3 (Summer 1984), pp. 179–197.

32. Damon Darden, "Faced with More Competition, P & G Sees New Products as Crucial to Earnings Growth," *The Wall Street Journal* (September 13, 1983), pp. 37 and 53. For discussion of the general problems of overcontrolling the marketing effort in test markets, see "How to Keep Well-Intentioned Research from Misleading New-Product Planners" and "How to Improve Your Chances for Test-Market Success," *Marketing News*, 18 (January 6, 1984), pp. 1 and 8, and pp. 12 and 13, respectively.

33. Problems 1–8 are discussed in Jay E. Klompmaker, G. David Hughes, and Russell I. Haley, "Test Marketing in New Product Development," *Harvard Business Review*, 54 (May–June 1976), pp. 135–136; Problem 9 is found in Lynn G. Reiling, "Consumer Misuse Mars Sampling for Sunlight Dishwashing Liquid," *Marketing News*, 16 (September 3, 1982), pp. 1 and 12; and Problem 10 is discussed in Annetta Miller and Dody Tsiantor, "A Test for Market Research," *Newsweek*, 110 (December 28, 1987), pp. 32–33.

34. On the basis of in-depth interviews with 31 marketing executives, Klompmaker, Hughes, and Haley, "Test Marketing in New Product Development," offer some specific suggestions regarding when a firm should conduct a test market, what can be learned from such a test, and how information from test markets should be used. See also "How to Improve Your Chances for Test Market Success."

35. For a full list of the research firms operating controlled test markets and the cities that they use, see Pat Seelig, "All Over the Map," *Sales and Marketing Management*, 142, (March 1989).

36. Jacob Kendathel, "The Advantages of Electronic Test Markets: An Advertiser View Based on Experience," *Journal of Advertising Research*, 25 (December 1985/January 1986), pp. RC11–RC12. See also Aimee L. Stern, "Test Marketing Enters a New Era," *Dun's Business Month*, 126 (October 1985), p. 86.

37. "Simulated Test Marketing Winning Acceptance," *Marketing News*, 19 (March 1, 1985), pp. 15 and 19. See also Henry P. Khost, "Pretesting to Avoid Product Postmortems," *Advertising Age*, 53 (February 22, 1982), pp. M10–M11; " 'Magic Town' Doesn't Exist for Test Marketers," *Marketing News*, 19 (March 1, 1985), pp. 5 and 18; and Allan D. Shocker and William G. Hall, "Pretest Market Models: A Critical Evaluation," *Journal of Product Innovation Management*, 3 (September 1986), p. 86–107.

38. Andrew M. Tarskis, "Natural Sell-In Avoids Pitfalls of Controlled Tests," *Marketing News*, 20 (October 14, 1986), p. 14.

39. John R. Blair, "Volumetric Estimation: Review of Approaches the Pros Use—Packaged Goods Emphasis," paper presented at American Marketing Association's 7th Annual Marketing Research Conference, Orlando, Florida, September 29, 1986; and Dwight R. Riskey, "Test Market Decisions . . . Under Pressure," *Jounal of Data Collection*, 27 (Spring 1987), pp. 9–13.

Suggested Additional Readings

For a review of the structure, purposes, and useful approaches of descriptive designs, see

Claire Selltiz, Lawrence S. Wrightsman, and Stuart W. Cook, *Research Methods in Social Relations*, 3rd ed. (New York: Holt, Rinehart and Winston, 1976).

For a discussion of the criteria of good hypotheses and the value of hypotheses in guiding research, see

Fred N. Kerlinger, *Foundations of Behavioral Research*, 3rd ed. (New York: Holt, Rinehart and Winston, 1986).

For a discussion of the operation of consumer panels, see

Seymour Sudman and Robert Ferber, *Consumer Panels* (Chicago: American Marketing Association, 1979).

For a discussion of methods for analyzing panel data, see

Gregory B. Markus, *Analyzing Panel Data* (Beverly Hills, Calif.; Sage Publications, 1979).

For general discussions regarding the design of experiments, see

Thomas D. Cook and Donald T. Campbell, *Quasi-Experimentation: Design and Analysis Issues for Field Settings* (Chicago: Rand McNally College Publishing Company, 1979).

Geoffrey Keppel, *Design and Analysis: A Researcher's Handbook*, 2nd ed. (Englewood Cliffs, N.J.: Prentice-Hall, 1982).

Part Two

Research Project

The second stage in the research process is to determine the research design. As we have seen in Chapters 5 and 6, the design may take one of three forms, depending on the objective of the research. In these chapters we discussed the three basic types of research: exploratory, descriptive, and causal.

You will recall that the major emphasis in exploratory research is on the discovery of ideas and insights. A descriptive study is typically concerned with determining the frequency with which something occurs or the relationship between two variables, and it is generally guided by an initial hypothesis. A causal research design is concerned with determining cause-and-effect relationships.

Researchers for the Centerville Area Radio Association (CARA) decided to begin their study by conducting some exploratory research. This research consisted primarily of two types: (1) a literature review and (2) experience surveys.

They began the literature review by reading articles dealing with the positive and negative perceptions held by users of television, radio, and newspaper advertising. This secondary information was found in marketing research studies, general articles, and reference works dealing with the three major advertising media.

They found "The Radio Marketing Consultants Guide to Media," published by the Radio Advertising Bureau, to be a particularly helpful source. This source provided extensive coverage of the advantages and problems associated with each of the three major media.

They supplemented what they had found in the literature review with an experience survey. They began by interviewing various people who had specialized knowledge and experience with these media and then used their input to develop a revised list of advantages and problems associated with each medium.

Next, they discussed each of the media attribute items on the list with a group of CARA advertising sales representatives in order to obtain their input. Although the sales reps' feedback and suggestions were valued highly and weighed heavily, researchers

also recognized that the group's opinions were not free of bias. Consequently, the final list of attribute items included in the study were determined by the researchers alone.

The resulting criteria decided upon were then discussed with three local retail businesses. This was done in order to determine the relevancy of each of the items and to make any appropriate additions, corrections, or deletions. In these interviews, it was obvious that individuals were going to have strong opinions and biases about the effectiveness of one medium versus another. However, there was virtually total agreement that the criteria chosen would be sufficient and broad enough in scope to assess the three media and respective sales representatives accurately.

The information gleaned from the literature review and experience survey were then used to develop the various hypotheses that would guide further research. A complete list of these hypotheses was given at the end of Part One. Among them were the hypotheses that there would be differences in business-peoples' attitudes toward television, radio, and newspaper, and that differences would also exist in attitudes toward sales representatives of each of the media.

As we pointed out in Chapter 3, the stages in the research process should not be viewed as discrete entities, but rather as elements in a continuous process. Information uncovered at one stage in the process is often used to refine decisions made earlier in the study. The information researchers for CARA discovered in the course of their exploratory research may well have been used to formulate the research problem more clearly.

In this case, once the hypotheses were formed, the decision was made to test them by examining the perceptions of a cross section of retailers.

Given the hypotheses, if you were one of the researchers for CARA,

- *What kinds of information would you attempt to secure from retailers?*
- *How would you go about selecting retailers to contact?*

Cases to Part Two

Case 2.1   Rumstad Decorating Centers (A)

In 1929, Joseph Rumstad opened a small paint and wallpaper supply store in downtown Rockford, Illinois. For the next 45 years the store enjoyed consistent, though not spectacular, success. Sales and profits increased steadily but slowly as, to keep pace with the competition, the original line of products was expanded to include unpainted furniture, mirrors, picture-framing materials, and other products. In 1974, because of a declining neighborhood environment, Jack Rumstad, who had taken over management of the store from his father in 1970, decided to close the downtown store and to open a new outlet on the far west side of the city. The west side was chosen because it was experiencing a boom in new home construction. In 1988, a second store was opened on the east side of the city, and the name of the business was changed to Rumstad Decorating Centers. The east-side store was staffed with sales clerks but was basically managed by Jack Rumstad himself from the west-side location. All ordering, billing, inventory control, and even the physical storage of excess inventory, was concentrated at the west-side store.

In 1989, the east-side store was made an independent profit center. Jack Rumstad personally took over the management of the outlet and hired a full-time manager for the west-side store. With the change in accounting procedures occasioned by this organizational change, it became possible to examine the profitability of each outlet separately.

Jack Rumstad conducted such an examination early in 1990, using the profit and loss figures in Table 1, and became very concerned with what he discovered. Both stores had suffered losses for 1989, and although he had anticipated incurring a loss during the first couple of years of operation of the east-side store, he was not at all prepared for a second successive loss at the west-side outlet. He blamed the 1988 loss on the disruptions caused by the change in organizational structure. Further, from 1988 to 1989, the east-side store had a 25-percent increase in net sales, a 25-percent increase in gross profits, and an 8-percent increase in total direct costs. Also, although the east-side store still showed a net loss, it was

80-percent less than the previous year's loss. The west-side store, on the other hand, had shown a 21-percent decrease in net sales, a 31-percent decrease in gross profit, an 11-percent decrease in direct costs, and a 136-percent increase in net loss.

Mr. Rumstad is very concerned about the survival of the business and particularly concerned with the west-side store. He has called you in as a research consultant to help him pinpoint what is happening so that he might take corrective action.

West-Side Store

The west-side store is located in the heart of the census tract with the highest per capita income in the city. Most of the residents in the area are professional people or white-collar workers. The store is a freestanding unit located on a frontage road and has "Rumstad" printed across the front. Since Jack Rumstad's transfer to the east-side store, there has been a succession of managers at the west-side store. The first one lasted for six months and the second and third for four months. The current manager, previously a sales clerk at the store for four years, has held the job for ten months. Even though the products carried and the prices charged are the same in both stores, there is some difference in advertising emphasis. The west-side store does all of its advertising in the *Shopper's World*, a weekly paper devoted exclusively to advertising, which is distributed free to all households in the community. Delivery is by and large door-to-door, although it is quite typical for a group of newspapers to be placed at the entrance to apartment buildings and for residents to pick up a copy if they so choose.

East-Side Store

The east-side store is located in a predominantly blue-collar area. Most of the residents in the immediate vicinity work for one of the various machine tool manufacturers that compose one of the basic industries in Rockford. The store is located in a small

Table 1   **Profit and Loss Statement for Rumstad Decorating Centers**

	East-Side Store		West-Side Store	
	1989	1988	1989	1988
Total Sales	$114,461	$ 91,034	$ 67,703	$108,497
Cash sale discounts	4,347	2,971	4,165	2,930
Net sales	110,114	88,063	83,538	105,567
Beginning inventory	53,369	49,768	1,936	0
Purchases	64,654	56,528	163,740	59,366
Total	118,023	106,206	165,676	59,366
Ending inventory	51,955	53,369	115,554	1,936
Cost of sales	66,068	52,837	50,122	57,430
Gross profit or loss	44,046	35,226	33,416	48,137
Direct Costs				
Salaries	24,068	19,836	24,549	26,583
Payroll taxes	2,025	1,814	1,764	2,060
Depreciation—furniture and fixtures	92	92	92	92
Freight	6	43	511	800
Store supplies	694	828	607	4,153
Accounting and legal expenses	439	433	439	433
Advertising	2,977	4,890	4,820	5,252
Advertising—yellow pages	1,007	618	1,387	956
Convention and seminar expenses	0	33	83	216
Insurance	226	139	1,271	1,643
Office expense and supplies	4,466	4,393	5,327	5,010
Personal property tax	139	139	140	140
Rent	7,000	7,000	4,900	4,900
Utilities	2,246	1,651	2,746	2,359
Total direct costs	45,385	41,909	48,636	54,597
Profit or loss	(1,339)	(6,683)	(15,220)	(6,460)

shopping center. It has a large window display area with a readily visible "Rumstad Decorating Center" sign above the store. The east-side store advertises periodically in the *Rockford Morning Star* in addition to its yellow pages advertising.

address: (1) why is WS doing worse ES ?
(2) what should Rumstad do now?
Specific

Question

1. How would you proceed to answer Mr. Rumstad's problem?

Case 2.2   HotStuff Computer Software (A)[1]

Simpson, Edwards and Associates has had considerable success with a computer software package that it designed to enable government agencies to manage their data-base systems. The firm is currently developing a second product, a more specialized version of

its first endeavor. Called HotStuff, its latest computer software concept is targeted at the firefighting industry. Researchers at Simpson, Edwards and Associates have a hunch that fire departments are a prime market for data-base software because of their extensive information-handling responsibilities—equipment inventories, building layouts, hazardous materials data, budget records, personnel files, and so on.

[1]The contributions of Jacqueline C. Hitchon to the development of this case are gratefully acknowledged.

At this embryonic stage in the new product's development, the company is following the same game plan that helped it launch its previous success. Responsibilities have been broadly divided; Jean Edwards has assumed command of the production side, and Craig Simpson has taken charge of marketing and promotion. Simpson's first move was to reassemble the original team of staff members who had researched the market for government-agency software. At their first orientation meeting, he submitted the following objectives for their deliberation:

1. Determine market potential.
2. Identify important product attributes.
3. Develop an effective promotional strategy.
4. Identify competitors in the market.

By the close of discussion, the group decided that its first task would be exploratory research. Specifically, it decided to conduct experience surveys involving local fire chiefs, informal telephone interviews with state and national fire officials, and a literature search. Based on findings from the exploratory research effort, it hoped to be able to pursue descriptive research to fulfill the four objectives.

Exploratory Research

The first finding to emerge from the exploratory research affected the target market for HotStuff. There are two broad categories of fire departments: municipal departments, with full staffs of paid firefighters, and volunteer departments, consisting of a paid chief and remaining members who are either all volunteers or part paid and part volunteers. The team quickly discovered that the two kinds of departments differ in two important ways. First, from the point of view of funding, municipal departments receive the majority of their funds from taxes, so the money is tightly controlled and tends to be earmarked for specific uses. Volunteer fire departments, on the other hand, rely heavily on donors and special events as sources of income, to the extent that fund-raising may account for more than 50 percent of their total receipts. Since money obtained through fund-raising is not technically part of the budget, it is not subject to budgetary controls per se.

The second key difference between municipal and volunteer departments concerned purchasing procedures. Local municipal departments were observed to route all purchases through a central purchasing agent, who would then apply for approval from the data-processing center at city hall before acquiring computer hardware and software. Fire chiefs interviewed in volunteer departments, however, reported that they had sole authority to purchase any hardware or software required.

Telephone calls to out-of-state fire officials indicated that these differences were consistent across the nation. As a result, Simpson, Edwards and Associates decided to restrict its target market to volunteer fire departments only.

A second finding uncovered in the exploratory research concerned the extent to which the needs of the target market were already being met. Inquiries within the state revealed that only a few volunteer departments had already purchased computers. Further, those with computers had not possessed them long and were still in the process of automating manual data bases. The general feeling among fire officials was that computerization would be an inevitable development in the industry in the near future. Indeed, four specialized software packages were already being advertised in fire-prevention journals: Chief's Helper, Fire Organizer, Spread Systems, and JLT Software. Spread Systems differed from the others in that it consisted of separate programs, each of which sold individually and covered a particular information type, such as inventory records or hazardous materials. The strategy followed by Spread Systems allowed fire departments to reduce their expenditure on software because they could select only those programs that they needed. It was conjectured at Simpson, Edwards and Associates that specific programs for specific functions might help overcome initial consumer caution toward spending several thousand dollars for computer software, because the expenditure would not be made all at one time. It was also believed that some makers of generic software packages that perform spreadsheet or database management analysis should be included in the list of competitors, although users of generic software packages needed some proficiency with computers in order to tailor these basic packages to their specific applications.

A third finding of interest from the exploratory research was that the term *volunteer* was offensive to departments officially classified as volunteer because they thought that it implied a lack of professionalism. In fact, their staffs were as well trained as members of municipal departments. This sentiment led the researchers to conclude that the label *volunteer* should not be used in future promotion of HotStuff.

Based on what it had learned from the exploratory research, Simpson, Edwards and Associates decided to conduct a more formal investigation to address the following objectives:

1. Determine the market potential for its new software by
   (a) establishing the incidence of computer use and planned computer purchases in volunteer fire departments, and
   (b) obtaining more information about volunteer fire departments' funding and authority structures.
2. Identify important product attributes–that is, the types of information that need to be handled by volunteer fire departments and that therefore need to be incorporated into the software.
3. Secure ideas for promotional strategy by
   (a) determining which fire publications are read by the target market, and
   (b) determining which association conventions are most well attended by the target market.
4. Identify competitors in the market by
   (a) establishing which brands of software are currently used in volunteer fire departments, and
   (b) establishing how satisfactory existing software packages are perceived to be.

Study Design

Simpson, Edwards and Associates' researchers believed that the best way to address these objectives was through a national survey of volunteer fire departments. They decided on a telephone survey using team members as interviewers. The state fire marshall informed the group that most volunteer fire departments were located in communities with populations under 25,000. Consequently, it was decided to sample towns with populations under 25,000 that were situated within a 20-mile radius of cities of at least 100,000 people. Volunteer fire departments within those towns could then be contacted by telephone by means of directory assistance. Two large cities were randomly selected from each state, excluding Alaska and Hawaii, and then a town located near each city was randomly selected. An atlas and the 1990 Census were used to identify cities and towns of the right specification.

A questionnaire was devised and pretested twice. The first pretest was conducted through personal interviews and was meant to test the questionnaire; the second pretest was performed by telephone and was meant to test the mode of administration. In each case, inquiries were directed to the fire chiefs as representatives of the departments. The actual survey was conducted between April 13 and April 24. It would have taken less time to administer the survey had there not been a national fire convention the week that the phone survey began. Because the national fire convention coincided with Easter week, many fire chiefs were not at their departments; they attended the convention with their families, as their children did not have school. Nonetheless, the interviewers were able to increase the response rate to 85 percent by numerous callbacks.

Questions

1. Evaluate Simpson, Edwards and Associates' decision to focus on volunteer fire departments as its target market, based on the exploratory research.
2. Do you consider that exploratory research was productive in this case? Do you think that further useful insights could have been gained without significantly greater expenditure of resources? If so, what and how?
3. Comment on the differences between the four objectives as originally formulated and as reformulated after exploratory research.
4. Was the choice of phone interviews a good one?

Case 2.3   Gibbons College Library[1]

The library staff of Gibbons College in Iowa is deeply committed to serving the needs of the college's undergraduate student body. The library offers its students an attractive atmosphere in which to conduct individual or group study and provides numerous workshops and seminars designed to improve student study, writing, and test-taking skills. Of special

[1]The contributions of David M. Szymanski to the development of this case are gratefully acknowledged.

significance has been the administration's commitment to meeting the information needs of library patrons. For example, during the past academic year the library received some 70,000 requests for information and reference referral, and it had more than 169,000 library items checked out to registered students.

Because of the diversity in student backgrounds, meeting patron information demands is a very difficult and challenging activity. The facilities and installations must be specific enough to serve individual student needs, yet targeted to reach as large an audience as possible. Thus, careful staff consideration must be given continually to the establishment of new library policies and procedures.

Recently, the library staff contemplated the installation of a computer data base of bibliographic references to replace the manual methods of searching indexes and abstracts for information on research topics. The need for a computer search facility at the library had become especially acute in the last several years because

- Library users had become more sophisticated in their awareness of the potential resources available to them
- Library users and staff had become increasingly cognizant of the use and application of computers in educational and library settings
- Library staff had become aware of the ways in which reference questions and search-strategy problems could be solved through on-line data bases

By having computer search facilities available, students could—for a relatively small fee that would be based on the amount of computer time used and the length of the computer printout—quickly access information and coordinate research activities.

Because of the large number of data bases on the market, the library staff decided to conduct a study that would provide information directly related to decisions on choosing a computer data-base searching service. First, the staff wanted to learn more about who currently used the library and to what extent, what the characteristics of people using the library were, and what differences existed between heavy- and low-level users of library facilities. Second, the staff wanted to focus on preferred features of a data-base searching service. For example, how large

was the potential user population for the service, and what characteristics of the service would best meet the needs of an undergraduate student body?

Sampling Procedure

To obtain information necessary for making an informed judgment on the best data base to install, the library staff conducted a survey of library patrons. The population was defined to be all undergraduate users of the college's library.

Because a list of known sampling units was not available, a nonprobability sample was used for the study. The staff decided to draw the sample from individual users of the library during one particular day. A sample of 300 subjects was projected as being (1) necessary to be representative of the user population and (2) needed to do cross-tabulation analysis. Because the sample was dependent on volunteer returns, it was considered important that researchers secure an adequate response by sampling morning, afternoon, and evening library patrons. A questionnaire (see Figure 1) was therefore distributed to students entering the building during three periods: 9 to 11 a.m., 2 to 4 p.m., and 7 to 9 p.m. A large sign was posted informing patrons about the survey, and a questionnaire return box was placed near the library exits to facilitate survey returns.

The number of questionnaires distributed and returned for each period is listed in Table 1. Questionnaires lacking responses to major questions and questionnaires appearing to be carelessly done (for example, all 4s being checked) were eliminated from the analysis. For the final tabulations, 100 arbitrarily chosen responses from each of the three surveyed time frames were used, making the total number of subjects included in the analysis 300.

Questions

1. Using the research objectives as guidelines, construct dummy tables that can be used to help analyze the results obtained from the questionnaire.
2. Critique the research design. Will the research study as presented here lead to an "ideal" marketing research study of users' needs for a computer data base? Why or why not?

Figure 1   **Gibbons College Library Survey**

The College Library needs information from you in order to improve library service. We would appreciate it if you could answer the following questions and place the completed survey in one of the questionnaire return boxes (located at all exits) when you leave the library.

1. *What one thing do you like most about the College Library?*
   _____

2. *What one thing do you like least about the College Library?*
   _____

3. *Approximately how many times per week have you used the College Library this semester?*
   _____ this is my first visit to the College Library
   _____ less than once a week
   _____ once a week
   _____ 2–4 times a week
   _____ 5 or more times a week

4. *For what purpose do you most often use the College Library?*
   _____ to study
   _____ to do homework (nonresearch-work homework)
   _____ to do research work
   _____ other: please specify _____

5. *Have you used the* **Reader's Guide to Periodical Literature, The Magazine Index, Business Periodicals Index,** *or any other index to find magazine and journal articles this semester?*

   _____ yes   _____ no

   If yes, how often during the current school year have you used such indexes?
   _____ 1–2 times   _____ 3–4 times   _____ 5 or more times

6. *A computer data-base searching service finds references to magazine and journal articles as in a printed index but retrieves them from an on-line computer data base. Have you ever used such a service before?*

   _____ yes   _____ no

   If yes, how often have you used such a service before?
   _____ 1–2 times   _____ 3–4 times   _____ 5 or more times

   If yes, did you find these indexes:
   _____ very easy to use   _____ difficult to use
   _____ easy to use   _____ very difficult to use

7. *If a computer data-base service were available at the College Library, would you use it?*

   _____ yes   _____ no   _____ don't know

   If yes, how often would you anticipate having a need for such a service?
   _____ 1–2 times a year   _____ 3–4 times a year
   _____ 5 or more times a year

8. *When using a computer data-base service, the user must pay the library a fee based on the amount of computer time used and the length of the computer printout. How important would the cost of the service be in your decision to use a computer data base?*
   _____ not at all important
   _____ somewhat unimportant
   _____ neither important nor unimportant
   _____ somewhat important
   _____ very important

(continued)

Figure 1   *(Continued)*

9. *One of the advantages of a computer data base is that it can provide many bibliographic references in a short period of time. How important is this factor in your decision to use a computer data base?*

_____ not at all important
_____ somewhat unimportant
_____ neither important nor unimportant
_____ somewhat important
_____ very important

10. *Of the many types of data bases available to library users, which would you find most useful (check all relevant categories)?*

_____ psychological abstracts
_____ business & economic abstracts
_____ science abstracts
_____ engineering abstracts
_____ health-related abstracts
_____ general periodical indexes
_____ other: please specify _____

11. *What is your current class standing?*

_____ freshman   _____ junior
_____ sophomore   _____ senior
_____ special student
_____ other: please specify _____

12. *What is your declared or intended major area of study?*

_____ agriculture and life sciences
_____ allied health fields
_____ business
_____ education
_____ engineering
_____ family resources
_____ letters & sciences
_____ nursing
_____ other: please specify _____

13. *What is your sex?*

_____ male   _____ female

Table 1   ***Questionnaires Distributed and Returned During Each of the Time Periods Surveyed***

Time Period	Questionnaires Distributed	Questionnaires Returned	Response Rate
7–9 a.m.	855	317	.37
2–4 p.m.	600	217	.36
7–9 p.m.	790	237	.30
TOTAL	2,245	771	.34

Case 2.4   Chestnut Ridge Country Club (A)[1]

The Chestnut Ridge Country Club has long maintained a distinguished reputation as one of the outstanding country clubs in the Elma, Tennessee area. The club's golf facilities are said by some to be the finest in the state, and its dining and banquet facilities are highly regarded as well. This reputation is due in part to the commitment by the board of directors of Chestnut Ridge to offer the finest facilities of any club in the area. For example, several negative comments by club members regarding the dining facilities prompted the board to survey members to get their feelings and perceptions of the dining facilities and food offerings at the club. Based on the survey findings, the board of directors established a quality-control committee to oversee the dining room, and a new club manager was hired.

Most recently, the board became concerned about the number of people seeking membership to Chestnut Ridge. Although no records are kept on the number of membership applications received each year, the board sensed that this figure was declining. They also believed that membership applications at the three competing country clubs in the area—namely, Alden, Chalet, and Lancaster—were not experiencing similar declines. Because Chestnut Ridge had other facilities, such as tennis courts and a pool, that were comparable to the facilities at these other clubs, the board was perplexed as to why membership applications would be falling at Chestnut Ridge.

To gain insight into the matter, the board of directors hired an outside research firm to conduct a study of the country clubs in Elma, Tennessee. The goals of the research were (1) to outline areas in which Chestnut Ridge fared poorly in relation to other clubs in the area, (2) to determine people's overall perception of Chestnut Ridge, and (3) to provide recommendations for ways to increase membership applications at the club.

Research Method

The researchers met with the board of directors and key personnel at Chestnut Ridge to gain a better understanding of the goals of the research and the types of services and facilities offered at a country club. A literature search of published research relating

to country clubs uncovered no studies. Based solely on their contact with individuals at Chestnut Ridge, therefore, the research team developed the survey contained in Figure 1. Because personal information regarding demographics and attitudes would be asked of those contacted, the researchers decided to use a mail questionnaire.

The researchers thought it would be useful to survey members from Alden, Chalet, and Lancaster country clubs in addition to those from Chestnut Ridge for two reasons. One, members of these other clubs would be knowledgeable about the levels and types of services and facilities desired from a country club, and two, they had at one time represented potential members of Chestnut Ridge. Hence, their perceptions of Chestnut Ridge might reveal why they chose to belong to a different country club.

No public documents were available that contained a listing of each club's members. Consequently, the researchers decided to contact each of the clubs personally to try to obtain a mailing list. Identifying themselves as being affiliated with an independent research firm conducting a study on country clubs in the Elma area, the researchers first spoke to the chairman of the board at Alden Country Club. The researchers told the chairman that they could not reveal the organization sponsoring the study but that the results of their study would not be made public. The chairman was not willing to provide the researchers with the mailing list. The chairman cited an obligation to respect the privacy of the club's members as the primary reason for turning down the research team's request.

The researchers then made the following proposal to the board chairman: in return for the mailing list, the researchers would provide the chairman a report on Alden members' perceptions of Alden Country Club. In addition, the mailing list would be destroyed as soon as the surveys were sent. The proposal seemed to please the chairman, for he agreed to give the researchers a listing of the members and their addresses in return for the report. The researchers told the chairman they had to check with their sponsoring organization for approval of this arrangement.

The research team made similar proposals to the chairmen of the boards of directors of both the Chalet and the Lancaster country clubs. In return for a mailing list of the club's members, they promised each chairman a report outlining their members' percep-

[1]The contributions of David M. Szymanski to the development of this case are gratefully acknowledged.

Figure 1   **Questionnaire Used to Survey Country Club Members**

1. In which club are you currently a member? _____

2. How long have you been a member of this club? _____

3. How familiar are you with each of the following country clubs?

Alden Country Club?
_____ very familiar (I am a member or have visited the club as a guest)
_____ somewhat familiar (I have heard about the club from others)
_____ unfamiliar

Chalet Country Club?
_____ very familiar
_____ somewhat familiar
_____ unfamiliar

Chestnut Ridge Country Club?
_____ very familiar
_____ somewhat familiar
_____ unfamiliar

Lancaster Country Club?
_____ very familiar
_____ somewhat familiar
_____ unfamiliar

4. The following is a list of factors that may be influential in the decision to join a country club. Please rate the factors according to their importance to you in joining your country club. Circle the appropriate response, where 1 = not at all important and 5 = extremely important.

Golf facilities	1	2	3	4	5
Tennis facilities	1	2	3	4	5
Pool facilities	1	2	3	4	5
Dining facilities	1	2	3	4	5
Social events	1	2	3	4	5
Family activities	1	2	3	4	5
Number of friends who are members	1	2	3	4	5
Cordiality of members	1	2	3	4	5
Prestige	1	2	3	4	5
Location	1	2	3	4	5

5. The following is a list of phrases pertaining to Alden Country Club. Please place an X in the space that best describes your impressions of Alden. The ends represent extremes; the center position is neutral. Do so even if you are only vaguely familiar with Alden.

Club landscape is attractive.	:___:___:___:___:___:___:	Club landscape is unattractive.
Clubhouse facilities are poor.	:___:___:___:___:___:___:	Clubhouse facilities are excellent.
Locker room facilities are excellent.	:___:___:___:___:___:___:	Locker room facilities are poor.
Club management is ineffective.	:___:___:___:___:___:___:	Club management is effective.
Dining room atmosphere is pleasant.	:___:___:___:___:___:___:	Dining room atmosphere is unpleasant.

Figure 1   **(Continued)**

Left	Scale	Right
Food prices are unreasonable.	:—:—:—:—:—:—:	Food prices are reasonable.
Golf course is poorly maintained.	:—:—:—:—:—:—:	Golf course is well maintained.
Golf course is challenging.	:—:—:—:—:—:—:	Golf course is not challenging.
Membership rates are too high.	:—:—:—:—:—:—:	Membership rates are too low.

6. *The following is a list of phrases pertaining to Chalet Country Club. Please place an X in the space that best describes your impressions of Chalet. Do so even if you are only vaguely familiar with Chalet.*

Left	Scale	Right
Club landscape is attractive.	:—:—:—:—:—:—:	Club landscape is unattractive.
Clubhouse facilities are poor.	:—:—:—:—:—:—:	Clubhouse facilities are excellent.
Locker room facilities are excellent.	:—:—:—:—:—:—:	Locker room facilities are poor.
Club management is effective.	:—:—:—:—:—:—:	Club management is ineffective.
Dining room atmosphere is pleasant.	:—:—:—:—:—:—:	Dining room atmosphere is unpleasant.
Food prices are unreasonable.	:—:—:—:—:—:—:	Food prices are reasonable.
Food quality is excellent.	:—:—:—:—:—:—:	Food quality is poor.
Golf course is poorly maintained.	:—:—:—:—:—:—:	Golf course is well maintained.
Golf course is challenging.	:—:—:—:—:—:—:	Golf course is not challenging.
Tennis courts are in excellent condition.	:—:—:—:—:—:—:	Tennis courts are in poor condition.
There are too many tennis courts.	:—:—:—:—:—:—:	There are too few tennis courts.
Membership rates are too high.	:—:—:—:—:—:—:	Membership rates are too low.

7. *The following is a list of phrases pertaining to Chestnut Ridge Country Club. Please place an X in the space that best describes your impressions of Chestnut Ridge. Do so even if you are only vaguely familiar with Chestnut Ridge.*

Left	Scale	Right
Club landscape is attractive.	:—:—:—:—:—:—:	Club landscape is unattractive.
Clubhouse facilities are poor.	:—:—:—:—:—:—:	Clubhouse facilities are excellent.
Locker room facilities are excellent.	:—:—:—:—:—:—:	Locker room facilities are poor.
Club management is ineffective.	:—:—:—:—:—:—:	Club management is effective.
Dining room atmosphere is pleasant.	:—:—:—:—:—:—:	Dining room atmosphere is unpleasant.
Food prices are unreasonable.	:—:—:—:—:—:—:	Food prices are reasonable.
Food quality is excellent.	:—:—:—:—:—:—:	Food quality is poor.
Golf course is poorly maintained.	:—:—:—:—:—:—:	Golf course is well maintained.

(continued)

Figure 1   *(Continued)*

Tennis courts are in poor condition.	:—:—:—:—:—:—:—	Tennis courts are in excellent condition.
There are too many tennis courts.	:—:—:—:—:—:—:—	There are too few tennis courts.
Swimming pool is in poor condition.	:—:—:—:—:—:—:—	Swimming pool is in excellent condition.
Membership rates are too high.	:—:—:—:—:—:—:—	Membership rates are too low.

8. *The following is a list of phrases pertaining to Lancaster Country Club. Please place an X in the space that best describes your impression of Lancaster. Do so even if you are only vaguely familiar with Lancaster.*

Club landscape is attractive.	:—:—:—:—:—:—:—	Club landscape is unattractive.
Clubhouse facilities are poor.	:—:—:—:—:—:—:—	Clubhouse facilities are excellent.
Locker room facilities are excellent.	:—:—:—:—:—:—:—	Locker room facilities are poor.
Club management is ineffective.	:—:—:—:—:—:—:—	Club management is effective.
Dining room atmosphere is pleasant.	:—:—:—:—:—:—:—	Dining room atmosphere is unpleasant.
Food prices are unreasonable.	:—:—:—:—:—:—:—	Food prices are reasonable.
Food quality is excellent.	:—:—:—:—:—:—:—	Food quality is poor.
Golf course is poorly maintained.	:—:—:—:—:—:—:—	Golf course is well maintained.
Tennis courts are in poor condition.	:—:—:—:—:—:—:—	Tennis courts are in excellent condition.
There are too many tennis courts.	:—:—:—:—:—:—:—	There are too few tennis courts.
Swimming pool is in poor condition.	:—:—:—:—:—:—:—	Swimming pool is in excellent condition.
Membership rates are too high.	:—:—:—:—:—:—:—	Membership rates are too low.

9. *Overall, how would you rate each of the country clubs? Circle the appropriate response, where 1 = poor and 5 = excellent.*

Alden	1	2	3	4	5
Chalet	1	2	3	4	5
Chestnut Ridge	1	2	3	4	5
Lancaster	1	2	3	4	5

10. *The following questions are designed to give a better understanding of the members of country clubs.*

Have you ever been a member of another club in the Elma area?

_____ yes   _____ no

Approximately what is the distance of your residence from your club in miles?

_____ 0–2 miles   _____ 3–5 miles   _____ 6–10 miles
_____ 10+ miles

Age: _____ 21–30   _____ 31–40   _____ 41–50
_____ 51–60   _____ 61 or over

Figure 1   **(Continued)**

Sex: _____ male   _____ female

Marital status: _____ married _____ single _____ widowed
_____ divorced

Number of dependents including yourself?
_____ 2 or less   _____ 3–4   _____ 5 or more

Total family income:
_____ Less than $20,000
_____ $20,000–$29,999
_____ $30,000–$49,999
_____ $50,000–$99,999
_____ $100,000 or more
_____ Do not know/Refuse to answer

Thank you for your cooperation!

tions of his club, contingent on their securing approval from their sponsoring organization. Both agreed to supply the requested list of members.

The researchers subsequently met with the Chestnut Ridge board of directors. In their meeting, the researchers outlined the situation and asked for the board's approval to provide each of the clubs with a report in return for the mailing lists. The researchers emphasized that the report would contain no information regarding Chestnut Ridge nor information by which each of the other clubs could compare itself with any of the other clubs in the area, in contrast to the information to be provided to the Chestnut Ridge board of directors. The report would only contain a small portion of the overall study's results. After carefully considering the research team's arguments, the board of directors agreed to the proposal.

Membership Surveys

A review of the lists subsequently provided by each club showed Alden had 114 members, Chalet had 98 members, and Lancaster had 132 members. The researchers believed that 69 to 70 responses from each membership group would be adequate. Anticipating a 70- to 75-percent response rate because of the unusually high involvement and familiarity of each group with the subject matter, the research team decided to mail 85 to 90 surveys to each group, and a simple

Table 1   *Average Overall Ratings of Each Club by Club Membership of the Respondent*

	Club Membership			Composite Ratings across All Members
Club Rated	Alden	Chalet	Lancaster	
Alden	4.57	3.64	3.34	3.85
Chalet	2.87	3.63	2.67	3.07
Chestnut Ridge	4.40	4.44	4.20	4.35
Lancaster	3.60	3.91	4.36	3.95

Table 2   ***Average Ratings of the Respective Country Clubs across Dimensions***

| | Country Club | | | |
Dimension	Alden	Chalet	Chestnut Ridge	Lancaster
Club landscape	6.28	4.65	6.48	5.97
Clubhouse facilities	5.37	4.67	6.03	5.51
Locker room facilities	4.99	4.79	5.36	4.14
Club management	5.38	4.35	5.00	5.23
Dining room atmosphere	5.91	4.10	5.66	5.48
Food prices	5.42	4.78	4.46	4.79
Food quality	a	4.12	5.48	4.79
Golf course maintenance	6.17	5.01	6.43	5.89
Golf course challenge	5.14	5.01	a	4.77
Condition of tennis courts	b	5.10	4.52	5.08
Number of tennis courts	b	4.14	4.00	3.89
Swimming pool	b	b	4.66	5.35
Membership rates	4.49	3.97	5.00	4.91

[a]Question not asked.
[b]Not applicable.

Table 3   ***Attitudes toward Chestnut Ridge by Members of the Other Country Clubs***

Dimension	Alden	Chalet	Lancaster
Club landscape	6.54	6.54	6.36
Clubhouse facilities	6.08	6.03	5.98
Locker room facilities	5.66	5.35	5.07
Club management	4.97	5.15	4.78
Dining room atmosphere	5.86	5.70	5.41
Food prices	4.26	4.48	4.63
Food quality	5.52	5.75	5.18
Golf course maintenance	6.47	6.59	6.22
Condition of tennis courts	4.55	4.46	4.55
Number of tennis courts	4.00	4.02	3.98
Swimming pool	5.08	4.69	4.26
Membership rates	5.09	5.64	4.24

random sample of members was chosen from each list. In all, 87 members from each country club were mailed a questionnaire (348 surveys in total). Sixty-three usable surveys were returned from each group (252 in total) for a response rate of 72 percent.

Summary results of the survey are presented in Tables 1 through 3. Table 1 gives people's overall ratings of the country clubs, and Table 2 shows people's ratings of the various clubs on an array of dimensions. Table 3 is a breakdown of attitudes toward Chestnut Ridge by the three different membership groups: Alden, Chalet, and Lancaster. The data are average ratings of respondents. Table 1 scores are based on a five-point scale, where one is poor and five is excellent. Tables 2 and 3 are based on seven-point scales, in which one represents an extremely negative rating and seven an extremely positive rating.

Questions

1. What kind of research design is being used? Is it a good choice?

2. Do you think it was ethical for the researchers not to disclose the identity of the sponsoring organization? Do you think it was ethical for the other clubs' chairmen of the board to release the names of their members in return for a report that analyzed their members' perceptions toward their own club?

3. Overall, how does Chestnut Ridge compare with the three country clubs: Alden, Chalet, and Lancaster?

4. In what areas might Chestnut Ridge consider improvements to attract additional members?

Part
Three

Data-Collection Methods

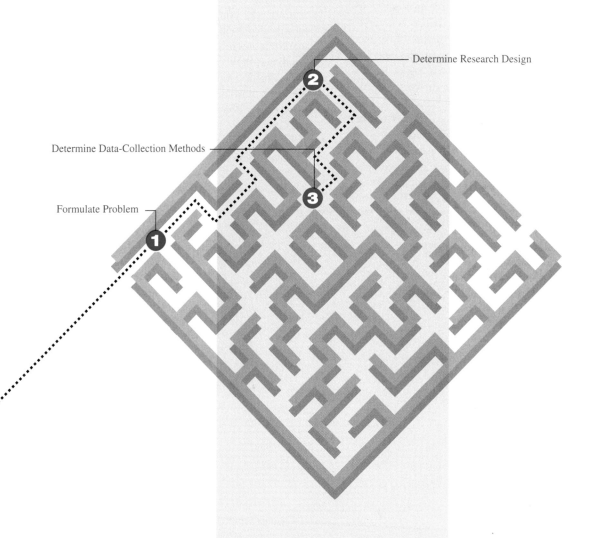

Determine Research Design

Determine Data-Collection Methods

Formulate Problem

Part Three covers the third stage in the research process, determination of the methods used to collect data. Chapter 7 focuses on secondary data as an information resource; and Chapter 8, on the data available from commercial suppliers. Chapter 9 compares the two methods marketing researchers have available for collecting marketing data — communication and observation. Chapter 10 then discusses the main alternatives if communication methods are used, and Chapter 11 explains the alternatives if observation methods are used.

MARY ANN WESTELL

Vice-President — Account Executive
Burke Marketing Research

When some of America's biggest corporations speak, Mary Ann Westell and Burke Marketing Research listen. As a vice-president and account executive working for Burke for the past 13 years, Westell has worked with many of Burke's clients, who number among the Fortune 100. They span both packaged goods manufacturing and service industries. Westell's first step in custom designing marketing research for any of her clients is to listen hard to what they're saying.

"Clients ask us to design research to help them tackle a wide range of problems: They may have a new concept they're considering for product development or a new product they'd like tried and evaluated in the home; they may have an ad they want to know the reaction to; sometimes they want to segment their market. Whatever the problem, my first job is to listen and try to figure out their specific objectives."

Once Westell feels she has a handle on the issue to be tackled, she can begin to recommend an approach. "In terms of data collection," she reports, "all studies fall into one of two categories—qualitative or quantitative. The difference is in the number of people you survey and the amount of detail you specify in the questioning sequence. Qualitative research is more seeking—we might improvise or change the study as we go along. With quantitative research you detail the questions in advance."

Data collection for qualitative studies usually takes one of several forms—most often a series of one-on-one in-depth interviews lasting from 30 minutes to an hour, or a two-hour focus-group discussion with a moderator. Sometimes Westell recommends the use of mini-groups—smaller versions of the traditional focus group. "Mini-groups are good if you want to give the respondents more time to speak—if your interview group consists of doctors or lawyers, for example, or if it's a group where you feel there might be too much disagreement if they congregate in a larger group. With children, we use even smaller groups, mostly pairs or triads."

Westell says that in specialized circumstances, most often when the decision whether or not to buy a client's product or use its service is made by a group, she sets up a team interview. "A good example would be a company that sells computer systems. No single person is going to make the decision whether their company is going to buy a particular system—the decision process is going to be shared by a committee. In a team interview, a team from the client company and a team from the respondent company, for example, people from sales, research and development, marketing, and production, *all* sit down in a room with a moderator." For some studies, observation replaces or augments direct questioning. "There are firms that watch people shop," reports Westell, "but we often record our observations of respondents, especially when we're dealing with someone trying a product.

Quantitative research tends to involve some form of set questionnaire and a much larger group of respondents. "With a quantitative study," says Westell, "the first thing you have to consider is who you're going to try to talk to and how available and cooperative they are. Then you have to think about how you want to approach them. Do you need to talk to them in person? Do you need to mail them something? How much data do you have to collect? The general rule is that 20 minutes is the limit in terms of interest and courtesy for a telephone interview. Do you need to expose them to something? Have them taste something? Can you mail it to them and then get their response, or would you prefer that they not have an unlimited amount of time to decide whether or not they like it?"

According to Westell, for any given problem there may be a number of data-collection options. One of the most important parts of her job is to work with the client to find the best one to fit all of the parameters of the problem. I can always design the optimal study from a research viewpoint, but if the client can't afford it, he's not going to do it."

Westell works in Burke Marketing Research's Chicago office, one of the firm's ten regional sales offices. "Burke is a very decentralized company," she explains. "That way we stay close to our clients. Our corporate headquarters are in Cincinnati.

"I love my job," she says. "My territory covers Illinois, Wisconsin, Minnesota, and Indiana. Between traveling to clients and spending time at the Cincinnati headquarters, I'm on the road almost three days a week. My job is 50-percent sales and 50-percent research consulting. I find the mix of sales and research very exciting. My job performance is evaluated on sales, but you can't sell research if you can't design it!"

7

*Chapter
Seven*

Secondary Data

Learning Objectives

Upon completing this chapter, you should be able to

1. Explain the difference between primary and secondary data.

2. Cite two advantages offered by secondary data.

3. Specify two problems common to secondary data.

4. List the three criteria researchers should use in judging the accuracy of secondary data.

5. State the most fundamental rule in using secondary data.

6. Explain the difference between internal and external data.

7. List some of the key sources researchers should consider in conducting a search process.

8. Describe the roles of the data-base producer, data-base vendor, and data user in the operations of on-line computer search services.

Case in Marketing Research

No one was more surprised than Bud Hendricks by the avalanche of criticism that news of Tyro Computer Company's new product had caused. As Tyro's new director of marketing, Hendricks had hoped to generate a lot of interest in the company's new offering. The product—called Markets!—was a software package designed to be used by small and medium-size businesses that wanted to do inexpensive, targeted mass mailings.

Available for use in all the major personal computing formats and to be sold for under $1,000, Markets! would list the names, addresses, shopping habits, and likely income levels of more than 80 million U.S. households. It would also provide profiles of the households, showing ages and incomes by ranges and placing each household in one of 50 "psychographic" categories. These groupings were created by blending data on individuals with census data (by cross matching block census data with individual addresses through the ZIP+4 postal-service listings, which carve Zip Codes into areas as small as individual streets). The 50 categories ranged from "accumulated wealth" through "cautious young couples" to "inner-city singles."

Hendricks had been excited about the prospect of such a hot new product. The trouble was, he had had no idea of just how "hot" Markets! was going to be. Now he and the Markets! team had been summoned by Jonathan Karling, Tyro's CEO, to be raked over the coals.

"The problem," said Karling, "is that while we saw no reason to keep our plans for Markets! a secret, no one expected this level of controversy. And with the product launch six months away, we have to decide how to handle the issues that have been raised—some of which call into question whether we should even continue with our plans to put the software on the market."

"It's that bad?" asked Amy Griffith, from new product development.

"Let's put it this way," replied Karling. "An attorney for the ACLU has been widely quoted as saying that a product like Markets! will cause people to lose control of how, and by whom, personal information is being used. He says sales of the program raise serious legal and ethical questions."

"What's that supposed to mean?" snapped someone from sales. "Markets! is just the logical extension of the information explosion that computers have made possible. The truth is that anytime anybody in this country takes part in a commercial transaction, the chances are that the information will be recorded and sold to others. Most people don't even think about it. Markets! isn't creating new information. It's just using new technology to make the information that already exists available to more people at a cheaper price."

"That's exactly what's got everybody up in arms," replied Hendricks. "All of the critics so far have acknowledged that Markets! doesn't offer much more than what is already available from established mailing-list brokers—"

"You'd think they'd be the ones screaming," quipped Griffith.

"But the problem is that we're going to make this stuff so much more widely available. The big consumer data bases rent tailored mailing lists to retailers for one-time use. The information we're selling is permanent. Also, the critics are saying that the way Markets! is designed—to allow users to ask a series of increasingly specific questions—makes it easy to abuse."

"I don't get it. That's what makes it easy to use," said Griffith.

"To use *and* abuse," replied Hendricks. "If you're planning on marketing gourmet dog treats to upscale consumers, Markets! is a godsend. It lets you target dog owners of a certain income who fit your profile of potential dog-treat buyers. But, if you're a con man who preys on lonely older women, Markets! lets you pinpoint the unmarried wealthy women over age 65 in any given neighborhood."

"What a mess," groaned Griffith.

"It sure is a mess," growled Karling. "And not one of us is going to leave this room until we've figured out how to get it cleaned up."

Discussion Issues

1. Suppose that you are part of the Markets! team. Which of the issues raised by the critics do you think the company should address? Which issues do you consider to be unavoidable?
2. Are there any safeguards that could be built into the product, or into the way it will be sold, that would address the privacy concerns?
3. What about the concern that the data are being sold versus being rented? Is that a meaningful distinction?

Secondary data
Information not gathered for the immediate study at hand but for some other purpose.

Primary data
Information collected specifically for the purpose of the investigation at hand.

Once the research problem is defined and clearly specified, the research effort logically turns to data collection. The natural temptation among beginning researchers is to advocate some sort of survey among appropriate respondent groups. This should be a last, rather than a first, resort. "A good operating rule is to consider a survey akin to surgery—to be used only after other possibilities have been exhausted."[1] First attempts at data collection should logically focus on **secondary data,** which are statistics not gathered for the immediate study at hand but previously gathered for some other purpose. Information originated by the researcher for the purpose of the investigation at hand is called **primary data.** The purpose therefore defines the distinction.

If General Electric conducted a survey on the demographic characteristics of refrigerator purchasers to determine who buys the various sizes of refrigerators, this would be primary data. If, instead, the company used its existing files and compiled the same data from warranty cards its customers had returned, or if it used already-published industry statistics on refrigerator buyers, the information would be considered secondary data.

Beginning researchers are apt to underestimate the amount of secondary data available. Table 7.1, for example, lists some of the information on people and households that has already been collected by the U.S. Government Census and is readily available for use by researchers. It is important for researchers to know what is available in secondary sources, not just to avoid "reinventing the wheel," but because secondary data possess some significant advantages over primary data. Further, because of the recent "information explosion," such an oversight will have even greater consequences in the future.

Advantages of Secondary Data

The most significant advantages of secondary data are the time and money they save the researcher. If the information being sought is available as secondary data, the researcher need simply go to the library, locate the appropriate source or sources, and extract and record the information desired. This should take no more than a few days and involve little cost. If instead the information were to be collected in a sample survey, the following steps would have to be taken: data-collection form designed and pretested; field interviewing staff selected and trained; sampling plan devised; data gathered and then checked for accuracy and omissions; data coded and tabulated. As a conservative estimate, this process would take two to three months and could cost several thousand dollars, since it would include expenses and wages for a number of additional field and office personnel. For fledgling businesses, cost savings are especially critical. Not only is secondary data useful as a way of conducting a preliminary assessment of the marketplace, but as Walter Kearns, director of Arthur D. Little Enterprises, so delicately put it, " 'Entrepreneur' generally translates as 'poor' "[2] If you're launching the next Apple Computer Corporation in your garage, secondary data may be the only data you can afford!

With secondary data, the expenses incurred in collecting the data have already been paid by the original compiler of the information. Even if there is a charge for using the data (unlike statistics compiled by government or trade associations, commercial data are not free), the cost is still substantially less than if the firm collected the information itself.

Given the substantial amount of time and money at stake, we offer this advice: *Do not bypass secondary data.* Begin with secondary data, and only when the secondary data are exhausted or show diminishing returns, proceed to primary data. Sometimes the

Table 7.1 *Information Items Available from the 1990 Census of Population*

Population	Housing
100-Percent Component	
Household relationship	Number of units in structure
Sex	Number of rooms in unit
Race	Tenure—owned or rented
Age	Vacancy characteristics
Marital status	Value of owned unit or rent paid
Hispanic origin	
Sample Component	
Education—enrollment and attainment	Source of water and method of sewage
Place of birth, citizenship, and year of	disposal
entry	Autos, light trucks, and vans
Ancestry	Kitchen facilities
Language spoken at home	Year structure built
Migration	Year moved into residence
Disability	Number of bedrooms
Fertility	Farm residence
Veteran status	Shelter costs, including utilities
Employment and unemployment	Condominium status
Occupation, industry, and class of	Plumbing
worker	Telephone
Place of work and commuting to work	Utilities and fuels
Work experience and income in 1989	

Note: Subjects covered in the 100-percent component will apply to all persons and housing units. Those covered by the sample component will apply to a portion of the population and housing units.
Source: "OMB and Census Agree on Decennial Questionnaires, Sample Size," *Census and You*, 23 (April–May 1988), p. 3.

secondary data are sufficient, especially when all the analyst needs is a ballpark estimate, which is often the case. For example, a common question that confronts marketing research analysts is, what is the market potential for the product or service? Are there enough people or organizations interested in it to justify providing it?

Entrepreneur George Campos, for example, thought there might be enough of a market to start a darkroom rental business. To validate his instinct, he bought a copy of *The Wolfman Report*, a national survey of the photographic industry, for $75. He also consulted local market surveys published by various photography magazines. By the time he was ready to approach potential financial backers for his business, Campos had amassed a convincing body of research to support his idea. Campos now has two photography centers in operation, and a third in the works.[3]

Table 7.2 illustrates how secondary data were used to advantage by a manufacturer of pet foods to assess the potential demand for a dog food that included both moist chunks and hard, dry chunks. As the example indicates, when using secondary data, it is often necessary to make some assumptions in order to use the data effectively (e.g., the number of owners who were good prospects). The key is to make reasonable assumptions and then to vary these assumptions to determine how sensitive a particular conclusion is to variations in them. In the dog food example, "altering the assumption regarding the number of owners who were good prospects for the new product to include as few as one-tenth of the original number did not alter

Table 7.2   *Use of Secondary Data by a Manufacturer of Pet Foods to Assess the Potential Demand for a Dog Food That Included Both Moist Chunks and Hard, Dry Chunks*

The question was, "Is there currently a significant number of persons who mix moist or canned dog food with dry dog food?" At this early stage in the exploration of this product concept, the firm did not want to expend funds for primary research. While an actual survey of pet owners would have yielded the best answer, such a survey would have required the expenditure of several thousand dollars. In addition, further development of the idea would have required a delay of several weeks to obtain the survey results. An effort to develop an acceptable first answer to the question of demand using secondary sources was initiated.

The firm identified the following information:

1. From published literature on veterinary medicine, the firm identified the amount (in ounces) of food required to feed a dog each day by type of food (dry, semimoist, moist), age, size, and type of dog.
2. From an existing survey conducted annually by the firm's advertising agency the firm obtained information on

(a) the percentage of U.S. households owning dogs;
(b) the number, sizes, and types of dogs owned by each household in the survey;
(c) the type(s) of dog food fed to the dogs; and
(d) the frequency of use of various types of dog food.

It was assumed that dog owners who reported feeding their dogs two or more different types of dog food each day were good prospects for a product that provided premixed moist and dry food. Combining the information in the survey with the information from the literature on veterinary medicine and doing some simple multiplication produced a demand figure for the product concept. The demand exceeded 20 percent of the total volume of dog food sales, a figure sufficiently large to justify proceeding with product development and testing.

Source: David W. Stewart, *Secondary Research: Information Sources and Methods* (Beverly Hills, Calif.: Sage Publications, 1984), p. 112.

the decision to proceed with the product. Under such circumstances, the value of additional information would be quite small."[4]

While it is rare that secondary data completely solve the particular problem under study, they usually will (1) help the investigator to better state the problem under investigation, (2) suggest improved methods or further data that should be collected, and/or (3) provide comparative data by which primary data can be more insightfully interpreted.

Disadvantages of Secondary Data

Two problems that commonly arise with secondary data are (1) they do not completely fit the problem, and (2) they are not totally accurate.

Problems of Fit

Since secondary data are collected for other purposes, it is rare when they perfectly fit the problem as defined. In some cases, the fit will be so poor as to render them completely inappropriate. Usually the poor fit is due to unsuitable (1) units of measurement, (2) class definitions, or (3) publication currency.

The size of a retail store, for instance, can be expressed in terms of gross sales, profits, square feet, and number of employees. Consumer income can be expressed by individual, family, household, and spending unit. So it is with many variables, and a recurring source of frustration in using secondary data is that the source containing the basic information desired presents that information in units of measurement different from that needed.

Assuming the units are consistent, we find that the class boundaries presented are often different from those needed. If the problem demands income by individual in increments of $5,000 (0–$4,999, $5,000–$9,999, and so on), it does the researcher little good if the data source offers income by individual using boundaries $7,500 apart (0–$7,499, $7,500–$14,999, and so on).

Finally, secondary data are often out of date. The time from data collection to data publication may be long. Government Census data, for example, take three years to get into print. Although Census data have great value while current, this value diminishes rapidly with time. Most marketing decisions require current, rather than historical, information.

Problems of Accuracy

The accuracy of much secondary data is also questionable. As this book should indicate, there are a number of sources of error possible in the collection, analysis, and presentation of marketing information. When a researcher is collecting primary data, firsthand experience helps in judging the accuracy of the information being collected. But when using secondary data, the researcher's task in assessing accuracy is more difficult.[5] It may help in this task to consider the primacy of the source, the purpose of publication, and the general quality of the data-collection methods and presentation.[6]

Primary source The originating source of secondary data.

Secondary source A source of secondary data that did not originate the data but rather secured them from another source.

Primacy of Source   Consider the source first. Secondary data can be secured from either a primary source or a secondary source. A **primary source** is the source that originated the data. A **secondary source** is a source that in turn secured the data from a primary source. The *Statistical Abstract of the United States*, for example, which is published each year and contains a great deal of useful information for many research projects, is a secondary source of secondary data: All of its data are taken from other government and trade sources. The researcher who *terminated* a search for secondary data with the *Statistical Abstract* would violate the most fundamental rule in using secondary data—*always use the primary source of secondary data.*

There are two main reasons for this rule. First and foremost, the researcher will need to search for general evidence of quality (e.g., the methods of data collection and analysis). The primary source will typically be the only source that describes the process of collection and analysis, and thus it is the only source by which this judgment can be made. Second, a primary source is usually more accurate and complete than a secondary source. Secondary sources often fail "to reproduce significant footnotes, or textual comments, by which the primary source had qualified the data or the definition of units."[7] Errors in transcription can also occur in copying the data from a primary source. Once made, transcription errors seem to hold on tenaciously, as the following example illustrates.

In 1901 Napoleon Lajoie produced the highest batting average ever attained in the American League when he batted .422 on 229 hits in 543 times at bat. In setting the type for the record book after that season, a printer correctly reported Lajoie's .422 average, but incorrectly reported his hits, giving him 220 instead of 229. A short time later, someone pointed out that 220 hits in 543 at-bats yields a batting average of .405, and so Lajoie's reported average was changed. The error persisted for some fifty years, until an energetic fan checked all the old box scores and discovered the facts.[8]

Purpose of Publication   A second criterion by which the accuracy of secondary data can be assessed is the purpose of publication. Suppose you encountered the following news item when making plans for an upcoming trip: "Airline passengers

When a new location for a General Nutrition Center store is being considered, franchisees use demographic and mall-traffic information to make their decision.

Source: Courtesy of General Nutrition Franchising, Inc.

who fly Northwest appear to have a lot to complain about—and they did so in droves last year. . . . Complaints against Northwest increased 1,418 percent in the past year." Faced with such information, how likely is it that you would make Northwest your carrier of choice? Would it make any difference if you were told that the news item resulted from press releases prepared by the Tobacco Institute, which was upset over Northwest Airlines' announced ban on smoking on all of its North American flights?[9] Alternatively, given the information in Research Window 7.1, how do you feel about fiberglass insulation in your home? Do you feel any differently after learning that Mr. Munson sells a competitive type of insulation? The examples illustrate the insights that can be gained by using the purpose as a criterion for evaluating the accuracy of secondary data.

> Sources published to promote sales, to advance the interests of an industrial or commercial or other group, to present the cause of a political party, or to carry on any sort of propaganda, are suspect. Data published anonymously, or by an organization which is on the defensive, or under conditions which suggest a controversy, or in a form which reveals a strained attempt at "frankness," or to controvert inferences from other data, are generally suspect.[10]

This is not to say that such data cannot be used by the researcher. A person may still wish to fly with Northwest or to insulate a home with fiberglass. Rather, it is simply to suggest that such data should be viewed most critically. A source that has no ax to grind but, rather, publishes secondary data as its primary function deserves confidence. If a source's business is to publish data, high quality must be maintained. Such a firm would gain no competitive advantage by publishing inaccurate data.

Research Window 7.1
Using the Source to Evaluate the Accuracy of Secondary Data

As if asbestos weren't scary enough, now we hear that fiberglass insulation, installed in millions of homes, may pose a cancer threat, too.

One reason we hear this is that Richard W. Munson keeps saying it. Running a group he founded called Victims of Fiberglass, Munson writes letters by the hundreds to labor unions, manufacturers, consumer advocates, and government officials, telling of the perils the material holds for America's health. He travels and gives speeches about it. Quick with a quote, he appears on TV news programs as an expert on fiberglass's dangers.

Some of the things Munson has done include the following:

1. Sending letters to every resident in Licking County, Ohio, 16,700 letters in all, warning them that there was a "death dust cloud" above the community. He did so after learning that the area had an unusually high rate of death from lung cancer. He blamed the deaths on fiber emissions from Owens-Corning Fiberglass Corporation's oldest and largest fiberglass plant, which is located there.

2. Telling the Environmental Protection Agency that fiberglass insulation gives off dangerous levels of hydrogen cyanide when it catches fire and that "the fiberglass industry stands accused of having turned every home in America into a gas chamber."

3. Suggesting to reporters that a former Owens-Corning pollution-control officer has damaging information on fiberglass, while the man expresses annoyance at calls from the press, suggests he can provide no such thing, and has never even met Munson, a claim with which Munson agrees.

Would it make any difference in your reaction to this information if you were told Munson sells a competing type of insulation, wood-based cellulose?

Source: Rick Wartzman, "A Foe of Fiberglass Tells All Who Listen It's Dangerous Stuff," *The Wall Street Journal* (February 26, 1988), pp. 1 and 6.

Indeed, the success of any organization whose primary function is to supply data depends on its reputation for accuracy and its customers' satisfaction to ensure that it stays in business.

General Evidence of Quality   The third criterion by which the accuracy of secondary data can be assessed is through the general evidence of quality. One way of determining this quality is to evaluate the ability of the supplying organization to collect the data. The Internal Revenue Service, for example, has greater leverage in securing income data than an independent marketing research firm. However, researchers also have to weigh whether this additional leverage may introduce bias. Would a respondent be more likely to hedge in estimating his income in completing his tax return or in responding to a consumer survey?

In judging the quality of secondary data, a user also needs to understand how the data were collected. A primary source should provide a detailed description of the data-collection process, including definitions, data-collection forms, method of sampling, and so forth. If it does not, researcher beware! Such omissions are usually indicative of sloppy methods.

When the details of data collection are provided, the user of secondary data should examine them thoroughly. Was the sampling plan sound? Was this type of data best collected through questionnaire or by observational methods? What about the quality of the field force? What kind of training was provided? What kinds of checks of the fieldwork were employed? What was the extent of nonresponse, due to refusals, not at homes, and by item? Are these statistics reported? Is the information presented in a well-organized manner? Are the tables properly labeled, and are the data within them internally consistent? Are the conclusions supported by the data? As these questions suggest, the user of secondary data must be familiar with the research process and the potential sources of error. The remainder of this book should provide much of the needed insight for evaluating secondary data. For the moment, though, let us examine some of the main types of secondary data.

Ethical
Dilemma 7.1   An independent marketing research firm was hired by a manufacturer of power equipment, including lawn mowers, snowblowers, and chain saws, to study the Minneapolis market. The manufacturer wanted to determine (1) whether there was sufficient market potential to warrant opening a new dealership, and (2) if so, where the dealership should be located in the metropolitan area. The research firm went about the task by scouring secondary data on the Minneapolis market, particularly statistics published by the Census Bureau. In less than two months, the research firm was able to develop a well-documented recommendation as to what the power equipment manufacturer should do.

Approximately six months after completing this study, the research firm has been approached by a manufacturer of electric power tools to do a similar study concerning the location of a distribution center through which it could more effectively serve the many hardware stores in the area.

- Is it ethical for the research firm to use the information it collected in the first study to reduce its cost quote to the client in the second?
- Does it make any difference if the firm making electric power tools also manufactures electric lawn mowers and chain saws?
- Suppose some of the data were collected through personal interviews that the first client paid for. Should that affect the situation in any way?

Types of Secondary Data: Internal and External

The most common way of classifying data is by source, whether internal or external. **Internal data** are those found within the organization for whom the research is being done, while **external data** are those obtained from outside sources. The external sources can be further split into those that regularly publish statistics and make them available to the user at no charge (e.g., the U.S. government), and those commercial organizations that sell their services to various users (e.g., the A. C. Nielsen Company). In the remainder of this chapter and its appendix we will review some of the main types and sources of published statistics, while in the next chapter we will review some of the more important sources of commercial statistics. Together they represent some of the most commonly used sources of secondary data, the ones with which the researcher would typically begin a search.

Internal data Data that originate within the organization for which the research is being done.

External data Data that originate outside the organization for which the research is being done.

Internal Secondary Data

Internal data that were collected for some purpose other than the study at hand are *internal secondary data*. For example, the sales and cost data compiled in the normal accounting cycle represent promising internal secondary data for many research problems—such as evaluation of past marketing strategy or assessment of the firm's competitive position in the industry. Such data are less helpful in guiding future-oriented decisions, such as evaluating a new product or a new advertising campaign, but even here they can serve as a foundation for planning other research.

Generally, the one most productive source document is the sales invoice. From this, the following information can usually be extracted:

- Customer name and location
- Product(s) or service(s) sold
- Volume and dollar amount of the transaction
- Salesperson (or agent) responsible for the sale
- End use of the product sold
- Location of customer facility where product is to be shipped and/or used
- Customer's industry, class of trade, and/or channel of distribution
- Terms of sale and applicable discount
- Freight paid and/or to be collected
- Shipment point for the order
- Transportation used in shipment

Other documents provide more specialized input. Some of the more important of these are listed in Table 7.3. Most companies are likely to use only two or three of these sources of sales information in addition to the sales invoice. The particular ones used depend on the company and the types of analyses used to plan and evaluate the marketing effort. Even something as simple as a product registration card can be used to advantage for marketing intelligence, as Research Window 7.2 indicates.

Another useful, but often overlooked, source of internal secondary data is prior marketing research studies on related topics. While each study typically addresses a number of specific questions, most also involve only one or two key learnings. There can be great synergy when these key learnings are studied and combined. As Larry Stanek, the director of marketing research at Kraft, comments:

> Combining key learnings can help you develop a competitive advantage for your company. By examining your combined learnings you may discover things that other companies have yet to learn. Or you can learn to be more productive or cost effective and lower your research costs. Or you may learn something that helps you skip steps or speeds your development process. . . .[11]

Internal secondary data are the least costly (and most readily available) of any type of marketing research. If maintained in an appropriate form, internal sales data can be used to analyze the company's past sales performance by product, geographic location, customer, channel of distribution, and so on, while cost data help in determining how profitable these segments of the business are. This type of information typically forms the basis of a firm's marketing intelligence system. We shall not go into the details of this type of analysis here because it is a somewhat specialized topic and is extensively reported elsewhere.[12] Most studies should begin with internal secondary data.

Searching for Published External Secondary Data

There is such a wealth of published external data that beginning researchers typically underestimate what is available. The statement that there is *some relevant* external secondary data on almost any problem a marketer might confront is not an

Table 7.3   **Some Useful Sources of Internal Secondary Data**

Document	Information Provided
Cash register receipts	Type (cash or credit) and dollar amount of transaction by department by salesperson
Salespeople's call reports	Customers and prospects called on (company and individual seen; planned or unplanned calls) Products discussed Orders obtained Customers' product needs and usage Other significant information about customers Distribution of salespeople's time among customer calls, travel, and office work Sales-related activities: meetings, conventions, etc.
Salespeople's expense accounts	Expenses by day by item (hotel, meals, travel, etc.)
Individual customer (and prospect) records	Name and location and customer number Number of calls by company salespeople (agents) Sales by company (in dollars and/or units, by product or service, by location of customer facility) Customer's industry, class of trade, and/or trade channel Estimated total annual usage of each product or service sold by the company Estimated annual purchases from the company of each such product or service Location (in terms of company sales territory)
Financial records	Sales revenue (by products, geographic markets, customers, class of trade, unit of sales organization, etc.) Direct sales expenses (similarly classified) Overhead sales costs (similarly classified) Profits (similarly classified)
Credit memos	Returns and allowances
Warranty cards	Indirect measures of dealer sales Customer service

exaggeration. The fundamental problem is not availability; it is identifying and accessing what is there. Even those researchers who do have an inkling of how much valuable secondary data there is are typically unsure of how to go about searching for it. Figure 7.1 provides some general guidelines that can be used to get started on a search of secondary data on a particular topic.[13]

Step 1   The first step in the process is to identify what you wish to know and what you already know about your topic. This may include relevant facts, names of researchers or organizations associated with the topic, key papers and other publications with which you are already familiar, and any other information you may have.

Step 2   A useful second step is to develop a list of key terms and authors. These terms and names will provide access to secondary sources. Unless you have a very specific topic of interest, it is better to keep this initial list long and quite general.

Research Window 7.2
Targeting: It's in the Cards

When the Skil Corporation was launching a cordless power screwdriver, management was worried. It believed that the company had designed a useful product, but it wondered whether consumers would think the new tool was just a gimmick. Using information from product registration cards and follow-up interviews, Skil was quickly able to prove to itself that the screwdriver was not a fad.

The registration card research revealed something else, however. Although do-it-yourselfers were the primary market for the new product, a substantial portion of the purchasers were elderly people for whom the screwdriver's ease of operation was the chief advantage. "We hadn't realized the arthritis implications," says Skil's Ron Techter. In response, Skil began advertising in publications geared to older Americans.

Almost everyone has filled out a product registration card. As they slip the card into the mailbox, few consumers realize that they have just completed a questionnaire. Yet for National Demographics & Lifestyles (NDL), the information from product registration cards has been pure gold. NDL compiles information from these "mini-questionnaires" to feed its comprehensive data base, which includes demographics and participation information covering 57 activities, interests, and lifestyles.

According to Jock Bickert, the company's founder, NDL data offer no special advantage at a national level, because a marketer can survey 1,500 or 2,000 consumers to obtain national projections. However, NDL's data base is very powerful when one moves down to individual markets, neighborhoods, or even postal routes.

One company that has made effective use of NDL's data ia Amana Appliance. One day Bill Packard, domestic sales manager for an independent Amana Appliance distributor in Fort Lauderdale was talking with Amana's manager of marketing services, Dave Collins. Collins mentioned that Amana could provide Packard with profiles of Amana purchasers from his territory for the past year and a half based on NDL product-registration cards. When the NDL profile arrived, Packard got an idea.

He took the information to the marketing director of a Boca Raton real estate developer who was trying to decide what brand of appliances to put into his $200,000 homes. Packard pointed out that the purchaser profile of high-end Amana products perfectly matched the developer's profile of potential customers. Initially skeptical, the marketing director polled 100 potential home buyers himself. These home-buyer profiles so closely matched Amana's that the developer decided to use Amana appliances in the kitchens.

"If you look at one of our completed questionnaires," says NDL's Bickert, "you really begin to get a picture of the individual. You are able to say, 'This person is a likely candidate for these kinds of offers and promotions and appeals and is very unlikely for other kinds.' You can't do that if you are looking at demography alone."

Source: Wally Wood, "Targeting: It's In the Cards," *Marketing & Media Decisions*, 23 (September 1988), pp. 121–122.

Step 3   In Step 3, you are ready to use the library for the first time. It is useful to begin your search with several of the directories and guides listed in Appendix 7A.

Step 4   Now it is time to compile the literature you have found. Is it relevant to your needs? Perhaps you are overwhelmed by information. Perhaps you have found little that is relevant. If so, rework your list of key words and authors and expand your search to include a few more years and a few additional sources. Once again evaluate your findings. By the end of Step 4, you should have a clear idea of the nature of the information you are seeking and sufficient background to use more specialized sources.

Figure 7.1   ***How to Get Started When Searching Published Sources of Secondary Data***

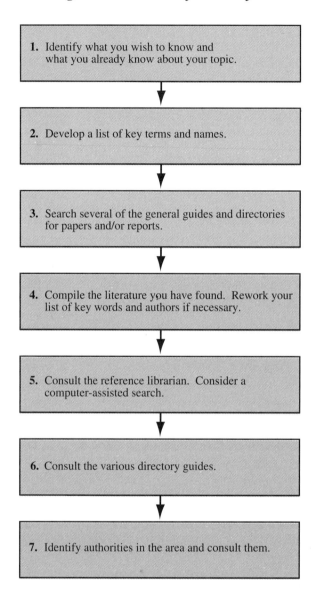

1. Identify what you wish to know and what you already know about your topic.

2. Develop a list of key terms and names.

3. Search several of the general guides and directories for papers and/or reports.

4. Compile the literature you have found. Rework your list of key words and authors if necessary.

5. Consult the reference librarian. Consider a computer-assisted search.

6. Consult the various directory guides.

7. Identify authorities in the area and consult them.

Step 5   One very useful specialized source is a reference librarian. Reference librarians are specialists who have been trained to know the contents of many of the key information sources in a library, as well as how to search those sources most effectively. It is a rare problem indeed for which a reference librarian cannot uncover some relevant published information. The reference librarian can help you if you wish to consider a computer-assisted information search. The librarian will need your help, though, in the form of a carefully constructed list of key words. Some librarians will prefer to produce their own lists of key words or descriptors, but it is a good idea to verify that such a list is reasonably complete. The librarian may be able to suggest specialized sources related to the topic. You need to remember that the reference librarian cannot be of much help until you can provide some rather specific details about what you want to know.

Step 6   If you have had little success or your topic is highly specialized, consult one of the general guides to information listed in Appendix 7A. These are really directories of directories, which means that this level of search will be very general. You will first need to identify potentially useful primary directories, which will then lead you to other sources.

Step 7   If you are unhappy with what you have found or are otherwise having trouble, and the reference librarian has not been able to identify sources, use an authority. Identify some individual or organization that might know something about the topic. The various *Who's Who* publications, *Consultants and Consulting Organizations Directory*, *Encyclopedia of Associations*, *Industrial Research Laboratories in the United States*, or *Research Centers Directory* may help you identify sources. The Bureau of the Census puts out a list of department specialists who users can contact for information on any of the bureau's studies. These people are often quite knowledgeable about related studies in their areas of expertise. Faculty at universities, government officials, and business executives can also be useful sources of information.

Some Key General Sources of External Secondary Data

In addition to the key role played by reference librarians, some other particularly important sources of external secondary data are associations, general guides to useful marketing information, and on-line computer searches.

Associations   Most associations gather and often publish detailed information on such things as industry shipments and sales, growth patterns, environmental factors affecting the industry, operating characteristics, and the like. Trade associations are often able to secure information from members that other research organizations cannot, because of the working relationships that exist between the association and the firms that belong to it. Two useful sources for locating associations serving a particular industry are the *Directory of Directories* and the *Encyclopedia of Associations*, described in Appendix 7A.

General Guides to Secondary Data   Other useful sources for locating information on a particular topic are the general guides to secondary data described in Appendix 7A. Table 7.4, for example, lists what the *Encyclopedia of Business Information Sources* has to say about data sources on the electric appliance industry. Aspiring researchers are also well advised to acquaint themselves with the more general sources of marketing information so that they know what statistics are available and where they can be found. Many of the most important of these are listed and briefly described in Appendix 7A.

On-Line Computer Searches

On-line computer searches have become increasingly popular for locating published information and data in the last 20 years, as computer-readable storage systems for data bases have come into their own. Many public libraries, as well as college and university libraries, have invested in the equipment and personnel that are

Table 7.4   **Sources of Data on the Electric Appliance Industry**

General Works

The Last Hundred Years: Household Technology. Daniel Cohen. M. Evans and Co., 216 E. 49th St., New York, NY 10017. (212) 688–2810. 1982. $8.95.

Modern Household Equipment. Ruth E. Brasher and Carolyn L. Garrison. Macmillan Publishing Co., 866 Third Ave., New York, NY 10022. (800) 257-5755 or (212) 702-2000. 1982. Price on application.

Directories

Appliance Manufacturer—Annual Directory Issue. Corcoran Communications, Inc., 6200 S.O.M. Center Rd., Solon, OH 44139. (216) 349-3060. Annual. $10.00.

Appliance—Purchasing Directory Issue. Dana Chase Publications, 1000 Jorie Blvd., Oakbrook, IL 60521. (708) 990-3484. Annual. $30.00.

Directory of Consumer Electronics, Photography & Major Appliance Retailers & Distributors. Chain Store Guide Information Services, Lebhar-Friedman, Inc., 425 Park Ave., New York, NY 10022. (212) 371-9400. Annual. $189.00. Firms with a minimum of $500,000 in annual sales. Generally includes product lines, sales volume, year founded, key personnel, and related information.

Financial Ratios

Cost of Doing Business Survey. National Association of Retail Dealers of America, Two N. Riverside Plaza, Chicago, IL 60606. Annual. Members, $10.00; nonmembers, $25.00.

Expenses in Retail Business. NCR Corporate Education—Learning Systems, Dayton, OH 45479. Annual. $1.25.

On-Line Data Bases

Trinet Databases. Trinet, Inc., 9 Campus Dr., Parsippany, NJ 07054. (800) 874-6381 or (201) 267-3000. Current data on nonmanufacturers and manufacturers in the business sector. Updated several times a year. Inquire as to on-line cost and availability.

Periodicals and Newsletters

Appliance. Dana Chase Publications, 1000 Jorie Blvd., Oakbrook, IL 60521. (708) 990-3484. Monthly. $60.00 per year.

Appliance Manufacturer. Corcoran Communications, Inc., 6200 S.O.M. Center Rd., Solon, OH 44139. (216) 349-3060. Monthly. $45.00 per year.

Appliance Service News. Gamit Enterprises, Inc., 110 W. Saint Charles Rd., Box 789, Lombard, IL 60148. (708) 932-9550. Monthly. $9.25.

NARDA News. National Association of Retail Dealers of America, Two N. Riverside Plaza, Chicago, IL 60606. (312) 454-0944. Monthly. $12.00

Product Design and Development. Chilton Book Co., Chilton Way, Radnor, PA 19089. (800) 345-1214 or (215) 964-4000. Monthly. $35.00 per year.

Statistics Sources

Major Household Appliances. U.S. Bureau of the Census, Washington, DC 20233. (202) 783-3238. Annual.

Merchandising. Billboard Publications, Inc., One Astor Plaza, New York, NY 10036. Monthly. $30.00 per year.

Trade Associations and Professional Societies

Appliance Parts Distributors Association, 228 E. Baltimore St., Detroit, MI 48202. (313) 875-8455.

Association of Home Appliance Manufacturers, 20 N. Wacker Dr., Chicago, IL 60606. (312) 984-5800.

National Appliance Service Association, 1308 Pennsylvania St., Kansas City, MO 64105. (816) 221-1808.

National Association of Retail Dealers of America, 10 E. 22nd St., Lombard, IL 60148. (708) 953-8950.

Other Sources

Value Line Investment Survey. Value Line, Inc., 711 Third Ave., New York, NY 10017. (212) 687-3965. Weekly. $425.00 per year. Published in three parts: (I) Summary & Index, (II) Selection & Opinion, (III) Ratings & Reports. Part III contains analyses of specific industries.

Source: James Woy, ed., *Encyclopedia of Business Information Sources* (Detroit: Gale Research, Inc., 1988), p. 325.

necessary to make data-base searching available to their patrons. Currently, there are more than 3,000 data bases to pick from, with 200 to 300 of them applying to business.

The operation of the on-line services is as follows: There are a data-base producer, a data-base vendor, and a data user. The data-base producer collects the information and edits it according to its own criteria. The producer then puts it on tape or compact disk and sells it to the vendor for a fee. The vendor mounts the tape or disk on a computer. The vendor might combine or split the information to fit his or her own needs. Thus, the same data base from different vendors might have different structures. The vendor also pays a fee every time the data base is used and pays a fee for all citations from it.

The user pays when accessing the data base, whether he or she gets the answer or not. The more information one gets, the more one pays. The user also pays for the use of the telephone lines, connect charges, and printing charges. Printing charges vary as a function of how much is printed and whether the printing occurs on-line or off-line at a more convenient time, in which case the output is mailed to the user. In sum, the costs of using a data base include: (1) planning and executing the search, (2) telephone-line charges, (3) connect charges, and (4) citation and printing charges. The big advantage of on-line searching is time savings. Some of the more well-known data-base vendors are BRS, Compuserve, Data-Star, Dialog, Easynet, Mead Data Central, Orbit, The Source, and Vu/Text.

Data bases are typically defined by the type of information they contain. For example, bibliographic data bases provide references to magazine or journal articles. They will list the name of the article, the author, the title of the journal, and the date of publication. They are also likely to include some key words that describe the contents of the article. Most bibliographic data bases also provide an abstract or summary of the article. Some of the useful data bases for marketers are those that contain the following:

- *Specific company or industry information*—The information in these data bases comes primarily from reports filed with the Securities and Exchange Commission, stockholder reports, and stock market information. The data bases cover financial, marketing, and product information, some company profiles, and the usual directory information, such as name of an organization, its address, and its phone number. Typical examples are *Moody's Corporate Profiles* and *Standard and Poor's Corporate Descriptions.*

- *Mergers, affiliations, ownership information*—These data bases typically list the institutions and people that own a stock by name, and the ownership changes, including the mergers and acquisitions, that have taken place in the recent past or are pending. Typical examples are *Disclosure/Spectrum Ownership* and *Insider Trading Monitor.*

- *Company directory information*—There are a number of directories. These differ in the types of companies they cover (e.g., public or private), the size of the companies covered, and their geographic coverage. In addition to the name, address, and telephone number, many of the directories will list the primary and secondary Standard Industrial Classification (SIC) codes for the business. Typical examples are *D&B's Dun's Market Identifiers* and *Standard and Poor's Corporate Register.*

- *U.S. government contract information*—These data bases are particularly useful to businesses dealing with the government. They contain information on whether a specific company has any government contracts and recent contract awards. Typical examples are *Commerce Business Daily* and *DMS Contract Awards.*

- *Economic information*—These data bases contain general economic and demographic information. Some of it comes from U.S. Census materials and some from the private sector. Many of these data bases contain forecasts of future economic activity. Typical examples are *Cendata* and *PTS U.S. Forecasts.*

- *General business information*—These data bases cover companies, industries, people, and products. The information from them comes primarily from trade

---

Table 7.5   *How to Conduct a Data-Base Search*

Step 1: Discuss the information sought with the specialist who will be doing the search, to develop a "search strategy." The search strategy is a set of words that will be entered into the computer for the actual search.

Step 2: Once a search strategy is determined, the specialist uses a telephone to dial the number of the particular data base to be used. When the connection is made, the search specialist hooks up his or her terminal to the data-base computer via a modem.

Step 3: The data-base computer will then ask for identification to determine whether the search specialist is an authorized user of the system. The search specialist will reply by typing in a code. If it is accepted, the data-base computer will then ask for the name of the data base or file to be searched.

Step 4: If the file is available, the computer will ask the user to input a search strategy. When the search strategy has been entered, the computer will begin the search.

Step 5: The computer will then inform the user of the number of matches made by the search. If the number of matches made is large, the user may wish to add further qualifiers of the terms used in the search to find the specific information he or she needs.

Step 6: If the results are satisfactory, the user must decide the level of detail he or she wants to see for each match made. Choices range from a simple bibliography, an annotated bibliography, a bibliography with abstracts, or even a copy of the references themselves.

Step 7: The user must also decide whether to have the information printed at the computer site and delivered later by mail or United Parcel Service, or printed immediately at the user's terminal. Having the results delivered by mail or UPS is usually cheaper, since charges for the services are generally based on the amount of time the computer is connected to the user's terminal. Printers are considered slow devices in computer terms.

Source: Based on H. Webster Johnson, Anthony J. Faria, and Ernest L. Maier, *How to Use the Business Library: With Sources of Business Information*, 5th ed. (Cincinnati: South-Western Publishing Co., 1984), pp. 29–32.

and business-oriented journals, selected newspapers, and various reports. Typical examples are *ABI/Inform* and *Harvard Business Review*.

- *Brand name information*—These data bases contain information on specific products, including what competitors might be doing with respect to new product introductions or expenditures on advertising and what company owns a specific trademark. Typical examples are *New Product Announcements* and *Thomas Register Online*.

- *People information*—These data bases contain information on people who have been noted in the literature for their accomplishments in the arts, sciences, business, or other fields of endeavor. These data bases are used to track people in the business world or inventors and the patents they hold. Typical examples are *American Men & Women of Science* and *Standard & Poor's Register-Biographical*.

As the preceding list indicates, companies use on-line data bases to search for journal articles, reports, speeches, marketing data, economic trends, legislation, inventions, and many other types of information on a particular topic. Some especially useful guides to on-line data bases are described in Appendix 7A. Table 7.5 explains how to conduct a data-base search.

Ethical
Dilemma 7.2   A marketing manager for a dog food manufacturer stumbled onto an important piece of competitive intelligence while visiting a local printer near his company's plant. While waiting to speak with the salesperson that handled his company's account, the manager noticed some glossy advertising proofs for one of its competitor's products. The ad highlighted some new low prices. When he mentioned the prices to the printer, he was told that they were part of a new advertising

campaign. On his return to headquarters, the marketing manager called a meeting of his own company's management. As a result of that meeting, the company initiated a preemptive, price-cutting campaign of its own that effectively neutralized the competitor's strategy.

- Did the marketing manager act ethically in reporting the information back to his own company?
- Would your judgment be different if the proofs were in a folder and the marketing manager casually and somewhat inadvertently opened the folder while standing there? What if he did so on purpose after noticing that the folder pertained to the competitor?
- Should information like this be entered into the firm's decision support system?

Back to the Case

Tyro's CEO hadn't lied when he said no one was leaving the room until they figured out how to deal with the public relations mess that their yet-to-be launched new product, Markets! had landed them in. It was a tired and rumpled group that was busily dictating a revised plan for making the new product as privacy-sensitive as possible.

The group agreed that no phone numbers would be included in the available data and that Markets! should not be available in retail stores. Further, it would be sold only to "legitimate" businesses at verified addresses; sales would be checked against a "fraud file." In addition, a contract was planned that would specifically limit the uses of Markets! and provide penalties for abuses.

Bud Hendricks had also suggested that anyone who didn't want their name to be included in the Markets! list should be able to write to Tyro and have their name removed from subsequent versions.

"The bottom line," Jonathan Karling concluded as they all sighed with exhaustion and relief, "is that Markets! will lower the threshold for small-business people who want to use targeted direct mail but can't afford to rent conventional lists. This isn't going to change the world. It's just going to mean that the average consumer will be as likely to get direct mail from the dentist around the corner as from the big corporation that's already using targeted-mail technology."

Source: Based on the case of Lotus Development Corporation's new product Marketplace, as reported by John R. Wilke, "Lotus Product Spurs Fears about Privacy," *The Wall Street Journal* (November 13, 1990), p. B1. Partially because of the controversy it sparked, the product was never introduced.

Summary

Learning Objective 1: Explain the difference between primary and secondary data.

Secondary data are statistics not gathered for the immediate study at hand, but for some other purpose. Primary data are originated by the researcher for the purpose of the investigation at hand.

Learning Objective 2: Cite two advantages offered by secondary data.

The most significant advantages offered by secondary data are time savings and money savings for the researcher.

Learning Objective 3: Specify two problems common to secondary data.

Two problems that commonly arise when secondary data are used are (1) they do not completely fit the problem, and (2) they are not completely accurate.

Learning Objective 4: List the three criteria researchers should use in judging the accuracy of secondary data.

The three criteria researchers should use in judging the accuracy of secondary data are (1) the source, (2) the purpose of publication, and (3) general evidence regarding the quality of the data.

Learning Objective 5: State the most fundamental rule in using secondary data.

The most fundamental rule in using secondary data is to always use the primary source of secondary data.

Learning Objective 6: Explain the difference between internal and external data.

Internal data are those found within the organization for which the research is being done, while external data are those obtained from outside sources.

Learning Objective 7: List some of the key sources researchers should consider in conducting a search process.

The key sources researchers should keep in mind in conducting a search process are reference librarians, associations, on-line computer searches, and general guides to useful marketing information.

Learning Objective 8: Describe the roles of the data-base producer, data-base vendor, and data user in the operations of on-line computer search services.

The data-base producer collects the information and edits it according to its own criteria, puts it on a computer tape or disk, and sells it to the vendor for a fee. The vendor mounts the tape or disk on a computer and sells access to it to the data user. The data user pays for citation and printing charges, connect charges, telephone-line charges, and also incurs the cost of planning and executing the computer search. The vendor also pays the data-base producer a fee every time the data base is used and a fee for all citations from it.

Discussion Questions, Problems, and Projects

1. List some major secondary sources of information for the following situations.
   (a) The marketing research manager of a national soft drink manufacturer has to prepare a comprehensive report on the soft drink industry.
   (b) Mr. Baker has several ideas for instant cake mixes and is considering entering this industry. He needs to find the necessary background information to assess its potential.
   (c) The profit margins in the fur business are high! This is what Mr. Adams has heard. The fur industry has always intrigued him, so he decides to do some research to determine if the claim is true.
   (d) A recent graduate hears that condominiums are the homes of the nineties. He decides to collect some information on the condominium market.
   (e) Owning a grocery store has been Mrs. Smith's dream. She finally decides to make this into a reality. The first step she wishes to take is to collect information on the grocery business in her hometown.
2. Assume you are interested in opening a fast food Italian restaurant in Kansas City, Missouri. You are unsure of its acceptance by consumers and are considering doing a marketing research study to evaluate their attitudes and opinions. In your search for information you find the following studies:
   Study A was recently conducted by a research agency. In order to secure a copy of this study you would be required to pay the agency $225. The study evaluated

consumers' attitudes toward fast food in general. The findings—based on a sample of 500 housewives from the cities of Springfield, Illinois; St. Louis and Kansas City, Missouri; and Topeka, Kansas—indicated that respondents did not view fast food favorably. The major reason for the unfavorable attitude was the low nutritional value of the food.

Study B was completed by a group of students as a requirement for an M.B.A. marketing course. This study would not cost you anything, as it is available in your university library. The study evaluated consumers' attitudes toward various ethnic fast foods. The respondents consisted of a convenience sample of 200 students from St. Louis. The findings indicated a favorable attitude toward two ethnic fast foods, Italian and Mexican. Based on these results, one of the students had planned to open a pizza parlor in 1985, but instead accepted a job as sales representative for General Foods Corporation.

(a)   Critically evaluate the two sources of data.

(b)   Which do you consider better? Why?

(c)   Assume you decide that it will be profitable to become a franchisee in fast food. Identify five more specific secondary sources of data and evaluate the data.

3.   Interior Decor Products for many years had been a leading producer of paint and painting-related equipment such as brushes, rollers, turpentine, and so on. The company is now considering adding wallpaper to its line. At least initially, it does not intend to manufacture the wallpaper but rather to subcontract the manufacturing. Interior Decor will, however, assume the distribution and marketing functions.

Before adding the wallpaper to its product line, the company secures some secondary data assessing the size of the wallpaper market. One mail survey made by a trade association showed that, on the average, families in the United States wallpapered two rooms in their homes each year. Among these families, 60 percent did the task themselves. Another survey, which had also been done by mail, but by one of the major home magazines, found that 70 percent of the subscribers answering the questionnaire had wallpapered one complete wall or more during the last twelve months. Among this 70 percent of the families, 80 percent had done the wallpapering themselves. Interior Decor thus has two sets of secondary data on the same problem, but the data are not consistent.

Discuss the data in terms of the criteria one would use to determine which set, if either, is correct. Assuming that you are forced to make the determination on the basis of the information in front of you, which would you choose?

4.   Using the 1990 *Statistical Abstract of the United States*, answer the following questions.

(a)   Which consolidated metropolitan statistical area in the United States has the largest population as of 1988?

(b)   What is the population of this consolidated metropolitan statistical area?

(c)   What was the estimated median age of the U.S. population as of 1988?

(d)   Complete the following table:

Marital Status of U.S. Population	1988 (million)	Percent of Total
Single		
Married		
Widowed		
Divorced		

(e)   What percent of households consisted of five persons as of 1988?

(f)   Complete the following table on school enrollment for 1988. What do the percentages indicate?

	18–19 Years Old	20–21 Years Old	22–24 Years Old
Percent of blacks enrolled in school			
Percent of hispanics enrolled in school			

(g) Which of the following recreational products and/or services had the highest personal consumption expenditures in 1988?
(1) magazines and newspapers
(2) admissions to specified spectator amusements
(3) radio and television receivers, records, and musical instruments
(4) nondurable toys and sport supplies

(h) Complete the following table:

Income Category	Percent of All Families (1987)
Under $5,000	
$5,000 to $9,999	
$10,000 to $14,999	
$15,000 to $24,999	
$25,000 to $34,999	
$35,000 to $49,999	
$50,000 to $74,999	
$75,000 and over	

(i) What was the Consumer Price Index for all items in 1988? What was the base year? What does this indicate?

(j) Complete the following table:

Industry Group	Ratio of Profits to Equity (1988) (percent)	Profits per Dollar of Sales (1988) (cents)
Nondurable Good Industries		
Food and kindred products		
Textile mill products		
Paper and allied products		

5. The *Statistical Abstract* is a secondary source of secondary data. As it is always better to use the primary source, identify the primary source for the following data that were referred to in the previous question.
(a) The estimated median age of the U.S. population.
(b) Personal consumption expenditures for recreation.
(c) The Consumer Price Indexes by major groups.
(d) The manufacturing corporations' profits to stockholders' equity and profits per dollar of sales.

6. John Smith is interested in becoming a wholesaler in household appliances. He has collected some general information but requires your help in finding answers to the following questions.
   (a) What is the SIC code for household appliance manufacturers?
   (b) How many retail establishments sell household appliances in the United States?
   (c) What are the total sales of all the retail establishments?
   Instead of attempting to handle all household appliances, Smith is considering specialization in household refrigerators and freezers.
   (d) What are the total number of establishments manufacturing household refrigerators and freezers?
   (e) How many wholesale establishments are there in the United States dealing in this category?
   Smith thinks that Dayton, Ohio, would be a profitable place to locate. He needs to know the following:
   (f) What is the total population of Dayton, Ohio?
   (g) What is the total civilian labor force in Dayton, Ohio?
   (h) How many persons are employed in Dayton, Ohio?
   (i) What are the total number of home furnishing and equipment stores that have a payroll in Dayton, Ohio?
   (Hint: In order to complete the above exercise, refer to the *Census of Manufactures*, *Census of Retail Trade*, *Census of Wholesale Trade*, and *County and City Data Book*.)

7. Suppose you are interested in introducing a four-by-two-inch FM/AM radio that could be carried in a person's pocket.
   (a) What data would be useful in making your decision?
   (b) Identify the specific secondary sources and the data they would provide that would assist you in making your decision.
   (c) Develop a brief report on the data you find.

8. In addition to on-line computer searches, many university and public libraries now offer off-line data-base search capability, using CD-ROM technology. Prepare a brief report outlining availability of both types of these information resources (on-line and off-line) in your area. Be sure to include the following information for each available service in your report:
   (a) name of service and type of information (e.g., bibliographic, statistical) available
   (b) location(s) of access point(s)
   (c) times available for use
   (d) name of contact person(s) for further information
   (e) any special skills required for use and availability of training, if needed
   (f) access fees, if any
   (g) report formats available (e.g., hard copy, transfer to diskette)

9. Assume that your school is interested in developing a marketing plan to boost sagging attendance at major athletic events, in particular home football games. As an initial step in developing the new marketing plan, the athletic department has decided that it needs a demographic and life-style profile of people who currently attend games on a regular (season-ticket) basis. Fortunately, the ticket office maintains a listing of all season-ticket purchasers (name and address) from year to year. What potential sources of internal secondary data might the athletic department first investigate before considering the collection of primary data?

Endnotes

1. Robert Ferber and P. J. Verdoorn, *Research Methods in Economics and Business* (New York: Macmillan, 1962), p. 208.

2. Joanne Kelleher, "Getting to Know Your Market," *Venture*, 35 (May 1983), pp. 70–74.

3. Ibid.

4. David W. Stewart, *Secondary Research: Information Sources and Methods* (Beverly Hills, Calif.: Sage Publications, 1984), p. 113. See also *Measuring Markets: A Guide to the Use of Federal and State Statistical Data* (Washington, D.C.: U.S. Department of Commerce, 1979) for discussion of the marketing-related information that is available from the federal and state governments and how that information can be used for such marketing tasks as market potential estimation, establishing sales quotas, allocating advertising budgets, locating retail outlets, and so on.

5. Jacob has a particularly helpful discussion on the various errors that are present in published data and what remedies are available to the analyst for treating these errors. See Herbert Jacob, *Using Published Data: Errors and Remedies* (Beverly Hills, Calif.: Sage Publications, 1984).

6. For an alternative list of criteria, see Stewart, *Secondary Research*, pp. 23–33.

7. Erwin Esser Nemmers and John H. Myers, *Business Research: Text and Cases* (New York: McGraw-Hill, 1966), p. 38.

8. *The Chicago Tribune*, September 19, 1960. If there had not been a cult of "baseball superfans whose passion is to dig up obscure facts about the erstwhile national pastime," the error might never have been discovered. See "You May Not Care but 'Nappie' Lajoie Batted .422 in 1901," *The Wall Street Journal* (September 13, 1974), p. 1.

9. "If You Can't Lick 'Em, Just Call 'Em Names," *The Wall Street Journal* (March 30, 1988), p. 21.

10. Nemmers and Myers, *Business Research*, p. 43. For other illustrations of how knowledge of the source provides insights into the accuracy of the data, see Marilyn Chose, "Mixing Science,

Stocks Raises Question of Bias in the Testing of Drugs," *The Wall Street Journal* (January 26, 1989), p. A1, and Michael Miller, "High-Tech Hype Reaches New Heights," *The Wall Street Journal* (January 12, 1989), p. B1.

11. Larry P. Stanek, "Keeping Focused on the Consumer While Managing Tons of Information," in *Presentations from the 9th Annual Marketing Research Conference* (Chicago: American Marketing Association, 1988), pp. 66–67. Kraft has assigned a group of very experienced people to the task of developing key learnings. While the group has only been in existence for a short while, it's already issued key learnings documents on three major areas: advertising testing, concept testing, and in-market testing.

12. See, for example, Charles H. Sevin, *Marketing Productivity Analysis* (New York: McGraw-Hill, 1965), or Sanford R. Simon, *Managing Marketing Profitability* (New York: American Management Association, Inc., 1969), for two of the best treatments of sales and profitability analysis.

13. The figure and surrounding discussion are adapted from Stewart, *Secondary Research*. See also Jac L. Goldstucker, *Marketing Information: A Professional Reference Guide* (Atlanta: College of Business Administration, Georgia State University, 1982).

Suggested Additional Readings

For general discussions of secondary data sources and how to go about finding secondary data, see

H. Webster Johnson, Anthony J. Faria, and Ernest L. Maier, *How to Use the Business Library: With Sources of Business Information*, 5th ed. (Cincinnati: South-Western Publishing Co., 1984).

David W. Stewart, *Secondary Research: Information Sources and Methods* (Beverly Hills, Calif.: Sage Publications, 1984).

For discussion of the marketing-related information that is available from the federal and state govern-

ments and how that information can be used for such marketing tasks as market potential estimation, establishing sales quotas, allocating advertising budgets, locating retail outlets, and so on, see

Measuring Markets: A Guide to the Use of Federal and State Statistical Data (Washington, D.C.: U.S. Department of Commerce, 1979).

P. T. Zeisset, *Teachers' Guide: Approaches to Census Data* (Washington, D.C.: U.S. Department of Commerce, 1977).

Appendix
7A

Secondary Data

There is so much published secondary data that it is impossible to mention all of it in a single appendix. For this reason, only a representative cross section of the available material is presented.[1] These secondary sources are organized into six sections, according to the type of information they contain. Several sources of electronic on-line search services are included. First, however, a brief discussion of governmental sources of secondary data is presented.

Census Data and Other Government Publications: Overview

The Bureau of the Census of the United States Department of Commerce is the largest gatherer of statistical information in the country. The original census was the Census of Population, which was required by the Constitution to serve as a basis for apportioning representation in the House of Representatives. The first censuses were merely head counts. Not only has the Census of Population been expanded, but the whole census machinery has also been enlarged. At this point there are nine different censuses, all of which are of interest to the marketing researcher. Table 7.1, for example, listed some of the most useful data on population and housing that are available in the Census of Population. Table 7A.1 lists some of the most useful data that are collected in the various economic censuses described in the following sections.

Census data are of generally high quality. Further, they are quite often available on the detailed level that the researcher needs. When not available in this form, researchers can purchase either computer tapes or flexible diskettes from the Bureau of the Census for a nominal fee to create their own tabulations. Alternatively, researchers can contract with one of the private companies that market census-related products for information on a particular issue. Not only does this allow getting the information tailored to one's own needs, but it is also one of the fastest ways to get census data. Further, many of the private providers update the census data at a detailed geographic level for the between-census years.

There are two major drawbacks to the use of census data: (1) censuses are not taken every year, and (2) the delay from time of collection to time of publication is quite substantial, often two years or more. This last weakness, however necessary because of the massive editing, coding, and tabulation tasks involved, renders the data obsolete for many research problems. The first difficulty requires that the researcher supplement the census data with current data. Unfortunately, current data are rarely available in the detail the researcher desires. This is particularly true with respect to detailed classifications by small geographic area, unless one takes advantage of the services of a private provider with update capability.

The federal government also collects and publishes a great deal of statistical information in addition to the censuses. Some of this material is designed to supplement the various censuses and is gathered and published for this purpose (e.g., *Current Population Reports*), whereas other data are generated in the normal course of operations, such as collecting taxes, social security payments, claims for unemployment benefits, and so forth. Some publications also result from the desire to make the search for information more convenient.

Company and Industry Information

Almanac of Business and Industrial Financial Ratios **(Englewood Cliffs, N.J.: Prentice-Hall)** This publication contains the number of establishments, sales, and selected operating ratios for various industries (e.g., food stores). The figures are derived from tax-return data supplied by the Internal Revenue Service and are reported for twelve categories, based on assets, within each industry. The data thus allow the comparison of a particular company's financial ratios with competitors of similar size.

Census of Agriculture **(U.S. Bureau of the Census: Government Printing Office)** The *Census of Agriculture* was formerly taken in the years ending in "4" and "9." Since 1982, it is taken in years ending in "2" and "7." This census offers detailed breakdowns by state and county on the number of farms, farm types, acreage, land-use practices, employment, livestock produced and products raised, and value of products. It is supplemented by the annual publications *Agriculture Statistics* and *Commodity Yearbook*. In addition, the Department of Agriculture issues a number of bulletins, which often contain data not otherwise published.

Census of Construction Industries **(U.S. Bureau of the Census: Government Printing Office)** Taken every five years (in the years ending with "2" and "7"), this census covers establishments primarily engaged in contract construction, in construction for sale, or in subdividing real property into lots. Statistics are provided for such things as value of inventories, total assets, and employment by state.

Table 7A.1   **Information Available from Economic Censuses**

Major Data Items	Retail Trade	Wholesale Trade	Service Industries	Construction Industries	Manufactures	Mineral Industries
Number of Establishments and Firms						
All establishments	X			X		
Establishments with payroll	X	X	X	X	X	X
Establishments by legal form of organization	X	X	X	X	X	X
Firms	X	X	X		X	X
Single-unit and multi-unit firms	X	X	X		X	X
Concentration by major firms	X	X	X		X	
Employment						
All employees	X	X	X	X	X	X
Production (construction) workers				X	X	X
Employment size of establishments	X	X	X	X	X	X
Employment size of firms	X	X	X			
Production (construction) worker hours				X	X	X
Payrolls						
All employees, entire year	X	X	X	X	X	X
All employees, first quarter	X	X	X	X	X	
Production (construction) workers				X	X	X
Supplemental labor costs, legally required and voluntary	X	X	X	X	X	X
Sales Receipts, or Value of Shipments						
All establishments	X			X	X	X
Establishments with payroll	X	X	X	X		
By product or line or type of construction	X	X	X	X	X	X
By class of customer	X	X				
By size of establishments	X	X	X	X	X	X
By size of firm	X	X	X			
Operating Expenses						
Total	X	X	X			
Cost of materials, etc.	X	X		X	X	X
Specific materials consumed (quantity and cost)	X	X			X	X
Cost of fuels	X	X	X	X	X	X

Source: Adapted from *Guide to the 1982 Economic Censuses and Related Statistics* (Washington, D.C.: Bureau of the Census, U.S. Department of Commerce, 1984), p. 3.

Census of Government (U.S. Bureau of the Census: Government Printing Office)
The *Census of Government* presents information on the general characteristics of state and local governments, including such things as employment, size of payroll, amount of indebtedness, and operating revenues and costs. The census is authorized in the years ending in "2" and "7."

Table 7A.1   *(Continued)*

Major Data Items	Retail Trade	Wholesale Trade	Service Industries	Construction Industries	Manufactures	Mineral Industries
Operating Expenses						
Electric energy consumed (quantity and cost)	X	X	X		X	X
Contract work		X		X	X	X
Products bought and sold					X	X
Advertising	X	X	X			
Rental payments, total	X	X	X	X	X	X
Buildings and structures	X	X	X	X	X	X
Machinery and equipment	X	X	X	X	X	X
Communications services	X	X	X	X	X	X
Purchased repairs	X	X	X	X	X	
Capital Expenditures						
Total	X	X	X	X	X	X
New, total	X	X	X	X	X	X
Buildings/equipment	X	X	X	X	X	X
Used, total	X	X	X	X	X	X
Buildings/equipment				X		X
Depreciable Assets, Gross Value Buildings/Equipment						
End of 1981	X	X	X	X	X	X
End of 1982	X	X	X	X	X	X
Depreciation (total and detail for buildings/equipment)	X	X	X	X	X	X
Retirements (total and detail for buildings/equipment)	X	X	X	X	X	X
Inventories						
End of 1981	X	X		X	X	X
End of 1982	X	X		X	X	X
Other						
Value added	X	X		X	X	X
Specialization by type of construction/ manufacturing				X	X	
Central administrative offices and auxiliaries	X	X	X	X	X	X
Water use					X	X

Census of Manufactures (**U.S. Bureau of the Census: Government Printing Office**)   The *Census of Manufactures* has been taken somewhat irregularly in the past, but is now authorized for the years ending in "2" and "7." It categorizes manufacturing establishments by type, using some 450 classes, and contains detailed industry and geographic statistics for such items as the number of establishments, quantity of output, value added in manufacture, capital expenditures, employment, wages, inventories, sales by customer class, and fuel, water, and energy consumption. The *Annual Survey of Manufactures* covers the years between publications of the census, and *Current Industrial Reports* contains the monthly and annual production figures for some commodities.

Census of Mineral Industries (U.S. Bureau of the Census: Government Printing Office)

The *Census of Mineral Industries* is taken in the years ending in "2" and "7." The information here parallels that for the *Census of Manufactures* but is for the mining industry. The census offers detailed geographic breakdowns for some 50 mineral industries on such things as the number of establishments, production, value of shipments, capital expenditures, cost of supplies, employment, payroll, power equipment, and water use. The *Minerals Yearbook*, published by the Bureau of Mines of the Department of the Interior, supplements the *Census of Mineral Industries* by providing annual data, although the two are not completely comparable because they employ different classifications—an industrial classification for the Census Bureau data and a product classification for the Bureau of Mines data.

Census of Retail Trade (U.S. Bureau of the Census: Government Printing Office)

The *Census of Retail Trade* is taken every five years, in the years ending in "2" and "7." Retail stores are classified by type of business, and statistics are presented on such things as the number of stores, total sales, employment, and payroll. The statistics are broken down by small geographic areas such as counties, cities, and standard metropolitan statistical areas. Current data pertaining to some of the information can be found in *Monthly Retail Trade*.

Census of Service Industries (U.S. Bureau of the Census: Government Printing Office)

The *Census of Service Industries* is taken every five years, in the years ending in "2" and "7." The service trade census provides data on receipts, employment, type of business (for example, hotel, laundry, and so on), and number of units by small geographic areas. Current data can be found in *Monthly Selected Services Receipts*.

Census of Transportation (U.S. Bureau of the Census: Government Printing Office)

The *Census of Transportation*, too, is taken in the years ending in "2" and "7." It covers three major areas: passenger travel, truck and bus inventory and use, and the transport of commodities by the various classes of carriers.

Census of Wholesale Trade (U.S. Bureau of the Census: Government Printing Office)

The *Census of Wholesale Trade* is taken every five years, in the years ending in "2" and "7." It classifies wholesalers into over 150 business groups and contains statistics on the functions they perform, their sales volume, warehouse space, expenses, and so forth. It presents these statistics for counties, cities, and standard metropolitan statistical areas. Current data can be found in *Monthly Wholesale Trade*.

Commodity Yearbook (New York: Commodity Research Bureau)

Published annually, this publication contains data on prices, production, exports, stocks, and so on, for approximately 100 individual commodities.

Merchandising, "Statistical and Marketing Report" (New York: Billboard Publications)

This annual report, contained in the March issue, includes statistical information related to sales, shipments, imports, exports, and more for certain consumer durables, including home electronics and major appliances.

Moody's Manuals (New York: Moody's Investors Service)

Published annually, these manuals—*Banks and Finance, Industrials, Municipals and Governments, Public Utilities,* and *Transportation*—contain balance sheets and income statements for individual companies and government units.

Predicasts Forecasts (Cleveland: Predicasts, Inc.)   The quarterly *Predicasts Forecasts* provides short- and long-term forecasts for economic indicators, industries, and products and also serves as a guide to statistical information about companies and industries.

Standard & Poor's Corporate Records (New York: Standard & Poor's Corporation)   *Corporate Records* provides current financial statistics for companies as well as background information and news items.

Standard & Poor's Industry Surveys (New York: Standard & Poor's Corporation) These surveys provide analyses of all major domestic industries, including outlooks for the industry, trends and problems, and statistical tables and charts. A basic analysis is published yearly and offers a comparative company analysis of the leading companies in an industry. Current analyses are published three times per year and include important developments and available statistics for the industry, market, and company, as well as investment outlook for the industry.

Standard & Poor's Statistical Service (New York: Standard & Poor's Corporation)   This publication presents monthly statistical data (current and historical) for several areas, including banking and finance, production and labor, and income and trade.

U.S. Industrial Outlook (Industrial Trade Administration, U.S. Department of Commerce: Government Printing Office)   Produced annually, this publication covers the recent trends and five-year outlook for more than 350 manufacturing and service industries.

Worldcasts (Cleveland: Predicasts, Inc.)   Published quarterly, *Worldcasts* provides worldwide forecast information for regions and for products. Forecast data are drawn from over 800 publications.

Related Indexes, Directories, and Guides

Business Organizations, Agencies, and Publications Directory (Detroit: Gale Research)   This directory serves as a guide to approximately 20,000 organizations, agencies, and publications related to business, trade, and industry in the areas of marketing, accounting, administration, human resources, and much more.

Directory of Corporate Affiliations (Wilmette, Ill.: National Register Publishing Company)   An annual publication, the *Directory of Corporate Affiliations* provides a listing of more than 4,000 major U.S. companies and their 48,000 subsidiaries, divisions, and affiliates. Both private and public firms are broken down by Standard Industrial Classification (SIC) code, by state (geography), and alphabetically. The publication includes a listing of mergers, acquisitions, and name changes since 1976.

Fortune Directory (New York: Time, Inc.)   Published annually by the editors of *Fortune* magazine, this directory provides information on sales, assets, profits, invested capital, and employees for the 500 largest industrial corporations in the United States.

Guide to Industrial Statistics (Washington, D.C.: U.S. Bureau of the Census) The *Guide to Industrial Statistics* is a guide to the Census Bureau's programs relating to industry, including the type of statistics gathered and where these statistics are published.

How to Find Information about Companies: The Corporate Intelligence Source Book, **6th ed. (Washington, D.C.: Washington Researchers, 1988)**   A useful guide to locating information about specific companies.

International Directory of Corporate Affiliations **(Wilmette, Ill.: National Register Publishing Company)**   Similar to the *Directory of Corporate Affiliations*, this annual publication contains information about the holdings of parent companies. However, it provides listings of the holdings of foreign companies by U.S. parent companies, as well as the U.S. holdings of foreign parent companies.

Million Dollar Directory **(New York: Dun and Bradstreet)**   Published annually by Dun & Bradstreet, this reference source lists the offices, products, sales, and number of employees for companies with assets of $500,000 or more.

Predicasts F & S Index — United States **(Cleveland: Predicasts, Inc.)**   This index includes company, product, and industry information from over 750 sources, including financial publications, business newspapers, trade magazines, and special reports. Information is included on new products, technological developments, corporate acquisitions and mergers, and more. The index is published weekly, with monthly, quarterly, and annual compilations.

Standard Industrial Classification Manual **(Springfield, Va.: Office of Management and Budget, National Technical Information Service)**   The *Standard Industrial Classification Manual* provides the basic system used for classifying industries into 11 major divisions. The SIC system is used for federal economic statistics classified by industry.

Standard & Poor's Register of Corporations, Directors, and Executives **(New York: Standard & Poor's Corporation)**   This annual publication lists officers, products, sales, addresses, telephone numbers, and employees for more than 50,000 U.S. and Canadian corporations.

Thomas Register of American Manufacturers and Thomas Register Catalog File **(New York: Thomas Publishing Company)**   Published annually, this multi-volume publication lists the specific manufacturers of individual products and provides information on their addresses, branch offices, and subsidiaries.

Many of the listed sources are general. They contain information applicable to a wide number of research problems. They will typically provide a productive start in the search for secondary data. If this search results in a dead end, all is not lost by any means. The required secondary data may still be available in industry trade publications. The amount of data available on an industry-by-industry basis is extensive indeed, and researchers are well advised not to finish their search without reviewing the appropriate industry sources. Often the source of industry statistics will be the industry trade association; in other cases, it may be trade journals serving the industry.

Market and Consumer Information

Aging America — Trends and Projections **(U.S. Senate Special Committee on Aging and the American Association of Retired Persons: Government Printing Office)**   This chartbook describes the sustained growth in America's elderly population expected during the next 30 years. Graphs and tables cover areas such as demographics, employment, health, and income.

Census of Housing (U.S. Bureau of the Census: Government Printing Office)

The *Census of Housing* is published decennially for the years ending in "0." It was first taken in 1940 in conjunction with the *Census of Population* and lists such things as type of structure, size, building condition, occupancy, water and sewage facilities, monthly rent, average value, and equipment, including stoves, dishwashers, air conditioners, and so on. For large metropolitan areas, it provides detailed statistics by city block. The periods between publications of the *Census of Housing* are covered by the bureau's annual *American Housing Survey*.

Census of Population (U.S. Bureau of the Census: Government Printing Office)

The *Census of Population* is taken every ten years, in the years ending with "0." The census reports the population by geographic region. It also provides detailed breakdowns on such characteristics as sex, marital status, age, education, race, national origin, family size, employment and unemployment, income, and other demographic characteristics. The *Current Population Reports*, which are published annually and make use of the latest information on migrations, birth and death rates, and so forth, update the information in the *Census of Population*.

County and City Databook (U.S. Bureau of the Census: Government Printing Office)

Published once every five years, the *County and City Databook* serves as a convenient source of statistics gathered in the various censuses and provides breakdowns on a city and county basis. Included are statistics on such things as population, education, employment, income, housing, banking, manufacturing output and capital expenditures, retail and wholesale sales, and mineral and agricultural output.

County Business Patterns (U.S. Department of Commerce: Government Printing Office)

This annual publication contains statistics on a number of businesses by type and their employments and payrolls, broken down by county. These data are often quite useful in industrial market-potential studies.

Editor and Publisher Market Guide (New York: Editor and Publisher Magazine)

Published annually, this guide contains data on some 265 metropolitan statistical areas, including location, population, number of households, principal industries, retail sales and outlets, and climate.

A Guide to Consumer Markets (New York: The Conference Board)

Issued annually, this publication contains data on the behavior of consumers in the marketplace. It includes statistics on population, employment, income, expenditure, and prices.

Marketing Economics Guide (New York: Marketing Economics Institute)

Published annually, this publication provides detailed operating information on 1,500 retailing centers throughout the country on a regional, state, county, and city basis. It contains information on population, percent of households by income class, disposable income, total retail sales, and retail sales by store group.

Rand McNally Commercial Atlas and Marketing Guide (Chicago: Rand McNally Company)

Published annually, this atlas contains marketing data and maps for some 100,000 cities and towns in the United States. Included are such things as population, auto registrations, and retail trade.

Sales and Marketing Management Survey of Buying Power **(New York: Sales and Marketing Management)**   Published annually, this survey contains market data for states, a number of counties, cities, and standard metropolitan statistical areas. Included are statistics on population, retail sales, and household income and a combined index of buying power for each reported geographic area.

State and Metropolitan Area Data Book **(U.S. Department of Commerce: Government Printing Office)**   This book is a *Statistical Abstract of the United States* supplement put out by the Department of Commerce. It contains information on population, housing, government, manufacturing, retail and wholesale trade, and selected services by state and standard metropolitan statistical areas.

Related Indexes, Directories, and Guides

Data Sources for Business and Market Analysis, **3rd ed., Nathalie D. Frank (Metuchen, N.J.: Scarecrow Press, 1983)**   An annotated guide to original statistical sources arranged by source of information rather than by topic.

Directory of Federal Statistics for Local Areas: A Guide to Sources **(Washington, D.C.: U.S. Bureau of the Census, 1978)**   A guide to the sources of federal statistics for local areas on such topics as population, health, education, income, and finance.

Directory of Federal Statistics for States: A Guide to Sources **(Washington, D.C.: U.S. Bureau of the Census, 1976)**   Similar to the guide for local sources, above, this guide outlines the sources of federal statistics for states on such topics as population, income, education, and so on.

Directory of Nonfederal Statistics for State and Local Areas: A Guide to Sources **(Washington, D.C.: U.S. Bureau of the Census, 1970)**   Similar to the preceding two census guides, this guide details the private, local, and state organizations collecting and publishing data on economic, political, and social subjects for state and local areas.

Guide to 1980 Census Data on the Elderly **(Washington, D.C.: U.S. Bureau of the Census and U.S. Administration on Aging, 1986)**   This report specifies where to look in the 1980 census publications and other reports for data on the older population, with references covering all of the main sources.

Measuring Markets: A Guide to the Use of Federal and State Statistical Data **(Washington, D.C.: U.S. Department of Commerce, 1979)**   This book serves as an excellent guide to both federal and state statistical data.

1980 Census of Population and Housing: User's Guide **(U.S. Bureau of the Census: Government Printing Office)**   The *User's Guide* provides information about how the data were collected and the scope of every subject, discusses how to locate all the statistics for a given geographical area, and provides a glossary of terms used in the census. An index to summary tape files is also available.

State Data and Database Sourcebook **(Chevy Chase, Md.: Information USA, Inc., 1989)**   This volume contains information on how to obtain data (including information that might be useful from a marketing perspective) from state offices. Information about available data, their cost, and so on, are provided for each state.

General Economic and Statistical Information

Business Statistics **(U.S. Department of Commerce: Government Printing Office)**   Published every two years, this publication provides a historical record of the data series appearing monthly in the *Survey of Current Business.*

Economic Indicators **(Council of Economic Advisers: Government Printing Office)**   This monthly publication contains charts and tables of general economic data such as gross national product, personal consumption expenditures, and other series important in measuring general economic activity. An annual supplement presenting historical and descriptive material on the sources, uses, and limitations of the data is also issued.

Economic Report of the President **(U.S. Government: Government Printing Office)**   This publication results from the president's annual address to Congress about the general economic well-being of the country. The back portion of the report contains summary statistical tables using data collected elsewhere.

Federal Reserve Bulletin **(Washington, D.C.: Federal Reserve System Board of Governors)**   Published monthly, this publication is an important source of financial data, including statistics on banking activity, interest rates, savings, the index of industrial production, an index of department store sales, prices, and international trade and finance.

The Handbook of Basic Economic Statistics **(Washington, D.C.: Economic Statistics Bureau of Washington, D.C.)**   This monthly publication provides a compilation of more than 1,800 statistical series related to the national economy, condensed from the volumes of information released by the federal government.

Handbook of Cyclical Indicators **(Washington, D.C.: U.S. Department of Commerce)**   Published monthly, this publication contains at least 70 indicators of business activity designed to serve as a key to general economic conditions.

Historical Statistics of the United States from Colonial Times to 1970 **(U.S. Bureau of the Census: Government Printing Office)**   This volume was prepared by the Bureau of the Census to supplement the *Statistical Abstract of the United States.* The *Statistical Abstract* is one of the more important general sources for the marketing researcher, since it contains data on many social, economic, and political aspects of life in the United States. One problem a user of the *Statistical Abstract* data faces is incomparability of figures at various points in time because of the changes in definitions and classifications occasioned by a dynamic economy. *Historical Statistics* contains annual data on some 12,500 different series using consistent definitions and going back to the inception of the series.

Monthly Labor Review **(U.S. Bureau of Labor Statistics: Government Printing Office)**   Published monthly, this publication contains statistics on employment and unemployment, labor turnover, earnings and hours worked, wholesale and retail prices, and work stoppages.

Statistical Abstract of the United States **(U.S. Bureau of the Census: Government Printing Office)**   This annual publication reproduces more than 1,500 tables originally published elsewhere that cover such areas as the economic, demographic, social, and political structure of the United States. The publication is intended to serve as a convenient statistical reference and as a guide to more detailed statistics. The latter function is fulfilled through references to the original sources in the introductory comments to each section, the table footnotes, and a bibliography of sources. The *Statistical Abstract* is a source with which many researchers begin the search for external secondary data.

Statistics of Income (Internal Revenue Service: Government Printing Office)
Published annually, this publication is prepared from federal income tax returns of corporations and individuals. There are different publications for each type of tax report—one for corporations, one for sole proprietorships and partnerships, and one for individuals. The *Corporate Income Tax Return* volume, for example, contains balance sheet and income statement statistics compiled from corporate tax returns and broken down by major industry, asset size, and so on.

Survey of Current Business (U.S. Bureau of Economic Analysis: Government Printing Office)
This monthly publication provides a comprehensive statistical summary of the national income and product accounts of the United States. There are some 2,600 different statistical series reported, covering such topics as general business indicators, commodity prices, construction and real-estate activity, personal consumption expenditures by major type, foreign transactions, income and employment by industry, transportation and communications activity, and so on. Most of the statistical series present data on the last four years.

United Nations Statistical Yearbook (New York: United Nations)
This annual United Nations publication contains statistics on a wide range of foreign and domestic activities, including forestry, transportation, manufacturing, consumption, and education.

World Almanac and Book of Facts (New York: Newspaper Enterprise Association)
Issued annually by the Newspaper Enterprise Association, this publication serves as a well-indexed handbook on a wide variety of subjects. Included are industrial, financial, religious, social, and political statistics.

General Guides to Business Information

In addition to the following sources, see "Related Indexes, Directories, and Guides," earlier in this appendix.

American Marketing Association Bibliography Series (Chicago: American Marketing Association)
Published periodically, each of the publications in the series provides an in-depth annotated bibliography of a topic of interest in marketing.

Business Information: How to Find It, How to Use It (Phoenix, Ariz.: Oryx Press, 1987)
A general guide to searching for business information, this book provides useful information for the development of search strategies.

Business Information Sources, revised ed., Lorna M. Daniells (Berkeley: University of California Press, 1985)
A guide to the basic sources of business information, organized by subject area.

Census Catalog and Guide (U.S. Bureau of the Census: Government Printing Office)
This catalog is an annual, cumulative publication describing all products

(reports, maps, microfiche, computer tapes, diskettes, and on-line items) that the Census Bureau has issued since 1980, including information about how to order the information. Also, the catalog provides an appendix that includes, among other things, a directory of telephone numbers of Census Bureau specialists by area of expertise.

***Encyclopedia of Business Information Sources*, 7th ed. (Detroit: Gale Research, 1988)**   A guide to the information available on various subjects, including basic statistical sources, associations, periodicals, directories, handbooks, and general literature.

***Factfinder for the Nation* (U.S. Bureau of the Census: Government Printing Office)**   Issued irregularly, this series of publications describes the range of Census Bureau materials that are available on a variety of subjects and suggests some of their uses. A few of the subjects included are population statistics, housing statistics, statistics on race and ethnicity, availability of census records about individuals, and more.

***The Federal Database Finder* (Chevy Case, Md.: Information USA, Inc.)**   This useful resource provides a directory of over 4,200 no-cost and fee-based data bases and data files that are available through the federal government.

***Guide to American Directories*, 11th ed., Bernard Klein (Coral Springs, Fla.: B. Klein Publications, 1982)**   This guide provides information on directories published in the United States, categorized under 300 technical, mercantile, industrial, scientific, and professional headings.

***Guide to Foreign Trade Statistics* (Washington, D.C.: U.S. Bureau of the Census, 1983)**   A guide to the published and unpublished sources of foreign trade statistics.

***Guide to the 1987 Economic Censuses and Related Statistics* (U.S. Bureau of the Census: Government Printing Office)**   This reference provides general information about the uses, scope, content, coverage, legal authority and confidentiality, classification system, and geographic detail of the 1987 economic censuses. It describes each of the censuses, their related surveys, and special programs, with cross-references to other Census Bureau statistics.

***A Handbook on the Use of Government Statistics* (Charlottesville, Va.: Tayloe Murphy Institute)**   This publication is designed to assist the businessperson with the use of government statistics. A series of brief case descriptions are presented.

***How to Win With Information or Lose Without It*, Andrew P. Garven and Hubert Bermont (Washington, D.C.: Bermont Books, 1980)**   This publication, written in nontechnical language especially for executives, discusses data banks and information retrieval services.

***The Library and Information Manager's Guide to Online Services*, Ryan E. Hoover et al. (White Plains, N.Y.: Knowledge Industry Publication, 1980)**   A guide for on-line information searches. See also *Online Search Strategies*, by the same author, which contains practical tips on the effective use of bibliographic data bases and search systems.

***Statistics Sources*, 12th ed., Paul Wasserman et al. (Detroit: Gale Research, 1989)**   A guide to federal, state, and private sources of statistics on a wide variety of subjects.

A User's Guide to BEA Information **(U.S. Bureau of Economic Analysis: Government Printing Office)**   This booklet provides a directory for Bureau of Economic Analysis publications, computer tapes, diskettes, and other information sources.

Where to Find Business Information: A Worldwide Guide for Everyone Who Needs the Answers to Business Questions, **2nd ed., David M. Brownstone and Gorton Carruth (New York: John Wiley, 1982)**   This publication lists over 5,000 books, periodicals, or data bases of current interest and contains subject, title, and publisher indexes.

Indexes

In addition to the following sources, see "Related Indexes, Directories, and Guides," earlier in this appendix.

American Statistics Index **(Washington, D.C.: Congressional Information Service)**   Published annually and updated monthly, the publication is intended to serve as a comprehensive index of statistical data available to the public from any agency of the federal government.

Business Index **(Foster City, Calif.: Information Access Company)**   The *Business Index* is a microform index to over 460 business periodicals, *The Wall Street Journal*, *Barrons*, the *New York Times*, and business information from more than 1,100 general and legal periodicals. Index entries are arranged by subject and author in alphabetic order.

Business Periodicals Index **(Bronx, N.Y.: The H. W. Wilson Company)**   The *Business Periodicals Index* is a general-purpose business index published monthly (with quarterly and annual compilations) and is composed of subject entries covering about 350 business periodicals.

Communications Abstracts **(Beverly Hills, Calif.: Sage Publications)**   Issued quarterly, *Communications Abstracts* provides an index to communications-related articles, books, and reports. Such topics as marketing, advertising, and mass communication are covered.

Dissertation Abstracts International **(Ann Arbor, Mich.: University Microfilms International)**   Issued monthly, this publication contains descriptions of doctoral dissertations from nearly 500 participating institutions in North America and around the world. The approximately 35,000 annual entries are divided into three divisions: the humanities and social sciences, the sciences and engineering, and European abstracts.

The Information Catalog **(New York: FIND/SVP)**   *The Information Catalog* is a bimonthly publication of FIND/SVP, a business information and research firm. This resource contains overviews of reports, directories, reference works, and so on, that may be of interest to businesses. The reports have been produced by FIND/SVP and other research companies, publishers, and brokerage firms.

Journal of Marketing, **"Marketing Literature Review" (Chicago: American Marketing Association)**   Each quarterly issue of the *Journal of Marketing* includes a "Marketing Literature Review" section, which indexes a selection of article abstracts related to marketing from the business literature. Abstracts are drawn from over 125 business journals; entries are indexed under a variety of marketing subject headings.

Social Sciences Citation Index (**Philadelphia: Institute for Scientific Information**)
Published three times yearly, with annual cumulations, this publication indexes all articles in about 1,400 social science periodicals and selected articles in approximately 3,300 periodicals in other disciplines.

Statistical Reference Index (**Washington, D.C.: Congressional Information Service**)   Published monthly (with annual cumulations), this publication is intended to serve as a selective guide to American statistical publications from private organizations and state government sources.

The Wall Street Journal Index (**Princeton, N.J.: Dow Jones Books**)   Published monthly, *The Wall Street Journal Index* provides a subject index of information appearing in *The Wall Street Journal*. The index consists of two sections—general news and corporate news.

Directories

In addition to the following sources, see "Related Indexes, Directories, and Guides," earlier in this appendix.

American Marketing Association International Membership Directory & Marketing Services Guide (**Chicago: American Marketing Association**)   This directory, produced annually, contains an international directory of AMA members and member companies as well as a guide to providers of marketing services.

Business Organizations, Agencies, and Publications Directory (**Detroit: Gale Research**)   This directory serves as a guide to approximately 20,000 organizations, agencies, and publications related to business, trade, and industry in the areas of marketing, accounting, administration, human resources, and many more fields.

Consultants and Consulting Organizations Directory, **9th ed. (Detroit: Gale Research, 1989)**   This directory lists approximately 14,000 firms and individuals who are active in consulting and briefly describes their services and fields of interest.

Directories in Print, **6th ed. (Detroit: Gale Research, 1989)**   This directory, which is arranged by subject, lists, among other things, commercial and manufacturing directories; directories of individual industries, trades, and professions; and rosters of professional and scientific societies.

Directory of American Research and Technology, **23rd ed. (New York: Bowker, 1989)**   The *Directory of American Research and Technology* is a guide to research and development capabilities of more than 11,000 industrial organizations in the United States. It contains an alphabetical listing of the organizations, addresses of facilities, sizes of staffs, and fields of research and development.

Directory of Online Databases (**Santa Monica, Calif.: Cuadra Associates, Inc.**)
Published quarterly, this publication describes more than 4,000 bibliographic and nonbibliographic data bases.

Encyclopedia of Associations (**Detroit: Gale Research**)   Published annually, this encyclopedia lists the active trade, business, and professional associations, briefly describes each organization's activities, and lists their publications.

Encyclopedia of Information Systems and Services, **9th ed., Amy Lucas and Nan Soper, editors (Detroit: Gale Research, 1989)**   This encyclopedia lists and describes over 2,500 organizations involved in data storage and retrieval. Included are data-base producers and publishers, on-line vendors, information centers, research centers, and data banks.

Federal Statistical Directory: The Guide to Personnel and Data Sources **(Phoenix, Ariz.: Oryx Press)**   The directory lists, by subject and by organizational unit within each agency, the names, office addresses, and telephone numbers of key personnel working with statistical programs and related activities of agencies in the executive branch of the federal government.

FINDEX, The Directory of Market Research Reports, Studies and Surveys **(Bethesda, MD.: Cambridge Information Group)**   This publication provides a directory of more than 10,000 research reports produced by 500 top U.S. and international research firms.

International Directory of Marketing Research Houses and Services **(New York: American Marketing Association, New York Chapter)**   This publication provides an alphabetic listing of domestic and international marketing research companies. A geographic listing is also provided, along with an index of principal personnel.

Standard Directory of Advertisers **(Wilmette, Ill.: National Register Publishing Company)**   This annual directory lists over 25,000 companies with annual advertising allotments for advertising of more than $75,000. Included are individual listings containing information on type of business, address, key personnel, advertising agency relationship, products advertised, media utilized, and so on. The directory is published in two editions, one by product classification and one by geographic location.

Standard Directory of Advertising Agencies **(Wilmette, Ill.: National Register Publishing Company)**   The *Standard Directory of Advertising Agencies* lists approximately 5,000 advertising agencies and provides information such as personnel by title, key accounts, addresses, and telephone numbers for the agencies. The directory is published three times each year.

Who's Who in Consulting **(Detroit: Gale Research, 1983)**   This directory provides biographical information on consultants in a variety of fields, including their subject area and geographical location.

Endnote

1. For more detailed treatment, see H. Webster Johnson, Anthony J. Faria, and Ernest L. Maier, *How to Use the Business Library: With Sources of Business Information*, 5th ed. (Cincinnati: South-Western Publishing Co., 1984); Eleanor G. May, *A Handbook for Business on the Use of Federal and State Statistical Data* (Washington, D.C.: U.S. Department of Commerce, 1979); and David W. Stewart, *Secondary Research: Information Sources and Methods* (Beverly Hills, Calif.: Sage Publications, 1984).

8

Chapter Eight

Standardized Marketing Information Services

Learning Objectives

Upon completing this chapter, you should be able to

1. List three common uses of the information supplied by standardized marketing information services.

2. Define *geodemography*.

3. Describe the operation of a diary panel.

4. Describe the operation of store audits.

5. Define *UPC*.

6. Define *single-source measurement*.

7. Discuss the purpose and operation of people meters.

Case in Marketing Research

Ruth Seidel was dying to find out about the purchasers of Wheat Crisps—how old they were, how often they shopped, how many kids they had, whether they clipped coupons, and whether they made their living behind a desk or on the factory floor. Most important Seidel wanted to know if, once they had bought one box of Wheat Crisps, they would buy them again.

The snack food division of Archer Foods had been test marketing Wheat Crisps in the Milwaukee area for the past ten months. Wheat Crisps was a new product, a hybrid between a chip and a cracker, designed to appeal to buyers of traditional chips who were becoming increasingly health conscious. While salty and crunchy like chips, Wheat Crisps were lower in fat and calories than other snacks.

Seidel had been in on the product's development from the beginning. Her research department had experimented with 50 different shapes, hundreds of names, and all kinds of flavors. They had talked to more than 10,000 consumers nationwide to find out what they liked and disliked about different versions of the snack. After extensive focus-group testing, the hands-down winner had been a thin rectangular cracker with ridges and a salty, nutty flavor. Wheat Crisps had been born.

To find out how Wheat Crisps would fare in the real world of the supermarket, Seidel had turned to scanner data. By using scanner data from one of the companies that specialized in supplying and interpreting such information, Seidel hoped to get the clearest picture yet of who would buy Wheat Crisps. She wanted to know not only how many shoppers were buying them in the test market and who these shoppers were, but who went back a second and a third time. It was this critical, "depth of repeat" information that Seidel was anxiously awaiting. It was, she felt, the single most important indicator of whether Wheat Crisps had mass market potential.

Discussion Issues

1. If you were Seidel, what would you want to know about the people in the test market who purchased Wheat Crisps?
2. Why do you think depth of repeat is of such importance in the test of a new product?
3. Besides telling Seidel whether enough people in the test market bought the product to justify launching it nationwide, what applications could the scanner data have?

The many standardized marketing information services that are available are another important source of secondary data for the marketing researcher. These services are available at some cost to the user and in this respect are a more expensive source of secondary data than published information. However, they are also typically much less expensive than primary data, because purchasers of these data share the costs incurred by the supplier in collecting, editing, coding, and tabulating them. Because it must be suitable for a number of users, though, what is collected and how the data are gathered must be uniform. Thus, the data may not always ideally fit the needs of the user, which is their main disadvantage over primary data.

This chapter describes some of the main types and sources of standardized marketing information service data.

Profiling Customers

Market segmentation is common among businesses seeking to improve their marketing efforts. Effective segmentation demands that firms group their customers into relatively homogeneous groups. That enables them to tailor marketing programs to the individual groups, thereby making the programs more effective. A common segmentation base for firms selling industrial goods takes into account the industry designation or designations of its customers, most typically by means of the Standard Industrial Classification (SIC) codes. The SIC codes are a system developed by the U.S. Census Department for organizing the reporting of business information, such as employment, value added in manufacturing, capital expenditures, and total sales. Each major industry in the United States is assigned a two-digit number, indicating the group to which it belongs. The types of businesses making up each industry are further identified by additional digits. Figure 8.1 displays a partial breakdown of the construction industry.

One of the commercial services that is especially popular among industrial goods and service suppliers is Dun's Market Identifiers (DMI), a special name given by Dun and Bradstreet to its marketing information service. DMI is a roster of over 4 million establishments that is updated monthly so that the record on each company is accurate and current. The records are available in hard copy or as computer files. Figure 8.2 is an example of a three-by-five-inch card record. Note its contents, particularly the ability to identify, by means of the SIC codes, the industries that the company or plant serves. A recent innovation has made the identification task even more precise. Called the *2 + 2 Enhancement*, the new system builds on the revised 1987 SIC codes with a two-tiered expansion. The expansion is structured similarly to the way the third and fourth digits of the current code refine the basic two-digit major groups. Table 8.1 shows how the system works. The upshot of the additional digits is a dramatic expansion in the number of types of businesses. There are 1,006 four-digit categories as defined by the government's 1987 revisions, some 2,500 six-digit codes, and more than 15,000 eight-digit codes with the 2 + 2 Enhancement.

The enhanced system allows much more precise customer targeting. Suppose, for example, "that one of your targeted markets is food products machinery, and the product you sell into that segment is heat gauges, which are used on only three specific types of food machines—milk-pasteurizing machinery, bakery ovens, and brewing equipment. By utilizing the 2 + 2 Enhancement of that one market segment, food products machinery can now be separated into the three distinct areas you need to target, with each measured and analyzed on its own merits. Conversely, you can

Figure 8.1   *Partial Breakdown of Standard Industrial Classification (SIC) Codes*

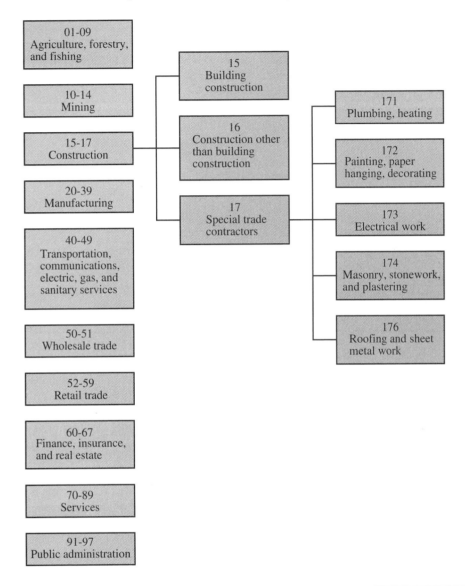

easily combine the performance of these three segments into one by using the first four digits of each, thereby allowing you to produce growth trends or compare sales performance with data from previous years."[1]

The DMI records on a company-by-company basis allow sales management to construct sales prospect files, define sales territories and measure territory potentials, and isolate potential new customers with particular characteristics. They allow advertising management to select potential customers by size and location; to analyze and select the media to reach them; to build, maintain, and structure current mailing

Figure 8.2   ***Dun's Market Identifiers (DMI)***

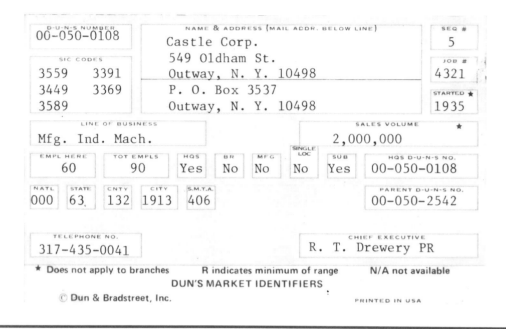

lists; to generate sales leads qualified by size, location, and quality; and to locate new markets for testing. Finally, they allow marketing research professionals to assess market potential by territory, to measure market penetration in terms of numbers of prospects and numbers of customers, and to make comparative analyses of overall performance by districts and sales territories and in individual industries.

Firms selling consumer goods can ill afford to target individual customers, because no single customer is likely to buy much of any product or service. Rather, firms need to target groups of customers. Their ability to do this has increased substantially since the 1970 census, which was the first electronic census. Since that time, the Census Bureau has made available computer tapes of the facts that have been gathered and, more recently, optical disks, which also make the data usable by those with personal computers. Having the data available in electronic form allows their tabulation by arbitrary geographic boundaries, and an entire industry has developed since 1970 to take advantage of this capability. The **geodemographers,** as they are most typically called, combine census data with their own survey data or data that they gather from administrative records, such as motor vehicle registrations or credit transactions, to produce customized products for their clients. For example: "R. L. Polk and Urban Decision Systems, [UDS] . . . have a product for retailers called the Vehicle Origin Survey. Polk gathers license plate numbers from cars parked in shopping centers and uses motor vehicle registration files to find out where the owners live; UDS then retrieves detailed demographics about the neighborhood characteristics. Another kind of link has been pioneered by Donnelley Marketing. ACES (Automated Customer Evaluation Service) ties Donnelley's data with monthly MasterCard and Visa sales tickets, on contract with Citicorp Credit Services, Inc. Clients get reports summarizing the profiles of their customers. Then they can go to Donnelley to rent lists of people having the same characteristics."[2]

Geodemography The availability of demographic, consumer-behavior, and life-style data by arbitrary geographic boundaries that are typically quite small.

Table 8.1   *How the DMI 2 + 2 Enhancement System Works*

To better explain how this system works, let's examine one of the two-digit manufacturing codes: SIC 35—Industrial & Commercial Machinery and Computer Equipment.

This particular two-digit major group represents all machinery manufacturers, with a third digit defining the specific type of machinery—engines, farm machinery, construction, metal working, special industry machinery, office machinery, and so on. In this example, we'll use SIC 355—Special Industry Machinery. By adding a fourth digit, we can further refine the type of machinery within the three-digit Special Industry category (food products, textiles, woodworking, paper, printing, etc.). For example, if we want to identify manufacturers of Food Products Machinery, we would look at SIC 3556. But this is as far as the government's system goes in its standard codings.

DMI's 2 + 2 Enhancement adds two additional two-digit codes to the four-digit SIC. Thus, continuing with this same example, we find that within SIC 3556 there are numerous types of food products machinery—dairy machinery, beverage machinery, meat-processing machinery, and more. The first two-digit extension would divide these other types of industries into major subgroups of six digits, with a second two-digit extension further refining each line of business, which, in the case of dairy machinery, would break down into cheese-making machinery, ice cream machinery, milk-processing machinery, and other highly specific categories.

These subgroups are all identified and categorized independently, yet they are related at both the six-digit and four-digit levels, because each is a refinement of the previous code. What this means is that all food products machinery can be collapsed back into the three-digit category and even further back into the two-digit major group, which makes it possible to compare data on shipments and establishments with those produced by the federal government and other sources.

Source: Jerry Reisberg, "The Next Generation in Direct Marketing," *Sales & Marketing Management*, 142 (May 1989), pp. 60–62.

Another thing that the geodemographers do is regularly update the census data through statistical extrapolation. The data can consequently be used with much more confidence during the years intervening between the censuses. Another value-added feature that has had a great deal to do with the success of the industry has been the analysis performed on the census data. Firms supplying geodemographic information have cluster-analyzed the census-produced data to produce "homogeneous groups" that describe the American population. For example, Claritas (the first firm to do this and still one of the leaders in the industry) used over 500 demographic variables in its Prizm (Potential Ratings for Zip Markets) system when classifying residential neighborhoods. This system breaks the 250,000 neighborhood areas in the United States into 40 types based on consumer behavior and life-style. Each of the types has a fancy name that theoretically describes the type of people living there, such as Urban Gold Coast, Shotguns and Pickups, Pools and Patios, and so on. Claritas or the other suppliers will do a customized analysis for whatever geographic boundaries a client specifies. Alternatively, a client can send a tape listing the Zip Code addresses of some customer data base, and the geodemographer will attach the cluster codes. Figure 8.3 shows the type of colored maps that can be produced by these services.

Ethical

Dilemma 8.1   Maps, Inc., is the marketing research division of a large credit card company. The division specializes in the preparation of geodemographic maps. To prepare these maps, it combines information from customers' credit card transactions with the demographic data it collected when the customers applied for a credit card. Then, with its profiles of who is purchasing what, in combination with Census data on small geographic areas, Maps, Inc., is able to develop maps that display by zip

Figure 8.3   ***Sample Geodemographic Map***

This map shows the 1989 estimated median household income per square mile in Atlanta, Georgia.

Source: Urban Decision Systems.

code area the potential market for various types of products and services. The company in turn sells this information to various manufacturers, wholesalers, and retailers after customizing the data to the geographic boundaries specified by the client.

- Is it ethical to use credit card transaction information in this way?
- Do the credit card users have a right to know this research is being conducted?
- Should it be necessary for Maps, Inc., to get signed releases from individual card holders before incorporating the individuals' purchase transactions in the data base? What might happen to the quality of the data with the requirement of signed releases?

Measuring Product Sales and Market Share

A critical need in today's increasingly competitive environment is for firms to have an accurate assessment of how they are doing. A common yardstick for that assessment is sales and market share. Firms selling industrial goods or services typically track their own sales and market shares through analyses of their sales invoices. They also obtain feedback from the sales department in terms of how they did in various product or system proposal competitions. An alternative source that companies use to measure their market share is one of the on-line bibliographic data sources discussed in the last chapter. Many times a search of an appropriate data base will turn up published studies containing product, company, and market information, including market share statistics.

Manufacturers of consumer goods also monitor their sales by account through the examination of sales invoices. For them, though, that is only part of the equation to determine how they are doing. Using factory shipments as a sales barometer neglects the filling or depleting of distribution pipelines that may be occurring. The other part of the equation involves the measurement of sales to final consumers. Historically there are several ways that such measurements have been handled, including the use of diary panels of households and store audits.

Diary Panels

All diary panels operate similarly. For example, the National Purchase Diary (NPD) consumer panel, which is the largest in the United States, comprises more than 15,000 reporting households, who use a preprinted diary to record their monthly purchases in approximately 50 product categories. Figure 8.4 illustrates the sample diary for Toys & Games. Note that the diary asks for considerable detail about the toy purchased, including the price paid, store where purchased, age and sex of both the recipient and the purchaser, as well as other specific characteristics of the purchase.

The households composing NPD are geographically dispersed. The total panel contains 29 miniature panels, each representative of a local market. Panel members are recruited quarterly and are added to the active panel after they have satisfactorily met NPD's reporting standards. Households are recruited so that the composition of the panel mirrors the population of the United States. The panel is balanced with respect to size, age of female head of household, household income, and geography. Panel members are compensated for their participation with gifts, and families are dropped from the panel at their request or if they fail to return three of their last six diaries.

The diaries are returned to NPD monthly, the purchase histories are aggregated, and reports prepared. Using these reports, the subscribing company is able to assess (among other things) the following:

The size of the market, the proportion of households buying over time, and the amount purchased per buyer
- Manufacturer and brand shares over time
- Brand loyalty and brand-switching behavior
- Frequency of purchase and amount purchased per transaction
- Influence of price and special price deals, as well as average price paid
- Characteristics of heavy buyers
- Impact of a new manufacturer or brand on the established brands
- Effect of a change in advertising or distribution strategy[3]

Figure 8.4 **Sample Page from National Purchase Diary**

TOYS & GAMES/HOBBY & CRAFT PURCHASES FOR CHILDREN & ADULTS
Be sure to include ALL ELECTRONIC AND VIDEO GAMES AND TOYS

STORE CODES

01 BOOK STORE	50 ELECTRONICS STORE
10 DEPARTMENT STORE	60 5&10/VARIETY
20 MAIL ORDER HOUSE	70 GROCERY/FOOD/SUPERMARKET
21 HOBBY STORE	80 DRUG
22 STATIONERY/CARD/GIFT SHOP	85 CATALOG SHOWROOM
28 HARDWARE	90 DOOR TO DOOR
30 DISCOUNT	95 PRICE CLUB
40 VIDEO STORE	97 HOME SHOPPING VIA TV
45 TOY STORE	99 OTHER

CATEGORY CODES

10 **Infant Toys:** Rattles, Teethers, Crib Toys, Activity Centers, Mobiles, Parenting Aids (Intercoms, Exercise Sets)
14 **Role Playing/Home Making:** Doctor/Nurse Kits, Play Kitchens, Gardening Tools, Play Cosmetics & Dress Up Sets, Play Appliances, Etc.
18 **Talking/Sound Toys:** Slide Viewers, Tape Recorders & Play Telephones, Musical Instruments/Radios
22 **Dolls & Accessories:** Fashion Dolls, Baby Dolls, Mini Dolls, Talking Dolls, Clothes & Accessories
26 **Stuffed Toys:** Stuffed Animals & Toys Including Talking, Musical & Animated Plush
30 **Action Figures/Accessories:** Robots, Warriors, Monsters, Military & Space Figures
34 **Guns:** Laser Guns, Water Pistols, All Other Guns
38 **Building & Construction Toys:** Wood, Metal, Plastic Blocks/Interlocking Pieces
42 **Remote Controlled Vehicles:** Cars, Boats, Trucks, Aircraft Operated By A Remote Mechanism
46 **Radio Controlled Vehicles:** Cars, Boats, Trucks, Aircraft That Are Radio Operated
48 **Battery Powered Vehicles:** Cars, Boats, Trucks, Aircraft That Require A Battery
54 **Wind Up/Friction-Powered Vehicles:** Cars, Boats, Trucks, Aircraft Powered By Rubber Bands, Wind Up Mechanism or Friction
58 **Other Vehicles:** Non-Powered Cars, Boats, Trucks, Planes (Plastic, Wood, Metal)
62 **Electric Cars/Trains & Accessories**
66 **Games/Puzzles:** Trivia, Board, Word, Card & Puzzle Games, Chess, Checkers, Backgammon, Brain Teasers & Jigsaw Puzzles
70 **Electronic & Video Games/Learning Aids:** Include Educational Electronics, Electronic Games, Video Game Cartridges & Players, Interactive TV Games & Software
74 **Learning & Scientific Toys:** (Non Electronic) Flash Cards, Alphabet Boards, Globes, Telescopes & Lab Sets
78 **Creative Toys:** Paint, Crayons, Sewing/Knitting Sets & Supplies, Models & Other Design Toys
82 **Activity Toys:** Jacks, Marbles, Kites, Yo-Yos, Bubbles, Balloons
86 **Sports Equipment:** (Indoor/Outdoor) Bats, Balls, Skates, Skateboards & Aerobic/Exercise Items
90 **Ride Ons:** Riding Toys Including Bikes, Trikes, Wagons, Scooters, Rocking Horses, Sleds
99 **All Other Toys:** Children's Furniture, Pools, Etc. & All Other Toys Not In Any Other Category

N2 1990 J F M A M J J A S O N D

WHERE DID YOU PURCHASE? — NAME OF STORE OR COMPANY IF PURCHASED FROM DOOR-TO-DOOR OR HOME DELIVERY SALESPERSON

FOR WHAT AGE WAS ITEM PURCHASED? (IF UNDER 2 YEARS REPORT AS MONTHS) — MALES / FEMALES

SPECIAL QUESTIONS (See List Below) A, B, C & D Only

TOTAL PRICE PAID (Do Not Include Tax)

HOW MANY OF EACH KIND DID YOU BUY? (Write In Number)

DESCRIPTION OF TOY OR GAME — TYPE OF TOY OR GAME SUCH AS GAME WITH BOARD, BUILDING BLOCKS, PUZZLE, DOLL, ETC. / CATEGORY CODE (See List at Right)

MANUFACTURER'S CODE — Example 48001 296502

MODEL NUMBER — Please Fill In

MANUFACTURER (Write In)

FULL NAME OF TOY OR GAME — Copy From Label or Box

DATE OF PURCHASE

SPECIAL QUESTIONS: ENTER CORRECT CODES IN FAR RIGHT COLUMNS ABOVE

A. HOW IS THE RECEIVER(S) OF THIS TOY/BOOK RELATED TO THE BUYER? (Write in all numbers that apply)

CODE		CODE	
01 Son(s)	07 Nephew	13 Wife	
02 Daughter(s)	08 Brother	14 Friend (No Relation)	
03 Grandson(s)	09 Sister	15 Do Not Know Recipient Yet	
04 Granddaughter(s)	11 Bought for Myself/Ourselves	17 Grandson(s) and Granddaughter(s)	
05 Cousin	12 Husband	99 Other	
06 Niece	10 Bought for Entire Family		

B. WHAT WAS THE OCCASION?
CODE
1 Christmas/Chanukah
2 Birthday
3 Other Special Occasion
4 No Special Occasion

C. DID YOU PLAN TO BUY THIS SPECIFIC ITEM WHEN YOU WENT TO THE STORE?
CODE
1 Yes
2 No

D. DID RECIPIENT INFLUENCE PURCHASE?
CODE
1 Asked For This Toy/Book By Name
2 Asked For This Type of Toy/Book
3 Had No Direct Influence

ANSWER E and F for JUVENILE BOOKS ONLY

E. IS THE BOOK...
CODE
1 Hard Covered With Paper Pages Inside?
2 Hard Covered With Board Pages Inside?
3 Soft Covered?
4 A Boxed Set?

F. IS THE ITEM...
CODE
1 A Book?
2 A Book And Record Set?
3 A Book And Cassette Set?

ANSWER **ALL** SPECIAL QUESTIONS FOR JUVENILE BOOKS ON TOP OF FACING PAGE

Source: Courtesy of The NPD Group, Inc., Port Washington, NY.

For example, the Toy Manufacturers of America, the industry trade group, found through analysis of NPD data that there is a fundamental shift occurring in where toys are purchased. There has been a decline in use of toy departments in department and discount stores and an increasing use of toy supermarkets like Toys "R" Us and Child World.[4]

Ethical
Dilemma 8.2
Toys-4-Kids, a major toy manufacturer, wishes to monitor changes in its sales, market share, and household penetration through the establishment and maintenance of a panel of households having children ages 12 and under. The households will be asked to record their purchases of all toys and games. Jean Blue, the marketing research director, believes it will be best to withhold the sponsor's name when recruiting households for the panel. She thinks that if the panel members know the research is being conducted by Toys-4-Kids, their reporting behavior could be biased.

- If the panel members are volunteers, do they have a right to know who is sponsoring the panel?
- If they are compensated for their participation, do they have a right to know who is sponsoring the panel?
- Do you think a household's reporting behavior will be biased if the household knows Toys-4-Kids is sponsoring the research?

Store Audits

Another historically popular way of measuring sales to ultimate customers involves store audits. The basic concept of a store audit is very simple. The research firm sends field workers, called auditors, to a select group of retail stores at fixed intervals. On each visit the auditors take a complete inventory of all products designated for the audit. The auditors also note the merchandise moving into the store by checking wholesale invoices, warehouse withdrawal records, and direct shipments from manufacturers. Sales to consumers are then determined by the following calculation:

Beginning inventory + Net purchases (from wholesalers and manufacturers) − Ending inventory = Sales.

The store audit was pioneered by the A. C. Nielsen Company and served as the backbone of the *Nielsen Retail Index* for many years. The method is still used to measure sales and to gather information on retail prices, store displays, and promotional activity for the drugstores, mass merchandisers, and liquor stores among the sample of outlets used to construct the *Nielsen Retail Index*. Sales of food stores in the sample of outlets, however, are now monitored by scanner. The company takes the auditing records and generates the following information for each of the brands for each of the products audited:

- Sales to consumers
- Purchases by retailers
- Retail inventories
- Number of days' supply
- Out-of-stock stores
- Prices (wholesale and retail)

- Special factory packs
- Dealer support (displays, local advertising, coupon redemption)

Subscribers to the Nielsen service can get these data broken down by competitor, geographic area, or store type. Nielsen will also provide special reports to clients for a fee. These special reports include such things as the effect of shelf facings on sales, the sales impact of different promotional strategies, premiums or prices, or the analysis of sales by client-specified geographic areas. The stores pinpointed for inclusion in the panel are contacted personally to secure their cooperation. Further, the stores are compensated for their cooperation on a per-audit basis.

Scanners

Scanner An electronic device that automatically reads the imprinted Universal Product Code as a product is pulled across the scanner, looks up the price in an attached computer, and instantly prints the description and price of the item on the cash register tape.

Since the late 1970s, Nielsen has been supplementing its *Retail Index* service with its SCANTRACK service. The SCANTRACK service emerged from the revolutionary development in the grocery industry brought about by the installation of scanning equipment to read Universal Product Codes. Universal Product Codes are 11-digit numbers imprinted on each product sold in a supermarket. The first digit, called the number system character, indicates the type of product it is (e.g., grocery or drug). The next five digits identify the manufacturer and the last five a particular product of the manufacturer, be it a different size, variety, or flavor (Figure 8.5).

There is a unique 11-digit code for each product in the supermarket. As the product with its bar code is pulled across the **scanner**, the scanner identifies the

Figure 8.5   ***Universal Product Codes***

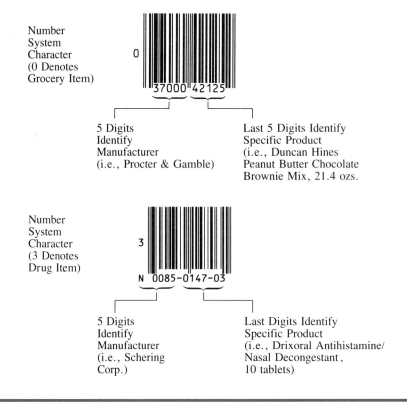

Scanner technology allows manufacturers to specifically target consumers. In this case, if a shopper purchases one of up to 180 different brands, once its UPC code is read by the store's computer, a coupon for a competitive or complementary brand is printed on a printer installed next to the cash register and is handed to the consumer with her receipt.

Source: Courtesy of Catalina Marketing Corporation.

11-digit number, looks up the price in the attached computer, and immediately prints the description and price of the item on the cash register receipt. At the same time, the computer can keep track of the movement of every item that is scanned. The SCANTRACK service provides weekly sales data from a nationwide sample of scanner-equipped stores. The data allow clients to evaluate the effectiveness of short-term promotions, to evaluate pricing changes, to follow new product introductions, and to monitor unexpected events, such as product recalls and shortages.

Scanners' effect on the collection of sales and market share data has been profound. For one thing, they have changed the locus of power in distribution channels. Research Window 8.1 describes the nature of the change. Another important change wrought by scanners is an increased ability to link purchase behavior with demographic information. Before the advent of scanners, the link was made using diaries. A problem with diaries is that they depend for their accuracy on the conscientiousness of those in the panel to record their purchases as they occur. Scanner data are not subject to such recording biases. Several firms have developed systems over the last few years to take advantage of this fact, including Information Resources and Nielsen. A key feature of the new systems is the ability to link television-viewing behavior with product-purchasing behavior to produce what has become known as *single-source* data.

The basics of single-source research are straightforward. As an example, consider the operation of the Information Resources BehaviorScan system. In each of the markets in which BehaviorScan operates, more than 2,500 households have been recruited by Information Resources to present identification cards at each of the grocery stores every time their members make a purchase. Almost all the supermarkets in each area are provided scanners by Information Resources. Each

Research Window 8.1
Scanners Shift Balance of Power in Marketplace

The marketplace has always been a battleground. Manufacturers clamoring for shelf space are pitted against retailers struggling to offer a wide range of products to their customers. Until recently, manufacturers dominated the fray. They could extend their product line with new sizes, new flavors, and so on, relatively secure in the knowledge that retailers would willingly stock the new items. However, the widespread use of optical scanners has recently tipped the balance in the other direction.

Scanners at the checkout read the universal product codes (UPCs), which describe the brand, item, manufacturer, and pricing of each item sold. Wal-Mart, Sears, and K-Mart have begun to install scanners in their stores. All Toys "R" Us stores are equipped with scanners, and the toy chain, which controls roughly one-quarter of the U.S. toy market, refuses to stock any item not marked with a UPC code.

Although the impact of scanning information is just beginning in most retail markets, it has already transformed the grocery store. Let's say that you have developed a new brand of yogurt that you would like to introduce nationally. The problem is that the grocer's shelves are already bursting with products, and by using scanner data the grocer knows pretty closely to the penny how much money can be made on each of the products on the shelves. However, the grocer has no evidence that your new product will sell half as much as the product that has to be removed from the shelf to make room for it.

To deal with this problem, retailers have begun charging slotting allowances, which are fees that retailers charge manufacturers for each space or slot on the shelf that a new product will occupy. A major retailer in Los Angeles might charge a slotting fee of $4,000 for the chain, per slot. If your brand of yogurt has 14 flavors, distribution in that one chain alone would cost $56,000, and shelf space in all five of L.A.'s major chains would cost a whopping $280,000.

But slotting fees are only one aspect of the new technology. One very powerful application of optical scanner data is direct product profitability (DPP), which is just beginning to be applied in the marketplace. DPP is a financial model that allocates all the retailer's costs, item by item, to every item on the shelf to determine the net profit of each. The model factors in costs associated with purchasing, transportation, shelf inventory, and marketing as well as the general overhead of the store.

A good way to see what a powerful tool DPP can be is to look at a single product—for example, sugar. On a gross-profit basis, sugar looks like an important and profitable category, but by using DPP it becomes clear that on a net-profit basis, sugar is a money-loser for the retailer. Sugar is a big, bulky package, heavy and easily damaged, and the space it consumes in the warehouse and on the shelf, as well as the labor expenses for stocking it, cost more than the return the retailer is getting based on price and sales turnover. Retailers are obviously not going to pull sugar from their shelves. However, it seems reasonable that retailers will take a close look at how much space is devoted to sugar and which brands perform better than others.

Retailers have up until now been the primary beneficiary of optical scanner information, but some are beginning to also help manufacturers while improving their own margins. For example, Safeway Stores, Inc., one of the world's leading food stores, has launched an optical scanner checkout network to help manufacturers evaluate promotion effectiveness and identify potential new markets.

Safeway Scanner Marketing Research Service (SMRS) uses scanner data to track sales of items stocked in two locations in a single store to see, for example, whether chewing gum sells better at the checkout stand or in the candy aisle. The company downloads summaries of weekly sales items onto floppy disks so that manufacturers can analyze the data. SMRS tracks coupon redemptions and helps manufacturers determine the effect of in-store sampling on sales and the most effective types of in-store displays. By using scanner data, SMRS can also track the effect on unit sales of a change in price. SMRS sells this information to manufacturers willing to use the service.

Sources: Spencer L. Hapoienu, "The Struggle for a Place on the Shelf," *Viewpoint* (July/August 1988), pp. 3–9; "Safeway Stores Double as Research Lab," *Marketing News*, 21 (August 28, 1987), p. 36; and Brent H. Felgner, "Retailers Grab Power, Control Marketplace," *Marketing News*, 23 (January 16, 1989), pp. 1–2.

household member presents his or her identification card when checking out. The card is scanned along with the purchases, allowing Information Resources to relate a family's purchases by brand, size, and price to the family's demographic characteristics and the household's known exposure to coupons, newspaper ads, free samples, and point-of-purchase displays.

Information Resources also is able to direct different TV advertising spots to different households through the "black boxes" that have been attached to the television sets in each test household, in cooperation with the cable television systems serving the markets. This allows Information Resources to monitor the buying reactions to different advertisements or to the same advertisement in different types of households (e.g., whether the buying reactions to a particular ad are the same or different among past users and nonusers of the product). This targetable television capability allows Information Resources to balance the panel of members for each ad test within each market according to the criteria the sponsor chooses (e.g., past purchases of the product), thereby minimizing the problem of having comparable experimental and control groups.

The Nielsen system operates similarly, although there are differences in the measurement of both viewing and behavior. The Nielsen system is not restricted to cable television households but can direct the target ads to previously specified households using normal broadcast signals. The system measures purchases through the use of a wand that participating household members are asked to pass over the UPC codes on products brought into the house.

The impact of single-source measurement on the conduct of marketing activities has been, and promises to be, so profound that it may "ultimately rival the importance of the microscope to scientists," according to a report by J. Walter Thompson USA.[5]

> A Campbell Soup Co. single-source experiment with its V-8 juice shows how the system works. Using an index of 100 for the average household's V-8 consumption, Campbell found that demographically similar TV audiences can consume vastly different amounts of V-8. In early 1987, for example, "General Hospital" had a below-average 80 index, while "Guiding Light" had an above-average 120 index. The results were surprising, because "General Hospital" actually had a slightly higher percentage of women 25 to 54 years old—the demographic groups most predisposed to buy V-8—and so would ordinarily have been expected to be a better advertising forum to reach V-8 drinkers.[6]

Measuring Advertising Exposure and Effectiveness

Another area in which there is a great deal of commercial information available for marketers relates to the assessment of exposure to, and effectiveness of, advertising. Most suppliers of industrial goods advertise most heavily in trade publications. To sell space more effectively, the various trade publications typically sponsor readership studies that they make available to potential advertisers. Suppliers of consumer goods and services also have access to media-sponsored readership studies. In addition, a number of services have evolved to measure consumer exposure to the various media.

Television and Radio

The Nielsen Television Index is probably the most generally familiar commercial information service. The most casual television watcher has probably heard of the Nielsen ratings and their impact on which television shows are canceled by the networks and which are allowed to continue. The index itself is designed to provide

Research Window 8.2
Grousing about People Meters

When ABC chairman Tom Murphy addressed more than 100 television critics, he asked a leading question: "How many of you would conscientiously be pushing a people meter's buttons after you'd had one in your home for several weeks?" Only two of the professional tube-watchers raised their hands. They aren't the only ones expressing skepticism about the A. C. Nielsen Company's switch from diaries and passive Audimeters to a technology dependent on button-pushers.

In the past, Nielsen measured television audiences on the basis of written diaries filled out by scientifically selected families twice a year during "sweeps" month. Now these data are being gathered by high-tech people meters, and the change has a lot of broadcasters grousing. Many think that the new system is biased in favor of yuppies or "techies" and against those who feel uncomfortable with high-tech gadgetry. There is also widespread concern that the system underrepresents teens and kids.

Nickelodeon and MTV have been especially hard hit by the disinclination of young people to punch people-meter buttons. People-meter viewing levels for the two networks are routinely 20 to 40 percent below those shown by the Nielsen diary. MTV sales reps actually show a people meter to prospective advertisers to demonstrate how hard the device is to operate. According to Marshall Cohen, senior vice-president for MTV Networks, telephone coincidentals are the most consistently accurate form of kid and teen measurement. But this process, which involves calling each and every household in the people-meter sample, is very expensive.

Yet people meters aren't without their supporters. Many smaller independent stations have found their market share boosted by the new people-meter data. With the old diary system, Nielsen families usually sat down at the end of the week and filled in the diary. When they wrote down what shows they watched, they tended to remember the most popular shows—most of which are shown on the networks. The rerun of "Happy Days" they may have watched while they folded laundry was less likely to make it into the diary.

In addition, some researchers believe that people meters more accurately differentiate between "core" viewers, who actively seek out a particular show, and "peripheral" viewers, who end up watching whatever happens to be on when they walk into the room. Thus, MTV may show more adult viewers, CNN more young people, and ESPN more women than before.

Although industry insiders may disagree about the relative merits of people meters, they do agree about one thing: a passive audience-measurement device is the only solution to accurately measuring an increasingly fragmented audience. Nielsen has been field testing an infrared-based passive meter, but no commercial use of that device has yet been scheduled.

"The desire is there on behalf of nearly everyone involved in TV buying to have access to a reliable passive-measurement system," says David Marans of J. Walter Thompson in New York. "It's just a matter of making the new technology less cumbersome."

Source: Richard Mahler, "Grousing about People Meters," *Adweek* (December 5, 1988), pp. F.K. 10–11; and Chuck Ross, "How Meters Matter in the Sweeps," *Adweek* (June 20, 1988), pp. B.T. 10–12.

People meter A device used to measure when a television is on, to what channel it is tuned, and who in the household is watching it.

estimates of the size and nature of the audience for individual television programs. Until recently, the basic data were gathered through the use of Audimeter instruments, which were electronic devices attached to the television sets in cooperating households. Each Audimeter was connected to a central computer, which recorded when the set was on and to what channel it was tuned. Beginning in the fall of 1988, Nielsen started measuring television audiences through the use of people meters. The switch was not without controversy, however, as Research Window 8.2 indicates. **People meters** attempt to measure not only the channel to which a set is tuned, but who in the household is watching. Each member of the family has his or her own viewing number. Whoever turns on the set, sits down to watch, or changes the channel is supposed to enter his or her number into the people meter. All of this information is transmitted immediately to the central computer for processing.

Through the data provided by these basic records, Nielsen develops estimates of the number and percentage of all television households viewing a given television show. Nielsen also breaks down these aggregate ratings by ten socioeconomic and demographic characteristics, including territory, education of head of house, county size, time zones, household income, age of woman of house, color-television ownership, occupation of head of house, presence of nonadults, and household size. These breakdowns assist the network, of course, in selling advertising on particular programs, while they assist the advertiser in choosing to sponsor programs that reach households with the desired characteristics.[7]

Advertisers buying radio time are also interested in the size and demographic composition of the audiences they will be reaching. Radio-listening statistics are typically gathered using diaries that are placed in a panel of households. Arbitron, for example, generates telephone numbers randomly to ensure that it is reaching households with unlisted numbers. Those household members who agree to participate when called are sent diaries in which they are asked to record their radio-listening behavior for a short period. Most radio markets are rated only once or twice a year, although some of the larger ones are rated four times a year. The April/May survey is conducted in every Arbitron market and consequently is known as the "sweeps" period. Radio ratings are typically broken down by age and sex and focus more on individual than household behavior, in contrast with television ratings.

Print Media

There are several services that measure exposure to, and readership of, print media. For example, the Starch Readership Service measures the reading of advertisements in magazines and newspapers. Some 75,000 advertisements in 1,000 issues of consumer and farm magazines, business publications, and newspapers are assessed each year using over 100,000 personal interviews.

The Starch surveys employ the *recognition method* to assess a particular ad's effectiveness. With the magazine open, the respondent is asked to indicate whether he or she has read each ad. Four degrees of reading are recorded:

1. Nonreader—a person who did not remember having previously seen the advertisement in the issue being studied.
2. Noted—a person who remembered seeing the advertisement in that particular issue.
3. Associated—a person who not only noted the advertisement but also saw or read some part of it that clearly indicates the brand or advertiser.
4. Read most—a person who read 50 percent or more of the written material in the ad.[8]

During the course of the interview, reading data are also collected on the component parts of each ad, such as the headlines, subheadings, pictures, copy blocks, and so forth.

Interviewing begins a short time after the issue of the magazine is placed on sale. For weekly and biweekly consumer magazines, interviewing begins three to six days after the on-sale date and continues for one to two weeks. For monthly magazines, interviewing begins two weeks after the on-sale date and continues for three weeks.

The interviews are conducted by a trained staff of field interviewers, who have the responsibility of selecting those to be interviewed, since a quota sample is employed. Each interviewer must locate within a particular area an assigned number of readers who are 18 years of age and over, with various occupations, family sizes, and marital and economic statuses. The quotas are determined so that different characteristics will be represented in the sample in proportion to their representation in the population. Readers are included in the sample when they conform to the specified demographic characteristics and when they reply in the affirmative when asked if they have read the particular magazine issue in question. The size of the sample varies by publication. Most Starch studies are based on 100 to 150 interviews per sex.

Because newspaper and magazine space-cost data are also available, a *readers-per-dollar variable* can be calculated. The final summary report from Starch shows for each ad (one-half page or larger) overall readership percentages, readers per dollar, and rank when grouped by product category. The summary sheet is attached to a labeled copy of the issue in which each ad is marked to show the readership results for the ad as a whole and for each component part. The data allow the magazine or newspaper advertiser to compare (with respect to readership) his or her ads with those of competitors, current ads with prior ads, and current ads against product averages. This process can be effective in assessing changes in theme, copy, layout, use of color, and so on.

Multimedia Services

The Simmons Media/Marketing Service uses a national probability sample of some 19,000 respondents and serves as a comprehensive data source allowing the cross-referencing of product usage and media exposure. Four different interviews are conducted with each respondent so that magazine, television, newspaper, and radio can all be covered by the Simmons Service. Information is reported for total adults and for males and females separately.[9]

The service conducts two personal interviews, which obtain measures of respondent readership of individual magazines and newspapers. During the second personal interview, respondents are also asked about their radio-listening behavior. A self-administered questionnaire is used to gather product purchase and use information for over 800 product categories, which remain relatively fixed from year to year. Finally, television-viewing behavior is ascertained by means of a personal viewing diary, which each respondent is asked to keep for two weeks.

A probability sample is used in selecting respondents for the study. High-income households are sampled more than proportionately, while low-income households are sampled less than proportionately, to their number. All households receive a premium for participating, and a minimum of six calls is made in the attempt to interview previously unavailable respondents. A large number of demographic characteristics are gathered from each respondent included in the study.

Simmons determines magazine readership using the *through-the-book*, or editorial-interest, method for 43 major magazines and by the *recent-reading* method for 95 smaller monthly magazines. In the through-the-book method, respondents are screened to determine which magazines they might have read during the past six months. They are then shown actual issues of magazines stripped of confusing material (for identification purposes), such as advertising pages and recurring columns and features. Ten feature articles unique to the issue are exhibited, and an indirect approach, asking respondents to select the articles they personally find especially interesting, is employed. At the end, a qualifying question is asked: "Now that you have been through this magazine, could you tell me whether this is the first time you happened to look into this particular issue, or have you looked into it before?" Respondents must affirm prior exposure to the issue to qualify as readers. Expressions of doubt or uncertainty would disqualify them.

The recent-reading method operates by having respondents physically sort a deck of four-color magazine logo cards. First, respondents are asked to sort the cards into two piles, representing magazines read and not read in the past six months. For all the cards in the "read pile," respondents are asked to indicate which ones they have read in the past month. The following types of information are gathered from the more than 800 products included in the annual Simmons study:

- Users of products, brands, or services
- Ownership of products
- Price paid for selected items
- Brand used most often
- Volume/frequency of use
- Store at which purchased

This product information can then be tabulated against such things as magazines read, television programs viewed, newspapers read, and radio-listening behavior and simultaneously against a number of demographic characteristics that enable a client to identify target groups and to determine the combinations of media vehicles required to reach them most efficiently and with the desired frequency.

Mediamark Research also makes available information on exposure to various media and household consumption of various products and services. Its annual survey of 20,000 adult respondents covers more than 250 magazines, newspapers, radio stations, and television channels and over 450 products and services.[10] Information is gathered from respondents by two methods. First, a personal interview is used to collect demographics and data pertaining to media exposure. Magazine readership is measured by a recent-reading method that asks respondents to sort a deck of magazine logo cards according to whether they (1) are sure they have read, (2) are not sure they have read, and (3) are sure they have not read, a given magazine during its most recent publication period. Newspaper readership is measured using a *yesterday-reading* technique in which respondents are asked which of the daily newspapers on the list of papers that circulate in the area were read or looked into within the previous seven days. For Sunday and weekend papers, a four-week time span is used. Radio listening is determined through a *yesterday-recall* technique in which respondents are asked how much time was spent listening to a radio during each time period on the previous day. They are then asked what stations were listened to. Television-audience data are collected in a similar manner.

On completion of the interview, interviewers then leave a questionnaire booklet with respondents. The booklet, which covers personal and household usage of approximately 450 products and services and 5,700 brands, is personally picked up by the interviewer after a short time period. The 20,000 respondents for the Mediamark reports are selected using probability sampling methods.

The difference in the procedures used by Simmons and Mediamark to measure media exposure, particularly magazine readership, can create a real dilemma for advertisers. Both firms interview approximately 20,000 people for each study, but the figures reported by them can be very different, as Figure 8.6 indicates. In general, it seems that Mediamark's figures of readership are about 10 percent higher for weeklies and 35 percent higher for monthlies, but that can vary dramatically by publication.[11] This difference, of course, creates havoc for those attempting to buy media space in which to place ads.

Figure 8.6   ***A Controversy as to the Top Five Magazines Based on Total Adult Readership***

	In Millions
The Simmons List	
1. TV Guide	43.2
2. Reader's Digest	37.5
3. People	24.6
4. National Geographic	23.6
5. Time	23.2
The Mediamark List	
1. Reader's Digest	50.9
2. TV Guide	46.8
3. Better Homes and Gardens	35.5
4. People	30.4
5. National Geographic	30.3

Source: Joanne Lipman, "Readership Figures for Periodicals Stir Debate in Publishing Industry," *The Wall Street Journal* (September 2, 1987), p. 21.

Customized Measurements

In addition to the services mentioned previously, some firms supply customized rather than standardized marketing information. To discuss all of these suppliers of marketing intelligence would take us too far afield. We do wish to discuss mail panels, though, to give readers a sense of their operation. Although they are not a true source of secondary data, because the data collected using them are specifically designed to meet the client's needs, the studies are sufficiently standardized and have enough features in common to warrant their inclusion here.

NFO Research, Inc., is one of the major independent research firms specializing in custom-designed consumer surveys using mail panels. NFO maintains representative panels drawn from a sampling frame of more than two million consumers who have agreed to cooperate without compensation in completing self-administered questionnaires on a variety of subjects. The topics may include specific product usage; reaction to the product or advertising supporting it; reaction to a product package; attitude toward or awareness of some issue, product, service, or ad; and so on.

The national panel is dissolved and rebuilt every two years so that it matches current family-population characteristics with respect to income, population density, age of homemaker, and family size for the continental United States and each of the nine geographic divisions in the census.

A current demographic profile is maintained for each family in the data bank. Included are such characteristics as size of family, education, age of family members, presence and number of children by sex, occupation of the principal wage earner, race, and so on. This information is used to generate highly refined population segments. If the user's needs require it, NFO can offer the client panels composed exclusively of mothers of infants, teenagers, elderly people, dog and cat owners, professional workers, mobile home residents, multiple-car owners, or other specialized types. Each of these panels can be balanced to match specific quotas dictated by the client.[12]

The Consumer Mail Panel (CMP), operated as part of Market Facts, Inc., also represents a sample of households that have agreed to respond to mail questionnaires and product tests. Samples of persons for each product test or use are drawn from the 275,000 households in the CMP pool. The pool is representative of the geographical divisions in the United States and Canada and is broken down, within these divisions, according to census data on total household income, population density and degree of urbanization, and age of panel member.

According to CMP, its mail panel is ideally suited for experimental studies because the samples are matched with respect to demographic characteristics. In particular, CMP is believed to be particularly valuable when

1. Large samples are required at low cost because the size of the subgroups is large or there are many subgroups to be analyzed.
2. Large numbers of households must be screened to find eligible respondents.
3. Continuing records are to be kept by respondents to report such data as products purchased, how products are used, television programs viewed, magazines read, and so on.

CMP has recorded a number of other characteristics with respect to each participating household that allow for cross tabulation of the client's criterion variable against such things as place of residence (state, county, and standard metropolitan area), marital status, occupation and employment status, household size, age, sex, home ownership, type of dwelling, and ownership of pets, dishwashers, washing machines, dryers, other selected appliances, and automobiles.[13]

Back to the Case

Ruth Seidel opened the Wheat Crisps data binder that had just been delivered by messenger. The report's introduction showed that to get information on consumers in the Milwaukee test area, the research supplier had recruited 1,500 households to be part of a scanner panel. The panel members had been asked to provide information about the size of their family, their income, their marital status, how many televisions they owned, what types of newspapers and magazines they read, and who in the household did most of the shopping. The panel members had then been issued a special, bar-coded identification card to be presented at the cash register when buying groceries. Whenever the card had been passed over the scanner or its digits had been

manually entered into the register, the scanner had recorded everything the shopper was buying.

Seidel flipped impatiently to the summary page. Later she would spend hours pouring over the data. She would even perform her own analyses. But right now she wanted to see the depth-of-repeat figures, which would show how many Wheat Crisps purchasers bought the product at least four times during the ten-month test period. She looked at the page and found the appropriate column. Then she let out a cheer more appropriate for a football stadium than the marketing research office of a large corporation. Her secretary came in to see what had come over her usually sedate boss.

"Let's put it this way," explained

Seidel, grinning from ear to ear. "If 15 to 20 percent of the people who bought Wheat Crisps in Milwaukee once had gone back and bought them four more times, we'd say we were looking at a strong new product."

"And?" prompted her secretary.

"And we did a lot better than 20 percent," replied Seidel. "Better yet, now we can match the descriptions of the households from the panel to their purchasing patterns so that we can tailor our marketing efforts to potential customers."

Based on Frito-Lay's development of their new product Sun Chips, as reported by Ricardo Sookdeo, "What the Scanner Knows about You," *Fortune*, (December 3, 1990), pp. 51–52.

Summary

Learning Objective 1: List three common uses of the information supplied by standardized marketing information services.

The information supplied by standardized marketing information services is commonly used to (1) profile customers, (2) measure product sales and market share, and (3) measure advertising exposure and effectiveness.

Learning Objective 2: Define *geodemography*.

Geodemography refers to the availability of demographic, consumer-behavior, and life-style data by arbitrary geographic boundaries that are typically small.

Learning Objective 3: Describe the operation of a diary panel.

Diary panels are made up of families who use a preprinted diary to record the details of each purchase in a number of prespecified product categories. The details include the brand and amount bought, the price paid, whether the product was purchased on any deal and the type of deal if it was, the store where purchased, and so on. Families are recruited on a regular basis, often quarterly, to keep the panel balanced demographically.

Learning Objective 4: Describe the operation of store audits.

Store audits involve sending field workers, called auditors, to a select group of retail stores at fixed intervals. On each visit the auditors take a complete inventory of all products designated for the audit. The auditors also note the merchandise moving into the store by checking wholesale invoices, warehouse withdrawal records, and direct shipments from manufacturers, and from this information determine sales to consumers.

Learning Objective 5: Define *UPC*.

The Universal Product Code (UPC) is an 11-digit number imprinted on each product sold in a supermarket. The first digit, called the number system character, indicates the type of product (e.g., grocery or drug). The next five digits identify the manufacturer; and the last five, a particular product of the manufacturer, be it a different size, variety, or whatever.

Learning Objective 6: Define *single-source measurement*.

Single-source measurement refers to those organizations who have the capability to monitor product-purchase data and advertising-exposure data by household, and to relate that information to the demographic characteristics of the various households.

Learning Objective 7: Discuss the purpose and operation of people meters.

People meters attempt to measure which household members are watching which television channels at what times. Each member of the family has his or her own viewing number. Whoever turns on the set, sits down to watch, or changes the channel is supposed to enter his or her number into the people meter, which is an electronic device that stores and transmits this information to a central computer for processing.

Discussion Questions, Problems, and Projects

1. Several scenarios are presented below. In each case, there exists a need for standardized marketing information. Recommend a service or services that could provide the required information. Explain your choice.

   (a) As part of its advertising-sales strategy, radio station KZZD wants to stress the fact that their programming appeals to young adults between the ages of 19 and 25. The advertising salespeople need "numbers" to back up this claim.

   (b) Pulitzer Peanut Company has developed a unique couponing and television ad campaign for their 36-ounce container of Spanish peanuts. They need to know the following in order to evaluate the campaign:

(1) Are people more likely to use the coupon when they've also seen the television ad?

(2) What is the median size of the households using the coupon?

(3) What is the proportion of new purchasers to past purchasers among the users of the coupon?

(c) A national manufacturer of a nutritional supplement for children between the ages of two and four is considering changing the current packaging to a recyclable glass container. The change will necessitate a 10-percent price increase. The manufacturer wants to know if its target market (parents with children between two and four years of age) will perceive the price increase as justified since the new package is more environmentally sound.

(d) EMM Advertising Agency assured one of its clients that despite the $200,000 cost of placing a half-page ad in one issue of a national magazine, the actual cost per reader of the ad would be less than two cents. EMM is preparing a report to the client and needs data to back its assurance.

(e) Eco-Soft, Inc., is introducing a software package that will make long-range forecasts of contaminant buildup levels in plants that manufacture polyester fibers. They need a current listing of potential customers, organized by plant sales volume, in order to prioritize their sales calls for the new package.

(f) MidTowne Shopping Mall wishes to know the demographic characteristics of its patrons. However, the mall's retail tenants recently voted to ban marketing research interviews in or around the mall area, due to numerous customer complaints about harassment by interviewers. Where might the mall obtain the desired information?

2. Interview representatives of your local media outlets (e.g., radio stations, television stations, and newspapers) and determine the extent to which they utilize sources of standardized marketing information. You may wish to use the following questions as a guideline for your interviews.

(a) Which sources do they use?

(b) What specific types of information do they obtain from the source?

(c) How do they use the information?

(d) How important is the information in the conduct of their business?

(e) How do they rate the accuracy of the information?

(f) Do they supplement the standardized information with locally collected primary data?

Endnotes

1. Jerry Reisberg, "The Next Generation in Direct Marketing," *Sales & Marketing Management*, 142 (May 1989), p. 62.

2. Martha Farnsworth Riche, "The Business Guide to the Galaxy of Demographic Products and Services," *American Demographics*, 7 (June 1985), p. 25. See also Eugene Carlson, "Population-Data Firms Profit by Pinpointing Special Groups," *The Wall Street Journal* (October 15, 1985), p. 33; Betsy Morris, "Marketing Firm Slices U.S. into 240,000 Parts to Spur Clients' Sales," *The Wall Street Journal* (November 3, 1986), pp. 1, 23; Lisa Del Priore, "Geomapping Tools for Market Analysis," *Marketing Communications*, 12 (March 1987), pp. 91–94; and Joe Schwartz, "Why They Buy," *American Demographics*, 11 (March 1989), pp. 40–41.

3. See *Insights: Issues 1–13* (New York: NPD Research, Inc., undated) for discussion of these and other analyses using diary-panel data.

4. "Toy Departments Are Fading Away," *Wisconsin State Journal* (December 16, 1984), p. 12.

5. "Study Predicts Bigger Impact by Single-Source Data," *Marketing News*, 22 (February 1, 1988), p. 13.

6. Joanne Lipman, "Single-Source Ad Research Heralds Detailed Look at Household Habits," *The Wall Street Journal* (February 16, 1988), p. 35. For examples of these and other kinds of analyses that single-source measurement systems allow, see Gerald J. Eskin, "Applications of Electronic Single-Source Measurement Systems," *European Research*, 15 (No. 1, 1987), pp. 12–20.

7. Greater detail about the Nielsen television rating can be found in *The Nielsen Ratings in Perspective* (Northbrook, Ill.: A. C. Nielsen Company, undated). For discussion of the advantages and disadvantages of using people meters for television-audience measurement, see Richard Mahler, "Grousing about People Meters," *Adweek* (December 5, 1988), pp. F.K. 10–11; and Peter Barnes and Joanne Lipman, "Networks and Ad Agencies Battle over Estimates of TV Viewership," *The Wall Street Journal* (January 7, 1987), p. 21. For an investigation into their reliability, see Roland Soong, "The Statistical Reliability of People Meter Ratings," *Journal of Advertising Research*, 26 (February–March 1988), pp. 50–56.

8. *Starch Readership Report: Scope, Method, and Use* (Mamaroneck, N.Y.: Starch INRA Hooper, undated).

9. See *Dependable Data for Advertising and Marketing Decisions* (New York: Simmons Market Research Bureau, Inc., undated).

10. "Knowledge Is Power" (New York: Mediamark Research, Inc., 1987). See also "Winning the Marketing Game: How Syndicated Consumer Research Helps Improve the Odds" (New York: Mediamark Research, Inc., 1987) for description of the types of analyses the media exposure and product-uses data bases allow.

11. Joanne Lipman, "Readership Figures for Periodicals Stir Debate in Publishing Industry," *The Wall Street Journal* (September 2, 1987), p. 21.

12. More detailed information about the mail panel can be found in the company's publication *NFO* (Toledo, Ohio: NFO Research, Inc., undated).

13. More detail about the Market Facts mail panel can be found in *Why Consumer Mail Panel Is the Superior Option* (Chicago: Market Facts, Inc., undated) or *Market Facts, Inc.: Data Collection and Analysis for Reducing Business Decision Risks* (Chicago: Market Facts, Inc., undated).

Suggested Additional Readings

The best source of additional readings with respect to the operation of, and the possible analyses with, standardized marketing information services are the brochures describing their services put out by the companies themselves. Complimentary copies are often available for the asking.

Collecting Primary Data

Learning Objectives

Upon completing this chapter, you should be able to

1. List the kinds of demographic and socioeconomic characteristics that interest marketers.

2. Relate the premise on which life-style analysis rests.

3. Cite the three main approaches used to measure the effectiveness of magazine ads.

4. Give two reasons why researchers are interested in people's motives.

5. Describe the two basic means of obtaining primary data.

6. State the specific advantages of each method of data collection.

Case in Marketing Research

In the sleek 44th-floor conference room of Tillman and Skyr, a Chicago advertising agency, four people were eating corned beef sandwiches and complaining about a client. Peter Halpern, who was in charge of marketing research, had invited his cohorts on the Danes cigarette account for lunch. He hoped that by dessert they'd be able to get past the grousing and get on to some productive brainstorming.

Danes was Tillman and Skyr's newest account. Marketed under another name, the cigarette was the number-one seller in Scandinavia. The manufacturer, a Danish firm, was venturing across the Atlantic for the first time. The company proposed to target their brand to blue-collar males between the ages of 21 and 35, because it felt that the strong tobacco and full flavor of Danes would have the strongest appeal to that group. It had hired Tillman and Skyr to help the cigarettes appeal to that market.

"The problem is that they're just greedy," snapped Jill Toomey, who had just gone head-to-head with the people at Danes over the marketing research budget and was still smarting. "They drool at the size of the American market, but they don't understand that the scale of everything is bigger—including what it takes to do marketing research. You should have seen one guy's face when I told him that a moderate-size attitudes and usage survey for 800 to 1,000 respondents might run as high as $100,000. I thought he was going to have a stroke."

"I don't think they're necessarily greedy," said Halpern. "I think they're very successful in their established market and they don't see why they shouldn't be successful here. I even think they have the right idea in targeting the brand to blue-collar males in the 21-to-35 age bracket.

"The real problem," he said, "is that I don't think any of us in this room have anything more than a superficial understanding of what motivates a young man in a blue-collar job to choose one brand of cigarettes over another. And I think we know a lot more than the client does."

"What we need is to give the folks at Danes a crash course on the American consumer in general and on young, blue-collar males in particular," said Sherry Bergren, who had worked extensively with foreign clients in the past.

"And we need to do it for a bargain basement price," said Toomey, fresh from the Danes budget wars.

"The client has proposed using Little Rock, Arkansas, as a test market. Why don't we send a couple of people down there to do a quick and dirty qualitative study," she suggested. "I'm sure we can get a local recruiter to round up a dozen subjects who fit the profile of a Danes purchaser."

"You guys know that the words 'quick and dirty' fill me with fear," replied Halpern. "But a focus group in Little Rock is better than nothing, and it's certainly a start. Who knows—once we know what we're up against, we might be able to convince the Danes people that we need to do a more comprehensive study."

Discussion Issues

1. Do you think some types of secondary data might be useful to the group working on the Danes account?
2. If you were Halpern, what would you hope to find out from the Little Rock study?
3. What would your concerns be about doing such a limited study?

In Chapter 7 we emphasized the advantages of using secondary data. Such research information is usually fast, inexpensive, and fairly easy to obtain. We also noted that researchers who give secondary data only a casual look are being reckless. However, as we have seen, such data also have certain shortcomings and rarely will provide a complete solution to a research problem. The units of measurement or classes used to report the data may be wrong; the data may be nearly obsolete by the time of their publication; the data may be incomplete; and so on. When these conditions occur, the researcher logically turns to primary data.

This chapter is the first of three dealing with primary data, and it serves as an introduction to the subject. In this chapter we will discuss the various types of primary data researchers collect from and about subjects, and we will examine the two main means they employ to do it: communication and observation. In subsequent chapters we will explore each of these methods in more detail.

Types of Primary Data

Demographic/Socioeconomic Characteristics

One type of primary data of great interest to marketers is the subject's demographic and socioeconomic characteristics, such as age, education, occupation, marital status, sex, income, and social class. Researchers often match these variables with the data they have collected to gain greater insight into the subject under investigation. They might be interested, for example, in determining whether people's attitudes toward ecology and pollution are related to their level of formal education. Alternatively, they may ask whether the use of a particular product is in any way related to a person's age, sex, education, income, and so on, and if so, in what way. These are questions of market segmentation. Demographic and socioeconomic characteristics are often used to delineate market segments.

Until the early 1980s, American Express, for example, never made a serious effort to woo women or the young, according to one of the company's executives. The company's primary interest was in those it considered to be serious business travelers, who were largely men. But by 1982, the company determined that almost 40 percent of the American Express card's eligible universe had already been secured, and it cast about for ways to broaden the pool of potential users.

In focus groups, the marketing team discovered that although career women aged 25 to 40 knew and enjoyed the company's "Do you know me?" campaign, they never imagined that the cards were for them. They identified the American Express card as an almost exclusively male product.

Researchers also discovered that men and women see success differently—for women, it is not synonymous with business achievement. Focus groups told researchers that women put less value than men on career advancement and possessions and more on having interesting lives.

Based on that research, the "interesting lives" campaign was launched, in which women were portrayed taking their husbands to dinner, cross-country skiing with an infant in a Snugli, or disembarking a plane while toting a briefcase—and a teddy bear.

The campaign was wildly successful. In 1980 only 16 percent of cardholders were women; by 1985 that number had soared to 29 percent.[1]

Demographic and socioeconomic characteristics are sometimes called "states of being," in that they represent attributes of people. Some of these states of being, such

More babies were born in 1989 than in any year in the past three decades. This type of demographic information is critical for a multitude of industries ranging from baby food to life insurance.

Source: Courtesy of Ann Heath and Dave Theisen.

as a respondent's age, sex, and level of formal education, can be readily verified. Some, such as social class, cannot be verified except very crudely, since they are relative and not absolute measures of a person's standing in society.[2] A person's income can also be a fairly difficult piece of information to verify. Although the amount a person earns in a given year is an absolute, not a relative, quantity, in our society money is such a sensitive topic that exact numbers may be hard to determine.

Psychological/Life-Style Characteristics

Personality Normal patterns of behavior exhibited by an individual; the attributes, traits, and mannerisms that distinguish one individual from another.

Another type of primary data of interest to marketers is the subject's psychological and life-style characteristics in the form of personality traits, activities, interests, and values. **Personality** refers to the normal patterns of behavior exhibited by an individual—the attributes, traits, and mannerisms that distinguish one individual from another. We often characterize people by the personality traits—aggressiveness, dominance, friendliness, sociability—they display. Marketers are interested in personality because it seems as if it would affect the way consumers and others in the marketing process behave. Many marketers maintain, for example, that personality can affect a consumer's choice of stores or products, or an individual's response to an advertisement or point-of-purchase display. Similarly, they believe that successful salespeople are more likely to be extroverted and understanding of other people's feelings than are unsuccessful salespeople. While the empirical evidence regarding the ability of personality to predict consumption behavior or salesperson success is weak, personality remains a variable dear to the hearts of marketing researchers.[3] Typically, it is measured by one of the standard personality inventories that have been developed by psychologists.

Psychographic analysis A technique that investigates how people live, what interests them, and what they like; it is also called *life-style analysis*, since it relies on a number of statements about a person's AIO— activities (A), interests (I), and opinions (O).

Life-style analysis rests on the premise that the firm can plan more effective strategies to reach its target market if it knows more about it customers in terms of how they live, what interests them, and what they like. The general thrust of such research, which is often called **psychographic analysis,** has been to develop a number

Table 9.1   *Life-Style Dimensions*

	Activities	Interests	Opinions
	Work	Family	Themselves
	Hobbies	Home	Social issues
	Social events	Job	Politics
	Vacation	Community	Business
	Entertainment	Recreation	Economics
	Club membership	Fashion	Education
	Community	Food	Products
	Shopping	Media	Future
	Sports	Achievements	Culture

Source: Adapted from Joseph T. Plummer, "The Concept and Application of Life Style Segmentation," *Journal of Marketing*, 38 (January 1974), p. 34. Published by the American Marketing Association, Chicago, IL 60606.

of statements that reflect a person's AIO—activities (A), interests (I), and opinions (O)—and consumption behavior. The statements might include such things as "I like to watch football games on television," "I like stamp collecting," "I am very interested in national politics." Such a psychographic test would typically contain a great many such statements for respondents to choose from and would be administered to a large sample of respondents.[4]

For example, the advertising agency of Needham, Harper, and Steers conducts an annual life-style study that asks 3,500 respondents to answer 700 questions.[5] Table 9.1 contains the list of characteristics that are usually assessed with AIO inventories. The analysis attempts to identify groups of consumers who are likely to behave similarly toward a product, and who have similar life-style profiles. Research Window 9.1, for example, provides life-style descriptions of the seven most common shopper types.

While the idea seems like a good one in the abstract, marketers have discovered that in actual practice the technique has problems. One problem is that the categories of users, as identified by psychographics or AIO inventories, keep changing from product to product. This means that each product requires a new data-collection and analysis exercise. Because the profiles across products are so unstable, it is also impossible to develop demographic descriptions of the various groups that would be useful in planning marketing strategies for new products or brands.

Value and life-style research (VALS) was developed to avoid these problems by creating a standard psychographic framework that could be used for a variety of products. One particularly popular VALS classification scheme, for example, divides people into four main groups—need-driven, outer-directed, inner-directed, and combined outer- and inner-directed—and nine subgroups.[6]

Attitudes/Opinions

Attitude An individual's preference, inclination, views, or feelings toward some phenomenon.

Some authors distinguish between attitudes and opinions, while others use the terms interchangeably. Most typically **attitude** is used to refer to an individual's "preference, inclination, views or feelings toward some phenomenon," while

Research Window 9.1
Life-Style Descriptions of Seven Most Common Shopper Types

Inactive Shoppers (15% of all shoppers) have extremely restricted life-styles and shopping interests. Best characterized by their inactivity, Inactive shoppers do not engage in outdoor or do-it-yourself activities except for working in the yard or garden. They do not express strong enjoyment or interest in shopping, nor are they particularly concerned about such shopping attributes as price, employee service, or product selection.

Active Shoppers (12.8%) have demanding life-styles and are "tough" shoppers. They engage in all forms of outdoor activities and are usually do-it-yourselfers. Actives enjoy "shopping around," and price is a major consideration in their search. However, given their full range of interests outside of shopping, Actives appear to shop more as an expression of their intense life-styles than as an interest in finding bargains. Therefore, these shoppers probably balance price with quality, fashion, and selection in their search for value.

Service Shoppers (10%) demand a high level of in-store service when shopping. They usually seek convenient stores with friendly, helpful employees. Conversely, they quickly become impatient if they have to wait for a clerk to help them.

Traditional Shoppers (14.1%) share Active shoppers' preoccupation with outdoor activities but not their enthusiasm for shopping. They actively hike, camp, hunt, and fish and are do-it-yourselfers who often work on their cars. In general, though, Traditional shoppers are not price sensitive nor do they have other strong shopper requirements.

Dedicated Fringe Shoppers (8.8%) present clear motives for being heavy catalog shoppers. They are do-it-yourselfers and are more likely than average to try new products. They have almost a compulsion for being different. Dedicated Fringe shoppers are disinterested in extreme socializing. They have little interest in television and radio advertisements and exhibit limited brand and store loyalty. Therefore, the catalog represents a medium for obtaining an expanded selection of do-it-yourself and other products, and this reflects their individualism.

Price Shoppers (10.4%), as the name implies, are most identifiable by their extreme price consciousness. Price shoppers are willing to undertake an extended search to meet their price requirements, and they rely heavily on all forms of advertising to find the lowest prices.

Transitional Shoppers (6.9%) seem to be consumers in earlier stages of the family life cycle who have not yet formalized their life-style patterns and shopping values. They take an active interest in repairing and personalizing cars. Most participate in a variety of outdoor activities. They are more likely than average to try new products. Transitional shoppers exhibit little interest in shopping around for low prices. They are probably "eclectic shoppers" because they appear to make up their minds quickly to buy products once they become interested.

Source: Jack A. Lesser and Marie Adele Hughes, "The Generalizability of Psychographic Market Segments across Geographic Locations," *Journal of Marketing*, 50 (January 1986), p. 23.

Opinion Verbal expression of an attitude.

opinions are "verbal expressions of attitudes." We shall not make the distinction between the terms in this text but will treat attitudes and opinions interchangeably as representing a person's ideas, convictions, or liking with respect to a specific object or idea.

Attitude is one of the more important notions in the marketing literature, since it is generally thought that attitudes are related to behavior.

> Obviously, when an individual likes a product he will be more inclined to buy it than when he does not like it; when he likes one brand more than another, he will tend to buy the preferred brand. Attitudes may be said to be the forerunners of behavior.[7]

Thus, marketers are often interested in people's attitudes toward the product itself, their overall attitudes with respect to specific brands, and their attitudes toward specific aspects or features possessed by several brands. Attitude is such a pervasive notion in behavioral science, and particularly in marketing, that Chapter 14 is devoted to various types of instruments used to measure it.

But, as many a marketer has discovered, it is risky to assume that people's attitudes toward products will remain consistent. General Mills discovered this fact to its dismay when sales of its Izod brand knit shirts, with their distinctive alligator emblem, dropped dramatically when the "preppy" look went out of vogue.[8]

Awareness/Knowledge

Awareness/knowledge
Insight into, or understanding of facts about, some object or phenomenon.

Awareness/knowledge as used in marketing research refers to what respondents do and do not know about some object or phenomenon. For instance, an issue of considerable importance is the effectiveness of magazine ads. One indicator of effectiveness is the "awareness" generated by the ad, which is measured using one of the three approaches described in Table 9.2. All three approaches are aimed at assessing the respondent's awareness of and knowledge about the ad, although the three approaches can produce dramatically different results. Research Window 9.2 discusses the use of recall data to assess the value of getting products in film.

Retention rates are much higher when knowledge is measured by recognition rather than by recall and by aided rather than unaided recall. This, of course, raises the question of which method is the most accurate. There are problems with each method.[9] The important thing to note is that when marketers speak of a person's awareness, they often mean the individual's knowledge of the advertisement. A person "very much aware" or possessing "high awareness" typically knows a great deal about the ad.

Awareness and *knowledge* are also used interchangeably when marketers speak of product awareness. Marketing researchers are often interested in determining whether the respondent is aware of the following:[10]

- The product
- Its features
- Where it is available
- Its price
- Its manufacturer
- Where it is made
- How it is used, and for what purpose
- Its specific distinctive features

Table 9.2   Approaches Used to Measure Awareness

Unaided Recall Without being given any clues, consumers are asked to recall what advertising they have seen recently. Prompting is not used because, presumably, even if prompting for the general category were used (for example, laundry detergents), respondents would have a tendency to remember more advertisements in that product category.

Aided Recall Consumers are given some prompting, typically in the form of questions about advertisements in a specific product category. Alternatively, respondents might be given a list showing the names or trademarks of advertisers that appeared in a particular magazine issue, along with names or trademarks that did not appear, and would be asked to check those to which they were exposed.

Recognition Consumers are shown copies of actual advertisements and are asked whether or not they remember seeing each one.

Research Window 9.2
CinemaScore Tests Moviegoers' Recall

Crocodile Dundee II grossed more than $70 million for Paramount Pictures, but how did it do for the products that negotiated their way into the hands of its stars and onto the movie screen? Enter Ed Mintz, whose CinemaScore has surveyed opening-night audiences for more than a decade. After years of finding out whether people liked the movies they saw, Mintz became intrigued with the question of whether audiences remembered the products that were placed in motion pictures.

The CinemaScore system, which ultimately translates data into terms that a marketer can understand—cost per thousand—is based on an exit survey. The survey, designed to look like a ticket stub, has tabs that can quickly be torn to indicate the viewers' age, sex, those products they remembered seeing, and how well they liked the movie. CinemaScore runs the survey at different theaters across the country and at different show times to gather responses from a wide range of moviegoers.

From there, CinemaScore tallies it all up and applies a formula that uses audience recall and total box-office grosses to compute what the cost of that placement should be. The cost figure is then divided by the number of tickets sold to get a cost per thousand viewers.

In *Dundee II*, Mintz found a mixed bag of winners and losers. Both Coca-Cola and Pepsi were in the film. With Coke, an average of 26 percent of those surveyed remembered seeing the product, whereas only 6 percent of the audience remembered seeing Pepsi.

But it wasn't just a flat case of a cola battle. Coke, it seems, had more of a starring role. In one scene, the star, Paul Hogan, throws a rock at a Coke can—it's the focus of attention. In Pepsi's case, it was just another can in the background along with several other cans. All those elements are taken into CinemaScore's final analysis.

In *Dundee II*, sources say General Foods paid at least $40,000 to put Sanka Coffee in the film. Did it get what it paid for? CinemaScore found that although the product was in the movie and the brand name was visible, the image was hardly recognizable. The exit survey put recall at just 12 percent.

"Once and for all it gives studios and corporate America a yardstick to measure the value of product placement in a film," says Marvin Cohen, who represents both studios and production companies in certain product-placement projects. "[CinemaScore] gives us hard, black-and-white figures that we can relate to, measuring not just the product, but the performance of the product," Cohen says.

Source: Betsy Sharkey, "How Many Noticed Sanka in 'Dundee II'? CinemaScore Polls Moviegoers," *Adweek's Marketing Week*, 29 (June 20, 1988), pp. 33–34.

Although framed in terms of awareness, these questions, to a greater or lesser degree, aim at determining the individual's knowledge of or beliefs about the product. For our purposes, then, *knowledge* and *awareness* will be used interchangeably to refer to what a respondent believes about an advertisement, product, retail store, and so on.

Intentions

Intentions Anticipated or planned future behavior.

A person's **intentions** refer to the individual's anticipated or planned future behavior. Marketers are interested in people's intentions primarily with regard to purchase behavior. One of the better known studies regarding purchase intentions is that conducted by the Survey Research Center at the University of Michigan. The center regularly conducts surveys for the Federal Reserve Board to determine the general financial condition of consumers and their outlook with respect to the state of the economy in the near future. The center asks consumers about their buying intentions for big-ticket items such as appliances, automobiles, and homes during the next few

Some empty promises from Sunline.

If you stock SweeTARTS, you'll sell SweeTARTS. It's as simple as that.

Because SweeTARTS enjoy a 95% awareness level among consumers. They're the Number 1 selling sweet and tangy candy in America and are ranked sixth of all non-chocolate candies. Also, Sunline has an on-going quarterly promotional program to keep SweeTARTS top-of-mind.

So stock your shelves with SweeTARTS and other Sunline favorites—PIXY STIX and TANGY TAFFY, Sunline's Family Treat Line. In the new hot-selling grocery packs in 12-count cases.

We promise your shelves will empty. And your cash drawers will fill.

Source: Accutracks, November 1989

This ad, which is geared toward grocers making decisions about which brands to stock in their stores, cites a 95-percent awareness level among consumers.

months. The responses are then analyzed, and the proportion of the sample that indicates each of the following is reported:

- Definite intention to buy
- Probable intention to buy
- Undecided
- Definite intention not to buy

Intentions receive less attention in marketing than do other types of primary data, largely because there is often a great disparity between what people say they are going to do and what they actually do. This is particularly true with respect to purchase behavior. Figure 9.1, for example, describes the results of one investigation of the relationship. In the experiment, consumers were given a questionnaire that described a new pricing option for a service to which customers already subscribed. The questionnaire asked the respondents to circle a number that best indicated how likely they were to buy the service when it became available. The scale anchors ranged from 1 (definitely would not buy) to 10 (definitely would buy). As Figure 9.1 indicates, only 45 percent of those indicating that they definitely would buy the service did so within the first three months of its availability. Further, some of the respondents who indicated that they would not buy it did so. Researchers are most likely to use

Figure 9.1   ***Proportion of People Buying the Service versus Their Intention to Purchase It***

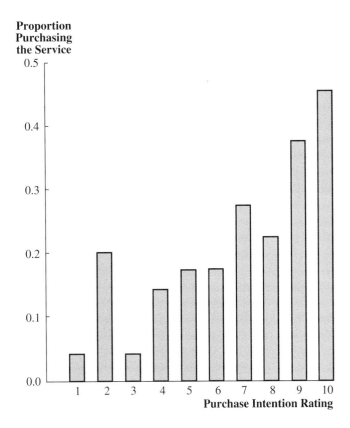

Source: William J. Infosino, "Forecasting New Product Sales from Likelihood of Purchase Ratings," *Marketing Science*, 5 (Fall 1986), p. 375.

purchasing intentions when investigating the likelihood of consumers' buying items that require a large sum of money. For a family this might be an automobile, a new house, or even a vacation trip. For a business, a study of purchase intentions would usually focus on a new plant or equipment.

The general assumption researchers make is that the more an item costs, the more time a consumer will spend in planning the purchase. If that assumption is true, then there should be a significant correlation between anticipated and actual behavior. Unfortunately, the evidence of such a correlation is weak.[11]

Motivation

The concept of motivation seems to contain more semantic confusion than most concepts in the behavioral sciences.

> Some writers insist that *motives* are different from *drives* and use the latter term primarily to characterize the basic physiological "tissue" needs (e.g., hunger, thirst, shelter, sex). Others distinguish between *needs* and *wants*, stating that needs are the basic motivating forces which translate themselves into more immediate wants which satisfy these needs (e.g., hunger needs give rise to wanting a good steak dinner).[12]

Motive A need, a want, a drive, a wish, a desire, an impulse, or any inner state that energizes, activates, or moves and that directs or channels behavior toward goals.

For our purposes, a **motive** may refer to a need, a want, a drive, an urge, a wish, a desire, an impulse, or any inner state that directs or channels behavior toward goals.

A marketing researcher's interest in motives typically involves determining *why* people behave as they do. There are several reasons that explain this interest. In the first place, researchers believe that a person's motives tend to be more stable than an individual's behavior and therefore offer a better basis for predicting future behavior than does past behavior. For example, a young couple living in an apartment may say that they want to buy a house. Just because they did not buy a house last year, or the year before, does not mean that their motives have changed. Once they have saved enough for a down payment, or once a baby is on the way, they may be spurred to act on their motives, and past behavior will have no bearing on this action.

The second reason researchers are interested in motives is that by understanding what drives a person's behavior, it is easier to understand the behavior itself. A desire for status may motivate one car buyer to purchase a Mercedes-Benz, while a concern for safety may send another to the local Volvo showroom. If researchers understand the forces underlying consumer behavior, they are in a better position to influence future behavior, or at least to design products consistent with what they anticipate that behavior to be.

Behavior

Behavior What subjects have done or are doing.

Behavior concerns what subjects have done or are doing. In marketing this usually means purchase and use behavior. Now, behavior is a physical activity. It takes place under specific circumstances, at a particular time, and involves one or more actors or participants. A marketing researcher investigating behavior would be interested in a description of the activity and its various components. Table 9.3 is a checklist of the key elements involved in purchase behavior. Researchers can use a checklist like this one to design data-collection instruments.[13]

As a researcher fills in each category, he or she must make a decision about what information to include or omit. Consider the "where" category, for example. The "where of purchase" may be specified with respect to kind of store, the location of the

Table 9.3   **Behavior Checklist**

	Purchase Behavior	Use Behavior
What		
How much		
How		
Where		
When		
In what situation		
Who		

Source: Fred L. Schreier, *Modern Marketing Research: A Behavioral Science Approach* (Belmont, Calif.: Wadsworth Publishing Company, 1963), p. 251.

store by broad geographic area or specific address, size of the store, or even the name of the store. So it is with each of the many categories. The study of behavior, then, involves the development of a description of the purchase or use activity, either past or current, with respect to some or all of the characteristics contained in Table 9.3.

Ethical
Dilemma 9.1   A national department store chain with a relatively sophisticated image is planning to open a store in an area inhabited by wealthy professionals. The marketing research director of the company wants a detailed profile of the residents' characteristics and life-styles in order to tailor the new store to the tastes of this lucrative new market. He suggests that you, a member of his staff, contribute to the research effort by spending a month observing the residents going about their daily affairs of eating in restaurants, attending church, shopping in other stores, socializing with one another, and so on. You are then to prepare a report on what expenditures support their life-styles.

■   Are there ethical problems involved in observing people in public places? Do the ethical problems become more serious if you socialize with your subjects?

■   Who has ethical responsibility for your behavior: the marketing research director? You? Both?

Obtaining Primary Data

The researcher attempting to collect primary data has a number of choices to make among the means that will be used. Figure 9.2 presents an overview of these choices. The primary decision is whether to employ communication or observation. **Communication** involves questioning respondents to secure the desired information, using a data-collection instrument called a questionnaire. The questions may be oral or in writing, and the responses may also be given in either form. **Observation** does not involve questioning. Rather, it means that the situation of interest is scrutinized and the relevant facts, actions, or behaviors are recorded. The observer may be one or more persons or a mechanical device. For instance, supermarket scanners may be used to determine how many boxes of a particular brand of cereal are sold in a given region in a typical week. Alternatively, a researcher interested in the brands of canned vegetables a family buys might arrange a pantry audit in which the family's shelves are checked to see which brands they have on hand.

Choosing a primary method of data collection necessitates a number of additional decisions. For example, should we administer questionnaires by mail, over the telephone, or in person? Should the purpose of the study be disguised or remain undisguised? Should the answers be open-ended, or should the respondent be asked to choose from a limited set of alternatives? While Figure 9.2 implies that these decisions are independent, they are actually intimately related. A decision with respect to method of administration, say, has serious implications regarding the degree of structure that must be imposed on the questionnaire.

Each method of obtaining primary data has its own advantages and disadvantages. For the remainder of this chapter we will review these general pluses and minuses. In the next chapter we will discuss the decisions that must be made when using the communication method; and in the chapter after that, the decisions involved in the observational method.

Communication A method of data collection involving questioning of respondents to secure the desired information, using a data-collection instrument called a questionnaire.

Observation A method of data collection in which the situation of interest is watched and the relevant facts, actions, or behaviors are recorded.

Figure 9.2   ***Basic Choices among Means for Collecting Primary Data***

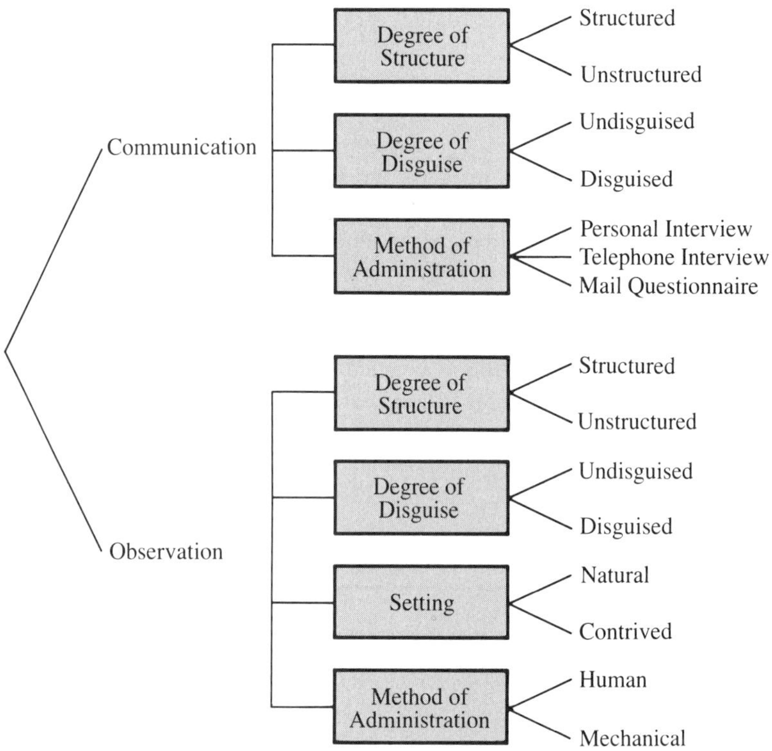

In general, the communication method of data collection has the general advantages of versatility, speed, and cost, while observational data are typically more objective and accurate.

Versatility

Versatility is the ability of a technique to collect information on the many types of primary data of interest to marketers. A respondent's demographic/socioeconomic characteristics and life-style, the individual's attitudes and opinions, awareness and knowledge, intentions, the motivation underlying the individual's actions, and even the person's behavior may all be ascertained by the communication method. All we need to do is ask, although the replies will not necessarily be truthful.

Not so with observation. Observational techniques can provide us only with information about behavior and certain demographic/socioeconomic characteristics and even here there are certain limitations. Our observations are limited to present behavior, for example. We cannot observe a person's past behavior. Nor can we observe the person's intentions as to future behavior. If we are interested in past behavior or intentions, we must ask.

Some demographic/socioeconomic characteristics can be readily observed. Sex is the most obvious example. Others can be observed but with less accuracy. A person's age and income, for example, might be inferred by closely examining the individual's mode of dress and purchasing behavior. Clearly, though, both of these observations may be in error, with income likely to be the farthest off. Still others, such as social class, cannot be observed with any degree of confidence about the accuracy of the recorded data.

The other basic types of primary data cannot be measured by observation at all. We simply cannot observe an attitude or opinion, a person's awareness or knowledge, or motivation. Certainly we can attempt to make some inferences about these variables on the basis of the individual's observed behavior. For instance, if a person is observed purchasing a box of new XYZ detergent, we might infer that the person has a favorable attitude toward XYZ. There is a real question, though, as to the accuracy of the inference. A great deal of controversy exists over whether attitudes precede behavior or behavior precedes attitude formation. If the latter explanation is correct, the person buying XYZ has no particular attitude toward it but has just decided to try it. He or she may not have even been aware of XYZ previously. Or he or she may have been induced to try XYZ by a sizable cents-off coupon from the local newspaper or by an attractive promotional price offered by the supermarket. Then again, the person might be buying the box for a neighbor. Generalizing from behavior to states of mind is clearly risky, and researchers need to recognize this. Questioning clearly affords a broader base of primary data.

Speed and Cost

The speed and cost advantages of the communication method are closely intertwined. Assuming the data lend themselves to either means, communication is a faster means of data collection than observation, because it provides a greater degree of control over data-gathering activities. With the communication method, researchers are not forced to wait for events to occur, as they are with the observation method. In some cases, it is impossible to predict when the event will occur precisely enough to observe it. For still other behaviors, the time interval between events can be substantial. For instance, an observer seeking to determine the brand purchased most frequently in one of several appliance categories might have to wait a long time to make any observations at all. Much of the time the observer would be idle. Such idleness is expensive, as the worker will probably be compensated on an hourly, rather than a per-contact, basis. Events that last a long time can also cause difficulty. An observational approach to studying the relative influence of a husband and a wife in the purchase of an automobile would be prohibitive in terms of both time and money.

Objectivity and Accuracy

Although the observation method has some serious limitations in terms of scope, time, and cost, it does have certain advantages with regard to objectivity and accuracy. Data that can be secured by either method will typically be more accurately secured by observation. This is because the observation method is independent of the respondent's unwillingness or inability to provide the information desired. For example, respondents are often reluctant to cooperate whenever their replies might place them in an unfavorable light. Sometimes respondents conveniently forget embarrassing events, while in other cases the events are not of sufficient importance for them to remember what happened. Since observation allows the recording of behavior as it occurs, it is not dependent on the respondent's memory or mood in reporting what occurred.

Observation typically produces more objective data than does communication. The interview represents a social interaction situation. Thus, the replies of the person being questioned are conditioned by the individual's perceptions of the interviewer. The same is true of interviewers' perceptions, but their training should afford a greater degree of control over their perceptions than would be true of the interviewee. With the observation method, the subject's perceptions play less of a role than in the communication method. Sometimes people are not even aware that they are being observed. Thus, they are not tempted to tell the interviewer what they think the interviewer wants to hear or to give socially acceptable responses that are not truthful. The problems of objectivity are concentrated in the observer's methods, and this makes the task easier. The observer's selection, training, and control, and not the subject's perceptions of the field worker, become the crucial elements.

Ethical
Dilemma 9.2

A marketing research firm was hired by a candy manufacturer to gather data on the alternatives consumers consider when deciding to buy a candy bar. Sue Samuelson, the person in charge of the research, believed that the best way to collect accurate information was through an observation study done in major supermarkets, drugstores, and discount stores in a number of large cities. Unfortunately, at that time the personnel of the firm were stretched to the limit because of a number of other assignments. The company simply did not have sufficient personnel available to do the study using personal observation and still meet the client's deadline. Samuelson consequently decided that she would propose to the client a mail study utilizing the research firm's panel of households. Not only would this place fewer demands on the research firm's personnel, but the cost to the client would be about 25 percent less than with personal observation.

- Does Samuelson have an obligation to the client to disclose why she is recommending the mail panel?
- Is it ethical for a research firm to use alternative methods of gathering data because of internal constraints? What if the alternatives reduce the charges to the client?
- Who should make the decision as to the best way to approach the project—the client or the research supplier?

Back to the Case

Peter Halpern lay on his bed in his hotel room in Little Rock, Arkansas. It had been a long, hard day at the end of a long, hard week. He had hired a local focus-group recruiter, but rounding up 12 subjects— "blue-collar but articulate"—turned out to be anything but easy. When he'd set the date for the study, he

had no idea that the research would coincide with the first weekend of deer-hunting season. Many of the prospects had turned down the offer of $50 for two to five hours of conversation and had taken to the woods instead.

Finally, they had managed to round up nine interview subjects.

Halpern had found the ensuing discussion, which he had watched from behind a one-way mirror, fascinating. The men who had participated in the study were poor, sexually frustrated, and seemed to feel particularly hemmed in by their lives. They worked in repetitive, low-paying jobs with little hope of advancement. But they valued their male friends and spent some of their best times with them. Lighting up together seemed an integral part of their buddy network.

Halpern was glad that he'd had the focus-group session videotaped.

It confirmed his feeling that both his client and his colleagues had a lot to learn about the market identified for Danes cigarettes. He just hoped that once the client had a chance to hear what these nine people had to say in the focus group, they'd be willing to

give him the go-ahead for a more comprehensive study.

Based on the case of Prince brand cigarettes, see Joshua Levine, "Desperately Seeking Jeepness," *Forbes* (May 15, 1989) pp. 134–136.

Summary

Learning Objective 1: List the kinds of demographic and socioeconomic characteristics that interest marketers.

Marketers are interested in such socioeconomic and demographic characteristics as age, education, occupation, marital status, sex, income, and social class.

Learning Objective 2: Relate the premise on which life-style analysis rests.

Life-style analysis rests on the premise that the firm can plan more effective strategies to reach its target market if it knows more about its customers in terms of how they live, what interests them, and what they like.

Learning Objective 3: Cite the three main approaches used to measure the effectiveness of magazine ads.

The three main approaches used to measure awareness of magazine ads are (1) unaided recall, in which the consumer is given no cues at all, (2) aided recall, in which the consumer is given some prompting, and (3) recognition, in which the consumer is actually shown an advertisement and asked whether or not he or she remembers seeing it.

Learning Objective 4: Give two reasons why researchers are interested in people's motives.

First, researchers believe that motives tend to be more stable than behavior and therefore offer a better basis for predicting future behavior than does past behavior. Secondly, researchers believe that by understanding what drives a person's behavior, it is easier to understand the behavior itself.

Learning Objective 5: Describe the two basic means of obtaining primary data.

The two basic means of obtaining primary data are communication and observation. Communication involves questioning respondents to secure the desired information, using a data-collection instrument called a questionnaire. Observation involves scrutinizing the situation of interest and recording the relevant facts, actions, or behaviors.

Learning Objective 6: State the specific advantages of each method of data collection.

In general, the communication method of data collection has the advantages of versatility, speed, and cost, while observation data are typically more objective and accurate.

Discussion Questions, Problems, and Projects

Should the communication or observation method be used in the situations captured in Questions 1 and 2? (Justify your choice.)

1. In 1989 the Metal Product Division of Miracle Ltd. devised a special metal container to store plastic garbage bags. Plastic bags pose household problems, as they give off unpleasant odors, look disorderly, and provide a breeding place for insects. The container overcomes these problems, as it has a bag-support apparatus that holds the bag open for filling and seals the bag when the lid is closed. In addition, there is

enough storage area for at least four full bags. The product is priced at $53.81 and is sold through hardware stores. The company has done little advertising and relies on in-store promotion and displays. The divisional manager is wondering about the effectiveness of these displays. She has called on you to do the necessary research.

2. Friendship is a national manufacturer and distributor of greeting cards. The company has recently begun distributing a lower-priced line of cards that is made possible by using a lower-grade paper. Quality differences between the higher- and lower-priced cards do not seem to be noticeable to consumers. The company follows a policy of printing its name and the price on the back of each card. The initial acceptance of the new line of cards has convinced the vice-president of production, Sheila Howell, that the company should use this lower-grade paper for all its cards and increase its profit margin from 12.3 percent to 14.9 percent. The sales manager is strongly opposed to this move and has commented, "Sheila, consumers are concerned abut the quality of greeting cards; a price difference of 5 cents on a card does not matter." The vice-president has called upon you to undertake the study.

3. Stop-Buy, Inc., recently opened a new convenience store in Galveston, Texas. The store is open every day from 7:00 a.m. to 11:00 p.m. Management is interested in determining the trading area from which this store draws its customers, so that it can better plan the location of other units in the Galveston area.

   How would you determine this information by the questionnaire method? By the observation method? Which method would be preferred? Be sure to specify in your answer how you would define "trading area."

4. Following are several objectives for marketing research projects. For each objective, specify the type(s) of primary data that would be of use and a possible method of data collection.
   (a) assess "people flow" patterns inside a shopping mall
   (b) gauge the effectiveness of a new advertisement
   (c) gauge a salesperson's potential for success
   (d) segment a market
   (e) identify the shopper types that patronize a particular store
   (f) discover how people feel about a new package design

5. Life-style, or psychographic, analysis collects data concerning three dimensions of a respondent's life-style. Compare and contrast these dimensions. Are the three dimensions exhaustive, or can you suggest others that should be included?

Endnotes

1. Bernice Kanner, "Think Plastic," *New York*, 18 (March 4, 1985), pp. 19–24.

2. See James H. Myers and William H. Reynolds, *Consumer Behavior in Marketing Management* (Boston: Houghton Mifflin, 1967), pp. 206–216, for a useful discussion of social class, its role in marketing-related phenomena, and the various ways in which it has been measured. See Charles M. Schaninger, "Social Class versus Income Revisited: An Empirical Investigation," *Journal of Marketing Research*, 18 (May 1981), pp. 192–208, for a comparison of the ability of social class and income to predict consumption of a number of household products; and see Gillian Stevens and Joo Hyun Cho, "Socioeconomic Indexes and the New 1980 Census Occupational Classification Scheme," *Social Science Research*, 14 (1985), pp. 142–168, for discussion of the measurement of socioeconomic status using occupation.

3. For a review of the evidence regarding the relationship of personality to consumer behavior, see Harold H. Kassarjian, "Personality and Consumer Behavior: A Review," *Journal of Marketing Research*, 8 (November 1971), pp. 409–418. For a review of the evidence regarding the relationship between personality characteristics and salesperson success, see Neil M. Ford, Orville

C. Walker, Jr., Gilbert A. Churchill, Jr., and Steven W. Hartley, "Selecting Successful Salespeople: A Meta-Analysis of Biographical and Psychological Selection Criteria," in Michael J. Houston, ed., *Review of Marketing 1987* (Chicago: American Marketing Association, 1987), pp. 98–134.

4. One of the more popular AIO inventories is the 300-question set that appears in William D. Wells and Douglas Tigert, "Activities, Interests, and Opinions," *Journal of Advertising Research*, 11 (August 1971), pp. 27–35. For a general review of the origins, development, and thrust of life-style and psychographic research, see William D. Wells, ed., *Life Style and Psychographics* (Chicago: American Marketing Association, 1974); and Emanuel H. Demby, "Psychographics Revisited: The Birth of a Technique," *Marketing News*, 23 (January 2, 1989), p. 21. For evidence regarding the reliability and validity of psychographic inventories, see Alvin C. Burns and Mary Carolyn Harrison, "A Test of the Reliability of Psychographics," *Journal of Marketing Research*, 16 (February 1979), pp. 32–38; John L. Lastovicka, "On the Validation of Lifestyle Traits: A Review and Illustration," *Journal of Marketing Research*, 19 (February 1982), pp. 126–138; and Ian Fenwick, D. A. Schellinck, and K. W. Kendall, "Assessing the Reliability of Psychographic Analyses," *Marketing Science*, 2 (Winter 1983), pp. 57–74.

5.   Cara S. Frazer, "Staying Afloat in Oceans of Data," *Advertising Age*, 54 (October 31, 1983), pp. m42–m43.

6.   Arnold Mitchell, *The Nine American Lifestyles* (New York: Macmillan, 1983). Other value-based classification schemes include Monitor, and The List of Values (LOV). For discussions of the use of value and life-style research, see Bickley Townsend, "Psychographic Glitter and Gold," *American Demographics*, 7 (November 1985), pp. 22–29; Lynn R. Kahle, Sharon E. Beatty, and Pamela Homer, "Alternative Measurement Approaches to Consumer Values: The List of Values (LOV) and Values and Life Style (VALS)." *Journal of Consumer Research*, 13 (December 1986), pp. 405–409; and John L. Lastovicka et al., "A Lifestyle Typology to Model Young Male Drinking and Driving," *Journal of Consumer Research*, 14 (September 1987), pp. 257–263.

7.   Fred L. Schreier, *Modern Marketing Research: A Behavioral Science Approach* (Belmont, Calif.: Wadsworth, 1963), p. 273. For a general review of the relationship between attitude and behavior, see Susan T. Fiske and Shelley E. Taylor, *Social Cognition* (Reading, Mass.: Addison-Wesley, 1984), pp. 369–399.

8.   Pamela G. Hollis, "Izod's Fall from Vogue a Drag on General Mills," *New York Times*, 133 (November 15, 1984), pp. D1 and D5.

9.   See Herbert E. Krugman, "Point of View: Measuring Memory—An Industry Dilemma," *Journal of Advertising Research*, 25 (August/September 1985), pp. 49–51; and Charles E. Young and Michael Robinson, "Guideline: Tracking the Commercial Viewer's Wandering Attention," *Journal of Advertising Research*, 27 (June/July 1987), pp. 15–22, for discussions of the controversy about which method to use. For measurement of the effectiveness of radio commercials using recall, see Murphy A. Sewall and Dan Sarel, "Characteristics of Radio Commercials and Their Recall Effectiveness," *Journal of Marketing*, 50 (January 1986), pp. 52–60.

10.   Schreier, *Modern Marketing Research*, pp. 269–273.

11.   Manohar U. Kalwani and Alvin J. Silk, "On the Reliability and Predictive Validity of Purchase Intention Measures" *Marketing Science*, 1 (Summer 1982), pp. 243–286; Murphy A. Sewall, "Relative Information Contributions of Consumer Purchase Intentions and Management Judgment as Explanations of Sales," *Journal of Marketing Research*, 18 (May 1981), pp. 249–253; Gary M. Mullett and Marvin J. Karson, "Analysis of Purchase Intent Scales Weighted by Probability of Actual Purchase," *Journal of Marketing Research*, 22 (February 1985), pp. 93–96. Those organizations that collect purchase-intentions data regularly often adjust the data based on their past experience as to how much bias a set of intentions data might contain.

12.   Myers and Reynolds, *Consumer Behavior*, p. 80.

13.   The checklist is adapted from Schreier, *Modern Marketing Research*, p. 251. Schreier also has a productive discussion of the many kinds of questions that need to be answered to complete the checklist.

Suggested Additional Readings

There are a number of guides to the various personality inventories. Three of the better ones for marketers are

C. M. Bonjean, R. J. Hill, and S. D. McLemore, *Sociological Measurement: An Inventory of Scales and Indices* (San Francisco: Chandler, 1974).

Ki-Taiek Chun, Sidney Cobb, and J. R. P. French, *Measures for Psychological Assessment* (Ann Arbor, Mich.: Institute for Social Research, University of Michigan, 1975).

D. G. Lake, M. B. Miles, and R. B. Earle, Jr., *Measuring Human Behavior: Tools for the Assessment of Social Functioning* (New York: Teachers College Press, Columbia University, 1973).

For a general review of the origins, development, and thrust of life-style and psychographic research, see

William D. Wells, ed., *Life Style and Psychographics* (Chicago: American Marketing Association, 1974).

For a general discussion of the purpose, procedures, and uses of life-style research, see

Arnold Mitchell, *The Nine American Lifestyles* (New York: Macmillan, 1983).

Bickley Townsend, "Psychographic Glitter and Gold," *American Demographics*, 7 (November 1985), pp. 22–29.

Collecting Information by Questionnaire

Learning Objectives

Upon completing this chapter, you should be able to

1. Explain the concept of *structure* as it relates to questionnaires.

2. Explain what is meant by *disguise* in a questionnaire.

3. Discuss why structured-undisguised questionnaires are the type most frequently used by marketing researchers.

4. Cite three drawbacks of fixed-alternative questions.

5. Explain the reason why researchers use projective methods in conducting some studies.

6. List three common types of stimuli used in projective techniques.

7. Differentiate among the three methods of administering questionnaires.

8. Cite the points researchers generally consider when they compare the various methods of administering questionnaires.

Case in Marketing Research

"Do you know who your customers *really* are?" asked Rick Shanahan, the domestic sales manager for Clean-Rite appliances. He was sitting in the office of Tom Karlin, a successful appliance distributor who had a nine-county Clean-Rite franchise in booming central Florida.

"What do you mean?" asked Karlin, obviously intrigued.

"I mean that demographically, I can tell you who in your region has bought a Clean-Rite appliance within the last two years. I can tell you how old they are, how much money they make, what they like to do in their free time, and why they bought Clean-Rite rather than the competition."

"That's neat," replied Karlin, "but where's the information from? I didn't think Clean-Rite did a lot of heavy demographic research, especially not anything specific to central Florida."

"Well, we don't—at least not directly. We've started using a company that specializes in providing a consumer data base that it generates from the information on product registration cards."

"You mean the cards the customers fill out and send back, saying where and when they bought their dishwasher and what the serial number is?"

"Yep. Not only does the registration card help us keep track of warranty information, but we also ask the consumers to answer some quick questions about their income, education, and interests. We already know their address. Most people don't even realize they're filling out a questionnaire."

"You're right, I never thought about product registration cards as questionnaires."

"Well," continued Shanahan, warming to his subject, "we pack a postage-paid registration card in with every appliance. The buyer fills it out and sends it directly to DLD, Demographics Life-Style Data, a company in Houston. DLD uses the information from the cards to generate a demographic data base similar to U.S. Census information, but much more current. In addition, DLD's data base has a lot more life-style information about the respondents. But the real beauty of the thing isn't in national projections—any marketer can send out 2,000 questionnaires and make national projections. DLD can break out *specific geographical regions*. They can make projections down to specific postal codes or neighborhoods. Like I said, I can tell you all about the consumers in your franchise area who, over the past two years, have bought an appliance from Clean-Rite."

"That's amazing." replied Karlin. "I'd love to see the information."

When the DLD computer printouts arrived several days later, Karlin spent some time studying the data. It really was interesting to see what kind of person bought Clean-Rite over other brands. Of course, he'd already had a picture of that customer in the back of his mind, based on his experience as a dealer. Clean-Rite had a reputation as a quality manufacturer and as a rule didn't go after the low end of the market. But this information was much more specific than just a salesman's gut response.

He learned that the typical Clean-Rite purchaser in his part of Florida had an income of $40,000 or greater, a college education, and a taste for outdoor recreation like golf, tennis, and boating.

"Great," thought Karlin as he tapped his pencil against the side of his coffee cup. "Now what?"

Discussion Issues

1. What are the limitations of product registration cards used as marketing research questionnaires?

2. Should someone make any major decisions based on the product registration data alone?

3. What kinds of additional research would you recommend?

In Chapter 9 we discussed the types of primary data that interest marketing researchers. We also briefly examined the two methods, communication and observation, that researchers employ to gather such data. In this chapter we will investigate communication techniques more closely, paying particular attention to the many types of questionnaires researchers use and the means by which they are administered.

Communication Methods

Structure The degree of standardization imposed on the data-collection instrument. A highly structured questionnaire, for example, is one in which the questions to be asked and the responses permitted subjects are completely predetermined, while a highly unstructured questionnaire is one in which the questions to be asked are only loosely predetermined, and respondents are free to respond in their own words and in any way they see fit.

Disguise The amount of knowledge hidden from the respondent by the data-collection method. An undisguised questionnaire, for example, is one in which the purpose of the research is obvious.

Fixed-alternative questions Questions in which the responses are limited to stated alternatives.

As we saw in Figure 9.2, if researchers choose to use the communication method of securing data, they must then decide on the kind of questionnaire that would best serve the problem at hand. They must determine the degree of **structure,** or standardization, to be imposed on the questionnaire, and the degree of **disguise** that is appropriate to the problem they are investigating.[1]

In a highly structured questionnaire, the questions to be asked and the responses permitted the subjects are completely predetermined. In a highly unstructured questionnaire, the questions to be asked are only loosely predetermined, and the respondents are free to respond in their own words. A questionnaire in which the questions are fixed but the responses are open-ended would represent an intermediate degree of structure. A disguised questionnaire attempts to hide the purpose of the study, whereas an undisguised questionnaire makes the purpose of the research obvious by the questions posed.

Structured-Undisguised Questionnaires

Marketing researchers often use structured-undisguised questionnaires in which questions are presented with exactly the same wording and in exactly the same order to all respondents when collecting data. The reason for standardizing the wording is to ensure that all respondents are replying to the same questions.[2] If one interviewer asked, "Do you drink orange juice?" and another asked, "Does your family use frozen orange juice?" the replies would not be comparable.

In the typical structured-undisguised questionnaire, the responses as well as the questions are standardized. **Fixed-alternative questions,** in which the responses are limited to the stated alternatives, are used. Consider the following question regarding the subject's attitude toward pollution and the need for more government legislation to control it.

Do you feel the United States needs more or less antipollution legislation?
- ☐   Needs more
- ☐   Needs less
- ☐   Neither more nor less
- ☐   No opinion

This question is a good example of a structured-undisguised question for two reasons. First, its purpose is clear: it seeks to discover the subject's attitudes toward antipollution legislation in a very straightforward manner. Second, it employs a highly structured format. Respondents are limited to only one of four stated replies.

Probably the greatest advantages of structured-undisguised questionnaires are that they are simple to administer and easy to tabulate and analyze.[3] Subjects should be reliable in that if they were asked the question again, they would answer in a similar fashion (assuming, of course, the absence of some attitude-changing event).

Magazines often poll their readers on subjects of interest. The results of these questionnaires are tabulated and then reported in future issues. The results are also often used to present a profile of readers' attributes when the magazine markets ad space.

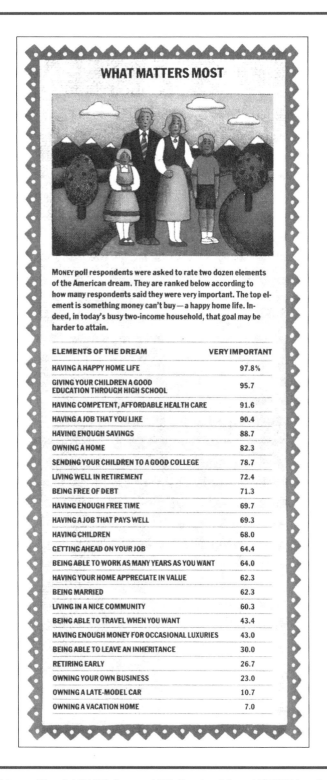

WHAT MATTERS MOST

MONEY poll respondents were asked to rate two dozen elements of the American dream. They are ranked below according to how many respondents said they were very important. The top element is something money can't buy—a happy home life. Indeed, in today's busy two-income household, that goal may be harder to attain.

ELEMENTS OF THE DREAM	VERY IMPORTANT
HAVING A HAPPY HOME LIFE	97.8%
GIVING YOUR CHILDREN A GOOD EDUCATION THROUGH HIGH SCHOOL	95.7
HAVING COMPETENT, AFFORDABLE HEALTH CARE	91.6
HAVING A JOB THAT YOU LIKE	90.4
HAVING ENOUGH SAVINGS	88.7
OWNING A HOME	82.3
SENDING YOUR CHILDREN TO A GOOD COLLEGE	78.7
LIVING WELL IN RETIREMENT	72.4
BEING FREE OF DEBT	71.3
HAVING ENOUGH FREE TIME	69.7
HAVING A JOB THAT PAYS WELL	69.3
HAVING CHILDREN	68.0
GETTING AHEAD ON YOUR JOB	64.4
BEING ABLE TO WORK AS MANY YEARS AS YOU WANT	64.0
HAVING YOUR HOME APPRECIATE IN VALUE	62.3
BEING MARRIED	62.3
LIVING IN A NICE COMMUNITY	60.3
BEING ABLE TO TRAVEL WHEN YOU WANT	43.4
HAVING ENOUGH MONEY FOR OCCASIONAL LUXURIES	43.0
BEING ABLE TO LEAVE AN INHERITANCE	30.0
RETIRING EARLY	26.7
OWNING YOUR OWN BUSINESS	23.0
OWNING A LATE-MODEL CAR	10.7
OWNING A VACATION HOME	7.0

Source: "What Matters Most," *MONEY*, January 1990. Reprinted from *MONEY* Magazine by special permission; copyright 1990 The Time Inc. Magazine Company.

Such reliability is facilitated by the consistency of fixed-alternative questions. These questions help standardize responses by providing subjects with an identical frame of reference. In contrast, consider the question, "How much television do you watch?" If no alternatives were supplied, one respondent might say "every day," another might say "regularly," and still another might respond with the number of hours per day. Responses from such an open-ended question would be far more difficult to interpret than those from a fixed-alternative question limiting replies to the categories of "every day," "at least three times a week," "at least once a week," or "less than once a week."

Providing alternative responses also often helps to make the question clear. "What is your marital status?" is less clear in its intent than "Are you married, single, widowed, or divorced?" The latter question provides the dimensions in which to frame the reply.

Although fixed-alternative questions tend to provide the most reliable responses, they may also elicit misleading answers. For example, fixed alternatives may force an answer to a question on which the respondent has no opinion. Even when a "no opinion" category is provided, interviewers often try to keep the number of "no opinions" to a minimum by pressing the respondent for a reply. The individual may agree, under pressure, to one of the other alternatives offered, but the alternative may not accurately capture the individual's true position on the issue. For example, the antipollution example presented earlier makes no allowance for those who feel that something probably should be done about pollution and that more legislation may possibly be one answer, but who fundamentally favor other approaches.

Fixed-alternative responses may also produce inaccuracies when the response categories themselves introduce bias. This is particularly true when a reasonable response is omitted because of an oversight or insufficient prior research as to the response categories that are appropriate. The provision of an "other" category does not eliminate this bias either, since subjects are often reluctant to respond in the "other" category. In posing a fixed-alternative question, one should make sure the alternatives offered adequately cover the range of probable replies.

The fixed-alternative question is thus most productive when possible replies are "well known, limited in number, and clear-cut. Thus they are appropriate for securing factual information (age, education, home ownership, amount of rent, and so on) and for eliciting expressions of opinion about issues on which people hold clear opinions."[4] They are therefore not very appropriate for securing primary data on motivations but certainly could be used (at least sometimes) to collect data on attitudes, intentions, awareness, demographic/socioeconomic characteristics, and behavior.

Unstructured-Undisguised Questionnaires

The unstructured-undisguised questionnaire is distinguished by the fact that the purpose of the study is clear but the response to the question is open-ended. Consider the following question:

"How do you feel about pollution and the need for more antipollution legislation?"

This initial question (which is often called a *stimulus* by researchers) is clear in its purpose. With it the interviewer attempts to get the subject to talk freely about his or her attitudes toward pollution. This is an **open-ended question,** because it leads to a very unstructured interview (called a **depth interview**). The respondent's initial reply, the interviewer's follow-up questions that seek elaboration, and the respon-

Open-ended question A question characterized by the condition that respondents are free to reply in their own words rather than being limited to choosing from among a set of alternatives.

Depth interview An unstructured personal interview in which the interviewer attempts to get the subject to talk freely and to express his or her true feelings.

dent's subsequent answers determine the direction of the interview. The interviewer may attempt to follow a rough outline. However, the order and the specific framing of the questions will vary from interview to interview, and the specific content will therefore vary.

The freedom permitted the interviewer in conducting these depth interviews reveals the major advantages and disadvantages of the method. By not limiting the respondent to a fixed set of replies, and by careful probing, an experienced interviewer should be able to derive a more accurate picture of the respondent's true position on some issue. This is particularly true with respect to sensitive issues in which there is social pressure to conform and to offer a "socially acceptable" response. Note, however, that we qualified our description of this method by specifying that "experienced interviewers" be used and "careful probing" be done. The depth interview requires highly skilled interviewers. They are hard to find and expensive to hire. But they are essential to accurate results with this type of questionnaire, in which the lack of structure allows the interviewer to strongly influence the result. Keen judgment as to when to probe and how to word the probes is required of the interviewer, and good depth interviews often take a long time to complete. This makes it difficult to secure the cooperation of respondents. It also means that a study using depth interviews, as opposed to fixed-alternative questions, will not only take longer to complete, but will involve fewer respondents or will require a greater number of interviewers. And the more interviewers there are, the more likely it will be that responses will vary based on each interviewer's personal technique in administering the questionnaire.[5]

The depth interview also causes severe problems in analysis. One or more skilled psychologists are typically required to interpret the responses—an expensive service. Further, the psychologist's own background and frame of reference will affect the interpretation. This subjectivity raises questions about both the reliability and validity of the results. It also causes difficulty in determining what the correct interpretation is and thus presents problems when tabulating the replies.[6]

Some of the problems with coding open-ended questions may be changing with new technology. Researchers today often feed respondents' answers into computers programmed to recognize a large vocabulary of words in their search for regularities in the replies. The computers are able to rank each word by the frequency of usage and then can print out sentences containing the key words. The detailed analysis of these sentences allows researchers to pick up on recurring themes.[7] While these systems automate the coding of unstructured interviews, they still leave interpretation to the individual analyst. Nevertheless, the systems can achieve in hours what a purely human review might take weeks to accomplish.

The depth interview is probably best suited to exploratory research, since it is productive with respect to just about all of the common purposes of exploratory research.

Unstructured-Disguised Questionnaires

Unstructured-disguised questionnaires lie at the heart of what has become known as motivation research.

> A person needs only limited experience in questionnaire-type surveys to realize that many areas of inquiry are not amenable to exploration by direct questions. Many important motives and reasons for choice are of a kind that the consumer *will not* describe because a truthful description would be damaging to his ego. Others he *cannot* describe, either because he himself does not have the words to

make his meaning clear or because his motive exists below the level of awareness. Very often such motives are of paramount importance in consumer behavior. If one tries to inquire into them with direct questions, especially categorical questions, one tends to get replies that are either useless or dangerously misleading.[8]

As evidence of the preceding observation, consider the following example: When consumers began complaining about the amount of salt in many prepared foods, a number of food companies flooded grocery store shelves with dozens of low-salt items. Sales of most of the items are either flat or declining. "All the market research showed that 60 percent of the people in this country were concerned about salt in their diet," said the marketing research director at Campbell Soup. "[But] in fact, only a fraction of those are willing to trade taste to get the salt out." Campbell's low-sodium soups never sold as well as the company had expected.[9]

Projective method The term used to describe questionnaires containing ambiguous stimuli that force subjects to rely on their own emotions, needs, motivations, attitudes, and values in framing a response.

Researchers have tried to overcome subjects' reluctance to discuss their feelings by developing techniques that are largely independent of the subjects' self-awareness and willingness to reveal themselves. The main thrust of these kinds of techniques, known as **projective methods,** has been to conceal the true subject of the study by using a disguised stimulus. Among the most common stimuli used are word association, sentence completion, and storytelling.

Though the stimulus is typically standardized, subjects are allowed to respond to it in a very unstructured form, which is why this method is known as an unstructured-disguised questionnaire. The basic assumption in projective methods is that the way an individual responds to a relatively unstructured stimulus provides clues as to how that person really perceives the subject under investigation and what his or her true reactions are to it.

> [T]he more unstructured and ambiguous a stimulus, the more a subject can and will project his emotions, needs, motivations, attitudes, and values. The *structure* of a stimulus . . . is the degree of choice available to the subject. A highly structured stimulus leaves very little choice: the subject has unambiguous choice among clear alternatives. . . . A stimulus of low structure has a wide range of alternative choices. It is ambiguous: the subject can "choose" his own interpretation.[10]

In general terms, then, a projective technique involves the use of a vague stimulus that an individual is asked to describe, expand upon, or build a structure around.

Word association A questionnaire containing a list of words to which respondents are instructed to reply with the first word that comes to mind.

Word Association   In the projective method of **word association,** subjects respond to a list of words with the first word that comes to mind. The test words are intermixed with neutral words to conceal the purpose of the study. In the study of pollution, some of the key words might be

- *Water*   _____
- *Air*   _____
- *Lakes*   _____
- *Industry*   _____
- *Smokestack*   _____
- *City*   _____

Responses to each of the key terms are recorded word-for-word and later analyzed for their meaning. The responses are usually judged in three ways: by the frequency with which any word is given as a response, by the average amount of time that elapses before a response is given, and by the number of respondents who do not respond at all to a test word after a reasonable period of time.

Any common responses that emerge are grouped to reveal patterns of interest, underlying motivations, or stereotypes. It is often possible to categorize the associations as favorable-unfavorable, pleasant-unpleasant, modern–old-fashioned, and so forth, depending upon the problem.

To determine the amount of time that elapses before a response is given to a test word, a stopwatch may be used or the interviewer may count silently while waiting for a reply. Respondents who hesitate (which is usually defined as taking longer than three seconds to reply) are judged to be sufficiently emotionally involved in the word so as to provide not their immediate reaction but rather what they consider to be an acceptable response. If they do not respond at all, their emotional involvement is judged to be so high as to block a response. An individual's pattern of responses, along with the details of the response to each question, are then used to assess the person's attitudes or feelings on the subject.

Sentence completion A questionnaire containing a number of sentences that subjects are directed to complete with the first words that come to mind.

Sentence Completion   The method of **sentence completion** requires that the respondent complete a number of sentences similar to the following:

- *Many people behave as if our natural resources were* _____.
- *A person who does not use our lakes for recreation is* _____.
- *The number-one concern for our natural resources is* _____.
- *When I think of living in a city, I* _____.

Again, respondents are instructed to reply with the first thoughts that come to mind. The responses are recorded word-for-word and are later analyzed.

> In one study, Kassarjian and Cohen asked 179 smokers who believed cigarettes to be a health hazard why they continued to smoke. The majority gave responses such as "Pleasure is more important than health," "Moderation is OK," "I like to smoke." One gets the impression that smokers are not dissatisfied with their lot. However, in a portion of the study involving sentence-completion tests, smokers responded to the question, "People who never smoke are _____," with comments such as "better off," "happier," "smarter," "wiser," "more informed." To the question, "Teenagers who smoke are _____," smokers responded with "foolish," "crazy," "uninformed," "stupid," "showing off," "immature," "wrong."
>
> Clearly the impression one gets from the sentence completion test is that smokers are anxious, uncomfortable, dissonant, and dissatisfied with their habit. This is quite different from the results of a probed open-end question.[11]

One advantage of sentence completion over word association is that respondents can be provided with a more directed stimulus. There should be just enough direction to evoke some association with the concept of interest. The researcher needs to be careful not to convey the purpose of the study or provoke the "socially acceptable" response. Obviously, skill is needed to develop a good sentence-completion or word-association test.

Storytelling A questionnaire method of data collection relying on a picture stimulus such as a cartoon, photograph, or drawing, about which the subject is asked to tell a story.

Thematic Apperception Test (TAT) A copyrighted series of pictures about which the subject is asked to tell stories.

Storytelling   Pictorial material such as cartoons, photographs, or drawings is often used in the **storytelling** approach, although other stimuli are also used. These pictorial devices are descendants of the psychologists' **Thematic Apperception Test (TAT).** The TAT consists of a copyrighted series of pictures about which the subject is asked to tell stories. Some of the pictures are of ordinary events and some of unusual events; in some of the pictures the persons or objects are clearly represented, and in others they are relatively obscure. The way a subject responds to these events helps researchers interpret that individual's personality. For example, the nature of

Responses to phone questionnaires like this one often influence network programming decisions.

How the new TV shows stack up

What they like

"Fresh Prince of Bel Air"

NBC-TV's "Fresh Prince of Bel Air" is this year's best-liked new TV program, according to a Gallup Organization survey. The 486 respondents who said they had watched at least one of this year's new shows were asked: "Which new TV show do you like the most?"

1	"Fresh Prince of Bel Air"	NBC
2	"The Flash"	CBS
3	"The Simpsons"*	Fox
4	"Cop Rock"	ABC
5	"Evening Shade"	CBS
6	"In Living Color"*	Fox
7	"Uncle Buck"	CBS
8	"The Fanelli Boys"	NBC
9	"Married People"	ABC
10	"Gabriel's Fire"	ABC
**	"Law & Order"	NBC

* Not a program new to the fall schedule. ** Tie.
Source: Gallup Organization

What they dislike

"Cop Rock"

ABC's "Cop Rock," a drama/comedy/musical hybrid, was voted the most disliked of the fall's new shows. The 486 respondents who said they had watched at least one of this year's new shows were asked: "Which new TV show do you dislike the most?"

1	"Cop Rock"	ABC
2	"The Simpsons"*	Fox
3	"Ferris Bueller"	NBC
4	"Roseanne"*	ABC
5	"Fresh Prince of Bel Air"	NBC
**	"Uncle Buck"	CBS
7	"True Colors"	Fox
8	"The Fanelli Boys"	NBC
**	"Evening Shade"	CBS
10	"Parenthood"	NBC
**	"The Flash"	CBS
**	"Married People"	ABC
**	"In Living Color"*	Fox

Source: John Heiland, "How the New TV Shows Stack Up," *Advertising Age*, November 5, 1990. Reprinted with permission from *Advertising Age*. Copyright 1990 Crain Communications, Inc. All rights reserved.

the response might show a subject to be impulsive or controlled, creative or unimaginative, and so on.

When used in a marketing situation, the same pattern is followed. Respondents are shown a picture and asked to tell a story about the picture. However, the responses are used to assess attitudes toward the phenomenon under investigation rather than to interpret the subject's personality. For example,

McCann-Erickson ad agency resorted to stick-figure sketches in research on its American Express Gold Card account. Focus group interviews hadn't made clear consumers' differing perceptions of gold-card and green-card holders.

The drawings, however, were much more illuminating. In one set, for example, the gold-card user was portrayed as a broad-shouldered man standing in an active position, while the green-card user was a "couch potato" in front of a TV set. Based on such pictures and other research, the agency decided to market the gold card as a "symbol of responsibility for people who have control over their lives and finances."[12]

With respect to the pollution example, the stimulus might be a picture of a city, and the respondent might be asked to describe what it would be like to live there. The analysis of the individual's response would then focus on the emphasis given to pollution in its various forms. If no mention were made of traffic congestion, dirty air, noise, and so on, the person would be classified as displaying little concern for pollution and its control.

Each of the projective methods we have discussed differs somewhat in how structured its stimulus is. In the word-association and sentence-completion methods, researchers present each respondent with the same stimulus in the same sequence, and in this sense these methods are quite structured. However, both methods are typically categorized with storytelling as unstructured techniques, because, like the storytelling techniques, they allow very unstructured responses. Respondents are free to interpret and respond to the stimuli with their own words and in terms of their own perceptions.

Many of the same difficulties encountered with the unstructured-undisguised methods of data collection are also encountered with projective methods. Although having a standardized stimulus is a distinct advantage in interpreting the replies, the interpretation often reflects the researcher's frame of reference as much as it does the respondent's. Different researchers often reach different conclusions about the same response. This wreaks havoc with the editing, coding, and tabulating of replies and suggests that projective methods are also more suited for exploratory research than for descriptive or causal research.

Structured-Disguised Questionnaires

Structured-disguised questionnaires are the least used in marketing research. They were developed as a way of combining the advantages of disguise in uncovering subconscious motives and attitudes with the advantages of structure in coding and tabulating replies. Those who favor the structured-disguised approach usually base their support on the importance of a person's attitudes in his or her mental and psychological makeup.

One theory holds, for example, that an individual's knowledge, perception, and memory of a subject are conditioned by his or her attitudes toward it. Thus, in order to secure information about people's attitudes when a direct question would produce a biased answer, this theory suggests we simply ask them what they know, not what their opinion is. Presumably greater knowledge reflects the strength and direction of an attitude. Democratic voters, for example, could be expected to know more about Democratic candidates and the Democratic platform than would those intending to vote Republican. This argument is consistent with what we have learned about the process that psychologists call *selective perception*. That concept holds that individuals tend to selectively expose themselves, selectively perceive, and selectively retain ideas, arguments, events, and phenomena that are consistent with their previously held beliefs. Conversely, people tend to avoid, see differently, and forget situations and items that are inconsistent with their previously held beliefs.

This theory would suggest that one way of discovering a respondent's true attitudes toward pollution and the need for antipollution legislation, for example, would be to ask the person what he or she knows about the subject. Thus, the researcher might ask, "What is the status of the antipollution legislation listed below?" and then present some actual and some hypothetical bills for the respondent to check: "In committee," "Passed by the House but not the Senate," "Vetoed by the President," and so on. Respondents' attitudes toward the need for more legislation would then be assessed by the accuracy of their responses.

The main advantages of this approach emerge in analysis. Responses are easily coded and tabulated and an objective measure of knowledge quickly derived. Whether this measure of knowledge can also be interpreted as a measure of the person's attitudes, though, is another matter. Is high legislative awareness indicative of a favorable or an unfavorable attitude toward the need for more antipollution legislation? Or is it simply indicative of someone who keeps abreast of current events? In general, the evidence suggests that it is possible to obtain results with a structured-disguised approach that are at least comparable to those obtained with unstructured-disguised approaches.

Ethical
Dilemma 10.1
Pharmaceutical Supply Company derived its major source of revenue from physician-prescribed drugs. For quite some time, Pharmaceutical Supply had maintained a dominant position in the market. A new competitor had entered the market, however, and was quickly gaining market share.

In response to competitive pressure, Pharmaceutical Supply's management decided that it needed to conduct an extensive study concerning physician decision making with regard to selection of drugs. Janice Rowland, the marketing research director, decided that the best way to gather this information would be through the use of personal and telephone interviews. Rowland directed the interviewers to represent themselves as employees of a fictitious marketing research agency, as she believed that a biased response would result if the physicians were aware that Pharmaceutical Supply was conducting the study. In addition, the interviewers were instructed to tell the physicians that the research was being conducted for the research agency's own purpose and not for a particular client.

- Was Rowland's decision to withhold the sponsor's true name and purpose a good one?
- Did the physicians have a right to know who was conducting the research?
- It has been argued that use of such deception prevents a respondent from making a rational choice about whether or not she or he wishes to participate in a study. Comment on this.
- What kind of results might have been obtained if the physicians had known the true sponsor of the study?
- What are the consequences for the research profession of using this form of deception?

Personal interview
Direct, face-to-face conversation between a representative of the research organization, the interviewer, and a respondent, or interviewee.

Telephone interview
Telephone conversation between a representative of the research organization, the interviewer, and a respondent, or interviewee.

Methods of Administering Questionnaires

Questionnaires can also be classified by the method that will be used to administer them. The main methods are by personal interview, telephone interview, and mail questionnaire.

A **personal interview** implies a direct face-to-face conversation between the interviewer and the respondent, as compared to the **telephone interview.** In both cases, the interviewer asks the questions and records the respondent's answers either

Mail questionnaire
A questionnaire administered by mail to designated respondents under an accompanying cover letter. The respondents return the questionnaire by mail to the research organization.

while the interview is in progress or immediately afterward. The **mail questionnaire** is sent to designated respondents with an accompanying cover letter. The respondents complete the questionnaire at their leisure and mail their replies back to the research organization.

A number of variations are possible on these so-called pure methods of administration. Questionnaires for a mail administration may simply be attached to products or printed in magazines and newspapers. Questionnaires in a personal interview may be self-administered, meaning the respondents complete the questionnaire themselves as opposed to having the interviewer ask the questions and fill in the respondents' answers. This might be done in the interviewer's presence, in which case there would be an opportunity for the respondents to ask the interviewer to clarify any points that may be confusing. Or the respondents might complete the questionnaire in private for later pickup by a representative of the research organization, in which case the interaction would resemble a personal interview even less. Another possibility is for the interviewer to hand the designated respondent the questionnaire personally, but then have the respondent complete it in private and mail it directly to the research organization. In this case, the personal interview is indistinguishable from the mail-questionnaire method.

Each of these methods of administration possess some advantages and disadvantages. When we discuss the various pros and cons of each method, we will use so-called pure cases as a frame of reference. By modifying the method of administration, researchers may also change some of the general advantages and disadvantages that normally characterize the method.

Other factors peculiar to a specific situation may also influence the strengths and weaknesses of each method. Nevertheless, a general discussion of advantages and disadvantages will help to clarify the various criteria that researchers must keep in mind when deciding on the method they will use to collect the data. Sampling control, information control, and administrative control are the points researchers generally consider when comparing the methods.

Sampling control The term applied to studies relying on questionnaires and concerning the researcher's dual abilities to direct the inquiry to a designated respondent and to secure the desired cooperation from that respondent.

Sampling Control

Sampling control involves the researcher's ability to direct the inquiry to a designated respondent and to get the desired cooperation from that respondent.

Sampling frame The list of sampling units from which a sample will be drawn; the list could consist of geographic areas, institutions, individuals, or other units.

The direction of the inquiry is guided by the **sampling frame,** that is, by the list of population elements from which the sample will be drawn. With the telephone method, for example, one or more phone books typically serve as the sampling frame. Respondents are selected by some random method from phone books serving the areas in which the study is to be done. Phone book sampling frames are inadequate because they do not include those without phones or those who have unlisted numbers.

Of course, a great percentage of the U.S. population has phones—93 percent of all households in 1985. Yet there is some variation by regions and by other factors. The regional range is from 94 percent in the Midwest to 92 percent in the South and West. There is very little variation between urban and rural households.[13]

The census data also indicate that telephone penetration is higher for whites than for blacks and hispanics. The proportion of households with telephones increases each year, however, and thus the problem of bias resulting from the exclusion of nontelephone households should diminish in the future.

Studies that rely on phone book sampling frames underrepresent transient households. Anywhere from 12 to 15 percent of the residential numbers in a typical telephone directory are found to be disconnected when called. Phone book sampling frames also do not include numbers that were assigned after the current directory was published, nor the segment of the population that has requested an unlisted telephone number. The voluntary unlisted segment has been growing steadily and now represents approximately 20 percent of all residential phones. The problem is particularly acute in urban areas in general and some urban areas in particular. Figure 10.1, for example, shows the fourteen metropolitan areas with over 40 percent of the telephones unlisted.

The empirical evidence suggests that people with unlisted numbers tend to be younger, nonwhite, living in a large city, not college graduates, and employed by someone else in an unskilled or semiskilled job.[14] These characteristics conflict with the stereotype that someone with an unlisted number is probably among the rich and famous!

Random-digit dialing A technique used in studies employing telephone interviews, in which the numbers to be called are randomly generated.

An attempt at overcoming the sampling bias of unlisted numbers is **random-digit dialing,** in which a computer generates a list of random numbers, and often dials them automatically as well. The calls are typically handled through the central interviewing facility using the Wide Area Telephone Service (WATS). This procedure allows geographically wide distribution or coverage.

One problem with the random generation of phone numbers is that it can increase survey costs. While there are approximately 340 million possible phone numbers that can be called in the continental United States, there are only about 80 million working residential telephone numbers. Hence, when using random dialing, interviewers may only make a residential contact in about one out of four calls. This makes random-digit dialing very costly both in dollars and in time.[15]

Plus-one sampling A technique used in studies employing telephone interviews, in which a single, randomly determined digit is added to numbers selected from the telephone directory.

An alternative scheme to random-digit dialing is **plus-one sampling,** where a probability sample of phone numbers is selected from the telephone directory and a single, randomly determined digit is added to each selected number.[16]

One or more mailing lists typically serve as the sampling frame in mail questionnaires. The quality of these lists determines the sampling biases. If the list is a reasonably good one, the bias may be small. For example, some firms have established panels, which can be used to answer mail questionnaires and which are representative of the population in many important respects. Further, some mailing lists that may be ideally suited for certain types of studies can be purchased.

Figure 10.1   ***Metro Areas in Which More than 40 Percent of the Phones Are Unlisted***

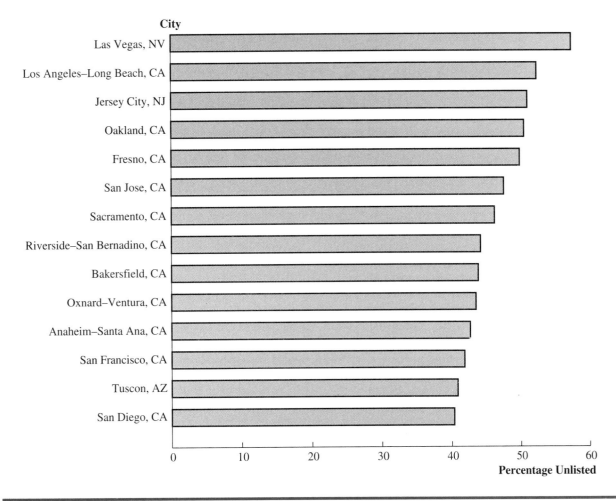

Source: Survey Sampling, Inc.

Say you run a direct-mail business that specializes in selling monogrammed baby bibs. For a fee at any given time you can obtain a mailing list containing the names and addresses of up to one million pregnant women. And if it should suit your purposes, it's easy enough to get the list limited to women whose babies are expected in a certain month or who are expecting their first child.[17]

Sometimes the list is internally generated. Spurred on by technical advances, a number of firms are developing greater capabilities to target questionnaires or other mailings to specific households. For example, American Express, with its new image-processing technology, now is able to select all of its cardholders who made purchases from golf pro-shops, or who traveled more than once to Europe, or who attended symphony concerts, or who made some other specific purchase using their American Express card.[18]

The fact remains, though, that the mailing list determines the sampling control in a mail study. If there is an accurate, applicable, and readily available list of

Research Window 10.1
Mail-Room Malady

The mail room at General Motors is saying no to bulk mail. GM's Flint Automotive Division has halted the delivery of bulk mail in an effort to reduce operating costs, and they are not alone. Hundreds of businesses nationwide are refusing to deliver third-class mail to their employees. As such decisions are becoming increasingly widespread, they are a source of real concern to direct marketers who want to reach employees where they work. Business-to-business advertisers whose mailings are targeted toward corporate managers are especially hard hit.

The Direct Marketing Association (DMA) has responded by setting up a task force to study the scope of the problem and devise possible solutions. The DMA recently surveyed mail-room supervisors of *Fortune 500* companies to determine mail-room practices. Preliminary results indicate that at least 30 percent of mail delivered to the companies is not received by the addressees.

Legally, there's nothing direct marketers can do about mail rooms' throwing away bulk mail and nonsubscription magazines. The U.S. Postal Service has a longstanding policy declaring that mail addressed to an individual at a business is the property of that business. Another problem is that many corporations are requiring incoming mail to have mail-stops, or internal delivery codes, that identify various departments and speed sorting.

To make sure that they're reaching the right person, direct marketers need to follow up initial mail directly, perhaps via first-class mail. Another solution is for direct marketers and mail-room supervisors to work more cooperatively. One way is to ask mail-room supervisors to have employees fill out cards indicating what types of mail are beneficial.

Most important, marketers can keep the situation from worsening by frequently updating their mailing lists, says Gene Del Polito, executive director of the Direct Mail Association. "When you have sloppy mail practices and a lot of your mail is directed to people who aren't there . . . you're not creating the impression that the nature of your mail is very important," concludes Mr. Del Polito.

Source: Patricia Strnad, "Mail-Room Malady," *Advertising Age*, 60 (March 20, 1989), p. 62.

population elements, the mail questionnaire allows a wide and representative sample, since it costs no more to send a questionnaire across country than it does to send one across town. Even ignoring costs, it is sometimes the only way of contacting the relevant population, such as busy executives who will not sit still for an arranged personal or telephone interview but may respond to a mail questionnaire.

A key here, though, is the ability to address the questionnaire to a specific respondent rather than a position. As Research Window 10.1 indicates, getting mail addressed to a person occupying a particular position is getting more difficult. It is estimated that the average consumer has his or her name on anywhere from 25 to 40 separate mailing lists and receives 80 pieces of unsolicited mail per year. All those who think unsolicited mail is a bother, however, can send one letter to the Direct Mail Marketing Association, a trade group of more than 2,600 direct mail marketers, and that organization will remove the name from every member's list. The statistics indicate, however, that for every person requesting to have his or her name removed, two more request that their names be added.[19]

Sampling control for personal interviewing is a bit more difficult than for telephone interviewing or mail questionnaires, but is still possible. For some populations, such as doctors, architects, or business firms, trade associations or directories will furnish names from which a sample can be drawn. For studies focused on consumers in which in-house interviews are to be conducted, however, there are few lists available, and those that are available are typically out-of-date. Instead of seeking names, researchers often choose their samples based on geographic areas and houses or apartments, termed *sampling units*, within that area. In this method, instead of inaccurate lists of people, interviewers use accurate, current lists of sampling units in the form of maps. In a later chapter we will discuss how such *area sampling*, as it is called, works.

While there is still the problem of ensuring that the field interviewer will contact the right household and person, the personal interview does provide some sampling control in directing the questionnaire to specific sampling units.

A currently popular alternative for conducting personal interviews among consumers is to use **mall intercepts.** The technique involves exactly what the name implies.[20] Interviewers intercept, or stop, those passing by and ask if they would be willing to participate in a research study. Those who agree are typically taken to the firm's interviewing facility that has been set up in the mall, where the interview is conducted.[21] With shopping mall intercepts, there are two issues affecting the ability to direct the inquiry to a randomly determined respondent. First, although a great many people do shop at malls, not everyone does. Only those who visit the particular mall in question have a chance of being included in the study. Second, a person's chances of being asked to participate depend on the likelihood of their being in the mall. That, in turn, depends on the frequency with which they shop there. One thing that is commonly done with respect to this second source of variation in the selection probabilities is to weight the replies of the respondent by the reciprocal of the number of visits made to the mall in a set amount of time.[22]

It is one thing to figure out whom to contact in a study; it is quite another to get that person to agree to participate. For example, of the three methods of data collection we have discussed, the personal interview affords the most sample control with respect to obtaining cooperation from the designated respondent. With a personal interview, the respondent's identity is known, and thus there is little opportunity for anyone else to reply. People are also less likely to refuse a personal interview than they are a telephone interview or a mail questionnaire. There is sometimes a problem with not-at-homes, but this can often be handled by calling back at a different time.

Telephone methods also suffer from not-at-homes or no-answers. In one very large study involving more than 259,000 telephone calls, it was found, for example, that over 34 percent of the calls resulted in a no-answer.[23] Even more disturbing was the fact that the probability of making contact with an eligible respondent on the first call was less than 1 in 10 (see Table 10.1). Of course, calling back by phone is much simpler and more economical than is trying to rearrange a personal interview. The relatively low expense of a telephone contact allows a number of follow-up calls to secure a needed response, while the high cost of field contact restricts the number of follow-ups that can be made in studies using personal interviews. However, making sure the intended respondent replies is somewhat more difficult with telephone interviews than with personal interviews, as is the problem of determining which person in the household should be interviewed.[24]

Mail questionnaires afford the researcher little control in securing a response from the intended respondent. Although the researcher can offer the individual some incentive for cooperating,[25] a great many subjects may nevertheless refuse to respond. In many cases, only those most interested in the subject will respond. In other cases subjects will be incapable of responding because they are illiterate. For example, the International Reading Association estimates that some 20 million English-speaking,

Mall intercept A method of data collection in which interviewers in a shopping mall stop or interrupt a sample of those passing by to ask them if they would be willing to participate in a research study; those who agree are typically taken to an interviewing facility that has been set up in the mall, where the interview is conducted.

Table 10.1   **Results of First Dialing Attempts**

Result	Number of Dialings	Probability of Occurrence
No answer	89,829	.347
Busy	5,299	.020
Out-of-service	52,632	.203
No eligible person	75,285	.291
Business	10,578	.041
At home	25,465	.098
Refusal	3,707	.014 (.146)[a]
Completion	21,758	.084 (.854)
Total	259,088	1.000

[a]Probability of occurrence given eligible individual is at home.

Source: Roger A. Kerin and Robert A. Peterson, "Scheduling Telephone Interviews," *Journal of Advertising Research*, 23 (April/May 1983), p. 44.

native-born American adults read or write so poorly that they have trouble holding jobs, and the author of *Illiterate America* suggests that 60 million adult Americans are illiterate.[26] Since many of these people have difficulty with everyday tasks such as reading job notices, making change, or getting a driver's license, it is no wonder that they might not respond to a mail questionnaire!

Whatever the reason for nonresponse, it causes a bias of unknown size and direction. Lack of control also exists in respect to identifying who is responding to the mail questionnaire. The researcher cannot even ensure that the preferred respondent from the household replies.

Information Control

Information control A term applied to studies using questionnaires and concerning the amount and accuracy of the information that can be obtained from respondents.

Information control, which involves the kinds of questions that can be asked and the amount and accuracy of the information that can be obtained from respondents, varies according to the method of data collection that is used. The personal interview, for example, can be conducted using almost any form of questionnaire, from structured-undisguised through unstructured-disguised. The personal nature of the interaction allows the interviewer to show the respondent pictures, examples of advertisements, lists of words, scales, and so on, as stimuli. In contrast, the telephone interview rules out most aids. The mail questionnaire, however, allows the use of some of them.

Personal interviews also allow the automatic sequencing of questions; for example, if the answer to question 4 is positive, ask questions 5 and 6, whereas if it is negative, ask questions 7 and 8. Although automatic sequencing is also possible with telephone interviews, mail questionnaires permit much less of it.

There is a greater danger of *sequence bias* with mail questionnaires than with questionnaires administered in person or over the phone. Respondents can see the whole questionnaire, and thus their replies to any single question may not be independently arrived at but are more likely to be conditioned by their responses to other questions than if either personal interviews or telephone interviews were used.

The mail questionnaire permits control of the bias caused by the interviewee's perception of the interviewer. With a mail questionnaire, respondents are also able to work at their own pace. This may produce better-thought-out responses than would be obtained in personal or telephone interviews, where there is a certain urgency associated with giving a response. A thought-out response, however, is no guarantee of an appropriate reply. If the question is ambiguous, the mail survey offers no opportunity for clarification. The question must succeed or fail on its own merits. Because researchers cannot decipher differences in interpretation among respondents, they cannot impose a consistent frame of reference on the replies. Thus the responses to an open-ended question in a mail questionnaire may be excessive or inadequate. With structured questions, the answers may simply reflect differences in the frame of reference being employed rather than any subject-to-subject variation in the particular characteristic being measured. The anonymity sometimes associated with a mail questionnaire does afford people an opportunity to be more frank on certain sensitive issues (for example, sexual behavior).

Both personal and telephone interviews can cause interviewer bias because of the respondent's perception of the interviewer or because different interviewers ask questions and probe in different ways. Both of these biases can be more easily controlled in telephone surveys. There are fewer interviewer actions to which the respondent can react, and a supervisor can be present during telephone interviews to ensure that they are being conducted consistently. It is typically more difficult, though, to establish rapport over the phone than in person. The respondent in a telephone interview often demands more information about the purposes of the study, the credentials of the interviewer and research organization, and so on.

With regard to the length of the questionnaire or the amount of information to be collected, the general rule of thumb is that long questionnaires can be handled best by personal interview and least well by telephone interview. So much, though, depends on the subject of inquiry, the form of the questionnaire, and the approach used to secure cooperation that a rigid interpretation of this advice would be unwarranted and hazardous.

As with so many things, computers are changing the way surveys are conducted. Computers were first used in the early 1970s to assist with telephone interviews. The early systems linked mainframe computers or minicomputers to cathode-ray tube terminals (CRTs). Their essential function was to present on the terminal the questions that normally would have been on a paper questionnaire. Interviewers would read the questions as they came up on the CRT and would enter respondents' answers directly on the keyboard. The early systems generated such substantial savings in time and resources that they spawned a virtual revolution in data collection. Partly because of the advantages that accrue with CRT administration of question-naires, telephone interviews have become the most popular data-collection technique (see Research Window 10.2). The revolution that CRT interviewing wrought was given further impetus with the development of the microcomputer.

Computer-assisted interviewing (CAI) The conduct of surveys using computers to manage the sequence of questions and where the answers are recorded electronically through the use of a keyboard.

Currently, there are at least four types of uses for micro-based, stand-alone, **computer-assisted interviewing (CAI)** software:

1. Telephone surveys in which each interviewer has a personal computer from which to ask questions.
2. In-person interviews in which the interviewer transports a portable lap-top computer to the interview site and uses it to interview the respondent, or places

Research Window 10.2
Percentage of People Participating in Various Types of Surveys by Year

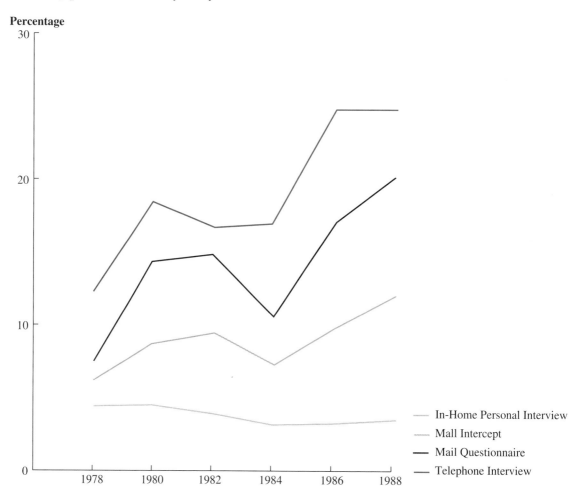

Source: Estimated from the information in *Industry Image Study: Research on Research*, 8th ed. (Indianapolis, Ind.: Walker Research, Inc., 1988), p. 3.

the computer in front of the respondent and lets the respondent answer questions as they appear on the screen.

3. Interviews in which the interviewee is sitting in front of the computer in a shopping mall or research laboratory and responds to questions as they are displayed on the monitor.

4. Mail administration in which the questionnaire is sent by mail on diskette to respondents, who answer the questions using their own microcomputer and return the completed diskette by mail.[27]

One of the most important advantages of computer-assisted interviewing is the information control it allows. First, the computer displays each question exactly as the researcher intended. It will show only the questions and information that the respondent needs to, or should, see. Further, it will display the next question only when an acceptable answer to the current one is entered on the keyboard. If a respondent says that she or he bought a brand that is not available in that particular locale, for example, the computer can be programmed to reject the answer. This greatly simplifies skipping or branching procedures. The interviewer does not have to grapple with selecting the next question given the response to the current one; the computer does this automatically. This saves considerable time and confusion in administering the questionnaire and permits a more natural flow of the interview. It also assures that there will be no variation in the sequence in which the questions are asked. Information control also manifests itself in the following:

1. *Personalization of the questions.* During the course of the interview, the computer is aware of all previous responses (e.g., name of wife, cars owned, supermarket patronized) and can customize the wording of future questions—for example, "When your wife, Ann, shops at the Acme, does she usually use the Fiat or the Buick?" Such personalized questions can enhance rapport and thus provide for higher-quality interviews.

2. *Customized questionnaires.* Key information elicited early in the interview can be used to customize the questionnaire for each respondent. For example, only product attributes previously acknowledged by respondents as determinants of their decisions would be used to measure their brand perceptions, rather than using an a priori list of attributes common to all respondents.

In addition to the enhanced branching abilities and personalization of the questionnaires that they allow, computer-assisted interviews often produce increased accuracy in the results. There is evidence to suggest that people are more truthful when responding to a computer than to an interviewer or even when completing a self-administered, paper-and-pencil questionnaire. They seem to think that the computer is less judgmental and provides them greater anonymity. For example, Chevron's Ortho Consumer Products unit in San Francisco asked salespeople in two separate studies to assess the company's marketing strategy. Although both studies promised anonymity, salespeople had only kind words for their bosses when asked in the paper-and-pencil survey. "When the questions were posed by computer, in contrast, 'not all the responses were so favorable to management,' says Edward Evans, manager of planning and analysis."[28]

Computer-assisted interviewing certainly speeds the data-collection and processing tasks. The preliminary tabulations of the answers are available at a moment's notice, because the replies are already stored in memory. One does not have the typical two- to three-week delay caused by coding and data entry that happens when questionnaires are completed by hand.

Respondents also seem to enjoy the interviewing experience more when the questionnaire is administered by computer. That, in turn, seems to help response rates. For example, the return rate in disk-by-mail surveys often exceeds 50 percent.[29] Further, the whole notion of involving computers in the interviewing process has opened up some other capabilities with respect to managing the interviewing process, including making it easier to write the questionnaire, schedule the people to be contacted, monitor what happens to each attempted call, and prepare the research report.[30]

Even though computers have had a profound effect on interviewing techniques, they are not a panacea.

> There are limits to what the machines can do. They can't win over respondents with social chitchat or explain questions that are misunderstood. Unless the interviewees are good typists, the computers can't elicit lengthy responses. They can't recognize fuzzy or superficial answers and prod respondents to elaborate. They can't ask follow-up questions of interviewees who drop unexpected leads. And, the ones that ask questions by phone with mechanical voices have raised the ire of some people who consider unsolicited, randomly dialed calls an invasion of privacy.[31]

Further, disk-by-mail administration can be used only among those likely to own or to have access to a microcomputer. Although they can be quite useful in industrial surveys, because most businesspeople have access to a machine, they are more limited in general consumer surveys unless the product or service at issue involves a population likely to own a microcomputer (e.g., a new software program).

Administrative Control

Administrative control
A term applied to studies relying on questionnaires and referring to the speed, cost, and control of the replies afforded by the mode of administration.

Administrative control involves the time and cost of administering the questionnaire, as well as the control of the replies afforded by the administrative method chosen. The telephone survey is one of the quickest ways of obtaining information. A number of calls can be made from a central exchange in a short period, perhaps as many as 15 or 20 per hour per interviewer if the questionnaire is short. An in-home personal interview affords no such time economies, since there is unproductive time between each interview in which the interviewer travels to the next respondent. If the researcher wishes to speed up the replies secured with in-home personal interviews, the size of the field force must be increased. However, as the number of interviewers increases, so do problems of interviewer-related variations in responses. By properly selecting and training interviewers, researchers can minimize some of the differences in approach that lead to variations, but personal interviews still present more problems of control than telephone interviews.

Personal interviews also give researchers little control over possible interviewer cheating. Since the researcher can supervise telephone interviewers directly when they are making their calls, problems of variation in administration and cheating should be minimized. Mall interviews are similar to telephone interviews in this regard.

While the mail questionnaire represents a standardized stimulus, and thus allows little variation in administration, it also affords little speed control. It often takes several weeks to secure the bulk of the replies, at which time a follow-up mailing is often begun. It, too, will involve a time lapse of several weeks for the questionnaires to reach the respondents, be completed, and find their way back. Depending on the number of follow-up mailings required, the total time needed to conduct a good mail study can often be substantial.[32] With a mail study it also takes as long to get replies from a small sample as it does from a large sample. This is not so with personal and telephone interviews, where there is a direct relationship between the number of interviews and the time required to complete them. In general, in-home personal interviews tend to be the most expensive per completed contact, and the mail questionnaire tends to be the cheapest. However, many factors can change the cost picture dramatically. For example, it costs relatively little, per contact, to mail a questionnaire; but if the response rate is very low, the cost per return may actually be quite high.

For the most part, the cost of the various methods hinges on the problem of assuring quality control. It is generally true that the larger the field staff is, the greater the problems of control. Mail surveys require the fewest staffers. Telephone, mall, and in-home personal interview methods require progressively larger field staffs. Hence, a personal interview in the home is typically the most expensive method of data collection.

Combining Administration Methods

Each method of data collection thus has its advantages and disadvantages, and none is superior in all situations. The research problem itself will often suggest one approach over the others, but the researcher should recognize that a combination of approaches is often the most productive. In one home product-use test, for example, interviewers distributed the product, self-administered questionnaires, and return envelopes to the respondents, while telephone interviews were used for follow-up. The combination of methods produced telephone cooperation from 97 percent of the testing families, while 82 percent of the mail questionnaires were returned.[33]

Another example demonstrating the advantages that can accrue through the creative use of a combination of data-collection techniques is the locked-box approach recommended for industrial surveys.[34] Surveying the industrial market is a relatively expensive proposition. One has to contend with busy executives who have better things to do with their time than answer questionnaires, and with efficient secretaries and receptionists who prescreen executive mail, telephone calls, and personal visitors. Industrial surveys consequently produce very low response rates. The locked box has proved to be effective in getting through the prescreens and in generating executive cooperation. It is nothing more than a metal, shoe-sized box that is locked with a three-digit combination lock and that contains flash cards, interview exhibits, concept statements, or other survey materials. It is accompanied by a cover letter explaining the purpose of the survey and telling the respondent that an interviewer will be contacting him or her in a few days. The box becomes the gift for cooperating. However, it is of no use unless one knows the combination, information that is given the executive after he or she cooperates in the follow-up telephone interview. Thus, mail is used to deliver the box; and the telephone, to conduct the actual interview. At the same time, the box provides an opportunity to use stimuli such as pictures, examples, lists of words, scales, and so on—stimuli that otherwise might be restricted to personal interviews.

Back to the Case

Tom Karlin had built a successful appliance distributorship by taking the initiative, so not surprisingly, it wasn't long before the information he received from Demographics Life-Style Data (DLD) gave him an idea.

He made an appointment to see Peter Haraldsen, a Tampa real estate developer.

Haraldsen specialized in luxury developments built around golf courses. The homes in Harald-

sen's latest development would start at around $200,000 when they were finished. Haraldsen had set up the meeting to take place at one of the finished model homes in that development.

"It really is beautiful," commented Karlin after he'd been given the tour.

"Thank you," replied Haraldsen, "but you know this is our fifth development, and I think we've really gotten the hang of what our clientele wants."

"What are your customers like?" asked Karlin.

"Successful businesspeople in their late 50s, early 60s. They're still active, still working. Often they buy a second home in Florida with the idea that within the next ten years they'll move down here permanently. These are active people, mind you. They could go anywhere. They come here for the golf and the tennis, the year-round good weather."

"Well," replied Karlin, launching into his pitch, "the reason I wanted to meet with you today was to have a chance to share some data with you. My data show that the profile of the high-end Clean-Rite appliances purchaser matches the profile of your potential customers perfectly."

Karlin and Haraldsen spent an hour going over the data, but in the end Haraldsen remained unconvinced. He'd had few complaints about the WasherMaid appliances he'd used in his previous developments, so even the sweet prices that Karlin was offering him didn't seem reason enough to change.

"I'll tell you what," Haraldsen concluded, "leave the data with me. I'll send the information over to my marketing director and let him take a look at it, and we'll get back to you."

Three weeks later, Karlin received a call from Haraldsen. "Tom, I've got to tell you—when I showed my marketing director that appliance-sale demographic data, he was a bit skeptical. So he asked 100 potential home buyers who came to one of our open houses to fill out a questionnaire about their appliance preferences. And you know what? Most of them preferred Clean-Rite. Let's set up a time this week to get together and talk dollars and cents."

Summary

Learning Objective 1: Explain the concept of *structure* as it relates to questionnaires.

The degree of structure in a questionnaire is the degree of standardization imposed on it. In a highly structured questionnaire the questions to be asked and the responses permitted the subjects are completely predetermined. In a highly unstructured questionnaire, the questions to be asked are only loosely predetermined, and the respondents are free to respond in their own words. A questionnaire in which the questions are fixed but the responses are open-ended would represent an intermediate degree of structure.

Learning Objective 2: Explain what is meant by *disguise* in a questionnaire.

The amount of disguise in a questionnaire is the amount of knowledge hidden from the respondent as to the purpose of the study. An undisguised questionnaire makes the purpose of the research obvious by the questions posed, while a disguised questionnaire attempts to hide the purpose of the study.

Learning Objective 3: Discuss why structured-undisguised questionnaires are the type most frequently used by marketing researchers.

Structured-undisguised questionnaires are the most popular type of data collection because they are simple to administer and easy to tabulate and analyze. They are also relatively reliable, since they typically use fixed-alternative questions.

Learning Objective 4: Cite three drawbacks of fixed-alternative questions.

Fixed-alternative questions may force a subject to respond to a question on which he or she does not really have an opinion. They may also prove inaccurate if none of the response categories allows the accurate expression of the respondent's opinion. The response categories themselves may introduce bias if one of the probable responses is omitted because of an oversight or insufficient prior research.

Learning Objective 5: Explain the reason why researchers use projective methods in conducting some studies.

Researchers use projective techniques as a way of overcoming subjects' reluctance to discuss their feelings. The main thrust of these techniques has been to conceal the true subject of the study by using a disguised stimulus. The basic assumption in projective methods is that the way an individual responds to a relatively unstructured stimulus provides clues as to how that person really perceives the subject under investigation and what his or her reactions are to it.

Learning Objective 6: List three common types of stimuli used in projective techniques.

Three common types of stimuli used in projective techniques are word association, sentence completion, and storytelling.

Learning Objective 7: Differentiate among the three methods of administering question-naires.

Personal interviews imply a direct face-to-face conversation between the interviewer and the respondent, as opposed to the *telephone interview*. In both types, the interviewer asks the questions and records the respondents' answers, either while the interview is in progress or immediately afterward. *Mail questionnaires* are sent to designated respondents with an accompanying cover letter. The respondents complete the questionnaire at their leisure and mail their replies back to the research organization.

Learning Objective 8: Cite the points researchers generally consider when they compare the various methods of administering questionnaires.

Sampling control, information control, and administrative control are the points researchers generally consider when comparing the methods of personal interviewing, telephone interviewing, and mail questionnaires.

Discussion Questions, Problems, and Projects

1. Pick three of your friends and conduct a depth interview with each one of them to determine their feelings toward purchasing designer jeans.
   (a) What factors were mentioned in the first interview?
   (b) What factors were mentioned in the second interview?
   (c) What factors were mentioned in the third interview?
   (d) Based on the findings for Questions a, b, and c, what specific hypotheses would you suggest?
   (e) Briefly discuss the strengths and weaknesses of depth interviews.
2. Design and administer a word-association test to determine a student's feelings toward eating out.
   (a) List ten stimuli and the subject's responses and the amount of time that elapsed before the subject reacted to each stimulus.

Stimulus	**Response**	**Time**
1.		
2.		
3.		
4.		
5.		
6.		
7.		
8.		
9.		
10.		

   (b) On the basis of your mini-survey, what tentative conclusions can you infer regarding the person's feelings toward eating out?
   (c) Briefly discuss the strengths and weaknesses of this technique.
3. Design and administer a sentence-completion test to determine a student's feelings toward coffee consumption.

(a) List at least eight sentences that are to be used in the sentence-completion exercise.

1.
2.
3.
4.
5.
6.
7.
8.

(b) On the basis of the respondent's reactions, how would you describe the person's attitudes toward drinking coffee?

(c) How would a researcher analyze the responses?

4. Design and administer a storytelling test to determine a student's reasons for not living in a residence hall, or dormitory.

(a) Develop a stimulus (verbal or pictorial) for the story-completion exercise. (Hint: It might be easier to use a verbal stimulus.)

(b) Based on this exercise, what are your findings as to the person's reasons for not living in a residence hall?

5. Suppose you were requested to design an appropriate communication method to find out students' feelings and opinions about the various food services available on campus.

(a) What degree of structure would be appropriate? Justify your choice.

(b) What degree of disguise would be appropriate? Justify your choice.

(c) What method of administration would be appropriate? Justify your choice.

Which survey method (mail, telephone, or personal) would you use for the situations listed in Questions 6 through 10? Justify your choice.

6. Administration of a questionnaire to determine the number of people who listened to the "100 Top Country Tunes in 1990," a program that aired on December 31, 1990.

7. Administration of a questionnaire to determine the number of households having a mentally ill individual in the household and the history of mental illness in the family.

8. Administration of a questionnaire by a national manufacturer of microwave ovens in order to test people's attitudes toward a new model.

9. Administration of a questionnaire by a local dry cleaner who wants to determine customers' satisfaction with a recent discount promotion.

10. Administration of a questionnaire by the management of a small local hotel that wants to assess customers' opinions of its service.

11. Arrange an interview with a professional researcher engaged in commercial marketing research. Discuss the objectives of the researcher's current project and what type of method(s) she or he is using to collect primary data. Report on the advantages and disadvantages of the data-collection method(s) used in relation to the research objective. Try to determine if trade-offs have been necessary (e.g., cost against speed; structure against disguise) in order to collect the data, and if so, the reasons for those trade-offs. Be sure to address the broad issues of structure, disguise, sampling control, information control, and administrative control in your report.

12. Arrange an interview with a member of the marketing faculty at your school (other than your instructor in this course) who is actively engaged in academic marketing research. Discuss the objectives of the faculty member's research and what type of method(s) she or he uses to collect primary data. Report on the advantages and disadvantages of the data-collection method(s) used in relation to the research objective. Try to determine if trade-offs have been necessary (e.g., cost against speed; structure against disguise) in order to collect the data, and if so, the reasons for those trade-offs. Be sure to address the broad issues of structure, disguise, sampling control, information control, and administrative control in your report.

Endnotes

1. The simultaneous treatment of structure and disguise was suggested by Donald T. Campbell, "The Indirect Assessment of Social Attitudes," *Psychological Bulletin*, 47 (January 1950), pp. 15–38. A similar treatment can be found in Harper W. Boyd, Jr., Ralph Westfall, and Stanley F. Stasch, *Marketing Research: Text and Cases*, 7th ed. (Homewood, Ill.: Richard D. Irwin, 1989), pp. 215–221.

2. Claire Selltiz, Lawrence S. Wrightsman, and Stuart W. Cook, *Research Methods in Social Relations*, 3rd ed. (New York: Holt, Rinehart and Winston, 1976), p. 309. See also Norman M. Bradburn and Seymour Sudman, *Improving Interview Method and Questionnaire Design: Response Effects to Threatening Questions in Survey Research* (San Francisco: Jossey-Bass, 1979).

3. This general discussion of advantages and disadvantages of the structured-undisguised question follows that of Selltiz, Wrightsman, and Cook, *Research Methods*, pp. 309–321.

4. Selltiz, Wrightsman, and Cook, *Research Methods*, p. 316.

5. Barbara Bailar, Leroy Bailey, and Joyce Stevens, "Measures of Interviewer Bias and Variance," *Journal of Marketing Research*, 14 (August 1977), pp. 337–343; and J. R. McKenzie, "An Investigation into Interviewing Effects in Market Research," *Journal of Marketing Research*, 14 (August 1977), pp. 330–331. A currently popular use of the depth interview is in laddering studies, in which the emphasis is on discovering the relationship between product attributes and consumer benefits and values, or means-ends chains. See, for example, Thomas J. Reynolds and Jonathan Gutman, "Laddering Theory, Method, Analysis and Interpretation," *Journal of Advertising Research*, 26 (February–March 1988), pp. 11–31. See also Jeffrey F. Durgee, "Depth Interview Techniques for Creative Advertising," *Journal of Advertising Research*, 25 (December 1985/ January 1986), pp. 29–37.

6. Martin Collins and Graham Kalton, "Coding Verbatim Answers to Open Questions," *Journal of the Market Research Society*, 22 (October 1980), pp. 239–247.

7. Jeffrey Zaslow, "A Maverick Pollster Promotes Verbosity That Others Disdain," *The Wall Street Journal* (February 13, 1985), pp. 1 and 23. Formally, the procedure is known as content analysis. For discussion of how to go about conducting a content analysis, see Robert P. Weber, *Basic Content Analysis* (Beverly Hills, Calif.: Sage Publications, 1985).

8. F. P. Kilpatrick, "New Methods of Measuring Consumer Preferences and Motivation," *Journal of Farm Economics* (December 1957), p. 1314. See also Dennis Rook, "The Ritual Dimension of Consumer Behavior," *Journal of Consumer Research*, 12 (December 1985), pp. 251–264.

9. Betsy Morris, "Study to Detect True Eating Habits Finds Junk-Food Fans in the Health-Food Ranks," *The Wall Street Journal*, (February 3, 1984), p. 19.

10. Fred N. Kerlinger, *Foundations of Behavioral Research*, 3rd ed. (New York: Holt, Rinehart and Winston, 1986), p. 471. For an overview of projective tests, see W. G. Klopfer and E. S. Taulkie, "Projective Tests," in M. R. Rosenweig and L. W. Porter, eds., *Annual Review of Psychology* (1976), pp. 543–567; and Sidney J. Levy, "Dreams, Fairy Tales, Animals, and Cars," *Psychology and Marketing*, 2 (Summer 1985), pp. 67–82.

11. Harold H. Kassarjian, "Projective Methods," in Robert Ferber, ed., *Handbook of Marketing Research* (New York: McGraw-Hill, 1974), p. 3–91.

12. Ronald Alsop, "Advertisers Put Consumers on the Couch," *The Wall Street Journal* (May 13, 1988), p. 17.

13. *American Housing Survey for the United States in 1985* (Washington, D.C.: U.S. Bureau of the Census, 1988).

14. Tyzoon T. Tyebjee, "Telephone Survey Methods: The State of the Art," *Journal of Marketing*, 43 (Summer 1979), pp. 68–78; A. B. Blankenship, "Listed versus Unlisted Numbers in Telephone-Survey Samples," *Journal of Advertising Research*, 17 (February 1977), pp. 39–42; and Patricia E. Moberg, "Biases in Unlisted Phone Numbers," *Journal of Advertising Research*, 22 (August–September 1982), pp. 51–55.

15. Albert G. Swint and Terry E. Powell, "CLUSFONE Computer-Generated Telephone Sampling Offers Efficiency and Minimal Bias," *Marketing Today* (Elrick and Lavidge), 21 (1983). There is some evidence to suggest that certain sampling schemes can produce a higher proportion of working residential numbers without introducing any appreciable bias in the process. See, for example, Joseph Waksberg, "Sampling Methods for Random Digit Dialing," *Journal of the American Statistical Association*, 73 (March 1978), pp. 40–46; Robert Groves and Robert L. Kahn, *Surveys by Telephone* (New York: Academic Press, 1979); and Richard Pothoff, "Some Generalizations of the Mitofsky-Waksberg Technique of Random Digit Dialing," *Journal of the American Statistical Association*, 82 (June 1987), pp. 409–418. More sophisticated sampling schemes have also been used with random-digit dialing to locate relatively rare segments of the population. See Johnny Blair and Ronald Czaja, "Locating a Special Population Using Random Digit Dialing," *Public Opinion Quarterly*, 46 (Winter 1982), pp. 585–590.

16. E. Laird Landon, Jr., and Sharon K. Banks, "Relative Efficiency and Bias of Plus-One Telephone Sampling," *Journal of Marketing Research*, 14 (August 1977), pp. 294–299; and Madhav N. Segal and Firooz Hekmat, "Random Digit Dialing: A Comparison of Methods," *Journal of Advertising*, 14 (No. 4, 1985), pp. 36–43.

17. "Mailing List Brokers Sell More than Names to Their Many Clients," *The Wall Street Journal* (February 19, 1974), pp. 1, 18; and Bob Davis, "Baby-Goods Firms See Direct Mail as the Perfect Pitch for New Moms," *The Wall Street Journal* (January 29, 1986), p. 31. For other discussions of how firms go about developing mailing lists and their value, see Jeffrey H. Birnbaum, "Firms Try Shredders, Special Tasks to Protect Valuable Mailing Lists," *The Wall Street Journal* (April 27, 1981), p. 27; "Lists Make Targeting Easy," *Advertising Age*, 55 (July 9, 1984), p. 20; and "Making a List, Selling It Twice," *The Wall Street Journal* (May 20, 1985), pp. 64–65.

18. Michael Finley, "Data-Base Marketing Alters Landscape," *Marketing News*, 22 (November 7, 1988), pp. 1–2.

19. Bruce Shawkey, "Mail Order Peddlers Pan Gold in Them Thar Lists," *Wisconsin State Journal* (July 31, 1983), pp. 1 and 4; and Melinda Grenier Guiles, "Why Melinda S. Gets Ads for Panty Hose, Melinda F., Porsches," *The Wall Street Journal* (May 6, 1988), pp. 1 and 4.

20. For general discussions of the mall intercept as a data-collection technique, see Roger Gates and Paul J. Solomon, "Research Using the Mall Intercept: State of the Art," *Journal of Advertising Research*, 22 (August/September 1982), pp. 43–50; and Alan J. Bush and Joseph F. Hair, Jr., "An Assessment of the Mall Intercept as a Data Collection Method," *Journal of Marketing Research*, 22 (May 1985), pp. 158–167.

21. "Mall Research Facilities Directory," *Quirk's Marketing Research Review* (October–November 1988), contains a list of all shopping centers that have research facilities.

22. The weighting technique was suggested by Seymour Sudman, "Improving the Quality of Shopping Center Sampling," *Journal of Marketing Research*, 17 (November 1980), pp. 423–431. For empirical assessments of the usefulness of the weighting, see Thomas D. Dupont, "Do Frequent Mall Shoppers Distort Mall-Intercept Survey Results?" *Journal of Advertising Research*, 27 (August/

September 1987), pp. 45–51; and John P. Murry, Jr., John L. Lastovicka, and Guarav Bhalla, "Demographic and Life-style Selection Error in Mall-Intercept Data," *Journal of Advertising Research*, 27 (February/March 1989), pp. 46–52.

23. Roger A. Kerin and Robert A. Peterson, "Scheduling Telephone Interviews," *Journal of Advertising Research*, 23 (April/May 1983), pp. 41–47. See also Michael F. Weeks, Richard A. Kulka, and Stephanie A. Pierson, "Optimal Call Scheduling for a Telephone Interview," *Public Opinion Quarterly*, 51 (1987), pp. 540–549.

24. Ronald Czaja, Johnny Blair, and Jutta P. Sebestik, "Respondent Selection in a Telephone Survey: A Comparison of Three Techniques," *Journal of Marketing Research*, 19 (August 1982), pp. 381–385; Diane O'Rourke and Johnny Blair, "Improving Random Respondent Selection in Telephone Interviews," *Journal of Marketing Research*, 20 (November 1983), pp. 428–432; and Terry L. Childers and Steven J. Skinner, "Theoretical and Empirical Issues in the Identification of Survey Respondents," *Journal of the Market Research Society*, 27 (January 1985), pp. 39–53.

25. See Paul L. Erdos, *Professional Mail Surveys* (Malabar, Fla.: Robert E. Kreiger, 1983), for a discussion of the problem of sample control in mail surveys and what can be done to overcome respondent resistance. For general references on conducting telephone or mail surveys, see A. B. Blankenship, *Professional Telephone Surveys* (New York: McGraw-Hill, 1977); Donald A. Dillman, *Mail and Telephone Surveys: The Total Design Method* (New York: Wiley-Interscience, 1978); Paul J. Lavrakas, *Telephone Survey Methods* (Newbury Park, Calif.: Sage Publications, 1987); and Robert M. Groves et al., eds., *Telephone Survey Methodology* (New York: Wiley-Interscience, 1988). For discussions on how to conduct industrial mail surveys, see Seymour Sudman, "Mail Surveys of Reluctant Professionals," *Evaluation Review*, 9 (June 1985), pp. 349–360; and Bruce J. Walker, Wayne Kirchmann, and Jeffrey S. Conant, "A Method to Improve Response to Industrial Mail Surveys," *Industrial Marketing Management*, 16 (November 1987), pp. 305–314.

26. Daniel Machalaba, "Hidden Handicap: For Americans Unable to Read Well, Life is a Series of Small Crises," *The Wall Street Journal* (January 17, 1984), pp. 1 and 12; and Chris Martell, "Illiteracy Hurts All, Author Says," *Wisconsin State Journal* (April 3, 1985), pp. 1–2; Jock Elliott, "Our Inadequate, Uncompetitive System of Education," *Viewpoint* (July–August 1987), pp. 31–35; Janice C. Simpson, "A Shallow Labor Pool Spurs Businesses to Act to Bolster Education," *The Wall Street Journal* (September 28, 1987), pp. 1 and 19; and Mogens Nygaard Christofferson, "The Educational Bias in Mail Questionnaires," *Journal of Official Statistics*, 3 (No. 4, 1987), pp. 459–464. The illiteracy problem is also severe in England. See *Journal of the Market Research Society*, 26 (April 1984), for a number of articles on the subject and its consequences for survey research.

27. Edwin H. Carpenter, "Software Tools for Data Collection: Microcomputer Assisted Interviewing," *Applied Marketing Research*, 29 (Winter 1988), pp. 23–32. This article also compares the available CAI software packages with respect to their capabilities.

28. Selwyn Feinstein, "Computers Replacing Interviewers for Personnel and Marketing Tasks," *The Wall Street Journal* (October 9, 1986), p. 35. See also Sara Kiesler and Lee T. Sproull, "Response Effects in the Electronic Survey," *Public Opinion Quarterly*, 50 (Fall 1986), pp. 402–413; and William Maher and Terry G. Vavra, "The PC vs. the Pencil," *Pharmaceutical Executive*, 7 (June 1987), pp. 32–38.

29. "Disks-by-Mail," *Sawtooth News*, 5 (Spring 1989), pp. 4–5.

30. See Joseph Curry, "Computer-Assisted Telephone Interviewing: Technology and Organizational Management" (Ketchum, Idaho: Sawtooth Software, 1987), pp. 7–9. For general overviews of the effect of computer-assisted telephone interviewing systems, see William L. Nicholls II and Robert M. Groves, "The Status of Computer-Assisted Telephone Interviewing: Part I—Introduction and Impact on Cost and Timeliness of Survey Data," *Journal of Official Statistics*, 2 (No. 2, 1986), pp. 93–115; and Robert M. Groves and William L. Nicholls II, "The Status of Computer-Assisted Telephone Interviewing: Part II—Data Quality Issues," *Journal of Official Statistics*, 2 (No. 2, 1986), pp. 117–134.

31. Feinstein, "Computers Replacing Interviewers."

32. Because of the need to send follow-up mailings to reduce the typically high incidence of nonresponse that occurs to any single mailing, researchers sometimes attempt to predict the ultimate response rate to a mailing based on the early returns. See Stephen J. Huxley, "Predicting Response Speed in Mail Surveys," *Journal of Marketing Research*, 17 (February 1980), pp. 63–68; and Richard W. Hill, "Using S-Shaped Curves to Predict Response Rates," *Journal of Marketing Research*, 18 (May 1981), pp. 240–242, for discussion of how this can be done.

33. Stanley L. Payne, "Combination of Survey Methods," *Journal of Marketing Research*, 1 (May 1964), p. 62.

34. David Schwartz, "Locked Box Combines Survey Methods, Helps End Some Woes of Probing Industrial Field," *Marketing News*, 11 (January 27, 1978), p. 18. For studies that used the locked box, see Jerome E. Scott and Stephen K. Keiser, "Forecasting Acceptance of New Industrial Products with Judgment Modeling," *Journal of Marketing*, 48 (Spring 1984), pp. 54–67; and Donald M. Fitch, "Combination Technique Unlocks Hesitant Responses," *Marketing News*, 22 (January 4, 1988), p. 10.

Suggested Additional Readings

For a useful discussion of the advantages and disadvantages of structured, unstructured, disguised, and undisguised questions, see

Claire Selltiz, Lawrence S. Wrightsman, and Stuart W. Cook, *Research Methods in Social Relations*, 3rd ed. (New York: Holt, Rinehart and Winston, 1976).

For a general discussion of projective research methods, see

Fred N. Kerlinger, *Foundations of Behavioral Research*, 3rd ed. (New York: Holt, Rinehart and Winston, 1986).

Sidney J. Levy, "Dreams, Fairy Tales, Animals, and Cars," *Psychology and Marketing*, 21 (Summer 1985), pp. 67–82.

For details as to how to go about conducting studies, especially using mail surveys or telephone interviews, see

A. B. Blankenship. *Professional Telephone Surveys* (New York: McGraw-Hill, 1977).

Donald A. Dillman, *Mail and Telephone Surveys: The Total Design Method* (New York: Wiley-Interscience, 1978).

Paul L. Erdos, *Professional Mail Surveys* (Malabar, Fla.: Robert E. Kreiger, 1983).

Paul J. Lavrakas, *Telephone Survey Methods* (Newbury Park, Calif.: Sage Publications, 1987).

Chapter Eleven

Collecting Information by Observation

Learning Objectives

Upon completing this chapter, you should be able to

1. List the different methods by which observational data can be gathered.

2. Cite the main reason researchers may choose to disguise the presence of an observer in a study.

3. Explain the advantages and disadvantages of conducting an observational experiment in a laboratory setting.

4. Discuss the principle that underlies the use of a galvanometer.

5. Explain the function of a tachistoscope.

6. Explain how researchers use eye cameras.

7. Define *response latency* and explain what it measures.

8. Define *voice-pitch analysis* and explain what it measures.

Case in Marketing Research

Edward Meyer was a man with a mission. As the director of U.S. marketing for a German fixture manufacturer, Meyer wanted to see a Tausch kitchen sink and faucet installed in every luxury new home or lavishly remodeled kitchen. Tausch fixtures were sleek, beautifully designed, and relatively expensive. While they sold well in urban markets where people were generally willing to pay a premium for style, Meyer was having a hard time getting Tausch into kitchens outside of New York and Los Angeles.

Meyer was in Chicago after a meeting with Tausch's midwestern sales reps. He had asked them how they thought Tausch might increase its share of the U.S. market. A few of the reps had counseled that the Midwest was just more traditional and conservative than the coasts and that Tausch's Eurostyle line would always hold a boutique position there. Others had stated that the line's hefty price tag turned off value-minded midwesterners, and those reps had argued for a more populist pricing strategy. The reps had certainly given Meyer a lot to think about.

He had a couple of hours to kill before his flight to New York. Instead of waiting at O'Hare, he decided to drop in at the Tausch showroom at the Merchandise Mart. The Mart, as it is referred to in the trade, is the largest decorator showroom in the United States. Just west of the Chicago River, every product connected to decorating is displayed under one roof. It is there that manufacturers of furniture, fabrics, wallpaper, lighting, and plumbing fixtures ply their wares to decorating professionals.

Tausch had a big showroom in the Mart, where its entire line of fixtures was displayed. The showroom manager had been flattered (and flustered) at Meyer's unheralded arrival and had quickly offered his own desk for the marketing director's use. It was in a tiny office tucked behind a one-way mirror at one side of the sales floor; nevertheless, Meyer was grateful for a quiet phone from which to tackle his long call list.

But the only call that Meyer ended up making was to the airline to book himself on a later flight. Instead of making calls he spent hours sitting behind the one-way mirror and watching decorators and their clients look at Tausch kitchen sinks. Several women brought wallpaper samples that they were trying to coordinate with the many different Tausch sink colors. But then they took the hands-on approach, turning the knobs on the faucets, standing at the displays and putting their hands in the sinks as if they were washing dishes. Often he saw a decorator and a client conferring over a sink; more often than not, the exchange ended with the client shaking his or her head no.

As the afternoon progressed, Meyer grew bolder and ventured out from behind the one-way mirror to talk to the decorators and their clients about what they liked and didn't like about the Tausch sinks. What he heard surprised him, but it also gave him an idea.

Discussion Issues

1. In what kind of observation did Meyer engage?
2. What are the advantages of this type of observation, and what are its limitations?
3. What would be the logical next step for whatever ideas occurred to Meyer in the Tausch showroom?

In Chapter 10 we examined how researchers use communication techniques to collect data, specifically by questioning respondents. In this chapter we will look at another method by which researchers gather information—observation.

Methods of Observation

Observation is a fact of everyday life. We are constantly observing other people and events as a means of securing information about the world around us. Admittedly, some people make more productive use of those observations than do others. One interesting story of a man who put his powers of observation to work is told about William Benton, one of the co-founders of the Benton and Bowles advertising agency. On a steamy day in 1929 Benton took a walk along a street in Chicago. Since it was hot, most of the windows in the apartments he passed were open, and he could hear the radios playing inside. As he strolled along, he repeatedly heard the voices of the actors in "Amos and Andy," one of the leading comedy programs at that time. Struck by this, Benton retraced his steps, this time counting the radios he could hear. He counted twenty-three of them in all and found that twenty-one were tuned to "Amos and Andy." Rushing back to his advertising firm, Benton suggested that they advertise one of their client's products, Pepsodent toothpaste, on "Amos and Andy." The sales of Pepsodent took off like a rocket, all because of Benton's first audience survey of radio listenership.[1]

Observation is also a tool of scientific inquiry. When used for that purpose, the observations are systematically planned and recorded so as to relate to the specific phenomenon of interest. While planned, they do not have to be sophisticated to be effective. They can be as basic as United Airlines' study of the garbage gathered from its various flights, which prompted the airline to discontinue serving butter on many

Response to some products is best measured by direct observation. Colleen, pictured at right, prepares to participate in a dog food taste test.

Figure 11.1   **Basic Choices among Observational Means for Collecting Data**

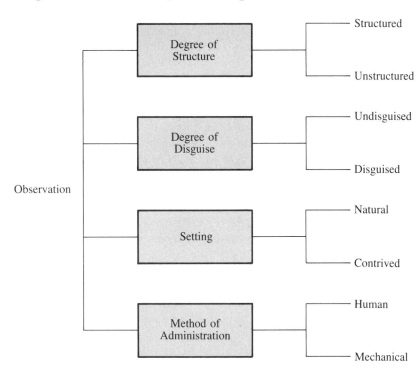

of its short-range flights because few people were eating it. Or take the method employed by the retailer who used a different color of promotional flyer for each Zip Code to which he mailed.[2] When customers came in the store with the flyers, he could then identify which trading areas the store was serving.

A more sophisticated scheme is used by many malls to determine their trading areas. People are hired to walk the parking lot of the mall and record every license number they find. A typical day yields 2,500 different numbers. The data are then fed into computers at R. L. Polk & Company of Detroit, specialists in auto industry statistics. Polk matches the license plates to Zip Code areas or census tracts and returns a color-coded map showing customer density from the various areas. At a cost of anywhere from $5,000 to $25,000, these studies are not only less expensive, but they are quicker and more reliable, than store interviews or examinations of credit card records.[3]

Like communication methods, observation methods may be structured or unstructured, disguised or undisguised. Further, as Figure 11.1 shows, the observations may be made in a contrived or a natural setting and may be secured by a human or a mechanical observer.

Structured versus Unstructured Observation

The distinction between structured and unstructured observation is similar to that between structured and unstructured communication methods. **Structured observation** applies when the problem has been defined precisely enough so that the

Structured observation
The problem has been defined precisely enough so that the behaviors that will be observed can be specified beforehand, as can the categories that will be used to record and analyze the situation.

Unstructured observation The problem has not been specifically defined, so a great deal of flexibility is allowed the observers in terms of what they note and record.

behaviors that will be observed can be specified beforehand, as can the categories that will be used to record and analyze the situation. **Unstructured observation** is used for studies in which the problem has not been so specifically defined, so that a great deal of flexibility is allowed the observers in terms of what they note and record.

Consider a study designed to investigate the amount of search and deliberation that a consumer goes through in buying a detergent. On the one hand, the observers could be told to stand at one end of a supermarket aisle and record whatever behavior they think is appropriate with respect to each sample customer's deliberation and search. This might produce the following record: "Purchaser first paused in front of ABC brand. He picked up a box of ABC, glanced at the price, and set it back down again. He then checked the label and price for DEF brand. He set that back down and after a slight pause, picked up a smaller box of ABC than originally looked at, placed it in his cart, and moved down the aisle." Alternatively, observers might simply be told to record the first detergent examined, the total number of boxes picked up by the customer, and the time in seconds that the customer spent in front of the detergent shelves—and to record these observations by checking the appropriate boxes on the observation form. The last situation represents a good deal more structure than the first.

To use the more structured approach, researchers must decide precisely which behaviors are to be observed and which specific categories and units will be used to record the observations. In order to make such decisions, researchers must have specific hypotheses in mind. Thus, the structured approach is again more appropriate for descriptive and causal studies than for exploratory research. The unstructured approach would be useful in generating insights about the various aspects of the search and deliberation behavior in the preceding example. But it is less appropriate for testing hypotheses about it. Since so many different kinds of behaviors could be recorded, it would be difficult for researchers to code and quantify the data in a consistent manner.

One way to develop consistency in coding is to make sure that the coders are well trained. A number of trained coders were used, for example, in an observational study examining the patterns of interactions between parents and children in choosing breakfast cereals. The observers in this study recorded word for word the verbal exchanges between parent and child when making the choice. The coders then tried to assess

1. Which party initiated the selection episode.
2. How the other party responded.
3. The content and tone of the communication.
4. The occurrence of unpleasant consequences such as arguments or unhappiness.

The ultimate aim of the study was to determine if the child was unhappy with the resolution of the situation.[4]

The advantages and disadvantages of structure in observation are very similar to those in communication. Structuring the observation reduces the potential for bias and increases the reliability of observations. However, the reduction in bias may be accompanied by a loss of validity, since the number of seconds spent in deliberation or the number of boxes of detergent picked up and examined may not represent the complete story of deliberation and search. What about the effort spent in simply looking at what is available but not picking them up, or the discussion between husband and wife as to which detergent to select? A well-trained, highly qualified observer might be able to interpret these kinds of behaviors and relate them in a meaningful way to search and deliberation.

> The major problem of behavioral observation is the observer himself. . . . In behavioral observation the observer is both a crucial strength and a crucial weakness. Why? The observer must digest the information derived from observations and then make inferences about constructs. . . . The strength and the weakness of the procedure is the observer's powers of inference. If it were not for inference, a machine observer would be better than a human observer. The strength is that the observer can relate the observed behavior to the constructs or variables of a study: he brings behavior and construct together.[5]

Nintendo, the computer game manufacturer, is one company that makes regular use of both structured and unstructured observation to keep abreast of playing trends and interests. The main mechanism by which it does this is through its Player-Support Program, which consists of "hotline" telephone numbers that provide tips on playing Nintendo games. In a typical week, some 16,000 people will call the toll-free number for recorded tips, and another 84,000 people will speak to more than 250 game counselors. In addition, the game counselors will respond to another 8,000 letters per week. Nintendo uses these hotlines not only to enhance customer satisfaction but also as a source of marketing intelligence. As Peter Main, the vice-president of marketing, comments: "It has kept us in close contact with the end user. . . . We use the data we collect to absolutely ensure that our game developers are aware of what's hot and what's not."[6] The game counselors and the unstructured observations they make, along with structured observations of the number of calls made to the recorded tips on each game, allow Nintendo to monitor changing player interests.

Disguised versus Undisguised Observation

Undisguised observation
The subjects are aware that they are being observed.

Disguised observation
The subjects are not aware that they are being observed.

In **undisguised observation,** the subjects know they are being observed; in **disguised observation,** they do not. In the search and deliberation study just described earlier, observers could assume a position well out of the way of shoppers' notice. Or the disguise could be accomplished by observers' becoming part of the shopping scene. One firm, for example, uses observers disguised as shoppers to assess package designs by recording how long shoppers spend in the display area, whether they have difficulty finding the product, and whether the information on the package appears hard to read. Other retailers are increasingly turning to on-site cameras, not only to assess packaging designs but also to determine what general improvements in counter space and floor displays are needed and to study traffic flows.[7] Still others are using paid observers disguised as shoppers to evaluate the attitude, courtesy, and promptness of service provided by their own employees.[8] Motel 6 uses its own representatives, who pose as soap salespeople, to stop guests at Motel 6 locations; they inform the guests that they are trying to sell soap to the chain, "but, by the way, what do you think of the place?"[9]

The reason the observer's presence is disguised, of course, is to control the tendency for people to behave differently when they know their actions are being watched. At least two disadvantages are entailed in disguised observation, though. First, it is often very difficult to disguise an observation completely, and second, one cannot obtain other relevant information, such as background data, that can often be obtained by identifying oneself as a research worker. There is also an ethical question associated with disguised observation.

> [T]he investigator who proposes to enter a situation without revealing his research purpose has an obligation to ask himself whether there is any possibility that his disguised activities will harm any of the people in the situation and if so, whether the potential results of his research are valuable enough to justify their acquisition under these circumstances.[10]

Disguised observations may be *direct* or *indirect*. A direct observation, for example, might be a person at the checkout counter counting the number of boxes of each brand of detergent being purchased. An indirect observation might involve counting the inventory on hand by brand at the end of each day and adjusting the results for shipments received to determine how much of each brand was sold. The key difference is that the behavior itself is observed in direct observation, whereas the *effects* or *results* of that behavior are observed in indirect observation.

There are many types of indirect observation.[11] One could, for example, determine the market share held by each brand of detergent by conducting pantry audits. In a pantry audit, researchers would visit respondents' homes and ask permission to examine the "pantry inventory." Their goal would be to determine what brands the family had on hand and the amount of each. While it is rare that researchers would go to the expense of a pantry audit for one product, they might use this method if they wanted to determine consumption of a number of products at once.

Over the years a number of innovative, indirect measures of behavior have been developed. For example, a car dealer in Chicago checked the position of the radio dial of each car brought in for service. The dealer then used this as a way of determining the appropriate share of the listening audience each station held, and used that information to decide where to advertise. As further examples, the number of different fingerprints on a page has been used to assess the readership of various ads in a magazine, and the age and condition of the cars in the parking lot have been used to gauge the affluence of the group patronizing a given business establishment.

Observation is often more useful than surveys in sorting fact from fiction with respect to desirable behaviors. For example, a group of electric utilities had been accustomed to using pollsters' reports of consumer interviews to project energy usage. Despite their attempt to forecast demand scientifically, they found their projections continually fell short of reality. They asked a marketing research firm to investigate. The research firm put television cameras focused on the thermostat in 150 homes. The cameras revealed that what people said they did and what they actually did were vastly different. Many people claimed they set the thermostat at 68 degrees and left it there. It turned out that they fiddled with it all day. "Older relatives and kids—especially teenagers—tended to turn [it] up, and so did cleaning ladies. Even visitors did it. In a lot of homes, it was guerrilla warfare over the thermostat between the person who paid the bill and everyone else."[12]

For its Breyers' ice cream account, Young & Rubicam, the advertising agency, also used cameras, along with personal observation, to get a sense of what ice cream means to people. "They photographed people lounging in their favorite chairs and taking that first scrumptious lick. They snooped in freezers, inspected bowls and utensils, watched people spoon on toppings and listened to one woman describe how she dims the lights and flips on her stereo before digging in. We learned about people's emotional response to ice cream and found that it's a very sensual, inner-directed experience," comments Robert Baker, marketing director for Breyers.[13]

Natural versus Contrived Setting for Observation

Observations may be obtained in either **natural** or **contrived settings.** Sometimes the natural setting is altered to some degree for experimental purposes. In the search and deliberation study mentioned earlier, for example, researchers may choose to keep the setting completely natural and study only the extent of the activities that

Natural setting Subjects are observed in the environment where the behavior normally takes place.

Contrived setting Subjects are observed in an environment that has been specially designed for recording their behavior.

When using a people meter to monitor television viewing, each member of the family has a viewing number, which he or she enters into the meter before watching a program.

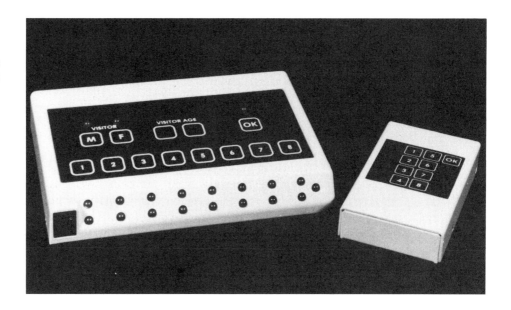

Source: Courtesy of Nielsen Media Research.

normally go into the purchase of detergents. Alternatively, they may wish to introduce some point-of-purchase display materials and measure their effectiveness. One measure of effectiveness might be the amount of search and deliberation the materials stimulate for the particular brand being promoted.

If a contrived setting is desired, the researcher could bring a group of people into a very controlled environment such as a multi-product display in a laboratory and ask them to engage in some simulated shopping behavior. This controlled environment might contain, for example, a detergent display that would enable researchers to study the degree of search and deliberation each participant goes through as he or she decides what to buy.

The advantage of the laboratory environment is that researchers are better able to control outside influences that might affect the interpretation of what happened. For example, shoppers in a natural setting might pause to chat with neighbors in the midst of deciding what detergent to buy. If researchers were measuring the time spent in deliberation, this interruption could raise havoc with the accuracy of the measurement. The disadvantage of the laboratory setting is that the contrived setting itself may cause differences in behavior and thus raise real questions about the external validity of the findings.

A contrived setting also tends to speed the data-collection process, result in lower-cost research, and allow the use of more objective measurements. For example, Fisher-Price, which used to take toy prototypes to local homes to test reactions, now runs a free nursery at its corporate headquarters. The nursery handles five groups of children who come for six-week periods. Designers watch as children play with Fisher-Price toys and those of competitors.[14] Another advantage of the contrived setting is that the researcher does not need to wait for events to occur but can instruct the participants to engage in the needed kind of behavior. This means that a great many observations can be made in a short period of time; perhaps an entire study can be completed in a couple of days or a week. This can substantially reduce costs.

The laboratory also allows the greater use of electrical and/or mechanical equipment than the natural setting does and thereby frees the measurement from the observer's selective processes. For example, IBM has set up "usability labs," in which customers try out software while programmers observe through a one-way mirror and "video cameras tape everything from fingers on keyboards to screens to facial expressions of participants."[15]

Ethical

Dilemma 11.1   A leading manufacturer of breakfast cereals was interested in learning more about the kinds of processes that consumers go through when deciding to buy a particular brand of cereal. To gather this information, an observational study was conducted in the major food chains of several large cities. The observers were instructed to assume a position well out of the shoppers' way, because it was thought that the individuals would change their behavior if they were aware of being observed.

- Was it ethical to observe another person's behavior systematically without that person's knowledge? What if the behavior had been more private in nature? What if the behavior had been recorded on videotape?
- Does use of this method of data collection invade an individual's privacy?
- Even if there is no harm done to the individual, is there harm done to society?
- Does the use of such a method add to the concern over Big Brotherism?
- Can you suggest alternative methods for gathering the same information?

Human versus Mechanical Observation

Human observation
Individuals are trained to systematically observe a phenomenon and to record on the observational form the specific events that take place.

Mechanical observation
A mechanical device observes a phenomenon and records the events that take place.

Much scientific observation is of the pencil-and-paper variety. One or more individuals are trained to observe a phenomenon systematically and to record on the observational form the specific events that took place—this is **human observation** as opposed to **mechanical observation.** DuPont, for example, relies on a human observer to deal with one of the most difficult problems it faces in its automotive paint division: color matching. It seems that no matter how much time and energy goes into the metal repair work after an accident, slight differences in color shading can occur, greatly upsetting the customer. There is no problem in matching colors for domestic cars, since new models are introduced each fall in an orderly fashion, and factory color information is available well before the vehicles reach the showrooms. However, new models of imported cars tend to reach dealer showrooms on a random basis throughout the year, and having paint shades available for their repair is a much greater problem.

DuPont handles this problem via Charlie Smith, color matcher par excellence. Smith operates out of a dockside laboratory in Jacksonville, Florida, the port of entry for thousands of imported cars each month. He not only has all the equipment necessary to mix the colors that will match the cars outside, but he also has a direct computer hookup to DuPont's Troy, Michigan, laboratory, where the formulas for 17,000 different colors are stored. "DuPont has formulas to match almost any color I see coming ashore," reports Smith. "As each new color arrives, I spray out the DuPont formula on a test panel and compare it to the new car. If the spray-out matches the color, I report this to our Troy lab to verify the formula already in the computer. If it doesn't match, I go back to my lab and make adjustments in the formula."

This process may take a few hours or a few days. Once satisfied with the match, Smith relays the new formula directly to the Troy computer, and the new information is distributed to body shops through DuPont's "refinish sales" network.[16]

Electrical and/or mechanical observation also has its place in marketing research. Although it has been used for a long time, the development of new technologies is expanding the role and importance of electrical/mechanical observation. Some of the earliest uses focused on copy research and involved the *galvanometer, tachistoscope*, and *eye camera*.

Galvanometer A device used to measure the emotion induced by exposure to a particular stimulus, by recording changes in the electrical resistance of the skin associated with the minute degree of sweating that accompanies emotional arousal; in marketing research, the stimulus is often specific advertising copy.

The **galvanometer** is used to measure the emotional arousal induced by an exposure to specific advertising copy. It belongs to the class of instruments that measure autonomic reactions, or reactions that are not under an individual's voluntary control. Because these responses are not controlled, it is not possible for individuals to mask or hide their true reactions to a stimulus. The galvanometer operates on the same principle as the lie-detector apparatus used in criminal investigations. Galvanometers record changes in the electrical resistance of the skin associated with the minute degree of sweating that accompanies emotional arousal. The subject is fitted with small electrodes on the palms or forearms to monitor this electrical resistance. As different advertising copy is shown, the strength of the current that results is used to gauge the subject's attitude.[17]

Tachistoscope A device that provides the researcher timing control over a visual stimulus; in marketing research, the visual stimulus is often a specific advertisement.

The **tachistoscope** is a device that tells researchers how long it takes a subject to get the intended point of an ad. It does this by flashing the ad before the subject for an exposure interval that may range from less than a hundredth of a second to several seconds. After each exposure, the subject is asked to describe everything he or she saw and to explain what it meant. By systematically varying the exposure, the researcher is able to measure how quickly and accurately a particular stimulus—in this case, the ad—can be perceived and interpreted. Note, however, that since the subject is asked to respond verbally to what he or she saw, the tachistoscope is not a mechanical observer, but rather a mechanical means of presenting stimuli.

Eye camera A device used by researchers to study a subject's eye movements while he or she is reading advertising copy.

The **eye camera** is now used by researchers to study a subject's eye movements while he or she is reading advertising copy. The original eye cameras, which were introduced at the Chicago World's Fair in 1890, established the fact that people's eyes do not move smoothly along a line of type as they read and that people's reading habits differ widely. Until recently, eye cameras used a light that was positioned to bounce off the cornea of the subject's eye onto a moving film. The reflected light traced eye movements on the film. The researcher had to then project the film, frame by frame, while manually recording eye movements on a sheet of paper. Since the mid-1970s, computers have been developed that can automatically perform this analysis for videotape. There have also been significant advances in the cameras themselves. Some of the new videocameras weigh only a few ounces and are so small that they can be clipped to a respondent's eyeglasses. The visual record produced as an individual reads an advertisement allows researchers to study the person's behavior in great detail. See, for example, Research Window 11.1. The eye camera can reveal the part of the ad the subject noticed first, how long his or her eyes lingered on a particular item, and whether the subject read all the copy or only part of it. The small videocameras that follow the path of the eye have also been used to analyze package designs, billboards, and displays in the aisles of supermarkets.[18]

Some of the newer electrical/mechanical observation devices include the optical scanner, which has automated the checkout process at many retail stores and in the process revolutionized the marketing research function, and the people meter, which is used to develop television-viewing statistics. Both of these were discussed in earlier chapters.

Research Window 11.1
The Eyes Have It

As if advertisers didn't have enough to worry about, Perception Research Services, Inc., a firm that electronically measures consumers' reactions to ads, has found that readers notice the brand names in only six out of ten magazine ads.

The company discovered this information when it used beams of infrared light, computers, and cameras to track the movement of people's eyes as they glanced through magazines. "There's a lot of talk today about how people use remote-control devices to zap TV commercials," said Elliot Young, president of the Englewood Cliffs, New Jersey, firm. "But advertisers forget sometimes how easy it is for readers to turn the page of a magazine."

Perception Research plans to conduct eye-tracking studies with 20 magazines on a regular basis. Young believes visual cues are more reliable than consumers' memories in judging whether an ad really attracted their attention.

Some of Perception Research's conclusions clash with commonsense notions about advertising. For example, the company says food marketers may be thwarting themselves by running mouth-watering photographs of cakes and cookies. Often in such ads,

the reader's eye lingers on the luscious illustration and overlooks the product name. The eye-tracking study also revealed that automobile ads catch readers' attention surprisingly well in women's magazines. And contrary to popular belief, Perception Research did not find that people were naturally more inclined to read ads on right-hand pages or in the front of magazines.

Some ad agency executives believe such research can help them decide which size ad to run in particular magazines and where to place headlines and copy for maximum impact. Yet, many also are suspicious of the artificial conditions in eye-tracking studies. Subjects don't leisurely browse through magazines as they would at home. Rather, they position their heads on chin rests and watch pictures of the magazine pages flash on a screen.

"I put this in the same dubious category as galvanic skin response measurement," said Morgan Neu, a vice-president at Starch INRA Hooper, Inc., another firm that does magazine readership research. "Just knowing someone's eye passed across an ad doesn't tell whether the message registered and had any meaning."

Source: Ronald Alsop, "Study of Magazine Ads Yields Some Eye-Opening Findings," *The Wall Street Journal*, 65 (December 5, 1985), p. 33

Response latency The amount of time a respondent deliberates before answering a question.

Two methods of mechanical observation that promise to provide useful supplementary information in telephone interviews—response latency and voice-pitch analysis—owe their current popularity to mechanical/electronic recorders and the computer's ability to diagnose what is recorded. **Response latency** is the amount of time a respondent deliberates before answering a question. Since response time seems to be directly related to the respondent's uncertainty in the answer, it assists in assessing the individual's strength of preference when choosing among alternatives. It helps researchers judge how strongly an individual prefers one brand over another when asked to choose between alternatives. It also provides an unobtrusive way of measuring a subject's ambiguity in responding to a particular question.

The measure of response depends upon a voice-operated relay that triggers an electronic stopwatch. When an interviewer approaches the end of a question, he or she simply presses a pedal that sets the stopwatch to zero and alerts the electronic mechanism to listen for the offset (end of the question) of the interviewer's voice. The stopwatch is automatically triggered at the offset. The moment the respondent begins answering, the watch is stopped by the voice-operated relay system, and a digital readout system indicates response latency to the interviewer, who can then record the deliberation time on the interview form.

There are several advantages in such a system. First, the method provides an accurate response latency measure without respondents' being aware that this dimension of behavior is being recorded. Second, since the time is measured by an automatic device, the technique does not make the interviewer's task any more difficult, nor does it appreciably lengthen the interview.[19]

In an otherwise routine research study, and with little additional effort, DuPont, for example, used response latency to assess potential users' brand awareness and perception of quality of an industrial product compared to many competing brands.[20]

Voice-pitch analysis
Analysis that examines changes in the relative frequency of the human voice that accompany emotional arousal.

Voice-pitch analysis relies on the same basic premise as the galvanometer. Subjects experience a number of involuntary physiological reactions, such as changes in blood pressure, rate of perspiration, or heart rate when emotionally aroused by external or internal stimuli. Voice-pitch analysis examines changes in the relative vibration frequency of the human voice that accompanies emotional arousal. All individuals function at a certain physiological pace, called the *baseline*. The baseline in voice analysis is established by recording the respondent's speech while he or she is engaged in unemotional conversation. Deviations from the baseline level indicate that the respondent has reacted to the stimulus question. These deviations can be measured by special computer equipment adapted to hear abnormal frequencies in the voice caused by changes in the nervous system. Such changes may not be discernable to the human ear. The amount the individual was affected by the stimulus can be measured by comparing the person's abnormal frequency to his or her normal one. The greater the difference, the greater the emotional intensity of the subject's reaction is said to be.

Voice-pitch analysis has at least two advantages over other physiological-reaction techniques. First, unlike the other techniques, it measures not only the intensity but also the direction of the individual's feeling, since subjects are asked the nature of their opinions while the intensity of their emotions is being measured mechanically. Second, voice-pitch analysis allows a natural interaction between researcher and participant because subjects do not need to be connected to any equipment. This also tends to make it less time-consuming and expensive to use.[21]

Brain-wave research
Subjects are fitted with electrodes that monitor the electrical impulses emitted by the brain as the subject is exposed to various stimuli.

At the other extreme, **brain-wave research,** which is still in its infancy and surrounded by a good deal of controversy, requires a rather elaborate hookup of the subject to equipment. The purpose of this technique is to assess the stimuli that subjects find arousing or interesting. To do this, subjects are fitted with electrodes that monitor the electrical impulses emitted by the brain as the subject is exposed to various stimuli. The evidence suggests that the two hemispheres of the brain respond differently to specific stimuli, with the right hemisphere responding more to emotional stimuli and the left to rational stimuli.[22]

Two other electrical/mechanical observation techniques that are still in their infancy but that seem to have the potential to significantly affect the measurement of particular consumer behaviors are Information Resources' VideoCart and Nielsen's videocassette ratings system, described in Research Window 11.2. Further, there are other potentially important developments in electronic measurement on the horizon.[23]

As mentioned, electrical/mechanical equipment frees the observation from the observer's selective process. This is both its major strength and its major weakness. Certainly recording when a television set is turned on, to what channel it is tuned, and who is "watching" can be accomplished much more accurately by a people meter

Research Window 11.2
VideoCarts and Video Ratings

Market researchers want to know *everything*—what foods you pick up at the grocery store to snack on and what you're watching while you eat them. Not only that, but some new technology is helping them get the information faster and more efficiently than ever before. Information Resources, Inc., has just launched VideoCart, which will gather data as shoppers push it around the store, and A. C. Nielsen has begun testing an electronic videocassette rating system that will measure not only who's watching what but whether they fast-forward through the credits and coming attractions.

VideoCart, about the size of a lap-top computer, is mounted on the handles of a shopping cart. Although designed primarily as an advertising medium, the carts also gather data as shoppers push them down the aisles. As a shopper pushes a VideoCart through the store, the manufacturers' ads for brands on the shelves being passed at that moment are triggered and appear on the flat, 6″ × 8″ liquid-crystal display. Tie-in promotion ads are also used; for instance, a hot-dog bun ad appears when the cart is near the hot dogs. Yet only 15 percent of VideoCart's display time is devoted to ads. The rest includes recipes, a continually changing video news magazine, store maps, and video games to play while waiting to check out.

Among data gathered are the VideoCart's own path through the store, the time spent in various parts of the store, and shoppers' opinions. For some applications, shoppers can interact with VideoCart through its touch-screen capability. Data obtained from "interrogating" each cart enables the grocer to analyze shopping patterns and the time spent shopping in each product category, for optimal product placement and traffic management.

While VideoCart tracks shopping patterns in the grocery store, A. C. Nielsen, the company that monitors television viewing in the home, is expanding its rating services to include videocassettes. The company's new videocassette rating system will be piggybacked onto Nielsen' existing electronic television rating system. Currently 4,000 homes across the country are wired with people meters, electronic devices that record which family members are watching television. About half of those homes also have videocassette recorders, which will be wired with a small box attached to the VCR. The box "reads" an electronic code on the videocassettes and tracks what part of the tape is—and isn't—viewed. Meanwhile, the people meter records who is watching the film. The box also kicks in when a television program is taped, encoding the tape with information identifying what station is being watched at what time. Thus, the device can be used to track how often videotaped television programs are watched and whether viewers fast-forward through the commercials.

Sources: "VideoCart Shopping Cart with Computer Screen Creates New Ad Medium that Also Gathers Data," *Marketing News*, 22 (May 9, 1988), pp. 1–2; and Joanne Lipman, "Nielsen to Test Videocassette Rating System," *The Wall Street Journal* (August 17, 1988), p. 21.

than by some other means. The fact that the set is tuned to a particular channel and that someone pushed the button indicating that he or she was in the room does not say anything, however, about the person's level of interest. A trained human observer's record might be more difficult to analyze, and it might be less objective, but his or her powers of integration could certainly produce a more valid assessment of what occurred. The essential point is that marketing researchers need to be aware of the electrical/mechanical equipment that is available so that they can make an informed choice as to the best technique for a particular study. Would a piece of equipment make a better observer than a human in a given instance, or vice versa? Or would a combination approach be more productive? These are difficult decisions that can greatly affect the quality of a study. A researcher who keeps abreast of the developments in the field is in the best position to make those decisions.

Ethical
Dilemma 11.2   You are running a laboratory experiment for the promotion manager of a soft drink company. The promotion manager has read a journal article indicating that viewers' responses to upbeat commercials are more favorable if the commercials follow very arousing film clips, and he is interested in testing this proposition with respect to his firm's commercials. To establish whether film clips that induce high levels of arousal result in more extreme evaluations of ensuing commercials than film clips that induce low levels of arousal, you are pretesting film clips for their arousing capacity. To do this, you are recording subjects' blood pressure levels as they watch various film clips. The equipment is not very intrusive, consisting of a finger cuff attached to a recording device. You are satisfied that the procedure does not threaten the subject's physical safety in any way. In addition, you have made the subjects familiar with the equipment, with the result that they are relaxed and comfortable and absorbed in the film clips. On getting up to leave at the end of the session, one subject turns to you and asks, "Is my blood pressure normal, then?"

■   Is it ethical to give respondents information about their physiological responses that they can interpret as an informed comment on the state of their health?

■   What might be the result if you do not tell the subject the function of the equipment?

Back to the Case

Edward Meyer was a happy man. Hanging in his office were the schematic drawings for four different styles of Tausch kitchen sinks and faucets. They made up the beginning of a new Tausch line of sinks designed specifically for the U.S. market. Meyer was happy because he thought the new line was going to be a big success and because he had been directly responsible for its coming into existence.

From his observation of consumers at the Merchandise Mart in Chicago, he had begun to suspect that while high price and modern styling might have contributed to Tausch's poor sales in the Midwest, they were not the main obstacles. That afternoon in the Tausch showroom, decorators had told him that they loved the Tausch look and always steered

their clients into the showroom to see the gorgeous Eurostyle fixtures. But their clients confessed that they decided against Tausch before they even thought of asking about the price. It wasn't the Eurostyle look they didn't like—it was the design.

The customers who were remodeling their kitchens were also the people who were going to be doing the dishes, and while they found the Tausch products attractive, they worried that they were impractical. Tausch had taken its best-selling European models and transplanted them directly to the United States. The faucet stem was lower than that on most U.S. fixtures, and as a rule there were two knobs, one for hot water and one for cold. In addition, while the sinks were deeper than standard U.S. sinks, they were also a

little shorter from front to back. Tausch had been counting on Americans' liking the sleek look of its fixtures and being willing to pay a little more for them. What Tausch hadn't counted on was that the way Americans washed dishes was different from the way Europeans did.

After his Chicago trip, Meyer had hired a marketing research company to recruit a panel of families who would consent to having a closed-circuit television camera mounted above their kitchen sink, so that their dishwashing habits could be observed. Twenty midwestern American families had been studied by Tausch, and the results were surprising.

While Europeans generally filled their sinks with soapy water and washed their dishes submerged,

Americans tended to hold each item under running water. They then either rinsed it and put it in the dishwasher or squirted a little dish soap directly on the item and washed it with a sponge. While the typical European turned the water on and off four times while doing the dinner dishes, the American turned it on and off more than fifteen. No wonder the Americans had balked at two knobs instead of one.

The fledgling Tausch American line had been made up in prototype and photographed. Meyer flipped through the glossy brochure. While the fixtures still bore the unmistakable Tausch look, the sinks had high faucets, and the faucets had a single control. The basins were as deep as the European counterparts, only larger. Meyer smiled to himself. First production was still six weeks away, but he had talked to the showroom manager in Chicago that morning and already the orders were coming in.

Summary

Learning Objective 1: List the different methods by which observational data can be gathered.

Observational data may be gathered using structured or unstructured methods that are either disguised or undisguised. The observations may be made in a contrived or a natural setting and may be secured by a human or an electrical/mechanical observer.

Learning Objective 2: Cite the main reason researchers may choose to disguise the presence of an observer in a study.

Most often an observer's presence is disguised in order to control the tendency of people to behave differently when they know their actions are being watched.

Learning Objective 3: Explain the advantages and disadvantages of conducting an observational experiment in a laboratory setting.

The advantage of a laboratory environment is that researchers are better able to control outside influences that might affect the interpretation of what happened. The disadvantage of the laboratory setting is that the contrived setting itself may cause differences in behavior and thus threaten the external validity of the findings. A contrived setting, however, usually speeds the data-collection process, results in lower-cost research, and allows the use of more objective measurements.

Learning Objective 4: Discuss the principle that underlies the use of a galvanometer.

The galvanometer records changes in the electrical resistance of the skin associated with the minute degree of sweating that accompanies emotional arousal. When the subject is shown different advertising copy, the strength of the current that results is used to gauge his or her attitude toward the copy.

Learning Objective 5: Explain the function of a tachistoscope.

The tachistoscope is a device that tells researchers how long it takes a subject to get the intended point of an ad. It does this by flashing the ad before the subject for a short interval of time and then asking that subject to describe everything he or she saw and to explain what it meant.

Learning Objective 6: Explain how researchers use eye cameras.

Eye cameras are used by researchers to study a subject's eye movements while he or she is reading advertising copy. The visual record produced can allow researchers to determine the part of the ad the subject noticed first, how long his or her eyes lingered on a particular item, and whether the subject read all the copy or only part of it.

Learning Objective 7: Define *response latency* and explain what it measures.

Response latency is the amount of time a respondent deliberates before answering a question. Since response time seems to be directly related to the respondent's uncertainty in the answer, it assists in assessing the individual's strength of preference when choosing among alternatives.

Learning Objective 8: Define *voice-pitch analysis* and explain what it measures.

Voice-pitch analysis examines changes in the relative vibration frequency of the human voice that accompany emotional arousal. The amount an individual is affected by a stimulus question can be measured by comparing the person's abnormal frequency to his or her normal one. The greater the difference, the greater the emotional intensity of the subject's reaction is said to be.

Discussion Questions, Problems, and Projects

1. Next time you go shopping (grocery or otherwise) do the following disguised observation study with a fellow student. The objective is to assess the service provided to customers while checking out purchases. One of you should complete the following structured observation table. The other should conduct an unstructured observation study by observing and recording all that seems relevant to the objective.

    (a) Store _____   Date _____
         Location _____   Time _____

Too few checkout counters	Yes	No
Long wait in line	Yes	No
Cashier: Quick and efficient	Yes	No
Cashier: Prices well recorded	Yes	No
Cashier: Friendly and pleasant	Yes	No
Purchases packed quickly	Yes	No
Purchases packed poorly	Yes	No
Bags carried to car	Yes	No
Bags provided were flimsy	Yes	No
Bags provided were attractive	Yes	No
Other facts _____		

    (b) Compare the two sets of results and discuss the strengths and weaknesses of structured versus unstructured observation.

2. Discuss the ethical ramifications of disguised observation versus undisguised observation.

3. Discuss the strengths and weaknesses of a natural setting versus a contrived setting.

4. What advantages does the people meter have over the more traditional diary panel for measuring television-viewing audiences?

5. Describe how each of the following instruments work and in what area of marketing they are most useful.
    (a) Galvanometer
    (b) Tachistoscope
    (c) Eye camera

6. If you were the product manager of a leading brand of toothpaste, how would observational studies in a retail store help you do your job?

7. The Better Business Bureau (BBB) has received several complaints over the past six months that certain local automobile dealers are engaging in subtle forms of racial discrimination. The alleged discrimination concerns things such as overly restrictive credit terms, lack of salesperson assistance, and refusals to perform routine maintenance services in a timely manner. The BBB has surveyed the firms in question and found no evidence of discriminatory practices, yet complaints continue to be received. The BBB decided to call in professional researchers and has contracted with your marketing research firm to collect data for use in their investigation of these allegations.
    (a) Briefly outline the manner in which you would collect information for the BBB using observation techniques. Be sure to address the issues of structure, disguise, setting, and mechanical versus human observers in your answer. Do you think an observational study will yield information as good as, better than, or worse than, the survey?

(b) Is it ethical and/or proper for a marketing research firm to conduct this type of research project? Why or why not?

8. Discuss the advantages and disadvantages of using electrical/mechanical methods of data collection versus using human observers. What criteria should the researcher consider when deciding which method to use for a particular project?

Endnotes

1. Edward Cornish, "Telecommunications: What's Coming," paper delivered at the American Marketing Association's 1981 Annual Conference held in San Francisco, California, June 14–17, 1981.

2. "Business Bulletin," *The Wall Street Journal* (August 11, 1983), p. 1.

3. See James G. Barnes, G. A. Pym, and A. C. Noonan, "Marketing Research: Some Basics for Small Business," *Journal of Small Business Management*, 20 (July 1982), pp. 62–66; Steve Raddock, "Follow That Car," *Marketing and Media Decisions*, 16 (January 1981), pp. 70–71, 103; "I've Got Your Number," *The Wall Street Journal* (February 5, 1981), p. 21; and Martha Farnsworth Riche, "The Business Guide to the Galaxy of Demographic Products and Services," *American Demographics*, 7 (June 1985), pp. 22–33.

4. Charles K. Atkin, "Observation of Parent-Child Interaction in Supermarket Decision Making," *Journal of Marketing*, 42 (October 1978), pp. 41–45. Diaries have also been used to get at parent-child interactions when purchasing products and services. See Leslie Isler, Edward T. Popper, and Scott Ward, "Children's Purchase Requests and Parental Responses: Results from a Diary Study," *Journal of Advertising Research*, 27 (October/November 1987), pp. 28–39.

5. Fred N. Kerlinger, *Foundations of Behavioral Research*, 3rd ed. (New York: Holt, Rinehart and Winston, 1986), p. 487.

6. Joe Mandese, "Power Plays," *Marketing & Media Decisions*, 24 (March 1989), p. 104.

7. David A. Schwartz, "Research Can Help Solve Packaging Functional and Design Problems," *Marketing News*, 9 (January 16, 1976), p. 8. For a general, how-to guide on participant observation, see Danny L. Jorgensen, *Participant Observation: A Methodology for Human Studies* (Newbury Park, Calif.: Sage Publications, 1989).

8. Larry Gulledge, "Evaluation Services Pay Off in Bigger Bottom Lines," *Marketing News*, 18 (October 12, 1984), p. 30; and Karen Gershowitz, "Research Design Is Used to Evaluate Sales Reps," *Marketing News*, 21 (January 2, 1987), p. 6.

9. Carol Hall, "King of the Road," *Marketing & Media Decisions*, 24 (March 1989), p. 86.

10. Claire Selltiz, Lawrence S. Wrightsman, and Stuart W. Cook, *Research Methods in Social Relations*, 3rd ed. (New York: Holt, Rinehart and Winston, 1976), p. 218. See also Martin Bulmer, ed., *Social Research Ethics: An Examination of the Merits of Covert Participant Observation* (New York: Holmes & Meier Publishers, 1982).

11. For insight into some of the many ingenious ways that have been developed to make indirect measurements by observation, see Eugene J. Webb et al., *Unobtrusive Measures: Nonreactive Research in the Social Sciences* (Chicago: Rand McNally, 1966); Lee Sechrest, *New Directions for Methodology of Behavior Science: Unobtrusive Measurement Today* (San Francisco: Jossey-Bass, 1979); and Thomas J. Bouchard, Jr., "Unobtrusive Measures: An Inventory of Uses," *Sociological Methods and Research* (February 1976), pp. 267–301.

12. Frederick C. Klein, "Researcher Probes Consumers Using 'Anthropological Skills,'" *The Wall Street Journal* (July 7, 1983), p. 21.

13. Ronald Alsop, "'People Watchers' Seek Clues to Consumers' True Behavior," *The Wall Street Journal* (September 4, 1986), p. 25.

14. "Fisher-Price Built on Reputation," *Wisconsin State Journal* (March 17, 1986), p. B3.

15. Aaron Bernstein, "Big Changes at Big Blue," *Business Week* (February 15, 1988), p. 96.

16. "Mixing and Matching," *Special Report News from DuPont of Interest to the College Community*, 76 (November–December 1982), p. 18.

17. A review of 118 studies on involuntary responses to advertising found that pupil dilation, skin moisture, and heart rate are the most commonly used. See Paul J. Watson and Robert J. Gatchel, "Autonomic Measures of Advertising," *Journal of Advertising Research*, 19 (June 1979), pp. 15–26. See also David W. Stewart and David H. Furse, "Applying Psychophysiological Measures to Marketing and Advertising Research Problems," in James H. Leigh and Claude R. Martin, Jr., eds., *Current Issues and Research in Advertising* (Ann Arbor: University of Michigan, 1982), pp. 1–38; and Joanne M. Klebba, "Physiological Measures of Research: A Review of Brain Activity, Electrodermal Response, Pupil Dilation and Voice Analysis Methods and Studies," in James H. Leigh and Claude R. Martin, Jr., eds., *Current Issues and Research in Advertising* (Ann Arbor: University of Michigan, 1985), pp. 53–76.

18. For discussions of the operation and use of eye camera technology to study the effectiveness of ads, packages, and displays, see J. E. Russo, "Eye Fixation Can Save the World," in H. K. Hunt, ed., *Advances in Consumer Research* (Ann Arbor, Mich.: Association for Consumer Research. 1978), pp. 561–570; J. Treistman and J. P. Gregg. "Visual, Verbal, and Sales Response to Print Ads," *Journal of Advertising Research*, 19 (August 1979), pp. 41–47; "Determining How Ads Are Seen," *Dun's Business Month*, 119 (February 1982), pp. 85–86; "Recall Scores Are Given Short Shrift to Outdoor Ads, Study Finds," *Marketing News*, 18 (November 23, 1984), p. 16; and Ronald Alsop, "Study of Magazine Ads Yields Some Eye-Opening Findings," *The Wall Street Journal* (December 5, 1985), p. 31.

19. For general discussions of the use of response latency measures in marketing research, see James MacLachlan, John Czepiel, and Priscilla LaBarbera, "Implementation of Response Latency Measures," *Journal of Marketing Research*, 16 (November 1979), pp. 573–577; James MacLachlan and Priscilla LaBarbera, "Response Latency in Telephone Interviews," *Journal of Advertising Research*, 19 (June 1979), pp. 49–56; Tyzoon T. Tyebjee, "Response Latency: A New Measure for Scaling Brand Preference," *Journal of Marketing Research*, 16 (February 1979), pp. 96–101; and W. Jefferey Burroughs and Richard A. Feinberg, "Using Response Latency to Assess Spokesperson Effectiveness," *Journal of Consumer Research*, 14 (September 1987), pp. 295–299.

20. Robert C. Grass, Wallace H. Wallace, and Samuel Zuckerkandel, "Response Latency in Industrial Advertising Research," *Journal of Advertising Research*, 20 (December 1980), pp. 63–65.

21. Nancy Nischwonger and Claude R. Martin, "On Using Voice Analysis in Marketing Research," *Journal of Marketing Research*, 18 (August 1981), pp. 350–355. For general discussions of the use of voice-pitch analysis in marketing research, see Ronald G. Nelson and David Schwartz, "Voice Pitch Analysis," *Journal of Advertising Research*, 19 (October 1979), pp. 55–59; Glen A. Buckman, "Uses of Voice-Pitch Analysis," *Journal of Advertising Research*, 20 (April 1980), pp. 69–73; Linda Edwards, "Hearing What Consumers

Really Feel," *Across the Board*, 17 (April 1980), pp. 62–67; and James Grant and Dean E. Allman, "Voice Stress Analyzer Is a Marketing Research Tool," *Marketing News*, 22 (January 4, 1988), p. 22.

22. For general discussions of the status of brain-wave research, see F. Hansen, "Hemispherical Lateralization: Implications for Understanding Consumer Behavior," *Journal of Consumer Research*, 8 (June 1981), pp. 23–36; A. Weinstein, "A Review of Brain Hemisphere Research," *Journal of Advertising Research*, 22 (June/July 1982), pp. 59–63; Michael L. Rothschild et al., "Hemispherically Lateralized

EEG as a Response to Television Commercials," *Journal of Consumer Research*, 15 (September 1988), pp. 185–198; and Michael L. Rothschild and Yong J. Hyun, "Micro Information Processing: Predicting Memory for Components of TV Commercials from EEG," *Journal of Consumer Research*, 16 (December 1989), pp. 7–16.

23. See, for example, Gregg Cebrzynski, "New Research Tools Provide 'Accurate' Attention Data," *Marketing News*, 20 (April 11, 1986), p. 1; and "Big Boom in Electronic Research is Predicted," *Marketing News*, 22 (July 4, 1988), pp. 11 and 17.

Suggested Additional Readings

For general discussion of the strengths and weaknesses of observation as a data-collection method, see

Fred N. Kerlinger, *Foundations of Behavioral Research*, 3rd. ed. (New York: Holt, Rinehart and Winston, 1986).

For discussion and examples of unobtrusive measurement techniques, see

Thomas J. Bouchard, Jr., "Unobtrusive Measures: An Inventory of Uses," *Sociological Methods and Research* (February 1976), pp. 267–301.

Lee Sechrest, *New Directions for Methodology of Behavioral Science: Unobtrusive Measurement Today* (San Francisco: Jossey-Bass, 1979).

For discussion of physiological measures to assess respondents' reactions to stimuli, see

Joanne M. Klebba, "Physiological Measures of Research: A Review of Brain Activity, Electrodermal Response, Pupil Dilation and Voice Analysis Methods and Studies," in James H. Leigh and Claude R. Martin, Jr., eds., *Current Issues and Research in Advertising* (Ann Arbor: University of Michigan, 1985), pp. 53–76. David W. Stewart and David H. Furse, "Applying Psychophysiological Measures to Marketing and Advertising Research Problems," in James H. Leigh and Claude R. Martin, Jr., eds., *Current Issues and Research in Advertising* (Ann Arbor: University of Michigan, 1982), pp. 1–38.

Research Project

The third stage in the research process is to determine the data-collection method. As we have seen from the chapters in this section, two types of data may be useful in addressing the research problem: secondary data and primary data. While a beginning researcher's initial impulse may be to advocate a survey among respondent groups, the prudent and experienced researcher will always begin the study by investigating available secondary data first. Only if the answer the decision maker is seeking is unavailable in the secondary data should the researcher consider gathering primary data.

If a research study seems to be warranted, many other decisions must be made. In the data-collection stage, one of the primary decisions is whether to collect information by questionnaire or by observation.

Researchers for CARA sought to determine whether differences existed in the attitudes of local businesspeople toward the advertising media of television, radio, and newspaper, and toward the sales representatives of those media. They also wanted to test the hypothesis that differences in attitudes were associated with differences in annual advertising budgets.

As the researchers told their clients, when the purpose of a study is to determine the association between variables, the most common research design is descriptive. Descriptive designs presuppose a good deal of knowledge about the phenomenon to be studied, and they are guided by one or more hypotheses. Knowledge about the phenomenon under investigation was gleaned from the exploratory research phase of the study. The hypotheses mentioned here and discussed in earlier parts of this textbook guided the descriptive design.

Researchers used secondary data—existing data gathered for some purpose other than the study at hand—during the exploratory research phase to help in understanding the topic of advertising and its perceived strengths and weaknesses.

The information gained from the descriptive phase of the study, however, was based on primary data (data collected to solve the particular problem under investigation) and was secured with a structured-undisguised questionnaire. This type of data-collection instrument is characterized by standardized questions and responses, which simplify administration, make the purpose of the study clear, facilitate easy tabulation and analysis of the data, and provide reliable responses.

The researchers chose to administer the questionnaire by mail. This method was chosen partly to avoid the disadvantages posed by telephone and personal interviews and also because researchers wanted a tangible form that would allow a respondent to view all of the alternative responses. The mail questionnaire's format was designed with standardized questions and responses for reporting attitudes.

While the mail questionnaire format had many advantages, researchers were also aware of its possible drawbacks. For one, researchers often find it difficult to get individuals to respond to this type of questionnaire. In many studies researchers find that offering respondents an incentive of some sort may help to increase the response rate. Nonetheless, the problem of determining how those who do respond differ from those who do not remains.

Despite these problems, mail questionnaires are often the least expensive method of administration per completed contact. Researchers for CARA estimated that the cost per contact for personal interviews would be about $25; the cost per contact for mail questionnaires was $1.70. When the cost of an incentive for return was added in, the cost jumped to between $4.50 and $5.50. While substantially higher than the base cost per contact, this cost was still much lower than the cost of a personal interview.

Besides lower cost and the opportunity for the respondent to mull over a list of possible alternative answers, what other advantages might the mail questionnaire have had over personal or telephone interviews in this study?

Cases to Part Three

Case 3.1   Suchomel Chemical Company

Suchomel Chemical Company was an old-line chemical company that was still managed and directed by its founder, Jeff Suchomel, and his wife, Carol. Jeff served as president and Carol as chief research chemist. The company, which was located in Savannah, Georgia, manufactured a number of products that were used by consumers in and around their homes. The products included waxes, polishes, tile grout, tile cement, spray cleaners for both windows and other surfaces, aerosol room sprays, and insecticides. The company distributed its products regionally. It had a particularly strong consumer following in the northern Florida and southern Georgia areas.

The company had not only managed to maintain, but had increased, its market share in several of its key lines in the past half-dozen years, in spite of increased competition from the national brands. Suchomel Chemical had done this largely through product innovation, particularly innovation that emphasized modest product alterations rather than new technologies or dramatically new products. Jeff and Carol both believed that the company should stick to the things it knew best rather than try to be all things to all people and in the process get the company's resources spread too thin, particularly given its regional nature. One innovation the company was now considering was a new scent for its insect spray, which was rubbed or sprayed on a person's body. The new scent had undergone extensive testing in both the laboratory and in the field. The tests indicated that it repelled insects, particularly mosquitos, as well as or even better than the two leading national brands. One of the things that the company was particularly concerned about as it considered the introduction of the new brand was what to call it.

The Insecticide Market

The insecticide market had become a somewhat tricky one to figure out over the past several years. Although there had been growth in the purchase of insecticides in general, much of this growth had occurred in the

tank liquid market. The household spray market had decreased slightly during the same time span. Suchomel Chemical had not suffered from the general sales decline, however, but had managed to increase its sales of spray insecticides slightly over the past three years. The company was hoping that the new scent formulation might allow it to make even greater market share gains.

The company's experience in the industry led it to believe that the name given to the new product would be a very important element in the product's success, because there seemed to be some complex interactions between purchase and usage characteristics among repellent users. Most purchases were made by married women for their families. Yet repeat purchase was dependent on support by the husband that the product worked well. Therefore, the name had to appeal to both the buyer and the end user, even though the two people were not typically together at the time of purchase. To complicate matters further, past research indicated that a product with a name that appealed to both purchaser and end user would be rejected if the product's name and scent did not match. In sum, naming a product like this, to be used on a person's body, was a complex task.

Research Alternatives

The company followed its typical procedures in developing possible names for the new product. First, it asked those who had been involved in the product's development to suggest names. It also scheduled some informal brainstorming sessions among potential customers. Subjects in the brainstorming sessions were simply asked to throw out all the names they could possibly think of with respect to what a spray insecticide could or should be called. A panel of executives, mostly those from the product group but a few from corporate management as well, then went through the names and reduced the large list down to a more manageable subset based on their personal reactions to the names and subsequent discussion about what the names connoted to them. The subset of names was then submitted to the corporate legal staff, who checked them for possible copyright infringement. Those that survived this check were discussed again by the panel, and a list of 20 possibles was generated. Those in the product group were charged with the responsibility of developing a research design by which the final name could be chosen.

The people in the product group were considering two different alternatives for finding out which name was preferred. Both alternatives involved personal interviews at shopping malls. More specifically, the group was planning to conduct a set of interviews at one randomly determined mall in Atlanta, Savannah, Tallahassee, and Orlando. Each set of interviews would involve 100 respondents. The target respondents were married females, ages 21 to 54, who had purchased the product category during the past year. Likely looking respondents would be approached at random and would be asked if they had used any insect spray at all over the past year and then would be asked their age. Those who qualified would be asked to complete the insecticide-naming exercise using one of the two alternatives being considered.

Alternative 1 involved a sort of the 20 tentative names by the respondents. The sort would be conducted in the following way. First, respondents would be asked to sort the 20 names into two groups based on their appropriateness for an insect repellent. Group 1 was to consist of the ten best names and Group 2 the ten worst. Next, respondents would be asked to select the four best from Group 1 and the four worst from Group 2. Then they would be asked to pick the one best from the subset of the four best

and the one worst from the subset of the four worst. Finally, all respondents would be asked why they picked the specific names they did as the best and the worst.

Alternative 2 also had several stages. All respondents would first be asked to rate each of the 20 names on a seven-point scale with end anchors "Extremely inappropriate name for an insect repellent" and "Extremely appropriate name for an insect repellent." After completing this rating task, they would be asked to spray the back of their hand or arm with the product. They would then be asked to repeat the rating task using a similar scale, but this time it would be one in which the polar descriptors referred to the appropriateness of the name with respect to the specific scent. Next they would be asked to indicate their interest in buying the product by again checking one of the seven positions on a scale that ranged from "Definitely would not buy it" to "Definitely would buy it." Finally, each respondent would be asked why she selected each of the names she did as being most appropriate for insect repellents in general and the specific scent in particular.

Questions

1. Evaluate each of the two methods being considered for collecting the data. Which would you recommend and why?
2. How would you use the data from each method to decide what the brand name should be?
3. Do you think that personal interviews in shopping malls are a useful way to collect these data? If not, what would you recommend as an alternative?

Case 3.2   QUIN (A)[1]

QUIN is a nonprofit, listener-sponsored community radio station. More than 70 percent of its $300,000 annual budget comes directly from listener support, accrued during on-air fund drives and direct-mail campaigns. The remainder of its budget is derived from government grants, special events, and underwriting. When businesses underwrite (i.e., contribute

to QUIN as a form of community service), the station acknowledges their generosity with on-air credits. Apart from providing publicity for its patrons, however, QUIN does not offer airtime for promotional purposes and is essentially a noncommercial venture. Needless to say, funding is problematic, and, like other nonprofit organizations, the station is constantly seeking alternative means of generating income.

With a mixture of nostalgic sadness and joyful anticipation, QUIN recently moved from a cozy but

[1]The contributions of Jacqueline C. Hitchon to the development of this case are gratefully acknowledged.

antiquated studio to a new location, which contains state-of-the-art equipment for audio production work. The new equipment is currently being used primarily for on-air broadcasting and for training volunteers in various aspects of production. As such, it is evident to QUIN staff that the facility is shamefully underutilized. Untapped potential for audio production and an ongoing search for alternative sources of funding have led QUIN to consider establishing a commercial audio production studio in its new facility.

QUIN staff members wish to know if their new studio can serve a local need for audio production services with minimal investment in new equipment. As a basis for making a judgment, they would like answers to the eight following questions:

1. Who in the area uses audio production services?
2. How many users select services available locally?
3. Which local services do they use?
4. Why do they select those services?
5. Are they satisfied with the service they receive?
6. How often do they use an audio production service?
7. What type of audiovisual work do they require?
8. Is there a growing market for audiovisual services in the area?

One of the DJs at QUIN has a friend, Rob Heidenreich, who is studying for an MBA at the local university and is eager to obtain some consulting experience during summer vacation. QUIN staff members are happy to have someone research their problem at a reduced rate, and Heidenreich is delighted to have the opportunity to exercise his newly acquired skills outside the classroom. As soon as final exams for the spring semester were over, Heidenreich started collecting background information on the general status of audio production in the region. He also made a note of the apparatus available at the new facility, with a view to assessing how QUIN's capabilities compare to user requirements for audio production and to the capabilities of other audio production services.

Background Information on Audio Production

Heidenreich found that for present purposes, audio production work could be profitably classified into four categories, reflecting the operational distinction between voice and music production and the technical distinction between simple and multichannel recording. Simple recording, he learned, refers to recordings on one through four channels using a ¼-inch-format tape recorder, whereas multichannel recording requires larger-format recording equipment that typically offers eight channels.

I. Voice Production

A. *Simple voice production* uses one to four channels to combine voice, prerecorded music, and sound effects on ¼-inch reel-to-reel audiotapes. The two-channel recording of voice over a "bed" of music is most commonly used for commercials and public service announcements (PSAs).

B. *Multichannel voice production* uses more than four channels on ½-inch or larger reel-to-reel audiotapes. It is relatively rare for more than four channels to be used to record voice production, however. (Regardless of the number of channels used during recording, it is standard practice for recording studios to rerecord final versions of voice projects on ¼-inch audiotape. This is the format on which clients receive their commercials or PSAs, unless they specifically request otherwise.)

II. Music Production

A. *Simple music production* is sometimes done in the studio but is most often done on location for recording of live performances. On-location production requires ¼-inch tape-recording equipment and typically entails using just three microphones—stereo left and right and a back microphone. Sound is usually mixed live on two tracks.

B. *Multichannel music production* encompasses the great majority of music recordings. Usually undertaken in the studio, it requires one or more microphones per instrument plus microphones to record stereo left and right. To accommodate such production, multichannel projects must typically be recorded on at least eight tracks. On those occasions when multichannel music production is undertaken on location, it obviously necessitates transporting more equipment than simple music production does. Another function of multichannel production is to allow overdubbing (i.e., the recording of sound over a prerecorded piece by recording on channels not previously used).

Having gained some insight into the kinds of audio production work undertaken in the industry, Heidenreich subsequently turned his attention to the capabilities of QUIN's new facility.

QUIN's New Production Facility

QUIN's production facility contains two combo rooms (containing both production and on-air equipment), a master control room, a large studio, and a small studio.

The two combo rooms are used primarily for on-air music programs, in which the program host is also the engineer, and for preparation of prerecorded news stories and PSAs. Each room has a mixing board and a 96-plug "port" to interface the equipment, two turntables, two ¼-inch stereo reel-to-reel tape recorders, a cassette player, a cartridge machine, and at least three microphones. One combo room has a compact disk player.

The master control room contains the equipment used for sending the on-air transmission to the station's transmitter. It also contains a 16-channel mixing board, an equalizer, and a four-channel ½-inch reel-to-reel tape recorder intended for use with the large studio.

The large studio has 16 microphone input plugs that run directly to the mixing board in the master control room, and it is large enough for a dozen or more performers. The small studio has four microphones and is presently used primarily for on-air voice production. The microphones are connected to mixing boards in both combo rooms, and an audio engineer is required to run the board.

Being neither an engineer nor even a moderate stereo enthusiast, it was with some relief that Heidenreich closed his file on QUIN's new facility and turned to an investigation of existing audio production services in the area. So far, he had been able to obtain information by means of interviews with QUIN staff and a conducted tour of the station. But now he broadened his methodology to include interviews with service users and local businesses.

Audio Production Services in the Area

Heidenreich's investigation of local services had two basic thrusts. First, he needed to establish the number and types of services available. Second, he needed to determine the kind of work that production facilities undertook.

His inquiries indicated that there are three types of production facilities available in the area. First, the 16 local radio stations regularly accept outside audio production work, most of which consists of recording 30- and 60-second radio commercial spots. Both quality and cost expectations among clients for audio production by radio stations are low. In contrast, the second type of facility, represented by the 27 commercial producers in the region, is typically perceived as high cost and high quality. The third type of production facility consists of firms that do their own production work in-house. There are many firms in this last category, particularly with respect to simple audio production, since the equipment is relatively inexpensive, durable, and easy to operate.

Production of radio and television commercials seems to be the most prevalent type of project undertaken by audio producers. Even for television commercials, the sound tracks tend to be recorded on audiotape because speakers are not to be seen on-screen. The sound track is dubbed onto ¼-inch tape and then rerecorded onto videotape. This procedure also facilitates the task of editing while taking advantage of the relatively low cost of audio production. PSAs, as opposed to commercials per se, do not generate a great deal of audio production work, however, as they are generally read by announcers live on the air rather than being prerecorded.

Other kinds of audio production work mentioned in the discussions were music recordings; sound tracks for slide presentations; prerecorded news; dramatic readings; and audiotape for film, which, unlike videotape, requires separate recording of sound from the picture.

It was discovered that when commercials and PSAs are recorded at radio stations, the client is offered a package deal that includes airtime in the price of the commercial's production. The stations then distribute the commercials or PSAs (usually on ¼-inch tape or cassette) to any other stations from which the client decides to purchase airtime. Unfortunately, QUIN, as a noncommercial station, would be unable to air the commercials it produces. And, although the station does air PSAs, there is only a very small market for prerecorded PSAs. In a similar vein, news and public information programming for radio are usually recorded at the station that will air the program. Furthermore, dramatic readings are generally produced and provided for national distribution by the public radio system.

Research Orientation

Heidenreich pondered the information that he had accumulated and concluded that commercial voice production would be an obvious direction for QUIN to pursue. As a radio station, simple voice production is already one of its main functions. Moreover, it could handle multichannel voice production by submixing background sound sources (i.e., combining sound effects and music onto one tape) before adding foreground sound (such as narration). Submixing would allow the final mixing of the project on ½-inch or ¼-inch tape, from which it could be dubbed to the client's specifications.

Technically, QUIN also has the capacity for music production. Indeed, some simple music production could be undertaken in the present facilities. The microphones used for voice in the small studio and combo rooms are sufficiently versatile; and the recording equipment, together with the 16 microphone inputs in the large studio, offers a great deal of potential. Live mixing would be required to record on the four-channel reel-to-reel tape recorder, but this would suffice for many purposes. Unfortunately, the large studio would require better sound insulation for some types of music production, and the station would need to purchase a piano because the instrument could not be transported practically by the artists. All in all, Heidenreich believed that music production was a complex marketing area that would require a separate study and that voice production should be QUIN's first commercial venture.

Methodology

To provide firm answers to the list of questions developed by QUIN staff, Heidenreich decided that primary data should be collected in a descriptive study of the population identified as potential customers for voice production services. Based on his exploratory research, he divided the population of actual and potential users into four segments: (1) businesses, (2) nonprofit organizations, (3) state government agencies, and (4) advertising agencies. Since the smaller segments (advertising and government agencies) would not yield a sufficient number of responses for analytical purposes if not heavily sampled, these segments were to be sampled more heavily than the others.

Two questionnaires were developed for telephone administration; (1) a general survey of mass-media use designed for businesses, government agencies, and nonprofit organizations (see Figure 1), and (2) a questionnaire designed for advertising agencies, which included specific questions about cost and technical aspects of production, since such inquiries fall within the expertise of the agencies' personnel (see Figure 2).

Figure 1   ***Survey for Businesses, Government Agencies, and Nonprofit Organizations***

Hello, my name is _____, and I am a graduate business student at the university. I'm conducting a survey to see how local (businesses/nonprofit organizations/government agencies) use mass media (for advertising, public service announcements, or other educational purposes). Do you use the mass media for (advertising/those purposes)?

_____ Y   _____ N

- (If NO, *END*): Thank you for your time.
- (If YES): Do you have time to answer a few questions? The survey will take about 10 minutes, and your answers are confidential.

1. *I'll read you a list of different types of mass media. Which of the following mass media do you use for advertising?*

	YES	NO	
(PRINT):	_____	_____	Newspapers
	_____	_____	Magazines
	_____	_____	Posters and handbills

(continued)

Figure 1   *(Continued)*

(BROADCAST):

———— ———— Television commercials
———— ———— Radio commercials
———— ———— Television PSAs
Do you prerecord those PSAs, or send written copies of your
PSAs to television stations?
———— Prerecord ———— Written ———— Both
———— ———— Radio PSAs
Do you prerecord those PSAs, or send written copies of your
PSAs to radio stations?
———— Prerecord ———— Written ———— Both

(IN HOUSE):

———— ———— Slide presentations
Do your slide presentations include prerecorded sound?
———— Y   ———— N
———— ———— Video presentations
———— ———— Anything else? ————————————————

■ **(If PRINT ONLY, OR NOT PRERECORDED): Thank you for your time.**

2(a). You said that you use ————. Who produced your last one for you? (LEAVE
OPEN-ENDED)
———— In-house
———— Ad agency
———— Commercial production facility
———— Radio station
———— Television station
———— Other ————————————————

■ **(If IN-HOUSE, go to 2(b).)**

Was it produced locally? ———— *Y*   ———— *N*

(If YES): Where? ————————————————————————

(b). You also use ————. Who produced your last one for you?
———— In-house
———— Ad agency
———— Commercial production facility
———— Radio station
———— Television station
———— Other ————————————————

■ **(If IN-HOUSE, go to 2(c).)**

Was it produced locally? ———— *Y*   ———— *N*

(If YES): Where? ————————————————————————

(c). You also use ————. Who produced your last one for you?
———— In-house
———— Ad agency
———— Commercial production facility
———— Radio station
———— Television station
———— Other ————————————————

Figure 1   *(Continued)*

■ (If IN-HOUSE, go to #3.)

Was it produced locally? _____ Y   _____ N

(If YES): Where? _____

3(a). How many (commercials/PSAs/slide-tapes/videotapes) do you produce each year?
(LEAVE OPEN-ENDED)

_____

(b). Also, how many (commercials/PSAs/slide-tapes/videotapes) do you produce each year?
(LEAVE OPEN-ENDED)

_____

(c). Finally, how many (commercials/PSAs/slide-tapes/videotapes) do you produce each
year? (LEAVE OPEN-ENDED)

_____

4(a). (If response to #1 was MORE THAN ONE A/V OUT-OF-HOUSE MEDIUM):
Was your most recent media project a _____, _____, or _____? (LIST
FROM #1)
(go to #5.)

(b). (If response to #1 was ONE A/V MEDIUM, or AFTER 5(a)): Was your most recent
media project a _____, _____, or _____? (LIST FROM #1)

_____

5.   *Would you please comment on some aspects of that production? Imagine a ruler with*
five points on it; 1 stands for "not satisfied at all," and 5 stands for "very satisfied."
Using the ruler image, what number would you assign the following:

1	2	3	4	5	
____	____	____	____	____	Cost of production
____	____	____	____	____	Quality of sound in the audio portion
____	____	____	____	____	Amount of time it took to produce the project
____	____	____	____	____	Quality of voice talent
____	____	____	____	____	Quality of music and special effects

6.   *Do you expect that next year you will produce (commercials/PSAs/slide-tapes/*
videotapes):

_____ more often
_____ less often
_____ about the same as this year

7.   *In your opinion, which of the following aspects of a commercial production studio are*
the most important for your purposes? Please rate them from 1 to 5, with 1 being
"not important at all," to 5 being "very important."

1	2	3	4	5	
____	____	____	____	____	Low cost
____	____	____	____	____	High-quality production
____	____	____	____	____	Availability of good voice talent
____	____	____	____	____	Selection of music and special effects
____	____	____	____	____	Convenient location
____	____	____	____	____	Well-established relationship with the studio
____	____	____	____	____	Anything else? _____

Thank you for your time.

Figure 2   **Survey for Ad Agencies**

Hello, my name is _____, and I am a graduate business student at the university. I'm conducting a survey to learn about audio production work done by local advertising agencies. Does your agency do audio production work?

_____ Y   _____ N

■ (If NO, *END*): Thank you for your time.
■ (If YES): Do you have time to answer a few questions? The survey will take about 10 minutes, and your answers are confidential.

1. *Which of the following audio or audiovisual media does your agency produce? Please answer yes or no to each.*

   YES   NO
   _____ _____ Television commercials
   _____ _____ Radio commercials
   _____ _____ Television PSAs
   _____ _____ Radio PSAs
   _____ _____ Slide/tape presentations
   _____ _____ Videotape presentations
   _____ _____ Anything else?_____

2(a). *You said that you produce _____. What production facilities do you use? (LEAVE OPEN-ENDED; CHECK ALL THAT APPLY)*
   _____ In-house
   _____ Commercial production facility _____
   _____ Radio station _____
   _____ Local television station _____

   Where do you have your work done? (Fill in blank.)

(b). *You also said that you produce _____. What production facilities do you use? (LEAVE OPEN-ENDED; CHECK ALL THAT APPLY)*
   _____ In-house
   _____ Commercial production facility _____
   _____ Radio station _____
   _____ Local television station _____

   Where do you have your work done? (Fill in blank.)

(c). *Finally, you said that you produce _____. What production facilities do you use? (LEAVE OPEN-ENDED; CHECK ALL THAT APPLY)*
   _____ In-house
   _____ Commercial production facility _____
   _____ Radio station _____
   _____ Local television station _____

   Where do you have your work done? (Fill in blank.)

3(a). *How many _____ do you produce each month?*
   _____

(b). *Also, how many _____ do you produce each month?*
   _____

(c). *Finally, how many _____ do you produce each month?*
   _____

4(a). *(FOR RADIO) Please think back to the last radio (commercial/PSA) you produced. How much time was spent recording and editing that project?*
   _____

Figure 2   **(Continued)**

About how much did it cost to record and edit that project? Don't include the cost of airtime. $ _____

Does that include the cost of voice talent? ____ Y ____ N ____ Don't Know
Does that include the cost of music?   ____ Y ____ N ____ Don't Know

(b). *(FOR TELEVISION) Please think back to the last television (commercial/PSA) you produced. Did you record the audio portion of your project separately from the video portion?* _____ Y _____ N _____ Don't Know

(If YES): How much time was spent recording and editing the audio track of that project? _____

About how much did it cost to record and edit the audio portion of that project? Don't include the cost of airtime. $ _____

Does that include the cost of voice talent? ____ Y ____ N ____ Don't Know
Does that include the cost of music?   ____ Y ____ N ____ Don't Know

(c). *(FOR SLIDE/TAPE) Please think back to the last slide/tape program you produced. How much time was spent recording and editing the audio portion of that project?*

_____

*About how much did it cost to record and edit the audio portion of that project?*____ *Don't include the cost of airtime. $* _____

Does that include the cost of voice talent? ____ Y ____ N ____ Don't Know
Does that include the cost of music?   ____ Y ____ N ____ Don't Know

(d). *(FOR VIDEOTAPES) Please think back to the last videotape you produced. Did you record the audio portion of your project separately from the video portion?* _____ Y _____ N _____ Don't Know

(IF YES): How much time was spent recording and editing the audio track of that project? _____

About how much did it cost to record and edit the audio portion of that project? $ _____

Does that include the cost of voice talent? ____ Y ____N ____ Don't Know
Does that include the cost of music?   ____ Y ____ N ____ Don't Know

5(a). *Would you please comment on some aspects of your last (television commercial, radio commercial, television PSA, radio PSA, slide presentation, videotape presentation, other* _____*)? Imagine a ruler with five points on it; 1 stands for "not satisfied at all," and 5 stands for "very satisfied." Using the ruler image, what numbers would you assign the following:*

    1   2   3   4   5
____ ____ ____ ____ ____ Cost of production
____ ____ ____ ____ ____ Quality of sound in the audio portion
____ ____ ____ ____ ____ Amount of time it took to produce the project
____ ____ ____ ____ ____ Quality of voice talent
____ ____ ____ ____ ____ Quality of music and special effects

(b). *Would you comment now on those same aspects for your last* _____*? Again, 1 stands for "not satisfied at all," and 5 stands for "very satisfied."*

    1   2   3   4   5
____ ____ ____ ____ ____ Cost of production
____ ____ ____ ____ ____ Quality of sound in the audio portion
____ ____ ____ ____ ____ Amount of time it took to produce the project
____ ____ ____ ____ ____ Quality of voice talent
____ ____ ____ ____ ____ Quality of music and special effects

(continued)

Figure 2   *(Continued)*

(c). *Finally, would you please comment on those aspects for your last _____? Again, 1 stands for "not satisfied at all," and 5 stands for "very satisfied."*

1	2	3	4	5	
____	____	____	____	____	Cost of production
____	____	____	____	____	Quality of sound in the audio portion
____	____	____	____	____	Amount of time it took to produce the project
____	____	____	____	____	Quality of voice talent
____	____	____	____	____	Quality of music and special effects

6. *In your opinion, which of the following aspects of a production studio are the most important for your audio work? Please rate them from 1 to 5 with 1 being "not important at all" to 5 being "very important."*

1	2	3	4	5	
____	____	____	____	____	Low cost
____	____	____	____	____	High-quality production
____	____	____	____	____	Availability of good voice talent
____	____	____	____	____	Selection of music and special effects
____	____	____	____	____	Convenient location
____	____	____	____	____	Well-established relationship with the studio
____	____	____	____	____	Anything else? _____

7. *Finally, do you expect that next year you will use audio production studios*
   _____ more often
   _____ less often
   _____ about the same as this year

Thank you for your time.

Questions

1. Do you think that Heidenreich's decision to focus on voice production was sensible? Why or why not?
2. Based on your knowledge of the advantages and disadvantages of telephone surveys compared with other data-collection techniques and on the information available in the case, why do you think Heidenreich chose to use a telephone survey?
3. Do you consider it a good idea to develop and administer two questionnaires, one for advertising agency personnel and one for personnel of other organizations? Why or why not?
4. Evaluate the questionnaires.

Case 3.3   Premium Pizza, Inc.[1]

The 1980s saw a sharp increase in the use of promotions (coupons, cents-off deals marked on the package, free gifts, etc.) because of their manifest success at increasing short-term purchase behavior. In fact, sales promotion is now estimated to represent 65 percent of the typical marketing budget, compared with 35 percent for advertising.[2] The initial benefit of increased sales, however, has in many industries resulted in long-term escalation of competition. As firms are forced to "fight fire with fire," special offer

[1]The contributions of Jacqueline C. Hitchon to this case are gratefully acknowledged.

[2]Courtland L. Bovee and William F. Arens, *Contemporary Advertising*, 3rd ed., (Homewood, Ill.: Richard D. Irwin, Inc., 1989).

Table 1	**Five Promotional Concepts**
Coupon A:	Get a medium soft drink for 5 cents with the purchase of any slice.
Coupon B:	Buy a slice and get a second slice of comparable value free.
Coupon C:	Save 50 cents on the purchase of any slice and receive one free trip to our salad bar.
Coupon D:	Buy a slice and a large soft drink and get a second slice free.
Coupon E:	Get a single-topping slice for only 99 cents.

follows special offer in a never-ending spiral of promotional deals.[3]

The fast food industry has been one of the most strongly affected by this trend. Pizzas come two for the price of one; burgers are promoted in the context of a double-deal involving cuddly toys for the kids; tacos are reduced in price some days—but not others. It is within this fiercely competitive, erratic environment that Premium Pizza Corporation has grown from a small local chain into an extensive midwestern network with national aspirations. Over the past few years, Jim Battaglia, vice-president of marketing, has introduced a number of promotional offers, and Premium Pizza parlors have continued to flourish. Nevertheless, as the company contemplates further expansion, Battaglia is concerned that he knows very little about how his customers respond to his promotional deals. He believes that he needs a long-term strategy aimed at maximizing the effectiveness of dollars spent on promotions. And, as a first step, he thinks that it is important to assess the effectiveness of his existing offers.

Specific Objectives

In the past, Battaglia has favored the use of five types of coupons, and he now wishes to determine their independent appeal, together with their relation to several identifiable characteristics of fast food consumers. The five promotional concepts are listed in Table 1. The consumer characteristics that Battaglia's experience tells him warrant investigation include number of children living at home, age of youngest child,

propensity to east fast food, propensity to eat Premium Pizza in particular, preference for slices over pies, propensity to use coupons, and occupation.

The specific objectives of the research study can therefore be summarized as follows:

1. To evaluate the independent appeal of the five promotional deals to determine which deals are most preferred.
2. To gain insight into the reasons that certain deals are preferred.
3. To examine the relationships between the appeal of each promotional concept and various consumer characteristics.

Proposed Methodology

After much discussion, Battaglia's research team finally decided that the desired information could best be gathered by means of personal interviews, using a combination of open-ended and close-ended questions. A medium-size shopping mall on the outskirts of a metropolitan area in the Midwest was selected as the research site. Shoppers were intercepted by professional interviewers while walking in the mall and were asked to participate in a survey requiring five minutes of their time.

The sampling procedure employed a convenience sample in which interviewers were instructed to approach anyone passing by, provided that they met certain criteria (see Figure 1). In sum, the sample of respondents was restricted to adult men and women between the ages of 18 and 49 who had both purchased lunch, dinner, or carry-out food at a fast food restaurant in the past seven days and had eaten restaurant pizza within the last thirty days, either at a restaurant or delivered to the home. In addition, interviewers were warned not to exercise any bias

---

[3]Alan G. Sawyer and Peter R. Dickson, "Psychological Perspectives on Consumer Response to Sales Promotions," in Katherine E. Jocz, ed., *Research on Sales Promotion: Collected Papers* (Cambridge, Mass.: Marketing Science Institute, 1984), pp. 1–21.

Figure 1   ***Interviewer Instructions***

Below are suggestions for addressing each question. Please read all of the instructions before you begin questioning people.

Interviewer Instructions

Approach shoppers who appear to be between 18–49 years of age. Since we would like equal numbers of respondents in each age category and a 50-percent male-female ratio, please do not select respondents based on their appeal to you. The interview should take approximately five minutes. When reading questions, read answer choices *if indicated.*

Question 1:   Terminate interview with any respondent who has not eaten lunch or dinner from any fast food restaurant in the last seven days.

Question 2:   Terminate interview with any respondent who has not eaten retaurant pizza within the last thirty days. This includes carry-out, drive-thru, or dining in.

Question 3:   Terminate interview with respondent if not between 18–49 years of age. If between 18–49, circle the appropriate number answer. For this question, please read the question and the answer choices.

After completing questions 1 through 3, hand respondent the coupon booklet. *Make sure that the booklet and the response sheets are the same color.* Also check to see that the coupon booklet number indicated on the upper right-hand corner of the response sheet matches the coupon book number.

Question 4:   Ask the respondent to open the coupon booklet and read the first coupon concept. Read the first section of question 4, showing the respondent that the scales are provided on the page above the coupon concept. Enter his or her answer in the box provided.

Read the second section of the question and enter respondent's answer in the second box provided.

When asking the respondent, "Why did you respond as you did for use," please record the first reason mentioned and use the lines provided to probe and clarify the reasons.

during the selection process, as they would do, for example, if they approached only those people who looked particularly agreeable or attractive. Finally, interviewers were asked to obtain as close as possible to a 50-50 split of male and female participants.

The questionnaire was organized into three sections (see Figure 2). The first section contained the screening questions aimed at ensuring that respondents qualified for the sample. In the second section, respondents were asked to evaluate on ten-point scales the appeal of each of the five promotional concepts based on two factors: perceived value and likelihood of use. After they had evaluated a concept, interviewees were asked to give reasons for their likelihood-of-use rating. The third and final section consisted of the questions on consumer characteristics that Battaglia believed to be pertinent.

The questionnaire was to be completed by the interviewer based on the respondent's comments. In other words, the interviewer read the questions aloud and wrote down the answer given in each case by the interviewee. It was decided to show respondents an example of each coupon before they rated it. For this purpose, enlarged photographs of each coupon were produced. It was also thought necessary to depict the ten-point scales that consumers should use to evaluate the promotional offer. Coupons and scales were therefore assembled in a booklet so that, as the interviewer showed each double-page spread, the respondent would see the scales on the top page and the coupon in question on the bottom page (see Figure 3, page 322).

Because the researcher wished to counterbalance the order in which the coupons were viewed and rated, the five coupons were organized into booklets of

For questions 5 through 8, periodically remind the respondent to look at the scales provided on the page above the coupon concept that he or she is looking at.

Question 9:   Enter number of children living at home. If none, enter the number zero and proceed to question 11.

Question 10:   Enter age of *youngest* child living at home in the box provided.

Question 11:   Read the question and each answer slowly. Circle the number corresponding to the appropriate answer.

Question 12:   Read the question and each answer slowly. Circle the number corresponding to the appropriate answer. If answer is never, proceed to question 14. Otherwise continue to question 13.

Question 13:   Circle the number corresponding to the appropriate answer. Do not read answer choices.

Question 14:   Circle the number corresponding to the appropriate answer. Do not read answer choices.

Question 15:   Read the question and each answer slowly. Circle the number corresponding to the appropriate answer.

Question 16:   Read the question and each answer slowly. Circle the number corresponding to the appropriate answer.

Question 17:   If an explanation is requested for occupation, please tell respondent that we are looking for a broad category or title. "No occupation" is not an acceptable answer. If this should happen, please probe to see if the person is a student, homemaker, retired, unemployed, etc.

At the end of the questionnaire, you are asked to indicate whether the respondent was male or female. Please circle the appropriate answer. This is not a question for the respondent.

Figure 2   ***Questionnaire***

Response Number   _____
Coupon Book #   _____

(Approach shoppers who appear to be between the ages of 18–49 and say . . .)

Hi, I'm _____ from Midwest Research Services. Many companies like to know your preferences and opinions about new products and promotions. If you have about 5 minutes, I'd like to have your opinions in this market research study.

(If refused, terminate interview)

1. *Have you eaten lunch or dinner in, or carried food away from, a fast food restaurant in the last seven days?*

    . . . (must answer yes to continue)

2. *Have you eaten restaurant pizza within the last thirty days, either at the restaurant or by having it delivered?*

    . . . (must answer yes to continue)

(continued)

Figure 2   **(Continued)**

3. *Which age-group are you in?* (read answers, circle number)

    1 18–24   2 25–34   3 35–49   4 Other — Terminate interview

I am now going to show you five different coupon concepts and ask you three questions for each. Please respond to each coupon independently of the others. Look at the next coupon only when I ask you to.

4. *Please read the first coupon concept. Using a ten-point scale as shown on the page above, how would you rate this concept if one represents very poor value and ten represents very good value?*

    enter value

    Looking at the second scale, how would you rate this concept if one represents definitely would not use and ten represents definitely would use?

    enter value

    Why did you respond as you did for use? _____

    _____

5. *Please turn the page and read the next coupon concept. Ignoring the last coupon and using the same scale, how would you rate this concept in terms of value?*

    enter value

    Referring to the second scale, how would you rate this concept in terms of your level of use?

    enter value

    Why did you respond as you did for use? _____

    _____

6. *Please turn the page and read the next coupon concept. Ignoring the last coupon and using the same scale, how would you rate this concept in terms of value?*

    enter value

    Referring to the second scale, how would you rate this concept in terms of your level of use?

    enter value

    Why did you respond as you did for use? _____

    _____

7. *Please turn the page and read the next coupon concept. Ignoring the last coupon and using the same scale, how would you rate this concept in terms of value?*

    enter value

    Referring to the second scale, how would you rate this concept in terms of your level of use?

    enter value

    Why did you respond as you did for use? _____

    _____

8. *Please turn the page and read the next coupon concept. Ignoring the last coupon and using the same scale, how would you rate this concept in terms of value?*

    enter value

    Referring to the second scale, how would you rate this concept in terms of your level of use?

    enter value

Figure 2   *(Continued)*

Why did you respond as you did for use? _____
_____
_____

Thank you. The following questions will help us classify the preceding information.

9. *How many children do you have living at home?*
   If answer is none, proceed to question 11.

   [enter number]
   none = 0

10. *What is the age of your youngest child?*

    [   ]

11. *How often do you eat fast food for lunch or dinner?*
    (read answers, circle number) 1 Once per month or less
                                        2 Two to three times per month
                                        3 Once or twice a week
                                        4 More than twice a week

12. *How often do you eat at Premium Pizza?*
    (read answers, circle number) 1 Never visited Premium Pizza
                                        2 Once per month or less
                                        3 Two to three times per month
                                        4 Once a week or more

    If answer is never, proceed to question 14.

13. *Do you* yourself *usually buy whole pies or slices at Premium Pizza?*

    1 whole pies
    2 slices
    (circle one)

14. *Have you used fast food or restaurant coupons in the last thirty days?*

    1 yes
    2 no
    (circle one)

15. *Have you ever used coupons for Premium Pizza?*
    (read answers, circle number) 1 Never
                                        2 I sometimes use them when I have them.
                                        3 I always use them when I have them.

16. *What is your marital status?*
    (read answers, circle number) 1 Single
                                        2 Married
                                        3 Divorced, separated, widowed

17. *What is your occupation?* _____

Thank you for your participation — Terminate interview at this time.

This is **not** *a question for the respondent.*
Please circle appropriate answer — respondent was: 1 male
                                                       2 female
                                                       (circle number)

six different sequences. Each sequence was subsequently bound in one of six distinctly colored binders. A total of 96 questionnaires were then printed in six different colors to match the binders. In this way, there were 16 questionnaires of each color, and the color of the respondent's questionnaire indicated the sequence that he or she had seen.

The questionnaire and procedure were pretested at a mall similar to the target mall and were found to be satisfactory.

Figure 3   *Stimuli*

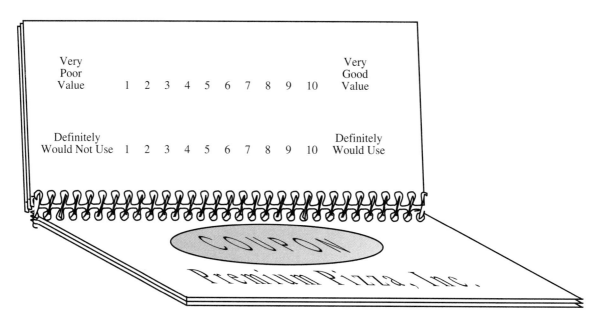

Questions

1. Is the choice of mall intercept interviews an appropriate data-collection method given the research objectives?
2. Do you think that there are any specific criteria that the choice of shopping mall should satisfy?
3. Evaluate the instructions to interviewers (Figure 1).
4. Evaluate the questionnaire (Figure 2).
5. Do you think that it is worthwhile to present the coupons in a binder, separate from the questionnaire? Why or why not?
6. Do you consider it advisable to rotate the order of presentation of coupons? Why or why not?

Part
Four

Data-Collection Forms

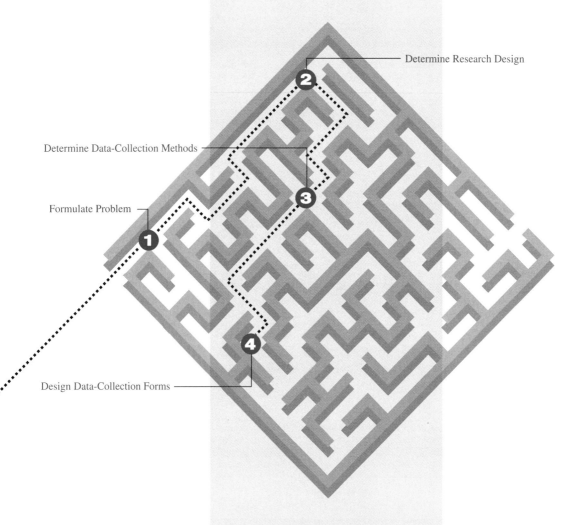

— Determine Research Design

2

Determine Data-Collection Methods —

3

Formulate Problem —

1

Design Data-Collection Forms —

4

Once the data-collection method has been decided, the researcher needs to design the data-collection forms that will be used. Chapter 12 discusses the construction of questionnaires and observation forms. Chapter 13 provides some measurement basics that researchers need to be aware of so that they do not mislead others. Chapter 14 then discusses the measurement of attitudes, perceptions, and preferences.

RON CONLIN
Manager of Consumer Market Planning and Research
Goodyear Tire & Rubber Company

"The biggest problem in my job," says Ron Conlin, manager of Consumer Market Planning and Research at the Goodyear Tire & Rubber Company, "is that people aren't very articulate about tires. It is easy to ask them questions about tires, but hard to get meaningful answers. Tires are a low-involvement product category," concedes Conlin, "so we have to be ingenious and persistent in developing ways to find out what consumers want out of a tire."

According to Conlin, Goodyear uses the full spectrum of data-collection instruments in order to gauge consumer preferences. "We do face-to-face interviews, mall intercepts, we have a consumer mail panel, where we monitor 25,000 households for a tire or auto-service purchase every quarter," he reports. Since there are almost 5,000 Goodyear retail outlets nationwide, the company has created mock-up stores to do observational research on how consumers relate to different retail store formats.

"We own our own state-of-the-art telephone interviewing facility," says Conlin. "We do thousands of phone interviews every year." Conlin thinks that the technological advances in phone interviewing have caused a trend away from mail questionnaires.

"Computer-assisted telephone interviewing offers a flexible means of data collection, and it's very exciting," says Conlin. At Goodyear, telephone interviewers sit in front of computer screens that display the questions to be asked. The interviewers, talking to the interview subject on a headset phone, enter the answers directly into the computer. "It is possible to develop very sophisticated skip patterns," reports Conlin. "If someone gives a particular answer, it prompts the computer to bring up a specific question. It allows us to follow a number of branch inquiries. The interview can be really fine-tuned so that you end up asking the right people the right questions."

Asking the right people the right questions is not an easy goal to achieve. "We always, always, always pretest the questions," reports Conlin. "I don't think I've ever developed the perfect questionnaire the first time."

A big problem is ambiguously worded questions. Even if everyone understands the question, that doesn't mean that person A is going to understand it the same way as person B. "If respondents don't take away the same thing from a question, it's a disaster," says Conlin.

To ensure high-quality data collection, Conlin not only pretests questions, but he also listens to live interviews, reviews videotape of personal interviews, checks entered responses from the phone interviews, and debriefs both interviewer and interviewee in the early stages of a research study. "Raw data look the same whether the questionnaire was poorly designed or well designed. But if it was poorly designed, you've got a classic case of 'garbage in, garbage out.'"

Because tires are such a low consumer-involvement product category, Conlin says that he's a "big fan" of conjoint analysis. "A tire is a bundle of attributes," reports Conlin. "What you gain in tread wear you lose in traction. It's only logical that you'd present the consumer with a list of tire alternatives to identify what is important to them."

Conlin says that while the trend is definitely away from mail questionnaires, the proliferation of telephone interviewing makes Goodyear very sensitive to its responsibility to the members of the general public who may prefer to eat their dinner rather than answer questions about tires. "We try hard not to be annoying," says Conlin. "We don't push too hard for completes."

Conlin says that it's exciting to work for a company like Goodyear that is a brand manufacturer and a retailer. "The number of issues in the marketing mix is huge," he says. "It is a very competitive industry, and Goodyear is pushing hard to become market oriented. It's very exciting, but it's also a big challenge. The hardest thing, believe it or not, is to dot all the *i*'s and cross all the *t*'s. It's easy to do poor research. It takes a lot of discipline to do good research."

Chapter Twelve

Designing the Questionnaire or Observation Form

Learning Objectives

Upon completing this chapter, you should be able to

1. Explain the role of research hypotheses in developing a questionnaire.

2. Define *telescoping error* and *recall loss* and explain how they affect a respondent's ability to answer questions accurately.

3. Cite some of the techniques researchers use to secure respondents' cooperation in answering sensitive questions.

4. Explain what an open-ended question is.

5. Name two kinds of fixed-alternative questions and tell the difference between them.

6. List some of the primary rules researchers should keep in mind in trying to develop bias-free questions.

7. Explain what the funnel approach to question sequencing is.

8. Explain what a branching question is and discuss when it is used.

9. Explain the difference between basic information and classification information and tell which should be asked first in a questionnaire.

Case in Marketing Research

Bill Hershey, a young staffer at Wright Communications Research, was leafing through the first batch of questionnaires that had been returned on the MedAccounts study. To anyone passing his desk, he presented a picture of frustration and bewilderment. This was supposed to be a very straightforward survey, and Hershey didn't understand what could have gone wrong.

MedAccounts was a company that provided specialized computer systems for doctors' offices. Its systems centralized all record-keeping and billing functions, which cut down on the cost and time devoted to updating charts and sending bills. However, when there was a service problem with the MedAccounts system, a doctor's office could be paralyzed. That was why the people at MedAccounts had hired Wright Communications Research to find out how quickly and effectively their service department was handling service calls.

It had been decided that the most cost-efficient method for the study would be to send out a questionnaire. Hershey had been picked to help draft it. He had taken the questionnaire through several versions and had fine-tuned it with more experienced staffers. Then the final version had been printed and mailed to the sample of 900 physicians listed by MedAccounts as using its system.

Hershey had thought that the hard part was over; all that remained was to tabulate the responses from the completed questionnaires. The stack of completed forms on his desk, however, constituted a rude surprise.

For one thing, it represented a much lower response rate than he'd counted on. He had expected that many of the physicians surveyed would be too busy to reply to the questionnaire, but he'd expected more responses than this.

Even more perplexing was the Jekyll and Hyde quality of the replies. About half of the questionnaires were intelligently completed. The other half were full of sketchy answers and questions left blank.

Hershey had no idea what was going on, but he was determined to find out. He picked up the phone and began dialing the number of one of the physicians whose half-filled-out questionnaire sat on the desk in front of him.

Discussion Issues

1. Do you think that a mail questionnaire was a good choice for the MedAccounts study? Why or why not?
2. Do you think that Hershey might have avoided some of his problems with a pretest of his questionnaire?
3. What are some of the possible explanations for the kinds of initial results Hershey received?

In the previous chapters we discussed the various types of questionnaires and observation forms researchers use and how they are administered, as well as the pros and cons of the specific types of questionnaires and observation methods. We also examined the various advantages and disadvantages of using communication and observation research techniques.

In this chapter we will build on that discussion by reviewing the procedures researchers can follow in developing a questionnaire or observation data-collection form.

Questionnaire Design

Although much progress has been made, designing questionnaires is still an art and not a science. Much of the progress has been simply an awareness of what to avoid, namely, leading questions and ambiguous questions. Few guidelines exist, however, on how to develop questions that are not leading or ambiguous.

Figure 12.1 offers a method the beginning researcher might find helpful to develop questionnaires.[1] More experienced researchers would be expected to develop their own patterns, although the steps listed in Figure 12.1 would certainly be part of that pattern.

While the stages of development are presented in the figure in sequence, researchers will rarely be so fortunate as to develop a questionnaire in that step-by-step fashion. A more typical development will involve circling back to clarify some aspects of earlier steps after they have been found to be faulty later on in the questionnaire's design. The researcher may find, for example, that the way a question is worded tends to elicit unhelpful responses. Researchers should not be surprised, then, if they find themselves working back and forth among some of the stages. That is natural.

Researchers should also be warned not to take the stages too literally. They are presented as a guide or a checklist. With questionnaires, the proof of the pudding is very much in the eating. Does the questionnaire produce accurate data of the kind needed? Blind adherence to procedure is no substitute for creativity in approach, nor is it any substitute for a pretest (Step 9 of Figure 12.1), with which one can discover if the typical respondent indeed understands each question and is able and willing to supply the information sought.

Step 1: Specify What Information Will Be Sought

The first step in questionnaire design, deciding what information will be sought, is easy, provided that researchers have been meticulous and precise at earlier stages in the research process. Careless earlier work will make this decision difficult.

Both descriptive and causal research require that researchers have enough knowledge about the problem to frame some specific hypotheses to guide the research. The hypotheses also guide the questionnaire. They determine what information will be sought, and from whom, because they specify what relationships will be investigated. If researchers have already established dummy tables to structure the data analysis, their job of determining what information is to be collected is essentially complete. You may remember that a dummy table is a table designed to catalog the data that will be collected. It is identical to the one that will be used in the actual research, but in this early stage it has no numbers.

Researchers must collect information on the variables specified in the dummy tables in order to investigate the hypotheses. Further, researchers must collect this

Figure 12.1 **Procedure for Developing a Questionnaire**

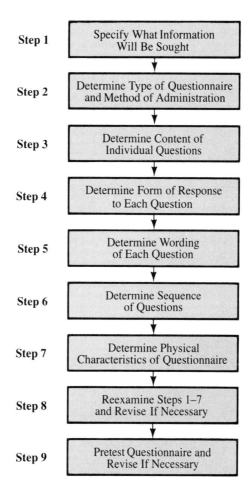

Step 1	Specify What Information Will Be Sought
Step 2	Determine Type of Questionnaire and Method of Administration
Step 3	Determine Content of Individual Questions
Step 4	Determine Form of Response to Each Question
Step 5	Determine Wording of Each Question
Step 6	Determine Sequence of Questions
Step 7	Determine Physical Characteristics of Questionnaire
Step 8	Reexamine Steps 1–7 and Revise If Necessary
Step 9	Pretest Questionnaire and Revise If Necessary

information from the right people and in the right units. Hence, it is clear that hypotheses are not only guides to what information will be sought, but also affect the type of question and form of response used to collect it.

Of course, the preparation of the questionnaire may itself suggest further hypotheses and other relationships that might be investigated at slight additional effort and cost. A most important warning is in order here: If the new hypothesis is indeed vital to understanding the phenomenon, by all means include it and use it to advantage when designing the questionnaire. On the other hand, and we are repeating ourselves, if it simply represents one of those potentially "interesting findings" but is not vital to the research effort, forget it. The inclusion of interesting but not vital items simply lengthens the questionnaire, causes problems in administration and analysis, and often increases nonresponse. For example, Figure 12.2, which is based on data from over one million interviews, shows what happens to refusal rates as the length of the interview increases.

The exploratory research effort is, of course, aimed at the discovery of ideas and insights and not at their systematic investigation. The questionnaire for an

Figure 12.2   **Refusal Rate as a Function of Length of the Interview**

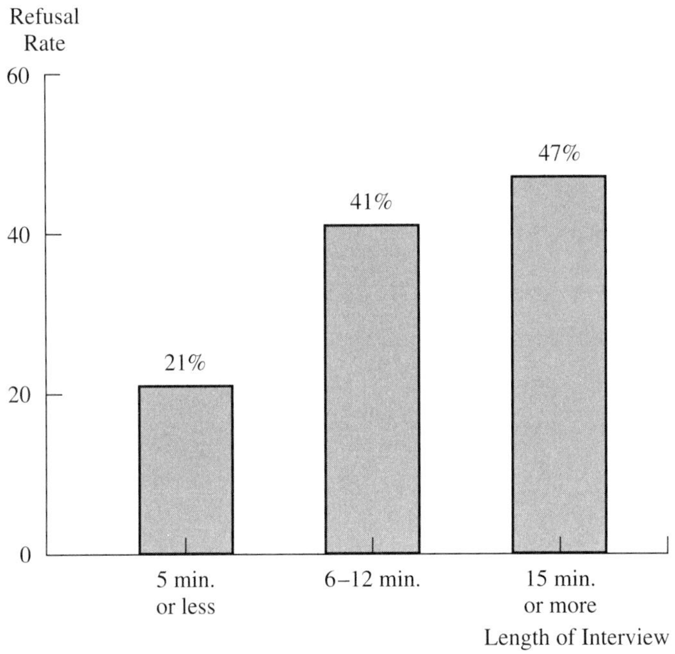

Source: Developed from information in *Industry Image Study*, 8th ed. (Indianapolis, Ind.: Walker Research, Inc., 1988).

exploratory study is therefore loosely structured, with only a rough idea of the kind of information that might be sought. This is particularly true at the earliest stages of exploratory research. It is also true, but to a lesser extent, at the later stages of exploratory research, when the emphasis is on determining the priorities that should be given to various hypotheses in guiding future research.

Step 2: Determine Type of Questionnaire and Method of Administration

After specifying the basic information that will be sought, the researcher needs to specify how it will be gathered. Decisions on the type of questionnaire and method of administering it constitute the second step. Such decisions center on the structure and disguise to be used in the questionnaire and whether it will be administered by mail, telephone, or personal interviews. We saw previously that these decisions are not independent of one another. If the researcher decides on a disguised-unstructured questionnaire in which subjects will be shown a picture and asked to tell a story about it, a telephone interview would be out of the question, and even a mail survey might pose serious problems.[2] Similarly, it is probably not a good idea to use a mail survey for an unstructured-undisguised questionnare that asks open-ended questions.

The type of data to be collected will have an important effect, of course, on these questions. A researcher investigating the relationship between some behavior and a series of demographic characteristics (for example, How is dishwasher ownership related to income, age, family size, and so on?) might use mail, telephone, or in-home or mall personal interviews to gather the data. The methods would not be equally attractive because of cost and other considerations, but they all could be used. On the other hand, a researcher interested in measuring attitudes could not use all of the methods. The method that would be most appropriate would be largely determined by decisions made earlier about structure and disguise. If researchers decided to use a lengthy attitude scale, for example, they would probably have to rule out telephone interviews. Such data could be gathered best either by mail or in personal interviews. Likewise, an open-ended questionnaire on attitudes might be unsuitable for mail administration. Thus, the researcher must specify precisely what primary data are needed, how these data might be collected, what degree of structure and disguise will be used, and then how the questionnaire will be administered.

Figure 12.3 offers an example of a questionnaire and its cover letter. The primary data at issue are the use of caffeinated ground coffee and attitudes toward various brands. The questions are all very structured and undisguised. The questionnaire is to be administered by mail, using part of the National Family Opinion panel. Note the ease with which the responses could be tabulated.

Step 3: Determine Content of Individual Questions

The researcher's previous decisions regarding information needed, the structure and disguise to be imposed on its collection, and the method for administering the questionnaire will largely control the decisions regarding individual question content, which is the third step. But the researcher can and should ask some additional questions.[3]

Is the Question Necessary?   Suppose an issue is important. Then the researcher needs to ask whether the point has been adequately covered by other questions. If not, a new question is in order. The question should then be framed to secure an answer with the required detail, but not an answer with more detail than needed. Very often in marketing, for example, we employ the concept of *stage in the life cycle* to explore family consumption behavior. Stage in the life cycle is a variable made up of several elements, including marital status, presence of children, and the ages of children. The presence of children is an important factor, because it most often indicates a dependency relationship. This is especially true if the youngest child is under six years old and thus represents one type of responsibility, whereas children over six but under seventeen represent another type of responsibility for the parents. In a study using stage in the life cycle as a variable, there is no need to ask the age of each child. Rather, all that is needed is one question aimed at securing the age of the youngest child if there are any children. Once again, the roles of the hypotheses and dummy tables are obvious when designing the questionnaire.

Are Several Questions Needed Instead of One?   There will often be situations in which several questions are needed instead of one. Consider the question, "Why do you use Crest?" One respondent may reply, "To reduce cavities," while another may reply, "Because our dentist recommended it." Obviously two different frames of reference are being employed to answer this question. The first respondent is replying in terms of why he is using it now, while the second is replying in terms of how she started using it. It would be better to break this one question down into

Figure 12.3   *Cover Letter and Mail Questionnaire for Caffeinated Ground Coffee Study*

''MARKET RESEARCH THROUGH REPRESENTATIVE HOUSEHOLDS''

NATIONAL FAMILY OPINION, INC.

P. O. Box 474   Toledo, OH 43654

TOLL-FREE NUMBERS
OUTSIDE OHIO: 1-800-537-4097
INSIDE OHIO: 1-800-472-4000

MONDAY THROUGH FRIDAY
8:00 A.M. TO 4:30 P.M.
EASTERN TIME

11519

Dear NFO Member,

Please give this questionnaire to the person in your household who is the Primary Coffee Drinker (this may be you). Thank you!

TO THE HOUSEHOLD MEMBER ANSWERING THIS QUESTIONNAIRE:

Today's questionnaire is about **caffeinated ground coffee**. Most of my questions can be answered by simply checking a box. However, where I've asked you to write in your opinions, please be as specific as possible.

When you have completed the questionnaire, please return it to me in the postage-paid envelope I've provided.

Thanks so much for your cooperation with this important study.

Sincerely,

Carol

Carol Adams

MEMBER OF AMERICAN MARKETING ASSOCIATION TOLEDO CHAMBER OF COMMERCE

Figure 12.3   **(Continued)**

1. What type of coffeemaker do you usually use to prepare your ground coffee at home? **(CHECK** *ONE* **BOX)**

    1 ☐ Automatic drip
    2 ☐ Electric percolator
    3 ☐ Stove top percolator
    4 ☐ Stove top dripolator
    ☐ Other (Specify): _____

2. **a.** Check all the brands of regular ground coffee that you have **ever used** at home. **(CHECK** *ALL* **THAT APPLY)**

    b. Check the **one** brand you **use most often.** **(CHECK** *ONE* **BOX)**

    c. Check all the brands you currently **have on hand.** **(CHECK** *ALL* **THAT APPLY)**

    d. Check the **one** brand you will probably **buy next.** **(CHECK** *ONE* **BOX)**

    e. For each brand please indicate how much you like the brand overall on a scale of **1** to **10** with "**1**" meaning **dislike it extremely** and "**10**" meaning **like it extremely.** Rate each brand, whether you have used the brand or not.

	"A" Ever Used	"B" Use Most Often	"C" Have On Hand	"D" Will Buy Next	Brand Rating "1" Dislike It Extremely ◄------------------► "10" Like It Extremely
Folgers	1☐	1☐	1☐	1☐	01☐ 02☐ 03☐ 04☐ 05☐ 06☐ 07☐ 08☐ 09☐ 10☐
Hills Brothers	2☐	2☐	2☐	2☐	01☐ 02☐ 03☐ 04☐ 05☐ 06☐ 07☐ 08☐ 09☐ 10☐
Maxwell House Regular	3☐	3☐	3☐	3☐	01☐ 02☐ 03☐ 04☐ 05☐ 06☐ 07☐ 08☐ 09☐ 10☐
Maxwell House Master Blend	4☐	4☐	4☐	4☐	01☐ 02☐ 03☐ 04☐ 05☐ 06☐ 07☐ 08☐ 09☐ 10☐
Yuban	5☐	5☐	5☐	5☐	01☐ 02☐ 03☐ 04☐ 05☐ 06☐ 07☐ 08☐ 09☐ 10☐
Other (Specify): _____	6☐	6☐	6☐	6☐	01☐ 02☐ 03☐ 04☐ 05☐ 06☐ 07☐ 08☐ 09☐ 10☐

3. What do you usually add to the coffee you drink? **(CHECK** *ALL* **THAT APPLY)**

    1 ☐ Nothing (I drink it black)
    2 ☐ A dairy creamer, like milk, cream, or Half and Half
    3 ☐ A non–dairy creamer, powdered or liquid
    4 ☐ Sugar
    5 ☐ Artificial sweetener
    ☐ Something else (Specify): _____

4. Are you the principal coffee **purchaser** for your household?

    1 ☐ Yes
    2 ☐ No

(continued)

Figure 12.3   *(Continued)*

6.   On a scale of **0** to **10** with "**0**" meaning **does not describe at all** and "**10**" meaning **describes completely**, please indicate how well the following statements describe **each** of the coffee brands listed below. Rate each brand, whether you have used the brand or not. Please write in the number which indicates your answer on the lines provided.

	Folgers	Hills Brothers	Maxwell House Regular	Maxwell House Master Blend	Yuban
Rich taste	____	____	____	____	____
Always fresh	____	____	____	____	____
Gets the day off to a good start	____	____	____	____	____
Full–bodied taste	____	____	____	____	____
Rich aroma in the cup	____	____	____	____	____

	Folgers	Hills Brothers	Maxwell House Regular	Maxwell House Master Blend	Yuban
Good value for the money	____	____	____	____	____
The best coffee to drink in the morning	____	____	____	____	____
Rich aroma in the can/bag	____	____	____	____	____
Smooth taste	____	____	____	____	____
Highest quality coffee	____	____	____	____	____

	Folgers	Hills Brothers	Maxwell House Regular	Maxwell House Master Blend	Yuban
Premium brand	____	____	____	____	____
Not bitter	____	____	____	____	____
The coffee that brightens my day the most	____	____	____	____	____
Costs more than the other brands	____	____	____	____	____
Strong taste	____	____	____	____	____

	Folgers	Hills Brothers	Maxwell House Regular	Maxwell House Master Blend	Yuban
Has no aftertaste	____	____	____	____	____
Economy brand	____	____	____	____	____
Rich aroma while brewing	____	____	____	____	____
The best ground coffee available	____	____	____	____	____
Enjoy drinking with a meal	____	____	____	____	____
Costs less than other brands	____	____	____	____	____

7.   Please indicate your **sex** and **age**.

1 ☐ Male
2 ☐ Female   Age:_____

Figure 12.3   *(Continued)*

5.   Please indicate how important it is to you that a ground coffee have each of the following characteristics. (CHECK *ONE* BOX FOR *EACH* CHARACTERISTIC)

	Not At All Important									Extremely Important
Rich taste	01☐	02☐	03☐	04☐	05☐	06☐	07☐	08☐	09☐	10☐
Always fresh	01☐	02☐	03☐	04☐	05☐	06☐	07☐	08☐	09☐	10☐
Gets the day off to a good start	01☐	02☐	03☐	04☐	05☐	06☐	07☐	08☐	09☐	10☐
Full–bodied taste	01☐	02☐	03☐	04☐	05☐	06☐	07☐	08☐	09☐	10☐
Rich aroma in the cup	01☐	02☐	03☐	04☐	05☐	06☐	07☐	08☐	09☐	10☐

	Not At All Important									Extremely Important
Good value for the money	01☐	02☐	03☐	04☐	05☐	06☐	07☐	08☐	09☐	10☐
The best coffee to drink in the morning	01☐	02☐	03☐	04☐	05☐	06☐	07☐	08☐	09☐	10☐
Rich aroma in the can/bag	01☐	02☐	03☐	04☐	05☐	06☐	07☐	08☐	09☐	10☐
Smooth taste	01☐	02☐	03☐	04☐	05☐	06☐	07☐	08☐	09☐	10☐
Highest quality coffee	01☐	02☐	03☐	04☐	05☐	06☐	07☐	08☐	09☐	10☐

	Not At All Important									Extremely Important
Premium brand	01☐	02☐	03☐	04☐	05☐	06☐	07☐	08☐	09☐	10☐
Not bitter	01☐	02☐	03☐	04☐	05☐	06☐	07☐	08☐	09☐	10☐
The coffee that brightens my day the most	01☐	02☐	03☐	04☐	05☐	06☐	07☐	08☐	09☐	10☐
Costs more than the other brands	01☐	02☐	03☐	04☐	05☐	06☐	07☐	08☐	09☐	10☐
Strong taste	01☐	02☐	03☐	04☐	05☐	06☐	07☐	08☐	09☐	10☐

	Not At All Important									Extremely Important
Has no aftertaste	01☐	02☐	03☐	04☐	05☐	06☐	07☐	08☐	09☐	10☐
Economy brand	01☐	02☐	03☐	04☐	05☐	06☐	07☐	08☐	09☐	10☐
Rich aroma while brewing	01☐	02☐	03☐	04☐	05☐	06☐	07☐	08☐	09☐	10☐
The best ground coffee available	01☐	02☐	03☐	04☐	05☐	06☐	07☐	08☐	09☐	10☐
Enjoy drinking with a meal	01☐	02☐	03☐	04☐	05☐	06☐	07☐	08☐	09☐	10☐
Costs less than other brands	01☐	02☐	03☐	04☐	05☐	06☐	07☐	08☐	09☐	10☐

Source: Contributed by NFO Research, Inc.

separate questions that reflect the possible frames of reference that could be used. For example:

How did you first happen to use Crest? _____

What is your primary reason for using it? _____

Do Respondents Have the Necessary Information?   The researcher should carefully examine each issue to determine whether the typical respondent can be expected to have the information sought. Respondents will give answers; whether the answers mean anything, though, is another matter. In one public opinion survey, the following question was asked:[4]

Which of the following statements most closely coincides with your opinion of the Metallic Metals Act?

- ☐   It would be a good move on the part of the United States.
- ☐   It would be a good thing, but it should be left to the individual states.
- ☐   It is all right for foreign countries, but it should not be required here.
- ☐   It is of no value at all.
- ☐   No opinion.

The proportion of respondents checking each alternative was, respectively, 21.4 percent, 58.6 percent, 15.7 percent, 4.3 percent, and 0.3 percent. The second alternative captures the prevailing sentiment, right? Wrong! There was no Metallic Metals Act, and the point of the example is that *most questions will get answers, but the real concern is whether the answers mean anything.*[5] In order for the answers to mean anything, the questions need to mean something to the respondent. This means that, first, the respondent needs to be informed with respect to the issue addressed by the question, and, second, the respondent must remember the information.

Consider the question, "How much does your family spend on groceries in a typical week?" Unless the respondent does the grocery shopping or the family operates with a fairly strict budget, he or she is unlikely to know. In a situation like this, it might be helpful to ask "filter questions" before this question to determine if the individual is indeed likely to have this information. A filter question might be, "Who does the grocery shopping in your family?" It is not unusual, for example, to use filter questions of the sort, "Do you have an opinion on . . . ?" before asking about the specific issue in question in opinion surveys. The empirical evidence indicates that providing a filter like this will typically increase the proportion responding "no opinion" by 20 to 25 percentage points.[6]

Not only should the individual have the information sought, but he or she should remember it. Our ability to remember various events is influenced by the event itself and its importance, the length of time since the event, and the presence or absence of stimuli that assist in recalling it. Important events are more easily remembered than are unimportant events. While many people might be able to remember who shot President John F. Kennedy or the make of the first car they ever owned, many of them will be unable to recall the particular television shows they watched last Wednesday evening. Returning to our toothpaste example, many people will be unable to recall the first brand they ever used, when they switched to their current brand, or why they switched. While the switching and use information might be very important to a *brand manager for toothpastes*, it is unimportant to most individuals, a condition we have to keep in mind continually when designing questionnaires. We need to put ourselves in the shoes of the respondent, not those of the product manager, when deciding whether the information is important enough for the individual to remember.

We also need to recognize that an individual's ability to remember an event is influenced by how long ago it happened. While we might recall the television programs we watched last evening, we might have much greater difficulty remembering those we watched last week on the same evening, and might find it all but impossible to recall our viewing pattern of a month ago. The moral of this is that if the event could be considered relatively unimportant to most individuals, we should ask about very recent occurrences of it.[7] For more important events, there are two forces, operating in opposite directions, that affect a respondent's ability to provide accurate answers to questions referring to some specified time period. **Telescoping error** is one; it is the tendency to remember an event as having occurred more recently than it did. **Recall loss** is the other; it is the tendency to forget the relatively important event entirely. The degree to which the two sources of error affect the accuracy of the reported information depends on the length of the period in question. For long periods, the telescoping effect is smaller, while the recall loss is greater. For short periods, the reverse is true: "Thus, for short reference periods, the telescoping error may outweigh the recall loss, while for long periods the reverse will apply; in between there will be a length of reference periods at which the two effects counterbalance each other."[8] Unfortunately, there is no single reference period that can be used to frame questions for all events, because what is optimal depends on the importance of the event to those involved.

Will Respondents Give the Information?   A situation sometimes arises in which respondents have the necessary information, but they will not give it. Their unwillingness may be a function of the amount of work involved in producing an answer, their ability to articulate an answer, or the sensitivity of the issue.

While a purchasing agent may be able to determine to the penny how much the company spent on cleaning compound last year, or the relative amount spent on each brand bought, the agent is unlikely to take the time to look up these data to reply to an unsolicited questionnaire. Questionnaire developers need to be constantly mindful of the amount of effort it might take respondents to give the information sought. When the effort is excessive, the respondent may either ignore the question or give only an approximate answer. It may be wiser to omit these types of questions, since they tend to irritate respondents and lessen their cooperation in responding to the rest of the survey.

Otherwise, the researcher needs to use a good deal of creative energy designing a mechanism that allows respondents to articulate their views. While respondents might not be able to express their preferences in car styling, for example, they should be able to indicate the style they like best when shown pictures of different body styles. General Motors used this picture scheme to determine preferences for grill designs when it found that respondents could not articulate their likes and dislikes.[9]

When an issue is embarrassing or otherwise threatening to respondents, they are also apt to refuse to cooperate. Such issues should be avoided whenever possible. If that is impossible because the issue is very significant to the study, then the researcher needs to pay close attention to how the issue is addressed, particularly with respect to question location and question phrasing. Income, for example, is often a sensitive issue. Respondents' willingness to cooperate depends on how and when the researcher asks for income data.

In general, it is better to address sensitive issues later, rather than earlier, in the survey. Most surveys will produce some initial mistrust in respondents. One has to

Telescoping error A type of error resulting from the fact that most people remember an event as having occurred more recently than it did.

Recall loss A type of error caused by a respondent's forgetting that an event happened at all.

overcome this skepticism and establish rapport. This is made easier when respondents have the opportunity to warm to the task by answering nonthreatening questions early in the interview, particularly questions that establish the legitimacy of the project.

When sensitive questions must be asked, it helps to consider ways to make them less threatening. Some helpful techniques in this regard follow:[10]

1. Hide the question in a group of other, more innocuous, questions.
2. Before asking the specific question, state that the behavior or attitude is not unusual; for example, "Recent studies show that one of every four households has trouble meeting its monthly financial obligations." This technique, known as the use of counterbiasing statements, makes it easier for the respondent to admit the potentially embarrassing behavior.
3. Phrase the question in terms of others and how they might feel or act; for example, "Do you think most people cheat on their income taxes? Why?" While respondents might readily reveal their attitudes toward cheating on income tax forms when asked this type of question, they might be very reluctant to do so if they were asked outright if they ever cheat on their taxes and why.
4. State the response in terms of a number of categories that the respondent may simply check. Instead of asking women for their age, for example, one could simply hand them a card with the age categories,

    A: 20–29   D: 50–59
    B: 30–39   E: 60+
    C: 40–49

    and ask them to respond with the appropriate letter.

5. Use the **randomized-response model,** in which the respondent answers one of several paired questions at random.[11] For example, the respondent may draw colored balls from an urn, being instructed to answer Question A if the ball is blue and Question B if the ball is red. The interviewer is unaware of the question being answered by the respondent, because he or she never sees the color of the ball drawn. Under these conditions the respondent is less likely to refuse to answer or to answer untruthfully. A study to investigate the incidence of shoplifting might pair the sensitive question, "Have you ever shoplifted?" with the innocuous question, "Is your birthday in January?" The incidence of shoplifting can still be estimated by using an appropriate statistical model, since the percentage of respondents answering each question is controlled by the proportion of red and blue balls in the urn. Since the researcher cannot determine specifically which respondents have admitted to shoplifting by this technique, though, there is no opportunity to examine such questions as whether shoplifting behavior was associated with any particular demographic characteristics.

Randomized-response model An interviewing technique in which potentially embarrassing and relatively innocuous questions are paired, and the question the respondent answers is randomly determined but is unknown to the interviewer.

Step 4: Determine Form of Response to Each Question

If a fixed-alternative format is chosen, researchers must decide whether to use questions that are open-ended or that have multiple choices, two choices, or perhaps represent a scale.

Open-ended question A question that respondents are free to answer in their own words rather than being limited to choosing from among a set of alternatives.

Open-Ended Questions   Respondents are free to reply to **open-ended questions** in their own words rather than being limited to choosing from a set of alternatives. The following are examples:

How old are you? _____

Do you think laws requiring passengers in motor vehicles to wear seat belt
needed? _____

Who sponsors the Monday-night football games? _____

Do you intend to purchase an automobile this year? _____

Why did you purchase a Zenith brand color television set? _____

Do you own a sewing machine? _____

These questions span the gamut of the types of primary data that could be collected—from demographic characteristics, through attitudes and intentions, to behavior. The open-ended question is indeed a versatile device.

Open-ended questions are often used to begin a questionnaire. The general feeling is that it is best to proceed from the general to the specific in constructing questionnaires. So an opening question like, "When you think of television sets, which brands come to mind?" gives some insight into the respondent's frame of reference and could be most helpful in interpreting the individual's replies to later questions. The open-ended question is also often used to probe for additional information. The probes "Why do you feel that way?" and "Please explain" are often used to seek elaboration of a respondent's reply.

In a fixed-alternative format, respondents choose their answer from a predetermined number of responses. Researchers generally use one of three types of fixed-alternative formats.

Multichotomous Questions   Despite the daunting name, every college student is probably familiar with the **multichotomous question.** From grade school to graduate school, students answer questions in the same format on multiple-choice exams. In a multichotomous question, respondents are asked to choose the one alternative from several choices that most closely reflects their position on the subject. Table 12.1, for example, presents some of the open-ended questions from the preceding list as multichotomous questions. Respondents would be instructed to check the box or boxes that apply.

The examples in Table 12.1 illustrate some of the difficulties encountered in using multiple-choice questions. None of the alternatives in the seat belt question, for example, may correctly capture the respondent's true feeling on the issue. The individual's opinion may be more complex. He may feel that seat belts should be required on school buses but not in private vehicles. Or she may think that seat belts should be required but that tickets for noncompliance should be issued only in conjunction with another traffic violation. The multiple-choice question does not permit individuals to elaborate on their true position but requires them to condense their complex attitude into a single statement. Of course, a well-designed series of multiple-choice questions could allow for such elaborations. Researchers must be careful, however, not to allow so many possible choices that the questionnaire becomes too long to be used effectively.

The seat belt question also illustrates a general problem in question design: should respondents be provided with a "don't know" or "no opinion" option? If a respondent truly does not know an answer, or has no opinion on an issue, he or she should obviously be allowed to state so. But should the option be *explicitly* provided to the respondent in the form of a "don't know" or "no opinion" category or by asking

Multichotomous question A fixed-alternative question in which respondents are asked to choose the alternative that most closely corresponds to their position on the subject.

les of Multichotomous Questions

	Television Purchase

Why did you purchase a Zenith brand color TV?

- ☐ Price was lower than other alternatives
- ☐ Feel it represents the highest quality
- ☐ Availability of local service
- ☐ Availability of a service contract
- ☐ Picture is better
- ☐ Warranty is better
- ☐ Other

20 – 29
- ☐ 30 – 39
- ☐ 40 – 49
- ☐ 50 – 59
- ☐ 60 or over

Seat Belt Legislation   **Telephone Use**

Do you think laws requiring passengers in motor vehicles to wear seat belts are needed?

- ☐ Definitely needed
- ☐ Probably needed
- ☐ Probably not needed
- ☐ Definitely not needed
- ☐ No opinion

How many long-distance telephone calls do you make in a typical week?

- ☐ Less than 5
- ☐ 5 – 10
- ☐ More than 10

a filter question like, "Do you have an opinion on . . . "? The arguments about the desirability of a neutral point or "no opinion" category center on the need for data accuracy versus the desire to have as many respondents as possible answer the question at issue.

Those against including a "no opinion" answer argue that most respondents are unlikely to be truly neutral on an issue. Instead of providing them an easy way out, critics say, it is much better to have them think about the issue so that they can frame their preference, however slight it may be. That is much better than allowing the researcher to infer the majority opinion from the responses of those taking a stand on the issue. The argument for including a neutral or "no opinion" category among the responses claims that forcing a respondent to make a choice when his or her preference is fuzzy or nonexistent simply introduces response error into the results. Further, it makes it harder for respondents to answer, and it may turn them off to the whole survey. The jury is still out with respect to which form better captures respondents' true position on an issue. There is no question, however, that the two alternatives can produce widely differing proportions regarding the number holding a neutral view, potentially in the range of 10 to 50 percent.[12]

For example, in one fairly large study using four-point versus five-point purchase-intention scales, which were the same except for the provision of the neutral category in the five-point scale, it was found that if one used only the extreme points (i.e., definitely will buy/definitely will not buy) for evaluating a new product or idea, *either* scale could be used. On the other hand, the researcher who wanted to use two categories as the percentage likely to buy the product (i.e., definitely will buy or probably will buy) would find a difference in the two scales, with the four-point scale providing more positive responses than the five-point scale.[13]

The television set purchase question in Table 12.1 illustrates a number of problems associated with multiple-choice questions. First, the list of reasons cited for purchasing a Zenith color television may not exhaust the reasons that could have been used by the respondent. The person may have purchased a Zenith out of loyalty to a friend who owns the local Zenith distributorship or because she really supports the "buy locally" plea advanced by many small-town chambers of commerce. The "other" response category attempts to solve this problem. If a great many respondents check the "other" category, however, they could render the study useless. Thus, the burden is on the researcher to make the list of alternatives in a multiple-choice question exhaustive. This may entail a good deal of prior research into the phenomenon that is to serve as the subject of a multiple-choice question.

Unless the respondent is instructed to check all alternatives that apply, or is to rank the alternatives in order of importance, the multiple-choice question also demands that the alternatives be mutually exclusive. The income categories of $5,000–$10,000 and $10,000–$15,000 violate this principle. A respondent with an income of $10,000 would not know which alternative to check. A legitimate response with respect to the color television purchase question might include several of the alternatives listed. The respondent thought the picture, warranty, and price were all more attractive on the Zenith than they were on other makes. Thus, the instructions would necessarily have to be, "Check the most important reason," "Check all those reasons that apply," or "Rank all the reasons that apply from most important to least important."

A third difficulty with the television purchase question is its great number of alternative responses. The list should be exhaustive. Yet the number of alternative statements an individual can process simultaneously appears to be limited. In one early study, the researchers presented each respondent with a card with six alternative statements. After each respondent had made his or her choice, the card was immediately replaced with another. On the second card, two of the six statements had been changed, and one statement from the original list was omitted. Yet only one-half of the respondents "could identify the changes, and a mere handful located the omission."[14] The meaning of all this is that in designing multiple-choice questions, the researcher should remain aware of human beings' limited data-processing capabilities. Perhaps a series of questions is more appropriate than one question. If there are a great many alternatives to a single question, then they should be shown to respondents using cards, and not simply read to them.

The fourth weakness of the television purchase question in Table 12.1 is that it is susceptible to order bias. That is, the responses are likely to be affected by the order in which the alternatives are presented. Research Window 12.1, for example, shows how the distribution of responses to the same questions was affected by the order in which the alternatives were listed on two versions of a mail questionnaire. That the three questions produced statistically significant distributions of replies is especially noteworthy because order bias is least likely to occur in mail questionnaires, because respondents can see all the response categories. In point of fact, response order bias is typically much greater in telephone surveys or interviews in which the structured responses are read to the respondents. The recommended procedure for combating this order, or position, bias is to prepare several forms of the questionnaire, or several cards, if cards are used to list the alternatives. The order in which the alternatives are listed is then altered from form to form. If each alternative appears once at the extremes of the list, once in the middle, and once somewhere in between, the researcher can feel reasonably comfortable that the possible effects of position bias have been neutralized.[15]

Research Window 12.1
How the Order in Which the Alternatives Are Listed Affects the Distribution of Replies

[Compared to a year ago] the amount of time spent watching television by my household is . . .

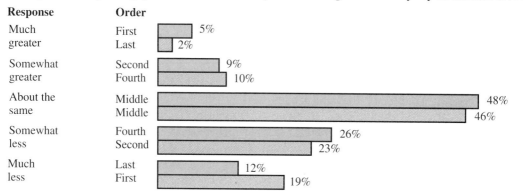

[Compared to a year ago] my household eats out at restaurants . . .

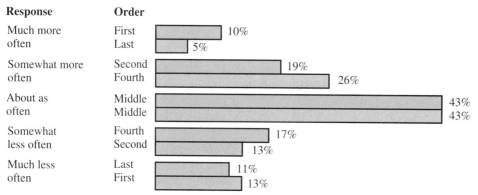

Most home repair or improvement projects completed in my home during the past years have been completed by . . .   [Base: Those completing a project.]

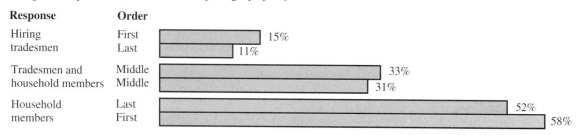

Source: "An Examination of Order Bias," *Research on Research*, No. 1 (Chicago: Market Facts, Inc., undated). Reprinted with permission.

The long-distance telephone call example in Table 12.1 illustrates another problem with multiple-choice questions when they are used to get at the frequency of various behaviors. The range of the categories used in the question seems to cue respondents about how they should reply. That is, the response scale categories themselves affect subjects' reports of the frequency with which they engage in the behavior. A scale with the three categories,

☐   Less than 10
☐   10–20
☐   More than 20

would likely produce a different picture of the frequency with which these same respondents make long-distance telephone calls. It seems that respondents make judgments about the researcher's knowledge or expectations from the categories and then respond accordingly. Specifically, they seem reluctant to report behaviors that are unusual in the context of the response scale—namely, those that constitute the extreme categories.[16] A general strategy for combating this tendency is to use open-ended answer formats when obtaining data on behavioral frequencies.

Dichotomous question
A fixed-alternative question in which respondents are asked to indicate which of two alternative responses most closely corresponds to their position on a subject.

Dichotomous Questions   Also a fixed-alternative question, the **dichotomous question** is one in which there are only two alternatives listed, as in the following examples:

Do you think laws requiring passengers in motor vehicles to wear seat belts are needed?
☐   Yes
☐   No

Do you intend to purchase an automobile this year?
☐   Yes
☐   No

We have already seen how the first of these questions could also be handled as a multiple-choice question. The second could also be given a multichotomous structure. Instead of simply presenting the yes-no alternatives, the list could be framed as "Definitely intend to buy," "Probably will buy," "Probably will not buy," "Definitely intend not to buy," and "Undecided." Dichotomous questions can often be framed as multichotomous questions, and vice versa. (The two possess similar advantages and disadvantages, which were reviewed earlier when discussing structured questions. The advantages and disadvantages will not be repeated here.) The dichotomous question offers the ultimate in ease of coding and tabulation, and this probably accounts for its being the most commonly used type of question in communication studies.

One special problem with the dichotomous question is that the response can well depend on how the question is framed. This is true, of course, of all questions, but with the dichotomous question it represents a special problem. Consider two alternative questions:

Do you think that gasoline will be more expensive or less expensive next year than it is now?
☐   More expensive
☐   Less expensive

Do you think that gasoline will be less expensive or more expensive next year than it is now?

☐   Less expensive
☐   More expensive

Now the questions appear identical, and certainly we might want to expand each to include categories for "no opinion" and "about the same." The fact remains, though, that the two questions will elicit different responses.[17] The simple switching of the positions of "More expensive" and "Less expensive" can affect the response an individual gives. Which, then, is the correct wording?

As mentioned earlier, one generally accepted procedure for combating this order bias is to employ a split ballot. One phrasing is used on one-half of the questionnaires, and the alternative phrasing is employed on the other one-half of the questionnaires. The averaged percentages from the two forms should then cancel out any biases.

Scales   Another type of fixed-alternative question is the question that employs a scale to capture the response. For instance, when inquiring about the various sewing machine features that home seamstresses use, the following question might be asked:

How often do you use the zigzag stitch on your machine?

☐   Never
☐   Occasionally
☐   Sometimes
☐   Often

In this form, the question is a multichotomous question. However, the responses also represent a scale of use. The scale nature of the question would be more obvious, perhaps, if the following form were used to secure the replies:

Never	Occasionally	Sometimes	Often

The advantage of this scheme is that the descriptors or categories could be presented at the top of the page, and a number of possible features could be listed along the left margin, for example, decorative stitch, blind stitch, built-in button-holer, and so on. The respondent would then be instructed to designate the frequency of use for each feature. The instruction would need to be given only once, at the beginning, and thus a great deal of information could be secured from the respondent in a short period of time.

Step 5: Determine Wording of Each Question

Step 5 in the questionnaire development process involves the phrasing of each question. This is a critical task, in that poor phrasing of a question can cause respondents to refuse to answer it even though they agreed to cooperate in the study. Poor phrasing may also cause respondents to answer a question incorrectly, either on purpose or because of misunderstanding. The first condition, known as **item nonresponse,** can create a great many problems in analyzing the data. The second condition produces measurement error in that the recorded or obtained score does not equal the respondent's true score on the issue.[18]

Item nonresponse
A source of nonsampling error that arises when a respondent agrees to an interview but refuses, or is unable, to answer specific questions.

Experienced researchers know that the phrasing of a question can directly affect the responses to it. One humorous anecdote in this regard involves two priests, a Dominican and a Jesuit, who are discussing whether it is a sin to smoke and pray at the same time. "After failing to reach a conclusion, each goes off to consult his respective superior. The next week they meet again. The Dominican says, 'Well, what did your superior say?' The Jesuit responds, 'He said it was all right.' 'That's funny,' the Dominican replies, 'my superior said it was a sin.' Jesuit: 'What did you ask him?' Reply: 'I asked him if it was all right to smoke while praying.' 'Oh,' says the Jesuit, 'I asked my superior if it was all right to pray while smoking.' "[19]

While researchers recognize that question wording can affect the answers obtained, there are, unfortunately, few basic principles researchers can rely upon to develop bias-free ways of framing a question. Instead, the literature is replete with rules of thumb. Although these rules of thumb are often easier to state than to practice, researchers need to be aware of them.

Use Simple Words   Because most researchers are more highly educated than the typical questionnaire respondent, they tend to use words with which they themselves are familiar but that are not understood by many respondents. This is a difficult problem because it is not easy to dismiss what one knows and put oneself instead in the respondent's shoes when trying to determine appropriate vocabulary. A significant proportion of the population, for example, does not understand the word *Caucasian*, although most researchers do.[20] The researcher needs to be constantly aware that the average person in the United States has a high school, not a college, education and that many people have difficulty in coping with such routine tasks as making change, reading job notices, or completing a driver's license application blank. Even common words can cause difficulty on questionnaires as Research Window 12.2 indicates. The best advice is to keep the words simple.

Avoid Ambiguous Words and Questions   Not only should the words and questions be simple, they should also be unambiguous. Consider again the multichotomous question:

How often do you use the zigzag stitch on your machine?
- ☐   Never
- ☐   Occasionally
- ☐   Sometimes
- ☐   Often

For all practical purposes, the replies to this question would be worthless. The words *occasionally*, *sometimes*, and *often* are ambiguous. For example, to one respondent, the word *often* might mean "every time I sew." To another it might mean, "yes, I use it when I have the specific need. This happens on about one of every four projects." Thus, while the question would get answers, it would generate little real understanding of the frequency of use of the zigzag stitch. A much better strategy would be to provide concrete alternatives for the respondent, such as the following:

- ☐   Never use
- ☐   Use on approximately one of ten projects
- ☐   Use on approximately one of three projects
- ☐   Use on almost every project

Research Window 12.2
A Rogues' Gallery of Problem Words

"Use Simple Words!" "Use unambiguous words!" Students of questionnaire design are accustomed to hearing those rules cited loudly and often. But, unfortunately, some of the simplest words may still be ambiguous in meaning. Here's a short list of words that may cause trouble if you're not sensitive to their possibilities for misinterpretation.

You

"You" is extremely popular with question worders, since it is implicated in every question they ask. In most cases "you" gives no trouble, since it is clear that it refers to the second person singular. However, and here is the problem, the word sometimes may have a collective meaning. Consider the question:

> How many television sets did you repair last month?

The question seems to be straightforward, until it is asked of a repairman in a large shop, who counters with, "Who do you mean, me or the whole shop?"

Sometimes "you" needs the emphasis of "you yourself," and sometimes it just isn't the word to use, as in the above situation, where the entire shop is meant.

All

"All" is one of those dead-giveaway words. From your own experience with true-false exams, you probably know that it is safe to count almost every all-inclusive statement as false. That is, you have learned that in such tests it is safe to follow the idea that all statements containing "all" are false, including this one. Some people have the same negative reaction to opinion questions that hinge upon all-inclusive or all-exclusive words. They may be generally in agreement with a proposition, but nevertheless hesitate to accept the extreme idea of *all*, *always*, *each*, *every*, *never*, *nobody*, *only*, *none*, or *sure*.

Bad

In itself the word "bad" is not at all bad for question wording. It conveys the meaning desired and is satisfactory as an alternative in a "good or bad" two-way question. Experience seems to indicate, however, that people are generally less willing to criticize than they are to praise. Since it is difficult to get them to state their negative views, sometimes the critical side needs to be softened. For example, after asking, "What things are good about your job?" it might seem perfectly natural to ask, "What things are bad about it?" But if we want to lean over backwards to get as many criticisms as we can, we may be wise not to apply the "bad" stigma, but to ask, "What things are not so good about it?"

Dinner

"Dinner," the main meal of the day, comes at noon with some families and in some areas. Elsewhere it is the evening meal. The question should not assume that it is either the one or the other.

Government

"Government" is one of those words heavily loaded with emotional concepts. It is sometimes used as a definite word meaning the federal government, sometimes as an inclusive term for federal, state, and local government, sometimes as an abstract idea, and

Source: Stanley L. Payne, *The Art of Asking Questions* (Princeton: Princeton University Press, 1979), pp. 158–176.

When designing a questionnaire, one must be aware of words like "dinner," which mean one thing to some people (the noon meal in this case) and something else to others (the evening meal).

Source: Grant Wood, American, 1891–1942; Dinner for Threshers, 1934; Oil on masonite, 20″ × 81″. Gift of Mr. and Mrs. John D. Rockefeller 3rd, 1979.7.105. Reproduced by permission of The Fine Arts Museums of San Francisco.

sometimes as the party in power as distinct from the opposition party. The trouble is that the respondent does not always know which "government" is meant. One person may have a different idea from another. It is best to specify if we want all respondents to answer with the same government in mind.

Like

"Like" is on the problem list only because it is sometimes used to introduce an example. The problem with bringing an example into a question is that the respondent's attention may be directed toward the particular example and away from the general issue which it is meant only to illustrate. The use of examples may sometimes be necessary, but the possible hazard should always be kept in mind. The choice of an example can affect the answers to the question—in fact, it may materially change the question, as in these two examples:

Do you think that leafy vegetables like spinach should be in the daily diet?
Do you think that leafy vegetables like lettuce should be in the daily diet?

Where

The frames of reference in answers to a "where" question may vary greatly. Consider the possible answers from this simple question:

Where did you read that?

Three of the many possible answers are,

In the *New York Times*.
At home in front of the fire.
In an advertisement.

Despite the seemingly wide variety of these three answers, some respondents could probably have stated them all: "In an ad in the *New York Times* while I was at home sitting in front of the fire."

Another way to avoid ambiguity in asking about the frequency of behavior is to ask when the behavior last occurred. Our earlier question might be framed in the following way:

When you last sewed, did you use the zigzag stitch?
- ☐ Yes
- ☐ No
- ☐ Can't recall

The proportion responding yes would then be used to infer the frequency with which the zigzag stitch was used, while the follow-up question among all those responding yes, "For what purpose?" would give insight as to how respondents are using it. Among the people responding, there will be some who normally use the zigzag stitch but did not use it the last time they sewed. There will be others who do not normally use that particular stitch but did use it the last time they sewed. These variations should cancel each other out if a large enough sample of respondents is used.

The total sample should provide a good indication of the proportion of times the zigzag stitch is used, and for what purposes. The researcher, in effect, relies on the sample to provide insight into how frequently the phenomenon occurs, rather than relying on a specific question that may contain ambiguous alternatives. In such cases it is important that the sample be large enough so that the proportions can be estimated with the appropriate degree of confidence.

Leading question
A question framed so as to give the respondent a clue as to how he or she should answer.

Avoid Leading Questions   A question framed so as to give the respondent a clue as to how he or she should answer is a **leading question.** Consider this question:

Do you feel that limiting taxes by law is an effective way to stop the government from picking your pocket every payday?
- ☐ Yes
- ☐ No
- ☐ Undecided

This was one of three questions in an unsolicited questionnaire that the author received as part of a study sponsored by the National Tax Limitation Committee. The committee intended to make the results of the poll available to Congress and to state legislators. Given the implied purpose, it is probably not surprising to see the leading words "picking your pocket" being used in this question, or the leading word "gouge" being used in another question. What is especially unfortunate is that it is unlikely that the questions themselves accompanied the report to Congress. Rather, it is more likely that the report suggested that some high percentage (e.g., 90 percent of those surveyed) favored laws limiting taxes. Conclusion: Congress should pay attention to the wishes of the people and pass such laws.

One sees instances of this phenomenon every day in the newspaper. The public is treated to a discussion of the results of this or that study with respect to how the American people feel on issues but is not shown the questionnaire. One interesting report in this regard was published during New York City's financial crisis.

Question: What percentage of the American public favors federal aid for New York City? Choose one of the following: a. 69; b. 55; c. 42; d. 15; e. all of the above.

The correct answer is "all of the above," because each of these results represented an outcome of a survey taken at the time.

One apparent key to the different responses was whether the aid was described as a "bailout," "federal funds," or "the federal government guaranteeing loans."[21]

The correct phrasing of this or almost any question could of course be argued. The important point for both researchers and managers to remember is that the phrasing finally chosen will affect the responses secured. If one truly wants an accurate picture of the situation, one needs to avoid leading the respondent as to how he or she should answer.

Avoid Implicit Alternatives   An alternative that is not expressed in the options is an **implicit alternative.** In one study, researchers wanted to know the attitudes of nonworking wives toward the idea of having a job outside the home. They asked two random samples of housewives the following two questions:[22]

*Would you like to have a job, if this were possible?*_____

*Would you prefer to have a job, or do you prefer to do just your housework?*_____

While the two questions appear very similar, they produced dramatically different responses. In the first version, 19 percent of the housewives said they would not like to have a job. In the second version, 68 percent said they would prefer not to have one—over three and one-half times as many as in the first version. The difference in the two questions is that the second version makes explicit the alternative only implied in the first version. As a general rule, one should avoid implicit alternatives unless there is a special reason for including them. Thus, the second version is better than the first. Further, because the order in which the alternatives appear can affect the responses, one should rotate the order of the options in samples of questionnaires.

Avoid Implicit Assumptions   Questions are frequently framed so that there is an **implicit assumption** as to what will happen as a consequence. The question, "Are you in favor of placing price controls on crude oil?" will elicit different responses from individuals, depending on whether they think price controls will result in rationing, long lines at the pump, or lower prices. A better way of stating this question is to make explicit the possible consequence(s). For example, the question could be altered to ask, "Are you in favor of placing price controls on crude oil if it would produce gas rationing?"

Figure 12.4 shows what can happen when the consequences are explicitly stated in a question. Version B makes the implied consequence in Version A explicit; the only way the seat belt law could be effective would be if there were some penalty for not complying with it. Yet, when there was no explicit statement about what would happen if a person did not comply with the proposed law, 73 percent were in favor of it. When people faced the prospect of a fine for noncompliance, only 50 percent favored a mandatory seat belt law.

Avoid Generalizations and Estimates   Questions should always be asked in specific, rather than general, terms. Consider the question, "How many salespeople did you see last year?" which might be asked of a purchasing agent. To answer the question, the agent would probably estimate how many salespeople call in a typical week and would multiply this estimate by 52. This burden should not be placed on the agent. Rather, a more accurate estimate would be obtained if the purchasing agent were asked, "How many representatives called last week?" and the researcher multiplied the answer provided by 52.

Implicit alternative
An alternative answer that is not expressed in a question's options.

Implicit assumption
A problem that occurs when a question is not framed so as to explicitly state the consequences, and thus it elicits different responses from individuals who *assume* different consequences.

Figure 12.4   *Illustration of What Can Happen When an Implied Assumption Is Made Explicit*

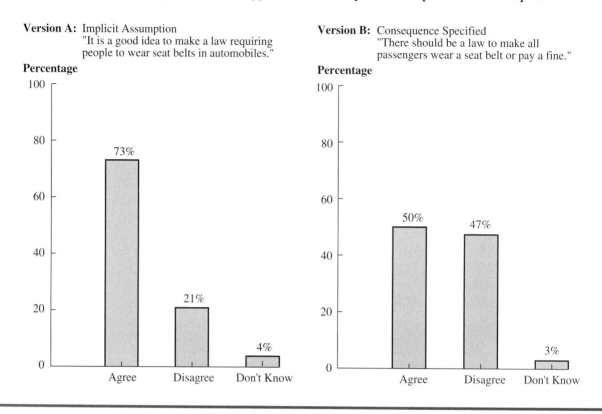

Version A: Implicit Assumption
"It is a good idea to make a law requiring people to wear seat belts in automobiles."

Version B: Consequence Specified
"There should be a law to make all passengers wear a seat belt or pay a fine."

Source: Albert J. Ungar, "Projectable Surveys: Separating Useful Data from Illusions," *Business Marketing*, 71 (December 1986), p. 90.

Double-barreled question A question that calls for two responses and thereby creates confusion for the respondent.

Avoid Double-Barreled Questions   A question that calls for two responses and thereby creates confusion for the respondent is a **double-barreled question.** The question, "What is your evaluation of the price and convenience offered by XYZ's catalog showroom?" is asking respondents to react to two separate attributes by which the showroom could be described. The respondent might feel the prices are attractive but the location is not, for example, and thereby is placed in a dilemma as to how to respond. The problem is particularly acute if the individual must choose an answer from a fixed set of alternatives. One can and should avoid double-barreled questions by splitting the initial question into two separate questions. A useful indicator that two questions might be needed is the use of the word *and* in the initial wording of the question.

Step 6: Determine Question Sequence

Once the form of response and specific wording for each question have been decided, the researcher is ready to begin putting them together into a questionnaire. The researcher needs to recognize immediately that the order in which the questions are presented can be crucial to the success of the research effort. Again, there are no hard-and-fast principles but only rules of thumb to guide the researcher in this activity.

Use Simple and Interesting Opening Questions   The first questions asked the respondent are crucial. If respondents cannot answer them easily or if they find them uninteresting or threatening in any way, they may refuse to complete the remainder of the questionnaire. Thus, it is essential that the first few questions be simple, interesting, and in no way threatening to respondents. Questions that ask respondents for their opinion on some issue are often good openers, as most people like to feel their opinion is important. Sometimes it is helpful to use such an opener even when responses to it will not be analyzed, since opinion questions are often effective in relaxing respondents and securing their cooperation.

Funnel approach
An approach to question sequencing that gets its name from its shape, starting with broad questions and progressively narrowing down the scope.

Use Funnel Approach   One approach to question sequencing is the **funnel approach,** which gets its name from its shape, starting with broad questions and progressively narrowing down the scope. If respondents are to be asked, "What improvements are needed in the company's service policy?" and also, "How do you like the quality of service?" the first question needs to be asked before the second. Otherwise, quality of service will be emphasized disproportionately in the responses simply because it is fresh in the respondents' minds.

There should also be some logical order to the questions. This means that sudden changes in topics and jumping around from topic to topic should be avoided. Transitional devices are sometimes necessary to smooth the flow when a change in subject matter occurs. Sometimes researchers will insert filter questions as a way to change the direction of the questioning. Most often, however, researchers will insert a brief explanation as a way of bridging a change in subject matter.

Branching question
A technique used to direct respondents to different places in a questionnaire, based on their response to the question at hand.

Design Branching Questions with Care   A direction as to where to go next in the questionnaire based on the answer to a preceding question is called a **branching question.** For example, the initial question might be, "Have you bought a car within the last six months?" If the respondent answers yes, he or she is then instructed to go to another place in the questionnaire, where questions are asked about specific details of the purchase. Someone replying no to the same question would be directed to skip the question relating to the details of the purchase. The advantage to branching questions is that they reduce the number of alternatives that are needed in individual questions, while ensuring that those respondents capable of supplying the needed information still have an opportunity to do so. Those for whom a question is irrelevant are simply directed around it.

Branching questions and directions are much easier to develop for telephone or personal interviews, especially for these administered through computer-assisted interviewing, than for mail surveys. With mail questionnaires the number of branching questions needs to be kept to an absolute minimum so that respondents do not become confused when responding, or refuse to cooperate because the task becomes too difficult. While they can be used more liberally with telephone and personal interview surveys, branching questions still need to be designed with care, since the evidence indicates that branching instructions increase the rate of item nonresponse for items immediately following the branch.[23] When using branching questions, it is generally good practice to (1) develop a flow chart of the logical possibilities and then prepare the branching questions and instructions to follow the flow chart, (2) place the question that follows the branch as close as possible to the original question, so as to minimize the amount of page-flipping that is necessary, and (3) order the branching questions so that respondents cannot anticipate what additional information is required.[24]

The last point can be illustrated by a questionnaire seeking information about small appliance ownership. A skillfully designed questionnaire might begin by asking if a respondent owns any of a certain list of small appliances. If she answers yes to any, the researcher may then go on to ask the brand name, the store where purchased, and so on, for each. If instead the researcher had begun by asking, "Do you own a food processor?" and followed up with questions about brand, price, and so on, the respondent would soon recognize that "yes" answers to subsequent questions about the ownership of other appliances would inevitably lead to many other questions, and she may decide it is less taxing to say no in the first place.

Ask for Classification Information Last   The typical questionnaire contains two types of information: basic information and classification information. *Basic information* refers to the subject of the study, for example, intentions or attitudes of respondents. *Classification information* refers to the other data we collect to classify respondents so as to extract more information about the phenomenon of interest. For instance, we might be interested in determining if a respondent's attitudes toward the need for seat belt legislation are in any way affected by the person's income. Income here would be a classification variable. Demographic/socioeconomic characteristics of respondents are often used as classification variables for understanding the results.

The proper questionnaire sequence is to present questions securing basic information first and those seeking classification information last. There is a logical reason for this. The basic information is most critical. Without it, there is no study. Thus, the researcher should not risk alienating the respondent by asking a number of personal questions before getting to the heart of the study, since it is not unusual for personal questions to alienate respondents most. Respondents who readily offer their opinions about television programming may balk when asked about their income. An early question aimed at determining their income may affect the whole tone of the interview or other communication. It is best to avoid this possibility by placing the classification information at the end.

Place Difficult or Sensitive Questions Late in the Questionnaire   The basic information itself can also present some sequence problems. Some of the questions may be sensitive. Early questions should not be, for the reasons we mentioned earlier. If respondents feel threatened, they may refuse to participate in the study. Thus, sensitive questions should be placed in the body of the questionnaire and intertwined and hidden among some not-so-sensitive ones. Once respondents have become involved in the study, they are less likely to react negatively or refuse to answer when delicate questions are posed.

Step 7: Determine Physical Characteristics of Questionnaire

The physical characteristics of the questionnaire can affect the accuracy of the replies that are obtained. In one study, researchers asked consumers if they had purchased certain products. If they answered yes, they were then asked the specific brand of the product they had purchased. Two versions of the question seeking brand information were used, Form A and Form B. The only significant difference in the questions was that a set of parentheses was provided in Form B for the "other brand" category, whereas Form A had a line where respondents wrote in the name of those brands not on the original list. The difference in results regarding the percentage of households owning the two brands, F and G, among the 4,000 households surveyed was remarkable for all three products, as Table 12.2 indicates. Form B results were within

Table 12.2   *Brand Share among Owners*

| | Percentage Owning Brand | | |
	Form A	Form B	Net Difference
Product X			
Brand F	30	3	27
Brand G	47	71	24
Product Y			
Brand F	18	2	16
Brand G	27	41	14
Product Z			
Brand F	27	3	24
Brand G	35	58	23

a couple of percentage points of the results from the survey conducted one year earlier. It seems that respondents counted up from the bottom of the question when checking the brand category, and that the line on which the other brand was to be entered in Form A was too close to the ruled line separating this question from the next one.[25] In sum, the physical layout in Form A created confusion and produced inaccurate data.

The physical characteristics of a questionnaire can also affect how respondents react to it and the ease with which the replies can be processed. In determining the physical format of the questionnaire, a researcher wants to do those things that help get the respondent to accept the questionnaire, and facilitate handling and control by the researcher.

Securing Acceptance of the Questionnaire   The physical appearance of the questionnaire can influence respondents' cooperation. This is particularly true with mail questionnaires, but it applies as well to questionnaires used in personal interviews. If the questionnaire looks sloppy, respondents are likely to feel the study is unimportant and hence refuse to cooperate despite researchers' assurance that it is important. If the study is important, and there is no reason to conduct it if it is not, make the questionnaire reflect that importance. This means that good-quality paper should be used for the questionnaires. It also means that the questionnaires should be printed, not mimeographed or otherwise photocopied.

The introduction to the research can also affect acceptance of the questionnaire. With mail questionnaires, the cover letter serves to introduce the study. It is very important that the cover letter convince the designated respondent to cooperate. Good cover letters are rarely written in a hurry; rather, they usually require a series of painstaking rewrites to get the wording just so. Research Window 12.3 lists important content considerations in the construction of cover letters.[26] With personal and telephone interviews, the introduction to the research is necessarily shorter. Nonetheless, the introduction needs to convince respondents about the importance of the research and the importance of their participation. Typically, this means

Research Window 12.3
Contents of and Sample Cover Letter for a Mail Questionnaire

Panel A: Contents

1. Personal communication.
2. Asking a favor.
3. Importance of the research project and its purpose.
4. Importance of the recipient.
5. Importance of the replies in general.
6. Importance of the replies when the reader is not qualified to answer most questions.
7. How the recipient may benefit from this research.
8. Completing the questionnaire will take only a short time.
9. The questionnaire can be answered easily.
10. A stamped reply envelope is enclosed.
11. How recipient was selected.
12. Answers are anonymous or confidential.
13. Offer to send report on results of survey.
14. Note of urgency.
15. Appreciation of sender.
16. Importance of sender.
17. Importance of the sender's organization.
18. Description and purpose of incentive.
19. Avoiding bias.
20. Style.
21. Format and appearance.
22. Brevity.

Source: Paul L. Erdos, *Professional Mail Surveys* (Melbourne, Fla: Robert E. Krieger Publishing Co., Inc., 1983), pp. 102–103. Reprinted with permission.

describing how they can benefit from it, the fact that their replies will be confidential, and the incentive, if any, that they will receive for participating.

It is also a good idea to include the name of the sponsoring organization and the name of the project on the first page or on the cover if the questionnaire is in book form. Both of these lend credibility to the study. However, since awareness of the sponsoring firm may bias respondents' answers, many firms use fictitious names for the sponsoring organization. This practice also helps eliminate phone calls or other inquiries from respondents asking for the results of the study.

Facilitate Handling and Control   Several steps that facilitate handling and control by the researcher also contribute to acceptance of the questionnaire by respondents. These include questionnaire size and layout and question sequencing.

Questionnaire size is important.[27] Smaller questionnaires are better than larger ones if—and this is a big "if"—they do not appear crowded. Smaller questionnaires seem easier to complete; they appear to take less time and are less likely to cause respondents to refuse to participate. They are easier to carry in the field and are easier to sort, count, and file in the office than are larger questionnaires.

If, on the other hand, smaller size is gained at the expense of an uncluttered appearance, these advantages are lost. A crowded questionnaire has a bad appearance, leads to errors in data collection, and results in shorter and less informative replies for both self-administered and interviewer-administered questionnaires. Researchers have found, for example, that the more lines or space left for recording the response to open-ended questions, the more extensive the reply will be. Similarly, the more information a respondent is given about the kind of information being sought, the better the reply is apt to be.[28] Both of these techniques, however, increase the physical size of the questionnaire needed for the study.

Research Window 12.3 (*Continued*)

The numbers refer to the corresponding items in Panel A.

Panel B: Sample

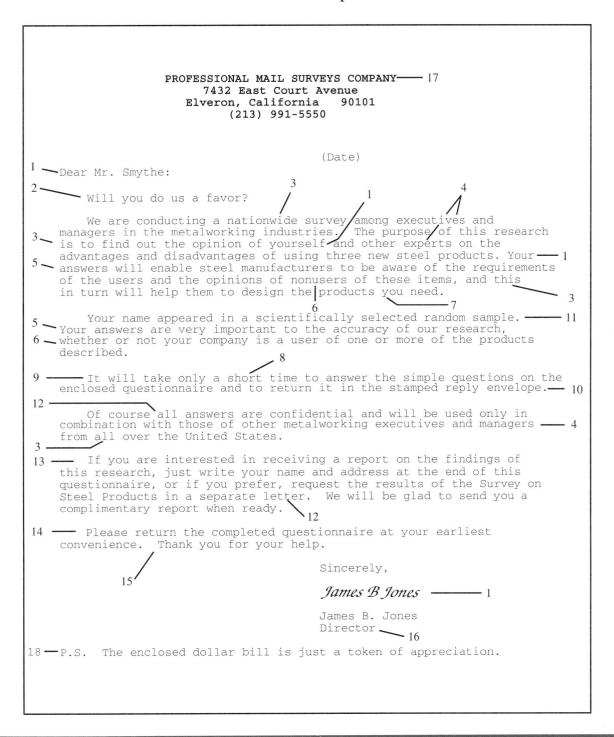

PROFESSIONAL MAIL SURVEYS COMPANY —— 17
7432 East Court Avenue
Elveron, California   90101
(213) 991-5550

(Date)

1 —— Dear Mr. Smythe:

2 ——— Will you do us a favor?

      3   1   4

We are conducting a nationwide survey among executives and
3 — managers in the metalworking industries. The purpose of this research
is to find out the opinion of yourself and other experts on the
5 — advantages and disadvantages of using three new steel products. Your —— 1
answers will enable steel manufacturers to be aware of the requirements
of the users and the opinions of nonusers of these items, and this
in turn will help them to design the products you need. —— 3

      6   7

5 — Your name appeared in a scientifically selected random sample. —— 11
Your answers are very important to the accuracy of our research,
6 — whether or not your company is a user of one or more of the products
described.

      8

9 ——— It will take only a short time to answer the simple questions on the
enclosed questionnaire and to return it in the stamped reply envelope.—— 10

12 ———

Of course all answers are confidential and will be used only in
combination with those of other metalworking executives and managers —— 4
from all over the United States.

3 ———

13 —— If you are interested in receiving a report on the findings of
this research, just write your name and address at the end of this
questionnaire, or if you prefer, request the results of the Survey on
Steel Products in a separate letter. We will be glad to send you a
complimentary report when ready. —— 12

14 —— Please return the completed questionnaire at your earliest
convenience. Thank you for your help.

Sincerely,

15 /

James B Jones ——— 1

James B. Jones
Director —— 16

18 — P.S. The enclosed dollar bill is just a token of appreciation.

While post-card size probably represents the lower limit, letter size probably represents the upper limit to the size of an individual page in a questionnaire. When the questions will not all fit on the front and back of one sheet, multiple sheets need to be used. When this happens, one should make the questionnaire into a booklet rather than stapling or paper-clipping the pages together. The method of binding not only facilitates handling but also reinforces an image of quality. So does numbering the questions, which also promotes respondent cooperation, particularly when branching questions are employed. Without numbered questions, instructions as to how to proceed (e.g., "If the answer to Question 2 is yes, please go to Question 5") cannot be used. Even with numbered questions, though, it is helpful if the respondent can be directed by arrows to the appropriate next question after a branching question. Another technique researchers have found useful with branch-type questions is the use of color coding on the questionnaire, where the next question to which the respondent is directed matches the color of the space in which the answer to the branching or filter question was recorded.

Numbering the questions also makes it easier to edit, code, and tabulate the responses.[29] It also helps if the questionnaires themselves are numbered. This makes it easier to keep track of the questionnaires and to determine which ones, if any, are lost. It also makes it easier to monitor interviewer performance and to detect interviewer biases, if any. The research director will be able to develop a log listing which questionnaires were assigned to which interviewers. Mail questionnaires are an exception to the principle that the questionnaires themselves be numbered. Respondents often interpret an assigned number on a mail questionnaire as a mechanism by which their responses can be identified as theirs. The possible loss in anonymity is threatening to many of them, and they may refuse to cooperate or even distort their answers.

Step 8: Reexamine and Revise Steps 1 Through 7 If Necessary

A researcher should not expect that the first draft will result in a usable questionnaire. Rather, reexamination and revision are staples in questionnaire construction. Each question should be reviewed to ensure that the question is easy to answer and not confusing, ambiguous, or potentially offensive to the respondent. Neither should any question be leading or bias-inducing. How can one tell? An extremely critical attitude and good common sense should help. The researcher should examine each word in each question. The literature on question phrasing is replete with examples of how some seemingly innocuous questions produced response problems.[30] When a potential problem is discovered, the question should be revised. After examining each question, and each word in each question, for its potential meanings and implications, the researcher might test the questionnaire in some role-playing situations, using others working on the project as subjects. This role playing should reveal some of the most serious shortcomings and should lead to further revision of the questionnaire.

Pretest Use of a questionnaire (or observation form) on a trial basis in a small pilot study to determine how well the questionnaire (or observation form) works.

Step 9: Pretest Questionnaire and Revise If Necessary

The real test of a questionnaire is how it performs under actual conditions of data collection. For this assessment, the questionnaire **pretest** is vital. The questionnaire pretest serves the same role in questionnaire design that test marketing serves in new product development. While the product concept, different advertising appeals, alternative packages, and so on, may all have been tested previously in the product development process, test marketing is the first place where they all come together. Thus, test marketing provides the real test of customer reactions to the product and the accompanying marketing program. Similarly, the pretest provides the real test of the questionnaire and the mode of administration.

There are a number of interesting examples in the literature of questions with unintended implications that could have been avoided with an adequate pretest of the questionnaire. In one life-style study, for example, the following question was asked: "How would you like to be living two years from now?" While the question was intended to get at hoped-for life-styles, a large group of the respondents simply replied "yes." In another study, a question about brands of deodorant was used on a self-administered questionnaire. It was only when a number of replies came back with the written response "AirWick" that the researchers realized that putting the word *personal* in front of *deodorant* would have eliminated the confusion caused by the question.[31]

Data collection should never begin without an adequate pretest of the questionnaire. The pretest can be used to assess both individual questions and their sequence.[32] It is best if there are two pretests. The first pretest should be done by personal interview, regardless of the actual mode of administration that will be used. An interviewer can watch to see if people actually remember data requested of them, or if some questions seem confusing or produce resistance or hesitancy among respondents for one reason or another. The pretest interviews should be conducted among respondents similar to those who will be used in the actual study, by the firm's most experienced interviewers.

The personal interview pretest should reveal some questions in which the wording could be improved or the sequence changed. If the changes are major, the revised questionnaire should again be pretested employing personal interviews. If the changes are minor, the questionnaire can be pretested a second time using mail, telephone, or personal interviews, whichever is going to be used for the full-scale study. This time, though, less experienced interviewers should also be used in order to determine if typical interviewers will have any special problems with the questionnaire. The purpose of the second pretest is to uncover problems unique to the mode of administration.

Finally, the responses that result from the pretest should be coded and tabulated. We have previously discussed the need for the preparation of dummy tables prior to the development of the questionnaire. The tabulation of pretest responses can check on our conceptualization of the problem and the data and method of analysis necessary to answer it.

> [T]he tables will confirm the need for various sets of data. If we have no place to put the responses to a question, either the data are superfluous or we omitted some contemplated analysis. If some part of a table remains empty, we may have omitted a necessary question. Trial tabulations show us, as no previous method can, that all data collected will be put to use, and that we will obtain all necessary data.[33]

The researcher who avoids a questionnaire pretest and tabulation of replies is either naive or a fool. The pretest is the most inexpensive insurance the researcher can buy to ensure the success of the questionnaire and the research project. A careful pretest along with proper attention to the do's and don'ts presented in this chapter and summarized in Table 12.3 should make the questionnaire development process successful.

Table 12.3   Some Do's and Don'ts When Preparing Questionnaires

Step 1: Specify What Information Will Be Sought

1. Make sure that you have a clear understanding of the issue and what it is that you want to know (expect to learn). Frame your research questions, but refrain from writing questions for the questionnaire at this time.
2. Make a list of your research questions. Review them periodically as you are working on the questionnaire.
3. Use the dummy tables that were set up to guide the data analysis to suggest questions for the questionnaire.
4. Conduct a search for existing questions on the issue.
5. Revise existing questions on the issue, and prepare new questions that address the issues you plan to research.

Step 2: Determine Type of Questionnaire and Method of Administration

1. Use the type of data to be collected as a basis for deciding on the type of questionnaire.
2. Use the degree of structure and disguise as well as cost factors to determine the method of administration.
3. Compare the special capabilities and limitations of each method of administration and the value of the data collected from each with the needs of the survey.

Step 3: Determine Content of Individual Questions

1. For each research question ask yourself, "Why do I want to know this?" Answer it in terms of how it will help your research. "It would be interesting to know" is not an acceptable answer.
2. Make sure each question is specific and addresses only one important issue.
3. Ask yourself whether the question applies to all respondents; it should, or provision should be made for skipping it.
4. Split questions that can be answered from different frames of reference into multiple questions, one corresponding to each frame of reference.
5. Ask yourself whether respondents will be informed about, and can remember, the issue that the question is dealing with.

6. Make sure the time period of the question is related to the importance of the topic. Consider using aided-recall techniques like diaries or written records.
7. Avoid questions that require excessive effort, that have hard-to-articulate answers, and that deal with embarrassing or threatening issues.
8. If threatening questions are necessary,
   (a) hide the questions among more innocuous ones.
   (b) make use of a counterbiasing statement.
   (c) phrase the question in terms of others and how they might feel or act.
   (d) ask respondents if they have ever engaged in the undesirable activity, and then ask if they are presently engaging in such an activity.
   (e) use categories or ranges rather than specific numbers.
   (f) use the randomized-response model.

Step 4: Determine Form of Response to Each Question

1. Determine which type of question—open-ended, dichotomous, or multichotomous—provides data that fit the information needs of the project.
2. Use structured questions whenever possible.
3. Use open-ended questions that require short answers to begin a questionnaire.
4. Try to convert open-ended questions to fixed-response questions to reduce respondent work load and coding effort for descriptive and causal studies.
5. If open-ended questions are necessary, make the questions sufficiently directed to give respondents a frame of reference when answering.
6. When using dichotomous questions, state the negative or alternative side in detail.
7. Provide for "don't know," "no opinion," and "both" answers.
8. Be aware that there may be a middle ground.
9. Be sensitive to the mildness or harshness of the alternatives.
10. When using multichotomous questions, be sure the choices ae exhaustive and mutually exclusive, and if combinations are possible, include them.

11. Be sure the range of alternatives is clear and that all reasonable alternative answers are included.
12. If the possible responses are very numerous, consider using more than one question to reduce the potential for information overload.
13. When using dichotomous or multichotomous questions, consider the use of a split-ballot procedure to reduce order bias.
14. Clearly indicate if items are to be ranked or if only one item on the list is to be chosen.

Step 5: Determine Wording of Each Question

1. Use simple words.
2. Avoid ambiguous words and questions.
3. Avoid leading questions.
4. Avoid implicit alternatives.
5. Avoid implicit assumptions.
6. Avoid generalizations and estimates.
7. Use simple sentences and avoid compound sentences.
8. Change long, dependent clauses to words or short phrases.
9. Avoid double-barreled questions.
10. Make sure each question is as specific as possible.

Step 6: Determine Question Sequence

1. Use simple, interesting questions for openers.
2. Use the funnel approach, first asking broad questions and then narrowing them down.
3. Ask difficult or sensitive questions late in the questionnaire, when rapport is better.
4. Follow chronological order when collecting historical information.
5. Complete questions about one topic before moving on to the next.
6. Prepare a flow chart whenever branching questions are being considered.
7. Ask filter questions before asking detailed questions.
8. Ask demographic questions last so that if respondent refuses, the other data are still usable.

Step 7: Determine Physical Characteristics of Questionnaire

1. Make sure the questionnaire looks professional and is relatively easy to answer.
2. Use quality paper and print; do not photocopy the questionnaire.
3. Attempt to make the questionnaire as short as possible while avoiding a crowded appearance.
4. Use a booklet format for ease of analysis and to prevent lost pages.
5. List the name of the organization conducting the survey on the first page.
6. Number the questions to ease data processing.
7. If the respondent must skip more than one question, use a "go to."
8. If the respondent must skip an entire section, consider color coding the sections.
9. State how the responses are to be reported, such as a check mark, number, circle, etc.

Step 8: Reexamine Steps 1–7 and Revise If Necessary

1. Examine each word of every question to ensure that the question is not confusing, ambiguous, offensive, or leading.
2. Get peer evaluations of the draft questionnaire.

Step 9: Pretest Questionnaire and Revise If Necessary

1. Pretest the questionnaire first by personal interviews among respondents similar to those to be used in the actual study.
2. Obtain comments from the interviewers and respondents to discover any problems with the questionnaire, and revise it if necessary. When the revisions are substantial, repeat Steps 1 and 2 of Step 9.
3. Pretest the questionnaire by mail or telephone to uncover problems unique to the mode of administration.
4. Code and tabulate the pretest responses in dummy tables to determine if questions are providing adequate information.
5. Eliminate questions that do not provide adequate information, and revise questions that cause problems.

Ethical
Dilemma 12.1   A candy manufacturer tells you that he wants to raise the price of his gourmet chocolates and he needs you to establish the greatest price increase that shoppers will stand. He suggests that you interview patrons of gourmet candy shops without informing them of the sponsor or purpose of the research, describe the candy to them in general terms, and suggest prices that they might find acceptable, starting with the highest price.

- Is it ethical to ask people questions when their answer may be detrimental to their self-interest?
- Is it ethical not to reveal the purpose or sponsor of the research? If you did reveal the purpose of the research, would survey respondents give the same answers as otherwise?

Observation Forms

There are generally fewer problems in constructing observation forms than in constructing questionnaires, because the researcher is no longer concerned with the fact that the question and the way it is asked will affect the response. Through proper training of observers, the researcher can create the necessary expertise so that the data-collection instrument is handled consistently. Alternatively, the researcher may simply use a mechanical device to measure the behavior of interest and secure complete consistency in measurement. This is not to imply that observation forms offer no problems of construction. Rather, the researcher needs to make very explicit decisions about what is to be observed and the categories and units that will be used to record this behavior. Figure 12.5, which is the observation form used by a bank to evaluate the service provided by its employees having extensive customer contact, shows how detailed some of these decisions can be. In this case the observers posed as shoppers.

The statement that "one needs to determine what is to be observed before one can make a scientific observation" seems trite. Yet this is exactly the case. Almost any event can be described in a number of ways. When we watch someone making a cigarette purchase, we might report that (1) the person purchased one package of cigarettes; (2) the woman purchased one package of cigarettes; (3) the woman purchased a package of Tareyton cigarettes; (4) the woman purchased a package of Tareyton 100s; (5) the woman, after asking for and finding that the store was out of Virginia Slims, purchased a package of Tareyton 100s; and so on.

A great many additional variations are possible, such as adding the type, name, or location of the store where this behavior occurred. In order for this observation to be productive for scientific inquiry, we must predetermine which aspects of this behavior are relevant. In this particular example, the decision as to what to observe requires that the researcher specify the following:

- Who should be observed? Anyone entering the store? Anyone making a purchase? Anyone making a cigarette purchase?
- What aspects of the purchase should be reported? Which brand they purchased? Which brand they asked for first? Whether the purchase was of king-size or regular cigarettes? What about the purchaser? Is the person's sex to be recorded? Is the individual's age to be estimated? Does it make any difference if the person was alone or in a group?

Figure 12.5   *Form Used by Observer Acting as Shopper to Evaluate Service Provided by Bank Employees*

Bank _____

Date _____ Time _____ Shopper's Name _____

Nature of Transaction: ☐ Personal   ☐ Telephone

Details _____

_____

_____

_____

- -

A. For Personal Transactions

Bank Employee's Name _____

1. How was name obtained?	☐ Employee had name tag
	☐ Nameplate on counter or desk
	☐ Employee gave name
	☐ Shopper had to ask for name
	☐ Name provided by other employee
	☐ Other _____
	_____

B. For Telephone Transactions

Bank Employee's Name _____

1. How was name obtained?	☐ Employee gave name upon answering the telephone
	☐ Name provided by other employee
	☐ Shopper had to ask for name
	☐ Employee gave name during conversation
	☐ Other _____
	_____

C. Customer Relations Skills	Yes	No	Does Not Apply
1. Did the employee notice and greet you immediately?	☐	☐	☐
2. Did the employee speak pleasantly and smile?	☐	☐	☐
3. Did the employee answer the telephone promptly?	☐	☐	☐
4. Did the employee find out your name?	☐	☐	☐
5. Did the employee use your name during the transaction?	☐	☐	☐
6. Did the employee ask you to be seated?	☐	☐	☐
7. Was the employee helpful?	☐	☐	☐

(continued)

Figure 12.5   *(Continued)*

8. *Was the employee's desk or work area neat and uncluttered?*   ☐   ☐   ☐

9. *Did the employee show a genuine interest in you as a customer?*   ☐   ☐   ☐

10. *Did the employee thank you for coming in?*   ☐   ☐   ☐

11. *Did the employee enthusiastically support the bank and its services?*   ☐   ☐   ☐

12. *Did the employee handle any interruptions (phone calls, etc.) effectively?*   ☐   ☐   ☐

Comment on any positive or negative details of the transaction that you found particularly noticeable.

_____

_____

_____

_____

_____

D. Sales Skills	Yes	No	Does Not Apply
1. *Did the employee determine if you had any accounts with this bank?*	☐	☐	☐
2. *Did the employee use "open-ended" questions in obtaining information about you?*	☐	☐	☐
3. *Did the employee listen to what you had to say?*	☐	☐	☐
4. *Did the employee sell you on the bank services by showing you what the service could do for you?*	☐	☐	☐
5. *Did the employee ask you to open the service which you inquired about?*	☐	☐	☐
6. *Did the employee ask you to bank with this particular bank?*	☐	☐	☐
7. *Did the employee ask you to contact him/her when visiting the bank?*	☐	☐	☐

■ When should the observation be made? On what day of the week? At what time of the day? Should day and time be reported? Should the observation be recorded only after a purchase occurs, or should an approach by a customer to a salesclerk also be recorded even if it does not result in a sale?

■ Where should the observation be made? In what kind of store? How should the store be selected? How should it be noted on the observation form—by type, by location, by name? Should vending-machine purchases also be noted?

Figure 12.5   **(Continued)**

8. *Did the employee ask you if you had any questions or if you understood the service at the end of the transaction?*   ☐   ☐   ☐

9. *Did the employee give you brochures about other services?*   ☐   ☐   ☐

10. *Did the employee give you his/her calling card?*   ☐   ☐   ☐

11. *Did the employee indicate that you might be contacted by telephone, engraved card, or letter as a means of follow-up?*   ☐   ☐   ☐

12. *Did the employee ask you to open or use other services? Check the following if they were mentioned.*   ☐   ☐   ☐

   ☐ savings account

   ☐ checking account

   ☐ automatic savings

   ☐ Mastercharge

   ☐ Master Checking

   ☐ safe-deposit box

   ☐ loan services

   ☐ trust services

   ☐ automatic payroll deposit

   ☐ bank-by-mail

   ☐ automatic loan payment

   ☐ bank hours

   ☐ other _____

Comment on the overall effectiveness of the employee's sales skills.

_____

_____

_____

_____

_____

Source: Courtesy of Neil M. Ford.

The careful reader will note that these are the same kinds of who, what, when, and where decisions that need to be made in selecting the research design. The why and how are also implicit. The research problem should dictate the why of the observation, while the how involves choosing the observation device or form that will be used. A paper-and-pencil form should be very simple to use. It should parallel the logical sequence of the purchase act (for example, a male approaches the clerk, asks for a package of cigarettes, and so on, if these behaviors are relevant) and should permit the recording of observations by a simple check mark if possible. Again, careful attention to detail, exacting examination of the preliminary form, and an adequate pretest should return handsome dividends with respect to the quality of the observations made.

Ethical Dilemma 12.2   As you supervise the sending out of a mail survey from a client's place of business, you notice some numbers printed on the inside of the return envelopes. You point out to the client that the cover letter promises survey respondents anonymity, which is not consistent with a policy of coding the return envelopes. She replies that she needs to identify those respondents who have not replied so that she can send a follow-up mailing. She also suggests the information might be useful in the future in identifying those who might react favorably to a sales call for the product.

- Is it ethical to promise anonymity and then not adhere to your promise?
- Is it healthy for the marketing research profession if legitimate research becomes associated with subsequent sales tactics?

Back to the Case

It wasn't really funny, but Bill Hershey had to laugh. He had spent the afternoon on the phone with a random sample of the physicians that MedAccounts had earmarked to reply to its service questionnaire. The poor overall response to the questionnaire now made perfect sense. And while the whole situation was quite a screwup, he could laugh about it because his boss had taken it philosophically, and it was at least as much the client's fault as it was Hershey's.

In a nutshell, the problem was that MedAccounts didn't have a clear idea of who its customers were, at least in terms of service. True, its sales reps called on the physicians in a practice, and some physicians purchased the MedAccounts billing system. But in reality, the doctors spent

their days treating patients, not billing them. While the doctors might have been the purchasers of the system, they were certainly not the users. Most of the doctors who purchased the MedAccounts system didn't even know where it was located in their office. They weren't the ones who called the service department: they had no idea of whether the service rep was punctual, polite, or quick to spot the problem.

It was the office manager who called MedAccounts when there was a problem, who knew the service rep's name and whether his or her appearance was neat and demeanor professional. Hershey's informal phone research explained a lot. Many of the doctors to whom the questionnaire had been sent had just thrown it

away. Some of the doctors had given the questionnaire to their office manager or had filled it out with the office manager's assistance. Other doctors had taken a couple of minutes and filled it out as best they could with their limited knowledge and had sent it off half finished.

In school Hershey had been taught the importance of checking one's hypothesis when formulating a questionnaire. Still, it had never occurred to him to question whether a client knew who its own customers were. As a result, the research firm and the client had wasted some money, and they'd wasted some time. Hershey was more than a little embarrassed, but he recognized that he'd learned an important lesson, albeit the hard way.

Summary

Learning Objective 1: Explain the role of research hypotheses in developing a questionnaire.

Research hypotheses guide the questionnaire by determining what information will be sought and from whom (since the hypotheses specify what relationships will be investigated). Hence, research hypotheses also affect the type of question and the form of response used to collect it.

Learning Objective 2: Define *telescoping error* and *recall loss* and explain how they affect a respondent's ability to answer questions accurately.

Telescoping error refers to people's tendency to remember an event as having occurred more recently than it did. *Recall loss* means they forget it happened at all. The degree to which the two types of error affect the accuracy of the reported information depends on the length of the period in question. For long periods, the telescoping effect is smaller, while the recall loss is larger. For short periods, the reverse is true.

Learning Objective 3: Cite some of the techniques researchers use to secure respondents' cooperation in answering sensitive questions.

When asking sensitive questions, researchers may find it helpful to (1) hide the question in a group of other, more innocuous, questions; (2) state that the behavior or attitude is not unusual before asking the specific question of the respondent; (3) phrase the question in terms of others and how they might feel or act; (4) state the response in terms of a number of categories that the respondent may simply check; (5) use the randomized-response model.

Learning Objective 4: Explain what an open-ended question is.

An open-ended question is one in which respondents are free to reply in their own words rather than being limited to choosing from a set of alternatives.

Learning Objective 5: Name two kinds of fixed-alternative questions and tell the difference between them.

Two types of fixed-alternative questions are multichotomous and dichotomous questions. In a multichotomous question respondents are asked to choose from a list of alternatives the one that most closely reflects their position on the subject. In a dichotomous question, only two alternatives are listed.

Learning Objective 6: List some of the primary rules researchers should keep in mind in trying to develop bias-free questions.

Among the rules of thumb that researchers should keep in mind in developing bias-free questions are (1) use simple words, (2) avoid ambiguous words and questions, (3) avoid leading questions, (4) avoid implicit alternatives, (5) avoid implicit assumptions, (6) avoid generalizations and estimates, and (7) avoid double-barreled questions.

Learning Objective 7: Explain what the funnel approach to question sequencing is.

The funnel approach to question sequencing gets its name from its shape, starting with broad questions and progressively narrowing down the scope.

Learning Objective 8: Explain what a branching question is and discuss when it is used.

A branching question is one that contains a direction as to where to go next on the questionnaire based on the answer given. Branching questions are used to reduce the number of alternatives that are needed in individual questions, while ensuring that those respondents capable of supplying the needed information still have an opportunity to do so.

Learning Objective 9: Explain the difference between basic information and classification information and tell which should be asked first in a questionnaire.

Basic information refers to the subject of the study, classification information refers to the other data we collect to classify respondents so as to extract more information about the phenomenon of interest. The proper questionnaire sequence is to present questions securing basic information first and those seeking classification information last.

Discussion Questions, Problems, and Projects

1. Evaluate the following questions.
   (a) *Which of the following magazines do you read regularly?*
       _____ Time
       _____ Newsweek
       _____ Business Week
   (b) *Are you a frequent purchaser of Birds Eye Frozen vegetables?*
       _____ Yes   _____ No
   (c) *Do you agree that the government should impose import restrictions?*
       _____ Strongly agree
       _____ Agree
       _____ Neither agree nor disagree
       _____ Disagree
       _____ Strongly disagree
   (d) *How often do you buy detergent?*
       _____ Once a week
       _____ Once in two weeks
       _____ Once in three weeks
       _____ Once a month
   (e) *Rank the following in order of preference:*
       _____ Kellogg's Corn Flakes
       _____ Quaker's Life
       _____ Post Bran Flakes
       _____ Kellogg's Bran Flakes
       _____ Instant Quaker Oatmeal
       _____ Post Rice Krinkles
   (f) *Where do you usually purchase your school supplies?*
   (g) *When you are watching television, do you also watch most of the advertisements?*
   (h) *Which of the following brands of tea are most similar?*
       _____ Liptons Orange Pekoe
       _____ Turnings Orange Pekoe
       _____ Bigelow Orange Pekoe
       _____ Salada Orange Pekoe
   (i) *Do you think that the present policy of cutting taxes and reducing government spending should be continued?*
       _____ Yes   _____ No
   (j) *In a seven-day week, how often do you eat breakfast?*
       _____ Every day of the week
       _____ 5–6 times a week
       _____ 2–4 times a week
       _____ Once a week
       _____ Never
2. Make the necessary corrections to the above questions.
3. Evaluate the following multichotomous questions. Rephrase them as dichotomous or open-ended questions if you think it would be more appropriate.

(a) *Which one of the following reasons is most important in your choice of stereo equipment?*
_____ Price
_____ In-store service
_____ Brand name
_____ Level of distortion
_____ Guarantee/warranty

(b) *Please indicate your education level.*
_____ Less than high school
_____ Some high school
_____ High school graduate
_____ Technical or vocational school
_____ Some college
_____ College graduate
_____ Some graduate or professional school

(c) *Which of the following reflects your views toward the issues raised by ecologists?*
_____ Have received attention
_____ Have not received attention
_____ Should receive more attention
_____ Should receive less attention

(d) *With which of the following statements do you most strongly agree?*
_____ Delta Airlines has better service than Northwest Airlines.
_____ Northwest Airlines has better service than United Airlines.
_____ United Airlines has better service than Delta Airlines.
_____ United Airlines has better service than Northwest Airlines.
_____ Northwest Airlines has better service than Delta Airlines.
_____ Delta Airlines has better service than United Airlines.

4. Evaluate the following open-ended questions. Rephrase them as multichotomous or dichotomous questions if you think it would be more appropriate.
   (a) *Do you go to the movies often?*
   (b) *Approximately how much do you spend per week on groceries?*
   (c) *What brands of cheese did you purchase during the last week?*

5. Assume you are doing exploratory research to find out people's opinions about television advertising.
   (a) Specify the necessary information that is to be sought.
   You have decided to design a structured-undisguised questionnaire and employ the personal interview method.
   (b) List the individual questions on a separate sheet of paper.
   (c) Specify the form of the response for each question (i.e., open-ended, multichotomous, dichotomous, scale). Provide justification for selecting a particular form of response.
   (d) Determine the sequence of the questions. Reexamine and revise the questions.
   (e) Attach the final version of the questionnaire.
   (f) Pretest the questionnaire on a convenience sample of five students, and report the results of your pretest.

6. The objective of this study is to determine whether brand names are important for mothers purchasing children's clothing.
   (a) Specify the necessary information that is to be sought.
   You have decided to use a structured-undisguised questionnaire and to employ the telephone interview method.
   (b) List the individual questions on a separate sheet of paper.
   (c) Specify the form of the response for each question. Provide justification for selecting a particular form of response.
   (d) Determine the sequence of the questions. Reexamine and revise the questions.

(e) Attach the final version of the questionnaire.

(f) Using the phone book as a sampling frame, pretest the questionnaire on a sample of five respondents, and report the results of your pretest.

7. A small brokerage firm was concerned with its declining number of customers and decided to do a quick survey. The major objective was to find out the reasons for patronizing a particular brokerage firm and to find out the importance of customer service. The following questionnaire was to be administered by telephone.

Good Afternoon, Sir/Madam:

We are doing a survey on attitudes toward brokerage firms. Could you please answer the following questions? Thank you.

1. Have you invested any money in the stock market?
_____ Yes   _____ No
If respondent replies "yes" continue; otherwise terminate interview.

2. Do you manage your own investments, or do you go to a brokerage firm?
_____ Manage own investments   _____ Go to a brokerage firm
If respondent replies "go to a brokerage firm," continue; otherwise terminate interview.

3. How satisfied are you with your brokerage firm?

Very Satisfied	Satisfied	Neither Satisfied nor Dissatisfied	Dissatisfied	Very Dissatisfied
____	____	____	____	____

4. How important is personal service to you?

Very Important	Important	Not Particularly Important	Not at All Important
____	____	____	____

5. Which of the following reasons is the most important in patronizing a particular firm?
_____ The commission charged by the firm
_____ The personal service
_____ The return on investment
_____ The investment counseling

6. Approximately how long have you been investing through the brokerage firm you are currently using?
_____ about 3 months   _____ about 9 months
_____ about 6 months   _____ about 1 year or more

7. How much capital do you have invested?
_____ $500–$750   _____ $1,000–$1,500
_____ $750–$1,000   _____ $1,500 or more

Good-bye, and thank you for your cooperation.

Evaluate the above questionnaire.

8. Assume that a medium-size manufacturer of candy employs you to conduct an observation study in determining children's influence on adults in the purchase of candy.

    (a)   List the variables that are relevant in determining this influence.

    (b)   List the "observations" that might reflect each of these variables.

    (c)   Develop an observation form that will be able to collect the needed information.

    (d)   Observe three such purchases in a store/supermarket or the location that you specified above.

    (e)   Report your findings.

9.   This observation task can be conducted near the vending machines in the cafeteria, library, or business school: The objective is to observe the deliberation time taken at the various machines and determine the factors that influence the deliberation time.

    (a)   List the variables that would be relevant in achieving the above objective.

    (b)   List the "observations" that would reflect each of these variables.

    (c)   Develop an observation form that will be able to collect the needed information.

    (d)   Do five such observations and report your findings.

10.   Your employer, a commercial marketing research firm, has contracted to perform a study whose objective is the investigation of usage patterns and brand preferences for premixed infant formula among migrant farm workers in the southeastern United States. You have been assigned to develop a suitable questionnaire and method of administration to collect the desired information. What potential problems might arise in design and administration due to the unique nature of the population in question? List these problems and provide solutions. What method of administration will you recommend?

11.   Discuss various reasons that a researcher might have for using an observation form as opposed to a questionnaire.

Endnotes

1. This procedure is adapted from one suggested by Arthur Kornhauser and Paul B. Sheatsley, "Questionnaire Construction and Interview Procedure," in Claire Selltiz, Lawrence S. Wrightsman, and Stuart W. Cook, *Research Methods in Social Relations*, 3rd ed. (New York: Holt, Rinehart and Winston, 1976), pp. 541–573.

2. The two methods of administration might possibly be used in combination through the locked-box approach.

3. These questions were suggested by Kornhauser and Sheatsley, "Questionnaire Construction." For a systematic treatment of questionnaire construction, see the classic work by Stanley L. Payne, *The Art of Asking Questions* (Princeton, N.J.: Princeton University Press, 1951). Other good general sources are Douglas R. Berdie and John F. Anderson, *Questionnaires: Design and Use* (Metuchen, N.J.: Scarecrow Press, 1974); Seymour Sudman and Norman M. Bradburn, *Asking Questions: A Practical Guide to Questionnaire Design* (San Francisco: Jossey-Bass, 1982); and Jean M. Converse and Stanley Presser, *Survey Questions: Handcrafting the Standardized Questionnaire* (Beverly Hills, Calif.: Sage Publications, 1986).

4. Sam Gill, "How Do You Stand on Sin?" *Tide*, 21 (March 14, 1947), p. 72.

5. In a subsequent replication of the study on the Metallic Metals Act almost 40 years later, 64 percent of those interviewed had a definite opinion on the nonexistent act. See Daniel T. Seymour, "Numbers Don't Lie—Do They?" *Business Horizons*, 27 (November/December 1984), pp. 36–37. There are a number of other examples in the literature that report findings of people having opinions about totally fictional issues like the Metallic Metals Act. See, for example, Del I. Hawkins and Kenneth A. Coney, "Uninformed Response Error in Survey Research," *Journal of Marketing Research*, 18 (August 1981), pp. 370–374; Kenneth C. Schneider, "Uniformed Response Rates in Survey Research: New Evidence," *Journal of Business Research*, 13 (August 1985), pp. 153–162; and George F. Bishop, Alfred J. Tuchfarber, and Robert W. Oldendick, "Opinions on Fictitious Issues: The Pressure to Answer Survey Questions," *Public Opinion Quarterly*, 50 (Summer 1986), pp. 240–250. The phenomenon is not unique to opinions. It also applies when measuring brand awareness, where it has been observed that the more plausible sounding a brand name, the more likely consumers are to claim they are aware of it even though it does not exist. See " 'Spurious Awareness' Alters Brand Tests," *The Wall Street Journal* (September 13, 1984), p. 29.

6. Howard Schuman and Stanley Presser, "The Assessment of 'No Opinions' in Attitude Surveys," in Karl F. Schnessler, ed., *Sociological Methodology, 1979* (San Francisco: Jossey-Bass, 1979), pp. 241–275. See also George F. Bishop, Robert W. Oldendick, and Alfred J. Tuchfarber, "Effects on Filter Questions in Public Opinion Surveys," *Public Opinion Quarterly*, 47 (Winter 1983), pp. 528–546.

7. Bruce Buchanan and Donald G. Morrison, "Sampling Properties of Rate Questions with Implications for Survey Research," *Marketing Science*, 6 (Summer 1987), pp. 286–298.

8. Graham Kalton and Howard Schuman, "The Effect of the Question on Survey Responses: A Review," *Journal of the Royal Statistical Society*, Series A, 145 (Part I, 1982), pp. 44–45. See also William A. Cook, "Telescoping and Memory's Other Tricks," *Journal of Advertising Research*, 27 (February/March 1987), pp. RC5–RC8; and Norman M. Bradburn, Lance J. Rip, and Steven K. Shevell, "Answering Autobiographical Questions: The Impact of Memory and Inference on Surveys," *Science*, 236 (April 10, 1987), pp. 157–161.

9. Harper W. Boyd, Jr., Ralph Westfall, and Stanley F. Staasch, *Marketing Research: Text and Cases*, 6th ed. (Homewood, Ill.: Richard D. Irwin, 1985), p. 272.

10. For more extensive treatments on how to handle sensitive questions, see Kent H. Marquis et al., *Response Errors in Sensitive Topic Surveys: Estimates, Effects, and Correction Options* (Santa Monica,

Calif.: Rand Corporation, 1981); Thomas W. Mangione, Ralph Hingson, and Jane Barrett, "Collecting Sensitive Data: A Comparison of Three Survey Strategies," *Sociological Methods and Research*, 10 (February 1982), pp. 337–346; and Anton J. Nederhof, "Methods of Coping with Social Desirability Bias: A Review," *European Journal of Social Psychology*, 15 (1985), pp. 263–280.

11. James E. Reinmuth and Michael D. Geurts, "The Collection of Sensitive Information Using a Two-Stage Randomized Response Model," *Journal of Marketing Research*, 12 (November 1975), pp. 402–407. For an elementary overview of the randomized response model, see Cathy Campbell and Brian L. Joiner, "How to Get the Answer Without Being Sure You've Asked the Question," *American Statistician*, 26 (December 1973), pp. 229–231. For discussion of randomization devices and methodologies for self-administered and telephone interview applications of the randomized-response method, see Donald E. Stem, Jr., and R. Kirk Steinhorst, "Telephone Interview and Mail Questionnaire Applications of the Randomized Response Model," *Journal of the American Statistical Association*, 79 (September 1984), pp. 555–564. For general treatments, see James Alan Fox and Paul E. Tracy, *Randomizing Response: A Method for Sensitive Surveys* (Beverly Hills, Calif.: Sage Publications, 1986); and Arijit Chaudhuri and Rahul Mukerjee, *Randomized Response: Theory and Techniques* (New York: Marcel Dekker, Inc., 1987).

12. Kalton and Schuman, "The Effect of the Question on Survey Responses: A Review," pp. 51–52.

13. "Measuring Purchase Intent," *Research on Research, No. 2* (Chicago: Market Facts, Inc., undated). See also Gregory J. Spagna, "Questionnaires: Which Approach Do You Use?" *Journal of Advertising Research*, 24 (February/March 1984), pp. 67–70; and George F. Bishop, "Experiments with the Middle Response Alternative in Survey Questions," *Public Opinion Quarterly*, 51 (Summer 1987), pp. 220–232.

14. Hadley Cantril and Edreta Fried, *Gauging Public Opinion* (Princeton, N.J.: Princeton University Press, 1944), Chapter 1, as reported in Payne, *The Art of Asking Questions*, p. 93. For a discussion of people's limited information-processing abilities, see Jacob Jacoby, "Perspectives on Information Overload," *Journal of Consumer Research*, 10 (March 1984), pp. 432–435.

15. Although it is commonly done, Niels J. Blunch, "Position Bias in Multiple-Choice Questions," *Journal of Marketing Research*, 21 (May 1984), pp. 216–220, argues to the contrary that position bias in multiple-choice questions cannot be eliminated by rotating the order of the alternatives.

16. Norbert Schwarz, Hans J. Hippler, Brigitte Deutsch, and Fritz Strack, "Response Scales: Effect of Category Range on Reported Behavior and Comparative Judgments," *Public Opinion Quarterly*, 49 (Fall 1985), pp. 388–395; and Norbert Schwarz et al., "The Range of Response Alternatives May Determine the Meaning of the Question: Further Evidence on Information Functions of Response Alternatives," *Social Cognition*, 6 (No. 2, 1988), pp. 107–117.

17. Two of the best discussions of this are to be found in Payne, *The Art of Asking Questions*, and Howard Schuman and Stanley Presser, *Questions and Answers in Attitude Surveys* (Orlando, Fla.: Academic Press, 1981), especially pp. 56–77.

18. For a review of the literature on the quality of questionnaire data, including item omission, see Robert A. Peterson and Roger A. Kerin, "The Quality of Self-Report Data: Review and Synthesis," in Ben Enis and Kenneth Roering, eds., *Annual Review of Marketing 1981* (Chicago: American Marketing Association, 1981), pp. 5–20.

19. Sudman and Bradburn, *Asking Questions*, p. 1.

20. Alan E. Bayer, "Construction of a Race Item for Survey Research," *Public Opinion Quarterly*, 36 (Winter 1972–1973), p. 596.

Payne, *The Art of Asking Questions*, has a list of the recommended words, while John O'Brien, "How Do Market Researchers Ask Questions?" *Journal of the Market Research Society*, 26 (April 1984), pp. 93–107, reports on the relative frequency with which Payne's recommended words are used on a sample of British questionnaires.

21. "Why the Polls Get Differing Results on Aid to New York," *Capital Times* (November 8, 1975), p. 2. See also Tom Smith, "That Which We Call Welfare By Any Other Name Would Smell Sweeter: An Analysis of the Impact of Question Wording on Response Patterns," *Public Opinion Quarterly*, 51 (Spring 1987), pp. 75–83.

22. E. Noelle-Neumann, "Wanted: Rules for Wording Structured Questionnaires," *Public Opinion Quarterly*, 34 (Summer 1970), p. 200.

23. Donald J. Messmer and Daniel T. Seymour, "The Effects of Branching on Item Nonresponse," *Public Opinion Quarterly*, 46 (Summer 1982), pp. 270–277.

24. Sudman and Bradburn, *Asking Questions*, pp. 223–227.

25. Charles S. Mayer and Cindy Piper, "A Note on the Importance of Layout in Self-Administered Questionnaires," *Journal of Marketing Research*, 19 (August 1982), pp. 390–391.

26. Each of the parts listed in Research Window 12.3 is discussed in detail in Paul L. Erdos, *Professional Mail Surveys* (Melbourne, Fla.: Robert E. Krieger Publishing Co., 1983), pp. 101–117. See also Bruce J. Walker, Wayne Kirchmann, and Jeffrey S. Conant, "A Method to Improve Response to Industrial Mail Surveys," *Industrial Marketing Management*, 16 (November 1987), pp. 305–314.

27. A. Regula Herzog and Jerald G. Bachman, "Effects of Questionnaire Length on Response Quality," *Public Opinion Quarterly*, 45 (Winter 1981), pp. 549–559.

28. Charles F. Cannell, Lois Oksenberg, and Jean M. Converse, "Striving for Response Accuracy: Experiments in New Interviewing Techniques," *Journal of Marketing Research*, 14 (August 1977), pp. 306–315; Ed Blair, Seymour Sudman, Norman M. Bradburn, and Carol Stocking, "How to Ask Questions about Drinking and Sex: Response Effects in Measuring Consumer Behavior," *Journal of Marketing Research*, 14 (August 1977), pp. 316–321; and Andre Laurent, "Effects of Question Length on Reporting Behavior in the Survey Interview," *Journal of the American Statistical Association*, 67 (June 1972), pp. 298–305.

29. These elementary steps, which are involved in the processing of all questionnaires, are discussed in Chapter 19.

30. Payne's book, *The Art of Asking Questions*, is particularly good in this regard. Chapter 13, for example, is devoted to the development of a passable question. When one considers that an entire chapter can be devoted to the development of one passable question (not a great question, mind you), one can appreciate the need for reexamining each question under a microscope for its potential implications. A condensed treatment of the things to be avoided in a question is to be found in Lyndon O. Brown and Leland L. Beik, *Marketing Research and Analysis*, 4th ed. (New York: Ronald, 1969), pp. 242–262. Sudman and Bradburn, *Asking Questions*, have recommendations specific to the type of question being asked (e.g., opinions versus demographic characteristics).

31. Linda Kirby, "Bloopers," *Newspaper Research Council* (January/February 1989), p. 1.

32. An empirical examination of the usefulness of the pretest in uncovering various problems can be found in Shelby D. Hunt, Richard D. Sparkman, Jr., and James B. Wilcox, "The Pretest in Survey Research: Issues and Preliminary Findings," *Journal of Marketing Research*, 19 (May 1982), pp. 265–275.

33. Brown and Beik, *Marketing Research and Analysis*, pp. 265–266.

Suggested Additional Readings

For more elaborate treatments of how to go about constructing questionnaires, see

Patricia J. Labaw, *Advanced Questionnaire Design* (Cambridge, Mass.: Abt Books, 1981).

Stanley L. Payne, *The Art of Asking Questions* (Princeton, N.J.: Princeton University Press, 1979).

Howard Schuman and Stanley Presser, *Questions and Answers in Attitude Surveys* (Orlando, Fla.: Academic Press, 1981).

Seymour Sudman and Norman M. Bradburn, *Asking Questions: A Practical Guide to Questionnaire Design* (San Francisco: Jossey-Bass, 1982).

Chapter Thirteen

Measurement Basics

Learning Objectives

Upon completing this chapter, you should be able to

1. Define the term *measurement* as it is used in marketing research.

2. List the four types of scales that can be used to measure an attribute.

3. Explain the primary difference between a ratio scale and an interval scale.

4. Cite some of the factors that may cause differences in two measures of the same attribute.

5. Name the two types of error that may affect measurement scores and define each.

6. Explain the concept of validity as it relates to measuring instruments.

7. Specify the two types of inferences a researcher makes in attempting to establish the validity of an instrument.

8. Cite the three types of direct assessment techniques used to infer the validity of a measure.

9. Outline the sequence of steps to follow in developing valid measures of marketing constructs.

Case in Marketing Research

On the first day that Teen Sport deodorant was being test marketed in Middlefield, Ernie Henderson, the research analyst in charge of the project, had a meeting with Todd Whalen, from marketing. Henderson found Whalen in his office, feet up on his desk, looking at some of the promotional materials that had been produced for Teen Sport, Reliance Cosmetics' new deodorant, which was targeted to girls aged 12 to 17.

When Henderson entered the room, Whalen leapt to his feet and greeted the researcher with a hearty handshake.

"Well, Ernie," he said jovially, "I've done my job. Now it's your turn to do yours. The advertising is ready, the promotional coupons are in the pipeline, and we've got a lock on our shelf space in the retail outlets. As we speak, samples are being mailed to all the teenaged girls in Middlefield."

"I'm all set to go, too," replied Henderson. "We'll be running qualitative studies to find out what consumers like and dislike about Teen Sport. We'll also be doing awareness studies of both print and television advertising."

"So when do we get to hear whether we have the winner I think we have?"

"I know you're excited about the test market," answered Henderson cautiously, "and I'm not saying that we're not going to hit a home run with this one, but I think it's more likely that we're going to have to make some adjustments after we get the results from Middlefield."

"Don't be a wet blanket, Ernie," replied Whalen. "You don't know teenagers like I know teenagers. I handed out samples at my 14-year-old's slumber party, and the girls said Teen Sport was great."

"Teenagers are a very fickle and segmented market," countered Henderson. "Their tastes vary widely from one part of the country to the other, and what they think is great one day is passé six months later."

"So, then, how long is it going to be before we get results from the test market?"

"I figure we need to measure at 8, 14, and 20 weeks to get any valid reading. I'm also worried that we're going to run into problems with Christmas. . . ."

"Ernie, I think you're just a born worrier."

"Not really," replied Henderson. "You came here from snack foods. Wait until you've been in personal consumer products as long as I have—you'll be a worrier, too."

Discussion Issues

1. What kinds of problems might a marketer encounter in trying to measure consumers' attitudes toward a new product?

2. What assumption is Whalen making that could prove faulty? Why could it prove faulty?

3. What kinds of questions should Henderson ask to determine consumers' attitudes toward the new deodorant?

Without realizing it, most of us spend the day engaging in various forms of measurement. We stagger out of bed and hop onto the bathroom scale, hoping our midnight foray to the refrigerator will fail to register. We measure coffee into the coffee maker, or stir a teaspoonful of instant coffee into a cup of water. We keep an eye on the clock so that we will not miss the bus or leave too little time to negotiate the rush-hour traffic on our way to class. We check the sports page for the score of the previous night's game—and perhaps the business section for the closing price on a favorite investment.

Most of the things we measure are fairly concrete: pounds on a scale, teaspoons of coffee, the amount of gas in a tank. But how does one measure a person's attitude toward bubble gum? The likelihood of a teenager's using a certain brand of acne medication? A family's social class? Marketers are interested in measuring many attributes that laypeople rarely think of in terms of numerical values. In this chapter and the next, we will discuss how marketing researchers go about assigning numbers to various objects and phenomena.

Scales of Measurement

Measurement Rules for assigning numbers to objects to represent quantities of attributes.

Measurement consists of "rules for assigning numbers to objects in such a way as to represent quantities of attributes."[1] Note two things about the definition. First, it indicates that we measure the attributes of objects and not the objects themselves. We do not measure a person, for example, but may choose to measure the individual's income, social class, education, height, weight, attitudes, or whatever, all of which are attributes of this person. Second, the definition is broad in that it does not specify how the numbers are to be assigned. In this sense, the rule is too simplistic and conveys a false sense of security, because there is a great temptation to read more meaning into the numbers than they actually contain. We often incorrectly attribute all the properties of the scale of numbers to the assigned numerals.

Consider the properties of the scale of numbers for a minute. Take the numbers 1, 2, 3, and 4. Now let the number 1 stand for one object, 2 for two objects, and so on. The scale of numbers possesses a number of properties. For example, we can say that 2 is larger than 1, and 3 is larger than 2, and so on. Also, we can say that the interval between 1 and 2 is the same size as the interval between 3 and 4, which is the same as that between 2 and 3, and so on. We can say still further that 3 is three times greater than 1, while 4 is four times greater than 1 and two times greater than 2, and so on.

When we assign numbers to attributes of objects, we must beware of the temptation to make these same arguments with the numbers in that it is unlikely that these relationships hold. We must determine what the properties of the attribute are and assign numbers in such a fashion that they accurately reflect the properties of the attribute. Errors at this point could mislead both the researchers and the users of the research.

There are four types of scales on which an attribute can be measured, namely, nominal, ordinal, interval, and ratio.[2] Table 13.1 summarizes some of the more important features of these scales.

Nominal Scale

Nominal scale Measurement in which numbers are assigned to objects or classes of objects solely for the purpose of identification.

One of the simplest properties of the scale of numbers is *identity*. A person's social security number is a **nominal scale,** as are the numbers on football jerseys, lockers, and so on. These numbers simply identify the individual assigned the number.

Table 13.1   **Scales of Measurement**

Scale	Basic Comparisons[a]	Typical Examples	Measures of Average[b]
Nominal	Identity	Male/female	Mode
		User/nonuser	
		Occupations	
		Uniform numbers	
Ordinal	Order	Preference for brands	Median
		Social class	
		Hardness of minerals	
		Graded quality of lumber	
Interval	Comparison of intervals	Temperature scale	Mean
		Grade point average	
		Attitude toward brands	
Ratio	Comparison of absolute magnitudes	Units sold	Geometric mean
		Number of purchasers	Harmonic mean
		Probability of purchase	
		Weight	

[a]All the comparisons applicable to a given scale are permissible with all scales above it in the table. For example, the ratio scale allows the comparison of intervals and the investigation of order and identity, in addition to the comparison of absolute magnitudes.

[b]The measures of average applicable to a given scale are also appropriate for all scales below it in the table; i.e., the mode is also a meaningful measure of the average when measurement is on an ordinal, interval, or ratio scale.

Similarly, if in a given study males are coded 1 and females 2, we have again made use of a nominal scale. The individuals are uniquely identified as male or female. All we need to determine an individual's sex is to know whether the person is coded as a 1 or as a 2. Note further that there is nothing implied by the numerals other than identification of the sex of the person. Females, although they bear a higher number, are not necessarily "superior" to males, or "more" than males, or twice as many as males—as the numbers 2 and 1 might indicate—or vice versa. We could just as easily reverse our coding procedure so that each female is a 1 and each male a 2.

The reason we could reverse our codes is that the only property conveyed by the numbers is identity. With a nominal scale, the only permissible operation is counting. Thus, the mode is the only legitimate measure of central tendency or average. It does not make sense in a sample consisting of sixty men and forty women to say that the average sex is 1.4, given males were coded 1 and females 2, even though the calculation 0.6 (1) + 0.4 (2) yields the number 1.4. All we can say is that there were more males in the sample than females, or that 60 percent of the sample was male.

Ordinal Scale

A second property of the scale of number is that of *order*. Thus, we could say that the number 2 is greater than the number 1, that 3 is greater than both 2 and 1, and that 4 is greater than all three of these numbers. The numbers 1, 2, 3, and 4 are ordered, and the larger the number, the greater the property. Note that the **ordinal scale** implies identity, since the same number would be used for all objects that are the same. An example would be the assignment of the number 1 to denote freshmen, 2 to denote sophomores, 3 juniors, and 4 seniors. We could just as well use the numbers 10 for freshmen, 20 for sophomores, 25 for juniors, and 30 for seniors. This assignment would still indicate the class level of each person and the *relative standing* of two persons when compared in terms of who is further along in the academic program. Note that this is all that is conveyed by an ordinal scale. The difference in ranks says nothing about the difference in academic achievement between two ranks.

This is perhaps easier to see if we talk about the three top people in a graduating class. Assume that the top-ranked person's average grade is 3.85 on a four-point scale, the second-ranked person's average is 3.74, and the third-ranked person's is 3.56. While an ordinal scale will tell us that one person was ranked first and another was ranked second, it tells us nothing about the difference in academic achievement between the two. Nor does an ordinal scale imply that the difference in academic achievement between the first- and second-ranked people equals the difference between the second- and third-ranked people, even though the difference between 1 and 2 equals the difference between 2 and 3.

As suggested, we can transform an ordinal scale in any way we wish as long as we maintain the basic ordering of the objects. Again, whether we can use the ordinal scale to assign numerals to objects depends on the attribute in question. The attribute itself must possess the ordinal property to allow ordinal scaling that is meaningful. With ordinal scales, both the median and the mode are permissible, or meaningful, measures of average. Thus, if twenty people ranked Product A first in comparison with Products B and C, while ten ranked it second and five ranked it third, we could say that (1) the average rank of Product A as judged by the median response was 1 (with thirty-five subjects, the median is given by the eighteenth response when ranked from lowest to highest) and that (2) the modal rank was also 1.

Interval Scale

A third property of the scale of numbers is that the *intervals* between the numbers are meaningful in the sense that the numbers tell us how far apart the objects are with respect to the attribute. This means that the differences can be compared. The difference between 1 and 2 is equal to the difference between 2 and 3. Further, the difference between 2 and 4 is twice the difference that exists between 1 and 2.

One classic example of an **interval scale** is the temperature scale, since it indicates what we can and cannot say when we have measured an attribute on an interval scale. Suppose the low temperature for the day was 40°F and the high was 80°F. Can we say that the high temperature was twice as hot (that is, represented twice the heat) as the low temperature? The answer is an unequivocal no. To see the folly in claiming 80°F is twice as warm as 40°F, one simply needs to convert these temperatures to their centigrade equivalents, where $C = (5F - 160)/9$. Now we see that the low was 4.4°C and the high was 26.6°C, a much different ratio between low and high than was indicated by the Fahrenheit scale.

The example illustrates that we cannot compare the absolute magnitude of numbers when measurement is made on the basis of an interval scale. The reason is

---

Ordinal scale
Measurement in which numbers are assigned to data on the basis of some order (for example, more than, greater than) of the objects.

Interval scale
Measurement in which the assigned numbers legitimately allow the comparison of the size of the differences among and between members.

that in an interval scale, the zero point is established arbitrarily. For example, the same natural phenomenon, the freezing point of water, is represented by zero on the Celsius scale but 32 on the Fahrenheit scale.[3] The zero position is therefore arbitrary.

What, then, can we say when measurement is made on an interval scale? First, we can say that 80°F is warmer than 40°F. Second, given a third temperature, we can compare the intervals; that is, we can say the difference in heat between 80°F and 120°F is the same as the difference between 40°F and 80°F, and that the difference between 40°F and 120°F is twice the difference between 40°F and 80°F. To see that this conclusion is legitimate, we can simply resort to the centigrade equivalents: the difference between 4.4°C (40°F) and 26.6°C (80°F) is the same as that between 26.6°C (80°F) and 48.8°C (120°F), namely, 22.2°. Further, the difference of 44.4°C between 4.4°C and 48.8°C is twice as great as that between 4.4°C and 26.6°C, as it was when the Fahrenheit scale was used. The comparison of intervals is legitimate with an interval scale because the relationships among the differences hold regardless of the particular constants chosen. With an interval scale, the mean, median, and mode are all meaningful measures of average.

Ratio Scales

Ratio scale Measurement that has a natural, or absolute, zero and therefore allows the comparison of absolute magnitudes of the numbers.

The **ratio scale** differs from an interval scale in that it possesses a *natural*, or *absolute*, zero, one for which there is universal agreement as to its location. Height and weight are obvious examples. Because there is an absolute zero, comparison of the *absolute magnitude* of the numbers is legitimate. Thus, a person weighing 200 pounds is said to be twice as heavy as one weighing 100 pounds, and a person weighing 300 pounds is three times as heavy.

In a ratio scale, zero has an absolute empirical meaning—that is, that none of the property being measured exists. Further, we have already seen that the more powerful scales include the properties possessed by the less powerful ones. This means that with a ratio scale we can compare intervals, rank objects according to magnitude, or use the numbers to identify the objects (everything that interval, ordinal, and nominal scales do). And the geometric mean, as well as the more usual arithmetic mean, median, and mode, is a meaningful measure of average when attributes are measured on a ratio scale.

Scaling of Psychological Attributes

Researchers decide which scale to use based on the attribute being measured, in that the characteristic or qualities being measured may preclude use of a more powerful scale. For example, we may have to use a nominal rather than an ordinal scale because the qualities being measured may not lend themselves to a numerical ranking. That is, the properties implied by the numbers used for ranking may not correlate with the properties of the attribute being measured. Also, we cannot use an interval scale for an attribute that is only ordinal in nature. We introduce a serious error into our scale if we try to exceed the basic nature of the attribute with our measure. Therefore it is critical to know something about the attribute itself before we assign numbers to it using some measurement procedure.

Further, the procedure used in constructing the scale determines the type of scale actually generated. The more powerful scales allow stronger comparisons and conclusions to be made. Thus, we can make certain types of comparisons that allow particular conclusions when measurement is on a ratio scale, say, that we cannot make when measurement is on an interval, ordinal, or nominal scale. There is a great temptation to assume that our measures have the properties of the ratio or at least the interval scale. Whether they do in fact is another question, and the simple condition that the attributes of the objects have been assigned numbers should not delude us. Rather, we should critically ask: What is the basic nature of the attribute? Have we captured this basic nature by our measurement procedure?

It is rare that a psychological construct can reasonably be assumed to have a natural, or absolute, zero.

> For example, what would an absolute zero of intelligence be? Or what is the absolute zero of attitude toward the Republican Party? There can be neutrality of feeling, and neutral position is often used as the zero point on the scale, but it does not represent an absolute lack of the attitude.[4]

The problem is no less real in marketing. Many of our constructs, borrowed from psychology and sociology, possess no more than interval measurement, and some possess even less. We have to be very careful in conceptualizing the construct or characteristic so as not to delude ourselves or mislead others with our measures and, more important, *with our interpretation of those measures*.

The second problem we must face squarely is the ability of our measures to capture the construct as conceptualized. Even if an absolute zero logically exists, for example, do our measures determine it? The procedures used to generate the measure in large part determine the answer. If all we require is that the respondent rank five objects in terms of their overall desirability, we need to recognize that we have generated only an ordinal scale in the absence of further assumptions.

Ethical
Dilemma 13.1
Jose Cardenas, a research analyst for Quality Surveys, was working on a study attempting to assess the image of the various automobile dealers in a metropolitan area. The survey instrument asked about such things as the quality and promptness of the dealer's repair service; the courteousness, knowledge, and helpfulness of the dealership's salespeople; how competitive the dealer was with respect to its automobile assortment and prices; and so on. Altogether there were 35 items that addressed the various attributes by which customers might evaluate automobile dealers. Respondents were asked to evaluate the dealer with whom they were most familiar, on each attribute using one of the four categories: poor (1), fair (2), good (3), or excellent (4). Thus, the range of scores could run from 35 to 140. In presenting the results to the client, a Ford dealership, Cardenas stated that, on average, people in town had twice as favorable an attitude toward the Ford dealer as toward its nearest Chevrolet dealer. This was based on the average scores of 120 for the Ford dealership and 60 for the Chevrolet dealership.

- Could Cardenas rightly make such a claim? If not, what could he say?
- What were Cardenas' responsibilities to the client with respect to understanding measurement-scale issues?
- Did Cardenas' superiors have any responsibility in this regard?

Introduction to Psychological Measurement

As suggested earlier, part of the difficulty in measuring attitudes stems from the general difficulty in measuring any psychological construct or concept. Since we cannot physically see psychological constructs such as attitude, awareness, inten-

Research Window 13.1
Controversy Surrounding the Measurement of Newspaper Readership

Roy Megarry, publisher of the *Toronto Globe and Mail*, has had beefs for years with the Audit Bureau of Circulations (ABC), the agency that verifies newspaper circulation figures. Finally last October, he got so fed up that he pulled his paper out of the ABC. The last straw? The ABC's decision to count sales to juvenile detention centers as regular paid circulation.

Megarry, who describes the ABC as "a dinosaur," also quibbles with rules that permit publishers to include as paid circulation some of the copies stolen from vending boxes and papers distributed to children in classroom reading programs. "And yet," he complains, "the ABC refused to count bulk sales to hotels that hand out newspapers free to their guests. Somehow I think advertisers would rather reach travelers in first-class hotels than inmates and school kids."

The *Globe and Mail*'s surprising defection from the audit bureau, followed by the resignations of 14 Gannett Company newspapers, brings to the forefront a long-simmering debate about how papers should be measured for advertising purposes. Both publishers and advertisers question audit-bureau rules on what qualifies as honest-to-goodness paid circulation. Critics also believe that much more attention should be given to the total number of readers rather than simply the tally of papers sold.

Many advertisers argue that bulk sales should continue to be listed separately because people are less inclined to read a paper they receive as a freebie.

"Readers who seek out a publication become more engrossed in its stories and advertising," says Stephen Fajen, media director at the Saatchi & Saatchi Compton ad agency.

More important than bulk sales is the issue of audience data. Audience figures make a publication look better than circulation because, typically, more than one person reads a single copy of a newspaper or magazine.

Marketers are leery, however, of much audience research because it is based on interviews with relatively small samples of readers. Depending on who is counting, there can be great discrepancies. Consider *Newsweek*, which last year became the first major magazine to base ad rates on audience rather than circulation. It says one syndicated research firm estimates that it has more than 20 million readers, whereas another puts the total at 16.9 million.

"I look at audience research but prefer audited circulation figures to projections based on consumers' recollections," says George Mahrlig, director of media services at Campbell Soup Company. Understandably so. Campbell learned from its research that some people consider a quick skim of the paper to be reading, others devote 20 minutes or more to the paper, and still others page through it just to clip coupons. "It kept us mindful," Mahrlig says, "that the noses being counted are real people with real distractions."

Source: Ronald Alsop, "To Some Papers, Readership Is Not as Elementary as ABC," *The Wall Street Journal* (January 16, 1986), p. 25.

tions, and so on, it is difficult to gauge whether our measures have measured them accurately. Even if we could see them, though, there would still be a question as to whether the measure we were using captured adequately the construct it was supposed to reflect. Research Window 13.1, for example, discusses the controversy in measuring something so basic to advertisers as newspaper readership. This problem is common to all scientific measurement.

The essence of the measurement problem is presented in Figure 13.1. The basic researcher or scientist uses theories in an attempt to explain phenomena. These theories or models consist of constructs (denoted by the circles with *C*'s in them), linkages among and between the constructs (single lines connecting the *C*'s), and data that connect the constructs with the empirical world (double lines). The single lines

Figure 13.1   *Schematic Diagram Illustrating the Structure of Science and the Problem of Measurement*

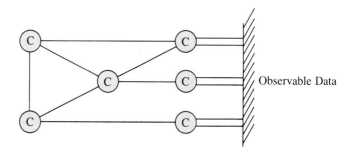

Constitutive (conceptual) definition
A definition in which a given construct is defined in terms of other constructs in the set, sometimes in the form of an equation that expresses the relationship among them.

Operational definition
A definition of a construct that describes the operations to be carried out in order for the construct to be measured empirically.

represent **conceptual** or **constitutive definitions,** in that a given construct is defined in terms of other constructs in the set. The definition may take the form of an equation that precisely expresses the interrelationship of the construct to the other constructs, such as the equation in mechanics that suggests that force equals mass times acceleration. Alternatively, the relationship may be only imprecisely stated, which is typically the case in the social sciences.

The double lines represent operational definitions. An **operational definition** describes how the construct is to be measured. It specifies the activities that the researcher must complete in order to assign a value to the construct (e.g., sum the scores on the ten individual statements to generate a total score). In essence, the operational definition tells the investigator what to do and in what manner to measure the concept. Table 13.2, for example, shows how consumer sentiment toward marketing was assessed in one large study using Market Facts' mail panel by measuring respondents' reactions to product quality, product prices, advertising, and retailing and personal selling. Conceptual definitions logically precede operational definitions and guide their development, for we must specify what a construct is before we can develop rules for assessing its magnitude.

The role of scientific inquiry is to establish the relationships that exist among the constructs of a model. It is necessary that some of the constructs be related to observable data if scientists are to accomplish their task. Otherwise, the model will be circular, with given unobservable constructs being defined in terms of other unobservable constructs. Since a circular model cannot be supported or refuted by empirical data, it is not legitimately considered a theory. Rather, a theory or system of explanation rests upon the condition that at least some of the constructs can be operationalized sufficiently so as to allow their measurement. Recall that measurement is defined as "rules for assigning numbers to objects to represent quantities of attributes." The rigor with which these rules are defined and the skill with which they are implemented determine whether the construct has been captured by the measure.

You would undoubtedly scoff at the following measurement procedure: John has blue eyes and Bill has brown eyes; therefore, John is taller than Bill. You might reply that the color of a person's eyes has nothing to do with the person's height and, further, that if you wanted to see who was taller, the best procedure would be to measure them with a yardstick or to stand them side by side and compare their heights. You would be right on both counts. If I measured both John and Bill by

Table 13.2   ***Illustration of Operational Definitions***

Concept	Measurement[a]
	Sum of responses to the following items, each measured on a five-point disagree-agree scale.
Product Quality	The quality of most products I buy today is as good as can be expected.
	I am satisfied with most of the products I buy.
	Most products I buy wear out too quickly. (R)
	Products are not made as well as they used to be. (R)
	Too many of the products I buy are defective in some way. (R)
	The companies that make products I buy don't care enough about how well they perform. (R)
	The quality of products I buy has consistently improved over the years.
Price of Products	Most products I buy are overpriced. (R)
	Business could charge lower prices and still be profitable. (R)
	Most prices are reasonable considering the high cost of doing business.
	Competition between companies keeps prices reasonable.
	Companies are unjustified in charging the prices they charge. (R)
	Most prices are fair.
	In general, I am satisfied with the prices I pay.
Advertising for Products	Most advertising provides consumers with essential information.
	Most advertising is very annoying. (R)
	Most advertising makes false claims. (R)
	If most advertising were eliminated, consumers would be better off. (R)
	I enjoy most ads.
	Advertising should be more closely regulated.
	Most advertising is intended to deceive rather than to inform consumers. (R)
Retailing or Selling	Most retail stores serve their customers well.
	Because of the way retailers treat me, most of my shopping is unpleasant. (R)
	I find most retail salespeople to be very helpful.
	Most retail stores provide an adequate selection of merchandise.
	In general, most middlemen make excessive profits. (R)
	When I need assistance in a store, I am usually *not* able to get it. (R)
	Most retailers provide adequate service.

[a]An (R) indicates that scoring of the item needs to be reversed so that higher scores indicate more positive attitudes.

Source: Developed from the information in John F. Gaski and Michael J. Etzel, "The Index of Consumer Sentiment Toward Marketing," *Journal of Marketing*, 50 (July 1986), pp. 71–81.

asking them how tall they were, you would have probably voiced less objection to my procedure—unless John said he was taller while your observation of the two men showed that Bill was definitely the taller.

Now the interesting thing about most psychological constructs is that we cannot rely on visual comparisons to either confirm or refute a measure. We cannot see an attitude, a personality characteristic, a person's knowledge about or awareness of a particular product, or other psychological characteristics such as intelligence, mental anxiety, or whatever. These characteristics are all part of the consumer's black box. Their magnitude must be inferred from our measurements. Since we cannot resort to a visual check on the accuracy of our measures, we must rely on evaluating the procedures we used to determine the measure. Eye color is certainly not height, but can we capture sales representatives' satisfaction with their job if we ask them directly how satisfied they are? Probably not, for reasons that will become obvious as we continue our discussion.

Note that the problem of measuring the constructs is not unique to the researcher interested in scientific explanation. The practitioner shares this concern. The deodorant manufacturer in our opening case will need to know that the research is actually measuring consumers' attitudes toward the new product and that the accuracy of the data is not being influenced by the interviewers asking the questions or by one of the many other factors with which research must contend. The ability to make these assessments relies heavily on an understanding of measurement, measurement error, and the concepts of reliability and validity. Understanding these concepts is the task to which we now turn.

Variations in Measured Scores

You will recall that when we engage in measurement we are measuring the attributes of objects, not necessarily the objects themselves. Most measurement tasks present problems, but psychological measurement is particularly difficult at times since it usually involves a complex situation in which there are a great many factors that affect the attribute being measured. In addition, the measurement process itself may influence the results. For example, assume that certain tobacco companies are interested in measuring people's attitudes toward smoking in public places such as restaurants, office buildings, and medical waiting areas. An attitude scale to measure these feelings has been administered to a sample of respondents. A high score (maximum: 100) means that the respondent has a strong objection to smoking in public areas, while a low score (minimum: 25) indicates the opposite. If Mary scored 75 and Jane scored 40, we might conclude that Mary has a much more negative attitude toward smoking in public places than does Jane. But the validity of that conclusion would depend on the quality of the measurement. Let us consider some of the possible causes for the difference in the two scores.[5]

1. *A true difference in the characteristic we are measuring.* In an ideal situation, the difference in scores would reflect true differences in the attitudes of Mary and Jane and nothing else. This situation will rarely, if ever, occur. More likely, the different scores will also reflect some of the intruding factors that follow.
2. *True differences in other relatively stable characteristics of the individual.* Not only does a person's position on an issue affect his or her score, but other characteristics can also be expected to have an effect. Perhaps the difference between Mary's and Jane's scores is simply due to the greater willingness of Mary to express negative feelings. Jane, by contrast, follows the adage, "If you can't say something nice, don't say anything at all." Her cooperation in the study has been requested, so she responds, but not truthfully.
3. *Differences due to transient personal factors.* A person's mood, state of health, fatigue, and so on, may all affect his or her responses. Yet these factors are temporary and

can vary. Thus, if Mary, a nonsmoker, has just returned from a long wait in her dentist's smoke-filled waiting room, her responses may be decidedly different than if she had been interviewed several days earlier.

4. *Differences due to situational factors.* The situation surrounding the measurement also can affect the score. Mary's score might be different if her husband were there while the scale was being administered. Incidentally, this problem is the bane of researchers studying the decision-making process of married couples. When the husband is asked for the respective roles of husband and wife in purchasing a new automobile, for instance, one set of responses is secured; when the wife is asked, the responses are different; when the two are asked together, still a third set is obtained. Which is correct? It is hard to say, since the fact remains that the situation surrounding a measurement can affect the scores that are obtained.

5. *Differences due to variations in administration.* Much measurement in marketing involves the use of questionnaires administered by phone or in person. Since interviewers can vary in the way they ask questions, the responses also may vary as a function of the interviewer. The same interviewer may even handle two interviews differently enough to trigger a variance in recorded answers, although the respondents do not really differ on the characteristic.

6. *Differences due to the sampling of items.* As we attempt to measure any construct, we typically tap only a small number of the items relevant to the characteristic being measured. Thus, our attitude scale for the tobacco companies will contain only a sample of all the items or statements we could possibly have included. In fact, often we will not even know what all the relevant items are. If we added, deleted, or changed the wording of some items, we would undoubtedly change the outcome with respect to the scores of Mary and Jane. We must constantly be aware that our instrument reflects our interpretation of the construct and the items we use to measure it and that the resulting scores will vary according to the way in which items are chosen and the way those items are expressed.

   Our final score is also influenced by the number of items presented. A man's height can serve as an indicator of his "size," but so can his weight, the size of his waistline, chest, and so on. We certainly could expect to have a better measure of a man's size if we included all these items. So it is with psychological measurements. Other things being equal, a one-item scale is a less adequate sample of the universe of items relevant to a characteristic than is a twenty-five-item scale.

7. *Differences due to lack of clarity of the measuring instrument.* Sometimes a difference in response to a questionnaire or an item on a scale may represent differences in interpretation of an ambiguous or complex question rather than any fundamental differences in the characteristic one is attempting to measure. We saw in the last chapter how even simple words can be open to misinterpretation. In measuring complex concepts such as attitudes, the possibilities for misunderstanding increase greatly. One of the researcher's main tasks is to generate items or questions that mean the same thing to all respondents, so that the observed differences in scores are not caused by differences in interpretation.

8. *Differences due to mechanical factors.* "Circumstances such as broken pencils, check marks in the wrong box, poorly printed instructions, and lack of space to record responses fully, play their role in preventing the most effective functioning of a measuring instrument."[6]

Research Window 13.2
Marketing Researchers Face the *Real* Pepsi Challenge: Interpreting Taste Tests

When the Coca-Cola Company uncorked its formula for the "New" Coke, executives boasted that it was the surest move they had ever made. They described as "overwhelming" the results of taste tests with 190,000 consumers, the majority of whom preferred the new recipe over old Coke.

History now records the introduction of the "New" Coke right up there with the debut of the Edsel as one of the greatest marketing debacles of all time. But what went wrong? If a marketer can't count on the results from 190,000 taste tests, then what is the role of research in the marketing mix?

Analysts now agree that what Coke failed to measure was the psychological impact of tampering with a 99-year-old soft drink. "When you have a product with a strong heritage that people could always count on being there, the mind becomes more important than physiological responses," said the research director for a rival cola.

Few products could stir as much emotion as all-American Coke, but other factors can also dilute the significance of taste tests. Certainly the image created by advertising affects people's perceptions of taste. That's why researchers often do both blind taste tests and tests in which brand names are revealed. "We did blind tests in the Pepsi Challenge commercials to eliminate brand influences," said an executive at one advertising firm. "But then we had to be very careful to say that people preferred the taste of Pepsi, not that they preferred Pepsi."

The color of a product also may make it seem tastier. When light-colored beer gets a shot of food coloring, consumers tend to describe it as heartier.

Market researchers also say that 7-Up often beats colas in taste tests partly because people like its clear, light color. Yet, when the same people are asked what they take along on picnics or order at fast food restaurants, they usually say a cola.

Measuring taste preferences is further confounded because the ability to discriminate between flavors varies greatly from one person to the next. Coca-Cola's marketing research director says that only about half the population has taste buds sensitive enough to distinguish between Coke and Pepsi. Indeed, "if you remove the caramel color from Coke, a lot of people won't be able to tell it from one of the clear drinks like Sprite," he said.

Testing conditions and procedures can also distort the results of taste studies. Researchers note that responses may be influenced by how hungry or thirsty a subject is, how questions are phrased, and even how the test samples of competing brands are numbered. Typically, companies choose numbers like 697 and 483 to label products because 1 and 2 and A and B carry definite connotations.

Other marketing consultants criticize taste tests as unrealistic because they often compare only two products, when in reality consumers have many more choices in supermarkets. In addition, taste tests are conducted in the unnatural setting of a shopping mall. But research firms try to screen out as many other distorting influences as possible. They make sure test samples are kept at precisely the same temperature, and they serve only one sample from a can or bottle. To neutralize interviewee's palates, they usually feed people a cup of water and an unsalted cracker.

Source: Ronald Alsop, "Coke's Flip-Flop Underscores Risks of Consumer Taste Tests," *The Wall Street Journal*, (July 18, 1985), p. 27.

Classification and Assessment of Error

Systematic error Error in measurement that is also known as *constant error* since it affects the measurement in a systematic way.

The ideal in any scale is to generate a score that reflects true differences in the characteristic one is attempting to measure, without interference from irrelevant factors. What we may in fact obtain is often something else. One type of error that may appear in our scores is, **systematic error,** which is also called **constant error** since it affects the measurement in a constant way. Examples would be the measurement of a man's height with a poorly calibrated wooden yardstick or differences in stable characteristics that affect the person's score.

Random error Error in measurement due to the transient aspects of the person or measurement situation and which affects the measurement in irregular ways.

Another type of error, **random error,** is not constant but is instead due to transient aspects of the person or measurement situation, and which affects the measurement in irregular ways. A random error is present when we repeat a measurement on an individual or group of individuals and do not get the same scores as the first time we did the measurement, even though the characteristic being measured has not changed. For instance, if, unbeknownst to the researcher, a man who was measured once changes his shoes before being measured again, the two measures may not agree even though the man's actual height has not changed.

Validity The extent to which differences in scores on a measuring instrument reflect true differences among individuals, groups, or situations in the characteristic that it seeks to measure, or true differences in the same individual, group, or situation from one occasion to another, rather than constant or random errors.

The distinction between systematic error and random error is critical because of the way the **validity,** or correctness, of a measure is assessed. Any scale or other measurement instrument that accurately measures what it was intended to measure is said to have validity. The validity of a measuring instrument is defined as "the extent to which differences in scores on it reflect true differences among individuals on the characteristic we seek to measure, rather than constant or random errors."[7] To accomplish this is a very difficult task. It is not accomplished by simply making up a set of questions or statements to measure a person's attitude toward smoking in public places, for example. The researcher must take the necessary steps to ensure the questionnaire does actually measure a person's attitude on this subject. This is never established unequivocally, but is always inferred. There are two types of inferences we make as we try to establish the validity of an instrument: (1) direct assessment of validity and (2) indirect assessment using reliability.[8]

Direct Assessment of Validity

There are three types of direct assessment techniques we can use to infer the validity of a measure. We can look for evidence of its pragmatic validity, content validity, and construct validity.

Pragmatic validity The usefulness of the measuring instrument as a predictor of some other characteristic or behavior of the individual; it is sometimes called *predictive validity* or *criterion-related validity.*

Pragmatic Validity   How well the measure actually predicts the criterion, whether it be a characteristic or specific behavior of the individual, is its **pragmatic validity.** An example would be the Graduate Management Admissions Test. The fact that this test is required by most of the major schools of business attests to its pragmatic validity; it has proved useful in predicting how well a student with a particular score on the exam will do in an accredited M.B.A. program. The test score is used to predict the criterion of performance. An attitude-scale example might be to use scores that sales representatives achieve on a measuring instrument designed to assess their job satisfaction in predicting their likelihood of quitting. Both of these examples illustrate *predictive validity* or *criterion-related validity,* which are alternate terms for pragmatic validity, in that the attitude scores are used to predict a future behavior.

Concurrent validity The correlation between the predictor variable and the criterion variable when both are assessed at the same point in time.

However, there is another type of pragmatic validity known as **concurrent validity,** which is concerned with the relationship between the predictor variable and the criterion variable when both are assessed at the same point in time. For example, the common tuberculin tine test, which is a routine part of many physical exams, is not meant to predict whether a person is apt to contract tuberculosis at some point in the future, but whether the person has tuberculosis now.

Pragmatic validity is determined strictly by the correlation between the measuring instrument and the characteristic or behavior being measured. If the correlation is high, the measure is said to have pragmatic validity.

Thus if it were found that accuracy in horseshoe pitching correlated highly with success in college, horseshoe pitching would be a valid measure for predicting success in college. This is not meant to imply that sound theory and common sense are not useful in selecting predictor instruments for investigation, but after the investigations are done, the entire proof of the pudding is in the correlations.[9]

Pragmatic validity is relatively easy to assess. It requires, to be sure, a reasonably valid way of measuring the criterion with which the scores on the measuring instrument are to be compared. Given that such scores are available, though (for example, the grades the student actually achieves in an M.B.A. program or a tally of how many sales representatives actually quit), all that the researcher needs to do is to establish the degree of relationship, usually in the form of some kind of correlation coefficient, between the scores on the measuring instrument and the criterion variable. While easy to assess, pragmatic validity is rarely the most important kind of validity. We are often concerned with "what the measure in fact measures" rather than simply whether it predicts accurately or not.

Content Validity   If the measurement instrument adequately covers the most important aspects of the construct that is being measured, it has **content validity.** Consider, for example, the characteristic of "spelling ability," and suppose that the following list of words was used to assess an individual's spelling ability: *catcher, shortstop, foul, strike, walk, pitcher.* Now, you would probably take issue with this spelling test. Further, the basis for your objection probably would be the fact that all the words relate to the sport of baseball. Therefore, you could argue that an individual who is basically a very poor speller could do well on this test simply because he or she is a baseball fan. You would be right, of course. A person with a good basic ability for spelling but little interest in baseball might, in fact, do worse on this spelling test than one with less native ability but a good deal more interest in baseball. The test could be said to lack content validity, since it does not properly sample the range of all possible words that could be used but is instead very selective in its emphasis.

Theoretically, to capture a person's spelling ability (in English) most accurately, we would have to administer a test that includes all the words in the English language. The person who spelled the greatest number of these words correctly would be said to have the most spelling ability. This is an unrealistic procedure. It would take several lifetimes to complete. We therefore resort to sampling the range of the characteristic by constructing spelling tests that consist of samples of all the possible words that could be used. Different samples of items can produce different comparative performances by individuals. We need to recognize that whether we have assessed the true characteristic depends on how well we have sampled the range of the characteristic. This is true not only for spelling ability, but also holds for psychological characteristics.

How can we ensure that our measure will possess content validity? We can never guarantee it, because it is partly a matter of judgment. We may feel quite comfortable with the items included in a measure, for example, while a critic may argue that we have failed to sample from some relevant aspect of the characteristic. While we can never guarantee the content validity of a measure, we can minimize the objections of the critics. The key to content validity lies in the *procedures* that are used to develop the instrument.

One way to define an appropriate domain, for example, is to search the literature and see how other researchers have defined the domain. The next step is to formulate a large number of items that broadly represent the range of attitudes that could be

Content validity
The adequacy with which the domain of the characteristic is captured by the measure; it is sometimes called *face validity.*

related to the topic in question. At this stage, the researcher may wish to include a wide variety of items with slightly different shades of meaning, since this original list will be narrowed down to produce the final instrument.

The collection of items must be large, so that after refinement the measure still contains enough items to adequately sample the entire range of the variable. In the example cited previously, a measure of a sales representative's job satisfaction would need to include items about each of the components of the job (duties, fellow workers, top management, sales supervisor, customers, pay, and promotion opportunities) if it is to be content-valid.

Construct validity
Assessment of how well the instrument captures the construct, concept, or trait it is supposed to be measuring.

Construct Validity   The measurement of constructs is a vital task, and **construct validity** is the most difficult type of validity to establish. Not only must the instrument be internally consistent, but it must also measure what it was intended to measure. That is, each item in the instrument must reflect the construct and must also show a correlation with other items in the instrument.[10]

Thus, a measuring instrument designed to measure attitude would be said to have construct validity if it indeed measured the attitude in question and not some other underlying characteristic of the individual that affects his or her score. Construct validity lies at the very heart of scientific progress. Scientists need constructs with which to communicate. So do you and I. In marketing we speak of people's socioeconomic class, their personality, their attitudes, and so on, because these are all constructs for explaining marketing behavior. And while vital, they also are unobservable. We can observe behavior related to these constructs but not the constructs themselves. Rather, we try to operationally define a construct in terms of things we can observe. When we agree on the operational definition, precision in communication is advanced. Instead of saying that what is measured by these 75 items is the person's brand loyalty, we can speak of the notion of brand loyalty.

Once researchers have specified the domain of the construct, generated a set of items relevant to the breadth of the domain, refined the items, and ensured that the remaining items are internally consistent, the final step is to see how well the measure relates to measures of other constructs to which the construct in question is theoretically related. Does it behave as expected? Does it fit the theory or model relating this construct to other constructs?

For example, consider our earlier example relating job satisfaction to job turnover among sales representatives. Suppose we had developed a measure to assess a sales representative's job satisfaction. The construct validity of the measure could be assessed by determining if there is indeed a relationship between job-satisfaction scores and company turnover. Those companies in which the scores are low (indicating less job satisfaction) should experience more turnover than those with high scores. If they do not, one would question the construct validity of the job-satisfaction measure. In other words, the construct validity of a measure is assessed by whether the measure confirms or denies the hypotheses predicted from the theory based on the constructs.

The problem, of course, is that the failure of the hypothesized relationship to hold true for the phenomenon being observed may be due either to a lack of construct validity or to incorrect theory. We often try to establish the construct validity of a measure, therefore, by relating it to a number of other constructs rather than only one. We also try to use those theories and hypotheses that have been tested by others and found to be sound.

If the trait or construct exists, it also should be measurable by more than one method. These methods should be independent insofar as possible. If they are all measuring the same construct, though, the measures should have a high level of

Convergent validity
Confirmation of the
existence of a construct
determined by the
correlations exhibited by
independent measures of
the construct.

Discriminant validity
Criterion imposed on a
measure of a construct
requiring that it not
correlate too highly with
measures from which it is
supposed to differ.

Method variance The
variation in scores
attributable to the method
of data collection.

Reliability Similarity of
results provided by
independent but
comparable measures of
the same object, trait, or
construct.

correlation. This provides evidence of **convergent validity,** which is defined as "the confirmation of a relationship by independent measurement procedures." Another evidence of construct validity is **discriminant validity,** which requires that a measure not correlate too highly with measures from which it is supposed to differ.[11] Correlations that are too high suggest that the measure is not actually capturing an isolated trait or that it is simply reflecting **method variance,** which is the variation in scores attributable to the method of data collection. "The assumption is generally made . . . that what the test measures is determined by the content of the items. Yet the final score . . . is a composite of effects resulting from the content of the items and effects resulting *from the form of the items used*"[12] (emphasis added).

Indirect Assessment via Reliability

Reliability refers to the ability to obtain similar results by measuring an object, trait, or construct with independent but comparable measures. If we gave a group of people two different measures of intelligence, and the two sets of scores from the two measures correlated highly with each other, we would say that the measures are reliable in that each is able to replicate the scores of the other.

Evaluating the reliability of any measuring instrument consists of determining how much of the variation in scores is due to inconsistencies in measurement.[13] The reliability of the instrument should be established before it is used for a substantive study and not after.

Before discussing how evidence of reliability is obtained, we need to make a few points. If a measure is reliable, it is not influenced by transitory factors. However, a measure could be reliable but not necessarily valid. For example, let us assume we have devised a measure of upper body strength. The measure requires that subjects do a series of different exercises with some weights. Now suppose that the results from the various exercises agree. This would mean the measure was reliable. Suppose, though, that the weights used were mismarked. While reliable, then, the measure of body strength would be systematically off the mark, meaning it would be invalid.

Figure 13.2 illustrates the concept pictorially. The old rifle is unreliable. The new rifle is relatively reliable, but its sights are set incorrectly in the center diagram. The right-hand diagram shows the new rifle with its sights set correctly. Only in the right-hand diagram could a user of any of the rifles be expected to hit the center of the target with regularity.

Although a measure that is reliable may or may not be valid, if it is not reliable, it is surely not valid. Conversely, if it is valid, it is surely reliable. A valid measure of height will be reliable, since it is actually measuring the trait in question. Reliability thus provides only negative evidence; it can prove the lack of validity but not the presence of it. Reliability is more easily determined than validity, however, so there has been a greater emphasis on it historically for inferring the quality of measures.

Stability Evidence of the
reliability of a measure;
determined by measuring
the same objects or
individuals at two
different points in time
and then correlating the
scores; also known as test-
retest reliability
assessment.

Stability   One of the more popular ways of establishing the reliability of a measure is to measure the same objects or individuals at two different points in time and to correlate the obtained scores. Assuming that the objects or individuals have not changed in the interim, the two scores should correlate perfectly. To the extent that they do not, random disturbances were operating in either one or both of the test situations to produce random error in the measurement. The procedure is known as *test-retest reliability assessment*, and it establishes a measure's **stability.**

Figure 13.2   ***Illustration of Difference between Random and Systematic Error***

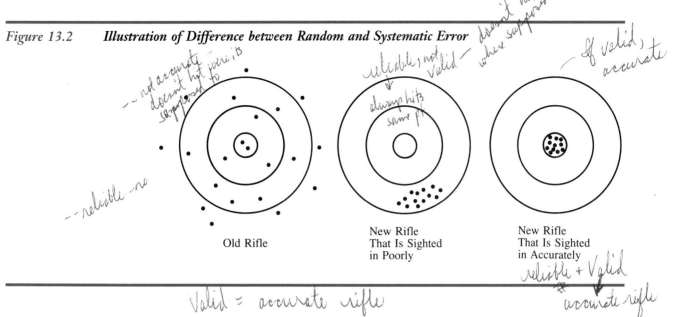

Old Rifle

New Rifle
That Is Sighted
in Poorly

New Rifle
That Is Sighted
in Accurately

Equivalence Evidence of
the reliability of a
measure; determined in
both single instruments
and measurement
situations. When applied
to instruments, the
equivalence measure of
reliability is the internal
consistency or internal
homogeneity of the set of
items forming the scale;
when applied to
measurement situations,
the equivalence measure
of reliability focuses on
whether different
observers or different
instruments used to
measure the same
individuals or objects at
the same point in time
yield consistent results.

One of the critical decisions the researcher must face in determining the stability
of a measure is how long to wait between successive administrations of the
instrument. Suppose the researcher's instrument is an attitude scale. If the researcher
waits too long, the person's attitude may change, thus producing a low correlation
between the two scores. On the other hand, a short wait will likely produce test
bias—people may remember how they responded the first time and be more
consistent in their responses than is warranted by their attitudes.

To handle this problem, many researchers will use alternative forms for the two
administrations. Instead of putting all the items in one form, the researcher generates
two instruments that are as identical as possible in content. That is, each form should
contain items from the same domains, and each domain of content should receive
approximately the same emphasis in each form. Ideally, there would be a one-to-one
correspondence between items on each of the two forms so that the means and
standard deviations of the two forms would be identical and the intercorrelations
among the items would be the same in both versions.[14] While it is next to impossible
to achieve the ideal, it is possible to construct forms that are roughly parallel, and
parallel forms can be correlated across time to measure stability. The recommended
time interval between administrations is two weeks.[15]

Equivalence   In an attitude scale, every item is theoretically acting as a measure of
the attitude, and a subject's score on one part of the scale should correlate with his or
her score on another part of the scale. The **equivalence** measure of reliability focuses
on the internal consistency of the set of items forming the scale.

The earliest measure of the internal consistency of a set of items was the *split-half
reliability* of the scale. In assessing split-half reliability, the total set of items is divided
into two equivalent halves; the total scores for the two halves are correlated; and this
is taken as the measure of reliability of the instrument. Sometimes the division of
items is made randomly, while at other times the even items are assumed to form one
half and the odd the other half of the instrument. The total score on the even items
is then correlated with the total score obtained from the odd items.

Pointed criticism is increasingly being directed at split-half reliability as the
measure of the internal consistency of a scale. The criticism focuses on the necessarily

arbitrary division of the items into equivalent halves. Each of the many possible divisions can produce different correlations between the two halves or different reliabilities. Which division is correct or, alternatively, what is then the reliability of the instrument? For example, a ten-item scale has 126 possible splits or 126 possible reliability coefficients.[16]

A more appropriate way to assess the internal homogeneity of a set of items is to look at all of the items simultaneously, using coefficient alpha. One reason is that coefficient alpha has a direct relationship to the most accepted and conceptually appealing measurement model, the *domain sampling model*. The domain sampling model holds that the purpose of any particular measurement is to estimate the score that would be obtained if *all* the items in the domain were used. The score that any subject would obtain over the whole sample domain is the person's true score, X_T.

In practice, one typically does not use all of the items that could be used, but only a sample of them. To the extent that the sample of items correlates with true scores, it is good. According to the domain sampling model, then, a primary source of measurement error is the inadequate sampling of the domain of relevant items.

Basic to the domain sampling model is the concept of a very large correlation matrix showing all correlations among the items in the domain. No single item is likely to provide a perfect representation of the concept, just as no single word can be used to test for differences in subjects' spelling abilities and no single question can measure a person's intelligence.

The average correlation among the items in this large matrix, $\bar{r}$, indicates the extent to which some common core is present in the items. The dispersion of correlations about the average indicates the extent to which items vary in sharing the common core. The key assumption in the domain sampling model is that all items, *if they belong to the domain of the concept*, have an equal amount of common core. This statement implies that the average correlation in each column of the hypothetical matrix is the same, and in turn equals the average correlation in the whole matrix. That is, if all the items in a measure are drawn from the domain of a single construct, responses to those items should be highly intercorrelated. Low inter-item correlations, in contrast, indicate that some items are not drawn from the appropriate domain and are producing error and unreliability.

Coefficient alpha provides a summary measure of the intercorrelations that exist among a set of items. Alpha is calculated as[17]

$$\alpha = \left(\frac{k}{k-1}\right)\left(1 - \frac{\sum_{i=1}^{k}\sigma_i^2}{\sigma_t^2}\right)$$

where k = number of items in the scale,
   σ_i^2 = variance of scores on item i across subjects and
   σ_t^2 = variance of total scores across subjects where the total score for each respondent represents the sum of the individual item scores.

Coefficient alpha routinely should be calculated to assess the quality of measure. It is pregnant with meaning because the *square root* of coefficient alpha is the *estimated correlation of the k-item test with errorless true scores*.

If alpha is low, what should the analyst do? If the item pool is sufficiently large, this outcome suggests that some items do not share equally in the common core and should be eliminated. The easiest way to find them is to calculate the correlation of

Figure 13.3   ***A Situation in Which the Judgments of Two Observers Did Not Agree***

Source: Reprinted with special permission of King Features Syndicate, Inc.

each item with the total score and to plot these correlations by decreasing order of magnitude. Items with correlations near zero would be eliminated. Further, items that produce a substantial or sudden drop in the item-to-total correlations would also be deleted.

If the construct had, say, five identifiable dimensions or components, coefficient alpha would be calculated for each dimension. The item-to-total correlations used to delete items would also be based on the items in the component and the total score for that dimension.

The preceding discussion deals with the equivalence measure of reliability when applied to a single instrument. An alternate equivalence measure is used when different observers or different instruments measure the same individuals or objects at the same point in time. Do these methods produce consistent results? Are they equivalent as measured by the correlations among the total scores? An example would be a beauty contest. Do the judges, using the established criteria of beauty, talent, poise, and so on, rank the women in the same order in terms of winner, first runner-up, second runner-up, and so on? The reliability of the measure is greater to the extent that the judges agree. Figure 13.3, for example, depicts a situation in which the judgments of two different observers do not agree. This type of equivalence is the basis of convergent validation when the measures are independent.[18]

Developing Measures

For a beginning researcher, it is easy to get confused over the issue of how one goes about developing measures of marketing constructs. How does one contend with the basic issues of reliability and validity, and how does one make the choices among the various coefficients that can be computed? Figure 13.4 diagrams a sequence of steps that can be followed to develop valid measures of marketing constructs.[19]

Step 1 in the process involves specifying the domain of the construct that is to be measured. Researchers need to be careful in specifying what is included in the domain of the construct and what is excluded. Consider measuring customer satisfaction with a new space heater the family recently purchased, for example. What attributes of the product and the purchase should be measured to assess accurately the family's satisfaction? Certainly one would want to be reasonably exhaustive in the list of

Figure 13.4   ***Suggested Procedure for Developing Measures***

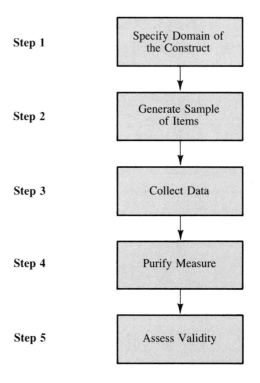

Step 1 — Specify Domain of the Construct

Step 2 — Generate Sample of Items

Step 3 — Collect Data

Step 4 — Purify Measure

Step 5 — Assess Validity

Source: Adapted from the procedure suggested by Gilbert A. Churchill, Jr., "A Paradigm for Developing Better Measures of Marketing Constructs," *Journal of Marketing Research*, 16 (February 1979), p. 66.

product features to be included, incorporating such facets as cost, durability, quality, operating performance, and aesthetic features. But what about purchaser's reaction to the sales assistance received? What about the family members' reactions to subsequent advertising for a competitor's product offering the same features at lower cost? Or what about the family's reactions to news of some negative environmental effects of using the product? To detail which of these factors should be included or how customer satisfaction should be operationalized is beyond the scope of this book. But, obviously, researchers need to be very careful in specifying what is to be included in the domain of the construct being measured and what is to be excluded.

Step 2 in the process is to generate items that capture the domain as specified. Those techniques that are typically productive in exploratory research, including literature searches, experience surveys, and insight-stimulating examples, are generally productive here. The literature should indicate how the variable has been defined previously and how many dimensions or components it has. The search for ways to measure customer satisfaction would include product brochures, articles in trade magazines and newspapers, or results of product tests such as those published by *Consumer Reports*. The experience survey might include discussions with people in the product group responsible for the product, sales representatives, dealers, persons in marketing research, consumers, and outsiders who have a special expertise in heating equipment. The insight-stimulating examples could involve a comparison of competitors' products or a detailed examination of some particularly vehement complaints in unsolicited letters about the performance of the product. Examples that reveal sharp contrasts or having striking features would be most productive. Focus groups also could be used to advantage at the item-generation stage.

Step 3 involves collecting data about the concept from a relevant sample of the target population—for example, all those who have purchased a space heater within the last six months.

Step 4 uses the data collected in Step 3 to purify the original set of items. The purification involves eliminating items that seemed to create confusion among respondents and items that do not discriminate between subjects with fundamentally different positions on the construct. The fundamental criterion that is used to eliminate items is how each item goes together with the other items. If all the items in a measure are drawn from the domain of a single construct, responses to those items should be highly correlated. If they are not, that is an indication that some of the items are not drawn from the appropriate domain and are producing error and unreliability, and those items should be eliminated. Several of the equivalence reliability coefficients mentioned earlier can be used to make this assessment, as can other statistical techniques.[20]

Step 5 in the process involves determining the validity of the purified measure. This involves assessing primarily its convergent, discriminant, and construct validity, since its content validity will have largely been addressed in Steps 1 through 4; and the assessment of its construct validity involves determining whether it behaves as expected, which in turn involves determining its pragmatic validity.

Ethical
Dilemma 13.2   Susan Black has been given the assignment of measuring the quality of service provided by her employer, Valley Bank. She welcomes the assignment for several reasons. One important reason is that she saw a scale for measuring a bank's image in a recent issue of a bank trade magazine. She plans to use the scale as is. That will take care of the measurement issues, leaving only the sampling issues (e.g., who to sample, how many, how, and so on) with which to grapple, thereby simplifying the task.

- Before using a scale of this type, does Black have any responsibility to investigate its reliability and validity properties?
- Can she simply assume that because the scale has been published it is good? What are the publisher's responsibilities in this regard?
- What if Black has no formal training in measurement? What should she do?

Back to the Case

"Cheer up, Todd," urged Ernie Henderson. "It's not the end of the world. It's not even the end of Teen Sport. We just have to make some changes, that's all."

"I can't believe it," replied Todd Whalen, shaking his head. "I know that Teen Sport's a winner. I simply can't believe these test market results. I think you just ran into so much

trouble with the holidays that it screwed up all of the results."

"It's true, we did run into problems with the holidays. At that time of year the stores are so full of promotional items that people tend to be distracted from everyday products like deodorant. We also had a lower response rate on our phone interviews than we usually like to have. People are very tense and busy during the holidays and are much less likely to say yes when a phone interviewer asks them for 10 minutes of their time."

"Like I said," snapped Whalen, "the test results are suspect."

"I don't think so," said Henderson calmly. "Besides, the test market study has turned up another problem that's completely unrelated to the holidays."

"I don't want to hear it."

"Well, here it is anyway: I think we're going to have to dump all the Teen Sport we have on hand and reformulate. Remember how I pushed for an additional round of open-ended focus groups when we were testing for packaging preferences?"

"We just didn't have time," replied Whalen. "You yourself said that teenagers are fickle. We needed to get the product on the shelves before they changed their minds about what they liked."

"Well, the problem is that while we addressed the usual issues of smell, odor protection, packaging, and price in the initial round of focus groups, we never considered one variable that's going to turn out to be very important."

"What's that?" asked Whalen.

"Color."

"Color? All your studies showed that teenaged girls love hot, neon colors. I thought that making the deodorant shocking pink would be the perfect way to get the message across that Teen Sport wasn't their mother's deodorant. It ties in perfectly with the advertising campaign."

"Yes, but maybe teenaged girls love neon colors only for the package," replied Henderson. "There's a lot of environmental awareness among kids this age. Maybe the girls don't want to use a product that contains artificial colors. Besides, I think that the neon craze has already peaked. . . ."

Not only should researchers be careful to not let their own biases affect the instrument, but they also need to be careful to design attitude scales that measure the total potential domain of the construct being measured. Only if the total domain is covered can the instrument be said to provide content validity.

Summary

Learning Objective 1: Define the term *measurement* as it is used in marketing research.

Measurement consists of rules for assigning numbers to objects in such a way as to represent quantities of attributes.

Learning Objective 2: List the four types of scales that can be used to measure an attribute.

The four types of scales on which an attribute can be measured are nominal, ordinal, interval, and ratio scales.

Learning Objective 3: Explain the primary difference between a ratio scale and an interval scale.

In an interval scale, the zero point is established arbitrarily. The ratio scale possesses a natural, or absolute, zero—one for which there is universal agreement as to its location.

Learning Objective 4: Cite some of the factors that may cause differences in two measures of the same attribute.

Some of the factors that may cause differences in two measures of the same attribute are (1) true differences in the characteristic being measured, (2) true differences in other relatively stable characteristics of the individual that affect the score, (3) differences due to transient personal factors, (4) differences due to situational factors, (5) differences due to variations in administration, (6) differences due to the sampling of items, (7) differences due to lack of clarity of the measuring instrument, and (8) differences due to mechanical factors.

Learning Objective 5: Name the two types of error that may affect measurement scores and define each.

Two types of error may affect scores. The first type is systematic error, which affects the measurement in a constant way. The second type is random error, which is due to transient aspects of the person or measurement situation, and which affects the measurement in irregular ways.

Learning Objective 6: Explain the concept of validity as it relates to measuring instruments.

Any scale or other measurement instrument that actually measures what it was intended to measure is said to have validity. The validity of a measuring instrument is defined as "the extent to which differences in scores on it reflect true differences among individuals on the characteristic we seek to measure, rather than constant or random errors."

Learning Objective 7: Specify the two types of inferences a researcher makes in attempting to establish the validity of an instrument.

The two types of inferences we make as we try to establish the validity of an instrument are based on (1) direct assessment of its validity and (2) indirect assessment of its validity using reliability.

Learning Objective 8: Cite the three types of direct assessment techniques used to infer the validity of a measure.

The three types of validity that can be directly assessed in a measure are pragmatic validity, content validity, and construct validity.

Learning Objective 9: Outline the sequence of steps to follow in developing valid measures of marketing constructs.

The following sequence of steps are helpful in developing better measures of marketing constructs: (1) specify the domain of the construct, (2) generate a sample of items, (3) collect data, (4) purify the measure, and (5) assess validity.

Discussion Questions, Problems, and Projects

1. Identify the type of scale (nominal, ordinal, interval, ratio) being used in each of the following questions. Justify your answer.
   (a) *During which season of the year were you born?*
       ____ winter   ____ spring   ____ summer   ____ fall
   (b) *What is your total household income?* _____
   (c) *Which are your three most preferred brands of cigarettes? Rank them from 1 to 3 according to your preference, with 1 as most preferred.*
       ____ Marlboro   ____ Salem
       ____ Kent   ____ Kool
       ____ Benson and Hedges   ____ Vantage
   (d) *How much time do you spend on traveling to school every day?*
       ____ under 5 minutes   ____ 16–20 minutes
       ____ 5–10 minutes   ____ 30 minutes and over
       ____ 11–15 minutes
   (e) *How satisfied are you with* **Newsweek** *magazine?*
       ____ very satisfied   ____ dissatisfied
       ____ satisfied   ____ very dissatisfied
       ____ neither satisfied nor dissatisfied
   (f) *On an average, how many cigarettes do you smoke in a day?*
       ____ over 1 pack   ____ less than ½ pack
       ____ ½ to 1 pack
   (g) *Which one of the following courses have you taken?*
       ____ marketing research   ____ sales management
       ____ advertising management ____ consumer behavior
   (h) *What is the level of education for the head of the household?*
       ____ some high school   ____ some college
       ____ high school graduate ____ college graduate and/or graduate work
2. The analysis for each of the above questions is given below. Is the analysis appropriate for the scale used?
   (a) About 50 percent of the sample was born in the fall, while 25 percent of the sample was born in the spring, and the remaining 25 percent was born in the

winter. It can be concluded that the fall is twice as popular as the spring and the winter seasons.

(b) The average income is $25,000. There are twice as many individuals with an income of less than $9,999 than individuals with an income of $40,000 and over.

(c) Marlboro is the most preferred brand. The mean preference is 3.52.

(d) The median time spent on traveling to school is 8.5 minutes. There are three times as many respondents traveling less than 5 minutes as respondents traveling 16–20 minutes.

(e) The average satisfaction score is 4.5, which seems to indicate a high level of satisfaction with *Newsweek* magazine.

(f) Ten percent of the respondents smoke less than one-half pack of cigarettes a day, while three times as many respondents smoke over one pack of cigarettes a day.

(g) Sales management is the most frequently taken course, since the median is 3.2.

(h) The responses indicate that 40 percent of the sample have some high school education, 25 percent of the sample are high school graduates, 20 percent have some college education, and 10 percent are college graduates. The mean education level is 2.6.

3. You have developed a questionnaire designed to measure attitudes toward a set of television ads for a new snack food product. The respondents, as a group, will view the ads on a television set and then complete the questionnaire. Due to logistical circumstances beyond your control, you must split your sample of respondents into three groups and collect data on three separate days. What steps might you take in an effort to minimize possible variance in scores caused by the three separate administrations?

4. Many areas of marketing research rely heavily on measures of psychological constructs. What characteristics inherent in these constructs make them so difficult to measure? What tools can the marketing researcher bring to bear when evaluating the "correctness" of his or her measure? In other words, what things can we do that allow us to state with some degree of confidence that we are indeed measuring the construct of interest?

5. Discuss the notion that a particular measure could be reliable and still not be valid. In your discussion, distinguish between reliability and validity.

6. Find the following articles from the periodical section of your library: (i) G. A. Churchill, Jr., N. M. Ford, and O. C. Walker, Jr., "Measuring Job Satisfaction of Industrial Salesmen," *Journal of Marketing Research*, 11 (August 1974), pp. 254–260; and (ii) W. J. Lundstrom and L. M. Lamont, "The Development of a Scale for Measuring Consumer Discontent," *Journal of Marketing Research*, 13 (November 1976), pp. 373–381. For each of the articles, answer the following questions:

(a) How was the reliability assessed? What techniques were specifically used?

(b) What kinds of validity were assessed (predictive, content, and so forth)?

7. Feather-Tote Luggage is a producer of cloth-covered luggage, one of the primary advantages of which is its light weight. The company distributes its luggage through major department stores, mail-order houses, clothing retailers, and other retail outlets such as stationery stores, leather good stores, and so on. The company advertises rather heavily, but it also supplements this promotional effort with a large field staff of sales representatives, numbering around 400. The number of sales representatives varies, and one of the historical problems confronting Feather-Tote Luggage has been the large number of sales representatives' resignations. It is not unusual for 10 to 20 percent of the sales force to turn over every year. Since the cost of training a new sales representative is estimated at $5,000 to $10,000, not including the lost sales that might result because of a personnel switch, Mr. Harvey, the sales manager, is rightly concerned. He has been concerned for some time and therefore has been conducting exit interviews with each departing sales representative. On the basis of these interviews, he has formulated the opinion that the major reason for this high turnover is general sales representatives' dissatisfaction with company policies, promotional

opportunities, and pay. But top management has not been sympathetic to Harvey's pleas regarding the changes needed in these areas of corporate policy. Rather, it has tended to counter Harvey's pleas with arguments that too much of what he is suggesting is based on his gut reactions and little hard data. Before it would be willing to change things, top management desires more systematic evidence that job satisfaction, in general, and these dimensions of job satisfaction, in particular, are the real reasons for the high turnover.

Describe the procedures you would employ in developing a measure by which the job satisfaction of Feather-Tote Luggage sales representatives could be assessed. Indicate the type of scale you would use and why, and detail the specific steps you would undertake to assure the validity and reliability of this measure.

Endnotes

1. Jum C. Nunnally, *Psychometric Theory*, 2nd ed. (New York: McGraw-Hill, 1978), p. 3.

2. Our classification follows that of Stanley S. Stevens, "Mathematics, Measurement and Psychophysics," in Stanley S. Stevens, ed., *Handbook of Experimental Psychology* (New York: John Wiley, 1951), the most accepted classification in the social sciences.

3. The zero point on the Fahrenheit scale was originally established by mixing equal weights of snow and salt.

4. Wendell R. Garner and C. D. Creelman, "Problems and Methods of Psychological Scaling," in Harry Helson and William Bevan, eds., *Contemporary Approaches to Psychology* (New York: Van Nostrand, 1967), p. 4.

5. These differences are adapted from Claire Selltiz, Lawrence S. Wrightsman, and Stuart W. Cook, *Research Methods in Social Relations*, 3rd ed. (New York: Holt, Rinehart and Winston, 1976), pp. 164–168. See also Duane F. Alwin and David J. Jackson, "Measurement Models for Response Errors in Surveys: Issues and Applications," in Karl F. Schuessler, ed., *Sociological Methodology 1980* (San Francisco: Jossey-Bass, 1979), pp. 69–119; and Frank E. Saal, Ronald G. Downey, and Mary Anne Lakey, "Rating the Ratings: Assessing the Psychometric Quality of Ratings Data," *Psychological Bulletin*, 88 (September 1980), pp. 413–428.

6. Selltiz, Wrightsman, and Cook, *Research Methods*, p. 168.

7. Selltiz, Wrightsman, and Cook, *Research Methods*, p. 169.

8. For detailed discussion of the conceptual relationships that should exist among the various indicants of reliability and validity and an empirical assessment of the evidence, see J. Paul Peter and Gilbert A. Churchill, Jr., "The Relationship among Research Design Choices and Psychometric Properties of Rating Scales: A Meta-Analysis," *Journal of Marketing Research*, 23 (February 1986), pp. 1–10.

9. Nunnally, *Psychometric Theory*, p. 88.

10. See Gilbert A. Churchill, Jr., "A Paradigm for Developing Better Measures of Marketing Constructs," *Journal of Marketing Research*, 16 (February 1979), pp. 64–73, for a procedure that can be used to construct scales having construct validity. See J. Paul Peter, "Construct Validity: A Review of Basic Issues and Marketing Practices," *Journal of Marketing Research*, 18 (May 1981), pp. 133–145, for an in-depth discussion of the notion of construct validity.

11. One convenient way of establishing the convergent and discriminant validity of a measure is through the multitrait-multimethod matrix of Campbell and Fiske. See Donald T. Campbell and Donald W. Fiske, "Convergent and Discriminant Validation by the Multitrait-Multimethod Matrix," *Psychological Bulletin*, 56 (1959), pp. 81–105. See also Neal Schmitt, Bryan W. Coyle, and Bruce B. Saari, "A Review and Critique of Analyses of Multitrait-Multimethod Matrices," *Multivariate Behavioral Research*, 12 (October 1977), pp. 447–478; and Donald P. Schwab, "Construct Validity in Organizational Behavior," in B. Staw and L. L. Cummings, eds., *Research in Organizational Behavior*, Vol. 2 (Greenwich, Conn.: JAI Press, 1980), pp. 3–43.

12. L. J. Cronbach, "Response Sets and Test Validity," *Educational and Psychological Measurement*, 6 (1946), p. 475. See also Joseph A. Cote and M. Ronald Buckley, "Estimating Trait, Method, and Error Variance: Generalizing Across 70 Construct Validation Studies," *Journal of Marketing Research*, 24 (August 1987), pp. 315–318.

13. See J. Paul Peter, "Reliability: A Review of Psychometric Basics and Recent Marketing Practices," *Journal of Marketing Research*, 16 (February 1979), pp. 6–17, for a detailed treatment of the issue of reliability in measurement. See Gilbert A. Churchill, Jr., and J. Paul Peter, "Research Design Effects on the Reliability of Rating Scales: A Meta-Analysis," *Journal of Marketing Research*, 21 (February 1984), pp. 360–375, for an empirical assessment of the factors that seem to affect the reliability of rating scales.

14. George W. Bohrnstedt, "Reliability and Validity Assessment in Attitude Measurement," in Gene F. Summers, ed., *Attitude Measurement* (Chicago: Rand McNally, 1970), p. 85.

15. Nunnally, *Psychometric Theory*, p. 234, presents a rather scathing argument against test-retest reliability when alternative forms of the instrument are not available. See pages 232–236 in particular.

16. In general, for a scale with $2n$ items, the total number of possible splits of the items into two halves is $(2n!)/2(n!)(n!)$. See Bohrnstedt, "Reliability and Validity," p. 86.

17. See Nunnally, *Psychometric Theory*, Chapters 6 and 7, pp. 190–255, for the rationale behind coefficient alpha and more detailed discussion of the formula for computing it.

18. For a general discussion of the measurement of interjudge reliability, see William D. Perreault, Jr., and Laurence E. Leigh, "Reliability of Nominal Data Based on Qualitative Judgments," *Journal of Marketing Research*, 26 (May 1989), pp. 135–148.

19. The procedure is adapted from Gilbert A. Churchill, Jr., "A Paradigm," pp. 64–73.

20. See Churchill, "A Paradigm," for detailed discussion of which coefficients should be used and the rationale for their use.

Suggested Additional Readings

For a procedure that can be used to construct scales having construct validity, see

Gilbert A. Churchill, Jr., "A Paradigm for Developing Better Measures of Marketing Constructs," *Journal of Marketing Research*, 16 (February 1979), pp. 64–73.

For a treatment of the various types of reliability and the role of reliability in measurement, see

Gilbert A. Churchill, Jr., and J. Paul Peter, "Research Design Effects on the Reliability of Rating Scales: A Meta-Analysis," *Journal of Marketing Research*, 21 (February 1984), pp. 360–375.

J. Paul Peter, "Reliability: A Review of Psychometric Basics and Recent Marketing Practices," *Journal of Marketing Research*, 16 (February 1979), pp. 6–17.

For in-depth discussions of the notions of validity, see

J. Paul Peter, "Construct Validity: A Review of Basic Issues and Marketing Practices," *Journal of Marketing Research*, 18 (May 1981), pp. 133–145.

J. Paul Peter and Gilbert A. Churchill, Jr., "The Relationship among Research Design Choices and Psychometric Properties of Rating Scales: A Meta-Analysis," *Journal of Marketing Research*, 23 (February 1986), pp. 1–10.

14

Chapter
Fourteen

Measuring Attitudes, Perceptions, and Preferences

Learning Objectives

Upon completing this chapter, you should be able to

1. List the various ways by which attitudes can be measured.

2. Name the most widely used attitude scaling techniques in marketing research and explain why researchers prefer them.

3. Explain how a Stapel scale differs from a semantic-differential scale.

4. Cite the one feature that is common to all ratings scales.

5. List three of the most common types of ratings scales.

6. Explain the difference between a graphic-ratings scale and an itemized-ratings scale.

7. Explain how the constant-sum scaling method works.

8. Identify the key decisions an analyst must make in order to complete a multidimensional-scaling analysis.

9. Explain the basic principle behind conjoint analysis.

Case in Marketing Research

For years Marvell Toys had been the only consistent performer in the volatile toy industry. In a business known for its big hits and even bigger busts, Marvell had avoided the go-for-broke mentality of the rest of the industry by carving out a comfortable niche for itself: Marvell had stuck to basic preschool toys that lasted forever and never went out of style.

But then Marvel had been challenged by a pack of competitors eager to enter the growing preschool market. Deciding that a good offense was the best defense, Marvell had decided to move aggressively into the market for children five and over. These school-age children were the target for Marvell's newly designed line of Flight Ranger toys.

Phil Baxter, a relative newcomer to Marvell's marketing department, was meeting with Susan Muskie, from Dale & Barnett, a firm that specialized in conducting marketing research with children. Marvell, so confident in the preschool market, was palpably nervous about venturing outside of what it knew best. It was certainly not going to launch the new product line without first conducting extensive marketing research.

"How long have you been involved in selling to kids, Phil?" asked Muskie after the preliminaries were over.

"Before signing on with Marvell, I worked in the marketing department at Heineman Beer," confessed Baxter.

"Well, as you've probably noticed since you've come to Marvell, marketing to kids is a lot less straightforward than selling beer to adults."

"Selling beer to adults isn't always that straightforward. . . ."

"Maybe not, but kids are a tough market. For one thing, they're fickle. What they loved last Christmas isn't necessarily going to rate a second look this Christmas. To make matters worse, when it comes right down to it, they're not the ones making the decisions to buy the toys. It's a two-pronged sales problem. First you have to convince the kids to want the toy; then you have to convince the parents that the kids should have what they want. And we haven't even touched on all the problems in trying to measure kids' attitudes toward a product while the product's still in its developmental stages. So, why don't you tell me about Flight Ranger before I succeed in getting you too depressed?"

"Well, Flight Ranger is a total departure for Marvell. It's a line of toys geared toward boys aged five to seven, which is the first time we've ventured past kindergarten. Also, it's a television tie-in, which we've never done before. The launch of the line is timed to coincide with a new Saturday-morning cartoon series called Flight Ranger, which is about pilot cowboys who patrol the Australian outback. There are two components to the line: full-sized costumes and weapons to be worn by the child, so that he can actually look like a Flight Ranger, and miniature Flight Ranger action figures and vehicles."

"I'm glad you came to me," said Muskie. "This is a very competitive segment of the toy market, and I wonder how people will feel seeing the Marvell label on guns and planes after all these years of associating Marvell with preschool push toys. Why don't you send me several complete sets of samples and I'll get right to work."

Discussion Issues

1. What problems might researchers expect to encounter in measuring children's attitudes?

2. How might children's attitudes and parents' attitudes differ on the same toy? On the Marvell brand name?

3. What other information about the new products does Muskie need before getting started on her research?

One of the most pervasive notions in all of marketing is that attitudes play a pivotal role in consumer behavior. Consequently, an attempt to measure attitudes is incorporated in most of the major marketing models and in many, if not most, investigations of consumer behavior that do not rely on formal integrated models.[1] Marketers tend to emphasize the importance of attitudes. "Attitudes directly *affect* purchase decisions and these, in turn, *directly affect* attitudes through experience in using the product or service selected. In a broad sense, purchase decisions are based *almost solely* upon attitudes existing at the time of purchase, however these attitudes might have been formed"[2] (emphasis added).

Practitioners are also interested in people's attitudes and use them for a variety of purposes, including: (1) The appliance manufacturer's interest in present dealer and prospective dealer attitudes toward the company's warranty policy. If the dealers support the policy, the company feels they are more likely to give adequate, courteous service and, in the process, produce more satisfied customers. (2) The cosmetic manufacturer's interest in consumers' attitudes toward the company's new shampoo as it debuts in test market. Based on an early assessment of consumers' reactions, the company may decide to revise or fine-tune its introductory marketing strategy before going national. (3) The industrial marketer's interest in the general job satisfaction of its highly trained, highly skilled field staff of sales representatives.

These examples indicate some of the many groups of people in whose attitudes the marketer typically is interested: the company's employees, its intermediaries, and its customers. Their attitude, stance, or predisposition to act can be important determinants of the company's success, and the marketer needs devices for measuring these attitudes. This chapter reviews some of the those devices.

While the attitude concept is one of the most widely used in social psychology, it is used inconsistently. Both researchers and practitioners have trouble agreeing on interpretations of its various aspects. However, there does seem to be substantial agreement on the following points:

1. Attitude represents a predisposition to act but does not guarantee that the actual behavior will occur. It merely indicates that there is a readiness to respond to an object. It is still necessary to do something to trigger the response.
2. Attitudes are relatively persistent and consistent over time. They can be changed, to be sure, but alteration of an attitude that is strongly held requires substantial intervention.
3. There is a consistency between attitudes and behavior, and people act in such a fashion as to maintain this consistency.
4. Attitudes connote a preference and evaluation of an idea or object. They result in either positive or neutral or negative feelings for the idea or object.

The consistencies noted in this list led to our definition of attitude as representing a person's ideas, convictions, or liking with regard to a specific object or idea, presented in Chapter 9.

In addition to attitudes, marketers also have a keen interest in perceptions and preferences, and in this chapter we will examine some of the techniques researchers use to measure attitudes, perceptions, and preferences.

Attitude-Scaling Procedures

There are a number of ways in which attitudes have been measured, including self-reports, observation of overt behavior, indirect techniques, performance of objective tasks, and physiological reactions.[3] By far the most common approach has

Self-report A method of assessing attitudes in which individuals are asked directly for their beliefs about or feelings toward an object or class of objects.

been **self-reports,** in which people are asked directly for their beliefs or feelings toward an object or class of objects. For example, Research Window 14.1 depicts the results of a study that used self-reports, which was conducted by Ogilvy & Mather to help the agency select media in various countries. A number of scales and scaling methods using self-reports have been devised to measure these feelings. The main types will be reviewed here, but first let us briefly review the other approaches to attitude determination.

Observation of Behavior

The observation approach to attitude determination rests on the presumption that a subject's behavior is conditioned by his or her attitudes, and that we can therefore use the observed behavior to infer these attitudes. The behavior that the researcher wishes to observe is often elicited by creating an artificial situation. For example, to assess a person's attitude toward mandatory seat belt legislation, the subject might be asked to sign a strongly worded petition in favor of making seat belt usage a law. The individual's attitude toward seat belts would be inferred based on whether or not he or she signed. Alternatively, subjects might be asked to participate in a group discussion of the seat belt issue, and the researcher would note whether the individuals supported or opposed seat belt legislation in the discussion.

Indirect Techniques

Indirect techniques Methods of assessing attitudes that use unstructured or partially structured stimuli such as word-association tests, sentence-completion tests, storytelling, and so on.

The **indirect techniques** of attitude assessment use some unstructured or partially constructed stimuli as discussed in Chapter 10, such as word-association tests, sentence-completion tests, storytelling, and so on. Since the arguments concerning the use of these devices were detailed there, they will not be repeated here.

Performance of Objective Tasks

Performance of objective tasks A method of assessing attitudes that rests on the presumption that a subject's performance of a specific assigned task (for example, memorizing a number of facts) will depend on the person's attitude.

On the theory that people's **performance of objective tasks** will reflect their attitudes, one might ask a person to memorize a number of facts about an issue and then assess his or her attitude toward that issue from the facts that were successfully memorized. Thus, to assess a person's attitude toward seat belt legislation, one might ask him or her to memorize such facts as (1) the number of lives saved by seat belt usage, (2) the number of people who died in accidents because they could not remove their seat belts in time, and (3) the number of states that have adopted a mandatory seat belt law. The material should reflect both sides of the issue. The researcher then would determine what facts the person remembered. The assumption is that subjects would be more apt to remember those arguments that are most consistent with their own position.

Physiological Reaction

Physiological reaction A method of assessing attitudes in which the researcher monitors the subject's response, by electrical or mechanical means, to the controlled introduction of some stimuli.

Another approach to attitude measurement involves **physiological reaction,** which was discussed in Chapter 11. Here, through electrical or mechanical means, such as the galvanic skin response technique, the researcher monitors the subject's response to the controlled introduction of some stimuli. One problem that arises in using these measures to assess attitude is that, with the exception of voice-pitch analysis, the individual's physiological response indicates only the intensity of the individual's feelings and not whether they are negative or positive.

Research Window 14.1
Opinions in Various Countries about Advertising in Different Media

	Hong Kong, % Agree	Brazil, % Agree	Colombia, % Agree	UK, % Agree	U.S., % Agree	West Germany, % Agree
Newspapers						
Informative	32	71	74	45	57	46
Entertaining	39	11	11	8	10	14
Boring	22	13	15	34	25	35
Irritating	7	5	—	13	8	5
Radio						
Informative	23	51	19	23	33	17
Entertaining	39	21	30	18	28	31
Boring	22	19	32	30	23	45
Irritating	16	9	19	29	16	7
TV						
Informative	26	48	18	19	29	18
Entertaining	61	32	75	51	29	39
Boring	6	15	5	13	22	38
Irritating	7	5	2	17	20	5
Billboards						
Informative	24	51	36	33	32	21
Entertaining	50	20	43	33	21	21
Boring	22	20	15	26	26	52
Irritating	24	9	6	8	21	6
Magazines						
Informative	33	71	31	41	52	32
Entertaining	40	14	62	22	19	21
Boring	23	10	6	25	18	40
Irritating	4	5	1	12	11	7
Direct Mail						
Informative	24	62	60	10	16	19
Entertaining	18	2	17	3	5	7
Boring	24	26	19	23	35	57
Irritating	34	10	4	64	44	17

Informative, entertaining, boring, or irritating—pick *one* to describe advertising in each medium: newspapers, magazines, radio, TV, billboards, and direct mail.

If you're American, you're most likely to say newspaper and magazine advertising is "informative," and direct mail is "irritating." After that you can't decide. If you're British, you feel much the same, except you do also grant that TV advertising is "entertaining." For the West Germans, though, it's *all* pretty "boring." By complete contrast, unless you're talking about direct mail, it's all "entertaining" in Hong Kong; and in Brazil, advertising, no matter where you find it, is likely to be "informative." The Colombians are more discriminating—newspaper and direct mail advertising is "informative"; TV, billboard and magazine advertising is "entertaining"; and radio advertising in Colombia is just as likely to be "boring" as "entertaining."

Source: *Listening Post, Number 64,* (September 1987) (New York: Ogilvy & Mather), pp. 3 and 5. Reprinted with permission from Ogilvy & Mather.

Figure 14.1   **Example of Summated-Ratings Scale**

	Strongly Disagree	Disagree	Neither Agree nor Disagree	Agree	Strongly Agree
1. The bank offers courteous service.	____	____	____	____	____
2. The bank has a convenient location.	____	____	____	____	____
3. The bank has convenient hours.	____	____	____	____	____
4. The bank offers low-interest-rate loans.	____	____	____	____	____

Although self-report techniques for attitude assessment are the most widely used in marketing research studies because they are easy to administer, one should be aware of these other approaches, particularly when attempting to establish the validity of a self-report measure. They can provide useful insight into how the method of measurement, rather than differences in the basic attitudes of subjects, caused the scores to vary. This is consistent with the notion of using multiple indicators to establish the convergent and discriminant validity of a measure.

Self-Report Attitude Scales

Since attitude is one of the most pervasive concepts in all of social psychology, it is natural that researchers would devise a number of methods to measure it. Although many of the methods use self-reports, each method uses them in different ways. In this section, we shall review some of these self-report scales, particularly those that have novel features or have been used extensively in marketing studies. The discussion should give you an appreciation of the main types and their construction and use. Incidentally, in following the arguments, you will find it helpful to distinguish between how a scale is constructed and how it is used.

Summated-Ratings Scale

Summated-ratings scale A self-report technique for attitude measurement in which the subjects are asked to indicate their degree of agreement or disagreement with each of a number of statements; a subject's attitude score is the total obtained by summing over the items in the scale.

The *Likert scale*, also called a **summated-ratings scale,** is one of the most widely used attitude-scaling techniques in marketing research. It is particularly useful since it allows respondents to express the intensity of their feelings.[4]

Scale Construction   In developing a Likert, or summated-ratings scale, researchers devise a number of statements that relate to the issue or object in question. Subjects are asked to indicate their degree of agreement or disagreement with each statement in the series. Figure 14.1 is an example of a scale that might be used by a bank interested in comparing its image with that of its competitors.

In developing this type of scale, the researcher tries to generate statements about the characteristics of the object that could influence a person's attitude toward it. Each statement is then classified as either favorable or unfavorable.

Subjects are asked to indicate their degree of agreement or disagreement with each statement, and the various degrees of agreement are assigned scale values. For our purposes, let's assume the values 1, 2, 3, 4, and 5 are assigned to the respective response categories. Now, a subject could be considered to feel positively about the bank if he or she either agreed with a favorable statement or disagreed with an unfavorable statement. Consequently, it is necessary to reverse the scaling with negative statements; a "strongly agree" response to a favorable statement and a "strongly disagree" response to an unfavorable statement would both receive a score of 5.

Using this scoring procedure, a total attitude score is then calculated for each subject. Researchers then evaluate the responses to determine which of the items discriminate most clearly between the high scorers and low scorers on the total scale. Those statements that generate mixed responses are weeded out, since they may tend to produce ambiguous results or, at the very least, may not be discriminating of attitude. In this way, the questionnaire is made internally consistent, so that every item relates to the same general attitude.[5]

Scale Use   Once the list of statements has been refined, the remaining items are randomly ordered on the scale form so as to mix positive and negative statements. The scale is then ready to be administered to the desired sample of respondents. Once again, subjects are asked to indicate their degree of agreement with each statement. Subjects generally find it easy to respond, because the response categories allow the expression of the intensity of the feeling. The subject's total score is generated as the simple sum of the scores on each statement.

Unfortunately, interpretation of these summed scores is rarely simple. If, for example, the maximum favorable score on a particular twenty-item scale is 100, what do we say about a score of 78? Can we assume that the person's attitude toward the bank is favorable? We cannot, since the raw scores only assume meaning when we compare them with some standard. This problem is not unique to psychological scaling. It arises every day of our lives in a variety of ways. We are always making judgments on the basis of comparisons with some standard. Most typically the standard is established via our experiences and rarely is rigorously defined. Thus, when we say, "The man is very tall," we are in effect saying that on the basis of the experience we have, the man is taller than average.

In psychological scaling, this is formalized somewhat by clearly specifying the standard. Very often the standard is taken as the average score for all subjects, although averages are also computed for certain predefined subgroups. The procedure is called *developing norms*. Comparisons can then be made against the norms to determine whether the person has a positive or negative attitude toward the object. Norms are not, of course, necessary for comparing subjects to determine which person has the more favorable attitude. Here one can simply compare the raw scores of the subjects. Nor are norms necessary when attempting to determine whether an individual's attitude has changed over time or whether a person likes one object better than another. One can simply compare the later and earlier scores or the difference in scores for the two objects.

Semantic-differential scale A self-report technique for attitude measurement in which subjects are asked to check which cell between a set of bipolar adjectives or phrases best describes their feelings toward the object.

Semantic-Differential Scale

One of the most popular techniques for measuring attitudes in marketing research is the **semantic-differential scale.** It has been found to be particularly useful in corporate, brand, and product-image studies.

Figure 14.2 **Example of Semantic-Differential Scaling Form**

Service is discourteous.	:——:——:——:——:——:——:	Service is courteous.
Location is convenient.	:——:——:——:——:——:——:	Location is inconvenient.
Hours are inconvenient.	:——:——:——:——:——:——:	Hours are convenient.
Loan interest rates are high.	:——:——:——:——:——:——:	Loan interest rates are low.

This scale grew out of some research by Charles Osgood and his colleagues at the University of Illinois concerning the underlying structure of words.[6] The technique has been adapted, however, to make it suitable for measuring attitudes.

The original semantic-differential scale consisted of a great many bipolar adjectives, which were used to determine people's reactions to the objects of interest. Osgood found that most reactions could be categorized into one of three basic dimensions: (1) an *evaluation* dimension, represented by adjective pairs such as good-bad, sweet-sour, helpful-unhelpful; (2) a *potency* dimension, represented by adjective pairs such as powerful-powerless, strong-weak, deep-shallow; and (3) an *activity* dimension, represented by adjective pairs such as fast-slow, alive-dead, noisy-quiet. The same three dimensions tended to emerge regardless of the object being evaluated. Thus, the general thrust in using the semantic-differential technique to form scales was to select an appropriate sample of the accepted or basic adjective pairs so that a score could be generated for the object for each of the evaluation, potency, and activity dimensions. The object could then be compared to other objects using these scores.

Marketers have taken Osgood's general idea and adapted it to fit their own needs. First, instead of applying the *basic* adjective pairs to the objects of interest, marketers have generated pairs of their own. These pairs have not always been antonyms, nor have they been single words. Rather, marketers have used phrases to anchor the ends of the scale, and some of these phrases have been attributes possessed by the product. For example, one end of the scale may be "good value for the money," and its opposite end, "poor value for the money." Second, instead of attempting to generate evaluation, potency, and activity scores, marketers have been more interested in developing profiles for the brands, stores, companies, or whatever is being compared, and total scores by which the objects could be compared. In this respect, the use of the semantic-differential approach in marketing studies has tended to follow the summated-ratings approach to scale construction rather than the semantic-differential tradition.

Let us again use the bank attitude-scaling problem to illustrate the semantic-differential method. First, a researcher would generate a large list of bipolar adjectives or phrases. Figure 14.2 parallels Figure 14.1 in terms of the attributes used to describe the bank, but it is arranged in a semantic-differential format. All we have done in Figure 14.2 is try to express the things that could be used to describe a bank, and thus serve as a basis for attitude formation, in terms of positive and negative statements. Note that the negative phrase sometimes appears at the left side of the scale and other times at the right. This is to prevent a respondent with a positive attitude from simply checking either the right- or left-hand sides without even bothering to read the descriptions.

Figure 14.3   **Contrasting Profiles of Banks A and B**

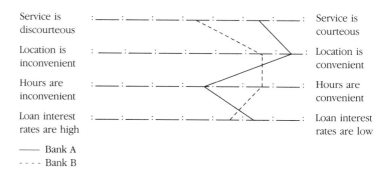

The scale would then be administered to a sample of subjects. Each respondent would be asked to read each set of bipolar phrases and to check the cell that best described his or her feelings toward the object. Respondents are usually instructed to consider the end positions in the scale as being *very descriptive* of the object, the center position as being *neutral*, and the intermediate positions as *slightly descriptive* and *quite descriptive*. Thus, for example, if the subject felt that Bank A's service was courteous, but only moderately so, he or she would check the sixth position reading from left to right.

The subject could be asked to evaluate two or more banks using the same scale. When several banks are rated, the different profiles can be compared. Figure 14.3, for example (which is sometimes referred to as a **snake diagram** because of its shape), illustrates that Bank A is perceived as having more courteous service and a more convenient location and as offering lower interest rates on loans, but as having less convenient hours than Bank B. Notice that in constructing these profiles, all positive descriptors were placed on the right. This practice makes it much easier to interpret the results. The plotted values represent the average score of all subjects on each descriptor. The profile that emerges gives a clear indication of how respondents perceive the differences between the two banks.

Rather than developing a profile, one can also total the scores on a semantic-differential scale in order to compare attitudes toward different objects (for example, alternative package designs). This score is arrived at by totaling the scores for the individual descriptors.

The popularity of semantic-differential scales in marketing research may be due to the ease with which they can be developed and the clarity with which they reveal results. The technique also has the advantage of allowing subjects to express the intensity of their feelings toward company, product, package, advertisement, or whatever. When combined with proper item-analysis techniques, the semantic-differential technique offers the marketing researcher a most valuable research tool.

Stapel Scale

A modification of the semantic-differential scale that has received some attention in marketing literature is the **Stapel scale.** It differs from the semantic-differential scale in that (1) adjectives or descriptive phrases are tested separately instead of simultaneously as bipolar pairs, (2) points on the scale are identified by number, and

Snake diagram
A diagram (so called because of its shape) that connects with straight lines the average responses to a series of semantic-differential statements, thereby depicting the profile of the object or objects being evaluated.

Stapel scale A self-report technique for attitude measurement in which respondents are asked to indicate how accurately each of a number of statements describes the object of interest.

Figure 14.4   *Example of Stapel Scale*

	−5	−4	−3	−2	−1	+1	+2	+3	+4	+5
Service is courteous.	☐	☐	☐	☐	☐	☐	☐	☐	☐	☐
Location is convenient.	☐	☐	☐	☐	☐	☐	☐	☐	☐	☐
Hours are convenient.	☐	☐	☐	☐	☐	☐	☐	☐	☐	☐
Loan interest rates are high.	☐	☐	☐	☐	☐	☐	☐	☐	☐	☐

(3) there are ten scale positions rather than seven. Figure 14.4 casts the same four attributes previously used to measure attitudes toward banks in a Stapel scale format. Respondents would be told to rate how accurately each of a number of statements describes the object of interest, Bank A. Instructions such as the following are given to respondents:

> You would select a *plus* number for words that you think describe (Bank A) accurately. The more accurately you think the word describes it, the larger the *plus* number you would choose. You would select a *minus* number for words you think do not describe it accurately. This less accurately you think a word describes it, the larger the *minus* number you would choose. Therefore, you can select any number from +5, for words that you think are very accurate, all the way to −5, for words that you think are very inaccurate.[7]

Proponents of the Stapel scale point out that this method not only frees the researcher from the sometimes difficult task of developing bipolar adjectives for each of the items on the test, but also permits finer discriminations in measuring attitudes. Despite these advantages, the Stapel scale has not been as warmly embraced as the semantic-differential scale, judging by the number of published marketing studies using each.[8] One problem with the Stapel scale is that many of the descriptors used to evaluate an object can be phrased one of three ways—positively, negatively, or neutrally—and the particular choice of phrasing seems to affect the results as well as subjects' ability to respond. Nevertheless, it is a useful addition to the researcher's equipment arsenal, especially since it can be administered over the telephone.[9]

It should be pointed out that a total score on both the semantic-differential and Stapel scales is like a total score on a summated-ratings scale. The score 48, for example, is meaningless by itself but takes on meaning when compared with some norm or other score. There is a good deal of controversy as to whether semantic-differential, Stapel, or even summated-ratings total scores represent interval scaling, or, in actuality, ordinal scaling. While the controversy rages, marketers, like many psychological scaling specialists, have opted to assume that the scores represent interval scaling. While this assumption may not be entirely correct, it does allow researchers to use more powerful methods of analysis on the data generated.

Further, from a statistical point of view, the assumption of intervality often makes sense. Statistical tests of significance, for example, "do not care from where the numbers come" as long as the assumptions underlying the use of a particular statistical test are satisfied.[10] It is not necessary, therefore, to be overly concerned about the level of measurement from a *statistical* point of view. What we must be careful about, though, is the *interpretation* of the results (for example, arguing that a person with a score of 80 has twice as favorable an attitude toward an object as a person with a score of 40—unless, of course, the measurement scale is ratio).

Ethical

Dilemma 14.1   An independent researcher was hired by a national chain of department stores to develop a scale by which the chain could measure the image of each of its stores. The researcher thought that the best way to do this was through a semantic-differential scale. Since she was interested in establishing her credentials as an expert on store-image research, however, she decided to also develop items for a Likert scale and to administer both of the scales to designated participants. She realized that this might induce greater respondent fatigue and perhaps lower-quality responses, but she was willing to take the chance because she knew that the client would not sanction nor pay for administering the second survey to an independent sample of respondents.

- Was it ethical for the researcher to accept the risk of lowering the quality of the data addressing the client's issue so that she could further her own goals and career?
- What if the data collected by the two instruments provided stronger evidence that store image had indeed been measured adequately than if data had been collected through the sole use of the semantic-differential scale?
- Would it make any difference if there had been a reasonable chance that the Likert format would produce a better instrument for measuring retail image than a semantic-differential format?

Other Ratings Scales

The previous discussion dealt with some of the main scaling methods that have been used to measure attitudes. The treatment was by no means exhaustive. Particularly conspicuous by its absence was a discussion of the importance of the various attributes to the individual. That is, in the bank example, even though the individual believes the bank has convenient hours, the person may not value this attribute, and, therefore, it may not affect his or her attitude toward the bank. On the other hand, if the individual places a strong emphasis on the convenience of a bank's location, and if he or she perceives the bank as being inconveniently located, this will have a negative, and perhaps a strongly negative, impact on his or her feelings toward the bank. To capture the differing emphases people place on specific attributes, researchers often try to measure their importance. Research Window 14.2, for example, depicts the importance of various attributes to people when shopping for microwave ovens, console color televisions, and portable video cameras or camcorders.

Admittedly, there is a good deal of controversy about how the importance of various attributes should be incorporated in determining a person's attitude toward an object. We shall not delve into this controversy, because it involves some very complex arguments as to how one determines which attributes are salient (that is, used in forming an attitude) and how they should be measured. Rather, we shall simply use importance values as a way of focusing on the differences among the general types of ratings scales.[11] Knowledge of the basic types should help in developing special scales for particular purposes.

Research Window 14.2
Most Important Considerations When Shopping for Selected Appliances

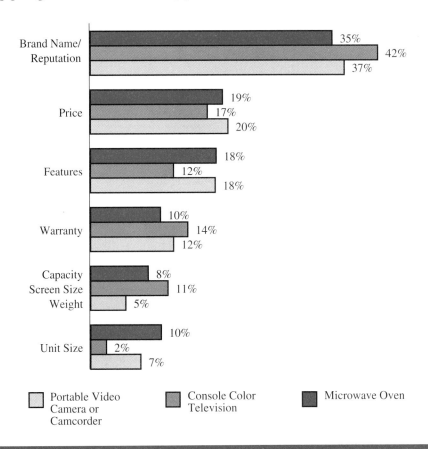

Source: Margaret Steele, "Major Appliances—The Top Shopping Consideration," *TeleNation Reports* (Fall 1987), p. 1. Published by Market Facts, Inc.

There is one feature that is common to all ratings scales: "The rater places the person or object being rated at some point along a continuum or in one of an ordered series of categories; a numerical value is attached to the point or the category."[12] The scales differ, though, in the fineness of the distinctions they allow and in the procedures involved in assigning objects to positions. Three of the most common ratings scales are the graphic, the itemized, and the comparative.

Graphic-Ratings Scale

Graphic-ratings scale
A scale in which individuals indicate their ratings of an attribute by placing a check at the appropriate point on a line that runs from one extreme of the attribute to the other.

When using **graphic-ratings scales** individuals indicate their rating by placing a check at the appropriate point on a line that runs from one extreme of the attribute to the other. Many variations are possible. The line may be vertical or horizontal; it may be unmarked or marked; if marked, the divisions may be few or many as in the case of a *thermometer scale*, so called because it looks like a thermometer. Figure 14.5 is an

Figure 14.5   *Graphic-Ratings Scale*

Please evaluate each attribute, in terms of how important the attribute is to you personally, by placing an "X" at the position on the horizontal line that most reflects your feelings.

Attribute	Not Important	Very Important
Courteous service		
Convenient location		
Convenient hours		
Low-interest-rate loans		

example of a horizontal, end-anchored only, graphic-ratings scale. Each individual would be instructed to indicate the importance of the attribute by checking the appropriate position on the scale. The importance value would then be inferred by measuring the length of the line from the left origin to the marked position.

One of the great advantages of graphic-ratings scales is the ease with which they can be constructed and used. They provide an opportunity to make fine distinctions and are limited in this regard only by the discriminatory abilities of the rater. Yet, for their most effective use, the researcher is advised to avoid making the ends of the continuum too extreme, since extremes tend to force respondents into the center of the scale, resulting in little useful information.

Itemized-Ratings Scale

Itemized-ratings scale
A scale distinguished by the fact that individuals must indicate their ratings of an attribute or object by selecting one from among a limited number of categories that best describes their position on the attribute or object.

The **itemized-ratings scale** is similar to the graphic-ratings scale except that the rater must select from a limited number of categories instead of placing a mark on a continuous scale. In general, five to nine categories work best in that they permit fine distinctions and yet seem to be readily understood by respondents. Of course, more can be used.[13]

There are a number of possible variations with itemized scales. Figure 14.6, for example, depicts three different forms of itemized-ratings scales that have been used to measure customer satisfaction. Note that the categories are ordered in terms of their scale positions, and that while in some cases the categories have verbal descriptions attached, in other cases they do not. Category descriptions are not absolutely necessary in itemized-ratings scales, although their presence and nature does seem to affect the responses.[14] When they are used, it is important to ensure that the descriptors mean similar things to those responding. When they are not used, it is tempting to conclude that a graphic-ratings scale is being used. That is an erroneous conclusion, however. The distinguishing feature of an itemized scale is that the possible response categories are limited in number. Thus, a set of faces varying systematically in terms of whether they are frowning or smiling used to capture a person's satisfaction or preference (appropriately called a *faces scale*) would be considered an itemized scale, even when no descriptions are attached to the face categories.

A summated-ratings statement is an example of a five-point itemized-ratings scale, while a semantic-differential adjective pair is an example of a seven-point scale.

Figure 14.6   ***Three Different Forms of Itemized-Ratings Scales Used to Measure Satisfaction***

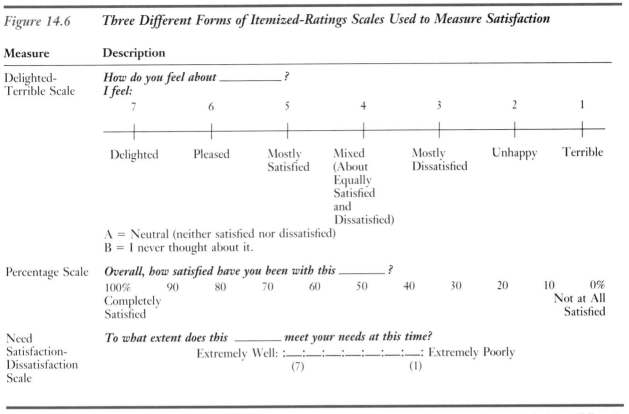

Measure	Description
Delighted-Terrible Scale	*How do you feel about _____ ?* *I feel:* 7 6 5 4 3 2 1 Delighted Pleased Mostly Satisfied Mixed (About Equally Satisfied and Dissatisfied) Mostly Dissatisfied Unhappy Terrible A = Neutral (neither satisfied nor dissatisfied) B = I never thought about it.
Percentage Scale	*Overall, how satisfied have you been with this _____ ?* 100% 90 80 70 60 50 40 30 20 10 0% Completely Satisfied Not at All Satisfied
Need Satisfaction-Dissatisfaction Scale	*To what extent does this _____ meet your needs at this time?* Extremely Well: :__:__:__:__:__:__:__: Extremely Poorly (7) (1)

Source: Adapted from Robert A. Westbrook, "A Rating Scale for Measuring Product/Service Satisfaction," *Journal of Marketing*, 44 (Fall 1980), p. 69. Published by the American Marketing Association, Chicago, IL 60606.

Figure 14.7   ***Itemized-Ratings Scale Used to Measure Importance Values***

Please evaluate each attribute, in terms of how important the attribute is to you personally, by placing an "X" in the appropriate box.

Attribute	Not Important	Somewhat Important	Fairly Important	Very Important
Courteous service	☐	☐	☐	☐
Convenient location	☐	☐	☐	☐
Convenient hours	☐	☐	☐	☐
Low-interest-rate loans	☐	☐	☐	☐

Figure 14.7 is an itemized-ratings scale used to measure importance values; this four-point scale has the descriptor labels attached to the categories.

The itemized-ratings scale is also easy to construct and use, and although it does not permit the fine distinctions possible with the graphic-ratings scale, the clear definition of categories generally produces more reliable ratings.

Figure 14.8   *Comparative-Ratings Scale*

Please divide 100 points between the following two attributes in terms of the relative importance of each attribute to you.

Courteous service   _____

Convenient location   _____

Comparative-Ratings Scale

Comparative-ratings scale A scale requiring subjects to make their ratings as a series of relative judgments or comparisons rather than as independent assessments.

In graphic and itemized scales, respondents are not asked to compare two attributes with each other or with a standard given by researchers. For example, respondents may be asked to indicate how important convenient location is to them in choosing a bank, but not if convenient location is more or less important than convenient hours. In **comparative-ratings scales,** however, respondents are asked to judge each attribute with direct reference to the other attributes being evaluated.

Constant-sum method A type of comparative-ratings scale in which an individual is instructed to divide some given sum among two or more attributes on the basis of their importance to him or her.

The constant-sum scaling method is an example of a comparative-ratings scale that can be used to measure importance values. In the **constant-sum method,** the individual is instructed to divide some given sum among two or more attributes on the basis of their importance to him or her. Thus, in Figure 14.8, if the subject assigned 50 points to courteous service and 50 points to convenient location, the attributes would be judged to be equally important; if the individual assigned 80 to courteous service and 20 to convenient location, courteous service would be considered to be four times as important. Note the difference in emphasis with this method. All judgments are now made in comparison to some other alternative.

Respondents are generally asked to compare two attributes in this method, although it is possible to compare more. The individual could also be asked to divide 100 points among three or more attributes.

Halo effect A problem that arises in data collection when there is carryover from one judgment to another.

Although comparative scales require more judgments from the individual than either graphic or itemized scales, they do tend to eliminate the **halo effect** that so often manifests itself in scaling. A halo effect occurs when there is carryover from one judgment to another.

The problem researchers may encounter in using graphic or itemized scales to measure importance values is that respondents may be inclined to indicate that all, or nearly all, of the attributes are important. Yet empirical research indicates that when individuals are confronted by decisions that are complex because many alternatives or attributes are involved, they tend to simplify the decision by reducing the number of alternatives or attributes they actually consider.[15] This is consistent with the notion that only certain attributes are salient when forming attitudes. The comparative scaling methods do allow more insight into the relative ranking, if not the absolute importance, of the attributes to each individual.

Determining Which Scale to Use

When making the choice among scale types, number of scale points to use, whether or not to reverse some of the items, and so on, readers might find help in the findings of a very extensive study of the marketing measurement literature that examined these questions, and others, with respect to their impact on the reliability of measures.

The study, which reviewed the marketing literature over a 20-year period, examined measures for which at least two indicators of quality were reported, and it quantitatively assessed the impact of a measure's features on its reliability.[16] As you may recall from Chapter 13, reliability gauges whether different measures of the same object, trait, or construct produce similar results. It is an important indicator of a measure's quality because it determines the impact of inconsistencies in measurement on the results. The general conclusion that emerged from the study is that many of the characteristics do not seem to affect the quality of the measure in any significant way. The exceptions are the number of items and the number of scale points. For both of these characteristics, the reliability of the measure increases as they increase. For the other characteristics, though, no choices are superior in all instances. Many of the choices are, and will probably remain, in the domain of researcher judgment, including the choice among semantic-differential, summated-ratings, or other ratings scales. All the scales have proven useful at one time or another. All rightly belong in the researcher's measurement tool kit. The nature of the problem, the characteristics of the respondents, and the planned mode of administration of the questionnaire will—and should—all affect the final choice. The respondents' commitment to the task will also be a factor in the measure's reliability.

Ethical
Dilemma 14.2   The Samuelson Research Firm was contacted by Larkin Electronics, a manufacturer of small electronic radio parts, to conduct a survey of Larkin's employees. The purpose of the research was to determine the state of worker morale and the importance of certain employee grievances so that Larkin's management could gauge the strength of its position in collective bargaining with the employee union. Samuelson Research agreed to conduct the study.

■   What are the consequences for employees who participate in such a survey?
■   Would cooperating in this research be detrimental to the employee's immediate self-interest?
■   Do researchers have the right to ask questions concerning this issue?
■   Does this research undercut the position of labor's representatives inasmuch as they have no corresponding way of gauging the intensity of management's opinions?
■   If you had been director of the research, what kind of questions might you have asked of Larkin's management?
■   Would you have agreed to conduct such a survey?
■   In general, should a researcher be concerned with the uses of the research that he or she conducts or its effects on the research participants?

Perceptual Scaling

Thus far in this chapter, we have emphasized the measurement of people's attitudes toward objects. Marketing managers are also interested in determining how people perceive various objects, be they products or brands. In its constant quest for a differential advantage, a firm needs to correctly position its products against competitive offerings. In order to do this, the product manager needs to identify the following:[17]

1.   The number of dimensions consumers use to distinguish products.
2.   The names of these dimensions.

Research Window 14.3
Product Positioning in the Automotive Industry

Exasperated by the growing similarity of cars on the road, a former Detroit auto executive recently remarked that if all of today's models were lined up end to end, even the top officers of the Big Three car makers would have a hard time telling them apart at a respectable distance.

The comment addresses an increasing challenge for automotive stylists and marketers. As fuel-efficiency requirements have narrowed design and performance characteristics for cars, the auto companies have had to turn to more subtle ways of drawing distinctions between different models. An example of how that is done is the "brand image" map shown in the figure.

According to Mr. R. N. Harper, Jr., manager of product marketing plans and research, Chrysler draws up a series of such maps about three times a year, using responses to customer surveys. The surveys ask owners of different makes to rank their autos on a scale of 1 to 10 for such qualities as "youthfulness," "luxury," and "practicality." The answers are then worked into a mathematical score for each model and plotted on a graph that shows broad criteria for evaluating customer appeal.

The accompanying figure uses the technique to measure the images of the major divisions of U.S. auto makers, plus a few import companies. Using it, Chrysler would conclude, for instance, that the position of its Plymouth division in the lower left-hand quadrant means that cars carrying the Plymouth name generally have a practical, though somewhat stodgy, image. The Chrysler nameplate, by contrast, is perceived as more luxurious—though not nearly as luxurious as its principal competitors, Cadillac and Lincoln.

The map has other strategic significance, as well. By plotting on the map strong areas of customer demand, an auto maker can calculate whether its cars are on target. It can also tell from the concentration of dots representing competing models how much opposition it is likely to get in a specific territory on the map. Presumably, cars higher up on the graph should also fetch a higher price than models ranked toward the bottom, where the stress is on economy and practicality.

After viewing the results for its divisions, Chrysler concluded that Plymouth, Dodge and Chrysler all needed to present a more youthful image.

3. The positioning of existing products along these dimensions.
4. Where consumers prefer a product to be on the dimensions.

One way in which managers can grasp the positioning of their brand versus competing brands is through the study of perceptual maps. In a perceptual map, each product or brand occupies a specific point. Products or brands that are similar lie close together, and those are different lie far apart. Perceptual maps provide managers with meaningful pictures of how their products and brands compare with other products and brands. Research Window 14.3, for example, depicts the situation in the automobile industry.

There are several ways by which perceptual maps can be created. The fundamental distinction is between nonattribute-based and attribute-based approaches. The attribute-based approaches rely on characteristic-by-characteristic assessments of the various objects using, for example, summated-ratings or semantic-differential scales. The ratings of the objects on each of the items are subsequently analyzed using various statistical techniques to identify the key dimensions or attributes consumers use to distinguish the objects.

Perceptual Map of Automobiles

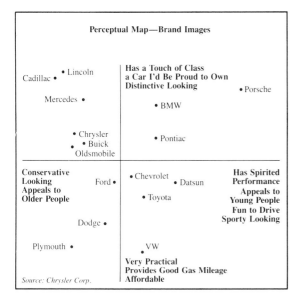

Perceptual Map—Brand Images

Cadillac • • Lincoln

Mercedes •

Has a Touch of Class
a Car I'd Be Proud to Own
Distinctive Looking

• Porsche

• BMW

• Chrysler
  • Buick
Oldsmobile

• Pontiac

Conservative
Looking
Appeals to
Older People

Ford •

• Chevrolet
      • Datsun
  • Toyota

Has Spirited
Performance
Appeals to
Young People
Fun to Drive
Sporty Looking

Dodge •

Plymouth •

• VW

Very Practical
Provides Good Gas Mileage
Affordable

Source: Chrysler Corp.

It also decided that Plymouth and Dodge needed to move up sharply on the luxury scale.

Similarly, General Motors Corporation might find after looking at the map that its Chevrolet division, traditionally for entry-level buyers, ought to move down in practicality and more to the right in youthfulness. Another problem for GM on the map: the close proximity of its Buick and Oldsmobile divisions, almost on top of each other in the upper left-hand quadrant. That would suggest the two divisions are waging a marketing war more against each other than the competition.

Chrysler also uses its marketing map to plot individual models—both those it sells currently and those it plans for the future. By trying to move a model into an unoccupied space on the map through changes in styling, price or advertising, the company believes it can better hope to carve out a distinctive niche in the market.

"The real advantage of the map," says Mr. Harper, "is that it looks at cars from a consumer perspective while also retaining some sort of tangible product orientation." He says, for example, that his bosses were delighted when, on a recent map, Chrysler's forthcoming Lancer and Commander models showed up on the map next to the Honda Accord. . . . "That told us that consumers think of our two new cars exactly the way we hoped they would," says Mr. Harper. "It was tangible evidence of where the car would compete in the market. And frankly, that can be hard to get these days."

Multidimensional scaling An approach to measurement in which people's perceptions of the similarity of objects and their preferences among the objects are measured, and these relationships are plotted in a multidimensional space.

In the nonattribute-based approaches, instead of asking a subject to rate objects on designated attributes (such as convenience, friendliness, or value for the money), one asks the individual to make some *summary* judgments about the objects. Then the researcher attempts to infer which characteristics were used to form those judgments. The reason for using this indirect approach is that in many cases the attributes may be unknown and the respondents unable or unwilling to represent their judgments accurately.

Typically, subjects are asked for their *perceptions of the similarity* between various objects and their *preferences* among these objects. An attempt is then made to locate the objects in a multidimensional space where the number of dimensions corresponds to the number of characteristics the individual used in forming the judgments. **Multidimensional-scaling** analysis is the label that is used to describe the similarity- and preference-based approaches.

The preference-based approaches for perceptual mapping are not used nearly as much as the similarity-based approaches. Our discussion, therefore, will concentrate on the similarity-based approaches, and in particular on the decisions that must be made in order to conduct multidimensional analysis.

Figure 14.9   *Key Decisions When Conducting a Multidimensional Scaling Analysis*

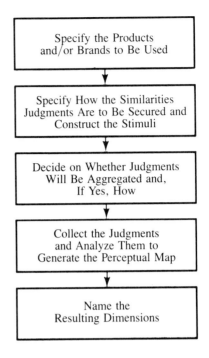

The attribute-based approaches are discussed only briefly later in this chapter because a full appreciation of them requires understanding of the essential purposes and operation of factor and discriminant analyses, topics that are not discussed in this book.[18]

Key Decisions in Multidimensional Scaling

In order to complete a multidimensional-scaling analysis, an analyst must make a variety of decisions. Several of the key ones are pictured in Figure 14.9. The first of these is to specify the products or brands that will be used. While the purpose of the study will determine some of them, others will be left to the analyst to choose. In choosing, an analyst needs to recognize that the dimensions that appear in the perceptual map will be a direct result of the objects (known as a *stimulus set*) used to secure the judgments.

Suppose the study was being conducted to determine respondents' perceptions of various soft drinks. If no unsweetened or low-calorie soft drinks were included in the stimulus set, this very important dimension may not appear in the results. So as not to run such a risk, analysts may be tempted to include every conceivable product or brand in the stimulus set. This strategy, though, can place such a burden on respondents that their answers may be meaningless.

The burden on respondents is going to depend partly on the number of judgments each has to make and partly on the difficulty of each judgment. Both of these issues in turn depend on how the similarity judgments are to be secured. There are two main alternatives and a number of options under each alternative. The two major options are *direct* or *indirect similarity judgments,* two terms that are to some extent self-explanatory. The direct methods rely on data-collection mechanisms in which respondents compare stimuli using whatever criteria they desire and, on the basis of that comparison, state which of the stimuli are most similar, least similar, and so on.

In our soft drink example, for instance, respondents might evaluate brands on the basis of their "colaness" or "dietness." All possible pairs of the brands being evaluated could be formed, and respondents could be asked to rank-order the various pairs from most similar to least similar using their own criteria. (For example, which pair is more similar: Pepsi-Coke, 7-Up–Coke, or Pepsi–7-Up?) Alternatively, a brand could be singled out as a focal brand, and respondents could be asked to rank-order each of the other brands in terms of their similarity to the focal brand (if, for example, Coke were the focal brand, respondents might be asked to rank-order Pepsi, RC Cola, 7-Up, and Tab as to their similarities to Coke.) Each brand could serve, in turn, as the focal brand. While there are a number of alternative ways of collecting these judgments, they all have one thing in common: the respondents are asked to judge directly how similar the various alternatives are using criteria that they choose.

The indirect methods operate differently. Instead of respondents' selecting the criteria on which to compare the alternatives, they are asked to evaluate each brand using prespecified criteria chosen by the analyst. Some kind of measure of similarity is then calculated for each pair of brands (for example, the correlation between the ratings of the brands).

The third decision analysts have to make is whether the judgments of individual respondents will be aggregated, or grouped together, so that group perceptual maps can be developed, or whether individual maps will be generated. The problem with individual maps is that they become very difficult for the marketing manager to use to develop marketing strategy. Managers typically look at marketing planning questions in terms of market segments, not individuals. Yet, as soon as the segment issue is raised, the question becomes one of deciding how the individual judgments will be aggregated. Is it likely that individuals used the same number of criteria (say, colaness, dietness, and sweetness) when evaluating the various brands? Even if they used the same number, are the criteria themselves likely to be the same? (What if some used colaness, dietness, and value for the money instead?) If they are not, what criteria should be used to group respondents? One of the most popular algorithms, INDSCAL, for example, assumes that all subjects use the same criteria to judge the similarity of objects but that they weight the dimensions differently when forming their judgments.[19]

Step 4 in Figure 14.9 involves the actual collection of the judgments and their processing. The processing involves two steps. First, an initial configuration must be determined for each of the dimensions. Different programs use different routines to generate an initial solution. Second, the points must be moved around until the fit is the best it can be in that dimensionality, using the criterion under which the program operates.

The last decision analysts have to make when conducting a similarity-based multidimensional-scaling analysis involves what to call the dimensions. There are several procedures for naming the dimensions. The respondent can be asked to evaluate each of the objects (for instance, soft drinks) in terms of several attributes (colaness, dietness, price) determined by the researcher. The researcher then correlates the attribute scores each object receives with the coordinates for each object on the plotted diagram. In this method, the size of the respective correlation coefficients between attributes and dimensions is used to attach labels.

Another approach is to have the manager or researcher interpret the dimensions using his or her own experience and the visual configuration of points. Still a third approach is to attempt to relate the dimensions to the physical characteristics of the soft drinks such as sweetness, color, or calories.

The practical fact is, however, that difficulty in naming the dimensions is one of management's major concerns with similarity-based multidimensional-scaling analysis.

Attribute-Based Approaches

One of the advantages of the attribute-based approaches to the development of perceptual maps is that they do make the naming of dimensions easier.[20] They also seem to be easier for respondents to use. As mentioned earlier, the attribute-based approaches rely on having individuals rate various brands using (usually) either semantic-differential or summated-ratings scales. These judgments are usually then inputted to either discriminant analysis or factor analysis.

The emphasis in discriminant analysis is upon determining the combinations of attributes that best discriminate between the objects or brands. The dependent measures are the products rated (Coke, Pepsi, 7-Up), and the predictor variables are the attribute ratings. The analysis is typically run across groups of respondents to find a common structure. The dimensions are named by examining the weightings of the attributes that make up a discriminant dimension or by computing the correlations between the attributes and each of the discriminant scores. The use of discriminant analysis to develop perceptual maps seems to work particularly well when one is concerned with product design attributes that can be clearly and unequivocally perceived by consumers.[21]

Factor analysis relies on the assumption that there are only a few basic dimensions that underlie the attribute ratings. It examines the correlations among the attributes to identify these basic dimensions. The correlations are typically computed across brands and groups of consumers. The dimensions usually are named by examining the factor loadings that represent the correlations between each attribute and each factor. The use of factor analysis in the development of perceptual maps seems to be particularly useful when the marketing emphasis is on the formulation of communications strategy in which the linguistic relations between the attributes are key.

Comparison of Approaches to Perceptual Mapping

The advantages of the attribute-based approach versus the nonattribute-based approach to multidimensional scaling are summarized in Table 14.1. Most of the nonattribute-based applications in marketing use similarity judgments. Similarity measurement has the advantage of not depending on a predefined attribute set. But this feature is a two-edged sword. Although it allows respondents to use only those dimensions they normally use in making judgments among objects, it creates difficulties in naming the dimensions. Further, different consumers may use different dimensions, and then one must grapple with how best to combine consumers when forming maps. Constructing a separate map for each individual is prohibitively costly. Aggregating all the responses and then developing one map distorts reality in that it implies a homogeneity in perceptions that probably does not exist. The middle ground of grouping consumers into segments raises the whole issue of how the aggregation should be effected. Even individual consumers have been known to vary the criteria they use when making a series of judgments, indicating that the criteria depend on the products or brands in the stimulus set.

Table 14.1   ***Comparison of the Nonattribute- and Attribute-Based***
Approaches for Developing Perceptual Maps

Technique	Respondent Measures	Advantages	Disadvantages
Nonattribute-based similarity judgments	Judged similarity of various products and/or brands	Does not depend on a predefined attribute set. Allows respondents to use their normal criteria when judging objects. Allows for condition that perception of the "whole" may not be simply the sum of the perceptions of the parts.	Difficult to name dimensions. Difficult to determine if, and how, the judgments of individual respondents should be combined. Criteria respondents use depend on the stimuli being compared. Requires special programs. Provides oversimplified view of perceptions when few objects are used.
Attribute-based discriminant or factor anaysis	Ratings on various products and/or brands on prespecified attributes	Facilitates naming the dimensions. Easier to cluster respondents into groups with similar perceptions. Easy and inexpensive to use. Computer programs are readily available.	Requires a relatively complete set of attributes. Rests on the assumption that overall perception of a stimulus is made up of the individual's reactions to the attributes making up the stimulus.

The fact that the criteria can change as the series of similarity judgments are made makes the already difficult problem of naming the dimensions even harder. One must be especially careful in using the similarity-based programs if the number of objects being judged is less than eight, as it is then very easy to develop an oversimplified picture of the competitive environment.

As previously mentioned, the attribute-based approaches make naming the dimensions easier and they also make the task of clustering respondents into groups with similar perceptions easier to deal with. They presume, however, that the list of attributes used to secure the ratings are relatively accurate and complete and that a person's perception or evaluation of a stimulus is some combination of the individual's reactions to the attributes making up the stimulus. Yet, people may not perceive or evaluate objects in terms of underlying attributes but may instead perceive them as some kind of whole that is not decomposable in terms of separate attributes. (For example, Corvette owners may not buy the car because of its handling, gas mileage, or even styling, but because of some undefinable attribute, or attributes—status, image, sexiness, playfulness, power?—that together make up a quality uniquely held by Corvette.)

Further, the measures used to group people imply some assumptions about how consumers' reactions to the various attribute scales should be combined. The attribute-based approaches are easier to use than the similarity method, since the programs employed are more readily available and less expensive to run.

Regardless of the approach taken, the appeal of multidimensional scaling lies in the maps produced by the technique. These maps can be used to provide insight into some very basic questions about markets, including, for product markets, the following:

1.   The salient product attributes perceived by buyers in the market.
2.   The combination of attributes buyers most prefer.

3. The products that are viewed as substitutes and those that are differentiated from one another.
4. The viable segments that exist in a market.
5. Those "holes" in a market that can support a new product venture.

Further, the technique also appears suited for product life-cycle analysis, market segmentation, vendor evaluation, the evaluation of advertisements, test marketing, sales representative–image and store-image research, brand-switching research, and attitude scaling.[22]

Conjoint Analysis

Conjoint analysis
A technique in which respondents' utilities or valuations of attributes are inferred from the preferences they express for various combinations of these attributes.

Like multidimensional-scaling analysis, **conjoint analysis** relies on the ability of respondents to make judgments about stimuli. In multidimensional-scaling analysis, the stimuli are products or brands, and respondents are asked to make judgments about their relative *similarity*. In conjoint analysis, the stimuli represent some *predetermined combinations of features, benefits, and attributes* offered by a product, and respondents are asked to make judgments about their *preference* for these various combinations. In essence, conjoint analysis seeks to determine which benefits or attributes buyers are willing to trade off to retain others. The basic aim is to determine which combinations of features respondents prefer most.

Respondents might use, for example, such attributes as miles per gallon, seating capacity, price, length of warranty, and so on, in making judgments about which automobile they prefer. Yet, if asked to do so directly, many respondents might find it very difficult to state which attributes they were using and how they were combining them to form overall judgments. Conjoint analysis attempts to handle this problem by estimating how much each of the attributes are valued on the basis of the choices respondents make among product concepts that are varied in systematic ways. In this type of analysis, researchers attempt to infer respondents' value systems based on their choices rather than on the respondents' own estimations.

Conjoint analysis presumes that the relative values of things considered jointly can be measured when they might not be measurable if taken one at a time. Quite often respondents are asked to express the relative value to them of various alternatives by ordering the alternatives from most desirable to least desirable. Researchers then attempt to assign values to the levels of each of the attributes in a way that is consistent with the respondents' rank-order judgments.

Example of Conjoint Analysis

Suppose we were considering introducing a new drip coffee maker and wished to assess how consumers evaluated the following levels of each of these product attributes:

- Capacity—4, 8, and 10 cups
- Price—$18, $22, and $28
- Brewing time—3, 6, 9, and 12 minutes

All three of these attributes are *motherhood* attributes, meaning that, other things being equal, most consumers would prefer either the most or least of each property—in this instance, the largest-capacity maker with the shortest brewing time and the lowest price. Unfortunately, life is not that simple. The larger coffee maker will cost more; faster brewing means a larger heating element for the same pot

Table 14.2   **Respondent Ordering of Various Product Descriptions**

Capacity	4 Cups			8 Cups			10 Cups		
Price	$18	$22	$28	$18	$22	$28	$18	$22	$28
Brewing Time									
3 minutes	17	15	6	30	26	24	36	34	28
6 minutes	16	12	5	29	25	22	35	33	27
9 minutes	9	8	3	21	20	8	32	31	23
12 minutes	4	2	1	14	13	7	19	18	11

capacity, which also raises the cost. And a larger-capacity maker with no change in the heating element will require increased brewing time. In sum, a consumer is going to have to trade off one property to secure more of another. What the manufacturer is interested in determining is how consumers value these specific attributes. Is low price most valued, or are consumers willing to pay a higher price to secure some of the other properties? Which price? Which properties?

One way to answer these questions is to develop a set of index cards containing all possible combinations of these product attributes. If each card contained a combination of one possible aspect of each category (e.g., 4-cup capacity, $22 price, 6-minute brewing time), there would be thirty-six possible combinations.

Suppose we then asked a respondent to order these product descriptions or cards from least desirable (ranked 1) to most desirable (ranked 36), so that higher numbers reflected greater preference. The respondent could be instructed, for example, to sort the cards first into four categories labeled "very undesirable," "somewhat undesirable," "somewhat desirable," and "very desirable," and then, after completing the sorting task, to order the cards in each category from least to most desirable. Suppose the ordering contained in Table 14.2 resulted from this process.

Note several things about these entries. First, the respondent least preferred the $28 maker with 4-cup capacity and 12-minute brewing time (ranked 1) and most preferred the 10-cup maker with 3-minute brewing time priced at $18 (ranked 36). Second, if the respondent cannot have her first choice, she is willing to trade off the short brewing time for a longer brewing time so that she could still get the 10-cup maker for $18 (ranked 35). She is not willing to trade off too much, however, as reflected by her third choice (ranked 34). Rather, she is willing to pay a little more to secure the faster 3-minute brewing time rather than having to endure an even slower 9-minute brewing time. In effect, she is willing to trade off price for brewing time.

The type of question that conjoint analysis attempts to answer is, What are the individual's utilities for price, brewing time, and pot capacity in determining her choices? How much value does the individual place on each of these attributes in making her choice of products?

Procedure in Conjoint Analysis

The procedure for determining the individual's *utilities*, or values, for each of several product attributes followed in conjoint analysis is quite similar to that followed in multidimensional-scaling analysis. Again the technique is dependent on the availabil-

When Sunbeam decided to redesign its entire line of small appliances, it used conjoint analysis to pinpoint optimal attribute trade-offs.

Source: Courtesy of Sunbeam Housewares.

ity of a high-speed computer. Just as in multidimensional scaling, the computer program's emphasis is on generating an initial solution and subsequently on modifying that solution through a series of iterations to improve the goodness of fit.[23] More specifically, given a set of input judgments, the computer program will

1. Assign arbitrary utilities to each level of each attribute.
2. Calculate the utilities for each alternative by somehow combining, most typically adding, the individual utility values.

Research Window 14.4
Use of Conjoint Analysis by Western Oceanic to Improve Its Competitive Bidding Process

Western Oceanic was concerned about its success ratio in making bids. In this situation, as in many others involving major purchases, oil companies send out requests for proposals to a prescreened list of qualified contractors. The assignment is to drill in a certain location to reach a targeted depth.

During recent years, this market has been quite weak, resulting in severe price competition. Many clients' rigs were idle, a most expensive overhead cost. In February 1987, the rigs' rate of use was dragging the bottom at 39 percent.

The challenge was to better understand how the oil companies were selecting among the bidders. A small sample of drilling superintendents and purchasing agents for the oil companies was polled to learn which factors they evaluated. These personal interviews also revealed how foremen rating sheets were used for comparison of the proposals.

In offshore drilling, the prices are daily rates. In the exploratory phase, we learned that prices varied by depth of water, location offshore, distance from supply points, and other performance factors. This allowed us to construct "prices" that were described as "deviations from the average daily rate," such as 15

percent higher than the average for all bids, 10 percent higher, at parity, 10 percent lower, and 15 percent lower.

The safety record of the bidding company's rigs was found to be an important evaluation issue. In exploratory interviews, we learned how safety was evaluated on a numerical scale and, thus, how it should be presented in the conjoint package.

Results indicated that a driller's operational structure may not be consistent with the type of operation that the client wants. The trade-off analysis led Western Oceanic to decide not to install very expensive ancillary equipment on some of its rigs, to move other rigs to different parts of the world, and to make better decisions about manning rigs and setting work schedules. This helped it match its resources to the lease operators' priorities.

As a result of the actions taken by Western Oceanic, its rig utilization rate jumped from 39 percent at the beginning to 93 percent at the end of 1987. In the Gulf of Mexico, Western now enjoys the highest number of average jobs per rig among all drilling contractors.

Source: Excerpted from Gabriel M. Gelb, "Conjoint Analysis Helps Explain the Bid Process," *Marketing News*, 22 (March 14, 1988), pp. 1 and 31. Excerpted with permission from *Marketing News*, published by the American Marketing Association, Chicago, IL 60606.

3. Calculate the goodness of fit between the ranking of the alternatives using these derived utility values and the original ordering of the input judgments.
4. Modify the utility values in a systematic way until the derived utilities produce evaluations that, when ordered, correspond as closely as possible to the order of the input judgments.

Based on the results determined by the computer, the researcher can determine the relative importance of each attribute. It is important to keep in mind that the importance values are dependent on the particular attributes chosen to structure the analysis. Thus, if higher prices had been used, the respondents' values may have been different, suggesting that price was relatively more important to the individual than if lower prices had been used.

An analysis such as this can be used to identify the optimal levels and importance of each attribute in structuring product and service offerings. Research Window 14.4, for example, describes how conjoint analysis was used by Western Oceanic to improve its competitive bidding process.

General Comments on Conjoint Analysis

One can see that vital marketing questions in product design are being addressed by conjoint analysis. Further, the technique is not restricted to product evaluations. It can be used whenever one is making a choice among multi-attribute alternatives. With multi-attribute alternatives, one typically does not have the option of having more of everything that is desirable and less of everything that is not desirable. Instead, most decisions involve trading off part of something in order to get more of something else. Conjoint analysis attempts to mirror the trade-offs one is willing to make. Consequently, while it has most often been used for product-design issues, including concept evaluation, it is also used quite regularly as an aid in pricing decisions, market-segmentation questions, or advertising decisions. It has been used less frequently for making distribution decisions, for evaluating vendors, for determining the rewards that salespeople value, and for determining consumer preferences for various attributes of health organizations, among other things.

Back to the Case

"Phil, I have some of the preliminary results of our tests on Flight Ranger with me today, but I wanted to talk to you about them for a few minutes before I left them with you," said Susan Muskie. "As we discussed earlier, measuring kids' attitudes is an art, not a science. That's why I'm a little nervous about your just looking at the results and making hard-and-fast decisions on that basis alone."

"What are you getting at? Is Flight Ranger a loser?" asked Phil Baxter apprehensively.

"It's strange, but I wish I could say for certain it was. The truth is that our test results were very mixed. Some of the kids liked some of the Flight Ranger toys very much. Some of the kids hated some of the toys. It's fair to say that Flight Ranger has almost no appeal to girls in the target age-group.

"We also ran a test to compare the responses of children with those of their parents on similar sets of questions. For example, we asked the kids, 'Who in your family decides what toys you get? Would you say you do? Or do your mother and father?' Then we asked the parents, 'Who decides what toys to buy the children?' and we gave them the following choices: 'child decides, parents decide, or parents and child decide together.'"

"The children's question was dichotomous; the parents' was multichotomous. Naturally, the children's answers were not as statistically clean as the parents', but I think that if you interpret them carefully, you'll find some interesting comparisons."

"What else?" asked Baxter, who was hoping for more definitive findings.

"We found that you have a very interesting image problem. Marvell is the preeminent preschool and infant brand. It is not a brand for older children. Traditionally Marvell has aimed all of its advertising efforts at parents, to whom its brand name is gold. Our tests showed that kids have

less preference for, or even awareness of, the Marvell name than parents do. Ironically, when kids do have an association with the Marvell name, it's negative. They associate it too closely with babies for it to be cool. Some parents also found it disturbing to see the Marvell name associated with a mature toy—and in the toy business, a product for seven-year-olds is a mature toy. One parent said seeing the name Marvell on the Flight Ranger rifle was like seeing the Gerber name on a can of beer. . . ."

"Susan, this is all very well and good, but do we go ahead and make the Flight Ranger toys or not?" demanded Baxter.

"That's for more powerful heads than ours to decide, don't you think, Phil? I mean, ultimately it's Marvell's decision. Read the report; weigh the information. Decide what level of risk you're willing to incur. You can see in the report that my firm feels the biggest unknown is the success of the Flight Ranger cartoon show.

When selling to kids, you first have to win the hearts and minds of your consumers. Television goes a long way toward doing that. . . ."

Proper data-analysis techniques can overcome many of the unique problems inherent in measuring children's attitudes. The real problem arises when marketers attempt to take data from children's attitude studies and assume that the data are "truth."

It is especially important in such studies for researchers to point out clearly to marketing decision makers that children's attitudes are hard to measure and that children's attitude data must be used with caution.

This case is based very loosely on Fisher-Price's foray into the "mature" toy market.

Summary

Learning Objective 1: List the various ways by which attitudes can be measured.

Attitudes can be measured by self-reports, observation of overt behavior, indirect techniques, performance of objective tasks, and physiological reactions.

Learning Objective 2: Name the most widely used attitude scaling techniques in marketing research and explain why researchers prefer them.

The Likert scale, or summated-ratings scale, and the semantic-differential scale are the most widely used attitude scaling techniques in marketing research. Both are particularly useful because they allow respondents to express the intensity of their feelings.

Learning Objective 3: Explain how a Stapel scale differs from a semantic-differential scale.

A Stapel scale differs from a semantic-differential scale in that (1) adjectives or descriptive phrases are tested separately instead of simultaneously as bipolar pairs, (2) points on the scale are identified by number, and (3) there are ten scale positions rather than seven. Respondents are told to rate how accurately each of a number of statements describes the object of interest.

Learning Objective 4: Cite the one feature that is common to all ratings scales.

The one feature common to all ratings scales is that the rater places the person or object being rated at some point along a continuum or in one of an ordered series of categories; a numerical value is attached to the point or the category.

Learning Objective 5: List three of the most common types of ratings scales.

Three of the most common ratings scales are the graphic, the itemized, and the comparative scales.

Learning Objective 6: Explain the difference between a graphic-ratings scale and an itemized-ratings scale.

The itemized-ratings scale is similar to the graphic-ratings scale except that the rater must select from a limited number of categories instead of placing a mark on a continuous scale. In general, five to nine categories work well.

Learning Objective 7: Explain how the constant-sum scaling method works.

In the constant-sum method of comparative rating, the individual is instructed to divide some given sum among two or more attributes on the basis of their importance to him or her. Respondents are generally asked to compare two attributes in this method, although it is possible to compare more.

Learning Objective 8: Identify the key decisions an analyst must make in order to complete a multidimensional-scaling analysis.

In order to complete a multidimensional-scaling analysis, an analyst must (1) specify the products and/or brands to be used; (2) specify how the similarities judgments are to be secured and construct the stimuli; (3) decide on whether judgments will be aggregated and, if so, how; (4) collect the judgments and analyze them to generate the perceptual map; and (5) name the resulting dimensions.

Learning Objective 9: Explain the basic principle behind conjoint analysis.

In conjoint analysis, the stimuli represent some predetermined combinations of features, benefits, and attributes offered by a product, and respondents are asked to make judgments about their preference for these various combinations. In essence, conjoint analysis seeks to determine which benefits or attributes buyers are willing to trade off to obtain others. The basic aim is to determine which combinations of features respondents prefer most.

Discussion Questions, Problems, and Projects

1. (a) List at least eight attributes that students might use in evaluating bookstores.
    (b) Using these attributes, develop eight summated-ratings items and eight semantic-differential items by which attitudes toward (i) the university bookstore and (ii) some other bookstore can be evaluated.
    (c) Administer each of the scales to ten students.
    (d) What are the average sample scores for the two bookstores using the scale of summated ratings? What can be said about students' attitudes toward the two bookstores?
    (e) Develop a profile analysis or snake diagram for the semantic-differential scale.
    (f) Based on the semantic-differential scale, what can be said about students' attitudes toward the two bookstores?

2. (a) Assume that a manufacturer of a line of cheese products wanted to evaluate customer attitudes toward the brand. A panel of 500 regular consumers of the brand responded to a questionnaire that was sent to them and that included several attitude scales, which produced the following results:
    (i) The average score for the sample on a 25-item summated-ratings scale was 105.
    (ii) The average score for the sample on a 20-item semantic-differential scale was 106.
    (iii) The average score for the sample on a 15-item Stapel scale was 52.
    The vice-president has requested you to indicate whether his customers have a favorable or unfavorable attitude toward the brand. What will you tell him? Please be specific.
    (b) Following your initial report, the vice-president has provided you with some more information. The following memo has been given to you: "The company has been using the same attitude measures over the past eight years. The results of the previous studies are as follows:

Year	Summated Ratings	Semantic Differential	Stapel
1983	86	95	43
1984	93	95	48
1895	97	98	51
1986	104	101	55
1987	110	122	62
1988	106	112	57
1989	104	106	53
1990	105	106	52

We realize that there may not be any connection between attitude and behavior, but it must be pointed out that sales peaked in 1987 and since then have been gradually declining." With this information, do your conclusions change? Can anything more be said about customer attitudes?

3. Generate eight attributes that assess students' attitudes toward "take-home exams." Use (i) graphic-, (ii) itemized-, and (iii) comparative-ratings scales to determine the importance of each of these attributes in students' evaluation of take-home exams. (Note: In the case of the comparative-ratings scale, use only five of the attributes.) Administer each of these scales to separate samples of five students.
   (a) What are your findings with the graphic-ratings scale? Which attributes are important?
   (b) What are your findings with the itemized-ratings scale? Which attributes are important?
   (c) What are your findings with the comparative-ratings scale? Which attributes are important?

4. Assume that you are a staff researcher for a manufacturer of three nationally branded laundry detergents. The research and development department has formulated a new type of detergent that the company has decided to introduce under a new brand name. The product manager for the laundry detergent line has expressed concern that the new brand, unless it is carefully positioned, may cannibalize sales of the firm's current brands. You have been assigned to provide research-based information that will assist management in properly positioning the new brand in order to minimize the possibility of cannibalization. What method of analysis should you employ and why? Given your choice of method, what are some fundamental decisions that you must make?

5. Find six print advertisements for different types of medium-size automobiles (for example, Ford, Toyota, Dodge, etc.). Append the six advertisements to this exercise.
   (a) Form all possible pairs of these models. Using the advertisements as input, rank the pairs in decreasing order of similarity (rank the most similar pair as 1) according to the way you perceive them.
   (b) Complete the following table:

| Model | **Perceived Similarity Judgments** | | | | | |
	1	2	3	4	5	6
1. ———						
2. ———						
3. ———						
4. ———						
5. ———						
6. ———						

   (c) List the criteria that you used in determining the similarity of the models.
   (d) Now, rate the models on the following two attributes, (i) style and (ii) features, using a seven-point semantic-differential scale. For example, if you think that a particular model has a lot of style, you should give it a rating of 6 or 7, and so on. Do this for all six models on both the attributes.
   (e) Complete the following distance matrix by computing the distances between each pair of objects. The distances can be computed with the following formula:

$$D_{ij} = \sqrt{(x_i - x_j)^2 + (y_i - y_j)^2}$$

where

$$x_i = \text{rating of Model } i \text{ on Attribute 1} \quad i = 1 \ldots 6$$
$$y_i = \text{rating of Model } i \text{ on Attribute 2}$$
$$x_j = \text{rating of Model } j \text{ on Attribute 1} \quad j = 1 \ldots 6 \, i \neq j$$
$$y_j = \text{rating of Model } j \text{ on Attribute 2}$$

For example, the distance between Model 1 and Model 2 is

$$D_{12} = \sqrt{(x_1 - x_2)^2 + (y_1 - y_2)^2}$$

Distance Matrix

Model	1	2	3	4	5	6
1. ___						
2. ___						
3. ___						
4. ___						
5. ___						
6. ___						

Note: The pairs that are most similar on the two attributes have smaller distances. The pairs that are most dissimilar on the two attributes have larger distances.

(f) Convert the above distances to similarity values by assigning the rank of 1 to the two closest objects, the rank of 2 to the next closest objects, and so on. Assign the average of the ranks to those pairs in which the distances between the two objects are the same.

Calculated Similarity Judgments

Model	1	2	3	4	5	6
1.						
2.						
3.						
4.						
5.						
6.						

(g) Compare the perceived similarity in part (b) of this question and the calculated similarity in part (f).

6. Suppose you are interested in introducing a new toaster oven and decide to use conjoint analysis to determine how people value different attributes.
    (a) List three product attributes that would be relevant to you.
    (b) List three levels of each of these product attributes you might use to assess respondents' utilities.
    (c) Assign utilities to each of these levels. For example, suppose size is one of the attributes. One might then assign higher utilities to each of the larger sizes.

Attribute I		Attribute II		Attribute III	
Levels	Utility	Levels	Utility	Levels	Utility
1.					
2.					
3.					

(d) Calculate the utilities for each alternative by assuming that the utilities for each attribute will combine additively. Complete the following table:

Utilities for the Feature Combinations Given the Assumed Values

Attribute I	*(1)*			*(2)*			*(3)*		
Attribute II	*(1)*	*(2)*	*(3)*	*(1)*	*(2)*	*(3)*	*(1)*	*(2)*	*(3)*
	___	___	___	___	___	___	___	___	___
Attribute III									
(1)									
(2)									
(3)									

(e) Request a respondent to rank-order these product descriptions from least desirable (rank of 1) to most desirable (rank of 27).
Note: (i) There are 27 combinations.
(ii) Writing each combination on a separate index card would ease the task.

(f) Now, complete the following table:

Respondent's Ordering of Various Product Descriptions

Attribute	*(1)*			*(2)*			*(3)*		
Attribute II	*(1)*	*(2)*	*(3)*	*(1)*	*(2)*	*(3)*	*(1)*	*(2)*	*(3)*
	___	___	___	___	___	___	___	___	___
Attribute III									
(1)									
(2)									
(3)									

(g) Plot the original order of the input judgments against the assigned utilities.
(h) Are the assigned utilities appropriate?

7. Questionnaire design is, at best, guided by only generalized rules and procedures. As a result, two researchers with the same objective may design very different questionnaires. With this in mind, critically review the CARA questionnaire presented in the Part Four Research Project, on the following pages. What are its good points? What features would you change? Provide specific examples and justify them if you feel an alternative technique would provide more useful information.

Endnotes

1. See, for example, James F. Engel, Roger D. Blackwell, and Paul Miniard, *Consumer Behavior*, 6th ed. (Hinsdale, Ill.: Dryden Press, 1990); and J. Paul Peter and Jerry C. Olson, *Consumer Behavior: Marketing Strategy Perspectives*, 2nd ed. (Homewood, Ill.: Richard D. Irwin, Inc., 1990).

2. James H. Myers and William H. Reynolds, *Consumer Behavior and Marketing Management* (Boston: Houghton Mifflin, copyright © 1967), p. 146. For discussion of the role of attitudes and their effect on consumer behavior, see Robert A. Peterson, Wayne D. Hoyer, and William R. Wilson, eds., *The Role of Affect in Consumer Behavior: Emerging Theories and Applications* (Lexington, Mass.: D.C. Heath, 1986).

3. This classification of approaches is taken from Stuart W. Cook and Claire Selltiz, "A Multiple Indicator Approach to Attitude Measurement," *Psychological Bulletin*, 62 (1964), pp. 36–55.

4. The scale was first proposed by Rensis Likert, "A Technique for the Measurement of Attitudes," *Archives of Psychology*, No. 140 (1932).

5. For a generalizable procedure on how to go about constructing scales, see Gilbert A. Churchill, Jr., "A Paradigm for Developing Better Measures of Marketing Constructs," *Journal of Marketing Research*, 16 (February 1979), pp. 64–73.

6. Charles E. Osgood, George J. Suci, and Percy H. Tannenbaum, *The Measurement of Meaning* (Champaign, Ill.: University of Illinois Press, 1957).

7. Irving Crespi, "Use of a Scaling Technique in Surveys," *Journal of Marketing*, 25 (July 1961), p. 71.

8. One study that compared the performance of the Stapel scale with that of the semantic-differential found basically no difference between the results produced by, or respondents' ability to use, each. See Del I. Hawkins, Gerald Albaum, and Roger Best, "Stapel Scale or Semantic Differential in Marketing Research," *Journal of Marketing Research*, 11 (August 1974), pp. 318–322.

9. Gregory D. Upah and Steven C. Cosmas, "The Use of Telephone Dials as Attitude Scales," *Journal of the Academy of Marketing Science* (Fall 1980), pp. 416–426; and Barbara Loken et al., "The Use of 0–10 Scales in Telephone Surveys," *Journal of the Market Research Society*, 29 (July 1987), pp. 353–362.

10. There is evidence that demonstrates, for example, that there is little difference in results when ordinal data are analyzed by procedures appropriate to interval data. See Sanford Labovitz, "Some Observations on Measurement and Statistics," *Social Forces*, 46 (1967), pp. 151–160; Sanford Labovitz, "The Assignment of Numbers to Rank Order Categories," *American Sociological Review*, 35 (1970), pp. 515–524; and John Gaito, "Measurement Scales and Statistics: Resurgence of an Old Misconception," *Psychological Bulletin*, 87 (1980), pp. 564–567.

11. For empirical comparisons involving various forms of self-report scales of attribute importance, see "Measuring the Importance of Attributes," *Research on Research*, No. 28 (Chicago: Market Facts, Inc., undated); and "The Use of Concern Scales as an Alternative to Importance Ratings," *Research on Research*, No. 44 (Chicago: Market Facts, Inc., undated).

12. Claire Selltiz, Lawrence S. Wrightsman, and Stuart W. Cook, *Research Methods in Social Relations*, 3rd ed. (New York: Holt, Rinehart and Winston, 1976), pp. 403–404.

13. Eli P. Cox III, "The Optimal Number of Response Alternatives for a Scale: A Review," *Journal of Marketing Research*, 17 (November 1980), pp. 407–422.

14. Albert R. Wildt and Michael B. Mazis, "Determinants of Scale Response: Label versus Position," *Journal of Marketing Research*, 15 (May 1978), pp. 261–267; H. H. Friedman and J. R. Liefer, "Label versus Position in Rating Scales," *Journal of the Academy of Marketing Science* (Spring 1981), pp. 88–92.

15. Jerome S. Bruner, Jacqueline J. Goodnow, and George R. Austin, *A Study of Thinking* (New York: John Wiley, 1956); James G. Miller, "Sensory Overloading," in Bernard E. Flaherty, ed., *Psychophysiological Aspects of Space Flight* (New York: Columbia University Press, 1961), pp. 215–224; and Jacob Jacoby, "Perspectives on Information Overload," *Journal of Consumer Research*, 10 (March 1984), pp. 432–435.

16. Gilbert A. Churchill, Jr., and J. Paul Peter, "Research Design Effects on the Reliability of Rating Scales: A Meta-Analysis," *Journal of Marketing Research*, 21 (November 1984), pp. 360–375.

17. Glen L. Urban and John R. Hauser, *Design and Marketing of New Products* (Englewood Cliffs, N.J.: Prentice-Hall, 1980), p. 195.

18. See John R. Hauser and Frank S. Koppelman, "Alternative Perceptual Mapping Techniques: Relative Accuracy and Usefulness," *Journal of Marketing Research*, 16 (November 1979), pp. 495–506; and Joel Huber and Morris B. Holbrook, "Using Attribute Ratings for Product Positioning: Some Distinctions Among Compositional Approaches," *Journal of Marketing Research*, 16 (November 1979), pp. 507–516, for illustrations of the factor and discriminant analysis approaches to the generation of perceptual maps.

19. For an overview of some marketing studies that have used various algorithms, see Lee G. Cooper, "A Review of Multidimensional Scaling in Marketing Research," *Applied Psychological Measurement*, 7 (Fall 1983), pp. 427–450. For a review of algorithms generally available for microcomputers, including INDSCAL, see Paul E. Green, Frank J. Carmone, Jr., and Scott M. Smith, *Multidimensional Scaling: Concepts and Applications* (Boston: Allyn and Bacon, 1989).

20. Hauser and Koppelman, "Alternative Perceptual Mapping Techniques."

21. Huber and Holbrook, "Using Attribute Ratings for Product Positioning."

22. For a review of these applications, see Cooper, "A Review of Multidimensional Scaling in Marketing Research." 23.

23. There are several programs available. One of the historically more popular is MONANOVA. See J. B. Kruskal, "Analysis of Factorial Experiments by Estimating Monotone Transformations of the Data," *Journal of the Royal Statistical Society*, Series B, 27 (1965), pp. 251–263; and J. B. Kruskal and F. Carmone, "Use and Theory of MONANOVA, a Program to Analyze Factorial Experiments by Estimating Monotone Transformations of the Data," unpublished paper, Bell Laboratories, 1968. For an empirical comparison involving MONANOVA versus other prediction schemes, see Dick R. Wittink and Philippe Cattin, "Alternative Estimation Methods for Conjoint Analysis: A Monte Carlo Study," *Journal of Marketing Research*, 18 (February 1981), pp. 101–106.

Suggested Additional Readings

For a general discussion of how to ask questions in attitude surveys, see

Howard Schuman and Stanley Presser, *Questions and Answers in Attitude Surveys* (Orlando, Fla.: Academic Press, 1981).

For discussion of a general procedure that can be followed to develop attitude scales having desirable qualities, see

Gilbert A. Churchill, Jr., "A Paradigm for Developing Better Measures of Marketing Constructs," *Journal of Marketing Research*, 16 (February 1979), pp. 64–73.

For discussion of the various alternatives for conducting a multidimensional-scaling analysis, see

Glen L. Urban and John R. Hauser, *Design and Marketing of New Products* (Englewood Cliffs, N.J.: Prentice-Hall, 1980), especially pp. 185–234.

For discussion of the various issues surrounding conjoint analysis, see

Paul E. Green and V. Srinivasan, "Conjoint Analysis in Consumer Research: Issues and Outlook," *Journal of Consumer Research*, 5 (September 1978), pp. 103–123.

Part Four

Research Project

The fourth stage in the research process is to design the data-collection form. As we learned from the chapters in this part, designing a questionnaire is still an art, not a science. Nonetheless, as we saw in Chapter 12, there is a pattern of steps that beginning researchers often find useful in developing questionnaires. The method outlined begins with specifying what information will be sought, and it ends with pretesting the questionnaire and revising it if necessary. As was pointed out in the chapter, however, only rarely will actual questionnaire development be so orderly. More often, researchers will find themselves circling back to revise an earlier part of the questionnaire after subsequent development has proven it to be faulty in some respect.

We also learned in these chapters that the typical questionnaire contains two types of information: basic information and classification information. Basic information refers to the subject of the study, while classification information refers to the data collected about respondents, such as demographic and socioeconomic characteristics, that help in understanding the results. As we saw, the proper questionnaire sequence is to secure basic information first and classification information last, since without the basic information, there is no study.

Researchers for CARA decided to use a self-report attitude scale to measure local businesspeople's feelings toward various advertising media and their sales representatives. In the chosen format, respondents were asked to indicate the extent to which they agreed or disagreed with statements about sales representatives and advertising media by checking one of the blanks ranging from strong agreement to strong disagreement. This format allowed the researers two advantages: they could measure a respondent's intensity of feeling, and responses could be easily scored.

In the CARA study, the various degrees of agreement were assigned the values of 5, 4, 3, 2, and 1, with "strongly agree" representing the value of 5 and "strongly disagree" representing the value of 1. A total attitude score for each respondent could thereby be calculated by summing the ratings of the individual items.

Respondents were asked to rate the importance of the attributes and characteristics used to describe sales representatives and advertising media by checking the three most important items in each category. Researchers thought this was important because an individual may strongly agree or disagree with an item but may not value that characteristic or attribute.

Each of the three categories of sales representatives contained 12 descriptive attributes. The attributes were ordered randomly, and the identical order was then used in each category. By using identical items in identical order, researchers could compare total attitude scores between the sales representative categories. If different items, or a different ordering of items, within each category had been used, variation in the testing instrument might have been responsible for differences in resulting scores.

Respondents were also asked to indicate which 3 of the 12 attributes they felt were the most important. These attributes were listed in the same order as the items in the sales representatives' scales.

The advertising media of television, radio, and newspaper were also described by 12 characteristics. These characteristics were randomly ordered, and each category used the identical order of items for the reason just cited. The 12 attributes were also listed in an importance scale in the same order as the items in the media categories, and respondents were asked to select the 3 attributes they believed to be most important.

Questions regarding the sales representatives were asked first so as to generate interest in the questionnaire. This section was followed by questions about attitudes toward the various media. Finally, researchers added a section requesting classification information. This section was last because, while important, it was the least critical to the study.

Researchers chose the 12 specific attributes used to describe the sales representatives and the advertising media based on their review of the literature, discussions with CARA members, and experience surveys with local retailers.

CARA   Questionnaire

Section 1

Please indicate your opinion as to the extent to which you agree or disagree with the following statements for your television, radio, and newspaper sales representatives by placing an "X" in the appropriate blank. If you have more than one sales representative in any of these media, your opinions should include your general impressions of the sales representatives calling on you. If you have never been in contact with a sales representative in one or more of these media, please omit that section (or those sections) and proceed to the next. Don't worry over individual responses. It is your first impression on each item that is important.

Television Sales Representative

The television sales representatives calling on me are	Strongly Agree	Agree	Neither Agree nor Disagree	Disagree	Strongly Disagree
1. Creative	_____	_____	_____	_____	_____
2. Reliable	_____	_____	_____	_____	_____
3. Sincere	_____	_____	_____	_____	_____
4. Results oriented	_____	_____	_____	_____	_____
5. Knowledgeable about my business	_____	_____	_____	_____	_____
6. Cooperative	_____	_____	_____	_____	_____
7. Available when needed	_____	_____	_____	_____	_____
8. Hardworking	_____	_____	_____	_____	_____
9. Concerned about my particular advertising needs	_____	_____	_____	_____	_____
10. Able to get my ads placed quickly	_____	_____	_____	_____	_____
11. Aware of who my customers are	_____	_____	_____	_____	_____
12. Concerned about follow-through after the service	_____	_____	_____	_____	_____

Radio Sales Representative

The radio sales representatives calling on me are	Strongly Agree	Agree	Neither Agree nor Disagree	Disagree	Strongly Disagree
1. Creative	_____	_____	_____	_____	_____
2. Reliable	_____	_____	_____	_____	_____
3. Sincere	_____	_____	_____	_____	_____
4. Results oriented	_____	_____	_____	_____	_____

(continued)

CARA   Questionnaire   *(Continued)*

The radio sales representatives calling on me are	Radio Sales Representative				
	Strongly Agree	Agree	Neither Agree nor Disagree	Disagree	Strongly Disagree
5. Knowledgeable about my business	_____	_____	_____	_____	_____
6. Cooperative	_____	_____	_____	_____	_____
7. Available when needed	_____	_____	_____	_____	_____
8. Hardworking	_____	_____	_____	_____	_____
9. Concerned about my particular advertising needs	_____	_____	_____	_____	_____
10. Able to get my ads placed quickly	_____	_____	_____	_____	_____
11. Aware of who my customers are	_____	_____	_____	_____	_____
12. Concerned about follow-through after the service	_____	_____	_____	_____	_____

The newspaper sales representatives calling on me are	Newspaper Sales Representative				
	Strongly Agree	Agree	Neither Agree nor Disagree	Disagree	Strongly Disagree
1. Creative	_____	_____	_____	_____	_____
2. Reliable	_____	_____	_____	_____	_____
3. Sincere	_____	_____	_____	_____	_____
4. Results oriented	_____	_____	_____	_____	_____
5. Knowledgeable about my business	_____	_____	_____	_____	_____
6. Cooperative	_____	_____	_____	_____	_____
7. Available when needed	_____	_____	_____	_____	_____
8. Hardworking	_____	_____	_____	_____	_____
9. Concerned about my particular advertising needs	_____	_____	_____	_____	_____
10. Able to get my ads placed quickly	_____	_____	_____	_____	_____
11. Aware of who my customers are	_____	_____	_____	_____	_____
12. Concerned about follow-through after the service	_____	_____	_____	_____	_____

Please indicate what you believe are the three most important characteristics of a sales representative by placing an "X" in the appropriate blank. For example, if you feel Items 4, 8, and 10 are the most important characteristics, you would place an "X" in the blank next to each of these items.

The three most important characteristics of a media sales representative are

1. Creativity   _____

2. Reliability   _____

3. Sincerity   _____

CARA   *Questionnaire*   *(Continued)*

4. An orientation toward results   _____

5. A knowledge about my business   _____

6. Cooperation   _____

7. Availability when needed   _____

8. A willingness to work hard   _____

9. A concern about my particular advertising needs   _____

10. The ability to quickly place my ads   _____

11. Awareness of who my customers are   _____

12. Concern about follow-through after the service   _____

Section 2

Please indicate your opinion as to the extent to which you agree or disagree with the following statements about television, radio, and newspaper advertising, regardless of whether you use that form of advertising or not. Place an "X" in the appropriate blank. Again, don't worry over individual responses, since it is your first impression on each item that is important.

Television Advertising	Strongly Agree	Agree	Neither Agree nor Disagree	Disagree	Strongly Disagree
1. People pay attention to the ads.	___	___	___	___	___
2. The ads reach my target market.	___	___	___	___	___
3. The ads do not cost too much.	___	___	___	___	___
4. The ads improve my sales volume.	___	___	___	___	___
5. The ads are creative.	___	___	___	___	___
6. The ads do not have to be repeated frequently to be effective.	___	___	___	___	___
7. The ads reach a large number of people.	___	___	___	___	___
8. The ads build up recognition of my business.	___	___	___	___	___
9. There is evidence that ads reach a known market.	___	___	___	___	___
10. Buying the ads is not a difficult process.	___	___	___	___	___
11. It is easy to monitor when the ads are being run.	___	___	___	___	___
12. The quality of the ads is high (good).	___	___	___	___	___

Radio Advertising	Strongly Agree	Agree	Neither Agree nor Disagree	Disagree	Strongly Disagree
1. People pay attention to the ads.	___	___	___	___	___
2. The ads reach my target market.	___	___	___	___	___
3. The ads do not cost too much.	___	___	___	___	___
4. The ads improve my sales volume.	___	___	___	___	___

(continued)

CARA   Questionnaire   (Continued)

Radio Advertising	Strongly Agree	Agree	Neither Agree nor Disagree	Disagree	Strongly Disagree
5. The ads are creative.	___	___	___	___	___
6. The ads do not have to be repeated frequently to be effective.	___	___	___	___	___
7. The ads reach a large number of people.	___	___	___	___	___
8. The ads build up recognition of my business.	___	___	___	___	___
9. There is evidence that ads reach a known market.	___	___	___	___	___
10. Buying the ads is not a difficult process.	___	___	___	___	___
11. It is easy to monitor when the ads are being run.	___	___	___	___	___
12. The quality of the ads is high (good).	___	___	___	___	___

Newspaper Advertising	Strongly Agree	Agree	Neither Agree nor Disagree	Disagree	Strongly Disagree
1. People pay attention to the ads.	___	___	___	___	___
2. The ads reach my target market.	___	___	___	___	___
3. The ads do not cost too much.	___	___	___	___	___
4. The ads improve my sales volume.	___	___	___	___	___
5. The ads are creative.	___	___	___	___	___
6. The ads do not have to be repeated frequently to be effective.	___	___	___	___	___
7. The ads reach a large number of people.	___	___	___	___	___
8. The ads build up recognition of my business.	___	___	___	___	___
9. There is evidence that the ads reach a known market.	___	___	___	___	___
10. Buying the ads is not a difficult process.	___	___	___	___	___
11. It is easy to monitor when the ads are being run.	___	___	___	___	___
12. The quality of the ads is high (good).	___	___	___	___	___

Please indicate what you believe are the three most important attributes of advertising by placing an "X" in the appropriate blank. For example, if you feel Items 4, 8, and 10 are the most important attributes, you would place an "X" in the blank next to each of those items.

The three most important attributes of advertising are that

1. People pay attention to the ads.   ___

2. The ads reach my target market.   ___

3. The ads do not cost too much.   ___

4. The ads improve my sales volume.

CARA   *Questionnaire*   *(Continued)*

5. The ads are creative. _____

6. The ads do not have to be repeated frequently to be effective. _____

7. The ads reach a large number of people. _____

8. The ads build up recognition of my business. _____

9. There is evidence that the ads reach a known market. _____

10. Buying the ads is not a difficult process. _____

11. It is easy to monitor when the ads are being run. _____

12. The quality of the ads is high (good). _____

Section 3: Classification Data

1. What types of advertising have you used over the last 12 months?

Outdoor _____

Radio _____

Television _____

Newspaper _____

Magazine _____

Yellow Pages _____

Direct Mail _____

Shoppers _____

Other _____

2. Approximately what proportion of your total yearly advertising budget is spent on each of the following types of advertising?

Outdoor _____

Radio _____

Television _____

Newspaper _____

Magazine _____

Yellow Pages _____

Direct Mail _____

Shoppers _____

Other _____

Total = 100%

3. How much do you spend annually on advertising?

0–$9,999 _____

$10,000–$24,999 _____

$25,000–$49,999 _____

$50,000 and over _____

(continued)

CARA *Questionnaire*   *(Continued)*

4. *Which category best describes your position?*
Manager   _____

Owner/Manager   _____

Secretary   _____

Clerk   _____

Other   _____

5. *Do you make decisions regarding advertising expenditures?*
Yes   _____

No   _____

6. *Do you use an advertising agency?*
Yes   _____

No   _____

handwritten notes:
- Location
- advertising
exploratory research data.
these 2 reasons.

Case 4.1   Rumstad Decorating Centers (B)

Rumstad's was an old-line Rockford, Illinois, business. The company was originally founded as a small paint and wallpaper supply store in 1929 by Joseph Rumstad, who managed the store until his retirement in 1970, at which time Jack Rumstad, his son, took over. In 1974, the original downtown store was closed and a new outlet was opened on the city's rapidly expanding west side. In 1988, a second store was opened on the east side of the city, and the name of the business was changed to Rumstad Decorating Centers.

Jack Rumstad's review of 1989 operations proved disconcerting. Both stores had suffered losses for the year (see Rumstad Decorating Centers (A)). The picture was far more dismal at the west-side store. Losses at the east-side store were 80 percent less than the previous year's, which was partially due to some major organizational changes. Further, the east-side store had experienced a 25-percent increase in net sales and a 25-percent increase in gross profits over 1988. The west-side store, in contrast, had shown a 21-percent decrease in net sales and a 31-percent decrease in gross profit.

Some preliminary research by Mr. Rumstad suggested that the problem at the west-side store might be traced to the store's location or its advertising. Was the location perceived as convenient? Were potential customers aware of Rumstad Decorating Centers, the products they carried, and where they were located? Did people have favorable impressions of Rumstad? How did attitudes toward Rumstad compare with those toward Rumstad's major competitors? *[handwritten: awareness & attitudes & knowledge]*

Jack Rumstad realized that he did not have the expertise to answer these questions. Consequently, he called in Mrs. Sandra Parrett, who owned and managed a marketing research service in the Rockford area. Mrs. Parrett handled all liaison work with the client and assisted in the research design. In addition to Mrs. Parrett, Lisa Parrett, her daughter, supervised the field staff of four, analyzed data, and prepared research reports. Although the company was small,

[handwritten margin: research objectives]

it had an excellent reputation within the business community.

Research Design

Jack Rumstad agreed with Mrs. Parrett's suggestion that the best way to investigate Rumstad's concerns would be to use a structured, somewhat disguised questionnaire (see Figure 1). The sponsor of the research was to be hidden from the respondents to prevent them from answering "correctly" instead of honestly, so questions about two of Rumstad's main competitors, the Nina Emerson Decorating Center and the Wallpaper Shop, were introduced. Both of these stores offered products and services similar to those carried by Rumstad, and they were located in the same area as Rumstad's west-side store. The study was to be confined to the west-side store because of cost; loss of profits for the last several years had severely constrained Rumstad's ability to engage in research of this sort. However, the west-side store was so critical to the very survival of Rumstad Decorating Centers that Jack Rumstad was willing to commit funds to this investigation, although he repeatedly stressed to Mrs. Parrett the need to keep the cost as low as possible.

Even though the Nina Emerson Decorating Center and the Wallpaper Shop were similar to Rumstad, there were differences in their marketing strategies. Both stores seemed to advertise more than Rumstad, for example, although the exact amounts of their advertising budgets were not available. Emerson advertised in the *Shopper's World* (a weekly paper devoted exclusively to advertising that was distributed free), ran ads four times a year in the *Rockford Morning Star*, and did a small amount of radio and outdoor advertising. The Wallpaper Shop also advertised regularly in the *Shopper's World* but ran small ads daily in the *Morning Star* and daily radio commercials as well. Rumstad had formerly advertised in the *Morning Star* but now relied exclusively on the *Shopper's World*.

...ple Questionnaire – Rumstad Decorating Centers

...s 1–8, please indicate your opinion about the importance of the following ...osing a decorating center. Place an "X" in the appropriate blank.

	Not Important	Slightly Important	Fairly Important	Very Important
1. Saw or heard an advertisement	_____	_____	_____	_____
2. Special sale	_____	_____	_____	_____
3. Convenient location	_____	_____	_____	_____
4. Convenient hours	_____	_____	_____	_____
5. Knowledgeable sales personnel	_____	_____	_____	_____
6. Good-quality products	_____	_____	_____	_____
7. Additional services (e.g., matching paints, decorator services, etc.)	_____	_____	_____	_____
8. Reasonable prices in relation to quality	_____	_____	_____	_____

Below is a list of abbreviations for the three west-side stores that will be referred to throughout the questionnaire:

Nina Emerson Decorating Center—"Emerson"
Rumstad Decorating Center—"Rumstad"
Wallpaper Shop—"Wallpaper Shop"

Please indicate your response with an "X" in the appropriate blank.

9. *Do you know where any of the following west-side stores are located? (i.e., could you find any of these stores without referring to another source?)*

	Yes	No
Emerson	_____	_____
Rumstad	_____	_____
Wallpaper Shop	_____	_____

10. *When was the last time you heard or saw any advertisements for the following stores?*

	Never	Within the Last Month	1–6 Months Ago	More than 6 Months Ago
Emerson	_____	_____	_____	_____
Rumstad	_____	_____	_____	_____
Wallpaper Shop	_____	_____	_____	_____

11. *Please indicate the source(s) of any advertisements you have seen or heard.*

	Have Not Seen/Heard	Shopper's World	Rockford Morning Star	Radio	TV	Other	Don't Recall
Emerson	_____	_____	_____	_____	_____	_____	_____
Rumstad	_____	_____	_____	_____	_____	_____	_____
Wallpaper Shop	_____	_____	_____	_____	_____	_____	_____

12. *Do you know which of the following items are available in these stores? If so, check the item(s) that apply.*

	Don't Know	Paint	Paneling	Carpeting	Draperies	Other
Emerson	_____	_____	_____	_____	_____	_____
	_____	_____	_____	_____	_____	_____
Rumstad						
Wallpaper Shop	_____	_____	_____	_____	_____	_____

Figure 1   *(Continued)*

13. Which name brands of paint, if any, do you associate with the following stores?

	Benjamin Moore	Dutch Boy	Glidden	Pittsburgh	Do not associate any listed
Emerson	——	——	——	——	——
Rumstad	——	——	——	——	——
Wallpaper Shop	——	——	——	——	——

14. Have you ever visited any of these west-side stores?

	Never	Within the Last Year	1–5 Years Ago	More than 5 Years Ago
Emerson	——	——	——	——
Rumstad	——	——	——	——
Wallpaper Shop	——	——	——	——

Section II

If you have visited or have knowledge of *one or more* of the stores listed below, please indicate the extent to which you agree or disagree with the following statements for each store. For instance, if you have knowledge of only one store, please answer each question for that particular store. If you have not visited or have no knowledge of any of these stores, omit this section and proceed to Section III.

	Strongly Agree	Agree	Neither Agree nor Disagree	Disagree	Strongly Disagree

15. The location of the store is convenient.

	Strongly Agree	Agree	Neither Agree nor Disagree	Disagree	Strongly Disagree
Emerson	——	——	——	——	——
Rumstad	——	——	——	——	——
Wallpaper Store	——	——	——	——	——

16. The sales personnel are knowledgeable.

Emerson	——	——	——	——	——
Rumstad	——	——	——	——	——
Wallpaper Store	——	——	——	——	——

17. The store lacks additional services (e.g., matching paint, decorator services, etc.).

Emerson	——	——	——	——	——
Rumstad	——	——	——	——	——
Wallpaper Store	——	——	——	——	——

18. The store carries good-quality products.

Emerson	——	——	——	——	——
Rumstad	——	——	——	——	——
Wallpaper Store	——	——	——	——	——

19. The prices are reasonable in relation to the quality of the products.

Emerson	——	——	——	——	——
Rumstad	——	——	——	——	——
Wallpaper Store	——	——	——	——	——

20. The store hours are inconvenient.

Emerson	——	——	——	——	——
Rumstad	——	——	——	——	——
Wallpaper Store	——	——	——	——	——

(continued)

Figure 1   **(Continued)**

Section III

1. Your sex: ____ Male   ____ Female

2. Your age: ____ Under 25   ____ 25–29 years   ____ 30–39 years   ____ 40–54 years
      ____ 55 or over

3. How long have you lived in Rockford?
      ____ Less than 1 year   ____ 1–3 years   ____ 4 or more years

4. Do you ____ Own a home or condominium   ____ Rent a house
      ____ Rent an apartment   ____ Other

5. When was the last time you painted or remodeled your residence?
      ____ Never   ____ Within past year   ____ 1–5 years ago
      ____ More than 5 years ago

6. Approximately how many times have you received the weekly **Shopper's World** *in the past 3 months?*
      ____ Never   ____ 1–5 times   ____ 6–12 times

7. Do you read or page through the **Shopper's World?**
      ____ Do not receive it   ____ Never   ____ Less than ½ the time
      ____ About ½ the time   ____ More than ½ the time

Sample

Because of the financial constraints imposed on the study by Jack Rumstad, it was decided to limit the study to households within a two-mile radius of Rumstad, Emerson, and the Wallpaper Shop. Aldermanic districts within the two-mile radius were identified; there were four in all, and the wards within each district were listed. Two of the 12 wards were then excluded because they were outside of the specified area. Blocks within each of the 10 remaining wards were enumerated, and five blocks were randomly selected from each ward. An initial starting point for each block was determined, and the questionnaires were then administered by the Parrett field staff at every sixth house on the block. All interviews were conducted on Saturday and Sunday. If there was no one at home or if the respondent refused to cooperate, the next house on the block was substituted; there was no one at home at 39 households, and 18 others refused to participate. The field work was completed within one weekend and produced a total sample of 123 responses.

Questions

1. Evaluate the questionnaire. Do you think the questionnaire adequately addresses the concerns of Jack Rumstad?
2. How would you suggest the data collected be analyzed to best solve Rumstad's problem?
3. Do you think personal administration of the questionnaires was called for in this study, or would you have suggested an alternative scheme? Why or why not?

Case 4.2   Young Ideas Publishing Company[1]

How does a company go about marketing products to a specified niche of the teenage market? That is the question confronting Linda Halley, co-owner of Young Ideas Publishing Company. Halley is convinced that her unconventional novels for young people would be very attractive to at least a segment of the teenaged market. She is unsure, however, about how to reach this "nonconformist" segment of the market.

Background

Three years ago, Halley wrote her first novel, a youth-oriented book entitled *Illusions of Summer*. None of the major publishers would publish the book, however, primarily because it dealt with several controversial social and political concerns. Most publishers simply felt that such topics would not be of interest to enough high school teenagers to justify publication, although many agreed that the novel was of publication quality in other respects.

Frustrated in her efforts to publish her novel, Halley and a business partner, Teresa Martinez, decided to form their own publishing company and publish the book themselves. Both believed that teenagers would be interested in social and political topics and would buy the book. Thus, Young Ideas Publishing Company was born. Halley hoped that effective marketing of the book on a local basis by the company might encourage national distributors to alter their positions toward the novel.

When *Illusions of Summer* was released, it was very well-received by several literary critics, winning promising reviews and awards. Despite its critical success, however, commercial acceptance was much harder to find. During the first 24 months after publication, only about 1,500 copies of the book were sold, mostly through local bookstores and mail orders. Most distributors were unwilling to handle the book because it was not from an established publisher. With few channels through which to market the product, it remained virtually unknown outside of a limited local market.

Even with this poor showing from a commercial standpoint, Halley continued to believe that so-called nonconformist teenagers would be willing to buy books of this nature. Accordingly, she wrote and published a second novel, *Ultimate Choices*. Once again, the novel dealt with several controversial issues for teens and social and political concerns; once again, the critics reacted favorably. Initial sales for *Ultimate Choices* were better than they were for *Illusions of Summer;* two months after publication, about 250 copies had been sold. By talking to clerks in local bookstores, Halley was able to learn that most of the books were being sold to teenagers.

Nature of the Problem

Although encouraged by the good reviews and increased sales of the second book, Halley and Martinez were concerned about the future of Young Ideas Publishing Company. Even though the company had managed to break even during the past two years by contracting for outside printing jobs, Martinez indicated that the survival of the company might well depend on the success of the new novel.

Both partners were still convinced that a market existed for the novels. They recognized, however, that they might not know enough about the teenage market to effectively market the novels. For example, they believed that insights were needed in the following areas:

- Will high school teenagers specifically select young-adult novels, or do they think that these are written for younger teens?
- Are teenagers interested in social and political issues?
- Where do high school teenagers usually obtain books for pleasure reading?
- Do teens purchase books for themselves, or do parents purchase books for them?
- What types of promotional items do high school teens enjoy most?
- What advertising media are most effective in reaching teens?
- How do nonconformist teens differ on these issues from other teens?

In an effort to generate insight into these issues, Halley retained the services of a young marketing researcher. The researcher prepared a questionnaire that was administered to 166 teens in the target age-group. A portion of the questionnaire is shown in Figure 1; note that a scale to measure the nonconformity construct is included.

[1]The contributions of Tom J. Brown to the development of this case are gratefully acknowledged.

Figure 1   **Partial Questionnaire/Coding**

The following is a portion of a questionnaire administered to teens ages 15 to 18 years. The questionnaire was designed to gather information and opinions pertaining to reading habits, subject matter preferences, and related issues.

NOTE: Nonresponses were coded as "9" or "99."

For the first group of questions, respondents were asked to check the appropriate box.

1. *On average, how many books do you read for pleasure outside of school in one month?*

   □ Less than one   □ Four
   □ One   □ Five
   □ Two   □ Six
   □ Three   □ I never read any.

2. *In the last 12 months, where have you usually gotten the books you have read for pleasure?*

   □ I never read any.   □ Store other than bookstore
   □ Public library   □ Book club
   □ School library   □ Mail order other than book club
   □ Home   □ Received as gifts
   □ Borrowed from another person   □ Other
   □ Bookstore

3. *On average, what would you pay for a new paperback book?*

   □ Less than $3.00   □ $6.00 to $6.99
   □ $3.00 to $3.99   □ $7.00 to $7.99
   □ $4.00 to $4.99   □ $8.00 or more
   □ $5.00 to $5.99

In the following section, the teens were asked to judge the importance of various features of books in their decision process of purchasing a book.

	Very Important	Somewhat Important	Neither Important nor Unimportant	Somewhat Unimportant	Very Unimportant
4. *The story description*	□	□	□	□	□
5. *The author*	□	□	□	□	□
6. *The price*	□	□	□	□	□

Next, respondents were asked to circle the appropriate number corresponding to how likely they were to read books within various subject matter categories.

	Extremely Likely		Neither Likely nor Unlikely		Extremely Unlikely		
7. *Science fiction*	1	2	3	4	5	6	7
8. *Humor/ comedy*	1	2	3	4	5	6	7
9. *Mystery/ suspense*	1	2	3	4	5	6	7

Figure 1   *(Continued)*

	Extremely Likely			Neither Likely nor Unlikely			Extremely Unlikely	
10. Politics	1	2	3	4	5	6	7	
11. Romance	1	2	3	4	5	6	7	
12. Social issues/ problems	1	2	3	4	5	6	7	

To determine the degree to which a teen was nonconformist, respondents were asked to indicate their level of agreement with each of the following statements.

	Strongly Agree	Agree	Disagree	Strongly Disagree
13. When I make decisions, I like to get other people's opinions.	1	2	3	4
14. I would lead a demonstration for a social cause if I felt strongly about it.	1	2	3	4
15. I fit in well with society.	1	2	3	4
16. I respect the opinons of most adults.	1	2	3	4
17. I like to try to change society.	1	2	3	4
18. It's important to me that I fit in well with other students my age.	1	2	3	4
19. I would participate in a local/national campaign to promote a candidate who represented my views.	1	2	3	4
20. My life-style is different than that of most students my own age.	1	2	3	4
21. I keep up with current events.	1	2	3	4
22. I don't like to call attention to myself.	1	2	3	4
23. If I feel strongly about something, I need to make my statement even if my friends disagree.	1	2	3	4
24. I try to avoid conflict with my parents.	1	2	3	4
25. Keeping up with the trends is important to me.	1	2	3	4

Finally, two of the classification questions from the questionnaire are presented.

26. *What is your age?* _____ years old
   [Actual age was coded.]

27. *Are you male or female?*
   ☐   Male
   ☐   Female

Questions

1. Items 13 through 25 in Figure 1 attempt to measure nonconformity. Define "nonconformity" based on these items. How well do these items tap into the construct? What other items could (or should) have been included?

Case 4.3   Calamity-Casualty Insurance Company[1]

Calamity-Casualty is an insurance company located in Dallas, Texas, that deals exclusively with automobile coverage. Its policy offerings include the standard features offered by most insurers, such as collision, comprehensive, emergency road service, medical, and uninsured motorist. The unique aspect of Calamity-Casualty Insurance is that all policies are sold through the mail. Agents do not make personal calls on clients, and the company does not operate district offices. As a result, Calamity-Casualty's capital/labor requirements are greatly reduced, at a substantial cost savings to the company. A great portion of these savings are passed on to the consumer in the form of lower prices. The data indicate that Calamity-Casualty offers its policies at 20 to 25 percent below the average market rate.

The company's strategy of selling automobile insurance by mail at low prices has been very successful. Calamity-Casualty has traditionally been the third largest seller of automobile insurance in the Southwest. During the past five years, the company has consistently achieved an average market share of some 14 percent in the fours states it serves— Arizona, New Mexico, Nevada, and Texas. This compares favorably with the 19-percent and 17-percent market shares realized by the two leading firms in the region. However, Calamity-Casualty has never been highly successful in Arizona. The largest market share gained by Calamity-Casualty in Arizona for any one year was 4 percent, which placed the company seventh among firms competing in that state.

The company's poor performance in Arizona greatly concerns Calamity-Casualty's board of executives. Demographic experts estimate that during the next six to ten years, the population in Arizona will increase some 10 to 15 percent, the largest projected growth rate of any state in the Southwest. Thus, for Calamity-Casualty to remain a major market force in the area, the company needs to improve its sales performance in Arizona.

In response to this matter, Calamity-Casualty sponsored a study that was conducted by the Automobile Insurance Association of America (AIAA), the national association of automobile insurance executives, to determine Arizona residents' attitudes toward and perceptions of the various insurance companies selling policies in that state. The results of the AIAA research showed that Calamity-Casualty was favorably perceived across most categories measured. Calamity-Casualty received the highest ratings with respect to service, pricing, policy offering, and image. Although these findings were well received by the company's board of executives, they provided little strategic insight into how Calamity-Casualty might increase sales in Arizona.

Since the company was committed to obtaining information useful for developing a more effective Arizona sales campaign, the executive board sought the services of Aminbane, Pedrone, and Associates, a marketing research firm specializing in insurance consulting, to help with the matter. After many discussions between members of the research team and executives at Calamity-Casualty, it was decided that the most beneficial approach toward designing a more appropriate sales campaign would be to ascertain the psychographic profiles of nonpurchasers and direct mail purchasers of Calamity-Casualty insurance. This would help the company better understand the personal factors influencing people's decision to respond or not respond to direct mail solicitation.

Research Design

To learn more about which psychographic factors are important in describing purchasers of automobile insurance, some exploratory research was undertaken.

[1]The contributions of David M. Szymanski to the development of this case are gratefully acknowledged.

Table 1   *Calamity-Casualty Marketing Research Questionnaire Items*

Risk Aversion

1. It is always better to buy a used car from a dealer than from an individual.
2. Generally speaking, I avoid buying generic drugs at the drugstore.
3. It would be a disaster to be stranded on the road due to a breakdown.
4. It would be important to me to plan a long road trip very carefully and in great detail.
5. I would like to try parachute jumping sometime.
6. Before buying a new product, I would first discuss it with someone who had already used it.
7. Before deciding to see a new movie in a theater, it is important to read the critical reviews.
8. If my car needed even a minor repair, I would first get cost estimates from several garages.

Powerlessness

1. Persons like myself have little chance of protecting our personal interests when they conflict with those of strong pressure groups.
2. A lasting world peace can be achieved by those of us who work toward it.
3. I think each of us can do a great deal to improve world opinion of the United States.
4. This world is run by the few people in power, and there is not much the little guy can do about it.
5. People like me can change the course of world events if we make ourselves heard.
6. More and more, I feel helpless in the face of what's happening in the world today.

Convenience Orientation

1. I like to buy things by mail or catalog because it saves time.
2. I think that it is not worth the extra effort to clip coupons for groceries.
3. I would rather wash my own car than pay to have it washed at a car wash.
4. I would prefer to have an automatic transmission rather than a stick shift in my car.
5. When choosing a bank, I believe that location is the most important factor.
6. When shopping for groceries, I would be willing to drive a longer distance in order to buy at lower prices.

Note: Each item requires one of the following responses:

Responses	Code
S.A.—Strongly Agree	5
A.—Agree	4
N.—Neither Agree nor Disagree	3
D.—Disagree	2
S.D.—Strongly Disagree	1

In-depth interviews were held with two insurance salespersons, who offered various insights on the subject. These experience interviews were followed by a focus-group meeting with Arizona residents who had received a direct mail offer from Calamity-Casualty. Finally, the research team consulted university professors in both psychology and mass communications to uncover other determinants of buyer behavior. Output from these procedures revealed three primary factors that could be used to describe purchasers of insurance by mail—namely, risk aversion, powerlessness, and convenience orientation. It was believed that people who were risk averse, had a sense of powerlessness, and were convenience oriented would be more favorably disposed toward direct mail marketing efforts and thus would be more likely to purchase Calamity-Casualty automobile insurance.

Method of Data Collection

Given these factors of interest, the list of items contained in Table 1 was generated to form the basis of a questionnaire to be administered to Arizona residents. Two samples of subjects were to be used—one of direct mail buyers and one of nonbuyers. The research team estimated that 175 subjects would be required from both samples to adequately assess the three constructs. Because a mail questionnaire dealing with psychographic subject matter might have a very low response rate, and because attitude toward direct mail was one of the attributes being measured, a telephone interview was believed to be best suited to the needs at hand.

Questions

1. Conceptually, what are the constructs risk aversion, convenience, and powerlessness?
2. Do you think that the sample of items adequately assesses each construct? Can you think of any additional items that could or should be used?

Sampling and Data Collection

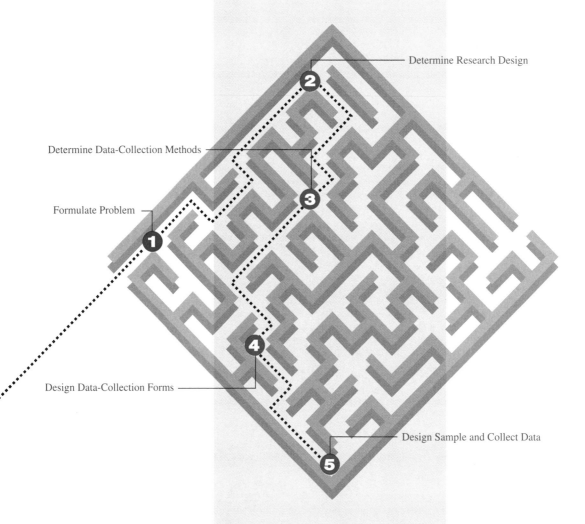

Determine Research Design

Determine Data-Collection Methods

Formulate Problem

Design Data-Collection Forms

Design Sample and Collect Data

Part Five focuses on the collection of data needed to answer a problem. **Chapter 15** overviews the various types of sampling plans that can be used to determine the population elements from which data should be collected. It also describes non-probability sampling and simple random sampling, one of the probability sampling plans. **Chapter 16** then discusses two popular, but more complex, probability sampling schemes — stratified and cluster sampling. **Chapter 17** treats the question of how many of the population elements are needed to answer the problem with precision and confidence in the results. **Chapter 18** discusses the many nonsampling errors that can arise in completing the data-collection task.

Larry Widi wishes he had a list of all the companies in the market to purchase, lease, or rent construction equipment. As worldwide manager of Marketing Research at J. I. Case Company's construction equipment division, almost all of his research begins with lists—lists of companies that have bought construction equipment, companies that currently use construction equipment, companies that might be interested in someday purchasing construction equipment. . . . And while Widi may not ever get his wish of having a list of all the companies in the construction equipment universe, he does a good job of keeping track of many of them.

For example, J. I. Case Company was recently interested in designing a new high-capacity wheel loader. One of the uses of wheel loaders is to move feed and manure in beef and cattle feedlots. To ensure the new wheel loader had the design features necessary for the feedlot application, Widi needed to survey some of the people who purchase and operate wheel loaders for feedlots.

To draw a representative sample of feedlots, a list of the total feedlot universe needed to be compiled. Widi started with a list of feedlots from Dun & Bradstreet. To this he added a list of feedlots that had purchased one or more similar sized wheel loaders during the past five years. Widi had two more list sources to combine with the previous lists: lists provided by beef and cattle feedlot associations and names of feedlots that had purchased Case wheel loaders, generated from the Case warranty system.

In the end, Widi had a combined list of 16,500 feedlots, 6,500 of which had purchased one or more wheel loaders in the past five years. "That kind of list makes me very efficient,"

says Widi. He estimates this list included 85 to 90 percent of his universe. "This coverage level is quite common for the studies I work on. We're still missing 10 to 15 percent, but 85 percent is pretty darn good."

The next step in the wheel loader study was for Widi to identify which segments of the feedlot market needed to be represented. He decided to break it down by size and geography. Once he identified the size and geographical segments that needed to be represented, he used a computer program to draw a random sample of feedlots from each segment. Then he sent the list of people to be contacted and the questionnaire he had developed to a telephone interviewing company to conduct the interviews.

"Throughout the research process, nonresponse is always a big problem," concedes Widi. "I can pull a representative sample from the data base of names I've compiled, but if I get a high nonresponse level, there could be a major impact on the representativeness of the input."

"From the list I provide for telephone interviews, we may have a nonresponse rate ranging from 5 to 40 percent. This is a very big issue because it adds a potential error to what we're trying to do."

As a result, Widi is a self-described stickler for bringing down the nonresponse rate. "We absolutely

make every effort. Often we need to talk to the equipment manager, who may be very hard to reach. We start calling at 6:00 a.m. all the way through to 10:00 p.m. If we can't get in touch with the appropriate person, we set up callback appointments that are convenient for their schedule."

"If it isn't possible to find a phone number, we'll send the company a card indicating that we'd like to talk to them and ask for their phone number; we get 40 percent of those back, which helps bring the nonresponse rate down."

Keeping tabs on all the companies that are in the market for construction equipment keeps Widi very busy. He says that while there's no such thing as a typical day in his job, most of his days are spent in one of three ways: He is in the field at least a third of the time, at one of the company's proving grounds, setting up end-user evaluations of his company's products or those of the competition; on the customers' job sites, observing equipment in action and talking to operators; or conducting focus groups on any number of issues. Then there are the office days, when he designs research studies and receives and evaluates results, spending the bulk of his day at his desk in front of his computer terminal. The third kind of day is spent in meetings, communicating results and participating in business decisions within the organization.

"The thing I like most about my work," says Widi, "is to contribute high-quality end-user input that helps J. I. Case make a quality product that meets the customer's needs and exceeds his expectations. To me, that's what my job is. When you come right down to it, companies that meet the customers' needs are going to be in business for a long time. Those that don't, won't."

453

Types of Samples and Simple Random Sampling

Learning Objectives

Upon completing this chapter, you should be able to

1. Distinguish between a census and a sample.

2. List the six steps researchers use to draw a sample of a population.

3. Define *sampling frame.*

4. Explain the difference between a probability sample and a nonprobability sample.

5. Distinguish between a fixed and a sequential sample.

6. Explain what a judgment sample is and describe its best use and its hazards.

7. Define *quota sample.*

8. Explain what a parameter in a sampling procedure is.

9. Explain what the derived population is.

10. Explain why the concept of sampling distribution is the most important concept in statistics.

Case in Marketing Research

"Here's the problem," sighed Judy Moon, of B. C. Patterson's. "We have a great product concept and terrific marketing ideas, but we can't figure out how to identify, much less test, our market."

"Well, you've certainly got my interest," replied Millicent Conway, who worked for a large marketing research firm that had done work for Patterson's and other clothing retailers in the past. "What's the product?"

'We've developed an entire line of fashion clothing especially designed for women with arthritis and other movement-limiting conditions. The clothes are stylish and feature Velcro fasteners hidden beneath purely decorative buttons."

"That is a great idea," Conway interjected. "As the fashion business becomes more specialized, there's a real trend by retailers to focus on specialized conditions. Research shows that a full third of all adults fall into the "hard-to-fit" category, which covers everyone from dwarfs to the obese. In addition, 20 percent of Americans are disabled—that's almost 43 million people. Do you have any idea how many women there are with arthritis who might constitute your market?"

"Actually, that's why I'm here today," replied Moon. "At Patterson's we've talked ourselves through this until we're blue in the face. We need fresh input and your research expertise. We know that half of American women over 45 have arthritis, but we have no idea how to reach them. We considered using the list of contributors to the Arthritis Foundation as a start, at least for some test marketing, but when we looked at the list, we realized that most of the contributors either weren't women or weren't arthritis sufferers."

"I try to never, never, ever talk myself out of work," said Conway, "but I'm surprised you haven't just taken the traditional retailing route of offering a specialty section in your retail stores or sending out a mini-catalog to your charge customers."

"I'm not going to say we haven't thought about it," answered Moon, "but we feel that marketing to these women is going to be tricky. Women with fingers too stiff to button buttons don't want their problem known outside the privacy of the dressing room. That makes it imperative that we pitch our marketing efforts just right. As you know, that means

trying out a couple of different strategies on sample groups. But that gets us back to our original problem. How can we come up with a representative sample if we can't get a handle on who our target population is? I tell you, Millicent, this one has really got us tearing our hair out."

Discussion Issues

1. If you were Conway, how would you define the target population for the B. C. Patterson's study?
2. If all shoppers who entered a B. C. Patterson's store on a given day were polled to see whether they might be potential purchasers for Moon's line of easy-to-wear clothing, would that constitute a probability or a nonprobability sample? If the female respondents with arthritis were then asked to fill out a questionnaire, would they constitute a probability or a nonprobability sample?
3. Name at least two potential criteria that could be used to develop a procedure for sampling shoppers at B. C. Patterson's stores.

Census A complete canvass of a population.

Sample Selection of a subset of elements from a larger group of objects.

Population The totality of cases that conform to some designated specifications.

Sampling frame The list of sampling units from which a sample will be drawn; the list could consist of geographic areas, institutions, individuals, or other units.

Once the researcher has clearly specified the problem and developed an appropriate research design and data-collection instruments, the next step in the research process is to select those elements from which the information will be collected. One way to do this is to collect information from each member of the population of interest by completely canvassing this population. A complete canvass of a population is called a **census.** Another way would be to collect information from a portion of the population by taking a **sample** of elements from the larger group and, on the basis of the information collected from the subset, to infer something about the larger group. One's ability to make this inference from subset to larger group depends on the method by which the sample of elements was chosen. A major part of this chapter is devoted to the "why" and "how" of taking a sample.

Incidentally, **population** here refers not only to people but also to manufacturing firms, retail or wholesale institutions, or even inanimate objects such as parts produced in a manufacturing plant; it is defined as the totality of cases that conform to some designated specifications. The specifications define the elements that belong to the target group and those that are to be excluded. A study aimed at establishing a demographic profile of frozen-pizza eaters requires specifying who is to be considered a frozen-pizza eater. Anyone who has ever eaten a frozen pizza? Those who eat at least one such pizza a month? A week? Those who eat a certain minimum number of frozen pizzas per month? Researchers need to be very explicit in defining the target group of interest. They also need to be very careful that they have actually sampled the target population and not some other population due to an inappropriate or incomplete **sampling frame,** which is the listing of the elements from which the actual sample will be drawn.

One might choose to sample rather than to canvass a whole population for several reasons. First, complete counts on populations of even moderate size are very costly and time consuming. Often the information will be obsolete by the time the census is completed and the information processed. In some cases, a census is impossible. If, for example, researchers sought to test the life a company's electric light bulbs by leaving all of its inventory of bulbs on until they burned out, they would have reliable data, but no product to sell.

Finally—and to novice researchers, surprisingly—one might choose a sample over a census for purposes of accuracy. Censuses involve larger field staffs, which in turn introduce greater potential for nonsampling error. This is one of the reasons the Bureau of the Census uses sample surveys to check the accuracy of various censuses. That is correct; samples are used to infer the accuracy of the census.[1]

Required Steps in Sampling

Figure 15.1 outlines a useful six-step procedure that researchers can follow when drawing a sample of a population. Note that it is first necessary to define the population, or the collection of elements, about which the researcher wishes to make an inference. The researcher must decide if the relevant population consists of individuals, households, business firms, other institutions, credit card transactions, or whatever. In making these decisions, the researcher also has to be careful to specify what units are to be excluded. Geographic boundaries and a time period for the study must always be specified, although additional restrictions are often placed on the elements. When the elements are individuals, for example, the relevant population may be defined as all those over eighteen years of age, or females only, or those with a high school education only.

Figure 15.1   Six-Step Procedure for Drawing a Sample

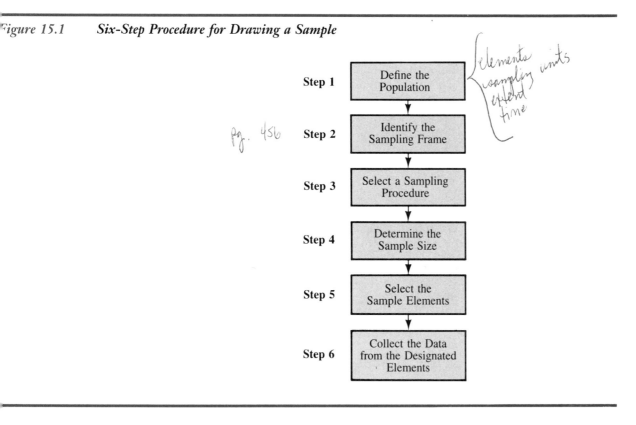

Handwritten note (top right): elements (sampling) units extend time

Handwritten note (left of Step 2): Pg. 456

In general, the simpler the definition of the target population, the higher the incidence and the easier and less costly it is to find the sample.[2] **Incidence** refers to the percent of the population or group that qualifies for inclusion in the sample using some criteria. Incidence has a direct bearing on the time and cost it takes to complete studies. When incidence is high (i.e., most population elements qualify for the study because only one or very few easily satisfied criteria are used to screen potential respondents), the cost and time to collect data are minimized. Alternatively, as the number of criteria used to describe what constitutes eligible respondents for the study increases, so do the cost and time necessary to find them. The most important thing is that the researcher be precise in specifying exactly what elements are of interest and what elements are to be excluded. A clear statement of research purpose helps immeasurably in determining the appropriate elements of interest.

The second step in the sample-selection process is identifying the sampling frame, which, you will recall, is the listing of the elements from which the actual sample will be drawn. Say that the target population for a particular study is all the households in the metropolitan Dallas area. At first glance, the Dallas phone book would seem an easy and good example of a sampling frame. However, upon closer examination it becomes clear that the telephone directory provides an inaccurate listing of Dallas households, omitting those with unlisted numbers (and, of course, those without phones) and double-counting those with multiple listings. People who have recently moved and thus received new phones not yet listed are also omitted.

Experienced researchers have found that only rarely is there a perfect correspondence between the sampling frame and the target population in which they are interested. One of the researcher's more creative tasks in sampling is developing an appropriate sampling frame when the list of population elements is not readily available. Sometimes this means sampling geographic areas or institutions and then subsampling within these units when, say, the target population is individuals but a current, accurate list of appropriate individuals is not available.

The third step in the procedure for drawing a sample is closely intertwined with the identification of the sampling frame. Choosing a sampling method or procedure depends largely on what the researcher can develop for a sampling frame. Different types of samples require different types of sampling frames. This chapter and the next review the main types of samples employed in marketing research. The connection between sampling frame and sampling method should become obvious from these discussions.

The fourth step in the sample-selection process requires that sample size be determined. Chapter 17 discusses this question. The fifth step indicates that the researcher needs to actually pick the elements that will be included in the study. How this is done depends upon the type of sample being used, and consequently we will explore the topic of sample selection when we discuss sampling methods. Finally, the researcher needs to actually collect data from the designated respondents. A great many things can go wrong with this task. These problems are reviewed, and some methods for handling them are discussed, in Chapter 18.

Types of Sampling Plans

Sampling techniques can be divided into the two broad categories of **probability and nonprobability samples.** In a probability sample, each member of the population has a *known, nonzero* chance of being included in the sample. The chances of each member of the population being included in the sample may not be equal, but everyone has a known probability of inclusion. That probability is determined by the specific mechanical procedure that is used to select sample elements.

With nonprobability samples, on the other hand, there is no way of estimating the probability that any population element will be included in the sample. Thus, there is no way of ensuring that the sample is representative of the population. For example, all registered voters have a chance of being called for jury duty. If all the people who were called ultimately served on juries, and jurors were assigned to cases randomly, juries could be said to represent a probability sample. However, as any fan of courtroom dramas can tell you, an amazing amount of fancy footwork and folklore goes into the process of jury selection. One of the things a defendant pays an attorney for is his or her skill and judgment in picking a potentially sympathetic jury. Hence, a jury represents a nonprobability sample.

All nonprobability samples rely on personal judgment somewhere in the sample-selection process rather than on a mechanical procedure to select sample members. While these judgments may sometimes yield good estimates of a population characteristic, there is no way of determining objectively if the sample is adequate. It is only when the elements have been selected with known probabilities that one is able to evaluate the precision of a sample result. For this reason, probability sampling is usually considered to be the superior method, in terms of being able to estimate the amount of sampling error present.

Samples can also be categorized by whether they are **fixed** or **sequential samples.** In fixed samples, the sample size is decided before the study begins, and all the needed information is collected before the results are analyzed. In our discussion

---

Probability sample A sample in which each population element has a known, nonzero chance of being included in the sample.

Nonprobability sample A sample that relies on personal judgment somewhere in the element selection process and therefore prohibits estimating the probability that any population element will be included in the sample.

Fixed sample A sample for which size is determined *a priori* and needed information is collected from the designated elements.

Sequential sample A sample formed on the basis of a series of successive decisions. If the evidence is not conclusive after a small sample is taken, more observations are taken; if it is still inconclusive after these additional observations, still more observations are taken. At each stage, then, a decision is made as to whether more information should be collected or whether the evidence is sufficient to draw a conclusion.

The target population for the U.S. Census is every individual residing in the United States. Advertisements like this one are used to encourage participation.

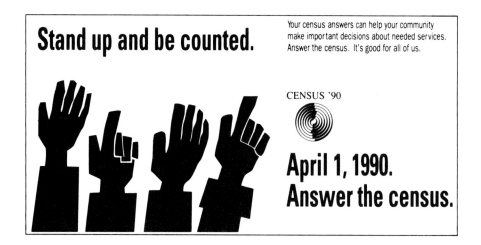

we shall emphasize fixed samples since they are the type most commonly used in marketing research. Nevertheless, you should be aware that sequential samples can also be taken, and they can be used with each of the basic sampling plans we will discuss.

In a sequential sample, the number of elements to be sampled is not decided in advance but is determined by a series of decisions as the data are collected. For example, if, after a small sample is taken, the evidence is not conclusive, more observations will be made. If the results are still inconclusive, the size of the sample will be expanded further. At each stage, a decision is made as to whether more information should be collected or whether the evidence is now sufficient to permit a conclusion. The sequential sample allows trends in the data to be evaluated as the data are being collected, and this affords an opportunity to reduce costs when additional observations show diminishing usefulness.

Both probability and nonprobability sampling plans can be further divided by type. Nonprobability samples, for instance, can be classified as *convenience*, *judgment*, or *quota*, while probability samples can be *simple random*, *stratified*, or *cluster*, and some of these can be further divided. Figure 15.2 shows the types of samples we shall discuss in this chapter and the next. You should be aware that the basic sample types can be combined into more complex sampling plans. If you understand the basic types, though, you should well understand the more complex designs.

Nonprobability Samples

As we stated earlier, nonprobability samples involve personal judgment somewhere in the selection process. Sometimes this judgment is imposed by the researcher, while in other cases the selection of population elements to be included is left to individual field workers. Since the elements are not selected by a mechanical procedure, it is impossible to assess the probability of any population member's being included and, thus, the degree of sampling error involved. Without knowing how much error results from a particular sampling procedure, researchers cannot gauge the accuracy of their estimates with any precision.

Figure 15.2   ***Classification of Sampling Techniques***

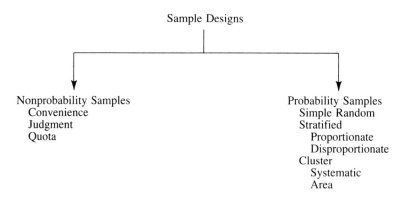

Convenience Samples

Convenience sample
A nonprobability sample sometimes called an *accidental sample* because those included in the sample enter by accident, in that they just happen to be where the study is being conducted when it is being conducted.

Convenience samples are sometimes called *accidental samples* because those composing the sample enter by "accident"—they just happen to be where the information for the study is being collected. Examples of convenience samples abound in our everyday lives. We talk to a few friends, and on the basis of their reactions, we infer the political sentiment of the country; our local radio station asks people to call in and express their reactions to some controversial issue, and the opinions expressed are interpreted as prevailing sentiment; we ask for volunteers in a research study and use those who come forward.

The problem with convenience samples, of course, is that we have no way of knowing if those included are representative of the target population. And while we might hesitate to infer that the reactions of a few friends indicate prevailing political sentiment, we are often tempted to conclude that large samples, even though selected conveniently, are representative. The fallacy of this assumption is illustrated by a personal incident.

One of the local television stations in the city where the author resides conducted a daily public opinion poll several years ago on topics of interest to the local community. The polls were labeled the "Pulse of Madison" and were conducted in the following way. During the six o'clock news every evening, the station would ask a question about some controversial issue to which people could reply with a yes or no. Persons in favor would call one number; persons opposed would call another. The number of viewers calling each number was recorded electronically. Percentages of those in favor and opposed would then be reported on the ten o'clock news. With some 500 to 1,000 people calling in their opinions each night, the local television commentator seemed to interpret these results as reflecting the true state of opinion in the community.

On one six o'clock broadcast, the following question was posed: "Do you think the drinking age in Madison should be lowered to 18?" The existing legal limit was 21. Would you believe that almost 4,000 people called in that night and that 78 percent were in favor of lowering the age requirement? Clearly, 4,000 responses in a community of 180,000 people "must be representative"! Wrong. As you may have suspected, certain segments of the population were more vitally interested in the issue

Research Window 15.1
The Problem of Representativeness of Convenience Samples

So, what's the best rock radio station in the country?

Don't even try to guess. For the *ninth* consecutive year, Cleveland's WMMS has been voted number one by *Rolling Stone* magazine readers. That's quite a coup, considering that Cleveland is only the country's 11th largest radio market.

What is WMMS's secret? Its with-it disc jockeys? Its mix of hard rock with the Top 40 hits? How about its ballot-box stuffing?

The truth is in the stuffing.

Management at WMMS, a Malrite Communications Group station, says that it bought some 800 copies of the magazine that contained the poll and distributed many of them to fans and station employees. "We urge employees to fill them out, but we don't know who they voted for," says station manager Lonnie Gronek. He says the station has done this for many years.

WMMS won this year's contest with 1,000 votes, beating New York's WNEW by 30 votes. About 23,000 votes were cast.

Rolling Stone probably wouldn't have uncovered the ploy if the Cleveland *Plain Dealer*'s rock editor hadn't gotten a tip. The paper published a station memo to employees asking them to pick up the hundreds of copies at a local store.

"WMMS has always urged its own employees to participate in the balloting—all at the station's expense," WMMS responded in a full-page ad in the Cleveland paper. Besides, it added, "positive recognition of the station translated as a source of pride for Cleveland."

So far WMMS's admission has rocked its hometown more than it has New York. Mark D. Chernoff, WNEW's program director, says he won't insist that his station be declared the winner. "That's up to *Rolling Stone*," he says, quickly adding, "But we'd gladly accept it."

Cleveland broadcasters aren't so kind. John Lanigan, disc jockey at competing station WMJI, suggests that WMMS "should buy a billboard that says: 'We bought more *Rolling Stone* magazines than any other station.'" He also maintains that WMMS's actions "tell kids it's right to lie and cheat to be number one."

At *Rolling Stone*, managing editor James Henke says the annual contest hasn't barred stations from voting for themselves. "Obviously they went against the spirit of the contest," he says.

For its part, the magazine is considering stripping WMMS of the once-coveted award. And it has pulled the plug on future radio-popularity votes.

Source: Gregory Stricharchuk, "Repeat After Me: I Like WMMS, I Like WMMS, I Like WMMS," *The Wall Street Journal* (March 2, 1988), p. 25. See also Martha Brannigan, "Pseudo Polls: More Surveys Draw Criticisms for Motives and Methods," *The Wall Street Journal* (January 29, 1987), p. 27, which discusses the use of phone-in polls using AT&T's 900 area code.

than others. Thus, it was no surprise, when discussing the issue in class a few weeks later, to find that students had taken half-hour phone shifts on an arranged basis. Each person would call the yes number, hang up, call again, hang up, and so on, until it was the next person's turn. Thus, neither the size of the sample nor the proportion favoring the age change was surprising. The sample was simply not representative.

Further, increasing a sample's size does not make it representative. The representativeness of a sample must be ensured by the sampling procedure. When participation is voluntary or sample elements are selected because they are convenient, the sampling plan provides no assurance that the sample is representative. Empirical evidence, as a matter of fact, is much to the contrary. Rarely do samples selected on a convenience basis, regardless of size, prove representative. Research Window 15.1, for example, depicts what can be wrong with convenience samples, even when they are large. Convenience samples are not recommended, therefore, for descriptive or causal research. They may be used with exploratory designs in which the emphasis is on generating ideas and insights, but even here the judgment sample seems superior.

Judgment Samples

Judgment sample
A nonprobability sample that is often called a *purposive sample;* the sample elements are handpicked because they are expected to serve the research purpose.

Judgment samples are often called *purposive samples;* the sample elements are handpicked because it is expected that they can serve the research purpose. Most typically, the sample elements are selected because it is believed that they are representative of the population of interest. One example of a judgment sample is seen every four years at presidential election time, when television viewers are treated to in-depth analyses of the swing communities. These communities are thought to be representative, since in previous elections the local winner has been the next president. Thus, by monitoring these pivotal communities, election analysts are able to offer an early prediction of the eventual winner. While election analysis and prediction have become much more sophisticated in recent years, the judgment sample of representative communities is still used.

As mentioned, the key feature of judgment sampling is that population elements are purposively selected. In some cases, sample elements are chosen not because they are representative but rather because they can offer researchers the information they need. When the courts rely on expert testimony, they are in a sense using judgment samples. The same kind of philosophy may prevail in creating exploratory designs. When searching for ideas and insights, the researcher is not interested in sampling a cross section of opinion but rather in sampling those who can offer some perspective on the research question.

Snowball sample
A judgment sample that relies on the researcher's ability to locate an initial set of respondents with the desired characteristics; these individuals are then used as informants to identify still others with the desired characteristics.

The **snowball sample** is a judgment sample that is sometimes used to sample special populations.[3] This sample relies on the researcher's ability to locate an initial set of respondents with the desired characteristics. These individuals are then used as informants to identify others with the desired characteristics.

Imagine, for example, that a company wanted to determine the desirability of a certain product that would enable deaf people to communicate over telephone lines. Researchers might begin by identifying some key people in the deaf community and asking them for names of other deaf people who might be used in the study. Those asked to participate would also be asked for names of others who might cooperate.[4] In this way the sample "snowballs" by getting larger as participants identify still other possible respondents.

Quota sample
A nonprobability sample chosen in such a way that the proportion of sample elements possessing a certain characteristic is approximately the same as the proportion of the elements with the characteristic in the population; each field worker is assigned a quota that specifies the characteristics of the people he or she is to contact.

As long as the researcher is at the early stages of research when ideas or insights are being sought—and when the researcher realizes its limitations—the judgment sample can be used productively. It becomes dangerous, though, when it is employed in descriptive or causal studies and its weaknesses are conveniently forgotten. The Consumer Price Index (CPI) provides a classic example of this. As Sudman points out, "the CPI is in only fifty-six cities and metropolitan areas selected judgmentally and to some extent on the basis of political pressure. In reality, these cities represent *only themselves* although the index is called the *Consumer Price Index for Urban Wage Earners and Clerical Workers*, and most people believe the index reflects prices everywhere in the United States. Within cities, the selection of retail outlets is done judgmentally, so that the *possible size of sample bias is unknown*" (emphasis added).[5]

Quota Samples

A third type of nonprobability sample, the **quota sample,** attempts to be representative of the population by including the same proportion of elements possessing a certain characteristic as is found in the population (see Research Window 15.2). Consider, for example, an attempt to select a representative sample of

Research Window 15.2
The Ad Is Slick, Clever, Expensive— But Is Anybody Reading It?

Every year advertisers spend millions of dollars producing the ads that appear in publications ranging from *Advertising Age* to *Yankee* magazine. While a certain amount of copy and art testing can be done in-house at the agency before the ad is published, the real test of its success is when it appears in a publication, alongside dozens of other ads designed equally carefully, and fights for a reader's attention.

Starch INRA Hooper is a company that measures advertising readership in consumer, business, trade, and professional magazines and newspapers and reports its findings to advertisers and agencies—for a fee, of course. Since large sums are being gambled daily by advertisers seeking to get their message across to consumers, the Starch organization has been careful to design a sample for its research that can give subscribers fast—and accurate—information about the success of its advertising. Each year Starch interviews more than 100,000 people on their reading of over 75,000 advertisements. Approximately 1,000 individual issues are studied annually.

Starch uses a quota sample comprised of a minimum of 100 readers per sex. Starch has determined that at this sample size, major fluctuations in readership levels stabilize. Adults, eighteen years and older, are personally interviewed face-to-face for all publications except those that are directed exclusively to special groups (e.g., for *Seventeen* magazine they would interview teenaged girls).

Interviews are arranged to parallel the publication's geographic circulation. For *Los Angeles* magazine, for example, the study would focus on readers in southern California. A study of *Time* magazine would parallel its national circulation. Interviews are conducted in between 20 and 30 cities for each issue under study.

Each interviewer is assigned only a small quota of interviews in order to minimize interviewer bias.

Interviews are distributed among people of varied ages, income levels, and occupations so that collectively each study is broadly representative of the publication's audience. For certain business, trade, and professional publications, interviewing assignments are also designed to parallel the circulation by field of industry and job responsibility. For publications with small circulations, subscriber lists are used to help locate eligible respondents.

In each interview, interviewers ask respondents, who are permitted to look through the publication at the time of the interview, if they have seen or read any part of a particular advertisement. If the respondent answers yes, the interviewer follows up with more questions to determine the extent to which the respondent has read the ad.

Based on the respondent's answers, the interviewer classifies him or her as one of the following:

- *Noted reader:* a person who remembered having previously seen the advertisement in the issue being studied
- *Associated reader:* a person who not only "noted" the advertisement, but also saw or read some part of it that clearly indicated the brand or advertiser
- *Read-most reader:* a person who read half or more of the written material in the ad

After all the ads are asked about, interviewers record basic classification data on sex, age, occupation, marital status, race, income, family size and composition, so that sampling can be checked and cross tabulations of readership can be made.

Properly used, Starch data help advertisers and agencies to identify the types of advertisement layouts that attract and retain the highest readership and those that result in average or poor readership. For advertisers, this kind of information can be invaluable in designing an effective campaign for their products.

Source: "Starch Readership Report: Scope, Method, and Use," *Starch INRA Hooper*, Mamaroneck, NY 10543.

undergraduate students on a college campus. If the eventual sample of 500 contained no seniors, one would have serious reservations about the representativeness of the sample and the generalizability of the conclusions beyond the immediate sample group. With a quota sample, the researcher could ensure that seniors would be included and in the same proportion as they occur in the entire undergraduate student body.

Assume that a researcher was interested in sampling the undergraduate student body in such a way that the sample would reflect the composition of the student body by class and sex. Suppose further that there were 10,000 undergraduate students in total and that 3,200 were freshmen, 2,600 sophomores, 2,200 juniors, and 2,000 seniors, and further that 7,000 were males and 3,000 females. In a sample of 1,000, the quota sampling plan would require that 320 sample elements be freshmen, 260 sophomores, 220 juniors, and 200 seniors, and further that 700 of the sample elements be male and 300 be female. The researcher would accomplish this by giving each field worker a quota—thus the name *quota sample*—specifying the types of undergraduates he or she is to contact. Thus, one field worker assigned 20 interviews might be instructed to find and collect data from

- Six freshmen—five male and one female
- Six sophomores—four male and two female
- Four juniors—three male and one female
- Four seniors—two male and two female

Note that the specific sample elements to be used would not be specified by the research plan, but would be left to the discretion of the individual field worker. The field worker's personal judgment would govern the choice of specific students to be interviewed. The only requirement would be that the interviewer diligently follow the established quota and interview five male freshmen, one female freshman, and so on.

Note further that the quota for this field worker accurately reflects the sex composition of the student population, but does not completely parallel the class composition; 70 percent (fourteen of twenty) of the field worker's interviews are with males but only 30 percent (six of twenty) are with freshmen, whereas freshmen represent 32 percent of the undergraduate student body. It is not necessary or even usual with a quota sample that the quotas per field worker accurately mirror the distribution of the control characteristics in the population; usually only the total sample has the same proportions as the population.

Note finally that quota samples still rely on personal, subjective judgment rather than objective procedures for the selection of sample elements. Here the personal judgment is that of the field worker rather than the designer of the research, as it might be in the case of a judgment sample. This raises the question of whether quota samples can indeed be considered representative even though they accurately reflect the population with respect to the proportion of the sample possessing each control characteristic. Three points need to be made in this regard.

First, the sample could be very far off with respect to some other important characteristic likely to influence the result. Thus, if the campus study is concerned with racial prejudice existing on campus, it may very well make a difference whether field workers interview students from urban or rural areas. Since a quota for the urban-rural characteristic was not specified, it is unlikely that those participating will accurately reflect this characteristic. The alternative, of course, is to specify quotas for all potentially important characteristics. The problem is that increasing the number of control characteristics makes specifications more complex. This in turn makes the location of sample elements more difficult—perhaps even impossible—and certainly more expensive. If, for example, geographic origin and socioeconomic status were also important characteristics in the study, the field worker might be assigned to find an upper-middle-class male freshman from an urban area. This is obviously a much more difficult task than simply locating a male freshman.

Also, it is difficult to verify whether a quota sample is representative. Certainly one can check the distribution of characteristics in the sample not used as controls to determine whether the distribution parallels that of the population. However, this type of comparison provides only negative evidence. It can indicate that the sample does not reflect the population if the distributions on some characteristics are different. If the sample and population distributions are similar for each of these characteristics, it is still possible for the sample to be vastly different from the population on some characteristic not explicitly compared.

Finally, interviewers left to their own devices are prone to follow certain practices. They tend to interview their friends in excessive proportion. Since their friends are often similar to themselves, this can introduce bias. Interviewers who fill their quotas by stopping passersby are likely to concentrate on areas where there are large numbers of potential respondents, such as business districts, railway and airline terminals, and the entrances to large department stores. This practice tends to overrepresent the kinds of people who frequent these areas. When home visits are required, interviewers often succumb to the lures of convenience and appearance. They may conduct interviews only during the day, for example, resulting in an underrepresentation of working people. They often avoid dilapidated buildings and the upper stories of buildings without elevators.

Depending on the subject of the study, all of these tendencies have the potential for bias. They may or may not in fact actually bias the result, but it is difficult to correct them when analyzing the data. When the sample elements are selected objectively, on the other hand, researchers have certain tools they can rely on to make the question of whether a particular sample is representative less difficult. In these probability samples, one relies on the sampling procedure and not the composition of the specific sample to solve the problem of representation.

Ethical

Dilemma 15.1   You are designing an experiment to compare the effectiveness of different types of commercials and need to recruit a large group of subjects of varying ages to watch television for an hour every night for a week. You approach your local church minister and tell her that you will make a donation to the church restoration fund for every member of the congregation who agrees to participate.

- When might incentives be coercive?
- Is it ethical to coerce people to participate in research?
- Will the quality of the data suffer from the coercive recruitment of participants?

Probability Samples

In a probability sample, researchers can calculate the likelihood that any given population element will be included, because the final sample elements are selected objectively by a specific process and not according to the whims of the researcher or field worker. Since the elements are selected objectively, researchers are then able to assess the reliability of the sample results, something not possible with non-probability samples regardless of the careful judgment exercised in selecting individuals.

This is not to say that probability samples will always be more representative than nonprobability samples. Indeed, a nonprobability sample may be more representative. The advantage of probability samples is that they allow an assessment of the amount of sampling error likely to occur, because a sample rather than a census was employed when gathering the data. Nonprobability samples, on the other hand, allow the investigator no objective method for evaluating the adequacy of the sample.

Simple Random Sampling

Most people have had experience with simple random samples either in beginning statistics courses or in reading about the results of such samples in newspapers or magazines. In a simple random sample, each unit included in the sample has a known and equal chance of being selected for study, and every combination of population elements is a sample possibility. For example, if we wanted a simple random sample of all students enrolled in a particular college, we might assign a number to each student on a comprehensive list of all those enrolled and then have a computer pick a sample randomly.

Parent Population

Parent population The totality of cases that conform to some designated specifications; also called a *target population*.

Parameter A fixed characteristic or measure of a parent, or target, population.

The **parent population,** or *target population*, is the population from which the simple random sample will be drawn. This population can be described by certain **parameters,** which are characteristics of the parent population, each representing a fixed quantity that distinguishes one population from another. For example, suppose the parent population for a study were all adults in Cincinnati. A number of parameters could be used to describe this population: the average age, the proportion with a college education, the range of incomes, and so on. Note that these quantities are fixed in value. Given a census of this population, we can readily calculate them. Rather than relying on a census, we usually select a sample and use the values calculated from the sample observations to estimate the required population values.

To see how this is done, consider the hypothetical population of 20 individuals shown in Table 15.1. There are several advantages in working with a small hypothetical population like this. First, the population's small size makes it easy to calculate the population parameters that might be used to describe it. Second, its size makes it relatively easy to see what might happen under a particular sampling plan. Both of these features make it easier to compare the sample results to the "true," but now known, population value than would be the case in the typical situation where the actual population value is unknown. The comparison of the estimate with the "true" value is thus more vivid than it otherwise would be.

Suppose we wanted to estimate the average income in this population from two elements selected randomly. Then the *population mean income* would be a parameter. To estimate a population mean, denoted by μ, we would divide the sum of all the values by the number of values making up the sum. That is,

$$\text{population mean} = \mu = \frac{\text{sum of population elements}}{\text{number of population elements}}.$$

Table 15.1   **Hypothetical Population**

Element	Income (Dollars)	Education (Years)	Newspaper Subscription	Element	Income (Dollars)	Education (Years)	Newspaper Subscription
1 A	5,600	8	X	11 K	9,600	13	X
2 B	6,000	9	Y	12 L	10,000	13	Y
3 C	6,400	11	X	13 M	10,400	14	X
4 D	6,800	11	Y	14 N	10,800	14	Y
5 E	7,200	11	X	15 O	11,200	15	X
6 F	7,600	12	Y	16 P	11,600	16	Y
7 G	8,000	12	X	17 Q	12,000	16	X
8 H	8,400	12	Y	18 R	12,400	17	Y
9 I	8,800	12	X	19 S	12,800	18	X
10 J	9,200	12	Y	20 T	13,200	18	Y

In this case the calculation yields

$$\frac{5,600 + 6,000 + \ldots + 13,200}{20} = 9,400.$$

Another parameter that might be used to describe the incomes in this population would be the *population variance*, which is one measure of the spread of incomes. To compute the population variance, we would calculate the deviation of each value from the mean, square these deviations, sum them, and divide by the number of values making up the sum. Letting σ^2 denote the population variance, the calculation yields

$$\text{population variance } \sigma^2 = \frac{\text{sum of squared differences of each population element from the population mean}}{\text{number of population elements}}$$

$$= \frac{(5,600 - 9,400)^2 + (6,000 - 9,400)^2 + \ldots + (13,200 - 9,400)^2}{20}$$

$$= 5,320,000.$$

Derived Population

Derived population
A population of all possible distinguishable samples that could be drawn from a parent population under a specific sampling plan.

Statistic A characteristic or measure of a sample.

The **derived population** consists of all the possible samples that can be drawn from the parent population under a given sampling plan. A **statistic** is a characteristic or measure of a sample. The value of a statistic used to estimate a particular parameter depends on the particular sample selected from the parent population under the sampling plan specified. Different samples yield different statistics and different estimates of the same population parameter.

Consider the derived population of *all* the possible samples that could be drawn from our hypothetical parent population of 20 individuals, under a sampling plan that specifies that a sample size of $n = 2$ be drawn by simple random sampling without replacement.

Let us assume, for the time being, that the information for each population element—in this case, the person's name and income—is written on a disk, placed in a jar, and shaken thoroughly. The researcher then reaches into the jar, pulls out one disk, records the information on it, and puts it aside. She does the same with a second disk. Then she places both disks back in the jar and repeats the process. Table 15.2 shows the many possible results of following this procedure. There are 190 possible combinations of the 20 disks.

For each combination, one could calculate the sample mean income. Thus, for the sample AB, ($k = 1$),

$$k^{\text{th}} \text{ sample mean} = \frac{\text{sum of sample elements}}{\text{number of elements in sample}} = \frac{5{,}600 + 6{,}000}{2} = 5{,}800.$$

Figure 15.3 displays the estimates of population mean income and the amount of error in each estimate when samples $k = 25, 62, 108, 147,$ and 189 are drawn.

Before discussing the relationship between the sample mean income (a statistic) and the population mean income (the parameter to be estimated), a few words are in order regarding the notion of derived population. First, note that, in practice, we do not actually generate the derived population. This would be extremely wasteful of time and data. Rather, the practitioner merely generates one sample of the needed size. But the researcher will make use of the *concept* of a derived population and the associated notion of sampling distribution in making inferences. We shall see how in just a moment.

Second, note that the derived population is defined as the population of all possible distinguishable samples that can be drawn under a *given sampling plan*. Change any part of the sampling plan, and the derived population will also change. Thus, when selecting disks, if the researcher is to replace the first disk drawn, the derived population will include the sample possibilities *AA*, *BB*, and so on. With samples of Size 3 instead of 2, drawn without replacement, *ABC* is a sample possibility, and there are a number of additional possibilities as well—1,140 versus the 190 with samples of Size 2. Change the method of selecting elements by using something other than simple random sampling, and the derived population will also change.

Finally, note that picking a sample of a given size from a parent population is equivalent to picking a single element (1 of the 190 disks) out of the derived population. This fact is basic in making statistical inferences.

Sample Mean versus Population Mean

If we want to evaluate the income of those in a simple random sample, can we assume that the sample mean will equal the parent population mean? To a large extent we generally assume there is a relationship; otherwise, it would be senseless to use the sample value to estimate the population value. But how much error is there likely to be?

Suppose we added up all the sample means in Table 15.2 and divided by the number of samples; that is, suppose we were to average the averages. By doing this, we would get the following:

$$\frac{5{,}800 + 6{,}000 + \ldots + 13{,}000}{190} = 9{,}400.$$

Table 15.2   ***Derived Population of All Possible Samples of Size* n = 2 *with Simple Random Selection***

k	Sample Identity	Mean	k	Sample Identity	Mean	k	Sample Identity	Mean	k	Sample Identity	Mean
1	AB	5,800	51	CQ	9,200	101	GI	8,400	151	KQ	10,800
2	AC	6,000	52	CR	9,400	102	GJ	8,600	152	KR	11,000
3	AD	6,200	53	CS	9,600	103	GK	8,800	153	KS	11,200
4	AE	6,400	54	CT	9,800	104	GL	9,000	154	KT	11,400
5	AF	6,600	55	DE	7,000	105	GM	9,200	155	LM	10,200
6	AG	6,800	56	DF	7,200	106	GN	9,400	156	LN	10,400
7	AH	7,000	57	DG	7,400	107	GO	9,600	157	LO	10,600
8	AI	7,200	58	DH	7,600	108	GP	9,800	158	LP	10,800
9	AJ	7,400	59	DI	7,800	109	GQ	10,000	159	LQ	11,000
10	AK	7,600	60	DJ	8,000	110	GR	10,200	160	LR	11,200
11	AL	7,800	61	DK	8,200	111	GS	10,400	161	LS	11,400
12	AM	8,000	62	DL	8,400	112	GT	10,600	162	LT	11,600
13	AN	8,200	63	DM	8,600	113	HI	8,600	163	MN	10,600
14	AO	8,400	64	DN	8,800	114	HJ	8,800	164	MO	10,800
15	AP	8,600	65	DO	9,000	115	HK	9,000	165	MP	11,000
16	AQ	8,800	66	DP	9,200	116	HL	9,200	166	MQ	11,200
17	AR	9,000	67	DQ	9,400	117	HM	9,400	167	MR	11,400
18	AS	9,200	68	DR	9,600	118	HN	9,600	168	MS	11,600
19	AT	9,400	69	DS	9,800	119	HO	9,800	169	MT	11,800
20	BC	6,200	70	DT	10,000	120	HP	10,000	170	NO	11,000
21	BD	6,400	71	EF	7,400	121	HQ	10,200	171	NP	11,200
22	BE	6,600	72	EG	7,600	122	HQ	10,400	172	NQ	11,400
23	BF	6,800	73	EH	7,800	123	HS	10,600	173	NR	11,600
24	BG	7,000	74	EI	8,000	124	HT	10,800	174	NS	11,800
25	BH	7,200	75	EI	8,200	125	IJ	9,000	175	NT	12,200
26	BI	7,400	76	EK	8,400	126	IK	9,200	176	OP	11,400
27	BJ	7,600	77	EL	8,600	127	IL	9,400	177	OQ	11,600
28	BK	7,800	78	EM	8,800	128	IM	9,200	178	OR	11,800
29	BL	8,000	79	EN	9,000	129	IN	9,800	179	OS	12,000
30	BM	8,200	80	EO	9,200	130	IO	10,000	180	OT	12,200
31	BN	8,400	81	EP	9,400	131	IP	10,200	181	PQ	11,800
32	BO	8,600	82	EQ	9,600	132	IQ	10,400	182	PR	12,000
33	BP	8,800	83	ER	9,800	133	IR	10,600	183	PS	12,200
34	BQ	9,000	84	ES	10,000	134	IS	10,800	184	PT	12,400
35	BR	9,200	85	ET	10,200	135	IT	11,000	185	QR	12,200
36	BS	9,400	86	FG	7,800	136	JK	9,400	186	QS	12,400
37	BT	9,600	87	FH	8,000	137	JL	9,600	187	QT	12,600
38	CD	6,600	88	FI	8,200	138	JM	9,800	188	RS	12,600
39	CE	6,800	89	FJ	8,400	139	JN	10,000	189	RT	12,800
40	CF	7,000	90	FK	8,600	140	JO	10,200	190	ST	13,000
41	CG	7,200	91	FL	8,800	141	JP	10,400			
42	CH	7,400	92	FM	9,000	142	JQ	10,600			
43	CI	7,600	93	FN	9,200	143	JR	10,800			
44	CJ	7,800	94	FO	9,400	144	JS	11,000			
45	CK	8,000	95	FP	9,600	145	JT	11,200			
46	CL	8,200	96	FQ	9,800	146	KL	9,800			
47	CM	8,400	97	FRM	10,000	147	KM	10,000			
48	CN	8,600	98	FS	10,200	148	KN	10,200			
49	CO	8,800	99	FT	10,400	149	KO	10,400			
50	CP	9,000	100	GH	8,200	150	KP	10,600			

Figure 15.3   ***Several Possible Samples and Their Respective Errors When***
Estimating the Population Mean

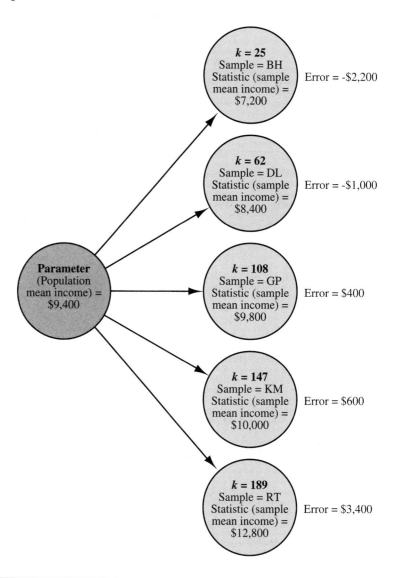

This is the mean of the parent population also. And this is what is meant by an
unbiased statistic; its average value equals the population parameter that it is supposed
to estimate. Note that the fact that it is unbiased says nothing about any particular
value of the statistic. Even though unbiased, a particular estimate may be very far
from the true population value, for example, if either sample *AB* or sample *ST* were
selected. In some cases, the true population value may even be impossible to achieve
with any possible sample even though the statistic is unbiased; this is not true in the
example, though, since a number of sample possibilities—for example, *AT*—yield a
sample mean that equals the population average.

Figure 15.4   **Distribution of Variable in Parent Population and Distribution of Estimates in Derived Population**

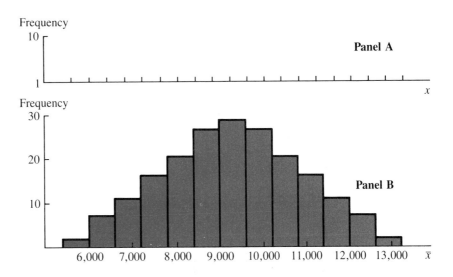

Next it is useful to take a look at the spread of these sample estimates, and particularly the relationship between this spread of estimates and the dispersion of incomes in the population. We saw previously that in order to compute the population variance, we needed to calculate the deviation of each value from the mean, square these deviations, sum them, and divide by the number of values making up the sum.

The variance of mean incomes could be calculated similarly. That is, we could calculate the variance of mean incomes by taking the deviation of each mean around its overall mean, squaring and summing these deviations, and then dividing by the number of cases.

Alternatively, we could determine the variance of mean incomes indirectly by using the variance of incomes in the parent population, since there is a direct relationship between the two quantities. More specifically, it turns out that when the sample is only a small part of the parent population, the variance of sample mean incomes is equal to the parent population variance divided by the sample size. In symbols, this means that

$$\sigma_{\bar{x}}^2 = \frac{\sigma^2}{n}$$

where $\sigma_{\bar{x}}^2$ is the variance of sample mean incomes, while σ^2 is the variance of incomes in the population, and n is the sample size.[6]

Third, consider the distribution of the estimates in contrast to the distribution of the variable in the parent population. Figure 15.4 indicates that the parent population distribution, depicted by Panel A, is spiked—each of the twenty values occurs once—and is symmetrical about the population mean value of 9,400. The distribution of estimates, displayed in Panel B, was constructed from Table 15.3,

Table 15.3   ***Classification of Estimates by Size***

Sample Mean	Number of Samples
$6,000 or less	2
$6,100 to 6,600	7
$6,700 to 7,200	11
$7,300 to 7,800	16
$7,900 to 8,400	20
$8,500 to 9,000	25
$9,100 to 9,600	28
$9,700 to 10,200	25
$10,300 to 10,800	20
$10,900 to 11,400	16
$11,500 to 12,000	11
$12,100 to 12,600	7
$12,700 or more	2

Sampling distribution
The distribution of values of some statistic calculated for each possible distinguishable sample that could be drawn from a parent population under a specific sampling plan.

which in turn was generated by placing each of the estimates in Table 15.2 in categories according to size and then counting the number contained in each category. Panel B is the traditional histogram discussed in beginning statistics courses and represents the **sampling distribution** of the statistic. Note this: The notion of sampling distribution is the single most important notion in statistics; it is the cornerstone of statistical inference procedures. If one knows the sampling distribution for the statistic in question, one is in a position to make an inference about the corresponding population parameter. If, on the other hand, one knows only that a particular sample estimate will vary with repeated sampling and has no information as to *how* it will vary, then it will be impossible to devise a measure of the sampling error associated with that estimate. Since the sampling distribution of an estimate describes how that estimate will vary with repeated sampling, it provides a basis for determining the reliability of the sample estimate. This is why probability sampling plans are so important to statistical inference. With known probabilities of inclusion of any population element in the sample, statisticians are able to derive the sampling distribution of various statistics. Researchers then rely on these distributions—be they for a sample mean, sample proportion, sample variance, or some other statistic—in making their inferences from single samples to population values. Note also that the distribution of sample means is mound-shaped and symmetrical about the population mean with samples of Size 2.

Recapitulating, we have shown that

1. The mean of all possible sample means is equal to the population mean.
2. The variance of sample means is related to the population variance.
3. The distribution of sample means is mound-shaped, whereas the population distribution is spiked.

Central-limit theorem
A theorem that holds that if simple random samples of size n are drawn from a parent population with mean μ and variance σ^2, then when n is large, the sample mean $\bar{x}$ will be approximately normally distributed with mean equal to μ and variance equal to σ^2/n. The approximation will become more and more accurate as n becomes larger.

Central-Limit Theorem   The mound-shaped distribution of estimates provides preliminary evidence of the operation of the **central-limit theorem,** which holds that if simple random samples of a given size n are drawn from a parent population with mean equal to μ, and variance equal to σ^2, then when the sample size n is large, the *distribution of sample means* will be approximately normally distributed with its mean equal to the population mean and its variance equal to the parent population variance divided by the sample size; that is,

$$\sigma_{\bar{x}}^2 = \frac{\sigma^2}{n}.$$

The approximation will become more and more accurate as n becomes larger. Note the impact of this. It means that regardless of the shape of the parent population, the distribution of sample means *will be normal* if the sample is large enough. How large is large enough? If the distribution of the variable in the parent population is normal, then the distribution of means of samples of size $n = 1$ will be normal. If the distribution of the variable is symmetrical but not normal, then samples of very small size will produce a distribution in which the means are normally distributed. If the distribution of the variable is highly skewed in the parent population, then samples of a larger size will be needed.

The fact remains, though, that the distribution of the statistic, sample mean, can be assumed normal only if we work with a sample of sufficient size. We do not need to rely on the assumption that the variable is normally distributed in the parent population in order to make inferences using the normal curve. Rather, we rely on the central-limit theorem and adjust the sample size according to the population distribution so that the normal curve can be assumed to hold. Fortunately, the normal distribution of the statistic occurs with samples of relatively small size, as Figure 15.5 indicates.

Confidence Interval Estimates   How does all of the preceding help us in making inferences about the parent population mean? After all, in practice we do not draw all possible samples of a given size, but only one, and we use the results obtained in it to infer something about the target group. It all ties together in the following way.

It is known that with any normal distribution, a specific percentage of all observations is within a certain number of standard deviations of the mean; for example, 95 percent of the values are within ± 1.96 standard deviations of the mean. The distribution of sample means is normal if the central-limit theorem holds and thus is no exception. Now, the mean of this sampling distribution is equal to the population mean μ, and its standard deviation is given by the square root of the variance of means, which is called the standard error of the mean, specifically $\sigma_{\bar{x}} = \sigma/\sqrt{n}$. Therefore, it is true that

- 68.26 percent of the sample means will be within $\pm 1\ \sigma_{\bar{x}}$ of the population mean
- 95.45 percent of the sample means will be within $\pm 2\ \sigma_{\bar{x}}$ of the population mean
- 99.73 percent of the sample means will be within $\pm 3\ \sigma_{\bar{x}}$ of the population mean

and in general that $\mu \pm z\sigma_{\bar{x}}$ will contain some certain proportion of all sample means depending on the selected value of z. This expression can be rewritten as an inequality relation that

$$\begin{pmatrix}\text{population}\\\text{mean}\end{pmatrix} - z\begin{pmatrix}\text{standard error}\\\text{of the mean}\end{pmatrix} \leq \begin{matrix}\text{sample}\\\text{mean}\end{matrix} \leq \begin{pmatrix}\text{population}\\\text{mean}\end{pmatrix} + z\begin{pmatrix}\text{standard error}\\\text{of the mean}\end{pmatrix}$$

Figure 15.5   ***Distribution of Sample Means for Samples of Various Sizes and Different Population Distributions***

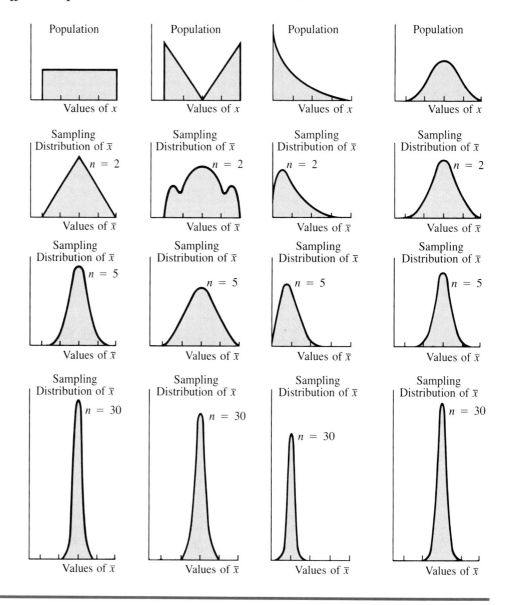

Source: Ernest Kurnow, Gerald J. Glasser, and Frederick R. Ottman, *Statistics for Business Decisions* (Homewood, Ill.: Richard D. Irwin, Inc., © 1959), pp. 182–183. Used with permission.

or

$$\mu - z\sigma_{\bar{x}} \le \bar{x} \le \mu + z\sigma_{\bar{x}} \tag{15.1}$$

which is held to be true a certain percentage of the time, and which implies that the sample mean will be in the interval formed by adding and subtracting a certain number of standard deviations to the mean value of the distribution. This inequality can be transferred to the equivalent inequality:

Table 15.4   ***Confidence Intervals for First Ten Samples Assuming the Distribution of Sample Means Was Normal***

Sample Number	Sample Identity	Mean	Confidence Interval Lower Limit	Confidence Interval Upper Limit	Pictorial True μ = 9,400 (represented by vertical line)
1	AB	5,800	2,689	8,911	
2	AC	6,000	2,889	9,111	
3	AD	6,200	3,089	9,311	
4	AE	6,400	3,289	9,511	
5	AF	6,600	3,489	9,711	
6	AG	6,800	3,689	9,911	
7	AH	7,000	3,889	10,111	
8	AI	7,200	4,089	10,311	
9	AJ	7,400	4,289	10,511	
10	AK	7,600	4,489	10,711	

$$\frac{\text{sample}}{\text{mean}} - (z)\left(\frac{\text{standard error}}{\text{of the mean}}\right) \leq \frac{\text{population}}{\text{mean}} \leq \frac{\text{sample}}{\text{mean}} + (z)\left(\frac{\text{standard error}}{\text{of the mean}}\right)$$

or

$$\bar{x} - z\sigma_{\bar{x}} \leq \mu \leq \bar{x} + z\sigma_{\bar{x}}. \tag{15.2}$$

And if Equation 15.1 is true, say, 95 percent of the time (z = 1.96), then Equation 15.2 is also true 95 percent of the time. *When we make an inference on the basis of a single sample mean, we make use of Equation 15.2.*

It is important to note that Equation 15.2 says *nothing about the interval constructed from a particular sample as including the population mean.* Rather, the interval addresses the *sampling procedure.* The interval around a single mean may or may not contain the true population mean. Our confidence in our inference rests on the property that 95 percent of all the intervals we could construct under that sampling plan would contain the true value. We trust or hope that our sample is one of those 95 out of 100 that does (when we are 95-percent confident) include the true value.

To illustrate this important point, suppose for the moment that the distribution of sample means of size n = 2 for our hypothetical example was normal. Table 15.4 illustrates the outcome pictorially for the first 10 out of the possible 190 samples that could be drawn under the specified sampling plan. Note that only 7 of the 10 intervals contain the true population mean. Confidence in the estimate arises because of the *procedure,* therefore, and not because of a particular estimate. The procedure suggests that with, say, a 95-percent confidence interval, if 100 samples were to be drawn and the sample mean and the confidence interval computed for each, 95 of the constructed intervals would include the true population value. The accuracy of a specific sample is evaluated only by reference to the procedure by which the sample was obtained. A sampling plan that is representative does not guarantee that a particular sample i representative. Statistical inference procedures rest on the representativeness of the sampling plan, and this is why probability samples are so critical to those procedures Probability samples allow an estimate of the *precision* of the results in terms of how closely the estimates will tend to cluster about the true value. The greater the standard error of the statistic, the more variable the estimates and the less precise the procedure.

If it disturbs you that the confidence level applies to the procedure and not a particular sample result, you can take comfort in the fact that you can control the level of confidence with which the population value is estimated. Thus, if you do not wish to take the risk that you might have 1 of the 5 sample intervals in 100 that does not contain the population value, you might employ a 99-percent confidence interval, in which the risk is that only 1 in 100 sample intervals will not contain the population mean. Further, if you are willing to increase the size of the sample, you can increase your confidence and at the same time maintain the precision with which the population value is estimated. This will be explored more fully in Chapter 17.

There is one other perhaps disturbing ingredient in our procedure: The confidence interval estimate made use of three values: $\bar{x}$, z, and $\sigma_{\bar{x}}$. Now the sample mean $\bar{x}$ is computed from the selected sample, and z is specified to produce the desired level of confidence. But what about the standard error of the mean, $\sigma_{\bar{x}}$? It is equal to $\sigma_{\bar{x}} = \sigma/\sqrt{n}$, and thus in order to calculate it, we need to know the standard deviation of the variable in the population, that is, σ. What do we do if the population standard deviation, σ, is unknown? There is no problem, for two reasons. First, variation typically changes much more slowly than level for most variables of interest in marketing. Thus if the study is a repeat, we can use the previously discovered value for σ. Second, once the sample is selected and the information gathered, we can calculate the sample variance to estimate the population variance. The unbiased sample variance $\hat{s}^2$ is calculated as

$$\text{sample variance} = \hat{s}^2 = \frac{\begin{array}{c}\text{sum of deviations around}\\\text{sample mean squared}\end{array}}{\text{sample size} - 1}.$$

To compute the sample variance, then, we first calculate the sample mean. We then calculate the difference between each of our sample values and the sample mean, square these differences, sum them, and divide the sum by one less than the number of sample observations. The sample variance not only provides an estimate of the population variance, but it can also be used to secure an estimate of the standard error of the mean. When the population variance, σ^2, is known, the standard error of the mean, $\sigma_{\bar{x}}$, is also known, since $\sigma_{\bar{x}} = \sigma/\sqrt{n}$. When the population variance is unknown, the standard error of the mean can only be estimated. The estimate is given by $s_{\bar{x}}$, which equals the sample standard deviation divided by the square root of the sample size, that is, $\hat{s}/\sqrt{n}$. The estimate calculation parallels that for the true value with the sample standard deviation substituted for the population standard deviation. Thus, if we draw sample AB, with a mean of 5,800,

$$\hat{s}^2 = \frac{(5,600 - 5,800)^2 + (6,000 - 5,800)^2}{1} = 80,000$$

Table 15.5   *Symbols and Formulas Used for Means and Variances with Simple Random Samples*

	Mean	**Variance**
Population	$\mu = \dfrac{\text{sum of population elements}}{\text{number of population elements}}$	$\sigma^2 = \dfrac{\begin{array}{c}\text{sum of squared differences of}\\\text{each population element from the}\\\text{population mean}\end{array}}{\text{number of population elements}}$
Sample	$\bar{x} = \dfrac{\text{sum of sample elements}}{\text{number of sample elements}}$	$\hat{s}^2 = \dfrac{\begin{array}{c}\text{sum of squared differences of}\\\text{each sample element from the}\\\text{sample mean}\end{array}}{\text{number of sample elements} - 1}$
Derived Population of Sample Means	average value = unknown population mean	$\sigma_{\bar{x}}^2 = \dfrac{\sigma^2}{n}$ (when population variance is known) $s_{\bar{x}}^2 = \dfrac{\hat{s}^2}{n}$ (when population variance is unknown)

and thus $\hat{s} = 283$ and $s_{\bar{x}} = \hat{s}/\sqrt{n} = 283/\sqrt{2} = 200$, and the 95-percent confidence interval is now

$$5{,}800 - 1.96(200) \le \mu \le 5{,}800 + 1.96(200) = 5{,}408 \le \mu \le 6{,}192,$$

which is somewhat smaller than before.

Table 15.5 summarizes the computational formulas for the various means and variances used in this chapter.

Drawing the Simple Random Sample   Although it was useful for illustrating the concepts of derived population and sampling distribution, the selection of sample elements from a jar containing all the population elements is not particularly recommended because of its great potential for bias. It is unlikely that the disks would be exactly uniform in size or feel, and slight differences here could affect the likelihood that any single element would be drawn. The national draft during the Vietnam war using a lottery serves as an example. Draft priorities were determined by drawing disks with birth dates stamped on them from a large container in full view of a television audience. Unfortunately, the dates of the year had initially been poured into the bowl systematically, January first and December last. Although the bowl was then stirred vigorously, December dates tended to be chosen first and January dates last. The procedure was later revised to produce a more random selection process.

The preferred way of drawing a simple random sample is through the use of a table of random numbers. Using a random-number table involves the following sequence of steps: First, the elements of the parent population are numbered serially from 1 to N; for the hypothetical population, the element A would be numbered 1, B as 2, and so on. Next, the numbers in the table are treated so as to have the same number of digits as N. With $N = 20$, two-digit numbers would be used; if N were between 100 and 999, three-digit numbers would be required, and so on. Third, a starting point is determined randomly. We might simply open the table to some arbitrary place and point to a position on the page with our eyes closed. Since the

Table 15.6   *Abridged List of Random Numbers*

10 09 73 25 33	76 52 01 35 86	34 67 35 48 76	80 95 90 91 17	39 29 27 49 45
37 54 20 48 05	64 89 47 42 96	24 80 52 40 37	20 63 61 04 02	00 82 29 16 65
08 42 26 89 53	19 64 50 93 03	23 20 90 25 60	15 95 33 47 64	35 08 03 36 06
99 01 90 25 29	09 37 67 07 15	38 31 13 11 65	88 67 67 43 97	04 43 62 76 59
12 80 79 99 70	80 15 73 61 47	64 03 23 66 53	98 95 11 68 77	12 17 17 68 33
66 06 57 47 17	34 07 27 68 50	36 69 73 61 70	65 81 33 98 85	11 19 92 91 70
31 06 01 08 05	45 57 18 24 06	35 30 34 26 14	86 79 90 74 39	23 40 30 97 32
85 26 97 76 02	02 05 16 56 92	68 66 57 48 18	73 05 38 52 47	18 62 38 85 79
63 57 33 21 35	05 32 54 70 48	90 55 35 75 48	28 46 82 87 09	83 49 12 56 24
73 79 64 57 53	03 52 96 47 78	35 80 83 42 82	60 93 52 03 44	35 27 38 84 35
98 52 01 77 67	14 90 56 86 07	22 10 94 05 58	60 97 09 34 33	50 50 07 39 98
11 80 50 54 31	39 80 82 77 32	50 72 56 82 48	29 40 52 42 01	52 77 56 78 51
83 45 29 96 34	06 28 89 80 83	13 74 67 00 78	18 47 54 06 10	68 71 17 78 17
88 68 54 02 00	86 50 75 84 01	36 76 66 79 51	90 36 47 64 93	29 60 91 10 62
99 59 46 73 48	87 51 76 49 69	91 82 60 89 28	93 78 56 13 68	23 47 83 41 13
65 48 11 76 74	17 46 85 09 50	58 04 77 69 74	73 03 95 71 86	40 21 81 65 44
80 12 43 56 35	17 72 70 80 15	45 31 82 23 74	21 11 57 82 53	14 38 55 37 63
74 35 09 98 17	77 40 27 72 14	43 23 60 02 10	45 52 16 42 37	96 28 60 26 55
69 91 62 68 03	66 25 22 91 48	36 93 68 72 03	76 62 11 39 90	94 40 05 64 18
09 89 32 05 05	14 22 56 85 14	46 42 75 67 88	96 29 77 88 22	54 38 21 45 98
91 49 91 45 23	68 47 92 76 86	46 16 28 35 54	94 75 08 99 23	37 08 92 00 48
80 33 69 45 98	26 94 03 68 58	70 29 73 41 35	53 14 03 33 40	42 05 08 23 41
44 10 48 19 49	85 15 74 79 54	32 97 92 65 75	57 60 04 08 81	22 22 20 64 13
12 55 07 37 42	11 10 00 20 40	12 86 07 46 97	96 64 48 94 39	28 70 72 58 15
63 60 64 93 29	16 50 53 44 84	40 21 95 25 63	43 65 17 70 82	07 20 73 17 90

numbers in a random-number table are in fact random, that is, without order, it makes little difference where we begin.[7] Finally, we proceed in some arbitrary direction, for example, up, down, or across, and select those elements for the sample for which there is a match of serial number and random number.

To illustrate, consider the partial list of random numbers contained in Table 15.6. Since $N = 20$, we need work with only two digits, and therefore we can use the entries in Table 15.6 as is, instead of having to combine columns to produce numbers covering the range of serial numbers. Suppose we had previously decided to read down and that our arbitrary start indicated the eleventh row, fourth column,

Table 15.6   **(Continued)**

61 19 69 04 46	26 45 74 77 74	51 92 43 37 29	65 39 45 95 93	42 58 26 05 27
15 47 44 52 66	95 27 07 99 53	59 36 78 38 48	82 39 61 01 18	33 21 15 94 66
94 55 72 85 73	67 89 75 43 87	54 62 24 44 31	91 19 04 25 92	92 92 74 59 73
42 48 11 62 13	97 34 40 87 21	16 86 84 87 67	03 07 11 20 59	25 70 14 66 70
23 52 37 83 17	73 20 88 98 37	68 93 59 14 16	26 25 22 96 63	05 52 28 25 62
04 49 35 24 94	75 24 63 38 24	45 86 25 10 25	61 96 27 93 35	65 33 71 24 72
00 54 99 76 54	64 05 18 81 59	96 11 96 38 96	54 69 28 23 91	23 28 72 95 29
35 96 31 53 07	26 89 80 93 54	33 35 13 54 62	77 97 54 00 24	90 10 33 93 33
59 80 80 83 91	45 42 72 68 42	83 60 94 97 00	13 02 12 48 92	78 56 52 01 06
46 05 88 52 36	01 39 09 22 86	77 28 14 40 77	93 91 08 36 47	70 61 74 29 41
32 17 90 05 97	87 37 92 52 41	05 56 70 70 07	86 74 31 71 57	85 39 41 18 38
69 23 46 14 06	20 11 74 52 04	15 95 66 00 00	18 74 39 24 23	97 11 89 63 38
19 56 54 14 30	01 75 87 53 79	40 41 92 15 85	66 67 43 68 06	84 96 28 52 07
45 15 51 49 38	19 47 60 72 46	43 66 79 45 43	59 04 79 00 33	20 82 66 95 41
94 86 43 19 94	36 16 81 08 51	34 88 88 15 53	01 54 03 54 56	05 01 45 11 76
98 08 62 48 26	45 24 02 84 04	44 99 90 88 96	39 09 47 34 07	35 44 13 18 80
33 18 51 62 32	41 94 15 09 49	89 43 54 85 81	88 69 54 19 94	37 54 87 30 43
80 95 10 04 06	96 38 27 07 74	20 15 12 33 87	25 01 62 52 98	94 62 46 11 71
79 75 24 91 40	71 96 12 82 96	69 86 10 25 91	74 85 22 05 39	00 38 75 95 79
18 63 33 25 37	98 14 50 65 71	31 01 02 46 74	05 45 56 14 27	77 93 89 19 36
74 02 94 39 02	77 55 73 22 70	97 79 01 71 19	52 52 75 80 21	80 81 45 17 48
54 17 84 56 11	80 99 33 71 43	05 33 51 29 69	56 12 71 92 55	36 04 09 03 24
11 66 44 98 83	52 07 98 48 27	59 38 17 15 39	09 97 33 34 40	88 46 12 33 56
48 32 47 79 28	31 24 96 47 10	02 29 53 68 70	32 30 75 75 46	15 02 00 99 94
69 07 49 41 38	87 63 79 19 76	35 58 40 44 01	10 51 82 16 15	01 84 87 69 38

Source: This table is reproduced from page 1 of The Rand Corporation, *A Million Random Digits with 100,000 Normal Deviates* (New York: The Free Press, 1955). Copyright © 1955 and 1983 by The Rand Corporation. Used by permission.

specifically the number 77. This number is too high and would be discarded. The next two numbers would also be discarded, but the fourth entry, 02, would be used, since 2 corresponds to one of the serial numbers in the list, Element *B*. The next five numbers would also be passed over as too large, whereas the number 05 would designate the inclusion of Element *E*. Elements *B* and *E* would thus represent the sample of two from whom we would seek information on income.

You should note that a simple random sample requires a serial numbered list of population elements. This means that the identity of each member of the population must be known. For some populations this is no problem, for example, if the study is to be conducted among *Fortune* magazine's list of the 500 largest corporations in the United States. The list is readily available, and a simple random sample of these firms could be easily selected. For many other populations of interest (for example, all families living in a particular city), the list of universe elements is much harder to come by, and applied researchers often resort to other sampling schemes.

Back to the Case

After three weeks of working on B. C. Patterson's "unassisted dressing" account—as it had been dubbed at her firm—Millicent Conway was beginning to understand why the Patterson's people had felt like pulling out their hair. She agreed with them that the concept was a winner. Segmentation of the retail market, the aging population—both pointed to potentially big sales. But the problem of how to reach the market was indeed a thorny one.

Conway's job, however, wasn't to wring her hands over problems, but to solve them. She'd just finished roughing out a plan that she thought might get Patterson's past at least some of the first obstacles. She'd asked her colleague, Clayton Parks, to come to her office and listen to her plan.

"Do you mind if I just talk you through my proposal?" Conway asked him.

"Go ahead," replied Parks.

"The main stumbling block that we need to get around is the fact that while up to 50 percent of the women over age 45 in this country have arthritis, we don't know how to identify them. In addition, even if we could identify them, we wouldn't be able to tell which ones are affected severely enough to be potential buyers for the "unassisted dressing" line. Worse, women who aren't interested in the clothes might be insulted that Patterson's thinks they are. No retailer needs that kind of negative response."

"So," prompted Parks, "what do you propose to do about it?"

"From the beginning, Patterson's has wanted use a large probability sample to test its promotional ideas. Since coming up with that kind of sample would be incredibly time consuming and expensive, I propose we use a much smaller, judgment sample. We can recruit women who fit the target parameters, and we

can use them in focus groups and in-depth interviews. Who knows, we may get some ideas from them about how best to target the great number of women who have trouble dressing themselves. If not, Patterson's might have to focus on producing ads that reach potential consumers without turning off everybody else."

"Well, it certainly seems worth presenting to the client," remarked Parks, "but I sure wish we could think of some way to target arthritic women who have a hard time with buttons and zippers."

"Me too," replied Conway. "If you have any brainstorms on the subject, please be sure to share them with me."

This fictional case is based on the efforts of JC Penney, Sears, and other retailers to target fashion-conscious consumers who have special physical conditions. See Kevin Helliker, "Fashion Catalogs Focus on Consumers' Special Physical Needs," *The Wall Street Journal* (November 29, 1990), p. B1.

Summary

Learning Objective 1: Distinguish between a census and a sample.

A complete canvass of a population is called a census. A sample is a portion of the population taken from the larger group.

Learning Objective 2: List the six steps researchers use to draw a sample of a population.

The six steps researchers use in drawing a sample are (1) define the population, (2) identify the sampling frame, (3) select a sampling procedure, (4) determine the sample size, (5) select the sample elements, and (6) collect the data from the designated elements.

Learning Objective 3: Define *sampling frame*.

A sampling frame is the listing of the elements from which the actual sample will be drawn.

Learning Objective 4: Explain the difference between a probability sample and a nonprobability sample.

In a probability sample, each member of the population has a known, nonzero chance of being included in the sample. The chances of each member of the population being included in the sample may not be equal, but everyone has a known probability of inclusion.

With nonprobability samples, on the other hand, there is no way of estimating the probability that any population element will be included in the sample. Thus, there is no way of ensuring that the sample is representative of the population. All nonprobability samples rely on personal judgment at some point in the sample-selection process. While these judgments may yield good estimates of a population characteristic, there is no way of determining objectively if the sample is adequate.

Learning Objective 5: Distinguish between a fixed and a sequential sample.

In a fixed sample, the sample size is decided before the study begins, and all the needed information is collected before the results are analyzed. In a sequential sample, the number of elements to be sampled is not decided in advance but is determined by a series of decisions as the data are collected.

Learning Objective 6: Explain what a judgment sample is and describe its best use and its hazards.

A judgment sample is that in which sample elements are handpicked because it is expected that they can serve the research purpose. Sometimes, the sample elements are selected because it is believed that they are representative of the population of interest.

As long as the researcher is at the early stages of research, when ideas or insights are being sought—or when the researcher realizes its limitations—the judgment sample can be used productively. It becomes dangerous, though, when it is employed in descriptive or causal studies and its weaknesses are conveniently forgotten.

Learning Objective 7: Define *quota sample*.

The quota sampling technique attempts to ensure that the sample is representative of the population by selecting sample elements in such a way that the proportion of the sample elements possessing a certain characteristic is approximately the same as the proportion of the elements with the characteristic in the population. This is accomplished by assigning each field worker a quota that specifies the characteristics of the people the interviewer is to contact.

Learning Objective 8: Explain what a parameter in a sample procedure is.

A parameter is a characteristic of the parent population; it is a fixed quantity that distinguishes one population from another.

Learning Objective 9: Explain what the derived population is.

The derived population consists of all the possible samples that can be drawn from the parent population under a given sampling plan.

Learning Objective 10: Explain why the concept of sampling distribution is the most important concept in statistics.

The notion of the sampling distribution of the statistic is the cornerstone of statistical inference procedures. If one knows the sampling distribution for the statistic in question, one is in a position to make an inference about the corresponding population parameter. If, on the other hand, one knows only that a particular sample estimate will vary with repeated sampling and has no information as to *how* it will vary, then it will be impossible to devise a measure of the sampling error associated with that estimate. Since the sampling distribution of an estimate describes how that estimate will vary with repeated sampling, it provides a basis for determining the reliability of the sample estimate.

Discussion Questions, Problems, and Projects

1. For each of the following situations identify the appropriate target population and sampling frame.
   (a) A local chapter of the American Lung Association wants to test the effectiveness of a brochure titled "12 Reasons for Not Smoking" in the city of St. Paul, Minnesota.
   (b) A medium-size manufacturer of cat food wants to conduct an in-home usage test of a new type of cat food in Sacramento, California.
   (c) A large wholesaler dealing in household appliances in the city of New York wants to evaluate dealer reaction to a new discount policy.
   (d) A local department store wants to assess the satisfaction with a new credit policy offered to charge account customers.
   (e) A national manufacturer wants to assess whether adequate inventories are being held by wholesalers in order to prevent shortages by retailers.
   (f) Your school cafeteria wants to test a new soft drink manufactured and sold by the staff of the cafeteria.
   (g) A manufacturer of cake mixes selling primarily in the Midwest wants to test market a new brand of cake mix.

2. The management of a popular tourist resort on the West Coast had noticed a decline in the number of tourists and length of stay over the past three years. An overview of industry trends indicated that the overall tourist trade was expanding and growing rapidly. Management decided to conduct a study to determine people's attitudes toward the particular activities that were available at the resort. It wanted to cause the minimum amount of inconvenience to its customers and hence adopted the following plan: A request was deposited in each hotel room of the two major hotels in the resort, indicating the nature of the study and encouraging customers to participate. The customers were requested to report to a separate desk located in the lobby of the hotels. Personal interviews, lasting 20 minutes, were conducted at this desk.
   (a) What type of sampling method was used?
   (b) Critically evaluate the method used.

3. A national manufacturer of baby food was planning to enter the Canadian market. The initial thrust was to be in the provinces of Ontario and Quebec. Prior to the final decision of launching the product, management decided to test market the products in two cities. After reviewing the various cities in terms of external criteria such as demographics, shopping characteristics, and so on, the research department settled on the cities of Hamilton, Ontario, and Sherbrooke, Quebec.
   (a) What type of sampling method was used?
   (b) Critically evaluate the method used.

4. The Juno Company, a manufacturer of clothing for large-size consumers, was in the process of evaluating its product and advertising strategy. Initial efforts consisted of a number of focus-group interviews. The focus groups consisted of ten to twelve large men and women of different demographic characteristics who were selected by the company's research department using on-the-street observations of physical characteristics.
   (a) What type of sampling method was used?
   (b) Critically evaluate the method used.

5. The Hi-Style Company is a chain of beauty salons in San Diego, California. During the past five years the company has witnessed a sharp increase in the number of outlets it operates and in the company's gross sales and net profit margin. The owner

plans to offer a free service of hair analysis and consultation, a service for which competing salons charge a substantial price. In order to offset the increase in operating expenses, the owner plans to raise the rates on other services by 5 percent. Prior to introducing this new service and increasing rates, the owner wants to do a survey using her customers as a sample and employing the method of quota sampling. Your assistance is required in planning the study.

(a) On what variables will you suggest the quotas be based? Why? List the variables with their respective levels.

(b) The owner has kept close track of the demographic characteristics of her customers over a five-year period and decides that these would be most relevant in identifying the sample elements to be used.

Variable	Level	Percent of Customers
Age	0–15 years	5
	16–30 years	30
	31–45 years	30
	46–60 years	15
	61–75 years	15
	76 years and over	5
Sex	Male	24
	Female	76
Income	$0–$9,999	10
	$10,000–$19,999	20
	$20,000–$29,999	30
	$30,000–$39,999	20
	$40,000 and over	20

Based on these three quota variables, indicate the characteristics of a sample of 200 subjects.

(c) Discuss the possible sources of bias with the sampling method.

6. A simple random sample of the 1989 *Fortune* 500 Largest Industrial Corporations was drawn from the listing published in *Fortune* (April 23, 1990, pp. 346–365), using the table of random numbers contained in this chapter. Selected values for annual sales (in millions of dollars) are listed below:

Company	Sales	Company	Sales
A	2,090.9	I	36,156.0
B	2,826.1	J	991.6
C	1,351.2	K	10,053.2
D	1,312.0	L	3,888.5
E	2,423.3	M	4,498.0
F	2,001.0	N	1,722.8
G	622.1	O	2,403.0
H	779.2		

(a) What is the sample mean?

(b) What is the sample variance?

(c) What is the estimated standard error of the mean?

(d) Construct a 95-percent confidence interval for the mean.

(e) Construct a 90-percent confidence interval for the mean. (Hint: Use $z = 1.65$.)

(f) What effect does lowering the confidence level to 90 percent have on the confidence interval? Why?

7. Repeat the above exercise after drawing your own simple random sample (of size $n = 20$) from the *Fortune* listing. Combine your findings with those of your classmates and construct a histogram of the sample means. What type of distribution is formed by the histogram? What cornerstone concept of inferential statistics does the histogram illustrate?

Endnotes

1. The fact that sample information is used to gauge the accuracy of the census has embroiled the Census Bureau in a debate about whether census counts should be adjusted on the basis of the sample results. For discussion of the controversy surrounding adjustment, see Eugene Carlson, "Census Debate: Is an Estimate More Accurate than a Count?" *The Wall Street Journal* (August 4, 1987), p. 35; Eugene Carlson, "Backers of an Adjusted Census Won't Take No for an Answer," *The Wall Street Journal* (November 3, 1987), p. 35; and "Census Bureau Will Not Adjust '90 Census Data," *Data User News*, 22 (December 1987), p. 3.

2. Seymour Sudman, "Applied Sampling," in Peter H. Rossi, James D. Wright, and Andy B. Anderson, eds., *Handbook of Survey Research* (Orlando: Academic Press, 1983), pp. 145–194.

3. The technique was originally suggested by Leo A. Goodman, "Snowball Sampling," *Annals of Mathematical Statistics*, 32 (1961), pp. 148–170.

4. AT&T used such a process for this communications problem, according to Robert Whitelaw, division manager for market research, in a speech "Research Solutions and New High Technology Service Concepts," which was delivered at the American Marketing Association's 1981 Annual Conference, held in San Francisco, California, June 14–17, 1981.

5. Seymour Sudman, *Applied Sampling* (San Francisco: Academic Press, 1976), p. 10. For discussion of the makeup of the CPI, see John R. Dorfman, "U.S. to Give More Emphasis to Costs of Housing in the Consumer Price Index," *The Wall Street Journal* (February 26, 1987), p. 8.

6. In the example at hand, the sample is 10 percent of the population, since the procedure specifies samples of size $n = 2$ be drawn from a population of size $n = 20$. In a situation such as this, in which the sample is a relatively large part of the population, the correct formula relating the two variances contains an additional term. Specifically it equals

$$\sigma_{\bar{x}}^2 = \frac{\sigma^2}{n} \frac{N - n}{N - 1}.$$

The additional term $\frac{N - n}{N - 1}$ is called the *finite population correction factor*. It is, of course, close to 1 when the population is very large in comparison to the sample, and can then safely be ignored. The variance of mean incomes for the example using the formula turns out to be

$$\sigma_{\bar{x}}^2 = \frac{5,320,000}{2} \frac{20 - 2}{20 - 1} = 2,520,000.$$

7. There are two major errors to avoid when using random-number tables: (1) starting at a given place because one knows the distribution of numbers at that place, and (2) discarding a sample because it does not "look right" in some sense and continuing to use random numbers until a "likely looking" sample is selected. Sudman, "Applied Sampling," p. 165.

Suggested Additional Readings

For a good exposition of the principles and advantages of sequential sampling versus fixed samples, see

E. J. Anderton and R. Tudor, "The Application of Sequential Analysis in Market Research," *Journal of Marketing Research*, 17 (February 1980), pp. 97–105.

For a discussion of the use of snowball samples, see

Patrick Biernacki and Dan Waldorf, "Snowball Sampling: Problems and Techniques of Chain Referred Sampling," *Sociological Methods and Research*, 10 (November 1981), pp. 141–163.

For a more in-depth discussion of some of the more fundamental issues in sampling, see

Martin Frankel, "Sampling Theory," in Peter H. Rossi, James D. Wright, and Andy B. Anderson, eds., *Handbook of Survey Research* (Orlando: Academic Press, 1983), pp. 21–67.

Chapter
Sixteen

Stratified and Cluster Sampling

Learning Objectives   Upon completing this chapter, you should be able to

1. Specify the two procedures that distinguish a stratified sample.

2. Cite two reasons why researchers might opt to use a stratified sample rather than a simple random sample.

3. Note what points investigators should keep in mind when dividing a population into strata for a stratified sample.

4. Explain what a proportionate stratified sample is.

5. Explain what a disproportionate stratified sample is.

6. List the steps followed in drawing a cluster sample.

7. Explain the difference between a one-stage cluster sample and a two-stage cluster sample.

8. Explain why cluster sampling, though far less statistically efficient than comparable stratified samples, is the sampling procedure used most in large-scale field surveys employing personal interviews.

9. Distinguish between one-stage area sampling and simple two-stage area sampling.

10. Note the quality that distinguishes probability-proportional-to-size sampling and explain when it is used.

Case in Marketing Research

Gary Heisler looked across the table at the two marketing researchers whose efforts had been instrumental in bringing the company so quickly to the verge of a new product launch. He had the highest respect for their judgment. The only problem was that each favored a totally different approach to test marketing.

Heisler and the two researchers, Terry Shapiro and Jim Lovesey, worked for Brigham Products in its personal-care products division. They had scrambled over the last six months to formulate and test a new two-in-one dandruff shampoo to challenge their competitor's dominance of that growing market segment.

Two-in-ones are shampoo and conditioner combinations aimed at the convenience segment of the shampoo market—consumers who want to save time by applying only one product to their hair while still receiving the benefits of using a hair conditioner. The convenience segment was the fastest-growing segment in the shampoo category, and in the cutthroat personal-care market, Brigham had to bring a new product into the market.

The result was Free 'n' Soft, a dandruff shampoo plus conditioner that Brigham hoped would be a way to target male consumers who don't traditionally use conditioners. Heisler sighed. They had developed a good product, they knew who they wanted to sell it to. . . . "Now," he thought to himself, "it really starts getting complicated."

"As you know," began Heisler, addressing the researchers, "the time has come to test market Free 'n' Soft. I know that there are several ways to do this. I also know that there is never one right way. Terry, why don't you tell me why you think we should go with a national sample."

"I think that live test markets are best for products that are 'nichey,' and that's what Free 'n' Soft is. We're targeting a very specific market—appearance-conscious men who presently use a dandruff shampoo. We've done extensive focus-group testing on the product formula and packaging. I think we can go ahead with what amounts to a mini-launch and then use data from a national sample to fine-tune our marketing efforts. We followed a similar strategy quite successfully with our launch of Summit Deodorant.

"As you recall, for Summit we used a research supplier called Insta-Track. They have a lot of experience using retail audit data to track new product introductions. They use a carefully designed national sample that reflects an accurate picture of retail food, drug, and mass-merchandise stores. The sample is not only the proper overall size, but internally it also reflects the proper structure, including different sizes and types of stores in urban, suburban, and rural areas of the country. This structure makes area-by-area and store-by-store analyses possible. That way we can measure the effects of special marketing efforts on sales performance."

"Isn't this going to cost a fortune?" asked Heisler.

"A test market of a national market is never going to be cheap," replied Shapiro, "but we can certainly keep costs under control by using disproportionate sampling. In the simplest terms, that means that we'd relate the sample selection to the store's volume rather than the number of stores of each type, which would result in more large-volume stores and fewer small stores. That way we'd end up with a sample that's equivalent to a much larger and more expensive sample."

"You know I think that disproportionate samples can be very useful and cost efficient," countered Lovesey, "but it works best when there's a great deal of variability among the stores in a category. It also assumes that we know enough about the population of interest to be able to judge the degree of variability among the stores in a category."

"Before we get into too much detail," Heisler interjected, "I'd like to take a coffee break and then let Jim present his proposal for a simulated test market. Then, I promise, I'll give each of you a chance to make my head spin with technical arguments."

Discussion Issues

1. If you were Heisler, what would you want to know about the sample proposed by each of the marketing researchers?
2. What might be the advantages of using a national sample?
3. What might be the advantages of using a simulated test market?

In the preceding chapter we discussed the basic types of samples and how they are drawn. Simple random samples were used to illustrate the basis of statistical inference in which a parameter is estimated from a statistic. In this chapter we will take these concepts a bit further to explore two other types of probability samples: stratified samples and cluster samples.

Stratified Sample

Stratified sample
A probability sample that is distinguished by the two-step procedure where (1) the parent population is divided into mutually exclusive and exhaustive subsets, and (2) a simple random sample of elements is chosen independently from each group or subset.

A **stratified sample** is a probability sample that is distinguished by the following two-step procedure:

1.   The parent population is divided into mutually exclusive and exhaustive subsets.
2.   A simple random sample of elements is chosen independently from each group or subset.

Note that the definition says nothing about what criteria are used to separate the universe elements into subsets. That is because it is not the criteria that determine whether or not a stratified sample has been drawn. Admittedly, those criteria will make a difference as to the ultimate usefulness of the particular sample in question. But as long as the sample reflects the two-stage process, it is a stratified sample. Keep this distinction in mind. It will be useful later when distinguishing cluster samples from stratified samples.

The subsets into which the universe elements are divided are called *strata* or *subpopulations*. Note that our definition specified that this division be mutually exclusive and exhaustive. This means that every population element must be assigned to one, and only one, stratum and that no population elements are omitted in the assignment procedure.

To illustrate the process, suppose we again used the hypothetical population of 20 people used in the last chapter and shown again in Table 16.1. That population

Table 16.1   **Hypothetical Population**

Element	Income (Dollars)	Educational (years)	Newspaper Subscription	Element	Income (Dollars)	Education (Years)	Newspaper Subscription
1 A	5,600	8	X	11 K	9,600	13	X
2 B	6,000	9	Y	12 L	10,000	13	Y
3 C	6,400	11	X	13 M	10,400	14	X
4 D	6,800	11	Y	14 N	10,800	14	Y
5 E	7,200	11	X	15 O	11,200	15	X
6 F	7,600	12	Y	16 P	11,600	16	Y
7 G	8,000	12	X	17 Q	12,000	16	X
8 H	8,400	12	Y	18 R	12,400	17	Y
9 I	8,800	12	X	19 S	12,800	18	X
10 J	9,200	12	Y	20 T	13,200	18	Y

Table 16.2   **Stratification of Hypothetical Population by Education**

Stratum I Elements		Stratum II Elements	
A	F	K	P
B	G	L	Q
C	H	M	R
D	I	N	S
E	J	O	T

could be described by several parameters, such as the average income, the range in education, and the proportion subscribing to various newspapers. Now assume we divide the group into two strata on the basis of educational level. Table 16.2 shows the results of this stratification procedure. Elements A through J form the *first stratum* (education of 12 years or less) and Elements K through T form the *second stratum* (education of more than 12 years). There is no particular reason to choose two strata. The parent population can be divided into any number of strata. We chose two as a convenient way of illustrating the technique.

The second step in the process requires that a simple random sample be drawn independently from *each* stratum. Let us again work with samples of Size 2, formed in this case by selecting one element from each stratum. (The number of elements from each stratum does not have to be equal, however.)

The procedure that would be used to select the two elements for the stratified sample would be the same as that used in drawing a simple random sample. Within each stratum, the population elements would be serially numbered from 1 to 10. A table of random numbers would be consulted. The first number encountered between 1 and 10 would designate the element from the first stratum. The element from the second stratum could be selected after another independent start or by continuing from the first randomly determined start. In either case, it would again be designated by the first encounter with a number between 1 and 10.

Derived Population

Although only one sample of Size 2 will in fact be selected, let us look briefly at the derived population of all possible samples of Size 2 that could be selected under this sampling plan. This derived population along with the mean of each sample is displayed in Table 16.3.

Note that in this sampling plan there are only 100 possible sample combinations of elements, whereas with simple random sampling there were 190 possible combinations. That is because this type of sampling specified that one element be drawn from each stratum. In simple random sampling, you will recall, any two elements could be drawn from the population of items. In this sense, stratified sampling is always more restrictive than simple random sampling. Note further that every element has an equal chance of being included in the sample—1 in 10—since each can be the single element selected from the stratum which it is in. This explains why we specified an additional requirement to define a simple random sample. Although simple random samples provide each element an equal chance of selection, other techniques can also. Thus, equal probability of selection is a necessary but not

Table 16.3   *Derived Population of All Possible Samples of Size 2 with Stratified Sampling*

k	Sample Identity	Mean	k	Sample Identity	Mean	k	Sample Identity	Mean	k	Sample Identity	Mean
1	AK	7,600	26	CP	9,000	51	FK	8,600	76	HP	10,00
2	AL	7,800	27	CQ	9,200	52	FL	8,800	77	HQ	10,20
3	AM	8,000	28	CR	9,400	53	FM	9,000	78	HR	10,40
4	AN	8,200	29	CS	9,600	54	FN	9,200	79	HS	10,60
5	AO	8,400	30	CT	9,800	55	FO	9,400	80	HT	10,80
6	AP	8,600	31	DK	8,200	56	FP	9,600	81	IK	9,20
7	AQ	8,800	32	DL	8,400	57	FQ	9,800	82	IL	9,40
8	AR	9,000	33	DM	8,600	58	FR	10,000	83	IM	9,60
9	AS	9,200	34	DN	8,800	59	FS	10,200	84	IN	9,80
10	AT	9,400	35	DO	9,000	60	FT	10,400	85	IO	10,00
11	BK	7,800	36	DP	9,200	61	GK	8,800	86	IP	10,20
12	BL	8,000	37	DQ	9,400	62	GL	9,000	87	IQ	10,40
13	BM	8,200	38	DR	9,600	63	GM	9,200	88	IR	10,60
14	BN	8,400	39	DS	9,800	64	GN	9,400	89	IS	10,80
15	BO	8,600	40	DT	10,000	65	GO	9,600	90	IT	11,00
16	BP	8,800	41	EK	8,400	66	GP	9,800	91	JK	9,40
17	BQ	9,000	42	EL	8,600	67	GQ	10,000	92	JL	9,60
18	BR	9,200	43	EM	8,800	68	GR	10,200	93	JM	9,80
19	BS	9,400	44	EN	9,000	69	GS	10,400	94	JN	10,00
20	BT	9,600	45	EO	9,200	70	GT	10,600	95	JO	10,20
21	CK	8,000	46	EP	9,400	71	HK	9,000	96	JP	10,40
22	CL	8,200	47	EQ	9,600	72	HL	9,200	97	JQ	10,60
23	CM	8,400	48	ER	9,800	73	HM	9,400	98	JR	10,80
24	CN	8,600	49	ES	10,000	74	HN	9,600	99	JS	11,00
25	CO	8,800	50	ET	10,200	75	HO	9,800	100	JT	11,20

a sufficient condition for simple random sampling; in addition, each combination o n elements must be a sample possibility and as likely to occur as any othe₁ combination of n elements.

Sampling Distribution

Table 16.4 contains the classification of sample means by size, and Figure 16.1 displays the plot of this sample statistic. Note that in relation to Figure 15.4, fo₁ simple random sampling, stratified sampling can produce a more concentrated distribution of estimates. This suggests one reason why we might choose a stratified sample; stratified samples can produce sample statistics that are more precise, or tha₁ have smaller error due to sampling, than simple random samples. With education a₁ a stratification variable, there is a marked reduction in the number of sample mean₁ that deviate widely from the population mean.

A second reason for drawing a stratified sample is that stratification allows the investigation of the characteristic of interest for particular subgroups. Thus, by stratifying, one is able to guarantee representation of those with a high schoo₁ education or less, and those with more than a high school education. This can be extremely important when sampling from populations with rare segments. Suppose for example, that a manufacturer of diamond rings wants to conduct a study of sale

Table 16.4   **Classification of Sample Means by Size with Stratified Sampling**

Sample Mean	Number of Samples
7,300 to 7,800	3
7,900 to 8,400	12
8,500 to 9,000	21
9,100 to 9,600	28
9,700 to 10,200	21
10,300 to 10,800	12
10,900 to 11,400	3

Figure 16.1   **Distribution of Sample Means with Stratified Sampling**

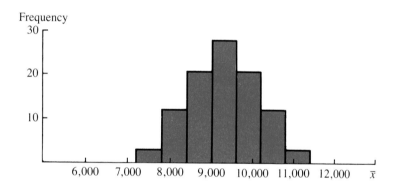

of the product by social class. Unless special precautions are taken, it is likely that the upper class—which represents only 3 percent of the total population—will not be repesented at all, or will be represented by too few cases. Yet this may be an extremely important segment to the ring manufacturer. It is often true in marketing that a small subset of the population of interest will account for a large proportion of the behavior of interest—for example, consumption of the product. It then becomes critical that this subgroup be adequately represented in the sample. Stratified sampling is one way of ensuring adequate representation from each subgroup of interest.

Confidence Interval Estimate

In establishing a confidence interval with a simple random sample, we saw that we need three things to complete the confidence interval specifications given by

$$\bar{x} - zs_{\bar{x}} \leq \mu \leq \bar{x} + zs_{\bar{x}}.$$

1. The degree of confidence desired so that a z value can be selected.
2. A point estimate of the population mean given by the sample mean $\bar{x}$.
3. An estimate of the amount of sampling error associated with the sample mean, which was given by the standard error of the mean, $s_{\bar{x}} = \hat{s}/\sqrt{n}$, when the population variance was unknown.

The same three quantities are required for making inferences with a stratified sample. The only difference in the procedure occurs in the way Items 2 and 3 are generated. With stratified sampling, the sample estimate of the population mean and the standard error of estimate associated with this statistic are determined by weighting the individual strata results.

More specifically, the analyst needs to compute the sample mean and the sample variance for each stratum. These would be calculated exactly as before, since a simple random sample is being taken from each stratum. The mean for the sample as a whole is then determined by weighting each of the respective strata means by the relative proportion of elements in the population that belong to the stratum. For example, if the population is divided into groups in such a way that one stratum contains one-fourth of all the population members, the sample mean for that stratum receives a weight of .25 when one is determining the mean for the total sample. Similarly, the sample mean for a stratum that contains 10 percent of the population elements is weighted .10 when one is estimating the overall sample mean.

The process to get the overall standard error of the mean is slightly more complex. The relative sizes of the respective strata are again used but the ratios are squared; for example, a stratum containing 10 percent of the population members would be weighted $(.10)^2 = .01$. Further, one needs to weight the variances of means by strata to get the overall variance of the mean. Then one takes the square root of the overall result to get the standard error of the mean for the overall sample. The variance of means for each stratum are obtained just as they were for a simple random sample, that is, by dividing the sample variance for the stratum by the sample size from that stratum.

Table 16.5 illustrates the procedure assuming Elements B and E were randomly selected from the first stratum and Elements N and S from the second stratum. Since each stratum contains 10 of the 20 population elements, the sample mean for each stratum is weighted by one-half ($10 \div 20$) when one is determining the overall sample mean, while each variance of estimate is weighted .25. With the overall sample mean of 9,200 and standard error of estimate of 583, the 95-percent confidence interval ($z = 1.96$) is $9,200 \pm (1.96)583$ or $8,057 \leq \mu \leq 10,343$. This interval is interpreted as before. The true mean may or may not be in the interval, but since 95 of 100 intervals constructed by this process will contain the true mean, we are 95-percent confident that the true population mean income is between \$8,057 and \$10,343.[1]

Increased Precision of Stratified Samples   We mentioned previously that one of the reasons one might choose a stratified sample is that such samples offer an opportunity for reducing sampling error or increasing precision. When estimating a mean, sampling error is given by the size of the standard error of the mean, $s_{\bar{x}}$; the smaller $s_{\bar{x}}$ is, the less the sampling error and the more precise the estimate will be, as indicated by the narrower confidence interval associated with a specified degree of confidence.

Consider the example in Table 16.1 again. The total size of the population and the population within each stratum are fixed. The only way, therefore, for total

Table 16.5   **Computation of Mean and Standard Error of Estimate for Stratified Sample**

Stratum 1			**Stratum 2**	
Element	**Income**		**Element**	**Income**
B	6,000		N	10,800
E	7,200		S	12,800

Mean: $\bar{x}_1 = \dfrac{6,000 + 7,200}{2} = 6,600$ $\bar{x}_2 = \dfrac{10,800 + 12,800}{2} = 11,800$

Variance: $\hat{s}_1^2 = \dfrac{(6,000 - 6,600)^2 + (7,200 - 6,600)^2}{2 - 1}$ $\hat{s}_2^2 = \dfrac{(10,800 - 11,800)^2 + (12,800 - 11,800)^2}{2 - 1}$

$= 720,000$ $= 2,000,000$

Variance of estimate: $s_{\bar{x}_1}^2 = \dfrac{\hat{s}_1^2}{n_1} = \dfrac{720,000}{2} = 360,000$ $s_{\bar{x}_2}^2 = \dfrac{\hat{s}_2^2}{n_2} = \dfrac{2,000,000}{2} = 1,000,000$

Overall Sample

Mean: $\bar{x} = \dfrac{10}{20}(6,600) + \dfrac{10}{20}(11,800) = 9,200$

Variance of estimate: $s_{\bar{x}}^2 = \left(\dfrac{10}{20}\right)^2 (360,000) + \left(\dfrac{10}{20}\right)^2 (1,000,000) = 340,000$

Standard error of estimate: $s_{\bar{x}} = \sqrt{s_{\bar{x}}^2} = 583$

sampling error to be reduced is for the variance of the estimate within each stratum to be made smaller. Now the variance of the estimate by strata in turn depends on the variability of the characteristic within the strata. Thus, the estimate of the mean can be made more precise to the extent that the population can be partitioned so that there is little variability within each stratum, that is, to the extent the strata can be made internally homogeneous.

A characteristic of interest will display a certain amount of variation in the population. The investigator can do nothing about this total variation because it is a fixed characteristic of the population. In the population in Table 16.1, for example, there is a variation in incomes which the investigator can do nothing about. But the analyst can do something when dividing the elements of the population into strata so as to increase the precision with which the average value of the characteristic (i.e., average income) can be estimated. Specifically, the goal is to divide the population into strata so that the elements within any given stratum are as similar in value as possible and the values between any two strata are as disparate as possible. In this case, the division of the population between those who have more than a high school education and those who do not was a good way of separating the population into two strata since the elements within each stratum have similar incomes.

In the limit, if the investigator is successful in partitioning the population so that the elements in each stratum are exactly equal, there will be no error associated with the estimate of the population mean. That is right! The population mean could then be estimated without error because *the variability that exists between strata does not enter into the calculation of the standard error of estimate with stratified sampling.*

One can see this readily in a simple case with a limited number of values. Suppose that in a population of 1,000 elements, 200 had the value 5; 300 had the value 10; and 500 had the value 20. Now the mean of this population is $\mu = 14$, and the variance is $\sigma^2 = 39$. If a simple random sample of size $n = 3$ is employed to estimate this mean, then the standard error of estimate is

$$\sigma_{\bar{x}} = \frac{\sigma}{\sqrt{n}} = \frac{\sqrt{39}}{\sqrt{3}} = 3.61$$

and the width of confidence interval would be $\pm z$ times this value, 3.61. Suppose, on the other hand, a researcher employed a stratified sample and was successful in partitioning the total population so that all the elements with a value of 5 on the characteristic were in one stratum, those with the value 10 in the second stratum, and those with the value 20 in the third stratum. To generate a completely precise description of the mean of each stratum, the researcher would then need only to take a sample of one from each stratum. Further, when the investigator combined these individual results into a global estimate of the overall mean, the standard error of the estimate would be zero, since each stratum standard error of estimate is zero. The population mean value would be determined exactly.

Bases for Stratification   The fact that variation among strata does not enter into the calculation of the standard error of estimate suggests the kinds of criteria that should be used to partition the population. The values assumed by the characteristic will be unknown, for if they were known, there would be no need to take a sample to estimate their mean level. What the investigator attempts to do, therefore, is to partition the population according to one or more criteria that are expected to be related to the characteristic of interest. It was no accident, therefore, that in our hypothetical example education was employed to divide the population elements into strata. As Table 16.1 indicates, there is a relationship between educational level and income level: the more years of school, the higher the income tends to be. Newspaper subscriptions, on the other hand, would have made a poor variable for partitioning the population into segments, since there is almost no relation between the paper to which a person subscribes and the individual's income. Whether one selects a "good" or a "bad" variable to partition the population does not affect whether a stratified sample is selected or not. It is significant in determining whether a good or poor sample is selected, but the two features defining a stratified sample are still (1) the partitioning of the population into subgroups and (2) the random selection of elements from each subgroup.

The calculation of the standard error of estimate provides some clue as to the number of strata that should be employed. Since the standard error of estimate depends only on variability within strata, the various strata should be made as homogeneous as possible. One way of doing this is to employ many, very small strata. In our education example, for instance, additional strata could be grade school education or less, some high school education, some college education, and graduate school education. Or even finer distinctions could be made. There are practical limits, though, to the number of strata that should be and are used in actual research studies. First, the creation of additional strata is often expensive in terms of sample design, data collection, and analysis. Second, there is an upper limit to the amount of variation that can be accounted for by any practical stratification. Regardless of the criteria by which the population is partitioned, a certain amount of variation is likely to remain unaccounted for, and thus the additional strata will serve no productive purpose.

Proportionate and Disproportionate Stratified Samples

Whether one chooses a stratified sample over a simple random sample depends in part on the trade-off between cost and precision. Although stratified samples typically produce more precise estimates, they also usually cost more than simple random samples. If the decision is made in favor of a stratified sample, the researcher must still decide whether to select a proportionate or disproportionate one.

Proportionate stratified sample A stratified sample in which the number of observations in the total sample is allocated among the strata in proportion to the relative number of elements in each stratum in the population.

Disproportionate stratified sample A stratified sample in which the individual strata or subsets are sampled in relation to both their size and their variability; strata exhibiting more variability are sampled more than proportionately to their relative size, while those that are very homogeneous are sampled less than proportionately.

With a **proportionate stratified sample,** the number of observations in the total sample is allocated among the strata in proportion to the *relative* number of elements in each stratum in the population. A stratum containing one-fifth of all the population elements would account for one-fifth of the total sample observations, and so on. Proportionate sampling was employed in our education example, since each stratum contained one-half of the population and they were sampled equally.

One advantage of proportionate allocation is that the investigator needs to know only the relative sizes of each stratum in order to determine the number of sample observations to select from each stratum with a given sample size. A **disproportionate stratified sample,** however, can produce still more efficient estimates. It involves balancing the two criteria of strata size and strata variability. With a fixed sample size, strata exhibiting more variability are sampled more than proportionately to their relative size. Conversely, those strata that are very homogeneous are sampled less than proportionately. Research Window 16.1, for example, describes the disproportionate stratified sampling scheme used by Nielsen in developing the *Nielsen Retail Index*, described in Chapter 8.[2]

While a full discussion of how the sample size for each stratum should be determined would take us too far afield and would be much too technical for our purpose, some feel for the rationale behind disproportionate sampling is useful. Consider at the extreme a stratum with zero variability. Since all the elements are identical in value, a single observation tells all. On the other hand, a stratum that is characterized by great variability will require a large number of observations to produce a precise estimate of the stratum mean. One would expect, for example, great variability among the income levels of those people subscribing to *Newsweek* but much less among people subscribing to the glossy society magazine *Town and Country*. One can expect greater precision when the various strata are sampled proportionate to the relative variability of the characteristic under study rather than proportionate to their relative size in the population.

A disproportionate stratified sample requires more knowledge about the population of interest than does a proportionate stratified sample. To sample the strata in relation to their variability, one needs knowledge of relative variability. Sampling theory is a peculiar phenomenon in that knowledge begets more knowledge. Disproportionate sampling can produce more efficient estimates than proportionate sampling, but the former method also requires that some estimate of the relative variation within strata be known. One can sometimes anticipate the relative homogeneity likely to exist within a stratum on the basis of past studies and experience. Sometimes the investigator may have to rely on logic and intuition in establishing sample sizes for each stratum. For example, one might expect that large retail stores would show greater variation than small stores in sales of some products. That is one reason why the large stores are sampled more heavily in the *Nielsen Retail Index*.

Research Window 16.1
Disproportionate Stratified Sampling Scheme Used by Nielsen

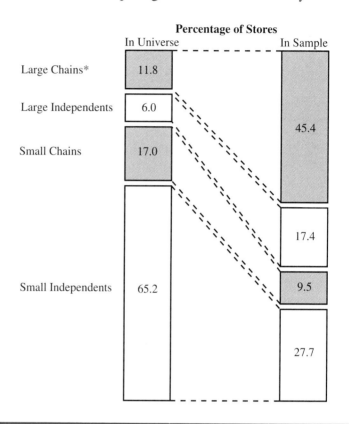

Source: Developed from information supplied by Nielsen Marketing Research.

Cluster sample
A probability sample distinguished by a two-step procedure in which (1) the parent population is divided into mutually exclusive and exhaustive subsets, and (2) a random sample of subsets is selected. If the investigator then uses all of the population elements in the selected subsets for the sample, the procedure is one-stage cluster sampling; if a sample of elements is selected probabilistically from the subsets, the procedure is two-stage cluster sampling.

Stratified versus Quota Sample

Inexperienced researchers sometimes confuse stratified samples with quota samples. There are similarities. In each case, the population is divided into segments, and elements are selected from each segment. There is one key difference, though. In stratified samples, sample elements are selected by probability methods; in quota samples, elements are chosen based on a researcher's judgment. This difference has important implications. Since elements in a stratified sample are selected probabilistically, researchers can establish the sampling distribution of the statistic in question, and hence a confidence interval judgment. In a quota sample there is no objective way to assess the degree of sampling error. Therefore there is also no way to arrive at confidence interval estimates and statistical tests of significance.

Cluster Sample

Cluster samples are another probability sampling technique often used by researchers. Cluster sampling shares some similarities with stratified sampling, but also has some key differences. Cluster sampling involves the following steps:

1.   The parent population is divided into mutually exclusive and exhaustive subsets.
2.   A random sample of the subsets is selected.

If the investigator then uses all of the population elements in the selected subsets for the sample, the procedure is one-stage cluster sampling. If, on the other hand, a sample of elements is selected probabilistically from the selected subsets, the procedure is known as two-stage cluster sampling.

Note the similarities and differences between cluster sampling and stratified sampling. Although in each case the population is divided into mutually exclusive and exhaustive subgroups, in stratified sampling a sample of elements is selected *from each subgroup*. With cluster sampling, one chooses a *sample of subgroups*.

Remember that in stratified sampling, the goal is to separate the population into strata that are fairly homogeneous for a certain characteristic. In cluster sampling, the goal is to form subgroups that are similar to each other and are each small-scale models of the population. Each cluster should reflect the diversity of the whole population.

In our earlier example relating income to level of education, we noted that dividing the population into subgroups based on newspaper subscriptions was probably not a good idea for stratified sampling because that characteristic is not a good predictor of income. However, since the goal in cluster sampling is to form subgroups that are as heterogeneous as possible, newspaper subscriptions might be a good basis for dividing the population for this form of sample.

If all those subscribing to Paper X were considered to form one subgroup and all those subscribing to Paper Y a second subgroup, then one could be relatively safe in randomly selecting either subgroup to estimate the mean income in the population. While the distribution of incomes within each subgroup is not exactly the same as it is in the population, the range of incomes is such that there would be only a slight error if one were to estimate the mean income and variance of incomes of the population with the elements from either subset.

Admittedly, in practice clusters are not always formed to be as heterogeneous as possible. Because of the way cluster samples are often drawn, the defined clusters are homogeneous rather than heterogeneous in regard to the characteristic of interest. Beginning researchers often mistakenly then call the procedure *stratified sampling*, since it involves the construction of homogeneous subgroups of population elements. But as long as subgroups are subsequently selected for investigation randomly, the procedure is *cluster sampling* regardless of how the subgroups are formed. Admittedly, however, homogeneous subgroups produce less ideal cluster samples from a statistical efficiency viewpoint than do heterogeneous subgroups.

Statistical efficiency
A measure used to compare sampling plans; one sampling plan is said to be superior (more statistically efficient) to another if, for the same size sample, it produces a smaller standard error of estimate.

Statistical efficiency is a relative notion by which sampling plans can be compared. One sampling plan is said to be more statistically efficient than another if, for the same size sample, it produces a smaller standard error of estimate. When the characteristic of interest is the mean, for example, the sampling plan that produces the smallest value of the standard error of the mean, $s_{\bar{x}}$, for a given-size sample is most statistically efficient. Cluster samples are typically much less statistically efficient than comparable stratified samples or even simple random samples because the probable margin of error with a fixed-size sample is often greatest with cluster sampling.

Even with its typically lower statistical efficiency, cluster sampling is probably the sampling procedure used most in large-scale field surveys employing personal interviews. Why? Simply because cluster sampling is often more *economically efficient* in that the cost per observation is less. The economies permit the selection of a larger sample at a smaller cost. Since cluster sampling allows researchers to secure so many more observations for a given cost than they would be able to secure with stratified sampling, the margin of error associated with the estimate may actually be smaller for cluster sampling. That is, cluster sampling is often more *efficient overall* than the other forms of sampling. Although it requires a larger sample for the same degree of precision, and is thus less statistically efficient, the smaller cost per observation allows samples so much larger that estimates with a smaller standard error can be produced for the same cost.

Systematic Sample

Systematic sample
A form of cluster sampling in which every kth element in the population is designated for inclusion in the sample after a random start.

The **systematic sample** is a form of cluster sampling that offers one of the easiest ways of sampling many populations of interest. It involves selecting every kth element after a random start. Consider again the hypothetical population of twenty individuals, and suppose a sample of five is to be selected from this population. Number the elements from one to twenty. With twenty population elements and a sample size of five, the sampling fraction is $f = n/N = 5/20 = 1/4$, meaning that one element in four will be selected. The sampling interval $i = 1/f$ will be 4. This means that after a random start, every fourth element will be chosen. The random start, which must be some number between 1 and 4—1 and i in general—is determined from a random-number table. Thus if the random start were 1, the first, fifth, ninth, thirteenth, and seventeenth items would be the sample. If it were 2, the second, sixth, tenth, fourteenth, and eighteenth items would be the sample, and so on.

Systematic sampling is one-stage cluster sampling since the subgroups are not subsampled, but rather all of the elements in the selected clusters are used. The subgroups or clusters in this case are

- Cluster I: A, E, I, M, Q
- Cluster II: B, F, J, N, R
- Cluster III: C, G, K, O, S
- Cluster IV: D, H, L, P, T

and one of these clusters is selected randomly for investigation. The random start, of course, determines the cluster that is to be used.

One can readily see the ease with which a systematic sample can be drawn. It is much easier to draw a systematic sample than it is to select a simple random sample of the same size, for example. With a systematic sample one needs to enter the random-number table only once. The problem of checking for the duplication of elements, which is cumbersome with simple random samples, does not occur with systematic samples. All the elements are uniquely determined by the selection of the random start.[3]

A systematic sample can often be made more representative than a simple random sample. With our hypothetical population, for example, we are guaranteed representation from the low-income segment and the high-income segment with our systematic sampling plan. Regardless of which of the four clusters is chosen, one element must have an income of $6,800 or less; another must have an income of $12,000 or more; and the remaining three elements must have incomes between these two values. A simple random sample of Size 5 might or might not include low-income or high-income people.

The same is true when sampling from other populations. Thus, if we are sampling retail stores, we can guarantee representation of both small and large stores by employing a systematic sample, if the stores can be arrayed from smallest to largest according to some criteria such as annual sales or square footage. The ability to guarantee representation from each size segment depends on the availability of knowledge about the size of each store so that they can be arrayed from smallest to largest and numbered serially. A simple random sample of stores would be apt to represent large stores inadequately since there are fewer large stores than small stores. Yet the fewer large stores account for a great proportion of all sales.

The degree to which the systematic sample will be more representative than a simple random sample thus depends on the clustering of objects within the list from which the sample will be drawn. The ideal list for a systematic sample will have elements similar in value on the characteristic (for example, similar levels of income, sales, education, and so on) close together and elements diverse in value spread apart.

At least one danger with systematic samples is that if there is a natural periodicity in the list of elements, the systematic sample can produce estimates seriously in error. For example, suppose we have the annual ticket sales of an airline by day and wish to analyze these sales in terms of length of trip. To analyze all 365 days may be prohibitively costly, but suppose the research budget does allow the investigation of 52 days of sales. A systematic sample of days using a sampling interval of 7 (365 ÷ 52) would obviously produce some misleading conclusions, since the day's sales would reflect all Monday trips, Friday trips, or Sunday trips, for example.[4] Of course, any other sampling interval would be acceptable, and in general, an enlightened choice of the sampling interval can do much to eliminate the problems associated with natural periodicities in the data. An appropriate choice of sampling interval, of course, depends on knowledge of the phenomenon and the nature of the periodicity.

Area Sample

In every probability sampling plan discussed so far, the investigator needs a list of population elements in order to draw the sample. A list identifying each population element is a necessary requirement for simple random samples, stratified samples, and systematic samples. The latter two procedures also require knowledge about some other characteristic of the population if they are to be designed optimally. For many populations of interest, however, such detailed lists are unavailable. Further, it will often prove prohibitively costly to construct them. When this condition arises, the cluster sample offers the researcher another distinct benefit—he or she only needs the list of population elements for the selected clusters.

Suppose, for example, that an investigator wishes to measure certain characteristics of industrial sales representatives, such as their earnings, attitudes toward the job, hours worked, and so on. It would be extremely difficult, if not impossible, and certainly costly to develop an up-to-date roster listing each industrial sales representative. Yet such a list would be required for a simple random sample. A stratified sample would further require that the investigator possess knowledge about some additional characteristics of each sales representative, for example, education or age, so that the population could be divided into mutually exclusive and exhaustive subsets. With a cluster sample, on the other hand, one could use the companies as sampling units. The investigator would generate a sample of business firms from the population of firms of interest. The business firms would be primary **sampling units** where a sampling unit is defined as "that element or set of elements considered for selection in some stage of sampling."[5] The investigator could then compile a list of sales representatives working for each of the selected firms, a much more realistic assignment. If the investigator then studied each of the sales representatives in each of the selected firms, it would be one-stage cluster sampling. If the researcher

Sampling units
Nonoverlapping collections of elements from the population.

Table 16.6   **Possible Clusters to Use to Sample Various Types of Population Elements**

Population Elements	Possible Clusters
College seniors	Colleges
Elementary school students	Schools
Manufacturing firms	Counties Localities Plants
Airline travelers	Airports Planes
Hospital patients	Hospitals

Source: Adapted from Seymour Sudman, *Applied Sampling* (San Francisco: Academic Press, 1976), 70.

Area sampling A form of cluster sampling in which areas (for example, census tracts, blocks) serve as the primary sampling units. The population is divided into mutually exclusive and exhaustive areas using maps, and a random sample of areas is selected. If all the households in the selected areas are used in the study, it is one-stage area sampling, while if the areas themselves are subsampled with respect to households, the procedure is two-stage area sampling.

subsampled sales representatives from each company's list, it would be two-stage cluster sampling. Table 16.6 lists some possible clusters that could be used to sample various types of population elements.

The same principle underlies **area sampling.** Current, accurate lists of population elements are rarely available. Directories of all those living in a city at a particular moment simply do not exist for many cities, and when they do exist, they are obsolete when published: people move, others die, new households are constantly being formed.[6] While lists of families are nonexistent, relatively accurate lists of primary sampling units are available in the form of city maps, if the area divisions of the city serve as the primary sampling units. While the complex details of area sampling are not relevant here, an appreciation for the rationale underlying the various approaches is.

One-Stage Area Sample   Suppose the investigator is interested in estimating the amount of wine consumed per household in the city of Chicago, and how consumption is related to family income. An accurate listing of all households is unavailable for the Chicago area. A phone book when published is already somewhat obsolete, in addition to having the other inadequacies previously mentioned. One approach to this problem would be to

1. Choose a simple random sample of n city blocks from the population of N blocks.
2. Determine wine consumption and income for all households in the selected blocks and generalize the sample relationships to the larger population.

The probability of any household being included in the sample can be calculated. It is given simply as n/N since it equals the probability that the block on which it is located will be selected. Since the probabilities are known, the procedure is indeed probability sampling. Here, though, blocks have been substituted for households when selecting primary sampling units. The substitution is made because the list of blocks in the Chicago area can be developed from city maps. Each block can be identified, and the existence of this universe of blocks permits the calculation of the necessary probabilities.

Since each household on the selected blocks is included in the sample, the procedure is one-stage area sampling. Note that the blocks serve to divide the parent population into mutually exclusive and exhaustive subsets. Note further that the blocks do not serve very well as ideal subsets statistically for cluster samples; households on a given block can be expected to be somewhat similar with respect to their income and wine consumption rather than heterogeneous as desired. On the other hand, the data-collection costs will be very low because of the concentration of households within each block.

Two-Stage Area Sample   The distinguishing feature of the one-stage area sample is that all of the households in the selected blocks (or other areas) are enumerated and studied. It is not necessary to employ all items in a selected cluster; the selected areas themselves can be subsampled, and it is often quite advantageous to do so. Two types of two-stage sampling need to be distinguished:

1.   Simple, two-stage area sample.
2.   Probability-proportional-to-size area sample.

Simple two-stage area sampling A form of cluster sampling in which a certain proportion of second-stage sampling units (e.g., households) is selected from each first-stage unit (e.g., a block).

With **simple two-stage area sampling,** a certain proportion of second-stage sampling units (e.g., households) is selected from each first-stage unit (e.g., a block). Consider a universe of 100 blocks; suppose there are 20 households per block; assume that a sample of 80 households is required from this total population of 2,000 households. The overall sampling fraction is thus $80/2{,}000 = 1/25$. There are a number of ways by which the sample can be completed, such as by (1) selecting 10 blocks and 8 households per block, (2) selecting 8 blocks and 10 households per block, (3) selecting 20 blocks and 4 households per block, or (4) selecting 4 blocks and 20 households per block. The last alternative would, of course, be one-stage area sampling, while the first three would all be two-stage area sampling.

The probability with which the blocks are selected is called the *block*, or *first-stage, sampling fraction* and is given as the ratio of n_B/N_B, where n_B and N_B are the number of blocks in the sample and in the population, respectively. For the first three schemes illustrated above, the first-stage sampling fractions would be, in order, 1 in 10, 1 in 12.5, and 1 in 5.

The probability with which the households are selected is the *household*, or *second-stage, sampling fraction*. Since there must be a total of 80 households in the sample, the second-stage sampling fraction differs for each alternative. The second-stage sampling fraction is given as $n_{H/B}/N_{H/B}$, where $n_{H/B}$ and $N_{H/B}$ are the number of households per block in the sample and in the population. For the first sampling scheme, the household sampling fraction is calculated to be $8/20 = 2/5$, while for the second scheme, it is $10/20 = 1/2$, and for the third scheme, $4/20 = 1/5$. Note that the product of the first-stage and second-stage sampling fractions in each case equals the overall sampling fraction of $1/25$.

Which scheme would be preferable? Although it is beyond the scope of this text to present the detailed calculation for determining this, we would like to illustrate the general principle. Economies of data collection would dictate that the second-stage sampling fraction be high. This means that a great many households would be selected from each designated block, as with the second scheme. Statistical efficiency would dictate a small second-stage sampling fraction, since it can be expected that the blocks would be relatively homogeneous and thus it would be desirable to have a very few households from any one block. The third scheme would be preferred on statistical grounds. Statistical sampling theory would suggest the balancing of these two criteria. There are formulas for this purpose that reflect essentially the cost of data collection and the variability of the characteristic within and between clusters, although a useful rule of thumb is that clusters of three to eight households per block or segment are near optimum for most social science variables.[7]

Table 16.7   ***Illustration of Probability-Proportional-to-Size Sampling***

Block	Households	Cumulative Number of Households
1	800	800
2	400	1,200
3	200	1,400
4	200	1,600
5	100	1,700
6	100	1,800
7	100	1,900
8	50	1,950
9	25	1,975
10	25	2,000

Probability-proportional-to-size sampling A form of cluster sampling in which a fixed number of second-stage units is selected from each first-stage unit. The probabilities associated with the selection of each first-stage unit are in turn variable because they are directly related to the relative sizes of the first-stage units.

Simple two-stage area sampling is quite effective when there is approximately the same number of second-stage units (e.g., households) per first-stage unit (e.g., a block). When the second-stage units are decidedly unequal, simple two-stage area sampling can cause bias in the estimate. To pursue our hypothetical example, some blocks in Chicago may contain multistoried low-income housing. Blocks in more affluent parts of the city may contain relatively few, single-family houses. In such a case, the number of second-stage units per first-stage unit would be vastly different. Sometimes this problem can be overcome by combining areas. When this option is not available or is cumbersome to implement, *probability-proportional-to-size sampling* can be employed.

Consider, for example, the data of Table 16.7 and suppose a sample of 20 elements is to be selected from this population of 2,000 households. With **probability-proportional-to-size sampling,** a *fixed* number of second-stage units is selected from each first-stage unit.[8] Suppose after balancing economic and statistical considerations that the number of second-stage units per first-stage unit is determined to be 10. Two first-stage units must be selected to produce a total sample of 20. The procedure gets its name from the way these first-stage units are selected. The probability of selection is variable in that it depends on the size of the first-stage unit. In this particular case, a table of four-digit random numbers will be consulted. The first two numbers encountered between 1 and 2,000 will be employed to indicate the blocks that will be used. All numbers between 1 and 800 will indicate the inclusion of Block 1; those from 801 to 1,200, Block 2; from 1,201 to 1,400, Block 3; and so on.

The probability that any particular household is included in the sample is equal, since the unequal first-stage selection probabilities are balanced by unequal second-stage selection probabilities. Consider, for example, Blocks 1 and 10, the two extremes. The first-stage selection probability for Block 1 is $800/2,000 = 1/2.5$, since 800 of the permissible 2,000 random numbers correspond to Block 1. Only 25 of the permissible random numbers (1,976 to 2,000) correspond to Block 10, on the other hand, and thus the first-stage sampling fraction for Block 10 is $25/2,000 = 1/80$. Since 10 households are to be selected from each block, the second-stage sampling fraction for

Block 1 is $^{10}\!/\!_{800} = ^{1}\!/\!_{80}$, while for Block 10 it is $^{10}\!/\!_{25} = ^{1}\!/\!_{2.5}$. The products of the first- and second-stage sampling thus compensate, since

$$\frac{800}{2,000} \times \frac{10}{800} = \frac{25}{2,000} \times \frac{10}{25}$$

which is also true for the remaining blocks.

Probability-proportional-to-size sampling is another illustration of how information begets information with applied sampling problems. One can avoid the bias of simple two-stage area sampling and can also produce estimates that are more precise when there is great variation in the number of second-stage units per first-stage unit. The price one pays, of course, is that probability-proportional-to-size sampling requires that one have detailed knowledge about the size of each first-stage unit. This is not quite as high a price as it might be since the Census Bureau has reported the number of households per block for all cities of over 50,000 in population as well as for a number of other urbanized areas.[9] Maps are included in each report. While somewhat obsolete when published, these map and block statistics can be updated. The local electrical utility will have records of connections current to the day, and so will the telephone company. In many cases, these statistics will be broken down by blocks.

Ethical
Dilemma 16.1   Raphael Martinez is investigating conflict development and resolution in channels of distribution. Because of the difficulty of accessing actual channel members, he decides to run an experiment on a convenience sample of undergraduate students. Student samples are tolerated in consumer behavior research but have met with more severe criticism in channels research because although a student is also a consumer, a student is not also a channel member. Determined to present his research endeavor in the best possible light, however, Martinez ignores the large fraction of arts students included in his sample of introductory marketing students and refers to his sample as "business students with an average of three years' work experience in jobs in which bargaining and interpersonal skills were required and developed to a level comparable with most channel members."

■   Is it ethical to misrepresent an inappropriate sample as an appropriate sample?

Summary Comments on Probability Sampling

As you can probably begin to appreciate, sample design is a very detailed subject. Our discussion has concentrated on only a few of the fundamentals and, in particular, the basic types of probability samples. You should be aware, though, that the basic types can be, and are, combined in large-scale field studies to produce some very complex designs.

The Gallup Poll, for example, is probably one of the best known of all the polls. The sample for the Gallup Poll for each survey "consists of 1,500 adults selected from 320 locations, using area sampling methods. At each location the interviewer is given a map with an indicated starting point and is required to follow a specified direction. At each occupied dwelling unit, the interviewer must attempt to meet sex quotas."[10] In sum, the Gallup Poll uses a combination of area and quota sampling. Further, it is not uncommon to have several levels of stratification, such as by geographic area and density of population, precede several stages of cluster sampling. Thus, you cannot expect to be a sampling expert with the brief exposure to the subject contained here.[11] But you should be able to communicate effectively about the sample design and use effectively the available microcomputer software for selecting samples.[12] Further, while you may not understand completely, say, why n_1 observations were taken from one stratum and n_2 from another, you should appreciate the basic considerations determining the choice.

Back to the Case

"A simulated test market is fast and inexpensive, and it will let us see how Free 'n' Soft is going to do without letting the competition know we've run the test," began Jim Lovesey confidently. "As soon as we do live market testing, the folks at Tangle-Free will come after us. We don't have patented chemistry. They can rip us off and beat us to the national launch. In short, there are three very strong reasons for using a simulated test market—cost efficiency, speed, and secrecy."

"So how would the sample work?" asked Gary Heisler.

"We'd hire a marketing research firm to recruit a sizable panel of consumers in eight regionally dispersed markets that post standard sales index figures for hair-care products. The consumers would then be paid to come to the testing location. There, participants would be asked to fill out a questionnaire about their usage of dandruff shampoo. Then

they'd be shown a television sitcom interspersed with Free 'n' Soft advertising, competitive advertising, and advertising from noncompetitive products. Following the show, they'd fill out another questionnaire, seeking their recall of the ads. Then they'd be ushered into a model store with a hair-care department and sent on a mock shopping expedition. Finally, they'd be asked why they 'bought' each of the products they selected."

"So how would the eight markets be selected?" asked Heisler.

"We would choose cities that are typical of the regions in which they are located. That way the results from the simulated test markets could be generalized fairly accurately for the rest of the region. In addition, the individual panel members would be selected to represent a broad spectrum of the population. In essence, the city would be a microcosm of the region it represented, and the indi-

viduals would represent the city in microcosm."

"This all sounds very contrived," remarked Terry Shapiro pointedly.

"It is," replied Lovesey, "but the people who put together these kinds of tests have normative data, so they know how to weight the results. All the information from the simulated test markets plus our marketing strategy would go into a mathematical model, and out of that would come a year-one marketing plan with estimated results."

"I don't know, Jim," retorted Shapiro. "I put more faith in information about how real people shop in real stores."

"I do too," replied Heisler thoughtfully, "but Jim's points about secrecy and cost efficiency have to be taken into consideration. This is not going to be an easy decision to make."

Summary

Learning Objective 1: Specify the two procedures that distinguish a stratified sample.

A stratified sample is a probability sample that is distinguished by the following two-step procedure: (1) the parent population is divided into mutually exclusive and exhaustive subsets, and (2) a simple random sample of elements is chosen independently from each group or subset.

Learning Objective 2: Cite two reasons why researchers might opt to use a stratified sample rather than a simple random sample.

Stratified samples can produce sample statistics that are more precise, meaning they have smaller error due to sampling, than simple random samples. Stratification also allows the investigation of the characteristic of interest for particular subgroups.

Learning Objective 3: Note what points investigators should keep in mind when dividing a population into strata for a stratified sample.

Investigators should divide the population into strata so that the elements within any given stratum are as similar in value as possible and so that the values between any two strata are as disparate as possible.

Learning Objective 4: Explain what a proportionate stratified sample is.

With a proportionate stratified sample, the number of observations in the total sample is allocated among the strata in proportion to the *relative* number of elements in each stratum in the population.

Learning Objective 5: Explain what a disproportionate stratified sample is.

Disproportionate stratified sampling involves balancing the two criteria of strata size and variability. With a fixed sample size, strata exhibiting more variability are sampled more than proportionately to their relative size. Conversely, those strata that are very homogeneous are sampled less than proportionately.

Learning Objective 6: List the steps followed in drawing a cluster sample.

Cluster sampling involves the following steps: (1) the parent population is divided into mutually exclusive and exhaustive subsets, and (2) a random sample of the subsets is selected.

Learning Objective 7: Explain the difference between a one-stage cluster sample and a two-stage cluster sample.

If an investigator uses all of the population elements in the selected subsets for the sample, the procedure is one-stage cluster sampling. If, on the other hand, a sample of elements is selected probabilistically from the selected subsets, the procedure is known as two-stage cluster sampling.

Learning Objective 8: Explain why cluster sampling, though far less statistically efficient than comparable stratified samples, is the sampling procedure used most in large-scale field surveys employing personal interviews.

Cluster sampling is the sampling procedure used most in large-scale field surveys using personal interviews because it is often more economically efficient in that the cost per observation is less. The economies permit the selection of a larger sample at a smaller cost. Although cluster sampling requires a larger sample for the same degree of precision, and is thus less statistically efficient, the smaller cost per observation allows samples so much larger that estimates with a smaller standard error can be produced for the same cost.

Learning Objective 9: Distinguish between one-stage area sampling and simple two-stage area sampling.

The distinguishing feature of the one-stage area sample is that all of the households in the selected blocks (or other areas) are enumerated and studied. With simple two-stage area sampling, a certain proportion of second-stage sampling units is selected from each first-stage unit.

Learning Objective 10: Note the quality that distinguishes probability-proportional-to-size sampling and explain when it is used.

With probability-proportional-to-size sampling, a fixed number of second-stage units is selected from each first-stage unit. This type of sampling is particularly useful when the number of second-stage units is unequal and simple two-stage area sampling could cause bias in the estimate.

Discussion Questions, Problems, and Projects

1. The Minnesota National Bank, headquartered in Minneapolis, Minnesota, has some 400,000 users of its credit card scattered throughout the state of Minnesota. The application forms for the credit card asked for the usual information on name, address, phone, income, education, and so on, that is typical of such applications. The bank is now very much interested in determining if there is any relationship between the uses to which the card is put and the socioeconomic characteristics of the using party; for example, is there a difference in the characteristics of those people who use the credit card for major purchases only, such as appliances, and those who use it for minor as well as major purchases?
    (a) Identify the population and sampling frame that would be used by Minnesota National Bank.
    (b) Indicate how you would draw a simple random sample from the above sampling frame.
    (c) Indicate how you would draw a stratified sample from the above sampling frame.
    (d) Indicate how you would draw a cluster sample from the above sampling frame.
    (e) Which method would be preferred? Why?
2. Exclusive Supermarkets is considering entering the Boston market. Before doing so, though, management wishes to estimate the average square feet of selling space among potential competitors, so as to plan better the size of the proposed new outlet. A stratified sample of supermarkets in Boston produced the following results:

Size	Total Number in City	Number of This Size in Sample	Mean Size of Stores in Sample	Standard Deviation of Stores in Sample
Small supermarkets	1,000	20	4,000 sq. ft.	2,000 sq. ft.
Medium supermarkets	600	12	10,000 sq. ft.	1,000 sq. ft.
Large supermarkets	400	8	60,000 sq. ft.	3,000 sq. ft.

    (a) Estimate the average-size supermarket in Boston. Show your calculations.
    (b) Develop a 95-percent confidence interval around this estimate. Show your calculations.
    (c) Was a proportionate or disproportionate stratified sample design used in determining the number of sample observations for each stratum? Explain.
3. Store-More is a large department store located in Lansing, Michigan. The manager is worried about the constant overstocking of a number of items in the various departments. Approximately 3,000 items ranging from small multipurpose wrenches to lawn mowers are overstocked every month. The manager is uncertain whether the surpluses are primarily due to poor purchasing policies or poor store layout and shelving practices. The manager realizes the difficulty of scrutinizing the purchase orders, invoices, and inventory cards for all the items that are overstocked. He decides on choosing a sample of items but does not know how to proceed.
    (a) Identify the population elements and sampling frame.
    (b) What sampling method would you recommend? Why? Be specific.
    (c) How would you draw the sample based on this sampling method?
4. The university housing office has decided to conduct a study to determine what influence living in dormitories versus off-campus housing has on the academic performance of the students. You are required to assist the housing office.
    (a) What sampling method will you recommend? Why? Be specific.
    (b) How will you draw the sample based on this sampling method?

5. Maxwell Federated operates a chain of department stores in the greater Chicago metropolitan area. The management of Maxwell Federated has been concerned of late with tight money conditions and the associated deterioration of the company's accounts receivable. It appears on the surface that more and more customers are becoming delinquent each month. Management wishes to assess the current state of delinquencies, to determine if the delinquencies are concentrated in any stores, and to determine if they are concentrated among any particular types of purchases or purchasers.
   (a) What type of sampling method would you recommend? Why? Be specific.
   (b) How would you draw the sample based on this sampling method?

6. A retailer of household appliances is planning to introduce a new brand of dishwashers to the local market and wishes to estimate demand for the product. He has decided to use two-stage area sampling and has secured an up-to-date map of your area, but he does not know how to proceed and requires your assistance. Outline a step-by-step approach you will recommend for conducting the study.

7. In February 1991, a midwestern city instituted a mandatory recycling plan for certain types of household waste. A marketing research firm was hired to evaluate the progress of the plan in July 1991. Among several measures of effectiveness to be employed, the researchers wished to compare the weight of recyclables collected per household per week with a pre-implementation estimate of ten pounds per week. In order to do this, the following sampling procedure was used. First, the city was divided into 840 blocks. The blocks were then arrayed from largest to smallest based on the estimated number of households they contained and, based on the selection of a random number, every twelfth block was selected. Researchers then accompanied collectors on their weekly round and weighed each bag of recyclables collected on the specified blocks. (Assume each household puts out one bag per week.)
   (a) What are the population elements and the sampling frame?
   (b) What is the primary sampling unit?
   (c) Describe the sampling plan used by the researchers.
   (d) What is the approximate probability that a household will be included in the sample?

8. A researcher is interested in studying the job satisfaction of salespeople in the automatic milking machine industry. She has decided to use probability-proportional-to-size sampling to select a sample. Preliminary work has identified only eight companies that manufacture automatic milkers. Each company is considered to be one first-stage unit. The researcher has determined that she wants to draw four second-stage units per first-stage unit. The total sample size desired is sixteen. The following table has been generated:

Unit	Salespeople	Cumulative Salespeople
1	6	6
2	10	16
3	7	23
4	12	35
5	8	43
6	8	51
7	14	65
8	9	74

   (a) How many first-stage units must be selected?
   (b) Refer to Table 15.6, "Abridged List of Random Numbers," in the preceding chapter. Entering at the first column, first row and moving downward, which first-stage units will be selected for second-stage sampling?

(c) Demonstrate that the probability of any salesperson's being included in the sample is equal.

Endnotes

1. Note that we are again assuming that the normal distribution applies in making this inference. While this assumption is not strictly correct in this instance because of the size of the sample taken from each stratum, we are making it to allow more direct comparison with the interval constructed using simple random sampling. In most situations the normal distribution would hold because the central-limit theorem also applies to the individual strata means, and the linear combination of these means produces a normally distributed overall sample mean.

2. The Census Bureau also uses disproportionate stratified sampling in its surveys. For descriptions of the strata and the sampling rates, see "Eighteen Million Households Will Receive Sample Questionnaire in '90 Census," *Census and You*, 24 (January 1989), p. 2.

3. For an example of the use of systematic sampling, see Mark E. Slama and Armen Tashchian, "Selected Socioeconomic and Demographic Characteristics Associated with Purchasing Involvement," *Journal of Marketing*, 49 (Winter 1985), pp. 72–82.

4. Sudman suggests that when the "sampling interval i is not a whole number, the easiest solution is to use as the interval the whole number just below or above i. Usually, this will result in a selected sample that is only slightly larger or smaller than the initial sample required, and this new sample size will have no noticeable effect on either the accuracy of the results or the budget. For samples in which the interval i is small (generally for i less than 10), so that the rounding has too great an effect on the sample size, it is possible to add or delete the extra cases. . . . It is usually easier to round down in computing i so that the sample is larger, and then to delete systematically." Seymour Sudman, *Applied Sampling* (San Francisco: Academic Press, 1976), p. 54.

5. Earl R. Babbie, *The Practice of Social Research*, 2nd ed. (Belmont, Calif.: Wadsworth Publishing, 1979), p. 167.

6. R. L. Polk and Company, in Taylor, Michigan, publishes some 1,400 directories for most medium-size cities in the range of 50,000 to 800,000 people. The directories contain both an alphabetical list of names and businesses and a street address directory of households. While the alphabetic list can contain a large percentage of inaccurate listings at any one time, the address directory is reasonably accurate since it only omits new construction after the directory is published and the directories are revised every two or three years.

7. Sudman, *Applied Sampling*, p. 81.

8. For an empirical example that uses probability-proportional-to-size cluster sampling, see Johnny Blair and Ronald Czaja, "Locating a Special Population Using Random Digit Dialing," *Public Opinion Quarterly* 46 (Winter 1982), pp. 585–590.

9. *U.S. Census of Housing: 1990, Vol. III, City Blocks*, HC(3)—No. (city number).

10. Sudman, *Applied Sampling*, p. 71.

11. Those interested in pursuing the subject further should see one of the excellent books on the subject, such as F. J. Chaudhary and Daroga Singh, *Theory and Analysis of Sample Survey Design* (New York: John Wiley, 1986); William G. Cochran, *Sampling Techniques*, 3rd ed. (New York: John Wiley, 1977); Morris H. Hansen, William N. Hurwitz, and William G. Madow, *Sample Survey Methods and Theory, Vol. I, Methods and Applications* (New York: John Wiley, 1953); R. L. Jensen, *Statistical Survey Techniques* (New York: John Wiley, 1978); Graham Kalton, *Introduction to Survey Sampling* (Beverly Hills, Calif.: Sage Publications, 1982); Leslie Kish, *Survey Sampling* (New York: John Wiley, 1965); Richard L. Schaeffer, William Mendenhall, and Lyman Ott, *Elementary Survey Sampling*, 2nd ed. (North Scituate, Mass.: Duxbury Press, 1979); or Bill Williams, *A Sampler on Sampling* (New York: John Wiley, 1978). The little book by John Monroe and A. L. Finkner, *Handbook of Area Sampling* (Philadelphia: Chilton, 1959), provides an easy-to-read discussion of the design of an area sample. The books by Sudman, *Applied Sampling*, and A. C. Rosander, *Case Studies in Sample Design* (New York: Marcel Dekker, Inc., 1977), illustrate ways these sampling principles were applied to actual problems, whereas the articles by Seymour Sudman, "Improving the Quality of Shopping Center Sampling," *Journal of Marketing Research*, 17 (November 1980), pp. 423–431, and Edward Blair, "Sampling Issues in Trade Area Maps Drawn from Shopper Surveys," *Journal of Marketing*, 47 (Winter 1983), pp. 98–106, illustrate how the principles of sampling can be applied to improve sampling in shopping center studies. For a historical perspective on the development of survey sampling, see Martin R. Frankel and Lester R. Frankel, "50 Years of Survey Sampling in the United States," *Public Opinion Quarterly*, 51 (Winter 1987), pp. S127–S138.

12. For discussion of the available software, see Thomas L. Pilon, "A Review of PC-Based Software for Marketing Research," paper presented at the 9th Annual Marketing Research Conference in Arlington, Virginia, October 9–12, 1988.

Suggested Additional Readings

There are a number of excellent books that discuss in more detail than here the rationale for and various types of stratified and cluster samples. Three of the better and more extensive treatments are

William Cochran, *Sampling Techniques*, 3rd ed. (New York: John Wiley, 1977).

Morris H. Hansen, William N. Hurwitz, and William G. Madow, *Sample Survey Methods and Theory, Vol. 1, Methods and Applications* (New York: John Wiley, 1953).

Leslie Kish, *Survey Sampling* (New York: John Wiley, 1965).

For more abbreviated but still useful treatments of the principles underlying survey sampling, see

Graham Kalton, *Introduction to Survey Sampling* (Beverly Hills, Calif.: Sage Publications, 1982).

Richard L. Schaeffer, William Mendenhall, and Lyman Ott, *Elementary Survey Sampling*, 2nd ed. (North Scituate, Mass.: Duxbury Press, 1979).

Seymour Sudman, *Applied Sampling* (San Francisco: Academic Press, 1976).

Bill Williams, *A Sampler on Sampling* (New York: John Wiley, 1978).

Sample Size

Learning Objectives

Upon completing this chapter, you should be able to

1. Specify the key factor a researcher must consider in estimating sample size using statistical principles.

2. Cite two other factors researchers must also take into account when estimating a sample size and explain their relationship.

3. Explain in what way the size of the population influences the size of the sample.

4. Specify the circumstances under which the finite population correction factor should be used.

5. Explain the impact that cost has on sample size in stratified or cluster samples.

6. Cite the general rule of thumb for calculating sample size when cross-classification tables are used.

Case in Marketing Research

"How was your dinner this evening?" inquired Rosemary Malgieri of William and Emily Bader as they finished off their veal Picata.

"It was wonderful, as always," answered Emily. Her husband, still chewing, nodded appreciatively.

"I've asked Vincent to bring you some cannoli and cappuccino for dessert, with my compliments."

"How lovely, thank you," replied Emily.

"I feel a little bit awkward intruding on your dinner," began Rosemary, "But I remember Mr. Bader telling me one evening that he works for a marketing research company. I was wondering if there might be a time that I could discuss a little idea of mine. . . ."

"No time like the present," replied William, wiping his mouth and motioning to the empty chair next to him. "That is, if you can manage to leave your duties in the restaurant for a few minutes."

Rosemary motioned to the busboys to clear the Baders' table while she sat down. Vincent appeared at double speed with frothing cups of hot cappuccino and crisp tubes of pastry filled with ricotta cream.

"As I'm sure you know, the restaurant business is a very competitive one. Customer satisfaction is everything. Careless service, a change in the kitchen, can spell death for a restaurant. We have been very lucky here at Malgieri's. We have done very well ever since we opened three years ago. We've had very little turnover in our wait staff, and our chef, while temperamental, has been very loyal to us."

"So what is it you want my help with?" asked William.

"You know that my husband, Michael, and I are partners in this restaurant. I manage the dining room and oversee the kitchen. He handles the financial end. We both agree that it is time to expand. He would like to see us open a second location. He has his eye on a restored storefront in Bentleyville."

"On the west side?" asked Emily. "Where they're doing all the renovations in the old warehouse district?"

"Exactly. Michael feels that the area has a big potential for attracting the after-work crowd from downtown. He's probably right. On the other hand, I'm not convinced that another location is the right way to expand. I feel that Michael and I are the reason Malgieri's is a success. One of us is in the restaurant at all times. With two locations some distance apart, we will have to hire a manager, which will dilute our level of personal control."

"So how would you like to expand?" inquired Emily. "Do you want to increase the size of the existing restaurant?"

"No. I'd like to start a take-out and delivery service. When I was in Chicago for the restaurant show, I noticed that there is a big trend toward restaurant meals at home. I'd like to see us tap into that market. The problem is, I don't know whether to gear the service toward young professionals who don't have time to cook and want an elegant, restaurant-style meal at home or toward busy families who would see our take-out and delivery service as an alternative to a home-cooked meal."

"Well, one way to find out what people want and are willing to pay is to do a survey. A good start would be to survey people who've dined at Malgieri's during the past six months," William replied.

"But how many people would you want to survey?" asked the restauranteur. "I can't afford to spend a lot of money on marketing research. Restaurants operate on a very slim margin. Besides, my husband is determined to open a second restaurant. While solid marketing research might convince him that my plan is the better one, he's not going to agree to invest a lot of money in studying an option he's not particularly interested in."

Discussion Issues

1. What factors might influence sample size for a study that William Bader would do for Malgieri's Restaurant?
2. If you were William Bader, what information might you want to have about the patrons of Malgieri's Restaurant?

Thus far, our discussion of sampling has concentrated on sample type. Another important consideration is sample size. Unless the researcher is going to use a sequential sample, he needs some means of determining the necessary size of the sample before beginning data collection.

Beginning researchers might suppose that the sample should be as large as the client can afford, but the question of sample size is complex. It depends on, among other things, the type of sample, the statistic in question, the homogeneity of the population, and the time, money, and personnel available for the study. We cannot discuss all of these issues adequately in one chapter, but we will present the important statistical principles that determine sample size, using only simple random samples and a few of the more popular statistics. Readers interested in how sample size is determined for stratified or cluster samples should consult one of the standard references on sampling theory. Readers who would like to be able to use a simple random sample to estimate such things as population variance, which is beyond the scope of this chapter, will find help in a good intermediate-level statistics text. The principles are the same in each case, but the formulas differ since they depend on the sampling plan and the statistic in question.

Basic Considerations in Determining Sample Size

Not surprisingly, the sampling distribution of the statistic is the key to determining sample size. You will recall that the sampling distribution of the statistic indicates how the sample estimates vary as a function of the particular sample selected. If a researcher knows the spread of the sampling distribution, he or she can then determine the amount of error that can be associated with any estimate. For instance, in Chapter 15, we saw that the error associated with the estimation of a population mean by a sample mean was given by the standard error of the mean $\sigma_{\bar{x}} = \sigma/\sqrt{n}$, or the population standard deviation divided by the square root of the sample size when the population variance was known, and $s_{\bar{x}} = \hat{s}/\sqrt{n}$, or the sample standard deviation divided by the square root of the sample size when the population variance was unknown. The first factor one must consider in estimating sample size, then, is the standard error of the estimate obtained from the known sampling distribution of the statistic.

A second consideration is how precise the estimate must be. For example, a researcher investigating mean income might want the sample estimate to be within ±\$100 of the true population value. Or a less precise estimate might be required— say, one within ±\$500 of the true value. When the problem involves estimating a population parameter, **precision** can be said to be measured by the magnitude of error, or the size of the estimating interval involved.

Precision The degree of error in a study, or the size of the estimating interval. *Absolute precision* is expressed as within plus or minus so many units. *Relative precision* is expressed relative to the level of the estimate of the parameter.

The degree of precision required will be greatly influenced by the importance of the decision involved in the study from a managerial perspective. If millions of dollars and hundreds of employees' jobs ride on the results of the study, the acceptable range of error is likely to be small. *Absolute precision* is expressed as within plus or minus so many units. *Relative precision* is expressed relative to the level of the estimate of the parameter.

Confidence The degree to which one can feel confident that an estimate approximates the true value.

Another factor that affects sample size is the degree of **confidence** the researcher requires in the estimate. With a sample of fixed size, there is a trade-off between degree of confidence and degree of precision. One can specify either the degree of precision or the degree of confidence, but not both. It is only when sample size is allowed to vary that one can achieve both a specified precision and a specified degree of confidence in the result. Actually, the determination of sample size using statistical principles involves balancing the two considerations against each other.[1]

To understand the distinction between confidence and precision, suppose that we need to know the mean income of a certain population. The most precise measure of that particular parameter would be a point estimate of the mean, which is an estimate that involves a single value with no associated bounds of error. In the case of our study, calculations may show that the population mean income as estimated by the sample mean is $19,243. This point estimate is most assuredly wrong, and thus we can have no confidence in it despite its preciseness. On the other hand, we can have complete confidence in an estimate that the population mean income is between zero and $1 million, but that estimate is too imprecise to be of value.

The U.S. Census Bureau got even more caught up than usual with the issues surrounding precision and confidence after it published the results of the 1980 Census. Accurate Census data are important because they are used to determine representation in the U.S. House of Representatives and are used as a basis for distribution of a variety of funds from federal and state governments. Many people questioned the accuracy of the 1980 count, and some felt so certain that it was flawed that they filed suit against the Census Bureau. Research Window 17.1 describes some of the measures the bureau was taking to assure that the 1990 Census would reflect the accuracy that user groups require.

Ethical Dilemma 17.1

Researchers in the laboratory of a regional food manufacturer recently developed a new dessert topping. This topping was more versatile than those currently on the market because it came in a variety of flavors and thus had more potential uses than a product like Dream Whip, for instance. Although the manufacturer believed that the product had great promise, management also thought it would be necessary to convince the trade of its sales potential in order to get wholesalers and retailers to handle it. The manufacturer consequently decided to test market the product in a couple of areas where it had especially strong distribution. It selected several stores with which it had a long working relationship to carry the product. During the planned two-month test period, product sales did not begin to compare with sales of other dessert toppings. Feeling that such evidence would make it very difficult to gain distribution, the manufacturer decided to do two things: (1) run the test for a longer period, and (2) increase the number of accounts handling the test product. Four months later, the results were much more convincing and management felt more comfortable in approaching the trade with the test market results.

■ Is it ethical to conduct a test market in an area where a firm's distribution or reputation is especially strong?

■ Is it ethical not to report this fact to the trade, thereby causing it to misinterpret the market response to the item?

■ Is it ethical to increase the size of the sample until one secures a result one wants? What if the argument for increasing sample size was that the product was so novel that two months simply was not enough time for consumers to become sufficiently familiar with it?

■ Would it have been more ethical to plan initially for a larger and longer test than to adjust the length and scope of the test on the basis of early results? Why or why not?

Research Window 17.1
Steps the Census Bureau Took to Count the Undercounted

The goal of the U.S. Census is to count every single American every ten years. But not all Americans have a home, speak English, can read, or are eager to cooperate with the government. To make the 1990 Census the most comprehensive ever, the Census Bureau conducted several small-scale "dry runs." During one of these, the 1988 St. Louis Dress Rehearsal Census, several ethnographic studies were carried out to help tackle the specific problems faced by Census enumerators in counting those Americans who have traditionally been undercounted.

Ethnography is a social research method that relies on the researcher's participation in the daily lives of the persons or culture being studied. The ethnographer participates over an extended period of time, watching, listening, and asking questions. Ethnographic behavioral research differs from traditional behavioral research by placing the researcher inside the communities being studied. Rather than studying hard-to-count populations as independent observers, the researchers try to understand them by joining in community life.

As part of the St. Louis Dress Rehearsal Census, a group of sociologists at the University of Missouri at St. Louis, who were engaged in long-term ethnographic study of the homeless, attempted to measure how successful the Dress Rehearsal Census was at counting the homeless. The sociologists observed Census operations from 6 p.m. to 6 a.m. on three nights when enumerators tried to accurately count homeless people at various shelters. The St. Louis researchers placed participant observers among the homeless population to observe and evaluate the Census takers. The group also conducted its own independent count of the street population.

The St. Louis study helped the Census Bureau gain an understanding of the problems Census enumerators are likely to experience when trying to count the homeless. As a result of the study and in order to prepare for the 1990 Census, awareness specialists in the regional offices are boosting their efforts to ensure that every community has good lists of shelters and street locations where homeless people congregate.

Although the inability to read and understand Census Bureau forms is an additional obstacle to measuring the homeless, illiteracy and language barriers are problems that plague many other segments of the population as well. During the St. Louis Dress Rehearsal, a study was conducted to evaluate census coverage of the Laotian community. What the researchers discovered was that when many Laotian families received the Census form, they had no idea what it was; many thought it was a magazine subscription offer, and they threw it out. Others recognized that it was a government form and sought out translators in social service agencies and churches to assist them in responding. The report recommended community "drop-in" assistance centers, where Lao speakers would be available to help.

Several Census Bureau studies deal with the problem of underreporting of household residents among blacks and Hispanics. Since the early seventies, researchers have found that blacks and Hispanics as groups tend to report not the actual number of people living in any one household but the number who "officially" live there. There are several possible explanations for this. For example, there may be more people actually living in a public housing unit than the housing authority allows, or private housing leases may specify who is supposed to live in the house.

The Census Bureau is conducting three simultaneous studies of nonsampling errors of this kind. One focuses on black and Hispanic households in New York City, another examines participation of blacks and Hispanics in "underground economies" (business dealings outside the law) and public-assistance economies, and a third looks at recidivism among black, Hispanic, and Native American parolees and focuses on the difficulty of counting them when they are outside of prison.

Source: "Behavior Studies Look at Groups Traditionally Undercounted," *Census and You*, 24 (July 1989), pp. 3–4.

Figure 17.1   ***Sampling Distribution of Sample Means***

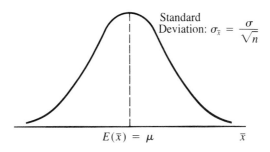

Standard
Deviation: $\sigma_{\bar{x}} = \dfrac{\sigma}{\sqrt{n}}$

$$E(\bar{x}) = \mu \qquad\qquad\qquad \bar{x}$$

Sample Size Determination When Estimating Means

We can best see the interrelationship of the basic factors affecting the determination of sample size by looking at an example. Imagine that the Division of Tourism in a certain midwestern state wants to know the average amount that fishermen spend each year on food and lodging while on fishing trips within the state. Our job as researchers is to use a simple random sample to estimate the mean annual expenditure of those fishermen, using a list of all those who applied for fishing licenses within the year.[2] The central-limit theorem suggests that the distribution of sample means will be normal for samples of reasonable size regardless of the distribution of expenditures in the population of fishermen. Consider, then, the sampling distribution of sample means in Figure 17.1 and distinguish two cases: Case I, in which the population variance is known, and Case II, in which the population variance is unknown.

Case I: Population Variance Known

The population variance, σ^2, might be known from past studies, even though the average expenditures for food and lodging might be unknown, since variation typically changes much more slowly than level.[3] This means that the spread of the distribution given by the standard error of estimate, $\sigma_{\bar{x}}$, as shown in Figure 17.1, is also known up to a proportionality constant, the square root of the sample size, since $\sigma_{\bar{x}} = \sigma/\sqrt{n}$. Thus we have some idea of the first ingredient in sample size determination, the standard error of estimate.

Suppose the director of tourism wanted the estimate to be within ±$25 of the true population value. Total precision would thus be $50, and half-precision, call it *H*, would be $25. The reason we work with *H* instead of the full length of the interval is that the normal curve is symmetrical about the true population mean, and it simplifies the calculations to work with only one-half of the curve.

The remaining item that needs to be specified is the degree of confidence desired in the result. Suppose the director of tourism wants to be 95-percent confident that the interval the researcher constructs will contain the true population mean. This implies that *z* is approximately equal to 2.[4]

Now we have all we need for determining sample size, since it is known that a number of standard deviations on each side of the mean will include a certain proportion of all observations with a normal curve and, in particular, that two standard deviations will include 95 percent of all observations. In Figure 17.1, each observation is a sample mean; the distribution of these sample means is centered about

Suppose that one wished to estimate the mean annual expenditure of fishermen in a certain state. The central-limit theorem suggests that the distribution of sample means will be normal for samples of reasonable size regardless of the distribution of expenditures in the population of fishermen.

Source: General Development Corporation.

the population mean; and two standard deviations are $2\sigma_{\bar{x}}$, or $z\sigma_{\bar{x}}$ in the general case. Note that the standard deviation for this distribution is the standard error of the mean since the distribution at issue is the distribution of sample means. Since we want our estimate to be no more than $25 (= H$) removed from the true population value, we can simply equate the size of the specified half-interval with the number of standard deviations ($= z\sigma_{\bar{x}}$) to yield

$$H = z\sigma_{\bar{x}} \tag{17.1}$$
$$= z\frac{\sigma}{\sqrt{n}}.$$

This equation can be solved for n, since H and z have been specified and σ is known from past studies. Specifically, n can be shown to be equal to

$$n = \frac{z^2}{H^2}\sigma^2 \tag{17.2}$$

or, in words,

$$\text{sample size} = \frac{\begin{array}{c} z, \text{ corresponding to desired} \\ \text{degree of confidence, squared} \times \text{population variance} \end{array}}{\text{desired level of precision squared}}.$$

To illustrate, suppose the historic variation in expenditures on food and lodging as measured by the population standard deviation, σ, was \$100. Then

$$n = \frac{(2)^2}{(25)^2}(100)^2$$

and $n = 64$. Thus only a relatively small sample needs to be taken to estimate the mean expenditure level when the population standard deviation is \$100 and the allowed precision is \$50.

Another way to solve estimation problems is to develop a *nomograph* for the equation and read off the sample size rather than calculate it. A nomograph, or *alignment chart*, is simply a graphical solution to an equation. When values of all but one of the variables in the equation are specified, the value of the remaining variable can be read from the graph. Figure 17.2 is a nomograph for Equation 17.2 when a 95-percent confidence level is desired. By placing a ruler, preferably a clear plastic ruler, on the values $H = 25$ and $\sigma = 100$, we can read the sample size from the column of sample sizes. For a 95-percent confidence level, the nomograph shows that $n = 64$.

Note what happens, however, if the estimate must be twice as precise: \$25 is the total width of the desired interval and $H = 12.5$. Reading from Figure 17.2 or substituting in Equation 17.2,

$$n = \frac{(2)^2}{(12.5)^2}(100)^2$$

and $n = 256$; doubling the precision (halving the total width of the interval) increased the required sample size by a factor of 4. This is the basic trade-off between precision and sample size. Whenever precision is increased by a factor, c, sample size is increased by a factor of c^2. Thus, if the desired precision were \$10 instead of \$50—the estimate must be five times more precise ($c = 5$)—the sample size would be 1,600 instead of 64 ($c^2 = 25$).

One also pays dearly for increases in the degree of confidence. Suppose, for example, that 99-percent confidence is desired rather than 95-percent. We could use the nomograph for a 99-percent confidence interval as shown in Figure 17.3, or we could calculate the result directly, using Equation 17.2, but now letting $z = 3$ instead of 2 as before. Suppose $H = 25$ and $\sigma = 100$ as in the original situation. Then

$$n = \frac{(3)^2}{(25)^2}(100)^2$$

and $n = 144$, whereas $n = 64$ when $z = 2$. When z was increased by a factor of $d(d = \frac{3}{2}$ in the example), sample size increased by a factor of d^2 ($d^2 = \frac{9}{4}$ in the example).

The bottom line in all these calculations is that you should be well aware of the price that must be paid for increased precision and confidence. While we often desire very precise estimates in which we have a great deal of confidence, in the real world somebody must foot the bill incurred by each added degree of precision and confidence.

Figure 17.2   **Nomograph to Determine Sample Size to Estimate a**
Mean with 95-Percent Confidence Level

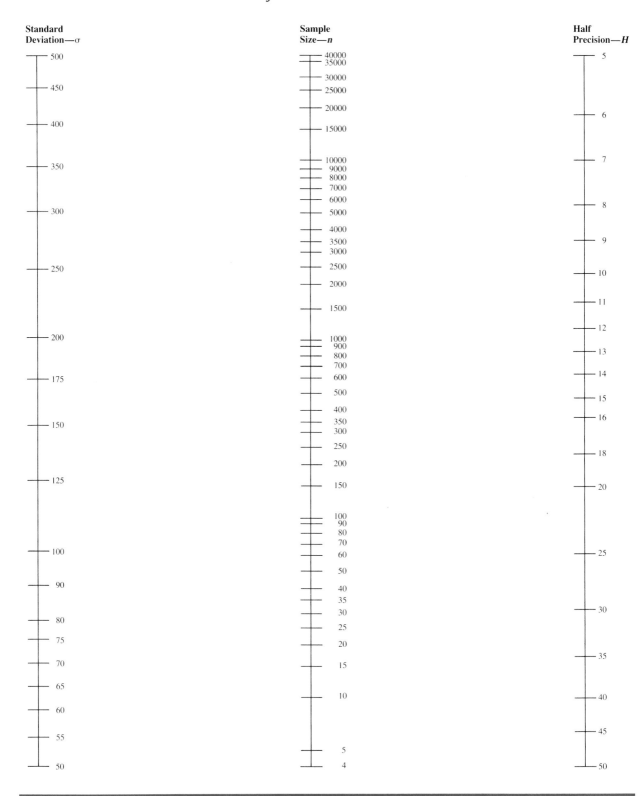

Figure 17.3   **Nomograph to Determine Sample Size to Estimate a**
Mean with 99-Percent Confidence Level

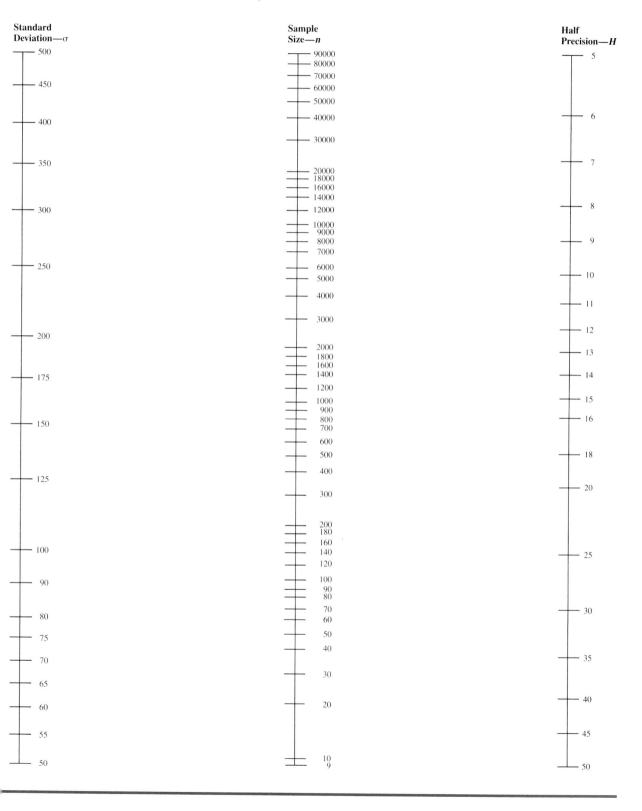

Research Window 17.2
Guidelines for Estimating Variance for
Data Obtained Using Rating Scales

Rating scales are doubly bounded: on a 5-point scale, for instance, responses cannot be less than 1 or greater than 5. This constraint leads to a relationship between the mean and the variance. For example, if a sample mean is 4.6 on a 5-point scale, there must be a large proportion of responses of 5, and it follows that the variance must be relatively small. On the other hand, if the mean is near 3.0, the variance can be potentially much greater. The nature of the relationship between the mean and the variance depends on the number of scale points and on the "shape" of the distribution of responses (e.g., approximately normal or symmetrically clustered around some central scale value, or skewed, or uniformly spread among the scale values). By considering the types of distribution shapes typically encountered in practice, it is possible to estimate variances for use in calculating sample size requirements for a given number of scale points.

The table lists ranges of variances likely to be encountered for various numbers of scale points. The low end of the range is the approximate variance when data values tend to be concentrated around some middle point of the scale, as in a normal distribution. The high end of the range is the variance that would be obtained if responses were uniformly spread across the scale points. Although it is possible to encounter distributions with larger variances than those listed (such as distributions with modes at both ends of the scale), such data are rare.

In most cases, data obtained using rating scales tend to be more uniformly spread out than in a normal distribution. Hence, to arrive at conservative sample size estimates (i.e., sample sizes that are *at least* large enough to accomplish the stated objectives), it is advisable to use a variance estimate at or near the high end of the range listed.

Table 1

Number of Scale Points	Typical Range of Variances
4	0.7 – 1.3
5	1.2 – 2.0
6	2.0 – 3.0
7	2.5 – 4.0
10	3.0 – 7.0

Source: *Research on Research*, No. 37 (Chicago: Market Facts, Inc., undated).

Case II: Population Variance Unknown

In our first case we used examples in which the population variance was known. What happens in the more typical case, when the population variance is unknown? The procedure in estimating the sample size is the same except that an *estimated* value of the population standard deviation, σ, is used in place of the previously known value. Once the sample is selected, the variance calculated from the sample is *used in place of the originally estimated variance* when establishing confidence intervals.

Suppose, for example, that there were no past studies on which to base an estimate of the population standard deviation of σ. How does one then generate an estimate of the population standard deviation? One could do a pilot study.[5] Alternatively, sometimes the variance can be estimated from the conditions surrounding the approach to the problem. Research Window 17.2, for example, discusses the estimation of the variance when rating scales are being used to measure the important variables. Still a third possibility is to take into account the fact that for a normally distributed variable, the range of the variable is approximately equal to plus or minus three standard deviations. Thus, if one can estimate the range of variation, one can estimate the standard deviation by dividing by 6. A little a priori knowledge of the phenomenon is often enough to estimate the range. If the estimate is in error, the consequence is a confidence interval more or less precise than desired. Let us illustrate.

Certainly there would be some licensed fishermen who would spend zero dollars on food and lodging while on fishing trips, since they would only be making one-day trips. Some might also be expected to go on several one-week trips a year. Suppose that fifteen days a year were considered typical of the upper limit, and food and lodging expenses were calculated at $30 per day; the total dollar upper limit would be $450. The range would also be 450 (since they could not spend less than zero); and the estimated standard deviation would then be 450/6 = 75.

With desired precision of ±$25 and a 95-percent confidence interval, the calculation of sample size is now

$$n = \frac{z^2}{H^2} (\text{est. } \sigma)^2$$

$$= \frac{(2)^2}{(25)^2} (75)^2$$

and $n = 36$. The nomograph in Figure 17.2 could also be used to get the same result.

A sample of size 36 would then be selected and the information collected. Suppose these observations generated a sample mean, $\bar{x} = 35$, and a sample standard deviation, $\hat{s} = 60$. The confidence interval is calculated as before,[6] using the expression sample mean $\pm z$ (standard error of the mean), where now the standard error of the mean is estimated using the sample standard deviation, or in symbols, $\bar{x} \pm z s_{\bar{x}}$, or

$$35 \pm 2\frac{\hat{s}}{\sqrt{n}} = 35 \pm 2\frac{60}{\sqrt{36}} = 35 \pm 20$$

or

$$15 \leq \mu \leq 55.$$

Note what has happened. The desired precision was ±$25; the obtained precision is ±$20. The interval is narrower than planned (a bonus) because we overestimated the population standard deviation as judged by the sample standard deviation. If we had underestimated the standard deviation, the situation would have been reversed, and we would have ended up with a wider confidence interval than desired.

Case of Multiple Objectives

Researchers rarely conduct a study to determine only one parameter. It is much more typical for a study to involve multiple objectives. Let us assume more realistically, therefore, that in our study the researcher has been asked also to estimate the annual mean level of expenditures on tackle and equipment by licensed fishermen, and the

Table 17.1   ***Sample Size Needed to Estimate Each of Three Means***

	Variable		
	Expenditures on Food and Lodging	Expenditures on Tackle and Equipment	Miles Traveled
Confidence level	95 percent ($z = 2$)	95 percent ($z = 2$)	95 percent ($z = 2$)
Desired precision	±$25	±$10	±100 miles
Estimated standard deviation	±$75	±$20	±500 miles
Required sample size	36	16	100

number of miles traveled in a year on fishing trips. There are now three means to be estimated. Suppose each is to be estimated with 95-percent confidence and that the desired absolute precision and estimated standard deviation are as given in Table 17.1. Table 17.1 also contains the sample sizes needed to estimate each variable, which were calculated using Equation 17.2.

The three requirements produce conflicting sample sizes. Depending on the variable being estimated, n should equal 36, 16, or 100. The researcher must somehow reconcile these values to come up with a sample size suitable for the study as a whole. The most conservative approach would be to choose $n = 100$, the largest value. This would ensure that each variable would be estimated with the required precision, assuming that the estimates of the standard deviations were accurate.

However, let us assume that of the three means to be determined, the estimate of miles traveled is the least critical. In such a case, it would be wasteful of resources to use a sample size of 100. A better approach would be to focus on those variables that are most critical and to select a sample sufficient in size to estimate them with the required precision and confidence. The variables for which a larger sample size is needed would then be estimated with either a lower degree of confidence or less precision than planned. Suppose in this case that the expenditure data are most critical and that the analyst, therefore, decides on a sample size of 36. Suppose also that the information from this sample of thirty-six fishermen produced a sample mean of $\bar{x} = 300$ and a sample standard deviation of $\hat{s} = 500$ miles traveled. The sample result is thus seen to agree with the original estimate of the population standard deviation, and so the confidence interval estimate will not be affected by inaccuracies here.

Using the standard expression, sample mean $\pm z$ (standard error of the mean), the confidence interval for miles traveled is calculated as

$$\bar{x} \pm z s_{\bar{x}} = \bar{x} \pm z \frac{\hat{s}}{\sqrt{n}} = 300 \pm 2 \frac{500}{\sqrt{36}}$$

or $133.3 \leq \mu \leq 466.7$. Whereas the desired precision was ±100 miles, the obtained precision is ±166.7 miles. In order to produce an estimate with the desired precision, the degree of confidence would have to be lowered from its present 95-percent level.

Sample Size Determination When Estimating Proportions

The preceding examples all concern mean values. Marketers are also often interested in estimating other parameters, such as the population proportion, π. In our example, the researcher might be interested in determining the proportion of licensed fishermen who are from out of state, or from rural areas, or who took at least one overnight trip.

At the beginning of this chapter we suggested three things were needed to determine sample size: a specified degree of confidence, specified precision, and knowledge of the sampling distribution of the statistic. As we noted earlier, the specific requirements of the research problem determine how the first two items will be specified. With percentages, though, precision means that the estimate will be within plus or minus so many percentage points of the true value, as, for example, within ±5 percentage points of the true value.

The remaining consideration then is the sampling distribution of the sample proportion. If the sample elements are selected independently, as can reasonably be assumed if the sample size is small relative to the population size, then the theoretically correct distribution of the sample proportion is the binomial. But the binomial becomes indistinguishable from the normal with large samples or when the population proportion is close to one-half.[7] It is convenient to use the normal approximation when estimating sample size. After the sample is drawn and the sample proportion determined, the researcher can always fall back on the binomial distribution to determine the confidence interval if the normal approximation proves to be in error.

The distribution of sample proportions is centered about the population proportion (Figure 17.4). The sample proportion is an unbiased estimate of the population proportion. The standard deviation of the normal distribution of sample proportions, that is, the standard error of the proportion, denoted by σ_p, is equal to $\sqrt{\pi(1-\pi)/n}$. Since we are working again with the normal curve, the level of precision is again equated to the number of standard deviations the estimate can be removed from the mean value. But now the mean value is the population proportion, while the standard deviation is the standard error of the proportion, that is,

$$H = z\sigma_p. \tag{17.3}$$

Substituting $\sqrt{\pi(1-\pi)/n}$ for σ_p and solving for n yields

$$n = \frac{z^2}{H^2}\pi(1-\pi) \tag{17.4}$$

or, in words,

$$\text{sample size} = \frac{\begin{array}{c}z,\text{ corresponding to desired}\\ \text{degree of confidence, squared}\end{array} \times \begin{array}{c}\text{population}\\ \text{proportion}\end{array} \times \begin{array}{c}(1-\text{population}\\ \text{proportion})\end{array}}{\text{desired level of precision squared}}.$$

Suppose the Division of Tourism is interested in knowing the proportion of all fishermen who took at least one overnight fishing trip in the past year. Suppose also that they wanted this estimate within ±2 percentage points, and they wanted to be

Figure 17.4   ***Approximate Sampling Distribution of the Sample Proportion***

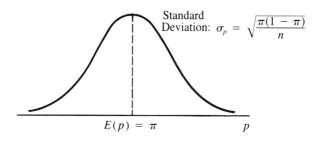

95-percent confident ($z = 2$) in the result. Substituting these values in the formula (Equation 17.4) yields

$$n = \frac{(2)^2}{(.02)^2} \pi(1 - \pi).$$

This equation contains two unknowns: the population proportion being estimated and the sample size. Thus, it is not solvable as it stands. In order to determine sample size, the researcher needs to estimate the population proportion. That is right! *The researcher must estimate the very quantity the study is being designed to discover in order to determine sample size.*

This fact is often bewildering, and certainly disconcerting, to decision makers and beginning researchers alike. Nevertheless, it is true that with proportions one is forced to make some judgment about the approximate value of the parameter in order to determine sample size. This is another example of how information begets information in sample design. To arrive at an initial estimate, researchers might consult past studies or other published data. Alternatively, they might conduct a pilot study. If neither of these options is available, they might simply use informed judgment—a best guess—as to the approximate likely value of the parameter.

A poor estimate will make the confidence interval more or less precise than desired. Suppose, for example, that the best considered judgment was that 20 percent of all licensed fishermen could be expected to take an overnight fishing trip during the year. Sample size is then calculated to be

$$n = \frac{(2)^2}{(.02)^2} (.20)(1 - .20)$$

and $n = 1,600$. After data are collected from the designated 1,600 fishermen, suppose that the sample proportion, p, actually turns out to be equal to 0.40. The confidence interval is then established, employing the sample standard error of the proportion, s_p, to estimate the unknown population standard error of the proportion, σ_p, where

$$s_p = \sqrt{\frac{pq}{n}}$$

where p is the proportion engaging in the behavior in the particular sample selected, and $q = 1 - p$. In the example,

$$s_p = \sqrt{\frac{0.40(0.60)}{1,600}} = \sqrt{\frac{0.24}{1,600}} = 0.012.$$

The confidence interval for the population proportion is given by the expression sample proportion $\pm$ (z) (standard error of the proportion) or

$$p \pm zs_p = 0.40 \pm 2(0.012)$$

or

$$0.376 \le \pi \le 0.424.$$

Note the interval is wider than desired. This is because the sample proportion turned out to be larger than the *estimated* population proportion.

Suppose a wider interval than planned was unacceptable. One way of preventing it is to choose the sample size so as to reflect the "worst of worlds." Note from the formula that the largest sample size will be obtained when the product $\pi(1 - \pi)$ is greatest, since sample size is directly proportional to this quantity. This product is in turn greatest when the population proportion is $\pi = 0.5$, as might be intuitively expected, since if one-half of the population behaves one way and the other half the other way, then one would require more evidence for a valid inference than if a substantial proportion all behaved in the same way.

In the absence of any other information about the population proportion, then, one can always conservatively assume that π is equal to 0.5. The established confidence interval will simply be more precise to the extent that the sample estimate deviates from the assumed 0.5 value. Figures 17.5 and 17.6 are the nomographs for determining sample size to estimate a population proportion with 95-percent confidence level and 99-percent confidence level, respectively.

Population Size and Sample Size

Although you may not have noticed it before, note it now: *The size of the population does not enter into the calculation of the size of the sample.* Except for one slight modification we will discuss shortly, the size of the population has *no direct effect* on the size of the sample.

Although this statement may initially seem strange, consider it carefully and you will see why it is true. When estimating a mean, if all population elements have exactly the same value of the characteristic (for example, if each of our fishermen spent exactly $74 per year on food and lodging), then a sample of one is all that is needed to determine the mean. This is true whether there are 1,000, 10,000, or 100,000 elements in the population. What directly affects the size of the sample is the variability of the characteristic in the population.

Suppose that our example state offered some of the best fishing in the country and drew fishermen from across the nation as well as happy locals. If the parameter we sought to measure was mean number of miles traveled annually on fishing trips, there would be great variation in the characteristic. The more variable the characteristic, the larger the sample needed to estimate it with some specified level of precision. This

Figure 17.5   ***Nomograph to Determine Sample Size to Estimate a Proportion with 95-Percent Confidence Level***

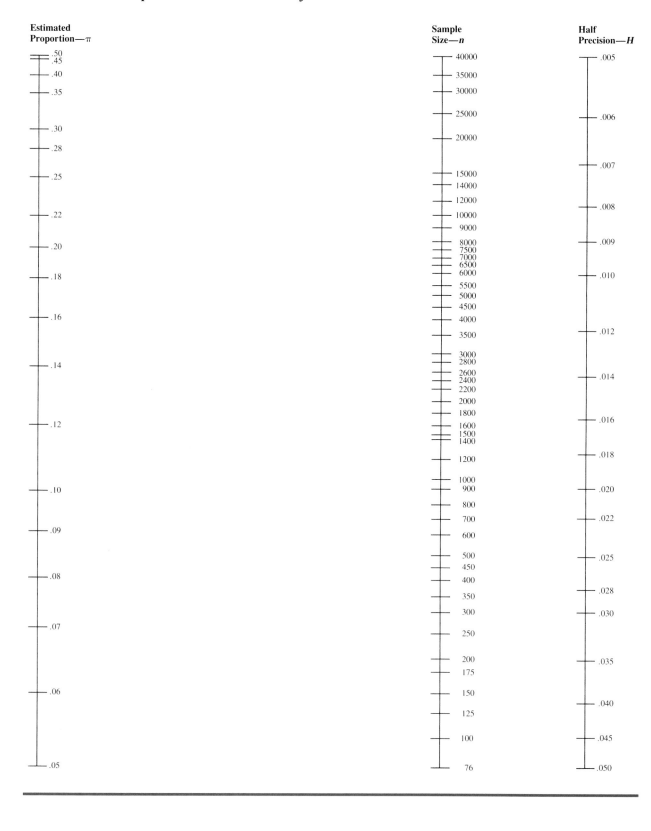

Figure 17.6 **Nomograph to Determine Sample Size to Estimate a Proportion with 99-Percent Confidence Level**

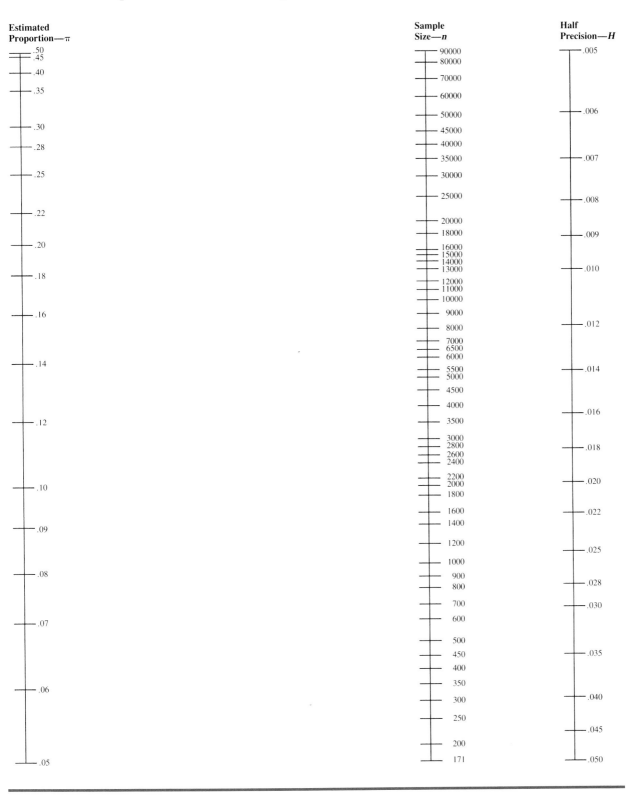

idea not only makes intuitive sense, but we can see it directly expressed in the formulas for determining sample size to estimate a population mean. (See Equation 17.2.) Thus, population size affects sample size only indirectly through variability. In most cases, the larger the population, the greater the *potential* for variation of the characteristic.

It is also true that population size does not affect sample size when estimating a proportion. With a proportion, the determining factor, as we have seen, is the estimated proportion of the population possessing the characteristic; the closer the proportion is to 0.5, the larger the sample that will be needed, regardless of the size of the population. A value of 0.5 signifies greatest variability because one-half of the population possesses the characteristic and one-half does not.

The procedures we have discussed so far apply to situations where the target population is essentially infinite. This is the case in most consumer goods studies. However, when we first began our discussion, we mentioned that there was one modification to the general rule that population size has no direct effect on sample size. In cases where the sample represents a large portion of the population, the formulas must be altered or they will overestimate the required sample. Since the larger the sample, the more expensive the study, the finite population correction factor should be employed.

As we have seen previously, the formula for the standard error of the mean is $\sigma_{\bar{x}} = \sigma/\sqrt{n}$ for most sampling problems. When the finite population correction factor is required, the formula becomes

$$\sigma_{\bar{x}} = \frac{\sigma}{\sqrt{n}} \sqrt{\frac{N - n}{N - 1}}$$

where N denotes the size of the population and n denotes the size of the sample. The factor $(N - n)/(N - 1)$ is the finite population correction factor.

When the estimated sample represents more than 5 percent of the population, the calculated size should be reduced by the finite population correction factor.[8] If, for example, the population contained 100 elements and the calculation of sample size indicated that a sample of 20 was needed, fewer than 20 observations would, in fact, be taken if the finite population correction factor were employed.

The required sample would be given as $n' = nN/(N + n - 1)$, where n was the originally determined size and n' was the revised size. Thus, with $N = 100$ and $n = 20$, only 17 sample elements would, in fact, be employed.

Other Probability Sampling Plans

So far, the discussions of sample size have been based on simple random samples. You should be aware, though, that there are also formulas for determining sample size when other probability sampling plans are used. The formulas are more complex, to be sure, but the same underlying principles apply. One still needs a knowledge of the sampling distribution of the statistic in addition to the research specifications regarding level of precision and degree of confidence.

The issue of sample size is compounded, though, by the fact that one now has a number of strata or a number of clusters with which to work. This means that one must deal with within-strata variability and within- and between-cluster variability in calculating sample size, whereas with simple random sampling only total population variability entered the picture. As before, the more variable the stratum or cluster, the larger the sample that needs to be taken from it, other things being equal. This is precisely the basis for disproportionate stratified sampling discussed in Chapter 16.

Something else that must be equal, though, is cost. Cost did not enter directly into the calculation of sample size with simple random sampling, although it often does affect sample size. If the cost of data collection with a sample of the calculated size would exceed the research budget, the cost could be the factor keeping the sample size below what was indicated by the formulas. In fact, it is not unusual for the size of a simple random sample to be determined by dividing the data-collection budget by the estimated cost per observation. From a strictly statistical viewpoint, however, cost per observation does not enter into the formulas for calculating sample size with simple random samples.

With stratified or cluster samples, cost exerts a direct impact. In calculating sample size, one has to allow for unequal costs per observation by strata or by cluster, and in implementing the sample size calculation, one has to have some initial estimate of these costs. The task then becomes one of balancing variability against costs and assessing the trade-off function relating the two. With a stratified sample, for example, if cost were the same by strata, one would want to sample most heavily the stratum that was most variable. On the other hand, if there were little variation within strata, one might choose to sample more heavily those strata in which the cost per observation was less. Since it is unlikely that the cost per observation or variability will be the same for each stratum, the challenge becomes one of determining sample size by considering the precision likely to result from sampling each stratum at a given rate. Formulas are available for this purpose, as for cluster samples. We shall not go into these formulas here, as they are readily available in the standard works on sampling theory and fall largely in the domain of the sampling specialist.[9] You should be aware, though, that when dealing with stratified or cluster samples, cost per observation by subgroup enters directly into the calculation of sample size.

You should also be aware that there are formulas for determining sample size when the problem is one of hypothesis testing and not confidence interval estimation. Once again, the principles are the same, although there are some additional considerations such as the levels of Type I and Type II errors to be tolerated and the issue of whether it is necessary to detect subtle differences or only obvious differences. We shall not deal with these formulas, since they are also readily available in standard statistical works and their discussion would take us too far afield.[10]

Sample Size Determination Using Anticipated Cross Classifications

Thus far, our discussion of how sample size is determined has been based primarily on the use of statistical principles, with a particular focus on the sampling error involved and the trade-off between degree of confidence and degree of precision. Until now we have limited ourselves to a discussion of these considerations since they are the most important ones theoretically. But in applied problems, the size of the sample is also going to be affected by certain practical considerations. In our discussion of stratified and cluster samples we already mentioned that the size of the budget for the study and the anticipated cost per observation would affect sample size. In addition to that, the size of the sample may also be affected by other, quite subjective factors. For example, researchers may find themselves increasing the size of the sample beyond what is required statistically in order to convince skeptical

| *Table 17.2* | **Number and Proportion of Fishermen Staying Overnight as a Function of Age and Income** |

Income	Age				
	Younger than 20	20–29	30–39	40–49	50 and older
Less than $10,000					
$10,000–$19,999					
$20,000–$29,999					
$30,000–$39,999					
$40,000 and over					

executives, who have little understanding of sampling theory, that they can have confidence in the results of the study.

One of the more important practical bases for determining the size of sample that will be needed is the cross classifications to which researchers plan to subject the data. Suppose that in our task of estimating the proportion of all fishermen who took at least one overnight fishing trip in the past year, we also proposed to determine whether this pattern of behavior was somehow related to an individual's age and income. Assume that the age categories of interest were as follows: younger than 20, 20–29, 30–39, 40–49, and 50 and older. Assume the income categories of interest were as follows: less than $10,000, $10,000–$19,999, $20,000–$29,999, $30,000–$39,999, and $40,000 and over. There are thus five age categories and five income categories for which the proportion of fishermen taking an overnight trip would be estimated.

While we could estimate proportions for each of these variables separately, we should also recognize that the two variables are interrelated in that increases in incomes are typically related to increases in age. To allow for this interdependence, we need to consider the impact of the two variables simultaneously. The way to do this is through a cross-classification table in which age and income jointly define the cells or categories in the table.[11]

Table 17.2, for instance, is a cross-classification table that could be used for the example at hand. Note that this dummy table is complete in all respects except for the numbers that actually go in each of the cells. These would, of course, be determined by the data actually collected on the number and proportion of all those samples who actually made at least one overnight trip. In the table there are twenty-five cells that need estimation. It is unlikely, however, that the decision maker for whom our study is designed is going to be comfortable with an estimate based on only a few cases of the phenomenon. Yet even with a sample of, say, 500 fishermen, there is only a potential of 20 cases per cell (i.e., 500 cases divided by 25 cells) if the sample is evenly divided with respect to the age and income levels considered. Further, it is very unlikely that the sample would split this way, which would put the researcher in the awkward position of estimating the proportion in a cell engaging in this behavior on the basis of fewer than 20 cases.

One can reverse this argument to estimate how large a sample should be taken. First, the researcher would calculate the number of cells in the intended cross classifications. That number can be found by multiplying the number of levels of the characteristics forming each of the cross classifications. In our study, researchers would multiply five levels of income by five levels of age to get twenty-five cells. If it was felt that the decision maker might need at least thirty observations per cell in order to feel comfortable with the cell's estimate, that would mean a sample of 750 subjects would be needed. However, the sample of 750 is unlikely to be evenly distributed across the cells of the table, so the researchers would need to determine how the variables are likely to be distributed. Once the most important cells have been identified, the researcher can compute a sample size large enough to satisfy concerns about sufficient sampling. One general rule of thumb is that "the sample should be large enough so that there are 100 or more units in each category of the major breakdowns and a minimum of 20 to 50 in the minor breakdowns."[12] Major breakdowns refer to the cells in the most critical cross tabulations for the study, and minor breakdowns refer to the cells in the less important cross classifications.

Through all of this one has to make allowances for nonresponses, since some individuals designated for inclusion in the sample will be unavailable and others will refuse to participate. The researcher "builds up" the sample, so to speak, from the size of the cross-classification table with due allowance for these considerations.

Perhaps cross classification will not be the basic method used to analyze the data. Perhaps, instead, other statistical techniques will be used. If so, the same arguments for determining sample size apply. That is, one needs a sufficient number of cases to satisfy the requirements of the technique, so as to inspire confidence in the results. Different techniques have different sample size requirements, often expressed by the degrees of freedom required for the analysis. Readers interested in using a particular statistical technique for analysis should pay close attention to the sample size requirements for the techniques to be used safely. For now, we merely wish to reiterate the important point made earlier when introducing the research process— that the stages are very much related, and a decision with respect to one stage can affect all of the other stages. In this case a decision with respect to Stage 6 regarding the method of analysis can have an important impact on Stage 5, which precedes it, with respect to the size of the sample that should be selected. Therefore, the researcher needs to think through the entire research problem, including how the data will be analyzed, before beginning the data-collection process.

Ethical
Dilemma 17.2
A recent discussion between the account manager for an independent research agency and the marketing people for the client left the account manager feeling perplexed. After numerous discussions, the account manager believed that she had a good handle on the client's problem and major concerns. On the basis of this understanding, she had developed a set of dummy tables by which the client's concerns could be investigated. During the most recent meeting, she had presented these to the client. The client had completely accepted the account manager's recommendation about how the data would be viewed, and closed the meeting by asking how large a sample the account manager would recommend and how much the study would cost. The account manager's anxiety was caused by the fact that she believed from the earlier discussions and some preliminary investigation that two of the seven hypotheses were especially promising. The sample size that was needed to investigate these two hypotheses was almost 60-percent smaller than that needed to address some of the other hypotheses because of the fewer cells in the cross-

Table 17.3   ***Typical Sample Sizes for Studies of Human and Institutional Populations***

Number of Subgroup Analyses	People or Households		Institutions	
	National	Regional or Special	National	Regional or Special
None or few	1,000–1,500	200–500	200–500	50–200
Average	1,500–2,500	500–1,000	500–1,000	200–500
Many	2,500+	1,000+	1,000+	500+

Source: Seymour Sudman, *Applied Sampling* (San Francisco, Academic Press, 1976), p. 87.

classification table. The account manager was in a dilemma about whether she should take the safe route and recommend the larger sample size to the client and thereby assure that all of the planned cross-classifications could be completed or whether she should go with her instinct and recommend the smaller sample size and save the client some money.

- What would you recommend that the account manager do?
- Is it ethical for the account manager to recommend the larger sample size when she is fairly certain that the smaller one will provide the answers the client needs? Is it ethical to do the reverse and recommend the smaller sample when there is some risk that the smaller sample will not adequately answer the problem that the firm was hired to solve?
- What are the account manager's responsibilities to the client in a case like this?

Determining Sample Size Using Historic Evidence

A final method by which an analyst can determine the size of the sample to employ is to use the size that others have used for similar studies in the past. While this may be different from the ideal size in a given problem, the fact that the contemplated sample size is in line with that used for similar studies is psychologically comforting, particularly to inexperienced researchers. Table 17.3, which summarizes the evidence, provides a crude yardstick in this respect. Note that national studies typically involve larger samples than regional or special studies. Note further that the number of subgroup analyses has a direct impact on sample size.

Back to the Case

At 3:00 in the afternoon Malgieri's Restaurant looked very different than it did at night when it was filled with people. Without tablecloths, the tables were revealed to be pitted and worn. In one corner, busboys in shirtsleeves sat folding napkins while they watched soap operas on a small black-and-white television.

Michael and Rosemary Malgieri were seated at another table going over what looked like receipts. They greeted William Bader warmly, and if Michael objected to his wife's exploring a business alternative that he didn't support, he certainly didn't show it.

"I've been giving Rosemary's idea of a take-out and delivery service a good deal of thought," began William. "In order to know whether it would be a profit-making venture for you, I think the single most important thing to find out is where your customers live relative to the restaurant. People won't go too far to pick up food, for fear that it'll be cold when they get home and because the whole idea of takeout is convenience. And if you're going to add a delivery service, you'll have the same con-cerns about hot food, as well as time and fuel costs for deliveries far away."

"So how about if tonight we instruct the wait staff to ask all patrons where they live and how far it is from the restaurant? They can ask when the patrons pay their check. We'll serve at least a hundred people tonight: that should give us a pretty good idea," suggested Michael.

"It would be a start, but not a particularly accurate one. I'd feel more comfortable if you would let me write out a little question-and-answer sheet for each waiter to read to the patrons on a given night. That way we'd be sure that everyone was re-sponding to the same questions, and I'd be able to tabulate the results with some confidence. Also, I know that a hundred people sounds like a lot, but I'm not sure of how reliable an estimate of average miles traveled would be, based on that number of respondents. I'd feel much more comfortable if you'd be willing to repeat the survey on one or two more nights if it turned out to be necessary."

"That seems reasonable," replied Rosemary.

"Then, I propose that if the simple location survey shows enough patrons clustered within a comfort-able radius of the restaurant, we do another patron survey. The focus of this one would be to explore age, income, and interest in a take-out and delivery service. That way we'd be able to see whether it would be better to gear your out-of-restaurant menu toward people wanting restaurant meals or those wanting family-style meals."

"How many people would you like to survey in the second stage?" asked Michael.

"Again, I'd like to keep that open-ended," replied William. "In any sample there's a trade-off be-tween degree of confidence and de-gree of precision. If we allow our-selves to vary the sample size to produce an estimate with precision and confidence levels that we want, then you're going to feel confident putting your time and dollars behind the decision you make."

Summary

Learning Objective 1: Specify the key factor a researcher must consider in estimating sample size using statistical principles.

The key factor a researcher must consider in estimating sample size is the standard error of the estimate obtained from the known sampling distribution of the statistic.

Learning Objective 2: Cite two other factors researchers must also take into account when estimating a sample size and explain their relationship.

When estimating a sample size, researchers must consider both how precise the estimate must be and the degree of confidence that is required in the estimate. With a sample of fixed size, there is a trade-off between degree of confidence and degree of precision. One can specify either the degree of precision or the degree of confidence, but not both. It is only when sample size is allowed to vary that one can achieve both a specified precision and a specified degree of confidence in the result. The determination of sample size involves balancing the two considerations against each other.

Learning Objective 3: Explain in what way the size of the population influences the size of the sample.

In most instances, the size of the population has no direct effect on the size of the sample but only affects it indirectly through the variability of the characteristic; and sample size is directly proportional to variability.

Learning Objective 4: Specify the circumstances under which the finite population correction factor should be used.

In general, when the estimated sample represents more than 5 percent of the population, the calculated sample size should be reduced by the finite population correction factor.

Learning Objective 5: Explain the impact that cost has on sample size in stratified or cluster samples.

With stratified or cluster samples, cost exerts a direct impact. In calculating sample size, one has to allow for unequal costs per observation by strata or by cluster; and in implementing the sample size calculation, one has to have some initial estimate of these costs. The task, then, becomes one of balancing variability against costs and assessing the trade-off function relating the two.

Learning Objective 6: Cite the general rule of thumb for calculating sample size when cross-classification tables are used.

When calculating sample size by using cross-classification tables, the general rule of thumb is that the sample should be large enough so that there are 100 or more units in each category of the major breakdowns and a minimum of 20 to 50 in the minor breakdowns.

Discussion Questions, Problems, and Projects

1. A survey was being designed by the marketing research department of a medium-size manufacturer of household appliances. The general aim was to assess customer satisfaction with the company's dishwashers. As part of this general objective, management wished to measure the average maintenance expenditure per year per household, the average number of malfunctions or breakdowns per year, and the number of times a dishwasher is cleaned within a year. Management wished to be 95-percent confident in the results. Further, the magnitude of the error was not to exceed ±$4 for maintenance expenditures, ±1 for malfunctions, and ±4 for cleanings. The research department noted that while some households would spend nothing on maintenance expenditures per year, others might spend as much as $120. Also, while some dishwashers would experience no breakdowns within a year, the maximum expected would be no more than three. Finally, while some dishwashers might not be cleaned at all during the year, others might be cleaned as frequently as once a month.
    (a) How large a sample would you recommend if each of the three variables were considered separately? Show all your calculations.
    (b) What size sample would you recommend *overall* given that management felt that the expenditure on repairs was most important and the number of cleanings least important to know accurately?
    (c) The survey indicated that the average maintenance expenditure was $30, and the standard deviation was $15. Estimate the confidence interval for the population parameter μ. What can you say about the degree of precision?
2. The management of a major dairy wanted to determine the average ounces of milk consumed per resident in the state of Montana. Past trends indicated that the

variation in milk consumption (σ) was 4 ounces. A 95-percent confidence level is required and the error is not to exceed $\pm\frac{1}{2}$ ounce.

 (a) What sample size would you recommend? Show your calculations.

 (b) Management wanted to double the level of precision and increase the level of confidence to 99 percent. What sample size would you recommend? Show your calculations. Comment on your results.

3. The manager of a local recreational center wanted to determine the average amount each customer spent on traveling to and from the center. On the basis of the findings, the manager was planning on raising the entrance fee. The manager noted that customers living near the center would spend nothing on traveling. On the other hand, customers living at the other side of town had to travel about 15 miles and spent about 20 cents per mile. The manager wanted to be 95-percent confident of the findings and did not want the error to exceed ±10 cents.

 (a) What sample size should the manager use to determine the average travel expenditure? Show your calculations.

 (b) After the survey was conducted, the manager found the average expenditure to be $1.00, and the standard deviation was $0.60. Construct a 95-percent confidence interval. What can you say about the level of precision?

4. A large manufacturer of chemicals recently came under severe criticism from various environmentalists for its disposal of industrial effluent and waste. In response, management launched a campaign to counter the bad publicity it was receiving. A study of the effectiveness of the campaign indicated that about 20 percent of the residents of the city were aware of the campaign and the company's position. In conducting the study, a sample of 400 was used and a 95-percent confidence interval was specified. Three months later, it was believed that 30 percent of the residents were aware of the campaign. However, management decided to do another survey and specified a 99-percent confidence level and a margin of error of ±2 percentage points.

 (a) What sample size would you recommend for this study? Show all your calculations.

 (b) After doing the survey it was found that 50 percent of the population was aware of the campaign. Construct a 99-percent confidence interval for the population parameter.

5. Score-It, Inc., is a large manufacturer of video games. The marketing research department is designing a survey in order to determine attitudes toward the products. Additionally, the percentage of households owning video games and the average usage rate per week are to be determined. The department wants to be 95-percent confident of the results and does not want the error to exceed ±3 percentage points for video game ownership and ±1 hour for average usage rate. Previous reports indicate that about 20 percent of the households own video games and the average usage rate is 15 hours with a standard deviation of 5 hours.

 (a) What sample size would you recommend, assuming only the percentage of households owning video games is to be determined? Show all your calculations.

 (b) What sample size would you recommend, assuming only the average usage rate per week is to be determined? Show all your calculations.

 (c) What sample size would you recommend, assuming both the above variables are to be determined? Why?

After the survey was conducted, the results indicated that 30 percent of the households owned video games and the average usage rate was 13 hours with a standard deviation of 4 hours.

 (d) Compute the 95-percent confidence interval for the percentage of individuals owning video games. Comment on the degree of precision.

 (e) Compute the 95-percent confidence interval for the average usage rate. Comment on the degree of precision.

6. The local gas and electric company in a city in the northeast United States recently started a campaign to encourage people to reduce unnecessary use of gas and

electricity. To assess the effectiveness of the campaign, management wanted to do a survey to determine the proportion of people that had adopted the recommended energy-saving measures.

(a) What sample size would you recommend if the error was not to exceed ±.025 percentage points and the confidence level was to be 90 percent? Show your calculations.

(b) The survey indicated that the proportion adopting the measures was 40 percent. Estimate the 90-percent confidence interval. Comment on the level of precision. Show your calculations.

7. Assume you are a marketing research analyst for TV Institute, and you have just been given the assignment of estimating the percentage of all American households that watched the ABC movie last Sunday night. You have been told that your estimate should have a precision of ±1 percentage point and that there should be a 95-percent "probability" of your being "correct" in your estimate. Your first task is to choose a sample of the appropriate size. Make any assumptions that are necessary.

(a) Recast the problem in a statistical format.

(b) Compute the sample size that will satisfy the required specifications.

(c) What is the required sample size if the precision is specified as ±2 percentage points?

(d) What would be the sample size if the probability of being "correct" were decreased to 90 percent, keeping the precision at ±1 percentage point?

(e) If you had only enough time to take a sample of Size 100, what precision could you expect from your estimate? (Assume a 95-percent confidence interval.)

(f) Assume that instead of taking a sample from the entire country (60 million households), you would like to restrict yourself to one state with one million households. Would the sample size computed in (b) be too large? Too small? Explain.

8. Assume TV Institute has hired you to do another study, this time estimating the average number of hours of television viewing per week per family in the United States. You are asked to generate an estimate within ±5 hours. Further, there should be 95-percent confidence that the estimate is correct. Make any assumptions that are necessary.

(a) Compute the sample size that will satisfy the required specifications.

(b) What would be the required sample size if the precision were changed to ±10 hours?

9. The manager of a local bakery wants to determine the average expenditure per household on bakery products. Past research indicates that the standard deviation is $10.

(a) Calculate the sample size for the various levels of precision and confidence. Show your calculations:

	Desired Precision (±)	Desired Confidence	Estimated Sample Size
1	0.50	0.95	
2	1.00	0.99	
3	0.50	0.90	
4	0.25	0.90	
5	0.50	0.99	
6	0.25	0.95	
7	1.00	0.90	
8	1.00	0.95	
9	0.25	0.99	

(b)   Which alternative gives the largest estimate for sample size? Explain.

10.   A manufacturer of liquid soaps wishes to estimate the proportion of individuals using liquid soaps as opposed to bar soaps. Prior estimates of the proportions are listed below.

(a)   For the various levels of precision and confidence indicated, calculate the needed size of the sample.

	Desired Precision in Percentage Points(±)	Desired Confidence	(%) Estimated Proportion	Estimated Sample Size
1	6	0.99	20	
2	2	0.90	10	
3	6	0.99	10	
4	4	0.95	30	
5	2	0.90	20	
6	2	0.99	30	
7	6	0.90	30	
8	4	0.95	10	
9	4	0.95	20	

(b)   Which alternative gives the largest estimate of the sample size? Explain.

11.   Your World, Inc., is a large travel agency located in Cincinnati, Ohio. Management is concerned about its declining leisure travel-tour business. It believes that the profile of those engaging in leisure travel has changed in the past few years. To determine if that is indeed the case, management decides to conduct a survey to determine the profile of the current leisure travel-tour customer. Three variables are identified that require particular attention. Prior to conducting the survey, the following three dummy tables are developed.

	Age			
Income	18–24	25–34	35–54	55+
0–$9,999				
$10,000–$19,999				
$20,000–$29,999				
$30,000–$39,999				
$40,000 and over				

	Education			
Age	Some High School	High School Graduate	Some College	College Graduate
18–24				
25–34				
35–54				
55+				

	Education			
Income	Some High School	High School Graduate	Some College	College Graduate
0–$9,999				
$10,000–$19,999				
$20,000–$29,999				
$30,000–$39,999				
$40,000 and over				

(a) How large a sample would you recommend be taken? Justify your answer.

(b) The survey produced the following incomplete table for the variables of age and education. Complete the table on the basis of the assumption that the two characteristics are independent (even though that assumption is wrong). On the basis of the completed table, do you think an appropriate sample size was used? If yes, why? If no, why not?

	Education				
Age	Some High School	High School Graduate	Some College	College Graduate	Total
18–24					100
25–34					200
35–54					350
55+					350
Total	200	400	300	100	1,000

12. You are the assistant director of political research for the ABC television network. It is 1996, and Marge Simpson and Ethan Martin are running for president of the United States of America. You need to furnish a prediction of the percentage of the vote going to Martin, assuming the election was held today, for tomorrow's evening newscast. You want to be 95-percent confident in your prediction and desire a total precision of 6 percent.

(a) Assume that you have no reliable information concerning the percentage of the population that prefers Martin. What sample size will you use for the project?

(b) Assume that a similar poll, taken 30 days ago, revealed that 40 percent of the respondents would vote for Martin. Taking this information into account, what sample size will you use for the project?

(c) Which of the two sample sizes you have just calculated would you prefer to use for your study? Why?

(d) Most polls of this type are conducted by telephone. When a potential respondent answers the phone, what is the *first* question you should ask? Why?

13. A city is considering implementing a "pay as you throw" billing system for residential garbage pickup. Under the plan, a household would be charged by the pound for garbage removal. As part of its proposal to the city council, the sanitation department needs to calculate an average monthly bill per household under the proposed system. To do so, the sanitation department plans to weigh the garbage collected from a random sample of households over the next two months. Based on an informal poll of route drivers, the department estimates that a household throws away between 30 and 90 pounds of garbage a month. The department wants the estimate to be within ±2 pounds of the true population average, and the city council insists that it will accept only a figure that has a 99-percent probability of being correct.

(a) What sample size would you recommend?

(b) You have just been informed that the budget has been cut and the size of the sample must be cut by 20 percent. However a 99-percent confidence level must be maintained. What is the new sample size? What does this mean in terms of the precision of the estimate?

Endnotes

1. Bayesian analysts also consider the cost of wrong decisions when determining sample size. For a comparison of classical and Bayesian procedures for determining sample size, see Seymour Sudman, *Applied Sampling* (San Francisco: Academic Press, 1976), pp. 85–105.

2. The problem would be of interest to the tourist industry, and it also could be of interest to the division of state government concerned with economic development. The problem was chosen because the availability of a list of population elements allows a simple random sample to be selected.

3. See Morris H. Hansen, William N. Hurwitz, and William G. Madow, *Sample Survey Methods and Theory: Vol. 1, Methods and Applications* (New York: John Wiley, 1953), for one of the best treatments on securing variance estimates from past data, especially pp. 450–455.

4. The variable z more correctly equals 1.96 for a 95-percent confidence interval. The approximation $z = 2$ is used since it simplifies the calculations.

5. See Raphael Gillett, "Confidence Interval Construction by Stein's Method: A Practical and Economical Approach to Sample Size Determination," *Journal of Marketing Research*, 26 (May 1989), pp. 237–240, for discussion of how the pilot study results can be used not only to develop an estimate of the population variance but also to produce an estimate of the population mean corresponding to the specified confidence level and desired interval size.

6. One would more strictly use the t distribution to establish the interval, since the population variance was unknown. The example was framed using the approximate $z = 2$ value for a 95-percent confidence interval so as to better illustrate the consequences of a poor initial estimate of σ.

7. The strict requirement is that $n\pi$ must be above a certain level if the normal curve is to provide a good approximation to the binomial, where π is the population proportion and n is the sample size. Some books hold that $n\pi$ must be greater than 5, while others suggest that the product must be greater than 10.

8. The 5-percent correction factor is not a hard-and-fast rule. Some books contend that the finite population correction factor should be ignored if the sample includes no more than 10 percent of the population. Cochran suggests that the finite population correction can be ignored whenever the "sampling fraction does not exceed 5 percent and for many purposes even if it is as high as 10 percent." William G. Cochran, *Sampling Techniques*, 3rd ed. (New York: John Wiley, 1977), p. 25. Ignoring the finite population correction will result in overestimating the standard error of estimate.

9. See, for example, Cochran, *Sampling Techniques;* Hansen, Hurwitz, and Madow, *Sample Survey Methods;* Leslie Kish, *Survey Sampling* (New York: John Wiley, 1965); R. L. Jensen, *Statistical Survey Techniques* (New York: John Wiley, 1978); Richard L. Schaeffer, William Mendenhall, and Lyman Ott, *Elementary Survey Sampling*, 2nd ed. (North Scituate, Mass.: Duxbury Press, 1979); Bill Williams, *A Sampler on Sampling* (New York: John Wiley, 1978); or Richard M. Jaeger, *Sampling in Education and the Social Sciences* (New York: Longman, 1984).

10. Computer-based expert systems that rely on artificial intelligence techniques also exist for determining sample size. These systems guide the researcher through a series of questions about the needed degree of confidence, precision, variability, and so on, and, based on the answers, perform the tedious computations concerning the needed sample size. See, for example, Ex-Sample,™ which is available from the Idea Works, in Columbia, Missouri.

11. Chapter 19 discusses the procedures for setting up and analyzing cross-classification tables so that the proper inferences can be drawn.

12. Sudman, *Applied Sampling*, p. 30.

Suggested Additional Readings

For a more thorough discussion of the estimation of sample size for different types of samples and characteristics other than the mean and proportion, see

William Cochran, *Sampling Techniques*, 3rd ed. (New York: John Wiley, 1977).

Morris H. Hansen, William N. Hurwitz, and William G. Madow, *Sample Survey Methods and Theory, Vol. 1, Methods and Applications* (New York: John Wiley, 1953).

Leslie Kish, *Survey Sampling* (New York: John Wiley, 1965).

Richard L. Schaeffer, William Mendenhall, and Lyman Ott, *Elementary Survey Sampling*, 2nd ed. (North Scituate, Mass.: Duxbury Press, 1979).

Chapter Eighteen

Collecting the Data: Field Procedures and Nonsampling Errors

Learning Objectives

Upon completing this chapter, you should be able to

1. Explain what sampling error is.

2. Cite the two basic types of nonsampling errors and describe each.

3. Outline several ways in which noncoverage bias can be reduced.

4. Explain what error due to nonresponse is.

5. Cite the standard definition for *response rate.*

6. Identify the two main sources of nonresponse bias.

7. Define *contact rate.*

8. Cite some of the factors that may contribute to a respondent's refusal to participate in a study.

9. Identify three factors that may be a source of bias in the interviewer-interviewee interaction.

10. Discuss the types of interviewer behaviors that may lead to response bias.

Case in Marketing Research

Lucy Lindenbloom was dressed for combat, or at least that's how she thought of it as she prepared herself to go to work. Lindenbloom was employed by the U.S. government, but not as a soldier. She was an official field interviewer for the U.S. Census Bureau, and her years on the job had taught her to be prepared for the worst.

She was dressed neatly but plainly, incorporating several layers because of the uncertain March weather. She had a raincoat in the trunk of her car and comfortable shoes on her feet. On the front seat of her aging Honda lay a map of the greater Plainfield area, a dozen No. 2 pencils, a ponderous manual of instructions, and a box of Kleenex tissues.

While most people thought that all the Census Bureau did was count noses every ten years, Lindenbloom had been involved in any number of other information-collection operations. Presently, she was gathering data for the Current Population Survey, a continuing program on which national unemployment figures are based. She had a list of people to contact that week in order to ask them about their work status during the previous week.

Her assignment that day was to interview a list of people in one of the city's most affluent suburbs, Moreland Heights. Early on in her career she might have looked forward to a day spent in a neighborhood where large houses were set back on deep, manicured lawns. Instead, she now foresaw a day filled with trekking up long driveways.

The first address on her list was 2720 Shelley Drive. Lindenbloom parked her car at the end of the block and set off up the drive of 2720. She hadn't gone more than a couple of yards when two huge black Labradors came charging toward her. Instinctively she reached for the can of canine repellent that she kept taped to the back of her clipboard. She stopped walking and spoke quietly to the dogs, who, after a while, seemed content enough to let her continue.

When she rang the doorbell, she heard the sound of more dogs barking within, but there was no response. Seeing cars parked behind the house and lights on in the upstairs windows, Lucy went around to the side door and rang the bell. After still receiving no response, she opened the storm door and made vigorous use of the door knocker. Inside, the dogs were getting hysterical.

Finally, the face of a young woman appeared at the window and she opened the door.

"Oh, hi," she said. "I hope you haven't been at the door long. I was upstairs riding the exercise bike and I didn't hear the bell. What can I do for you?"

"I'm a field interviewer for the U.S. Census Bureau," said Lindenbloom, showing her official ID card, "and I'm trying to locate Suzanne Cooper to ask her some questions about her employment during the last week."

"Suzanne—employed?" asked the young woman with a laugh. "Not unless you count tennis and shopping as employment."

"I take it you're not Mrs. Cooper," said Lindenbloom.

"No, I'm her sister. I'm just staying here to keep an eye on the dogs."

"Could you tell me when I might be able to find Mr. or Mrs. Cooper at home?"

"I'm not sure. They're in Italy right now. Rick had some business there, and Suzanne went along. I don't know—I think they're due back the middle of April."

Lindenbloom thanked the young woman for her time and continued down the street to 2722. When an older woman in a white uniform came to the door, Lindenbloom introduced herself and asked to speak to Mr. or Mrs. Evans.

"Mr. Evans doesn't live here anymore," said the woman. "He ran off with some woman from his office. He and Mrs. Evans are getting a divorce."

"I see," replied Lindenbloom. "Is Mrs. Evans at home?"

"No, she's at work. She's a lawyer downtown."

"Do you know when I might be able to catch her at home?"

"It's hard to say. Some nights she's back home by supper time; other nights she's got a meeting. I know the baby-sitter's coming tonight, so I guess she won't be home."

"Thanks for your time," replied Lindenbloom.

By midafternoon Lindenbloom had been to every house on Shelley. She had talked to six housekeepers, one window cleaner and three nannies. She felt as if she'd walked about 20 miles.

Discussion Issues

1. Besides not-at-homes and problems in coverage of the specified sampling areas, what other problems might field interviewers expect to encounter when gathering data?
2. What procedures might be helpful in alleviating such problems?
3. What problems might interviewers encounter in personal or telephone surveys that may not be a problem in mail surveys? What particular problems might mail surveys pose?

The data-collection task is the one that most often comes to mind when people think of marketing research. At this stage in the research process, some kind of a field force is used, operating either in the field or from an office as in a phone or mail survey. In this chapter we will focus on the various things that can go wrong in conducting a field study, with a special emphasis on sources of error we have not discussed in earlier chapters. A person who understands the potential sources of error in data collection will have insights that will be useful in evaluating the research information upon which decisions must be based.

Impact and Importance of Nonsampling Errors

Sampling error The difference between the observed values of a variable and the long-run average of the observed values in repetitions of the measurement.

Two basic types of errors arise in research studies: *sampling errors* and *nonsampling errors*. The concept of **sampling error** underlies much of the discussion in Chapters 15, 16, and 17. Basic to that discussion was the concept of the sampling distribution of some statistic, be it the sample mean, sample proportion, or whatever. The sampling distribution arises because of sampling error. The sampling distribution reflects the fact that the different possible samples that could be drawn under the sampling plan will produce different estimates of the parameter. The statistic varies from sample to sample simply because we are only sampling part of the population in each case. Sampling error then is "the difference between the observed values of a variable and the long-run average of the observed values in repetitions of the measurement."[1] As we saw, sampling errors can be reduced by increasing sample size. The distribution of the sample statistic becomes more and more concentrated about the long-run average value, as the sample statistic is more equal from sample to sample, when it is based on a larger number of observations.

Nonsampling error Error that arises in research and that is not due to sampling; nonsampling error can occur because of errors in conception, logic, interpretation of replies, statistics, arithmetic, tabulating, coding, or reporting.

Nonsampling errors reflect the many other kinds of error that arise in research, even when the survey is not based on a sample. They can be random or nonrandom. Nonrandom nonsampling errors are the more troublesome of the two. Random errors produce estimates that vary from the true value; sometimes these estimates are above and sometimes below the true value, but on a random basis. The result is that, if there are no sampling errors, the sample estimate will equal the population value. Nonrandom nonsampling errors, on the other hand, tend to produce mistakes only in one direction. They tend to bias the sample value away from the population parameter. Nonsampling errors can occur because of errors in conception, logic, interpretation of replies, statistics, arithmetic, tabulation, coding, or reporting. They are so pervasive that they have caused one writer to lament:

> The roster of possible troubles seems only to grow with increasing knowledge. By participating in the work of a specific field, one can, in a few years, work up considerable methodological expertise, much of which has not been and is not likely to be written down. *To attempt to discuss every way a study can go wrong would be a hopeless venture.*[2] (Emphasis added.)

Not only are nonsampling errors pervasive, but they are not as manageable as sampling errors. Sampling errors decrease with increases in sample size. Nonsampling errors do not necessarily decrease with increases in sample size. They may, in fact, increase. Also, sampling errors can be estimated if probability sampling procedures are used. With nonsampling errors, it is difficult even to predict the direction, much less the size, of the error.

True, nonsampling errors bias the sample value away from the population parameter, but in many studies it is hard to see whether they cause underestimation or overestimation of the parameter. Nonsampling errors also distort the reliability of sample estimates. The bias they cause may increase the standard error of estimates of particular statistics to such an extent that the confidence interval estimates turn out to be faulty.

One study, the Consumer Savings Project, conducted at the University of Illinois, demonstrated striking evidence of this phenomenon. In that study, researchers contrasted consumers' reports of financial assets and debts with known data.

> The empirical studies presented . . . indicate in striking fashion that nonsampling errors are not simply a matter of theory, but do in fact exist and are mainly responsible for the pronounced tendency of survey data to understate aggregates. . . . Not only was this bias present in the survey data, but in many instances the contribution of nonsampling errors to the total variance in the data was so large as to *render meaningless confidence intervals computed by the usual statistical formulas*. . . . The magnitude of this type of error *tends, if anything, to increase with sample size*.[3] (Emphasis added.)

Further, more sophisticated samples are not the answer to eliminating nonsampling errors.

> If the findings of this project are any indication, increasing attention must be given to the detection and correction of nonsampling errors. Such attention will be needed particularly in the conduct of large-scale, well-designed probability samples, for as the efficiency of a sample design increases and the size of sampling variances decreases, the effect of nonsampling errors becomes progressively more important. Since nonsampling variances are virtually unaffected by sample size, we are faced with the paradoxical situation that the more efficient is the sample design, the more important are nonsampling errors likely to be and the more meaningless are confidence interval computations based on the usual error formulas.[4]

In the University of Illinois study, the amount of nonsampling error could be calculated since the reports consumers gave of their financial assets and debts could be contrasted with actual data regarding their financial condition. But suppose such data were not available. Researchers may suspect that the responses they are eliciting are not accurate, but how are they to predict the direction of the error? Should they assume consumers are overstating their assets, for example, to impress the interviewer, or understating them for fear the IRS may get wind of the information? And if they are misrepresenting their assets, how is a researcher to determine the magnitude of this amount? Is it $10,000 over the real figure or $2,000 under? Or vice versa?

As you can begin to see, nonsampling errors are frequently the most important errors that arise in research. In special Census Bureau investigations of their size, for example, nonsampling errors were found to be ten times the magnitude of sampling errors.[5] This is not an unusual finding. Rather, a consistent finding is that nonsampling error is the major contributor to total survey error, while random sampling error has minimal impact.[6] Nonsampling errors can be reduced, but their reduction depends on improving method rather than increasing sample size. By understanding the sources of nonsampling errors, the analyst is in a better position to reduce them.

Types of Nonsampling Errors

Nonobservation error
Nonsampling error that arises because of nonresponse from some elements designated for inclusion in the sample.

Figure 18.1 offers a general overview of nonsampling errors.[7] They are of two basic types—errors due to nonobservation or to observation. **Nonobservation errors** result from a failure to obtain data from parts of the survey population. Nonobservation errors can happen because part of the population of interest was not included,

Figure 18.1   *Overview of Nonsampling Errors*

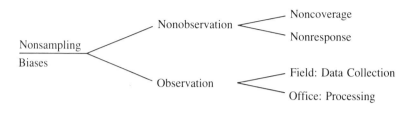

Source: Leslie Kish, *Survey Sampling* (New York: John Wiley & Sons, Inc., © 1965), p. 519.

Observation error
Nonsampling error that arises because inaccurate information is secured from the sample elements or because errors are introduced in the processing of the data or in reporting the findings.

or because some elements designated for inclusion in the sample did not respond. **Observation errors** occur because inaccurate information is secured from the sample elements or because errors are introduced in the processing of the data or in reporting the findings. In many ways, they are more troublesome than nonobservation errors. With nonobservation errors, we at least know we have a problem because of noncoverage or nonresponse. With observation errors, we may not even be aware that a problem exists. The very notion of an observation error rests on the presumption that there is indeed some "true" value for the variable or variables. An observation error, then, is simply the difference between the reported value and the "true" value. You can readily see that detection of an observation error places the researcher in the awkward position of knowing the very quantity the study is designed to estimate.

Nonobservation Errors

As is evident from Figure 18.1, there are two types of nonobservation errors: noncoverage errors and nonresponse errors. Each is capable of introducing significant bias in the results of a study, but analysts skilled enough to recognize the potential problem have several options for compensating for, or adjusting for, possible error.

Noncoverage error
Nonsampling error that arises because of a failure to include some units, or entire sections, of the defined survey population in the sampling frame.

Noncoverage Errors   A source of significant error in a study can be noncoverage, but **noncoverage error** does not refer to sections of a population that are deliberately excluded from the survey, but only those that were mistakenly excluded. Noncoverage, then, is essentially a sampling frame problem.

For a general survey, for instance, noncoverage error might result from using a telephone directory for the sampling frame. Not every family has a phone, and some who have phones do not have them listed in the directory. Further, there are some important demographic differences between those having and not having phones.

In a mail survey, where the mailing list dictates the sampling frame, noncoverage error can result from a mailing list that inadequately represents segments of the population. Experienced researchers know that rare is the mailing list that exactly captures the population that they wish to study, even though mailing lists are available for very specific population groups, as Table 18.1 indicates.

When the data are to be collected by personal interview in the home, some form of area sample is typically used to pinpoint respondents. In this case, the sampling frame is one of areas, blocks, and dwelling units, rather than a list of respondents. However, this does not eliminate the incomplete frame problem. Maps of the city may not be totally current, and so the newest areas may not have a proper chance of being included in the sample. The instructions to the interviewer may not be sufficiently detailed. The direction, "Start at the northwest corner of the selected blocks, generate a random start, and take every fifth dwelling unit thereafter," may be inadequate to handle those blocks with a number of apartment units. The evidence indicates, for example, that lower-income households are avoided when the selection of households is made by the field staff rather than the home office. Further, interviewers typically select the most accessible individuals within the household, contrary to instructions for random selection. This again means that a portion of the intended population is underrepresented in the study, while the accessible segment is overrepresented.

There are also sampling frame problems when personal interviews in shopping malls are to be used to collect the data. For one thing, there is no list of population elements. Rather, only those who shop in a particular mall have a chance of being included in the study, and their chances of being included depend on how often they shop there. That is why quota samples are often used in mall intercept studies.

However, noncoverage bias is not eliminated in quota samples, whether conducted in a mall or elsewhere. Rather, the interviewers' flexibility in choosing respondents can open the door to substantial noncoverage bias. Interviewers typically underselect in both the high- and low-income classes. The research director may not discover this bias, since field staffers also have a tendency to falsify characteristics so that it appears that they interviewed the appropriate number of cases per cell. Further, the more elaborate and complex the quota sample, the more critical this "forcing" problem becomes. With three or four variables defining the individual cells, the interviewer may find it difficult to locate respondents who have all the prescribed characteristics, so he or she may "cheat" a little bit on the characteristics defining difficult cells to fill.

Overcoverage error

Nonsampling error that arises because of the duplication of elements in the list of sampling units.

Overcoverage error can arise because of duplication in the list of sampling units. Units with multiple entries in the sampling frame—for example, families with several phone listings—have a higher probability of being included in the sample than do sampling units with one listing. For most surveys, though, noncoverage is much more common and troublesome than overcoverage.

Noncoverage bias is not a problem in every survey. For some studies, clear, convenient, and complete sampling frames exist. For example, the department store wishing to conduct a study among its charge-account customers should have little trouble with frame bias. The sampling frame is simply those with charge accounts. There might be some difficulty in distinguishing active accounts from inactive accounts, but this problem can be addressed during the design stage of the study.

Similarly, the credit union in a firm should experience little noncoverage bias in conducting a study among its potential clientele. The population of interest here would be the firm's employees, and it could be expected that the list of employees would be current and accurate since it is needed to generate the payroll.

Noncoverage bias raises two questions for the researcher: (1) How pervasive is it likely to be? (2) What can be done to reduce it? One difficulty is that its magnitude can be estimated only by comparing the sample survey results with some outside criterion. The outside criterion can in turn be established through an auxiliary quality check of a portion of the results, or it may be available from another reliable and current study, such as the population census. Comparison with the census or another large sample, though, means that the basic sampling units must be similar in terms of operational definitions. If researchers plan to make such comparisons, they may want to plan the study in such a way that the bases used (e.g., dwellings or persons) lend themselves to effective comparisons.

Table 18.1   **Some Population Groups for Which Mailing Lists Are Available**

Quantity		Price	Quantity		Price
12,900	Babies' Wear Retail $45/M		11,030	Banks, Loan Offices $45/M	
800	Bagel Shops...................................$85		243	Bankruptcy, Judges $85	
30,200	Bakeries, Retail $45/M		8,400	Barber & Beauty Supplies.................$45/M	
2,400	Bakery Products Mfrs.....................$45/M		64,200	Barber Shops..................................$45/M	
600	Ballet/Dance Companies $85		81,900	Bars, Taverns, Cocktail Lounges $45/M	
2,450	Balloon (Hot Air) Owners.................$45/M		2,800	Beauty Schools...............................$45/M	
10,500	Band Directors, High School.............$45/M		200,000	Beauty Shops..................................$45/M	
16,100	Bankers, Mortgage, Executives...........$45/M		315	Beekeepers $85	
4,100	Bankers, Mortgage, Firms................$45/M		90	Beer Brewers $85	
			11,900	Beer Distributors $45/M	
Banks			37,000	Behavioral Scientists $45/M	
13,790	Banks, Main Offices $45/M		170	Better Business Bureaus $85	
324	Banks with Assets $1 Billion or more ..$85		4,000	Beverage Bottlers & Distributors $45/M	
538	Banks with Assets $500 Million		26,000	Beverage Industry Executives $45/M	
	or more $85		11,700	Bicycle Dealers & Repairs..................$45/M	
1,278	Banks with Assets $200 Million		2,500	Billard Parlors & Poolrooms $45/M	
	or more $85		1,380	Billion Dollar Companies...................$85	
3,582	Banks with Assets $75 Million		5,700	Biological Chemists $45/M	
	or more $45/M		23,700	Biologists $45/M	
8,835	Banks with Assets $25 Million		3,900	Birth Control Centers $45/M	
	or more $45/M		6,400,000	Black Families...............................Inquire	
12,400	Banks with Assets $10 Million		4,600	Blood Banks $45/M	
	or more $45/M		3,000,000	Blue Collar Workers ....Inquire	
13,245	Banks with Assets $5 Million				
	or more $45/M		**Boats**		
200	Banks with Assets less than		5,250	Boat Basins (Marinas).......................$45/M	
	$5 Million $85		12,350	Boat Dealers $45/M	
40,100	Banks, Branches $45/M		21,000	Boat & Marine Supplies $45/M	
20,000	Banks, Cashiers $45/M		567,400	Boat Owners	
209,600	Banks, Executives $45/M			(Select by Type, Length, Power)....$50/M	
66,700	Banks, Executives, Women $45/M		10,000	Boat Yards, Building & Repairing $45/M	
3,490	Banks, Savings & Loans (HQ) $45/M		14,000	Boards of Education $45/M	
16,800	Banks, Savings & Loans (Branches).....$45/M		67,700	Body & Top Repair, Automobile $45/M	
6,000	Banks, Trust Officers $45/M		5,000	Boiler Contractors $45/M	

Given that noncoverage bias is likely, what can the researcher do to lessen its effect? The most obvious step, of course, is to improve the quality of the sampling frame. This may mean taking the time to bring available city maps up to date, or it may mean taking a sample to check the quality and representativeness of a mailing list with respect to a target population. The unlisted-number problem common to telephone surveys can be handled by random-digit or plus-one dialing, although this will not provide adequate sample representation of those without phones.

There are usually limits to the degree to which an imperfect sampling frame can be improved. Once these limits are reached, the researcher can attempt to reduce noncoverage bias still further through the selection of sampling units or the adjustment of the results. When sampling from lists, for example, analysts often encounter the problem that unwanted ineligibles and duplicates are included on the list, while some members of the target population are excluded. The first corrective

Quantity		Price	Quantity		Price
Boats			17,000	Brokers, Securities, Registered Representatives	$85/M
135	Book Clubs	$85	276,000	Building Contractors	$45/M
6,300	Book Publishers	$45/M	53,900	Building Materials & Supplies Dealers	$45/M
1,725	Book Publishers (Major)	$85	46,600	Building Materials & Supplies Wholesalers	$45/M
850	Book Wholesalers	$85	31,300	Building & Office Cleaners	$45/M
24,000	Bookkeeping Services	$45/M	13,600	Burglar Alarm Installers	$45/M
20,100	Bookstores	$45/M	19,000	Burners, (Oil & Furnace) Dealers & Distributors	$45/M
588	Bookstores, Chains	$85	9,000	Bus Companies (All)	$45/M
3,100	Bookstores, College	$45/M	5,200	Bus Companies (Charter & Retail)	$45/M
3,300	Bookstores, Religious	$45/M	3,550	Bus Companies (Inter-City)	$45/M
132	Botanical Gardens	$85	4,700	Bus Company Executives	$45/M
2,700	Botanists	$45/M			
2,600	Bottlers, Soft Drink	$45/M	**Business Execs./Owners**		
4,600	Boutiques	$45/M	3,600	Business Brokers	$45/M
7,500	Bowling Alleys	$45/M	3,100	Business Economists	$45/M
6,000	Box & Container Mfrs	$45/M	2,000,000	Business Executives	Inquire
530	Boy Scout Councils	$85	200,000	Business Executives, Home Address	Inquire
2,400	Bread, Baker Goods Mfrs	$45/M	60,000	Business Executives, Top Salaried, Home Address	$50/M
14,500	Bricklayers, Stonemasons	$45/M	4,600	Business Forms Mfrs	$45/M
8,290	Bridal Shops	$45/M	9,300	Business Machine Dealers	$45/M
30,100	Broadcasting Executives	$45/M	1,000,000	Business Owners, Home Address	Inquire
4,798	Broadcasting Stations—Radio AM	$45/M	2,000,000	Business Owners (Small)	Inquire
4,428	Broadcasting Stations—Radio FM	$45/M	525	Business Schools (Collegiate)	$85
1,050	Broadcasting Stations—TV	$85	2,000	Business, Secretarial Schools	$45/M
211,000	Brokers & Agents, Insurance	$45/M	3,700	Business & Trade Organization	$45/M
207,200	Brokers & Agents, Insurance (Offices)	$45/M	4,530	Business & Trade Publications	$45/M
3,600	Brokers, Business	$45/M	20,400	Butcher Shops	$45/M
300,000	Brokers & Agents, Real Estate (Individuals)	$45/M	8,900	Butchers, Wholesale	$45/M
170,000	Brokers & Agents, Real Estate (Offices)	$45/M	200	Buyers, Resident, Offices	$85
47,800	Brokers, Securities—Executives	$45/M			
28,400	Brokers, Securities—Offices	$45/M			

Source: Alvin B. Zeller, Inc., 37 East 28th Street, New York, NY 10016. Reprinted with permission.

step for this problem is to update the list, using supplementary sources if possible. While this would help reduce one aspect of the problem (excluded members), it might do little to eliminate ineligibles and duplicates. When the sample is drawn, however, all ineligibles can be ignored. Beware of the temptation to substitute the next name on the list, since this would bias selection toward those elements that follow ineligible listings. The correct procedure is to draw another element randomly, if simple random selection procedures are being used. If systematic sampling procedures are being used, the sampling interval should be adjusted before the fact to allow for the percentage of ineligibles.

The problem of duplicates is handled by adjustment. Specifically, the results are weighted by the inverse of the probability of selection. In a study using a list of car registrations, for example, each contacted respondent would be asked, "How many cars do you own?" The response of someone who said two would be weighted by $\frac{1}{2}$, while that of someone who said three would be weighted by $\frac{1}{3}$.[8]

Figure 18.2   Possible Outcomes When Attempting to Contact Respondents for Telephone Surveys

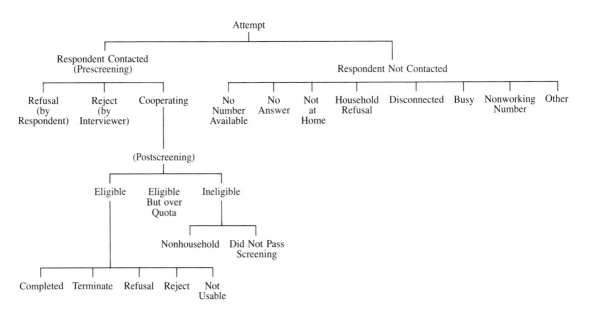

Source: Frederick Wiseman and Philip McDonald, *Toward the Development of Industry Standards for Response and Nonresponse Rates* (Cambridge, Mass.: Marketing Science Institute, 1980), p. 29. Reprinted with permission.

The appropriate sampling and adjustment procedures to account for inadequate sampling frames can become quite technical in complex sample designs and fall largely in the domain of the sampling specialist. We shall consequently not delve into these processes but shall simply note that noncoverage bias

1. Is a nonsampling error and is therefore not dealt with in our standard error formulas.
2. Is not likely to be eliminated by increasing the sample size.
3. Can be of considerable magnitude.
4. Can be reduced, but not necessarily eliminated, by recognizing its existence, working to improve the sampling frame, and employing a sampling specialist to help reduce, through the sampling procedure, and adjust, through analysis, the remaining frame imperfections.

Nonresponse error
Nonsampling error that represents a failure to obtain information from some elements of the population that were selected and designated for the sample.

Nonresponse Errors   Another source of nonobservation bias is **nonresponse error,** which represents a failure to obtain information from some elements of the population that were selected and designated for the sample. The first hurdle to overcome in dealing with nonresponse errors is simply anticipating all the things that can go wrong with an attempt to contact a designated respondent. Figure 18.2, for example, depicts the various outcomes of an attempted telephone contact. There is such a bewildering array of alternatives that even calculating a measure of the extent of the nonresponse problem becomes difficult.

In the late 1970s, several researchers became concerned that the marketing research industry had no uniform standard for measuring rates of response and nonresponse. Because the various research organizations used widely differing definitions and methods for calculating nonresponse, it was impossible to get an

Table 18.2   Response Rate Calculations for Telephone Directory Sample

Panel A: Outcome of Telephone Call

Disconnected/nonworking telephone number	426
Household refusal	153
No answer, busy, not at home	1,757
Interviewer reject (language barrier, hard of hearing . . .)	187
Respondent refusal	711
Ineligible respondent	366
Termination by respondent	74
Completed interview	501
Total	4,175

Panel B: Most Frequent, Minimum, and Maximum Response Rates

Most frequent

$$\frac{\text{Household refusals} + \text{Rejects} + \text{Refusals} + \text{Ineligibles} + \text{Terminations} + \text{Completed interviews}}{\text{All}} = \qquad (1)$$

$$\frac{153 + 187 + 711 + 366 + 74 + 501}{4,175} = 48\%$$

$$\frac{\text{Rejects} + \text{Refusals} + \text{Ineligibles} + \text{Terminations} + \text{Completed interviews}}{\text{All}} = \qquad (2)$$

$$\frac{187 + 711 + 366 + 74 + 501}{4,175} = 44\%$$

$$\frac{\text{Completed interviews}}{\text{All}} = \frac{501}{4,175} = 12\% \qquad (3)$$

Minimum

$$\frac{\text{Completed interviews}}{\text{All}} = \frac{501}{4,175} = 12\%$$

Maximum

$$\frac{\text{Refusals} + \text{Ineligibles} + \text{Termination} + \text{Completed interviews}}{\text{Rejects} + \text{Refusals} + \text{Ineligibles} + \text{Termination} + \text{Completed interviews}} =$$

$$\frac{711 + 366 + 74 + 501}{187 + 711 + 366 + 74 + 501} = 90\%$$

Source: Frederick Wiseman and Philip McDonald, *Toward the Development of Industry Standards for Response and Nonresponse Rates* (Cambridge, Mass.: Marketing Science Institute, 1980), pp. 12 and 19. Reprinted with permission.

accurate assessment of the nonresponse problem. In an attempt to get a handle on the problem, the researchers conducted a study among a sample of members of the Council of American Survey Research Organizations (CASRO) and leading user companies. Each member was mailed a questionnaire that displayed actual contact and response data from three different telephone surveys, a telephone directory sample, a random-digit sample, and a list sample. Respondents were asked to calculate the response, contact, completion, and refusal rates for each of the three surveys.[9] (Each of these rates is defined later in this chapter.) The difference in results was rather startling. The upper part of Table 18.2 displays the raw data from the telephone directory sample. Using the very same data, one responding organization

Response rate
The number of completed interviews with responding units divided by the number of eligible responding units in the sample.

reported the **response rate**—which is the number of interviews divided by the number of contacts—as 12 percent, while another reported 90 percent. Nor was there agreement among the other firms. No more than three firms out of forty agreed on any single definition of the response rate, and those firms used three different definitions to arrive at their answers. The lower part of Table 18.2 displays the three most frequently used definitions and the definitions producing the minimum and maximum response rates.

Not only does the variation in definitions cause confusion when nonresponse rates are reported for a survey, but it also makes the treatment of the nonresponse error problem more difficult. It becomes hard to discern, for instance, whether a particular method proved effective, or whether a different definition was responsible for a lower nonresponse error in a particular study. In an attempt to help to standardize findings so as to improve the practice of survey research, a special CASRO task force developed a definition of response rate that the industry is being encouraged to embrace as the standard definition. It follows:[10]

$$\text{response rate} = \frac{\text{number of completed interviews with responding units}}{\text{number of eligible responding units in the sample}}$$

The key requirement in accurately calculating the response rate is to properly handle eligibles. Table 18.3 shows how to calculate the response rate properly depending on whether there is or is not an eligibility requirement for inclusion in the sample.

Nonresponse is a problem in any survey in which it occurs because it raises the question of whether those who did respond are different in some important way from those who did not respond. This is, of course, a question we cannot answer, although study after study has indicated that the assumption that those who did not respond were in fact equal to those who did is risky.

The two main sources of nonresponse bias are not-at-homes and refusals. Nonresponse bias can arise with studies using personal interviews, telephone, or mail surveys to secure the data. With mail surveys, though, the not-at-home problem becomes one of nonreceipt of the questionnaire. The questionnaire may simply have been lost in the mail, in which case the nonsampling error could be considered random and nonbiasing, or there may be more fundamental reasons for nonreceipt: the addressee may have moved or died. These latter conditions would be a source of systematic nonsampling error.

Not-at-homes
Nonsampling error that arises when replies are not secured from some designated sampling units because the respondents are not at home when the interviewer calls.

Not-at-Homes   Replies will not be secured from some designated sampling units because the respondent will not be at home when the interviewer calls. The empirical evidence indicates that the percentage of **not-at-homes** has been increasing for a long time.[11] Obviously, much depends upon the nature of the designated respondent and the time of the call. Married women with young children are more apt to be at home during the day on weekdays than are men, married women without children, or single women. The probability of finding someone at home is also greater for low-income families and for rural families. Seasonal variations, particularly during the holidays, occur, as do weekday-to-weekend variations.[12] Further, it is much easier to find a "responsible adult" at home than a specific type of respondent, and thus the choice of the elementary sampling unit is key in the not-at-home problem.

Several things can be done to reduce the incidence of not-at-homes. For example, in some studies the interviewer might make an appointment in advance with the

Table 18.3   *The Impact of an Eligibility Requirement on the Calculation of the Response Rate*

Example 1. *Single-Stage Sample, No Eligibility Requirement*

Suppose a survey is conducted to obtain 1,000 interviews with subscribers of a particular magazine. A random sample of $n = 1,000$ is selected, and the initial data-collection effort produces the following results:

$$\text{Completed interviews} \quad = 660$$

$$\text{Refusals} \quad = 115$$

$$\text{Respondents not contacted} = 225$$

For each of the 340 nonrespondents, substitute subscribers are selected until a completed interview is obtained. Assume that in this follow-up data-collection effort 600 substitute names are required to secure the 340 interviews. The recommended response rate is

$$660/1,000 = 66.0\%$$

and not

$$1,000/1,600 = 62.5\%.$$

Example 2. *Single-Stage Sample, Eligibility Requirement*

From a list of registered voters, a sample of $n = 900$ names is selected. Eligible respondents are defined as those planning to vote in an upcoming election. Assume the data-collection effort produces the following results:

$$\text{Completed interviews} \quad = 300$$

$$\text{Not contacted} \quad = 250$$

$$\text{Refused, eligibility not determined} = 150$$

$$\text{Ineligible} \quad = 200$$

The recommended response rate is

$$\frac{300}{300 + \left[\dfrac{300}{300 + 200}\right](250+150)} = \frac{300}{300 + 240} = 55.5\%.$$

As indicated, when using an eligibility requirement one first must estimate the number of eligibles among the nonrespondents. This is done by using the eligibility percentage, $(300/500) = 60\%$, obtained among persons successfully screened and applying this percentage to the nonrespondents. Thus, of the 400 nonrespondents, 60% (240) are estimated to have been eligible and the estimated response rate becomes 300/540, or 55.5%.

Source: Frederick Wiseman and Maryann Billington, "Comment on a Standard Definition of Response Rates," *Journal of Marketing Research*, 21 (August 1984), p. 337. Reprinted from *Journal of Marketing Research*, published by the American Marketing Association, Chicago, IL 60606.

respondent. While this approach is particularly valuable in surveys of busy executives, it may not be justifiable in an ordinary consumer survey. A commonly used technique in the latter instance is the callback, which is particularly effective if the callback (preferably callbacks) is made at a different time than the original call. As a matter of fact, the nonresponse problem due to not-at-homes is so acute and so important to the accuracy of most surveys that one leading expert has suggested that small samples with four to six callbacks are more efficient than large samples without callbacks, unless the percentage of initial response can be increased considerably above normal levels.[13] Some data indicate, for example, that four to five calls are often needed to reach three-fourths of the sample of households (see Table 18.4).

Table 18.4   *Percentage of Sample Homes Reached with Each Call in*
Personal Interview and Telephone Surveys

Call	Personal Interview		Telephone	
	Percent	Cumulative Percent	Percent	Cumulative Percent
1	25	25	24	24
2	25	50	18	42
3	18	68	14	56
4	11	79	11	67
5	7	86	8	75
6	5	91	6	81
7	3	94	5	86
8	6	100	3	89[a]

[a]It took 17 calls to reach all the homes in the telephone survey.

Source: Robert M. Groves and Robert L. Kahn, *Surveys by Telephone* (Orlando, Fla.: Academic Press, 1979), pp. 56 and 58.

An alternative to the *straight callback* is the *modified callback*. If the initial contact attempt and first few callbacks were made by an interviewer and a contact was not established, the interviewer might simply mail a self-administered questionnaire with a stamped, self-addressed envelope (or leave one at the door if an in-person survey is being made). If the not-at-home is simply a "designated-respondent-absent" rather than a "nobody-at-home," the interviewer can use the opportunity to inquire about the respondent's hours of availability.

One technique that is sometimes naively suggested for handling the not-at-homes is to substitute the neighboring dwelling unit or, in a telephone survey, to call the next name on the list. This is a very poor way of handling the not-at-home condition. All it does is substitute more at-homes (who may be different from the not-at-homes in a number of important characteristics) for the population segment the interviewer is in fact trying to reach. This increases the proportion of at-homes in the sample and, in effect, aggravates the problem instead of solving it.

The proportion of reported not-at-homes is likely to depend on the interviewer's skill and the judgment used in scheduling initial contacts and callbacks. This suggests that one way of reducing not-at-home nonresponse bias is by better interviewer training, particularly with respect to how to schedule callbacks more efficiently.

The fact that interviewer effectiveness affects the number of not-at-homes also suggests one measure by which interviewers themselves can be compared and evaluated: by calculating the **contact rate (K),** which is the percentage of the eligible assignments in which the interviewer makes contact with the designated respondent; that is,

Contact rate (K)
A measure used to evaluate and compare the effectiveness of interviewers in making contact with designated respondents; K = number of sample units contacted divided by total number of eligible sample units approached.

$$K = \frac{\text{number of sample units contacted}}{\text{total number of eligible sample units approached}}.$$

The contact rate measures the interviewer's persistence. Interviewers can be compared with respect to their contact rates, and corrective measures can often be taken on that basis. The field supervisor may want to investigate the reasons for any individual interviewer's low contact rate. Perhaps this interviewer is operating in a traditionally high not-at-home area, such as a high-income section of an urban area. Alternatively, by examining the call reports for the time of each call, the trouble may be traced to poor follow-up procedures. This condition would suggest additional training is necessary, which might then be provided by the field supervisor while the study is still in progress. The contact rate can also be used to evaluate an entire study with respect to the potential nonresponse caused by not-at-homes.

Refusals   In almost every study, some respondents will refuse to participate. In one of the most extensive investigations of the magnitude of this problem, 46 field research companies sponsored a study called "Your Opinion Counts," which involved almost 1.4 million phone and personal interviews. The study indicated that 38 percent of the people asked to participate declined to do so, with 86 percent of those people refusing to participate before or during the introduction. The rest of those who declined broke away before the survey was completed.[14] Research Window 18.1 depicts what is happening to refusal rates in general and some of the major reasons respondents give for having refused to participate in surveys. The rate of **refusals** depends, among other things, on the nature of the respondent, the nature of the organization sponsoring the research, the circumstances surrounding the contact, the nature of the subject under investigation, and the skill of the interviewer.

The method used to collect the data also makes a difference. The empirical evidence indicates, for example, that personal interviews are most effective, and mail questionnaires least effective, in generating response. Telephone interviews are somewhat less successful on the average (about 10 percent less successful) than personal interviews in getting target respondents to cooperate.[15]

Although different data-collection techniques will influence the types of people likely to cooperate in a survey, there does seem to be a tendency for females, nonwhites, those who are less well-educated, who have lower incomes, and who are older, to be more likely to refuse to participate.[16]

The type of organization sponsoring the research can also make a difference in the number of refusals. People not only report differently to different sponsors, but they may also make their decision on whether or not to respond on the basis of who the sponsor is.

Sometimes the circumstances surrounding the contact can cause a refusal. A respondent may be busy, tired, or sick when contacted. And the subject of the research also affects the refusal rate. Those interested in the subject are most likely to respond. On the other hand, nonresponse tends to increase with the sensitivity of the information being sought.

Finally, interviewers themselves can have a significant impact on the number of refusals they obtain. Their approach, manner, and even their own demographic characteristics can affect a respondent's willingness to participate.

What can be done to correct the nonresponse bias introduced when designated respondents refuse their participation? There seem to be three available strategies:

1. The initial response rate can be increased.
2. The impact of refusals can be reduced through follow-up.
3. The obtained information can be extrapolated to allow for nonresponse.

Refusals Nonsampling error that arises because some designated respondents refuse to participate in the study.

Research Window 18.1
Trends in Refusal Rates and Reasons Given for Refusing to Participate

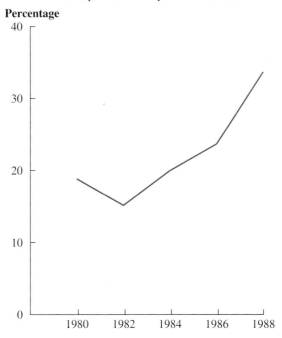

Panel A: Percentage of Those Contacted Who Had Refused to Participate in a Survey in the Past Year

Increasing Initial Response Rate Improving the circumstances surrounding an interview or increasing the training of interviewers are logical ways to increase the response rate, but the nature of the respondent would seem to be one factor strictly beyond the researcher's control. After all, the problem dictates the target population, and this population is likely to contain households with different education levels, income levels, cultural and occupational backgrounds, and so forth. However, the task is not as hopeless as it might seem. As will be shown later when we examine a model for interviewer-interviewee interaction, the interviewee's cooperation can be encouraged by an "appropriate choice" of interviewer. Cooperation can also be

Panel B: Reasons Given for Having Refused to Participate*

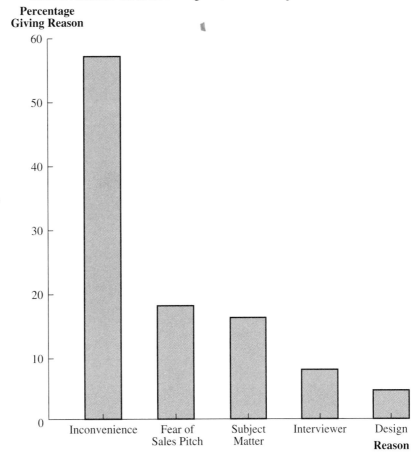

*1988 survey results.
Source: *Walker Industry Image Study: Research on Research*, 8th ed. (Indianapolis, Ind.: Walker Research, Inc., 1988), p. 4.

encouraged by convincing respondents of the value of the research and the importance of their participation. Advance notice may help, too.

If the identification of the organization sponsoring the research is likely to increase nonresponse, researchers can overcome this bias by concealing that information or by hiring a professional research organization to conduct the field study. This is one reason why companies with established, sophisticated research departments of their own sometimes employ research firms to collect data.

Evidence suggests that the more information interviewers provide about the content and purpose of the survey, the higher the response rate will be in both

Table 18.5   **Impact of Selected Techniques on Response Rates**

Techniques	Number of Response Rates Included in the Averages	Average Net Difference in Response Rates
Monetary Incentives		
Used/not used	49/30	15.3
Prepaid/not used	33/22	15.6
Promised/not used	13/7	5.8
Nonmonetary Incentives		
Premium/no premium	5/5	9.2
Offer of survey results/no offer	12/12	−2.6[a]
Response Facilitators		
Prior notification of survey/no prior notification	10/9	8.1
Foot-in-the-door/no prior request for respondent to do an initial task	34/12	18.3
Personalized cover letter/cover letter not personalized	35/32	6.6
Respondent promised anonymity/anonymity not promised	8/7	−0.4[a]
Deadline for responding specified/deadline not specified	7/7	−0.7[a]
Return postage provided/return postage not provided	6/5	1.3[a]
Follow-up letter sent/follow-up letter not sent	16/14	17.9

[a]Not a statistically significant difference.

Source: Developed from the data in Julie Yu and Harris Cooper, "A Quantitative Review of Research Design Effects on Response Rates to Questionnaires," *Journal of Marketing Research*, 20 (February 1983), pp. 36–44.

personal and telephone interviews. A guarantee of confidentiality will secure further responses, since some individuals refuse to participate because they do not wish to be identified with their responses. Moreover, the research suggests that monetary incentives are effective in increasing response rates in mail surveys.[17] Interestingly, they are not effective when personal interviews are being used, except when the interviewing is being conducted at shopping malls.[18]

It is difficult to generalize about the effectiveness of various inducements in increasing the response rate, because the effects of each technique are different from survey to survey. The data in Table 18.5 are interesting in this regard. In this quantitative analysis of the published literature on response rates from 1965 to 1981, some studies reported response rates for several different survey techniques. Each response rate was treated as one observation when this occurred. The table looks at the average net difference in response rates when the technique was used versus when it was absent. It suggests that on average, the three most effective ways to increase the response rate in a given study are (1) to get a "foot in the door" by having respondents comply with some small request before presenting them with the larger survey, (2) to follow up the initial request for cooperation with a letter to those who did not respond to the initial request, and (3) to offer a monetary incentive. Unfortunately, the study did not investigate whether the effectiveness of certain inducement techniques depended upon the method of data collection being used.

Increasing Response Rate by Follow-up   In some cases, the circumstances surrounding a contact are responsible for a respondent's refusal to participate. Since these circumstances may be temporary or changeable, follow-up actions may elicit a later response and thus increase the overall response rate. If a respondent declined participation because he or she was busy or sick, a callback at a different time or using a different approach may be enough to secure cooperation. In a mail survey, this may mean a follow-up mailing at a more convenient time. The key to the success of this follow-up may be appropriate training and control of the field staff.

Less can be done with the subject of the research itself if it is the source of nonresponse bias, since it is dictated by the problem to be solved. A sensitive research subject or one of little interest to the respondents is likely to elicit a high rate of refusals. However, the researcher should not overlook any opportunities for making the study more interesting—for example, by eliminating unnecessary questions.

If a respondent has refused to participate in a personal interview or a telephone survey for reasons other than circumstances, callbacks will be less successful. This is not so with mail surveys. Frequently responses are obtained with the second and third mailings from those who did not respond to the initial mailing. Of course, follow-up in a mail survey requires identification of those not responding earlier, which in turn requires identification of those who did respond, and we have already seen that reluctance to be identified may cause a refusal. Thus, identification of the respondents, which may serve to decrease one source of nonresponse, may increase another. The alternative, which is to send each new mailing to each designated sample member without screening those who have responded previously, can be expensive for the research organization and frustrating for the respondent.

Adjusting Results to Correct for Nonresponse   A third strategy for correcting nonresponse bias involves estimating its effects and then adjusting the results.[19] Suppose that in estimating the mean income for some population, one secured responses from only a portion (p_r) of some designated sample. The proportion not responding could then be denoted p_{nr}. If $\bar{x}_r$ is the mean income of those *responding*, and $\bar{x}_{nr}$ the mean income of those *not responding*, then the overall mean would be

$$\bar{x} = p_r \bar{x}_r + p_{nr} \bar{x}_{nr}.$$

This computation, of course, assumes that $\bar{x}_{nr}$ is known or at least can be estimated. An intensive follow-up of a sample of the nonrespondents is sometimes used to generate this estimate. The follow-up may be a modified callback (described earlier). While this rarely generates a response from each nonrespondent designated for the follow-up, it does allow a crude adjustment of the initial results. Ignoring the initial nonresponse is equivalent to assuming that $\bar{x}_{nr}$ is equal to $\bar{x}_r$, which is usually incorrect.

A second way to adjust the results is to keep track of those responding to the initial contact, the first follow-up, the second follow-up, and so on. The mean of the variable (or other appropriate statistic) is then calculated, and each subgroup is compared to determine whether any statistically significant differences emerge as a function of the difficulty experienced in making contact. If not, the variable mean for the nonrespondents is assumed equal to the mean for those responding. If a discernible trend is evident, the trend is extrapolated to allow for nonrespondents. This method is particularly valuable in mail surveys, where it is an easy task to identify those responding to the first mailing, the second mailing, and so on.

A third way by which the results from personal interviews can be adjusted is to use the scheme developed by Politz and Simmons that does not involve callbacks at all.[20] Rather, it relies on a single attempted contact with each sample member at a randomly determined time. During this contact, the respondent is asked if he or she was home at the time scheduled for the interview for the preceding five days. These five answers together with the time of contact provide information on the time the respondent was at home for six different days. The responses from each informant are then weighted by the reciprocal of their self-reported probability of being at home; for example, the answers of a respondent who was home one out of six times would receive a weight of 6. The basic rationale is that people who are usually not at home are more difficult to catch for an interview and therefore will tend to be underrepresented in the survey. Consequently, the less a subject reports being at home, the more the subject's responses would be weighted.

Evidence accumulated in past surveys also sometimes serves as the basis of the adjustment for nonresponse. Organizations that frequently conduct surveys using similar sampling procedures find this approach particularly useful. While no method of adjustment is perfect, any of them is better than assuming that nonrespondents are similar to respondents on the characteristics of interest. Yet this is the very assumption we make if no attempt is made to correct for nonresponse.

Item Nonresponse   The preceding discussions all deal with *total nonresponse*. *Item nonresponse*, which can also be a problem, occurs when the respondent agrees to the total interview but refuses, or is unable, to answer some specific questions because of the content or form of the questions, or the amount of work required to produce the requested information. As we discussed earlier, researchers usually attempt to address these problems when developing the questionnaire and planning the methods for administering it. Sometimes, however, item nonresponses occur in spite of researchers' best efforts to avoid them.

Whether anything can then be done about item nonresponse depends on its magnitude. Here we must distinguish between flagrant item nonresponse and isolated or sporadic nonresponse. If too many questions are left unanswered, the reply becomes unusable, and the treatment, or at least adjustment, is the same as that for a complete nonresponse. On the other hand, if only a few items are left unanswered on any questionnaire, the reply can often be made usable. At the very minimum, the "don't know" and "no answers" can be treated as separate categories when reporting the results. In many ways this is the best strategy because the little evidence that is available on item nonresponse suggests that the problem is extensive and nonrandom. Alternatively, the information from the missing item or items can sometimes be inferred from other information in the questionnaire. This is especially true if there are other questions on the questionnaire that relate to the same issue. The other questions are checked, and a consistent answer is formulated for the unanswered item. In the absence of such consistency checks, the statistical technique known as *regression analysis*, which measures the relationship between two or more variables, is sometimes used. The missing item is treated as the criterion variable, and the functional relationship is established between it and a priori related questions through regression analysis for those cases for which the item was answered. The equation is then used to estimate a response for the remaining questionnaires given the information they contain on the predictor variables.

Finally, a third way by which item nonresponse is handled is by substituting the average response for the item of those who did respond. This technique, of course, carries the assumption that those who did not respond to the item are similar to those who did. As we have suggested many times, this assumption may be risky, and therefore substituting the average should be done with caution.

Response Rates versus Completeness Rate   Just as the contact rate can be used to compare and evaluate interviewers with respect to not-at-homes, at least two ratios have been suggested for comparing interviewers with respect to refusals: the response rate, *R*, and the **completeness rate, *C*.** As explained earlier, the response rate equals the ratio of the number of completed interviews with responding units divided by the number of eligible responding units in the sample. The response rate reflects the interviewer's effectiveness at the door or on the phone.

Completeness rate*(C)* A measure used to evaluate and compare interviewers with respect to their ability to secure needed information from contacted respondents; the completeness rate measures the proportion of complete contacts by interviewer.

The completeness rate applies to the individual items in the study. Most typically it will be used to evaluate interviewers with respect to the crucial questions involved in the study, for example, a respondent's income, debt, or asset position, although it can also be used to evaluate the whole contact. The completeness rate simply determines whether the response is complete or not, either with respect to the crucial questions or the whole questionnaire.

Observation Errors

Observation errors, defined earlier, may be more insidious than nonobservation errors, since the research analyst may not even be aware that they exist.

Field error Nonsampling error that arises during the actual collection of the data.

Field Errors   By far the most prevalent type of observation error is the **field error,** which arises after the individual has agreed to participate in a study. Instead of cooperating fully, the individual refuses to answer specific questions or provides an untruthful response. These errors have been referred to, respectively, as *errors of omission* and *errors of commission*.[21] In the last section we discussed errors of omission and item nonresponse. Now we wish to turn our attention to errors of commission, which are usually categorized as response errors.

When considering response errors, it is useful to keep in mind what occurs when respondents answer questions. First, they need to understand what is being asked. Second, they need to engage in a reasoning process to arrive at an answer. Typically, the respondent will try to assess the information needed for an accurate answer and then remember the attitudes, facts, or experiences that would be relevant to the question. He or she will then try to organize a response based on this information. Third, respondents need to evaluate the response in terms of its accuracy. Fourth, they need to evaluate the response in terms of other goals they might have, such as preserving their self-image or attempting to please the interviewer. Finally, they need to put into words the response that results from all of this mental processing. Reaching the final step is the object of the survey process. However, breakdowns can occur at any of the preceding steps, resulting in an inaccurate answer, a response error.

The factors that can cause response errors are so numerous that they almost defy categorization. One seemingly useful scheme for dealing with data-collection errors, though, is the interviewer-interviewee interaction model proposed by Kahn and

Sometimes direct questions produce misleading answers from consumers. For example, marketing research indicated more of an interest in low-salt or salt-free products than actually existed. Among the flood of items introduced to the market, only a few were successful, including Mrs. Dash. Misleading answers are an example of field, data-collection errors.

Source: Courtesy of Alberto Culver; model: Kate O'Connor.

Cannell (Figure 18.3).[22] The model suggests several things. First, each person brings certain background characteristics and psychological predispositions to the interview. While some of the background characteristics (such as age and sex) are readily observable, others are not, nor can the psychological state of the other person be seen. Yet both interviewer and interviewee will form some attitudes toward, and expectations of, the other person on the basis of their initial perceptions. Second, the interview is an interactive process, and both interviewer and interviewee are important determinants of the process. Each party perceives and reacts to the specific behaviors of the other. Note, though, that there is no direct link between the boxes labeled behavior. Rather, the linkage is more complicated, "involving a behavior on the part of the interviewer or respondent, the perception of this behavior by the other principal in the interview, a cognitive or attitudinal development from that perception, and finally a resultant motivation to behave in a certain way. Only at this point is a behavioral act carried out, which in turn may be perceived by and reacted to by the other participant in the interview."[23]

The perceptions of this behavior may not be correct, just as the initial perceptions of each party may be in error. Nevertheless, such inferences will inevitably be made

Figure 18.3   ***A Model of Bias in the Interview***

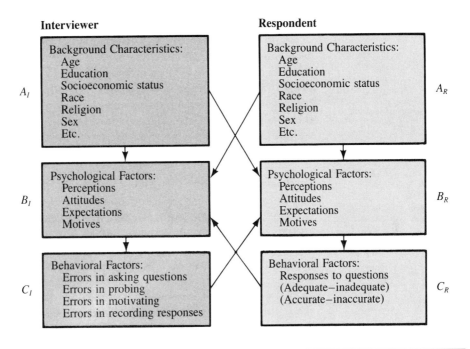

Source: Robert L. Kahn and Charles F. Cannell, *The Dynamics of Interviewing* (New York: John Wiley & Sons, Inc., © 1957), p. 193.

as both interviewer and respondent search for cues to help them understand each other and carry out the requirements imposed by the interview situation. In sum, not only do the specific behaviors of each party to the interaction affect the outcome, but so do the background characteristics and psychological predispositions of both interviewer and respondent.

The interviewer-interviewee interaction model is appealing for several reasons. One, it is consistent with the empirical evidence. Two, it offers some valuable insight on how response errors (as well as nonresponse errors due to refusals) can potentially be reduced. The model also applies to telephone and mail surveys, thereby further increasing its value. For example, the respondent's perceptions of the background characteristics and behavior of a telephone interviewer will likely affect the answers he or she provides. The respondent's background is certainly going to affect his or her reported responses. So will the person's suspicions regarding the true purpose of the study, or the individual's assumption of how confidential his or her responses will truly be. These factors can distort the respondent's answers regardless of the manner used to collect the data, and it is unlikely these distortions would be random. At any rate, the model suggests certain actions that the researcher can take to generate accurate information.

Background Factors   The empirical evidence supports the notion that background factors affect reported responses. More specifically, the evidence suggests that the interviewer is likely to get better cooperation and more information from the respondent when the two share similar backgrounds than if they are different. This is particularly true for readily observable characteristics, such as race, age, and sex, but applies as well to more unobservable characteristics, such as social class and income. Consequently, it may be prudent to match the background characteristics of the interviewer and respondent as closely as possible, since the more characteristics the two have in common, the greater the probability of a successful interview.

Unfortunately, researchers have found it difficult to implement this practice. Most interviewers are housewives who use interviewing as a way to supplement their family income. The job by no means attracts a balanced demographic cross section of people. So what can the researcher do to minimize such biases? He or she may be restricted to merely computing a measure of interviewer variability when analyzing the results. Possibly the field supervisor could revise interviewers' schedules in a specific project so as to improve background matches, but the most effective measure would be to recruit interviewers with diverse socioeconomic backgrounds.

Psychological Factors   The evidence regarding the impact of psychological factors on responses tends to support the notion that interviewers' opinions, perceptions, expectations, and attitudes affect the responses they receive.[24] Certainly these attitudes, opinions, expectations, and so on, are going to be conditioned by the interviewers' backgrounds, and since that is something we cannot control, how are we to control for these psychological factors? The primary way is through training. The fact that interviewers will have psychological predispositions is not critical, since these psychological factors are not observed by the respondent. What is critical is that these factors not be allowed to affect interviewers' behavior during the interview and thereby contaminate the responses.

Most surveys, therefore, are conducted using a rather rigid set of procedures that interviewers must follow. The instructions should be clear and should be written. Further, they should state the purpose of the study clearly. They should describe the materials to be used, such as questionnaires, maps, time forms, and so on. They should describe how each question should be asked, the kinds of answers that are acceptable, and the kinds and timing of probes that are to be used, if any. The instructions should also specify the number and identity of respondents that interviewers need to contact and the time constraints under which they will be operating. It is also important that the instructions be well organized and unambiguous.

The instructions must be clearly articulated; however, it is even more important that interviewers understand and can follow them. This suggests that practice training sessions will be necessary. It might also be necessary to actually examine the interviewers with respect to study purposes and procedures. Finally, interviewers might also be required to complete the questionnaire so that if there is a pattern between the interviewers' answers and the answers they get when administering the questionnaire, it can be discerned.

Behavioral Factors   The respondents' background, attitudes, motives, expectations, and so on, are also potentially biasing. Whether they actually do introduce bias depends on how the interviewer and respondent interact. In other words, the predispositions to bias become operative only in behavior.

Unfortunately the evidence indicates that even when the rules are rigid and the questionnaires relatively simple and structured, interviewers do not follow the rules. They thereby introduce bias. In one classic study, 15 college-educated interviewers interviewed the same respondent, who had previously been instructed to give identical answers to all 15 interviewers.[25] All the interviews were recorded and were later analyzed for the incidence of errors by type and frequency. One of the most startling findings of the study was the sheer number of errors. For example, there were 66 failures to ask supplementary questions when inadequate responses were given, and the number of errors per interviewer varied from 12 to 36. In another, more recent study, it was found that ". . . one-third of the . . . interviewers deviated frequently and markedly from their instructions, sometimes failing to explain the key terms or to repeat them as required, sometimes leaving them out altogether, shortening questions, or failing to follow up certain ambiguous answers in the manner required."[26]

At least three interviewer behaviors led to response bias: (1) errors in asking questions and in probing when additional information is required, (2) errors in recording the answers, and (3) errors due to cheating.

While errors in asking questions can arise with any of the basic question types, the problem is particularly acute with open-ended questions where probing follows the initial response. No two interviewers are likely to employ the same probes. The content, as well as the timing, of the probes may differ. This raises the possibility that the differences in answers may be due to the probes that are used rather than any "true" differences in the position of the respondents.

The manner in which the initial question is phrased can also introduce error. Interviewers often reword the question to fit their perceptions of what the respondent is capable of understanding. They may also change the wording in a way that reflects their own opinion of what constitutes an appropriate answer.

Surprisingly, questions that include alternative answers possess great potential for interviewer bias. This bias occurs because the interviewer places undue emphasis on one of the alternatives in stating the question. Slight changes in tone can change the meaning of the entire question. In one of the most comprehensive studies to investigate interviewer errors in asking questions, it was found, for example, that the average number of errors per question by type was[27]

- Reading error   0.293
- Speech variations   0.116
- Probes   0.140
- Feedbacks to respondents   0.161

One of the interviewer's main tasks is keeping the respondent interested and motivated. At the same time, the interviewer must try to record what the respondent is saying by dutifully writing down the person's answers to open-ended questions or checking the appropriate box with closed questions. These dual, sometimes incompatible, responsibilities can also be a source of error. Interviewers may not correctly "hear" what the respondent is actually saying. This may be because the respondent is inarticulate and the response is garbled, or because an interviewer's own selective processes are operating. Interviewers may hear what they want to hear and retain what they want to retain. This is a common failing with all of us, and, in spite of interviewer training, recording errors in the interview are all too common.

Lest we be too hard on interviewers, we need to recognize that their job is a difficult one. It demands a good deal of ingenuity, creativity, and dogged determination. Research Window 18.2 highlights, for example, what an interviewer for the Census Bureau must do to complete the work assigned.

Interviewer cheating can also be a source of response error. Cheating may range from the fabrication of a whole interview to the fabrication of one or two answers to make the response complete. The Advertising Research Foundation (ARF), for example, conducts validation studies for its members upon request by reinterviewing a sample of those who were reported to have been interviewed previously. Foundation researchers check to see if the interview actually took place and the designated questions were asked. For the years 1972 and 1973, ARF found that 5.4

Research Window 18.2
Adventures of a Census Interviewer

Allie Sanborn held up the questionnaire. "You go in as information, but come out as a statistic," she said and then launched into the questions that make up the Census Bureau's Survey of Income and Program Participation (SIPP). Sanborn is one of the Census Bureau's 3,000 field representatives, a hardy band of adventurers who scour the streets for their target households and conduct the interviews that give us the data we release.

On this day, Sanborn was visiting three households. In two cases, she was meeting her respondents for the first time. She would tell them she would be visiting them every four months over the next two and one-half years to ask about their income and employment.

In one household, she interviewed a single parent living on disability. The householder fought off weakness to answer Sanborn's questions and expressed pleasure at participating in the survey. Here Sanborn asked the basic SIPP questions on income and labor force participation. In future interviews, she would be asking questions on these and other subjects.

Sanborn arrived at the second household and managed to persuade the woman of the house to answer questions while frying salmon cakes for dinner. This interview proved to be more difficult since the household consisted of several adults.

No, the woman told Sanborn, she couldn't give her all the information needed. She gave what she could and called her son-in-law to complete his portion of the interview. None of her daughters were home. Sanborn tried unsuccessfully to interview the woman's husband, but agreed to come back two days hence to continue the interview.

"I have a feeling . . ." Sanborn said as she left. Sure enough, when she returned two days later, no one was home. Missed appointments were a way of life.

"The larger households are tough," Sanborn explained. "Some of the respondents may be out, and those you talk to may not be able to answer for those who aren't there, especially if the people aren't related. Over the two-and-one-half-year interviewing cycle, people will come and go, move out of state—and we make an attempt to follow them. We have to question each adult about recent work and income. We ask what's happened over the past four months. The more adults, the more difficult it is to get all the information from everyone.

"We become a part of the family history. We see births, deaths, divorces; we see children grow up and leave. I had one respondent tell me that I knew the family better than anyone else in the world.

"We walk in as a stranger, but after two and one-half years we leave practically a member of the family."

The third household Sanborn visited that day had been in the survey for two years. It housed an older couple with grown children away at school. In this household, Sanborn asked the basic SIPP questions on income and several supplemental questions on assets, work disability, and other topics. (After the first interview, households are asked additional questions on various topics ranging from family background to taxes.)

Sanborn finally returned home at 10 p.m.; even so, she still wasn't finished. She had to review the questionnaires to see if she had conducted the interviews properly. The next day she shipped the questionnaires off to the Philadelphia regional office.

Source: "Census Field Representatives Meet Statistics Face to Face," *Census and You*, 24 (April 1989), pp. 6–8.

"Interviewer's Interviewer"

Sanborn is a supervisory field representative, the interviewer's interviewer. She trains new field representatives, rates them, handles problem cases, and in general provides on-the-spot support for an army of field representatives.

Most representatives work in their own counties. Supervisory field representatives have a much larger territory; Sanborn's is particularly large. She generally works in Baltimore and Annapolis but routinely drives to Delaware and Pennsylvania.

The first two weeks of the month she works on SIPP. She sees 10 to 15 households. In this survey, the representative must contact all households in person. The third week she works on the Current Population Survey; the work load is heavier, about 35 households. Many of these are telephoned. The last week of the month is used for reinterviews or solving other problems.

The representatives are on the road a good bit and work odd hours—nights and weekends. "We have to go when people are most likely to be home," Sanborn explains.

Sanborn receives her assignments from the Philadelphia regional office. After that, it's up to her. She sends new households a standard introductory letter to break the ice. "I always try to add a personal note."

Occasionally one household member may be cooperative, another much less so. "In one case, the wife greeted me and we proceeded into the living room, where the husband was sprawled out in his recliner. He was a steelworker who had just lost his job. And he wasn't feeling kindly toward the government.

"He refused the interview and made me leave. I arranged to call the wife at work in order to continue. But that didn't work, and when I stopped by to see her again, he came out and became very abusive. I tried to explain the value of the survey, but he got angrier and louder. I was afraid he'd become violent. It was quite frightening. About 90 to 95 percent of the people I meet are cooperative. It takes some ingenuity and persistence to deal with the others. But I take it as a real challenge to get the interview."

Tales from the Trenches

Just Horsing Around   Calling at a rural address, one field representative found a locked gate. The house was out of sight up an entrance road behind a nearby hill. No one came to the gate to let her in, and there were no neighbors nearby. She wrote a note explaining her visit and setting a time at which she would return later that day.

When she returned, the note was gone, the gate was ajar, and there was a horse standing just inside the gate. There was also a note addressed to "Census representative." The note instructed the field representative to mount the horse, which would carry her up to the house, where the owner would be happy to see her.

Without hesitation, the interviewer, who had never ridden a horse before, clambered up on the horse, which then plodded up the hill and delivered her to the door of the house.

Sure enough, the respondent, gracious and congenial, was waiting, and the interview was completed.

At the end of the interview, the Census Bureau worker thanked the respondent and again mounted the horse, which, plodding carefully, delivered her to the gate.

percent of the interviews across thirty-three separate studies could not be verified, and that an additional 7.9 percent contained at least two performance errors.[28] What is especially disturbing about these results is that it is generally believed that the surveys submitted for verification are among the best executed in the advertising area.

Most commercial research firms validate 10 to 20 percent of the completed interviews through follow-up telephone calls or by sending postcards to a sample of "respondents" to verify that they have in fact been contacted. Generally, these follow-ups are most productive in detecting the flagrant cheating that occurs when a field worker fabricates the entire interview. They are much less effective in detecting more subtle forms of cheating in which (1) the interviewer asks only the key questions and fills in the remaining information later, (2) the interviewer interviews respondents in groups rather than separately as instructed, (3) the interviewer interviews the wrong respondent because the designated respondent is inaccessible or difficult to contact, or (4) the interviewer employs one contact for information for two separate studies and thereby introduces contamination through respondent fatigue.

Another form of cheating, which is not exactly response error but which has a strong effect on all nonsampling errors, is padding bills. The interviewer may falsify the number of hours worked or the number of miles traveled. The problem is widespread because of the nature of the interviewing situation. The interviewer works without direct supervision in a basically low-paying job. Further, the supervisor's pay is normally geared to the interviewer's charges, so that the higher the interviewer's bills, the higher the supervisor's compensation. Bill padding drains resources from other parts of the study and thereby decreases the efficiency (value) of the information because it is obtained at higher cost.

As suggested previously, it is much more difficult to adjust for response errors than for nonresponse errors. Both their direction and their magnitude are unknown because, in order to estimate their effects, the true value must be known. The researcher's main hope lies in prevention rather than subsequent adjustment of the results. The various sources of errors themselves suggest preventives. For example, training can help reduce errors in asking questions and recording answers. Similarly, the way interviewers are selected, paid, and controlled could reduce cheating. Overall interviewer performance can be assessed by rating the quality of the work with respect to appropriate characteristics such as costs, types of errors, ability to follow instructions, and so on. We shall not elaborate on the recommended procedures for assessing these factors, since that would be a book in its own right. For our purposes, we need to recognize the existence of response errors, their sources, and their potentially devastating impact. The interviewer-interviewee interaction model is helpful in visualizing these sources and in indicating some methods of prevention.

Office Errors   Our problems with nonsampling errors do not end with data collection. Errors can and do arise in the editing, coding, tabulating, and analyzing of the data.[29] For the most part, these errors can be reduced, if not eliminated, by exercising proper controls in data processing. These questions are discussed in the chapters dealing with analysis.

Ethical

Dilemma 18.1   A well-known car agency needed to make a decision about whether or not to import a relatively unknown line of foreign cars to complement its domestic line. To aid in its decision making, the agency contracted a research firm to conduct a study to determine potential consumer interest and demand for this foreign car line.

The results indicated that substantial awareness and interest existed, and consequently the decision was made to take on the new line.

To publicize the new line, a special preview was arranged for interested community members such as local newspaper and radio people, executives in related automotive industries, filling station and repair shop owners, and leaders of men's and women's clubs. The agency's owners also wanted to invite the survey participants who had expressed an interest in the car and consequently asked the research firm to make known to them the respondents' names. The research firm refused to comply with this request, arguing that to do so would be a violation of the respondents' promised anonymity.

- Should the research firm have complied with the agency's request?
- Did the car agency have the right to receive the participants' names since it had paid for the research?
- Would it have made a difference if the study had not been one to determine sales potential?
- What would be some of the consequences of making the respondents' names known to the car agency?
- If the question had been anticipated before the survey was begun, could the interview structure have avoided the dilemma in which the research company and the agency now find themselves?

Total Error Is Key

By this time the reader should understand the warning that total error, rather than any single type of error, is the key in a research investigation. The admonition particularly applies to sampling error. With a course in statistics behind them, students beginning their studies in research methods often argue for the "largest possible sample," reasoning that a large sample is much more likely to produce a statistic close to the population parameter being estimated than a small sample is. What the student fails to appreciate, though, is that the argument applies only to sampling error. Increasing the sample size does, in fact, decrease sampling error. However, it may also increase nonsampling error because the large sample requires more interviewers, for instance, and this creates additional burdens in selection, training, and control. Further, nonsampling error is a much more insidious and troublesome error than sampling error. Sampling error can be estimated. Many forms of nonsampling error cannot. Sampling error can be reduced through more sophisticated sample design or by using a larger sample. The path is clear and relatively well-traveled, so the researcher should have little difficulty keeping sampling error within bounds. Not so with nonsampling errors. The path is not paved. New sources of nonsampling error are being discovered all the time, and even though known, many of these sources defy reduction by any automatic procedure. "Improved method" is critical, but what this ideal method should be is unknown. This chapter has attempted to highlight some of the better-known sources of nonsampling error and ways of dealing with them.

Table 18.6 attempts to summarize what we have been saying about nonsampling errors and how they can be reduced and controlled. The table can be used as a sort of checklist for marketing managers and other users of research to evaluate the quality of the research prior to making substantive decisions on the basis of the research

Table 18.6   Overview of Nonsampling Errors and Some Methods for Handling Them

Type	Definition	Methods for Handling
Noncoverage	Failure to include some units or entire sections of the defined survey population in the sampling frame.	1. Improve basic sampling frame using other sources. 2. Select sample in such a way as to reduce incidence, for example, by ignoring ineligibles on a list. 3. Adjust the results by appropriately weighting the subsample results.
Nonresponse	Failure to obtain information from some elements of the population that were selected for the sample.	
Not-at-homes	Designated respondent is not home when the interviewer calls.	1. Have interviewers make advance appointments. 2. Call back at another time, preferably at a different time of day. 3. Attempt to contact the designated respondent using another approach (e.g., use a modified callback).
Refusals	Respondent refuses to cooperate in the survey.	1. Attempt to convince the respondent of the value of the research and the importance of his or her participation. 2. Provide advance notice that the survey is coming. 3. Guarantee anonymity. 4. Provide an incentive for participating. 5. Hide the identification of the sponsor by using an independent research organization. 6. Try to get a foot in the door by getting the respondent to comply with some small task before getting the survey. 7. Use personalized cover letters. 8. Use a follow-up contact at a more convenient time. 9. Avoid unnecessary questions. 10. Adjust the results to account for the nonresponse.

results. While not all of the methods for handling nonsampling errors will be applicable in every study, a systematic analysis of the research effort, using the table guidelines, should provide the proper appreciation for the quality of research information that is obtained.

Ethical Dilemma 18.2   "These new computer-voiced telephone surveys are wonderful!" your friend enthuses over lunch. "Because we don't have to pay telephone interviewers, we can afford to have target numbers automatically redialed until someone answers. Of course, the public finds the computer's voice irritating and the whole notion of being

Type	Definition	Methods for Handling
Field	Although the individual participates in the study, he or she refuses to answer specific questions or provides incorrect answers to them.	1. Match the background characteristics of interviewer and respondent as closely as possible. 2. Make sure interviewer instructions are clear and written down. 3. Conduct practice training sessions with interviewers. 4. Examine the interviewers' understanding of the study's purposes and procedures. 5. Have interviewers complete the questionnaire and examine their replies to see if there is any relationship between the answers they secure and their own answers. 6. Verify a sample of each interviewer's interviews.
Office[a]	Errors that arise when coding, tabulating, or analyzing the data.	1. Use a field edit to detect the most glaring omissions and inaccuracies in the data. 2. Use a second edit in the office to decide how data-collection instruments containing incomplete answers, obviously wrong answers, and answers that reflect a lack of interest are to be handled. 3. Use closed questions to simplify the coding, but when open-ended questions need to be used, specify the appropriate codes that will be allowed before collecting the data. 4. When open-ended questions are being coded and multiple coders are being used, divide the task by questions and not by data-collection forms. 5. Have each coder code a sample of the other's work to ensure that a consistent set of coding criteria is being employed. 6. Follow established conventions; for example, use numeric codes and not letters of the alphabet when coding the data for computer analysis. 7. Prepare a codebook that lists the codes for each variable and the categories included in each code. 8. Use appropriate methods to analyze the data.

[a]Steps to reduce the incidence of office errors are discussed in more detail in the analysis chapters.

interviewed by a machine rather humiliating. Nevertheless, we can overcome most people's reluctance to participate by repeatedly calling them until they give in and complete the questionnaire."

■ Is it ethical to contact respondents repeatedly until they agree to participate in a research study? How many contacts are legitimate?

■ If an industry is unable to constrain its members to behave ethically, should the government step in with regulations?

■ If the public reacts against this kind of telephone survey, what are the results likely to be for researchers using traditional, more considerate telephone surveys?

Back to the Case

Rosemont was not that far geographically from affluent Moreland Heights, but economically it was a world away. Rosemont was a low-income neighborhood with a high crime rate, and it was literally on the other side of the tracks. But to Lucy Lindenbloom, gathering information in Rosemont wasn't any worse than gathering it in Moreland Heights. As a Census interviewer, she was always faced with problems: in Rosemont the problems were just a little different. Besides, Lindenbloom always felt a special mission when she went into low-income neighborhoods. These were the people that many government programs were designed to help. If the government couldn't find these people to count them, then it would never be able to find them to help them.

Her first stop was a run-down brownstone with a broken doorbell and a busted lock on the front door. Lindenbloom stepped into the vestibule. It was crammed with strollers and smelled faintly of cabbage. On one wall was a bank of mailboxes. She found the name she was looking for on the box marked 4D. "Great,"

she thought to herself, "the fourth floor and no elevator."

Lindenbloom knew that it was buildings like this that sometimes drove interviewers to skip the stairs and just fill in the interview forms themselves. The temptation to cheat was always there, and interviewers had been known to fabricate data in a number of ways, from making up entire interviews to more subtle methods such as interviewing respondents in groups rather than separately. "But no matter how you did it," thought Lindenbloom as she plodded up the uneven stairs, "it would still be cheating. When one interviewer cheats, it affects the work of all the others by introducing response error into the data."

Lindenbloom, slightly out of breath, knocked on the door of apartment 4D.

"Who is it?" inquired a frightened voice.

"U.S. Census Bureau, ma'am," Lindenbloom responded. "I'm trying to locate Mary Porter to ask her some questions."

"Wait there," said the voice.

Lindenbloom waited and waited. After ten minutes, she knocked on the door again. "Ms. Porter?" she asked. "Are you all right?"

Just then Lindenbloom heard footsteps on the stairway. Two uniformed policemen approached her and demanded to know what she was doing.

"I'm a Census interviewer," Lindenbloom said, showing her ID.

"Sorry to trouble you," one of the officers said, "but there have been a lot of robberies in the neighborhood. It makes folks around here real suspicious of people trying to gain access to their apartments."

"It's okay, Mrs. Porter," one of the policemen shouted through the locked door. "This is Ms. Lindenbloom. She really is with the Census Bureau. She just wants to ask you a few questions."

Lindenbloom sighed as she heard the sound of the chain lock being slipped aside. She had been a Census interviewer for more than ten years. This wasn't the first time she had begun an interview with a police escort.

Summary

Learning Objective 1: Explain what sampling error is.

Sampling error is the difference between the observed values of a variable and the long-run average of the observed values in repetitions of the measurement.

Learning Objective 2: Cite the two basic types of nonsampling errors and describe each.

There are two basic types of nonsampling errors: errors due to nonobservation and errors due to observation. Nonobservation errors result from a failure to obtain data from parts of the survey population. They occur because part of the population of interest was not included or because some elements designated for inclusion in the sample did not respond. Observation errors occur because inaccurate information was secured from the sample elements or because errors were introduced in the processing of the data or in reporting the findings.

Learning Objective 3: Outline several ways in which noncoverage bias can be reduced.

Noncoverage bias can be reduced, although not necessarily eliminated, by recognizing its existence, working to improve the sampling frame, and employing a sampling specialist to help reduce (through the sampling procedure) and adjust (through analysis) the remaining frame imperfections.

Learning Objective 4: Explain what error due to nonresponse is.

Error due to nonresponse represents a failure to obtain information from some elements of the population that were selected and designated for the sample.

Learning Objective 5: Cite the standard definition for *response rate*.

Response rate may be defined as the number of completed interviews with responding units divided by the number of eligible responding units in the sample.

Learning Objective 6: Identify the two main sources of nonresponse bias.

The two main sources of nonresponse bias are not-at-homes and refusals.

Learning Objective 7: Define *contact rate*.

The contact rate is the percentage of eligible assignments in which the interviewer makes contact with the designated respondent; that is,

$$K = \frac{\text{number of sample units contacted}}{\text{total number of eligible sample units approached}}.$$

Learning Objective 8: Cite some of the factors that may contribute to a respondent's refusal to participate in a study.

The rate of refusals in a study will depend on, among other things, the nature of the respondent, the nature of the organization sponsoring the research, the circumstances surrounding the contact, the nature of the subject under investigation, and the skill of the interviewer. The method used to collect the data may also make a difference.

Learning Objective 9: Identify three factors that may be a source of bias in the interviewer-interviewee interaction.

The interviewer-interviewee interaction may be biased by background characteristics, psychological factors, and behavioral factors on the part of either the interviewer or the respondent, or both.

Learning Objective 10: Discuss the types of interviewer behaviors that may lead to response bias.

At least three interviewer behaviors can lead to response bias: (1) errors in asking questions and in probing when additional information is required, (2) errors in recording the answers, and (3) errors due to cheating.

Discussion Questions, Problems, and Projects

1. J. Hoffman was the owner of a medium-size supermarket located in St. Cloud, Minnesota. She was considering altering the layout of the store so that, for example, the frozen food section would be near the section with fresh fruit and vegetables. These changes were designed to better accommodate customer shopping patterns and thereby increase customer patronage. Prior to making the alterations, she decided to administer a short questionnaire in the store to a random sample of customers. For a period of two weeks, three of the store cashiers were instructed to stand at the end of selected aisles and conduct personal interviews with every fifth customer. Hoffman gave specific instructions that on no account were customers to be harassed or offended. Identify the major sources of noncoverage and nonresponse errors. Explain.

2. Tough-Grip Tires was a large manufacturer of radial tires located in New Orleans, Louisiana, and it was experiencing a problem common to tire manufacturers. The poor performance of the auto industry was having a severe negative impact on the tire industry. To try to maintain sales and competitive positions, the various manufacturers were offering wholesalers additional credit and discount opportunities. Tough-Grip's management was particularly concerned about wholesaler reaction to a new discount policy it was considering. The first survey the company conducted to explore this reaction was unsatisfactory to management. Management felt it was conducted in a haphazard manner and contained numerous nonsampling errors. Tough-Grip's management decided to conduct another study, containing the following changes:

- The sampling frame was defined as a list of 1,000 of the largest wholesalers that stocked Tough-Grip tires, and the sample elements were to be randomly selected from this list.
- A callback technique was to be employed, with the callbacks being made at different times than the original attempted contact.
- The sample size was to be doubled, from 200 to 400 respondents.
- The sample elements that were ineligible or refused to cooperate were to be substituted by the next element from the list.
- An incentive of $1.00 was to be offered to respondents.

Critically evaluate the steps that were being considered to prevent the occurrence of nonsampling errors. Do you think they were appropriate? Be specific.

3. A major publisher of a diverse set of magazines was interested in determining customer satisfaction with three of the company's leading publications: *Style Update*, *Business Profiles*, and *Hi-Tech Review*. The three magazines dealt, respectively, with women's fashions, business trends, and computer technology developments. Three sampling frames, consisting of lists of subscribers residing in Chicago, were formulated. Three random samples were to be chosen from these lists. Personal interviews using an unstructured-undisguised questionnaire were to be conducted. The publishing company had a regular pool of interviewers that it called upon whenever interviews were to be conducted. The interviewers had varying educational backgrounds, though 95 percent were high school graduates and the remaining 5 percent had some college education. In terms of age and sex, the range varied from eighteen years to forty-five years with 70 percent females and 30 percent males. The majority of interviewers were housewives and students. Prior to conducting a survey the company sent the necessary information and requested that the interviewers indicate whether they were interested. The questionnaires, addresses, and other details were then sent to those interviewers replying affirmatively. After an interviewer completed his or her quota of interviews, the replies were sent back to the company. The company then mailed the interviewer's remuneration.

(a) Using the guidelines in Table 18.6, critically evaluate the selection, training, and instructions given to the field interviewers.

(b) Using Kahn and Cannell's model (Figure 18.3), identify the major sources of bias that would affect the interviews.

4. The placement office at your university has asked you to assist it in the task of determining the size of starting salaries and the range of salary offers received by graduating seniors. The placement office has always gathered some information in this regard in that historically some seniors come in to report the name of the company for which they are going to work and the size of their starting salary. The office feels that these statistics may be biased, and thus it wishes to approach the whole task more systematically. This is why it has hired your expertise to determine what the situation was with respect to last year's graduating seniors.

(a) Describe how you would select a sample of respondents to answer the question of starting salaries. Why would you use this particular sample?

(b) What types of nonsampling errors might you expect to encounter with your approach, and how would you control for them?

5. An executive recruitment firm utilized a lengthy mail survey to gather information on the job mobility of midlevel managers. A sample of 500 eligible middle managers was selected, using a simple random sampling procedure. The firm used three waves of mailings. After the third mailing, each of the nonresponding sample units was contacted by phone and asked to answer only four questions regarding variables that the recruitment firm thought were particularly important, given the objective of the study. The table below gives mean values for these variables.

Wave	Number of Responses	Age	Income ($)	Years in Current Position	Total Years of Management Experience
1	125	30	22,000	1.2	5.1
2	100	37	27,000	4.0	9.4
3	75	42	32,500	5.1	15.1
N.R.	200	50	31,250	10.2	24.2

(a) What was the response rate for the completed questionnaire?
(b) Furnish some rough estimates for the *overall* sample means of the four variables. Show your work.
(c) Which variables seem to be most affected by potential nonresponse bias? Does this tell you anything about the sample selection procedure?

6. Arrange to interview a researcher at a local marketing research firm or in-house research department. How large a problem is nonresponse for the firm? What are typical response rates for the firm's research projects? Discuss the method(s) used to handle nonresponse bias. Does the firm compensate for nonresponse in ways that are not addressed in the text? Prepare a written report of your findings.

7. Prepare a brief questionnaire regarding the television-viewing habits of adults in your city. Administer this instrument to a sample of subjects using at least ten telephone interviews and ten personal interviews. Discuss the extent of the nonresponse bias with each method.

8. For this exercise you will need to use the questionnaire on television-viewing habits developed in Exercise 7. In addition, develop questions designed to measure a respondent's attitude toward the television medium. Add these questions to the questionnaire on television-viewing habits. Administer this new questionnaire to one of your classmates. Then request that this classmate administer the questionnaire so that you will be the interviewee. Refer to Figure 18.3, and discuss the background factors, psychological factors, and behavioral factors that might have led to bias in the interview. (Hint: After the interview it would be useful to discuss these aspects with your classmate. Explain what you meant by the various questions, and find out how your classmate interpreted these questions.)

Endnotes

1. Frederick Mosteller, "Nonsampling Errors," *Encyclopedia of Social Sciences* (New York: Macmillan, 1968), p. 113. See also the special issue of the *Journal of Official Statistics*, 4 (No. 3, 1987), edited by Lars Lyberg, which is devoted to nonsampling errors.

2. Mosteller, "Nonsampling Errors," p. 113.

3. Robert Ferber, *The Reliability of Consumer Reports of Financial Assets and Debts* (Urbana, Ill.: Bureau of Economic and Business Research, University of Illinois, 1966), p. 261. There was a series of studies with respect to the single objective. Ferber's monograph provides an overview of the studies and results, although there are six monographs in all.

4. Ibid., p. 266. Wiseman and McDonald make a similar point with the comment, "The use of very sophisticated sampling schemes when other aspects of the data collection effort are much less sophisticated may result in higher costs than are justified for the resultant data quality." See Frederick Wiseman and Philip McDonald, "Noncontact and Refusal Rates in Consumer Telephone Surveys," *Journal of Marketing Research*, 16 (November 1979), p. 483.

5. W. H. Williams, "How Bad Can 'Good' Data Really Be?" *The American Statistician*, 32 (May 1978), p. 61.

6. See, for example, Ronald Andersen, Judith Kasper, Martin R. Frankel, and Associates, *Total Survey Error* (San Francisco: Jossey-

Bass, 1979), or Henry Assael and John Keon, "Nonsampling vs. Sampling Errors in Survey Research," *Journal of Marketing*, 46 (Spring 1982), pp. 114–123.

7. Leslie Kish, *Survey Sampling* (New York: John Wiley, 1965), Chapter 13, "Biases and Nonsampling Errors," is particularly recommended for discussion of the biases arising from nonobservation.

8. The general adjustment procedure for dealing with the problem of duplicates on a list is to weight sample elements discovered to have been listed k times by $1/k$. Seymour Sudman, *Applied Sampling* (San Francisco: Academic Press, 1976), p. 63. Most of the standard computer packages for statistically analyzing the data contain mechanisms by which the analyst can specify the weight to be applied to each sample observation.

9. Frederick Wiseman and Philip McDonald, *Toward the Development of Industry Standards for Response and Nonresponse Rates* (Cambridge, Mass.: Marketing Science Institute, 1980).

10. "On the Definition of Response Rates," *CASRO Special Report* (Port Jefferson, N.Y.: The Council of American Survey Research Organizations, 1982).

11. Charlotte G. Steeh, "Trends in Nonresponse Rates," *Public Opinion Quarterly*, 45 (Spring 1981), pp. 40–57.

12. There are several studies that contain data about when particular types of individuals are likely to be home. See, for example, M. F. Weeks, B. L. Jones, R. E. Folsum, Jr., and C. H. Benrud, "Optimal Times to Contact Sample Households," *Public Opinion Quarterly*, 44 (Spring 1980), pp. 101–114; Michael F. Weeks, Richard W. Kulka, and Stephanie A. Pierson, "Optimal Call Scheduling for a Telephone Survey," *Public Opinion Quarterly*, 51 (Winter 1987), pp. 540–549; and Gideon Vigderhaus, "Scheduling Telephone Interviews: A Study of Seasonal Patterns," *Public Opinion Quarterly*, 45 (Summer 1981), pp. 250–259. The report "Identifying Monthly Response Rates Aids in Mail Planning," *Specialty Advertising Report*, 15 (4th Quarter, 1979), contains a useful table for scheduling mail studies to coincide with the months in which people are most likely to respond.

13. W. Edwards Deming, "On a Probability Mechanism to Attain an Economic Balance between the Resultant Error of Response and the Bias of Nonresponse," *Journal of the American Statistical Association*, 48 (December 1953), pp. 766–767. See also Benjamin Lipstein, "In Defense of Small Samples," *Journal of Advertising Research*, 15 (February 1975), pp. 33–40; and William C. Dunkelburg and George S. Day, "Nonresponse Bias and Callbacks in Sample Surveys," *Journal of Marketing Research*, 10 (May 1973), pp. 160–168, a study that provides "evidence on the rate at which sample values converge on their population distribution as the number of callbacks increases." See also Norman T. Bravold and James M. Comer, "A Model for Estimating the Response Rate to a Mailed Survey," *Journal of Business Research*, 16 (March 1988), pp. 101–116.

14. *Your Opinion Counts: 1986 Refusal Rate Study* (Chicago: Marketing Research Association, 1986).

15. Julie Yu and Harris Cooper, "A Quantitative Review of Research Design Effects on Response Rates to Questionnaires," *Journal of Marketing Research*, 20 (February 1983), pp. 36–44. The evidence also suggests that the method of data collection is becoming less important, while other factors, such as the number of follow-up contacts, are becoming more important. See John Goyder, "Face-to-Face Interviews and Mailed Questionnaires: The Net Difference in Response Rate," *Public Opinion Quarterly*, 49 (Summer 1985), pp. 234–252.

16. T. De Maio, "Refusals: Who, Where, and Why," *Public Opinion Quarterly*, 44 (Summer 1980), pp. 223–233. See also Jolene M. Strubbe, Jerome B. Kernan, and Thomas J. Grogan, "The Refusal

Problem in Telephone Surveys," *Journal of Advertising Research*, 26 (June/July 1986), pp. 29–37.

17. James R. Chromy and Daniel G. Horowitz, "The Use of Monetary Incentives in National Assessment Household Surveys," *Journal of the American Statistical Association*, 73 (September 1978), pp. 473–478; J. Duncan, "Mail Questionnaires in Survey Research: A Review of Response Inducement Techniques," *Journal of Management*, 5 (September 1979), pp. 39–55; *The Use of Monetary and Other Gift Incentives in Mail Surveys: An Annotated Bibliography* (Monticello, Ill.: Vance Bibliographies, 1979); and Lee Harvey, "Factors Affecting Response Rates to Mailed Questionnaires: A Comprehensive Literature Review," *Journal of the Market Research Society*, 29 (July 1987), pp. 341–353.

18. Frederick Wiseman, Marianne Schafer, and Richard Schafer, "An Experimental Test of the Effects of a Monetary Incentive on Cooperation Rates and Data Collection Costs in Central Location Interviewing," *Journal of Marketing Research*, 20 (November 1983), pp. 439–442.

19. *Statistical Adjustment for Nonresponse in Sample Surveys: A Selected Bibliography with Annotations* (Monticello, Ill.: Vance Bibliographies, 1979); J. Scott Armstrong and Terry S. Overton, "Estimating Nonresponse Bias in Mail Surveys," *Journal of Marketing Research*, 14 (August 1977), pp. 396–402; Michael J. O'Neil, "Estimating the Nonresponse Bias Due to Refusals in Telephone Surveys," *Public Opinion Quarterly*, 40 (Summer 1976), pp. 218–232; and David Elliott and Roger Thomas, "Further Thoughts on Weighting Survey Results to Compensate for Nonresponse," *Survey Methodology Bulletin*, 15 (February 1983), pp. 2–11.

20. The technique also could possibly be used with telephone interviews, but it was designed for personal interviews because of the tremendous expense of personal interview callbacks. Further, probing on the phone about when a respondent was home during the last five days can cause mistrust. See Alfred Politz and Willard Simmons, "An Attempt to Get the Not-at-Homes into the Sample Without Callbacks," *Journal of the American Statistical Association*, 44 (March 1949), pp. 9–32, for explanation of the technique. For an empirical investigation of the effect of weighting on bias, see James Ward, Bertram Russick, and William Rudelius, "A Test of Reducing Callbacks and Not-At-Home Bias in Personal Interviews by Weighting At-Home Respondents," *Journal of Marketing Research*, 22 (February 1985), pp. 66–73. See also Charles H. Alexander, "A Class of Methods for Using Personal Controls in Household Weighting," *Survey Methodology*, 13 (December 1987), pp. 183–198.

21. Robert A. Peterson and Roger A. Kerin, "The Quality of Self-Report Data: Review and Synthesis," in Ben Enis and Kenneth Roering, eds., *Annual Review of Marketing 1981* (Chicago: American Marketing Association, 1981), pp. 5–20.

22. Robert L. Kahn and Charles F. Cannell, *The Dynamics of Interviewing* (New York: John Wiley, © 1957), p. 193. The figure is used by permission of John Wiley & Sons, Inc.

23. Ibid., p. 194.

24. Seymour Sudman, Norman Bradburn, Ed Blair, and Carol Stocking, "Modest Expectations: The Effects of Interviewers' Prior Expectations and Response," *Sociological Methods & Research*, 6 (November 1977), pp. 177–182; Eleanor Singer and Luanne Kohnke-Aguirre, "Interviewer Expectation Effects: A Replication and Extension," *Public Opinion Quarterly*, 43 (Summer 1979), pp. 245–260; Eleanor Singer, Martin R. Frankel, and Marc B. Glassman, "The Effect of Interviewer Characteristics and Expectations on Response," *Public Opinion Quarterly*, 47 (Spring 1983), pp. 68–83; and Robert M. Groves and Lou J. Magilavy, "Measuring and Explaining Interviewer Effects in Centralized Telephone Surveys," *Public Opinion Quarterly*, 50 (Summer 1986), pp. 251–266.

25. L. L. Guest, "A Study of Interviewer Competence," *International Journal of Opinion and Attitude Research*, 1 (March 1947), pp. 17–30. See also Wil Dijkstra, "Interviewing Style and Respondent Behavior: An Experimental Study of the Survey Interview," *Sociological Methods & Research*, 16 (November 1987), pp. 309–334.

26. W. A. Belson, "Increasing the Power of Research to Guide Advertising Decisions," *Journal of Marketing*, 29 (April 1965), p. 38. See also Martin Collins and Bob Butcher, "Interviewer and Clustering Effects in an Attitude Survey," *Journal of the Market Research Society*, 25 (January 1983), pp. 39–58.

27. Norman M. Bradburn and Seymour Sudman, *Improving Interview Method and Questionnaire Design* (San Francisco: Jossey-Bass, 1979), p. 29.

28. Lipstein, "In Defense of Small Samples."

29. The reader who believes that analysis errors should be no problem should see Mosteller, "Nonsampling Errors," in which he devotes 9 of 19 pages to the discussion of potential errors in analysis. See also John G. Keane, "Questionable Statistics," *American Demographics*, 7 (June 1985), pp. 18–21. For an empirical example illustrating the potential extent of the problem, see David Elliot, "A Study of Variation in Occupation and Social Class Coding—Summary of Results," *Survey Methodology Bulletin*, 14 (May 1982), pp. 48–49.

Suggested Additional Readings

For general discussions of data quality, the differences between sampling and nonsampling error, and steps that can be taken to improve the quality of information gathered in marketing research studies, see

Ronald Andersen, Judith Kasper, Martin R. Frankel, and Associates, *Total Survey Error* (San Francisco: Jossey-Bass, 1979).

Henry Assael and John Keon, "Nonsampling vs. Sampling Errors in Survey Research," *Journal of Marketing*, 46 (Spring 1982), pp. 114–123.

Robert A. Peterson and Roger A. Kerin, "The Quality of Self-Report Data: Review and Synthesis," in Ben Enis and Kenneth Roering, eds., *Annual Review of Marketing 1981* (Chicago: American Marketing Association, 1981), pp. 5–20.

Frederick Wiseman, ed., *Improving Data Quality in Sample Surveys* (Cambridge, Mass.: Marketing Science Institute, 1983).

Research Project

The fifth stage in the research process is to design the sample and collect the data. As we learned from the chapters in this part, researchers generally prefer to use a sample of a population rather than a census of a population, not only because a sample is less costly to obtain, but because it is generally more accurate.

In these chapters we learned that researchers generally follow a six-step procedure for drawing a sample, which includes defining the population, identifying the sampling frame, selecting a sampling procedure, determining the sample size, selecting the sample elements, and collecting the data from the designated elements. We investigated the different types of samples that researchers use and the advantages and disadvantages of each.

In the last chapter we investigated the second type of error that affects research studies: nonsampling error. As we discussed, there are two types of nonsampling error: those due to nonobservation and those due to observation. Nonobservation errors include coverage errors and nonresponse errors, while observation errors include field errors and office errors.

The problem with nonsampling error, we learned, is that unlike sampling error, it generally cannot be accurately estimated and corrected for. Like viruses for the common cold, new sources of nonsampling error are being discovered all the time—and, again like the common cold, are proving resistant to cure. A researcher's best tactic is to know as much as possible about the types of nonsampling errors that can occur and try to design a study that will prevent them.

Researchers for CARA were interested in assessing the attitudes of local businesspeople for their study. They decided to define the *local area* as the Fairview County area. *Businesspeople* were defined as individuals who made decisions regarding advertising expenditures for their firms. The researchers decided to exclude from the sample any firms that used an advertising agency or showed minimal interest in using any of the three major advertising media. They excluded these firms because CARA was interested in obtaining responses from firms that were likely to be targeted directly by sales representatives. Companies that use advertising agencies will normally have little direct contact with sales representatives; very small companies offer little potential for ad revenues.

The researchers decided to use the latest Centerville Telephone Directory Yellow Pages as their sampling frame. Recall that a sampling frame is the list of elements from which the sample is drawn. They identified ten major categories of business from which to select the sample: building materials and hardware; automotive sales and service; apparel; furniture and home furnishings; eating and drinking establishments; health and fitness; financial institutions; home entertainment; professional services; and a miscellaneous category including florists, jewelers, printers, book dealers, and retail photographic sales and service.

By further winnowing the list to eliminate those firms employing advertising agencies or expressing little interest in advertising, the researchers compiled a final list of 3,086 businesses.

A systematic sampling plan was chosen for this study. Recall that in this type of sampling plan each element has a known a priori chance of inclusion in the sample. Each of the 3,086 businesses identified as a part of the sampling frame was classified as a member of one of the ten categories of business and was placed in alphabetical order within that category. The ten categories were then randomly ordered, and the businesses were numbered from 1 to 3,086.

The researchers decided on a sample size of 600 and then determined two measures: the sampling interval and a random start. The sampling interval involved dividing the number of elements in the population (3,086) by the desired sample size (600). This number (5.14) was then rounded down to 5. A random-number table was used to select the initial number between 1 and 5, and every fifth element was selected thereafter until the desired sample size was achieved. This process ensured that the sample was representative of the sampling frame; the proportion of various categories of business included in the sample equaled the proportion of these types of business in the sampling frame.

The researchers then pretested the questionnaire by mailing twenty questionnaires to businesses selected by the systematic sampling plan. Half of the respondents were given a dollar for their cooperation; half were given nothing except thanks. Eight of those receiving the incentive returned the questionnaire; only one of the others complied. Since eight of the nine questionnaires that were returned were fully completed, the researchers decided that no changes needed to be made to the questionnaire. Since CARA was interested in whether offering respondents an incentive would increase response similarly in the larger group, the researchers decided to offer half the sample a dollar for responding and nothing to the other half.

A general rule for selecting sample size is that there should be 100 or more units for each category of the major breakdowns and 20 to 50 for the minor breakdowns. The researchers assumed that the section of the questionnaire requesting attitudes toward sales representatives would have the highest percentage of incomplete subsections. Based on the responses to that section in the pretest, they estimated that 150 questionnaires were necessary to fulfill the requirement for the major breakdowns. They also assumed that if the returned forms were evenly distributed among the four categories of annual advertising budgets, 25 units per minor breakdown should result, thus fulfilling the second general rule.

Since there was no assurance that an even distribution would occur, they decided to increase the number of returns to increase the probability that the desired number of units in the minor breakdowns would approach the desired level. They estimated the rates of return conservatively at 10 percent for those individuals not receiving a dollar and 50 percent for those receiving a dollar. Hence, a sample size of 300 for each group should have resulted in 30 and 150 returns for the no-dollar and dollar groups, respectively, which would be enough to satisfy the general rules mentioned.

CARA researchers recognized the sources of nonsampling error in their study. They knew, for example, that coverage errors in their sampling frame were inevitable because the Centerville Yellow Pages was not a complete list of all local businesses. Some of the businesses listed were no longer in existence, others were too new to have been listed, and others may have chosen not to be listed. Nevertheless, no alternative offered a better list of businesses at a reasonable cost.

By using only ten major categories of businesses, the researchers also recognized that they had probably included some businesses that should not have been on the list and excluded others that should have been. Errors of inclusion and exclusion were also likely in their attempts to select only businesses not employing an advertising agency and businesses that would be interested in using the three major advertising media. Because of these biases, the researchers cautioned CARA representatives about generalizing the study's results to all businesses in Fairview County.

Nonresponse errors were evident in the response rates. Of the 600 questionnaires initially mailed, a total of 212 were returned. Of these, 165 were from the 300 that received a dollar, and 47 were from the 300 that received no incentive. Thirty-four of the returned questionnaires were unusable, however, either because none of the pages were completed or because only classification data were given.

The researchers were interested in sampling from among firms that did not use an advertising agency, individuals who were involved in making advertising decisions, and individuals who held the position of manager and/or owner. The results of the study seemed to indicate that the questionnaire generally secured responses from the population of interest. Of the 178 respondents submitting usable questionnaires, 149 companies (84 percent) did not use an advertising agency, 166 respondents (93 percent) were decision makers, and 160 respondents (90 percent) were owners and/or managers.

To further ensure that the data used for analyses were representative of the desired population, mean scores on attitudes toward the various advertising media and advertising media sales representatives were compared for those companies using an advertising agency versus those not using an advertising agency, those respondents who made decisions about advertising versus those who did not, and those who were owners and/or managers versus those who were not. No significant differences (alpha = .05) were found, except for the attitudes of those who used an advertising agency versus those who did not. Therefore, when analyzing the attitude scores, only those scores of those companies who did not use advertising agencies were considered.

Field errors occur when an individual who has agreed to participate in a study either refuses to answer specific questions or provides untruthful answers. CARA researchers noticed several instances of probable field error in the completed questionnaires. For example, on the scale measuring attitudes toward the advertising media of television, radio, and news-paper, 453 subsections were completed. Of this number, 133 were from the television category, 153 from the radio category, and 167 from the newspaper category. Since individuals were asked to fill out each subsection regardless of whether they used that type of advertising or not, there should not have been differences in these numbers. The researchers speculated that respondents may have been confused as to what their task was on this section, or they may merely have decided not to complete this section.

Respondents were also asked to approximate the proportion of their yearly advertising budget spent on nine different types of advertising. The researchers took the responses and determined the mean percentage scores for each category. The percentages did not add up to 100 percent, however, which indicated that some respondents had had difficulty determining these proportions.

Cases to Part Five

Case 5.1   St. Andrews Medical Center (B) [1]

The Eating Disorders Clinic of the St. Andrews Medical Center has been operating since 1985 to treat anorexia nervosa and bulimia. These conditions primarily strike women between the ages of 14 and 22. In recent years, the clinic has experienced a dramatic decline in patients, while, officials believe, a competing program offered by City Hospital has continued to grow. The programs are comparable in terms of staffing and cost of treatment. Patients are normally referred to an eating disorders program by their primary-care physician or another health-care professional.

Officials at St. Andrews were very concerned about the downward trend in the number of patients being referred to and treated at the Eating Disorders Clinic. Initially, they believed that the decrease might simply be a reflection of a decrease in the prevalence of anorexia nervosa and bulimia in the population. A review of the medical literature and discussions with administrators of eating disorders programs from across the country, however, strongly suggested that this was not the case. Furthermore, conversations with the medical director at City Hospital confirmed that the number of cases of the disorders treated by the City Hospital program has continued to increase during recent years.

St. Andrews officials next turned to the marketing department for the development and implementation of some type of research designed to uncover the reasons behind the decreasing enrollment in the eating disorders program.

Sampling Plan

Because more than 80 percent of the cases treated at the Eating Disorders Clinic are referred to the program by other health-care providers, the St. Andrews marketing staff believed that the research

should be directed at these health-care providers. In particular, they wanted to obtain attitudes and opinions about the St. Andrews program specifically and about eating disorders programs in general.

The population, then, for which a sampling frame was to be developed included all health-care professionals in the market area of St. Andrews Medical Center who may treat female patients between the ages of 14 and 22 years.

A review of admittance records showed that referrals are most likely to come from primary-care practitioners, including physicians in general medicine, family medicine, internal medicine, and gastroenterology. In addition, referrals have been received from pediatricians, obstetricians/gynecologists, psychiatrists, and psychologists. Although the names and addresses of physicians in these specialties were available from several sources, the marketing staff believed that the telephone directory provided the easiest and least expensive listing. The sampling frame thus included all physicians (or psychologists) from each of these specialties and was drawn from the yellow pages of the current telephone directory. Table 1 provides the breakdown of the number of

Table 1   Sampling Frame

Specialty	Number of Practitioners
Pediatricians	63
Obstetricians/Gynecologists	63
Psychiatrists	124
Psychologists	128
Primary-Care Practitioners*	321
Total	699

[1]The contributions of Tom J. Brown to the development of this case are gratefully acknowledged.

*Includes specialists in family medicine, general medicine, internal medicine, and gastroenterology.

professionals of each type included in the sampling frame. All health-care providers on the list were to be contacted.

Administration

The marketing department staff decided to conduct a mail survey and constructed a three-page structured questionnaire that was sent to the 699 health-care providers on the list, using the addresses obtained from the telephone directory. An appropriate cover letter was also included. Although neither the cover letter nor the questionnaire identified St. Andrews Medical Center as the sponsor of the survey, no attempt was made to disguise the purpose of the survey. In addition to questions related specifically to the St. Andrews program, the marketing staff included questions about City Hospital's competing program and about eating disorders programs in general.

Of the 699 questionnaires distributed, 56 (8 percent) were returned as undeliverable by the postal service, while 119 were completed and returned by respondents (a 17-percent response rate). Although St. Andrews officials were displeased with the low response rate—they had anticipated at least a 25-percent return rate—they thought that the data would provide useful information for the management of the Eating Disorders Clinic.

Questions

1. What is the appropriate target population, given the hospital's interest?
2. Evaluate the sampling frame, given the target population chosen by the hospital staff. What other sources might exist for use in developing the sampling frame?
3. Evaluate the use of a mail questionnaire for this research.

Case 5.2   PartyTime, Inc.[1]

Andrew Todd, chief executive officer of PartyTime, Inc., a manufacturer of specialty paper products, is preparing to make an important decision. In the 14 years since he founded the company, sales and profits have increased over tenfold to all-time highs of $7,000,000 and $1,150,000, respectively, during the current year. Industry analysts predict continued stable growth during the upcoming year. Despite his firm belief in the adage, "If it's not broken, don't fix it," Todd thinks that it might be time for the addition of a new channel of distribution, based on information he has recently received.

About the Company

PartyTime manufactures a variety of specialty paper products that can be grouped into three basic categories: gift wrap (all types), party goods (printed plates, cups, napkins, party favors, etc.), and other paper goods (specialty advertising, calendars, etc.). When Todd founded the company, he purchased and renovated an existing paper mill located in the Pacific

Northwest. Today, company headquarters and production facilities remain at the original location. During the heavy production season, the company employs approximately 200 people.

As shown in Table 1, gift wrap accounts for about 60 percent of revenues (50 percent of profits), and party goods amount to about 30 percent of sales (40 percent of profits). All other paper products sold by the company produce about 10 percent of revenues and an equivalent percentage of profits. Sales of gift wrap and other paper goods have been stable, increasing 3 to 4 percent per year during the previous five years. Interestingly (and as Todd is pleased to note), total sales of party goods have been increasing at about a 9-percent annual rate.

The Distribution Decision

Given the profitability of the party goods line and its substantial sales growth in recent years, Todd is very interested in further increasing sales of specialty party goods. A recent publication of the National Association of Paper and Party Retailers (NAPPR) indicated that industry-wide sales of party goods are expected to increase some 10 to 20 percent during the upcom-

---

[1]The contributions of Tom J. Brown to the development of this case are gratefully acknowledged.

Table 1   ***Current-Year Sales and Profit Breakdown by Category***

Category	Sales	Percentage	Profit	Percentage
Gift wrap	$4,302,300	61	$ 564,700	49
Party goods	2,045,500	29	472,300	41
Other paper goods	705,200	10	115,000	10
Total	$7,053,000	100	$1,152,000	100

ing year. Of particular interest is the projection that sales of party goods through independent party goods (IPG) shops will increase more than 25 percent. Currently, PartyTime party goods are distributed only through mass merchandisers and chain drugstores.

Although sales have been increasing steadily using existing channels, Todd wonders if the time is right to add the IPG channel. Any decision to include the new channel would have to be made early in the year, however, before orders for the holiday season begin arriving (a large percentage of total sales of party goods at the retail level occur during the holiday season).

Independent Party Goods (IPG) Shops

IPG retailers typically operate small to moderate-size stores that are often located in malls or strip shopping centers. The label "independent" indicates that the stores are not owned or franchised by major manufacturers such as Hallmark. In recent years, the number of IPG shops has grown tremendously, to the point where it is not unusual to have 15 to 20 shops in larger cities. Growth has been particularly strong in California, Florida, the upper Midwest, and the East.

Competitive Issues

Competition within traditional channels of distribution for party goods is intense. Within these channels, PartyTime must compete against major producers such as C.A. Reed, Beach Products, Unique, Hallmark, and Ambassador. The major competitors within the IPG channel, in contrast, are fewer in number; only AMSCAM, Contempo, and Paper Art serve as primary suppliers. Competition within the IPG channel is thought to be much less intense than that in the traditional channels.

(December 13)   Todd is leaning strongly toward committing the resources necessary to enter the IPG channel and calls a meeting of his managers to discuss the proposed move. He believes that there is room for at least one more supplier, because the competition is less intense than in the traditional distribution channels. In addition, he regards this as an opportunity to further expand the most profitable area of PartyTime's business.

At the meeting, most of PartyTime's managers seem to agree with Todd, although Kim Shinoda, the company's chief accountant, suggests that the company should learn more about IPG retailers before a decision is made. In a memorandum distributed at the meeting, she details the following areas on which more information is needed before a decision can be reached:

- *Competitive Products*   Are IPG retailers satisfied with current product offerings on the market? Do they receive a satisfactory level of service from the current suppliers?
- *Purchase Criteria*   In addition to price and product considerations, what other characteristics of suppliers and product lines do retailers think are important?
- *Supplier Loyalty*   To what extent are retailers willing to carry product lines of more than one supplier?

Todd agrees that more information would be useful in making a decision, but he realizes that time constraints will force him to make a decision within the next few weeks. Along with his managers, he decides to bring in a marketing research team.

(January 16)   The marketing research team is not ready to share the results of the research project with the managers at PartyTime. To obtain the information that Shinoda had suggested, as well as other information pertaining to the decision problem, the researchers developed an undisguised-semistructured telephone questionnaire. The survey document used by the interviewers is shown in Figure 1.

Officials at PartyTime are particularly interested in the responses of retailers located in those geographic areas in which growth is expected to be strongest over the next year; therefore, a sampling frame was developed using telephone directories in the major cities within these geographic regions. Because many types of stores could conceivably be considered IPG shops, two criteria were established for inclusion in the sampling frame: (1) the shop must devote more than 50 percent of its shelf space to paper and party goods, and (2) the shop must carry products from more than one supplier. A total of 110 shops were identified using the telephone directories. Although attempts were made to contact each of these shops during business hours, only 82 could be reached. Thirty-two of these met the two criteria, and 23 agreed to participate in the interview.

Figure 1   ***Survey Form***

Location:

Hello, may I speak with the store owner or purchasing agent, please?
My name is _____. My company is doing a study of the independent party shop channel for a private firm, and I would like to take a few minutes of your time to have you answer some questions. Any information you provide will be treated confidentially, and your name will not be used.

Do not pause.

Is this a convenient time? **If yes, continue.**

If, no: *Is there another time when you could be reached that would be more convenient for you, Mr./Ms. _____?*

Day and Time

_____

1. *In what category would your store fit?*
   [   ]   Gift shop
   [   ]   Card shop
   [   ]   Party goods shop
   [   ]   Combination. Please describe: _____
   [   ]   Other _____

If not a party goods shop or combination with party goods, stop, thank respondent for willingness to cooperate, and go on to the next call.

2. *What is the appropriate percentage of shelf space that your store devotes to paper and party goods?*
   Do not read off the categories.
   [   ]   0–20%
   [   ]   21–49%
   [   ]   50% or more

If less than 50%, stop survey here. Thank respondent for willingness to cooperate, and go on to the next call.

3. *Approximately how many suppliers of paper and party goods does your store deal with?* _____

Figure 1   *(Continued)*

If it carries only one line, stop survey here. Again, thank respondent for willingness to cooperate, and go on to the next call.

4. *Which of the following lines do you carry?*
   [   ]   C.A. Reed   [   ]   Contempo
   [   ]   AMSCAM   Others? _____
   [   ]   Paper Art

   The remaining questions refer to paper and party goods and the suppliers of these products.

5. *Concerning the suppliers of paper and party goods that you carry, how would you rate your satisfaction with the following (on a scale of 1 to 5, 5 being very satisfied and 1 being very dissatisfied)?*
   (a) Pricing and, in particular, discounts and markup capabilities _____
   (b) Sales representative service _____
   (c) Distribution (timeliness and completeness) _____
   (d) Product line_____

6. *Based on what you just said, you seem to be satisfied/dissatisfied with _____.
   What aspects of the suppliers' products or service have caused this?* **Probe for reasons.**
   _____

   Is there anything else that you think is important about your relationships with your suppliers? _____
   _____

7. *For each manufacturer, how would you rate the following in terms of importance (1 being most important and 4 being least important)?*

	C.A. Reed	**AMSCAM**	**Paper Art**	**Contempo**
Pricing	_____	_____	_____	_____
Promotion	_____	_____	_____	_____
Product line	_____	_____	_____	_____
Distribution	_____	_____	_____	_____

Repeat remaining options after each selection, if necessary.

Starting with most important and working down to least important, probe for reasons. Put responses for each supplier on the separate sheets that are attached.

   Pricing: (a) Wholesale pricing (discounts and allowances)
                    (b) Suggested retail prices
                    (c) Do you get credit for leftover seasonal merchandise?
   Promotion: (a) Display vehicles
                    (b) Manufacturer-sponsored consumer promotions
   Product Line: (a) Quality
                    (b) Dynamic product line (changing designs)
                    (c) Number of items/product categories
                    (d) Style
   Distribution: (a) Sales representative service (service calls, assistance)
                    (b) Timeliness of delivery
                    (c) Completeness of delivery (out-of-stocks)
                    (d) Ease of ordering

8. *Do any of your present suppliers offer a 1-800 number to process orders?*
   □   Yes   □   No   If yes, which ones? _____

(continued)

Figure 1   *(Continued)*

9. *Do you get advertising support from your suppliers?*
   ☐ Yes   ☐ No   If yes, which ones? _____

10. *Does a representative from your store attend paper and party goods trade shows regularly? How often? Which ones?* _____
    _____

11. *In general, do you feel that there is loyalty to suppliers from stores such as yours?* __
    _____
    _____

12. *What do you think is necessary for capturing loyalty?* _____
    _____

13. *How would your store react to additional suppliers attempting to enter the market?*
    _____
    _____

14. *What could a new supplier do to make your store aware of its existence and offerings?* _____
    _____

15. *Other than party goods, what are the best-selling products in your store now?* _____
    _____

16. *What are the worst-selling products in your store?* _____
    _____

Demographics

Now I'd like to ask you some general questions that will be used to help us classify the information given by all the people who have participated in this survey.

17. *In what type of area is your store located?*
    [ ] Mall   [ ] Free standing
    [ ] Strip shopping center   [ ] Outlet center
    [ ] Downtown

18. *How many stores do you have?*
    [ ] 1
    [ ] 2
    [ ] 3–5
    [ ] 6–10
    [ ] More

19. *What is the approximate size of your store in square feet?*
    Do not read off the categories.
    [ ] Less than 1,999   [ ] 5,000–5,999
    [ ] 2,000–2,999   [ ] 6,000–20,000
    [ ] 3,000–3,999   [ ] over 20,000
    [ ] 4,000–4,999

20. *What is your store's approximate level of annual sales? Is it*
    [ ] under $100,000?
    [ ] under $250,000?
    [ ] under $500,000?
    [ ] under $1,000,000?
    [ ] over $1,000,000 **[don't ask]**

Figure 1   *(Continued)*

21. *How many years has this particular store been in business?*
    [ ]   0–2 years
    [ ]   3–4 years
    [ ]   5–7 years
    [ ]   8–10 years
    [ ]   More than 10 years

22. *Compared with 1990, have sales in 1991 been up, down, or the same? What percentage?*
    _____

Thank you, Mr./Ms. _____, for your time and consideration. You have been very helpful.

(January 19) Based on the results of the marketing research project and the input of his managers, Todd has decided to increase production of party goods and market these products through the IPG channel.

Questions

1. Evaluate the research team's development of the sample of store owners. How would you have recommended the research team develop the sampling frame?
2. Do you think that a telephone survey was the best way to collect the needed information?
3. Evaluate the questionnaire used in the research project.

Case 5.3   HotStuff Computer Software (B) [1]

Simpson, Edwards and Associates, encouraged by its success with a computer software package for government agencies, is developing a second software product, HotStuff, which is tailored specifically for use in the firefighting industry. In the normal course of affairs, fire departments need to handle and store a considerable amount of information: building layouts, hazardous material characteristics and locations, equipment inventories, and so on. Further, although some exploratory research has suggested that some fire departments already own computers, it is generally recognized that the information-processing needs of the industry render computerization a future necessity. Based on preliminary inquiries into the composition of the industry, Simpson, Edwards and Associates decided to restrict its marketing efforts to volunteer fire departments only, at least initially, and

planned a national survey to determine the market potential of HotStuff. (See Case 2.2[A] for more background.)

Sampling Plan

The key issue in executing a national survey turned on sampling control: how could the researchers select and contract voluntary fire departments in a reliable, systematic fashion? After much deliberation and a few false starts, Craig Simpson's research staff finally presented him with two sampling plans.

Option 1 The first option that Simpson and his staff considered was a mail survey based on a sample drawn from a list of volunteer fire departments nationwide. The National Fire Protection Agency, like other national fire safety organizations, had a comprehensive mailing list of all 30,000 U.S. fire departments, but it did not distinguish between

[1]The contributions of Jacqueline C. Hitchon to the development of this case are gratefully acknowledged.

volunteer and municipal fire departments. Fortunately, the research team discovered that Alvin B. Zeller, Inc., of New York, sells listings of population groups. Moreover, the company could provide Simpson's team with an exhaustive mailing list of volunteer fire departments, organized by the state in which they were located. Recently updated, the total number of volunteer fire departments included on the list was almost 20,000, and the cost of sampling names from the list was $40 per 1,000 departments sampled. The names could be drawn according to whatever scheme Simpson, Edwards and Associates preferred.

The research team believed that a viable way to proceed to sample from the Zeller list would be to order the 48 states in the United States (excluding Alaska and Hawaii) according to the number of volunteer fire departments in each state. Once the states were ordered from smallest to largest in terms of incidence of volunteer fire departments, a sample could be drawn from all the departments on the list by selecting every k^{th} department after a random beginning. If it adopted a pessimistic perspective, expected only a 20-percent response rate, and were satisfied with only 100 completed surveys, Simpson, Edwards and Associates would need to mail 500 questionnaires. With 20,000 population elements and a sample of 500, every 40th volunteer fire station on the list would need to be selected, after a random start between 1 and 40.

Option 2   The second sampling plan being considered was founded on information received from the local state fire marshall and two assumptions. The marshall informed the researchers that most volunteer fire departments were located in communities with populations under 25,000. Based on the assumption that towns with a population under 5,000 would be too small to productively use a computer, the team decided that it should concentrate on two categories of towns: those with populations between 5,000 and 15,000 and those with populations between 15,000 and 25,000. In addition, it seemed logical to assume that volunteer fire departments located near large cities would be more progressive than those in more isolated areas and thus that they would be more likely to own or plan to purchase a computer.

Consistent with the preceding reasoning, the research team also considered drawing a sample in the following way:

- Step 1: Randomly select two cities of over 100,000 inhabitants from every state in the continental United States.
- Step 2: Randomly select a town of population 5,000–15,000 within 20 miles of one city, and a town of population 15,000–25,000 within 20 miles of the second city.
- Step 3: From directory assistance, obtain telephone numbers of the volunteer fire departments in each of the two towns selected in each state.

This strategy would provide a sample size of 96 volunteer fire departments from the 48 states.

After some discussion, Simpson decided to adopt the second option to use in conjunction with a telephone survey.

Questions

1. What kind of sampling plan was considered for sampling from the mailing list?
2. What kind of sampling plan was actually used to sample volunteer fire departments?
3. Evaluate the sampling plans.

Case 5.4   QUIN (B)[1]

Rob Heidenreich, while studying for his M.B.A., was looking for summer employment when a DJ friend suggested that he might like to take on a marketing research project for QUIN, a local nonprofit, listener-sponsored radio station. (See Case 3.2[A] for more details.) QUIN is considering marketing its audio production capabilities (e.g., recording music, sound tracks for commercials and films, dramatic readings, and slide presentations) to the local community. It is hoped that the income from the service will substantially improve the financial standing of the radio station, which, like most nonprofit organizations, is constantly seeking new sources of funding.

Based on some exploratory research, Heidenreich advised QUIN to focus on voice production rather

[1]The contributions of Jacqueline C. Hitchon to the development of this case are gratefully acknowledged.

than music production when marketing the service, since QUIN's existing experience is in voice production. QUIN's staff accepted his recommendation and instructed Heidenreich to plan a descriptive study of the local market for voice production services, with a view toward interviewing personnel in relevant organizations by telephone. A crucial step in designing the survey, therefore, was accessing existing or potential users of voice production services.

Target Population

From discussions with voice production service users, Heidenreich concluded that the population of actual and potential users consisted of four distinct segments: (1) advertising agencies, (2) state government agencies, (3) nonprofit organizations, and (4) other businesses.

Not all advertising agencies produce audio or audiovisual effects, but those that do are heavy users of production facilities, and, therefore, potentially valuable clients. Because QUIN is located in the state capital, which is the headquarters for many state government agencies, Heidenreich included state government agencies as potentially heavy users in the sample. Nonprofit organizations were listed because of the importance QUIN places on generating publicity for charitable agencies in the area. In turn, many nonprofits strongly support the station, even contributing funds during QUIN's pledge drives. They were therefore seen as possible customers for QUIN's recording facilities, although the extent to which they use prerecorded messages was unknown because many rely on public service announcements read live on-air. Finally, businesses were known to produce audio and audiovisual effects through numerous channels. Some organizations produce their own in-house, or they contract out to advertising agencies, local radio and television stations, or commercial production facilities; others are part of nationwide chains in which production is overseen by corporate headquarters. Since several local businesses support QUIN's endeavors, it seemed likely that they might be interested in the station's new venture.

Sampling Frames

The sampling frame for advertising agencies was developed from the yellow pages of the local telephone directory. Organizations that specialized in graphic art were deleted from the list, and the resulting edited version formed the final listing for research purposes. The population of government agencies was drawn from an index of these agencies in the 1990 *State Blue Book*. This list was purified to exclude the obvious nonusers or rare users of paid mass media, such as legislators and judges. The names of nonprofit organizations were taken from a recent study of local nonprofits and supplemented by the County Cultural Affairs Commission directory. Because of the nature of nonprofits, Heidenreich thought that organizations with annual budgets of less than $100,000 were unlikely to engage in paid advertising, and he therefore eliminated those from the sampling frame. Finally, a list of businesses in the area was acquired from the chamber of commerce.

Sampling Plan

Heidenreich decided to sample some segments more heavily than others. He selected the following proportions:

- 27 percent of the advertising agencies (15 of 55)
- 24 percent of the state government agencies (10 of 41)
- 23 percent of the nonprofit organizations (25 of 109)
- 10 percent of the area businesses (121 of 1,233)

Having identified the four segments and the number of elements he needed to sample in each, Heidenreich chose the individual elements from each group using a random-number table.

Questions

1. What type of sample is being used?
2. Is it a good choice?

Case 5.5   First Federal Bank of Bakersfield

The Equal Credit Opportunity Act, which was passed in 1974, was partially designed to protect women from discriminatory banking practices. It forbade, for example, the use of credit evaluations based on sex or marital status. While adherence to the law has changed the way many bankers do business, women's perception that there is a bias against them by a particular financial institution often remains unless some specific steps are taken by the institution to counter that perception.

Close to a dozen "women's banks"—that is, banks owned and operated by and for women—opened their doors during the 1970s with the specific purpose of targeting and promoting their services to this otherwise underdeveloped market. Today, although women's banks are evolving into full-service banks serving a wide range of clients, a number of traditional banks are moving in the other direction by attempting to develop services that are targeted specifically toward women. Many of these institutions see such a strategy as a viable way to attract valuable customers and to increase their market share in the short term while gaining a competitive advantage by which they can compete in the long term as the roles of women in the labor force gain in importance. One can find, with even the most cursory examination of the trade press, examples of credit card advertising that depicts single, affluent, and head-of-the-household female cardholders; financial seminar programs for wives of affluent professional men; informational literature that details how newly divorced and separated women can obtain credit; and entire packages of counseling, educational opportunities, and special services for women.

The First Federal Bank of Bakersfield was interested in developing its own program of this kind. The executives were curious about a number of issues. Were women's financial needs being adequately met in the Bakersfield area? What additional financial services would women especially like to have? How did Bakersfield's women feel about banks and bankers? Was First Federal in a good position to take advantage of the needs of women? What channels of communication would be best to reach women who might be interested in the services that First Federal had to offer?

The executives believed that First Federal might have some special advantages if it did try to appeal to women. For one thing, the Bakersfield community seemed to be quite sensitive to the issues being raised by the feminist movement. For another, First Federal was a small, personal bank. The executives thought that women might be more comfortable in dealing with a smaller, more personalized institution and that the bank might not have the traditional "image problem" among women that larger banks might have.

Research Objectives

One program the bank executives were considering that they believed might be particularly attractive to women was a series of financial seminars. The seminars could cover a number of topics, including money management, wills, trusts, estate planning, taxes, insurance, investments, financial services, and establishing a credit rating. The executives were interested in determining women's reactions to each of these potential topics. They were also interested to know what the best format might be in terms of location, frequency, length of each program, and so on, if there were a high level of interest. Consequently, they decided that the bank should conduct a research study that had the assessment of the financial seminar series as its main objective but that also shed some light on the other issues they had been debating. More specifically, the objectives of the research were as follows:

1. To determine the interest that exists among women in the Bakersfield area for seminars on financial matters.
2. To identify the reasons why Bakersfield women would change, or have changed, their banking affiliations.
3. To examine the attitudes of Bakersfield women toward financial institutions and the people who run them.
4. To determine if there is any correlation between the demographic characteristics of women in the Bakersfield area and the services they might like to have.
5. To analyze the media usage habits of Bakersfield-area women.

Method

The assignment to develop a research strategy by which these objectives could be assessed was given to the bank's internal marketing research department. The department consisted of only five members—Beth Anchurch, the research director, and four project analysts. As Anchurch pondered the assignment, she was concerned about the best way to proceed. She was particularly concerned with the relatively short time horizon she was given for the project. Top executives thought that there was promise in the seminar idea. If they were right, they wanted to get on with designing and offering the seminars before any of their competitors came up with a similar idea. Thus, they specified that they would like the results of the research department's investigation to be available within 45 to 50 days.

As Anchurch began to contemplate the data collection, she became particularly concerned with whether the study should use mail questionnaires or telephone interviews. She had tentatively ruled out personal interviews because of the short deadline that had been imposed. After several days of contemplating the alternatives, she finally decided that it would be best to collect the information by telephone. Further, she decided that it would be better to hire out the telephone interviewing than to use her four project analysts to make the calls.

Anchurch believed that the multiple objectives of the project required a reasonably large sample of women so that the various characteristics of interest would be sufficiently represented to enable some conclusions to be drawn about the population of Bakersfield as a whole. After pondering the various cross tabulations in which the bank executives would be interested, she finally decided that a sample of 500 to 600 adult women would be sufficient. The sample was to be drawn from the white pages of the Bakersfield telephone directory by the Bakersfield Interviewing Service, the firm that First Federal had hired to complete the interviews.

The sample was to be drawn using a scheme in which two names were selected from each page of the directory, first by selecting two of the four columns on the page at random and then by selecting the fifteenth name in each of the selected columns. The decision to sample names from each page was made so that each interviewer could operate with certain designated pages of the directory, since each was operating independently out of her home.

The decision to sample every fifteenth name in the selected columns was determined in the following way. First, there were 328 pages in the directory with four columns of names per page. There were 80 entries per column on average, or approximately 26,240 listings. Using Bureau of the Census data on household composition, it was estimated that 20 percent of all households would be ineligible for the study because they did not contain an adult female resident. This meant that only 20,992 ($0.80 \times 26,240$) of the listings would probably qualify. Since 500 to 600 names were needed, it seemed easiest to select two columns on each page at random and to take the same numbered entry from each column. The interviewer could then simply count or measure down from the top of the column. The number 15 was determined randomly; thus, the fifteenth listing in the randomly selected columns on each page was called. If the household did not answer or if the woman of the house refused to participate, the interviewers were instructed to select another number from that column through the use of an abbreviated table of random numbers that each was supplied. They were to use a similar procedure if the household that was called did not have an adult woman living there.

First Federal decided to operate without callbacks because the interviewing service charged heavily for them. Anchurch did think it would be useful to follow up with a sample of those interviewed to make sure that they indeed had been called, since the interviewers for Bakersfield Interviewing Service operated out of their own homes and it was impossible to supervise them more directly. She did this by selecting at random a handful of the surveys completed by each interviewer. She then had one of her project analysts call that respondent, verify that the interview had taken place, and check the accuracy of the responses to a few of the most important questions. This audit revealed absolutely no instances of interviewer cheating.

The completed interview forms were turned over to First Federal for its own internal analysis. As part of this analysis, the project analyst compared the demographic characteristics of those contacted with the demographic characteristics of the population in the Bakersfield area as reported in the 1980 Census. The comparison is shown in Table 1. The analyst also prepared a summary of the nonresponses and refusals by interviewer. This comparison is shown in Table 2.

Table 1   ***Selected Demographic Comparison of Survey Respondents with Bureau of Census Data***

Characteristic/ Category	Percentage of Women	
	Survey	Census
Marital Status		
Married	53	42
Single	30	40
Separated	1	2
Widowed	9	9
Divorced	7	7
Age		
18–24	23	23
25–34	30	28
35–44	16	14
45–64	18	21
65+	13	14
Income		
Less than $10,000	9	29
$10,000–$19,999	19	29
$20,000–$50,000	58	36
More than $50,000	2	6
Refused	12	

Questions

1. Compare the advantages and disadvantages of using telephone interviews as compared to personal interviews or mail questionnaires to collect the needed data.
2. Compare the advantages and disadvantages of using in-house staff versus a professional interviewing service to collect the data.
3. Do you think that the telephone directory provided a good sampling frame given the purposes of the study, or would you recommend an alternative sampling frame?
4. What type of sample is being used here? Still using the white pages of the telephone directory as the sampling frame, would you recommend some other sampling scheme? Why or why not?
5. If you were Anchurch, would you be happy with the performance of the Bakersfield Interviewing Service? Why or why not?

Table 2   **Results of Calls by Interviewer**

	Number of Nonresponses			Number of Refusals		
Interviewer	Line Busy	No Answer	Ineligibles*	Initial	After Partial Completion	Number of Completions
1	7	101	36	15	0	30
2	2	45	13	16	0	30
3	11	71	23	17	7	30
4	14	56	47	35	6	39
5	9	93	10	23	13	30
6	5	102	28	63	14	35
7	6	36	17	16	0	18
8	7	107	23	13	0	30
9	11	106	36	47	0	30
10	10	55	6	35	9	30
11	38	83	48	92	0	30
12	5	22	3	8	0	9
13	23	453	102	65	7	99
14	12	102	27	31	0	19
15	7	173	29	66	0	34
16	2	65	9	33	0	22
Total	169	1,670	457	575	56	515
		1,839			631	

*No adult female resident.

Case 5.6   Holzem Business Systems

Holzem Business Systems serviced a number of small business accounts in the immediate area surrounding its Madison, Wisconsin, location. The company, which was headed by Claude Holzem, a certified public accountant (CPA), specialized in the preparation of financial statements, tax forms, and other reports required by various governmental units. Since its founding in 1962, the company had experienced steady, and sometimes spectacular, growth. Holzem Business Systems, whose policy was high-quality service at competitive rates, was so successful in Dane County that it was far and away the dominant firm serving small businesses in the area. Further growth seemed to depend more on expansion into new areas than on further penetration of the Madison market.

Faced with such a prospect, Holzem conceived a plan that would capitalize on the substantial talent at the company's main office. What he envisioned was an operation in which area field representatives would secure raw data from clients. At the end of each day, they would transmit this information to headquarters using microcomputers with modems. There it would be coded and processed and the necessary forms prepared. These income statements, balance sheets, or tax forms would then be returned to the area representative. The field person would go over them with clients and would answer any questions that clients might have.

In Holzem's mind, the system had a number of advantages. First, it allowed Holzem Business Systems to capitalize on the substantial expertise it had in its Madison office. The quality control for which the company had become noted could be maintained, as could the company's record of quick service. Second, the company would not need to hire CPAs as field representatives, because these area managers would not actually be preparing financial statements. This was believed to be particularly crucial because, as a result of recent heavy demand, there was a current shortage of available CPAs. They were commanding premium salaries. The prospect of using business-college graduates who understood financial statements and could explain their significance to clients thus had substantial cost advantages.

The big question confronting Holzem was whether there would be a demand for such a service. There was no question in his mind that there was a need for accounting services among small businesses. His Madison experience had demonstrated this. But he was concerned that the physical distance between the client and the office might prove to be a psychological barrier for clients. If it proved to be necessary to establish full-service branches in each area, then geographic expansion was less attractive to him.

To help him decide whether to go ahead, Holzem commissioned a research study that had as its objectives identifying the perceived problems and the need for CPA services in general and, in particular, potential client attitudes toward the type of service arrangement he envisioned.

Hathaway Research Associates, headed by James and Nancy Hathaway, was retained to do the study. It was to be conducted using personal interviews among a representative sample of small businesses within the state. For purposes of the study, a small business was defined as one employing fewer than 50 people. The study was to be confined to small businesses in the industries designated as contract construction, manufacturing, wholesale trade, retail trade, and commercial services. These categories represented approximately 95 percent of all Holzem accounts, 85 percent of the total small businesses in the state, and 81 percent of all businesses in the state.

Sampling Plan

The businesses serving as the sample were to be selected in the following way. First, the state was to be divided into the three regions depicted in Figure 1. Next, five counties were to be selected from each region by the following scheme.

1. The cumulative number of businesses was to be calculated from Table 1. The accumulation for the first ten counties in Region 1, for example, is as follows:

County	Number of Businesses	Cumulative Number of Businesses
Douglas	668	668
Burnett	147	815
Polk	488	1,303
Washburn	282	1,585
Barron	565	2,150
Bayfield	178	2,328
Sawyer	324	2,652
Rusk	229	2,881
Ashland	307	3,188
Iron	122	3,310

2. A table of random numbers would be employed to determine which five counties would be selected. For example, if a number between 816 and 1,303 came up, Polk county would be used.

Hathaway Research Associates then planned to contact the state Department of Industry, Labor, and Human Relations (DILHR) for a list of individual firms within each county. DILHR used the unemployment computer tape to prepare such lists. This tape was compiled each year and reflected payments by firms into the state's unemployment compensation system. The records within the tape were maintained county by county, by SIC (Standard Industrial Classification) code within each county, and in alphabetical order within the SIC code. Since the number of employees of each firm was indicated, DILHR could screen the master list and print out only those firms that satisfied the location, industry, and geographic criteria Hathaway Research Associates specified. DILHR would sell these lists of firms to interested clients, but they would provide only the

Figure 1   **Regional Breakdown of Wisconsin Counties**

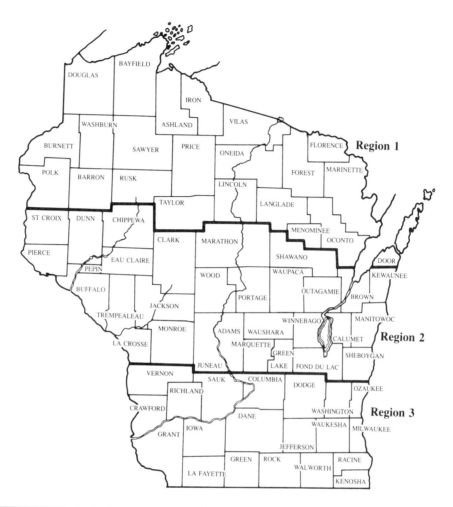

name, address, and phone number of the selected businesses.

Hathaway Research Associates proposed to select 40 businesses from each county by the following procedure:

1. The total number of businesses within the county was to be divided by 40 to get a sampling interval. The sampling interval would be different, of course, for each county.
2. A random start was to be generated for each county, using a table of random numbers. The random number was to be some number between 1 and the sampling interval, and this number was to be used to designate the first business to be included in the sample.

3. The sampling interval was to be added repeatedly to the random start, and every number generated in this manner was to designate a business to be included in the sample.

This procedure was to be followed for all counties except Milwaukee and Dane. Holzem believed that if he were to expand into the Milwaukee market at all, he wanted to do it with a completely self-sufficient branch and not with a satellite office tied to the Madison headquarters. He consequently instructed Hathaway Research Associates to exclude Milwaukee County from this part of the research investigation. Dane County was to be excluded because of the company's already successful penetration of this market.

Table 1   Number of Small Businesses by Major Industry Category

County	Contract Construction	Manufacturing	Wholesale Trade	Retail Trade	Commercial Services	Total
Adams	14	10	3	49	27	103
Ashland	26	37	26	127	91	307
Barron	88	52	82	295	48	565
Bayfield	20	25	8	85	40	178
Brown	387	187	330	871	804	2,579
Buffalo	23	14	22	92	47	198
Burnett	22	12	7	82	24	147
Calumet	62	47	48	162	128	447
Chippewa	105	67	94	300	216	782
Clark	60	76	82	203	101	522
Columbia	98	55	84	360	208	805
Crawford	33	25	32	119	64	273
Dane	638	314	493	1,800	1,705	4,950
Dodge	143	98	119	370	258	988
Door	76	27	27	206	168	504
Douglas	49	30	43	339	207	668
Dunn	37	21	55	187	110	410
Eau Claire	122	39	113	415	331	1,020
Florence	4	6	1	29	6	46
Fond du Lac	178	94	131	546	374	1,323
Forrest	9	25	8	116	27	185
Grant	88	60	125	341	200	814
Green	71	49	82	234	122	558
Green Lake	60	28	28	150	84	350
Iowa	41	23	55	135	65	319
Iron	11	15	10	60	26	122
Jackson	27	14	29	120	49	239
Jefferson	120	88	111	400	283	1,002
Juneau	38	28	27	172	79	344
Kenosha	159	75	105	624	167	1,130
Kewaunee	44	35	32	112	76	299
La Crosse	167	91	159	573	450	1,440
Lafayette	31	29	50	106	58	274
Langlade	29	53	59	135	92	368
Lincoln	50	43	38	184	109	424
Manitowoc	161	102	119	464	338	1,184
Marathon	244	148	196	520	432	1,540

Source: County Business Patterns.

Table 1   *(Continued)*

County	Contract Construction	Manufacturing	Wholesale Trade	Retail Trade	Commercial Services	Total
Marinette	63	75	56	253	153	600
Marquette	27	11	9	68	34	149
Menominee	1	5	2	4	6	18
Milwaukee	1,200	1,238	1,711	4,914	5,708	14,771
Monroe	49	37	67	235	115	503
Oconto	49	43	50	143	97	382
Oneida	101	40	45	305	180	671
Outagamie	273	117	227	697	568	1,882
Ozaukee	151	109	95	313	247	915
Pepin	12	7	18	61	31	129
Puerce	50	27	29	206	104	416
Polk	59	44	51	234	100	488
Portage	83	42	71	280	171	647
Price	19	44	32	92	59	246
Racine	292	285	178	853	738	2,346
Richland	29	20	35	108	67	259
Rock	236	118	148	811	570	1,883
Rusk	24	34	34	95	42	229
St. Croix	80	44	61	225	144	554
Sauk	104	58	91	376	223	852
Sawyer	36	25	16	128	119	324
Shawano	65	58	61	232	110	526
Sheboygan	204	151	118	523	433	1,429
Taylor	29	28	36	93	57	243
Trempealeau	51	43	60	192	98	444
Vernon	37	39	52	154	85	367
Vilas	72	30	17	175	113	407
Walworth	144	106	90	522	345	1,207
Washburn	41	27	18	136	60	282
Washington	173	110	97	369	262	1,011
Waukesha	694	506	501	1,147	1,097	3,945
Waupaca	81	70	72	328	201	752
Waushara	26	22	30	114	71	263
Winnebago	244	157	151	759	632	1,943
Wood	141	83	104	427	303	1,058
Totals	8,475	5,995	7,466	26,655	20,957	69,548

Once the total sample of 600 businesses had been specified, Hathaway Research Associates would contact each firm by phone to set up an appointment for a personal interview with one of its highly trained field interviewers.

Questions

1. What kind of sample was being proposed by Hathaway Research Associates? Was this a good choice?
2. Was the sample a true probability sample (i.e., did every small business in Wisconsin have a known chance of selection)?
3. What was the probability that a small business in Menominee County (the county with the fewest small businesses) would be included in the sample? What was the probability that a small business in Waukesha County (of those counties eligible, the one with the most small businesses) would be included in the sample? Would this discrepancy cause any problems in analysis?
4. Were businesses within each of the Standard Industrial Classifications likely to be represented properly in the sample?

Case 5.7   The Dryden Press

The Dryden Press was established in the mid-1960s by Holt, Rinehart and Winston, which had traditionally been a strong social science publisher, as a response to the growth in enrollments that business schools were experiencing and the explosion in enrollments that was predicted they would experience in the future. The venture represented one of the first forays by a traditional nonbusiness text publisher into the college business market. The experiment turned out to be very successful, and by the mid-1980s The Dryden Press was one of the top six publishers in the business area in sales. Company executives believed that one of the key reasons for Dryden's success was its ability to target books for specific market segments. The company was one of the first to recognize the potential growth in courses in consumer behavior and managerial economics, for example, and introduced the successful texts by Engel, Kollat, and Blackwell in consumer behavior and by Brigham and Pappas in managerial economics in response. Through careful management of the revisions, these books still maintained strong market positions more than 15 years after they had been introduced.

The Dryden Press editorial staff tried to maintain a posture of extreme sensitivity to changing market conditions brought about by the publication of new research findings or the changing demands placed on students as a result of changes in the environment and the needs of businesses. The editors made it a point to keep up with these changes so that the company would be prepared with new products when the situation demanded it. This was no small task,

because the lead time on a book typically ran from three to four years from the time the author was first signed to a contract to when the book was actually published. It seemed to take most authors almost two years to develop a first draft of a book manuscript. The typical manuscript was then reviewed by a sample of experts in the field. Based on those reviews, most manuscripts would undergo some revision before being placed into production. The production process, which included such things as copyediting the manuscript, setting type, drawing all figures, preparing promotional materials, proofreading, and so on, usually took about a year.

Research Questions and Objectives

So that it would not be caught short if the needs and desires of the market in consumer behavior texts changed, the editorial staff decided to find out the current level of use of the various texts in consumer behavior and the directions in which the market was moving. What were the market shares of the respective texts? What features of the various books were liked and disliked? Did the use of the various texts and the preference for the certain features vary by class of school? Did four-year colleges have different requirements for consumer behavior texts than two-year schools? After a good deal of discussion among the members of the editorial staff, these general concerns were translated into specific research objectives. More specifically, the staff decided to conduct a research investigation that attempted to determine the following:

1. The importance of various topical areas in the teaching of consumer behavior within the next two to five years.
2. The importance and treatment of managerial applications in consumer behavior courses.
3. The level of satisfaction with the textbooks currently in use.
4. The relative market shares of the major consumer behavior textbooks.
5. The degree of switching of texts that goes on in consumer behavior courses from year to year.
6. The importance of various pedagogical aids such as glossaries, cases, learning objectives, and so on, in the textbook selection decision.
7. The importance of supplementary teaching tools such as student study guides, overhead transparency masters, or an instructor's manual, among others, in the textbook selection decision.

The editorial staff thought it was important that the needed information be obtained from those who were actively involved in teaching consumer behavior courses. The staff also thought it imperative that only one respondent be used from any given school, even though the editors realized that some schools had multiple sections of the consumer behavior course and that different books might be used in different sections. For the most part, however, the editors believed that the same book would be used across sections, though not across courses, in the sense that the introductory courses at the undergraduate and graduate levels would use different books. The editors decided that it would be better to target the questionnaires to one individual at each of the selected institutions and to simply have that person indicate on the questionnaire whether he or she normally taught a graduate or undergraduate course. Dryden could then analyze the responses to determine if there were any differences in them that could be attributed to the level at which the course was taught.

Method

There were several reasons why the editorial staff decided to use a mail questionnaire to collect the data. For one thing, the target population was geographically dispersed. Even though it was decided to limit the study only to those actively involved in teaching consumer behavior domestically, that still meant respondents could come from all over the United States, which in turn meant that it would be prohibitive to collect this information by personal interview. At the same time, professors had no standard working schedule. Some might teach in the morning and some in the evening. When they were not teaching, some might work in their offices while others might work elsewhere. This variety of schedules and work conditions required that the questionnaires be available when the professors might be inclined to fill them out. Also, the objectives finally decided on allowed the use of a relatively structured and undisguised questionnaire.

The big question facing the Dryden staff was how to draw a sample from the target population of those actively teaching a consumer behavior course, at either the undergraduate or the graduate level. For purposes of the study, "actively teaching" was operationally defined as having taught a consumer behavior course at least once in the last two years or being scheduled to teach one within the next year.

The company was considering drawing the sample from one of two lists that it had at its disposal. One of the lists was an internal list consisting of all those professors whom the salespeople's reports indicated were interested in teaching specific courses such as financial planning, introductory accounting, marketing management, or consumer behavior. This meant that the salesperson had indicated on his or her report that the professor was to receive sample copies of all those books in, say, consumer behavior that The Dryden Press published. Most of the entries on the list were developed from salespeople's calls, although some of them arose at the national association meetings at which Dryden displayed its list of titles. Professors would often request sample copies of selected titles at the meetings so that they could review them before making an adoption decision. All requests for complimentary copies were sent for authorization to the salesperson serving the school. By approving the request, the salesperson was aware of the professor's interest and could follow it up in an attempt to get the adoption. Because of how it was developed and used, the internal list paralleled the salesperson territory structure.

Although most salespeople operated within one state and often within only part of a state, some operated across several states. Each salesperson was responsible for all the schools in his or her territory, including the universities with graduate programs, four-year colleges without graduate programs, and two-year institutions. The schools were listed alphabetically by salesperson, and each school had a computer code associated with it, designating its type. Each professor on the list had a set of computer codes associated with the name that identified his or her interest areas.

The alternate list The Dryden Press considered using was the printed membership directory of the Association for Consumer Research (ACR). ACR was formed in the late 1960s and was designed for the pursuit of knowledge in the area of consumer behavior. Its membership is dominated by marketing professors (almost 80 percent of the total), although it also includes interested members from business and government, as well as members representing other academic disciplines, such as sociology and psychology. The ACR directory was organized alphabetically by name of the member. Along with each member's

name, the directory provided either the office or the home address, depending on which the individual preferred to use, and both the office and the home phone numbers. While about one-half of the addresses listed only the college at which the individual worked, the other 50 percent also listed the department. There were 64 pages in the directory, and all pages except the last one had 16 names. A small percentage of the addresses were international.

Questions

1. Given the purposes of the study, how would you recommend a sample be drawn from
   (a) Dryden's internal computer list?
   (b) The ACR printed membership directory?
2. Which approach would you recommend and why?

Case 5.8   Canopy of Care (A)[1]

Canopy of Care is a nonprofit institution that raises money from the public and then allocates the funds to programs run by charitable agencies endeavoring to serve the human-care needs of the community. In this way, it functions as an umbrella, or canopy, for specialized charities, relieving them in large part of the need to market themselves and solicit donations. The campaign area encompasses a city with a population of half a million and its suburbs. In 1989, for example, Canopy of Care raised almost $17 million, which it distributed to 341 local health and social service programs. An efficient system for giving has been developed with the help of companies and government agencies, who solicit their employees on behalf of Canopy of Care and deduct donations corresponding to the employees' pledges directly out of their wages or salaries.

Despite the relative ease of administration, however, the percentage of solicited employees contributing to Canopy of Care has been decreasing. Only 50 percent of the employees at companies that agreed to participate contributed, for example, in 1989. Economic downturns in the area are thought to be

partially responsible for the reduction in employee contributions. The manufacturing industry, for example, one of Canopy of Care's largest targets, has recently experienced plant closings leading to employee cutbacks and wage freezes. Although Canopy of Care cannot control the effects of changes in the economy, its officials believe that the agency may be able to compensate for them by becoming more efficient in its approach to potential donors.

Study Objectives

Based on this reasoning, three broad research objectives were developed:

1. To determine why a large percentage of employees in companies solicited by Canopy of Care do not choose to contribute.
2. To assess both the information and the attitudes that givers and nongivers in solicited companies have about Canopy of Care.
3. To obtain general information that Canopy of Care can use in better planning its campaigns.

A local marketing research firm was asked to develop a study to investigate these issues.

[1]The contributions of Jacqueline C. Hitchon to the development of this case are gratefully acknowledged.

Data-Collection Procedure

The target population consisted of individuals employed in firms solicited by Canopy of Care. The marketing researcher advised Canopy of Care that there were two principal ways to access the population for research purposes:

1. Sample companies solicited by Canopy of Care, and then select a sample of employees within each selected company from a list of employees provided by the company. Once they were identified, the employees could be surveyed by mail or telephone. Since the desired information could be obtained through fixed-alternative questions without probing, personal interviews did not seem warranted.

2. Broaden the population of potential respondents to include all adults employed in the campaign area. This sample could be accessed by telephone, using plus-one sampling based on the local white pages and screening out unemployed respondents by means of an introductory question about employment. The survey could be administered either by volunteers from the Canopy of Care staff or by professional telephone interviewers.

After some deliberation, Canopy of Care selected the second option and decided to employ trained telephone interviewers to conduct the survey, although the budget for the project was very small and the sample size needed to be drastically reduced.

Plus-one dialing was used to generate a random sample that included unlisted numbers. Because of time and budget constraints, callbacks were not made; instead new numbers were generated and dialed until a valid response was obtained. The telephone interviewers were instructed in the correct manner to administer the survey and were monitored by supervisors both during a pretest and during the actual survey. The research took place between April 21 and April 25, 1990. Calls were placed between the hours of 4:00 p.m. and 9:00 p.m. in order to find a greater number of people at home. A total of 260 completed questionnaires was obtained.

Initial Results

As an initial step in analyzing the results of this survey, the researchers undertook two tasks. First, they examined the statistics on completed and uncompleted contacts (see Table 1). Second, they compared the demographic profile of their sample with projected 1988 census data, based on the 1980 census of the area, to evaluate the representativeness of their sample (see Tables 2, 3, and 4).

All in all, the sample demographic profiles were similar to the 1988 population projections based on the 1980 census with one or two differences. Both the nonwhite and lower-income groups were underrepresented in the sample (Tables 2 and 3). Further, all occupational categories were underrepresented except the service category, which appeared to be overrepre-

Table 1   **Numbers of Completed and Uncompleted Contacts**

Classification	Number of Individuals
Completed contacts	260
Contacts unemployed last year	271
Mid-survey terminations	22
Answering machine contacts	61
Refusals	235
No answers and busy signals	132
Nonworking numbers	419
Businesses contacted	90
Contacts with language/hearing barrier	13
No adult at home	30
Total dialings	1,533

Table 2   **Comparison of Household Income**

Income Category	Sample Percentage	1988 Projected Census Percentage
Less than $10,000	12.7	25.7
$10,000–$14,999	17.3	14.3
$15,000–$24,999	31.9	27.8
$25,000–$39,999	26.9	23.0
More than $40,000	11.2	9.2

Table 3   **Comparison of Race**

Racial Classification	Sample Percentage	1988 Projected Census Percentage
White	91.1	82.3
Black	6.5	13.9
Hispanic	0.8	2.4
Asian	0.4	0.8
Native American	1.2	0.6

Table 4   **Comparison of Occupation**

Type of Organization	Sample Percentage	1988 Projected Census Percentage
Manufacturing	22.4	28.5
Government	9.9	12.0
Wholesale/Retail	16.5	19.2
Service Industry	51.2	40.3

sented (Table 4). Nevertheless, the researchers were reasonably happy with these initial results.

Questions

1. What was the response rate?
2. Was the choice of plus-one telephone interviews judicious? Compare its advantages and disadvantages with those of the rejected sampling option.
3. Would you have selected professional interviewers over Canopy of Care volunteers, given the time and budget constraints? Why or why not?
4. Does the evidence indicate that the data-collection effort was of high quality?

Case 5.9   Rockway Publishing Company, Inc.

The Problem

Rockway Publishing Company publishes telephone directories for suburban and rural communities. Headquartered in a large midwestern metropolitan area, Rockway publishes directories for over 80 markets, mostly in the midwestern and southern parts of the United States. The telephone directories are published as an alternative to, and in competition with, directories published by the local telephone company serving these markets. Rockway has been very successful in offering yellow page advertisers a quality product at competitive rates. However, there have been some problems with distribution.

The distribution of the directories is handled in one of two ways. Winston Delivery Company has been under contract for the past two years to hand deliver directories in suburban areas and small cities. Winston hires college students, at minimum wage plus car expenses, to make the deliveries. Each student is given an assigned area of streets and rural routes to cover. For some locations, particularly where the households are heavily rural, the directories are sent through the mail. Recently, Rockway's salespeople have been receiving complaints from advertisers that some of their customers have not received a directory. It is believed by some of the salespeople that as much as 10 to 15 percent of households, in any given market, are not receiving a directory.

Survey Method

Faced with the prospect that not all of the directories intended for households are being delivered, Ron

Combs, president of Rockway, instituted a plan for measuring the discrepancy. Approximately three weeks after a directory is delivered in an area, a sample of households is telephoned, and respondents are asked if the directory has been received. The results are tabulated according to whether the household has a city or rural address. To be counted, the respondent must be sure that the book has been received or has not been received. Respondents who are uncertain or don't know are given more information about the time of delivery, what the face of the book looks like, and how it was delivered (by mail or by hand). If they are still uncertain, they are replaced in the sample and not included in the tally. The respondent may be anyone in the household who answers the phone or is available at the time of the call. Combs wants to ensure that sampling error is not greater than plus or minus two percentage points.

The Sampling Plan

The sampling frame is an internally produced cross directory of white-page listings by street. The interviewer goes through the pages, arbitrarily pulling names from the listings. If a respondent says a directory has not been received, additional calls are made on that street to determine if the entire street was missed. However, these additional calls are not included in the survey results.

Table 1 shows the results of the survey for areas distributed to in the most recent three months.

The total sample size for each area was determined by taking 1.5 percent of the area population.

Source: This case was prepared by Paul D. Boughton, Ph.D., Associate Professor of Marketing, Saint Louis University, 3674 Lindell Blvd., St. Louis, MO 63108. Reprinted with permission.

Table 1

	Hand Delivered			Mail Delivered	
	Area 1	**Area 2**	**Area 3**	**Area 4**	**Area 5**
Total area	35,000	50,000	69,000	85,000	155,000
Population					
City	24,000	45,700	52,000	43,000	100,000
Rural	11,000	4,300	17,000	42,000	55,000
Total Sample	525	750	1,035	1,275	2,325
City	325	650	775	685	1,325
Rural	200	100	260	590	1,000
Overall percentage receiving directory	88%	90%	95%	85%	92%

The breakdown between city and rural sample is arbitrary and the result of actual calls completed.

Combs wants to determine three things: (1) the overall soundness of the sampling plan; (2) the amount of sampling error in the results; and (3) the amount of response error by respondents.

Questions

1. What type of sample is being taken? Are city and rural residents being represented adequately? What other approach would you recommend and why?

2. What is the range of sampling error experienced from Area 1 to Area 5? (Assume 95 percent level of confidence.) How can Combs' error goal of plus or minus two percentage points be achieved?

3. What would you recommend as a sample size for each of the five areas?

4. Does Combs have enough information to determine respondent error? What would you recommend he do to obtain this information?

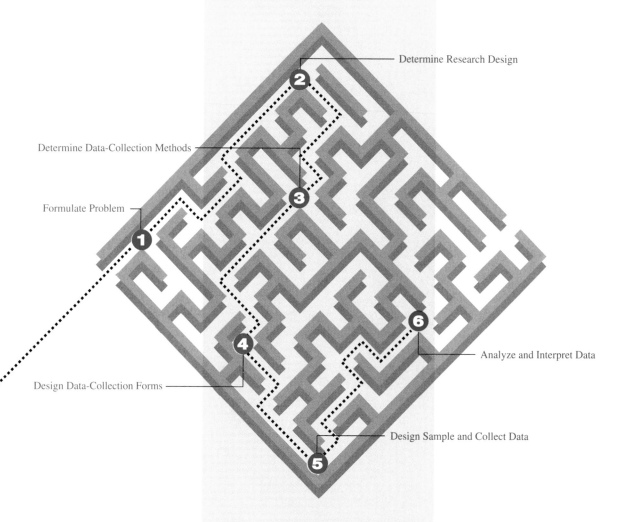

Part Six

Data Analysis

Determine Research Design

Determine Data-Collection Methods

Formulate Problem

Design Data-Collection Forms

Analyze and Interpret Data

Design Sample and Collect Data

After the data have been collected, the emphasis in the research process logically turns to analysis, which is the search for meaning in the collected information. This search involves many questions and several steps. Chapter 19 reviews the common steps of editing, coding, and tabulating the data. Some studies stop with these steps. Many involve additional analyses, however, particularly the testing for statistical significance, and Appendix 19A reviews some of the fundamentals regarding the testing for statistical significance. Chapter 20 and Appendix 20A then discuss the statistical procedures appropriate for determining whether some observed differences between and among groups are statistically significant. Finally, Chapter 21 and Appendix 21A discuss procedures for assessing the degree of association between variables.

Gretchen Vorlop would like you to know that market research analysts are not nerds who sit in front of the computer screen and crunch numbers all day long. "We are much more involved," declares Vorlop, a market research analyst at Helene Curtis. "At our company we have a team approach. My job is to be the link between the consumer and the company. I am the consumer's advocate with Brand Management."

Vorlop is a member of a marketing research department that includes 15 professionals. While her focus is on the consumer, other members of her department concentrate on how successful Helene Curtis brands are in competing with other products or on forecasting future product performance. Vorlop is involved in every aspect of brand management.

She worked recently on the introduction of a new product, Degree deodorant. "Marketing Research was involved in it from day one," she recalls. "We decided we wanted to introduce a new deodorant. We began with a broad strategic study that would help us define what needs were not being filled by products already in the market. As a result of our findings, we came up with the concept for Degree, a deodorant that works most when you need it most."

Once the concept for the new product was decided on, Vorlop worked closely with the research and development team in the lab to test and evaluate the product—the actual stuff that's in the package. "Deodorant is very tricky," she says. "Formulas appeal differently to men and women; there are aerosols, solids, and roll-ons. In addition, people tend to be very loyal to the particular brand that they use. We did several rounds of product testing. Did people like it? What did women like as opposed to men? Did people still like it when they knew that it was supposed to increase its protection when your need for it increased? Then we tested to make sure that the product actually filled the promise of its concept." In the end, the marketing research department recommended that the company go ahead with the product.

Vorlop believes that in order to use analytical tools to solve problems, you have to be able to grasp the big picture and then get really specific.

You have to design a test that answers the questions you want to ask. "It sounds so obvious," says Vorlop, "but when you get caught up in the process of trying to move a brand forward, it's often hard to see the trees for the forest. This is a very fast-paced work environment. Every day is just a different degree of busy. Sometimes I have 15 studies going on at once and the phone rings all day. We work in cubicles that are meant to encourage informal hallway meetings, but when things are moving so fast, it can be tough to be sure you've got all your bases covered."

Vorlop points out that in some sense, research has to be done in reverse. "You have to know what kind of information you hope to get out of a study so that when you do get your data back, you know how it's going to be tackled. You have to set up your test so that it will be statistically feasible to do it," says Vorlop. "For example, if you know you're going to need to do cluster analysis, you have to design the questionnaire so that what you end up with is appropriate for cluster analysis."

Vorlop enjoys every aspect of her job, but she concedes that "the fun part of analysis is not crunching numbers but looking at the numbers and asking, 'Why are consumers thinking this way?'"

Chapter Nineteen

Data Analysis: Preliminary Steps

Learning Objectives

Upon completing this chapter, you should be able to

1. Explain the purpose of the field edit.

2. Define what coding in the research process is.

3. List the three steps in the coding process.

4. Outline the conventions that are customarily followed when data are to be analyzed by a computer.

5. Describe the kinds of information contained in a codebook.

6. Define what tabulation is and distinguish between the two types of tabulation.

7. Explain the various ways in which one-way tabulation can be used.

8. Assess the particular importance of cross tabulation.

9. Describe a method by which a researcher can determine what impact one variable has on another in a cross-tabulation table.

10. Describe what banners are and how they are useful.

Case in Marketing Research

Rita McKenzie, a field supervisor with Delta Data Services, looked at the tired faces around her. She was looking at Delta's crack team of interviewers after a Saturday at Twin Pines Mall. Delta had been hired by Door's cafeteria to conduct a marketing research survey, and the interviewers had just spent the day polling Twin Pines shoppers to find out why they did or didn't dine at Door's. The same interviewers were scheduled for another day of polling on Sunday, and McKenzie wanted to make sure that everything had gone smoothly and to see if there were any misunderstandings or problems that needed to be cleared up.

"So how'd it go?" asked McKenzie as the interviewers helped themselves to coffee and doughnuts. "Did you get a lot of incompletes?"

"It's a long survey," replied a middle-aged woman who had worked for Delta for a number of years. "I had quite a few people, especially people with young kids, who initially agreed to be interviewed and then gave up about two-thirds of the way through it."

"I know," groaned a college student who worked part-time for Delta. "By the end of the day I was practically begging them to finish."

"Then tomorrow let's try to tell people when we approach them approximately how long it'll take," replied McKenzie. "How long would you guys say?"

"About 20 minutes," the interviewers chorused.

"Well, good," continued McKenzie. "Then up front just ask them whether they'd be willing to spend 20 minutes answering questions about Door's. We might get fewer people agreeing to be interviewed, but at least the ones who agree will finish."

The group around the table nodded in agreement.

"I've gone through some of the questionnaires that were finished this morning, and I've assembled some notes for each of you. I'm not trying to pick on anyone, but several of you have some real legibility problems. I know you're trying to take down what's being said as accurately as possible, but in your rush, your handwriting is really deteriorating. I'd like to remind you that survey results aren't meaningful if they aren't legible."

"One more thing," continued McKenzie. "There seems to be some confusion in regard to Question 11. The question is, 'How many times in the last three months have you eaten a meal in a shopping mall?' A lot of inconsistencies are turning up between the answers to this question and the answers to Question 12. People say they've eaten a meal in a shopping mall once in the last three months, and then they answer the next question, 'What did you eat?' with answers like 'popcorn' or 'ice cream.' You need to be sure that they understand Question 11, and you need to be on the lookout for inconsistencies."

Discussion Issues

1. What other types of things might McKenzie have looked for in her initial field edit of the Door's cafeteria questionnaire?

2. What should be done with the questionnaires that have already been completed but show inconsistencies in the replies?

Imagine yourself as the director of a marketing research project. For weeks you have supervised a massive field study in numerous shopping malls. Now the foot soldiers in your data-collecting army have moved on to other projects, and you are left in your office surrounded by stacks of completed questionnaires. The battle to get the information may be over, but you have not yet won the war until you can determine what all those data really mean.

In this chapter, we will begin to explore how analysts obtain meaning from raw data. All previous steps in the research process have been undertaken to support this search for meaning. The specific analytical procedures involved are closely related to the preceding steps, because the careful analyst looked ahead to this moment when he or she designed those other steps. The most astute researchers developed dummy tables as well, indicating how each item of information would be used. Thorough preparatory work probably revealed some undesirable data gaps and some "interesting" but not vital items that might have posed problems if they had not been dealt with at that time.

The search for meaning can take many forms. However, the preliminary analytical steps of editing, coding, and tabulating the data are common to most studies, so a review of what they are and how they are used is warranted.

Editing

The basic purpose of editing is to impose some minimum quality standards on the raw data. Editing involves the inspection and, if necessary, correction of each questionnaire or observation form. Inspection and correction are often done in two stages: the field edit and the central-office edit.

Field Edit

Field edit A preliminary edit, typically conducted by a field supervisor, which is designed to detect the most glaring omissions and inaccuracies in a completed data-collection instrument.

The **field edit** is a preliminary edit designed to detect the most glaring omissions and inaccuracies in the data. It is also useful in helping to control the behavior of the field force personnel and to clear up any misunderstandings they may have about directions, procedures, specific questions, and so on.

Ideally, the field edit is done as soon as possible after the questionnaire or other data-collection form has been administered. In that way, problems can be corrected before the interviewing or observation staff is disbanded, and while the particular contacts that were the source of trouble are still fresh in the interviewer's or observer's mind. The preliminary edit is usually conducted by a field supervisor. Some of the items checked are described in Table 19.1.[1]

Central-Office Edit

Central-office edit Thorough and exacting scrutiny and correction of completed data-collection forms, including a decision about what to do with the data.

The field edit is typically followed by a **central-office edit,** which involves more complete and exacting scrutiny and correction of the completed returns. The work calls for the keen eye of a person well versed in the objectives and procedures of the study. To ensure consistency of treatment, it is best if one individual handles all completed instruments. If the work must be divided because of length and time considerations, the division should be by parts of the data-collection instruments rather than by respondents. That is, one editor would edit Part A of all questionnaires while the other would edit Part B.

Unlike the field edit, the central-office edit depends less on follow-up procedures and more on deciding just what to do with the data. Accurate follow-up is now more

Table 19.1   ***Items Checked in the Field Edit***

1. **Completeness:** The check for completeness involves scrutinizing the data form to ensure that no sections or pages were omitted, and it also involves checking individual items. A blank for a specific question could mean that the respondent refused to answer; alternatively, it may simply reflect an oversight on the respondent's part or that he or she did not know the answer. It may be very important for the purposes of the study to know which reason is correct. It is hoped that by contacting the field worker while the interview is fresh in his or her mind, the field editor can obtain the needed clarification.

2. **Legibility:** It is impossible to code a questionnaire that cannot be deciphered because of illegible handwriting or obscure abbreviations. It is a simple matter to correct this now, whereas it is often extremely time-consuming later.

3. **Comprehensibility:** Sometimes a recorded response is incomprehensible to all but the field interviewer. By detecting this now, the field editor can obtain the necessary clarification.

4. **Consistency:** Marked inconsistencies within an interview or observation schedule typically indicate errors in collecting or recording the data and may indicate ambiguity in the instrument or carelessness in its administration. For instance, if a respondent indicated that he or she saw a particular commercial on television last night on one part of the questionnaire, and later indicated that he or she did not watch television last night, the analyst would indeed be in a dilemma. Such inconsistencies can often be detected and corrected in the field edit.

5. **Uniformity:** It is very important that the responses be recorded in uniform units. For instance, if the study is aimed at determining the number of magazines read per week per individual, and the respondent indicates the number of magazines for which he or she has monthly subscriptions, the response base is not uniform, and the result could cause confusion in the later stages of analysis. If the problem is detected now, perhaps the interviewer can recontact the respondent and get the correct answer.

difficult because of the time that has elapsed. The editor must decide how data-collection instruments containing incomplete answers, obviously wrong answers, and answers that reflect a lack of interest will be handled. Since such problems are more prevalent with questionnaires than with observation forms, we will discuss these difficulties from that perspective, although our discussion applies generally to all types of data-collection forms.

The study in which all the returned questionnaires are completely filled out is rare. Some will have complete sections omitted. Others will reflect sporadic item nonresponse. The editor's decision on how to handle these incomplete questionnaires depends on the severity of the omission. Questionnaires that omit complete sections are obviously suspect. Yet they should not automatically be thrown out. It might be, for example, that the omitted section refers to the influence of the spouse in some major durable purchase, whereas the respondent is not married. This type of reply is certainly usable in spite of the incomplete section. If there is no logical justification for the large number of unanswered questions, the total reply will probably be thrown out, increasing the nonresponse rate for the study. Questionnaires containing only isolated instances of item nonresponse will be retained, although they might undergo some *data cleaning* after coding, a subject discussed later in this chapter.

Careful editing of the questionnaire will sometimes show that an answer to a question is obviously incorrect. For example, respondents might first be asked for the type of store in which they purchased a camera and later be asked for the name of the store. If a person responds "department store" to the first question and then gives the name of a catalog showroom to answer the second, one of the answers is incorrect. The editor may be able to determine which of the two answers is correct from other information in the questionnaire. Alternatively, the editor may need to establish policies as to which answer, if either, will be treated as correct when these inconsistencies or other types of inaccuracies arise. These policies will reflect the purposes of the study.

Editors must also be on the alert to spot completed questionnaires that have failed to engage the respondent's interest. Evidence of this lack of interest may be obvious or quite subtle. Consider, for example, a subject who checked the "5" position on a five-point scale for each of forty items in an attitude questionnaire, even though some items were expressed negatively and some positively. Obviously, that person did not take the study seriously, and the editor should probably throw out such a response. A discerning editor might also be able to pick up more subtle indications of disinterest, such as check marks that are not within the boxes provided, scribbles, spills on the questionnaire, and so on. An editor may not want to throw out these responses, but they should be coded so that it is later possible to run separate tabulations for the questionable instruments and obviously good questionnaires. Then the two groups could be compared to see whether lack of interest makes any difference in the results.

Coding

Coding The technical procedure by which data are categorized; it involves specifying the alternative categories or classes into which the responses are to be placed and assigning code numbers to the classes.

Coding is "the technical procedure by which data are categorized. Through coding, the raw data are transformed into symbols—usually numerals—that may be tabulated and counted. The transformation is not automatic, however; it involves judgment on the part of the coder."[2]

The first step in coding is specifying the categories or classes into which the responses are to be placed.[3] There is no magic number of categories. Rather, the number will depend on the research problem being investigated and the specific items used to generate the information. Response choices should be mutually exclusive and exhaustive, so that every response logically falls into one and only one category. Multiple responses are legitimate for some questions—for example, if the question is, "For what purposes do you use Jell-O?" and the responses include such things as "a dessert item," "an evening snack," "an afternoon snack," and so on. On the other hand, if the question focuses on the person's age, then only one age category is, of course, acceptable, and the code should indicate clearly which category.

Coding closed questions and most scaling devices is simple because the coding is established when the data-collection instrument is designed. Respondents then code themselves with their responses, or the interviewer codes them in recording the responses on the checklist provided.

Coding open-ended questions can be very difficult and is often much more expensive than coding closed questions. The coder has to determine appropriate categories on the basis of answers that are not always anticipated.[4] Consider the following question, which was used in a study of the fast food franchise system of distribution.[5] "Please specify the product or service around which your franchise system is organized (for example, pancakes)." The expectation was that the respondents would reply with "hamburgers" or "chicken" or "pizza," and so on. Some did. Others responded with "hamburgers, hot dogs, and beverages." How should such a reply be treated? The decision, after much agonizing, was to establish the category of "multiple fast foods."

If there are so many questionnaires that several coders are needed, inconsistency in coding may be an additional problem. To assure consistency of treatment, the

One of the preliminary steps in data analysis is coding the data so that it can be entered into a computer.

Source: Courtesy of NCR Corporation.

work should be divided by task, not by dividing the questionnaires equally among the coders. By allowing coders to focus their energies on one or a few questions, researchers can ensure that a consistent set of standards is being applied to each question. This approach is also more efficient, because coders can easily memorize just a few codes and thus do not have to consult the codebook for each instrument. When several persons do, in fact, code the same question on different batches of questionnaires, it is important that they also code a sample of the other's work to ensure that a consistent set of coding criteria is being employed.[6]

The second step in coding involves assigning code numbers to the classes. For example, sex might be assigned the letter *M* for male and *F* for female. Alternatively, the classes could be denoted by 1 for male and 2 for female. Generally, it is better to use numbers rather than letters to denote the classes. It is also better at this stage to use numerical data as it was reported on the data-collection form, rather than to collapse it into smaller categories. For example, it is not advisable to code age as 1 = under 20 years, 2 = 20–29, 3 = 30–39, and so on, if actual ages of the people were provided. This would result in an unnecessary sacrifice of information in the original measurement and could just as easily be done at later stages in the analysis.

When a computer is being used to analyze the data, it is necessary to code the data so that they can be readily inputted to the machine. Regardless of how that input will be handled, whether by mark-sense forms or directly through a keyboard on a terminal, it is helpful to visualize the input in terms of a multiple-column record. Further, it is advisable to follow certain conventions when coding the data.

1. Locate only one character in each column. When the question allows multiple responses, allow separate columns in the coding for each answer. Thus in our Jell-O example, the coder should provide a separate column for those who use the product as a dessert item, those who use it as an evening snack, and so on.

2. Use only numeric codes, not letters of the alphabet or special characters, like @, or blanks. Most computer statistical programs have trouble manipulating anything but numbers.

3. Use as many columns for the field assigned to a variable as are necessary to capture the variable. Thus, if the variable is such that the ten codes from 0 to 9 are not sufficient to exhaust the categories, then one should use two columns, providing one hundred codes from 00 through 99. Moreover, no more than one variable should be assigned to any field.

4. Use standard codes for "no information." Thus, all "don't know" responses might be coded as 8, "no answers" as 9, and "does not apply" as 0. It is best if the same code is used throughout the study for each of these types of "no information."

5. Code in a respondent identification number on each record. This number need not, and typically will not, identify the respondent by name. Rather, the number simply ties the questionnaire to the coded data. This is often useful information in data cleaning (discussed later). If the questionnaire will not fit on one record, then code the respondent identification number and a sequence number into each record. Column 10 in the first record might then indicate how the respondent answered Question 2, while Column 10 in the second record might indicate whether the person is male or female.[7]

Codebook A book that describes each variable, gives it a code name, and identifies its location in the record.

The final step in the coding process is to prepare a **codebook,** which contains the general instructions indicating how each item of data was coded. It lists the codes for each variable and the categories included in each code. It further indicates where on the computer record the variable is located and how the variable should be read—for example, with a decimal point or as a whole number. The latter information is provided by the format specifications.

Tabulation

Simple tabulation A count of the number of cases that fall into each category when the categories are based on one variable.

Cross tabulation A count of the number of cases that fall into each of several categories when the categories are based on two or more variables considered simultaneously.

Tabulation consists simply of counting the number of cases that fall into the various categories. The tabulation may take the form of a *simple tabulation* or a *cross tabulation*. **Simple tabulation** involves counting a single variable. It may be repeated for each of the variables in the study, but the tabulation for each variable is independent of the tabulation for the other variables. In **cross tabulation,** two or more of the variables are treated simultaneously. For instance, coding the number of people who bought Campbell's soup at a Kroger store is an example of a cross tabulation, since it measures two related characteristics. The tabulations may be done entirely by hand, entirely by machine, or partially by machine and partially by hand. Which is more efficient depends both on the number of tabulations necessary and on the number of cases in each tabulation. The number of tabulations is a direct function of the number of variables, while the number of cases is a direct function of the size of the sample. The fewer the number of tabulations required and the smaller the sample, the more attractive hand methods become. However, the attractiveness of either alternative also is highly dependent on the complexity of the tabulations. Complexity increases as the number of variables receiving simultaneous treatment in a cross tabulation increases. Complexity also increases as the number of categories per variable increases.

For hand tabulation a tally sheet is typically used. Consider the question, "How many trips did you make to the grocery store this past week?" The tally for a sample of Size 40 might look like this:

0	⊥⊞T	1		6
1	⊥⊞T	⊥⊞T	11	12
2	⊥⊞T	⊥⊞T		10
3	⊥⊞T	111		8
4 or more	1111			4

The hand tally also can be used to create cross-classification tables. Suppose one of the study questions was the relationship between shopping behavior and family size. Table 19.2 shows the cross tabulation that might then be constructed. The cross tabulation indicates, for instance, that of the six families that made zero trips to the grocery store, four were composed of only one member, one family had two members, and one family had four members. The cross tabulation thus provides information on the *joint occurrence* of shopping trips and family size.

Note that the right-hand totals (sometimes referred to as the *marginal totals*) are identical to the results for the straight tabulation. This shows that it is unnecessary to make straight tabulations for individual variables that will be included in two-way tables.

While the hand tabulation might be useful in very simple studies involving a few questions and a limited number of responses, most studies rely on computer tabulation using packaged programs. A great many such programs are available.[8] Some will calculate summary statistics and will plot a histogram of the values in addition to reporting the number of cases in each category. The basic input to these statistical analyses will be the *data array*, which lists the value of each variable for each sample unit. Each variable occupies a specific place in the record for a sample unit, thereby making it easy to pick off the values for it from all of the cases. The location of each variable is given in the codebook.

Figure 19.1 shows an abbreviated version of a questionnaire that was sent to customers of a sporting goods retailer to determine their perceptions of buying sporting goods through the mail. Table 19.3 is an example of the data array that could result from such a study. Table 19.4 is the codebook to the study, describing what is contained in each column. Note that only one line had to be devoted to each sample unit or observation. If the amount of information sought from each sample unit were greater, so that it would not fit on one line, additional lines would be devoted to each

---

Table 19.2   ***Relationship between Family Size and Number of Shopping Trips***

Number of Trips	Number of Members					Total
	1	2	3	4	5 or more	
0	1111	1		1		6
1	111	1111	111	11		12
2	1	111	1111	11		10
3		1	⊥⊞T	1	1	8
4 or more				1	111	4
Totals	8	9	12	7	4	40

Figure 19.1   *Part of the Questionnaire for Avery Sporting Goods*

The following questionnaire was designed to give a well-known sporting goods company a better idea of people's perceptions of buying sporting goods and other general merchandise through catalogs. The first three columns of the data listed in Table 19.3 contain the customers' survey identification numbers.

1. During the past year, what percentage of the sporting goods you purchased were ordered through a catalog?

_____ 0 percent

_____ 1–10 percent

_____ 11–15 percent

_____ 16–20 percent

_____ 21+ percent

2. How willing are you to purchase merchandise offered through the Avery Sporting Goods catalog?

_____ Not at all willing

_____ Somewhat willing

_____ Very willing

3. Have you ever ordered any merchandise from the Avery Sporting Goods catalog?

_____ Never ordered

_____ Ordered before, but not within the last year

_____ Ordered within the last year

	Not at All Confident	Slightly Confident	Somewhat Confident	Confident	Very Confident
4. How confident are you that the following sporting goods purchased through a catalog would be of high quality?					
(a) Athletic clothing (shirts, warm-up suits, etc.)	___	___	___	___	___
(b) Athletic shoes	___	___	___	___	___
(c) Fishing equipment	___	___	___	___	___
(d) Balls (basketballs, footballs, etc.)	___	___	___	___	___
(e) Skiing equipment	___	___	___	___	___
5. How confident are you that the following sporting goods would be of high quality if purchased in a retail sporting goods store?					
(a) Athletic clothing (shirts, warm-up suits, etc.)	___	___	___	___	___
(b) Athletic shoes	___	___	___	___	___
(c) Fishing equipment	___	___	___	___	___
(d) Balls (basketballs, footballs, etc.)	___	___	___	___	___
(e) Skiing equipment	___	___	___	___	___

observation. The codebook would still indicate where the information for any particular variable was located.

There are a number of important questions concerning the analysis of data that can be illustrated using one-way tabulations and cross tabulations as vehicles. Consider, therefore, the data in Table 19.5. Suppose that the data were collected for

Table 19.3   **Listing of Raw Data**

0011115554344434

0021214455545453

0034135544245321

0043225543554324

0052115355453542

Table 19.4   **Portion of Codebook for Avery Sporting Goods Questionnaire**

Column(s)	Question Number	Variable (Variable Number)	Coding Specification
1–3	—	Questionnaire identification number (V1)	—
4	1	Percentage of products purchased through a catalog (V2)	1 = 0 percent 2 = 1–10 percent 3 = 11–15 percent 4 = 16–20 percent 5 = 21+ percent
5	2	Willingness to purchase merchandise from the Avery Sporting Goods catalog (V3)	1 = Not at all willing 2 = Somewhat willing 3 = Very willing
6	3	Ever ordered from the Avery Sporting Goods catalog (V4)	1 = Never ordered 2 = Ordered before, but not within the last year 3 = Ordered within the last year
			Coding Specifications 4(a)–5(e) 1 = Not at all confident 2 = Slightly confident 3 = Somewhat confident 4 = Confident 5 = Very confident
7	4(a)	Confidence in buying athletic clothing through a catalog (V5)	
8	4(b)	Confidence in buying athletic shoes through a catalog (V6)	
9	4(c)	Confidence in buying fishing equipment through a catalog (V7)	
10	4(d)	Confidence in buying balls through a catalog (V8)	
11	4(e)	Confidence in buying skiing equipment through a catalog (V9)	
12	5(a)	Confidence in buying athletic clothing in a retail store (V10)	
13	5(b)	Confidence in buying athletic shoes in a retail store (V11)	
14	5(c)	Confidence in buying fishing equipment in a retail store (V12)	
15	5(d)	Confidence in buying balls in a retail store (V13)	
16	5(e)	Confidence in buying skiing equipment in a retail store (V14)	

Table 19.5 Raw Data for Car Ownership Study

Family Identification No.	(1) Income in Dollars	(2) Number of Members in Family	(3) Education of Household Head in Yrs.	(4) Region Where Live N = North S = South	(5) Life-Style Orientation L = Liberal C = Conservative	(6) Number of Cars Family Owns	(7) Did Family Finance the Car Purchase?	(8) Does Family Own Station Wagon?	(9) Does Family Own Foreign Economy Car?	(10) Does Family Own Van?
1001	16,800	3	12	N	L	1	N	N	N	Y
1002	17,400	4	12	N	L	1	N	N	N	N
1003	14,300	2	10	N	L	1	N	N	N	N
1004	15,400	4	9	N	L	1	N	N	N	N
1005	14,000	3	8	N	L	1	N	N	N	N
1006	17,200	2	12	N	L	1	N	N	Y	N
1007	17,000	4	12	N	L	1	N	N	N	N
1008	16,900	3	10	N	L	1	N	N	N	N
1009	16,700	2	12	N	L	1	N	N	N	N
1010	13,800	4	6	N	C	1	Y	N	N	N
1011	14,100	3	8	N	C	1	N	N	N	N
1012	16,300	3	11	N	C	1	N	N	N	N
1013	14,700	2	12	N	C	1	N	N	N	N
1014	15,400	4	12	N	C	1	N	N	N	N
1015	15,400	4	12	N	C	1	N	N	N	N
1016	15,900	3	11	N	C	1	Y	N	N	N
1017	16,300	3	12	N	C	1	N	N	N	N
1018	17,400	2	12	N	C	2	N	N	N	N
1019	17,300	2	12	N	C	1	N	N	N	N
1020	13,700	3	8	N	C	1	N	N	N	N
1021	16,100	2	12	N	C	1	N	N	Y	N
1022	16,300	4	12	N	C	1	Y	N	N	N
1023	13,800	3	6	N	C	1	N	N	N	N
1024	14,400	4	8	N	C	1	Y	N	N	N
1025	15,300	2	9	N	C	1	Y	N	N	N

1026	15,900	3	12	N	C	1	N	Z	N	N
1027	15,100	4	12	S	L	1	Z	Z	Z	Y
1028	17,200	2	12	S	L	1	Z	Z	Y	N
1029	15,400	4	10	S	L	1	Z	Z	Z	Z
1030	15,600	3	12	S	L	1	Z	Z	Z	Z
1031	14,900	3	12	S	L	1	Z	Z	Z	Y
1032	14,800	4	11	S	C	1	Z	Z	Z	Z
1033	14,600	4	12	S	C	1	Z	Z	Z	Z
1034	13,100	3	9	S	C	1	Z	Z	Z	Y
1035	15,900	3	12	S	C	1	Z	Z	Z	Z
1036	16,700	4	12	S	C	1	Z	Z	Z	Y
1037	17,300	4	12	S	C	1	Z	Z	Z	Y
1038	17,100	3	12	S	C	1	Z	Z	Z	Z
1039	14,000	3	10	S	C	1	Z	Z	Z	Z
1040	13,600	3	10	S	C	1	Z	Z	Z	N
1041	16,200	3	12	S	C	1	Z	Z	Z	Z
1042	14,100	4	10	S	L	1	Z	Z	Y	N
1043	12,700	2	8	S	L	1	Y	Z	Z	N
1044	16,000	4	13	S	L	1	Y	Z	Z	N
1045	15,400	3	16	N	C	2	Z	Y	Y	N
1046	16,900	4	16	S	L	1	Y	Z	Z	N
1047	13,800	6	10	N	C	1	Y	Y	Z	Z
1048	17,100	8	16	S	L	2	Z	Y	Z	Z
1049	16,800	5	15	S	C	2	Y	Y	Z	Z
1050	12,900	5	8	S	L	1	Z	Z	Y	Y
1051	13,700	6	8	N	L	1	Y	Y	Y	Z
1052	16,800	8	12	S	C	2	Z	Z	Z	Z
1053	16,100	8	12	N	L	2	Z	Y	Z	Z
1054	15,700	6	12	N	C	1	Z	Z	Z	Z
1055	18,200	2	12	N	L	1	Z	Z	Z	Z

(continued)

Table 19.5 (Continued)

Family Identification No.	(1) Income in Dollars	(2) Number of Members in Family	(3) Education of Household Head in Yrs.	(4) Region Where Live N = North S = South	(5) Life-Style Orientation L = Liberal C = Conservative	(6) Number of Cars Family Owns	(7) Did Family Finance the Car Purchase?	(8) Does Family Own Station Wagon?	(9) Does Family Own Foreign Economy Car?	(10) Does Family Own Van?
1056	19,800	3	12	N	L	1	Y	N	N	N
1057	20,400	4	12	N	L	1	Y	N	N	N
1058	19,000	2	12	N	L	1	N	N	N	N
1059	17,600	4	12	N	L	1	Y	N	N	N
1060	32,000	3	12	N	L	1	N	N	N	N
1061	28,600	3	12	N	L	1	N	N	N	Y
1062	46,400	4	12	N	L	2	Y	N	Y	N
1063	21,200	2	12	N	L	1	Y	N	N	N
1064	19,300	4	10	N	C	1	Y	N	N	N
1065	17,700	4	10	N	C	1	Y	N	N	N
1066	32,400	3	12	N	C	2	N	N	Y	Y
1067	38,700	3	12	N	C	1	N	N	N	N
1068	24,200	2	12	S	L	1	Y	N	N	Y
1069	25,100	3	12	S	L	2	N	N	N	N
1070	23,300	4	12	S	L	1	N	N	N	Y
1071	20,200	2	12	S	L	1	Y	N	N	N
1072	19,300	3	10	S	C	2	N	N	N	Y
1073	18,200	4	12	S	C	1	N	N	N	N
1074	17,800	2	12	S	C	1	Y	N	N	N
1075	18,000	3	10	S	C	1	Y	N	N	Y
1076	31,300	4	16	N	L	1	N	Y	N	N

618

1077	N	N	N	N	2	L	N	16	4	26,900
1078	N	N	N	N	1	L	N	14	3	24,700
1079	N	N	N	N	1	L	N	17	3	27,300
1080	N	N	N	Y	2	L	N	13	2	18,100
1081	Y	N	N	N	1	L	N	14	2	104,200
1082	N	N	N	N	1	L	S	16	3	26,100
1083	N	N	N	N	1	L	S	13	4	19,300
1084	Y	N	N	N	9	L	S	16	4	20,800
1085	Y	N	N	Y	1	L	S	16	4	28,100
1086	N	N	N	Y	1	C	S	14	2	26,400
1087	N	N	N	Y	2	L	N	10	6	18,300
1088	N	N	Y	Y	2	L	N	10	5	17,800
1089	N	N	Y	Y	2	L	N	8	7	18,000
1090	Y	N	Y	Y	2	L	N	12	9	19,600
1091	Y	N	Y	Y	2	L	N	12	11	24,200
1092	Y	Y	Y	Y	2	L	N	10	6	22,100
1093	Y	Y	Y	Y	3	L	S	12	5	49,000
1094	Y	Y	Y	N	2	L	S	12	6	23,300
1095	Y	N	Y	Y	2	C	S	10	9	22,200
1096	Y	N	Y	Y	2	C	S	12	7	24,700
1097	N	Y	Y	Y	2	L	N	16	6	27,300
1098	N	Y	Y	N	3	L	N	18	10	26,900
1099	Y	N	N	Y	1	L	S	15	7	21,200
1100	N	Y	Y	Y	2	C	S	16	5	23,800

a study focusing on car ownership. Suppose, in particular, that the following questions were of research interest:

■ What characteristics distinguish families owning two or more cars from families owning one car?

■ What are the distinguishing characteristics of those who buy station wagons? Foreign economy cars? Vans?

■ Are there differences in the characteristics of families who financed their automobile purchase and those who did not?

Suppose that the data were collected from a probability sample of respondents using mailed questionnaires, and that the 100 people to whom the questionnaire was sent all replied. Thus, there are no problems of nonresponse with which to contend.

One-way Tabulation

The one-way tabulation, in addition to communicating the results of a study, can be used for several other purposes: (1) to determine the degree of item nonresponse, (2) to locate *blunders* (defined later), (3) to locate *outliers* (defined later), (4) to determine the empirical distribution of the variable in question, and (5) to calculate summary statistics. The first three of these are often referred to as *data cleaning*.

Item nonresponse is a significant problem in most surveys. Some percentage of the survey instruments invariably suffer from it. As a matter of fact, the degree of item nonresponse often serves as a useful indicator of the quality of the research. When it is excessive, it calls the whole research effort into question and suggests that the research objectives and procedures should be examined critically. When it is in bounds, it is still necessary for the research director to make a decision regarding what should be done about the missing items before analyzing the data. There are several possible strategies:

1. Leave the items blank, and report the number as a separate category. While this procedure works well for simple one-way and cross tabulations, it does not work well for a number of other statistical techniques.

2. Eliminate the case with the missing item in analyses using the variable. When using this approach, the analyst must continually report the number of cases on which the analysis is based, since the sample size is not constant across analyses. It also ignores the fact that a significant degree of nonresponse on a particular item might be informative in that it suggests respondents do not care very deeply about the issue being addressed by the question.

3. Substitute values for the missing items. Typically, the substitution will involve some measure of central tendency such as the mean, median, or mode. Alternatively, sometimes the analyst attempts to estimate the answer using other information contained in the questionnaire. The substitution of values makes maximum use of the data, since all the reasonably good cases are used. At the same time, it requires more work from the analyst, and it contains some potential for bias. It also raises the question of which statistical technique should be used to generate the estimate.[9]

There is no "right" or single answer as to how missing items should be handled. It all depends on the purposes of the study, the incidence of missing items, and the methods that will be used to analyze the data.

As mentioned earlier, another purpose of one-way tabulation is to locate **blunders,** which are simply errors that occur during editing, coding, or entering the data into the computer. Consider the one-way tabulation of the number of cars owned per family in Table 19.6. A check of the original questionnaire indicates the family

Blunder An error that arises when editing, coding, keypunching, or tabulating the data.

Table 19.6   ***Cars per Family***

Number of Cars per Family	Number of Families
1	74
2	23
3	2
9	1

reporting ownership of nine cars had, in fact, one car. The 9 is a blunder. The simple one-way tabulation has revealed the error, and it can now be corrected at a very early stage in the analysis with a minimum of difficulty and expense. Research Window 19.1 reveals how a one-way tabulation helped to uncover the true situation regarding the concentration of wealth, an issue with important public policy overtones.

Research Window 19.1
Are the Rich Really Getting Richer?

Headlines all over the country proclaimed the news: "Major Study Proves Rich Getting Richer." The results of a University of Michigan study released by Democrats on the Joint Economic Committee showed beyond a shadow of a doubt that the nation's wealthy were getting richer faster than ever, and faster than anyone else. The startling conclusion was that the richest 0.5 percent of Americans had 25 percent of the nation's wealth in 1963, but a full 35 percent by 1986.

The rich smiled and patted their Gold Cards, while the social reformers mounted plans to take up their cudgels and redistribute the wealth.

But there was something funny about the figures. Wealth is rarely measured, because it is such a loose concept, but census data have been showing a gradual *decline* in the concentration of income. How can wealth be getting more concentrated if income is getting less concentrated?

Noting this oddity, the Federal Reserve, which had commissioned the report, warned when it released the data that they seemed irregular. People in the Treasury looked at the numbers more closely and were amazed to learn that the study, if accurate, meant that the wealthy had huge new holdings in unincorporated business assets. The magnitude of those investments just didn't jibe with the Fed's own estimates.

Sensing that something had gone awry, the Fed took a closer look at the Michigan report and found a seemingly small error that shot the validity of all the data to smithereens. One wealthy family was reported as having $200 million in unincorporated business assets, when the family actually had $2 million in such assets. A key-puncher in Ann Arbor was probably to blame. This one error got compounded every time the figure was used, because the sample was so small. A correction subsequently issued by the Joint Economic Committee showed that once this error was fixed, the study showed a statistically insignificant increase in the concentration of wealth.

In this case, it was hard to say who was more disappointed with the corrected results: the rich, who found that their assets were growing at only the same rate as everyone else's, or the politicians, who had been delighted to use the report to make political hay.

Source: "Soak the Politicians," *The Wall Street Journal*, (August 22, 1986), p. 16.

Table 19.7   *Cars per Family*

Number of Cars per Family	Number of Families	Percent of Families
1	75	75
2	23	23
3	2	2
	100	100

The number of cases serving as a base for the one-way tabulation in Table 19.6 is 100, and thus the number entries are easily converted to percentages. In most cases, conversion will not be this simple. However, it is a good practice always to indicate percentages in the table, since they aid communication. Hence, a more typical way of presenting our car study data, corrected for blunders, is shown in Table 19.7.

Note that the percentages are presented to zero decimal places. In this case the percentages are whole numbers to begin with, because the sample size was 100, but in most cases they would have to be rounded off. Whole numbers should almost always be used, since they are easier to read and also because decimals may convey a greater accuracy than the figures can support, especially in a small sample. While in some cases the analyst might be justified in reporting percentages to one decimal place (rarely two decimal places, though), the general rule in reporting percentages is, *unless decimals have a special purpose, they should be omitted.*[10]

Sometimes the percentages are presented in parentheses (see Table 19.8) immediately to the right or below the actual count entry in the table. Sometimes only the percentages are presented. In this case it is imperative that the total number of cases on which the percentages are based be provided.

Outlier An observation so different in magnitude from the rest of the observations that the analyst chooses to treat it as a special case.

Still another use of the one-way tabulation is to locate **outliers,** which are not errors but rather observations so different in magnitude from the rest of the observations that the analyst chooses to treat them as special cases. This may mean eliminating the observation from the analysis or determining the specific factors that generate this unique observation. For instance, if the family in our earlier example had really owned nine cars, this figure would be considered an outlier, since it is highly unusual for a family to own that many cars.

For another case, consider the tabulation of incomes contained in Table 19.8, but ignore the right-hand column for the moment. The tabulation indicates there is only one family with an income greater than $55,400. Table 19.5 indicates that this family (Number 1081) had an annual income of $104,200. This is clearly out of line with the rest of the sample and is properly considered an outlier. What the analyst chooses to do with this observation depends on the objectives of the study. In this case, it is not unreasonable for a family to have such an income, and so the observation will be retained in the analysis.

A fourth use of the one-way frequency tabulation is to determine the *empirical distribution* of the characteristic in question. Some analysts ignore the distribution of the variables and automatically calculate summary statistics such as the mean. That can be a serious mistake. Consider the case of a new sauce product:

> On the average, consumers wanted it neither really hot nor really mild. The mean rating of the test participants was quite close to the middle of the scale, which had

Table 19.8   *Income Distribution of Respondents in Car Ownership Study*

Income	Number of Families		Cumulative Number of Families	
Less than $13,500	3	(3.0)	3	(3.0)
$13,500 to 15,400	23	(23.0)	26	(26.0)
$15,500 to 17,400	28	(28.0)	54	(54.0)
$17,500 to 19,400	14	(14.0)	68	(68.0)
$19,500 to 21,400	7	(7.0)	75	(75.0)
$21,500 to 23,400	4	(4.0)	79	(79.0)
$23,500 to 25,400	6	(6.0)	85	(85.0)
$25,500 to 27,400	6	(6.0)	91	(91.0)
$27,500 to 29,400	2	(2.0)	93	(93.0)
$29,500 to 55,400	6	(6.0)	99	(99.0)
More than $55,400	1	(1.0)	100	(100.0)
Total number of families	100	(100.0)		

Histogram A form of bar chart on which the values of the variable are placed along the abscissa, or X axis, and the absolute frequency or relative frequency of occurrence of the values is indicated along the ordinate, or Y axis.

Frequency polygon A figure obtained from a histogram by connecting the midpoints of the bars of the histogram with straight lines.

Cumulative distribution function A function that shows the number of cases having a value less than or equal to a specified quantity; the function is generated by connecting points representing the given combinations of X's (values) and Y's (cumulative frequencies) with straight lines.

"very mild" and "very hot" as its bipolar adjectives. This happened to fit the client's preconceived notion.

However, examination of the distribution of the ratings revealed the existence of a large proportion of consumers who wanted the sauce to be mild and an equally large proportion who wanted it to be hot. Relatively few wanted the in-between product, which would have been suggested by looking at the mean rating alone.[11]

It is always a good idea to get a sense for a variable's distribution before performing any analysis with it.

The distribution often is best visualized through a **histogram,** a form of bar chart in which the values of the variable are placed along the abscissa, or X axis, and the absolute frequency or relative frequency of occurrence of the values is indicated along the ordinate, or Y axis. The histogram for the income data in Table 19.8 appears as Figure 19.2, with the incomes over $29,500 omitted because their inclusion would have required an undue extension of the income axis. It is readily apparent that the distribution of incomes is skewed to the right. The actual distribution can be compared to some theoretical distribution to determine whether the data are consistent with some a priori model. Further insight into the empirical distribution of income can be obtained by constructing the **frequency polygon,** which is obtained from the histogram by connecting the midpoints of the bars with straight lines. The frequency polygon for incomes is superimposed on the histogram in Figure 19.2.

An alternative way of gaining insight into the empirical distribution is through the empirical **cumulative distribution function.** Once again, the one-way tabulation is the source of the data. In this case, though, the number of observations with a value less than or equal to a specified quantity is determined; that is, the cumulative frequencies are generated. Thus, in the right-hand column of Table 19.8, we see that there are three families with incomes less than $13,500, whereas there are twenty-six families (3 + 23) with incomes of $15,400 or less and fifty-four families (3 + 23 + 28)

Figure 19.2   *Histogram and Frequency Polygon of Incomes of Families in Car Ownership Study*

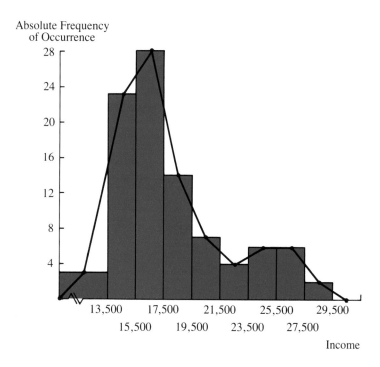

with incomes of $17,400 or less. These cumulative frequencies are denoted along the ordinate in Figure 19.3, while the abscissa again contains incomes. The empirical cumulative distribution function is generated by connecting the points representing the given combinations of X's (values) and Y's (cumulative frequencies) with straight lines.

The cumulative distribution function can also be used to determine whether the distribution of observed incomes is consistent with some theoretical or assumed distribution. In addition, it can be used to calculate some of the commonly used measures of location, such as the median, quartiles, and percentiles. These can simply be read from the plot once the cumulative relative frequencies are entered. In our case, the cumulative relative frequencies are equal to the cumulative absolute frequencies divided by 100, since there are 100 cases.

By definition, the sample median is that value for which 50 percent of the values lie below it and 50 percent are above it. To read the sample median from the plot of the cumulative distribution, simply extend a horizontal line from 0.50 on the relative frequency ordinate until it intersects the graph, and then drop a vertical line from the point of intersection to the X axis. The point of intersection with the X axis is the approximate sample median. In the case at hand, the sample median equals $17,300. The quality of the approximation could be checked by actually determining the median using the detailed data.

Sample quartiles could be determined in similar fashion. The first sample quartile (also known as the 25th percentile) is that value for which 25 percent of the observations are below it. The first sample quartile is determined by drawing a horizontal line from 0.25 on the relative frequency ordinate until it intersects the

Figure 19.3   **Cumulative Distribution of Incomes of Families in Car Ownership Study**

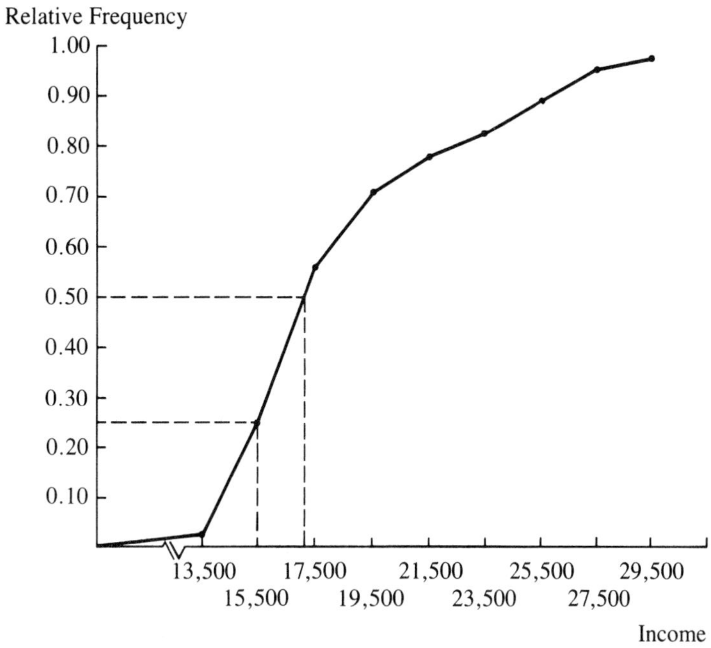

graph, dropping a vertical line from the point of intersection to the horizontal axis, and reading off the value of the first quartile at the point of intersection with the X axis. The first quartile is thus found to be \$15,300. The procedure for the third quartile (75th percentile) or any other percentile would be the same as that for the median or first quartile. The only change would be where the horizontal line began.

The one-way tabulation is also useful in calculating other summary measures, like the mode, mean, and standard deviation. The mode, or the most frequently occurring item, can be read directly from the one-way tabulation. Thus, Table 19.7 suggests that most families own one car. The mean, or "average" response, can be calculated from a one-way tabulation by weighting each value by its frequency of occurrence, summing these products, and dividing by the number of cases. The average number of cars per family given the data in Table 19.7 would thus be estimated as follows:

Value	Frequency	Value × Frequency
1	75	75
2	23	46
3	2	6
	100	127

The result is $127/100 = 1.27$ cars per family.

The standard deviation provides a measure of spread in the data. It is calculated from the one-way tabulation by taking the deviation of each value from the mean and squaring these deviations. The squared deviations are then multiplied by the frequency with which each occurs, these products are summed, and the sum is divided by one less than the number of cases to yield the sample variance. The square root of the sample variance then yields the sample standard deviation. The calculation of the standard deviation is thus very similar to that for ungrouped data, except for the fact that each value is weighted by the frequency with which it occurs. The standard deviation for the data in Table 19.7 is thus calculated as follows:

Value	Value − Mean	(Value − Mean)²	Frequency	Frequency Times Difference Squared
1	−.27	.0729	75	5.4675
2	.73	.5329	23	12.2567
3	1.73	2.9929	2	5.9858
				23.7100

This yields a variance of $23.7100/99 = .2395$ and a standard deviation of $\sqrt{.2395} = .4894$.

The one-way tabulation as a communication vehicle for the results has not been discussed. The reader needs only to look at Table 19.5 to see how much insight can be gathered about the variable income and then compare that with the insight generated in the one-way tabulation contained in Table 19.8. Considering that one-way tabulations also serve as a basic input to the histogram, frequency polygon, empirical cumulative distribution function, and in calculating summary statistics, it is an unwise analyst indeed who does not take the time to develop the one-way tabulations of the variables in the study and to plot the results so as to get a sense of how they are distributed.[12]

Cross Tabulation

While the one-way tabulation is useful for examining the variables of the study separately, cross tabulation is a most important mechanism for studying the relationships among and between variables. In cross tabulation the sample is divided into subgroups so as to learn how the dependent variable varies from subgroup to subgroup. It is clearly the most used data-analysis technique in marketing research. Some would call it the bread and butter of applied research. Most marketing research studies go no further than cross tabulation, while many of the studies that do use more sophisticated analytical methods still contain cross tabulation as a significant component. Thus, the analyst and the decision maker both need to understand how cross tabulations are developed and interpreted.

Consider the question of the relationship, if any, between the number of cars that a family owns and family income. To keep the example simple, suppose the analyst is simply interested in determining if a family above average in income is more likely to own two or more cars than a family below average in income. Suppose further that $17,500 is the median income in the population and that this figure is to be used to split the families in the sample into two groups, those with below-average and those with above-average incomes.

Table 19.9 presents the two-way classification of the sample families by income and number of cars. Looking at the marginal totals, we see that 75 families have one car or less, while 25 families have two cars or more. We also see that the sample is fairly representative of the population, at least as far as income is concerned; 54 families fall into the below-average income group using the $17,500 cutoff.

Table 19.9   ***Family Income and Number of Cars Family Owns***

| | Number of Cars | | |
Income	1 or Less	2 or More	Total
Less than $17,500	48	6	54
More than $17,500	27	19	46
Total	75	25	100

Table 19.10   ***Number of Cars by Family Income***

| | Number of Cars | | | |
Income	1 or Less	2 or More	Total	Number of Cases
Less than $17,500	89%	11%	100%	54
More than $17,500	59%	41%	100%	46

Table 19.11   ***Family Income by Number of Cars***

Income	1 or Less	2 or More
Less than $17,500	64%	24%
More than $17,500	36%	76%
Total	100%	100%
(Number of cases)	(75)	(25)

Does the number of cars depend on income? It certainly seems so on the basis of Table 19.9, since 19 of the families owning two or more cars are in the upper-income group. Is there anything that can be done to shed additional light on the relationship? The answer is yes. Compute percentages. Tables 19.10 and 19.11 are mathematically equivalent to Table 19.9, but are based on percentages calculated in different directions: horizontally in Table 19.10 and vertically in Table 19.11. The tables contain quite different messages. Table 19.10 suggests that multiple-car ownership is affected by family income; 41 percent of the families with above-average incomes had two or more automobiles, while only 11 percent of the below-average-income families did. This is an unambiguous finding. Table 19.11, on the other hand, conveys a different story. It suggests that 64 percent of those who owned one car had below-average incomes, while only 24 percent of those who owned two or more cars were below average in income. Does this mean that multiple-car ownership paves the

Table 19.12   **Number of Cars and Size of Family**

| Size of Family | Number of Cars | | |
	1 or Less	2 or More	Total
4 or less	70	8	78
5 or more	5	17	22
Total	75	25	100

Table 19.13   **Number of Cars by Size of Family**

| Size of Family | Number of Cars | | | Number of Cases |
	1 or Less	2 or More	Total	
4 or less	90%	10%	100%	(78)
5 or more	23%	77%	100%	(22)

Conditional probability
Probability that is assigned to Event A when it is known that Event B has occurred, or probability that would be assigned to Event A if it were known that Event B would occur.

way to higher incomes? Definitely not. Rather, it simply illustrates a fundamental rule of percentage calculations: *Always calculate percentages in the direction of the causal factor, or across the effect factor.* In this case, income is logically considered the cause, or independent variable, and multiple-car ownership the effect, or dependent variable. The percentages are correctly calculated, therefore, in the direction of income as in Table 19.10.[13]

One very useful way to determine the direction in which to calculate percentages is to think about the problem in terms of **conditional probabilities,** or the probability of one event occurring given that another event has occurred or will occur. Thus, the notion that a family is likely to have two or more cars *given* that it is a high-income family makes sense, while the notion that a family is likely to have a high income *given* that it has two or more cars does not.

The two-way cross tabulation, although it provides some insight into a dependency relationship, is not the final answer. Rather, it represents a start. Consider the relationship between multiple-car ownership and size of family. Table 19.12 indicates the number of small and large (five or more members) families that possess two or more cars. Now, analysts would logically consider family size a cause of multiple-car ownership, and not vice versa. Thus, the percentages would be properly computed *in the direction of size of family, or across number of cars.* Table 19.13 presents these percentages and suggests that the number of cars a family owns is affected by the size of the family—77 percent of the large families have two or more cars, while only 10 percent of the small families do.

This result raises the question, Does multiple-car ownership depend on family size or, as previously suggested, on family income? The proper way to answer this question is through the *simultaneous* treatment of income and family size. In effect, the two-way cross-classification table needs to be partitioned and a three-way table of

Table 19.14   ***Number of Cars by Income and Size of Family***

Income	4 Members or Less: Number of Cars			5 Members or More: Number of Cars			Total: Number of Cars		
	1 or Less	2 or More	Total	1 or Less	2 or More	Total	1 or Less	2 or More	Total
Less than $17,500	44	2	46	4	4	8	48	6	54
More than $17,500	26	6	32	1	13	14	27	19	46
Total	70	8	78	5	17	22	75	25	100

Table 19.15   ***Number of Cars by Income and Size of Family***

Income	4 Members or Less: Number of Cars			5 Members or More: Number of Cars			Total: Number of Cars		
	1 or Less	2 or More	Total	1 or Less	2 or More	Total	1 or less	2 or More	Total
Less than $17,500	96%	4%	100% (46)	50%	50%	100% (8)	89%	11%	100% (54)
More than $17,500	81%	19%	100% (32)	7%	93%	100% (14)	59%	41%	100% (46)

income, family size, and multiple-car ownership formed. One way of doing this is illustrated in Table 19.14. This table is, in one sense, two cross-classification tables of multiple-car ownership versus income—one for small families of four or fewer members, and one for large families of five or more members.

Once again we would want to compute percentages in the direction of income within each table. Table 19.15 contains these percentages, which indicate that multiple-car ownership depends both on income and on family size. For small families of four or less, 19 percent of those with above-average incomes have two or more cars, while only 4 percent of those with below-average incomes have more than one automobile. For large families, 93 percent of those with above-average incomes, and 50 percent of those with below-average incomes have more than one vehicle.

The preceding comparisons highlight the effect of income on multiple-car ownership, holding family size constant. We could also compare the effect of family size on multiple-car ownership, holding income constant. We would still find that each provides a partial explanation for multiple-car ownership. Now, you may have felt a bit uncomfortable with the presentation of the data in Tables 19.14 and 19.15. The information is there to be mined, but perhaps you may have wondered whether it could not be presented in a more revealing manner. It can, if you are willing to accept a couple of refinements in the manner of presentation. Look specifically at the first row of the first section of Table 19.15 as it is reproduced as Table 19.16. All of the information contained in this table can be condensed into one figure, 4 percent. This is the percentage of small, below-average-income families that have two or more

Table 19.16   **Car Ownership for Small, Below-Average-Income Families**

| | 4 Members or Less: Number of Cars | | |
Income	1 or Less	2 or More	Total
Less than $17,500	96%	4%	100% (46)

Table 19.17   **Percentage of Families Owning Two or More Cars by Income and Size of Family**

| | Size of Family | | |
Income	4 or Less	5 or More	Total
Less then $17,500	4%	50%	11%
More than $17,500	19%	93%	41%

cars. It follows that the complementary percentage, 96 percent, represents those that have one automobile or none.

Table 19.17 shows the rest of the data in Table 19.15 treated in the same way. The entry in each case is the percentage of families in that category that own two or more automobiles. Table 19.17 conveys the same information as Table 19.15, but it delivers the message with much greater clarity. The separate effect of income on multiple-car ownership, holding family size constant, can be determined by reading down the columns, while the effect of family size, holding income constant, can be determined by reading across the rows. Omitting the complementary percentages has helped reveal the structure of the data. Consequently, we will use this form of presentation whenever we attempt to determine the effect of several explanatory variables, considered simultaneously, in the pages that follow.

The original association between number of cars and family income reflected in Table 19.10 is called the **total** (or *zero-order*) **association** between the variables. Table 19.17, which depicts the association between the two variables within categories of family size, is called a *conditional table* that reveals the **conditional association** between the variables. Family size here is a *control variable*. Conditional tables that are developed on the basis of one control variable are called *first-order* conditional tables, while those developed using two control variables are called *second-order* conditional tables, and so on.

Which variable has the greater effect on multiple-car ownership: income or family size? A useful method for addressing this question is to calculate the difference in proportions as a function of the level of the variable.[14] This can be done for the zero-order tables as well as the conditional tables of higher order. Consider again Table 19.10, concentrating on the impact of income on the probability of the family's

Total association The association existing between the variables without regard to the levels of any other variables; also called the *zero-order association* between the variables.

Conditional association The association existing between two variables when the levels of one or more other variables are considered in the analysis; the other variables are called *control variables*.

having multiple cars. The proportion of low-income families that have two or more cars is 0.11, while the proportion of high-income families is 0.41. The probability of having multiple cars is clearly different depending on the family's income; specifically, high income increases the probability of having two or more cars by 0.30 (0.41 − 0.11) over low income. A similar analysis applied to Table 19.13 suggests the probability of multiple-car ownership is clearly different depending on family size. While 0.10 of the small families have multiple cars, 0.77 of the large families do. Thus, large family size increases the probability of having two or more cars by 0.67 (0.77 − 0.10) over small family size.

To determine whether income or family size has the greater impact, it is necessary to consider them simultaneously using a similar analysis. Table 19.17 contains the data that are necessary for this analysis. Let us first consider the impact of income. The proper way to determine the effect of income is to hold family size constant, which means, in essence, that we must investigate the relationship between income and multiple-car ownership for small families and then again for large families. Among small families, having high income increases the probability of having multiple cars by 0.15 (0.19 − 0.04). Among large families, having high income increases the probability of having multiple cars by 0.43 (0.93 − 0.50). The size of the associations between income and multiple-car ownership are different for different family sizes. This means there is a statistical interaction between the independent variables, and in order to generate a single estimate of the effect of income on car ownership, some kind of *average* of the separate effects needs to be computed. The appropriate average is a weighted average that takes account of the sizes of the groups on which the individual effects were calculated. There were 78 small families in the sample of 100 cases and 22 large families; the weight for small families is thus 0.78 and for large families 0.22. The weighted average is thus

$$0.15(0.78) + 0.43(0.22) = 0.21$$

which suggests that, on average, high versus low income increases the probability of owning multiple cars by 0.21.

To investigate the impact of family size, it is necessary to hold income constant, or alternatively, to investigate the impact of family size on multiple-car ownership for low-income families, then for high-income families, and then to generate a weighted average of the two results if they are not the same. Among low-income families, being large in size increases the probability of having multiple cars by 0.46 (0.50 − 0.04) compared with small size. Among high-income families, large size increases the probability by 0.74 (0.93 − 0.19) versus small size. Since there were 54 low-income families and 46 high-income families, the appropriate weights for weighting the two effects are 0.54 and 0.46, respectively. The calculation yields

$$0.46(0.54) + 0.74(0.46) = 0.59$$

as the estimate for the impact of family size on multiple-car ownership. Family size has a more pronounced effect on multiple-car ownership than does income. It increases the probability of having two or more cars by 0.59, whereas income increases it by 0.21.

The preceding example highlights an important application of cross tabulation—the use of an additional variable to refine an initial cross tabulation. In this case, family size was used to refine the relationship between multiple-car ownership and income. This is only one of the many applications of successive cross tabulation of

Table 19.18   **Conditions That Can Arise with the Introduction of an Additional Variable into a Cross Tabulation**

Initial Conclusion	With the Additional Variable	
	Change Conclusion	Retain Conclusion
Some relationship	I A. Refine explanation B. Reveal spurious explanation C. Provide limiting conditions	II
No relationship	III	IV

Table 19.19   **Van Ownership by Life-Style**

Life-Style	Own Van?		Total
	Yes	No	
Liberal	9(16%)	46(84%)	55(100%)
Conservative	11(24%)	34(76%)	45(100%)

variables, and, in fact, a number of conditions can occur when additional variables are introduced into a cross tabulation, as shown in the various panels of Table 19.18. The two-way tabulation may initially indicate the existence or nonexistence of a relationship between the variables. The introduction of a third variable may occasion no change in the initial conclusion, or it may indicate that a substantial change is in order.

Panel I: Initial Relationship Is Modified by Introduction of a Third Variable
Now that we have considered Panel I-A ("Refine explanation") in the preceding discussion, let us turn to an analysis of the alternative conditions. Consider Panel I-B ("Reveal spurious explanation"). One of the purposes of the automobile ownership study was to determine the kinds of families that purchase specific kinds of automobiles. Consider vans. It was expected that van ownership would be related to life-style and, in particular, that those with a liberal orientation would be more likely to own vans than would those who are conservative by nature. Table 19.19 was constructed, employing the raw data on car ownership in Table 19.5, to test this hypothesis. Contrary to expectation, conservatives are more apt than liberals to own vans; 24 percent of the conservatives and only 16 percent of the liberals in the sample owned vans.

Is there some logical explanation for this unexpected finding? Consider the addition of a third variable, the region of the country in which the family resides, to the analysis. A clear picture of the relationship among the three variables considered

Table 19.20   ***Van Ownership by Life-Style and Region of Country***

| | Region of Country | | |
Life-Style	North	South	Total
Liberal	5%	41%	16%
Conservative	5%	43%	24%

simultaneously can be developed employing our previously agreed-upon convention; that is, simply report the percentage in each category. The complement, 100 minus the percentage, then indicates the proportion not owning vans.

As Table 19.20 indicates, van ownership is not related to life-style. Rather, it depends on the region of the country in which the family resides. When region is held constant, there is no difference in van ownership between liberals and conservatives. Families living in the South are much more likely to own a van than are families who live in the northern states. It just so happens that people in the South are more conservative with regard to their life-style than people in the North. The original relationship is therefore said to be spurious.

While it seems counterproductive to calculate the difference in proportions to determine the impact of each variable for each of the potential conditions in Table 19.18, it does seem useful to do it for this case to demonstrate what is meant by a *main effect* without a statistical interaction. The example is also useful in reinforcing how the difference-in-proportions calculation can be used to isolate the causal relationships that exist in cross-tabulation data. Consider first the zero-order association between van ownership and life-style contained in Table 19.19. Being a conservative increases the probability of van ownership by 0.08 (0.24 − 0.16) compared to being liberal. Yet Table 19.20 shows that this is a spurious effect that is due to region of the country, since it disappears when region is held constant. Among those living in the North, the partial association between van ownership and life-style is 0.00 (0.05 − 0.05). Among those living in the South, there is a slightly higher probability of van ownership among conservatives, namely, 0.02 (0.43 − 0.41). This effect is so small that it can be attributed to rounding error, particularly since the proportions were carried to only two decimal places and the number of cases is so small. Regardless of the region of the country in which the family resides, their liberal or conservative orientation has no effect on whether or not they own a van.

Note, conversely, that the effect of region is pronounced and consistent. Among liberal families, living in the South increases the probability of van ownership 0.36 (0.41 − 0.05) compared to living in the North. Among conservative families, living in the South increases the probability by 0.38 (0.43 − 0.05). Within rounding error, the effect is the same for families with both philosophical orientations, which means there is no interaction among the two predictor variables. Rather, there is only a main effect of region on van ownership, and the best estimate of its size is given by either of these estimates or their average.

Consider now the question of ownership of foreign economy cars (Panel I-C, "Provide limiting conditions"). Does it depend on the size of the family? Table 19.21 suggests it does. Smaller families are *less* likely to own a foreign economy car than are

Table 19.21   **Foreign Economy Car Ownership by Family Size**

| | Own Foreign Economy Car? | | |
Size of Family	Yes	No	Total
4 or less	6 (8%)	72(92%)	78(100%)
5 or more	6(27%)	16(73%)	22(100%)

Table 19.22   **Foreign Economy Car Ownership by Family Size and Number of Cars**

| | Number of Cars | | |
Size of Family	1 or Less	2 or More	Total
4 or less	6%	25%	8%
5 or more	0%	35%	27%

larger families! Only 8 percent of the small families, but 27 percent of the large families, have such automobiles. This relationship is interesting because it runs counter to what we might intuitively expect to find. Can it be accounted for?

Let us expand this cross classification by adding a variable for the number of cars the family owns. Table 19.22 presents the percentage data, which indicate that it is only when large families have two or more cars that they own a foreign economy car. No large families with one car owned such an automobile. The introduction of the third variable has revealed a condition that limits foreign economy car ownership—multiple-car ownership where large families are concerned.

A study investigating the effectiveness of aspirin in treating blood clotting after surgery provides an interesting, important application of how the addition of a third variable to an analysis can reveal a limiting condition. The two-way tabulation of those treated with aspirin or a placebo versus the presence or absence of blood clots revealed aspirin was effective in reducing the incidence of clots. When the sample was broken down by sex of the patient, though, it was found that aspirin was very useful in preventing blood clotting in men but not at all useful in treating women.[15]

Panel II: Initial Conclusion of a Relationship Is Retained   Consider now the analysis of station wagon ownership based on the data in Table 19.5. At first, it would seem to be related to family size. A case could be made that larger families have a greater need for station wagons than smaller families.

The cross tabulation of these two variables in Table 19.23 suggests that larger families are indeed more likely to own stations wagons; 68 percent of the large families and only 4 percent of the small families own them.

Consider, however, whether income might also affect station wagon ownership. As Table 19.24 indicates, income has an effect over and above family size. As one

Table 19.23   *Station Wagon Ownership by Family Size*

| | Own Station Wagon? | | |
Size of Family	Yes	No	Total
4 or less	3 (4%)	75(96%)	78(100%)
5 or more	15(68%)	7(32%)	22(100%)

Table 19.24   *Station Wagon Ownership by Family Size and Income*

| | Income | | |
Size of Family	Less than $17,500	More than $17,500	Total
4 or less	4%	3%	4%
5 or more	63%	71%	68%

goes from a small to a large family, there is a substantial increase in the likelihood of owning a station wagon. With high-income families, however, the increase is larger. Alternatively, if one focuses solely on large families, there is an increase in station wagon ownership from below-average to above-average income groups. The initial conclusion, though, is retained: large families do display a greater tendency to purchase station wagons. Further, the effect of family size on station wagon ownership is much larger than the effect of income.

Panel III: Relationship Is Established with Introduction of a Third Variable
Suppose one of the purposes of the study is to determine the characteristics of families who financed the purchase of their automobile. Consider the cross tabulation of installment debt versus education of the household head. Table 19.25 results when the families included in Table 19.5 are classified into one of two educational categories—those with a high school education or less and those with some college training. As is evident, there is no relationship between education and installment debt; the percentage of families with outstanding car debt is 30 percent in each case.

Table 19.26 illustrates the situation when income is also considered in the analysis. For below-average incomes, the presence of installment debt increases with education. For above-average incomes, installment debt decreases with education. The effect of education was obscured in the original analysis because the effects canceled each other. When income is also considered, the relationship of installment debt to education is quite pronounced.

Panel IV: Conclusion of No Relationship Is Retained with Addition of a Third Variable   Consider once again the question of station wagon ownership. We have seen previously that it is related to family size. Let us forget this result for a minute and begin the analysis with the question, Is station wagon ownership affected by

Table 19.25   **Financed Car Purchase by Education of Household Head**

Education of Household Head	Financed Car Purchase?		Total
	Yes	No	
High school or less	24(30%)	56(70%)	80(100%)
Some college	6(30%)	14(70%)	20(100%)

Table 19.26   **Financed Car Purchase by Education of Household Head and Income**

Education of Household Head	Income		Total
	Less than $17,500	More than $17,500	
High school or less	12%	58%	30%
Some college	40%	27%	30%

Table 19.27   **Station Wagon Ownership by Region**

Region	Own Station Wagon?		Total
	Yes	No	
North	11(18%)	49(82%)	60(100%)
South	7(18%)	33(82%)	40(100%)

region of the country in which the family lives? Table 19.27 provides an initial answer. Station wagon ownership does not depend on region; 18 percent of the sample families living both in the North and in the South own wagons.

Let us now consider the relationship when family size is again taken into account. Table 19.28 presents the data. Once again the percentages are constant across regions. There is minor variation, but this is due to round-off accuracy. Small families display a low propensity to purchase station wagons, regardless of whether they live in the North or the South. Large families have a high propensity, and this, too, is independent of where they live. The original lack of relationship between station wagon ownership and region of residence is confirmed with the addition of the third variable, family size.

Summary Comments on Cross Tabulation   The previous examples should confirm the tremendous usefulness of cross tabulation as a tool in analysis. We have seen applications in which a third variable (1) helped to uncover a relationship not

Table 19.28   **Station Wagon Ownership by Region and Family Size**

| | Size of Family | | |
Region	4 or Less	More than 4	Total
North	4%	69%	18%
South	3%	67%	18%

Table 19.29   **The Researcher's Dilemma**

| | True Situation | |
Researcher's Conclusion	No Relationship	Some Relationship
No relationship	Correct decision	Spurious noncorrelation
Some relationship	Spurious correlation	Correct decision if concluded relationship is of proper form

immediately discernible and (2) triggered the modification of conclusions drawn on the basis of a two-variable classification. You may have paused to ask yourself, Why stop with three variables? Would the conclusion change with the addition of a fourth variable? A fifth? Indeed it might. The problem is that one never knows for sure when to stop introducing variables. The conclusion is always susceptible to change with the introduction of the "right" variable or variables. The analyst is always in the position of "inferring" that a relationship exists. Later research may demonstrate that the inference was incorrect. This is why the accumulation of studies, rather than a single study, supporting a particular relationship is so vital to the advancement of knowledge.

Table 19.29 is an overview of the dilemma the researcher faces. The true situation is always unknown. If it were known, there would be no need to research it. Instead, the researcher is always in the position of making statements about an unknown true situation. The analyst may conclude that there is no relationship, or that there is some relationship, between two or more variables when in fact there is none or there is some. Only one of the four possibilities in Table 19.29 *necessarily* corresponds to a correct conclusion—when the analyst concludes there is no relationship and in fact there is no relationship. Two of the other possibilities are necessarily incorrect, while one contains the possibility for error. That is, suppose the true situation is one of some relationship between or among the variables. The analyst has reached a correct conclusion only if he or she concludes that there is some relationship and, further, discovers its correct form.

Spurious noncorrelation means that the analyst concludes there is no relationship when, in fact, there is one. *Spurious correlation* occurs when there is no relationship among the variables but the analyst concludes that a relationship exists.

The opportunities for error are great. Consequently, one may be tempted to continue adding variables to the analysis ad infinitum. Fortunately, both theory and data will prevent the anxious—or overly ambitious—analyst from pursuing this course. Theory will constrain him or her because certain tabulations simply will not make any sense. The data will also act as a barrier to endless cross tabulations for several reasons. First, note that the analyst will want to add variables successively to the analysis in the form of higher-dimensional cross-classification tables. This can be accomplished only if the analyst has correctly anticipated the tabulations that would be desirable. This is most important. It is too late to say, "If only we had collected information on variable *X!*" once the analysis has begun. The relationships to be investigated, and thus the cross tabulations that should be appropriate, must be specified before the data are collected. Ideally, the analyst would construct dummy tables before beginning to collect the data. The dummy tables would be complete in all respects except for the number of observations falling in each cell. As a practical matter, it is usually impossible to anticipate all the cross tabulations one will want to develop. Nevertheless, careful specification of these tables at problem-definition time can return substantial benefits.

The analyst also is going to be limited by the size of the sample. In our example, since we started with 100 observations, the two-way tables were not particularly troublesome. Yet as soon as we introduced the third variable, cell sizes became extremely small. This occurred even though we treated all variables as dichotomies. Families were either below average or above average in income; they were either small or large; they lived either in the North or in the South, and so on. This was done purposely so as to simplify the presentation. Yet even here the three-way tabulation offers eight cells ($2 \times 2 \times 2$) into which the observations may be placed. Assuming an even allocation of the cases to the cells, this only allows 12.5 cases per cell. This is clearly a small number upon which to base any kind of conclusion.

The problem, of course, would have been compounded if a greater number of levels had been used for any of the variables. Consider what would have happened if the families had been divided into four income groups rather than two, given that the number of cells is the product of the number of levels for the variables being considered. For example, four income levels, three educational levels, and four family size levels would generate a cross-tabulation table with forty-eight separate cells ($4 \times 3 \times 4$). One would need a much larger sample than 100 to have any confidence in the suggested relationships.

Ethical
Dilemma 19.1
A manufacturer of aspirin had its marketing research department conduct a national survey among doctors to investigate what common household remedies doctors would be most likely to recommend when treating a patient with a cold. The question asked doctors to pick the one product they would most likely prescribe for their patients from among the choices Advil, Tylenol, aspirin, or none of the above. The distribution of responses was as follows:

Advil	100
Tylenol	100
Aspirin	200
None of the above	600
Total	1,000

The firm used the results of the survey as a basis for an extensive ad campaign that claimed, "In a national survey, doctors recommended aspirin two to one over

Advil and Tylenol as the medicine they would most likely recommend to their patients suffering from colds."

■ Was the firm's claim legitimate?
■ Was it ethical for the firm to omit reporting the number of doctors that expressed no preference?
■ What would be the fairest way to state the ad claim? Do you think stating the claim in this way would be as effective as stating it in the way the firm did?

Presenting Tabular Data

Banner A series of cross tabulations between a criterion, or dependent, variable and several (sometimes many) explanatory variables in a single table.

Tabular results for commercial marketing research studies are seldom presented using the tabulation and cross-tabulation procedure discussed so far in this chapter. Rather, the use of banners has become increasingly popular. A **banner** is a series of cross tabulations between a criterion or dependent variable and several, sometimes many, explanatory variables in a single table. The dependent variable, or phenomenon to be explained, typically serves as the row variable, which is also known as the *stub*. The predictor or explanatory variables serve as the column variables, with each category of these variables serving as a banner point. Table 19.30, for example, shows what the banner format might look like for the car ownership study. Although only two explanatory variables are shown, many more could be. The top line in each row of the table indicates the absolute number possessing the characteristic, whereas the second line indicates the percentage. All percentages have been rounded to zero decimal places in keeping with recommended practice.

The advantages of banner tables are several. In the first place, they allow a great amount of information to be conveyed in a very limited space. Second, their display format makes it easy for nonresearch managers to understand. Managers simply need to look at how the responses to the actual questions that were asked are distributed. A difficulty with these tables is that they tend to hide relationships in which it is necessary to consider several variables simultaneously (e.g., the joint effect of income

Table 19.30   Banner Format for Car Ownership Data

| | | Question: How many cars does your family own? | | | |
| | | Income | | Family Size | |
	Total Sample	Less than $17,500	More than $17,500	4 or Less	5 or More
Total	100 (100)	54 (100)	46 (100)	78 (100)	22 (100)
1	75 (75)	48 (89)	27 (59)	70 (90)	5 (23)
2	23 (23)	6 (11)	17 (37)	8 (10)	15 (68)
3	2 (2)	0 (0)	2 (4)	0 (0)	2 (9)

and family size on multiple car ownership). They consequently make it more difficult to probe alternative explanations for what is producing the results. Banners also make it more difficult to detect data errors caused by improper coding or editing. Although popular, they should not be considered as a substitute for careful cross-tabulation analysis but more as an efficient form of data presentation.

Ethical

Dilemma 19.2   Sarah Christopher is very happy on the whole with the project that she has just completed for the Crumbly Cookie Company. Most of her hypotheses were supported by the survey data. There were two hypotheses that did not work out, but she thought that she would just leave them out of the report.

- Is it ethical to omit information that does not tally with your beliefs?
- Can valuable information be lost through the omission?

Back to the Case

In Paula Karberg's office there was a huge folding table heaped with completed copies of the Door's cafeteria questionnaire. Karberg sat at one end of the table, methodically going through the forms as she tackled the formidable job of completing the central-office edit.

Karberg's first step was to separate the questionnaires into piles: One pile was of questionnaires that had been completely and correctly filled out. Another pile contained forms with omissions that Karberg felt were minor. Another pile was for questionnaires that were grossly incomplete or had major omissions. There was yet another pile for questionnaires from people who Karberg suspected were indifferent responders.

Once she'd gotten the questionnaires roughly sorted, then she'd proceed to the next step of editing them. Tackling each pile with greater attention, she'd try to decide which questionnaires could be used as they were, which ones would need to be cleaned up, and which would just have to be thrown out. Karberg hated to not include information that the field interviewer had taken time and effort to obtain, especially since not including it just added to the study's nonresponse rate. But as an editor, her job was to ensure that the information included in the study was complete and correct.

Summary

Learning Objective 1: Explain the purpose of the field edit.

The field edit is a preliminary edit designed to detect the most glaring omissions and inaccuracies in the data. It is also useful in helping to control the actions of the field force personnel and to clear up any misunderstandings they may have about directions, procedures, specific questions, and so on.

Learning Objective 2: Define what coding in the research process is.

Coding is the technical procedure by which data are categorized. Through coding, the raw data are transformed into symbols—usually numerals—that may be tabulated and counted. The transformation is not automatic, however; it involves judgment on the part of the coder.

Learning Objective 3: List the three steps in the coding process.

The coding process involves the three steps of (1) specifying the categories or classes into which the responses are to be placed, (2) assigning code numbers to the classes, and (3) preparing the codebook.

Learning Objective 4: Outline the conventions that are customarily followed when data are to be analyzed by a computer.

When data are to be analyzed by computer, a number of conventions should be followed in assigning the code numbers, including the following:

1. Locate only one character in each column.
2. Use only numeric codes.
3. Assign as many columns as are necessary to capture the variable.
4. Use the same standard codes throughout for "no information."
5. Code in a respondent identification number on each record.

Learning Objective 5: Describe the kinds of information contained in a codebook.

The codebook contains the general instructions indicating how each item of data was coded. It lists the codes for each variable and the categories included in each code. It further indicates where on the computer record the variable is located and how the variable should be read.

Learning Objective 6: Define what tabulation is and distinguish between the two types of tabulation.

Tabulation consists simply of counting the number of cases that fall into the various categories. The tabulation may take the form of a simple tabulation or a cross tabulation. Simple tabulation involves counting a single variable. In cross tabulation, two or more of the variables are treated simultaneously.

Learning Objective 7: Explain the various ways in which one-way tabulation can be used.

In addition to communicating the results of a study, one-way tabulation can be used (1) to determine the degree of item nonresponse, (2) to locate blunders, (3) to locate outliers, (4) to determine the empirical distribution of the variable in question, and (5) to calculate summary statistics.

Learning Objective 8: Assess the particular importance of cross tabulation.

Cross tabulation is one of the more useful devices for studying the relationships among and between variables since the results are easily communicated; further, cross tabulation can provide insight into the nature of a relationship since the addition of one or more variables to a two-way cross-classification analysis is equivalent to holding each of the variables constant.

Learning Objective 9: Describe a method by which a researcher can determine what impact one variable has on another in a cross-tabulation table.

A useful method for determining the impact one variable has on another variable in a cross-tabulation table is to compute the difference in proportions with which the dependent variable occurs as a function of the levels of the independent variable. This can be done for the zero-order tables as well as the conditional tables of higher order. The higher-order tables are used to remove the effects of other variables that might be affecting the dependent variable.

Learning Objective 10: Describe what banners are and how they are useful.

A banner is a series of cross tabulations between a criterion or dependent variable and several, sometimes many, explanatory variables in a single table. The dependent variable, or phenomenon to be explained, typically serves as the row variable, which is also known as the stub. The predictor or explanatory variables serve as the column variables, with each category of these variables serving as a banner point. Banners allow a great amount of information to be conveyed in a very limited space and are easy for managers to understand.

Discussion Questions, Problems, and Projects

1. The KIST television station was conducting research in order to help develop programs that would be well received by the viewing audience and would be considered dependable sources of information. A two-part questionnaire was administered by personal interviews to a panel of 3,000 respondents residing in the city of Houston. The field and office edits were simultaneously done, so that the deadline of May 1 could be met. A senior supervisor, Marlene Howe, was placed in charge of the editing tasks and was assisted by two junior supervisors and two field workers. The two field workers were instructed to discard instruments that were illegible or incomplete. Each junior supervisor was instructed to scrutinize 1,500 of the instruments for incomplete answers, wrong answers, and responses that indicated a lack of interest. They were instructed to discard instruments that had more than five incomplete or wrong answers (the questionnaire contained thirty questions). In addition, they were asked to use their judgment in assessing whether the respondent showed a lack of interest and, if so, to discard the questionnaire.
    (a)   Critically evaluate the above editing tasks. Please be specific.
    (b)   Make specific recommendations to George Kist, the owner of the KIST television station, as to how the editing should be done.
2. (a)   Establish response categories and codes for the question, "What do you like about this new brand of cereal?"
    (b)   Code the following responses using your categories and codes.
        (1) "$1.50 is a reasonable price to pay for the cereal."
        (2) "The raisins and nuts add a nice flavor."
        (3) "The sizes of the packages are convenient."
        (4) "I like the sugarcoating on the cereal."
        (5) "The container does not tear and fall apart easily."
        (6) "My kids like the cartoons on the back of the packet."
        (7) "It is reasonably priced compared with other brands."
        (8) "The packet is attractive and easy to spot in the store."
        (9) "I like the price; it is not so low that I doubt the quality, and at the same time it is not so high as to be unaffordable."
        (10) "The crispness and lightness of the cereal improve the taste."
3. (a)   Establish response categories and codes for the following question, which was asked of a sample of business executives: "In your opinion, which types of companies have not been affected by the present economic climate?"
    (b)   Code the following responses using your categories and codes.
        (1) Washington Post   (9) Marine Midlands Banks
        (2) Colgate Palmolive   (10) Zenith Radio
        (3) Gillette   (11) Holiday Inn
        (4) Hilton Hotels   (12) The Dryden Press
        (5) Chase Manhattan   (13) Singer
        (6) Prentice-Hall   (14) Saga
        (7) Hoover   (15) Bank America
        (8) Fabergé
4. A large manufacturer of electronic components for automobiles recently conducted a study to determine the average value of electronic components per automobile. Personal interviews were conducted with a random sample of 400 respondents. The following information was secured with respect to each subject's "main" vehicle when he or she had more than one.

Average Dollar Value of Electronic Equipment Per Automobile

Dollar Value of Electronic Equipment	Number of Automobiles
Less than or equal to $50	35
$51 to $100	40
$101 to $150	55
$151 to $200	65
$201 to $250	65
$251 to $300	75
$301 to $350	40
$351 to $400	20
More than $400	5
Total number of automobiles	400

(a) Convert the above information into percentages.
(b) Compute the cumulative absolute frequencies.
(c) Compute the cumulative relative frequencies.
(d) Prepare a histogram and frequency polygon with the average value of electronic equipment on the X axis and the absolute frequency on the Y axis.
(e) Graph the empirical cumulative distribution function with the average value on the X axis and the relative frequency on the Y axis.
(f) Locate the median, first sample quartile, and third sample quartile on the cumulative distribution function graphed in Part (e) of this project.
(g) Calculate the mean and standard deviation and variance for the frequency distribution. (Hint: Use the midpoint of each class interval and multiply that by the appropriate frequency. For the interval starting at $401, assume the midpoint is 425.5.)

5. Select a convenience sample of 50 students on your campus and ask them the following two questions: Are you a part-time or full-time student? How many hours did you spend studying last week?
(a) Compute the average number of hours spent studying. Show your calculations.
(b) Complete the following cross-classification table.

| | Hours Spent Studying | | |
Status	Less than Average	More than Average	Total
Full-time			
Part-time			
Total			

(c) Do your findings confirm the hypothesis that the hours spent studying depend on the status of the student? Compute the necessary percentages.

6. A social organization was interested in determining if there were various demographic characteristics that might be related to people's propensity to contribute to charities. The organization was particularly interested in determining if individuals above 40 years of age were more likely to contribute larger amounts than individuals below 40.

The average contribution in the population was $1,500, and this figure was used to divide the individuals in the sample into two groups: those that contributed large amounts or more than average versus those that contributed less than average. The following table presents a two-way classification of the sample of individuals by contributions and age.

Table 1   *Personal Contributions and Age*

Personal Contribution	Age		Total
	39 or Less	40 or More	
Less than or equal to $1,500	79	50	129
More than $1,500	11	60	71
Total	90	110	200

In addition, the social organization wanted to determine if contributions depended on income and/or age. The following table presents the simultaneous treatment of age and income. The median income in the population was $18,200, and this figure was used to split the sample into two groups.

Table 2   *Personal Contributions by Age and Income*

Personal Contributions	Income					
	Less than or Equal to $18,200		More than $18,200		Total	
	Age		Age		Age	
	39 or Less	40 or More	39 or Less	40 or More	39 or Less	40 or More
Less than or equal to $1,500	63	22	16	28	79	50
More than $1,500	7	18	4	42	11	60
Total	70	40	20	70	90	110

(a) Does the amount of personal contributions depend on age? Generate the necessary tables to justify your answer.
(b) Does the amount of personal contributions depend on age alone? Generate the necessary tables to justify your answer.
(c) Present the percentage of contributions of more than $1,500 by age and income in tabular form. Interpret the table.

7. A large toy manufacturer wants to determine the characteristics of families who have purchased a new electronic game that is designed and marketed for all age-groups. Management needs your assistance in interpreting the following two cross-classification tables.

Table 1   ***Purchased Electronic Games versus Number of Children***

| | Purchased Electronic Games | | |
Number of Children	Yes	No	Total
Less than or equal to 1	63	87	150
More than 1	21	29	50

Table 2   ***Purchased Electronic Games versus Number of Children and Age of Head of Household***

| | Age of Head of Household | | |
Number of Children	Less than or Equal to 45	More than 45	Total
Less than or equal to 1	14%	46%	42%
More than 1	38%	19%	42%

(a) What does Table 1 indicate? Explain and show calculations where necessary.
(b) What does Table 2 indicate? Have your conclusions changed or remained the same? Explain.

8. A local telephone company wants to determine the demographic characteristics of users of answering services. Management needs your help in interpreting the following two tables.

(a) What does Table 1 indicate? Explain and provide calculations where necessary.
(b) What does Table 2 indicate? Have your conclusions changed or remained the same? Explain.

Table 1   ***Use of Answering Services versus Education***

| | Use of Answering Service | | |
Education of Household Head	Yes	No	Total
High school or less	48	72	120
Some college or more	20	60	80

Table 2   ***Use of Answering Services versus Education and Income***

| | Income | | |
Education of Household Head	Less than $18,200	More than $18,200	Total
High school or less	15%	45%	40%
Some college or more	15%	42%	25%

9. A study on television ownership patterns, undertaken by your research firm, has produced the following zero-order tables, among others. You have been asked to make a presentation of your findings to the study sponsor's vice-president of marketing. Your supervisor has told you that "the guy hates to look at a bunch of little tables. Combine all the zero-order stuff on one transparency." Complete a table that will fulfill your supervisor's instructions.

10. Visit your school's library and find examples of banner, zero-order, first-order, and second-order tables. Look for these in publications such as *Business Week*, *Fortune*, *Newsweek*, and *The Wall Street Journal*. Make a copy of each of the tables you've found and analyze them, answering the following questions:
   (a) For the banner: What is the stub? What are the predictor variables? How many banner points are used for each predictor?

Table 1   ***Household Income and Number of Televisions Owned***

| | Number of Televisions | | | | |
Income	1 or Less	2	3	4 or More	Total
Less than $20,000	89	43	11	1	144
$20,000 or more	41	49	10	6	106
Total	130	92	21	7	250

Table 2   ***Household Size and Number of Televisions Owned***

| | Number of Televisions | | | | |
Household Size	1 or Less	2	3	4 or More	Total
2 or less people	116	34	10	0	160
3 or more people	14	58	11	7	90
Total	130	92	21	7	250

Table 3   ***Dwelling Size and Number of Televisions Owned***

Dwelling Size (sq. ft.)	Number of Televisions				Total
	1 or Less	2	3	4 or More	
1,500 or less	79	40	3	1	123
1,501 or more	51	52	18	6	127
Total	130	92	21	7	250

(b) For the zero-order table: List the variables named in the table.

(c) For the first-order table: List the variables named in the table. What is the control variable?

(d) For the second-order table: List the variables named in the table. What are the control variables?

(e) For each of the tables: Is the table presented in the format recommended in this textbook? How was the information presented in the table gathered? What table-based claims are made in the accompanying article? Does the table fully support these claims? Are there other variables that should have been considered? Are there alternative interpretations of the table that aren't mentioned in the article? If so, why aren't they mentioned in the article?

NFO Applications NFO Research, Inc. (NFO), recently conducted a study of the ground caffeinated coffee market because several of its clients operate in this market. The study was undertaken with several objectives in mind, including the identification of benefits that consumers seek and the comparison of consumer opinions regarding several of the brands offered in the market.

The questionnaire in Figure 12.3 (page 333) was designed to accomplish these objectives. This questionnaire was mailed to 400 individuals previously identified as consumers of ground caffeinated coffee (personally drinking at least one cup per day). Of those mailed out, 328 were returned; 299 of these were judged to be usable responses.

The data collected from these consumers are stored in a free-field format (space delimited) ASCII file named "coffee.dat" that is available from your instructor. The coding format for the data is shown below. Missing data are coded −99 for all items and should be disregarded for all analyses. While the data included are basically the data collected, some items or responses were generated to complete the data set.

Because this is a relatively large data file (103,168 bytes), it will probably be useful to conduct the analyses necessary to complete the following application problems using a personal computer with a hard disk drive or on a mainframe computer.

11. (a) Produce a histogram for the age variable. Does it appear that anything has been obviously miscoded? If so, explain.

(b) Produce a histogram for the variable "brand used most often." Determine an estimate of market share for the various brands based on this data set.

12. (a) Cross-tabulate "brand used most often" with "age," when the age variable has been recoded into the following categories:

35 years or less

36–45 years

46–59 years

60 years or more

Coding Format for NFO Coffee Study

Question Number	Variable (Variable Number)	Coding Specification
—	Questionnaire ID (VAR1)	—
1	Usual Method of Preparation (VAR2)	1 = automatic drip 2 = electric percolator 3 = stove-top percolator 4 = stove-top dripolator
2a	Ever Use: Folgers (VAR3) Hills Bros. (VAR4) Maxwell House Regular (VAR5) Maxwell House Master Blend (VAR6) Yuban (VAR7) Other (VAR8)	0 = no 1 = yes
2b	Brand Used Most Often (VAR9)	1 = Folgers 2 = Hills Bros. 3 = Maxwell House Regular 4 = Maxwell House Master Blend 5 = Yuban 6 = Other
2c	On Hand: Folgers (VAR10) Hills Bros. (VAR11) Maxwell House Regular (VAR12) Maxwell House Master Blend (VAR13) Yuban (VAR14) Other (VAR15)	0 = no 1 = yes
2d	Brand Will Buy Next (VAR16)	1 = Folgers 2 = Hills Bros. 3 = Maxwell House Regular 4 = Maxwell House Master Blend 5 = Yuban 6 = Other
2e	Overall Rating: Folgers (VAR17) Hills Bros. (VAR18) Maxwell House Regular (VAR19) Maxwell House Master Blend (VAR20) Yuban (VAR21) Other (VAR22)	Rating 1–10, where 1 = dislike it extremely 10 = like it extremely
3	Add Nothing (VAR23) Add Dairy Creamer (VAR24) Add Nondairy Creamer (VAR25) Add Sugar (VAR26) Add Artificial Sweetener (VAR27) Add Something Else (VAR28)	0 = no 1 = yes
4	Are You Primary Coffee Purchaser (VAR29)?	0 = no 1 = yes
5	Rich Taste (VAR30) Always Fresh (VAR31) Gets Day Off to Good Start (VAR32) Full-Bodied Taste (VAR33) Rich Aroma in the Cup (VAR34) Good Value for the Money (VAR35) Best Coffee in the Morning (VAR36) Rich Aroma in the Can/Bag (VAR37)	Importance Ratings, 0–10, where 0 = not at all important 10 = extremely important

Question Number	Variable (Variable Number)	Coding Specification
	Smooth Taste (VAR38)	
	Highest Quality Coffee (VAR39)	
	Premium Brand (VAR40)	
	Not Bitter (VAR41)	
	Coffee That Brightens Day Most (VAR42)	
	Cost More Than Other Brands (VAR43)	
	Strong Taste (VAR44)	
	Has No Aftertaste (VAR45)	
	Economy Brand (VAR46)	
	Rich Aroma While Brewing (VAR47)	
	Best Ground Coffee Available (VAR48)	
	Enjoy Drinking with Meal (VAR49)	
	Cost Less Than Other Brands (VAR50)	

Special Coding Instructions, Question 6:
All variables are rating scales coded 0–10, where
   0 = does not describe at all
   10 = describes completely

Variable	Folgers Var. No.	Hills Bros. Var. No.	Maxwell House Regular Var. No.	Maxwell House Master Blend Var. No.	Yuban Var. No.
Rich Taste	VAR51	VAR72	VAR93	VAR114	VAR135
Always Fresh	VAR52	VAR73	VAR94	VAR115	VAR136
Good Start	VAR53	VAR74	VAR95	VAR116	VAR137
Full-Bodied Taste	VAR54	VAR75	VAR96	VAR117	VAR138
Rich Aroma/Cup	VAR55	VAR76	VAR97	VAR118	VAR139
Good Value	VAR56	VAR77	VAR98	VAR119	VAR140
Best Coffee in a.m.	VAR57	VAR78	VAR99	VAR120	VAR141
Rich Aroma/Can	VAR58	VAR79	VAR100	VAR121	VAR142
Smooth Taste	VAR59	VAR80	VAR101	VAR122	VAR143
Highest Quality	VAR60	VAR81	VAR102	VAR123	VAR144
Premium Brand	VAR61	VAR82	VAR103	VAR124	VAR145
Not Bitter	VAR62	VAR83	VAR104	VAR125	VAR146
Brightens Day Most	VAR63	VAR84	VAR105	VAR126	VAR147
Costs More	VAR64	VAR85	VAR106	VAR127	VAR148
Strong Taste	VAR65	VAR86	VAR107	VAR128	VAR149
No Aftertaste	VAR66	VAR87	VAR108	VAR129	VAR150
Economy Brand	VAR67	VAR88	VAR109	VAR130	VAR151
Rich Aroma/Brewing	VAR68	VAR89	VAR110	VAR131	VAR152
Best Available	VAR69	VAR90	VAR111	VAR132	VAR153
Enjoy with Meal	VAR70	VAR91	VAR112	VAR133	VAR154
Costs Less	VAR71	VAR92	VAR113	VAR134	VAR155

Question Number	Variable (Variable Number)	Coding Specification
7a	Gender (VAR156)	1 = male 2 = female
7b	Age (VAR157)	Actual Age Coded

Generate percentages as well as frequency counts for each cell. What general conclusions might be drawn based on this information?

(b) How is the perceived relationship between brand used most often and age affected by the addition of a third variable, "sex of the respondent," to the analysis? Explain.

 13. Suppose that it is your job to compare Folgers with Maxwell House Regular. Produce a snake diagram profiling these brands on the 21 attributes included in question 6 of the questionnaire. What do your results indicate?

Endnotes

1. The classification of items to be checked in the field edit is taken from Claire Selltiz, Lawrence S. Wrightsman, and Stuart W. Cook, *Research Methods in Social Relations*, 3rd ed. (New York: Holt, Rinehart and Winston, 1976), pp. 475–476.

2. Selltiz, Wrightsman, and Cook, *Research Methods*, p. 473.

3. Some writers would make the specification of categories part of the editing rather than the coding function. Its placement in one or the other function is not nearly as important as the recognition that it is an extremely critical step with significant ramifications for the whole research effort.

4. In one study that explicitly compared the responses to open and closed questions, marked differences were found in the response distributions to the two types of questions. The authors concluded that the responses to closed questions are the more valid, because the responses to open questions are often so vague that they are misclassified by coders. See H. Schuman and S. Presser, "The Open and Closed Question," *American Sociological Review*, 44 (1979), pp. 692–712. To improve the consistency with which similar answers are coded, some researchers have attempted to develop systems by which computers can code open-ended responses. For an illustration, see Colin McDonald, "Coding Open-Ended Answers with the Help of a Computer," *Journal of the Market Research Society*, 24 (January 1982), pp. 9–27. For discussion of the problems and available methods for coding open-ended questions, see Rodger Knaus, "Methods and Problems in Coding Natural Language Survey Data," *Journal of Official Statistics*, 3 (No. 1, 1987), pp. 45–67.

5. Urban B. Ozanne and Shelby D. Hunt, *The Economic Effects of Franchising* (Madison, Wis.: Graduate School of Business, The University of Wisconsin, 1971).

6. For discussion of a set of indices that can be used to investigate coder reliability as well as to determine which questions might prove to be particularly troublesome, see Martin Collins and Graham Kalton, "Coding Verbatim Answers to Open Questions," *Journal of the Market Research Society*, 22 (October 1980), pp. 239–247; and William D. Perreault, Jr., and Laurence E. Leigh, "Reliability of Nominal Data Based on Qualitative Judgments," *Journal of Marketing Research*, 26 (May 1989), pp. 135–148.

7. Philip S. Siedl, "Coding," in Robert Ferber, ed., *Handbook of Marketing Research* (New York: McGraw-Hill, 1974), pp. 2-178 to 2-199. This article provides an excellent overview of the issues that arise in coding data and how they can be handled.

8. For a review of the features contained in the most popular statistical packages for microcomputers, see Robin Raskin, "Statistical Software for the PC: Testing for Significance," *PC Magazine*, 8 (March 14, 1989), pp. 103–255.

9. David W. Stewart, "Filling the Gap: A Review of the Missing Data Problem," unpublished manuscript, provides an excellent review of the literature on the problem of missing data, including various methods for eliminating cases and estimating answers. On the basis of this review, he concludes several things: missing data points should be estimated regardless of whether the data are missing randomly or nonrandomly; for very small amounts of missing data, almost any of the estimation procedures work reasonably well; when larger amounts of data are missing and the average intercorrelation of variables is .20 or less, the substitution of the mean seems to work best; and when the average intercorrelation of the variables exceeds .20, a regression or principal-components procedure is the preferred choice when linearity among the variables may be assumed. For a study that empirically examines the question of whether or not missing items are random, see Richard M. Durand, Hugh J. Guffey, Jr., and John M. Planchon, "An Examination of the Random versus Nonrandom Nature of Item Omissions," *Journal of Marketing Research*, 20 (August 1983) pp. 305–313. See also Roderick J. A. Little and Philip J. Smith, "Editing and Imputation for Quantitative Survey Data," *Journal of the American Statistical Association*, 82 (March 1987), pp. 58–68; and Naresh K. Malhotra, "Analyzing Marketing Research Data with Incomplete Information on the Dependent Variable," *Journal of Marketing Research*, 24 (February 1987), pp. 74–84.

10. See the classic book by Hans Zeisel, *Say It with Figures*, 5th ed. (New York: Harper and Row, 1968), pp. 16–17, for conditions that would support reporting percentages with decimal-place accuracy.

11. Robert J. Lavidge, "How to Keep Well-Intentioned Research from Misleading New-Product Planners," *Marketing News*, 18 (January 6, 1984), p. 8.

12. Box and whisker plots can also be used to get a sense for the distribution of the variable. They possess the attractive feature of including information about the variable mean, median, 25th and 75th percentiles, and outliers. For discussion of how they are constructed, see "Graphic Displays of Data: Box and Whisker Plots," *Research on Research*, No. 17 (Chicago: Market Facts, Inc. undated).

13. At times the direction of causation will not be straightforward and the calculation of percentages can logically proceed in either direction. Zeisel, *Say It with Figures*, pp. 30–32.

14. See Ottar Hellevik, *Introduction to Causal Analysis: Exploring Survey Data by Cross-tabulation* (London: George Allen & Unwin, 1984).

15. See Joann S. Lublin, "Aspirin Found to Cut Blood Clotting Risks in Men, Not Women," *The Wall Street Journal* (December 8 1977), p. 26.

Suggested Additional Readings

For useful discussion of the purposes and procedures to follow when editing and coding data, see

John A. Sonquist and William C. Dunkelberg, *Survey and Opinion Research: Procedures for Processing and Analysis* (Englewood Cliffs, N.J.: Prentice-Hall, 1977), especially pp. 41–196.

For especially insightful discussions of the use of cross-tabulation analysis to reveal the underlying patterns in data, see the classic works

Hans Zeisel, *Say It with Figures*, 5th ed. (New York: Harper and Row, 1968).

Ottar Hellevik, *Introduction to Causal Analysis: Exploring Survey Data by Cross-tabulation* (London: George Allen & Unwin, 1984).

Appendix
19A

Hypothesis Testing

In Chapter 19 we discussed the preliminary data-analysis steps of editing, coding, and tabulation. That chapter demonstrated the importance and potential value of these preliminary procedures, which are common to almost all research studies. Some studies stop with tabulation and cross tabulation. However, many others involve additional analyses, particularly the formal test of a statistical hypothesis or the establishment of a confidence interval. This appendix reviews these procedures.

When marketers prepare to launch a research study, they generally begin with a speculation, or guess, about a phenomenon in their environment. "I'll bet," the advertising manager might say to the marketing director, "that if we hired a sultry celebrity to promote our shampoo, sales would increase." Or the sales manager might say to the company's financial officer, "If my department only had more money to spend on training, our people would be more productive."

In marketing, as in other scientific fields, such unproven propositions are called hypotheses. Through the use of statistical techniques, we are often able to determine whether there is empirical evidence to confirm such hypotheses. Many of the procedures discussed in the next few chapters are used to test specific hypotheses. It is therefore useful to review some basic concepts that underlie hypothesis testing in classical statistical theory, such as framing the null hypothesis, setting the risk of error in making a wrong decision, and the general steps involved in testing the hypothesis.[1]

Null Hypothesis

Marketing research studies are unable to prove results. At best, they can indicate which of two mutually exclusive hypotheses are more likely to be true on the basis of observed results. The general forms of these two hypotheses and the symbols attached to them are as follows:[2]

- H_0, the hypothesis that our results do not show any significant differences between population groups over whatever factors have been measured
- H_a, the alternate hypothesis that differences shown in our results reflect real differences between population groups

The first of these hypotheses, H_0, is known as the *null hypothesis*. One simple fact underlies the statistical test of a hypothesis: A hypothesis may be rejected but can never be accepted except tentatively, since further evidence may prove it wrong. In other words, one *rejects* the hypothesis or *does not reject* the hypothesis on the basis of the evidence at hand. It is wrong to conclude, however, that since the hypothesis was not rejected, it can be *accepted* necessarily as valid.

A naive qualitative example should illustrate the issue.[3] Suppose we are testing the hypothesis that John Doe is a poor man. We observe that Doe dines in cheap restaurants, lives in the slum area of the city in a run-down building, wears worn and tattered clothes, and so on. Although his behavior is certainly consistent with that of a poor man, we cannot accept the hypothesis that he is poor. It is possible that Doe may in fact be rich, but extremely frugal. We can continue gathering information about him, but for the moment we must decide *not to reject* the hypothesis. One single observation, for example, that indicates he has a six-figure bank account or that he owns 100,000 shares of AT&T stock would allow the immediate rejection of the hypothesis and would lead to the conclusion that John Doe is rich.

Thus, researchers need to recognize that in the absence of perfect information (such as is the case when sampling), the best they can do is form hypotheses or conjectures about what is true. Further, their conclusions about these conjectures can be wrong, and thus there is always some probability of error in accepting any hypothesis. Statistical parlance holds that researchers commit a Type I error when they reject a true null hypothesis and thereby accept the alternative; they commit a Type II error when they do not reject a false null hypothesis, which they should, given that it is false. The null hypothesis is assumed to be *true* for the purpose of the test. Such an assumption is used to generate knowledge about how the various sample estimates produced under the sampling plan might vary. Further, researchers need to be aware that Type I errors can be specified to be no more than some specific amount (e.g., ≤ 0.05), whereas Type II errors are functions.[4]

The upshot of this discussion is that the researcher needs to frame the null hypothesis in such a way that its rejection leads to the acceptance of the desired conclusion, that is, the statement or condition he or she wishes to verify. For example, suppose a firm was considering introducing a new product if it could be expected to secure more than 10 percent of the market. The proper way to frame the hypotheses then would be

$$H_0: \pi \leq 0.10$$
$$H_a: \pi > 0.10$$

If the evidence led to the rejection of H_0, the researcher would then be able to "accept" the alternative that the product could be expected to secure more than 10 percent of the market, and the product would be introduced, since such a result would have been unlikely to occur if the null was indeed true. If H_0 could not be rejected, though, the product would not be introduced unless more evidence to the contrary became available. The example as framed involves the use of a *one-tailed* statistical test in that the alternate hypothesis is expressed directionally, that is, as being greater than 0.10. The one-tailed test is most commonly used in marketing research, although there are research problems that warrant a *two-tailed* test; for example, the market share achieved by the new formulation of Product X is no different from that achieved by the old formulation, which was 10 percent. A two-tailed test would be expressed as

$$H_0: \pi = 0.10$$
$$H_a: \pi \neq 0.10$$

There is no direction implied with the alternate hypothesis; the proportion is simply expressed as not being equal to 0.10.

The one-tailed test is more commonly used than the two-tailed test in marketing research for two reasons. First, there is typically some preferred direction to the outcome, for example, the greater the market share, the higher the product quality, or the lower the expenses, the better. The two-tailed alternative is used when there is no preferred direction in the outcome or when the research is meant to demonstrate the existence of a difference but not its direction. Second, the one-tailed test, when it is appropriate, is more powerful statistically than the two-tailed alternative.

Types of Errors

Since the result of statistically testing a null hypothesis is to reject it or not reject it, two types of errors may occur. First, the null hypothesis may be rejected when it is true. Second, it may not be rejected when it is false and, therefore, should have been rejected.

Table 19A.1   **Judicial Analogy Illustrating Decision Error**

	True Situation: Defendant Is	
Verdict	**Innocent**	**Guilty**
Innocent	Correct decision: probably $= 1 - \alpha$	Error: probability $= \beta$
Guilty	Error: probability $= \alpha$	Correct decision: probability $= 1 - \beta$

Table 19A.2   **Types of Errors in Hypothesis Testing**

	True Situation: Null Hypothesis Is	
Research Conclusion	**True**	**False**
Do not reject H_0	Correct decision Confidence level Probability $= 1 - \alpha$	Error: Type II Probability $= \beta$
Reject H_0	Error: Type I Significance level Probability $= \alpha$	Correct decision Power of test Probability $= 1 - \beta$

These two errors are, respectively, termed *Type I error* and *Type II error*, or α *error* and β *error*, which are the probabilities associated with their occurrence. The two types of errors are not complementary in that $\alpha + \beta \neq 1$.

To illustrate each type of error and to demonstrate that the errors are not complementary, consider a judicial analogy.[5] Since, under U.S. criminal law, a person is innocent until proven guilty, the judge and jury are always testing the hypothesis of innocence. The defendant may, in fact, be either innocent or guilty, but based on the evidence, the court may reach either verdict regardless of the true situation. Table 19A.1 displays the possibilities. If the defendant is innocent and the jury finds him innocent, or if the defendant is guilty and the jury finds him guilty, the jury has made a correct decision. If, however, the defendant truly is innocent and the jury finds the person guilty, they have made an error, and similarly if the defendant is guilty and they find him innocent. The jury must find one way or the other, and thus the probabilities of the jury's decision must sum vertically to 1. Thus if we let α represent the probability of incorrectly finding the person guilty when he is innocent, then $1 - \alpha$ must be the probability of correctly finding him innocent. Similarly, β and $1 - \beta$ represent the probabilities of findings of innocence and guilt when he is guilty. It is intuitively obvious that $\alpha + \beta$ is not equal to 1, although later discussion will indicate that β must increase when α is reduced if other things remain the same. Since our society generally holds that finding an innocent person guilty is more serious than finding a guilty person innocent, α error is reduced as much as possible in our legal system by requiring proof of guilt "beyond any reasonable doubt."

Table 19A.2 contains the corresponding research situation. Just as the defendant's true status is unknown to the jury, the true situation regarding the null hypothesis is unknown to the researcher. The researcher's dilemma parallels that of the jury in that the researcher has limited information with which to work. Suppose the null hypothesis is true. If the researcher concludes it is false, a Type I (α) error has been made. The

Research Window 19A.1
Typical Hypothesis-Testing Procedure

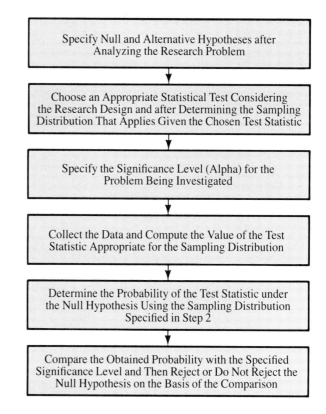

significance level associated with a statistical test indicates the probability with which this error may be made. Since sample information will always be somewhat incomplete, there will always be some α error. The only way it can be avoided is by never rejecting the null hypothesis (never finding anyone guilty, in the judicial analogy). The *confidence level* of a statistical test is $1 - \alpha$, and the more confident we want to be in a statistical result, the lower we must set α error. The *power* associated with a statistical test is the probability of correctly rejecting a false null hypothesis. One-tailed tests are more powerful than two-tailed tests because, for the same α error, they are simply more likely to lead to a rejection of a false null hypothesis. β error represents the probability of not rejecting a false null hypothesis. There is no unique value associated with β error.

Procedure

The relationship between the two types of errors is best illustrated through example, and the example would be most productive if developed following the general format of hypothesis testing. Research Window 19A.1 shows the typical sequence of steps that researchers follow in testing hypotheses. Suppose the problem was indeed one of investigating the potential for a new product and that the research centered around testing consumer preferences. Suppose that, in the judgment of management, the product should not be introduced unless at least 20 percent of the population could be expected to prefer it, and that the research calls for 625 respondents to be interviewed for their preferences.

Step 1   The null and alternate hypotheses would be

$$H_0: \pi \leq 0.20$$

$$H_a: \pi > 0.20$$

The hypotheses are framed so that if the null hypothesis is rejected, the product should be introduced.

Step 2   The appropriate sample statistic is the sample proportion, and the distribution of all possible sample proportions under the sampling plan is based on the assumption that the null hypothesis is true. Although the distribution of sample proportions is theoretically binomially distributed, the large sample size permits the use of the normal approximation.[6] The z test therefore applies. The z statistic in this case equals

$$z = \frac{p - \pi}{\sigma_p}$$

where p is the sample proportion preferring the product, σ_p is the standard error of the proportion, or the standard deviation of the distribution of sample p's. And σ_p in turn equals

$$\sqrt{\frac{\pi(1 - \pi)}{n}} = \sqrt{\frac{0.20(0.80)}{625}} = 0.0160$$

where n is the sample size. Note this peculiarity of proportions. As soon as we have hypothesized a population value, we have said something about the standard error of the estimate. The proportion is the most clear-cut case of "known variance," since the variance is specified automatically with an assumed π. The researcher thus knows all of the values for calculating z except p before ever taking the sample and further knows a priori the distribution to which the calculated statistic will be related. This is true in general, and the researcher should have these conditions clearly in mind before taking the sample.

Step 3   The researcher selects a significance level (α) using the following reasoning: In this situation α error is the probability of rejecting H_0 and concluding that $\pi > 0.2$, when in reality $\pi \leq 0.2$. This conclusion will lead the company to market the new product. However, since the venture will be profitable only if $\pi > 0.2$, a wrong decision to market would be financially unprofitable, possibly disastrous. The probability of Type I error should, therefore, be minimized as much as possible. The researcher recognizes, though, that the probability of a Type II error increases as α is decreased, other things being equal. Type II error in this case implies concluding $\pi \leq 0.2$ when in fact $\pi > 0.2$, which in turn suggests that the company would table the decision to introduce the product when it could be profitable. The opportunity lost from making such an error could be quite serious. Although, as explained later, the researcher does not know what β would be, he or she knows that α and β are interrelated and that an extremely low value of α, say, 0.01 or 0.001, would produce intolerable β errors. The researcher decides, therefore, on an α level of 0.05 as an acceptable compromise.[7]

Step 4   Since Step 4 involves the computation of the test statistic, it can be completed only after the sample is drawn and the information collected. Suppose 140 of the 625

Figure 19A.1   *Probability of z = 1.500 with a One-Tailed Test*

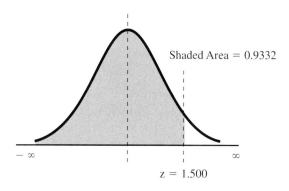

Shaded Area = 0.9332

$-\infty$ ∞

z = 1.500

sample respondents preferred the product. The sample proportion is thus $p = 140/625 = 0.224$. The basic question that needs to be answered is conceptually simple: "Is this value of p too large to have occurred by chance from a population with π assumed to be equal to 0.2?" Or, in other words, "What is the probability of getting $p = 0.224$ when $\pi = 0.2$?" The test statistic, z, equals

$$\frac{p - \pi}{\sigma_p} = \frac{0.224 - 0.20}{0.0160} = 1.500.$$

Step 5   The probability of occurrence of a z value of 1.500 can be found from standard tabled values of areas under the normal curve. (See Table 1 at the end of the book.) Figure 19A.1 shows the procedure. The shaded area between $-\infty$ and 1.500 equals 0.9332; this means the area to the right of $z = 1.500$ is $1.000 - 0.9332$, or 0.0668. This is the probability of securing a z value of 1.500 under a true situation of $\pi = 0.2$.

Step 6   Since the calculated probability of occurrence is higher than the specified significance level of $\alpha = 0.05$, the null hypothesis is not rejected. The product would not be introduced because, while the evidence is in the right direction, it is not sufficient to conclude beyond "any reasonable doubt" that $\pi > 0.2$. If the decision maker had been able to tolerate a 10-percent chance of committing a Type I error, the null hypothesis would have been rejected and the product marketed, since the probability of getting a sample $p = 0.224$ when the true $\pi = 0.20$, is, as we have seen, 0.0668.

Power

The example illustrates the importance of correctly specifying the risk of error. If a 10-percent chance of an α error were tolerable and the researcher specified $\alpha = 0.05$, a potentially profitable opportunity would have been bypassed. The choice of the proper significance level involves weighing the costs associated with the two types of error, which is unfortunately a procedure that most researchers ignore, choosing out of habit $\alpha = 0.10$ or 0.05. Perhaps this lapse is due to the difficulty encountered in specifying β error, or Type II error.

The difficulty arises because β error is not a constant. Recall that it is the probability of not rejecting a false null hypothesis. Therefore, the probability of committing a Type II error depends on the size of the difference between the *true*, but unknown, population value and the value assumed to be true under the null hypothesis. Other things being equal, we would prefer a test that minimized such errors. Alternatively, since the power of a test equals $1 - \beta$, we would prefer the test with the greatest power so that we would have the best chance of rejecting a false null hypothesis.[8] Now, clearly our ability to do this depends on "how false H_0 truly is." It could be "just a little bit false" or "way off the mark," and the probability of an incorrect inclusion would certainly be higher in the first case. The difference between the assumed value under the null and the true, but unknown, value is known as the *effect size*. As intuition suggests, large effects are easier to distinguish than small effects.

Consider again the hypotheses

$$H_0: \pi \leq 0.20$$

$$H_a: \pi > 0.20$$

where $\sigma_p = 0.0160$ and $\alpha = 0.05$, as before. Any calculated z value greater than 1.645 will cause us to reject this hypothesis, since this is the z value that cuts off 5 percent of the normal curve. The z value can be equated to the *critical* sample proportion through the formula

$$z = \frac{p - \pi}{\sigma_p}$$

$$1.645 = \frac{p - 0.20}{0.0160}$$

or $p = 0.2263$. Thus, any sample proportion greater than $p = 0.2263$ will lead to the rejection of the null hypothesis that $\pi \leq 0.2$. This means that if 142 or more $[0.2263(625) = 141.4]$ of the sample respondents prefer the new product, the null hypothesis will be rejected and the product introduced, while if 141 or less of the sample respondents prefer it, the null hypothesis will not be rejected and the new product will not be introduced.

The likelihood of a sample proportion of $p = 0.2263$ is much greater for certain values of π than for others. Suppose, for instance, that the true but unknown value of π is 0.22. The sampling distribution of the sample proportion is again normal, but now it is centered about 0.22. The probability of obtaining the critical sample proportion $p = 0.2263$ under this condition is found again from the normal curve table, where now[9]

$$z = \frac{p - \pi}{\sigma_p} = \frac{0.2263 - 0.22}{0.0166} = 0.380.$$

The shaded area between $-\infty$ and $z = 0.380$ is given in Table 1 at the end of the book as 0.6480, and thus the area to the right of $z = 0.380$ is equal to $1.000 - 0.6480 = 0.3520$ (see Panel B in Figure 19A.2). This is the probability that a value as large or larger than $p = 0.2263$ would be obtained if the true population proportion was $\pi = 0.22$. It is also the power of the test in that if π is truly equal to 0.22, the null hypothesis is false and 0.3520 is the probability that the null will be rejected. Conversely, the probability that $p < 0.2263$ equals $1 - 0.3520 = 0.6480$, which is β error. The null hypothesis is false, and yet the false null hypothesis is not rejected from any sample for which the proportion $p < 0.2263$.

Suppose that the true population condition was $\pi = 0.21$ instead of $\pi = 0.22$, and the null hypothesis was again $H_0: \pi \leq 0.20$. Since the null hypothesis is less false in this second case, we would expect power to be lower and the risk of β error to be higher because the null hypothesis is less likely to be rejected. Let us see if that is indeed the case. The z value corresponding to the critical $p = 0.2263$ is 1.000. Power given by the area to the right of $z = 1.000$ is 0.1587 (the β error is 0.8413), and the expected result is obtained (see Figure 19A.2, Panel C).

Figure 19A.2   **Computation of β Error and Power for Several Assumed True**
Population Proportions for the Hypothesis π ≤ 0.2

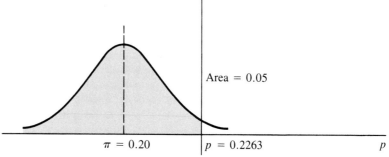

Area = 0.05

$\pi = 0.20$ $p = 0.2263$ p

Panel A: Critical Proportion under Null Hypothesis

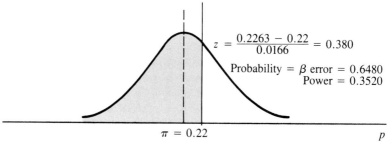

$z = \dfrac{0.2263 - 0.22}{0.0166} = 0.380$

Probability = β error = 0.6480
Power = 0.3520

$\pi = 0.22$ p

Panel B: Probability of Realizing Critical Proportion When $\pi = 0.22$,
Which Means Null Hypothesis Is False

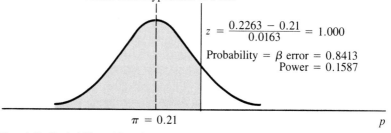

$z = \dfrac{0.2263 - 0.21}{0.0163} = 1.000$

Probability = β error = 0.8413
Power = 0.1587

$\pi = 0.21$ p

Panel C: Probability of Realizing Critical Proportion When $\pi = 0.21$,
Which Means Null Hypothesis Is False

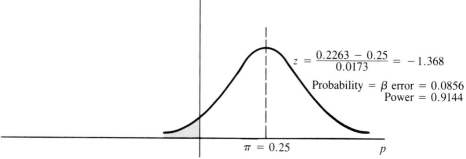

$z = \dfrac{0.2263 - 0.25}{0.0173} = -1.368$

Probability = β error = 0.0856
Power = 0.9144

$\pi = 0.25$ p

Panel D: Probability of Realizing Critical Proportion When $\pi = 0.25$,
Which Means Null Hypothesis Is False

Table 19A.3   β *Error and Power for Different Assumed True Values of* π *and the*
Hypotheses H_0: π ≤ 0.20 *and* H_a: π > 0.20

Value of π	Probability of Type II, or β, Error	Power of the Test: 1 − β
0.20	(0.950) = 1 − α	(0.05) = α
0.21	0.8413	0.1587
0.22	0.6480	0.3520
0.23	0.4133	0.5867
0.24	0.2133	0.7867
0.25	0.0856	0.9144
0.26	0.0273	0.9727
0.27	0.0069	0.9931
0.28	0.0014	0.9986
0.29	0.0005	0.9995
0.30	0.0000	1.0000

Consider one final value, true π = 0.25. The null hypothesis of π = 0.20 would be "way off the mark" in this case, and we would expect there would only be a small chance that it would not be rejected and a Type II error would be committed. The calculations are displayed in Figure 19A.2, Panel D; $z = -1.368$, and the are to the right of $z = -1.368$ is 0.9144. The probability of β error is 0.0856, and the a priori expectation is confirmed.

Table 19A.3 contains the power of the test for other selected population states, and Figure 19A.3 shows these values graphically. Figure 19A.3 is essentially the power curve for the hypotheses

$$H_0: \pi \le 0.20$$
$$H_a: \pi > 0.20$$

and it confirms that the farther away the true π is from the hypothesized value in the direction indicated by the alternate hypothesis, the higher the power. Note that power is not defined for the hypothesized value, because if the true value in fact equals the hypothesized value, a β error cannot be committed.

Note that since power is a function rather than a single value, the researcher attempting to balance Type I and Type II errors logically needs to ask how false the null hypothesis is likely to be and to establish his or her decision rule accordingly. The way to control both errors within predetermined bounds for a given size effect is to vary the sample size.[10] The need to specify all three items—α error (or degree of confidence), β error (or power), and the size of the effect it is necessary to detect—possibly explains why so many researchers content themselves with the specification of Type I, or α, error and allow β error to fall where it may. The example provides an excellent opportunity to illustrate the dangers in this approach.

The failure to even worry about, much less explicitly take into account, the power of the statistical test represents one of the fundamental problems with the classical statistics hypothesis-testing approach as it is commonly practiced in marketing research. Moreover,

Figure 19A.3   ***Power Function for Data of Table 19A.3***

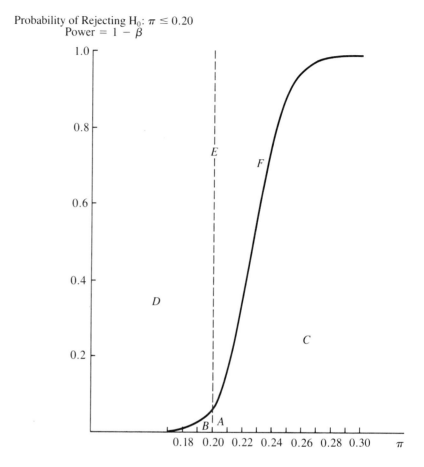

Probability of Rejecting H_0: $\pi \leq 0.20$
Power = $1 - \beta$

A—Type I error; true null hypothesis is rejected; significance level.
B—Type I error; true null hypothesis is rejected.
C—No error; false null hypothesis is rejected.
D—No error; true null hypothesis is not rejected.
E—No error; true null hypothesis is not rejected; confidence level.
F—Type II error; false null hypothesis is not rejected.

Type II errors are often more costly than Type I errors. Another common problem is the widespread tendency to misinterpret a "statistically significant result." There are several common misinterpretations.[11] One of the most frequent is to view a p value as representing the probability that the results occurred because of sampling error. Thus, the commonly used $p = 0.05$ is taken to mean that there is a probability of only 0.05 that the results were caused by chance, and thus there must be something fundamental causing them. In actuality, a p value of 0.05 means that if, and this is a big if, the null hypothesis is true, the odds are only 1 in 20 of getting a sample result of the magnitude that was observed. Unfortunately, there is no way in classical statistical significance testing to determine whether the null hypothesis is true.

A p value reached by classical methods is not a summary of the data. Nor does the p value attached to a result tell how strong or dependable the particular result is. . . . Writers and readers are all too likely to read .05 as $p(H/E)$, "the probability that the *Hypothesis* is true, given the *Evidence*." As textbooks on statistics reiterate almost in vain, p is $p(E/H)$, the probability that this *Evidence* would arise if the (null) *Hypothesis* is true.[12]

Another common misinterpretation is to equate statistical significance with practical significance. Many fail to realize that a difference can be of practical importance and not statistically significant if the power of the test is weak. Conversely, a result may be of no practical importance, even if highly significant, if the sample is very large.

A third very frequent misinterpretation is to hold that the α or p level chosen is in some way related to the probability that the research hypothesis, typically captured in the alternative hypothesis, is true. Most typically, this probability is taken as the complement of the α level. Thus, a p value of 0.05 is interpreted to mean that its complement, $1 - 0.05 = 0.95$, is the probability that the research hypothesis is true. "Related to this misinterpretation is the practice of interpreting p values as a measure or the degree of validity of research results, i.e., a p value such as $p < .0001$ is "highly statistically significant" or "highly significant" and therefore much more valid than a p value of, say, 0.05."[13] Both of these related interpretations are wrong.

The only logical conclusion that can be drawn when a null hypothesis is rejected at some predetermined p level is that sampling error is an unlikely explanation of the results, given that the null hypothesis is true. In many ways that is not saying very much, because, as was just argued, the null hypothesis is a weak straw man; it is set up to be false. The null, as typically stated, holds that there is no relationship between a certain two variables, say, or that the groups are equal with respect to some particular variable. Yet, we do not really believe that. Rather, we investigate the relationship between variables because we believe there is some association between them, and we contrast the groups because we believe they are different with respect to the variable. Further, we can control our ability to reject the null hypothesis simply by the power we built into the statistical test, primarily through the size of the sample used to test it. "Given sufficiently high statistical power, one would expect virtually *always* to conclude the exact null hypothesis is false."[14]

Marketing researchers, then, need to be wary when interpreting the results of their hypothesis-testing procedures so that they do not mislead themselves and others. They need constantly to keep in mind both types of errors that it is possible to make. Further, they need to make sure they do not misinterpret what a test of significance reveals. It represents no more than a test against the null hypothesis. One useful way of avoiding misinterpretation is to calculate confidence intervals when possible, as this gives decision makers a much better feel for how much faith they can have in the results.

A test of significance is very much a yes-no affair: either the sample result is statistically significant or it is not. On the other hand, "the confidence interval not only gives a yes or no answer, but also, by its width, gives an indication of whether the answer should be whispered or shouted."[15] While not every test of significance can be put in the form of a confidence interval estimate, many of them can, and it is advisable to put them in that form when the opportunity arises.[16]

Endnotes

1. Bayesian statistical theory assumes a different posture with respect to hypothesis testing than does classical statistics. Because classical statistical significance-testing procedures are much more commonly used in marketing research, though, only the basic elements underlying classical statistical theory are presented here.

2. E. J. Davis, "Appendix 2: Statistical Tests," in Margaret Crimp, *The Marketing Research Process* (Englewood Cliffs, N.J.: Prentice-Hall, 1981), p. 236.

3. The author expresses his appreciation to Dr. B. Venkatesh, of Burke Marketing Services, Inc., for suggesting this example to illustrate the rationale behind the framing of hypotheses.

4. We will have more to say about Type I and Type II errors later.

5. R. W. Jastram, *Elements of Statistical Inference* (Berkeley, Calif.: Book Company, 1947), p. 44.

6. The binomial distribution tends toward the normal distribution for a fixed π as sample size increases. The tendency is most rapid when $\pi = 0.5$. With sufficiently large samples, normal probabilities may be used to approximate binomial probabilities with π's in this range. As π departs from 0.5 in either direction, the normal approximation becomes less adequate, although it is generally held that the normal approximation may be used safely if the smaller of $n\pi$ or $n(1 - \pi)$ is 10 or more. If this condition is not satisfied,

binomial probabilities can either be calculated directly or found in tables that are readily available. In the example, $n\pi = 625(0.2) = 125$, and $n(1 - \pi) = 500$, and thus there is little question about the adequacy of the normal approximation to binomial probabilities.

7. We shall have more to say about the choice of $\alpha = 0.05$ and its interpretation after we have introduced the notion of power.

8. See Alan G. Sawyer and A. Dwayne Ball, "Statistical Power and Effect Size in Marketing Research," *Journal of Marketing Research*, 18 (August 1981), pp. 275–290, for a persuasive argument about why marketing researchers need to pay more attention to power in their research designs. The article also offers some suggestions on how to improve statistical power.

9. Note that σ_p is now $\sqrt{0.22(0.78)/625} = 0.0166$, because a different specification of π implies a different standard error of estimate.

10. See Helena Chumura Kraemer and Sue Thiemann, *How Many Subjects?* (Newbury Park, Calif.: Sage Publications, 1988), for discussion of the use of power to determine sample size.

11. For an excellent discussion of some of the most common misinterpretations of classical significance tests and some recommendations on how to surmount the problems, see Alan G. Sawyer and J. Paul Peter, "The Significance of Statistical Significance Tests in Marketing Research," *Journal of Marketing Research*, 20 (May 1983), pp. 122–133.

12. Lee J. Cronbach and R. E. Snow, *Aptitudes and Instructional Methods: A Handbook for Research on Interactions* (New York: Irvington, 1977), p. 52.

13. Sawyer and Peter, "The Significance," p. 123. For other useful discussions of what statistical tests of significance mean, see Mick Alt and Malcolm Brighton, "Analyzing Data or Telling Stories?" *Journal of the Market Research Society*, 23 (October 1981), pp. 209–219; and Norval D. Glenn, "Replications, Significance Tests and Confidence in Findings in Survey Research," *Public Opinion Quarterly*, 47 (Summer 1983), pp. 261–269.

14. Sawyer and Peter, "The Significance," p. 125.

15. Mary G. Natrella, "The Relation between Confidence Intervals and Tests of Significance," *American Statistician*, 14 (1960), p. 22. See also G. R. Dawling and P. K. Walsh, "Estimating and Reporting Confidence Intervals for Market and Opinion Research," *European Research*, 13 (July 1985), pp. 130–133.

16. For an excellent discussion of the relationship between tests of significance and confidence interval estimates, see Natrella, "The Relation between Confidence Intervals," pp. 20–22, 33.

20

Chapter Twenty

Data Analysis: Examining Differences

Learning Objectives

Upon completing this chapter, you should be able to

1. Explain the basic use of a chi-square goodness-of-fit test.

2. Discuss the similarities and differences between the chi-square goodness-of-fit test and the Kolmogorov-Smirnov test.

3. Specify which test is appropriate if one is testing a hypothesis about a single mean, given that the variance is known. Which is appropriate if the variance is unknown?

4. Identify the tests that are appropriate if the analysis involves two means from independent samples.

5. Specify the appropriate test if the analysis involves the difference between two parent-population proportions.

Case in Marketing Research

Angie Karlin followed Chuck Zellmer through the lunchtime crowd at the newest Omni Software store in Washington, D.C.

"The store is really sharp," remarked Karlin once they'd arrived at Zellmer's office, at the rear of the sales floor. "You certainly aren't having any trouble bringing in customers, not at this location anyway."

"Oh, no, we're doing a phenomenal business in the retail division. We're opening three more stores this year. Hopefully we'll be as successful at choosing the new locations as we were at choosing this one."

"So how's the catalog division doing?" asked Karlin. Zellmer was the director of catalog sales for Omni Software.

"Catalog sales are really flat. It's strange. You know that we started out as a catalog business and that the retail end was really an experiment that we could afford to make because we were doing so well in mail-order business. Now that we're making big bucks in retail, our mail orders are going nowhere. It troubles me because I can't explain it."

"Which is why you called me," filled in Karlin.

"Right. That is why I called you. We at Omni are committed to our catalog operation. It allows us to reach a national market at a fairly low cost. Besides, we think there is a fundamental difference between our catalog customers and our retail customers."

"What's that?" asked Karlin.

"You buy software from a catalog when you already know what you want. For example, if you're looking for a certain home finance program, let's say Thompson's Money Manager, then you look in the Omni catalog, call the 800 number, and order it. But if you're looking for a home finance program and you're not sure which one you need, then you go into an Omni store, where a salesperson can explain the different features of each program and help you decide."

"I understand why you see the market as being segmented," remarked Karlin.

"Our goal over the next year," continued Zellmer, "is to revitalize our catalog division. We'd like your firm to do a survey of our past customers so that we can gain an understanding of how to improve catalog sales."

"You know we'd love to do it," said Karlin. "It sounds like you guys have a pretty good idea of what you want."

"Yes. To begin with, we'd like to know what our mail-order customers think about our products and services. We'd also like to get a better feel for who our customers really are—how old they are, how much money they make, how computer literate they are," said Zellmer.

"I think that's a great start," replied Karlin. "But you know, there's a fixed cost to doing any kind of mail survey, and from my experience, I think we might as well take it one step further. I think we should take a look at how your customers feel about buying merchandise, especially computer software, through the mail as opposed to through a retail outlet. I think that perception might be important in how you subsequently formulate your marketing strategy."

"Great," said Zellmer. "Why don't you go ahead and draft a proposal for the study. I'll have Sid Green, at the mailing house, run out a list of the names of our catalog customers."

"Fine," answered Karlin. "How much have you budgeted for this study?"

"I don't know. How much is it going to cost?" asked Zellmer. "And don't think that by asking you that question I'm giving you a blank check. We're in a competitive business, and we're very sensitive to unnecessary expenditures. On the other hand, to do a study like this but not budget enough to do more than a half-baked job would be a total waste of money."

"Chuck," replied Karlin with feeling, "I wish all my clients were as intelligent as you are. . . ."

Discussion Issues

1. If you were the marketing research director on this survey, what variables would you want to investigate in the study?
2. How might some of those variables be interrelated?
3. Assuming a mail survey were to be used, what might you do to increase the response rate?

665

A question that arises regularly in the analysis of research data is, Are the research results statistically significant? Could the result have occurred by chance due to the fact that only a sample of the population was contacted, or does it actually indicate an underlying condition in the population? To answer, we use one of several tests of statistical significance. This chapter reviews some of the more important tests for examining the statistical significance of differences. The difference at issue might be the difference between some sample result and some expected population value, or the difference between two or more sample results. Different types of tests are applicable for different types of problems. The first part of the chapter reviews the χ^2 (chi-square) goodness-of-fit test, which is especially useful with nominal data. The second part reviews the Kolmogorov-Smirnov test, which is useful with ordinal data. The latter sections focus on the tests that are applicable when examining differences in means or proportions.

Goodness of Fit

It is often the case in marketing studies that an analyst must determine whether a certain pattern of behavior shown by the data corresponds to the pattern that was expected when the study was devised. As an illustration, consider a breakfast food manufacturer who has recently developed a new cereal called Score. The cereal will be packaged in the three standard sizes: small, large, and family size. In the past, the manufacturer has found that for every small package, three of the large and two of the family size are also sold. The manufacturer wishes to see if this same tendency will hold with this new cereal, since a change in consumption patterns could have significant production implications. The manufacturer therefore decides to conduct a market test to determine the relative frequencies with which consumers will purchase the various sizes.

Suppose that, in an appropriate test market, over a one-week period, 1,200 boxes of the new cereal are sold and that the distribution of sales by size is as follows:

Number Buying

Small	Large	Family	Total
240	575	385	1,200

As some quick multiplication would show, these figures do not match the pattern established earlier with other cereal brands. Does this preliminary evidence indicate that the firm should expect a change in the purchase patterns of the various sized packages with Score?

Chi-square goodness-of-fit test A statistical test to determine whether some observed pattern of frequencies corresponds to an expected pattern.

This is the type of problem for which the **chi-square goodness-of-fit test** is ideally suited. (Note that *chi* is a Greek letter that rhymes with *sky*.) The variable of interest has been broken into k mutually exclusive categories ($k = 3$ in the example), and each observation logically falls into one of the k classes or cells. The trials (purchases) are independent, and the sample size is large.

All that is necessary to employ the test is to calculate the *expected* number of cases that would fall in each category and to compare that with the *observed* number actually falling in the category, using the statistic

$$\chi^2 = \sum_{i=1}^{k} \frac{[O_i - E_i]^2}{E_i}$$

where

■ O_i is the observed number of cases falling in the ith category
■ E_i is the expected number of cases falling in the ith category
■ k is the number of categories

The expected number falling into a category is generated from the null hypothesis, which in this case is that the composition of sales of Score by package size will follow the manufacturer's normal sales (that is, for every small package, three large and two family sizes will be sold). In terms of the proportion of all sales, that means

$$\text{small size: } \frac{1}{1 + 3 + 2} = 1/6,$$

$$\text{large size: } \frac{3}{1 + 3 + 2} = 3/6, \text{ and}$$

$$\text{family size: } \frac{2}{1 + 3 + 2} = 2/6$$

or that one-sixth of the sales could be expected to be in the small package size, one-half in the large size, and one-third in the family size if sales of the new cereal follow traditional patterns. If the 1,200 boxes sold in test market followed the normal or expected pattern, then 200 (1/6 × 1,200) would have been the small size, 600 (1/2 × 1,200) would have been the large size, and 400 (1/3 × 1,200) would have been the family size. How does the observed pattern compare with the expected pattern? The appropriate χ^2 statistic is computed as

$$\chi^2 = \frac{(240 - 200)^2}{200} + \frac{(575 - 600)^2}{600} + \frac{(385 - 400)^2}{400} = 9.60.$$

The chi-square distribution is one of the statistical distributions that is completely determined by its degrees of freedom, v. The term *degrees of freedom* refers to the number of things that can vary independently. For example, suppose you had five numbers for which you calculated an average. Then, by knowing any four of the numbers and the average, you would be able to determine the fifth number. In effect, you have used up one degree of freedom in the numbers by calculating the average. The degrees of freedom in the chi-square test are determined by how many cells in a table are free to vary.[1] For example, suppose we had the following table,

	B_1	B_2	
A_1	x	x	5
A_2	x	x	7
	4	8	

and were given one of the cell values, say, the upper left value.

	B_1	B_2	
A_1	1	④	5
A_2	③	④	7
	4	8	

Then the circled values are all fixed, given that we know the marginal totals. If we know $A_1B_1 = 1$, then every other value is automatically determined. Because of this, we say that only one cell is free to vary.

In the cereal example, the number of degrees of freedom is one less than the number of categories (k), that is, $v = k - 1 = 2$, because the sum of the differences between the observed and expected frequencies is zero; both the expected and observed frequencies must sum to the total number of cases; given any $k - 1$ differences, the remaining difference is thus fixed, and this results in the loss of one degree of freedom.

Suppose the researcher has chosen a significance level of $\alpha = 0.05$ for this test. The tabled value of χ^2 for two degrees of freedom and $\alpha = 0.05$ is 5.99 (see Table 2 in the appendix at the end of the book). Since the calculated value ($\chi^2 = 9.60$) is larger, the conclusion is that the sample result would be unlikely to occur by chance alone. Rather, the preliminary market-test results suggest that sales of Score will follow a different pattern than is typical. The null hypothesis of sales in the ratio of 1:3:2 is rejected.

The chi-square test outlined here is an approximate test.[2] The approximation is relatively good if, as a rule of thumb, the expected number of cases in each category is five or more, although this value can be as low as 1 for some situations.[3]

The previous example illustrated the use of the chi-square distribution to test a null hypothesis regarding k population proportions, π_1, π_2, . . ., π_k. The proportions were needed to generate the expected number of cases in each of the k categories. Viewed in this light, the test of a single proportion discussed when reviewing the logic of hypothesis testing in the appendix to Chapter 19 is a special case; in the goodness-of-fit test, the single parameter π is replaced by the k parameters π_1, π_2, . . ., π_k.

Another use of the chi-square goodness-of-fit test is in determining whether a population distribution has a particular form. For instance, we might be interested in finding out whether a sample distribution of scores might have arisen from a normal distribution of scores. To investigate, we could construct the sample frequency histogram. The intervals would correspond to the k cells of the goodness-of-fit test. The observed cell frequencies would be the number of observations falling in each interval. The expected cell frequencies would be the number falling in each interval, if indeed the sample came from a normal distribution with mean μ and variance σ^2. If the population mean and variance were unknown, the sample mean and variance could be used as estimates. This would result in the loss of two additional degrees of freedom, but the basic test procedure would remain unchanged.

Ethical

Dilemma 20.1   A marketing researcher is perplexed at the results of his experiment—they do not tally at all with his a priori hypothesis! He immediately starts hunting through the literature for alternative hypotheses that will account for the findings.

Halfway through the stack of journal articles on his desk, he stops reading and leans back in his chair with a whistle of relief. "Thank goodness! That idea fits my findings pretty well." He reaches for a pad of paper to write his final report, in which his new hypothesis is presented a priori and is neatly upheld in the experiment.

- Is it ethical to select the first explanation that fits the existing data without considering all alternative explanations *and* without further testing?
- It is ethical to present a post hoc explanation as an a priori hypothesis?
- How often, in fact, are theories abandoned in the face of disconfirming evidence?

Kolmogorov-Smirnov Test

Kolmogorov-Smirnov test A statistical test employed with ordinal data to determine whether some observed pattern of frequencies corresponds to some expected pattern; also used to determine whether two independent samples have been drawn from the same population or from populations with the same distribution.

The **Kolmogorov-Smirnov test** is similar to the chi-square goodness-of-fit test in that it uses a comparison between observed and expected frequencies to determine whether observed results are in accord with a stated null hypothesis. But the Kolmogorov-Smirnov test takes advantage of the ordinal nature of the data.

Consider, for example, a manufacturer of cosmetics who is testing four different shades of a foundation compound: very light, light, medium, and dark. The company has hired a marketing research firm to determine whether any distinct preference exists toward either extreme. If so, the company will manufacture only the preferred shades. Otherwise, it will market all shades. Suppose that in a sample of 100, 50 persons prefer the very light shade, 30 the light shade, 15 the medium shade, and 5 the dark shade. Do these results indicate some kind of preference?

Since shade represents a natural ordering, the Kolmogorov-Smirnov test can be used to test the preference hypothesis. The test involves specifying the cumulative distribution function that would occur under the null hypothesis and comparing that with the observed cumulative distribution function. The point at which the two functions show the maximum deviation is determined, and the value of this deviation is the test statistic.

The null hypothesis for the cosmetic manufacturer would be that there is no preference for the various shades. Thus it would be expected that 25 percent of the sample would prefer each shade. The cumulative distribution function resulting from this assumption is presented as the last column of Table 20.1.

Kolmogorov-Smirnov D, which is equal to the *absolute value of the maximum deviation* between the observed cumulative proportion and the theoretical cumulative

Table 20.1   ***Observed and Theoretical Cumulative Distributions of Foundation Compound Preference***

Shade	Observed Number	Observed Proportion	Observed Cumulative Proportion	Theoretical Proportion	Theoretical Cumulative Proportion
Very light	50	0.50	0.50	0.25	0.25
Light	30	0.30	0.80	0.25	0.50
Medium	15	0.15	0.95	0.25	0.75
Dark	5	0.05	1.00	0.25	1.00

proportion, is $0.80 - 0.50 = 0.30$. If the researcher chooses an $\alpha = 0.05$, the critical value of D for large samples is given by $1.36/\sqrt{n}$, where n is the sample size. In our case of a sample size of 100, the critical value is 0.136. Calculated D exceeds the critical value, and thus the null hypothesis of no preference among shades is rejected. The data indicate a statistically significant preference for the lighter shades.

The careful reader will have noticed that the hypothesis of no preference could also have been tested with the chi-square goodness-of-fit test. When the data are ordinal though, the Kolmogorov-Smirnov test is the preferred procedure. It is more powerful than chi-square in almost all cases, is easier to compute, and does not require a certain minimum expected frequency in each cell as does the chi-square test.

The Kolmogorov-Smirnov test can also be used to determine whether two independent samples have been drawn from the same population or from populations with the same distribution. An example would be a manufacturer interested in determining whether consumer preference among sizes for a new brand of laundry detergent was the same as for the old brand. To apply the test, we would simply need to create a cumulative frequency distribution for each sample of observations using the same intervals. The test statistic would be the value of the maximum deviation between the two observed cumulative frequencies.[4]

Hypotheses about One Mean

A recurring problem in marketing research studies is the need to make some statement about the parent-population mean. Recall that when sampling from a parent population with known variance that the distribution of sample means is equal to the population mean, and the variance of the sample means, $\sigma_{\bar{x}}^2$, is equal to the population variance divided by the sample size; that is, $\sigma_{\bar{x}}^2 = \sigma^2/n$. Thus, it should not prove surprising to find that the appropriate statistic for testing a hypothesis about a mean when the population variance is *known* is

$$z = \frac{\bar{x} - \mu}{\sigma_{\bar{x}}}$$

where

- $\bar{x}$ is the sample mean
- μ is the population mean
- $\sigma_{\bar{x}}$ is the standard error of the mean, which is equal to $\sigma/\sqrt{n}$, where n is the sample size and σ is the population standard deviation

The z statistic is appropriate if the sample comes from a normal population, or if the variable is not normally distributed in the population but the sample is large enough for the central-limit theorem to be operative. What happens, though, in the more realistic case, in which the population variance is unknown?

When the parent-population variance is unknown, then, of course, the standard error of the mean, $\sigma_{\bar{x}}$, is unknown, since it is equal to $\sigma/\sqrt{n}$. The standard error of mean must then be estimated from the sample data. The estimate is $s_{\bar{x}} = \hat{s}/\sqrt{n}$, where $\hat{s}$ is the unbiased sample standard deviation; that is,

$$\hat{s} = \sqrt{\frac{\sum_{i=1}^{n} (X_i - \bar{x})^2}{n - 1}}.$$

Or, in words,

$$\hat{s} = \sqrt{\frac{\text{the sum of the deviations of the sample observations around the sample mean squared}}{\text{sample size} - 1}}.$$

The test statistic now becomes

$$\frac{\text{sample mean minus hypothesized value of population mean}}{\text{estimated standard error of the mean}}$$

or $(\bar{x} - \mu)/s_{\bar{x}}$, which is t distributed with $n - 1$ degrees of freedom if the conditions for the t test are satisfied.

To use the t statistic appropriately for making inferences about the mean, two basic questions need to be answered:

■ Is the distribution of the variable in the parent population normal, or is it asymmetrical?
■ Is the sample size large or small?

If the variable of interest is normally distributed in the parent population, then the test statistic $(\bar{x} - \mu)/s_{\bar{x}}$ is t distributed with $n - 1$ degrees of freedom. This is true whether the sample size is large or small. For small samples, we actually use t with $n - 1$ degrees of freedom when making an inference. Although t with $n - 1$ degrees of freedom is also the theoretically correct distribution for large n, the distribution approaches and becomes indistinguishable from the normal distribution for samples of 30 or more observations. The test statistic $(\bar{x} - \mu)/s_{\bar{x}}$ is therefore referred to a table of normal deviates when one is making inferences with large samples. Note, though, that this is because the theoretically correct t distribution (since σ is unknown) has become indistinguishable from the normal curve.

What happens if the variable is not normally distributed in the parent population when σ is unknown? If the distribution of the variable is symmetrical or displays only moderate skew, or asymmetry, there is no problem. The t test is quite robust to departures from normality. However, if the variable is highly skewed in the parent population, the appropriate procedure depends upon the sample size. If the sample is small, the t test is inappropriate. Either the variable has to be transformed so that it is normally distributed, or one of the distribution-free statistical tests must be used. If the sample is large, the normal curve could be used for making the inference, provided the following two assumptions are satisfied:

1. The sample size is large enough so that the sample mean, $\bar{x}$, is normally distributed because of the operation of the central-limit theorem. The greater the degree of asymmetry in the distribution of the variable, the larger the size of the sample that is needed to satisfy this assumption.
2. The sample standard deviation, $\hat{s}$, is a close estimate of the parent-population standard deviation, σ. The higher the degree of variability is in the parent population, the larger the size of the sample needed to justify this assumption.

Research Window 20.1 summarizes the situation for making inferences about a mean for known and unknown parent-population standard deviation, σ, and normally distributed and asymmetrical parent-population distributions.

Research Window 20.1
Testing Hypotheses about a Single Mean

	σ **Known**	σ **Unknown**
Distribution of variable in parent population is normal or symmetrical.	Small n: Use $z = \dfrac{\bar{x} - \mu}{\sigma_{\bar{x}}}$.	Small n: Use $$t = \frac{\bar{x} - \mu}{s_{\bar{x}}}$$ where $$s_{\bar{x}} = \hat{s}/\sqrt{n}$$ and $$\hat{s} = \sqrt{\frac{\sum_{i=1}^{n}(X_i - \bar{x})^2}{n - 1}}$$ and refer to t table for $n - 1$ degrees of freedom.
	Large n: Use $z = \dfrac{\bar{x} - \mu}{\sigma_{\bar{x}}}$.	Large n: Since the t distribution approaches the normal as n increases, use $$z = \frac{\bar{x} - \mu}{s_{\bar{x}}}$$ for $n > 30$.
Distribution of variable in parent population is asymmetrical.	Small n: There is no theory to support the parametric test. Either one must transform the variate so that it is normally distributed and then use the z test, or one must use a distribution-free statistical test.	Small n: There is no theory to support the parametric test. Either one must transform the variate so that it is normally distributed and then use the t test, or one must use a distribution-free statistical test.
	Large n: If the sample is large enough so that the central-limit theorem is operative, use $$z = \frac{\bar{x} - \mu}{\sigma_{\bar{x}}}.$$	Large n: If sample is large enough so that (1) the central-limit theorem is operative and (2) $\hat{s}$ is a close estimate of σ, use $$z = \frac{\bar{x} - \mu}{s_{\bar{x}}}.$$

To illustrate the application of the t test, consider a supermarket chain that is investigating the desirability of adding a new product to the shelves of its associated stores. Since many products must compete for limited shelf space, the store has determined that it must sell 100 units per week in each store in order for the item to be sufficiently profitable to warrant handling it. Suppose that the research department decides to investigate the item's turnover by putting it in a random

Table 20.2   ***Store Sales of Trial Product per Week***

Store i	Sales X_i	Store i	Sales X_i
1	86	6	93
2	97	7	132
3	114	8	116
4	108	9	105
5	123	10	120

sample of ten stores for a limited period of time. Suppose further that the average sales per store per week were as shown in Table 20.2.

Since the variance of sales per store is unknown and has to be estimated, the *t* test is the correct parametric test if the distribution of sales is normal. The normality assumption seems reasonable and could be checked using one of the goodness-of-fit tests. The little sales evidence available does not indicate any real asymmetry, so let us assume that the normality assumption is satisfied.

A one-tailed test is appropriate, since it is only when the sales per store per week reach at least 100 units that the product will be introduced on a national scale. The null and alternate hypotheses are

$$H_0: \mu \leq 100$$
$$H_a: \mu > 100$$

and suppose the significance level is to be $\alpha = 0.05$. From the data in Table 20.2,

$$\text{sample mean} = \frac{\text{sum of observations}}{\text{sample size}}$$

or

$$\bar{x} = \frac{\sum_{i=1}^{n} X_i}{n} = 109.4$$

and

$$\text{sample standard} \atop \text{deviation} = \sqrt{\frac{\text{square root of sum of deviations around sample mean squared}}{\text{sample size} - 1}}$$

or

$$\hat{s} = \sqrt{\frac{\sum_{i=1}^{n} (X_i - \bar{x})^2}{(n - 1)}} = 14.40$$

and therefore the estimated standard error of the mean is $s_x = \hat{s}/\sqrt{n} = 4.55$.

Calculations yield

$$t = \frac{\bar{x} - \mu}{s_{\bar{x}}} = \frac{109.4 - 100}{4.55} = 2.07.$$

Critical t as read from the t table with $v = n - 1 = 9$ degrees of freedom is 1.833 ($p = .95$). (See Table 3 in the appendix at the end of the book.) It is unlikely that the calculated value would have occurred by chance if the sales per store in the population were indeed less than or equal to 100 units per week.

Some insight into the sales per store per week that might be expected if the product were introduced on a national scale can be obtained by calculating the confidence interval. The appropriate formula is

sample mean $\pm$ t (estimated standard error of the mean)

or

$$\bar{x} \pm ts_{\bar{x}}.$$

For a 95-percent confidence interval and 9 degrees of freedom, $t = 1.833$, as we have already seen. The 95-percent confidence interval is thus $109.4 \pm (1.833)(4.55)$, or 109.4 ± 8.3, or, alternatively, $101.1 \le \mu \le 117.7$.

Suppose the product is placed in fifty stores and that the sample mean and sample standard deviation are the same, that is, $\bar{x} = 109.4$, $\hat{s} = 14.40$. The test statistic would now be $z = 4.62$, which would be referred to a normal table since the t is indistinguishable from the normal for samples of this size. Calculated z is greater than critical $z = 1.645$ for $\alpha = 0.05$, and, as expected, the same conclusion is warranted. The evidence is stronger now because of the larger sample of stores; the product could be expected to sell at a rate greater than 100 units per store per week.

The impact of the larger sample and the opportunity it provides to use the normal curve can also be seen in the smaller confidence interval the larger sample produces. When the normal curve rather than t distribution applies, the formula $\bar{x} \pm ts_{\bar{x}}$ for calculating the confidence interval changes to $\bar{x} \pm zs_{\bar{x}}$, where the appropriate z value is read from the normal curve table. Since for a 95-percent confidence interval, $z = 1.645$, the interval is $109.4 \pm (1.645)(4.55)$ or 109.4 ± 7.5, which yields the estimate $101.9 \le \mu \le 108.6$, a slightly narrower interval than that produced when 10 stores rather than 50 were in the sample.

Hypotheses about Two Means

Consider testing a hypothesis about the difference between two population means. Assuming the samples are independent, there are three cases to consider.

- The two parent-population variances are known
- The parent-population variances are unknown but can be assumed to be equal
- The parent-population variances are unknown and cannot be assumed to be equal

Variances Are Known

Experience has shown that the population variance usually changes much more slowly than does the population mean. This means that the "old" variance can often be used as the "known" population variance for studies that are being repeated. For example, we may have annually checked the per capita soft drink consumption of people living in different regions of the United States. If we were now to test a hypothesis about the differences in per capita consumption of a new soft drink, we could use the previously determined variances as "known" variances for our new soft drink. Consider that our problem is indeed one of determining whether there are any differences between northerners and southerners in their consumption of a new soft drink our company has recently introduced, called Spark. Further, past data indicate that per capita variation in the consumption of soft drinks is 10 ounces per day for northerners and 14 ounces per day for southerners as measured by the standard deviation, that is, $\sigma_N = 10$ and $\sigma_S = 14$.

The null hypothesis is that there is no difference between northerners and southerners in their consumption of Spark, or that their mean consumption is equal (H_0: $\mu_N = \mu_S$), while the alternate hypothesis is that there is a difference (H_a: $\mu_N \neq \mu_S$). It so happens that if $\bar{x}_N$ and $\bar{x}_S$, the sample means, are normally distributed random variables, then their sum or difference is also normally distributed. The two sample means could be normally distributed because per capita consumption is normally distributed in each region or because the two samples are large enough that the central-limit theorem is operative. In either case, the test statistic is z = the sample mean of the first sample minus the sample mean of the second sample minus the quantity, the hypothesized population mean in the first sample minus the hypothesized population mean in the second sample, all divided by the standard error of the difference in the two means; that is,

$$z = \frac{(\bar{x}_1 - \bar{x}_2) - (\mu_1 - \mu_2)}{\sigma_{\bar{x}_1 - \bar{x}_2}}$$

where

- $\bar{x}_1$ is the sample mean for the first (northern) sample
- $\bar{x}_2$ is the sample mean for the second (southern) sample
- μ_1 and μ_2 are the unknown population means for the northern and southern samples
- $\sigma_{\bar{x}_1 - \bar{x}_2}$ is the standard error of estimate for the difference in means and is equal to the square root of the sum of the two variances in means, specifically,

$$\sqrt{\sigma_{\bar{x}_1}^2 + \sigma_{\bar{x}_2}^2},$$

where, in turn, $\sigma_{\bar{x}_1}^2 = \sigma_1^2/n_1$ and $\sigma_{\bar{x}_2}^2 = \sigma_2^2/n_2$. Now σ_1^2 and σ_2^2 are the "known" population variances of $\sigma_1^2 = (10)^2 = 100$ and $\sigma_2^2 = (14)^2 = 196$.

Suppose that a random sample of 100 people from the North and 100 people from the South indicates that $\bar{x}_1 = 20$ ounces per day and $\bar{x}_2 = 25$ ounces per day. Does this result indicate a real difference in consumption rates? The standard error of estimate is

$$\sigma_{\bar{x}_1 - \bar{x}_2} = \sqrt{\frac{100}{100} + \frac{196}{100}} = \sqrt{2.96} = 1.720$$

and the calculated z is

$$z = \frac{(20 - 25) - (\mu_1 - \mu_2)}{1.720} = \frac{-5 - 0}{1.720} = -2.906.$$

Calculated z exceeds the critical tabled value of -1.96 for $\alpha = 0.05$, and the null hypothesis is rejected. There is a statistically significant difference in the per capita consumption of Spark by northerners and southerners.

The confidence interval for the difference in the two means is given by the formula

$$(\bar{x}_1 - \bar{x}_2) \pm z\sigma_{\bar{x}_1 - \bar{x}_2}.$$

For a 95-percent confidence interval, $z = 1.96$, and the interval estimate of the difference in consumption of Spark by the two groups is $-5 \pm (1.96)(1.720) = -5 \pm 3.4$. Northerners, on average, are estimated to drink 1.6 to 8.4 ounces less of Spark per day than southerners.

Variances Are Unknown

When the two parent-population variances are unknown, the standard error of the test statistic $\sigma_{\bar{x}_1 - \bar{x}_2}$ is also unknown, since $\sigma_{\bar{x}_1}$ and $\sigma_{\bar{x}_2}$ are unknown and have to be estimated. As was true with one sample, the sample standard deviations are used to estimate the population standard deviations;

$$\hat{s}_1^2 = \frac{\displaystyle\sum_{i=1}^{n_1} (X_{i1} - \bar{x}_1)^2}{(n_1 - 1)}$$

is used to estimate σ_1^2 and

$$\hat{s}_2^2 = \frac{\displaystyle\sum_{i=1}^{n_2} (X_{i2} - \bar{x}_2)^2}{(n_2 - 1)}$$

is used to estimate σ_2^2, and the estimates of the standard error of the means become

$$s_{\bar{x}_1} = \hat{s}_1/\sqrt{n_1} \text{ and } s_{\bar{x}_2} = \hat{s}_2/\sqrt{n_2}.$$

The general estimate of the standard error of the difference in two means, $\sigma_{\bar{x}_1 - \bar{x}_2}$, is then

$$s_{\bar{x}_1 - \bar{x}_2} = \sqrt{s_{\bar{x}_1}^2 + s_{\bar{x}_2}^2} = \sqrt{\frac{\hat{s}_1^2}{n_1} + \frac{\hat{s}_2^2}{n_2}}.$$

Although unknown, if the two parent-population variances *can be assumed equal*, a better estimate of the common population variance can be generated by pooling the samples to calculate

$$\hat{s}^2 = \frac{\displaystyle\sum_{i=1}^{n_1} (X_{i1} - \bar{x}_1)^2 + \sum_{i=1}^{n_2} (X_{i2} - \bar{x}_2)^2}{n_1 + n_2 - 2}$$

Table 20.3   ***Store Sales of Floor Wax in Units***

Store	Plastic Container	Metal Container	Store	Plastic Container	Metal Container
1	432	365	6	380	372
2	360	405	7	422	378
3	397	396	8	406	410
4	408	390	9	400	383
5	417	404	10	408	400

where s^2 is the pooled sample variance used to estimate the common population variance. Note that the calculation of the pooled sample variance involves summing the squares of the deviations of the first sample around their mean and adding that total to the sum of the squares of the deviations of the second sample around their mean. In this case the estimated standard error of the test statistic $s_{\bar{x}_1 - \bar{x}_2}$ reduces to

$$s_{\bar{x}_1 - \bar{x}_2} = \sqrt{\frac{s_1^2}{n_1} + \frac{s_2^2}{n_2}} = \sqrt{\frac{s^2}{n_1} + \frac{s^2}{n_2}} = \sqrt{s^2\left(\frac{1}{n_1} + \frac{1}{n_2}\right)}.$$

If the distribution of the variable in each population can further be assumed to be normal, the appropriate test statistic is

$$t = \frac{(\bar{x}_1 - \bar{x}_2) - (\mu_1 - \mu_2)}{s_{\bar{x}_1 - \bar{x}_2}}$$

which is t distributed with $\nu = n_1 + n_2 - 2$ degrees of freedom.

Suppose, for example, that a manufacturer of floor waxes has recently developed a new wax. The company is considering two different containers for the wax, one plastic and one metal. The company decides to make the final determination on the basis of a limited sales test in which the plastic containers are introduced in a random sample of ten stores and the metal containers are introduced in an *independent* random sample of ten stores. The test results are contained in Table 20.3.

$$\text{Calculated } t = \frac{(\bar{x}_1 - \bar{x}_2) - (\mu_1 - \mu_2)}{s_{\bar{x}_1 - \bar{x}_2}} = \frac{(403.0 - 390.3) - (0)}{8.15} = 1.56.$$

This value is referred to a t table for $\nu = n_1 + n_2 - 2 = 18$ degrees of freedom. The test is two-tailed because the null hypothesis is that the preferences for the containers are equal; there was no a priori statement in the alternate hypothesis that one was expected to sell better than the other. For $\alpha = 0.05$, say, and 18 degrees of freedom, critical $t = 2.101$. (One needs to look in the column headed $1 - \alpha = .975$ rather than at .95 in Table 3 in the appendix, since this is a two-tailed test.) Since calculated t is less than critical t, the null hypothesis of no difference would not be rejected. The sample data do not indicate that the plastic container could be expected to outsell the metal container in the total population, even though it did so in this limited experiment.

The example again demonstrates the importance of explicitly determining the statistical significance level by appropriately balancing Type I and Type II errors. Here α error was set arbitrarily equal to 0.05. This led to nonrejection of the null hypothesis and the conclusion that the plastic container would not be expected to outsell the metal container in the total population. Yet if the decision maker had been able to tolerate an α error of 0.20, say, just the opposite conclusion would have been warranted, since interpolating in Table 3 in the appendix for 18 degrees of freedom indicates that the probability of getting calculated $t = 1.56$ under an assumption of no difference in the population means is approximately 15 percent. Assuming the production and other costs were the same, it would clearly seem that the final packaging decision should favor the plastic container. If the production and other costs were not the same, then these costs should be reflected in the statistical decision rule.[5]

The preceding discussion assumes that the samples are independent and that the variable of interest is normally distributed in each of the parent populations. The normality assumption was again necessary to justify the use of the t distribution. What happens, though, if the variable is not normally distributed or the samples are not independent? The lower half of Research Window 20.2 summarizes the approach for non-normal parent distributions for known and unknown σ, while the next section treats the case of **related samples.**

Related samples Samples that are not drawn independently so that the observations are related in some way.

Samples Are Related

A manufacturer of camping equipment wished to study consumer color preferences for a sleeping bag it had recently developed. The bag was of medium quality and price. Traditionally, the high-quality, high-priced sleeping bags used by serious campers and backpackers came in the earth colors, such as green and brown. Previous research indicated that the low-quality, low-priced sleeping bags were frequently purchased for children, to be used at slumber parties. Vivid colors were preferred by this market segment, with bright reds and oranges leading the way. Production capacity restrictions would not allow the company to produce the new sleeping bag in both types of colors. To make the comparison, it selected a random sample of five stores into which it introduced bags of both types. The sales per store are indicated in Table 20.4. Do the data present sufficient evidence to indicate a difference in the average sales for the different colors of bags?

An analysis of the data indicates a difference in the two means of $(\bar{x}_1 - \bar{x}_2) = (50.2 - 45.2) = 5.0$. This is a rather small difference, considering the variability in sales that exists across the five stores. Further, application of the procedures of the last section suggests that the difference is not statistically significant. The pooled estimate of the common variance is

$$\hat{s}^2 = \frac{\sum_{i=1}^{n_1} (X_{i1} - \bar{x}_1)^2 + \sum_{i=1}^{n_2} (X_{i2} - \bar{x}_2)^2}{n_1 + n_2 - 2} = \frac{1512.8 + 1222.8}{8} = 341.95$$

and

$$s_{\bar{x}_1 - \bar{x}_2} = \sqrt{\hat{s}^2\left(\frac{1}{n_1} + \frac{1}{n_2}\right)} = \sqrt{341.95\left(\frac{1}{5} + \frac{1}{5}\right)} = 11.70.$$

Research Window 20.2

Testing Hypotheses about the Differences in Two Means

	σ Known	σ Unknown
Distribution of variables in parent populations is normal or symmetrical.	Small n: Use $z = \dfrac{(\bar{x}_1 - \bar{x}_2) - (\mu_1 - \mu_2)}{\sigma_{\bar{x}_1 - \bar{x}_2}}$ where $\sigma_{\bar{x}_1 - \bar{x}_2} = \sqrt{\dfrac{\sigma_1^2}{n_1} + \dfrac{\sigma_2^2}{n_2}}$. Large n: Use $z = \dfrac{(\bar{x}_1 - \bar{x}_2) - (\mu_1 - \mu_2)}{\sigma_{\bar{x}_1 - \bar{x}_2}}$.	Small n: Can you assume $\sigma_1 = \sigma_2$? 1. Yes: Use pooled variance t test where $t = \dfrac{(\bar{x}_1 - \bar{x}_2) - (\mu_1 - \mu_2)}{s_{\bar{x}_1 - \bar{x}_2}}$ and $s_{\bar{x}_1 - \bar{x}_2} =$ $\sqrt{\dfrac{\sum\limits_{i=1}^{n_1} (X_{i1} - \bar{x}_1)^2 + \sum\limits_{i=1}^{n_2} (X_{i2} - \bar{x}_2)^2}{n_1 + n_2 - 2} \left(\dfrac{1}{n_1} + \dfrac{1}{n_2}\right)}$ with $(n_1 + n_2 - 2)$ degrees of freedom. 2. No: Approach is shrouded in controversy. Several approaches have been suggested. Large n: Use $z = \dfrac{(\bar{x}_1 - \bar{x}_2) - (\mu_1 - \mu_2)}{s_{\bar{x}_1 - \bar{x}_2}}$ and use pooled variance if variances can be assumed equal, and unpooled variance if equality assumption is not warranted.
Distribution of variables in parent populations is asymmetrical.	Small n: There is no theory to support the parametric test. Either one must transform the variates so that they are normally distributed and then use the z test, or one must use a distribution-free statistical test. Large n: If the individual samples are large enough so that the central-limit theorem is operative for them separately, it will also apply to their sum or difference. Use $z = \dfrac{(\bar{x}_1 - \bar{x}_2) - (\mu_1 - \mu_2)}{\sigma_{\bar{x}_1 - \bar{x}_2}}$.	Small n: There is no theory to support the parametric test. Either one must transform the variates so that they are normally distributed and then use the t test, or one must use a distribution-free statistical test. Large n: One must assume that n_1 and n_2 are large enough so that the central-limit theorem applies to the individual sample means. Then it can also be assumed to apply to their sum or difference. Use $z = \dfrac{(\bar{x}_1 - \bar{x}_2) - (\mu_1 - \mu_2)}{s_{\bar{x}_1 - \bar{x}_2}}$ employing a pooled variance if the unknown parent-population variances can be assumed equal, and use an unpooled variance if the equality assumption is not warranted.

Table 20.4   ***Per-Store Sales of Sleeping Bags***

Store	Bright Colors	Earth Colors
1	64	56
2	72	66
3	43	39
4	22	20
5	50	45

Calculated t is thus

$$t = \frac{(\bar{x}_1 - \bar{x}_2) - (\mu_1 - \mu_2)}{s_{\bar{x}_1 - \bar{x}_2}} = \frac{(50.2 - 45.2) - 0}{11.70} = 0.427$$

which is less than the critical value $t = 2.306$ found in the table for $\alpha = 0.05$ and $v = n_1 + n_2 - 2 = 8$ degrees of freedom. The null hypothesis of there being no difference in sales of the two types of colors cannot be rejected on the basis of the sample data.

But wait a minute! A closer look at the data indicates a marked inconsistency with this conclusion. The bright-colored sleeping bags outsold the earth-colored ones in each store, and indeed an analysis of the per-store differences (the procedure is detailed further on) indicates that there is a statistically significant difference in the sales of the two bags. The reason for the seeming difference in conclusions—the difference is not significant versus it is significant—arises because the t test for the difference in two means is *not appropriate* for the problem. The difference-in-means test assumes that the samples are independent. These samples are not. Sales of bright-colored and earth-colored bags are definitely related, since they are both found in the same stores. Note how this example differs from the floor wax example, in which the metal containers were placed in one sample of stores and the plastic containers were located in an independent sample of stores. We need a procedure that takes into account the fact that the observations are related.

The appropriate procedure is the t test for related samples. The procedure is as follows. Define a new variable d_i, where d_i is the difference between sales of the bright-colored bags and the earth-colored bags for the ith store. Thus

$$d_1 = 64 - 56 = 8$$
$$d_2 = 72 - 66 = 6$$
$$d_3 = 43 - 39 = 4$$
$$d_4 = 22 - 20 = 2$$
$$d_5 = 50 - 45 = 5$$

Now calculate the mean difference by averaging the individual store-to-store differences

$$\bar{d} = \frac{\sum\limits_{i=1}^{n} d_i}{n} = \frac{8 + 6 + 4 + 2 + 5}{5} = 5.0$$

and the standard deviation of the difference by determining the sum of the deviations around the mean squared, specifically

$$s_d = \sqrt{\frac{\sum\limits_{i=1}^{n} (d_i - \bar{d})^2}{n - 1}} = \sqrt{\frac{20}{4}} = 2.24.$$

The test statistic is the sample mean difference minus the hypothesized population mean difference, divided by the standard deviation of the difference, divided by the square root of the sample size, or symbolically,

$$t = \frac{\bar{d} - D}{s_d/\sqrt{n}}$$

where D is the difference that is expected under the null hypothesis. Since there is no a priori reason why one color would be expected to sell better than the other, the appropriate null hypothesis is that there is no difference, while the alternate hypothesis is that there is; thus,

$$H_0: D = 0$$
$$H_a: D \neq 0$$

Calculated t is therefore

$$t = \frac{5.0 - 0}{2.24/\sqrt{5}} = 5.0.$$

This value is referred to a t table for ν = (number of differences minus 1) degrees of freedom; in this case, there are five paired differences, and thus $\nu = 4$. Critical t for $\nu = 4$ and $\alpha = 0.05$ is 2.776, and thus the hypothesis of no difference is rejected. The sample evidence indicates that the bright-colored sleeping bags are likely to outsell the earth-colored ones.

An estimate of how greatly the sales per store of the bright-colored sleeping bags would exceed those of the earth-colored bags can be calculated from the confidence interval formula, sample mean difference ± t(standard error of the mean difference), or

$$\bar{d} \pm t(s_d/\sqrt{n}).$$

The 95-percent confidence interval is

$$5.0 \pm (2.776)(2.24/\sqrt{5}) = 5.0 \pm 2.8$$

suggesting that sales of the bright-colored bags would be in the range of 2.2 to 7.8 bags greater per store on average.

Research Window 20.3
Caveat Emptor . . . or, Beware the Butchers!

Calvin Hoddock told this story about the possible pitfalls of marketing research:

"There are two types of research professionals playing with exotic techniques—the butchers and the surgeons (sometimes referred to as the technicians and the magicians). There are a lot more butchers around than surgeons.

"A butcher is statistically oriented—mesmerized with his exotic techniques but divorced from marketing reality. The surgeon is a sound statistician who is marketing-oriented. Surgeons are very hard to find in this business.

"Let me show you what a butcher can do to a research study. A large segmentation study was conducted in a health-oriented category. After substantial number crunching, there was an agonized meeting among the client, the advertising agency, and the supplier. Despite tons of numbers, the study did not discriminate. There were very few useful data in the study, a valid but unpalatable finding, after spending $75,000.

"It was decided to reanalyze the study with another supplier. Fortunately, the new supplier was a surgeon and discovered something that the butcher had overlooked. The homemaker purchased the product and tried to get other family members to use it. She was particularly unsuccessful in getting her husband to use the product. He resisted it for a number of 'macho reasons.'"

"Because the butcher did not understand this basic marketing dynamic, he merged the data of males and females together. The net result was to average everything out, leading to a lack of discrimination."

"Beware of the butchers in the business. We have too many of them. They have a high propensity to produce bad numbers. On the surface, however, their techniques are presumably statistically pristine and powerful."

Source: "Hoddock Cites 'Pitfalls' of Marketing Research," *Marketing News*, 12 (June 1, 1979), p. 1.

Hypotheses about Two Proportions

The appendix to Chapter 19 reviewed the essential nature of hypothesis testing, employing as an example the testing of a hypothesis about a single population proportion. In this section, we want to illustrate the procedure for testing for the difference between two population proportions.[6]

The test for the difference between two population proportions is basically a large sample problem. The samples from each population must be large enough so that the normal approximation to the exact binomial distribution of sample proportions can be used. As a practical matter, this means that np and nq should be greater than 10 for each sample, where p is the proportion of "successes" and q is the proportion of "failures" in the sample and n is the sample size.

To illustrate, suppose a cosmetics manufacturer is interested in comparing male college students and male nonstudents in terms of their use of hair spray. Suppose random samples of 100 male students and 100 male nonstudents in Austin, Texas, are selected and their use of hair spray in the last three months is determined. Suppose further that 30 of these students and 20 of these nonstudents have used hair spray within this period. Does this evidence indicate that a significantly higher percentage of male college students than male nonstudents use hair spray?

Since we are interested in determining whether the two parent-population proportions are different, the null hypothesis is that they are the same, that is,

$$H_0: \pi_1 = \pi_2$$
$$H_a: \pi_1 \neq \pi_2$$

where Population 1 is the population of male college students and Population 2 is the population of male nonstudents. The sample proportions are $p_1 = 0.30$ and $p_2 = 0.20$ and therefore $n_1 p_1 = 30$, $n_1 q_1 = 70$, $n_2 p_2 = 20$, $n_2 q_2 = 80$, and the normal approximation to the binomial distribution can be used. The test statistic is $z =$ first sample proportion minus second sample proportion minus the quantity, hypothesized proportion for the first population minus hypothesized proportion for the second population, divided by the standard error of the difference in the two sample proportions, or

$$z = \frac{(p_1 - p_2) - (\pi_1 - \pi_2)}{\sigma_{p_1 - p_2}}$$

where $\sigma_{p_1 - p_2}$ is the standard error of the difference in the two sample proportions. The one question that still remains in the calculation of z is, what does $\sigma_{p_1 - p_2}$ equal?

A general statistical result that is useful for understanding the calculation of $\sigma_{p_1 - p_2}$ is that *the variance of the sum or difference of two independent random variables is equal to the sum of the individual variances.* For a single proportion, the variance is $\pi(1 - \pi)/n$, and thus the variance of the difference is

$$\sigma_{p_1 - p_2}^2 = \sigma_{p_1}^2 + \sigma_{p_2}^2 = \frac{\pi_1(1 - \pi_1)}{n_1} + \frac{\pi_2(1 - \pi_2)}{n_2}.$$

Note that the variance of the difference is given in terms of the two unknown population proportions, π_1 and π_2. Although unknown, the two population proportions have been assumed equal, and thus we have a "natural" case of a *pooled variance* estimate; $s_{p_1 - p_2}^2$ is logically used to estimate $\sigma_{p_1 - p_2}^2$, where

$$s_{p_1 - p_2}^2 = pq\left(\frac{1}{n_1} + \frac{1}{n_2}\right)$$

and

$$p = \frac{\text{total number of successes in the two samples}}{\text{total number of observations in the two samples}}$$

$$q = 1 - p.$$

For the example,

$$p = \frac{30 + 20}{100 + 100} = \frac{50}{200} = 0.25,$$

$$s_{p_1 - p_2}^2 = (0.25)(0.75)\left(\frac{1}{100} + \frac{1}{100}\right) = 0.00375,$$

and

$$s_{p_1 - p_2} = 0.061.$$

Determining the proportion of people who like and who do not like a new product is a common problem faced by marketing researchers.

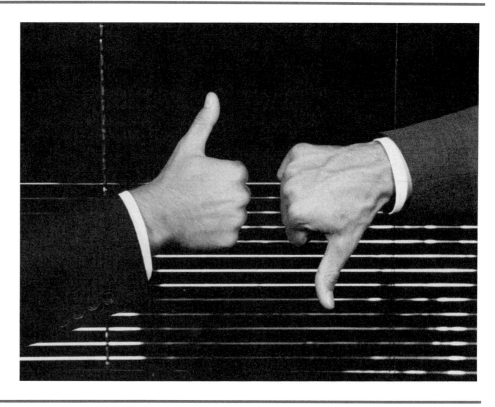

Source: Alan Tao/Photographer. Reprinted with permission from *Entrepreneur* Magazine, March 1991.

Calculated z is found as follows:

$$z = \frac{(0.30 - 0.20) - (0)}{0.061} = \frac{0.10}{0.061} = 1.64$$

while critical $z = 1.96$ for $\alpha = 0.05$. The sample evidence does not indicate that there is a difference in the proportion of male college students and male nonstudents using hair spray.

The 95-percent confidence interval is calculated by the formula, (first sample proportion − second sample proportion) ± z(estimated standard error of the difference in the two proportions), or $(p_1 - p_2) \pm z s_{p_1 - p_2}$, which is $(.30 - .20) \pm 1.96(0.061) = .10 \pm .12$, and which yields a similar conclusion. The interval includes zero, suggesting there is no difference in the proportions using hair spray in the two groups.

Ethical Dilemma 20.2

A field experiment was conducted to determine the most effective advertising appeal for an immunization program for a serious flu epidemic, one in which people had a chance of dying if they contracted the flu. The control communities received no appeal at all, whereas the experimental communities received varying appeals in different strengths. An analysis of the differences in the proportion of people with respiratory problems getting immunization shots clearly indicated the level of advertising that would be most cost effective for a national campaign.

- Is it ethical to withhold benefits (i.e., knowledge of an immunization program) from participants in the control group?
- What participant rights are being violated?
- How can this research be justified? Do the long-term benefits of the research outweigh the costs?

Back to the Case

"I know you didn't want to wait for a written report," said Angie Karlin, making herself comfortable in Chuck Zellmer's office, "So even though I've just finished analyzing the data, I'd be glad to fill you in on our findings so far."

"Wonderful," replied Zellmer. "What did you find?"

"Well, as you know, we mailed our questionnaire to 225 randomly chosen individuals from the mailing list Sid Green gave us. To encourage response, we offered these people a five-dollar coupon toward their next catalog purchase. We received 124 usable surveys, for a 55-percent response rate. To conduct the analysis, we used a program called SPSS, which is short for—"

"Statistical Package for the Social Sciences. Sure, I know the package," said Zellmer.

"Take a look at this," said Karlin, handing Zellmer a data sheet. "This is a table of two variables: the willingness of individuals on the Omni mailing list to purchase from the catalog, and whether or not those same individuals ever purchased from the catalog in the past. Willingness to buy through the Omni catalog is the dependent variable we are interested in explaining." (See Table 1.)

"Look at the column percentages," Karlin instructed. "They suggest that the 'most willing' group of purchasers among the catalog recipients are those who ordered from Omni within the last year. Over 75 percent of these people (40.5 plus 37.5 percent) are somewhat willing to order from Omni again. At the same time, almost 25 percent of those who bought within the last year are not willing to place another order.

"Now, take a look at the figure given where it says 'raw chi-square.' Basically, that figure measures whether the results of our analysis are statistically significant or just a matter of chance. In this case, the value is such that we can say with some certainty that the two variables we measured are indeed related. That is, a customer's willingness to purchase through the Omni catalog appears to be influenced by whether or not he or she has purchased from it before."

"That may be true," replied Zellmer, "but telling me that people who bought once from the Omni catalog are somewhat willing to do it again doesn't give me a tremendous amount of insight into how to revitalize my flat catalog sales."

"Wait, there's more," explained Karlin. "There's a lot of valuable information hidden in these questionnaires. For example, take a look at Question 11. We asked people how confident they felt purchasing various types of software by mail. Now the beauty of this is that we generated an index called CATCON— short for 'catalog confidence'— which is designed to measure the amount of confidence people have when purchasing products from a catalog. The CATCON index in this case is what you would get if you added up the scores assigned to the response categories regarding how confident subjects were in buying each type of software by mail. The scores by question ranged from 1 (not at all confident) to 5 (very confident). Look at this table," Karlin said, handing Zellmer a small chart. (See Table 2.)

"I assume you're going to tell me what this all means," Zellmer replied good-naturedly.

"Well, the really interesting thing we found is that the score differs based on the customer's sex. The table shows that the mean score for men is higher than it is for women. Since our sample was fairly small, you may well ask whether that difference is statistically significant," Karlin said.

Table 1   ***Cross Tabulation of Willingness to Purchase from Omni's Catalog (V3) with Whether Respondent Has Purchased from It Before (V4)***

Count Row Percent Column Percent Total Percent		V4			
		Never Ordered 1	Ordered before but Not within Past Year 2	Ordered within Past Year 3	Row Total
V3					
Unwilling	1	20 40.0 46.5 16.1	20 40.0 51.3 16.1	10 20.0 23.8 8.1	50 40.3
Somewhat Willing	2	7 20.0 16.3 5.6	11 31.4 28.2 8.9	17 48.6 40.5 13.7	35 28.2
Very Willing	3	16 41.0 37.2 12.9	8 20.5 20.5 6.5	15 38.5 35.7 12.1	39 31.5
Column Total		43 34.7	39 31.5	42 33.9	124 100.0

Raw chi-square = 10.997 with 4 degrees of freedom; significance = 0.027

Table 2   ***Difference in Means for CATCON Index between Males and Females***

Variable/Group	Number of Cases	Mean	Standard Deviation	Standard Error	Pooled Variance Estimate			Separate Variance Estimate		
					t Value	Degrees of Freedom	Two-Tail Probability	t Value	Degrees of Freedom	Two-Tail Probability
CATCON										
1. Males	65	21.462	2.001	.248	33.87	121	.000	33.87	119.42	.000
2. Females	58	9.224	2.000	.263						

"Sure," answered Zellmer. "The question was right on the tip of my tongue."

"It is significant," replied Karlin. "Just look at the value of t."

The CATCON index is an example of a hypothesis about two means, since its goal was to assess whether there was a difference in the degree of confidence between males and females when buying software from catalogs. A two-tailed test was used, since the alternate hypothesis was that they were unequal but there was no belief beforehand that one sex would be more confident than the other. In this case, the null hypothesis is rejected, since there indeed is a statistically significant difference between men's and women's confidence when buying computer software through catalogs.

Summary

Learning Objective 1: Explain the basic use of a chi-square goodness-of-fit test.

The chi-square goodness-of-fit test is appropriate when a nominally scaled variable falls naturally into two or more categories and the analyst wishes to determine whether the observed number of cases in each cell corresponds to the expected number.

Learning Objective 2: Discuss the similarities and differences between the chi-square goodness-of-fit test and the Kolmogorov-Smirnov test.

The Kolmogorov-Smirnov test is similar to the chi-square goodness-of-fit test in that it uses a comparison between observed and expected frequencies to determine whether observed results are in accord with a stated null hypothesis. But the Kolmogorov-Smirnov test takes advantage of the ordinal nature of the data.

Learning Objective 3: Specify which test is appropriate if one is testing a hypothesis about a single mean, given that the variance is known. Which is appropriate if the variance is unknown?

In testing a hypothesis about a single mean, the z test is appropriate if the variance is known, while the t test applies if the variance is unknown.

Learning Objective 4: Identify the tests that are appropriate if the analysis involves two means from independent samples.

In an analysis that involves two means from independent samples, the z test is used if the variances are known. If the variances are unknown but assumed equal, a t test using a pooled sample variance applies.

Learning Objective 5: Specify the appropriate test if the analysis involves the difference between two parent-population proportions.

The test of the equality of proportions from two independent samples involves a "natural" pooling of the sample variances. The z test applies.

Discussion Questions, Problems, and Projects

1. A large publishing house recently conducted a survey to assess the reading habits of senior citizens. The company published four magazines specifically tailored to suit the needs of senior citizens. Management hypothesized that there were no differences in the preferences for the magazines. A sample of 1,600 senior citizens interviewed in the city of Albuquerque, New Mexico, indicated the following preferences for the four magazines:

Publication	Frequency of Preference
1. *Golden Years*	350
2. *Maturation*	500
3. *High Serenity*	450
4. *Time for Living*	300
Total	1,600

Management needs your expertise to determine whether there are differences in senior citizens' preferences for the magazines.
(a) State the null and alternate hypotheses.
(b) How many degrees of freedom are there?
(c) What is the chi-square critical table value at the 5-percent significance level?

(d) What is the calculated χ^2 value? Show all your calculations.

(e) Should the null hypothesis be rejected or not? Explain.

2. Silken-Shine Company is a medium-size manufacturer of shampoo. During the past years the company has increased the number of product variations of Silken-Shine shampoo from three to five to increase its market share. Management conducted a survey to compare sales of Silken-Shine shampoo with sales of Rapunzel and So-Soft, its two major competitors. A sample of 1,800 housewives indicated the following frequencies with respect to most recent shampoo purchased:

Shampoo	Number Buying
1. Silken-Shine	425
2. Rapunzel	1,175
3. So-Soft	200
Total	1,800

Experience had indicated that three times as many households preferred Rapunzel to Silken-Shine and that, in turn, twice as many households preferred Silken-Shine to So-Soft. Management wants to determine if the historic tendency still holds, given that Silken-Shine Company has increased the range of shampoos available.

(a) State the null and alternate hypotheses.

(b) How many degrees of freedom are there?

(c) What is the chi-square critical table value at the 5-percent significance level?

(d) What is the calculated χ^2 value? Show all your calculations.

(e) Should the null hypothesis be rejected or not? Explain.

3. A manufacturer of music cassettes wants to test four different cassettes varying in tape length: 30 minutes, 60 minutes, 90 minutes, and 120 minutes. The company has hired you to determine whether customers show any distinct preference toward either extreme. If there is a preference toward any extreme, the company will manufacture only cassettes of the preferred length; otherwise, the company is planning to market cassettes of all four lengths. A sample of 1,000 customers indicated the following preferences:

Tape Length	Frequency of Preference
30 minutes	150
60 minutes	250
90 minutes	425
120 minutes	175
Total	1,000

(a) State the null and alternate hypotheses.

(b) Compute Kolmogorov-Smirnov D by completing the following table:

Tape Length	Observed Number	Observed Proportion	Observed Cumulative Proportion	Theoretical Proportion	Theoretical Cumulative Proportion
30 minutes					
60 minutes					
90 minutes					
120 minutes					

(c) Compute the critical value of D at $\alpha = 0.05$. Show your calculations.

(d) Would you reject the null hypothesis? Explain.

(e) What are the implications for management?

(f) Explain why the Kolmogorov-Smirnov test would be used in this situation.

4. Liberty Foods markets vegetables in six different sized cans: A, B, C, D, E, and F. Through the years the company has observed that sales of all its vegetables in the six can sizes are in the proportion 6:4:2:1.5:1.5:1, respectively. In other words, for every 1 case of size F that is sold, 6 cases of size A, 4 of size B, 2 of size C, 1.5 of size D, and 1.5 of size E are also sold.

The marketing manager would like the sales data for a new canned vegetable—pureed carrots—compared with the pattern for the rest of Liberty's product line to see if there is any difference. Based on a representative sample of 600 cases of pureed carrots, he observes that 30 percent were Size A, 20 percent B, 10 percent C, 10 percent D, 15 percent E, and 15 percent F.

(a) The marketing manager has asked you to determine whether the pureed carrots' sales pattern is similar to the pattern for other vegetables by using the chi-square goodness-of-fit test. Show all your calculations clearly.

(b) You are now asked to determine the above with the use of the Kolmogorov-Smirnov test. Show all your calculations clearly.

(c) What can you conclude from the use of the two test statistics? Are your results from the two tests conflicting or similar?

(d) Which test statistic would you prefer? Why?

5. A medium-size manufacturer of paper products was planning to introduce a new line of tissues, hand towels, and toilet paper. However, management had stipulated that the new products should be introduced only if average monthly purchases per household would be $2.50 or more. The product was market tested, and the diaries of the 100 panel households living in the test market area were checked. They indicated that average monthly purchases were $3.10 per household with a standard deviation of $0.50. Management is wondering what decision it should make and has asked for your recommendation.

(a) State the null and alternate hypotheses.

(b) Is the sample size considered large or small?

(c) Which test should be used? Why?

(d) At the 5-percent level of significance, would you reject the null hypothesis? Support your answer with the necessary calculations.

6. The president of a chain of department stores had promised the managers of the various stores a bonus of 8 percent if the average monthly sales per store increased $300,000 or more. A random sample of 12 stores yielded the following sales increases:

Store	Sales	Store	Sales
1	$320,000	7	$380,000
2	$230,000	8	$280,000
3	$400,000	9	$420,000
4	$450,000	10	$360,000
5	$280,000	11	$440,000
6	$320,000	12	$320,000

The president is wondering whether this random sample of stores indicates that the population of stores has reached the goal. (Assume the distribution of the variable in the parent population is normal.)

(a) State the null and alternate hypotheses.

(b) Is the sample size considered small or large?

(c) Which test should be used? Why?

(d) Would you reject the null hypotheses at the 5-percent level of significance? Support your conclusion with the necessary calculations.

7. Joy Forever is the owner of two jewelry stores located in Corpus Christi and San Antonio. Last year the San Antonio store spent a considerable amount on in-store displays as compared with the Corpus Christi store. Forever wants to determine if the in-store displays resulted in increased sales. The average sales for a sample of 100 days for the San Antonio and Corpus Christi stores were $21.8 million and $15.3 million. (Past experience has shown that $\sigma_{SA} = 8$ and $\sigma_{CC} = 9$ where σ_{SA} is the standard deviation in sales for the San Antonio store and σ_{CC} is the standard deviation for the Corpus Christi store.)

(a) State the null and alternate hypotheses.

(b) What test would you use? Why?

(c) What is the calculated value of the test statistic? Show your calculations.

(d) What is the critical tabled value at 5-percent significance level?

(e) Would you reject the null hypotheses? Explain.

(f) What can Forever conclude?

8. Come-and-Go Company, a large travel agency located in Portland, Oregon, wants to study consumer preferences for its packaged tours to the East. For the past five years Come-and-Go has offered two similarly priced packaged tours to the East which differ only in the places included in the tour. A random sample of five months' purchases from the past five years has been selected. The numbers of consumers that purchased the tours during these five months are listed below:

Month	Packaged Tour I	Packaged Tour II
1	90	100
2	70	60
3	120	80
4	110	90
5	60	80

The management of Come-and-Go needs your assistance to determine whether there is a difference in preferences for the two tours.

(a) State the null and alternate hypotheses.

(b) What test would you use? Why?

(c) What is the calculated value of the test statistic? Show your calculations.

(d) What is the critical tabled value at the 5-percent significance level?

(e) Would you reject the null hypothesis? Explain.

(f) What can the management of Come-and-Go Company conclude about preferences for the two tours?

9. Wet Noodle, a manufacturer of fresh refrigerated pasta products, is not happy with sales of its products. Management suspects that sales might improve if the product were displayed in a freestanding refrigerated case next to the dry pasta, rather than in the dairy case as it is now. To test this assumption, the marketing research department has arranged for six stores that currently carry Wet Noodle to allow placement of the freestanding case in addition to the regular display. Packages have been specially bar-coded so sales generated from each display can be tracked.

After a three-week trial period, the following sales figures are assembled:

Store	New Display	Old Display
1	230	195
2	187	185
3	250	220
4	157	130
5	99	80
6	295	245

(a) What is the appropriate test to determine if the two displays differ in effectiveness?
(b) State the null and alternate hypotheses.
(c) What is the value of the test statistic?
(d) If $\alpha = 0.05$, what is your conclusion?

10. The manager of the Budget Department Store recently increased the store's use of in-store promotions in an attempt to increase the proportion of entering customers who made a purchase. The effort was prompted by a study made a year ago that showed 65 percent of a sample of 1,000 parties entering the store made no purchase. A recent sample of 900 parties contained 635 who made no purchases. Management is wondering whether there has been a change in the proportion of entering parties who make a purchase.

(a) State the null and alternate hypotheses.
(b) What is the calculated value? Show your calculations clearly.
(c) Based on your results, would you reject the null hypothesis? Explain.

11. The creative shop at Impact Advertising developed two different approaches, labeled A and B, for a new direct mail solicitation for a major client. In order to test the effectiveness of the different solicitations, the research department was directed to conduct a test mailing. Two independent random samples of size $n = 2,000$ were selected, and after a one-month waiting period, the number of orders received from each sample was tabulated. Approach A resulted in 257 orders, and Approach B generated 230 orders.

(a) What is the appropriate test to determine if Approach A and Approach B differ in effectiveness?
(b) State the null and alternate hypotheses.
(c) What is the value of the test statistic?
(d) If $\alpha = 0.05$, what is your conclusion?

Refer to the NFO Research, Inc. coffee study described on pages 590–592 in Chapter 19 for the next two problems.

12. Compare the overall ratings (from question 2) of Folgers and Yuban. Is there a difference in the ratings for the two brands of coffee ($\alpha = 0.05$)? If so, which brand is rated more highly?

13. Compute a "taste" index score on the following features of question 6 for Maxwell House Regular: rich taste, always fresh, full-bodied taste, smooth taste, not bitter, has no aftertaste. Is there a difference in this overall score for individuals who add nothing to their coffee versus those who do add something ($\alpha = 0.05$)?

Endnotes

1. Paul R. Winn, Ross H. Johnson, *Business Statistics* (New York: Macmillan Publishing Co., Inc., 1978), pp. 274–275.

2. The correct distribution to test the hypothesis is the hypergeometric. The hypergeometric distribution, however, is unwieldy for anything but very small samples. The chi-square distribution approximates the hypergeometric for large sample sizes. For a discussion of this point, as well as the other conditions surrounding a goodness-of-fit test, see Leonard A. Marascuilo and Maryellen McSweeney, *Nonparametric and Distribution Free Methods for the Social Sciences* (Belmont, Calif.: Brooks/Cole, 1977), pp. 243–248.

3. W. G. Cochran, "The χ^2 Test of Goodness of Fit," *Annuals of Mathematical Statistics*, 23 (1952), pp. 315–345.

4. See Marascuilo and McSweeny, *Nonparametric and Distribution Free Methods*, pp. 250–251. See also Jean Dickinson Gibbons, *Nonparametric Statistical Inference*, 2nd ed. (New York: Marcel Dekker, Inc., 1985).

5. The Bayesian posture would be to introduce the plastic container even with the obtained sample results if the opportunity costs associated with each alternative were the same. If they were not the same, then the Bayesian approach would incorporate these costs directly into the decision rule regarding which container should be produced.

6. The tests for population proportions are logically considered with nominal data because they apply in situations in which the variable being studied can be divided into those cases *possessing* the characteristic and those cases lacking it, and the emphasis is on the number or proportion of cases falling into each category. Marketing examples abound: "prefer A" versus "do not prefer A"; "buy" versus "do not buy"; "brand loyal" versus "not brand loyal"; "sales representatives meeting quota" versus "sales representatives not meeting quota." The test for the significance of the difference between two proportions is treated here because the hypothesis is examined using the z test, and the procedure relies on an "automatic pooled sample variance" estimate. It was thought that these notions would be better appreciated after the discussion of the test of means rather than before.

Suggested Additional Readings

Most of the statistical tests discussed in this chapter can be found in any introductory statistics text, and readers are encouraged to refer to the text they used in their introductory statistics course for more details on any of the methods that are discussed.

A p p e n d i x
20A

Analysis of variance (ANOVA) A statistical test employed with interval data to determine if k ($k \geq 2$) samples came from populations with equal means.

Analysis of Variance

In Chapter 20 we used the example of packaging floor wax in plastic and metal containers to examine the statistical test of the difference in two population means. Let us now reconsider the data of Table 20.3 to demonstrate an alternate approach to the problem. Known as the **analysis of variance (ANOVA),** it has the distinct advantage of being applicable when there are more than two means being compared. The basic idea underlying the analysis of variance is that the parent-population variance can be estimated from the sample in several ways, and comparisons among these estimates can tell us a great deal about the population. Recall that the null hypothesis involving the two types of containers was that the two parent-population means were equal; that is, $\mu_1 = \mu_2$. If the null hypothesis is true, then, except for sampling error, the following three estimates of the population variance should be equal:

1. The *total variation*, computed by comparing each of the twenty sales figures with the grand mean.

2. The *between-group variation*, computed by comparing each of the two treatment means with the grand mean.

3. The *within-group variation*, computed by comparing each of the individual sales figures with the mean of its own group.

If, however, the hypothesis is not true, and there is a difference in the means, then the between-group variation should produce a higher estimate than the within-group variation, which considers only the variation within groups and is independent of differences between groups.

These three separate estimates of the population variation are computed in the following way when there are k treatments or groups.

1. Total variation: sum of squares total SS_T, given by the sum of the squared deviations of each observation from the grand mean. Now the grand mean of all n observations turns out to be equal to

$$\frac{432 + \ldots + 408 + 365 + \ldots + 400}{20} = 396.7$$

and the sum of squares total equals

$$SS_T = (432 - 396.7)^2 + \ldots + (408 - 396.7)^2$$
$$+ (365 - 396.7)^2 + \ldots + (400 - 396.7)^2.$$

The difference between *each observation* and the *grand mean* is determined; the differences are squared and then summed.

2.   Between-group variation: sum of squares between groups SS_B. To calculate between-group variation, it is first necessary to calculate the means for each group. The mean sales of the plastic container turn out to be equal to 403.0, and those for the metal container turn out to be equal to 390.3. The sum of squares between groups is thus

$$SS_B = 10(403.0 - 396.7)^2 + 10(390.3 - 396.7)^2.$$

The difference between each *group mean* and the *overall mean* is determined; the difference is squared; each squared difference is weighted by the number of observations making up the group, and the results are summed.

3.   Within-group variation: sum of squares within groups SS_W. The calculation of the sum of squares within groups involves calculating the difference between each observation and the mean of the group to which it belongs, specifically,

$$SS_W = (432 - 403.0)^2 + \ldots + (408 - 403.0)^2$$
$$+ (365 - 390.3)^2 + \ldots + (400 - 390.3)^2.$$

The difference between *each observation* and its *group mean* is determined; the differences are squared and then summed.

Let us take a closer look at the behavior of these three sources of variation. First, SS_T measures the overall variation of the n observations. The more variable the n observations, the larger SS_T becomes. Second, SS_B reflects the total variability of the means. The more nearly alike the k means are, the smaller SS_B becomes. If they differ greatly, SS_B will be large. Third, SS_W measures the amount of variation within each column or treatment. If there is little variation among the observations making up a group, SS_W is small. When there is great variability, SS_W is large.

It can be shown that $SS_T = SS_B + SS_W$ and that each of these sums of squares, when divided by the *appropriate number of degrees of freedom*, generates a mean square that is essentially an unbiased estimate of the population variance.[1] Further, if the null hypothesis of no difference among population means is true, they are all estimates of the same variance and should not differ more than would be expected because of chance. If the variance between groups is significantly greater than the variance within groups, the hypothesis of equality of population means will be rejected.

In other words, we can view the variance within groups as a measure of the amount of variation in sales of containers that may be expected on the basis of chance. It is the *error variance* or *chance variance*. The between-group variance reflects error variance plus any group-to-group differences occasioned by differences in popularity of the two containers. Therefore, if it is found to be significantly larger than the within-group variance, this difference may be attributed to group-to-group variation, and the hypothesis of equality of means is discredited.

But what are these degrees of freedom? The total number of degrees of freedom is equal to $n - 1$, since there is only a single constraint, the grand mean, in the computation of SS_T. For within-group sum of squares, there are n observations and k constraints, one constraint for each treatment mean. Hence, the degrees of freedom for the within group sum of squares equals $n - k$. There are k values, one corresponding to each treatment mean, in the calculation of SS_B, and there is one constraint imposed by the grand mean; hence, the degrees of freedom for the between-group sum of squares is $k - 1$.

The separate estimates of the population variance or the associated mean squares are

$$MS_T = \frac{SS_T}{df_T} = \frac{SS_T}{n - 1}$$

$$MS_B = \frac{SS_B}{df_B} = \frac{SS_B}{k - 1}$$

$$MS_W = \frac{SS_W}{df_W} = \frac{SS_W}{n - k}$$

The mean squares computed from the sample data are merely estimates of the true mean squares. The true mean squares are in turn given by the expected values of the corresponding sample mean squares. Given that the samples are independent, that the population variances are equal, and that the variable is normally distributed in the parent population, it can be shown that these expected values are

$$E(MS_W) = \sigma^2 = \text{error variance or chance variance}$$

and

$$E(MS_B) = \sigma^2 + \text{treatment effect.}$$

The ratio $E(MS)_B/E(MS_W)$ will equal 1 if there is no treatment effect. It will be greater than 1 if there is a difference in the sample means. Since the two expected values are not known, the sample mean squares are used instead to yield the ratio

$$\frac{MS_B}{MS_W} = F$$

which follows the F distribution. The F distribution depends on two degrees of freedom, one corresponding to the mean square in the numerator and one corresponding to the mean square in the denominator. Since MS_B and MS_W are only sample estimates of the true variances, one should not expect the ratio MS_B/MS_W to be exactly 1 when the treatment effect is zero, nor should one immediately conclude that there is a difference among the group means when the ratio is greater than 1. Rather, given a significance level and the respective degrees of freedom for the numerator and denominator, a critical value of F may be read from standard tables. The critical value indicates the magnitude of the ratio that can occur because of random sampling fluctuations, even when there is no difference in the group means, that is, $E(MS_B)/E(MS_W) = 1$. The entire analysis is conveniently handled in an analysis-of-variance table.

Table 20A.1 is the analysis-of-variance table for the plastic and metal container sales data. The calculated F value is referred to an F table for 1 and 18 degrees of freedom (see Table 4 in the appendix at the back of this textbook). Using the same α as before, $\alpha = 0.05$, critical F is found to be 4.41, and again the sample evidence is not sufficient to reject the hypothesis of the equality of the two means. This should not be surprising since it can be shown[2] that when the comparison is between two means (the degrees of freedom in the numerator of the F ratio are then $v_1 = k - 1 = 1$), $F = t^2 = (1.56)^2 = 2.43$. Both tests are identical in this special case, and if one test does not indicate a significant difference between the two means, neither will the other.[3]

Table 20A.1   ***Analysis of Variance of Sales of Plastic versus Metal Containers***

Source of Variation	Sum of Squares	Degrees of Freedom	Mean Square	F Ratio
Between group	806.5	1	806.5	2.43
Within group	5,978.1	18	332.1	
Total	6,784.6	19		

Randomized-Block Design

Imagine what might have happened if, by chance, the stores selected to handle the plastic containers were all substantially larger than those handling the metal containers. Any difference in sales between the two groups could have been because the larger stores routinely have more traffic and hence greater sales.

If a closer analysis of the situation shows that such outside influences may distort the results of an experiment, a **randomized-block design** can be employed. This design involves the grouping of "similar" test units into blocks and the random assignment of treatments to test units in each block. Similarity is determined by matching the test units on the expected extraneous source of variation, for example, store size in the container example. The hope is that the units within each block will be more alike than will units selected completely at random. Since the difference between blocks can be taken into account in the variance analysis for the same number of observations the error mean square should be smaller than it would be if a completely randomized design had been used. The test should therefore be more efficient.

Latin-Square Design

The **Latin-square design** is appropriate when there are two extraneous factors that can cause serious distortion in the results. Suppose a company wanted to test the effectiveness of three different plans for frequency of sales calls by their sales representatives on potential customers. The plans varied with regard to how often the sales rep would be required to call on various sizes of accounts. The manufacturer wanted to know which of the three would produce the most sales.

In order to test the plan, the firm chose a sample of 30 salespeople from among its sales staff of 500. The company was concerned that differences in sales ability might affect the results of the test. Consequently, it decided to match the sales representatives in terms of their ability, employing their past sales as the matching criterion. The company thus formed ten blocks of three relatively equal sales representatives each. The call-frequency plans were then assigned randomly to each of the sales representatives within a block, resulting in a randomized-block design.

Now suppose further that the firm decided to conduct the investigation not only with sales reps of different ability but also among sales representatives having different sizes of territories. Suppose, in fact, that it divided the sales representatives into three classes on the basis of ability—outstanding, good, and average—and three classes on the basis of territory size—large, average, and small. Thus there would be nine different conditions with which to cope. One way of proceeding would be to use randomized blocks and test each of the three call plans under each of the nine conditions. This would require a sample of 27 sales representatives. An alternative approach would be to try each call plan only once with each size of territory and each level of ability. This would require a sample of

Randomized-block design An experimental design in which (1) the test units are divided into blocks, or homogeneous groups, using some external criterion, and (2) the objects in each block are randomly assigned to treatment conditions. The randomized-block design is typically employed when there is one extraneous influence to be explicitly controlled.

Latin-square design An experimental design in which (1) the number of categories for each extraneous variable one wishes to control is equal to the number of treatments, and (2) each treatment is randomly assigned to categories according to a specific pattern. The Latin-square design is appropriate where there are two extraneous factors to be explicitly controlled.

only 9 test units or sales representatives. The primary gain in this case would be administrative control. In other cases, there may be cost advantages associated with the use of fewer test units. The interesting point is that if differences in territory size do indeed have an effect, the Latin-square design with 9 test units could be as efficient as the randomized-block design with many more test units.

The Latin-square design requires that the number of categories for each of the extraneous variables we wish to control be equal to the number of treatments. With three call plans to investigate, it was no accident that the sales representatives were divided into three ability levels and the territories into three size categories. The Latin-square design also requires that the treatments be randomly assigned to the resulting categories. This is typically accomplished by selecting one of the published squares at random and then randomizing the rows, columns, and treatments using this square.[4]

Factorial Designs

So far we have considered designs that involve only one experimental variable, although it may have had multiple levels, for example, three different call plans. It is often desirable to investigate the effects of two or more factors in the same experiment. For instance, it might be desirable to investigate the sales impact of the shape as well as the construction material of containers for floor wax. Suppose that in addition to packaging a new floor wax in metal or plastic containers, two shapes, A and B, were being considered for the containers. Package shape and package type would both be called *factors*. There would be two different levels of each factor, four different treatments in all since they can be used in combination, and a **factorial design** would be used. A factorial design is one in which the effects of two or more independent treatment variables are considered simultaneously.

Factorial design
An experimental design that is used when the effects of two or more variables are being simultaneously studied; each level of each factor is used with each level of each other factor.

There are three very good reasons why one might want to use a factorial design.[5] First, it allows the interaction of the factors to be studied. The plastic container might sell better in Shape A, while the metal container sells better in Shape B. This type of effect can be investigated only if the factors are considered simultaneously. Second, a factorial design allows a saving of time and effort since all the observations are employed to study the effects of each of the factors. Suppose separate experiments were conducted, one to study the effect of container type and another to study the effect of container shape. Then some of the observations would yield information about type and some about shape. By combining the two factors in one experiment, all the observations bear on both factors. "Hence one two-factor experiment is more economical than two one-factor experiments."[6] Third, the conclusions reached have broader application since each factor is studied with varying combinations of the other factors.[7] This result is much more useful than it would be if everything else had been held constant.

The factorial design may be used with any of the single-factor designs previously discussed—completely randomized, randomized-block, and Latin-square. The underlying model changes, as does the analysis of variance table, but the principle remains the same.

Endnotes

1. See Geoffrey Keppel, *Design and Analysis: A Researcher's Handbook*, 2nd ed. (Englewood Cliffs, N.J.: Prentice-Hall, 1982), pp. 24–64, for the derivation.

2. It can be shown mathematically that if a random variable is t distributed with v degrees of freedom, then t^2 is F distributed with $v_1 = 1$, $v_2 = v$ degrees of freedom; that is, if $t \sim t_v$, then $t^2 \sim F_{1,v}$.

3. For an insightful discussion of how one should set up hypotheses for analysis of variance, see Richard K. Burdick, "Statement of Hypotheses in the Analysis of Variance," *Journal of Marketing Research*, 20 (August 1983), pp. 320–324.

4. See R. A. Fisher and F. Yates, *Statistical Tables* (Edinburgh: Oliver and Boyd, 1948), for Latin squares from 4×4 to 12×12.

5. William C. Guenther, *Analysis of Variance* (Englewood Cliffs, N.J.: Prentice-Hall, 1964), pp. 99–100; and John Neter, William Wasserman, and Michael H. Kutner, *Applied Linear Statistical Models*, 2nd ed. (Homewood, Ill.: Richard D. Irwin, 1985), pp. 663–667.

6. Guenther, *Analysis of Variance*, p. 100. For examples of factorial experiments, see J. B. Wilkinson, J. Barry Mason, and Christie H.

Paksoy, "Assessing the Impact of Short-Term Supermarket Strategy Variables," *Journal of Marketing Research*, 19 (February 1982), pp. 72–86; and Susan M. Petroshius and Kent B. Monroe, "Effect of Product-Line Pricing Characteristics on Product Evaluations," *Journal of Consumer Research*, 13 (March 1987), pp. 511–519.

7. One can often use select combinations of factor levels rather than every possible combination, which greatly simplifies the experiment. See Charles W. Holland and David W. Cravens, "Fractional Factorial Experimental Designs in Marketing Research," *Journal of Marketing Research*, 10 (August 1973), pp. 270–276.

21

Data Analysis: Investigating Associations

Learning Objectives

Upon completing this chapter, you should be able to

1. Explain the difference between regression and correlation analysis.

2. List the three assumptions that are made about the error term in the least-squares solution to a regression problem.

3. Discuss what the Gauss-Markov theorem says about the least-squares estimators of a population parameter.

4. Define *standard error of estimate*.

5. Specify the relationship that a correlation coefficient is designed to measure.

6. Discuss the difference between simple regression analysis and multiple-regression analysis.

7. Explain what is meant by multicollinearity in a multiple-regression problem.

8. Describe when a partial-regression coefficient is used and what it measures.

9. Explain the difference between the coefficient of multiple determination and the coefficient of partial determination.

10. Describe how the use of dummy variables and variable transformations expands the scope of the regression model.

Case in Marketing Research

Lovelace Lingerie, Inc., had pioneered the sales of women's upscale lingerie—some called it "boudoir fashion"—by marketing it in tastefully decorated mall boutiques. But while women loved the lace curtains and antiques of the Lovelace retail outlets, most men were afraid to venture inside. That reluctance had given impetus for the company's mail-order catalog, which was geared toward men purchasing gifts.

Christmas catalog sales had been good, but Angela Spaulding, vice-president for Lovelace catalog sales, felt that the company was tapping into only a small segment of a potentially large market. She had hired Michael Wyse's marketing research firm to conduct a study of 400 men who had placed orders from the Christmas catalog. The idea was to find out about these men, in the hopes of finding ways to expand catalog sales.

Now Wyse was on his way to meet with Spaulding to discuss the results of the study. When he located the Lovelace boutique in the Plainview Mall, he understood why most men had second thoughts about venturing inside. The windows were heavily draped with chintz, providing a backdrop for a black lace negligee suspended from a padded satin hanger. Huge arrangements of orchids flanked the display. It wasn't that there was anything racy or offensive about the store; it was just that it was so . . . well, feminine.

But an intrepid researcher to the end, Wyse took a deep breath and entered the world of Lovelace Lingerie. He marched resolutely past racks of silk robes and satin nightgowns and, directed by one of the sales staff, located Spaulding in a surprisingly spacious conference room tucked behind the store. From behind a table stacked with computer printouts and lingerie, Spaulding rose to greet him.

"Michael, so glad you were able to meet me here," she said cheerfully, extending her hand. "We're just so busy putting together the merchandise for our spring catalog. What do you think of our store?"

"It's a lot different from my favorite place to shop," he replied apologetically.

"Where's that?" asked Spaulding.

"The hardware store around the corner from where I live," replied Wyse.

Spaulding laughed. "So tell me what you found in your study. We're having a big strategy meeting next week, and I'd really like to have a concrete plan for how best to expand our catalog sales."

"I know you're no slouch when it comes to numbers, Angela," said Wyse, "so I'd like to take you through some of the underlying statistical analyses, as well as the results of the study. I know you'll find the results interesting, but I think you'll have more confidence in our findings if you have an understanding on how we came up with them."

"I'm all ears," said Spaulding.

"In the survey we sent to our sample of 400 male catalog customers, Questions 7 through 11 were designed to get at how these men felt about making purchases from the Lovelace catalog. To determine that factor, we came up with an "Attitude toward Lovelace" index, called ATTLOVE, using responses to Questions 7 through 11." (See Table 1.)

Table 1   *Questions 7–11 from Lovelace Lingerie Questionnaire*

	Strongly Disagree	Disagree	Neither Agree nor Disagree	Agree	Strongly Agree
7. In general, Lovelace Lingerie sells a high-quality line of merchandise.	_____	_____	_____	_____	_____
8. Lovelace Lingerie carries a complete line of lingerie.	_____	_____	_____	_____	_____
9. Lovelace Lingerie has a very high-quality catalog.	_____	_____	_____	_____	_____
10. The Lovelace Lingerie catalog displays the merchandise attractively.	_____	_____	_____	_____	_____
11. It should be easy to find a nice gift in the Lovelace Lingerie catalog.	_____	_____	_____	_____	_____

Table 2   **Simple Regression Analysis of ATTLOVE versus Occupation**

Dependent variable . . . ATTLOVE
Variable(s) entered on step number 1: *V*41

		Analysis of Variance	DF	Sum of Squares	Mean Square	F
Multiple *R*	.869	Regression	1	4071.174	4071.174	374.512
R-squared	.754	Residual	122	1326.213	10.871	
Adjusted *R*-squared	.752					
Standard error	3.297					

Variables in the Equation

Variable	B	Beta	Standard Error β	F
*V*41	11.534	.869	.596	374.512
(Constant)	9.727			

"ATTLOVE was formed in such a way that higher scores implied more favorable attitudes about buying from Lovelace. The responses to the five questions were summed to produce the ATTLOVE score for each subject," Wyse said.

"We also wanted to know if that attitude was related to the respondent's demographic characteristics. This second table that we compiled shows whether the ATTLOVE index varies as a function of a person's occupation," he said, laying the relevant table in front of Spaulding.

"We coded blue-collar workers as 0 and white-collar workers as 1.

Using simple regression analysis, we determined that the results are both statistically and practically significant. You see where it says the adjusted *R*-squared value is .752?" Wyse asked, pointing to the third line in Table 2.

Spaulding nodded her head.

"That means that approximately 75 percent of the variation in the ATTLOVE index can be accounted for or explained by the variation in occupation. There is a positive relationship between the two variables (*B* equals 11.534)," Wyse said.

"So white-collar workers have a much more favorable attitude toward

Lovelace than blue-collar workers do," mused Spaulding. "Very interesting. Very interesting indeed."

Discussion Issues

1. In Wyse's study, regression analysis was used to study the relationship between two variables. What were they? Which was the dependent variable? Which was the independent?

2. While the regression analysis demonstrated a relationship between the two variables, did it demonstrate which one caused the other?

In the discussion of data analysis so far, we have been primarily concerned with testing for the significance of *differences* obtained under various research conditions, whether between a sample result and an assumed population condition or between two or more sample results. Quite often, however, the researcher must determine whether there is any *association* between two or more variables and, if so, the strength and functional form of the relationship.

Typically, we try to predict the value of one variable (for example, consumption of a specific product by a family) on the basis of one or more other variables (for example, income and number of family members). The variable being predicted is called the *dependent* or, more aptly, *criterion, variable*. The variables that form the basis of the prediction are called the *independent*, or *predictor, variables*.

Simple Regression and Correlation Analysis

Correlation analysis
A statistical technique used to measure the closeness of the linear relationship between two or more intervally scaled variables.

Regression analysis
A statistical technique used to derive an equation that relates a single criterion variable to one or more predictor variables; when there is one predictor variable, it is simple regression analysis, while it is multiple-regression analysis when there are two or more predictor variables.

Regression analysis and *correlation analysis* are widely used among marketing researchers for studying the relationship between two or more variables. Although the two terms are often used interchangeably, there is a difference in purpose. **Correlation analysis** measures the *closeness* of the relationship between two or more variables. The technique considers the joint variation of two measures, neither of which is restricted by the experimenter. **Regression analysis,** on the other hand, is used to derive an *equation* that relates the criterion variable to one or more predictor variables. It considers the frequency distribution of the criterion variable when one or more predictor variables are held fixed at various levels.[1]

It is perfectly legitimate to measure the closeness of the relationship between variables without deriving an estimating equation. Similarly, one can perform a regression analysis without investigating the closeness of the relationship between the variables. But, since it is common to do both, the body of techniques, rather than one or the other, is usually referred to as either regression or correlation analysis.

To save you endless frustration in trying to determine how the term *regression analysis* fits with the technique about to be discussed, we should pause to mention that, like many terms in our language, the name bears no useful relationship to the technique, although we will not delve into its semantic history here.[2]

As regards correlation analysis, we should also comment on the distinction between correlation and causation. The use of the terms *dependent* (criterion) and *independent* (predictor) *variables* to describe the measures in correlation analysis stems from the mathematical functional relationship between the variates and is in no way related to dependence of one variable on another in a causal sense. For example, while the techniques may show some correlation between high income and a tendency to take winter vacations to the Caribbean, it would be a mistake to assume that having a high income *causes* a person to head south when the thermometer plummets.

There is nothing in correlation analysis, or any other mathematical procedure, that can be used to establish causality. All these procedures can do is measure the nature and degree of *association* or *covariation* between variables. Statements of causality must spring from underlying knowledge and theories about the phenomena under investigation. They in no way spring from the mathematics.[3] In Research Window 21.1, the former director of marketing research at General Mills urges researchers to look beyond the welter of data they devote their energies to collecting and consider the theory that directs marketing inquiry. Without the theory, the mathematics are useless.

The subject of regression and correlation analysis is best discussed through example. Consider, therefore, the national manufacturer of a ballpoint pen, Click,

Research Window 21.1
The Importance of Theory in Marketing Research

If marketing researchers want to acquire true marketing "knowledge" they should devote more time and effort to developing and validating marketing theories, according to Lawrence D. Gibson, former director of marketing research, General Mills, Inc., Minneapolis.

"There's a funny notion around that theories are vague, ephemeral, and useless, and data are nice, hard, real things. And that somehow knowledge is associated with facts and data. This is nonsense. Knowledge is an interrelated set of validated theories and established facts, not just facts. In marketing, we are profoundly ignorant of what we're doing because we're woefully short on theory while we're drowning in data."

Deploring the lack of validated marketing theories and the overabundance of marketing "facts," Gibson quoted the scientist, R. B. Braithwaite: "The world is not made up of empirical facts with the addition of the laws of nature. What we call the laws of nature are simply theories, the conceptual devices by which we organize our empirical knowledge and predict the future."

And he quoted Albert Einstein: "The grand aim of all science is to cover the maximum number of empirical facts, by logical deduction, into the smallest number of axioms, axioms which represent that remainder which is not comprehended."

In other words, Gibson said, "the axioms and theories are not our knowledge, they are our ignorance. They're part of the problem we assume away." A theory, he said, is how "scientists choose to organize their knowledge and perceptions of the world. Theories are pretty well laid out, simplistic, general, have predicted usefulness, and fit the facts.

"Theory is basic to what data you choose to collect," he said. "You can't observe all the veins of all the leaves of all the branches of all the trees of all the forests in the world. You've got to choose what facts you choose to observe, and you're going to be guided in some sense by some kind of theory. And when you turn around to use the data, you're also going to be guided by theory. It will have a profound effect on what you do."

This shows up in the way researchers go about analyzing different kinds of data. For example, when working with observational data, people simply don't realize the weak theoretical ground on which they stand. They wander around the data, merrily trying to find out what makes sense.

"Perhaps you've seen some fairly typical versions of this. The creative analyst looks at the data and the survey and they don't make sense. 'Make sense' means the findings are congenial to his prior judgment. But the world isn't working the way he thought it was supposed to be working.

"So he cross-tabs by big cities versus little cities. Still doesn't make sense. But he is very creative, and observes there are more outer-directed people in big cities than in little cities, so he now cross-tabs by inner-directed versus outer-directed by city size, and—lo and behold—he finds out he was right all along!

"Now, obviously, as long as you keep analyzing when you don't like what you see, and stop analyzing when you do like what you see, the world always will look to you the way it's supposed to look. You'll never learn anything."

Source: "Marketing Research Needs Validated Theories," *Marketing News,* 17 (January 21, 1983), p. 14. Reprinted with permission from *Marketing News* published by the American Marketing Association, Chicago, IL 60606.

which is interested in investigating the effectiveness of the firm's marketing efforts. The company uses regional wholesalers to distribute Click and supplements their efforts with company sales representatives and spot television advertising. The company plans to use annual territory sales as its measure of effectiveness. These data and information on the number of sales representatives serving a territory are readily available in company records. The other characteristics to which the manufacturer seeks to relate sales—television spot advertising and wholesaler efficiency—are more difficult to determine. To obtain information on television spot advertising in a

Table 21.1   **Territory Data for Click Ballpoint Pens**

Territory	Sales (in Thousands) Y	Advertising (TV Spots per Month) X_1	Number of Sales Representatives X_2	Wholesaler Efficiency Index X_3
005	260.3	5	3	4
019	286.1	7	5	2
033	279.4	6	3	3
039	410.8	9	4	4
061	438.2	12	6	1
082	315.3	8	3	4
091	565.1	11	7	3
101	570.0	16	8	2
115	426.1	13	4	3
118	315.0	7	3	4
133	403.6	10	6	1
149	220.5	4	4	1
162	343.6	9	4	3
164	644.6	17	8	4
178	520.4	19	7	2
187	329.5	9	3	2
189	426.0	11	6	4
205	343.2	8	3	3
222	450.4	13	5	4
237	421.8	14	5	2
242	245.6	7	4	4
251	503.3	16	6	3
260	375.7	9	5	3
266	265.5	5	3	3
279	620.6	18	6	4
298	450.5	18	5	3
306	270.1	5	3	2
332	368.0	7	6	2
347	556.1	12	7	1
358	570.0	13	6	4
362	318.5	8	4	3
370	260.2	6	3	2
391	667.0	16	8	2
408	618.3	19	8	2
412	525.3	17	7	4
430	332.2	10	4	3
442	393.2	12	5	3
467	283.5	8	3	3
471	376.2	10	5	4
488	481.8	12	5	2

territory, researchers must analyze advertising schedules and study area coverage by channel to determine what areas each broadcast might reach. Wholesaler efficiency requires rating the wholesalers on a number of criteria and aggregating the ratings into an overall measure of wholesaler efficiency, where 4 is outstanding, 3 is good, 2 is average, and 1 is poor. Because of the time and expense required to generate these advertising and distribution characteristics, the company has decided to analyze only a sample of sales territories. The data for a simple random sample of 40 territories are contained in Table 21.1.

The effect of each of the marketing mix variables on sales can be investigated in several ways. One very obvious way is to simply plot sales as a function of each of the variables. Figure 21.1 contains these plots, which are called *scatter diagrams*. Panel A suggests that sales increase as the number of television spots per month increases. Panel B suggests that sales increase as the number of sales representatives serving the territory increases. Finally, Panel C suggests that there is little relationship between sales in a territory and the efficiency of the wholesaler serving the territory.

A close look at Panels A and B also suggests that it would be possible to summarize the relationship between sales and each of the predictor variables by drawing a straight line through the data points. One way to generate the relationship between sales and either television spots or number of sales representatives would be to "eyeball" it; that is, one could visually draw a straight line through the points in the graphs. Such a line would represent the line of "average" relationship. It would indicate the average value of the criterion variable, sales, for given values of either of the predictor variables, television spots or number of sales representatives. One could then enter the graph with, say, the number of television spots in a territory, and could read off the average level of sales expected in the territory. The difficulty with the graphic approach is that two analysts might generate different lines to describe the relationship. This simply raises the question of which line is more correct or fits the data better.

An alternative approach is to mathematically fit a line to the data. The general equation of a straight line is $Y = \alpha + \beta X$, where α is the Y intercept and β is the slope coefficient. In the case of sales Y and television spots X_1, the equation could be written as $Y = \alpha_1 + \beta_1 X_1$, while for the relationship between sales Y and number of sales representatives X_2, it could be written as $Y = \alpha_2 + \beta_2 X_2$, where the subscripts indicate the predictor variable being considered. As written, each of these models is a *deterministic model*. When a value of the predictor variable is substituted in the equation with specified α and β, a unique value for Y is determined, and no allowance is made for error.

When investigating social phenomena, there is rarely, if ever, zero error. Thus in place of the deterministic model, we might substitute a *probabilistic model* and make some assumptions about the error. For example, let us work with the relationship between sales and the number of television spots and consider the model

$$Y_i = \alpha_1 + \beta_1 X_{i1} + \epsilon_i$$

where Y_i is the level of sales in the ith territory, X_{i1} is the level of advertising in the ith territory, and ϵ_i is the error associated with the ith observation. This is the form of the model that is used for regression analysis. The error term is part and parcel of the model. It represents a failure to include all factors in the model, the fact that there is an unpredictable element in human behavior, and the condition that there are errors of measurement.[4] The probabilistic model allows for the fact that the Y value is not uniquely determined for a given X_i value. Rather, all that is determined for a given X_i value is the "average value" of Y. Individual values can be expected to fluctuate above and below this average.

The mathematical solution for finding the *line of best fit* for the probabilistic model requires that some assumptions be made about the distribution of the error term. The line of best fit could be defined in a number of ways. The typical way is in terms of the line that minimizes the sum of the deviations squared about the line (the *least-squares solution*). Consider Figure 21.2 and suppose that the line drawn in the figure is the estimated equation. Employing a caret (^) to indicate an estimated value,

Figure 21.1   ***Scatter Diagrams of Sales versus Marketing Mix Variables***

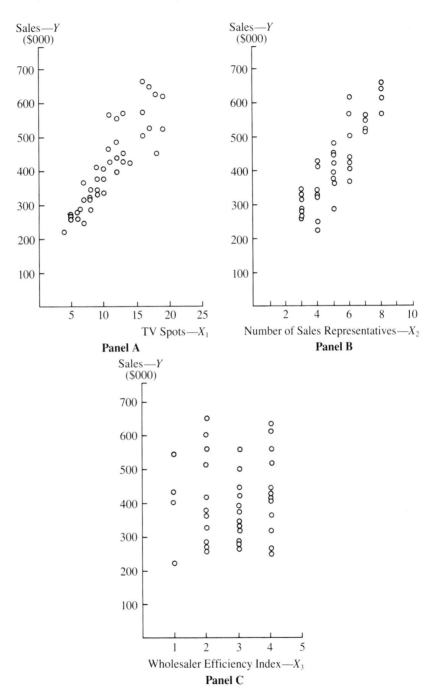

Figure 21.2   **Relationship between Y and X₁ in the Probabilistic Model**

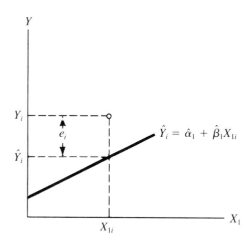

the error for the ith observation is the difference between the actual Y value, Y_i, and the estimated Y value, $\hat{Y}_i$; that is, $e_i = Y_i - \hat{Y}_i$. The least-squares solution is based on the principle that the sum of these squared errors should be made as small as possible; that is, $\Sigma_i^n e_i^2$ should be minimized. The sample estimates $\hat{\alpha}_1$ and $\hat{\beta}_1$ of the true population parameters α_1 and β_1 are determined so that this condition is satisfied.

There are three simplifying assumptions made about the error term in the least-squares solution:

1.   The mean or average value of the error term is zero.
2.   The variance of the error term is constant and is independent of the values of the predictor variable.
3.   The values of the error term are independent of one another.

Given these assumptions, it is possible to solve formulas to secure estimates for the population parameters, $\hat{\alpha}_1$, the intercept, and $\hat{\beta}_1$, the slope, by hand, although it is much more common to use a computer to estimate them.[5]

If we used the data in Table 21.1 for sales (Y) and television spots per month (X_1), it would turn out that the estimate for $\hat{\alpha}_1$ would be 135.4, and $\hat{\beta}_1$ would be 25.3.[6] The equation is plotted in Figure 21.3. The slope of the line is given by $\hat{\beta}_1$. The value 25.3 for $\hat{\beta}_1$ suggests that sales increase by \$25,300 for every unit increase in television spots. As mentioned previously, this is an estimate of the true population condition based on our particular sample of 40 observations. A different sample would most assuredly generate a different estimate. Further, we have not yet asked whether this is a statistically significant result or whether it could have occurred by chance. Nevertheless, it is a most vital item of information that helps in determining whether advertising expense is worth the estimated return. The estimate of the intercept parameter is $\hat{\alpha}_1 = 135.4$; this indicates where the line crosses the Y axis, since it represents the estimated value of Y when the predictor variable equals zero.

Standard Error of Estimate

An examination of Figure 21.3 shows that while the line seems to fit the points fairly well, there is still deviation in the points about the line. The size of these deviations measures the goodness of the fit. We can compute a numerical measure of the

Figure 21.3   *Plot of Equation Relating Sales to Television Spots*

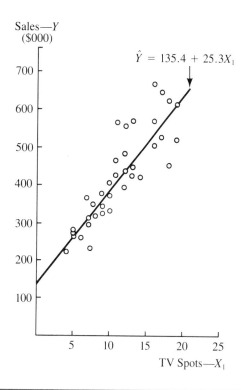

variation of the points about the line in much the same way as we compute the standard deviation of a frequency distribution.

Just as the sample mean is an estimate of the true parent-population mean, the line given by $\hat{Y}_i = \hat{\alpha}_1 + \hat{\beta}_1 X_{i1} + e_i$ is an estimate of the true regression line $Y_i = \alpha_1 + \beta_1 X_{i1} + \epsilon_i$. Consider the variance of the random error ϵ around the true line of regression, that is, σ_ϵ^2 or $\sigma_{Y/X}^2$. When the population variance σ^2 is unknown, an unbiased estimate is given by the square of the sample standard deviation, $\hat{s}$,

$$\hat{s} = \sqrt{\frac{\sum\limits_{i=1}^{n} (X_i - \bar{x})^2}{(n-1)}}.$$

Similarly, let $s_{Y/X}^2$ be an unbiased estimate of the population variance about the regression line, $\sigma_{Y/X}^2$. Now it can be shown that the sample estimate of the variance about the regression line is related to the sum of the squared errors, specifically, it equals

$$s_{Y/X}^2 = \frac{\sum\limits_{i=1}^{n} e_i^2}{(n-2)} = \frac{\sum\limits_{i=1}^{n} (Y_i - \hat{Y}_i)^2}{(n-2)}$$

where n is again the sample size, and $s_{Y/X}^2$ is an unbiased estimator of $\sigma_{Y/X}^2$, where Y_i and $\hat{Y}_i$ are, respectively, the observed and estimated values of Y for the ith

Figure 21.4   ***Rectangular Distribution of Error Term***

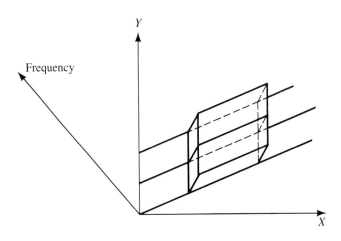

observation. The square root of the above quantity, $s_{Y/X}$, is often called the **standard error of estimate,** although the term *standard deviation from regression* is more meaningful.

The interpretation of the standard error of estimate parallels that for the standard deviation. Consider any X_{i1} value. The standard error of estimate means that for any such value of television spots X_{i1}, Y_i (sales) tends to be distributed about the corresponding $\hat{Y}_i$ value—the point on the line—with a standard deviation equal to the standard error of estimate. Further, the variation about the line is the same throughout the entire length of the line. The point on the line, the arithmetic mean, changes as X_{i1} changes, but the distribution of Y_i values around the line does not change with changes in the number of television spots. Figure 21.4 depicts the situation under the assumption that the error term is rectangularly distributed, for example.[7] Note that the assumption of constant $s_{Y/X}$, irrespective of the value of X_{i1}, produces parallel bands around the regression line.

The smaller the standard error of estimate, the better the line fits the data. For the line relating sales to television spots, it is $s_{Y/X} = 59.6$.

Inferences about the Slope Coefficient

Earlier we calculated the value of the slope coefficient, $\hat{\beta}_1$, to be 25.3. At that time we did not yet raise the question of whether that result was statistically significant or could have been due to chance. To deal with that question requires an additional assumption, namely, that the errors are normally distributed rather than rectangularly distributed as previously assumed. Before proceeding, though, let us emphasize that the least-squares estimators of the parent-population parameters are BLUE, that is, they are the *b*est, *l*inear, *u*nbiased *e*stimators of the true population parameters regardless of the shape of the distribution of the error term. All that is necessary is that the previous assumptions be satisfied. This is the remarkable result of the Gauss-Markov theorem. It is only if we wish to make statistical inferences about the regression coefficients that the assumption of normally distributed errors is required.

It can be shown that if the ϵ_i are normally distributed random variables, then $\hat{\beta}_1$ is also normally distributed. That is, if we were to take repeated samples from our population of sales territories and calculate a $\hat{\beta}_1$ for each sample, the distribution of these estimates would be normal and *centered* around the *true population* parameter β_1. Further, the variance of the distribution of $\hat{\beta}_1$'s, or $\sigma_{\hat{\beta}_1}^2$, can be shown to be equal to

$$\sigma_{\hat{\beta}_1}^2 = \frac{\sigma_{Y/X_1}^2}{\sum_{i=1}^{n} (X_{i1} - \bar{x}_1)^2}.$$

Since the population $\sigma_{Y/X}^2$ is unknown, $\sigma_{\hat{\beta}_1}^2$ is also unknown and has to be estimated. The estimate is generated by substituting the standard error of estimate $s_{Y/X}$ for $\sigma_{Y/X}$

$$s_{\hat{\beta}_1}^2 = \frac{s_{Y/X_1}^2}{\sum_{i=1}^{n} (X_{i1} - \bar{x}_1)^2}.$$

The situation so far is as follows: Given the assumption of normally distributed errors, $\hat{\beta}_1$ is also normally distributed with a mean of β_1 and unknown variance $\sigma_{\hat{\beta}_1}^2$. Since the variance of the distribution of the sample is unknown, we need to use a procedure similar to that used when making an inference about the mean when the population variance is unknown. That set of conditions requires a t test to examine statistical significance. The test for the significance of β_1 has a similar requirement. The null hypothesis is that there is no linear relationship between the variables, while the alternate hypothesis is that a linear relationship does exist, that is,

$$H_0: \beta_1 = 0$$
$$H_a: \beta_1 \neq 0$$

The test statistic is $t = (\hat{\beta}_1 - \beta_1)/s_{\hat{\beta}_1}$; that is, the slope estimated from the sample minus the hypothesized slope, divided by the standard error of estimate, which is t distributed with $n - 2$ degrees of freedom. In the example,

$$s_{\hat{\beta}_1}^2 = \frac{s_{Y/X_1}^2}{\sum_{i=1}^{n} (X_{i1} - \bar{x}_1)^2} = \frac{(59.6)^2}{723.6} = 4.91$$

$$s_{\hat{\beta}_1} = \sqrt{4.91} = 2.22$$

$$t = \frac{\hat{\beta}_1 - \beta_1}{s_{\hat{\beta}_1}} = \frac{25.3 - 0}{2.22} = 11.4.$$

For a 0.05 level of significance, the tabled t value for $v = n - 2 = 38$ degrees of freedom is 2.02. Since calculated t exceeds critical t, the null hypothesis is rejected; $\hat{\beta}_1$ is sufficiently different from zero to warrant the assumption of a linear relationship between sales and television spots. Now this does not mean that the true relationship between sales and television spots is *necessarily* linear, only that the evidence indicates that Y (sales) changes as X_1 (television spots) changes, and that we may obtain a better prediction of Y using X_1 and the linear equation than if we simply ignored X_1.

What if the null hypothesis is not rejected? As we have noted, β_1 is the slope of the assumed line over the region of observation and indicates the linear change in Y

Figure 21.5   ***Scatter of Points for Sample of* n *Observations***

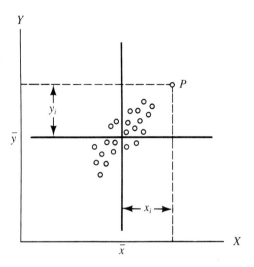

for a one-unit change in X_1. If we do not reject the null hypothesis that β_1 equals zero, it does not mean that Y and X_1 are unrelated. There are two possibilities. First, we may simply be committing a Type II error by not rejecting a false null hypothesis. Second, it is possible that Y and X_1 might be perfectly related in some curvilinear manner and we have simply chosen the wrong model to describe the physical situation.

Correlation Coefficient

Coefficient of correlation A term used in regression analysis to refer to the strength of the linear association between the criterion variable and a predictor variable.

So far we have been concerned with the functional relationship of Y to X. Suppose we were also concerned with the *strength of the linear relationship* between Y and X. This leads to the notion of the **coefficient of correlation.** Two additional assumptions are made when discussing the correlation model. First, X_i is also assumed to be a random variable. A sample observation yields both an X_i and Y_i value. Second, it is assumed that the observations come from a bivariate normal distribution, that is, one in which the X variable is normally distributed and the Y variable is also normally distributed.

Now consider the drawing of a sample of n observations from a bivariate normal distribution. Let ρ represent the strength of the linear association between the two variables in the parent population. Let r represent the sample estimate of ρ. Suppose the sample of n observations yielded the scatter of points shown in Figure 21.5 and consider the division of the figure into the four quadrants formed by erecting perpendiculars to the two axes at $\bar{x}$ and $\bar{y}$.

Consider the deviations from these bisectors. Take any point P with coordinates (X_i, Y_i) and define the deviations

$$x_i = X_i - \bar{x}$$
$$y_i = Y_i - \bar{y}$$

where the small letters indicate deviations around a mean. It is clear from an inspection of Figure 21.5 that the product $x_i y_i$ is

- Positive for all points in Quadrant I
- Negative for all points in Quadrant II
- Positive for all points in Quadrant III
- Negative for all points in Quadrant IV

Hence, it would seem that the quantity $\sum_{i=1}^{n} x_i y_i$ could be used as a measure of the linear association between X and Y,

- For if the association is positive so that most points lie in the Quadrants I and III, $\sum_{i=1}^{n} x_i y_i$ tends to be positive
- While if the association is negative so that most points lie in the Quadrants II and IV, $\sum_{i=1}^{n} x_i y_i$ tends to be negative
- While if no relation exists between X and Y, the points will be scattered over all four quadrants and $\sum_{i=1}^{n} x_i y_i$ will tend to be very small

The quantity $\sum_{i=1}^{n} x_i y_i$ has two defects, though, as a measure of linear association between X and Y. First, it can be increased arbitrarily by adding further observations, that is, by increasing the sample size. Second, it can also be arbitrarily influenced by changing the units of measurement for either X or Y or both, for example, by changing feet to inches. These defects can be removed by making the measure of the strength of linear association a dimensionless quantity and dividing by n. The result is the *Pearsonian*, or *product-moment*, *coefficient of correlation*, that is,

$$r = \frac{\sum_{i=1}^{n} x_i y_i}{n s_X s_Y}$$

where s_X is the standard deviation of the X variable and s_Y is the standard deviation of the Y variable.

The correlation coefficient computed from the sample data is an estimate of the parent-population parameter ρ, and part of the job of the researcher is to use r to test hypotheses about ρ. It is unnecessary to do so for the example at hand because the test of the null hypothesis H_0: $\rho = 0$ is equivalent to the test of the null hypothesis H_0: $\beta_1 = 0$. Since we have already performed the latter test, we know that the sample evidence leads to the rejection of the hypothesis that there is no linear relationship between sales and television spots; that is, it leads to the rejection of H_0: $\rho = 0$.

The product-moment coefficient of correlation may vary from -1 to $+1$. Perfect positive correlation, where an increase in X determines exactly an increase in Y, yields a coefficient of $+1$. Perfect negative correlation, where an increase in X determines exactly a decrease in Y, yields a coefficient of -1. Figure 21.6 depicts these situations and several other scatter diagrams and their resulting correlation coefficients. An examination of these diagrams will provide some appreciation of the size of the correlation coefficient associated with a particular degree of scatter. The square of the correlation coefficient is the **coefficient of determination.** By some algebraic manipulation, it can be shown to be equal to

Coefficient of determination A term used in regression analysis to refer to the relative proportion of the total variation in the criterion variable that can be explained or accounted for by the fitted regression equation.

$$r^2 = 1 - \frac{s_{Y/X}^2}{s_Y^2}$$

that is, $r^2 = 1$ minus the standard error of estimate squared, divided by the sample variance of the criterion variable. In the absence of the predictor variable, our best

Figure 21.6   ***Sample Scatter Diagrams and Associated Correlation Coefficients***

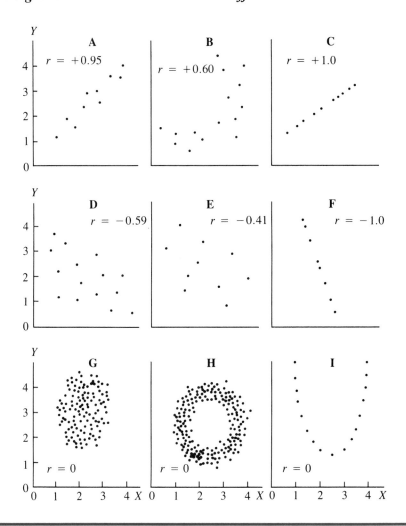

Source: Ronald E. Frank, Alfred A. Kuehn, and William F. Massy, *Quantitative Techniques in Marketing Analysis* (Homewood, Ill.: Richard D. Irwin, Inc., 1962), p. 71. Used with permission.

estimate of the criterion variable would be the sample mean. If there were low variability in sales from territory to territory, the sample mean would be a good estimate of the expected sales in any territory. However, high variability would render it a poor estimate. Thus, the variance in sales s_Y^2 is a measure of the "badness" of such an estimating procedure. The introduction of the covariate X might produce an improvement in the territory sales estimates. It depends on how well the equation fits the data. Since $s_{Y/X}^2$ measures the scatter of the points about the regression line, $s_{Y/X}^2$ can be considered a measure of the "badness" of an estimating procedure that takes account of the covariate. Now if $s_{Y/X}^2$ is small in relation to s_Y^2, the introduction of the covariate via the regression equation can be said to have substantially improved the predictions of the criterion variable, sales. Conversely, if $s_{Y/X}^2$ is approximately equal to s_Y^2, the introduction of the covariate X can be considered not to have helped in improving the predictions of Y. Thus, the ratio $s_{Y/X}^2/s_Y^2$ can be considered to be the ratio of variation left unexplained by the regression line divided by the total variation; that is,

$$r^2 = 1 - \frac{\text{unexplained variation}}{\text{total variation}}.$$

The right side of the equation can be combined in a single fraction to yield

$$r^2 = \frac{\text{total variation} - \text{unexplained variation}}{\text{total variation}}.$$

Total variation minus unexplained variation leaves "explained variation," that is, the variation in Y that is accounted for or explained by the introduction of X. Thus, the coefficient of determination can be considered to be equal to

$$r^2 = \frac{\text{explained variation}}{\text{total variation}}$$

where it is understood that total variation is measured by the variance in Y. For the sales and television spot example, $r^2 = 0.77$. This means that 77 percent of the variation in sales from territory to territory is accounted for, or can be explained, by the variation in television spot advertising across territories. Consequently, we can do a better job of estimating sales in a territory if we take account of television spots than if we neglect this advertising effort.

Ethical
Dilemma 21.1

The newly appointed analyst in the firm's marketing research department was given the responsibility of developing a method by which market potential for the firm's products could be estimated by small geographic areas. The analyst went about the task by gathering as much secondary data as he could. He then ran a series of regression analyses using the firm's sales as the criterion and the demographic factors as predictors. He realized that several of the predictors were highly correlated (e.g., average income in the area and average educational level), but he chose to ignore this fact when presenting the results to management.

- What is the consequence when the predictors in a regression equation are highly correlated?
- Is a research analyst ethically obliged to learn all he or she can about a particular technique before applying it to a problem in order to avoid incorrectly interpreting the results?
- Is a research analyst ethically obliged to advise those involved to be cautious in interpreting results because of violations of the assumptions in the method used to produce the results?
- What are the researcher's responsibilities if management has no interest in the technical details by which the results are achieved?

Multiple-Regression Analysis

The basic idea behind multiple-regression analysis is the same as that behind simple regression: to determine the relationship between independent and dependent, that is, predictor and criterion, variables. Multiple-regression analysis allows the

Research Window 21.2
Walkup's Laws of Statistics

Law No. 1

Everything correlates with everything, especially when the same individual defines the variables to be correlated.

Law No. 2

It won't help very much to find a good correlation between the variable you are interested in and some other variable that you don't understand any better.

Law No. 3

Unless you can think of a logical reason why two variables should be connected as cause and effect, it doesn't help much to find a correlation between them. In Columbus, Ohio, the mean monthly rainfall correlates very nicely with the number of letters in the names of the months!

Source: Lewis E. Walkup, "Walkup's First Five Laws of Statistics," *The Bent*, (Summer 1974), publication of Tau Beta Pi, National Engineering Honor Society, University of Missouri Alumni Magazine; as quoted in Robert W. Joselyn, *Designing the Marketing Research Project* (New York: Petrocelli/Charter, 1977), p. 175.

introduction of additional variables, so the equation constructed reflects the values of several rather than one predictor variable. The objective in introducing additional variables is to improve our predictions of the criterion variable.

A wry observer of many a research project once offered some astute insights on the behavior of variables and the way in which they may be correlated (see Research Window 21.2). You may want to keep them in mind while you read this section on multiple-regression analysis.

Revised Nomenclature

A more formal, revised notational framework is valuable for discussing multiple-regression analysis. Consider the general regression model with three predictor variables. The regression equation is

$$Y = \alpha + \beta_1 X_1 + \beta_2 X_2 + \beta_3 X_3 + \epsilon$$

which is a simplified statement of the more elaborate and precise equation,

$$Y_{(123)} = \alpha_{(123)} + \beta_{Y1.23}X_1 + \beta_{Y2.13}X_2 + \beta_{Y3.12}X_3 + \epsilon_{(123)}.$$

Coefficient of partial (or net) regression
A quantity resulting from a multiple-regression analysis, which indicates the average change in the criterion variable per unit change in a predictor variable, holding all other predictor variables constant; the interpretation applies only when the predictor variables are independent, as required for a valid application of the multiple-regression model.

In this more precise system, the following holds true:

- $Y_{(123)}$ is the value of Y that is estimated from the regression equation, in which Y is the criterion variable and X_1, X_2, and X_3 are the predictor variables
- $\alpha_{(123)}$ is the intercept parameter in the multiple-regression equation, in which Y is the criterion variable and X_1, X_2, and X_3 are the predictor variables
- $\beta_{Y1.23}$ is the coefficient of X_1 in the regression equation, in which Y is the criterion variable and X_1, X_2, and X_3 are the predictor variables. It is called the **coefficient of partial (or net) regression.** Note the subscripts. The two subscripts to the left of the decimal point are called *primary subscripts*. The first identifies the criterion variable, and the second identifies the predictor variable of which this β value is the coefficient. There are always two primary subscripts. The two

subscripts to the right of the decimal point are called *secondary subscripts*. They indicate which other predictor variables are in the regression equation. The number of secondary subscripts varies from zero for simple regression to any number, $k - 1$, where there are k predictor variables in the problem. In this case, the model contains three predictor variables, $k = 3$, and there are two secondary subscripts throughout.

■ $\epsilon_{(123)}$ is the error associated with the prediction of Y when X_1, X_2, and X_3 are the predictor variables

When the identity of the variables is clear, it is common practice to use the simplified statement of the model. The more elaborate statement is helpful, though, in interpreting the solution to the regression problem.

Multicollinearity Assumption

The assumptions that we made about the error term for the simple regression model also apply to the multiple-regression equation. And the multiple-regression model requires the additional assumption that the predictor variables are not correlated among themselves. When the levels of the predictor variables can be set by the researcher, the assumption is easily satisfied. When the observations result from a survey rather than an experiment, the assumption is often violated, because many variables of interest in marketing vary together. For instance, higher incomes are typically associated with higher education levels. Thus, the prediction of purchase behavior employing both income and education would violate the assumption that the predictor variables are independent of one another. **Multicollinearity** is said to be present in a multiple-regression problem when the predictor variables are correlated among themselves.

Multicollinearity
A condition said to be present in a multiple-regression analysis when the predictor variables are not independent as required but are correlated among themselves.

Coefficients of Partial Regression

Consider what would happen if we introduced a number of sales representatives into our problem of predicting territory sales. We could investigate the two-variable relationship between sales and the number of sales representatives. This would involve, of course, the calculation of the simple regression equation relating sales to number of sales representatives. The calculations would parallel those for the sales and television spot relationship. Alternatively, we could consider the simultaneous influence of television spots and number of sales representatives on sales using multiple-regression analysis. Assuming that is indeed the research problem, the regression model would be written

$$Y_{(12)} = \alpha_{(12)} + \beta_{Y1.2}X_1 + \beta_{Y2.1}X_2 + \epsilon_{(12)}$$

indicating that the criterion variable, sales in a territory, is to be predicted employing two predictor variables, X_1 (television spots per month) and X_2 (number of sales representatives).

Once again, the parameters of the model could be estimated from sample data employing least-squares procedures. Let us again distinguish the sample estimates from the true, but unknown, population values by using a caret to denote an estimated value. Let us not worry about the formulas for calculating the regression coefficients. They typically will be calculated on a computer anyway and can be found in almost any introductory statistics book. The marketing analyst's need is how to interpret the results provided by the computer.

For this problem, the equation turns out to be

$$\hat{Y} = \hat{\alpha}_{(12)} + \hat{\beta}_{Y1.2}X_1 + \hat{\beta}_{Y2.1}X_2 = 69.3 + 14.2X_1 + 37.5X_2.$$

This regression equation may be used to estimate the level of sales to be expected in a territory, given the number of television spots and the number of sales representatives serving the territory. Like any other least-squares equation, the line (a plane in this case, since three dimensions are involved) fits the points in such a way that the sum of the deviations about the line is zero. That is, if sales for each of the forty sales territories were to be estimated from this equation, the positive and negative deviations about the line would exactly balance.

The level at which the plane intercepts the Y axis is given by $\hat{\alpha}_{(12)} = 69.3$. Consider now the coefficients of partial regression, $\hat{\beta}_{Y1.2}$ and $\hat{\beta}_{Y2.1}$. *Assuming the multicollinearity assumption is satisfied*, these coefficients of partial regression can be interpreted as the average change in the criterion variable associated with a unit change in the appropriate predictor variable while holding the other predictor variable constant. Thus, assuming there is no multicollinearity, $\hat{\beta}_{Y1.2} = 14.2$ indicates that on the average, an increase of \$14,200 in sales can be expected with each additional television spot in the territory if the number of sales representatives is not changed. Similarly, $\hat{\beta}_{Y2.1} = 37.5$ suggests that each additional sales representative in a territory can be expected to produce \$37,500 in sales, on the average, if the number of television spots is held constant.

In simple regression analysis, we tested the significance of the regression equation by examining the significance of the slope coefficient employing the t test. Calculated t was 11.4 for the sales and television spot relationship. The significance of the regression could also have been checked with an F test. In the case of a two-variable regression, calculated F is equal to calculated t squared; that is, $F = t^2 = (11.4)^2 = 130.6$, while in general calculated F is equal to the ratio of the mean square due to regression to the mean square due to residuals. In simple regression, the calculated F value would be referred to an F table for $v_1 = n - 2$ degrees of freedom. The conclusion would be exactly equivalent to that derived by testing the significance of the slope coefficient employing the t test.

In the multiple-regression case, *it is mandatory that the significance of the overall regression be examined using an F test*. The appropriate degrees of freedom are $v_1 = k$ and $v_2 = n - k - 1$, where there are k predictor variables. Critical F for $v_1 = 2$ and $v_2 = 40 - 2 - 1 = 37$ degrees of freedom, and a 0.05 level of significance is 3.25. Calculated F for the regression relating sales to television spots and the number of sales representatives is 128.1. Since calculated F exceeds critical F, the null hypothesis of no relationship is rejected. There is a statistically significant linear relationship between sales and the predictor variables, number of television spots and number of sales representatives.

The slope coefficients can also be tested individually for their statistical significance in a multiple-regression problem, given the overall function is significant. The t test is again used, although the validity of the procedure is highly dependent on multicollinearity that exists within the data. If the data are highly multicollinear, there will be a tendency to commit Type II errors; that is, many of the predictor variables will be judged as not being related to the criterion variable when in fact they are. It is even possible to conclude that the overall regression is statistically significant but that none of the coefficients are significant. The difficulty with the t tests for the significance of the individual slope coefficients arises because the standard error of estimate of the least-square coefficients, $s_{\hat{\beta}_i}$, increases as the dependence among the predictor variables increases. And, of course, as the denominator of calculated t gets larger, t itself decreases, occasioning the conclusion of no relationship between the criterion variable and the predictor variable in question.

Is multicollinearity a problem in our example? Consider again the simple regression of sales on television spots; $\hat{\beta}_1$ ($\hat{\beta}_{Y1}$ in our more formal notation system) was equal to 25.3. Thus, when the number of sales representatives in a territory was not considered, the average change in sales associated with an additional television spot was $25,300. Yet when the number of sales representatives was considered, the average change in sales associated with an additional television spot was $14,200, $\hat{\beta}_{Y1.2} = 14.2$. Part of the sales effect that we were attributing to television spots was in fact due to the number of sales representatives in the territory. We were thus overstating the impact of the television spot advertising because of the way decisions have historically been made in the company. Specifically, those territories with the greater number of sales representatives have received more television advertising support (or vice versa). Perhaps this was logical since they contained a larger proportion of the consuming public. Nevertheless, the fact that the two predictor variables are not independent (the coefficient of simple correlation between television spots and number of sales representatives is 0.78) has caused a violation of the assumption of independent predictors. Multicollinearity is present within this data set.

A multicollinear condition within a data set reduces the efficiency of the estimates for the regression parameters. This is because the amount of information about the effect of each predictor variable on the criterion variable declines as the correlation among the predictor variables increases. The reduction in efficiency can be easily seen in the limiting case as the correlation between the predictor variables approaches 1 for a two-predictor model. Such a situation is depicted in Figure 21.7, where it is assumed that there is a perfect linear relationship between the two predictor variables, television spots and number of sales representatives, and also that there is a strong linear relationship between the criterion variable sales and television spots. Consider the change in sales from $75,000 to $100,000. This change is associated with a change in the number of television spots, from three to four. This change in television spots is also associated with a change in the number of sales representatives, from four to five. What is the effect of a television spot on sales? Can we say it is $100 - 75 = 25$, or $25,000? Most assuredly not, for historically a sales representative has been added to a territory whenever the number of television spots has been increased by one (or vice versa). The number of television spots and of sales representatives varies in perfect proportion, and it is impossible to distinguish their separate influences on sales, that is, their influence when the other predictor variable is held constant.

Very little meaning can be attached to the coefficients of partial regression when multicollinearity is present, as it is in our example. The "normal" interpretation of the coefficients of partial regression as "the average change in the criterion variable associated with a unit change in the appropriate predictor variable while holding the other predictor variables constant" simply does not hold.[8] The equation may still be quite useful for prediction, assuming conditions are stable. That is, it may be used to predict sales in the various territories for given levels of television spots and number of sales representatives *if* the historical relationship between sales and each of the predictor variables, and between or among the predictor variables themselves, can be expected to continue.[9] The partial-regression coefficients should not be used, though, as the basis for making marketing strategy decisions when significant multicollinearity is present.[10]

Figure 21.7   ***Hypothetical Relationship between Sales and TV Spots and between TV Spots and Number of Sales Representatives***

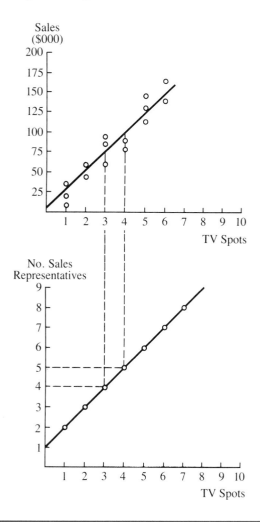

Coefficients of Multiple Correlation and Determination

Coefficient of multiple determination
In multiple-regression analysis, the proportion of variation in the criterion variable that is accounted for by the covariation in the predictor variables.

Coefficient of multiple correlation In multiple-regression analysis, the square root of the coefficient of multiple determination.

One item of considerable importance in simple regression analysis is the measure of the closeness of the relationship between the criterion and predictor variables. The coefficient of correlation and its square, the **coefficient of multiple determination,** are used for this purpose. In multiple regression, there are similar coefficients for the identical purpose.

The **coefficient of multiple correlation** is formally denoted by $R_{Y.123}$, where the primary subscript identifies the criterion variable and the secondary subscripts identify the predictor variables. When the variables entering into the relationship are obvious, the abbreviated form, R, is used. The coefficient of multiple determination is denoted formally by $R_{Y.123}^2$ and informally by R^2. It represents the proportion of variation in the criterion variable that is accounted for by the covariation in the predictor variables. In the investigation of the relationship between sales and television spots and number of sales representatives, $R_{Y.12}^2 = 0.874$. This means that 87.4 percent of the variation in sales is associated with variation in television spots and number of sales representatives. The introduction of the number of sales representatives has improved the fit of the regression line; 87.4 percent of the variation in sales is accounted for by the two-predictor variable model, whereas only 77.5 percent was accounted for by the one-predictor model. The square root of this quantity, $R_{Y.12} = 0.935$, is the coefficient of multiple correlation. It is always expressed as a positive number.

Coefficients of Partial Correlation

There are two additional quantities to consider when interpreting the results of a multiple-regression analysis that were not present in simple regression analysis: the coefficient of partial correlation and its square, the *coefficient of partial determination*.

Recall that in the simple regression analysis relating sales Y to television spots X_1 the coefficient of simple determination could be written

$$r_{Y.1}^2 = 1 - \frac{\text{unexplained variation}}{\text{total variation}}$$

and recall also that the unexplained variation was given by the square of standard error of estimate, $s_{Y.1}^2$, since the standard error of estimate measures the variation in the criterion variable that was unaccounted for by the predictor variable X_1. Total variation, of course, was given by the variation in the criterion variable s_Y^2. Thus,

$$r_{Y.1}^2 = 1 - \frac{s_{Y.1}^2}{s_Y^2}.$$

The last term in this formula is the ratio of the variation remaining in the criterion variable, after taking account of the predictor variable X_1, to the total variation in the criterion variable. It measures the relative degree to which the association between the two variables can be used to provide information about the criterion variable.

Now consider the multiple-regression case with two predictor variables, X_1 and X_2. Denote the standard error of estimate by $s_{Y.12}$ and its square by $s_{Y.12}^2$. The standard error of estimate measures the variation still remaining in the criterion variable Y after the two predictor variables X_1 and X_2 have been taken into account. Since $s_{Y.1}^2$ measures the variation in the criterion variable that remains after the first predictor variable has been taken into account, the ratio $s_{Y.12}^2/s_{Y.1}^2$ can be interpreted as measuring the relative degree to which the association among the three variables Y, X_1, and X_2 provides information about Y over and above that provided by the association between the criterion variable and the first predictor variable, X_1, alone. In other words, the ratio $s_{Y.12}^2/s_{Y.1}^2$ measures the *relative degree* to which X_2 adds to the knowledge about Y after X_1 has already been fully utilized. The ratio is the basis for the **coefficient of partial determination,** which in the sales (Y) versus television spots (X_1) and number of sales representatives (X_2) example is

Coefficient of partial determination
A quantity resulting from a multiple-regression analysis that indicates the proportion of variation in the criterion variable that is not accounted for by an earlier variable or variables and that is accounted for by the addition of a new variable into the regression equation.

$$r_{Y2.1}^2 = 1 - \frac{s_{Y.12}^2}{s_{Y.1}^2} = 1 - \frac{(45.2)^2}{(59.6)^2} = 1 - 0.576 = 0.424.$$

This means that 42.4 percent of the variation in sales that is not associated with television spots is incrementally associated with the number of sales representatives.

Alternatively, the errors made in estimating sales from television spots are, as measured by the variance, reduced by 42.4 percent when the number of sales representatives X_2 is added to X_1 as an additional predictor variable. The square root of the coefficient of partial determination is the **coefficient of partial correlation.**

Coefficient of partial correlation In multiple-regression analysis, the square root of the coefficient of partial determination.

In our example there were two predictors. Thus, we defined the coefficient of partial determination for the number of sales representatives X_2 as $r_{Y2.1}^2$. We could have simply defined a coefficient of partial determination for television spots. It would be denoted as $r_{Y1.2}^2$, and it would represent the percentage of the variation in sales not associated with X_2 that is incrementally associated with X_1; this latter coefficient would show the incremental contribution of X_1 after the association between Y and X_2 had already been considered.

When there are more than two predictors, we could define many more coefficients of partial determination. Each would have two primary subscripts indicating the criterion variable and the newly added predictor variable. There could be a great many secondary subscripts, as they always indicate which predictor variables have already been considered. Hence, if we had three predictor variables, we could calculate $r_{Y2.1}$, $r_{Y3.1}$, $r_{Y1.2}$, $r_{Y3.2}$, $r_{Y1.3}$, and $r_{Y2.3}$. These would all be *first-order* partial-correlation coefficients since they have one secondary subscript indicating that one other predictor variable is taken into account. We could also calculate $r_{Y1.23}$, $r_{Y2.13}$, and $r_{Y3.12}$. These are all *second-order* partial-correlation coefficients. Each has two secondary subscripts indicating that the incremental contribution of the variable is being considered after two other predictor variables have already been taken into account. Simple correlation coefficients, of course, have no secondary coefficients; they are, therefore, often referred to as *zero-order* partial-correlation coefficients.

Dummy Variables

The analysis of the sales data of Table 21.1 is still not complete. No attention has yet been given to the effect of distribution on sales, particularly as measured by the wholesaler efficiency index. One way of considering the effect of wholesaler efficiency on sales would be to introduce the index directly; that is, the X_3 value for each observation would simply be the value recorded in the last column of Table 21.1. Letting X_3 represent the wholesaler efficiency index, the multiple-regression equation, using the informal notation scheme, would be

$$Y = \alpha + \beta_1 X_1 + \beta_2 X_2 + \beta_3 X_3 + \epsilon.$$

The least-squares estimate of β_3 in this equation turns out to be $\hat{\beta}_3 = 11.5$. Note what this number implies if the predictor variables are independent. It means that the estimated average change in sales is $11,500 for each unit change in the wholesaler efficiency index. This means that a fair distributor could be expected to sell $11,500 more on the average than a poor one; a good one could be expected to average $11,500 more than a fair one; and an excellent one could be expected to sell $11,500 more on the average than a good one. The sales increments are assumed constant for each change in wholesaler rating. The implication is that the wholesaler efficiency index is an intervally scaled variable and that the difference between a poor and a fair wholesaler is the same as the difference between a fair and a good one. This is a questionable assumption with an index that reflects ratings.

Dummy (or binary) variable A variable that is given one of two values, 0 or 1, and that is used to provide a numerical representation for attributes or characteristics that are not essentially quantitative.

An alternative way of proceeding would be to convert the index into a set of **dummy variables** or, more appropriately, **binary variables.** A binary variable is one that takes on one of two values, 0 (zero) or 1. Thus, it can be represented by a single binary digit. Binary variables are used mainly because of the flexibility one has in defining them. They can provide a numerical representation for attributes or characteristics that are not essentially quantitative. For example, one could introduce sex into a regression equation using the dummy variable X_i, where

$$X_i = 0 \quad \text{if the person is a female}$$
$$X_i = 1 \quad \text{if the person is a male}$$

The technique is readily extended to handle multichotomous as well as dichotomous classifications. For instance, suppose one wanted to introduce the variable social class into a regression equation, and suppose there were three distinct class levels: upper class, middle class, and lower class. This could be handled using two dummy variables, say X_1 and X_2, as follows:

	X_1	X_2
■ If a person belongs to the upper class	1	0
■ If a person belongs to the middle class	0	1
■ If a person belongs to the lower class	0	0

There are several other logically equivalent coding schemes, for example, the following:

	X_1	X_2
■ If a person belongs to the upper class	0	0
■ If a person belongs to the middle class	1	0
■ If a person belongs to the lower class	0	1

It is therefore most important that the analyst interpreting the output from a regression run employing dummy variables pay close attention to the coding of the variables. It should be clear that an m category classification is capable of unambiguous representation by a set of $m - 1$ binary variables and that an mth binary would be entirely superfluous. As a matter of a fact, the use of m variables to code an m-way classification variable would render most regression programs inoperative.

Suppose that we were to employ three dummy variables to represent the four-category wholesaler efficiency index in the Click ballpoint pen example as follows:

	X_3	X_4	X_5
■ If a wholesaler is poor	0	0	0
■ If a wholesaler is fair	1	0	0
■ If a wholesaler is good	0	1	0
■ If a wholesaler is excellent	0	0	1

The regression model is

$$Y = \alpha + \beta_1 X_1 + \beta_2 X_2 + \beta_3 X_3 + \beta_4 X_4 + \beta_5 X_5 + \epsilon.$$

The least-squares estimates of the wholesaler efficiency parameters are as follows:

$$\hat{\beta}_3 = 9.2$$
$$\hat{\beta}_4 = 20.3$$
$$\hat{\beta}_5 = 33.3$$

These coefficients indicate that on the average a fair wholesaler could be expected to sell \$9,200 more than a poor one; a good wholesaler could be expected to sell \$20,300 more than a poor one; and an excellent wholesaler, \$33,300 more than a poor one. Note that all of these coefficients are interpreted with respect to the "null" state, that is, with respect to the classification for which all of the dummy variables are defined to be zero—the classification "poor" in this case.[11]

The analyst wishing to determine the difference in sales effectiveness between other classifications must look at coefficient differences. Thus, if the researcher wanted to calculate the estimated difference in expected sales from a good wholesaler and a fair wholesaler, the appropriate difference would be $\hat{\beta}_4 - \hat{\beta}_3 = 20.3 - 9.2 = 11.1$ thousand dollars (\$11,100). Similarly, an excellent wholesaler could be expected on the average to sell $\hat{\beta}_5 - \hat{\beta}_4 = 33.3 - 20.3 = 13.0$ thousand dollars (\$13,000) more than a good one.

The use of dummy variables indicates that the relationship between sales and the wholesaler efficiency index is not linear as was assumed when the index was introduced as an intervally scaled variable. Instead of an across-the-board increase of \$11,500 with each rating change, the respective increases are 9.2 (\$9,200) from poor to fair, 11.1 (\$11,100) from fair to good, and 13.0 (\$13,000) from good to excellent.

Variable Transformations

The use of dummy variables greatly expands the scope of the regression model. They allow the introduction of classificatory and rank-order variables in regression problems. As we have seen, they also allow nonlinear criterion variable/predictor variable relationships to be dealt with. Another technique that expands the obvious scope of the regression model is that of variable transformations.

Variable transformation
A change in the scale in which a variable is expressed.

A **variable transformation** is simply a change in the scale in which the given variable is expressed. Consider the model

$$Y = \alpha Y_1^{\beta_1} X_2^{\beta_2} X_3^{\beta_3} \epsilon$$

in which the relationship among the predictors and between the predictors and the error is assumed to be multiplicative. At first glance, it would seem that it would be impossible to estimate the parameters α, β_1, β_2, and β_3 using our normal least-squares procedures. Now consider the model

$$W = \alpha' + \beta_1 Z_1 + \beta_2 Z_2 + \beta_3 Z_3 + \epsilon'.$$

This is a linear model, and so it can be fitted by the standard least-squares procedures. But consider the fact that it is exactly equivalent to our multiplicative model if we simply let

$$\begin{aligned} W &= \ln Y & Z_2 &= \ln X_2 \\ \alpha' &= \ln \alpha & Z_3 &= \ln X_3 \\ Z_1 &= \ln X_1 & \epsilon' &= \ln \epsilon \end{aligned}$$

We have converted a nonlinear model to a linear model using variable transformations. To solve for the parameters of our multiplicative model, we simply (1) take the natural log of Y and each of the X's, (2) solve the resulting equation by the normal least-squares procedures, (3) take the antilog of α' to derive an estimate of α, and (4) read the values of the β_i since they are the same in both models.

The transformation to natural logarithms involves the transformation of both the criterion and predictor variables. It is also possible to change the scale of either the criterion or predictor variables. Transformations to the exponential and logarithmic are some of the most useful since they serve to relax the constraints imposed by the following assumptions:[12]

- The relationship between the criterion variable and the predictor variables is additive
- The relationship between the criterion variable and the predictor variables is linear
- The errors are *homoscedastic* (i.e., are equal to a constant for all values of the predictors)

Dummy variables are one form of transformation, and we have already seen how they allow the treatment of nonlinear relationships.

Ethical Dilemma 21.2

Sarah was absolutely convinced that there was a relationship between the firm's product sales to a household and the household's total disposable personal income. She was consequently very disappointed when her first pass through the diary panel data that she had convinced her superior to purchase revealed virtually no relationship between household purchases of the product and household income in the simple regression of one on the other. A series of additional passes in which a variety of transformations were tried proved equally disappointing. Finally, Sarah decided to break the income variable into classes through a series of dummy variables. When she regressed household purchases of the product against the income categories, she found a very irregular but strong relationship as measured by R^2. Purchases rose as income increased up to $24,999, then decreased as income went from $25,000 to $59,999, increased again for income between $60,000 and $104,999, and seemed to be unaffected by incomes greater than $105,000.

- How would you evaluate Sarah's approach?
- Do you think it is good procedure to continue searching data for support for a hypothesis that you absolutely believe is true, or would you recommend a single pass through the data with the procedure that a priori you thought was best?
- What are Sarah's ethical responsibilities when reporting the results of her analysis? Is she obliged to discuss all the analyses she ran, or is it satisfactory for her to report only the results of the dummy variable regression?

Summary Comments on Data Analysis

We have now come to the end of our section on data analysis. As we have seen, there are many sophisticated techniques analysts use to determine the meaning of collected data. While the computer has made data analysis much easier, and has provided researchers with many more opportunities for examining various facets of the data, we would be remiss if we did not close this chapter on a note of caution.

In Research Window 21.3 a well-known writer of the pre-computer era points out the hazards inherent in forecasting the future based on data collected in the past. For those of you who will be researchers, or even simply users of data, equations and statistical techniques will be important, but no more important than a heavy dose of common sense.

Research Window 21.3
Life on the Mississippi—742 Years from Now

Mark Twain may not have been a statistician, but he knew enough about the tricks numbers can play to write this little spoof for those who would predict "logical" outcomes based on past data.

"In the space of one hundred and seventy-six years the Lower Mississippi has shortened itself two hundred and forty-two miles. This is an average of a trifle over one mile and a third per year. Therefore, any calm person, who is not blind or idiotic, can see that in the Old Oölitic Silurian Period, just a million years ago next November, the Lower Mississippi River was upward of one million three hundred thousand miles long, and stuck out over the Gulf of Mexico like a fishing-rod. And by the same token any person can see that seven hundred and forty-two years from now the Lower Mississippi will be only a mile and three-quarters long, and Cairo and New Orleans will have joined their streets together, and be plodding comfortably along under a single mayor and a mutual board of aldermen. There is something fascinating about science. One gets such wholesale returns of conjecture out of such a trifling investment of fact."

Mark Twain knew about the tricks numbers can play.

Source: The Bettmann Archive.

Source: From *Life on the Mississippi*, p. 156, by Mark Twain.

Back to the Case

"The fact that white-collar men have a more favorable attitude about shopping through the Lovelace catalog is incredibly useful," said Angela Spaulding, "but there were other things I was interested in, too. For example, what's the breakdown of married versus nonmarried men?

What about how long they've been employed?"

"If you've got the stomach for some more tables, I've got the answers," declared Michael Wyse.

"Go ahead," replied Spaulding.

"Okay, you asked about marital status and years worked. Well, we

used a multiple-regression analysis to determine if the ATTLOVE index was related to those demographic characteristics.

"Since marital status can be broken into a variety of categories, we had to convert the categories into four dummy variables. Take a look at this table," he continued, handing Spaulding Table 3.

"Once again, we determined that the overall regression equation was statistically significant. Further, we discovered that the variables, taken together, account for 93 percent of the variation in the ATTLOVE index, as you can see from the adjusted *R*-squared value of .931," Wyse said.

"These results are particularly interesting, since they give us a chance to see the values for each of the categories of marital status, as they are keyed to the dummy variables. Look at this list," Wyse said,

handing a small table to Spaulding. (See Table 4 on page 726.)

"If we consider single people as the null state, we can see that marriage—even if it ends in divorce or the wife's death—seems to predispose men toward buying from Lovelace. Look at the *D2* value, for example. It shows that there is an increase in the ATTLOVE index of 2.85 on average if the man is married rather than single," Wyse said.

"What if I want to know the difference between married men and divorced men?" asked Spaulding.

"Easy," replied Wyse. "Just subtract one from the other. Divorced men have an ATTLOVE index approximately 4.16 higher on average than married men, since *D4* minus *D2* equals 4.155.

"This is great stuff, Michael," exclaimed Spaulding. "Now all I need to do is figure out the best way to get my hands on a huge list of divorced white-collar men, and I'll be all set!"

Table 3   ***Multiple-Regression Analysis of ATTLOVE Index versus Several Demographic Characteristics***

Dependent variable . . . ATTLOVE
Variable(s) entered on step number 1: *D2*
                                        V41
                                        V42
                                        D5
                                        D4
                                        D3

Analysis of Variance	DF	Sum of Squares	Mean Square	F
Regression	6	5042.459	840.410	277.036
Residual	117	354.928	3.034	

Multiple *R*	.967
R-squared	.934
Adjusted *R*-squared	.931
Standard error	1.742

Variables in the Equation

Variable	B	Beta	Standard Error B	F
D2	2.851	.165	.627	20.668
V41	3.753	.283	.600	39.081
V42	.213	.368	.029	55.626
D5	7.577	.550	.935	65.625
D4	7.006	.391	.948	54.618
D3	4.387	.267	.646	46.076
(Constant)	4.491			

Table 4   ***Relationship between ATTLOVE Index and Respondents' Marital Status When Converted to Dummy Variables***

$$D2 = 2.851$$
$$D3 = 4.387$$
$$D4 = 7.006$$
$$D5 = 7.577$$

where the various D's are defined thus:

$V43 =$	Implying	$D2$	$D3$	$D4$	$D5$
1	Single	0	0	0	0
2	Married	1	0	0	0
3	Separated	0	1	0	0
4	Divorced	0	0	1	0
5	Widowed	0	0	0	1

Summary

Learning Objective 1: Explain the difference between regression and correlation analysis.

Analysts use correlation analysis to measure the *closeness* of the relationship between two or more variables. The technique considers the joint variation of two measures, neither of which is restricted by the experimenter.

Regression analysis refers to the techniques used to derive an *equation* that relates the criterion variable to one or more predictor variables. It considers the frequency distribution of the criterion variable when one or more predictor variables are held fixed at various levels.

Learning Objective 2: List the three assumptions that are made about the error term in the least-squares solution to a regression problem.

There are three simplifying assumptions made about the error term in the least-squares solution:

1. The mean or average value of the error term is zero.
2. The variance of the error term is constant and is independent of the values of the predictor variable.
3. The values of the error term are independent of one another.

Learning Objective 3: Discuss what the Gauss-Markov theorem says about the least-squares estimators of a population parameter.

According to the Gauss-Markov theorem, the least-squares estimators are BLUE, that is, they are the *b*est, *l*inear, *u*nbiased *e*stimators of the true population parameters regardless of the shape of the distribution of the error term.

Learning Objective 4: Define *standard error of estimate*.

The standard error of estimate is an absolute measure of the lack of fit of the equation to the data.

Learning Objective 5: Specify the relationship that a correlation coefficient is designed to measure.

A correlation coefficient measures the strength of the linear relationship between Y and X.

Learning Objective 6: Discuss the difference between simple regression analysis and multiple-regression analysis.

The basic idea behind multiple-regression analysis is the same as that behind simple regression: to determine the relationship between independent and dependent, that is, predictor and criterion, variables. In multiple-regression analysis, however, several predictor variables are used to estimate a single criterion variable.

Learning Objective 7: Explain what is meant by multicollinearity in a multiple-regression problem.

Multicollinearity is said to be present in a multiple-regression problem when the predictor variables are correlated among themselves.

Learning Objective 8: Describe when a partial-regression coefficient is used and what it measures.

If the predictor variables are not correlated among themselves, each partial-regression coefficient indicates the average change in the criterion variable per unit change in the predictor variable in question, holding the other predictor variables constant.

Learning Objective 9: Explain the difference between the coefficient of multiple determination and the coefficient of partial determination.

The coefficient of multiple determination measures the proportion of the variation in the criterion variable accounted for, or "explained," by all the predictor variables, while the coefficient of partial determination measures the relative degree to which a given variable adds to our knowledge of the criterion variable over and above that provided by other predictor variables.

Learning Objective 10: Describe how the use of dummy variables and variable transformations expands the scope of the regression model.

Dummy, or binary, variables allow the introduction of classificatory or nominally scaled variables in the regression equation, while variable transformations considerably increase the scope of the regression model, since they allow certain nonlinear relationships to be considered.

Discussion Questions, Problems, and Projects

1. The chancellor of Enormous State University has decided that ESU needs to develop a new marketing plan in order to attract the best students. The objective is to attract students who will have the best chance of graduating within five years of their matriculation. The administration has assigned you, the associate vice-chancellor, the responsibility for carrying out this project. You have decided that, as part of the research to be performed in designing the new marketing plan, it would be helpful to know what, if any, characteristics possessed by high school seniors are associated with success in college. After devoting some thought to the problem, you decide that a multiple-regression approach seems to be the way to proceed. Your task is simplified by the existence of a large, comprehensive data base that contains the results of several broad-based surveys of high school seniors, many of whom later attended ESU. However, you know that simply mining the data base is not likely to be much help. Accordingly, your first task is to develop a theory of why students succeed in college. After explaining your theory, specify the criterion variable and predictor variables that you will use in the regression equation. How serious a problem is multicollinearity in the data likely to be, given your objective?

2. The Crystallo Bottling Company, which provides glass bottles to various soft drink manufacturers, has the following information pertaining to the number of cases per shipment and the corresponding transportation costs:

Number of Cases per Shipment	Transportation Costs in Dollars
1,500	200
2,200	260
3,500	310
4,300	360
5,800	420
6,500	480
7,300	540
8,200	630
8,500	710
9,800	730

The marketing manager is interested in studying the relationship between the number of cases per shipment and the transportation costs. Your assistance is required in performing a simple regression analysis.

(a) Plot the transportation costs as a function of the number of cases per shipment.
(b) Interpret the scatter diagram.
(c) Calculate the coefficients $\hat{\alpha}$ and $\hat{\beta}$ and develop the regression equation.
(d) What is the interpretation of the coefficients $\hat{\alpha}$ and $\hat{\beta}$?
(e) Calculate the standard error of estimate.
(f) What is the interpretation of the standard error of estimate you calculated?
(g) Compute the t value with $n - 2$ degrees of freedom with the use of the following formula for the square root of the variance of the distribution of β's

$$s_{\hat{\beta}} = \sqrt{\frac{s_{Y/X}^2}{\sum_{i=1}^{10} (X_i - \bar{x})^2}}$$

$$t = \frac{\hat{\beta}_1 - \beta_1}{s_{\hat{\beta}_1}}$$

where β is assumed to be zero under the null hypothesis of no relationship; that is,

$$H_0: \beta_1 = 0$$
$$H_a: \beta_1 \neq 0$$

(h) What is the tabled t value at a 0.05 significance level?
(i) What can you conclude about the relationship between transportation costs and number of cases shipped?
(j) The marketing manager wants to estimate the transportation costs for 18 cases.
(i) Use the regression model to derive the average value of Y_0.
(ii) Provide a confidence interval for the estimate using the following:

$$s_{\hat{Y}/X_{01}}^2 = s_{Y/X_1}^2 \left[\frac{1}{n} + \frac{(X_{01} - \bar{x})^2}{\sum_{i=1}^{10} (X_{i1} - \bar{x})^2} \right]$$

$$\hat{Y}_0 \pm t \, s_{\hat{Y}/X_{01}} =$$

3. The marketing manager of Crystallo Bottling Company wants to determine if there is an association between the size of cartons and the transportation costs per shipment. (The company follows a policy of including the same size cartons for any particular shipment.) The information pertaining to size of carton is given below.

Refer to the previous question for information on the transportation costs per shipment.

(a) Calculate the correlation coefficient.
(b) Interpret the correlation coefficient.
(c) Calculate the coefficient of determination.
(d) Interpret the coefficient of determination.

4. The marketing manager of Crystallo Bottling Company is considering multiple-regression analysis with the number of cartons per shipment and the size of cartons as predictor variables and transportation costs as the criterion variable (refer to the previous problem). He has devised the following regression equation:

$$\hat{Y} = \hat{\alpha}_{(12)} + \hat{\beta}_{Y1.2}X_1 + \hat{\beta}_{Y2.1}X_2 = -41.44 - 3.95X_1 + 24.44X_2$$

where X_1 is the number of cartons per shipment and X_2 is the size of the cartons.

(a) Interpret $\hat{\alpha}_{(12)}$, $\hat{\beta}_{Y1.2}$, and $\hat{\beta}_{Y2.1}$.
(b) Is multiple regression appropriate in this situation? If yes, why? If no, why not?

5. An analyst for a large shoe manufacturer developed a formal linear regression model to predict sales of its 122 retail stores located in different MSAs (Metropolitan Statistical Areas) in the United States. The model was as follows:

$$Y_{(123)} = \alpha_{(123)} + \beta_{1.23}X_1 + \beta_{2.13}X_2 + \beta_{3.12}X_3$$

where

$$X_1 = \text{population in surrounding area in thousands}$$
$$X_2 = \text{marginal propensity to consume}$$
$$X_3 = \text{median personal income in surrounding area in thousands of dollars}$$
$$Y = \text{sales in thousands of dollars}$$

Some empirical results were as follows:

Variable	Regression Coefficient	Coefficient Standard Errors ($s_{\beta i}$)
X_1	$\hat{\beta}_{1.23} = 0.49$	0.24
X_2	$\hat{\beta}_{2.13} = -0.40$	95
X_3	$\hat{\beta}_{3.12} = 225$	105
$R^2 = 0.47$	$\hat{\alpha} = -40$	225

(a) Interpret each of the regression coefficients.
(b) Are X_1, X_2, and X_3 significant at the 0.05 level? Show your calculations.
(c) Which independent variable seems to be the most significant predictor?
(d) Provide an interpretation of the R^2 value.
(e) The marketing research department of the shoe manufacturer wants to include an index that indicates whether the service in each store is poor, fair, or good. The coding scheme is as follows:

$$1 = \text{poor service}$$
$$2 = \text{fair service}$$
$$3 = \text{good service}$$

(i) Indicate how you would transform this index so that it could be included in the model. Be specific.

     (ii) Write out the regression model, including the preceding transformation.

     (iii) Suppose two of the parameters for the index are 4.6 and 10.3. Interpret these values in light of the scheme you adopted.

6. A survey was commissioned by Beyond the Blue Horizon (BBH) Travel Agency to help the agency better target its promotional efforts. BBH specializes in cruise ship tours that typically cost between seven and eight thousand dollars per couple. One objective of the research project is to predict the amount of money that couples spend on a vacation package, based on several socioeconomic characteristics (e.g., income level). BBH's rationale is that if such a relationship can be discovered, the agency can buy mailing lists designed to cover individuals that have the desired socioeconomic profile. One part of the survey asked respondents to indicate their type of employment. Given the following categories, respondents were asked to check the one category that best described their job or profession.

Attorney	Physician
Business Management	Accountant
Dentist	University Faculty
Sales	Other

    (a) Develop a coding scheme that will allow the employment variable to be introduced into a multiple-regression equation.

    (b) Assume that the analyst wishes to run a regression model that includes only the employment data. Write the regression model.

7. (a) List the assumptions underlying regression analysis.

    (b) List the possible limitations of regression analysis.

    (c) Identify one important practical application of regression analysis for a marketing manager.

8. Refer to the following article: William Qualls, Richard W. Olshavsky, and Ronald E. Michaels, "Shortening of the PLC—An Empirical Test," *Journal of Marketing*, 45 (Fall 1981), pp. 76–80.

    (a) What regression model have the authors used to derive Figure I of the study? What was the purpose of this model?

    (b) Was the regression coefficient found to be significant? What was the level of significance?

9. Refer to the following article: Lawrence A. Crosby and James R. Taylor, "Consumer Satisfaction with Michigan's Container Deposit Law: An Ecological Perspective," *Journal of Marketing*, 46 (Winter 1982), pp. 47–60.

    (a) Refer to Table 3 of the study. What does this table indicate?

    (b) What does the following footnote indicate: "Unless indicated otherwise, all r's are significant at the 95-percent confidence level"? What hypothesis is this a test of?

    (c) Which two variables have the highest correlation coefficient?

Refer to the NFO Research, Inc. coffee study described on pages 647 in Chapter 19 for the next three problems.

10. Use simple linear regression to investigate the association between the predictor variable age (as a continuous variable) and the criterion variable "value" index score composed of the following attributes from question 6 for Folgers: good value for the money, economy brand, costs less than other brands.

11. Repeat the previous analysis using dummy codes for age in the following categories:

35 years or less
36–45 years
46–59 years
60 years or more

Compare these results with those obtained previously.

12. Investigate the association between the "taste" index score for Yuban and the use (or nonuse) of the various additives from question 3 using multiple regression. The "taste" index will serve as the dependent variable and is composed of the following items from question 6: rich taste, always fresh, full-bodied taste, smooth taste, not bitter, has no aftertaste.

Endnotes

1. Although the regression model theoretically applies to fixed levels of the predictor variables (X's), it can also be shown to apply when the X's themselves are random variables, assuming certain conditions are satisfied. See John Neter, William Wasserman, and Michael H. Kutner, *Applied Linear Regression Models* (Homewood, Ill.: Richard D. Irwin, 1983), pp. 83–84; or Thomas H. Wonnacott and Ronald J. Wonnacott, *Regression: A Second Course in Statistics* (New York: John Wiley, 1981), pp. 49–50.

2. Donald R. Lehmann, *Market Research and Analysis*, 2nd ed. (Homewood, Ill.: Richard D. Irwin, 1985), p. 482.

3. See Darrell Huff, *How to Lie with Statistics* (New York: Norton, 1954), pp. 87–99, for a discussion of this point using some rather humorous anecdotes.

4. Strictly speaking, the regression model requires that errors of measurement be associated only with the criterion variable and that the predictor variables be measured without error. See Wonnacott and Wonnacott, *Regression*, pp. 293–299, for a discussion of the problems and solutions when the predictor variables also have an error component.

5. For those who would like to try solving for each of these values, the formulas are

$$\hat{\alpha} = \bar{y} - \hat{\beta}\bar{x},$$

$$\hat{\beta} = \frac{n\sum_{i=1}^{n} X_i Y_i - \left(\sum_{i=1}^{n} X_i\right)\left(\sum_{i=1}^{n} Y_i\right)}{n\sum_{i=1}^{n} X_i^2 - \left(\sum_{i=1}^{n} X_i\right)^2}$$

where

$$\bar{y} = \sum_{i=1}^{n} \frac{Y_i}{n} \text{ and } \bar{x} = \sum_{i=1}^{n} \frac{X_i}{n}.$$

6. Many of the results contained in the discussion were determined by computer and thus may differ slightly from those generated using hand calculations because of the rounding errors associated with the latter method.

7. This assumption will be modified shortly to that of normally distributed errors. It is made this way now in order to make more vivid the fact that the assumption of normally distributed errors is only necessary if statistical inferences are to be made about the coefficients.

8. M. G. Kendall, *A Course in Multivariate Analysis* (London: Charles Griffin, 1957), p. 74. See also Howard E. Doran, *Applied Regression Analysis in Econometrics* (New York: Marcel Dekker, Inc., 1989).

9. There are some things that the analyst faced with multicollinear data can do. See R. R. Hocking, "Developments in Linear Regression Methodology: 1959–1982," *Technometrics*, 25 (August 1983), pp. 219–230, and Ronald D. Snee, "Discussion," *Technometrics*, 25 (August 1983), pp. 230–237, for a discussion of the problem and some alternative ways of handling it.

10. There is another interpretation danger in the example that was not discussed. It is not unreasonable to assume that both the number of sales representatives serving a territory and the number of television spots per month were both determined on the basis of territorial potential. If this is the case, the implied causality is reversed or at least confused; instead of the number of sales representatives and number of television spots determining sales, sales in a sense (potential sales anyway) determine the former quantities, and they in turn could be expected to affect realized sales. If this is actually the case, the coefficient-estimating procedure needs to take into account the two-way "causation" among the variables. See Wonnacott and Wonnacott, *Regression*, pp. 284–292, for a discussion of the problems and the logic underlying the estimation of simultaneous equation systems.

11. For a useful discussion of some alternative ways to code dummy variables and the different insights that can be provided by the various alternatives, see Jacob Cohen and Patricia Cohen, *Applied Multiple Regression/Correlation Analysis for the Behavioral Sciences*, 2nd ed. (Hillsdale, N.J.: Lawrence Erlbaum, 1983), pp. 181–222.

12. See Ronald E. Frank, "Use of Transformations," *Journal of Marketing Research*, 3 (August 1966), pp. 247–253, for a discussion of these conditions and how the proper transformation can serve to fulfill them. See Leonard Jon Parsons and Piet Vanden Abeele, "Analysis of Sales Call Effectiveness," *Journal of Marketing Research*, 18 (February 1981), pp. 107–113, for an example that uses the log transformation.

Suggested Additional Readings

For a detailed discussion of regression and correlation analysis, see

Jacob Cohen and Patricia Cohen, *Applied Multiple Regression/Correlation Analysis for the Behavioral Sciences*, 2nd ed. (Hillsdale, N.J.: Lawrence Erlbaum, 1983).

John Neter, William Wasserman, and Michael H. Kutner, *Applied Linear Regression Models* (Homewood, Ill.: Richard D. Irwin, 1983).

Thomas H. Wonnacott and Ronald J. Wonnacott, *Regression: A Second Course in Statistics* (New York: John Wiley, 1981).

Nonparametric Measures of Association

Chapter 21 focused on the product-moment correlation as the measure of association. While the product-moment correlation coefficient was originally developed to deal with continuous variables, it has proven quite robust to scale type and can sometimes handle variables that are ordinal or dichotomous as well as those that are interval.[1] Though widely applicable, it is not universally applicable. This appendix therefore treats some alternate measures of association, namely, the contingency table and coefficient that are appropriate for nominal data and also the Spearman's rank-order correlation coefficient and the coefficient of concordance, which are suited to the analysis of rank-order data.

Contingency Table

One problem researchers often encounter in analyzing nominal data is the independence of variables of classification. In Chapter 19, for example, we examined a number of questions involving the relationship between automobile purchases and family characteristics. At that time, we conducted no statistical tests of significance, thus avoiding the question of whether the results reflected sample aberrations or represented true population conditions. If statistical tests had been run at that time, they would have been primarily of the chi-square contingency-table type, which is ideally suited for investigating the independence of variables in cross classifications.

Consider, for example, a consumer study involving the preferences of families for different sizes of washing machines. A priori, it would seem that larger families would be more prone to buy the larger units and smaller families the smaller units. To investigate this question, suppose the manufacturer checked a random sample of those purchasers who returned their warranty cards. Included on the warranty cards was a question on the size of the family. Although not a perfect population for analysis, the manufacturer felt it was good enough for this purpose since some 85 percent of all warranty cards are returned. Furthermore, it was a relatively economical way to proceed, since the data were internal. The study could be carried out by checking a random sample of warranty cards for family size and machine purchased.

A random sample of 300 of these cards provided the data in Table 21A.1. The assignment is to determine if family size affects the size of the machine that is purchased. The null hypothesis is that the variables are independent; the alternate is that they are not. Suppose a significance level of $\alpha = 0.10$ was chosen for the test. To calculate a χ^2 statistic, one needs to generate the expected number of cases likely to fall into each category. *The expected number is generated by assuming that the null hypothesis is indeed true*, that is, that there

---

Table 21A.1   *Size of Washing Machine versus Size of Family*

Size of Washing Machine Purchased	Size of Family in Members			Total
	1 to 2	3 to 4	5 or More	
8-lb. load	25	37	8	70
10-lb. load	10	62	53	125
12-lb. load	5	41	59	105
Total	40	140	120	300

is no relationship between size of machine purchased and family size. Suppose size of machine purchased is denoted by the variable A and size of family by the variable B and that

$$A_1 = \text{purchase of an 8-lb. load washing machine}$$
$$A_2 = \text{purchase of a 10-lb. load washing machine}$$
$$A_3 = \text{purchase of a 12-lb. load washing machine}$$
$$B_1 = \text{family of one to two members}$$
$$B_2 = \text{family of three to four members}$$
$$B_3 = \text{family of five or more members}$$

If variables A and B are indeed independent, then the probability of occurrence of the event A_1B_1 (a family of one to two members purchased an 8-lb. load machine) is given as the product of the separate probabilities for A_1 and B_1; that is,

$$P(A_1B_1) = P(A_1)P(B_1)$$

by the multiplication law of probabilities for independent events. Now $P(A_1)$ is given by the number of cases possessing the characteristic A_1, n_{A_1}, over the total number of cases n. $P(A_1)$ is thus

$$\frac{n_{A_1}}{n} = \frac{70}{300} = \frac{7}{30}.$$

Similarly, $P(B_1)$ is given by the number of cases having the characteristic B_1, n_{B_1}, over the total number of cases, or $P(B_1) = n_{B_1}/n = 40/300 = 2/15$. The joint probability $P(A_1B_1)$ is

$$P(A_1B_1) = P(A_1)P(B_1) = \left(\frac{7}{30}\right)\left(\frac{2}{15}\right) = \frac{7}{225}.$$

Given a total of 300 cases, the number expected to fall in the cell A_1B_1, E_{11} is given as the product of the total number of cases and the probability of any one of these cases falling into the A_1B_1 cell, that is,

$$E_{11} = nP(A_1B_1) = 300(7/225) = 9.33.$$

Although this is the underlying rationale for generating the expected frequencies, there is an easier computational form. Recall that $P(A_1) = n_{A_1}/n$ and that $P(B_1) = n_{B_1}/n$ and that $P(A_1B_1) = P(A_1)P(B_1)$. The formula for E_{11} upon substitution then reduces to

$$E_{11} = nP(A_1B_1) = nP(A_1)P(B_1)$$
$$= n\frac{n_{A_1}}{n}\frac{n_{B_1}}{n} = \frac{n_{A_1}n_{B_1}}{n}$$
$$= \frac{70 \times 40}{300} = 9.33.$$

Thus to generate the expected frequencies for each cell, one needs merely to multiply the marginal frequencies and divide by the total. The remaining expected frequencies, which are calculated in like manner, are entered in the lower right-hand corner of each cell in Table 21A.2. The calculated χ^2 value is thus

$$\chi^2 = \sum_{i=1}^{3} \sum_{j=1}^{3} \frac{(O_{ij} - E_{ij})^2}{E_{ij}}$$

$$= \frac{(25 - 9.33)^2}{9.33} + \frac{(37 - 32.67)^2}{32.67} + \frac{(8 - 28.00)^2}{28.00}$$

$$+ \frac{(10 - 16.67)^2}{16.67} + \frac{(62 - 58.33)^2}{58.33} + \frac{(53 - 50.00)^2}{50.00}$$

$$+ \frac{(5 - 14.00)^2}{14.00} + \frac{(41 - 49.00)^2}{49.00} + \frac{(59 - 42.00)^2}{42.00}$$

$$= 26.318 + 0.574 + 14.286 + 2.669 + 0.231 + 0.180 + 5.786 + 1.306 + 6.881$$

$$= 58.231$$

where O_{ij} and E_{ij}, respectively, denote the actual number and expected number of observations that fall in the $_{ij}$ cell. Now the expected frequencies in any row add to the marginal total. This must be true because of the way the expected frequencies were calculated. Thus, as soon as we know any two expected frequencies in a row, say, 9.33 and 32.67 in Row A_1, for example, the third expected frequency is fixed, because the three must add to the marginal total. This means that there are only $(c - 1)$ degrees of freedom in a row, where c is the number of columns. A similar argument applies to the columns; that is, there are $r - 1$ degrees of freedom per column, where r is the number of rows. The degrees of freedom in total in a two-way contingency table are thus given by

$$\nu = (r - 1)(c - 1).$$

In our problem $\nu = (3 - 1)(3 - 1) = 4$. Using our assumed $\alpha = 0.10$, the tabled critical value of χ^2 for four degrees of freedom is 7.78 (see Table 2 in the appendix). Computed $\chi^2 = 58.231$ thus falls in the critical region. The null hypothesis of independence is

Table 21A.2   **Size of Washing Machine versus Size of Family: Observed and Expected Frequencies**

Size of Washing Machine Purchased	Size of Family in Members			Total
	B_1 1 to 2	B_2 3 to 4	B_3 5 or More	
A_1—8-lb. load	25	37	8	70
	9.33	32.67	28.00	
A_2—10-lb. load	10	62	53	125
	16.67	58.33	50.00	
A_3—12-lb. load	5	41	59	105
	14.00	49.00	42.00	
Total	40	140	120	300

rejected. Family size is shown to be a factor in determining size of washing machine purchased.

In one form or another, the chi-square test is probably the most widely used test in marketing research, and the serious student is well advised to become familiar with its requirements.

Contingency Coefficient

While the χ^2 contingency-table test indicates whether two variables are independent, it does not measure the strength of association when they are dependent. The contingency coefficient can be used for this latter purpose. Since the contingency coefficient is directly related to the χ^2 test, it can be generated by the researcher with relatively little additional computational effort. The formula for the contingency coefficient, call it C, is

$$C = \sqrt{\frac{\chi^2}{n + \chi^2}}$$

where n is the sample size and χ^2 is calculated in the normal way.

Recall that calculated χ^2 for the data in Table 21A.1 was 58.23, and that since the calculated value was larger than the critical tabled value, the null hypothesis of independence was rejected. While the conclusion that naturally follows—that family size affects the size of washing machine purchased—is an interesting finding, it is only part of the story. Although the variables are dependent, what is the strength of the association between them? The contingency coefficient helps answer this question. The contingency coefficient is

$$C = \sqrt{\frac{58.23}{300 + 58.23}} = 0.403.$$

Does this value indicate strong or weak association between the variables? We cannot say without comparing the calculated value against its limits. When there is no association between the variables, the contingency coefficient will be zero. Unfortunately though, the contingency coefficient does not possess the other attractive property of the Pearsonian product-moment correlation coefficient of being equal to 1 when the variables are completely dependent or perfectly correlated. Rather, its upper limit is a function of the number of categories. When the number of categories is the same for each variable, that is, when the number of rows r equals the number of columns c, the upper limit on the contingency coefficient for two perfectly correlated variables is

$$\sqrt{(r - 1)/r}.$$

In the example at hand, $r = c = 3$, and thus the upper limit for the contingency coefficient is

$$\sqrt{\frac{2}{3}} = 0.816.$$

The calculated value is approximately halfway between the limits of zero for no association and 0.816 for perfect association, suggesting there is moderate association between size of family and size of washing machine purchased.

Spearman's Rank-Order Correlation Coefficient

The Spearman correlation coefficient, denoted r_s, is one of the best-known coefficients of association for rank-order data. The coefficient is appropriate when there are two variables per object, both of which are measured on an ordinal scale so that the objects may be ranked in two ordered series.[2]

Table 21A.3   *Distributor Performance*

Distributor	Service Ranking X_i	Overall Performance Ranking Y_i	Ranking Difference $d_i = X_i - Y_i$	Difference Squared d_i^2
1	6	8	−2	4
2	2	4	+2	4
3	13	12	+1	1
4	1	2	−1	1
5	7	10	−3	9
6	4	5	−1	1
7	11	9	+2	4
8	15	13	+2	4
9	3	1	+2	4
10	9	6	+3	9
11	12	14	−2	4
12	5	3	+2	4
13	14	15	−1	1
14	8	7	+1	1
15	10	11	−1	1

$$\sum_{i=1}^{15} d_i^2 = 52$$

Suppose, for instance, that a company wishes to determine whether there is any association between the overall performance of a distributor and the distributor's level of service. Again, there are many measures of overall performance: sales, market share, sales growth, profit, and so on. The company in our example feels that no single measure adequately defines distributor performance, but that overall performance is a composite of all of these measures. Thus, the marketing research department is assigned the task of developing an index of performance that effectively incorporates all of these characteristics. The department is also assigned the responsibility of evaluating each distributor in terms of the service he or she provides. This evaluation is to be based on customer complaints, customer compliments, service turnaround records, and so on. The research department feels that the indices it develops to measure these characteristics could be employed to rank-order the distributors with respect to overall performance and service.

Table 21A.3 contains the ranks of the company's 15 distributors with respect to each of the performance criteria. One way to determine whether there is any association between service and overall performance would be to look at the differences in ranks based on each of the two variables. Let X_i be the rank of the ith distributor with respect to service and Y_i be the rank of the ith distributor with regard to overall performance, and let $d_i = X_i - Y_i$ be the difference in rankings for the ith distributor. Now if the rankings on the two variables are exactly the same, each d_i will be zero. If there is some discrepancy in ranks, some of the d_i's will not be zero. Further, the greater the discrepancy, the larger will be some of the d_i's. Therefore, one way of looking at the association between the variables would be to examine the sum of the d_i's. The difficulty with this measure is that some of the negative d_i's would cancel some of the positive ones. To circumvent this difficulty, the differences are squared in calculating the Spearman rank-order correlation coefficient. The calculation formula is as follows:[3]

$$r_s = 1 - \frac{6 \sum_{i=1}^{n} d_i^2}{n(n^2 - 1)}.$$

In the example at hand,

$$\sum_{i=1}^{15} d_i^2 = 52$$

and

$$r_s = 1 - \frac{6(52)}{15(15^2 - 1)} = 1 - \frac{312}{3,360} = 0.907.$$

Now the null hypothesis for the example would be that there is no association between service level and overall distributor performance, while the alternate hypothesis would suggest there is a relationship. The null hypothesis that $r_s = 0$ can be tested by referring directly to tables of critical values of r_s or, when the number of sample objects is greater than 10, by calculating the t statistic

$$t = r_s \sqrt{\frac{n - 2}{1 - r_s^2}}$$

which is referred to a t table for $v = n - 2$ degrees of freedom. Calculated t is

$$t = 0.907 \sqrt{\frac{15 - 2}{1 - (0.907)^2}} = 7.77$$

while critical t for $\alpha = 0.05$ and $v = 13$ degrees of freedom is 2.16. Calculated t exceeds critical t, and the null hypothesis of no relationship is rejected. Overall distributor performance is related to service level. The upper limit for the Spearman rank-order correlation coefficient is 1, since if there were perfect agreement in the ranks, $\sum_{i=1}^{n} d_i^2$ would be zero. Thus the relationship is significant and relatively strong.

Coefficient of Concordance

So far we have been concerned with the correlation between *two* sets of rankings of n objects. There has been an X and Y measure in the form of ranks for each object. There will be cases in which we wish to analyze the association among three or more rankings of n objects or individuals. When there are k sets of rankings, Kendall's *coefficient of concordance*, W, can be employed to examine the association among the k variables.

One particularly important use of the coefficient of concordance is in examining interjudge reliability. Consider a computer equipment manufacturer interested in evaluating its domestic sales branch managers. Many criteria could be used: sales of the branch office, sales in relation to the branch's potential, sales growth, and sales representative turnover are just a few. Assume that the company feels that different executives in the company would place different emphasis on the various criteria and that a consensus with respect to how the criteria should be weighted would be hard to achieve. The company therefore decides that the vice-president in charge of marketing, the general sales manager, and the marketing research department should all attempt to rank the ten

Table 21A.4   **Branch Manager Rankings**

Branch Manager	Rank Advocated by			Sum of Ranks R_i
	Vice-President of Marketing	General Sales Manager	Marketing Research Department	
A	4	4	5	13
B	3	2	2	7
C	9	10	10	29
D	10	9	9	28
E	2	3	3	8
F	1	1	1	3
G	6	5	4	15
H	8	7	7	22
I	5	6	6	17
J	7	8	8	23

branch managers from best to worst, and that these rankings will be examined to determine whether there is agreement among them (see Table 21A.4).

The right-hand column of Table 21A.4 contains the sum of ranks assigned to each branch manager. Now if there were perfect agreement among the three rankings, the sum of ranks, R_i, for the top-rated branch manager would be $1 + 1 + 1 = k$, where $k = 3$. The second-rated branch manager would have sum of ranks $2 + 2 + 2 = 2k$, and the nth-rated branch manager would have the sum of ranks $n + n + n = nk$. Accordingly, when there is perfect agreement among the k sets of rankings, the R_i would be k, $2k$, $3k$, . . ., nk. If there is little agreement among the k ratings, the R_i would be approximately equal. Thus, the degree of agreement among the k rankings could be measured by the variance of the n sums of ranks; the greater the agreement, the larger would be the variance in the n sums.

The coefficient of concordance, W, is a function of the variance in the sums of ranks. It is calculated in the following way. First, the sum of the R_i for each of the n rows is determined. Second, the average R_i, $\bar{R}$, is calculated by dividing the sum of the R_i by the number of objects. Third, the sum of the squared deviations is determined; call this quantity s, where

$$s = \sum_{i=1}^{n} (R_i - \bar{R})^2.$$

The coefficient of concordance is then computed as

$$W = \frac{s}{\frac{1}{12}k^2(n^3 - n)}.$$

The denominator of the coefficient represents the maximum possible variation in sums of ranks if there were perfect agreement in the rankings. The numerator, of course, reflects the actual variation in ranks. The larger the ratio, the greater is the agreement among the evaluations.

$$\bar{R} = \frac{\sum_{i=1}^{n} R_i}{n} = \frac{13 + 7 + \ldots + 23}{10} = \frac{165}{10} = 16.5$$

$$s = (13 - 16.5)^2 + (7 - 16.5)^2 + \ldots + (23 - 16.5)^2 = 720.5$$

and

$$\frac{1}{12} k^2 (n^3 - n) = \frac{1}{12} (3)^2 (10^3 - 10) = 742.5.$$

Thus

$$W = \frac{720.5}{742.5} = 0.970.$$

The significance of W can be examined by using special tables when the number of objects being ranked is small, in particular, when $n \leq 7$. When there are more than seven objects, the coefficient of concordance is approximately chi-square distributed where $\chi^2 = k(n - 1) W$ with $\nu = n - 1$ degrees of freedom. The null hypothesis is that there is no agreement among the rankings, while the alternate hypothesis is that these is some agreement. For an assumed $\alpha = 0.05$, critical χ^2 for $\nu = n - 1 = 9$ degrees of freedom is 16.92, while calculated χ^2 is

$$\chi^2 = k(n - 1) W = 3 (9)(0.970) = 26.2.$$

Calculated χ^2 exceeds critical χ^2, and the null hypothesis of no agreement is rejected, because there indeed is agreement. Further, the agreement is good, as is evidenced by the calculated coefficient of concordance. The limits of W are zero with no agreement and 1 with perfect agreement among the ranks. The calculated value of W of 0.970 suggests that while the agreement in the ranks is not perfect, it is certainly good. The marketing vice-president, the general sales manager, and the marketing research department are applying essentially the same standards in ranking the branch managers.

Kendall has suggested that the best estimate of the true ranking of n objects is provided by the order of the various sums of ranks, R_i, when W is significant.[4] Thus, the best estimate of the true ranking of the sales managers is that F is doing the best job, B the next best job, and C the poorest job.

Endnotes

1. Jum Nunnally, *Psychometric Theory*, 2nd ed. (New York: Mc-Graw-Hill, 1978), especially pp. 117–150. For an empirical comparison of how various correlation coefficients perform with rating scale data, see Emin Babakus and Carl E. Ferguson, Jr., "On Choosing the Appropriate Measure of Association When Analyzing Rating Scale Data," *Journal of the Academy of Marketing Science*, 16 (Spring 1988), pp. 95–102.

2. The Spearman rank correlation coefficient is a shortcut version of the product-moment correlation coefficient, in that both coefficients produce the same estimates of the strength of association between two sets of ranks. The rank correlation coefficient is easy to conceptualize and calculate, so it is often used when the data are ranked. See Nunnally, *Psychometric Theory*, pp. 134–135.

3. See Leonard A. Marascuilo and Maryellen McSweeney, *Nonparametric and Distribution-Free Methods for the Social Sciences*, (Belmont, Calif.: Brooks/Cole, 1977), pp. 250–251. See also Jean Dickinson Gibbons, *Nonparametric Statistical Inference*, 2nd ed. (New York: Marcell Dekker, Inc., 1985).

4. M. G. Kendall, *Rank Correlation Methods* (London: Griffin, 1948), p. 87.

Research Project

The sixth stage in the research process is to analyze and interpret the data. All the earlier steps in the research process were undertaken to support this search for meaning. Most data analysis begins with the preliminary steps of editing, coding, and tabulating the data. The results are often analyzed further to determine if the differences are statistically significant, or if there is any correlation between the variables.

CARA researchers had begun their study with two objectives:

1. Identify business decision makers' attitudes toward the advertising media of newspaper, radio, and television.
2. Identify business decision makers' attitudes toward the advertising sales representatives of those media.

In analyzing the data collected from the questionnaires, researchers calculated the percentage of respondents who agreed that their sales representatives possessed the attributes listed on the questionnaire and who agreed that the categories of advertising media were characterized by the listed items. They calculated this by determining what proportion of the total number of respondents checked the "strongly agree" or "agree" category for each item.

Business Decision Makers' Attitudes toward Advertising Media

CARA researchers found that the characteristics of television advertising that garnered the highest percentage of agreement were (1) that the ads reached many people (86 percent), (2) that they built up recognition (80 percent), and (3) that people paid attention (67 percent). The highest categories for radio advertising were (1) that the ads reached many people (73 percent), (2) that they built up recognition (67 percent), and (3) that they were easy to buy (54

percent). Respondents agreed that newspaper ads (1) were easy to monitor (77 percent), (2) built up recognition (70 percent), (3) reached many people (70 percent), and (4) were easy to buy (70 percent). The items on which respondents expressed the lowest percentage of agreement for television advertising were (1) that few repeats were necessary (20 percent), and (2) that the ads were not costly (10 percent). For radio advertising, the items of lowest agreement were (1) that the ads were not costly (34 percent) and (2) that few repeats were necessary (17 percent). For newspaper advertising the lowest categories were (1) that the ads were creative (27 percent) and (2) that few repeats were necessary (27 percent).

Business Decision Makers' Attitudes toward Advertising Sales Representatives

When analyzing the data, CARA researchers found that 68, 62, and 62 percent of respondents felt their television sales representatives were cooperative, knowledgeable, and available, respectively, and these represented the items with the highest percentage of agreement in this category. For radio representatives, the highest percentage of agreement was found concerning their cooperation (72 percent), ability to quickly place ads (68) percent, and availability (64 percent). The highest rated items for newspaper representatives were cooperation (73 percent), the ability to place ads quickly (64 percent), and reliability (62 percent). The items with the lowest percent of agreement for television sales representatives were creativity (42 percent), awareness of client's customers (40 percent), and follow-through (37 percent). For radio representatives, the lowest items were follow-through (35 percent), awareness of client's customers (43 percent), and knowledgeability (28 percent). Follow-through, awareness, and knowledgeability were also the lowest items for newspaper representatives, with, respectively, 33 percent, 30 percent, and 29 percent of respondents agreeing.

Importance Scales

A chi-square test of independence was used to test whether respondents differed on the number of times they checked a given attribute or characteristic and to see whether these frequencies differed from the theoretical (expected) frequencies. Comparisons of the observed and expected frequencies for each individual attribute of sales representatives and characteristic of advertising media indicated that no significant differences existed between respondents who were decision makers and respondents who were not. The same type of comparison also revealed no significant differences between respondents who were owners and/or managers and those who were not.

A chi-square goodness-of-fit test was used to assess whether respondents ascribed different values to the attributes and characteristics listed in the sales-representatives and advertising-media sections of the study. Significant differences were found in the observed and expected frequencies of the attributes of sales representatives (see Table 1). Not all attributes were rated equally important. Figure 1 portrays graphically the number of times each attribute was chosen as one of the three most important attributes.

The most important attributes were creativity, knowledge about the client's business, concern about particular advertising needs, and an orientation toward results. The least important attributes were sincerity, concern about follow-through, a willingness to work hard, availability, ability to place ads quickly, and cooperation.

Significant differences were also noted when the observed and expected frequencies of the characteristics of advertising media were tested (see Table 2). The hypothesis that each of the characteristics was of equal importance was rejected. Figure 2 displays the observed frequencies associated with each characteristic. The most important characteristics were whether the ads improved sales volume, whether they build recognition of the business, whether they were costly, and whether people paid attention to them. The least important characteristics were whether the ads were of high quality, whether there was evidence that the ads reached a known market, whether they were creative, whether repetition was necessary for effectiveness, whether they were easy to monitor, and whether the ad-buying process was difficult.

Table 1   ***Chi-Square Test: Attributes of Sales Representatives***

Item No.	1	2	3	4	5	6	7	8	9	10	11	12
Observed Frequencies	75	98	28	122	15	8	47	99	17	1	5	23

Expected Frequencies   All cells = 43.83 $df = 11$ $\chi^2 = 444.35$[a]

[a]Statistically significant, $p < 0.001$.

Figure 1   **Number of Times an Attribute Was Chosen as One of the Three Most Important**

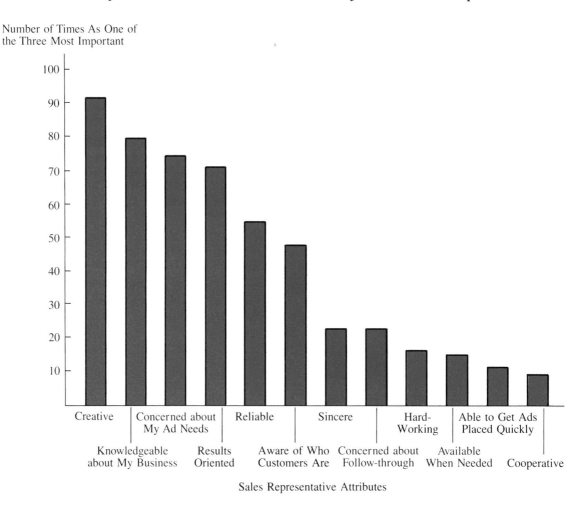

Table 2   **Chi-Square Test: Characteristics of Advertising**

Item No.	1	2	3	4	5	6	7	8	9	10	11	12
Observed Frequencies	91	54	23	73	80	11	17	18	75	13	48	23
Expected Frequencies	All cells = 43.83					$df = 11$			$\chi^2 = 222.67$[a]			

[a]Statistically significant, $p < 0.001$.

Figure 2   ***Number of Times a Characteristic Was Chosen as One of the Three Most Important***

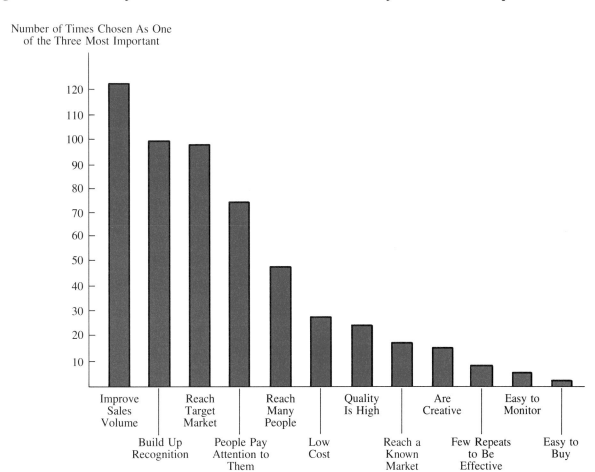

Number of Times Chosen As One
of the Three Most Important

Cases to Part Six

Case 6.1   University of Wisconsin–Extension: Engineering Management Program[1]

Introduction

The University of Wisconsin–Extension is the outreach campus of the University of Wisconsin System. It is responsible for offering high-quality continuing education to adults in a variety of professions from around the country.

The Management Institute is one of the many specialized departments within the UW-Extension. It conducts programs aimed at providing education and training in at least a dozen areas of business management and not-for-profit management. Extension Engineering is another of the specialized departments. Since 1901, it has grown from its summer school origins into one of the finest organizations of its kind. Extension Engineering has offered institutes and short courses annually since 1949. It has a dedicated full-time faculty of engineering and science professors, most of whom have extensive business and industrial experience.

Opportunity for an Engineering Management Program

In the spring of 1984, William Nitzke, the director of Extension Engineering client services, set out to explore the possibility of establishing a certificate program in engineering management. He recognized this opportunity after speaking with attendees of Extension Engineering seminars and reading several articles that made reference to the need for management training for engineers. Nitzke believed it would be feasible to develop a coordinated curriculum in engineering management by combining the strengths of the Management Institute and Extension Engineering. This new program would include a comprehensive series of management courses specifically created

to provide engineers with skills to better meet the challenges of management positions.

Background

More than half of the chief executives in major U.S. companies are engineers, and most of the middle management positions are filled by engineers.[2] Moreover, the American Association of Engineering Societies reports that about two-thirds of all engineers spend two-thirds of their careers in supervisory or management positions.[3] Yet the crowded engineering curricula at major colleges and universities allow little room for courses that prepare engineers for the types of problems they will have to face as managers. Thus, many engineers, as they evolve in their careers, find themselves promoted into management positions without formal training and unprepared to deal with a quite different set of challenges. One estimate suggests that nearly a million engineering supervisors and managers are currently not well prepared for their positions.[4]

Major corporations throughout the United States are becoming aware that their technically capable engineers are inadequately trained to handle the management-related problems they confront. As a result, the efficiencies of the corporations are affected, and the full potential of the engineers as managers is not realized.

In 1984, the Management Institute of the UW–Extension did provide programs for the nonmanagement manager. However, neither Extension

[1]The contributions of Maria Papas Heide to the development of this case are gratefully acknowledged.

[2]*Management for Engineers*, University of Kentucky and University of Missouri–Rolla joint sponsorship, October 5, 1983.
[3]Merrit A. Williamson, "Engineering Schools Should Teach Management Skills," *Professional Engineer*, 53 (Summer 1983), pp. 11–14.
[4]Ibid.

Engineering nor the Management Institute offered a coordinated or comprehensive series of programs specifically designed for engineers or similar professionals. Further, according to secondary data and direct client inquiry, few continuing education opportunities existed on a national level for engineers to gain specialized management training. The Extension Engineering department consequently decided that it would attempt to establish itself and the Management Institute as a leading-edge provider of professional-development programs in engineering management by being one of the first continuing-education institutes to offer a certificate program in Engineering Management.

The original conceptualization of the certificate program held that

> engineers would be granted a certificate only after successful completion of 10–12 seminars from the total set available. Each seminar would run 3–5 days. About 5–6 of these seminars would be required and the other 5–6 would be electives.

A study was undertaken to discover the degree of interest in this type of specialized management training among engineers who had previously attended Extension Engineering seminars. The thought was that the original conceptualization, described above, could be modified easily enough, depending on the findings from the study.

More specifically, the research was to address the following specific issues:

1. The overall general interest in an engineering management program offered by the UW–Extension.
2. The appeal of earning a certificate in contrast to taking selected seminars on an "as needed" basis.
3. The preferred design of a certificate engineering management program in terms of schedules of attendance, availability of correspondence seminars, and years to complete the certificate requirements.
4. The type of seminar topics that should comprise the certificate engineering management curriculum.

Research Method

The study had several stages. In the first preliminary stage, letters were sent to 212 recent attendees of UW–Extension engineering seminars, asking them to participate in a telephone interview regarding the proposed engineering management program. Reply postcards were received from 100 of the attendees, providing a response rate of 47 percent. The respondents fit into the following categories:

Percentage

38	agreed to participate in the telephone interview
49	did not wish to participate in the telephone interview but were willing to complete a written questionnaire and/or were interested in receiving information on the program when it was developed
$\frac{13}{100}$	were not interested in an engineering management program

The respondents contacted for the telephone interviews were very helpful in designing the written questionnaire, which was subsequently pretested on attendees of a current Extension Engineering seminar. After incorporating the changes suggested from the pretest, a final version of the written questionnaire was mailed to 2,000 randomly selected participants of Extension Engineering seminars within the past two years. A second mailing of the questionnaire to the same 2,000 respondents followed two weeks after the first mailing. The questionnaires for 123 of the names on the mailing list were returned as undeliverable. A total of 502 usable surveys, providing a response rate of 27 percent, was returned from the first and second mailings.

In the second mailing, a reply postcard was included along with the questionnaire. The postcard was provided to induce those contacted who were unwilling to complete an entire questionnaire to at least return a postcard answering the critical question about their interest in an engineering management program. One hundred ninety-one (191) usable postcards were returned. Including both the surveys and the postcards in which the single critical question about interest was answered, the response rate was 35 percent. It was found that 69 percent of all the respondents were interested in a program offering management seminars specifically designed for engineers.

One of the open-ended questions that was asked stated:

What are the three most important management-related problems you (or the engineers you supervise) face at work?

1. _____
2. _____
3. _____

The question was designed to gather some insights into the most common areas of management-related difficulties faced by all types of engineers. The question also specifically addressed the fourth research objective listed earlier—to determine the type of seminar topics that should comprise the certificate management curriculum. A representative sample of the responses to this question provided by the engineers is listed in Table 1.

Table 1   Sample of Verbatim Responses Regarding the Most Important Management-Related Problems Engineers Face

1. Increasing productivity
2. Management/union relationships
3. Management does not relate to employees
4. Quality of job performed
5. Dealing with changing priorities
6. Human relations
7. Client/public interactions and manipulation
8. Quality control of projects
9. Getting bogged down on minor items and losing sight of the big picture
10. Keeping employees happy
11. Communicating technical items to nontechnical persons
12. Utilization of time
13. The lack of ability of some to see the big picture
14. Motivation of subordinates to achieve consistent level of performance
15. Quality of workmanship
16. Obtaining appropriate information on a timely basis
17. Contract administration
18. Communications between scattered segments of company
19. Contractor performance
20. Designing job to be motivating
21. Effective sharing of information
22. Managing employees for maximum productivity
23. More efficient use of time
24. Management of information related to many projects in progress simultaneously
25. Personnel management
26. Communicating with other divisions of the company
27. Peer communications
28. Motivating those I supervise
29. Lack of defined career plan
30. Ability to communicate in nonengineering terms
31. Handling below-standard employees with union ties
32. Long-term motivation
33. Data exchange
34. Time constraints
35. Motivation of subordinates
36. Getting the most productivity out of subordinates
37. Information exchange with other departments
38. Cope with upcoming computers
39. Salary management
40. Understanding of contract management
41. Sometimes lack of enthusiasm
42. Correspondence
43. Determining accurate fee estimates
44. Evaluation/selection of "best" applicant for position
45. Satisfying the client
46. Problem identification and solving
47. Bureaucracy
48. Building confidence
49. Market entry/penetration
50. Timely responses from other departments
51. Bolstering morale
52. Lack of salary increases
53. Learning computer management tools
54. Holding effective meetings
55. Results tracking
56. Contract compliance
57. Interface with other project groups
58. Understanding and setting goals
59. Making sales contacts
60. Gaining recognition and promotion for qualified people
61. Conveying engineering problems to nontechnical management
62. Effective technical writing
63. Cost reduction
64. Follow-through on projects
65. Personal development with respect to career
66. Priority rank of assignments
67. Keeping good relationship with employees
68. Improving work habits
69. Figuring of project costs
70. Researching and compiling information to generate realistic cost proposal
71. Interdepartmental coordination of work efforts
72. Low productivity
73. Seeing the forest through the trees
74. Getting time to do my own work while supervising other workers
75. Dealing with hostile public
76. Lack of devotion of employees
77. Accomplish the volume of work in the given time
78. Skill in making sound management decisions
79. Politics within the company (how they affect decisions)
80. Estimating time to perform work
81. Budget control and forecasting
82. In-house cost estimating/tracking
83. Purchasing policies
84. Interpersonal relations
85. Scheduling

Table 1   (Continued)

86. Motivating others to contribute as a team toward a project goal
87. Data-base optimization and report use
88. Lack of supervisory training
89. Estimating engineering man-hours required
90. Knowing what the boss really wants
91. Meeting mandated deadlines
92. Motivating the people who work under you to try to achieve goals set
93. Upward communication
94. Business planning (growth projections, marketing plans, etc.)
95. Lack of initiative and curiosity
96. Understanding other people's work-related problems
97. Communications with upper-management
98. Discipline (self and principles of application)
99. Financial management of firm
100. Time management
101. Work load distribution
102. Unions
103. System bureaucracy
104. Sales and marketing of services
105. Work appropriation
106. Performance evaluation
107. Keeping employees interested, enthusiastic, and committed to job
108. Salary adjustments
109. Scheduling individual items in a project so project is completed on time
110. Information collection and dissemination
111. Project management—getting a project to run smoothly
112. Developing people
113. Task prioritization
114. Performance/salary structure relationship
115. Engineer performance review
116. Selling ideas
117. Politics
118. Effective presentation of the results
119. Cost analysis/control
120. Monitoring jobs in progress
121. Effective communications with associates
122. Providing opportunities for advancement
123. The inability to rate people properly
124. Achieving desired end results
125. Making effective use of computer-based systems
126. Training
127. Lack of coordination of effort
128. Keeping projects within budget
129. Reducing duplication of effort
130. Cost awareness
131. Conveying concise direct ideas to engineers in written form
132. Inefficient budgeting and financial expertise
133. Not getting continual feedback on my performance—feel like a machine expected to do a task
134. Public speaking
135. Distribution of assignments
136. Transfer of knowledge
137. Meeting budgets
138. Correcting those I supervise
139. Written communication
140. Establishing priorities
141. Management at meetings
142. Decision making
143. Application of appropriate disciplinary actions
144. Long-range planning
145. Conducting effective presentations
146. Creating and controlling project budgets
147. Employee handling
148. Making the right decision based on facts
149. Cross training in other departments
150. Manpower projection
151. Financial control
152. Work flow between departments
153. Getting ideas across
154. Distribution and best use of manpower
155. Communications
156. Management perception of engineers as people vs. tools
157. Commitment and performance
158. Rating of subordinates
159. Convincing top management of your ideas
160. Preparation and management of budgets
161. Managing people
162. Manpower allotment
163. Meeting schedules that change rapidly
164. Evaluation of employees
165. Failure of those in management positions to take control
166. To communicate more effectively
167. Clear division of responsibility between groups
168. Negotiating
169. Documenting
170. Conducting effective meetings
171. Keeping projects on schedule
172. Project administration
173. Understanding financial management
174. Understanding leadership roles
175. Keeping a project within the cost restrictions
176. Delegation of authority as well as responsibility
177. Lack of honest, constructive performance appraisal
178. Hiring/interviewing
179. Project work staffing
180. Counseling employees
181. Controlling employees
182. Supervisor does not aid me as he might in helping to pursue and achieve goals set down in annual performance review

Questions

1. Establish what you believe would be a relatively exhaustive and useful set of codes that could be used to code the responses to the question and to achieve the fourth objective for the study.
2. Use your a priori codes to code the verbatim responses listed in Table 1. Establish additional codes if needed to account for unanticipated categories of responses.
3. Summarize what the sample of data suggests about the problems faced by the engineers who responded to this survey. Recommend the types of seminars that should be included in the engineering management curriculum.

Case 6.2   Canopy of Care (B)[1]

Canopy of Care is a nonprofit organization that solicits donations on behalf of various local charities, thereby relieving them of the need to market themselves and raise funds on an individual basis (see Case 5.8[A] for more details). Fund-raising is accomplished with the cooperation of local businesses and government agencies, who approach their employees on behalf of Canopy of Care and, given employee pledges, deduct donations directly out of the employees' wages and salaries.

Recent statistics have shown that only 50 percent of the employees in participating companies agree to contribute, and with economic conditions in the community deteriorating, Canopy of Care officials believe that their approach to potential donors needs to be rendered more effective. To determine why solicited employees do not contribute, they decided to investigate differences in knowledge and attitudes about Canopy of Care between givers and nongivers. A marketing research firm was hired to tackle the problem, and based on interviews with Canopy of Care personnel and a review of secondary sources, the following summary of ideas was developed to guide the research:

1. The manner in which a firm conducts its Canopy of Care campaign may negatively affect employee giving. Employee reactions to the following issues could be important in this regard:
   (a) Employees are pressured to contribute by management.
   (b) Firms participate in Canopy of Care campaigns to enhance their image.
   (c) Employees would like to be more involved in their firms' Canopy of Care campaigns.
   (d) Employees think that the union should be involved in Canopy of Care campaigns.
2. Employees who have inaccurate information about Canopy of Care's functions and activities are less likely to give. Influential knowledge factors could be the following:
   (a) Employees think that Canopy of Care receives government funding.
   (b) Employees don't know about the donor option program.
   (c) Employees of firms conducting Canopy of Care campaigns have more accurate knowledge about Canopy of Care.
3. Employees who have negative attitudes toward and perceptions about Canopy of Care are less likely to give. Key negative attitudes and perceptions could include the following:
   (a) Canopy of Care is inefficient.
   (b) Canopy of Care programs are not useful to employees in general.
   (c) Canopy of Care funds programs that do not aid an employee and his or her family.
   (d) Canopy of Care helps only the poor.

Method

The previously outlined issues were addressed by means of a questionnaire (see Figure 1). Because lists of employees might be considered confidential by many businesses, it was decided that the research population would be broadened from employees of companies solicited by Canopy of Care to all adult employees in the area. The local white pages could

[1]The contributions of Jacqueline C. Hitchon to the development of this case are gratefully acknowledged.

Figure 1

Name of interviewer _____

{Interviewer – fill out for each person:}
First name _____
Time called _____
Date _____
Sex of respondent   M   or   F   **{Do not ask.}**
Telephone # _____

Hello, my name is _____
{If a child answers, ask:} *Could I please speak to someone over 16 who is employed?*

I am conducting a survey for Canopy of Care. I'd appreciate it if you would answer a few questions. I will not be soliciting donations.

1. *Which of the programs funded by Canopy of Care do you feel is the most important?*
   _____

2. *Have you been employed in the last year?*   Y   or   N

{If No, stop questionnaire.}

3. *Does your employer conduct a Canopy of Care campaign?*   Y   or   N
{If No, go to question #8.}

4. *How would you describe your company's attitude toward employee giving? Would you say:* {Read a – c.}
   (a) The company is against employee giving.
   (b) The company is neutral to the entire issue.
   (c) The company encourages employee giving.
   (d) Don't know.

5. *For the following statements, please indicate whether you Agree, have No opinion, or Disagree.*

The company should support Canopy of Care.	A, N, D
Pressure is put on me to contribute.	A, N, D
The Canopy of Care fund drive should be run by the company's executives.	A, N, D
The company wants to contribute in order to help its image.	A, N, D
More employees at all levels should be involved in the Canopy of Care fund and its fund drive.	A, N, D
Unions should not be involved in the Canopy of Care fund drive.	A, N, D
Canopy of Care should solicit people at home.	A, N, D

6. *Please answer the following question Yes or No.*
   Did you, personally, give money to Canopy of Care last year?   Y   or   N
{If Yes, go to #8.}

7. *We are interested in why people do not contribute. The following is a list of answers others have given. Please tell me which, if any, apply to you.*

{Read each and ask for a yes or a no.}
   (a) ____ Someone else in my household had already contributed.
   (b) ____ I did not have the money at the time.
   (c) ____ I gave to other charities.
   (d) ____ I volunteered my services to Canopy of Care instead of contributing money.
   (e) ____ I volunteered my services to other charities instead of contributing to Canopy of Care.

(continued)

Figure 1   *(Continued)*

(f) ＿＿ I did not give because Canopy of Care spends its money inefficiently.

(g) ＿＿ None of the above.

8. *To how many different charities do you think Canopy of Care gives money?*
{**Circle the appropriate response.**}

(a) 0–20

(b) 21–40

(c) 41–80

(d) 81–100

(e) More than 100

(f) Don't know

9. *For the following statements, please indicate whether you Agree, have No opinion, Disagree, or Don't Know.*

The programs funded by Canopy of Care are useful.	A, N, D, DK
The government should be responsible for the type of services Canopy of Care agencies provide.	A, N, D, DK
Canopy of Care programs are not useful to me or my family.	A, N, D, DK
Canopy of Care agencies help only the poor.	A, N, D, DK
Canopy of Care receives government funding.	A, N, D, DK
Canopy of Care can be viewed as a kind of insurance policy for everyone.	A, N, D, DK
Canopy of Care funds programs it should not support.	A, N, D, DK

10. *Respond True or False — you can specify which charity your money goes to when donating to Canopy of Care.*   T   or   F   or   DK

{**If False, or Don't Know, go to #12**}

11. *Again, True or False — the money donated really goes to the specific charity picked.*   T   or   F   or   DK

12. *I'm going to read to you a list that includes a number of organizations. Please tell me which of these groups, if any, you contributed to last year.*

{**Read the list and check the appropriate spaces.**}

＿＿＿ American Cancer Society

＿＿＿ Red Cross

＿＿＿ American Heart Association

＿＿＿ March of Dimes

＿＿＿ Easter Seals

＿＿＿ Multiple Sclerosis

＿＿＿ Salvation Army

＿＿＿ MACC Fund

＿＿＿ UPAF (United Performing Arts Funds)

＿＿＿ Other

＿＿＿ Did not contribute

13. *How many employees are there in the firm for which you work?*
{**Circle the appropriate response.**}

(a) Fewer than 100

(b) 100–500

(c) More than 500

(d) Don't know

14. *For what type of organization do you work?*
{**Read the list.**}

(a) Manufacturing

(b) Government

Figure 1   *(Continued)*

    (c) Wholesale/retail
    (d) Service industry—includes trades and professions
    (e) Other

15. *Are you employed full-time?*   Y or N

16. *In your present company, are you in a managerial position?*   Y or N

17. *Do you presently belong to a union?*   Y or N

18. *How long have you lived in the area?*
    (a) Less than 1 year
    (b) 1 year up to 3 years
    (c) 3 years up to 5 years
    (d) More than 5 years

19. *How many children do you have at home?*
    (a) None
    (b) 1
    (c) 2
    (d) 3
    (e) More than 3

20. *What is your marital status?*
    (a) Married
    (b) Single—never married
    (c) Separated
    (d) Divorced
    (e) Widowed
    (f) Other

21. *What is your zip code?* _____

22. *What is your race?* {**Read list.**}
    (a) White
    (b) Black
    (c) Hispanic
    (d) Native American
    (e) Asian
    (f) Other _____

23. *Please stop me when I come to the category that contains your age.*
    (a) 16–24
    (b) 25–34
    (c) 35–49
    (d) 50 and over

24. *Stop me when we get to your annual personal income level before taxes.*
    (a) Less than $10,000
    (b) $10,000 to under $15,000
    (c) $15,000 to under $25,000
    (d) $25,000 to under $40,000
    (e) More than $40,000

then be used as the sampling frame. Accordingly, professional interviewers were hired to complete the telephone survey using plus-one dialing. Because the target population was employed adults, the majority of whom work away from home during the day, phone calls were placed during evening hours.

Questions

1. Which items in the questionnaire correspond to each of the issues guiding the research?
2. How would you propose to analyze the data to investigate these issues? Be specific.

Case 6.3   WCOL-TV[1]

WCOL-TV is the local affiliate of the CBS network in Columbus, Ohio. The station is managed by Maurice Edward, who in 1986 commissioned an audience viewership study among the staff and students at Ohio State University. The study was done in November 1986 so as to coincide with the Nielsen and Arbitron ratings. The study was undertaken since these services, because of the transient nature of this community, did not include the university community in their viewership ratings of local news programs.

Edward believed that WCOL-TV had a much higher market share with its local news than either the ABC or the NBC affiliates, particularly among university staff and students, and he commissioned the study to either support or refute this conjecture. If it was true, it would provide one more weapon in the station's arsenal when it came to selling advertising time. At the same time he wished to determine the features of each network's local news broadcast that were liked and disliked, the channel switching that occurred between the programs broadcast immediately prior to the 6:00 p.m. local news and during the local news, and the channel switching that occurred between the 6:00 p.m. news and the 11:00 p.m. news.

Research Method and Results

The self-administered questionnaire was developed by the owner and founder of MEC Research Agency,

Mary Elizabeth Crosby, to address Edward's concerns. It was pretested on a judgment sample of staff and students. Other than needing a rewording of some of the Likert-type statements regarding features, the questionnaire developed by the agency proved satisfactory. The final questionnaire was subsequently mailed to a sample of faculty, staff, and students selected from the staff-student directory. The study team believed that this directory provided a reasonably good sampling frame, as it was published soon after fall registration.

The directory was organized into two parts, one listing students and the other, faculty and staff; 79 percent of the listings were students and 21 percent, faculty and staff. In order to select the desired sample of 800, a random start was generated and that name and every eightieth name thereafter was used. This produced a sample of 630 students and 170 staff. Of the 800 questionnaires sent with self-addressed, stamped return envelopes, 385 were returned.

The Likert-type statements on the questionnaire were coded 1 through 5, with 5 assigned to the "strongly agree" response category. The means and standard deviations of the ratings for each of the three local news broadcasts are shown in Table 1. The ratings were generated by asking respondents, "Which TV channel do you most often watch for the news?" and asking them to complete the scales with this channel in mind. The responses to the first three questions on the questionnaire and the questions that elicited these responses are contained in Table 2. Finally, Tables 3 and 4 contain, respectively, the cross tabulations of Questions 1 and 2 and Questions 1 and 3.

---

[1]The location and channels for this case are disguised for proprietary reasons at the request of the sponsor.

Table 1   **Mean Scores and Standard Deviations of Likert Statements Regarding Features**

Statement	WCOL-TV Channel 12	WRXY-TV Channel 4	WKLM-TV Channel 2
1. Newscasts cover topics of viewer concern.	3.698(.7825)	3.886(.6402)	3.727(.7887)
2. Pace of newscast is slow.	3.294(1.0203)	3.365(1.0054)	3.273(.9684)
3. Weather reports are timely.	3.560(.9788)	3.515(.9483)	3.870(.9914)
4. News team members take their work seriously and achieve credibility.	3.520(.9988)	3.788(.8323)	3.896(.7360)
5. Sports stories are up to date.	3.535(.7432)	3.743(.7075)	3.787(.7221)
6. Personalities frequently insert opinionated statements.	3.040(.9661)	3.154(.9929)	3.250(1.0344)
7. Friendliness of the personalties is evident.	3.770(.8501)	3.738(.8962)	3.724(.7933)
8. Weather report is not clear and understandable.	3.872(.8228)	3.721(.9395)	3.895(1.1025)
9. Newscasters and individuals interviewed are identified.	3.952(.6261)	3.976(.6982)	3.842(.6938)
10. Fast-breaking stories are given major importance in the newscast.	3.654(.8006)	3.721(.7563)	3.645(.8900)
11. Personalities are neatly dressed and have a well-groomed appearance.	3.866(.6565)	4.029(.6496)	4.000(.7297)
12. Field reports from the location of the news event are rare.	3.632(.9117)	3.743(.9202)	3.627(.7671)
13. Newscast mixes human interest stories with hard news (crimes, disasters).	3.748(.7450)	3.848(.5848)	3.649(.7908)
14. Newscast contains enough local news without undue emphasis on national news.	3.611(.9293)	3.713(.7528)	3.605(.8178)
15. There is too much emphasis on college sports.	3.177(1.1337)	3.419(.9485)	3.493(1.0827)
16. News is presented in an easily understood language.	4.016(.5511)	3.981(.6502)	4.093(.5244)
17. Visual aids used in the weather report are readable.	3.635(.9087)	3.740(.8243)	4.000(.8736)
18. Newscasts report happenings at the university.	3.419(.8397)	3.667(.8397)	3.632(.9379)
19. Transitions between segments of the news program seem abrupt.	3.389(.8576)	3.467(.8443)	3.307(.8216)
20. Weather report is accurate.	3.220(1.0229)	3.375(.7782)	3.636(.8722)
21. On-the-scene film reports are frequent.	3.581(.8751)	3.600(.8390)	3.613(.7692)
22. Quality of operational and technical production is low.	3.240(1.0806)	3.333(.9268)	3.526(.9306)
23. There are too many commercials.	2.157(.9954)	2.667(1.0712)	2.421(1.1805)
Total number	97	95	58

Table 2　**Response by Question**

1. *On which of the following originating stations do you watch the 6.00 p.m. news?*

　　97　12(CBS) WCOL-TV

　　95　4(NBC) WRXY-TV

　　58　2(ABC) WKLM-TV

　　135　I do not watch the 6:00 p.m. news on television.

2. *Prior to the 6:00 news, do you watch the following?*

　　129　12(CBS)—national news

　　63　4(NBC)—national news

　　44　2(ABC)—national news

　　149　I do not watch the 6:00 p.m. news on television.

3. *On which of the following stations do you watch the 11:00 p.m. news?*

　　69　12(CBS) WCOL-TV

　　75　4(NBC) WRXY-TV

　　57　2(ABC) WKLM-TV

　　184　I do not watch the 11:00 p.m. news on television.

Table 3　**Cross Tabulation of Question 1 versus Question 2**

Station Watched prior to 6:00 p.m. News	Station Watched for 6:00 p.m. News			Do Not Watch	Total
	12(WCOL-TV)	4(WRXY-TV)	2(WKLM-TV)		
12(WCOL-TV)	72	24	12	21	129
4(WRXY-TV)	4	48	8	3	63
2(WKLM-TV)	5	8	27	4	44
Do not watch	16	15	11	107	149
Total	97	95	58	135	385

Table 4　**Cross Tabulation of Question 1 versus Question 3**

Station Watched for 6:00 p.m. News	Station Watched for 11:00 p.m. News			Do Not Watch	Total
	12(WCOL-TV)	4(WRXY-TV)	2(WKLM-TV)		
12(WCOL-TV)	53	9	5	30	97
4(WRXY-TV)	6	48	11	30	95
2(WKLM-TV)	3	4	33	18	58
Do not watch	7	14	8	106	135
Total	69	75	57	184	385

Question

1. What would you tell Edward about how the local news on Channel 12 is perceived as opposed to perceptions of that on the NBC (Channel 4) and ABC (Channel 2) affiliates?

Case 6.4   Fabhus, Inc.

Fabhus, Inc., a manufacturer of prefabricated homes located in Atlanta, Georgia, had experienced steady, sometimes spectacular, growth since its founding in the early 1950s. In the late 1970s and into the early 1980s, however, inflation coupled with extremely high interest rates on mortgage loans caused a severe decline in the entire home building industry.

In an attempt to offset the dramatic decline in sales, company management decided to use marketing research to get a better perspective on their customers so that they could target their marketing efforts. After much discussion among the members of the executive committee, it was finally determined that the following would be important questions to address in this research effort.

1. What is the demographic profile of the typical Fabhus customer?
2. What initially attracts these customers to a Fabhus home?
3. Do Fabhus home customers consider other factory-built homes when making their purchase decision?
4. Are Fabhus customers satisfied with their homes? If they are not, what particular features are dissatisfactory?

Method

The research firm that was called in on the project suggested a mail survey to past owners. Preliminary discussions with management revealed that Fabhus had the greatest market penetration near its factory. As one moved further from the factory, the share of the total new housing business that went to Fabhus declined. The company suspected that this might result from the higher prices of the units due to shipping charges. Fabhus relied on a zone-price system in which prices were based on the product delivered at the construction site.

Local dealers actually supervised construction. Each dealer had pricing latitude and could charge more or less than Fabhus's suggested list price. Individual dealers were responsible for seeing that customers were satisfied with their Fabhus home, although Fabhus also had a toll-free number that customers could call if they were not satisfied with the way their dealer handled the construction or if they had problems moving in.

Considering the potential impact distance and dealers might have, the research team thought it was important to sample purchasers in the various zones as well as customers of the various dealers. Since Fabhus's records of houses sold were kept by zone and by date sold within zone, sample respondents were selected in the following way. First, the registration cards per zone were counted. Second, the sample size per zone was determined so that the number of respondents per zone was proportionate to the number of homes sold in the zone. Third, a sample interval, k, was chosen for each zone, a random start between 1 and k was generated, and every kth record was selected. The mail questionnaire shown in Figure 1 was sent to the 423 households selected.

A cover letter informing Fabhus's customers of the general purpose of the survey accompanied the questionnaire, and a new one-dollar bill was included with each survey as an incentive to respond. Further, the anonymity of the respondents was guaranteed by enclosing a self-addressed, postage-paid postcard in the survey. Respondents were asked to mail the postcard when they mailed their survey. All of those who had not returned their postcards in two weeks were sent a notice reminding them that their survey had not been returned. The combination of incentives, guaranteed anonymity, and follow-up prompted the return of 342 questionnaires for an overall response rate of 81 percent.

A complete list of the data is available from your instructor.

Figure 1   ***Factory-Built Home Owners Survey***

1. How did you first learn of the factory-built home that you bought? (Please check one.)

☐ Friend or relative   ☐ Direct mail
☐ Another customer   ☐ Newspaper
☐ Realtor   ☐ Radio
☐ Model home   ☐ TV
☐ Yellow pages   ☐ Don't remember
☐ National magazine   ☐ Other _____
                                     (please specify)

2. Did you own the land your home is on before you first visited your home builder?

☐ Yes   ☐ No

3. How long have you lived in your home? _____ years

4. Where did you live before purchasing your factory-built home? (Please check one.)

☐ Rented a house, apartment, or mobile home
☐ Owned a mobile home
☐ Owned a conventionally built home
☐ Owned another factory-built home
☐ Other _____
        (please specify)

5. Please rate your overall level of satisfaction with your home. (Please check one.)

☐ Very satisfied
☐ Somewhat satisfied
☐ Somewhat dissatisfied
☐ Very dissatisfied

6. How important to you were each of the following considerations in purchasing your factory-built home? (Please check a box for each item.)

Considerations	Extremely Important	Important	Slightly Important	Not Important
Investment value	☐	☐	☐	☐
Quality	☐	☐	☐	☐
Price	☐	☐	☐	☐
Energy features	☐	☐	☐	☐
Dealer	☐	☐	☐	☐
Exterior style	☐	☐	☐	☐
Floor plan	☐	☐	☐	☐
Interior features	☐	☐	☐	☐
Delivery schedule	☐	☐	☐	☐

7. Below, please list any other homes you looked at before purchasing the home you chose. Please state the reason you did not purchase the other home.

Name of Home	Factory-Built?	Reason for Not Purchasing
_____	☐ Yes ☐ No	_____
_____	☐ Yes ☐ No	_____
_____	☐ Yes ☐ No	_____
_____	☐ Yes ☐ No	_____

Now we would like you to please tell us about yourself and your family.

8. How many children do you have living at home? _____ children

Figure 1   *(Continued)*

9. *What is the age of the head of your household? (Please check one.)*
   - ☐ Under 20   ☐ 45–54
   - ☐ 20–24   ☐ 55–65
   - ☐ 25–34   ☐ 65 or over
   - ☐ 35–44

10. *What is the occupation of the head of the household? (Please check one.)*
    - ☐ Professional or official   ☐ Labor or machine operator
    - ☐ Technical or manager   ☐ Foreman
    - ☐ Proprietor   ☐ Service worker
    - ☐ Farmer   ☐ Retired
    - ☐ Craftsperson   ☐ Other _____
    - ☐ Clerical or sales   (please specify)

11. *Which of the following categories includes your family's total annual income? (Please check one.)*
    - ☐ Under $6,000   ☐ $24,000–29,999
    - ☐ $6,000–11,999   ☐ $30,000–35,999
    - ☐ $12,000–17,999   ☐ $36,000–41,999
    - ☐ $18,000–23,999   ☐ $42,000 or over

12. *Is the spouse of the head of the household employed? (Please check one.)*
    - ☐ Spouse employed full-time
    - ☐ Spouse employed part-time
    - ☐ Spouse not employed
    - ☐ Not married

One final question:

13. *Would you recommend your particular factory-built home to someone interested in building a new home?*
    - ☐ Yes   ☐ No

**Thank you very much for completing this survey.
Your help in this study is greatly appreciated.**

Questions

1. Using the data provided by your instructor and analytic techniques of your own choosing, address as best you can the objectives that prompted the research effort in the first place.

2. Do you think the research design was adequate for the problems posed? Why or why not?

Case 6.5   Como Western Bank[1]

Como Western Bank is one of several commercial lending institutions located in the Colorado community of Brentwood Hills. The bank maintains four branch offices, with one branch each located in the east, west, north, and south districts of town. Its main office is located in downtown Brentwood Hills.

During the past decade, changes in the banking industry in Brentwood Hills have paralleled those taking place nationally, in that the environment has become increasingly complex and competitive. Deregulation, technological innovation, and changing interest rates have all made it difficult for banks to attract and keep customers. Local banks must now compete with insurance companies, multiservice investment firms, and even the government for clients. As a result, lending institutions are focusing increased attention on meeting consumer needs and developing strategies to increase their client base. Como Western is no exception.

A 1972 study of commercial banking in Brentwood Hills showed Como Western to have an above-average proportion of older households, long-time residents of the community, and middle-income persons as customers. The bank appeared to be less successful in attracting younger households, college graduates, and new residents of Brentwood Hills. In addition, the study found noncustomers of Como Western to have a weak image of the bank, even though customers held a very positive image. Bank officials sensed that these results typified the current situation as well. However, because the officials were in the process of developing a comprehensive marketing plan, they desired more up-to-date and detailed information to aid in formulating an appropriate marketing strategy. Therefore, bank officials contracted with the Mestousis Research Agency to study current bank customers. The agency was a small, local one. It was led by its founder, Mike Mestousis, and Kathy Rendina, who served as the principal investigator on most projects. In addition, it employed six clerical people. The objectives of the study given to the Mestousis Agency were (1) to determine the demographic profiles of present bank customers; (2) to determine customer awareness, use, and overall perception of current bank services; and (3) to identify new bank services desired by customers.

Research Method

The Mestousis Agency proposed, and the bank's directors agreed, that the study should be conducted in two phases. The first phase was designed to increase the research team's familarity with Como Western's current clientele and service offerings. Several methods of inquiry were used. They included personal interviews with customers, bank employees, and members of the bank's board of directors, as well as a literature search of studies relating to the banking industry. Based on information gathered through these procedures, a questionnaire was developed to be used in the second portion of the project.

Because the information being sought was general yet personal in nature, the mail survey was deemed appropriate for data-collection purposes. To encourage a high response rate, a cover letter describing the research objectives and importance of responding was written by the bank president and mailed with each questionnaire, along with a stamped, self-addressed envelope. Furthermore, those who returned the questionnaire became eligible to participate in a drawing to win one of five $50 bills. To ensure anonymity, the name and address of the respondent was to be sealed in a separate envelope, which was supplied, and returned with the questionnaire.

The questionnaire itself was also designed to encourage high response. The instructions made it clear that the information would be held in strict confidence, and the more sensitive questions were asked last. In addition, the questionnaire was extensively pretested using bank customers of various ages and backgrounds.

Several weeks before the questionnaire was mailed, customers were notified by means of the bank's newsletter of the possibility that they would be receiving the questionnaire.

Sampling Plan

The relevant population for the study was defined as all noncommercial customers of Como Western Bank who lived in Brentwood Hills and who were not employees of the bank. The total number of customers meeting these requirements was 10,300. A printout of bank customers revealed that bank records listed customers in blocks according to zip codes.

The researchers were of the opinion that 500 survey responses were required to adequately perform

[1]The contributions of David M. Szymanski to the development of this case are gratefully acknowledged.

the analysis. Anticipating a 30- to 35-percent response rate, 1,500 to 1,600 surveys needed to be mailed. Given 10,300 population elements and the estimated sample size of 1,600, the researchers decided to send a questionnaire to one of every six names on the list. They generated the first name randomly using a table of random numbers. It was the fourth name on the list. They consequently sent questionnaires to the fourth, tenth, sixteenth, and so on, names on the list. In all, 1,547 questionnaires were sent and 673 were returned, for a response rate of approximately 44 percent. The questionnaire, coding form, and listing of the data are available from your instructor.

Question

1. Evaluate the general research design.
2. Evaluate the sampling plan.

3. What do the results suggest with respect to the following:
   (a) The demographic characteristics of Como Western's customers?
   (b) Customer awareness, use, and perceptions of the various services provided by Como Western?
   (c) The relationship, if any, between age and income of the respondents and their overall evaluation of the services provided by Como Western?
4. What new services, if any, should Como Western offer?

Case 6.6   Joseph Machine Company

The Joseph Machine Company, which was named after its founder and longtime owner/manager Gerald Joseph, produced pumps and air compressors. Joseph Machine had for some time been concerned with improving the procedures by which its sales force was selected. The company had always hired engineering graduates for this work because an equipment sale demanded some technical sophistication on the part of the sales representative. A sales representative simply had to be able to respond to a customer's technical questions about the equipment, and also to explain how the customer's processing system might be better designed. Assuming that a prospective sales candidate had an engineering degree (mechanical or electrical degrees were preferred, but others were accepted as well), the hiring decision was made primarily on the basis of a personal interview with several executives in the company. Those doing the interviewing often disagreed as to what kinds of credentials and candidates were acceptable.

The company was interested in determining whether there were some more objective criteria that could be employed in the hiring decision. An examination of sales performance literature suggested that a sales representative's personality and intellectual abilities are often primary determinants of success. The company therefore decided to administer personality and IQ tests to each of its sales representatives to determine whether there was any association between these characteristics and the representatives' performance. Total sales for the past year in relation to territory quota, expressed as an index, were to be employed as the performance criterion, and Joseph Machine wished to control for any differences in performance that might be attributable to time on the job.

The following data resulted from the investigation:

Sales Represen- tative	Performance Index	IQ Test	Personality Score	Time on the Job (in Months)	Sales Represen- tative	Performance Index	IQ Test	Personality Score	Time on the Job (in Months)
1	122	130	86	78	21	99	116	69	53
2	105	100	62	48	22	102	113	82	89
3	103	93	85	81	23	98	109	81	75
4	95	81	72	62	24	100	86	68	71
5	97	98	78	98	25	99	92	61	74
6	106	114	68	63	26	99	92	75	79
7	100	87	79	72	27	113	81	71	87
8	115	82	67	85	28	114	103	79	84
9	78	115	70	59	29	110	114	76	106
10	101	114	64	55	30	98	92	83	109
11	115	92	84	117	31	92	105	81	80
12	120	81	84	103	32	106	81	79	85
13	88	89	56	49	33	103	81	84	95
14	110	82	87	110	34	111	85	55	67
15	96	92	82	77	35	102	98	54	61
16	93	85	65	60	36	102	84	74	83
17	92	85	70	74	37	88	109	65	45
18	103	114	64	82	38	105	85	66	93
19	121	85	83	115	39	94	91	62	64
20	95	99	84	102	40	108	81	79	63
					41	84	101	59	41

Questions

1. Is there any relationship between a sales representative's performance and IQ? Performance and personality score?
2. Do the relationships change when time on the job is held constant?
3. What amount of performance can be attributed to all three factors considered simultaneously?
4. Evaluate your method of analysis and also evaluate the procedure being employed by Joseph Machine Company to improve its sales representative selection procedures.

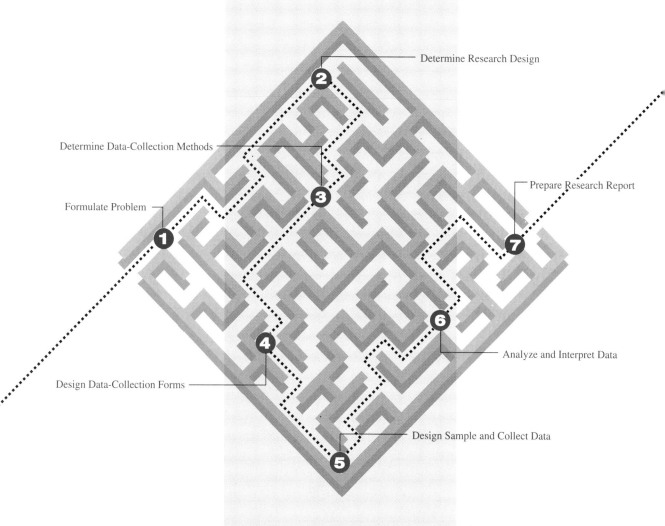

Part Seven

Research Reports

Part Seven consists of two chapters and an epilogue. Chapter 22 discusses one of the most important parts of the whole research process: the research report. The research report often becomes the standard by which the entire research effort is assessed, and it is important that the report contribute positively to the evaluation of the effort. Chapter 22 deals with the criteria a research report should satisfy and the form a research report can follow so that it does contribute positively to the research effort. Chapter 23 then discusses how to deliver effective oral reports and also reviews some of the graphic devices that can be employed to communicate important findings more forcefully. The epilogue ties together the parts of the research process. It reinforces the points made early in the text, that the steps in the research process are highly interrelated and a decision made at one stage has implications for the others, by demonstrating the nature of some of these interrelationships.

Steve Lauring believes that five or six heads are better than one. That's why, as manager of marketing research at Land O'Lakes, he tends to rely on oral presentations to communicate the results of his research efforts. "If I'm writing a research report," says Lauring, "it's just me in the room putting my thoughts and findings on paper. When I make a presentation, there are people there from research and development, sales, marketing—everyone who's involved. A lot of ideas get generated. We wind up making better decisions. In the end everyone wins."

Land O'Lakes is a cooperative owned by 300,000 dairy farmers. Lauring is responsible for the marketing research for consumer spreads (butter, margarine, blends) and dairy case cheese. He and five other professionals comprise the staff of the marketing research department.

The oral approach may not be best for every kind of company, but at Land O'Lakes, where the corporate culture is open and the free flow of ideas is the order of the day, most research results are presented orally in meetings. "It's just good to get everyone together in a room and discuss the results and status of the project," declares Lauring. "When you write a report, some people might not read it. Or, someone in research and development will read it and interpret what he or she has read quite differently from someone in

sales who read the same report. With an oral presentation, the take-away from the meeting is the same."

While the bulk of Lauring's work deals primarily with established products, he works on a very broad range of research projects. "We do it all," he says, "everything from custom focus-group studies, where we sit behind one-way mirrors while people talk about new cheese packages, all the way up to scanner data studies, modeling, and computer-generated research." Lauring also spends a good bit of time tracking the market performance of his company's various brands. He is interested in how Land O'Lakes products are doing relative to the competition as well as their own past performance.

"We work very closely with the marketing groups," reports Lauring. "We are very involved with their annual business plans. For example, if one group is planning an advertising program, we help them choose its direction based on our research data."

When Lauring is planning to present his research findings, he first considers what information he wants to communicate and who will be present at the meeting. Then he sits down with the data and tries to find the key nuggets of information to be presented. As a rule Lauring makes all of his presentations using an overhead projector, so the next step in his preparation is to pull together the overheads he will be using. "You don't want to overwhelm the group with charts and graphs," he says, "but you want to make sure that you have enough to make the point. I generally use a lot of graphics instead of number charts. Graphics are easier to understand quickly, and they tend to brighten things up."

Lauring points out that relying on oral presentations isn't without its drawbacks. "You need to be especially careful to create a written record of what went on or what was decided in a meeting." For each presentation he prepares a summary page and a recommendation page, which, in addition to the data, make up the research file. Lauring concedes that you also need to be the sort of person who feels comfortable thinking on your feet. "When you write a research report, you control what you put on the page. When you give an oral presentation, they can ask you *anything*."

Chapter
Twenty-Two

The Written Research Report

Learning Objectives

Upon completing this chapter, you should be able to

1. Specify the fundamental criterion by which all research reports are evaluated.

2. Identify and discuss the four criteria that a report should meet if it is to communicate effectively with readers.

3. Outline the main elements that make up a standard report form.

4. Explain the kind of information that is contained in the summary.

5. Distinguish between a conclusion and a recommendation.

6. Describe the kind of information that should be contained in the introduction.

7. Describe the kind of information that should be contained in the body.

8. Describe the kind of information that should be contained in the appendix.

Case in Marketing Research

Eric O'Donnell had spent a glorious summer weekend in the office, at his desk, working on the report for Oakhurst Hospital. To make matters worse, his boss, Caroline Sords, had asked him to drop off the first draft at her house when he'd finished. That was how he came to be sitting in his mentor's living room Sunday evening, studying her face for signs of a reaction.

"You know," said Sords, finally looking up from the report, "your writing has gotten a lot clearer since you first started, but you're still not writing to your audience. Tell me, who is going to read this report?"

"George Scanlon," replied O'Donnell promptly.

"And who else?"

"Probably Anthony Walsh."

"You'd better believe Walsh is going to read it," exclaimed Sords, "not to mention the hospital's chief financial officer, the board of directors, some of the trustees, the depart-ment heads, and, for all we know, the members of the Ladies Auxiliary."

"You think the report is too technical," groaned O'Donnell.

"You know it is," replied his boss kindly. "Eric, we're talking about a group of people—with the exception of Scanlon, who's got an M.B.A. in marketing—who think that a cross tab is something that holds your tie in place."

"I'll just scrap it and start over," said O'Donnell, determined to do a good job.

"You don't have to scrap the technical sections. Just move them into the appendix, where Scanlon can pore over them to his heart's content. And don't be discouraged. It's hard to keep in mind that most people are mystified by anything mathematical.

"But the truth is, our ultimate goal is to enable the hospital to improve its care delivery by acting on our findings. If they can't understand what we found out because they're confused by our complex analysis or turned off by our jargon, then we've failed—no matter how strong our research or how valid our findings."

"I don't know why I'm having such a hard time with this," said O'Donnell.

"You're having a hard time be-cause it is really hard. But it'll be a whole lot easier if you go home and get a good night's sleep. I know you'll get it right if you tackle it fresh tomorrow morning."

Discussion Issues

1. What is the primary danger of an overly technical research report?
2. How might a research report like the one that O'Donnell is writ-ing, which will be read by a wide audience with varying back-grounds, differ from one tar-geted to a smaller, more homo-geneous audience?

A frustrated executive of a large corporation once remarked that "he is convinced reports are devices by which the informed ensure that the uninformed remain that way."[1] To avoid creating the kind of report that executive was thinking of requires considerable amounts of knowledge, skill, and attention to detail. If length were the criterion of importance of a chapter, there would be an inverse relationship between this chapter and the criterion. This chapter is short, but its subject is vital to the success of the research effort. Regardless of the sophistication displayed in other portions of the research process, the project is a failure if the research report fails.

The empirical evidence indicates that the research report is one of the five most important variables affecting the use of research information.[2] The research steps discussed in the preceding chapters of this text determine the content of the research report, but since the report is all that many executives will see of the project, it becomes the yardstick for evaluation. The writer must ensure that the report informs without misinforming.

The report must tell readers what they need and wish to know. Typically, executives must be convinced of the usefulness of the findings. They are more interested in results than methods. However, to act on the report effectively, they must know enough about the methods that were used to recognize the methods' weaknesses and bounds of error. It is the researcher's responsibility to convey this information to the decision maker in sufficient detail and in understandable form.

In this chapter and the next, we will offer some guidelines for developing successful research reports. In this chapter we will focus on the criteria by which research reports are evaluated and the parts and forms of the written research report.

Research Report Criteria

Research reports are evaluated by one fundamental criterion—how well they communicate with the reader. The "iron law" of marketing research holds, for example, that "people would rather live with a problem they cannot solve than accept a solution they cannot understand."[3] The reader is not only the reason that the report is prepared, but also the standard by which its success is measured. This means that the report must be tailor-made for its reader or readers, with due regard for their technical sophistication, their interest in the subject area, the circumstances under which they will read the report, and the use they will make of it.

The technical sophistication of the readers determines their capacity for understanding methodological decisions, such as experimental design, measurement device, sampling plan, analysis technique, and so on. Readers with little technical sophistication will more than likely take offense at the use of unexplained technical jargon. "The readers of your reports are busy people, and very few of them can balance a research report, a cup of coffee, and a dictionary at one time."[4] Unexplained jargon may even make such persons suspicious of the report writer. Researchers should try to be particularly sensitive to this hazard, because, being technical people, they may fail to realize that they are using technical language unless they remind themselves to watch for it.

While the readers' backgrounds and need for methodological detail will determine the upper limit for the technical content of the report, it is the readers' individual preferences that must guide the report writer.

Some executives demand a minimum report; they want only the results—not a discussion of how the results were obtained. Others want considerable information on the research methods used in the study. Many executives place a premium on brevity, while others demand complete discussion. Some are interested only in the statistical results and not in the researcher's conclusions and recommendations.

Thus, *the audience determines the type of report*. Researchers must make every effort to acquaint themselves with the *specific preferences of their audience*. They should not consider these preferences as unalterable, but *any deviations from them should be made with reason and not from ignorance!*[5] (Emphasis added.)

The report writer's difficulties in tailoring the report are often compounded by the existence of several audiences. The marketing vice-president might have a different technical capacity and level of interest than the product manager responsible for the product discussed in the report. There is no easy solution to this problem of "many masters." The researcher must recognize the potential differences that may arise and may have to exercise a great deal of ingenuity to reconcile them. Occasionally, a researcher may find it necessary to prepare several reports, each designed for a specific audience, although more often the conflicting demands can be satisfied by one report that contains both technical and nontechnical sections for different readers.

Writing Criteria

A report that achieves the goal of communicating effectively with readers is generally one that meets the specific criteria of completeness, accuracy, clarity, and conciseness.[6] These criteria are intimately related. An accurate report, for example, is also a complete report. For discussion purposes, however, it is helpful to discuss the criteria as if they were distinct.

Completeness

Completeness A criterion used to evaluate a research report; specifically, whether the report provides all the information readers need in language they understand.

A report is **complete** when it provides all the information readers need in language they understand. This means that the writer must continually ask whether every question in the original assignment has been addressed. What alternatives were examined? What was found? An incomplete report implies that supplementary reports, which are annoying and delay action, will be forthcoming.

The report may be incomplete because it is too brief or too long. The writer may omit necessary definitions and short explanations. On the other hand, the report may be lengthy but not profound, due to a reluctance to waste any collected information. In a report full of nonvital information, the main issues are often lost in the clutter. Also, if the report is big, it may discourage readers from even attempting to digest its contents.

Readers are thus the key to determining completeness. Their interest and abilities determine what clarification should be added and what findings should be omitted. In general, the amount of detail should be proportionate to the amount of direct control users can exercise over the areas under discussion. For example, if the intended reader is a product's advertising manager, it would generally be wise to omit a lengthy discussion of possible improvements to production techniques.

Accuracy

Accuracy A criterion used to evaluate a research report; specifically, whether the reasoning in the report is logical and the information correct.

The previously discussed steps in the research process are obviously vital to accuracy, but, given accurate input, the research report may generate inaccuracies because of carelessness in handling the data, illogical reasoning, or inept phrasing.[7] Thus, **accuracy** is another writing criterion. Table 22.1 illustrates some examples of sources of inaccuracy in report writing.

Table 22.1   ***Some Examples of Sources of Inaccuracy in Report Writing***

A. Simple Errors in Addition or Subtraction

"In the United States, 14 percent of the population has an elementary school education or less, 51 percent has attended or graduated from high school, and 16 percent has attended college."

An oversight such as this (14 + 51 + 16 does not equal 100 percent) can be easily corrected by the author, but not so easily by the reader, because he or she may not know if one or more of the percentage values is incorrect or if a category might have been left out of the tally.

B. Confusion between Percentages and Percentage Points

"The company's profits as a percentage of sales were 6.0 percent in 1982 and 8.0 percent in 1987. Therefore, they increased only 2.0 percent in five years."

In this example, the increase is, of course, 2.0 percentage points, or 33 percent.

C. Inaccuracy Caused by Grammatical Errors

"The reduction in the government's price supports for dairy products has reduced farm income $600 million to $800 million per year."

To express a range of reduction, the author should have written, "The reduction in the government's price supports for dairy products has reduced farm income $600–800 million per year."

D. Confused Terminology Resulting in Fallacious Conclusions

"The Jones' household annual income increased from $10,000 in 1964 to $30,000 in 1989, thereby tripling the family's purchasing power."

While the Jones' household annual income may have tripled in the 25 years, the family's purchasing power certainly did not, as the cost of living, as measured by the consumer price index, more than tripled in the same period.

The possession of advanced degrees is no safeguard against the hazards detailed in Table 22.1. In fact, the more educated a person is, the more apt he or she may be to sink into the morass of excess verbiage. Consider the president of a major university who, in the late 1960s, wrote a letter to soothe anxious alumni after a spell of campus unrest. "You are probably aware," he began, "that we have been experiencing very considerable potentially explosive expressions of dissatisfaction on issues only partially related." He meant that the students had been hassling the university about different things.[8] In Research Window 22.1, Jock Elliott, chairman emeritus of the advertising agency Ogilvy & Mather, shows how one corporate vice-president also sank into the quicksand of his own words.

Inaccuracies also arise because of grammatical errors in punctuation, spelling, tense, subject and verb agreement, and so on.[9] Careful attention to detail in these areas is essential for any report writer.

Clarity

Clarity A criterion used to evaluate a research report; specifically, whether the phrasing in the report is precise.

The writing criterion of **clarity** is probably failed more than any other. Clarity is produced by clear and logical thinking and precision of expression. When the underlying logic is fuzzy or the presentation imprecise, readers experience difficulty in understanding what they read. They may be forced to guess, in which case the corollary to Murphy's law applies: "If the reader is offered the slightest opportunity to misunderstand, he probably will."[10] Achieving clarity, however, requires effort.

Research Window 22.1
How to Write Your Way Out of a Job

Jock Elliott, the chairman emeritus of the Ogilvy & Mather advertising agency, is a man who appreciates good writing. After all, his business is built on his employees' ability to communicate with clients and consumers.

Elliott makes no bones about the importance of being able to write well in order to advance in a career. "As you sail along on your career," he writes, "bad writing acts as a sea anchor, pulling you back, good writing as a spinnaker, pulling you ahead."

In the following excerpt from an article he wrote, he tells about one prospective employee who sank beneath the waves, weighed down by the anchor of his own words:

"Last month I got a letter from a vice-president of a major management consulting firm. Let me read you two paragraphs. The first:

> Recently, the companies of our Marketing Services Group were purchased by one of the largest consumer research firms in the U.S. While this move well fits the basic business purpose and focus of the acquired MSG units, it is personally restrictive. I will rather choose to expand my management opportunities with a career move into industry.

"What he meant was: The deal works fine for my company, but not so fine for me. I'm looking for another job.

"Second paragraph:

> The base of managerial and technical accomplishment reflected in my enclosed resumé may suggest an opportunity to meet a management need for one of your clients. Certainly my experience promises a most productive pace to understand the demands and details of any new situation I would choose.

"What he meant was: As you can see in my resumé, I've had a lot of good experience. I am a quick study. Do you think any of your clients might be interested in me?

"At least, that's what I think he meant.

"This fellow's letter reveals him as pompous. He may not *be* pompous. He may only be a terrible writer. But I haven't the interest or time to find out which. There are so many people looking for jobs who don't sound like pompous asses.

"Bad writing done him in—with me, at any rate."

Jock Elliott, "How Hard It Is to Write Easily," *Viewpoint: By, For, and About Ogilvy & Mather*, 2 (1980), p. 18.

The first, and most important, rule is that the report be well organized.[11] In order for this to happen, you must first clarify for yourself the purpose of your report and how you intend to accomplish it. Make an outline of your major points. Put the points in logical order and place the supporting details in their proper position. Tell the reader what you are going to cover in the report and then do what you said you were going to do. Use short paragraphs and short sentences. Do not be evasive or ambiguous; once you have decided what you want to say, come right out and say it. Choose your words carefully, making them as precise and understandable as possible. See Research Window 22.2 for some specific suggestions when choosing words.

Do not expect your first draft to be satisfactory. Expect to rewrite it several times. When rewriting, attempt to reduce the length by half. That forces you to simplify and remove the clutter. It also forces you to think about every word and its purpose, to evaluate whether each word is helping you say what you wish to say. Jock Elliott has some very pointed comments on writing clearly:

> Our written and spoken words reflect what we are. If our words are brilliant, precise, well ordered and human, then that is how we are seen.
> When you write, you must constantly ask yourself: What am I trying to say? If you do this religiously, you will be surprised at how often you don't know what you are trying to say.

Research Window 22.2
Some Suggestions When Choosing Words for Marketing Research Reports

1. *Use short words.* Always use short words in preference to long words that mean the same thing.

Use this	Not this
Now	Currently
Start	Initiate
Show	Indicate
Finish	Finalize
Use	Utilize
Place	Position

2. *Avoid vague modifiers.* Avoid lazy adjectives and adverbs and use vigorous ones. Lazy modifiers are so overused in some contexts that they have become clichés. Select only those adjectives and adverbs that make your meaning precise.

Lazy modifiers	Vigorous modifiers
Very good	Short meeting
Awfully nice	Crisp presentation
Basically accurate	Baffling instructions
Great success	Tiny raise
Richly deserved	Moist handshake
Vitally important	Lucid recommendation

3. *Use specific, concrete language.* Avoid technical jargon. There is always a simple, down-to-earth word that says the same thing as the show-off fad word or the vague abstraction.

You have to *think* before you start every sentence, and you have to *think* about every word.

Then you must look at what you have written and ask: Have I said it? Is it clear to someone encountering the subject for the first time? If it's not, it is because some fuzz has worked its way into the machinery. The clear writer is a person clearheaded enough to see this stuff for what it is: fuzz.

It is not easy to write a simple declarative sentence. Here is one way to do it. Think what you want to say. Write your sentence. Then strip it of all adverbs and adjectives. Reduce the sentence to its skeleton. Let the verbs and nouns do the work.

Jargon	Down-to-earth English
Implement	Carry out
Viable	Practical, workable
Net net	Conclusion
Suboptimal	Less than ideal
Proactive	Active
Bottom line	Outcome

4. *Write simply and naturally—the way you talk.* Use only those words, phrases, and sentences that you might actually say to your reader if you were face-to-face. If you wouldn't say it, if it doesn't sound like you, don't write it.

Stiff	Natural
The reasons are fourfold	There are four reasons
Importantly	The important point is
Visitation	Visit

5. *Strike out words you don't need.* Certain commonly used expressions contain redundant phrasing. Cut out the extra words.

Don't write	Write
Advance plan	Plan
Take action	Act
Study in depth	Study
Consensus of opinion	Consensus
Until such time as	Until
The overall plan	The plan

Source: Table adapted from Chapter 2 of *Writing That Works* by Kenneth Roman and Joel Raphaelson. Copyright © 1981 by Kenneth Roman and Joel Raphaelson. Reprinted by permission of HarperCollins Publishers Inc.

> If your skeleton sentence does not express your thought precisely, you've got the wrong verb or noun. Dig for the right one. Nouns and verbs carry the guns in good writing; adjectives and adverbs are decorative camp followers.[12]

Conciseness A criterion used to evaluate a research report; specifically, whether the writing in the report is crisp and direct.

Conciseness

Although the report must be complete, it must also be **concise.** This means that the writer must be selective in what is included. The researcher must avoid trying to impress the reader with all that has been found. If something does not pertain directly

"WE GOT THE ASPIRIN ACCOUNT! A STUDY SHOWED OUR ADS GIVE PEOPLE HEADACHES."

Source: Cartoon by Harley Schwadron; *Advertising Age*, January 7, 1991, p. 21. Reprinted with permission.

to the subject, it should be omitted. The writer must also avoid lengthy discussions of commonly known methods. Given that the material is appropriate, conciseness can still be violated by writing style. This commonly occurs when the writer is groping for the phrases and words that capture an idea. Instead of finally coming to terms with the idea, the writer writes around it, restating it several times, in different ways, hoping that repetition will overcome poor expression. Concise writing, on the other hand, is effective because "it makes maximum use of every word. . . . No word in a concise discussion can be removed without impairing or destroying the function of the whole composition. . . . To be concise is to express a thought completely and clearly in the fewest words possible."[13]

One helpful technique for ensuring that the report is concise is reading the draft aloud. This often reveals sections that should be pruned or rewritten.[14]

> Silent reading allows him [the writer] to skim over the familiar material and thus impose an artificial rapidity and structural simplicity on something that is in reality dense and tangled. The eye can grow accustomed to the appearance of a sentence, but it is much more difficult for the tongue, lips, and jaw to deal with what the eye might accept readily.

Ethical Dilemma 22.1   As a member of an independent research team, it is your job to write the final report for a client. One of your colleagues whispers to you in passing, "Make it sound very technical. Lots of long words and jargon—you know the sort of thing. We want to make it clear that we earned our money on this one."

■   Is it ethical to obscure the substance of a report beneath complex language?
■   Will some clients be impressed by words that they do not fully understand?

Form of Report

The organization of the report influences all the criteria of report writing. While good organization cannot guarantee clarity, conciseness, accuracy, and completeness, poor organization can preclude them. There is no single, acceptable organization for a report. Once again, the writer should be guided by the nature and needs of the reader in choosing the most appropriate format for the report. The following format is sufficiently flexible to allow the inclusion or exclusion of elements to satisfy particular needs:

1. Title page
2. Table of contents
3. Summary
    a. Introduction
    b. Results
    c. Conclusions
    d. Recommendations
4. Introduction
5. Body
    a. Methodology
    b. Results
    c. Limitations
6. Conclusions and recommendations
7. Appendix
    a. Copies of data-collection forms
    b. Detailed calculations supporting sample size, test statistics, and so on
    c. Tables not included in the body
    d. Bibliography

Title Page

The title page indicates the subject of the report, the name of the organization for whom the report is made, the name of the organization submitting it, and the date. If the report is done by one department within a company for another, the names of organizations or companies are replaced by those of individuals. Those for whom the report is intended are listed on the title page, as are the departments or people preparing the report. If a report is confidential, it is especially important to list on the title page the names of the individuals authorized to see it.

Table of Contents

The table of contents lists, in order of appearance, the divisions and subdivisions of the report with page references. In a short report, the table of contents may simply contain the main headings. The table of contents will also typically include tables and figures and the pages on which they may be found. For most reports, exhibits will be labeled as either tables or figures, with maps, diagrams, and graphs falling into the latter category.

Summary

The summary is the most important part of the report. It is the heart and core. Many executives will read only the summary. Others will read more, but even they will use the summary as a guide to those questions about which they would like more information.

The true summary is not an abstract of the whole report in which everything is restated in condensed form, nor is it a simple restatement of the subject, nor is it a brief statement of the significant results and conclusions. A true summary gives the high points of the entire body of the report. A properly written summary saves the time of busy executives without sacrificing their understanding. A good test of a summary is self-sufficiency. Can it stand on its own, or does it collapse without the full report?

A good summary contains the necessary background information, as well as the important results and conclusions. Whether it contains recommendations is determined to an extent by the reader. Some managers prefer that the writer suggest appropriate action, while others prefer to draw their own conclusions on the basis of the evidence contained in the study. Although the good summary contains the necessary information, it will rarely be broken down through the use of headings and subheadings. The summary that requires such subdivisions is, in all likelihood, too long.

The summary begins with an introduction that should provide the reader with enough background to appreciate the results, conclusions, and recommendations of the study. The introduction should state who authorized the research and for what purpose. It should state explicitly the problems or hypotheses that guided the research.

Following the introduction should be a section in which the study's significant findings or results are presented. The results presented in the summary must agree, of course, with those in the body of the report, but only the key findings are presented here. A useful approach is to include one or several statements reporting what was found with regard to each problem or objective mentioned in the introduction.

The final two sections of the summary are conclusions and recommendations, which follow a discussion of the results. Conclusions and recommendations are not the same. A conclusion is an opinion based on the results. A recommendation is a suggestion as to appropriate future action.

Conclusions should be included in the summary section. The writer is in a much better position to base conclusions on the evidence than is the reader, as the writer has greater familiarity with the methods used to generate and analyze the data. The writer is at fault if conclusions are omitted and readers are allowed to draw their own. Recommendations, though, are another matter. Some managers simply prefer to determine the appropriate courses of action themselves and do not want the writer to offer recommendations. Others hold that the writer, being closest to the research, is in the best position to suggest a course of action. For example, the Lipton Company has the philosophy that it is the responsibility of the marketing research people to interpret the findings. As Dolph von Arx, the executive vice-president, comments: "We feel strongly that our market research people must go beyond reporting the facts. We want them to tell us what *they* think the facts mean—both in terms of conclusions, and, if possible, indicated actions. Those who are responsible for making the decisions may or may not accept those conclusions or recommendations, but we want this input from our market research people."[15]

Introduction

Whereas in the summary the readers' interests are taken into account, in the report's formal introduction their education and experience are considered. The introduction provides the background information readers need to appreciate the discussion in the body of the report. Some form of introduction is almost always necessary. Its length and detail, though, depend upon the readers' familiarity with the subject, the report's approach to it, and the treatment of it.[16] As a general rule, a report with wide distribution will require a more extensive introduction than a report for a narrow audience.

The introduction often serves to define unfamiliar terms or terms that are used in a specific way in the report. For instance, in a study of market penetration of a new product, the introduction might be used to define the market and name the products and companies considered "competitors" in calculating the new product's market share.

The introduction may provide some pertinent history, answering such questions as the following: What similar studies have been conducted? What findings did they produce? What circumstances led to the present study? How was its scope and emphasis determined? Clearly, if readers are familiar with the history of this project and related research or the circumstances that inspired the current research, these items can be omitted. A report going to executives with little background in the particular product or service dealt with would probably have to include them.

The introduction should state the specific objectives of the research. If the project was part of a larger, overall project, this should be mentioned. Each of the subproblems or hypotheses should be explicitly stated. After reading the introduction, readers should know just what the report covers and what it omits. They should appreciate the overall problem and how the subproblems relate to it. They should be aware of the relationship between this study and other related work. And they should appreciate the need for the study and its importance. Through all of this, the introduction should serve to win the readers' confidence and dispel any prejudices they may have.

Body

The details of the research—its method, results, and limitations—are contained in the body of the report. One of the hardest portions of the report to write is that giving the details of the method. The writer has a real dilemma here. Sufficient information must be presented so that readers can appreciate the research design, data-collection methods, sample procedures, and analysis techniques that were used without being bored or overwhelmed. Technical jargon, which is often a succinct way of communicating a complex idea, should be omitted, since many in the audience will not understand it.

Readers must be told whether the design was exploratory, descriptive, or causal. They should also be told why the particular design was chosen and what its merits are in terms of the problem at hand. Readers should also be told whether the results are based on secondary or primary data. If primary, are they based on observation or questionnaire? And if the latter, were the questionnaires administered in person, or by mail or telephone? Once again it is important to mention why the particular method was chosen. What were its perceived advantages over alternative schemes? This may mean discussing briefly the perceived weaknesses of the other data-collection schemes that were considered.

Sampling is a technical subject, and the writer cannot usually hope to convey all the nuances of the sampling plan in the body of the report, but must be somewhat selective in this regard. At the very minimum, the researcher should answer the following questions:

1. How was the population defined? What were the geographical, age, sex, or other bounds?
2. What sampling units were employed? Were they business organizations or business executives? Where they dwelling units, households, or individuals within a household? Why were these particular sampling units chosen?
3. How was the list of sampling units generated? Did this produce any weaknesses? Why was this method used?
4. Were any difficulties experienced in contacting designated sample elements? How were these difficulties overcome, and was bias introduced in the process?
5. Was a probability or nonprobability sampling plan employed? Why? How was the sample actually selected? How large a sample was selected? Why was this size of sample chosen?

In essence, the readers need to understand at least three things with respect to the sample: What was done? How was it done? Why was it done?

There is very little that can be said about the method of analysis when discussing research methods, since the results tend to show what has been done in this regard. It often proves quite useful, though, to discuss the method in general before detailing the results. Thus, if statistical significance is established through chi-square analysis, the writer might provide the general rationale and calculation procedure for the chi-square statistic, as well as the assumptions surrounding this test and how well the data supported the assumptions. This enables readers to separate what was found from how it was determined. The distinction may not only help the readers' understanding but also prevent repetition in the report. The procedure is outlined with its key components once, and the results are then simply reported in terms of these components.

The results section of the body of the report presents the findings of the study in some detail, often including supporting tables and figures, and accounts for the bulk of the report. The results need to address the specific problems posed and must be presented with some logical structure.[17] The first of these requirements directs that information that is interesting but irrelevant in terms of the specific problems that guided the research be omitted. The second requirement directs that the tables and figures not be a random collection but reflect some psychological ordering.[18] This may mean ordering by subproblem, geographic region, time, or another criterion that served to structure the investigation.

Tables and figures should be used liberally when presenting the results. While the tables in the appendix are complex, detailed, and apply to a number of problems, the tables in the body of the report should be simple summaries of this information. Each table should address only a single problem, and it should be specially constructed to shed maximum light on this problem. Guidelines for constructing tables follow:[19]

1. Order the columns or rows of the table by the marginal averages or some other measure of size. If there are many similar tables, keep the same order in each one.
2. Put the figures to be compared into columns rather than rows, and, if possible, put the larger numbers at the top of the columns.
3. Round the numbers to two effective digits.

4. For each table, give a brief verbal summary that will guide the reader to the main patterns and exceptions.

Table 22.2 gives an example of how these guidelines can yield better tables.

Table 22.2 **Guidelines for Producing Better Tables**

Table A displays some sales figures for a product being sold in ten U.S. cities. At first glance it seems fairly laid out, but look again. How would you summarize the information in the table to someone over the phone?

Table A
Quarterly Sales of Product Y in Ten Cities

City	Quarter 1	Quarter 2	Quarter 3	Quarter 4
	Sales in Thousands of Dollars			
Atlanta	540.4	507.6	528.4	833.2
Chattanooga	68.9	64.0	55.4	64.5
Des Moines	65.7	61.1	52.9	61.5
Hartford	61.1	71.5	59.0	70.5
Indianapolis	153.2	162.8	122.8	185.7
Los Angeles	700.2	660.3	580.8	662.7
Miami	553.6	517.2	446.0	672.4
Omaha	78.3	72.8	63.0	73.3
Phoenix	196.8	227.6	198.5	235.2
San Antonio	168.2	179.3	166.9	207.1

The table seems to be a jumble when looked at more carefully. It appears that no thought was given to communicating what the numbers really mean. The main difficulty is that the cities for which the numbers are given are listed alphabetically. There is no apparent pattern in each column. Now look at the same information as presented in Table B.

Table B
Quarterly Sales of Product Y in Ten Cities Ordered by Population Size (Rounded and with Averages)

City	Quarter 1	Quarter 2	Quarter 3	Quarter 4	Average
Los Angeles	700	660	580	660	650
Miami	550	520	450	670	550
Atlanta	540	510	530	830	600
Phoenix	200	230	200	240	220
San Antonio	170	180	170	210	180
Indianapolis	150	160	120	190	160
Hartford	60	70	60	70	70

(continued)

Table B *(Continued)*

City	Quarter 1	Quarter 2	Quarter 3	Quarter 4	Average
Omaha	80	70	60	70	70
Chattanooga	70	60	60	60	60
Des Moines	70	60	50	60	60
Average	260	250	230	310	260

Note how ordering the information by following the recommended steps improves the table's readability.

Table B's heading informs the reader that the cities are ordered by population size. Having this information and examining the table as it's now laid out, we can begin to see major patterns emerge: the bigger the cities, the higher the sales, as might be expected. The single exception is Atlanta, where sales are relatively high given its population size.

Trends over time are also easier to see. Although not typical, the column averages help us see that sales in each city were relatively steady quarter by quarter, but that they were lower in Quarter 3 and higher in Quarter 4. We can also see that the fourth-quarter increases were largest in Miami and Atlanta.

The difference between Tables A and B is the difference between a good table and a poor one. In a good table, the patterns and exceptions should be obvious at a glance, at least once one knows what they are.

Next time you have trouble reading a table, ask yourself if the information could be better ordered. The fault may not be in your ability to comprehend the information but in the table itself.

Source: Adapted from A. S. C. Ehrenberg, "The Problem of Numeracy," *The American Statistician*, 35 (May 1981), pp. 67–71.

Figures, like tables, should address only one subproblem. Further, they should be chosen carefully for the type of message they can most effectively convey. This subject will be discussed in the next chapter.

It is impossible to conduct the "perfect" study, because every study has its limitations. The researcher knows what the limitations of his or her efforts are, and these limitations should not be hidden from the reader. Researchers sometimes fear that a frank admission of the study's limitations may diminish the reader's opinion of the quality of the research. Often the contrary is true. If some limitations are not stated and readers discover them, they may begin to question the whole report and assume a much more skeptical, critical posture than they would have had, had the limitations been stated explicitly. Stating them also allows the writer to discuss whether, and by how much, the limitations might bias the results. Their exclusion, and later discovery, encourages readers to draw their own conclusions in this regard.

When discussing the limitations, the writer should provide some idea of the accuracy with which the work was done. The writer should specifically discuss the sources of nonsampling error and the suspected direction of their biases. This often means that the researcher provides some limits by which the results are distorted due to these inaccuracies. Readers should be informed specifically as to how far the results can be generalized. To what populations can they be expected to apply? If the study was done in Miami, readers should be warned not to generalize the results to the southern states or all the states. The writer should provide the proper caveats for readers and not make readers discover the weaknesses themselves. However, the writer should not overstate the limitations either, but should assume a balanced perspective.

Conclusions and Recommendations

The results lead to the conclusions and recommendations. In this section, the writer shows the step-by-step development of the conclusions and states them in greater detail than in the summary. There should be a conclusion for each study objective or problem. As one book puts it, "readers should be able to read the objectives, turn to the conclusions section, and find specific conclusions relative to each objective."[20] If the study does not provide evidence sufficient to draw a conclusion about a problem, this should be explicitly stated.

Appendix

The appendix contains material that is too complex, too detailed, too specialized, or not absolutely necessary for the text. The appendix will typically contain as an exhibit a copy of the questionnaire or observation form used to collect the data. It will also contain any maps used to draw the sample as well as any detailed calculations used to support the determination of the sample size and sample design. The appendix may include detailed calculations of test statistics and will often include detailed tables from which the summary tables in the body of the report were generated. The writer should recognize that the appendix will be read by only the most technically competent and interested reader. Therefore, the writer should not put material in the appendix if its omission from the body of the report would create gaps in the presentation.

Synopsis

Table 22.3 can serve as a checklist of things to include in reports. The checklist reflects the guidelines that have been developed to evaluate research that is to be put to a public purpose. Public-purpose research can affect the interests of people and organizations who have had no part in its design, execution, or funding. Consequently, the criteria on which it is evaluated tend to be stricter than those applied to research done for private use. Still, the general issues and questions serve as useful criteria by which all research reports can be judged.

Table 22.3   *Checklist for Evaluating Research Reports*

A. Origin: What Is Behind the Research
Does the report identify the organizations, divisions, or departments that initiated and paid for the research?   _____
Is there a statement of the purpose of the research that says clearly what it was meant to accomplish?   _____
Are the organizations that designed and conducted the research identified?   _____

B. Design: The Concept and the Plan
Is there a full, nontechnical description of the research design?   _____
Is the design consistent with the stated purpose for which the research was conducted?   _____
Is the design evenhanded? That is, is it free of leading questions and other biases?   _____

(continued)

Table 22.3   *(Continued)*

Have precautions been taken to avoid sequence or timing bias or other factors that might prejudice or distort the findings?   _____

Does it address questions that respondents are capable of answering?   _____

Is there a precise statement of the universe or population that the research is meant to represent?   _____

Does the sampling frame fairly represent the population under study?   _____

Does the report specify the kind of sample used and clearly describe the method of sample selection?   _____

Does the report describe the plan for the analysis of the data?   _____

Are copies of all questionnaire forms, field and sampling instructions, and other study materials available in the appendix or on file?   _____

C. Execution: Collecting and Handling the Information
Does the report describe the data-collection and data-processing procedures?   _____

Is there an objective report on the care with which the data were collected?   _____

What procedures were used to minimize bias and ensure the quality of the information collected?   _____

D. Stability: Sample Size and Reliability
Was the sample large enough to provide stable findings?   _____

Are sampling error limits shown if they can be computed?   _____

Are methods of calculating the sampling error described, or, if the error cannot be computed, is this stated and explained?   _____

Does the treatment of sampling error limits make clear that they do not cover nonsampling error?   _____

For the major findings, are the reported error tolerances based on direct analysis of the variability of the collected data?   _____

E. Applicability: Generalizing the Findings
Does the report specify when the data were collected?   _____

Does the report say clearly whether its findings do or do not apply beyond the direct source of the data?   _____

Is it clear who is underrepresented by the research, or not represented at all?   _____

If the research has limited application, is there a statement covering who or what it represents and the time or conditions under which it applies?   _____

F. Meaning: Interpretations and Conclusions
Are the measurements described in simple and direct language?   _____

Does it make logical sense to use such measurements for the purpose to which they are being put?   _____

Are the actual findings clearly differentiated from the interpretation of the findings?   _____

Have rigorous objectivity and sound judgment been exercised in interpreting the research findings?   _____

G. Candor: Open Reporting and Disclosure
Is there a full and forthright disclosure of how the research was done?   _____

Has the research been fairly presented?   _____

Source: Adapted from *Guidelines for the Public Use of Market and Opinion Research*, © 1981 by the Advertising Research Foundation. Adapted with permission.

Ethical
Dilemma 22.2   A colleague confides in you: "I've just run a survey for a restaurant owner who is planning to open a catering service for parties, weddings, and the like. He wanted to know the best way to advertise the new service. In the questionnaire, I asked respondents where they would expect to see advertisements for catering facilities, and the most common source was the newspaper. I now realize that my question only established where people are usually exposed to relevant ads, not where they would like to see relevant ads or where they could most productively be exposed to an ad. All we know is where other caterers advertise! Yet I'm sure my client will interpret my findings as meaning that the newspaper is the most effective media vehicle. Should I make the limitations of the research explicit?"

■   What are the costs of making the limitations of the research explicit?
■   What are the costs of not doing so?
■   Isn't promoting the correct use of the research one of the researcher's prime obligations?

Back to the Case

"Eric, this is a 100-percent improvement," beamed Caroline Sords as she finished his latest draft of the research report for Oakhurst Hospital. "I think everyone, from the hospital's chief financial officer to the chairman of pediatrics, will be able to read it and understand it."

"Thanks, Caroline," replied Eric O'Donnell, breathing an internal sigh of relief.

"There is one thing that troubles me, though," said Sords. "I don't see any mention of the problems we had with data collection. In your first draft, they were mentioned in the results section."

"Yes, they were. I really went back and forth over whether to keep those in," responded O'Donnell. "Finally I thought they'd just confuse the people who read the report and erode their confidence in our findings."

"I admit our field interviewers had a lot of trouble reaching families in which both spouses worked," said Sords. "They also were turned down a good deal when they tried to interview the elderly. Now, I grant you that most of the people who are going to read this report wouldn't notice that we glossed over these problems, but George Scanlon's got a mind like a steel trap. He'd be sure to pick up on the fact that we failed to note the sources of nonsampling bias, and

it would make our whole report suspect."

"Of course, you're right, Caroline. All those late nights working on the report must have been clouding my judgment. Any other changes?"

"Just a couple of editing changes that I've penciled in here and there. Otherwise it looks great. By the way, would you like to come with me when I present the results to Scanlon on Thursday? I'd like to have you there as a resource, and it'll give me a chance to show you off a little."

Summary

Learning Objective 1: Specify the fundamental criterion by which all research reports are evaluated.

Research reports are evaluated by one fundamental criterion—communication with the reader. The reader is not only the reason that the report is prepared, but also the standard by which its success is measured.

Learning Objective 2: Identify and discuss the four criteria that a report should meet if it is to communicate effectively with readers.

A report that achieves the goal of communicating effectively with readers is generally one that meets the specific criteria of completeness, accuracy, clarity, and conciseness.

Learning Objective 3: Outline the main elements that make up a standard report form.

A standard report generally contains the following elements: title page, table of contents, summary, introduction, body, conclusions and recommendations, and appendix.

Learning Objective 4: Explain the kind of information that is contained in the summary.

A true summary gives the high points of the entire body of the report, including necessary background information, as well as important results and conclusions.

Learning Objective 5: Distinguish between a conclusion and a recommendation.

A conclusion is an opinion based on the results. A recommendation is a suggestion as to appropriate future action.

Learning Objective 6: Describe the kind of information that should be contained in the introduction.

An introduction provides background information, defines unfamiliar terms, outlines pertinent history, and states the specific objectives of the research. Through all this, the introduction should serve to win the readers' confidence and dispel any prejudices they may have.

Learning Objective 7: Describe the kind of information that should be contained in the body.

The details of the research are contained in the body of the report. This includes details of method, results, and limitations.

Learning Objective 8: Describe the kind of information that should be contained in the appendix.

The appendix contains material that is too complex, too detailed, too specialized, or not absolutely necessary for the text. The appendix will typically contain as an exhibit a copy of the questionnaire or observation form used to collect the data.

Discussion Questions, Problems, and Projects

1. It should be clear from your reading of this chapter that a professional marketing researcher must possess a well-developed ability to write effectively. Many colleges and universities offer a variety of programs designed to help students hone their writing skills. These programs may take a variety of forms, such as writing labs, special seminars, word-processing tutorials, one-on-one writing tutors, and regular written communication classes. Prepare a research report of the resources available at your school that can be used to enhance written communication skills. Assume that your report will be furnished to incoming first-year students as part of their orientation materials. Be sure to structure your report in the manner presented in this chapter.

2. The owner of a medium-size home-building center specializing in custom-designed and do-it-yourself bathroom supplies requested the Liska and Leigh Consulting Firm to prepare a report on the customer profile of the bathroom design segment of the home-improvement market. Evaluate the following excerpts from the report:

Research report excerpts

The customer market for the company can be defined as the do-it-yourself and bathroom design segments. A brief profile of each follows.

The do-it-yourself (DIY) market consists of individuals in the 25–45 age-group living in a single dwelling. DIY customers are predominantly male, although an increasing number of females are becoming active DIY customers. The typical DIY customer has an income in excess of $20,000 and the median income is $22,100 with a standard deviation of 86. The DIY customer has an increasing amount of leisure time, is strongly value- and convenience-conscious, and displays an increasing desire for self-gratification.

The mean age of the custom bathroom design segment is 41.26 and the annual income is in the range of $25,000 to $35,000. The median income is $29,000 with a standard deviation of 73. The custom bathroom design customers usually live in a single dwelling. The wife is more influential and is the prime decision maker about bathroom designs.

3. Discuss the difference between conclusions and recommendations in research reports.

4. Assume that Wendy's International, Inc., wants to diversify into another fast food area. You are required to prepare a brief report for the company executives outlining an attractive opportunity. In preparing the report, go through the following steps:
   (a) Decide on the particular fast food area you think is most appropriate.
   (b) Collect secondary data relating to the area and analyze consumption trends over the past five years (or ten years).
   (c) Decide on the outline of the report and its various sections.
   (d) Develop the appropriate tables and charts to support your analysis.
   (e) Write the report.

5. Describe the information that should be contained in the summary, and discuss why this is the most important part of the research report.

6. In presenting a report to a group of grocery store managers, a researcher stated the following: "The data from the judgment sample of 10 grocery stores was analyzed and the results show that the 95-percent confidence interval for average annual sales in the population of grocery stores is $1,000,000 ± $150,000."
   (a) As far as the audience is concerned, what is wrong with this statement?
   (b) Rewrite the statement. Be sure to include all of the relevant information while correcting the problem.

7. Your marketing research firm is preparing the final written report on a research project commissioned by a major manufacturer of lawn mowers. One objective of the project was to investigate seasonal variations in sales, both on an aggregate basis and by each of the company's sales regions individually. Your client is particularly interested in the width of the range between maximum and minimum seasonal sales. Table 1, on the next page, was submitted by one of your junior analysts. Critique the table and prepare a revision suitable for inclusion in your report.

Table 1   **Seasonal Sales Variation**

Sales Region	Sales in Thousands of Dollars			
	Spring	**Summer**	**Fall**	**Winter**
Northeast	120.10	140.59	50.90	30.00
East-central	118.80	142.70	61.70	25.20
Southeast	142.00	151.80	134.20	100.10
Midwest	100.20	139.42	42.90	20.00
South-central	80.77	101.00	90.42	78.20
Plains	95.60	120.60	38.50	19.90
Southwest	105.40	110.50	101.60	92.10
Pacific	180.70	202.41	171.54	145.60

Endnotes

1. Reprinted by special permission from William J. Gallagher, *Report Writing for Management*, p. 1. Addison-Wesley Publishing Company, Inc., Reading, Massachusetts. Copyright © 1969. All rights reserved. Much of this introductory section is also taken from this excellent book. See also Richard Hatch, *Business Communication*, 2nd ed. (Chicago: Science Research Associates, 1983).

2. The other variables are the extent of interaction that researchers have with managers, the research objectives, the degree of surprise in the results, and the stage of the product or service in its life cycle. See Rohit Deshpande and Gerald Zaltman, "A Comparison of Factors Affecting Researcher and Manager Perceptions of Market Research Use," *Journal of Marketing Research*, 21 (February 1984), pp. 32–38.

3. Walter B. Wentz, *Marketing Research: Management, Method, and Cases*, 2nd ed. (New York: Harper and Row, 1979), p. 61. David J. Smallen, director of marketing research at Fisher-Price, similarly argues that research reports must be easy to access, easy to understand, easy to use, and easy to believe. See David J. Smallen, "Little People to Puffalumps: Managing Information in an Emerging Marketing Research Environment," paper presented at the 9th Annual Marketing Research Conference of the American Marketing Association, Arlington, Virginia, October 9–12, 1988.

4. Stewart Henderson Britt, "The Communication of Your Research Findings," in Robert Ferber, ed., *Handbook of Marketing Research* (New York: McGraw-Hill, 1974), pp. 1–90.

5. Harper W. Boyd, Jr., Ralph Westfall, and Stanley F. Stasch, *Marketing Research: Text and Cases*, 7th ed. (Homewood, Ill.: Richard D. Irwin, 1989), p. 657.

6. Gallagher, *Report Writing*, p. 78.

7. See Gallagher, *Report Writing*, pp. 80–83, for a number of examples that display some of the inaccuracies that may arise. The examples are particularly interesting because they have been extracted from actual company reports. Frustrated by writing that is muddled and wastes time, firms are increasingly turning to writing consultants or in-house seminars to improve the writing skills of their employees. Some 34 percent of all organizations with 50 or more employees provide some writing training. See Cynthia F. Mitchell, "Firms Seek Cure for Dull Memos; Find Windy Writers Hard to Curb," *The Wall Street Journal* (October 4, 1985), p. 21.

8. Taken from William Zinsser, *On Writing Well*, 3rd ed. (New York: Harper and Row, 1985), pp. 7–8, a modern classic for writers that is as helpful as it is fun to read.

9. Gallagher, *Report Writing*, Chapter 10, "Reviewing for Accuracy: Grammar," pp. 156–177, has examples of how these inaccuracies can confuse and misinform. See also Charles T. Brusaw, Gerald J. Alred, and E. Watter Oliv, *The Business Writers Handbook*, 2nd ed. (New York: St. Martins Press, 1982).

10. Gallaher, *Report Writing*, p. 83.

11. Kenneth Roman and Joel Raphaelson, *Writing That Works* (New York: Harper and Row, 1981). This book gives some excellent advice on how to write more effective reports, memos, letters, and speeches. See also Kenneth Roman and Joel Raphaelson, "Don't Mumble and Other Principles of Effective Writing," *Viewpoint: By, For, and About Ogilvy & Mather*, 2 (1980), pp. 19–36. The little book by William Strunk, Jr., and E. B. White, *The Elements of Style*, 3rd ed. (New York: Macmillan, 1979), is a classic on how to write clearly.

12. Jock Elliott, "How Hard It Is to Write Easily," *Viewpoint: By, For, and About Ogilvy & Mather*, 2 (1980), p. 18.

13. Gallagher, *Report Writing*, p. 87.

14. Ibid., p. 84.

15. Dolph von Arx, "The Many Faces of Market Research," paper delivered at the meeting of the Association of National Advertisers, Inc., New York, April 3, 1985. The trend is for managers to seek recommendations from marketing research people. Stephen M. Matis, "The Marketing Research Organization in Transition," paper presented at the 9th Annual Marketing Research Conference of the American Marketing Association, Arlington, Virginia, October 9–12, 1988.

16. Gallagher, *Report Writing*, p. 54.

17. Some of the many structures and the conditions under which they can be used are contained in Jessamon Dawe, *Writing Business and Economic Papers: Theses and Dissertations* (Totowa, N.J.: Littlefield, Adams, 1975), pp. 75–86.

18. See Gallagher, *Report Writing*, pp. 50–68, for a discussion of the psychological order of things in research reports.

19. See A. S. C. Ehrenberg, "Rudiments of Numeracy," *Journal of the Royal Statistical Society*, Series A, 140 (1977), pp. 277–297, and A. S. C. Ehrenberg, "The Problem of Numeracy," *American Statistician*, 35 (May 1981), pp. 67–71, for particularly informative discussions using examples of how adherence to these principles can dramatically improve readers' abilities to comprehend the information being presented in tables.

20. Boyd, Westfall, and Stasch, *Marketing Research*, p. 663.

Suggested Additional Readings

For excellent, succinct treatments of how to write better, see

Kenneth Roman and Joel Raphaelson, *Writing That Works* (New York: Harper and Row, 1981).

William Strunk, Jr., and E. B. White, *The Elements of Style*, 3rd ed. (New York: Macmillan, 1979).

William Zinsser, *On Writing Well*, 3rd ed. (New York: Harper and Row, 1985).

Chapter
Twenty-Three

The Oral Research Report

Learning Objectives

Upon completing this chapter, you should be able to

1. Specify the first rule to keep in mind when preparing an oral report.

2. Describe the two most common forms of organization for oral reports.

3. Discuss the key points a presenter should keep in mind regarding the use of visual aids.

4. Explain how the time allotted for an oral presentation should be organized.

5. Describe the circumstances in which a pie chart is most effective.

6. Explain the best use of a line chart.

7. Describe the circumstances in which a stratum chart is most effective.

8. Cite the reason why bar charts are so widely used.

9. Describe the circumstances in which a grouped-bar chart is most effective.

Case in Marketing Research

Ann Stigler and Jim Thurow pulled into the parking lot of Berkshire Dairies at 8:30 on Monday morning. While Thurow was unloading a portfolio of flip charts and overhead transparencies from the trunk, Mark Friedman, Berkshire's director of marketing, pulled into an adjacent parking spot.

"Good morning, Ann," declared Friedman in surprise. "Good morning, Jim. Please tell me that you guys are just early and that I haven't made some terrible mistake about the time of your presentation."

"As far as I know, we're still on for ten," replied Stigler with a smile, "but I need some lead time to check out the room, set up my audiovisuals, and find the coffee machine before I'm ready to wow you with our results."

"In that case, let me help you with some of this stuff," volunteered Friedman. "Then I can also show you where we're going to be meeting."

"I thought we'd be making our presentation in the board room, where we had our meeting with Rob Samuelson," said Thurow.

"Well, you know Samuelson. The issue of how best to expand our consumer base for Berkshire Premium ice cream is on everyone's mind right now, so Samuelson's invited everyone. There will be people from production, sales, even heads of other divisions. I've had to reserve a much larger room."

"What fun," said Stigler in a less-than-cheerful voice. "Is there a copy machine we might be able to use?"

Discussion Issues

1. If you were in charge of delivering the final oral report on your company's research project, what kind of information would you want in advance?
2. How would you use that information in preparing your report?
3. How might your oral report differ from your written report?

In addition to the written report, most marketing research investigations require one or more oral reports. Often clients, or those in the company for whom the study is being undertaken, want progress reports during the course of the project. Almost always they require a formal oral report at the conclusion of the study. The principles surrounding the preparation and delivery of the oral report parallel those for the written report.

Preparing the Oral Report

As we emphasized in the preceding chapter, the first requirement is to know the audience. What is their technical level of sophistication? What is their involvement in the project? Their interest? Once again, researchers may want to present more detailed reports to those who are deeply involved in the project or who have a high level of technical sophistication than to those who are only slightly involved or interested.

In general, it is better to err on the side of too little technical detail rather than too much. Executives want to hear and see what the information means to them as managers of marketing activities. What do the data suggest with respect to marketing actions? They can ask for the necessary clarification with respect to the technical details if they want it.

Another important consideration is how the presentation is organized. There are two popular forms of organization. Both begin by stating the general purpose of the

Oral research reports often incorporate video and overhead presentations, as well as computer-generated graphics.

Source: Courtesy of Tingley Systems, Inc., Highway 52 West, P.O. Box 700, San Antonio, FL 33576.

Research Window 23.1
Ten Tips for Preparing Effective Presentation Visuals

Keep it simple. Deliver complex ideas in a manner that your audience can understand. Present one point per slide, with as few words and lines as possible.

Use lots of slides as you talk, rather than lots of talk per slide. Less is more when you are speaking.

Use one minute per visual. Slides and overheads should make their impact quickly; then move on. No more than ten words per slide.

Highlight significant points. Bullets work for black and white transparencies; slides are better suited for color and graphics.

Use a graphic on every page. One is usually enough. Take advantage of "white space," and don't overcrowd.

Build complexity. If you have a complicated concept to communicate, start with the ground level and use three or four slides to complete the picture.

Be careful with color. Color can add interest and emphasis. It can also detract if used without planning. Plan your color scheme and use it faithfully throughout.

Prepare copies of overheads or slides. Hand them to the audience before or after your presentation. If people have to take notes, they won't be watching or listening closely.

Number your pages. You will have a better reference for discussion or a question-and-answer period.

Make visuals easy to read. Use large, legible typefaces. You can use up to three sizes of type, but use only one or two typefaces. Bold and italics can be used freely for emphasis. With slides, use light type against a dark background.

Source: Colleen Paul, "You're in Show Biz! 10 Tips for Presenters," *Micro Monitor*, 6 (May 1989), pp. 12–13.

study and the specific objectives that were addressed. They differ, however, with respect to when the conclusions are introduced. In the most popular structure, the conclusions are introduced after all of the evidence supporting a particular course of action is presented. This allows the presenter to build a logical case in sequential fashion. By progressively disclosing the facts, the presenter has the opportunity to deal with audience concerns and biases as they arise, and thus lead them to the conclusion that the case builds.

In the alternative structure, conclusions are presented immediately after the purpose and main objectives. This structure tends to involve managers immediately in the findings. It not only gets them to think about what actions the results suggest, but also alerts them to pay close attention to the evidence supporting the conclusions. This format allows managers to evaluate the strength of the evidence supporting an action, since they know beforehand the conclusions that have been drawn from it.

The structure a presenter decides to use should depend on the particular company's style and preferences and on the presenter's own level of comfort with each form of organization. In either case, the evidence supporting the conclusions must be presented systematically, and the conclusions drawn must be consistent with the evidence.

A third important element in an effective oral presentation is the use of appropriate visual aids. Depending on the size of the group and the physical facilities in which the meeting is held, flip charts, transparencies, slides, and even chalkboards can all be used to advantage. Regardless of which type of visual is used, make sure it can be read easily by those in the back of the room. Keep the visuals simple so they can be understood at a glance. Whenever possible, use figures rather than tables to make the points, as figures are more easily understood. In addition, obey the other principles of effective visual aid design listed in Research Window 23.1.

Research Window 23.2
How to Use a Microphone Well

Bungling at the microphone can create a "sound barrier" between you and your audience. But using a sound system effectively can connect you and bring your ideas to the audience in a powerful, intimate way. Here's some useful advice:

- **The mike must be aimed at your mouth, about six to eight inches away from you.** Adjust the microphone height to mouth level quickly, before you say a word. Then point the mike toward your mouth. Don't hunch over to reach the mouthpiece; instead, as recording engineer David Satz says, "let the microphone address you."

- **Check out the sound system before you speak.** "You have a right to have someone there who knows the system," says Satz, "and you have a right to a few moments of practice." If possible, meet with the sound operator.

- **When you test a microphone, just talk into it normally and ask someone to listen.** Never blow into it.

- **Let the sound system work for you.** Let *it* do the broadcasting. Keep your volume, inflections, and pacing in your normal range. Listen to how well the system is working for those ahead of you and, when it's your turn, adjust your voice as necessary.

- **When using a hand-held microphone,** hold it in front of you, aimed at your mouth (not under your chin). Be careful that your handling of the microphone does not make noises—watch out for clunking finger rings.

- **In a question-and-answer session,** don't aim your microphone at the questioner. Instead, repeat the question over the sound system (following this procedure also gives you an extra moment to frame an answer).

- **Know when not to use a sound system.** If you can be heard comfortably by all the people in the room without amplification, by all means, talk without a microphone. Relying on a sound system for a few dozen people, or in a room with excellent acoustics, distances you from your audience. Check your audibility by stepping away from the mike and asking listeners in the back if they can hear you. Unless you see puzzled stares, proceed on your own steam.

Source: John Stoltenberg, "How to Use a Microphone Well," *Working Woman* (February 1986), p. 79.

Delivering the Oral Report

Honor the time limit set for the meeting. Use no more than a third to a half of the time for the formal presentation. But be careful not to rush the presentation of the information contained in the charts. Remember, the audience is seeing them for the first time. Order your presentation in such a way that there is enough time to both present and discuss the most critical findings. Reserve the remaining time for questions and further discussion.

One of the unique benefits of the oral presentation is that it allows interaction. A question-and-answer period may be the most important part of your presentation. It allows you to clear up any confusion that may have arisen during the course of your talk, to emphasize points that deserve special attention, and to get a feeling for the issues that are of particular concern or interest to your audience. The nature of the questions raised during a progress report may help you structure your final report to best advantage.

Use the time-honored principles of public speaking when delivering the message: Keep the presentation simple and uncluttered so that the audience does not have to backtrack mentally to think about what was said, and choose words and sentences that are appropriate for the tongue. That means spoken speech, your usual vocabulary, and simple phrases.[1] Finally, if the situation demands that you use a microphone, use it well. Research Window 23.2 offers some specific suggestions in this regard.

Ethical
Dilemma 23.1   The results of a research study you supervised are disappointing. Only one of the four basic questions motivating the study has been clearly answered. The answers to the other three questions are rather equivocal in spite of careful planning of the study and a sizable expenditure of money to carry it out. Unanticipated difficulties in contacting people by telephone raised the cost of each contact, which meant the obtained sample was smaller than the planned sample, which in turn made the evidence less clear-cut. You are concerned that you and your research team will be evaluated unfavorably because of this. Members of your research team are arguing that when you deliver the oral report to management, you should attempt to somewhat hide the fact that only one of the four basic questions has been answered satisfactorily. The team members propose a multimedia presentation with lots of glitz, with maximum time devoted to the formal presentation and minimum time allowed for questions.

- Is it ethical to hide disappointing results in this way?
- What are the consequences of doing so?
- Is it okay to use so much glitz to generate interest in the topic being presented that the glitz overwhelms the substance of the findings? Should you not use glitz at all?

Graphic Presentation of the Results

The old adage that a picture is worth a thousand words is equally true for business reports. A picture, called a *graphic illustration* in the case of the research report, can indeed be worth a thousand words when it is appropriate to the presentation and well designed. When inappropriate or poorly designed, such an illustration may actually detract from the value of the written or oral research report. In this section, we will review briefly some of the most popular forms of graphics and when each is best used.[2]

In a research report, graphic illustration generally involves the presentation of quantities in graph form. To be effective, it must be more than simply converting a set of numbers into a drawing; the picture must give the readers an accurate understanding of the comparisons or relationships that they would otherwise have to search for in the numbers in the report and perhaps fail to see. If well done, the graphic illustration will give the readers this understanding more quickly, more forcefully, more completely, and more accurately than could be done in any other way.[3]

Graphic presentation is not the only way to present quantitative information, nor is it always the best. Sometimes text and tables are better used. Graphics should be used only when they serve the purpose better than do these other modes. Written textual material is generally the most useful in explaining, interpreting, and evaluating results, while tables are particularly good for providing emphasis and for vivid demonstrations of important findings. Particularly since some readers tend to shy away from graphic presentation as "too technical," it should be used with discretion and designed with care.

At one time graphic presentation was expensive and often delayed the presentation of reports because the visuals had to be drawn by graphic artists. Computer graphics are changing that. The development of computer software for graphically portraying the results of a study now makes the preparation of visuals fast

As technological advances make video conferencing more convenient and affordable, oral reports will no longer be limited to those in one location.

Source: Courtesy of Noon & Pratt, 1-800-722-1235.

and inexpensive. There is no longer any excuse for not using graphics when appropriate.[4]

There are three basic kinds of graphics: charts that show how much, maps that show where, and diagrams that show how. Since charts are generally the most useful of the three types, the following discussion focuses on some of the more common chart types.

Pie Chart

Pie chart A circle representing a total quantity and divided into sectors, with each sector showing the size of the segment in relation to that total.

Probably one of the more familiar charts, the **pie chart** is simply a circle divided into sections, with each of the sections representing a portion of the total. Since the sections are presented as part of a whole, or total, the pie chart is particularly effective for depicting relative size or emphasizing static comparisons. Figure 23.1 (resulting from the data of Table 23.1), for instance, shows the breakdown of personal consumption expenditures by major category for 1988. The conclusion is obvious. Expenditures for services account for the largest proportion of total consumption expenditures. Further, expenditures for services and nondurable goods completely dwarf expenditures for durable goods.

Figure 23.1 has three slices, and it is easy to interpret. Had the information been broken into finer categories (for example, if the separate components of durable and nondurable goods had been depicted), a greater number of sections would have been required. Although more information would have been conveyed, emphasis would have been lost. As a rule of thumb, no more than six slices should be generated; the

Figure 23.1   *Personal Consumption Expenditures by Major Category for 1988*

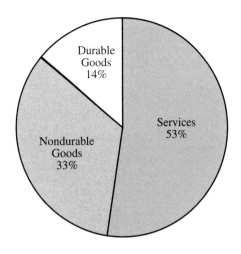

Table 23.1   **Personal Consumption Expenditures for 1970–1988 (Billions of Dollars)**

		Durable Goods			Nondurable Goods				Services
Year	Total Personal Consumption Expenditures	Total Durable Goods	Motor Vehicles & Parts	Furniture & Household Equipment	Total Nondurable Goods	Food	Clothing & Shoes	Gasoline & Oil	
1970	621.70	85.20	36.20	35.20	265.70	138.90	46.80	22.40	270.80
1971	672.20	97.20	45.40	37.20	278.80	144.20	50.60	23.90	296.20
1972	737.10	111.10	52.40	41.70	300.60	154.90	55.40	25.40	325.30
1973	812.00	123.30	57.10	47.10	333.40	172.10	61.40	28.60	355.20
1974	888.10	121.50	50.40	50.60	373.40	193.70	64.80	36.60	393.20
1975	976.40	132.20	55.80	53.50	407.30	213.60	69.60	40.40	437.00
1976	1,084.30	156.80	72.60	59.10	441.70	230.60	75.30	44.00	485.70
1977	1,204.40	178.20	84.80	65.70	478.80	249.80	82.60	48.10	547.40
1978	1,346.50	200.20	95.70	72.80	528.20	275.90	92.40	51.20	618.00
1979	1,507.20	213.40	96.60	81.80	600.00	311.60	99.10	66.60	693.70
1980	1,668.10	214.70	90.70	86.30	668.80	345.10	104.60	84.80	784.50
1981	1,849.10	235.40	101.90	92.30	730.70	373.90	114.30	94.60	883.00
1982	2,050.70	252.70	108.90	95.70	771.00	398.80	124.40	89.10	1,027.00
1983	2,234.50	289.10	130.40	107.10	816.70	421.90	135.10	90.20	1,128.70
1984	2,430.50	335.50	157.40	118.80	867.30	448.50	146.70	90.00	1,227.60
1985	2,629.00	372.20	179.10	129.90	911.20	471.60	156.40	90.60	1,345.60
1986	2,797.40	406.00	196.20	139.70	942.00	500.00	166.80	73.50	1,449.50
1987	3,010.80	421.00	195.50	149.10	998.10	529.20	177.20	75.20	1,591.70
1988	3,235.10	455.20	211.60	162.00	1,052.30	559.70	186.80	76.80	1,727.60

Source: Survey of Current Business (July 1989).

Figure 23.2   **Retail Sales of New Passenger Cars**

Millions of Units

Line chart showing retail sales of new passenger cars from 1970 to 1988, with Domestics and Imports series.

Line chart A two-dimensional chart constructed on graph paper with the X axis representing one variable (typically time) and the Y axis representing another variable.

Line Chart

The pie chart is a one-scale chart, which is why it is best used for static comparisons of a phenomena at a point in time. The **line chart** is a two-dimensional chart that is particularly useful in depicting dynamic relationships such as time-series fluctuations of one or more series. For example, Figure 23.2 (produced from the data of Table 23.2) shows that, for 1970–1988, new car sales of imports were subject to much less fluctuation than were domestic sales.

The line chart is probably used even more often than the pie chart. It is typically constructed on graph paper with the X axis representing time and the Y axis representing values of the variable or variables. When more than one variable is presented, it is recommended that the lines for different items be distinctive in color or form (dots and dashes in suitable combinations) with identification of the different forms given in a legend.[6]

Stratum chart A set of line charts in which quantities are aggregated or a total is disaggregated so that the distance between two lines represents the amount of some variable.

Stratum Chart

The **stratum chart** serves in some ways as a dynamic pie chart, in that it can be used to show relative emphasis by sector (for example, quantity consumed by user class) and change in relative emphasis over time. The stratum chart consists of a set of line charts whose quantities are grouped together (or a total that is broken into its components). It is also called a stacked line chart. For example, Figure 23.3 (resulting

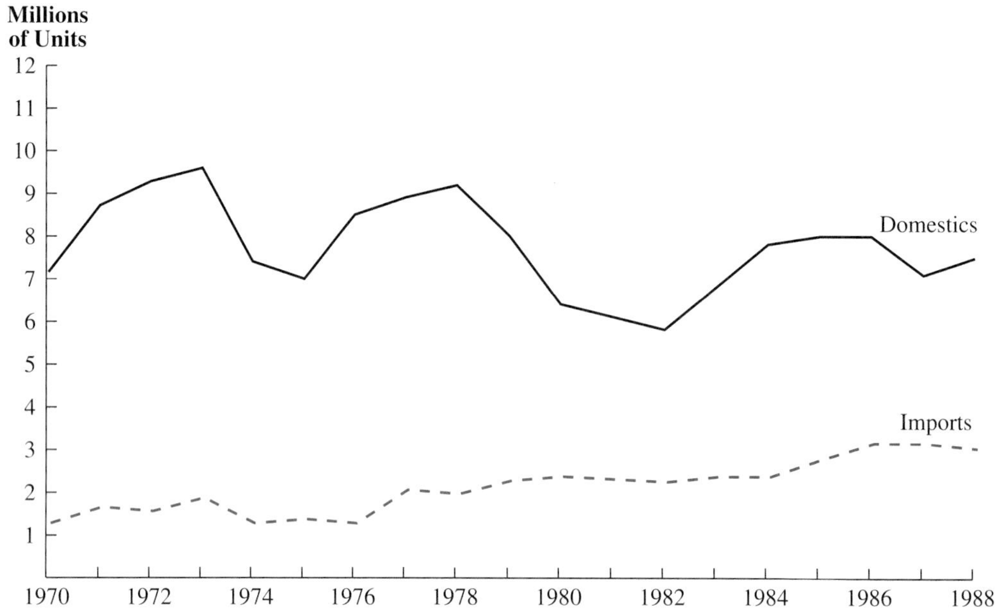

division of the pie should start at the twelve o'clock position; the sections should be arrayed clockwise in decreasing order of magnitude; and the exact percentages should be provided on the graph.[5]

Table 23.2   ***Retail Sales of New Passenger Cars (Millions of Units)***

Year	Domestics	Imports	Total
1970	7.10	1.30	8.40
1971	8.70	1.60	10.30
1972	9.30	1.60	10.90
1973	9.60	1.80	11.40
1974	7.40	1.40	8.80
1975	7.00	1.60	8.60
1976	8.50	1.50	10.00
1977	9.00	2.10	11.10
1978	9.20	2.00	11.20
1979	8.20	2.30	10.50
1980	6.60	2.40	9.00
1981	6.20	2.30	8.50
1982	5.80	2.20	8.00
1983	6.80	2.40	9.20
1984	8.00	2.40	10.40
1985	8.20	2.80	11.00
1986	8.20	3.20	11.40
1987	7.10	3.20	10.30
1988	7.50	3.10	10.60

Source: Economic Indicators.

from the data of Table 23.1) shows personal consumption expenditures by major category for the seventeen-year period of 1970–1988. The lowest line shows the expenditures just for durable goods, the second lowest line shows the total expenditures for durable plus nondurable goods. Personal consumption expenditures for nondurable goods are thus shown by the area between the two lines. So it is with the remaining areas. We would need seventeen pie charts (one for each year) to capture the same information, and the message would not be as obvious.

The X axis typically represents time in the stratum chart, and the Y axis again captures the value of the variables. The use of color or distinctive cross-hatching is strongly recommended to distinguish the various components in the stratum chart. As was true for the pie chart, no more than six components should be depicted in a stratum chart.

Bar Chart

Bar chart A chart in which the relative lengths of the bars show relative amounts of variables or objects.

The **bar chart** can be either a one-scale or a two-scale chart. This feature, plus the many other variations it permits, probably accounts for its wide use. Figure 23.4, for example, is a one-scale chart. It also shows personal consumption expenditures by

Figure 23.3   **Personal Consumption Expenditures by Major Category, 1970–1988**

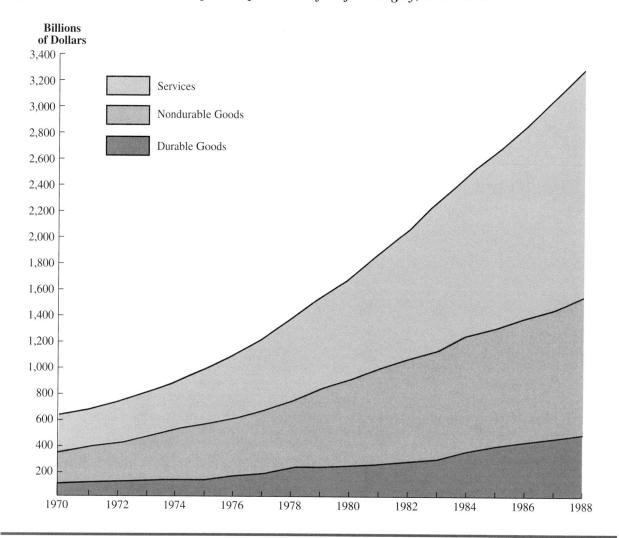

Figure 23.4   **Personal Consumption Expenditures by Major Category for 1988**

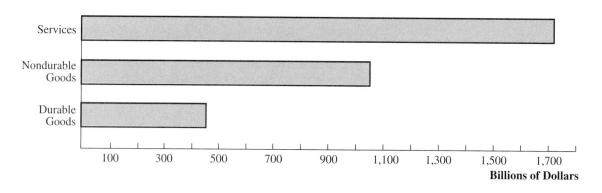

Figure 23.5   **Total Automobile Sales, 1970–1988**

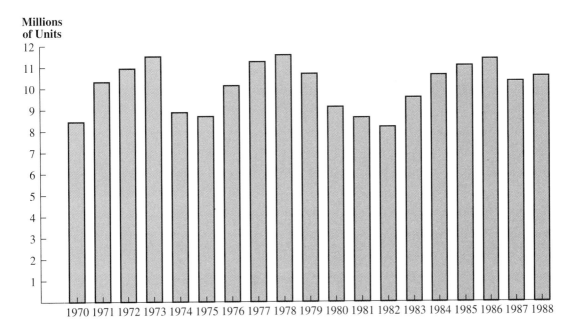

major category at a single point in time. Figure 23.4 presents the same information as Figure 23.1 but is, in at least one respect, more revealing; it not only offers some appreciation of the relative expenditures by major category, but also indicates the magnitude of the expenditures by category. Given the total amount of personal consumption expenditures for 1988, readers could, of course, also generate this information from the pie chart. However, it would involve additional calculations on their part.

Figure 23.5, on the other hand, is a two-scale bar chart. It uses the data contained in Table 23.2 and shows total automobile sales for the period 1970–1988. The *Y* axis represents quantity, and the *X* axis, time.

Figures 23.4 and 23.5 show that the bar chart can be drawn either vertically or horizontally. When emphasis is on the change in the variable through time, the vertical form is preferred, with the *X* axis as the time axis. When time is not a variable, either the vertical or the horizontal form is used.

Bar Chart Variations

As previously suggested, bar charts are capable of great variation. One variation is to convert them to **pictograms.** Instead of using the length of the bar to capture quantity, amounts are shown by piles of dollars for income, pictures of cars for automobile production, people in a row for population, and so on. This can be a welcome change of pace for the reader if there are a number of graphs in the report.[7]

A variation of the basic bar chart—the grouped-bar chart—can be used to capture the change in two or more series through time. Figure 23.6, for example, shows the change in consumption expenditures by the three major categories for the

Pictogram A bar chart in which pictures represent amounts—for example, piles of dollars for income, pictures of cars for automobile production, people in a row for population.

Figure 23.6   *Personal Consumption Expenditures by Major Category, 1980–1988*

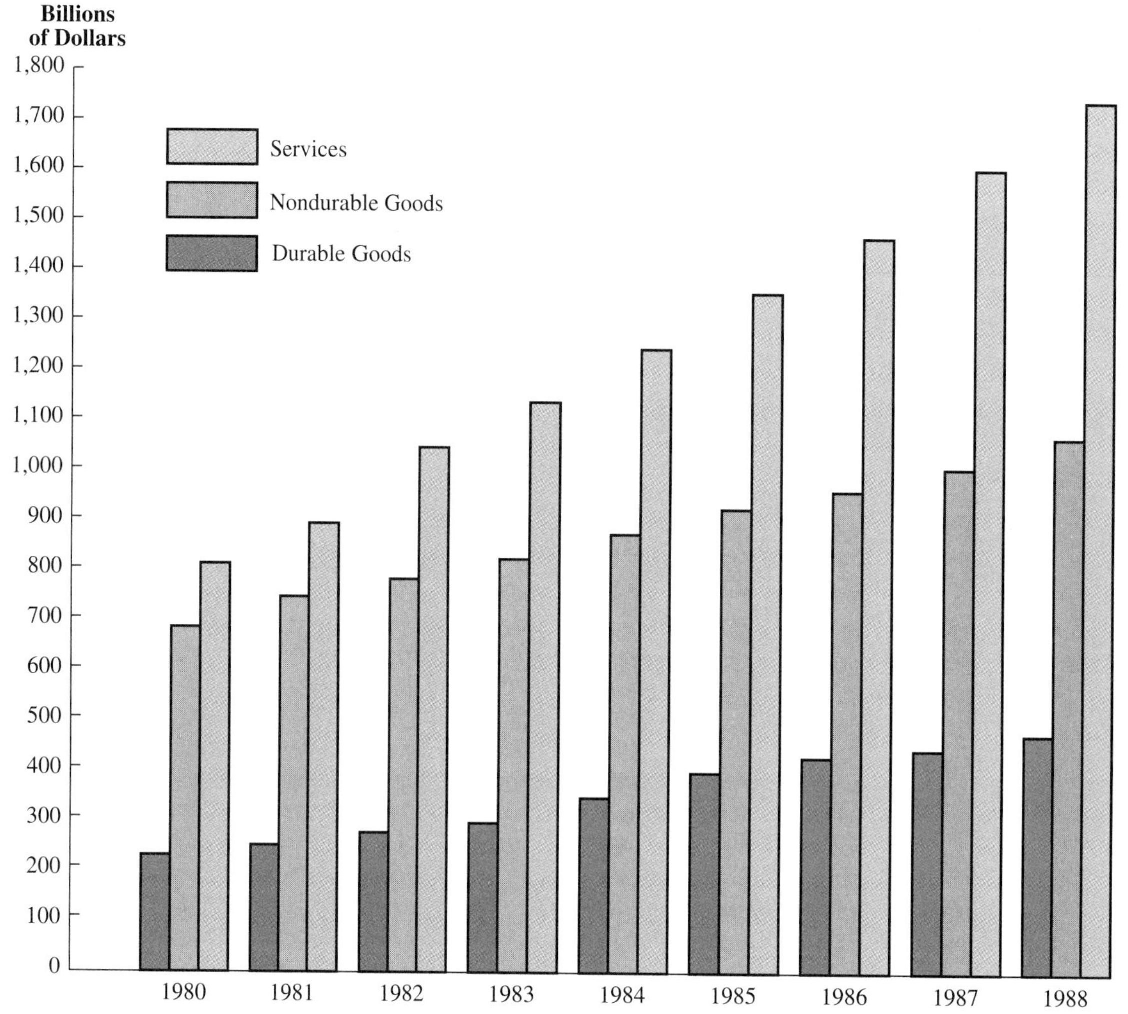

period 1980–1988. Just as distinctive symbols are effective in distinguishing the separate series in a line chart, distinctive coloring and/or cross-hatching is equally helpful in a grouped-bar chart.

There is also a bar chart equivalent to the stratum chart—the divided-bar chart or, as it is sometimes called, the stacked-bar chart. Its construction and interpretation are similar to those for the stratum chart. Figure 23.7, for example, is a divided-bar chart of personal consumption expenditures by major category. It shows both total and relative expenditures through time, and it makes use of distinctive color for each component.

Research Window 23.3 offers some suggestions on using graphics in slide presentations.

Figure 23.7 **Personal Consumption Expenditures by Major Category, 1970–1988**

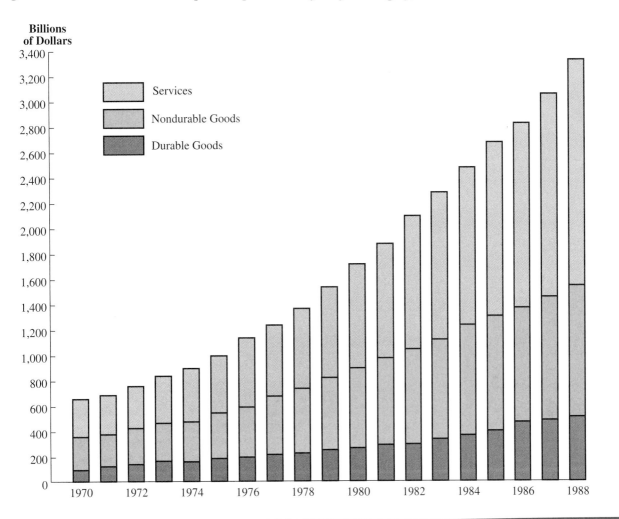

Research Window 23.3
Putting Slide Graphics to Use

Word slides

- Keep word slides brief: use key words only.
- Use bullets and color to highlight key points.
- Break up the information to make a series of slides (a progressive or "build" series). Use color to show the new line added to each slide.

Tabular slides

- Use tabular slides to show lists.
- Keep items as brief as possible; arrange them to fill the slide area so the type can be as large as possible.

Box charts

- Use box charts for organization charts, flow charts.
- Simplify to keep them legible.
- Break up complex charts into a series. (Show flow chart divided by time periods; show organization chart with the overall chart and departmental "close-up.")

Bar charts

- Use bar charts for data arranged in segments (by month, year, etc.).
- Choose vertical or horizontal bars (both within horizontal slide format).

- Add drop shadows for dimensional bars.
- Show complex facts clearly by using multiple or segmented bars.
- Divide extensive data into a progressive disclosure series.

Pie charts

- Use pie charts to emphasize the relationship of the parts to the whole.
- Select single pie or double pie.
- Consider options such as drop shadow for dimensional effect, pulled-out slices, etc.
- Arrange the slices to make your point most effectively.
- Divide the slice into a series if that improves effectiveness.

Line graphs and area graphs

- Use line graphs and area graphs to display trends or continuous data.
- Decide whether line graph or area graph shows your point better.
- Select baseline and scale for maximum effectiveness.
- Use call-outs to identify key points in graph.
- Divide extensive data into a series of graphs.

Source: Leslie Blumberg, "For Graphic Presentations, Managers Focus on Slides," *Data Management* (May 1983), p. 22.

Ethical
Dilemma 23.2   You are preparing to deliver the final report to top management to make the case that your new advertising campaign has increased sales dramatically in trial areas. Your conceptual arguments on behalf of the new campaign are very convincing, but although there has been a consistent rise in sales in trial areas, the bar charts look rather disappointing: 61,500 units the first month, 61,670 units the next, 61,820 the next. Why, the increase is barely visible! Then you realize how much more exciting your results would look if the Y axis were broken above the origin so that the plots started at 50,000 units.

- Where does salesmanship stop and deception start?

Back to the Case

Jim Thurow marveled at his colleague's poise. Ten minutes ago Ann Stigler had been running around with the rest of the group from AG Marketing Research, scrambling to adjust to a larger audience and a larger room for the presentation. They had made more copies of the handouts, secured an extension cord for the overhead projector, and found chalk for the blackboard. Stigler had quickly streamlined her remarks to accommodate a more diverse group and allow more time for questions. But despite her recent frenzy, Stigler now stood at the lectern and presented the conclusions of the research study with the composure of a professional.

"We at AG know that while Berkshire Premium ice cream burst onto the scene as the first premium brand of ice cream in 1982, its sales in the last few years have slipped between 3 and 4 percent a year. Some of the trends that have adversely affected all premium ice cream brands have also hurt Berkshire. For example, the young professionals who formed the core of Berkshire's market in the eighties and were so central to its success are now ten years older and much more conscious of their waistlines and their pocketbooks. While our study shows that the planned launch of a new 96-percent-fat-free frozen yogurt under the Berkshire label has strong market potential, we don't have such upbeat results when it comes to continued sales of Berkshire Premium ice cream."

"We know that at Berkshire Dairies there has been great interest in expanding sales of the premium ice cream by marketing it more strongly to the masses. Currently, Berkshire Premium is sold only in pint containers, and at $2.89 a pint, it is the most expensive ice cream on the market. But our research shows that while 67 percent of consumers surveyed said they thought it was a good idea to market Berkshire Premium in quart containers in order to serve families more conveniently, 85 percent of the survey respondents said they were cutting back on their nonessential grocery purchases. We've concluded that while the majority of people surveyed felt that selling Berkshire Premium in quarts was a good idea, almost 81 percent would not buy the larger size if it were priced at double the pint price, or $5.78 a quart."

As Stigler finished her presentation, Thurow looked at the audience. There wasn't a single happy face. He was glad he wasn't at the lectern looking out onto that grim group.

"I've left the last half hour of my talk for questions and answers," Stigler said. "Please feel free to ask questions to clear up any points that might be confusing or to expand on anything I may have touched on too briefly."

The room was absolutely quiet.

Thurow shifted nervously in his seat. Then Rob Samuelson, Berkshire's CEO, stood up.

"What makes you so sure that the people who think the larger size containers are such a good idea won't buy them?"

"That's a very good question, Mr. Samuelson," replied Stigler, "and one of the trickiest ones a marketing researcher must deal with. What we have here is the difference between attitudes and intentions. While most people had an attitude that the family-size container of Berkshire Premium would be a good idea, on average there wasn't enough money in the family grocery budget to include such a luxury. In spite of what they said about the concept, they themselves had no intention of purchasing the ice cream. We are very careful to design our research to go beyond what people say, to see what they plan to do and how those two relate."

Summary

Learning Objective 1: Specify the first rule to keep in mind when preparing an oral report.

As with written reports, the first rule when preparing an oral report is to know your audience.

Learning Objective 2: Describe the two most common forms of organization for oral reports.

There are two popular forms of organization for oral reports. Both begin by stating the general purpose of the study and the specific objectives that were addressed. In the most popular structure, the conclusions are introduced after all of the evidence supporting a particular course of action is presented. This allows the presenter to build a logical case in sequential fashion. In the alternative structure, conclusions are presented immediately after the purpose and main objectives. This format allows managers to evaluate the strength of the evidence supporting an action, since they know beforehand the conclusions that have been drawn from it.

Learning Objective 3: Discuss the key points a presenter should keep in mind regarding the use of visual aids.

The visual aids used in an oral report should be easily understood and should be easily seen by those in the back of the room.

Learning Objective 4: Explain how the time allotted for an oral presentation should be organized.

Honor the time limit set for the meeting. Use no more than a third to a half of the time for the formal presentation. Reserve the remaining time for questions and discussion.

Learning Objective 5: Describe the circumstances in which a pie chart is most effective.

A pie chart is a one-scale chart, which is particularly effective in communicating a static comparison.

Learning Objective 6: Explain the best use of a line chart.

A line chart is a two-dimensional chart that is particularly useful in depicting dynamic relationships such as time-series fluctuations of one or more series.

Learning Objective 7: Describe the circumstances in which a stratum chart is most effective.

A stratum chart is in some ways a dynamic pie chart, in that it can be used to show relative emphasis by sector and change in relative emphasis over time.

Learning Objective 8: Cite the reason why bar charts are so widely used.

The bar chart can be either a one-scale or a two-scale chart. This feature, plus the many other variations it permits, probably accounts for its wide use.

Learning Objective 9: Describe the circumstances in which a grouped-bar chart is most effective.

A variation of the basic bar chart, the grouped-bar can be used to capture the change in two or more series through time.

Discussion Questions, Problems, and Projects

1. The management of the Seal-Tight Company, a manufacturer of metal cans, has presented you with the following information:

The Seal-Tight Company:
A Comparative Statement of Profit and Loss for the Fiscal Years 1987–1991

	1987	1988	1989	1990	1991
Net sales	$40,000,000	$45,000,000	$48,000,000	$53,000,000	$55,000,000
Cost and expenses Cost of goods sold	$28,000,000	$32,850,000	$33,600,000	$39,750,000	$40,150,000
Selling and admin. expenses	4,000,000	4,500,000	4,800,000	5,300,000	5,500,000
Depreciation	1,200,000	1,350,000	1,440,000	1,590,000	1,650,000
Interest	800,000	900,000	960,000	1,060,000	1,100,000
	$34,000,000	$39,600,000	$40,800,000	$47,700,000	$48,400,000
Profits from operations	6,000,000	5,400,000	7,200,000	5,300,000	6,600,000
Estimated taxes	$ 2,400,000	$ 2,160,000	$ 2,880,000	$ 2,120,000	$ 2,640,000
Net profits	$ 3,600,000	$ 3,240,000	$ 4,320,000	$ 3,180,000	$ 3,960,000

(a). Develop a visual aid to present the company's distribution of sales revenues in 1991.

(b) Develop a visual aid that would compare the change in the net profit level with the change in the net sales level.

(c) Develop a visual aid that will present the following expenses (excluding cost of goods sold) over the five-year period: selling and administration expenses and depreciation and interest expenses.

(d) The management of Seal-Tight has the following sales data relating to its two major competitors:

	1987	1988	1989	1990	1991
Metalmax Co.	$35,000,000	$40,000,000	$42,000,000	$45,000,000	$48,000,000
Superior Can Co.	$41,000,000	$43,000,000	$45,000,000	$46,000,000	$48,000,000

You are required to prepare a visual aid to facilitate the comparison of the sales performance of Seal-Tight Company with its major competitors.

2. Most universities and colleges offer a wide variety of computer graphics software for student use in campus microcomputer labs. Investigate the availability of graphics software on your campus. Prepare a report outlining your findings. Be sure to include the following information for each available package:

(a) Name of package and basic capabilities

(b) Location(s) of access point(s)

(c) Times available for use

(d) Name of contact person(s) for further information

(e) Any special skills required for use and availability of training if needed

(f) Access fees, if any

(g) Hard-copy formats available (e.g., dot matrix printers, laser printers, color plotters, transparencies, slides)

3. Visit your school's library and find examples of each of the graphic illustrations described in this chapter. Look for these in publications such as *Business Week, Fortune, Newsweek, The Wall Street Journal*, and so on. Make a copy of each chart and critique it, using the criteria noted in the text. For example, does the pie chart you found exceed the recommended maximum number of divisions? Are the exact percentages displayed? In each case, is the chart appropriate for its intended purpose, or would another type of chart be more informative? Are there any changes you might recommend if the chart were to be used in an oral presentation?

Endnotes

1. There are a number of excellent books available on making effective oral presentations. See, for example, Dorothy Sarnoff, *Make the Most of Your Best: A Complete Program for Presenting Yourself and Your Ideas with Confidence and Authority* (Garden City, N.Y.: Doubleday, 1983).

2. The presentation should by no means include all the graph forms that could be used, but rather just some of the more common ones. Those interested in more detail should see Mary E. Spear, *Practical Charting Techniques* (New York: McGraw-Hill, 1969); and Edward R. Tufte, *The Visual Display of Quantitative Information* (Cheshire, Conn.: Graphics Press, 1983).

3. American Management Association, *Making the Most of Charts: An ABC of Graphic Presentation*, Management Bulletin, 28 (New York: American Telephone and Telegraph Company, 1960). See also J. M. Chambers, W. J. Cleveland, B. Kleiner, and P. A. Tukey, *Graphical Methods for Data Analysis* (Boston: Duxbury Press, 1983).

4. See Hirotaka Takeuchi and Allan H. Schmidt, "New Promise of Computer Graphics," *Harvard Business Review*, 58 (January–February 1980), pp. 122–131, for discussion of the elements necessary for generating report graphics by computer and the development trends concerning these elements.

5. Jessamon Dawe and William Jackson Lord, Jr., *Functional Business Communication*, 3rd ed. (Englewood Cliffs, N.J.: Prentice-Hall, 1983).

6. Idid.

7. Pictograms are especially susceptible to perceptual distortions. Report users have to be especially careful when reading them so that they are not led to incorrect conclusions. See Patricia Ramsey and Louis Kaufman, "Presenting Research Data: How to Make Weak Numbers Look Good," *Industrial Marketing*, 67 (March 1982), pp. 66, 68, 70, 74.

Suggested Additional Readings

For an excellent discussion of how to make effective oral presentations, see

Dorothy Sarnoff, *Make the Most of Your Best: A Complete Program for Presenting Yourself and Your Ideas with Confidence and Authority* (Garden City, N.Y.: Doubleday, 1983).

For discussion of how to develop effective graphics, see

Mary E. Spear, *Practical Charting Techniques* (New York: McGraw-Hill, 1969).

Edward R. Tufte, *The Visual Display of Quantitative Information* (Cheshire, Conn.: Graphics Press, 1983).

Leland Wilkinson, *SYGRAPH* (Evanston, Ill.: Systat, Inc., 1987), especially pp. 61–85.

Epilogue

The subject of marketing research can be approached in a number of ways. In this book we have used a *project emphasis* as the basis for our discussion. Using this perspective, we focused on how to define a problem and then develop the research needed to answer it. Because we have broken the research process down into components small enough to be discussed in the space of a chapter, it may seem to be a series of disconnected bits and pieces. However, as pointed out in Chapter 3, the research process is anything but a set of disconnected parts. All the steps are highly interrelated, and a decision made at one stage has implications for the others as well. Now that we have closely examined each of the individual components of the research process, in this epilogue we will look once again at how they work together. We will also review some of the key decisions that must be made as the process unfolds.

A research project should not be viewed as an end in itself. Projects arise because managerial problems need solving. The problems themselves may concern the identification of market opportunities, the evaluation of alternative courses of action, or control of marketing operations. Since these activities, in turn, are the essence of the managerial function, research activity can also be viewed from the broader perspective of the firm's marketing intelligence system. Chapter 2, therefore, focused on the nature and present status of the supply of marketing intelligence.

The Research Process Revisited

Earlier in this text, we suggested that marketing research involves the systematic gathering, recording, and analyzing of data about problems relating to the marketing of goods and services. We pointed out that these activities are logically viewed as a sequence of steps called the research process. The stages of the process were identified as follows:

1. Formulate the problem.
2. Determine the research design.
3. Determine the data-collection method.
4. Design the data-collection forms.
5. Design the sample and collect the data.
6. Analyze and interpret the data.
7. Prepare the research report.

The decision problem logically comes first. It dictates the research problem and design of the project. However, the transition from problem to project is not an automatic one. It is not unusual for a researcher to go from problem specification to tentative research design and then back to problem respecification and modified research design. This back-and-forth process is perfectly natural, and, in fact, reflects one of the researcher's more important roles: to help to define and redefine the problem so that it can be researched, and, more important, answer the decision maker's problem.

While this task might appear to be simple in principle, in practice it can be formidable, as it requires a clear specification of objectives, alternatives, and environmental constraints and influences. The decision maker may not readily provide these to the researcher, who then must dig them out in order to design effective research.

In some cases research may not even be necessary. If the decision maker's views are so strongly held that no amount of information might change them, the research will be wasted. It is up to the researcher to determine this before, rather than after, conducting the research. Often this can be accomplished by asking "what if" questions. What if consumer reaction to the product concept is overwhelmingly favorable? What if it is unfavorable? What if it is only slightly favorable? If the decision maker indicates that he or she will make the same decision in each case, there may be important objectives that have never been explicitly stated. This is a critical finding. Every research project should have one or more objectives, and one should not proceed to the other steps in the process until these can be explicitly stated.

It is also important to ask at this point whether the anticipated benefits of the research are likely to exceed the expected costs. It is a mistake to assume that simply because something might change as a result of the research, the research is warranted. It may be that the likelihood of finding something that might warrant a change in the decision is so remote that the research still will be wasted. Researchers and decision makers alike constantly need to ask: Why should this research be conducted? What could we possibly find out that we do not already know? Will the expected benefits from the research exceed its costs? If the answers indicate research, then the question logically turns to, what kind?

If the problem cannot be formulated as some specific "if-then" conjectural relationships, exploratory research is in order. The primary purpose of exploratory research is gathering some ideas and insights into the phenomenon. The output of an exploratory study will *not* be answers but more specific questions or statements of tentative relationships. The search for such insights demands a flexible research design. Structured questionnaires and probability sampling plans are not used in exploratory research, since the emphasis is not on gathering summary statistics but on gaining insight into the problem. The personal interview is much more appropriate than the telephone interview, and that in turn is more appropriate than a mail survey, since the unstructured question is most useful in the experience survey. Interviewees should be handpicked because they can provide the wanted information. In such cases, a convenience or judgment sample is very much in order, whereas it would be completely out of place in descriptive or causal research. Focus groups can also be productive.

The researcher may also want to conduct a survey of the literature or an analysis of selected cases. These steps can be advantageous in exploratory research, particularly if the researcher remembers that the goal of exploratory research is to discover ideas and tentative explanations of the phenomenon, and not to fix on one idea as being the sole definitive explanation. The analysis of published data may be particularly productive if it reveals sharp contrasts or other striking features that may help to illuminate the reasons behind the phenomenon under investigation.

If exploratory research has succeeded in generating one or more specific hypotheses to be investigated, the next research step would logically be descriptive or causal research. The design the researcher actually selects depends largely on how convinced he or she is that the tentative explanation is indeed the correct explanation for the phenomenon. Of course, the feasibility and cost of conducting an experiment are also important factors in determining research design. While experiments typically provide more convincing proof of causal relationships, they also usually cost more than descriptive designs. This is one of the reasons why descriptive designs are the most commonly employed type in marketing research.

Whereas exploratory designs are flexible, descriptive designs are rigid. Descriptive designs demand a clear specification of the who, what, when, where, how, and why of the research before data collection begins. They generally employ structured questionnaires or scales because these forms provide advantages in coding and tabulating. In descriptive designs, the emphasis is on generating an accurate picture of the relationships between and among variables. Probability sampling plans are desirable, but if the sample is to be drawn using nonprobabilistic methods, it is important that a quota sample be used. Descriptive studies typically rely heavily on cross-tabulation analysis or other means of investigating the association among variables, such as regression analysis, although the emphasis can also be on the search for differences. The great majority of descriptive studies are cross-sectional, although some do use longitudinal information.

Experiments are the best means we have for making inferences about cause-and-effect relationships, since, if designed properly, they provide the most compelling evidence regarding concomitant variation, time order of occurrence of variables, and elimination of other factors. A key feature of the experiment is that the researcher is able to control who will be exposed to the experimental stimulus (the presumed cause). Depending on the nature of the experiment, subjects may be individual consumers, members of panels, or other elements from the population of interest. Sampling plays little role in experiments other than in determining which objects are going to be assigned to which treatment conditions.

Because the goal is to test a specific relationship, causal designs also demand a clear specification of what is to be measured and how it is to be measured. Structured data-collection instruments such as questionnaires and scales are often used. Researchers also rely heavily on the observation method for collecting data, because this method tends to produce more objective and accurate information.

The major objective in analyzing experimental results is to determine if there are differences between those exposed to the experimental stimulus and those not exposed. Although researchers generally use analysis of variance to investigate and measure these differences, other techniques (for example, the t test for the difference in means of independent or correlated samples) are used as well.

The previous paragraphs should indicate how significantly the steps are interrelated and, in particular, how the basic nature of the research design implies a number of things with respect to the structure of the data-collection form, design of the sample, collection, and analysis of the data. A decision about appropriate research does not completely determine the latter considerations, of course, but simply suggests their basic nature. The analyst still has to determine their specific format. For example, is the structured questionnaire to be disguised or undisguised? Is the probability sample to be simple, stratified, or cluster? How large a sample is needed? Does the data-collection instrument dictate a data-analysis procedure for nominal, ordinal, interval, or ratio data? These questions, too, will be determined in large part by the way the research question is framed, although the ingenuity displayed by the designer of the research will determine their final form. The researcher will have to balance the various sources of error that can arise in the process when determining this final form. In effecting this balance, the researcher must be concerned with assessing and minimizing total error; this often means assuming additional error in one of the parts of the process so that total error can be decreased.

Research Project

The seventh and final stage in the research process is to prepare the research report. As we noted in the chapters in this part, despite the sophistication that may have been displayed in the earlier stages in the research process, the project will be a failure if the research report fails. Since the research report is all that most executives will see of the project, it is the yardstick by which the research will be evaluated.

A standard research report generally contains the following elements: title page, table of contents, summary, introduction, body, conclusions and recommendations, and appendix. Most marketing research projects also conclude with an oral report. Most effective oral presentations keep their technical detail to a minimum and make use of appropriate visual aids.

Both written and oral reports are judged by one fundamental criterion: how well they communicate with the audience, be it a reader or a listener. The report must be tailor-made for the reader or readers, with due regard for their technical sophistication, their interest in the subject area, the circumstances under which they will read the report, and the use they will make of it.

In the continuing case we have featured at the end of each part, we have discussed much of the material that would appear in a research report on such a project. For example, much of the information that would normally appear in an introduction appears at the end of Part One, where the first stage in the research process, problem formulation, is discussed. Information about the design of the study that would be included in the body of the report appears in subsequent sections that discuss the research design, the method of data collection, the design of the data-collection form, the design of the sample, and the data-collection process. Information that would generally appear in the section of the report devoted to conclusions was discussed at the end of Part Six. Certain items such as test statistics and calculations, tables, and a bibliography have been omitted because of length restrictions.

It is important, however, for students to see what the executive summary to such a research report would look like, since in many ways it encapsulates the rest of the document. A good executive summary contains necessary background information as well as the important results and conclusions, and it is thus the one part of the study that can truly stand alone.

This marketing research project was sponsored by the Centerville Area Radio Association (CARA). Its purpose was to identify specific problems that area businesses had with regard to advertising so that CARA advertising sales representatives could work to solve these through their marketing actions. The research objectives were as follows:

1. Identify business decision makers' attitudes toward the advertising media of newspaper, radio, and television.
2. Identify business decision makers' attitudes toward the advertising sales representatives of newspaper, radio, and television.

A five-page questionnaire was developed to measure these attitudes. The questionnaire was designed to test several hypotheses, the first being that different types of advertising media were perceived differently. CARA members were interested in investigating the different perceptions of newspaper, radio, and television as advertising media, since these three were the primary competitors for advertising budgets among Centerville-area businesses.

Another hypothesis was that the advertising sales representatives for the three types of media were also perceived differently from one another. Perceptions were measured through use of scaled ratings of itemized individual attributes of (1) the medium and (2) the sales representatives for each medium. It was hypothesized that attitudes would be further differentiated by the level of annual advertising expenditures made by the respondent's company. Moreover, the particular attributes of sales representatives and advertising media were tested to determine their importance to the respondents.

Also, it was hypothesized that the differences in business people's attitudes toward the three media would be reflected in the differences in their attitudes toward the sales representatives of each of the media.

The position title of the respondent, whether or not the respondent made advertising decisions, and whether or not the business used an advertising agency, were used to categorize and, if necessary, exclude individuals from the final data analysis.

The research method consisted of mailing a questionnaire to 600 area businesses. A systematic probability sample of 600 was drawn from a yellow pages listing of businesses identified by CARA as representative of those with which they did business or would have liked to do business. These businesses fell into ten broad categories: (1) building materials and hardware; (2) automotive sales and service; (3) apparel; (4) furniture and home furnishings; (5) eating and drinking establishments; (6) health and fitness; (7) financial institutions; (8) home entertainment; (9) professional services; and (10) a miscellaneous category consisting of florists, printers, bookstores, jewelers, and photographic sales and service.

In an effort to ensure an adequate response rate, a one-dollar bill was enclosed in 300 of the mailed questionnaires. The remaining 300 did not receive a dollar. The questionnaires were color coded (cream-colored for the ones that received the dollar bill and white for the others), so that response rates for the two groups could be calculated. Systematic probability sampling was also used to determine which businesses would receive a questionnaire with a one-dollar bill inside.

The questionnaires were mailed April 8th. The cutoff date for accepting returned questionnaires was April 24th. One hundred sixty-five (165) of the cream-colored questionnaires were returned, while 47 of the white ones were returned, for a total of 212. The results indicated that the inclusion of the dollar bill made a difference. Thirty-four (25 cream, 9 white) of the questionnaires returned were unusable due to incompleteness.

The hypothesis that there were differences in attitudes toward the three advertising media was not supported by the data. There were no significant differences in respondents' attitudes toward newspaper, radio, and television as advertising media.

With regard to the hypothesis that there were differences in attitudes toward newspaper, radio, and television sales representatives, there were no significant differences except when individuals whose business used an advertising agency were included with those who did not.

The classification of attitude scores by advertising expenditures revealed an inverse linear relationship: as advertising expenditures increased, attitudes toward advertising sales representatives became increasingly negative.

There were significant differences in the ratings of the *importance* of the different characteristics of the media and the various attributes of sales representatives. More particularly, the analysis of the item-importance scores indicated that it would be worthwhile for radio sales representatives to become more knowledgeable about their clients' areas of business and more aware and concerned about their clients' particular advertising needs. Radio representatives should make it clear to business clients that radio advertising can build up recognition of a business as well as, or better than, television advertising. Further, if radio advertising can improve a business's sales volume and can reach its target market better than television advertising, and as well as or better than newspaper advertising, this should be clearly indicated to business clients.

Appendix

Table 1 ***Cumulative Standard Unit Normal Distribution***

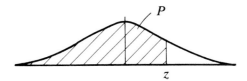

Values of P corresponding to Z for the normal curve. Z is the standard normal variable. The value of P for $-Z$ equals one minus the value of P for $+Z$, (e.g., the P for -1.62 equals $1 - .9474 = .0526$).

Z	.00	.01	.02	.03	.04	.05	.06	.07	.08	.09
.0	.5000	.5040	.5080	.5120	.5160	.5199	.5239	.5279	.5319	.5359
.1	.5398	.5438	.5478	.5517	.5557	.5596	.5636	.5675	.5714	.5753
.2	.5793	.5832	.5871	.5910	.5948	.5987	.6026	.6064	.6103	.6141
.3	.6179	.6217	.6255	.6293	.6331	.6368	.6406	.6443	.6480	.6517
.4	.6554	.6591	.6628	.6664	.6700	.6736	.6772	.6808	.6844	.6879
.5	.6915	.6950	.6985	.7019	.7054	.7088	.7123	.7157	.7190	.7224
.6	.7257	.7291	.7324	.7357	.7389	.7422	.7454	.7486	.7517	.7549
.7	.7580	.7611	.7642	.7673	.7704	.7734	.7764	.7794	.7823	.7852
.8	.7881	.7910	.7939	.7967	.7995	.8023	.8051	.8078	.8106	.8133
.9	.8159	.8186	.8212	.8238	.8264	.8289	.8315	.8340	.8365	.8389
1.0	.8413	.8438	.8461	.8485	.8508	.8531	.8554	.8577	.8599	.8621
1.1	.8643	.8665	.8686	.8708	.8729	.8749	.8770	.8790	.8810	.8830
1.2	.8849	.8869	.8888	.8907	.8925	.8944	.8962	.8980	.8997	.9015
1.3	.9032	.9049	.9066	.9082	.9099	.9115	.9131	.9147	.9162	.9177
1.4	.9192	.9207	.9222	.9236	.9251	.9265	.9279	.9292	.9306	.9319
1.5	.9332	.9345	.9357	.9370	.9382	.9394	.9406	.9418	.9429	.9441
1.6	.9452	.9463	.9474	.9484	.9495	.9505	.9515	.9525	.9535	.9545
1.7	.9554	.9564	.9573	.9582	.9591	.9599	.9608	.9616	.9625	.9633
1.8	.9641	.9649	.9656	.9664	.9671	.9678	.9686	.9693	.9699	.9706
1.9	.9713	.9719	.9726	.9732	.9738	.9744	.9750	.9756	.9761	.9767
2.0	.9772	.9778	.9783	.9788	.9793	.9798	.9803	.9808	.9812	.9817
2.1	.9821	.9826	.9830	.9834	.9838	.9842	.9846	.9850	.9854	.9857
2.2	.9861	.9864	.9868	.9871	.9875	.9878	.9881	.9884	.9887	.9890
2.3	.9893	.9896	.9898	.9901	.9904	.9906	.9909	.9911	.9913	.9916
2.4	.9918	.9920	.9922	.9925	.9927	.9929	.9931	.9932	.9934	.9936
2.5	.9938	.9940	.9941	.9943	.9945	.9946	.9948	.9949	.9951	.9952
2.6	.9953	.9955	.9956	.9957	.9959	.9960	.9961	.9962	.9963	.9964
2.7	.9965	.9966	.9967	.9968	.9969	.9970	.9971	.9972	.9973	.9974
2.8	.9974	.9975	.9976	.9977	.9977	.9978	.9979	.9979	.9980	.9981
2.9	.9981	.9982	.9982	.9983	.9984	.9984	.9985	.9985	.9986	.9986
3.0	.9987	.9987	.9987	.9988	.9988	.9989	.9989	.9989	.9990	.9990
3.1	.9990	.9991	.9991	.9991	.9992	.9992	.9992	.9992	.9993	.9993
3.2	.9993	.9993	.9994	.9994	.9994	.9994	.9994	.9995	.9995	.9995
3.3	.9995	.9995	.9995	.9996	.9996	.9996	.9996	.9996	.9996	.9997
3.4	.9997	.9997	.9997	.9997	.9997	.9997	.9997	.9997	.9997	.9998

Source: Paul E. Green, *Analyzing Multivariate Data* (Chicago: Dryden Press, 1978).

Table 2   Selected Percentiles of the χ² Distribution

Values of χ^2 corresponding to P

ν	$\chi^2_{.005}$	$\chi^2_{.01}$	$\chi^2_{.025}$	$\chi^2_{.05}$	$\chi^2_{.10}$	$\chi^2_{.90}$	$\chi^2_{.95}$	$\chi^2_{.975}$	$\chi^2_{.99}$	$\chi^2_{.995}$
1	.000039	.00016	.00098	.0039	.0158	2.71	3.84	5.02	6.63	7.88
2	.0100	.0201	.0506	.1026	.2107	4.61	5.99	7.38	9.21	10.60
3	.0717	.115	.216	.352	.584	6.25	7.81	9.35	11.34	12.84
4	.207	.297	.484	.711	1.064	7.78	9.49	11.14	13.28	14.86
5	.412	.554	.831	1.15	1.61	9.24	11.07	12.83	15.09	16.75
6	.676	.872	1.24	1.64	2.20	10.64	12.59	14.45	16.81	18.55
7	.989	1.24	1.69	2.17	2.83	12.02	14.07	16.01	18.48	20.28
8	1.34	1.65	2.18	2.73	3.49	13.36	15.51	17.53	20.09	21.96
9	1.73	2.09	2.70	3.33	4.17	14.68	16.92	19.02	21.67	23.59
10	2.16	2.56	3.25	3.94	4.87	15.99	18.31	20.48	23.21	25.19
11	2.60	3.05	3.82	4.57	5.58	17.28	19.68	21.92	24.73	26.76
12	3.07	3.57	4.40	5.23	6.30	18.55	21.03	23.34	26.22	28.30
13	3.57	4.11	5.01	5.89	7.04	19.81	22.36	24.74	27.69	29.82
14	4.07	4.66	5.63	6.57	7.79	21.06	23.68	26.12	29.14	31.32
15	4.60	5.23	6.26	7.26	8.55	22.31	25.00	27.49	30.58	32.80
16	5.14	5.81	6.91	7.96	9.31	23.54	26.30	28.85	32.00	34.27
18	6.26	7.01	8.23	9.39	10.86	25.99	28.87	31.53	34.81	37.16
20	7.43	8.26	9.59	10.85	12.44	28.41	31.41	34.17	37.57	40.00
24	9.89	10.86	12.40	13.85	15.66	33.20	36.42	39.36	42.98	45.56
30	13.79	14.95	16.79	18.49	20.60	40.26	43.77	46.98	50.89	53.67
40	20.71	22.16	24.43	26.51	29.05	51.81	55.76	59.34	63.69	66.77
60	35.53	37.48	40.48	43.19	46.46	74.40	79.08	83.30	88.38	91.95
120	83.85	86.92	91.58	95.70	100.62	140.23	146.57	152.21	158.95	163.64

Source: Adapted with permission from *Introduction to Statistical Analysis* (2nd ed.) by W. J. Dixon and F. J. Massey, Jr., © 1957 McGraw-Hill.

Table 3   **Upper Percentiles of the t Distribution**

ν	1 − α						
	.75	.90	.95	.975	.99	.995	.9995
1	1.000	3.078	6.314	12.706	31.821	63.657	636.619
2	.816	1.886	2.920	4.303	6.965	9.925	31.598
3	.765	1.638	2.353	3.182	4.541	5.841	12.941
4	.741	1.533	2.132	2.776	3.747	4.604	8.610
5	.727	1.476	2.015	2.571	3.365	4.032	6.859
6	.718	1.440	1.943	2.447	3.143	3.707	5.959
7	.711	1.415	1.895	2.365	2.998	3.499	5.405
8	.706	1.397	1.860	2.306	2.896	3.355	5.041
9	.703	1.383	1.833	2.262	2.821	3.250	4.781
10	.700	1.372	1.812	2.228	2.764	3.169	4.587
11	.697	1.363	1.796	2.201	2.718	3.106	4.437
12	.695	1.356	1.782	2.179	2.681	3.055	4.318
13	.694	1.350	1.771	2.160	2.650	3.012	4.221
14	.692	1.345	1.761	2.145	2.624	2.977	4.140
15	.691	1.341	1.753	2.131	2.602	2.947	4.073
16	.690	1.337	1.746	2.120	2.583	2.921	4.015
17	.689	1.333	1.740	2.110	2.567	2.898	3.965
18	.688	1.330	1.734	2.101	2.552	2.878	3.922
19	.688	1.328	1.729	2.093	2.339	2.861	3.883
20	.687	1.325	1.725	2.086	2.528	2.845	3.850
21	.686	1.323	1.721	2.080	2.518	2.831	3.819
22	.686	1.321	1.717	2.074	2.508	2.819	3.792
23	.685	1.319	1.714	2.069	2.500	2.807	3.767
24	.685	1.318	1.711	2.064	2.492	2.797	3.745
25	.684	1.316	1.708	2.060	2.485	2.787	3.725
26	.684	1.315	1.706	2.056	2.479	2.779	3.707
27	.684	1.314	1.703	2.052	2.473	2.771	3.690
28	.683	1.313	1.701	2.048	2.467	2.763	3.674
29	.683	1.311	1.699	2.045	2.462	2.756	3.659
30	.683	1.310	1.697	2.042	2.457	2.750	3.646
40	.681	1.303	1.684	2.021	2.423	2.704	3.551
60	.679	1.296	1.671	2.000	2.390	2.660	3.460
120	.677	1.289	1.658	1.980	2.358	2.617	3.373
∞	.674	1.282	1.645	1.960	2.326	2.576	3.291

ν = degrees of freedom

Source: Taken from Table III of R. A. Fisher and F. Yates: *Statistical Tables for Biological, Agricultural, and Medical Research*, published by Longman Group UK Ltd., London (previously published by Oliver & Boyd Ltd., Edinburgh, 1963), and used by permission of the authors and publishers.

Table 4   Selected Percentiles of the F Distribution

$F_{.90(v_1, v_2)}$ $\alpha = 0.1$

v_1 = degrees of freedom for numerator

v_2 = degrees of freedom for denominator

v_2 \ v_1	1	2	3	4	5	6	7	8	9	10	12	15	20	24	30	40	60	120	∞
1	39.86	49.50	53.59	55.83	57.24	58.20	58.91	59.44	59.86	60.19	60.71	61.22	61.74	62.00	62.26	62.53	62.79	63.06	63.33
2	8.53	9.00	9.16	9.24	9.29	9.33	9.35	9.37	9.38	9.39	9.41	9.42	9.44	9.45	9.46	9.47	9.47	9.48	9.49
3	5.54	5.46	5.39	5.34	5.31	5.28	5.27	5.25	5.24	5.23	5.22	5.20	5.18	5.18	5.17	5.16	5.15	5.14	5.13
4	4.54	4.32	4.19	4.11	4.05	4.01	3.98	3.95	3.94	3.92	3.90	3.87	3.84	3.83	3.82	3.80	3.79	3.78	3.76
5	4.06	3.78	3.62	3.52	3.45	3.40	3.37	3.34	3.32	3.30	3.27	3.24	3.21	3.19	3.17	3.16	3.14	3.12	3.10
6	3.78	3.46	3.29	3.18	3.11	3.05	3.01	2.98	2.96	2.94	2.90	2.87	2.84	2.82	2.80	2.78	2.76	2.74	2.72
7	3.59	3.26	3.07	2.96	2.88	2.83	2.78	2.75	2.72	2.70	2.67	2.63	2.59	2.58	2.56	2.54	2.51	2.49	2.47
8	3.46	3.11	2.92	2.81	2.73	2.67	2.62	2.59	2.56	2.50	2.50	2.46	2.42	2.40	2.38	2.36	2.34	2.32	2.29
9	3.36	3.01	2.81	2.69	2.61	2.55	2.51	2.47	2.44	2.42	2.38	2.34	2.30	2.28	2.25	2.23	2.21	2.18	2.16
10	3.29	2.92	2.73	2.61	2.52	2.46	2.41	2.38	2.35	2.32	2.28	2.24	2.20	2.18	2.16	2.13	2.11	2.08	2.06
11	3.23	2.86	2.66	2.54	2.45	2.39	2.34	2.30	2.27	2.25	2.21	2.17	2.12	2.10	2.08	2.05	2.03	2.00	1.97
12	3.18	2.81	2.61	2.48	2.39	2.33	2.28	2.24	2.21	2.19	2.15	2.10	2.06	2.04	2.01	1.99	1.96	1.93	1.90
13	3.14	2.76	2.56	2.43	2.35	2.28	2.23	2.20	2.16	2.14	2.10	2.05	2.01	1.98	1.96	1.93	1.90	1.88	1.85
14	3.10	2.73	2.52	2.39	2.31	2.24	2.19	2.15	2.12	2.10	2.05	2.01	1.96	1.94	1.91	1.89	1.86	1.83	1.80
15	3.07	2.70	2.49	2.36	2.27	2.21	2.16	2.12	2.09	2.06	2.02	1.97	1.92	1.90	1.87	1.85	1.82	1.79	1.76
16	3.05	2.67	2.46	2.33	2.24	2.18	2.13	2.09	2.06	2.03	1.99	1.94	1.89	1.87	1.84	1.81	1.78	1.75	1.72
17	3.03	2.64	2.44	2.31	2.22	2.15	2.10	2.06	2.03	2.00	1.96	1.91	1.86	1.84	1.81	1.78	1.75	1.72	1.69
18	3.01	2.62	2.42	2.29	2.20	2.13	2.08	2.04	2.00	1.98	1.93	1.89	1.84	1.81	1.78	1.75	1.72	1.69	1.66
19	2.99	2.61	2.40	2.27	2.18	2.11	2.06	2.02	1.98	1.96	1.91	1.86	1.81	1.79	1.76	1.73	1.70	1.67	1.63
20	2.97	2.59	2.38	2.25	2.16	2.09	2.04	2.00	1.96	1.94	1.89	1.84	1.79	1.77	1.74	1.71	1.68	1.64	1.61
21	2.96	2.57	2.36	2.23	2.14	2.08	2.02	1.98	1.95	1.92	1.87	1.83	1.78	1.75	1.72	1.69	1.66	1.62	1.59
22	2.95	2.56	2.35	2.22	2.13	2.06	2.01	1.97	1.93	1.90	1.86	1.81	1.76	1.73	1.70	1.67	1.64	1.60	1.57
23	2.94	2.55	2.34	2.21	2.11	2.05	1.99	1.95	1.92	1.89	1.84	1.80	1.74	1.72	1.69	1.66	1.62	1.59	1.55
24	2.93	2.54	2.33	2.19	2.10	2.04	1.98	1.94	1.91	1.88	1.83	1.78	1.73	1.70	1.67	1.64	1.61	1.57	1.53
25	2.92	2.53	2.32	2.18	2.09	2.02	1.97	1.93	1.89	1.87	1.82	1.77	1.72	1.69	1.66	1.63	1.59	1.56	1.52
26	2.91	2.52	2.31	2.17	2.08	2.01	1.96	1.92	1.88	1.86	1.81	1.76	1.71	1.68	1.65	1.61	1.58	1.54	1.50
27	2.90	2.51	2.30	2.17	2.07	2.00	1.95	1.91	1.87	1.85	1.80	1.75	1.70	1.67	1.64	1.60	1.57	1.53	1.49
28	2.89	2.50	2.29	2.16	2.06	2.00	1.94	1.90	1.87	1.84	1.79	1.74	1.69	1.66	1.63	1.59	1.56	1.52	1.48
29	2.89	2.50	2.28	2.15	2.06	1.99	1.93	1.89	1.86	1.83	1.78	1.73	1.68	1.65	1.62	1.58	1.55	1.51	1.47
30	2.88	2.49	2.28	2.14	2.05	1.98	1.93	1.88	1.85	1.82	1.77	1.72	1.67	1.64	1.61	1.57	1.54	1.50	1.46
40	2.84	2.44	2.23	2.09	2.00	1.93	1.87	1.83	1.79	1.76	1.71	1.66	1.61	1.57	1.54	1.51	1.47	1.42	1.38
60	2.79	2.39	2.18	2.04	1.95	1.87	1.82	1.77	1.74	1.71	1.66	1.60	1.54	1.51	1.48	1.44	1.40	1.35	1.29
120	2.75	2.35	2.13	1.99	1.90	1.82	1.77	1.72	1.68	1.65	1.60	1.55	1.48	1.45	1.41	1.37	1.32	1.26	1.19
∞	2.71	2.30	2.08	1.94	1.85	1.77	1.72	1.67	1.63	1.60	1.55	1.49	1.42	1.38	1.34	1.30	1.24	1.17	1.00

Source: Adapted with permission from *Biometrika Tables for Statisticians*, Vol. 1 (2nd ed.), edited by E. S. Pearson and H. O. Hartley, Cambridge University Press, 1958.

Table 4   Selected Percentiles of the F Distribution (Continued)

$$F_{.95}(v_1, v_2) \qquad \alpha = 0.05$$

v_1 = degrees of freedom for numerator

v_2 = degrees of freedom for denominator

v_2 \ v_1	1	2	3	4	5	6	7	8	9	10	12	15	20	24	30	40	60	120	∞
1	161.4	199.5	215.7	224.6	230.2	234.0	236.8	238.8	240.5	241.9	243.9	245.9	248.0	249.1	250.1	251.1	252.2	253.3	254.3
2	18.51	19.00	19.16	19.25	19.30	19.33	19.35	19.37	19.38	19.40	19.41	19.43	19.45	19.45	19.46	19.47	19.48	19.49	19.50
3	10.13	9.55	9.28	9.12	9.01	8.94	8.89	8.85	8.81	8.79	8.74	8.70	8.66	8.64	8.62	8.59	8.57	8.55	8.53
4	7.71	6.94	6.59	6.39	6.26	6.16	6.09	6.04	6.00	5.96	5.91	5.86	5.80	5.77	5.75	5.72	5.69	5.66	5.63
5	6.61	5.79	5.41	5.19	5.05	4.95	4.88	4.82	4.77	4.74	4.68	4.62	4.56	4.53	4.50	4.46	4.43	4.40	4.36
6	5.99	5.14	4.76	4.53	4.39	4.28	4.21	4.15	4.10	4.06	4.00	3.94	3.87	3.84	3.81	3.77	3.74	3.70	3.67
7	5.59	4.74	4.35	4.12	3.97	3.87	3.79	3.73	3.68	3.64	3.57	3.51	3.44	3.41	3.38	3.34	3.30	3.27	3.23
8	5.32	4.46	4.07	3.84	3.69	3.58	3.50	3.44	3.39	3.35	3.28	3.22	3.15	3.12	3.08	3.04	3.01	2.97	2.93
9	5.12	4.26	3.86	3.63	3.48	3.37	3.29	3.23	3.18	3.14	3.07	3.01	2.94	2.90	2.86	2.83	2.79	2.75	2.71
10	4.96	4.10	3.71	3.48	3.33	3.22	3.14	3.07	3.02	2.98	2.91	2.85	2.77	2.74	2.70	2.66	2.62	2.58	2.54
11	4.84	3.98	3.59	3.36	3.20	3.09	3.01	2.95	2.90	2.85	2.79	2.72	2.65	2.61	2.57	2.53	2.49	2.45	2.40
12	4.75	3.89	3.49	3.26	3.11	3.00	2.91	2.85	2.80	2.75	2.69	2.62	2.54	2.51	2.47	2.43	2.38	2.34	2.30
13	4.67	3.81	3.41	3.18	3.03	2.92	2.83	2.77	2.71	2.67	2.60	2.53	2.46	2.42	2.38	2.34	2.30	2.25	2.21
14	4.60	3.74	3.34	3.11	2.96	2.85	2.76	2.70	2.65	2.60	2.53	2.46	2.39	2.35	2.31	2.27	2.22	2.18	2.13
15	4.54	3.68	3.29	3.06	2.90	2.79	2.71	2.64	2.59	2.54	2.48	2.40	2.33	2.29	2.25	2.20	2.16	2.11	2.07
16	4.49	3.63	3.24	3.01	2.85	2.74	2.66	2.59	2.54	2.49	2.42	2.35	2.28	2.24	2.19	2.15	2.11	2.06	2.01
17	4.45	3.59	3.20	2.96	2.81	2.70	2.61	2.55	2.49	2.45	2.38	2.31	2.23	2.19	2.15	2.10	2.06	2.01	1.96
18	4.41	3.55	3.16	2.93	2.77	2.66	2.58	2.51	2.46	2.41	2.34	2.27	2.19	2.15	2.11	2.06	2.02	1.97	1.92
19	4.38	3.52	3.13	2.90	2.74	2.63	2.54	2.48	2.42	2.38	2.31	2.23	2.16	2.11	2.07	2.03	1.98	1.93	1.88
20	4.35	3.49	3.10	2.87	2.71	2.60	2.51	2.45	2.39	2.35	2.28	2.20	2.12	2.08	2.04	1.99	1.95	1.90	1.84
21	4.32	3.47	3.07	2.84	2.68	2.57	2.49	2.42	2.37	2.32	2.25	2.18	2.10	2.05	2.01	1.96	1.92	1.87	1.81
22	4.30	3.44	3.05	2.82	2.66	2.55	2.46	2.40	2.34	2.30	2.23	2.15	2.07	2.03	1.98	1.94	1.89	1.84	1.78
23	4.28	3.42	3.03	2.80	2.64	2.53	2.44	2.37	2.32	2.27	2.20	2.13	2.05	2.01	1.96	1.91	1.86	1.81	1.76
24	4.26	3.40	3.01	2.78	2.62	2.51	2.42	2.36	2.30	2.25	2.18	2.11	2.03	1.98	1.94	1.89	1.84	1.79	1.73
25	4.24	3.39	2.99	2.76	2.60	2.49	2.40	2.34	2.28	2.24	2.16	2.09	2.01	1.96	1.92	1.87	1.82	1.77	1.71
26	4.23	3.37	2.98	2.74	2.59	2.47	2.39	2.32	2.27	2.22	2.15	2.07	1.99	1.95	1.90	1.85	1.80	1.75	1.69
27	4.21	3.35	2.96	2.73	2.57	2.46	2.37	2.31	2.25	2.20	2.13	2.06	1.97	1.93	1.88	1.84	1.79	1.73	1.67
28	4.20	3.34	2.95	2.71	2.56	2.45	2.36	2.29	2.24	2.19	2.12	2.04	1.96	1.91	1.87	1.82	1.77	1.71	1.65
29	4.18	3.33	2.93	2.70	2.55	2.43	2.35	2.28	2.22	2.18	2.10	2.03	1.94	1.90	1.85	1.81	1.75	1.70	1.64
30	4.17	3.32	2.92	2.69	2.53	2.42	2.33	2.27	2.21	2.16	2.09	2.01	1.93	1.89	1.84	1.79	1.74	1.68	1.62
40	4.08	3.23	2.84	2.61	2.45	2.34	2.25	2.18	2.12	2.08	2.00	1.92	1.84	1.79	1.74	1.69	1.64	1.58	1.51
60	4.00	3.15	2.76	2.53	2.37	2.25	2.17	2.10	2.04	1.99	1.92	1.84	1.75	1.70	1.65	1.59	1.53	1.47	1.39
120	3.92	3.07	2.68	2.45	2.29	2.17	2.09	2.02	1.96	1.91	1.83	1.75	1.66	1.61	1.55	1.50	1.43	1.35	1.25
∞	3.84	3.00	2.60	2.37	2.21	2.10	2.01	1.94	1.88	1.83	1.75	1.67	1.57	1.52	1.46	1.39	1.32	1.22	1.00

Table 4   Selected Percentiles of the F Distribution (Continued)

$$F_{.975}(\nu_1, \nu_2) \qquad \alpha = 0.025$$

ν_1 = degrees of freedom for numerator

ν_2 = degrees of freedom for denominator

ν_2 \ ν_1	1	2	3	4	5	6	7	8	9	10	12	15	20	24	30	40	60	120	∞
1	647.8	799.5	864.2	899.6	921.8	937.1	948.2	956.7	963.3	968.6	976.7	984.9	993.1	997.2	1001	1006	1010	1014	1018
2	38.51	39.00	39.17	39.25	39.30	39.33	39.36	39.37	39.39	39.40	39.41	39.43	39.45	39.46	39.46	39.47	39.48	39.49	39.50
3	17.44	16.04	15.44	15.10	14.88	14.73	14.62	14.54	14.47	14.42	14.34	14.25	14.17	14.12	14.08	14.04	13.99	13.95	13.90
4	12.22	10.65	9.98	9.60	9.36	9.20	9.07	8.98	8.90	8.84	8.75	8.66	8.56	8.51	8.46	8.41	8.36	8.31	8.26
5	10.01	8.43	7.76	7.39	7.15	6.98	6.85	6.76	6.68	6.62	6.52	6.43	6.33	6.28	6.23	6.18	6.12	6.07	6.02
6	8.81	7.26	6.60	6.23	5.99	5.82	5.70	5.60	5.52	5.46	5.37	5.27	5.17	5.12	5.07	5.01	4.96	4.90	4.85
7	8.07	6.54	5.89	5.52	5.29	5.12	4.99	4.90	4.82	4.76	4.67	4.57	4.47	4.42	4.36	4.31	4.25	4.20	4.14
8	7.57	6.06	5.42	5.05	4.82	4.65	4.53	4.43	4.36	4.30	4.20	4.10	4.00	3.95	3.89	3.84	3.78	3.73	3.67
9	7.21	5.71	5.08	4.72	4.48	4.32	4.20	4.10	4.03	3.96	3.87	3.77	3.67	3.61	3.56	3.51	3.45	3.39	3.33
10	6.94	5.46	4.83	4.47	4.24	4.07	3.95	3.85	3.78	3.72	3.62	3.52	3.42	3.37	3.31	3.26	3.20	3.14	3.08
11	6.72	5.26	4.63	4.28	4.04	3.88	3.76	3.66	3.59	3.53	3.43	3.33	3.23	3.17	3.12	3.06	3.00	2.94	2.88
12	6.55	5.10	4.47	4.12	3.89	3.73	3.61	3.51	3.44	3.37	3.28	3.18	3.07	3.02	2.96	2.91	2.85	2.79	2.72
13	6.41	4.97	4.35	4.00	3.77	3.60	3.48	3.39	3.31	3.25	3.15	3.05	2.95	2.89	2.84	2.78	2.72	2.66	2.60
14	6.30	4.86	4.24	3.89	3.66	3.50	3.38	3.29	3.21	3.15	3.05	2.95	2.84	2.79	2.73	2.67	2.61	2.55	2.49
15	6.20	4.77	4.15	3.80	3.58	3.41	3.29	3.20	3.12	3.06	2.96	2.86	2.76	2.70	2.64	2.59	2.52	2.46	2.40
16	6.12	4.69	4.08	3.73	3.50	3.34	3.22	3.12	3.05	2.99	2.89	2.79	2.68	2.63	2.57	2.51	2.45	2.38	2.32
17	6.04	4.62	4.01	3.66	3.44	3.28	3.16	3.06	2.98	2.92	2.82	2.72	2.62	2.56	2.50	2.44	2.38	2.32	2.25
18	5.98	4.56	3.95	3.61	3.38	3.22	3.10	3.01	2.93	2.87	2.77	2.67	2.56	2.50	2.44	2.38	2.32	2.26	2.19
19	5.92	4.51	3.90	3.56	3.33	3.17	3.05	2.96	2.88	2.82	2.72	2.62	2.51	2.45	2.39	2.33	2.27	2.20	2.13
20	5.87	4.46	3.86	3.51	3.29	3.13	3.01	2.91	2.84	2.77	2.68	2.57	2.46	2.41	2.35	2.29	2.22	2.16	2.09
21	5.83	4.42	3.82	3.48	3.25	3.09	2.97	2.87	2.80	2.73	2.64	2.53	2.42	2.37	2.31	2.25	2.18	2.11	2.04
22	5.79	4.38	3.78	3.44	3.22	3.05	2.93	2.84	2.76	2.70	2.60	2.50	2.39	2.33	2.27	2.21	2.14	2.08	2.00
23	5.75	4.35	3.75	3.41	3.18	3.02	2.90	2.81	2.73	2.67	2.57	2.47	2.36	2.30	2.24	2.18	2.11	2.04	1.97
24	5.72	4.32	3.72	3.38	3.15	2.99	2.87	2.78	2.70	2.64	2.54	2.44	2.33	2.27	2.21	2.15	2.08	2.01	1.94
25	5.69	4.29	3.69	3.35	3.13	2.97	2.85	2.75	2.68	2.61	2.51	2.41	2.30	2.24	2.18	2.12	2.05	1.98	1.91
26	5.66	4.27	3.67	3.33	3.10	2.94	2.82	2.73	2.65	2.59	2.49	2.39	2.28	2.22	2.16	2.09	2.03	1.95	1.88
27	5.63	4.24	3.65	3.31	3.08	2.92	2.80	2.71	2.63	2.57	2.47	2.36	2.25	2.19	2.13	2.07	2.00	1.93	1.85
28	5.61	4.22	3.63	3.29	3.06	2.90	2.78	2.69	2.61	2.55	2.45	2.34	2.23	2.17	2.11	2.05	1.98	1.91	1.83
29	5.59	4.20	3.61	3.27	3.04	2.88	2.76	2.67	2.59	2.53	2.43	2.32	2.21	2.15	2.09	2.03	1.96	1.89	1.81
30	5.57	4.18	3.59	3.25	3.03	2.87	2.75	2.65	2.57	2.51	2.41	2.31	2.20	2.14	2.07	2.01	1.94	1.87	1.79
40	5.42	4.05	3.46	3.13	2.90	2.74	2.62	2.53	2.45	2.39	2.29	2.18	2.07	2.01	1.94	1.88	1.80	1.72	1.64
60	5.29	3.93	3.34	3.01	2.79	2.63	2.51	2.41	2.33	2.27	2.17	2.06	1.94	1.88	1.82	1.74	1.67	1.58	1.48
120	5.15	3.80	3.23	2.89	2.67	2.52	2.39	2.30	2.22	2.16	2.05	1.94	1.82	1.76	1.69	1.61	1.53	1.43	1.31
∞	5.02	3.69	3.12	2.79	2.57	2.41	2.29	2.19	2.11	2.05	1.94	1.83	1.71	1.64	1.57	1.48	1.39	1.27	1.00

Table 4   Selected Percentiles of the F Distribution (Continued)

$F_{.99}(\nu_1, \nu_2)$ α = 0.01

ν_1 = degrees of freedom for numerator

ν_2	1	2	3	4	5	6	7	8	9	10	12	15	20	24	30	40	60	120	∞
1	4052	4999.5	5403	5625	5764	5859	5928	5982	6022	6056	6106	6157	6209	6235	6261	6287	6313	6339	6366
2	98.50	99.00	99.17	99.25	99.30	99.33	99.36	99.37	99.39	99.40	99.42	99.43	99.45	99.46	99.47	99.47	99.48	99.49	99.50
3	34.12	30.82	29.46	28.71	28.24	27.91	27.67	27.49	27.35	27.23	27.05	26.87	26.69	26.60	26.50	26.41	26.32	26.22	26.13
4	21.20	18.00	16.69	15.98	15.52	15.21	14.98	14.80	14.66	14.55	14.37	14.20	14.02	13.93	13.84	13.75	13.65	13.56	13.46
5	16.26	13.27	12.06	11.39	10.97	10.67	10.46	10.29	10.16	10.05	9.89	9.72	9.55	9.47	9.38	9.29	9.20	9.11	9.02
6	13.75	10.92	9.78	9.15	8.75	8.47	8.26	8.10	7.98	7.87	7.72	7.56	7.40	7.31	7.23	7.14	7.06	6.97	6.88
7	12.25	9.55	8.45	7.85	7.46	7.19	6.99	6.84	6.72	6.62	6.47	6.31	6.16	6.07	5.99	5.91	5.82	5.74	5.65
8	11.26	8.65	7.59	7.01	6.63	6.37	6.18	6.03	5.91	5.81	5.67	5.52	5.36	5.28	5.20	5.12	5.03	4.95	4.86
9	10.56	8.02	6.99	6.42	6.06	5.80	5.61	5.47	5.35	5.26	5.11	4.96	4.81	4.73	4.65	4.57	4.48	4.40	4.31
10	10.04	7.56	6.55	5.99	5.64	5.39	5.20	5.06	4.94	4.85	4.71	4.56	4.41	4.33	4.25	4.17	4.08	4.00	3.91
11	9.65	7.21	6.22	5.67	5.32	5.07	4.89	4.74	4.63	4.54	4.40	4.25	4.10	4.02	3.94	3.86	3.78	3.69	3.60
12	9.33	6.93	5.95	5.41	5.06	4.82	4.64	4.50	4.39	4.30	4.16	4.01	3.86	3.78	3.70	3.62	3.54	3.45	3.36
13	9.07	6.70	5.74	5.21	4.86	4.62	4.44	4.30	4.19	4.10	3.96	3.82	3.66	3.59	3.51	3.43	3.34	3.25	3.17
14	8.86	6.51	5.56	5.04	4.69	4.46	4.28	4.14	4.03	3.94	3.80	3.66	3.51	3.43	3.35	3.27	3.18	3.09	3.00
15	8.68	6.36	5.42	4.89	4.56	4.32	4.14	4.00	3.89	3.80	3.67	3.52	3.37	3.29	3.21	3.13	3.05	2.96	2.87
16	8.53	6.23	5.29	4.77	4.44	4.20	4.03	3.89	3.78	3.69	3.55	3.41	3.26	3.18	3.10	3.02	2.93	2.84	2.75
17	8.40	6.11	5.18	4.67	4.34	4.10	3.93	3.79	3.68	3.59	3.46	3.31	3.16	3.08	3.00	2.92	2.83	2.75	2.65
18	8.29	6.01	5.09	4.58	4.25	4.01	3.84	3.71	3.60	3.51	3.37	3.23	3.08	3.00	2.92	2.84	2.75	2.66	2.57
19	8.18	5.93	5.01	4.50	4.17	3.94	3.77	3.63	3.52	3.43	3.30	3.15	3.00	2.92	2.84	2.76	2.67	2.58	2.49
20	8.10	5.85	4.94	4.43	4.10	3.87	3.70	3.56	3.46	3.37	3.23	3.09	2.94	2.86	2.78	2.69	2.61	2.52	2.42
21	8.02	5.78	4.87	4.37	4.04	3.81	3.64	3.51	3.40	3.31	3.17	3.03	2.88	2.80	2.72	2.64	2.55	2.46	2.36
22	7.95	5.72	4.82	4.31	3.99	3.76	3.59	3.45	3.35	3.26	3.12	2.98	2.83	2.75	2.67	2.58	2.50	2.40	2.31
23	7.88	5.66	4.76	4.26	3.94	3.71	3.54	3.41	3.30	3.21	3.07	2.93	2.78	2.70	2.62	2.54	2.45	2.35	2.26
24	7.82	5.61	4.72	4.22	3.90	3.67	3.50	3.36	3.26	3.17	3.03	2.89	2.74	2.66	2.58	2.49	2.40	2.31	2.21
25	7.77	5.57	4.68	4.18	3.85	3.63	3.46	3.32	3.22	3.13	2.99	2.85	2.70	2.62	2.54	2.45	2.36	2.27	2.17
26	7.72	5.53	4.64	4.14	3.82	3.59	3.42	3.29	3.18	3.09	2.96	2.81	2.66	2.58	2.50	2.42	2.33	2.23	2.13
27	7.68	5.49	4.60	4.11	3.78	3.56	3.39	3.26	3.15	3.06	2.93	2.78	2.63	2.55	2.47	2.38	2.29	2.20	2.10
28	7.64	5.45	4.57	4.07	3.75	3.53	3.36	3.23	3.12	3.03	2.90	2.75	2.60	2.52	2.44	2.35	2.26	2.17	2.06
29	7.60	5.42	4.54	4.04	3.73	3.50	3.33	3.20	3.09	3.00	2.87	2.73	2.57	2.49	2.41	2.33	2.23	2.14	2.03
30	7.56	5.39	4.51	4.02	3.70	3.47	3.30	3.17	3.07	2.98	2.84	2.70	2.55	2.47	2.39	2.30	2.21	2.11	2.01
40	7.31	5.18	4.31	3.83	3.51	3.29	3.12	2.99	2.89	2.80	2.66	2.52	2.37	2.29	2.20	2.11	2.02	1.92	1.80
60	7.08	4.98	4.13	3.65	3.34	3.12	2.95	2.82	2.72	2.63	2.50	2.35	2.20	2.12	2.03	1.94	1.84	1.73	1.60
120	6.85	4.79	3.95	3.48	3.17	2.96	2.79	2.66	2.56	2.47	2.34	2.19	2.03	1.95	1.86	1.76	1.66	1.53	1.38
∞	6.63	4.61	3.78	3.32	3.02	2.80	2.64	2.51	2.41	2.32	2.18	2.04	1.88	1.79	1.70	1.59	1.47	1.32	1.00

ν_2 = degrees of freedom for denominator

Index*

*Note: The lowercase n after a page number indicates the information can be found in a footnote; the lowercase s, in a source note; and the lowercase f, in a figure. Running glossary terms, and the page on which the terms are defined, appear in boldface type.